EUROPEAN YEARBOOK ON HUMAN RIGHTS 2021

This publication is supported by

PARIS LODRON UNIVERSITY SALZBURG | Austrian Human Rights Institute

Global Campus of Human Rights

United Nations Educational, Scientific and Cultural Organization

uniTwin

UNI GRAZ

UNESCO Chair in Human Rights and Human Security University of Graz, Austria

VIENNA FORUM FOR DEMOCRACY AND HUMAN RIGHTS

EUROPEAN YEARBOOK ON HUMAN RIGHTS 2021

Edited by
Philip CZECH
Lisa HESCHL
Karin LUKAS
Manfred NOWAK
Gerd OBERLEITNER

INTERSENTIA
Cambridge – Antwerp – Chicago

NWV
Vienna

Intersentia Ltd
8 Wellington Mews
Wellington Street | Cambridge
CB1 1HW | United Kingdom
Tel: +44 1223 736 170
Email: mail@intersentia.co.uk
www.intersentia.com | www.intersentia.co.uk

NWV Verlag GmbH
Seidengasse 9/OG 2/TOP 2.4
A-1070 Vienna
Tel.: +43 1 796 35 62-24 |
Fax: +43 1 796 35 62-25
Email: office@nwv.at
www.nwv.at

Distribution for the UK and
Rest of the World (incl. Eastern Europe)
NBN International
1 Deltic Avenue, Rooksley
Milton Keynes MK13 8LD
United Kingdom
Tel: +44 1752 202 301 | Fax: +44 1752 202 331
Email: orders@nbninternational.com

Distribution for Europe
Lefebvre Sarrut Belgium NV
Hoogstraat 139/6
1000 Brussels
Belgium
Tel: +32 (0)800 39 067
Email: mail@intersentia.be

Distribution for the USA and Canada
Independent Publishers Group
Order Department
814 North Franklin Street
Chicago, IL 60610
USA
Tel: +1 800 888 4741 (toll free) | Fax: +1 312 337 5985
Email: orders@ipgbook.com

European Yearbook on Human Rights 2021

ISBN (NWV) 978-3-7083-1385-6
ISBN (Intersentia) 978-1-83970-162-7
D/2021/7849/166
NUR 828

GPRC
Guaranteed
Peer Reviewed
Content

British Library Cataloguing in Publication Data. A catalogue record for this book is available from the British Library.

FOREWORD

2020 has been a particularly challenging year for human rights across the globe. The breadth of the issues faced by governments, civil society and individuals in Europe, and their complexity and interdependence, is thoroughly reflected in the selected contributions to this year's 13th edition of the European Yearbook on Human Rights.

2020 will always be viewed as the year of the great and global health crisis. Yet the health crisis also quickly developed into a human rights and rule of law crisis. In 2020, it became apparent that we can no longer rest on our laurels and pride ourselves on past achievements in the protection and promotion of human rights. While commitment to upholding human rights standards has been faltering across Europe for several years already, the COVID-19 pandemic has accelerated this erosion. On the symbolic day of 10 December 2020, Human Rights Day, I told the Member States of the Council of Europe that we are at a crossroads.[1] If we want to bolster individual freedoms rather than relinquishing them and empower people rather than marginalising them, we must show courage and firm commitment to the fundamental principles of post-war European solidarity: to human rights, democracy and the rule of law as ultimate guarantors of peace, justice and democratic security.

In 2020, we have been forced to focus our attention on an often overlooked, yet indispensable and fundamental human right: the right to health.[2] Without it, we cannot live in dignity, and our ability to exercise any other right, – to vote and enjoy civil and political freedoms, to work, learn and create – is significantly restricted. The COVID-19 pandemic has made us painfully aware that human rights, while individual rights, cannot be protected effectively at an individual level only. They need effective and inclusive systems, accessible to everyone and built on a robust sense of solidarity. This is especially true for social rights – which are often, however, still treated as an afterthought. It is exactly this nonchalance towards the right to health and its essential social determinants in the past that proved lethal in 2020.

---

1 D. Mijatović, Council of Europe Commissioner for Human Rights, 'The impact of COVID-19 on human rights and how to move forward', Speech, 10.12.2020, available at www.coe.int/en/web/commissioner/speeches, last accessed 14.07.2021.

2 D. Mijatović, Council of Europe Commissioner for Human Rights, 'Protecting the right to health through inclusive and resilient health care for all', Issue Paper, February 2021, available at www.coe.int/en/web/commissioner/issue-papers, last accessed 14.07.2021.

Even before the pandemic struck, health data demonstrated that disparities in access to preventive health care and treatment, based on gender, minority or socioeconomic background, were common across Europe.[3] Overall, the less advantaged in European societies have been experiencing worse health outcomes and reduced life expectancy. Alarmingly, the health gaps between socioeconomic groups have been increasing with age, demonstrating the shortcomings of European health and social care systems long before COVID-19. Yet the pandemic made more visible the painful truth of inequality that still afflicts our societies.

Following the 2008 financial crisis, many European states enacted austerity measures. These resulted in reduced public health financing and contributed to significant gaps in health services coverage. Austerity, as a general rule, strongly affects inclusivity, hitting the marginalised and vulnerable the hardest, with those on lower or fixed incomes, including older persons, children and persons with disabilities, suffering the most. Gaps in public health coverage lead to out-of-pocket payments and result in affordability problems as well as non-recourse or delayed recourse to health care, which can have disastrous consequences for both individual and public health. In the long term, it often leads to an increase in health expenditures. In many European countries, the pandemic tragically exposed the pre-existing weaknesses of health and social care systems that had been strained by years of austerity, economic difficulties and neglect. In some, past austerity measures heightened the need for early and particularly stringent lockdowns, which further limited access to non-COVID-related health care, severely restricted the enjoyment of other rights and had significant effects on mental health.

The right to health requires inclusive prevention, treatment and rehabilitation services for all, leaving no one behind and ensuring that structural inequalities are not magnified over time but pre-empted and addressed. Sustained efforts must be made to assure free access to high-quality health care for all, guided by the needs of patients rather than profit and regardless of gender, nationality, religion or socioeconomic status.[4] This is a complex but not an impossible task, involving in many European countries public and private actors working interdependently.

Moreover, the right to health cannot be addressed independently from the other social rights. In addition to inclusive and resilient health care systems that are based on strong primary care and universal health coverage, four essential

---

3 World Health Organization (WHO) 'Healthy, prosperous lives for all: the European Health Equity Status Report', 2019, available at www.euro.who.int/en/publications/abstracts/health-equity-status-report-2019, last accessed 14.07.2021.

4 Parliamentary Assembly of the Council of Europe (PACE) 'Lessons for the future for an effective and rights-based response to the COVID-19 pandemic', Resolution 2329(2020), June 2020, available at www.assembly.coe.int/nw/xml/XRef/Xref-XML2HTML-EN.asp?fileid=28676, last accessed 14.07.2021.

social determinants for the right to health for all have been determined: income security and social protection; adequate living conditions including housing; education; and decent labour and employment conditions. Remarkably, the WHO argued in 2019 that the most cost-effective means of closing the health divide in Europe would be the increased investment in housing and community amenities.[5] But unfortunately, affordable housing remains in short supply in Europe, and the overall average spending by governments on social housing has been decreasing over the last decade – while the number of homeless persons, including homeless children, has increased significantly.[6]

2020 dispelled all doubts. Health and social policymaking must be comprehensive, gender-sensitive and coherent. It must integrate economic, social and environmental governance dimensions at all levels of the process, based on participatory and rights-based budgeting. To ensure the best attainable standard of physical and mental health for all, we need a skilled health and social care workforce, adequate public financing and, crucially, effective leadership and governance. In addition, sustained efforts must be made to enhance equality and dignity for patients, promote transparency and accountability in relevant decision-making, and develop adequate health communication policies. It is also crucial that Council of Europe Member States ensure equitable global distribution of medical products and vaccines in all countries, rich or poor, invest in gender-inclusive bio-medical and pharmaceutical research that adequately addresses the health needs of men, women and children and adopt a 'One Health' approach in public health preparedness and global health security.

However, COVID-19 has not only been a health crisis. While the socioeconomic impact of the pandemic varies from state to state across Europe, large redundancies have made unemployment surge in all of them, prompting the risk that poverty will become an even greater challenge over the coming years. Social and economic rights support civil and political rights – and vice versa – as people who are forced to spend all their time trying to find ways to survive are prevented from taking part in public life and exercising their civil and political rights. But still today, the common perception lingers that social rights are a luxury – not important human rights obligations with immediate effect, whose non-observance has dire consequences not only at individual level but also for society as a whole. Their protection and equal enjoyment must therefore become a priority for all Council of Europe Member States.

Amid the pandemic's disastrous effects on multiple aspects of human rights protection across the globe, there is consensus in one area: children and young people have been particularly hard hit. While – thus far at least – they have

---

5 WHO (2019) 'Health status report', *supra* note 3.

6 D. Mijatović, Council of Europe Commissioner for Human Rights, 'The right to affordable housing: Europe's neglected duty', Human Rights Comment, 23.01.2020, available at www.coe.int/en/web/commissioner/blog-2020, last accessed 14.07.2021.

largely been spared from the direct health effects of COVID-19, the crisis has had a disproportionate, profound impact on their wellbeing. Virus containment measures have deprived them more than other groups of their usual routines, cutting them off from their social structures and support networks. During successive lockdowns, children across Europe have faced isolation, depression and a marked increase in domestic violence and abuse. OECD research revealed that young people's mental health has significantly declined since the onset of the COVID-19 crisis and remains higher than pre-crisis levels.[7] In addition, school closures – lasting many months in some European countries – have dramatically affected children's access to education and, in some cases, to healthy food. With schooling diminished to online learning models, the pre-existing digital divide has disproportionately limited the learning opportunities of children from less affluent families, further compounding inequality in European societies.

The pandemic has also exposed again the entrenched patterns of gender inequality across Europe. This is evident in the workplace, where deep-rooted societal attitudes keep women in a subordinate role, in the steady consistency of violence against women and in the increasing attempts to limit women's sexual and reproductive health and rights. Cases of domestic violence have increased exponentially across Europe during the lockdowns. Despite measures adopted by some governments to counter this alarming development, much remains to be done. This is especially so amid renewed attempts by ultra-conservative movements across Europe to undermine the Istanbul Convention and the progress made previously in the fight against gender-based violence. Under the pretext of defending family values and traditions, misrepresentations of the Convention continue to be disseminated, often hiding a misogynist and homophobic agenda. To those opponents, it is worth repeating: it is not a treaty combating domestic violence that destroys families, but rather, domestic violence itself.[8] LGBTI rights have also been under sustained attack in 2020, with a visible rise in hateful rhetoric, targeted stigmatisation and the propagation of homophobic narratives by public officials in some Member States.[9]

In 2020, we have witnessed substantial regression in other areas of human rights, as well. Of central concern is the worrying erosion of the rule of law in

---

7 Organisation for Economic Co-operation and Development (OECD) 'Supporting young people's mental health through the COVID-19 crisis', 12.05.2021, available at https://www.oecd.org/coronavirus/policy-responses/supporting-young-people-s-mental-health-through-the-covid-19-crisis-84e143e5/#section-d1e16, last accessed 14.07.2021.

8 D. Mijatović, Council of Europe Commissioner for Human Rights, 'European treaty against women's violence "saves lives"', Opinion, 11.05.2021, available at www.coe.int/en/web/commissioner/opinion-articles, last accessed 14.07.2021.

9 D. Mijatović, Council of Europe Commissioner for Human Rights, 'Pride vs. indignity: political manipulation of homophobia and transphobia in Europe', Human Rights Comment, 16.08.2021, available at www.coe.int/en/web/commissioner/blog-2021, last accessed 27.08.2021.

many Council of Europe Member States. The pandemic has been used by some governments as a welcome pretext to exploit fears and stifle dissent. Emergency legislation, often adopted without sunset clauses, has disproportionately restricted the exercise of rights, risking long-term consequences for human rights and the rule of law. In some Member States, the rights to information and media freedom have been particularly affected, curbing the most precious antidote against fear and distrust during times of crisis: the public's access to reliable and timely information and the possibility to freely exchange opinions. Measures restricting freedom of movement and freedom of assembly have been used to undercut the ability of human rights defenders and civil society to act in defence of human rights and aid the most vulnerable, with harsh and physical attacks against journalists and human rights defenders being particularly alarming. In addition, sustained attempts have been made to undermine the independence and impartiality of the judiciary and hamper the effectiveness of national human rights structures. European countries' failure to protect refugees and migrants trying to reach Europe via the Mediterranean has continued to cause thousands of avoidable deaths.

Clearly – and as also reflected by the range of serious challenges analysed in this book – Europe is thus facing multiple human rights crises in parallel. Crisis situations are always enormous tests for societies, for individuals, for communities and for governance, and they are times when human rights, democratic values and the rule of law become especially important. Thankfully, we have the European Convention on Human Rights and its protection system and a multitude of other ground-breaking legal tools to help us meet today's challenges. For decades, human rights have been instrumental in protecting individuals from state abuse and paving the way for major societal changes. They have served as benchmark and inspiration for institutions, human rights activists and countless individuals alike who pursued dignity, equality and justice throughout challenging times. Without them, we would doubtlessly be in a much worse situation.

State authorities must show renewed vigour today in implementing their human rights obligations and stand by the principles on which the Council of Europe was built. One lesson of 2020 is that societies are only as strong and resilient as their weakest members. The equal enjoyment of all human rights, including social and economic rights such as access to health care, housing and education for all, must be emphasised and robustly fought for, even if it takes an increase in public spending.

It is furthermore essential that we become more inclusive in the way we defend human rights. We must not only talk *about* but also *with* the victims of human rights violations, and we must listen to them carefully. Meaningful participation plainly leads to better outcomes. We have painfully learned in 2020 that decisions that are going to affect patients, women, school children or the health care work force are better taken in close consultation with representatives of these groups.[10] Lastly, it is imperative that cooperation and multilateralism be strengthened. The human rights challenges of today are too grave and too vast to be tackled at the national level only. We need international consultation and close collaboration to effectively address global challenges such as migration, the environment and current and future health crises. But we also need cooperation at the national level between government, civil society, independent institutions, media, community leaders and the private sector to ensure that human rights play a central role in public policymaking and in everyday life.

Dunja Mijatović
Council of Europe Commissioner for Human Rights

---

10 D. Mijatović (2021), 'Protecting the right to health', *supra* note 2.

EDITORS' PREFACE

Dear readers,

When COVID-19 hit the world, policy-makers and governments introduced a wide range of measures in the name of the pandemic. Their necessity might have been easily argued from a public health perspective justifying restrictions on some rights, such as those resulting from the imposition of quarantine or isolation limiting the freedom of movement and/or freedom of assembly. Additionally, as it was an unprecedented crisis, states authorities had to deploy maximum resources to combat the spread of the disease and had to take decisions at speed, which, while being well intended, might inadvertently have had a negative human rights impact. As the pandemic has now been going on for over a year in which the knowledge about the disease has considerably increased and vaccines have turned out to be an effective means to combat it, now seems to be the right moment to reflect on the impacts COVID-19 had on human rights and to assess the proportionality and necessity of state responses to the pandemic in light of human rights. COVID-19 measures disproportionally impacted certain groups of people, marginalised communities and certain individuals in society, exacerbating existing shortcoming in the protection of human rights and raising profound challenges with respect to non-discrimination laws, prevailing structural inequalities and the fragility of the rule of law. In order to ensure a resilient human rights system, there is a need to assess all these issues in order to ensure that in the future, responses to crisis not only pay respect to human rights but are rooted in them.

The European Yearbook on Human Rights has always been a platform for young and renowned scholars to raise, address and discuss important and topical human rights issues. It does not come as a big surprise, thus, that the 2021 EYHR is a special edition dedicated to 'Human Rights in Times of a Pandemic'. When selecting the final contributions, we, the editorial team, endeavored to cover a wide variety of topics, and we are proud to provide our readers with such a rich and intensive corpus of materials which clearly draws attention to important human rights aspects of the pandemic and contributes to the wider debate on state discretion in times of emergencies.

The 2021 EYHR is opened by a foreword by Dunja Mijatović, the Council of Europe Commissioner for Human Rights. In the last two years, Dunja Mijatović has constantly raised the need to find a human rights-based approach to the pandemic, particularly highlighting the importance of economic, social and cultural rights. We are therefore very grateful that she agreed to contribute to this year's edition, providing us with her insights and approaches to human rights in times of a pandemic.

Shifting to the international level, we are proud that Volker Türk, the Assistant Secretary-General for Strategic Coordination of the United Nations, opens our thematic section with a contribution on the responses by the UN to the pandemic, seen from a human rights perspective ('Early Lessons Learnt from the COVID-19 Pandemic and the United Nations Response').

Following the contribution by Volker Türk, the Yearbook moves to address the human rights impacts of the pandemic and states responses to it. In the first two contributions, important moral and philosophical questions raised by the pandemic are discussed. Accordingly, Laura Palazzani in her contribution 'The Pandemic and the Ethical Dilemma of Limited Resources: Who to Treat?' dives deep into the dilemma on how to distribute scarce resources in health care during emergency situations. The relationship between the state and its citizens, the bond between them and the mutual trust has been considerably stressed in the last years. Carinne Elion-Valter, in her contribution 'Social Contract in Public and Corporate Governance: Metaphor or New Morality?', addresses whether there is a need and potential for a new social contract between the state and civil society involving new actors, such as corporate businesses.

The human rights implications of the pandemic and the interplay between emergency situations and human rights is commonly understood in terms of negative human rights obligations and the interference of the state in human rights. However, Silvia Venier in her contribution 'Positive Obligations to Protect against Epidemic Outbreaks under Human Rights Law' takes a different perspective, focusing on states' positive human rights obligations as duties to take active steps to protect in all phases of the emergency cycle.

Moving to immediate COVID-19 induced interferences with human rights, Christina Binder and Adam Drnovsky in their contribution on 'Elections in Times of COVID-19: A Human Rights Perspective' analyse how democratic principles surrounding free and fair elections increasingly eroded during the pandemic. The concern for the rule of law is also at the heart of the contribution 'The Effects of COVID-19 on the EU Approach on the Rule of Law: Implications for the Commission and European Parliament' by Pietro de Perini, Paolo De Stefani and Marco Mascia, assessing whether the EU institutions have stepped up their efforts to protect the rule of law in Member States when the pandemic exposed the fragility of European values, including the rule of law.

Institutional responses to the pandemic are also subject to analysis in three further contributions: Heidi Suorsa asks whether the pandemic might have created a window of opportunity for the European Union to push for and finally create a European Health Union ('Creating a European Health Union in Times of COVID-19: A Trajectory Towards a Fundamental Right to Health Care?'). As the pandemic, the spread of the disease and its impact have also been connected to the environment and especially air pollution, Chiara Scissa in her contribution 'The Right to a Healthy Environment as an EU Normative Response to COVID-19: A Theoretical Framework' questions whether the pandemic might not help the right to a healthy environment to have more consideration and momentum. Lastly, Signe Andreasen Lysgaard and Jonas Grimheden in their contribution on 'The EU Sustainable Finance Agenda: A Strengthened Case for Human Rights in Times of COVID-19' assess the contributions of the taxonomy sector to creating social sustainability.

The next contributions deal with the human rights of particular vulnerable groups during the pandemic. Dragana Stöckel and Marina Pantelić dedicate their contribution to the difficult balance needed to protect the lives of people in long-term care facilities and respect their human rights to family life and freedom of movement ('Human Rights of Residents in Long-Term Care Facilities During COVID-19: Saving Lives at the Cost of Deprivation of Rights?'). Andrea Broderick and Silvia Favalli argue for increased efforts related to the transition from institutional care to community living of persons with disabilities. In institutional settings, the pandemic has not only resulted in increased risks of isolation and exploitation, but has also caused a disproportionate number of deaths amongst inhabitants of residential institutions and group homes, which fuels claims to increase efforts for different forms of living ('The Transition from Institutional Care to Community Living in the EU: Lessons Learned in the Shadows of the COVID-19 Pandemic').

Migration and asylum remain high on the political agenda despite – or because of – the pandemic. The contribution by Aphrodite Papachristodoulou on 'Migrants at Sea Amid the Coronavirus Pandemic: The Perfect Pretext for Endorsing *à la carte* Respect for Human Rights' is the first of three contributions dealing with the rights of migrants during the pandemic. While Papachristodoulou focuses on the rights of migrants intercepted and rescued at sea and subsequently detained under COVID-19 directives, Alan Desmond argues that the pandemic has been instrumentalised by states to maintain the restrictive approaches to migration which we have seen in particular since 2015/2016. ('The European Approach to Irregular Migration in Pandemic Times: The More Things Change, the More they Stay the Same?'). Elspeth Guild, Kathryn Allinson and Nicolette Busuttil subsequently assess whether the Global Compacts for Refugees and Migrants added to the protection of the rights of migrants in times of the pandemic ('Implementing the UN Global Compacts for Refugees and Migrants in Times of Pandemic: A View from the EUMS').

When Carinne Elion-Valter, in her contribution in the beginning of the Yearbook, raised the question of the need to discuss a new social contract involving big companies, tech companies have been clearly part of her considerations. These have played a central role during the pandemic, by assisting states, individuals, businesses and other entities to get through not only the public health crisis, but also a socio-economic one. The need to discuss their powers and human rights responsibilities is addressed by Sabrina Rau in her contribution on 'Technology Companies' Due Diligence and the Responsibility to Respect Amid COVID-19: What are Proportionate Means where there is Power and Reliance?'.

The thematic section on COVID-19 and human rights is brought to a close with a case study on 'Serbia's Compliance with Article 2(1) of the International Covenant on Economic, Social and Cultural Rights in Times of the COVID-19 Pandemic: Pandemic or Endemic?' by Danilo Ćurčić and Vlada Šahović, prescinding the need to protect economic and social rights.

The second part of the EYHR 2021 deals with other human rights developments in Europe and beyond, aside from the pandemic. It opens with a contribution by Claire Methven O'Brien on 'Business and Human Rights in Europe 2011–2021: A Decade in Review'. The need to strengthen corporate responsibilities is also subject to analysis in the contribution by Virginie Rouas on 'Towards Mandatory Human Rights Due Diligence in the European Union? Opportunities and Challenges for Corporate Accountability'.

A fairly new instrument adopted by the EU allowing for interventions against serious human rights abuses occurring beyond the Union's borders by adopting targeted sanctions is the Global Human Rights Sanctions Regime (GHRSR), which is analysed by Carmelo Danisi in his contribution on 'The European Union's Global Human Rights Sanctions Regime and the "Role Responsibility" of International Organisations'.

And lastly, Cristina Pugnale and Mathilde Bénard shed light on 'National Human Rights Institutions: An Emerging Human Rights Actor in The European Union'.

Courts play a crucial role in the protection of human rights in Europe and beyond. As it does every year, the EYHR includes a section on the relevant jurisprudence by the European Courts in the field of human rights. This year the jurisprudence part is opened by a contribution by Eirik Holmøyvik on 'The Right to an Effective (and Judicial) Examination of Election Complaints', which analyses recent developments in the case law of the ECtHR related to election complaints as essential guarantees of free and fair elections. Subsequently, Lorenzo Acconciamessa analyses relevant judgments of the ECtHR, while Christian Breitler and Martin Traussnigg focus on the relevant jurisprudence of the European Court of Justice.

The EYHR has always aimed to provide insights in the practical field of human rights. This year's edition is thus completed by a short contribution by Markus Möstl and Wanda Tiefenbacher from the UNESCO International Centre for the Promotion of Human Rights at the Local and Regional Levels on their efforts to promote human rights at the local level.

The pandemic brought about a number of changes for all of us. One positive change concerns the composition of the editorial team of the EYHR. The European Training and Research Centre on Human Rights and Democracy of the University of Graz (UNI-ETC), the Austrian Human Rights Institute of the University of Salzburg and the Global Campus of Human Rights Venice, which have acted as institutional bases from the outset, have been joined in 2021 by the Vienna Forum for Democracy and Human Rights. We would like to thank all our authors and reviewers, who bore the burden of another year of COVID-19 restrictions and still managed to submit all the contributions on time, allowing for a punctual publication of the EYHR. We would furthermore like to thank the Global Campus of Human Rights for its financial support, which makes this publication possible. Many thanks also go to Agnes Romanin for her excellent work and support. And lastly, particular thanks go to Ann-Christin Maak-Scherpe, Ahmed Hegazi and the wonderful Rebecca Moffat from Intersentia for their constant support, their availability and their flexibility during the entire publication process.

Graz, Salzburg, Venice, Vienna – August 2021
Philip Czech, Lisa Heschl, Karin Lukas,
Manfred Nowak and Gerd Oberleitner

CONTENTS

LIST OF ABBREVIATIONS

ACHR	American Convention on Human Rights
ADR	Alternative Dispute Resolution
AG	Advocate General
AI	Artificial Intelligence
ARSIWA	(Draft) Articles on the Responsibility of States for Internationally Wrongful Acts
ASGS	Annual Sustainable Growth Strategy
ATS	Alien Tort Statute
A&M	Asylum and Migration
BHR	Business and Human Rights
BID	Bail for Immigration Detainees
CCPR	Committee on Civil and Political Rights (Human Rights Committee)
CDDH	Steering Committee for Human Rights' (*Comité directeur pour les droits de l'homme*)
CEAS	Common European Asylum System
CEDAW	Convention/Committee on the Elimination of Discrimination against Women
CERD	UN Convention on the Elimination of All Forms of Racial Discrimination
CESCR	Committee on Economic, Social and Cultural Rights
CEU	Central European University
CFR	Charter of Fundamental Rights of the European Union
CILD	Italian Coalition for Civil Liberties and Rights
CJEU	Court of Justice of the European Union
CoE	Council of Europe
COMEST	World Commission for the Ethics of Scientific Knowledge and Technologies
CPR	Common Provisions Regulation
CRC	Convention on the Rights of the Child
CRII	Corona Response Investment Initiatives

CRPD	United Nations Convention on the Rights of People with Disabilities
CSOs	Civil Society Organisations
CSR	Corporate Social Responsibility/Country Specific Recommendations (European Commission)
CSRD	Corporate Sustainability Reporting Directive
CST	Civil Service Tribunal
DALY	Disability Adjusted Life Years
DARIO	Draft Articles on the Responsibility of International Organisations
DH-BIO	Committee on Bioethics of the Council of Europe
DPO	Person with Disabilities
DRR	Disaster Risk Reduction
EASO	European Asylum Support Office
EASPD	European Association of Service Providers for Persons with Disabilities
EAW	European Arrest Warrant
EC	European Commission
ECDC	European Centre for Disease Prevention and Control
ECE	Early Childhood Education
ECHR	European Convention on Human Rights
ECJ	European Court of Justice
ECRE	European Council for Refugees and Exiles
ECSR	European Committee of Social Rights
ECtHR	European Court of Human Rights
ED	Executive Director
EDAP	European Democracy Action Plan
EDPS	European Data Protection Supervisor
EdTech	Education Technology
EEA	European Economic Area/European Environmental Agency
EGC	European General Court
EGE	European Group on Ethics in Science and New Technologies
EHU	European Health Union
EMN	European Migration Network
ENNHRI	European Network of National Human Rights Institutions
EP	European Parliament

EPSR	European Pillar of Social Rights
ERDF	European Regional Development Fund
ERoLM	European Rule of Law Mechanism
ESC	European Social Charter
ESCR	European Committee on Social Rights
ESF	European Social Fund
ESG	Environmental, Social and Governance
ESIF	European Structural and Investment Funds
EU	European Union
EUBI	Emergency Universal Basic Income
EUMS	European Union Member States
EWRS	Early Warning and Response System
FRA	EU Agency for Fundamental Rights
FRO	Fundamental Rights Officer
FRONTEX	European Border and Coast Guard Agency
GA	United Nations General Assembly
GANHRI	Global Alliance of National Human Rights Institutions
GATS	General Agreement on Trade in Services
GC	General Comment, Grand Chamber
GCR	Global Compact on Refugees
GCSA	Group of Chief Scientific Advisors to the European Commission
GDP	Gross Domestic Product
GDPR	General Data Protection Regulation
GHRSR	Global Human Rights Sanctions Regime
HRBA	Human Rights Based Approach
HRC	Human Rights Committee/Human Rights Council
HRDD	Human Rights Due Diligence
HRIAs	Human Rights Impact Assessments
HRVP	High Representative for Foreign Affairs
HRW	Human Rights Watch
IACtHR	Inter-American Court of Human Rights
IBC	International Bioethics Committee
ICC	International Criminal Court/International Chamber of Commerce
ICCPR	International Covenant on Civil and Political Rights
ICESCR	International Covenant on Economic Social and Cultural Rights

ICJ	International Court of Justice
IHR	International Health Regulation
IHRL	International Human Rights Law
ILC	International Law Commission
ILO	International Labour Organization
IMO	International Maritime Organization
IOM	International Organization for Migration
IPCR	Integrated Political Crisis Response
LGBT+/I	Lesbian, Gay, Bisexual, Transgender/Transsexual plus/ Intersexual
LIBE	Committee on Civil Liberties, Justice and Home Affairs
LTCF	Long-term Care Facility
MC	Marrakesh Compact
MFF	Multiannual Financial Framework
MICS	Multiple Indicator Cluster Survey
MNE	Multinational Enterprise
MS	Member State
NAP	National Action Plan
NATO	North Atlantic Treaty Organization
NGO(s)	Non-governmental Organization(s)
NHRI	National Human Rights Institution
NVT	New Voting Technologies
ODIHR	Office for Democratic Institutions and Human Rights
OECD	Organisation for Economic Co-operation and Development
OHCHR	Office of the United Nations High Commissioner for Human Rights
OLP	Ordinary Legislative Procedure
OSCE	Organization for Security and Co-operation in Europe
PHEIC	Public Health Emergency of International Concern
PM	Particular Matter
QALY	Quality Adjusted Life Years
QMV	Qualified Majority Voting
RAMM	Regulation on Migration and Asylum Management
RBC	Responsible Business Conduct Working Group
RDR	Ranking Digital Rights
RoL	Rule of Law

RtP	Responsibility to Protect
SAR	Search and Rescue
SCA	Sub-Committee on Accreditation
SDGs	Sustainable Development Goals
SME	Small and Medium-Sized Enterprises
SOLAS	International Convention for the Safety of Life at Sea
SRSG	UN Special Representative of the Secretary-General (on the issue of human rights and transnational corporations and other business enterprises)
TCN	Third-Country Nationals
TEU	Treaty on European Union
TFEU	Treaty on the Functioning of the European Union
UDHR	Universal Declaration of Human Rights
UK	United Kingdom
UN	United Nations
UNCLOS	United Nations Convention on the Law of the Sea
UNCRPD	United Nations Convention on the Rights of Persons with Disabilities
UNESCO	United Nations Educational, Scientific and Cultural Organization
UNFCCC	UN Framework Convention on Climate Change
UNGA	United Nations General Assembly
UNGPs	United Nations Guiding Principles on Business and Human Rights
UNHCR	United Nations High Commissioner for Refugees
UNICEF	United Nations Children's Fund
UNWG	UN Working Group (on the issue of human rights and transnational corporations and other business enterprises)
US(A)	United States of America
VCLT	1969 Vienna Convention on the Law of Treaties
WG	Working Group on issues of human rights and transnational corporations and other business enterprises
WHA	World Health Assembly
WHO	World Health Organization

LIST OF CONTRIBUTORS

Lorenzo ACCONCIAMESSA
Lorenzo Acconciamessa is a PhD candidate in 'Human Rights: Evolution, Protection and Limits' at the University of Palermo, Italy, in partnership with the Department of International and European Law of the *École Doctorale de Droit de la Sorbonne, Université Paris 1, Panthéon-Sorbonne*. His research project deals with the balancing of principles technique in the case law of international courts and tribunals. More generally, his research fields are international human rights law, with special emphasis on the international protection of vulnerable individuals, the interpretation of international law and international procedural law. He is a Teaching Assistant of Public and Private International Law, International Human Rights Law, the Law of International Arbitration and Transnational Commercial Law at the Catholic University of Milan, Italy, where he obtained a Master's Degree in Law in 2019. He is the Content Manager of 'RAVEL – Repository of Documents of the Law and Practice Concerning the International Protection of Adults', a project of the Catholic University of Milan. He also works as a trainee lawyer.

Kathryn ALLINSON
Kathryn Allinson is a legal scholar researching in the field of state responsibility, human rights and migration. Her PhD on 'Establishing responsibility for causing displacement: An inquiry into the role of "Displacing Third States"' was awarded in January 2021 from Queen Mary University of London. She is a Lecturer in Law at the University of Bristol and Researcher on the Horizon 2020 PROTECT project. In this role she has contributed to a number of commentaries on the Global Compact on Migration, as well as publishing widely on the topic and producing a handbook for legal practitioners working in the UK. She is also the Managing Editor of the peer-reviewed journal *The International Community Law Review*.

Mathilde BÉNARD
Mathilde Bénard holds a BA in Law and an MA in European Studies, as well as an MA in Human Rights and Democratisation. She was granted the Global Campus of Human Rights Fellowship at the EU Delegation to the United Nations in Geneva, during which she worked for six months in the human rights section. She then joined the European Network of National Human Rights Institutions (ENNHRI)

in Brussels, to work on rule of law and economic and social rights for a year. In 2021 she started to collaborate with ENNHRI as an external consultant on rule of law matters.

Christina BINDER

Christina Binder holds the Chair for International Law and International Human Rights Law at the Bundeswehr University Munich since April 2017. Before, she was University Professor of International Law at the Department of European, International and Comparative Law at the University of Vienna and Deputy Director of the interdisciplinary Research Centre 'Human Rights'. She is member of the ILA Committee on Human Rights in Times of Emergency. Christina is member of the Executive Board and former Vice-President of the European Society of International Law (ESIL) and member of the Council of the Global Campus for Human Rights since 2019. Christina also served as legal and electoral expert for EU and OSCE/ODIHR election observation and assessment missions in several countries. She likewise acts as electoral expert for the Council of Europe Congress of Local and Regional Authorities.

Christian BREITLER

Christian Breitler is a Research and Teaching Assistant at the Institute of European Law at the University of Graz. Prior to that, he was a member of the Legal Service of the Austrian Foreign Ministry ('Office of the Legal Adviser', 'Völkerrechtsbüro'). His research interests include EU fundamental rights law, EU external relations law and the EU system of judicial protection.

Andrea BRODERICK

Andrea Broderick is an Assistant Professor at Maastricht University, having held a Marie Skłodowska-Curie scholarship to complete her PhD on international and comparative disability equality law. Andrea is the Dutch Director of the European Master's Programme in Human Rights and Democratisation, Venice. In addition, Andrea is a qualified lawyer. Andrea has published widely in peer-reviewed journals and edited books, and has written reports for the European Commission and Council of Europe. She has an interlinked research agenda in the fields of economic, social and cultural rights, including the rights to health and (inclusive) education; international and European disability and equality law; technology and human rights; and the European Court of Human Rights. She received the Edmond Hustinx Prize for Science in 2018. Andrea co-authored the first textbook on international and European disability law (Cambridge University Press, 2019) and the first Research Handbook on EU Disability Law (Edward Elgar, 2020). She has been invited as a senior expert in projects including European Disability Expertise, EU-CITZEN and PROLOG.

Nicolette BUSUTTIL

Nicolette Busuttil is a PhD candidate in the Department of Law, Queen Mary University of London where she researches states' fundamental rights obligations under EU law towards migrants with disabilities, particularly those with mental healthcare needs, in light of the UN Convention on the Rights of Persons with Disabilities. Nicolette is a Visiting Lecturer in International and European Refugee Law at the University of Westminster and was previously a Senior Teaching Fellow in EU Law at SOAS University of London.

Danilo ĆURČIĆ

Danilo Ćurčić attained an LLB from the Faculty of Law of the University of Belgrade, as well as an LLM in Economic, Social and Cultural Rights from the University of Essex. He is currently an Atlantic Fellow for Social and Economic Equity at the London School of Economics. He is the Programme Coordinator of the A 11 – Initiative for Economic and Social Rights, a Belgrade-based human rights NGO.

Philip CZECH

Philip Czech holds a JD and a PhD degree. Since 2002 he has been a Researcher at the Austrian Institute for Human Rights, which became a department of the University of Salzburg in 2014. He is editor of the 'Newsletter Menschenrechte', a periodical reporting in German on the current case law of the European Court of Human Rights. He is mainly engaged with publishing and teaching in the field of fundamental rights, especially with the case law of the ECtHR and its transposition in Austria. Further main fields of interest are asylum and migration law, the freedom of reproductive choice and family law as well as human rights in the penitentiary system.

Carmelo DANISI

Carmelo Danisi is Adjunct Professor and Research Fellow in Public International Law at the University of Bologna (Italy) and Visiting Research Fellow at the University of Sussex (UK). He collaborates with the Global Campus of Human Rights (ERMA programme) and the School of Advanced Studies of the University of London (MA in Refugee Protection). He was Endeavour Research Fellow at the Australian National University working on the principle of the best interests of the child in the context of migration (2015) and Research Fellow at the University of Sussex on International and European Refugee Law (2016–2020), where he was a member of the ERC-funded SOGICA project's research team. He is the author of a number of publications in the field of international human rights law, especially in the context of the ECHR and EU frameworks.

Pietro DE PERINI

Pietro de Perini, PhD in International Politics (City, University of London), is a Research Fellow at the University of Padova where he teaches Human Rights in International Politics. He is the Co-Editor-in-Chief of the *Italian Yearbook of Human Rights* (Bruxelles, Peter Lang), the Managing Editor of *Peace Human Rights Governance* (Padova University Press) and Associate Editor of the *International Journal of Human Rights* (London, Routledge).

Paolo DE STEFANI

Paolo De Stefani is Lecturer in International Law of Human Rights at the University of Padova, Vice-Coordinator of the International Joint Doctorate in Human Rights, Society and Multi-level Governance, National Director for Italy of the European master's programme in Human Rights and Democratisation and Editor-in-Chief of the *Italian Yearbook of Human Rights* (Bruxelles, Peter Lang).

Alan DESMOND

Alan Desmond has been a Lecturer in Law at the University of Leicester since September 2016. He is a member of the University's Migration, Mobility and Citizenship Network (MMCN). He has published widely on the topic of international migration and migrants' rights in leading international journals. Prior to Leicester, he taught at third-level institutions in Ireland, Italy and Poland. He has been a Visiting Researcher at the University of Warsaw in Poland, Yaşar University in Turkey, and Harvard Law School and UCLA School of Law in the US. He is Deputy Editor of the *Journal of Immigration, Asylum and Nationality Law.*

Adam DRNOVSKY

Adam Drnovsky is Election Observation Officer and currently also Co-Secretary of the Governance Committee at the Congress of Local and Regional Authorities of the Council of Europe in Strasbourg. He has observed a number of elections both in his current position in the Council of Europe as well as with the OSCE Office for Democratic Institutions and Human Rights (ODIHR). He holds MA degrees in Political Science from Masaryk University in Brno and in Human Rights and Democratisation from the Global Campus of Human Rights in Venice. He is also pursuing a PhD in International Human Rights Law at the Bundeswehr University Munich. His research interest centres around political science and international human rights law perspectives of various election-related topics.

Carinne ELION-VALTER

Carinne Elion-Valter is Assistant Professor at the Department of General Jurisprudence of Radboud University Nijmegen, the Netherlands. She holds a PhD in Law and Literature (Tilburg University). Her research is located on the crossroads of legal theory, political theory and literary theory with a special interest in the cultural and epistemological factors contributing to the legitimacy of rule of law and democracy. Literary texts are an important source for understanding questions of law and jurisprudence. Recent themes she dealt with are law and empathy, philosophy of recognition and legitimacy, Tocqueville's appeal to religion, quality of legislation, hope and the utopian dimensions of liberal philosophy. In line with her political activities and master in notarial law, she also reflects on issues of human rights in public governance and corporate law.

Silvia FAVALLI
Silvia Favalli is Post-Doctoral Research Fellow in international law at the Department of Political and Social Sciences of the University of Pavia (Italy). She is Principal Investigator of the research project 'RISID – Realising the rIght to Social Inclusion for persons with Disabilities through new tools of smart communication and sharing knowledge: from international to local effectiveness', financed by Fondazione Cariplo (February 2020-January 2023) and developed at the University of Pavia. She holds a PhD in Public Law, Criminal and International Justice from the Department of Law of the University of Pavia. She is the author of several articles and contributions covering various topics of public international law, human rights law, international disability law and policy, with a focus on access to justice for vulnerable groups in international law.

Jonas GRIMHEDEN
Jonas Grimheden was, at the time of writing the contribution to this Yearbook, a member of the EU Platform on Sustainable Finance on behalf of the European Union Agency for Fundamental Rights. Currently he is leading the independent fundamental rights monitoring of the European Border and Coast Guard Agency (Frontex). Since 2009 Dr. Grimheden has been an Associate Professor (*Docent*) at the Law Faculty of Lund University, Sweden.

Elspeth GUILD
Elspeth Guild is Jean Monnet Professor *ad personam* at the Queen Mary University of London, UK, as well as at the Radboud University Nijmegen, the Netherlands. Her interests and expertise lie primarily in the area of EU law – in particular, EU Justice and Home Affairs, including immigration, asylum, border controls, criminal law and police and judicial cooperation in criminal matters. She also researches EU privacy and data protection law and the nexus with human rights. Professor Guild provides regular advice to the European Parliament, the European Commission, the Council of Europe and other European and international organisations, such as the UNHCR, on the free movement of persons, migration and asylum. Professor Guild is also Co-Chair of the European Sub Committee, Immigration Law Practitioners Association, the UK legal profession's voice on immigration and asylum matters.

Lisa HESCHL
Lisa Heschl is a Post-Doctoral Research and Teaching Fellow at the European Training and Research Centre for Human Rights and Democracy at the University of Graz (UNI-ETC). She received her PhD in law from the University of Graz and holds a European Master's Degree in Human Rights and Democratization (EMA). She has been a Marie Curie Visiting Research Fellow at the University of Deusto, Bilbao and is a Visiting Lecturer at the University Oldenburg and the University of Padua. Her research focuses on the European migration and asylum policy and legislation, the extraterritorial application of international and European refugee and human rights law and its relation to European border policies and she has published widely in this field.

Eirik HOLMØYVIK
Eirik Holmøyvik is Professor of Law at the University of Bergen, Norway. He holds a PhD (2011) in law on a thesis on the separation of powers in the Norwegian 1814 constitution. His field of research is constitutional law and history and human rights. He has served as a legal expert for the Norwegian government and parliament on several constitutional and legal reforms and inquiries, including the drafting of a new election code for Norway (2020). Since 2016 he has been substitute member for Norway to the Council of Europe's Venice Commission, acting as rapporteur on numerous opinions on electoral law, constitutional reform, and judicial and democratic institutions. He acted as rapporteur on the Venice Commission's amicus curiae brief to the Grand Chamber of the European Court of Human Rights in the case of *Mugemengango v Belgium*.

Karin LUKAS
Karin Lukas is Senior Researcher and Head of Department at the Ludwig Boltzmann Institute of Human Rights. In January 2011, she joined the European Committee of Social Rights (ECSR) of the Council of Europe, and since 2017 she has been Vice-President of the ECSR. She has been a consultant for various national and international organisations, such as the UN Development Programme and the Austrian Ministry for Foreign Affairs. She has carried out research as well as project-related activities in the field of human rights – in particular women's rights, development cooperation and business. Ms. Lukas holds an LLM in Gender and the Law (American University), an EMA in Human Rights and Democratization (University of Padova) and a PhD in Legal Studies (University of Vienna). She currently works on the issue of labour rights in global production networks and international as well as company-based grievance mechanisms.

Signe Andreasen LYSGAARD
Signe Andreasen Lysgaard is a Strategic Advisor on Business and Human Rights at the Danish Institute for Human Rights. She has a background in Political Science from the University of Copenhagen. Her specialisation lies in human

rights and the financial sector and she serves as an expert advisor to a number of initiatives and bodies including the EU Platform on Sustainable Finance.

Marco MASCIA

Marco Mascia is Associate Professor of International Relations, UNESCO Chair 'Human Rights, Democracy and Peace' and Director of the Master's Degree Programme in Human Rights and Multi-Level Governance at the University of Padova.

Markus MÖSTL

Markus Möstl holds a doctoral degree in law and is a Senior Researcher at the European Training and Research Centre for Human Rights and Democracy, hosting the International Centre for the Promotion of Human Rights at the Local and Regional Levels under the auspices of UNESCO. He is a legal expert within the Austrian national focal point for the multidisciplinary research network of the European Union Agency for Fundamental Rights and Member of the Federal Commission for the Enforcement of Penalties and Measures of the Austrian National Preventive Mechanism.

Manfred NOWAK

Manfred Nowak is Professor of Human Rights and Scientific Director of the Vienna Master of Arts in Human Rights at Vienna University as well as Secretary General of the Global Campus of Human Rights, based in Venice. In 2016, he was appointed Independent Expert leading the UN Global Study on Children Deprived of Liberty, which he presented in October 2019 to the UN General Assembly. His former expert functions include UN expert on enforced disappearances, UN Special Rapporteur on Torture, Judge at the Human Rights Chamber for Bosnia and Herzegovina in Sarajevo and Vice-Chair of the EU Fundamental Rights Agency in Vienna. He was Director of the Netherlands Institute of Human Rights at the University of Utrecht, founder and Co-Director of the Ludwig Boltzmann Institute of Human Rights at the University of Vienna, and has held visiting chairs at the University of Lund, the Graduate Institute in Geneva and at Stanford University.

Claire Methven O'BRIEN

Claire Methven O'Brien is a Baxter Fellow and Lecturer in Law at the University of Dundee's School of Law and a Senior Researcher at the Danish Institute for Human Rights. Her research applies social-legal and governance approaches to the field of business and human rights. She has extensive experience of providing expert advice on business and human rights law and policy to the European Union, Council of Europe, national authorities and business enterprises. Claire's published works include the Council of Europe's *Business and Human Rights: A Handbook for Legal Practitioners* (2019), *Public Procurement and Human Rights. Opportunities, Risks and Dilemmas for the State as Buyer* (Edward Elgar, 2019) and *Research Methods in Human Rights* (2nd edition, forthcoming 2022).

Gerd OBERLEITNER

Gerd Oberleitner is UNESCO Chair in Human Rights and Human Security at the Faculty of Law, University of Graz, and Director of the European Training and Research Centre for Human Rights and Democracy at the University of Graz. He has been a Lecturer at the Centre for the Study of Human Rights of the London School of Economics and Political Science and Visiting Professor at the European Inter-University Centre Venice, the Université du Quebéc à Montréal, the Universities of Ljubljana and Bochum and Rutgers University. He teaches in the Global Campus of Human Rights.

Laura PALAZZANI

Laura Palazzani is Full Professor of Philosophy of law at Lumsa University, Rome; Deputy Vice-Chair of the Italian National Bioethics Committee at the Presidency of the Council of Ministers (since 2008); Italy's official delegate to the Committee on Bioethics DH-BIO, Council of Europe (since 2015); member of the European Group on Ethics in Science and New Technologies, European Commission (2011–2021); and member of the UNESCO International Bioethics Committee (2016–2023).

Marina PANTELIĆ

Marina Pantelić is an Assistant Professor at the University of Belgrade in the Faculty of Political Sciences, Department of Social Policy and Social Work. Her scientific and research fields of interest are Serbian social policy, particulary family-related policies and services, single parenthood and impact of new social risks on social welfare systems. She obtained her PhD degree on the following topic: 'Single-parent families and new social risks – Implications for social policy and practice in Republic of Serbia'.

Aphrodite PAPACHRISTODOULOU

Aphrodite Papachristodoulou is a PhD candidate at the Sutherland School of Law, University College Dublin (UCD), and she has recently (August 2021) submitted her thesis. She has tutored in contract law modules and lectured on international human rights at UCD. Aphrodite's research interests include human rights, refugee and migration law and law of the sea. In particular, her PhD project focuses on the protection of human life at sea against the backdrop of the European migration crisis. Her PhD thesis has been awarded the prestigious NUI E J Phelan Fellowship in International Law (2020). She is also a qualified lawyer and previously worked in legal practice.

Cristina PUGNALE

Cristina Pugnale holds a BA in International Diplomatic Sciences and an MA in Human Rights and Democratisation. Between 2014 and 2018, she has worked as a project assistant within the Italian reception system, as well as in migrants' countries of origin and transit. Since 2019, she has collaborated with the European Network of National Human Rights Institutions (ENNHRI) and the

UNHCR Liaison Office to Frontex. Today, she works for the European Asylum Support Office (EASO) as a Reception Information System Officer.

Sabrina RAU

Sabrina Rau is a Senior Research Officer in the Human Rights, Big Data and Technology (HRBDT) project based at the University of Essex. Her work focuses on rights, regulations and remedies and the role of business in the digital age. Sabrina holds a BA from the University of Toronto in political science and environmental studies and an LLM in international human rights and humanitarian law from the University of Essex.

Virginie ROUAS

Virginie Rouas is a Research Associate at the School of Oriental and African Studies (SOAS), University of London, and a Legal Advisor for Milieu, a multi-disciplinary consultancy providing legal and policy services to EU institutions. She holds a PhD in Law from SOAS and a Master's degree in Environmental Law from the University of Strasbourg (France). Her main areas of expertise include access to justice, business and human rights, global environmental law and EU law and policy.

Vlada ŠAHOVIĆ

Vlada Šahović is an Advocacy Associate at the A 11 – Initiative for Economic and Social Rights. He attained an MA in Communication and Art History from McDaniel College in Budapest, as well a Master's degree (Magister degree) in Sociology from Masaryk University and an LLM in Human Rights Law from the University of Nottingham.

Chiara SCISSA

Chiara Scissa is a PhD student in Law at Sant'Anna School of Advanced Studies in Pisa (Italy). Her research project deals with the recognition and protection of environmental migrants in international and EU law. She is also Visiting Researcher at the Division of Migration, Environment and Climate Change at IOM Regional Office for South-Eastern Europe, Eastern Europe and Central Asia in Vienna (Austria). Previously, she served as Migrant Protection Focal Point at the United Nations Major Group for Children and Youth, and collaborated on migration-related projects with the University of Bologna, the University Milano-Bicocca and the Global Campus of Human Rights. She holds an MA in International Cooperation and the Protection of Human Rights with honours from the University of Bologna.

Dragana STÖCKEL

Dragana Stöckel is an Assistant Professor at the University of Belgrade in the Faculty of Political Science, Department of Social Policy and Social Work. Her research interests are at the intersection of migration and disability studies, focusing particularly on integration and anti-discriminatory and anti-oppressive policies and practices. She obtained her PhD degree in disability studies, with an emphasis on the deinstitutionalisation process and development of community based services for people with intellectual and mental health disabilities in Serbia. She is currently engaged as a Researcher in the project 'Migration, Integration and Governance Research Centre (MIGREC)', funded by the European Union's Horizon 2020 Research & Innovation programme.

Heidi SUORSA

Heidi Suorsa is a Doctoral Researcher at the University of Antwerp, Faculty of Law. Her dissertation, 'Unity in Diversity of European Health Care Systems' explores, from a fundamental human rights perspective, the common values and organisational and financial principles that underpin health care in Europe. Her research interest falls at the intersection of social law and European socio-economic governance. Suorsa holds a degree in International Relations from Leiden University (MA) and a degree in International and European Law from the University of Amsterdam (LLM).

Wanda TIEFENBACHER

Wanda Tiefenbacher is a Researcher in social and political sciences at the International Centre for the Promotion of Human Rights at the Local and Regional Levels under the auspices of UNESCO and is also responsible for public relations and marketing. Her expertise is in civil society processes, political participation and youth engagement. She holds a Master's degree in Political Sociology from the London School of Economics as well as a Master's degree in Social Justice and Community Action from the University of Edinburgh.

Martin TRAUSSNIGG

Martin Traussnigg is a member of the scientific staff at the Constitutional Court of Austria. Prior to that, he was a Research and Teaching Assistant at the Institute of European Law at the University of Graz and a member of the Styrian Provincial Government Legal Service. He is a doctoral candidate at the University of Vienna in the field of constitutional and administrative law.

Volker TÜRK

Volker Türk is Assistant Secretary-General for Strategic Coordination in the Executive Office of the Secretary-General at the United Nations Headquarters in New York. Mr Türk chairs the Deputies Committee and serves as Secretary to the Executive Committee and the Senior Management Group. Prior to joining the Executive Office, he served as Assistant High Commissioner for Protection at the United Nations High Commissioner for Refugees (UNHCR) in Geneva. From April 2008 to September 2009, he was Director for Organizational Development and Management in Geneva and from 2000 to 2004 he was Chief of the Protection Policy and Legal Advice Section in Geneva. Before his time with UNHCR, he worked as a university assistant at the Institute of International Law at the University of Vienna in Austria, where he finished his doctoral thesis on UNHCR and its mandate. From 1985 to 1988, he was Research Assistant at the Institute of Criminal Law at the University of Linz.

Silvia VENIER

Silvia Venier, PhD, is Postdoctoral Researcher at the Institute of Law, Politics, Development at the Scuola Superiore Sant'Anna, Pisa, Italy. She is currently involved in the research project dealing with 'International Obligations related to CBRN risks and status of their implementation in Italy' (http://www.cbrn-italy.it/en, 2020–2023), funded under the prestigious PRIN Programme (research projects of high national interest) of the Italian Ministry of Research and University. Silvia's main area of expertise is international disaster law, with a particular focus on positive obligations under human rights law.

PART I

HUMAN RIGHTS IN TIMES OF A PANDEMIC

EARLY LESSONS LEARNT FROM THE COVID-19 PANDEMIC AND THE UNITED NATIONS RESPONSE

Volker TÜRK

As the world commemorated the 75th anniversary of the United Nations (UN) in 2020, it was hit by one of its most significant global challenges since its inception: a global pandemic triggered by a highly infectious respiratory pathogen, COVID-19. It felt like a harbinger of worse to come if we do not change course consciously, fundamentally and with determination.

The havoc wreaked by the COVID-19 pandemic is striking: over four million lives lost so far; some 131 million people pushed into extreme poverty; soaring unemployment, with the International Labour Organization (ILO) estimating some 114 million jobs lost in 2020 alone;[1] billions of livelihoods vanished overnight; a huge impact on gender equality following a stark increase in violence against women and girls, notably during lockdown situations; and a disproportionate loss of jobs among women, with a significant increase in unequally distributed care responsibilities. Nobody has been spared the direct or indirect consequences of the pandemic, except for a handful of billionaires who have benefited massively.[2]

Its effects have been felt in particular by the most vulnerable in our societies – older people, women and young people under certain circumstances, children, those living with disabilities, indigenous and minority groups, to name a few – as well as by most countries in the Global South.

Years, perhaps even decades of development progress have been reversed, making it both more complex and more urgent to keep the promise of the 2030 Agenda and the Sustainable Development Goals (SDGs).

---

1 ILO, 'ILO Monitor: COVID-19 and the world of work. Seventh edition', estimates and analysis, 25.01.2021, available at https://www.ilo.org/wcmsp5/groups/public/@dgreports/@dcomm/documents/briefingnote/wcms_767028.pdf, last accessed 30.07.2021.

2 OXFAM, 'The Inequality Virus', Oxfam Briefing Paper, 25.01.2021, available at https://policy-practice.oxfam.org/resources/the-inequality-virus-bringing-together-a-world-torn-apart-by-coronavirus-throug-621149/, last accessed 30.07.2021.

All of this put the UN system under huge pressure to rise to the challenge of a comprehensive pandemic response and to keep delivering. The UN has been there for everybody hit by the pandemic – from vulnerable populations in fragile settings to people in high-income countries who are not normally directly impacted by the work of the UN.

The UN managed to ensure business continuity literally overnight throughout its presences in all corners of the world, notably in fragile and conflict-affected countries. The pandemic has increased risks to peace everywhere and has posed an enormous threat to people caught up in conflict, which is why the UN Secretary-General made an immediate appeal for a global ceasefire in March 2020.[3] Unfortunately, this call was only partially heeded by various parties to violent conflicts around the world.

Very early on the decision was taken to make available the UN's widespread supply and logistics network – in particular, to ensure the delivery of vital protective equipment to countries most in need.

The overall UN response was essentially three-pronged: (i) strengthening of health systems and setting up of the Access to COVID-19 Tools (ACT) Accelerator and its COVID-19 Vaccines Global Access (COVAX) facility, which is the only global mechanism to ensure the distribution of vaccines to every country; (ii) humanitarian response in over 60 countries; and (iii) socio-economic recovery.

Through its various activities and operations on the ground, the UN supported some 160 countries in addressing the manifold impacts of the pandemic. More specifically, UN Country Teams rolled out 121 immediate socio-economic response plans covering 139 countries. More than three billion US dollars were repurposed, and an additional two billion was mobilised to prioritise immediate support to at-risk groups and those most affected by the crisis. Moreover, the UN helped more than 260 million children to access remote learning. Billions of personal protective equipment (PPE) items, other medical supplies and, eventually, over 152 million vaccine doses were shipped to over 180 countries.[4]

In an interesting development, the UN system also managed to make available its huge data set and expertise in a wide variety of areas by issuing 24 Secretary-General COVID-19 policy briefs on specific themes, population groups and regions.[5] These policy briefs were in effect a call to action to Member States and others, to learn from the mistakes of the pandemic and take effective

---

3 UN, 'Now is the Time for a Collective New Push for Peace and Reconciliation', appeal of António Guterres, 23.03.2020, available at https://www.un.org/en/globalceasefire, last accessed 30.07.2021.

4 The vaccines were shipped to 137 COVAX-participating countries. See GAVI, 'Covax Vaccine Roll-Out: Country Updates', available at https://www.gavi.org/covax-vaccine-roll-out, last accessed 30.07.2021.

5 UN Secretary-General, 'Policy Briefs', available at https://www.un.org/en/coronavirus/un-secretary-general, last accessed 30.07.2021.

action to address the fragilities and inequalities that COVID-19 has exposed. They were well received both by Member States, civil society partners and other stakeholders, providing important inspiration to policy choices at the national level.

One of the first policy briefs was dedicated to the human rights dimension of the crisis,[6] making it clear that human rights are at the centre of shaping the pandemic response, both for the public health emergency and the broader impact on people's lives and livelihoods. By its very nature, human rights put people at the centre and, importantly, focus our attention on who is suffering most, why and what can be done about it. The focus on human rights and a people-centred approach was a direct consequence and early manifestation of the Secretary-General's Call to Action for Human Rights,[7] which he launched at the Human Rights Council in Geneva in February 2020.[8]

The human rights policy brief essentially conveyed six messages: (i) a human rights lens on the COVID-19 response ensures better outcomes for everyone; (ii) health responses should be sensitive to unintended socio-economic impacts; (iii) a threat to one is a threat to all – do not discriminate or leave anyone behind and show international solidarity; (iv) inform people and be transparent for more impact; (v) emergency measures must be necessary, reasonable, time-bound and proportionate; and (vi) a recovery that respects human rights will get us closer to the SGDs and a better world.

Learning the lessons from the disproportionate impact of the pandemic on different segments of the population and countries is extremely important, from a human rights perspective. The following interlocking observations are intended to contribute to this crucial reflection process.

First, the pandemic has made everyone realise that all is connected and interdependent. The virus does not know borders or recognise nationality, and nor do its effects. They are all trans-boundary. The pandemic has also had the effect of connecting the Global North and the Global South in a different manner – with a vulnerability that is shared everywhere. This speaks directly to the universality of human rights as a base to address challenges of this nature.

Second, it became clear early on that existing global frameworks, such as the human rights framework and the SDGs – with their emphasis on universal

---

6 UN, 'Covid-19 and Human Rights. We are all in this together', report, April 2020, available at https://www.un.org/sites/un2.un.org/files/un_policy_brief_on_human_rights_and_covid_23_april_2020.pdf, last accessed 30.07.2021.

7 UN, 'Secretary-General's Call to Action for Human Rights', 2020, available at un.org/en/content/action-for-human-rights/index.shtml, last accessed 30.07.2021.

8 UN Secretary-General, 'Secretary-General's remarks to the UN Human Rights Council: "The Highest Aspiration: A Call to Action for Human Rights" [as delivered] – scroll down for all English', 2020, available at https://www.un.org/sg/en/content/sg/statement/2020-02-24/secretary-generals-remarks-the-un-human-rights-council-%E2%80%9Cthe-highest-aspiration-call-action-for-human-rights-delivered-scroll-down-for-all-english, last accessed 30.07.2021.

health coverage and their focus on livelihoods, education and social protection – were validated. Those countries, companies, cities, communities and individuals that had embraced an SDG and human rights outlook were faring much better in tackling the various facets of the crisis. This is yet another manifestation of the indivisibility of human rights and their adaptability to changing circumstances and emergency situations. It is equally a demonstration that we need to implement what has often been painstakingly thought through and agreed.

Third, beyond war zones, the pandemic is exposing and amplifying inequalities of all kinds. Based on the realisation that we are all interdependent – how the actions taken at home can resonate far beyond the borders of our communities and countries – we have been confronted with the stark realities and unimaginable choices that so many people face in zones of conflict or instability around the world. They help us to ask ourselves the difficult questions about where responsibilities lie for the making and unmaking of crises and inequalities, and how time and again we see what happens when segments of a population are marginalised, excluded, vilified and stigmatised – or simply ignored. Addressing inequalities, at the national and the global level, understanding the needs and aspirations of people and involving them in decisions that affect them is an important lesson to be gained and a key tenet of human rights in practice.

Fourth, it is clear that investment in strategic foresight, prevention and preparedness in relation to global risks is not a luxury but an absolute necessity. The crisis has also revealed weaknesses in the way public services are delivered, including unequal access to them. Similarly, it will be critical to invest in transforming core public systems, such as health services and universal health coverage, quality education, social protection and guarantees of decent work, with a shift towards more sustainability.

Fifth, the UN has argued that the socio-economic response will need to be human-centred, green and sustainable, making fiscal stimulus work for the most vulnerable and ensuring the recovery goes hand-in-hand with climate action.[9] When we recover, we must be able to bequeath to future generations a planet that is not on the brink of global disaster, by dint of the triple planetary crisis, artificial intelligence or deep-rooted inequalities that perpetuate conflict and violence. It is therefore key to consider the long term whilst tackling the short term. The human rights framework helps us to develop such strategies for the future.

Sixth, the pandemic has made clear (yet again) that we are all in this together and that no country can beat it alone. The COVID-19 crisis has therefore revealed the critical importance of international cooperation and multilateralism. In some areas, such as international financing solidarity and vaccine equity, massive

[9] UN, 'A UN framework for the immediate socio-economic response to COVID-19', report, April 2020, available at https://www.un.org/sites/un2.un.org/files/un_framework_report_on_covid-19.pdf, last accessed 30.07.2021.

shortcomings have been exposed, including from a broader human rights perspective. But in others, such as tackling the socio-economic impacts on the ground, we have seen the enormous potential of international cooperation for development and the resilience of people.

Looking ahead, the UN Secretary-General issued the so-called Common Agenda report in September 2021,[10] requested by the UN General Assembly in the UN75 Declaration.[11] This document constitutes the first major report of the UN that reflects on the future of multilateralism while heeding the lessons from the COVID-19 pandemic. It provides a rich analysis of the current state of affairs, describing the inflection point in history that we are facing: breakdown or breakthrough scenarios, depending on the leadership and choices we make. Importantly, the report sets forth a number of concrete proposals on the way forward in response to the UN75 Declaration, both more generically and in response to the 12 commitments contained therein.

The report essentially revolves around a reset of solidarity within societies, between them and in relation to future generations. It centres on renewing the social contract at country level and on crafting governance arrangements for the future through a better understanding of global public goods. The actions proposed are urgent, transformative and fill critical gaps, firmly underpinned by human rights. They neither supersede nor reopen existing agreements or the SDGs, but rather, seek to accelerate their implementation. This has to be the moment where we choose a positive path rather than a future of perpetual crisis.

---

10 UN Secretary-General, 'Our Common Agenda – Report of the Secretary-General', September 2021, available at https://www.un.org/en/content/common-agenda-report/assets/pdf/Common_Agenda_Report_English.pdf, last accessed 13.09.2021.

11 UN General Assembly, *Resolution adopted by the General Assembly on 21 September 2020*, UN Doc A/RES/75/1, 28.09.2020.

THE PANDEMIC AND THE ETHICAL DILEMMA OF LIMITED RESOURCES

Who to Treat?

Laura Palazzani

ABSTRACT

This contribution discusses different ethical perspectives on the issue of distribution of scarce resources in health care. While in an ideal situation with sufficient availability of resources for everyone, the problem of their distribution does not exist, in fact in the context of a pandemic the distribution of scarce resources reveals itself in a dramatic and urgent way. Concerning this issue, there is agreement on the fact that distribution should be 'fair', according to the shared meaning of justice as 'not to harm others' and to 'give each his own'. However, within the pluralist discussion there are different ways of conceiving justice on a theoretical level and applying it on a concrete level. This contribution examines classical bioethical theories that are reappearing in the discussion today – in different levels of intensity, or in different formulations – and this in the light of the international and national ethical guidelines of scientific societies of intensivists and recommendations of Committees for Bioethics, on national, European and international levels, on the distribution of resources during the COVID-19 pandemic.

1. INTRODUCTION

An element that immediately emerged and is still emerging in the second wave of the pandemic, in all the countries of the world affected by the pandemic (as a national, European, global problem), is the scarcity of the available health care resources (drugs, technologies, personnel, beds in intensive care and now vaccines). The issue of the distribution of health resources is certainly not a new topic in bioethics. For some time, medical ethics has raised the problem at different levels and in different areas. The problem lies in the 'macro-distribution' of resources, that is, the decisions taken in the context of health policies in the broad sense (how much to invest in health and in which sectors as a priority, compared to other investments). These decisions are shaped differently in the various countries of the world, in different political, economic and social contexts. It is also a problem of 'micro-distribution', that is, of decisions that health care facilities and doctors have to make when resources are limited in relation to the amount of patients' requests so that a selection of patients by priority of access is required.

Hence, when faced with the COVID-19-pandemic, the problem at the centre of bioethical debate is the allocation of scarce health care resources. In an ideal situation with sufficient availability of resources for everyone, the problem does not exist, but reality shows us, inexorably, the inevitability of the problem. Think of medicine in scenarios of war and disaster medicine, access for those waiting for organ transplants, the definition of priorities in the 'daily' management of emergency departments, hospitalisations, the use of expensive drugs or technologies.

The COVID-19 pandemic makes the existence of the problem evident in a dramatic and urgent way. On the one hand, the rapid and exponential growth of the infection (the high percentage of patients requiring hospitalisation, access to and even prolonged stay in intensive care units with the use of assisted ventilation, in the 'waves' that we are constantly monitoring), and on the other hand, the limits of the resources, which expose the alarming and dramatic possibility of such choices. All possible efforts are being made to expand distributable resources to avoid being faced with the tragic decision of whom to treat and whom not to treat: by increasing the number of beds in intensive care, transforming and setting up new wards, transferring patients to other facilities, buying necessary technologies, increasing staff, providing new facilities, urging citizens to be responsible in their behaviour to avoid getting sick and transmitting the infection and now also implementing vaccinations.

But if and when one is faced with the choice of whom to include and whom to exclude from hospitalisation, from access to intensive care or ventilation, is it possible to choose? And, on what basis does one choose? These are the main questions which arise. The 'random lottery' or draw as a criterion for solving the distribution dilemma seems unacceptable, even if, at times, given the impossibility of making a decision, it would seem to be the only possible solution.[1] The problem of allocating resources in health care is bound to remain

[1] The story '*The lottery in Babylon*' by J.L. Borges speaks of a society in which benefits and burdens are distributed by a periodic lottery: the extravagance of the story comes from the

unavoidably open. The task of bioethics in this regard is not to solve it, but only to indicate and justify the ethical criteria of reference on an inevitably abstract level with respect to the concreteness of the dramatic situation of those who are in the front line, the physicians and nurses. There is agreement on the fact that distribution should be 'fair', according to the shared meaning of justice as 'not to harm others' and to 'give each his own'. Within the pluralist discussion, however, there are different ways of conceiving of justice on a theoretical level and applying it on a concrete level.

2. THE LIBERAL THEORY

The theory of liberalism, starting from individualistic anthropology, interprets justice as the protection of self-determination. 'Not to harm' others assumes the meaning of not preventing, hindering or restricting the freedom of others, putting a strong emphasis therefore on commutative justice, which is limited to controlling the carrying out of exchanges, transactions and contracts between free individuals, owning property. 'Giving each his own' takes on the meaning of attributing resources to each individual according to his/her will, merits, abilities, the contribution he/she provides to society and free initiative.[2]

This perspective justifies on the level of health policies the minimisation of the intervention of the state, limited to protecting individuals from violence, theft and fraud, controlling the correctness of exchanges, with a prevalence of privatisation and the maximisation of the free market and market competition in the initiatives of free individuals.

The argument that is at the basis of the liberal theory is the consideration according to which nobody is responsible for natural and social inequalities. The results of the 'natural lottery' (or the unforeseeable changes in the fate of an individual due to natural forces, illnesses or natural damage) and the 'social lottery' (or the unforeseen changes due to social actions) are 'unlucky', not unjust. It follows that society is not forced to compensate the differences or to make up for damage due to natural causes or social circumstances. There is no 'direct obligation' to help the needy and compensate the weak. At the most one can 'sympathise' or have a philanthropic, charitable and empathetic benevolent attitude towards those who are more emarginated. But the principle of

fact that random selection does not take into account actions, merit, skills, needs or anything else. Only in some cases of unsolvable dilemmas, where there is no justification whatever the rational choice, can the fate and lottery criterion appear to be the only 'right' one. D. Dickenson, 'Is Efficiency Ethical? Resource Issues in Health Care', in B. Almond (ed.), *Introducing Applied Ethics*, Blackwell, Oxford 1995, pp. 229–246.

2 M. Charlesworth, *Bioethics in a Liberal Society*, Cambridge University Press, Cambridge 1993; T.H. Engelhardt, *Foundations of Bioethics*, Oxford University Press, New York 1996.

self-determination remains steadfast, by which the need of others must not encroach upon individual freedom, forcing sacrifices and limitations on it.

According to this theory, the individual has no legal entitlement to treatment and health care in the free market of private assistance: the rights of autonomy of individuals prevail over social obligations of beneficence. In the choice regarding patient selection, the rich are prioritised over the poor, individuals who hold important social positions over the unemployed, indigent or marginalised, those who are more autonomous over those who are less or no longer so. It is an economistic approach, according to which the selection of patients for treatment is based on individual free choice and the ability to pay ('the richest first'), as a requirement for participating in the free market.

Still present on the level of theoretical debate, this theory is not sparsely mentioned in the context of the discussion on the COVID-19 pandemic, and even the health systems of the countries inspired by this model have sought and are still seeking solutions to protect public health, due to the inevitable inequalities that the liberal model entails on the medical and socio-economic level. In some respects, the policies based on natural 'herd immunity' follows this approach, which accepts the exposure to the risks of COVID-19 of the most vulnerable people with the aim of immunising the whole community, with overall benefits and lower economic costs compared to lockdown policies, which are meant to protect first of all health and lives against the spread of the infection. This approach has been criticised both at scientific and ethical levels: on the scientific level since 'natural herd immunity' is neither proven nor subject of a broad consensus between scientists, and on the ethical level because of the foreseeable negative consequences for individuals and the inevitable increase in inequalities (because vulnerable people will inevitably die).

The German Ethics Council, in the opinion 'Solidarity and Responsibility during the Coronavirus Crisis, Ad Hoc Recommendation',[3] explicitly addresses the issue by distancing itself from the liberal model, in the specific context of COVID-19: 'Given the characteristics of the new virus, the distribution of risks, and the expectations of the impact on the health system, particularly on the hospital system, the laissez-faire strategy seems irresponsible'. The 'Recommendations on Improving Pandemic Preparedness and Management' (November 2020),[4]

---

3 German Ethics Council, 'Solidarity and Responsibility during the Coronavirus Crisis, Ad Hoc Recommendation', recommendation, 27.03.2020, available at https://www.ethikrat.org/fileadmin/Publikationen/Ad-hoc-Empfehlungen/englisch/recommendation-coronavirus-crisis.pdf, last accessed 06.05.2021.

4 European Commission, 'Recommendations on Improving Pandemic Preparedness and Management', 04.11.2020, available at https://ec.europa.eu/info/sites/info/files/research_and_innovation/groups/sam/joint_recommendations_on_pandemic_preparedness_and_management_v3.pdf, last accessed 06.05.2021.

written by the Group of Chief Scientific Advisors to the European Commission (GCSA), the European Group on Ethics in Science and New Technologies (EGE), together with the special advisor to the President of the European Commission, outlines the limits of herd immunity, considered to be a non-ethical concept.[5]

The United Nations Educational, Scientific and Cultural Organization (UNESCO) International Bioethics Committee (IBC) also expressed its opinion in this direction, which – together with the World Commission for the Ethics of Scientific Knowledge and Technologies (COMEST) in the document 'Statement on Covid-19: Ethical Considerations from a Global Perspective'[6] – affirmed a position against the notion of 'herd immunity', believing that it:

> needs a cautious ethical review, considering the impact on the number of lives exposed to threats and unsustainable medical conditions given the lack of availability of intensive care facilities even in developed countries. In a context of uncertainty with possible devastating negative consequences for the health and life of individuals and communities, it makes policies based on this notion 'unethical practices' because they act in an individualistic direction, against the effort to build a common global response to the pandemic.

The WHO declared 'the free circulation of the virus is immoral' (October, 2020).[7]

The liberal model is therefore the object of criticism for the human and social implications that it brings, in particular towards the weakest, the poor and the marginalised, who are exposed to risks and excluded from access to care. This model does not adequately take into account the social effects of individual actions, in the false hope that an 'invisible hand' will solve problems, accentuating subjective egoism, the cold logic of calculation and indifference to needs, denying the constitutive dimension of social responsibility towards oneself and responsibility and solidarity towards others.

---

5 The National Committees for Bioethics have the task to discuss on an interdisciplinary and pluralistic level emerging questions of bioethics in order to give advice to governments (with opinions). During pandemics the role of these committees has been very important as they interface with governments offering the ethical reasons for some political choices. In this sense it is interesting to notice that some of these committees (which include also members with liberal visions) approved opinions against natural herd immunity, considering it a 'non ethical' practice.

6 UNESCO International Bioethics Committee (IBC) and the World Commission for the Ethics of Scientific Knowledge and Technologies (COMEST), 'Statement on Covid-19: Ethical Considerations from a Global Perspective', 26.03.2020, available at https://www.unescobiochair.org/2020/03/31/statement-on-covid-19-ethical-considerations-from-a-global-perspective-ibccomest/, last accessed 06.05.2021.

7 WHO, 'Guidance for Managing Ethical Issues In Infectious Disease Outbreaks', 2016, available at https://apps.who.int/iris/handle/10665/250580, last accessed 06.05.2021.

3. THE UTILITARIAN THEORY

The theory of utilitarianism, in the search for the equal consideration of interests and the maximisation of benefits and minimisation of costs for the greatest number of individuals (that is, the best balance of benefits over costs, financial and human, for all concerned, according to the parameter of efficacy and efficiency), proposes a sharing of the resources so as to reach the best, most pragmatic result possible in relation to social productivity, with the same expenditure.[8] From this standpoint, justice takes on, in the commutative configuration, the meaning of not harming another person, where 'harming' means causing suffering or decreasing quality of life of individuals having interests. Collective utilitarianism identifies distributive justice with the necessity to give the greatest possible number of individuals the satisfaction of their interests to the greatest possible extent.

At the macro-allocation level, the financing of sectors that permit the increase of social wellbeing is privileged and the areas of health care that make it possible to recuperate the patient's activity in terms of efficiency and convenience are given priority. This would make possible a sort of economic return of investment, or of the costs of the treatment. Such objectives are pursued also at the cost of sacrificing those who are not yet able to or who are no longer able to produce for society, with the consequent marginalisation of the weaker subjects. At a micro-allocation level, this theory justifies the priority of access to patients having the greatest probability of returning to a productive life, with the consequent obligation of not treating those patients with no or low probability of recovery, in terms of quantity of number of years to live and quality of life. This theory is at the centre of the bioethical discussion in relation to the COVID-19 pandemic. This view applies the formula '*quality adjusted life years*' (QALY), that is, the number of years of life taking into account the quality and costs, for the greatest number of individuals. The allocation of limited resources in terms of access to care is deemed to be correct when it achieves, at the same expense, the best possible pragmatic result in relation to convenience and efficiency, therefore combining the number of patients who survive, the years of life left to live, with quality.

In this perspective, the right to access treatment and health care is recognised only to those who have a life 'worthy' of being lived in relation to the achievement or likelihood of achieving an expected number of years of life remaining and a certain standard of quality of life.[9] It is, however, a weak right, which is subject

---

[8] P. Singer and J. Harris, 'Qualifying the Value of Life', (1987) 13(3), *Journal of Medical Ethics*, pp. 117–123; J. Harris, *The Value of Life*, Routledge, London 1995; P. Singer, *Practical Ethics*, Cambridge University Press, Cambridge 1993.

[9] This approach, balanced with a call to equity, also in WHO (2020), 'Statement on Covid-19', *supra* note 7: 'total number of lives saved, the total number of life years saved, or the total number of quality-adjusted life years saved'.

to the maximisation of overall profit and may not allow for access to health care for the weaker social groups of our society, with the consequent marginalisation of the elderly, the disabled and the poor. It is in this context that the debate on so-called 'ageism', that is, discrimination based on age, emerges: the utilitarian approach is an approach that inevitably, explicitly or implicitly, correlates the maximum benefit obtainable with the prioritisation of younger people over older people, who have a shorter remaining life expectancy (in terms of the number of years left to live as well as the presumed level of quality of life) and, moreover, they have already lived years of life. For the same reason, 'able-ism' is introduced, as discrimination because of disability ('disability adjusted life years', DALY), as well as discrimination of poor people – as poverty is correlated to lower conditions of health and quality of life expectancy.

Along this line, some scientific societies of medicine, above all in the area of intensivist medicine, have expressed their views.[10] The Sociedad Española de Medicina Intensiva Crítica y Unidades Coronarias and the Sociedad Española de Enfermería Intensiva y Unidades Coronarias in the document 'Plan de Contingencia para los Servicios de Medicina Intensiva frente a la pandemic COVID-19' made an explicit reference to limit of treatments for elderly people (including age) and people with cognitive disabilities.[11] The same direction is also pursued in the document 'Ethical Principles concerning Proportionality of Critical Care during the 2020 COVID-19 Pandemic in Belgium', advice by the Belgian Society of Intensive Care Medicine,[12] where it is underlined that 'in elderly patients, cognitive impairment should be assessed and taken into account'. The Schweizerische Gesellschaft fur Intensivmedizin published the document 'Covid-19 Pandemie: Triage von intensivmedizinischen Behandlungen bei Ressourcenknappheit' (24 March, revised 4 November 2020),[13] where age

---

10 Scientific societies in medicine are organisations, generally recognised by high health institutions on a national level, which gather all the physicians in that area (for example: intensivists or paediatricians, etc.), and they discuss and approve guidelines on specific topics in order to give orientations in the practice. They are not ethical committees, but they may intervene also on ethical issues, as happened in this case.

11 Sociedad Española de Medicina Intensiva Crítica y Unidades Coronarias (Semicyuc) y Sociedad Española de Enfermería Intensiva y Unidades Coronarias (SEEIUC), 'Plan de Contingencia para los Servicios de Medicina Intensiva frente a la pandemia COVID-19', 2020, available at https://www.semicyuc.org/covid19_files/Plan_de_Contingencia_COVID-19.pdf, last accessed 06.05.2021.

12 Belgian Society of Intensive Care Medicine, 'Ethical principles concerning proportionality of critical care during the 2020 COVID-19 pandemic in Belgium: advice', 2020, available at https://www.zorgneticuro.be/sites/default/files/general/COVID-19-ethical_final_c.cleaned.pdf, last accessed 06.05.2021.

13 Schweizerische Gesellschaft für Intensivmedizin, 'Covid-19 Pandemie: Triage von intensivmedizinischen Behandlungen bei Ressourcenknappheit', 17.12.2020, available at https://www.samw.ch/dam/jcr:14cb0e53-eedb-4089-96dd-b49a1b388994/richtlinien_v3-1_samw_triage_intensivmedizinische_massnahmen_ressourcenknappheit_20201217.pdf, last accessed 14.10.2021.

is considered as a 'stringent criterion' for admission and discontinuation of treatment in triage, also justifying in certain cases the withdrawal of proportionate treatment (i.e. ventilators).

A discussion on this issue emerged in Italy with reference to the document by the Italian Society of Anesthesia Analgesia Resuscitation and Intensive Therapy (SIAARTI), 'Recommendations of Clinical Ethics for Admission to Intensive Treatments and for their Suspension, in Exceptional Conditions of Imbalance' (2020).[14] In the dramatic situation of COVID-19, this approach expresses some criteria for health professionals who are forced to make selective choices, with the aim of relieving them of the burden of responsibility of these decisions. The first point expressed in the document is that there is 'not necessarily a need to follow a criterion for access to intensive care, such as "first come, first served"': in other words, this approach seems to admit the possibility of not allowing a 'present' patient access, leaving open the possibility of treating a later arriving 'future' patient who may have a better prognosis. The second issue concerns the possibility of 'placing an age limit on entry into intensive care', firstly in order to allow access 'to those who have the most chance of survival and secondly to those who can have more years of life saved, with a view to maximising the benefits for the greatest number of people'. It should be acknowledged that the principle of the 'probability of survival' remains primary; however, the anagraphic data is also introduced (number of years of life saved) on equal terms. The document also states 'the presence of comorbidities and functional status should be carefully evaluated, in addition to age', which would seem to make age a primary criterion to which the clinical and prognostic criteria are added. The justification for this choice in the document is explained with reference to the fact that the same resources could be used for a shorter time for a patient in less serious conditions, saving money compared to their being used for elderly and frail patients. While recognising the exceptionality of the current dramatic situation, this approach introduces utilitarian criteria into 'normal' practice.

The criteria of the utilitarian vision are susceptible to a fundamental objection: these are criteria that deny the authentic meaning of justice, which recognises the dignity of every human being recognised as person without making extrinsic distinctions between lives with dignity or without dignity, or lives with greater dignity or lesser dignity, based on conditions regarding quality of life, number of years left to live or productivity. Moreover, the QALY criterion is susceptible to further scientific and philosophical objections: the uncertainty and difficulty

14 Società Italiana di Anestesia, Analgesia, Rianimazione e Terapia Intensiva (SIAARTI), 'Recommendations of Clinical Ethics for Admission to Intensive Treatments and for their Suspension, in Exceptional Conditions of Imbalance', 06.03.2020, available at https://www.fundaciogrifols.org/documents/4662337/1023429220/Italia/a0d1573f-fa74-443d-b5e4-55ce78d08410, last accessed 06.05.2021.

in calculating the probabilistic prediction of the number of years of life left to live; the subjectivity of the way of understanding and living the quality of life (not projectable on others); and the individual variability compared to the generalised 'average' referring to groups of individuals (for example, using age as a selection criterion does not consider the individual physiological variability of individual persons, regardless of age).

4. THE EGALITARIAN AND PERSONALIST THEORY

In bioethics there has been a reaction against the liberal and utilitarian vision applied to distribution of scarce health care resources, as it is incompatible with the shared fundamental value of equality among all human beings. Only the principle of justice based on equality is compatible with human rights, constitutions, deontological codes and the recognition of the fundamental right to health care: it is the minimum ethics in the context of the pluralistic discussion.

One path in this direction is outlined by the theory that echoes the egalitarianism of J. Rawls in the fictitious hypothesis of an 'original position' behind a 'veil of ignorance',[15] that is, if each of us ignored who he/she is (our own age, personal and social condition), we could not but accept the criterion of equality and difference as compensation of inequalities. The theory of social egalitarianism privileges social demands over individual freedom, the collective good over individual good – strengthening distributive justice (over commutative justice) in society, where 'giving each one his own' takes on the egalitarian value of giving 'to each individual equally' and the social value of 'giving according to need'. It is the theory of the 'minimum market' and the 'maximum state'. The maximum intervention from the state is ideally needed, thus reducing the spaces for private free initiative. The state and society must intervene to guarantee minimum standards of health care and assistance as fundamental rights (not giving them away to mere spontaneous and charitable donations). In this sense, individual freedom is subordinate to social ends. This theory maintains that society must take on the responsibility for the inequalities arising from the 'natural lottery' and the 'social lottery'. The natural and social inequalities, in a cooperative society, must be 'corrected', searching for compensation of the differences. In this context, health care and medical assistance are considered basic needs which must be guaranteed to each individual, 'maximising the minimum', or increasing the possibility and the opportunity of access to health care and medical assistance for the most vulnerable. At a micro-allocation level,

---

15 J. Rawls, *A Theory of Justice*, Belknap Press, Cambridge (Mass.) 1971.

an effort is made to guarantee equal access to treatment and an equal opportunity for everyone or a minimum of social security for everyone.[16]

The theorisation of egalitarian access is also supported by other theories, with different arguments. T.L. Beauchamp and J.F. Childress, based on the theorisation of 'principlism' (the application of the principles of autonomy, beneficence, non-maleficence and justice), believe that there is a right to a 'decent minimum of care' and that health care is an aspect of social protection against external threats from which the individual alone cannot protect himself, as in the case of the pandemic.[17]

This position is also shared by the personalist theory, which recognises the ontological primacy of the dignity of the human person.[18] This theory puts at the centre the common good and sociality, considering the intrinsic dignity of every human being and outlining justice as protection of the life of every human being. 'To give everyone their own' means to recognise what is ontologically 'due' to each human being at a personal and at a social level, on the basis of human nature itself. In this sense, 'to give' means to recognise the individual needs through reasoning, not to allocate with an act of subjective will or individual decision. This recognition means considering justice as solidarity and subsidiarity, based on the duty/right to act in view of the common good, and therefore in the obligation to cooperate for the good of society, helping the weakest, defenceless and needy. The criterion of justice, understood in the co-existential standpoint, is outlined in the inseparable consideration of the individual good of every human being and the common good of society. The search for common good takes place through the search for good in individual persons. At the macro-allocation level, this theory proposes sufficient investment in health care, in an inclusive way, leaving no one behind. At the micro-allocation level, this perspective considers that the main criterion of justice can be translated in the primary consideration of the dignity recognised in every human being.

According to the theories based on the principle of equality and non-discrimination, the criteria introduced by individualism, like the priority of the

16 N. Daniels, *Just Health Care: Studies in Philosophy and Health Policy*, Cambridge University Press, New York 1985; J.C. Moskop, 'Rawlsian Justice and a Human Right to Health Care', (1983) 8(4), *Journal of Medicine and Philosophy*, pp. 329–338; R. Green, Health Care and Justice in Contract Theory Perspective, in R. Veatch and R. Branson (eds.), *Ethics and Health Policy*, Ballinger, Cambridge 1976, pp. 111–126; N. Daniels, 'Health Care Needs and Distributive Justice', (1981) 10(2), *Philosophy and Public Affairs*, pp. 146–179; E.J. Emanuel, 'Justice and Managed Care. Four Principles for the Just Allocation of Health Care Resources', (2000) 30(3), *Hastings Center Report*, pp. 8–16.

17 T.L. Beauchamp and J.F. Childress, *Principles of Biomedical Ethics*, Oxford University Press, Oxford 2012; J.F. Childress, *Priorities in Biomedical Ethics*, Westminster Press, Philadelphia 1981.

18 E.D. Pellegrino and D.C. Thomasma, *A Philosophical Basis of Medical Practice*, Oxford University Press, New York 1987; C. Petrini, 'Triage in Public Health Emergencies: Ethical Issues', (2010) 5(2), *Internal Emergencies Medicine*, pp. 137–144.

young person over the elderly one, of the rich over the poor, the person with an important social position over the marginalised, are considered discriminatory. The criteria of utilitarianism, like the advantage of the subject with more probabilities of a happy life over whoever suffers, of the subject who recovers more easily for social productivity and of the subject that costs society less, are discriminatory as well. The criterion of age (or the preference for the less-lived life open to the future with respect to the more-lived life), the criterion of the social and economic role, quality of life, the productive ability or efficiency and the social cost are criteria that arbitrarily establish inequalities and asymmetries among human individuals. These criteria are founded on extrinsic and contingent elements, extra-medical and extra-clinical parameters, which forget, or even deny, the necessary consideration of human nature.

If we examine the problem of the selection of patients for access to care in search of the ethical criterion compatible with respect for dignity and justice, the only criterion is objective medical assessment, case by case, of the clinical condition, urgency, the severity of the illness, the possible presence of other diseases and the presumed prognostic efficacy of the treatment in terms of probable recovery, according to the criteria of proportionality and appropriateness.[19] Any deviation from this logic introduces arbitrary elements of discrimination.[20]

The starting point is the 'principle' recognition that everyone must be treated. If 'in fact' circumstances (such as scarcity of resources) inevitably force one not to be able to cure everyone, but to cure some and not others, the criterion cannot be defined on subjective or social (non-medical) grounds, but should be defined only on objective (medical) grounds, that is, on the basis of the patient's clinical condition. It is clear that scarce resources cannot be misused and wasted, but must be effective, that is, used to save lives. But we must not forget that the needs of every sick person must be placed at the centre. In the case of the pandemic, it should also be remembered that this criterion must be applied to all patients: the selection must not lead to a differentiated treatment between patients with infections and those with other pathologies, since vigilance is ethically due to the continuity of taking care of other patients. Those who are most vulnerable, such as elderly people or people with disabilities and poor people, must not be marginalised by selective logic inspired by individualism or social convenience. However, this does not mean treating 'at any cost' or implementing practices of clinical persistence, which must always be duly suspended when

---

[19] As in general in clinical practice, disproportion or unreasonable obstinacy in treatment (to be considered ineffective, futile and burdensome) is not ethically justifiable.

[20] Within the i-CONSENT project (that received funding from the European Union's Horizon 2020 research and innovation programme under Grant Agreement No 741856) it emerges that: fear and discomfort can compromise the understanding of information by patients; time constraints can reduce the opportunity for physicians to inform patients; but *transparent information* to *vulnerable patients* remains a fundamental requirement in emergency conditions (available at https://i-consentproject.eu/, last accessed 06.07.2021).

disproportionate, ineffective and burdensome, as well as the patient's autonomy of refusal or renunciation of treatments, with the verification of the awareness and full information of the consequences.

Ethics is left with a task: that of justifying and recalling health care professionals to values in their actions, values that must be interpreted and applied in specific contexts, at the 'patient's bedside'. It is at this stage that doctors should be able to consult clinical ethics committees, in order to facilitate discussion and provide support for their decisions, which are often complex to the point of being real 'dilemmas' (such that every choice seems wrong). In some cases there is no time for such consultation or there are no such committees in the facilities themselves, and doctors are left alone in the decisions they have to make. In this sense, the education of physicians (both at the university and/or specialisation) is also a very important mechanism by which to learn ethical theories and principles and to reflect about their interpretation and applications in practice, both in the framework of human rights and the intrinsic values of their profession.

This is the position expressed in many committees for bioethics, which have the institutional role of consultation and advice to politics/governments in decisions. The Comité Consultative National d'Etique (France) in the document 'Enjeux éthiques face à une pandémie' (2020), was the first to express a position on the topics, adhering on the medical criterion.[21] The Nuffield Council on Bioethics of the United Kingdom (UK), in the document 'Ethical Considerations in Responding to the Covid-19 Pandemic' (2020),[22] while focusing mainly on social policy issues, reiterates the need for an 'impartial' criterion for micro-distribution that recognises an equal moral worth to everyone. The Deutsche Ethikrat in Germany in the document 'Solidarity and Responsibility during the Coronavirus Crisis, Ad Hoc Recommendation',[23] – considers the criterion of human dignity to be the only guarantor of equality against all forms of discrimination (gender, ethnic origin, age, social role, disability), stating that any differentiation, direct or indirect, with reference to the protection of life is unacceptable.

---

21 The document incorporates principles outlined in the previous document *Questions éthiques soulevées par une possible pandémie grippale*, 2009. Comité consultative national d'Etique por le sciences de la vie et de la santé, 'Enjeux éthiques face à une pandémie', 2020, available at https://www.ccne-ethique.fr/sites/default/files/reponse_ccne_-_covid-19_def.pdf, last accessed 06.05.2021.

22 Nuffield Council on Bioethics, 'Ethical considerations in responding to the COVID-19 pandemic', 2020, available at https://www.nuffieldbioethics.org/assets/pdfs/Ethical-considerations-in-responding-to-the-COVID-19-pandemic.pdf, last accessed 06.05.2021.

23 German Ethics Council, 'Solidarity and Responsibility during the Coronavirus Crisis, Ad Hoc Recommendation', recommendation, 27.03.2020, available at https://www.ethikrat.org/fileadmin/Publikationen/Ad-hoc-Empfehlungen/englisch/recommendation-coronavirus-crisis.pdf, last accessed 06.05.2021.

In particular, a distinction is made between 'ex ante triage', which can also 'let some patients die' given the scarcity of resources and the factual impossibility of saving them (admitting that no one can be forced to do the impossible) and 'ex post triage', stating that discontinuity of treatment, namely, the suspension of a proportionate treatment, to save another patient by re-assigning resources, is never legitimate. The San Marino Bioethics Committee reiterated for COVID-19 a principle expressed in the document 'Bioethics of catastrophes' (2017) of the 'priority of treatments calculated on the basis of a correct application of triage, respecting all human life, regardless of age, gender, social or ethnic affiliation, ability'. In the document 'Response to the request for an urgent opinion on ethical aspects related to the use of assisted ventilation in patients of all ages with severe disabilities in relation to the Covid-19 pandemic' (16 March 2020),[24] the Committee reiterates that disability can never be an exclusion criterion, based on the principle of equality between every human being regardless of differences.

The Spanish Bioethics Committee, in 'Informe sobre los aspectos bioéticos de la priorizaciòn de recursos sanitarios en él contexto de la crisis del coronavirus' (25 March 2020),[25] takes a similar position, recognising in pandemics the need to maximising benefits, within limited resources, but it considers it a priority to respect the principles of equality and vulnerability. The Bioethics Commission of Austria, in the opinion 'Zum Umgang mit knappen Ressourcen in der Gesundheitsversorgung im Kontext der Covid-19-Pandemie' (March 2020),[26] defines the triage criterion with reference to the clinical and prognostic criterion. The Conselho Nacional de Etica para as Ciencias da Vida in Portugal in the document 'The Public Health Emergency caused by the Covid-19 Pandemics, Relevant Ethical Issues' (April 2020)[27] stresses necessity, effectiveness and proportionality as the criteria for the selection of care priorities. In the document produced by the National Committee of Luxembourg, 'Repères éthiques essentiels lors de l'orientation des patients dans un contexte de limitation des

---

[24] Comitato Sanmarinese di Bioetica, 'Response to the request for an urgent opinion on ethical aspects related to the use of invasive assisted ventilation in patients of all ages with serious disabilities in relation to the Covid-19 pandemic', 16.03.2020, available at http://www.sanita.sm/on-line/home/bioetica/comitato-sammarinese-di-bioetica/documents-in-english.html, last accessed 23.05.2021.

[25] Spanish Bioethics Committee, 'Informe sobre los aspectos bioéticos de la priorización de recursos sanitarios en él contexto de la crisis del coronavirus', 25.03.2020, available at http://assets.comitedebioetica.es/files/documentacion/Informe%20CBE-%20Priorizacion%20de%20recursos%20sanitarios-coronavirus%20CBE.pdf, last accessed 06.05.2021.

[26] Austrian Bioethics Commission, 'Management of scarce resources in healthcare in the context of the COVID-19 pandemic', 2020, available at https://www.bundeskanzleramt.gv.at/dam/jcr:3840b98e-667b-412d-ad5f-95cbcafe27d5/management_scarce.pdf, last accessed 06.05.2021.

[27] Conselho Nacional de Ética para as Ciências da Vida, 'The Public Health Emergency caused by the Covid-19 Pandemics, Relevant Ethical Issues', 2020, available at https://www.who.int/ethics/topics/outbreaks-emergencies/Pos-CNECV-Covid-19-EN.pdf?ua=1, last accessed 06.05.2021.

ressources thérapeutiques disponibles due à la crise pandémique du COVID-19' (31 March 2020),[28] the principle of intangible human dignity is affirmed, to deduce the principles of fairness and justice. The Swedish National Council on Medical Ethics, 'Ethical choices in a pandemic', expresses opinions which are in the same vein.[29] The Department of Health in Ireland, in 'Ethical Considerations Relating to Critical Care in the Context of Covid-19' (2020),[30] takes a view to minimising loss of life and maximising benefit, access for patients on the basis of urgency, severity and with a favourable prognosis.

The Italian Committee for Bioethics, in the COVID-19 opinion 'COVID-19: clinical decision-making in conditions of resource shortage and the "pandemic emergency triage" criterion' (8 April 2020),[31] starting from the constitutional principles (in particular Article 32 on protection of health, Article 2 on duties of solidarity and Article 3 on equality) and by Law 833 (1978), establishing the National Health Service, reaffirms that 'it is always necessary to do everything possible to guarantee all human beings, without exception', respecting 'the principles of justice, equity and solidarity, to offer all people equal opportunities to reach the maximum health potential allowed'. The clinical criterion is considered the most appropriate reference point for the allocation of resources, underlining that 'any other selection criteria defined a priori, such as age, sex, social status and role, belonging ethnicity, disability, responsibility for behaviors that induced the disease, costs, is considered by the Committee to be ethically unacceptable'. With reference to triage in pandemic emergencies, the document specifies the criteria of 'clinical appropriateness', understood as a medical evaluation of the efficacy of the treatment with respect to the clinical need of each individual patient, with reference to the urgency and severity of the onset of the disease and to the

---

28 Commission Nationale D'Éthique (CNE), 'Repères éthiques essentiels lors de l'orientation des patients dans un contexte de limitation des ressources thérapeutiques disponibles due à la crise pandémique du COVID-19', 2020, available at https://cne.public.lu/dam-assets/fr/publications/avis/Prise-de-position-COVID-19.pdf, last accessed 06.05.2021.

29 Swedish National Council on Medical Ethics, 'Ethical choices in a pandemic', 15.05.2020, available at https://smer.se/en/2020/05/15/report-ethical-choices-in-a-pandemic/, last accessed 06.05.2021.

30 Department of Health Ireland, 'Ethical Considerations Relating to Critical Care in the Context of Covid-19', 24.09.2020, available at https://www.gov.ie/en/publication/13ead5-ethical-considerations-relating-to-critical-care-in-the-context-of-c/, last accessed 06.05.2021.

31 Italian Committee for Bioethics, 'Bioethical Guidelines for Equal Access to Healthcare', 2001, available at http://bioetica.governo.it/en/opinions/opinions-responses/bioethical-guidelines-for-equal-access-to-healthcare/, last accessed 06.05.2021; Italian Committee for Bioethics, 'Covid 19: clinical decision-making in conditions of resource shortage and the "pandemic emergency triage" criterion', 08.04.2020, available at http://bioetica.governo.it/media/4008/p136_2020_covid-19-clinical-decision-making-in-conditions-of-resource-shortage-and-the-pandemic-emergency-triage-criterion_en.pdf, last accessed 06.05.2021; Italian Committee for Bioethics, 'Ethics, Health Care System and Resources', 1998, available at http://bioetica.governo.it/en/opinions/opinions-responses/ethics-health-care-system-and-resources/, last accessed 06.05.2021.

prognostic possibility of recovery and the criterion of the 'patient's community', which also includes, in addition to 'physically present' patients, the 'community of patients' (not only COVID-19 patients), allowing for the revision of waiting lists also including patients who have been clinically evaluated and observed, temporarily placed in sub-intensive wards or at home, but who suddenly worsen. A decision and planning, that of triage, which must always avoid the decisions on 'categories of people' but on 'individuals' and their specific needs.

The document 'The Ethical Framework for Health Care Institutions Responding to Novel Coronavirus SARS-CoV-2 (COVID-19) Guidelines for Institutional Ethics Services Responding to COVID-19 Managing Uncertainty, Safeguarding Communities, Guiding Practice of the Hastings Center (2020)'[32] follows a similar train of thought, which recalls the relevance of clinical ethics committees in support of complex decisions and reiterates the principle of equality and equity in the allocation of scarce resources.

The issue was also addressed by international bioethics committees, as the topic is closely connected to fundamental human rights, including the right to the protection of health, expressed in international constitutions and regulations. The Committee on Bioethics of the Council of Europe (DH-BIO) in the 'Statement in the Context of the Covid-19 Crisis' (April 2020),[33] affirms – recalling the basis of the Convention on Human Rights and Biomedicine (1997)[34] – the principle of equal access to care, without discrimination. The European Group on Ethics in Science and New Technologies of the European Commission, in the 'Statement on European Solidarity and the Protection of Fundamental Rights in the Covid-19 Pandemic' (2020),[35] although it does not address the specific problem of resource distribution, outlines the principles of dignity, justice and solidarity.

---

32 Hastings Center, 'The Ethical Framework for Health Care Institutions Responding to Novel Coronavirus SARS-CoV-2 (COVID-19) Guidelines for Institutional Ethics Services Responding to COVID-19 Managing Uncertainty, Safeguarding Communities, Guiding Practice', 2020, available at https://thehastingscenter.org/publications-resources/ethics-resources-on-the-coronavirus/, last accessed 23.05.2021; Kennedy Institute Pellegrino Center for Clinical Bioethics, Georgetown University Medical Center, 'Ethical principles of resource allocation in the event of an overwhelming surge of COVID-19 patients', 2020, available at https://kennedyinstitute.georgetown.edu/wordpress/wpcontent/uploads/2020/04/CovidEthicsPrinciples-Georgetown.pdf, last accessed 21.03.2021.

33 Committee for Bioethics (DH-BIO), 'DH-BIO Statement on human rights considerations relevant to the COVID-19 pandemic', 14.04.2020, available at https://rm.coe.int/inf-2020-2-statement-covid19-e/16809e2785, last accessed 06.07.2021.

34 Council of Europe, Convention for the Protection of Human Rights and Dignity of the Human Being with regard to the Application of Biology and Medicine: Convention on Human Rights and Biomedicine 1997, European Treaty Series (ETS) No. 164.

35 European Group on Ethics in Science and New Technologies (EGE), 'Statement on European Solidarity and the Protection of Fundamental Rights in the Covid-19 Pandemic', 2020, available at https://ec.europa.eu/info/sites/info/files/research_and_innovation/ege/ec_rtd_ege-statement-covid-19.pdf, last accessed 06.05.2021.

The International Bioethics Committee and the World Ethics Committee of Scientific Knowledge and New Technologies of UNESCO in the 'Statement on Covid-19: Ethical Considerations from a Global Perspective' stress that the ethical foundation of macro and micro-allocation must be based on principles of justice, charity and equity; 'In the case of patient selection in the context of scarcity of resources, the clinical need and the effectiveness of the treatment should be of primary consideration'. The reference is to human rights and health protection, Article 14 of the UNESCO Universal Declaration on Bioethics and Human Rights (2005), which states 'the highest attainable standard of health' is a fundamental human right. Vulnerable people 'become even more vulnerable in the period of the pandemic', in particular due to poverty, discrimination, gender, disease, loss of autonomy, age, disability, ethnicity, prison and migration and therefore must be adequately protected in their health needs.

5. LESSONS TO LEARN

It is essential to learn lessons from the crisis, both while the pandemic is ongoing and afterwards, when life has returned to something resembling normality. We have achieved awareness about the relatedness and interconnectedness of all individuals: the need for common values in bioethics in the framework of human rights.

We all know that inequalities already exist, but the challenges raised by COVID-19 tend to worsen them. We need to reduce injustice and try, as far as possible, to promote justice, in the intrinsic meaning of equality (non-discrimination) and equity, in the sense of inclusivity and 'inclusive health', considering that no one should be left behind or excluded and that we need to make every effort to guarantee affordable access for everyone, according to need.

In the pluralistic discussion in bioethics, a convergence emerges in the recognition of the relevance of putting at the centre human dignity, common good and our freedom, but also our responsibility towards the vulnerable. It should be highlighted that in times of pandemic the personalist and egalitarian approach, placing society and community before the individual, responds to the real sense of justice, 'giving to each his own' recognising the objective 'entitlement' that should be recognised to every human being to the protection of health, as an essential value and common good. The duty to act in pursuance of the common good and the obligation to cooperate for the good of society with particular attention to those most in need is the main lesson to be learned from this pandemic.

In a context of scarce resources, health care systems and professionals will need to balance their duty of care towards the individual patient with obligations to the wider population. Explicit and transparent shared ethical guidelines are essential. From the bioethical discussion within committees of bioethics, at national, European and international levels, it emerges that priorities in cases of scarce resources are set consistently on an ethical level only when they respect human dignity and the protection of human rights and fundamental freedoms as enshrined in international normative documents as well as in national constitutions. The principle of equitable access to health care has a very special ethical significance and is considered as the 'minimum ethics'.

This perspective underlines the fundamental link between human rights, equality, responsibility and solidarity, in a time of scarcity and severe public health crisis. It necessitates special efforts to improve access to health care for every individual, and particularly the most vulnerable, who are disadvantaged in accessing health care (such as the elderly, persons with disabilities and the poor). It also requires that in the context of constrained resources, existing disadvantages and inequalities should not continue or even be exacerbated. In this sense, preparedness, cooperation (beyond private competition/interests) and the benefits of sharing of knowledge need to be central starting points for public health in a society threatened by a pandemic, recognising 'health as common good' beyond pluralism and territorial borders, in a universal moral language.

We have a great moral responsibility to learn from the crisis that is currently playing out. This will help us to be better prepared for the next pandemic and to develop frameworks for providing guidance in the face of ethical choices that may have to be made in the future (including about the distribution of vaccines). This applies both nationally and internationally. Ethical analysis is therefore important in both the preparation and response phases. We all have a moral responsibility, during and after an ongoing pandemic, to gather knowledge, support research and learn lessons for the future.

SOCIAL CONTRACT IN PUBLIC AND CORPORATE GOVERNANCE

Metaphor or New Morality?

Carinne ELION-VALTER

ABSTRACT

The term 'social contract' is increasingly present in public and corporate governance discourse relative to social policy, sustainability goals and human rights. For instance, to promote corporate social responsibility (CSR), the call is made for a 'new social contract'. Are these references to the social contract mere slogans or do they express a new ideal and perspective on governance, whether public or corporate? How to qualify this discourse in light of the classic social contract theory and human rights? This contribution compares the calls for a 'new social contract' to the main positions in social contract theory and concludes that these calls express a normative ideal featuring a morality of reciprocity, shared responsibilities and recognition. Other than in some social contract theories, human rights are a core element of this call for a social contract. And while the classic social contract is based on the idea of a bargain, the modern social contract discourse's valuation of recognition and reciprocity reflects values inherent to the notion of the gift and the social contract of hospitality. However, a short analysis of the morality of hospitality shows its potential vulnerability for parasitism. Further research is therefore needed to assess the meaning of this vulnerability for modern social contract discourse in public and private governance.

1. INTRODUCTION

The term 'social contract' is increasingly present in public governance and corporate governance.[1] The discourse presents the social contract primarily as an ideal of shared responsibilities between state and civil society or between big companies and society in the execution of social policy, sustainability goals and human rights. For example, in 2017, Putters presented the term 'social contract' to indicate the desired relationship between government, societal organisations (in his case health organisations, like welfare organisations, hospitals, insurance companies) and citizens in the context of a changing Welfare State.[2] The proposed 'social contract' should ensure the rightful execution of policy goals tied to social rights like proper health care. It is presented as part of a new paradigm of public administration and governance to ensure cooperation and solidarity based on responsibility in the context of complexity and change.

The term also appears in business circles[3] and in legal debate related to company law, as can be illustrated by the following.[4] In the middle of the

---

1 A. Guterres, 'Tackling Inequality: A New Social Contract for a New Era', Nelson Mandela Lecture, 2020, available at https://www.un.org/en/coronavirus/tackling-inequality-new-social-contract-new-era, last accessed 12.07.2021; The New Social Contract Tour, aiming to bring national and local leaders together aimed at bringing a more equitable and liberated future for all, available at http://www.newsocialcontract.org/tour.html, last accessed 29.04.2021; M. Shafik, 'Covid and the climate crisis show why we need a new social contract between old and young', The Guardian, 25.02.2021, available at https://www.theguardian.com/commentisfree/2021/feb/25/covid-climate-crisis-new-social-contract-old-young, last accessed 29.04.2021.

2 K. Putters, '*Was Getekend. Op weg naar een vernieuw sociaal contract in de zorg*', report of University Rotterdam, 2017, p. 7, available at https://www.eur.nl/sites/corporate/files/2017-10/Putters_Oratie_Was_Getekend_170915.pdf, last accessed 12.07.2021.

3 F.I. G. Jakki, 'Five ways companies must redefine social contracts', *EY Bulletin*, available at https://www.ey.com/en_gl/megatrends/five-ways-companies-must-redefine-social-contracts, last accessed 29.04.2021; J. Manyika, A. Madgavkar and T. Tacke et al., 'The Social Contract in the 21st Century', McKinsey Global Institute, 2020, available at https://www.mckinsey.com/~/media/mckinsey/industries/public%20and%20social%20sector/our%20insights/the%20social%20contract%20in%20the%2021st%20century/mgi-the-social-contract-in-the-21st-century-full-report-final.pdf, last accessed 12.07.2021; pleading for overcoming many of today's gaps related to inequality of income and job security, housing, health care and regional differences.

4 J.W. Winter, J.M. de Jongh and J.B.S. Hijink et al., 'Naar een zorgplicht voor bestuurders en commissarissen tot verantwoorde deelname aan het maatschappelijk verkeer', (2020) 86,

COVID-19 crisis, a group of legal scientists specialised in company law argued that companies should be considered as partners in a social contract with society. Instead, big companies like Booking.com and Air France – KLM claimed large amounts of public funds in order to prevent these companies from going bankrupt. The public funding facilitated these companies to offload their entrepreneurial risks to the public domain. Briefly said, the profit is private, the losses are public. In line with developments in other countries, the proposal puts forward that companies, especially large companies, should demonstrate corporate social responsibility (CSR) and commit themselves to the effectuation of social and environmental sustainability goals. These goals are tied to human rights, like the right to a healthy environment, promotion of diversity, combating poverty and respecting participation rights. To this aim, the proposal is to make this social responsibility a formal objective of the company, a societal 'mission', for the execution of which board members should be held accountable. To this end, CSR should be codified in corporate law, stipulating that board members should act responsible in view of societal concerns. The proposal fits into a broader movement of stimulating companies to act in a more responsible way, observing long-term societal and environmental interests.[5] The proposal was inspired by the recently adopted French Loi PACTE, instigating companies to include a societal responsible purpose within their core statutory objective.[6]

1.1. ATTRACTIVE, BUT REALISTIC?

In short, the proposals in public and corporate governance offer the model of a social contract in order to ensure the meeting of social rights, sustainability goals and human rights. They call for responsibility, shared commitment and cooperation. From the perspective of human rights and sustainability, the proposals only seem to deserve full acclaim. However, the calls may also raise

Ondernemingsrecht [Towards a duty of care of directors and supervisory council members for corporate social responsibility, my translation, CEV]; J.M. de Jongh, 'Onderneming en maatschappij: naar een nieuw sociaal contract? De Loi PACTE als voorbeeld', (2020) 80, *Ondernemingsrecht* pp. 439–442.

5 N. Hsieh, 'The Social Contract Model of Corporate Purpose and Responsibility', (2015) 25(4), *Business Ethics Quarterly*, pp. 433–460; J. Kirkup, '*Returning the Favour, A new social contract for business*', report of the Social Market Foundation, 2020, p. 12, available at https://www.smf.co.uk/publications/returning-favour/, last accessed 12.07.2021.

6 Loi PACTE (Plan d'Action pour la Croissance et la Transformation des Entreprises), *JORF* no 0119 du 23 mai 2019, M.D. Repiquet, 'Report from France: Law Pacte 2019: A Successful Modernization of Company Law?' in *European Company Law* (2019) *16/5*, pp. 167–170, C. Bourgeois, X. Hollandts and B. Valiorgue, 'La Loi PACTE: Enjeux et Perspectives pour la Gouvernance des Sociétés Françaises', (2021) 22/23, *Revue Française de Gouvernance d'Entreprise*', pp. 4–29, J.M. de Jongh, 'Onderneming en maatschappij: naar een nieuw sociaal contract?' v. *supra* note 4.

some sceptical questions, of a practical, technical legal and more theoretical nature. The latter ones will be the focus of this contribution.

A critical question could be whether these calls for a social contract are realistic, certainly when viewed in light of earlier neo-liberal public governance approaches. From the 1970s onward, governments tried to counter the heavy bureaucracy, administrative ineffectiveness and inefficiency that resulted from their extensive welfare systems by resorting to a neo-liberal approach focused on efficiency, the so-called new public management (NPM).[7] Governmental obligations were considered as products and services, to be paid for and accounted for financially. Together with horizontalisation and decentralisation of government, this financial and organisational rationality has led to a very dense and complex structure of governmental and semi-governmental institutions, governed by procedures of accountability. It also led to a cutting-down on social security claims. This contributed to feelings of public distrust and diminishing legitimacy of governmental and non-governmental welfare institutions. The public governance calls for a social contract between the state and civil society aim to counter this distrust, to break with the former utilitarianism and to control complexity by appealing to responsibility, solidarity and social justice. However, the recent COVID-19 crisis raises doubts as to whether the idea of a social contract will be strong enough to revolve the existing governance structure. The freedom-limiting COVID-19 measures were instigated by the need to uphold a health care system that suffered cut downs on intensive care (IC) facilities for reasons of cost efficiency. So, the ideal of a social contract based upon solidarity seems attractive and legitimate, but will it be able to stop instrumental reason? Isn't it merely symbolic?

The call for a social contract between 'big companies' and civil society may raise criticism as well. Some of this criticism may be of a technical legal nature. For example, from the perspective of company law, the explicit mentioning of CSR in the board obligations might have negative side effects of enlarging liability claims, which might stifle investments and innovations. I leave this criticism for a more specialised company law debate. Other arguments might be that the implementation of CSR in company law is merely symbolic – certainly since the proposals are phrased in very broad terms. Implementation of CSR in company law might only lead to a practice of window dressing.

Nevertheless, the idea of a social contract is interesting enough to examine its potential implications. What is the theoretical basis of this call for a social

---

7 About NPM and various other philosophies of Public Administration, see E. Ongaro, 'Political Philosophy and public governance: the quest for justification in common good and in social contract arguments and their significance of the debate on the organisation of the public sector', in E. Ongaro, *Philosophy and Public Administration, An Introduction*, Edward Elgar Publishing, Cheltenham 2020, pp. 161–186, specifically p. 176 where NPM is qualified as a loose bundle of philosophies of public administration featured by utilitarian orientation.

contract? How does it relate to classic social contract theory? The questions are justified, since the governance discourse presents the social contract primarily as a normative model for relations of reciprocity and responsibility with regard to societal goals. In classic social contract theory, however, the social contract functions as a theoretical construction to account for and to legitimise (state) authority. It explains and theoretically justifies authority without having prescriptive value per se. Secondly, the modern social contract discourse calls for a morality of shared responsibilities and commitment to further human rights and the general interest. However, in classic social contract theory, the social contract is generally based upon a bargain founded in self-interest.[8] The idea of a bargain supported by self-interest does not seem to chime well with human rights.

1.2. QUESTION AND METHODOLOGY

In short, the calls for a social contract in the context of public and corporate governance seem to be attractive, but may disappoint as being too idealistic, too vague or even theoretically uncertain. The question thus arises as to how this call for a social contract in public and private governance relates to classic social contract theory and to what extent this discourse may be expected to truly further the case of human rights – and if so, what challenges and risks this would imply.

To answer this question, I will first qualify these calls for a social contract in light of the main classic political theoretical social contract positions and their relationship with human rights. In light of the confines of this contribution, I will limit myself to a comparison with the three main positions. The comparison will show that these calls for a social contract differ from the classic theoretical positions by their appeal to a morality of shared responsibility in a context of uncertainty. In order to explore the potential implications of this social contract of uncertainty I will draw a comparison with the concept of hospitality – since, as we will see, there are some interesting similarities. For this, I will draw upon some literary and anthropological insights. Within the limits of this contribution, I cannot be exhaustive. My aim is merely to offer food for thought. Further, my approach will be theoretical and critical, leaving technical legal issues to a more specialised public policy and legal debate. My contention is that the argument of a social contract of shared responsibilities opens up promising perspectives, but also raises some serious questions as to its implications.

[8] The classic theories are frequently indicated with capital letters, 'Social Contract' in contrast with informal uses such as calls that are discussed in this paper. In this paper the difference will be clear from the context.

2. THE NEW SOCIAL CONTRACT IN LIGHT OF CLASSICAL SOCIAL CONTRACT PHILOSOPHY AND ITS RELATION TO HUMAN RIGHTS

For classic social contract theory, a social contract is a construction to account for a political and/or legal order. The contract is hypothetical and is generally not meant as prescriptive. The social contract is held as a cooperative undertaking for mutual benefit. In its horizontal dimension, it is supposed to be closed between citizens regarding an authority or a specific political or social order. In some contexts it also has a vertical dimension. It is then the contract as closed between the people or society on the one hand and the political authority on the other. Social contract theory is broad and multifarious. For our purposes a short survey of the three main positions has to suffice.[9]

2.1. CLASSICAL VISIONS ON THE SOCIAL CONTRACT

According to the *interest-based tradition* (contractarian) going back to Hobbes' *Leviathan*,[10] the contract is based on a rational choice by the agreeing 'parties'.[11] This choice is based upon considerations of 'personal' interest. These interests can be various, such as personal gain, protection of property and safety or the protection of personal views, such as religion. The interest-based vision does not take it as evidence that cooperating parties act out of a common morality. The only thing that binds the cooperating parties is the shared need for protection of personal interests. For this, the parties are willing to moderate their proper interests and hand over some of their interests to a common authority that is deemed to offer this protection. By 'creating' this authority and handing over some of their interests, the parties assume they will be better off than just defending their private interests on their own. In the Hobbesian tradition, the contract has a horizontal and a vertical dimension.[12] Without the authority protecting their

---

9 See generally S. Freeman, 'Social Contract Approaches,' in D. Estlund, *The Oxford Handbook of Political Philosophy*, Oxford University Press, Oxford 2018, pp. 133–152, p. 137 et. seqq.

10 T. Hobbes, *Leviathan*, Penguin Books Harmondsworth/New York 1982, originally 1651, p. 227 et seqq.

11 For an oversight, see A. Cudd and S. Eftekhari, 'Contractarianism', in E.N. Zalta (ed.), *The Stanford Encyclopedia of Philosophy*, Stanford University, Stanford CA, 2018 summer edition, available at https://plato.stanford.edu/entries/contractarianism/, last accessed 29 April 2021. For an interest-based contractarian theory based on economic theory, see e.g. J. Buchanan and G. Tullock, *The Calculus of Consent*, Ann Arbor, The University of Michigan Press, Michigan 1965.

12 Compare: 'I Authorize and give up my Right of Governing my selfe, to this Man (…) on this condition, that thou give up thy Right to him (…)', Hobbes, *Leviathan*, ibid., p. 227.

interests, this state of nature would lead to brutish circumstances, a permanent war of all against all.

A second tradition goes back to Locke. Other than the Hobbesian tradition of an interest-based social contract, the theories standing in the tradition of Locke depart from a moral standpoint and are therefore qualified as contractualist and *right-based* conceptions. The constructed state of nature is based upon the natural law assumption that people have specific rights and are endowed with reason, not just interest-weighing rationality. By reason and awareness of their rights they consent to a social contract that protects and reflects these rights, and they thereby institute the authority to protect and promote these. This morality is self-evident (Locke) or can be deduced from principles of practical reason (Kant). For Locke, Rousseau and Kant, these rights are the right to equal freedom, life and property and the equal capacity to choose entrance in the political community by giving consent to the political authority instituted by the contract.[13] It therefore also has a horizontal and a vertical dimension.

The assumption of well-reasoned consent implies that the Lockean authority must be a *legitimate* authority, thereby underscoring the vertical dimension of the contract. In other words, a political authority is only legitimate and rightful because it can be reasoned that consent to handing over some of one's freedom to it could have been given on a reasoned basis. Locke's social contract theory legitimises a liberal constitution with political powers that can be evaluated upon whether it respects constitutional rights. For Locke, this authority could be a monarchy. For Rousseau, however, the political authority should be taken to embody the general will to make laws for the common good, a republican construction that may even force its laws upon the public to be free. While for Locke, the social contract legitimises the constitutional authority, for Rousseau, it constructs and legitimises simultaneously the democratic authority of the people as embodying the general will. In the Rousseauist position, the horizontal and vertical dimension could be said to be fused.[14]

13 J. Locke, 'Two Treatises of Government', in P. Laslett (ed.), *Two Treaties of Government*, Cambridge University Press, Cambridge 1988, p. 285 et. seqq; for Kant, see primarily: I. Kant, 'Against Hobbes', in I. Kant 'On the Proverb: That may be true in theory, but is of no practical use' in: I. Kant, *Perpetual Peace and other essays on Politics, History and Morals*, trans. T. Humphrey, Hackett Publishing Company, Indianapolis/Cambridge 1983, pp. 61–92, p. 70 et seqq., J.J. Rousseau, 'The Social Contract', in J.M. Dent & Sons (eds.), *The Social Contract and Discourses*, Everyman's Library, London 1973, pp. 175–176.

14 Rousseau speaks of the individual making the contract, 'with himself' and 'bound in a double relation; as a member of the Sovereign', he is bound to the individuals, and as a member of the state, to the Sovereign. J.J. Rousseau, ibid., pp. 175–176

For Rawls, who – due to his moral starting position[15] – also stands in the Lockean rights-based social contract tradition, although in a more limited sense,[16] it is primarily justice that is justified (or theoretically explained) by the social contract. Contrary to the aforementioned thinkers, Rawls' social contract results from a hypothetical situation, conceived as the original position without representing anything like 'natural', in which 'parties' do have rationality to choose, but do not have specific knowledge as to what this state amounts to or what the future holds.[17]

A third tradition consists of the empirical tradition that follows Hume. He did not believe in any social contract construction to justify authority (Hobbes) or to legitimise it as the rightful authority (Locke). The social contract as such never happened.[18] Hume admitted that a social contract may exist in empirical reality and a qualification of a specific situation as one of a social contract thus may help to recognise and explain political and economic practices. In other words, Humean social contract theory explains a certain institutional and societal order by understanding this as based upon a tacit agreement that people mutually agree to on the condition that others agree to it as well. This is not a theoretical justification by deduction from a construction, but a qualification of a situation perceived as empirical reality. The main rationales for people to come to such a tacit agreement may lie in habit, out of fear for disorder caused by the downfall of government or a certain concern for justice out of reflection and of public utility. The norms that are expressed in social practice and may be construed as part of the social contract consist of conventions of justice thought to be in everybody's interest. The Humean tradition stresses the horizontal dimension over the vertical. Due to its conventional and realist character, the Humean position is relativist. Its legitimising and prescriptive force depends on actual practice, not on some theoretical construction from which principles are deduced.

Summing up, the main social contract positions can be distinguished according to their theoretical function. In the Hobbesian and Humean tradition

---

15 I.e. that the contracting parties are morally obliged to accept regulatory social principles, J. Rawls, *A Theory of Justice*, Harvard University Press, Cambridge 1971, pp. 114–115; M. Lessnoff, *Social Contract*, MacMillan, London 1986, p. 134; but the scope and theoretical foundation of this supposed morality is doubted by R. Dworkin, *Taking Rights Seriously*, Harvard University Press, Cambridge 1978, p. 158 et. seqq.

16 I.e. primarily equal respect and concern related to the procedure of stipulating the kind of justice and ensuing political institutions, see Rawls, ibid., p. 118 referring to 'pure procedural justice'; cf. Dworkin, ibid., p. 182.

17 J. Rawls, *A Theory of Justice, revised edition,* The Belknap Press, Cambridge 1999, pp. 11, 102 et. seqq.

18 D. Hume, 'Of the Original Contract', in E.F. Miller (ed.), *Essays Moral, Political, and Literary*, Liberty Fund, Indianapolis 1963 (originally 1741), pp. 465–487. 'In vain, are we asked in what records this charter of our liberties is registered' (p. 468). Authority is not based on consent, but on necessity and custom. Society could not otherwise subsist' (p. 481).

the social contract is a means to explain and account for political authority and, for Hume, the normative practises people agree to. For Locke, the social contract is certainly explanatory, but also prescriptive, as it offers a framework for distinguishing constitutionally fit government from unconstitutional government. For Rawls, the social contract is meant as a justification of an order that meets certain principles of distributive justice.

In short, an analysis of present-day social contract discourse should pay attention to the objective of the discourse (whether it is meant as justification, descriptive or prescriptive), its relation to private or public interest, the kind of agreement that is implied (rationality, reason), the implications of the core dynamics of bargaining and whether it is focused on authority, distributive justice, democracy or something else. Finally, once a social contract is descriptively presented as a conventional agreement, critical scrutiny is needed as to the conventions and normative practises it is said to represent.

2.2. HUMAN RIGHTS IN CLASSICAL SOCIAL CONTRACT THEORY

Before I pursue evaluating the present social contract discourse in public and private governance, it is important to explore the relation between social contract thought and human rights. This relation is not evident, as we will see.

Human rights are generally considered as naturally tied to the human person. They are taken as reflecting universal, a-temporal and inalienable moral rights that are tied to equality of personhood and the human being as such. Compare the recognition of the 'inherent dignity and (...) the equal and inalienable rights of all members of the human family' in the Preamble of the Universal Declaration of Human Rights (UDHR) to which the European Convention of Human Rights (ECHR) refers.[19]

At the same time, human rights are part of a political and legal practice that constitutes the individual as a subject of law and a political subject. As declarations of pre-existing moral rights, human rights treaties create legal entitlements to be directed, first of all, to the state, although this does not exclude other addressees.[20] The state is pivotal for the protection and promotion of human rights. This protection consists of the obligation not to deprive people of their rights, but to protect human rights and to aid in realising these. The

19 R. Cruft, S.M. Liao and M. Renzo, 'The Philosophical Foundations of Human Rights: An Overview', in: R. Cruft, S.M. Liao and M. Renzo (eds.), *Philosophical Foundations of Human Rights*, Oxford University Press, Oxford 2015, pp. 1–41. Reference to the UDHR is made in the Preamble of the ECHR, see echr.coe.int full text p. 5.

20 Due to horizontal effect.

distinction between the classical liberal rights and political rights on the one hand and the social rights on the other is related to this obligation of the state to respect and to aid. Today we may notice an enlargement of entitlements and an extension of the circle of subjects liable for respecting human rights. By way of interpretation and adaptation, these rights have given implications that extend widely the ideas and images they were taken to stand for at the moment of their adoption in treaties and bills of rights.[21]

Human rights seem not to fit very well in the interest-based position of the Hobbesian tradition. Following a moral rights vision, not a contract, but human dignity itself should be taken as the first and final foundation for human rights.[22] Dignity cannot be bargained for – it should be recognised and taken as a self-evidence. Many human rights cannot be reduced to interests, but demand recognition per se – for instance the right not to be discriminated against.[23] Human rights might even be endangered in a Rousseaustic vision of the social contract. Rousseau's *volonté générale* can be taken as legitimising to force people to be free, and this may hurt foundational individual freedom rights.[24] Even in Rawls' theory, human rights flow only from the contract. They are not part of the original position as such, since the basic rights are limited to basic political liberties and procedural ones of equal respect and concern.[25] Instead, human rights should be thought to be presupposed to a social contract, which is not the case.[26]

The position of human rights is stronger in social contract conceptions standing in a Lockean or Kantian tradition. In this position, human rights are presupposed to the contract and are taken to be decisive for the legitimacy of a political authority.[27] This conception of the social contract supports a normative political conception of human rights. Finally, in the empirical tradition, the position of human rights depends on the practices themselves. They can be taken as part of and legitimised by the social contract in case and as long as they are effectively taken to be included in this contract. This shows that, from a

---

21 A good example is the concept of the right to family life (Article 8 ECHR). Other than may have been foreseen in 1951, it now includes stepparents, grandparents, and informal family members within its scope of protection.

22 P. Tiedemann, *Philosophical Foundation of Human Rights,* Springer, Cham in Switzerland 2020, p. 60.

23 Cf A. Buchanan, 'Human Rights', in D. Estlund (ed.), *The Oxford Handbook of Political Philosophy*, Oxford University Press, Oxford 2012, p. 288.

24 J.J. Rousseau, ibid., p. 177: 'Whoever refuses to obey the general will shall be compelled to do so by the whole body'.

25 See J. Rawls (1999), *A Theory of Justice, supra* note 15, pp. 10, 56 (basic political freedoms).

26 R. Dworkin, *Taking Rights Seriously,* Harvard University Press, Cambridge MA 1978, pp. 169, 177: these rights are so strong and fundamental that they trump rationalities of general utility and interest.

27 I. Kant, 'Perpetual Peace', *supra* note 13, p. 380: 'The rights of men must be held sacred, however great the cost of sacrifice may be to those in power. Here one cannot go halfway ...'.

theoretical point of view, this empirical, realist perspective offers human rights a foundation that is less strong than in the normative perspective of the Lockean position.

In short, human rights do not fit well with any non-normative and purely power-justifying and interest-based conceptions of the social contract. They are tied to normative visions and/or conventional understandings of the social contract. As we have seen, however, if a social contract is presented as a convention and a practice, a critical view is needed regarding the actual scope of this social contract in relation to these fundamental rights. This is relevant with respect to the current social contract discourse in public policy and corporate governance.

3. THE CALLS FOR A NEW CONTRACT PUT TO THE TEST

How, then, ought we to qualify the present calls for a social contract in public policy and corporate governance in light of classic social contract theory, and what do such calls imply for human rights?

In the classical theories the social contract first of all has an explanatory and/or legitimising function regarding a division of power (Hobbes), a constitutional order (Locke), rights, social justice (Rawls) and democracy (Rousseau). Some modern theories of business ethics use the social contract in comparable ways. For instance, to support his vision on corporate social responsibility, Donaldson applies the methodology of the state of nature to a state without productive organisations and concludes that 'from the standpoint of society, the goal of a productive organisation may be said to be *to enhance the welfare of society through a satisfaction of consumer and worker interests*.'[28] Palmer justifies companies' adherence to national laws and sustainability by applying Hobbes to companies.[29] Claassens also uses Hobbes to justify his concession theory of companies.[30] Corporations are not merely aggregates of shareholder interests, nor are they mere legal entities of their own. They owe their existence to the fact that the state, representing the general interest, has conceded corporations the power and means to maximise wealth in the general interest. This is done in two ways: first by instituting companies as corporations, in other words, by giving companies legal personhood; and second by creating and maintaining

28 Th. Donaldson, *Corporations and Morality*, Prentice Hall, Englewood Cliffs NJ 1982, p. 49.

29 E. Palmer, 'Multinational corporations and the social contract', (2001) 31(3), *Journal of Business Ethics*, pp. 245–258. For an overview, see: P. Neiman, 'A Social Contract for International Business Ethics', (2013) 114, *Journal of Business Ethics*, pp. 75–90.

30 See below section 3.2.

a legal system that allows companies to pursue their interests and claim their rights in courts. In other words, corporations cannot exist outside a legal system that allows them to protect their interests. In their turn, they may be expected to act in the general interest: 'When it grants incorporation, the State allows corporations to have private purposes, but requires that these purposes should be compatible with a specific public purpose.'[31] Others apply social contract to come to a Rawlsian vision on social justice.

However, the calls for a social contract in public and corporate governance to which I referred above, take another approach. They do not work out a new theory, but argue that businesses and governments actually adhere to a tacit social contract or should do so. With this, these calls seem to follow a Humean empirical perspective focusing on describing and/or prescribing a practice.[32] It is this kind of discourse that is of interest here since it gives an indication of changing views on the relation between companies, society and government. What then are the general features of the social contract in public and corporate governance discourse?

3.1. A SET OF PROSPECTIVE IDEALS OF COOPERATION AND RECIPROCITY

The social contract in current public policy and company law discourse generally functions as a set of broadly formulated prospective ideals, principles and norms meant to enhance the legitimacy of public authority and companies. The social contract provides a framework for value-based action guided by considerations of social justice, cooperation and responsibility. It is not a theoretical construction, but a broad ideal of a 'living social contract' that functions as a call for action.

This living social contract offers certain features that stand out if compared with the bargain for self-interest that is common to the classic theories. In summary, it promotes cooperation on a level of equality among various actors in conditions of uncertainty. So, first of all, this social contract in public policy includes governmental, non-governmental, societal organisations and citizens together in one horizontal network. It stresses the horizontal dimension of the social contract. In light of traditional, vertically organised control and accountability relations in the public domain, this horizontal character reflects a novel way of looking at responsibilities that is in line with the present horizontalised structures of public governance (at least in The Netherlands).

---

31 R. Claassens, 'Hobbes Meets the Modern Business Corporation', (2021) 53(1), *Polity*, pp. 101–131.

32 W. Cragg, 'Human Rights and Business Ethics: Fashioning a New Social Contract, (2000) 27, *Journal of Business Ethics*, pp. 205–214, p. 213: 'We need a new social contract to frame business activities in the emerging global market place.' See Neiman, *supra* note 29, for further references.

Connected with this horizontal feature of the social contract in current discourse is a second feature of *reciprocity*. Other than the bargain underlying the Hobbesian tradition, the reciprocity resides in a mutuality of interests and of shared responsibilities that are not carved in stone. The current discourse on social contract is rather vague as to the exact equality of responsibilities, as well as their interdependence and application. The social contract asks its adherents to take responsibility.[33]

This notion of reciprocity points to a third feature of the social contract in current discourses: to know its *open and dynamic character*. It is open for change. Tacit agreements may change into explicit ones. Power relations may shift and obligations may develop, as continually happens in health care or any other domain of governmental policy. The social contract is something that develops over time and, due to its vague circle of participants, also in space. In this way it should be able to cope with changing circumstances in the context of complexity.

In the fourth, as a call for action, this social contract has a strong symbolic and expressive function. The ideal expresses and creates a worldview and is meant to inspire. It is not harking backwards to some hypothetical contract underlying the current order, but is oriented towards the future.

A final feature of this social contract is the pivotal position of human rights. I will expand on that in the following section.

3.2. LICENCE TO GOVERN AND LICENCE TO OPERATE

In line with the above, the social contract in modern discourse is considered as a means to enhance the legitimacy of governments and companies. In other words, for their 'licence to govern' or (for companies) to operate it is not sufficient they can refer to a theoretical basis of authority or any other claim. Governments and companies have to continuously prove their legitimacy. Human rights play a pivotal role in this respect. Recent case law is illustrative of this. I discuss two cases.

The first case relates to the state's liability for the human right to a safe environment. A landmark case is the Urgenda climate case.[34] In 2018, the Dutch state was held liable for not following up sufficiently on the demands of the Paris Treaty. The state defended itself by referring to its discretionary power to decide on the measures to be taken. It should be held accountable to the Parliament,

33 For the aspects of reciprocity, see for now P. Serrand, 'Reciprocity', in D. Alland and S. Rials (eds.), *Dictionnaire de la Culture Juridique*, Presses Universitaires de France, Paris 2003, pp. 1299–1302.

34 Dutch Supreme Court d20.12.2019, ECLI:NL:HR:2019:2007.

not the judiciary. The judiciary would exceed its powers under the Trias Politica by judging the rightfulness of the state's implementation of the Paris Treaty. However, the Supreme Court did not follow the state's argumentation. Measures to prevent climate change are too important to be decided by arguments of formal power division. Furthermore, it would be inconsistent if on the one hand, a state binds itself to treaty obligations, while on the other hand it refuses to account for its execution of these treaty obligations.[35] The court held the state liable for infringing the active obligation it has to protect and aid the right to life and the right to privacy (and safe home) as laid down in the Articles 2 and 8 ECHR. The case confirms that actively protecting the human right to a safe environment is an integral part of a state's 'licence to govern'. Human rights treaties in particular function as a permanent critical lens for the duties of governments towards society as part of the 'living social contract' to which it is subject.

The second case relates to the enhanced liability of companies to protect and aid human rights. In principle, states are the primal party to which the responsibilities are assigned to maintain respect for human rights and implement social rights. However, recent case law confirms that it is no longer sufficient for companies to merely pay lip service to the law while focusing on serving the interests of their shareholders or affiliated stakeholders, such as employees. Recent cases witness enhanced liability for companies to take responsibility in respecting and aiding human rights. Two years after Urgenda, Shell, the British-Dutch oil company, has been held liable for societal and ecological damage in Nigeria under UK law as well as Dutch law. The Hague Court of Appeal judged that Shell might be liable for torts committed by one of its affiliates in Nigeria.[36] These torts may consist of infringements on important human rights regarding the environment, health and equitable treatment. As is true for states, following up on human rights is an integral part of the licence to operate, thereby confirming society and the environment are, to a certain extent, to be considered as stakeholders.

The call for a CSR implementation within company law fits in a broader development of holding companies publicly accountable for environmental issues, equitable labour circumstances, consumer law, governance, compliance and human rights.[37] The call for a social contract and social responsibility is supported by sources of hard law (ECHR, general principles of law and national

---

35 M. Loth, 'Eenheid in gelaagdheid, over formele en materiële rechtseenheid in een meergelaagde rechtsorde', 2018 *Ars Aequi*, pp. 335–342, referring to the importance of consistent interpretation, p. 337.

36 Court of Appeals The Hague 29.01.2021, ECLI:NL:GHDHA:2021:132 (breach of care in of parent company to prevent oil spills), UK Supreme Court allows Nigerians to sue Shell over oil spills, [2021] UKSC 3 12.02.2021.

37 See references under section 2.1. Also H.J. Zwalve-Erades, 'Maatschappelijk verantwoord ondernemen in Nederland', (2015) 1, *Tijdschrift voor Omgevingsrecht*, pp. 32–45.

bills of rights, regulations of the European Union (EU) calling for equitable employment protection, UK Modern Slavery Act) and follows in the footsteps of soft law such as corporate governance codes, the guidelines of the Organisation for Economic Co-operation and Development (OECD), Declaration Principles of the International Labour Organization (ILO), rules of the International Chamber of Commerce (ICC) and, indirectly, from the Paris Treaty.[38] The voluntary CSR approach tends to 'harden' by way of EU directives and national law.[39]

This development of hard law and soft law regarding CSR and the pursuance of human rights shows that companies cannot limit themselves to just making profit on their own behalf or on behalf of their shareholders or stakeholders. Merely obeying the law and following up on legal obligations seems to be insufficient to make them legitimate. The call for a social contract therefore underscores that a state's legitimacy and a company's licence to operate depend on their active responsibility-taking for the many obligations and principles as laid down in international law and codes of soft law, of which human rights form an important part.

In summary, the social contract as referred to in public and corporate governance distinguishes itself from the classic social contract theory by its open, dynamic and relational character, capable of coping with changing circumstances and uncertainty. The social contract does not function as a hypothetical bargain that accounts for legitimacy. Instead, the social contract is an ideal that must be followed up in order to prove legitimacy, be it by public or private institutions. Respecting and aiding human rights is not merely a consequence of this social contract, but the crucial element of the normative claim of this social contract. The calls set the framework for a living social contract that is meant as a normative guide for action. Due to this openness, flexibility and calls for actively taking responsibility in conditions of uncertainty, this living social contract shows certain similarities with, as will appear below, the social contract of hospitality. Although I cannot give an overview of all the strands and variations within this current of thought, I want at least to draw a few comparisons in order to probe the meaning of this social contract paradigm and the challenges and risks it offers for human rights.

---

38 See H.J. Zwalve-Erades (2015), ibid., p. 25 ff., see overview Policy Department for Citizens' Rights and Constitutional Affairs, Directorate-General for Internal Policies (2020), Corporate Social Responsibility and its implementation into EU Company Law, available at https://www.europarl.europa.eu/RegData/etudes/STUD/2020/658541/IPOL_STU(2020)658541_EN.pdf, last accessed 14.07.2021, see also OECD Overview of Selected Initiatives and Instruments Relevant to Corporate Social Responsibility, in Annual Report on the OECD Guidelines 2008, available at https://www.oecd.org/corporate/mne/40889288.pdf, last accessed 14.07.2021.

39 T. Szabados, 'Multilevel hardening in progress, Transition from soft towards hard regulation of CSR in the EU', (2021) 28(1), *Maastricht Journal of European and Comparative Law*, pp. 83–101.

4. RECIPROCITY AND PARASITISM IN THE SOCIAL CONTRACT

4.1. HOSPITALITY: A DANGEROUS RELATIONSHIP

The idea of hospitality is one of the most ancient kinds of social contract. For insight into its potential meaning and scope, the ancient myths offer some help. They make things concrete that we might otherwise forget. Think of the Ancient Greek sailors sailing the coast riddled with islands and cliffs to fish for a living, to transport goods and to investigate the world while searching for new land serving their economic and political needs. As nature and the gods confront man with bad surprises, these sailors have to seek a temporary safe haven on foreign grounds in strange households. Since those receiving the stranded men would be conscious that the same token, the same storms, could befall them, they would provide this hospitality, knowing that as long as each member of this imaginary community of hosts and sailors would conform to this social norm, the invisible chain of hospitality stands. Sooner or later, or maybe never at all, they or any of their descendants or village members or even no one directly connected could get their gift back. The stories show that providing hospitality is one of the oldest existing social norms rooted in religion and connected to the development of civilisation. Frequently hospitality comes in the form of a theoxeny (a god in disguise visiting the house of a human being, thereby testing his hospitality).[40] Infringement on this 'non droit' of hospitality is severely punished by, for instance, inundation or illness. The religious element confirms the universal and symbolic character of the relational laws of hospitality. Action is steeped in meaning.

The social contract of hospitality therefore revolves around notions of exchange and reciprocal recognition in conditions of uncertainty and is symbolically tied to the continuity of a group and humanity as a whole, subject to inscrutable nature. I will discuss each of these features briefly.

Reciprocity can take different forms. It covers the range among vengeance, the bargain and the gift. In other words, it can be vicious or virtuous.[41] Hospitality follows the logic of the exchange of gifts, a total social fact, according to Mauss in his seminal *Essai sur le don*.[42] The gift is voluntary in theory, but obligatory

---

40 A. Montandon, 'Mythes et représentations de l'hospitalité', in A. Montandon (ed.) *Mythes et représentations de l'hospitalité*, Presses Universitaires Blaise Pascal, Clermont-Ferrand 1999, p. 13.

41 See P. Ricoeur, *Parcours de la Reconnaissance*, Stock, Paris 2004, p. 331.

42 M. Mauss, *Essai sur le don, Forme et raison de l'échange dans les sociétés archaïques*, PUF, Paris 2007, p. 9, Engl. Edition, *The Gift, the form and reason for exchange in archaic societies*, Routledge, London 1990. I refer to the French edition.

in reality. It cannot be asked to be returned (as is reflected in positive law)[43] but creates an obligation to return it, if not an hierarchy of nobility.[44] The gift may also not be declined. Still, the reciprocity is set in uncertainty as to conditions of time, place, equivalence and participants.[45] It is part of a cyclical perception of time and asks to be continuously renewed and reconfirmed. The chain must not be broken. The social contract of hospitality realises itself in interaction. It is the doing that keeps the whole together.

Although hospitality is tied to communities, it also revolves around recognition of the other. The frame of hospitality admits recognising the other as fully human, while it simultaneous admits that the other is not and cannot be identical.[46] Hospitality does not demand that the stranger is considered as a member of a community. The stranger is an uncertain friend who should be accepted for what he or she is: similar, equal and yet different. Hospitality recognises the uniqueness of people and withstands the idea of total integration. The idea of offering hospitality to a stranger is part of the philosophy of recognition that is proper to human rights.[47] For Kant, hospitality is 'the right of an alien not to be treated as an enemy upon his arrival in another's country' and fundamental to his ideas of perpetual peace.[48] Hospitality offers a temporary solution to a potential conflict.[49] The notion of hospitality is therefore relevant to human rights, if not the core of it. For instance, the notion of hospitality is laying at the basis of offering citizens right to the city as promoted, for example, by Cities of Refuge.

Hospitality happens at the brink of spheres (inner/outer, common/strange). The social norms and ethics regulating this social contract of hospitality are finely tuned, but essentially unwritten and ambiguous.[50] They are 'founded upon ambivalence'.[51] They consist in providing shelter in one's own house for a limited

---

43 See for Article 175 3:175 Dutch Civil Code, following the Code Civil Français, the gift is a one-sided agreement; it can also only be retracted under strict conditions, cf. for a general overview A. Foubert, 'Don', in D. Alland and S. Rials (eds.), *supra* note 33, pp. 417–420.

44 Ibid., p. 10.

45 *Cf.* C. Hann, 'The Gift and Reciprocity: Perspectives from Economic Anthropology', in S.-CHR. Kolm and J.M. Ythier (eds.), *Handbook of the Economics of Giving, Altruism and Reciprocity*, Elsevier, Amsterdam 2006, pp. 207–223.

46 *Cf.* M. Agier, *The Stranger as my Guest, A Critical Anthopology of Hospitality*, Polity Press, Cambridge UK 2021, p. 23.

47 About recognition, see A. Honneth, *The Struggle for Recognition,* MIT Press, Cambridge MA 1996, see also P. Ricoeur, *Parcours de la Reconnaissance*, Stock, Paris 2004, see also, C. Elion-Valter, *De burger als ongelovige Thomas, geloofwaardigheid, legitimiteit en dialoog*, diss. Tilburg University 2017.

48 I. Kant (1983), *supra* note 13, p. 354, Third Definitive Article for a Perpetual Peace.

49 M. Agier, *supra* note 46, p. 3.

50 A. Montandon, 'Le non-dit de l'hospitalité ou les silences de l'hôte', in L. Gauvin, P. L'Herault and A. Montandon (eds.), *Le Dire de l'Hospitalité*, Presses Universitaires Blaise Pascal, Clermont-Ferrand 2004, pp. 19–32, p. 20.

51 *Cf.* J. Pitt-Rivers, *The Fate of shechem, or the Politics of Sex: Essays in the Anthropology of the Mediterranean*, Cambridge University Press, Cambridge 1977, p. 109.

amount of time. At the same time, the host definitively stays the master of the house. As to the guest, it is upon him or her to behave in a certain way, to 'respect the laws of the house', to be content with the shelter and food, not to complain, not to venture uninvited into the private part of the host's house and to leave after a certain while. In short, the guest must be respectful and maintain his or her distance from the host.[52]

Finally, as the old myths might be interpreted, the invisible contract of hospitality may potentially include more than just men. It is social, for sure, but nature and the gods participate in a certain way as well: nature as raw fact and a symbol of fate; and the gods as messenger, punisher and the bringer of redemption. They symbolise that man is to a certain extent a guest of nature and could be said to return the grace by being a host to society.

However, the myths show that the contract of hospitality is very vulnerable. The chain can be broken easily, certainly due to the ambivalent and unwritten norms. Furthermore, hospitality is potentially dangerous.[53] The host can turn out to be a cyclops intent upon murdering his guests (Ulysses and Polyphemos), or the guest can turn out to be a parasite, never to leave the house, exploiting his host for private profit and thereby introducing the logic of instrumentality within this vulnerable logic of the gift proper to hospitality. The comic tragedy of Tartuffe by Molière offers a good illustration of the many aspects that come into this phenomenon of parasitism. One of these is surely the naivety of the host himself. In short, parasitism always looms around the corner of hospitality. It is ingrained in the unwritten and flexible character of its norms, the 'non-dit' of hospitality – the tension between open house and privacy to be respected, between the search for familiarity and the confrontation with strangeness.

How does this social contract of hospitality behave if compared to the classic social contract (section 4.2), and what insight might this provide in the calls for a new social contract (section 4.3)?

4.2. A HIGHLY DEMANDING SOCIAL CONTRACT

If I compare the social contract of hospitality to the classic social contract, I come to the following. First of all, the classic social contract is generally grounded on the notion of the bargain that is theoretically assumed and is taken as a firm base for theoretical deduction. The mutual performance is a condition

---

52 See on this J. Derrida, 'Hospitality', (2000) 5(3), *Angelika: Journal of Theoretical Humanities*, pp. 3–18.

53 A. Montandon, 'Miroirs de l'hospitalité', in A. Montandon (ed.), *Le livre de l'hospitalité, Accueil de l'étranger dans l'histoire et les cultures*, Bayard, Paris 2004, pp. 6–14, p. 7; see also: M. Roman and A. Tomiche, 'Parasitisme', in A. Montandon (ed.), *Le livre de l'hospitalité*, Bayard, Paris 2004, pp. 1167–1189.

for the contract (and for the theory to hold). This frame of theoretical certainty stands in contrast with the notions of uncertainty and dynamic reciprocity of hospitality, for which returning the gift is a demand that may come true in the future. Secondly, other than the hospitality which is engrained in social reality, the classic social contract is based on an agreement between fictive and abstract individuals. In the third place, other than for hospitality, the social contract is instrumentalist. The fictive individual parties are instrumental to each other and to the agreement to hold. Recognition does not play a role. In other words, in the classic social contract solidarity is approached from an instrumentalist perspective, so to say to pacify a parasitism that is though inherent to man (following Hobbes). Fourthly, although the social contract is meant as a basis for society, the foundation of society is one of logical necessity, not of reciprocity tied to the existence of a social community or humanity as a whole. Society, peace and power are interest-based, not based on reflexive responsibility supported by values. The mediation is logical and devoid of the religious symbolism that is inherent to this social contract of hospitality. Finally, in contrast with the cyclical conception of time proper to hospitality, social contract thought is set in a linear and rational frame. It is not a 'living social contract' that asks to be renewed, reinterpreted and confirmed continuously, but a logical construction that supports claims for authority and reciprocity.

These features result in a different conception of authority and legitimacy. In the classical social contract, the state is entitled to the authority that it has been given by the contract. In the context of the living social contract of hospitality, there is no sole tangible entity to claim authority. There are only deities asking to be offered hospitality, in remembrance of the holy value of solidarity in the context of unpredictable nature that hosts man. The classic social contract theory, however, excludes nature and any (explicit) religious notions.

I admit that the comparison is schematic and somewhat speculative. It neglects the many differences between the several positions of social contract theory, as set out before. The comparison also neglects the Lockean and Kantian positions that offer a basis for recognition of rights and it ignores ideas of general interest as is present in the Rousseauist version of the social contract.[54] However, although sketchy, the comparison between the classic social contract and hospitality shows that the classic social contract is the result of a reduction by rationalistic individualistic thought of the fragile and complex mixture of exchange and mutual recognition that is part of the tradition of the social contract of hospitality. What does this imply for our understanding of the social contract in public and corporate governance discourse?

[54] See. L. Boltanski and L. Thévenot, *De la Justification*, Gallimard, Paris 1991, p. 140 et seqq.

4.3. THE 'NEW SOCIAL CONTRACT' AS A FORM OF HOSPITALITY

If we compare the social contract discourse in public policy and company governance to the social contract of hospitality, we may discover that the former shows certain parallels with the latter. Just like the social contract of hospitality, the social contract in public policy and corporate governance discourse revolves around reciprocity, mutuality and taking of one's responsibility, without expecting a one-to-one return of the act. The focus is thus on tacit obligations and counter-obligations under the condition of potentiality and willingness. The living social contract discourse also focuses on horizontal obligations and responsibilities.

Like the social contract of hospitality, the social contract in current public and corporate governance discourse potentially includes a wide circle of participants. The circle of participants and stakeholders might even include more stakeholders than the familiar ones. Sustainability goals, physical and societal goals, may be interpreted as confirming that in some respects nature might be considered a stakeholder of the contract. For illustration I refer to the granting of legal personhood to rivers (i.e. the Whanganui River in New Zealand). This stands in contrast with the biblical perspective on nature as subjugated to man. With this open character, the social contract discourse contrasts with the imaginary lying behind the classic social contract philosophy, in which nature is excluded.

In short, the living social contract discourse reflects many of the features of the living social contract of hospitality. It is as if the modern discourse tries to reconnect with this older underlying tradition that has been forgotten by modern political thought.[55] However, the comparison of both also makes us aware of some of the vulnerabilities and risks of this modern social contract discourse.

4.4. VULNERABILITIES OF THE SOCIAL CONTRACT DISCOURSE

Just like the contract of hospitality, this new social contract as used in modern public and private governance discourse might be very vulnerable. What are

[55] Cf. M. Mauss, *supra* note 42, p. 90. See also K. Polanyi, 'Le Sophisme économiciste', (2007) 1(29), *Revue du MAUSS*, pp. 63–79; in relation to economic thought and the conflation of the substantive understanding of economy as provision in human subsistence with the formal understanding of economy as market conditions, in other words the hypostasis of rationalism. Reconnecting the resurgence of a substantive vision on economical action of businesses merits more attention than I can give in this contribution however. Critically about this: L. Moncrieff, 'Karl Ponalyi and the Problem of Corporate Social Responsibility', (2015) 42, *Journal of Law and Society*, p. 434.

these vulnerabilities? I first go into the social contract in a public governance context. The first threat comes from parasitism or free ridership. As I analysed in the introduction, the public policy social contract discourse is a direct reaction to the utilitarian logic of effectiveness and risk management in public policy which led to a strong focus on accountability and protocols. Merely promoting a social contract does not automatically imply saying goodbye to this utilitarian logic. An open and living social contract as proposed in public and corporate governance may be vulnerable to the parasitism of free riders feeding on the open and flexible relation. As said, parasitism looms around the corner of every act of hospitality.

A second vulnerability may resort in loss of state authority and legitimacy due to the changing role of the state from guaranteeing authority into a participant. This may also be relevant for human rights. Although the call for a social contract in public policy is meant to serve social rights, a diminishing state authority may also endanger the position of these rights. An aggravating factor lies in the current secular context. As was shown by the comparison with hospitality, symbolic mediation is very important to uphold the contingent solidarity proper to the act of hospitality. The role was formerly fulfilled by mythical deities. However, although in some respects, the secular state is the successor of these deities, it lacks the persuasive (narrative) power to uphold the shared morality of reciprocal solidarity, certainly if 'brought down' to the position of a participant, instead of abstract guarantor. So, we have to be aware that a weakening of the state may also touch human rights.

Going now into the vulnerabilities of a social contract in corporate governance, the risk of being challenged by the utilitarian logic of 'parasitism' may be even greater. Although nowadays a company has to take the interests of a wide circle of stakeholders into consideration, and although a social contract with society may add to its 'licence to operate', a company still has to pursue its own interests and is part of a global playing field that is set in the logic of winners and losers. This shows that a societal mission is at least in tension with the economical mission of the company itself. With regard to human rights, a weakened position of the state – for example, if taken as partner to a social contract with a big company – may also potentially endanger the position of human rights.

In other words, after comparison with the living contract of hospitality, the social contract discourse of public policy and corporate governance comes forward as a promising retrieval of elements of a venerable tradition. The comparison however also demonstrates some of the vulnerabilities that come with that tradition, aggravated by secularity and utilitarianism. This makes that the calls for a new social contract, both in public policy as in corporate governance, offer promising perspectives, but may also turn out to be a mere metaphor.

4.5. A PROMISING BUT VULNERABLE SOCIAL CONTRACT

The modern social contract discourse in the context of public and corporate governance aims explicitly to advance human rights. Public governance is aimed at the execution of social rights. The idea of a social contract between big companies and civil society is inspired by human rights as laid down in several treaties, soft law regulations and increasingly in hard law. The question we asked was whether this social contract discourse can be qualified as an honest step forward in the advancement of human rights or whether it is primarily a metaphor covering an ongoing utilitarian logic.

To examine this question, this contribution first compared the modern discourse with the main classic positions in social contract theory with respect to human rights. As for classic social contract theory, the relation with human rights is somewhat dubious, since social contract theory is generally built upon the notion of a bargain made out of self-interest. Bargains and self-interest do not seem to chime well with rights which demand recognition for dignity's sake, not for self-interest. By comparison, the social contract as promoted in modern governance discourse diverges structurally from the classic social contract frame, as it stresses reciprocal responsibility of a wide circle of participants in a horizontal relationship, instead of limited relationship between fictive individuals acting out of self-interest. The public and private governance discourse offers the normative framework for a living social contract, instead of merely justifying a given order or authority. The modern contract offers a critical lens to evaluate a company's licence to operate or a government's licence to govern on a 'daily basis'. Due to these features of reciprocity and responsibility, the modern social contract discourse is a promising step forward for human rights.

But what risks and challenges does this modern social contract entail? To investigate the implications, I took inspiration from the social contract of hospitality. The comparison with hospitality reveals the 'high morality' of this modern social contract discourse. It is set in a morality of responsibility for the general interest, shared among a wide variety of stakeholders, among whom potentially nature.

However, the comparison of the social contract as promoted in public and corporate governance, also reveals some potential risks. The open and informal features of this living social contract make it vulnerable to parasitism. A morality of reciprocal respect hinges on the willingness of every participant to reflexively respect the unwritten code. This fragility is aggravated by the loss of symbolic mediating institutions like religion and the instrumentalist and utilitarian logic that is inherent to the public policy focus on effectiveness and the corporate logic of profit. These vulnerabilities should be taken into account by legal theory.

Still, COVID-19 as well as the climate crisis show that there is no society, nor public administration, nor any commercial activity that is free of charge.

Nature – supported by awareness of the vulnerability of societal ties – forces us to take responsibility. The climate crisis and the call for recognition and social justice show that reciprocal recognition as expressed by human rights is paramount and suggest that man ought to start to consider himself as a guest of nature instead of the reverse.

In short, the calls for a social contract in public and corporate governance should be taken very seriously, but also deserve to be critically analysed. With regard to human rights, such calls beg further exploration of issues like the meaning of recognition in the context of change, time and contingency and an ongoing utilitarian logic tied to globalisation.

POSITIVE OBLIGATIONS TO PROTECT AGAINST EPIDEMIC OUTBREAKS UNDER HUMAN RIGHTS LAW

Silvia Venier

ABSTRACT

The interplay between human rights law and emergency situations is generally understood in terms of negative obligations, that is, duties not to restrict rights in an unnecessary or disproportionate manner when implementing emergency response measures. This contribution argues for the importance of also looking at positive obligations, as duties to take active steps to protect in all phases of the emergency management cycle, from prevention and preparedness to response and recovery. It first outlines the content of positive obligations applicable to emergency situations as identified by the United Nations (UN) human rights Treaty Monitoring Bodies and Charter-based mechanisms and by the jurisprudence of the European Court of Human Rights (ECtHR). It also briefly discusses the interaction of requirements under human rights law with obligations enshrined in other branches of international law specifically governing epidemic outbreaks, such as the International Health Regulations (IHR). Public health measures adopted in Europe against the current pandemic outbreak are then assessed through the lenses of positive obligations and major gaps are identified. Some concluding remarks are offered on the role of positive obligations under human rights law to protect against emergency situations.

1. INTRODUCTION

At some point during the latter part of 2019, a new strain of coronavirus started to infect people in Wuhan, the 11-million-person capital of the Hubei province in central China. From the days when Chinese authorities notified the World Health Organization (WHO) about the first cases, the situation rapidly deteriorated so that the outbreak was first declared a Public Health Emergency of International Concern (PHEIC) under the terms of the International Health Regulations (IHR) on 30 January 2020 and a pandemic outbreak on 11 March 2020.[1] After more than a year, the outbreak's implications for international law continue to be widely debated, including in the human rights field, where debates have mainly focused on assessing the admissibility of restrictions of rights and freedoms imposed by public authorities to address this unprecedented situation. The traditional way of looking at human rights implications of emergency situations is indeed to consider negative obligations, that is, states' duties not to impact on human rights in a disproportionate or unnecessary manner when adopting and implementing emergency response measures.

As recently suggested by J.W. Nickel, there are many grounds for dissatisfaction in the different ways in which human rights law addresses emergencies, including that it is usually undifferentiated (not targeted to different hazards), mostly negative (focusing only on negative obligations) and rather simplistic (suggesting that the main danger is overreaction, while unpreparedness and inadequate response are never addressed).[2] During the current public health crisis, however, the attention has been slowly shifting towards more positive, differentiated and sophisticated models. Scholars have begun discussing positive obligations enshrined under human rights law, that is, requirements to take active steps to protect against (public health) emergencies, as highly relevant to this context.[3] Some authors have emphasised that the current pandemic outbreak

---

1 WHO, International Health Regulations, adopted 23 May 2005, entered into force 15 June 2007, 2509 UNTS 79 (hereinafter IHR).

2 J. W. Nickel, 'Two models of normative frameworks for Human Rights during Emergencies', in E. J. Criddle (ed.) *Human Rights in Emergencies*, Cambridge University Press, Cambridge 2016, pp. 56–79.

3 Examples include S. Joseph, 'International Human Rights Law and the Response to the Covid-19 Pandemic', (2020) 11(2), *Journal of International Humanitarian Legal Studies*, pp. 249–269; A. Coco and T. da Souza Dias, 'Prevent, Respond, Cooperate. States' Due Diligence Duties vis-à-vis the Covid-19 Pandemic', (2020) 11(2), *Journal of International*

offers 'a fertile ground for deepening our knowledge about the classification between negative and positive obligations',[4] while others have argued that it demonstrates that 'there is an urgent need to perceive public health emergencies as a matter of international human rights obligations and accountability'.[5]

Devoting more attention to positive obligations has many advantages. First, it sheds light on the fact that states' failure to act can limit freedom and endanger dignity as much as state action and that protection of human rights and emergency management can be mutually reinforcing. Second, positive obligations under human rights law are relevant to all the phases of the emergency management cycle, including not only emergency response, but also prevention, preparedness and recovery.[6] Indeed, the response phase is the moment when emergency measures' compliance with human rights law is traditionally assessed in terms of negative obligations, when a wide margin of discretion is usually left to public authorities and circumstances precluding wrongfulness or derogations from human rights treaties may be also evoked.[7] Third, by clarifying

---

Humanitarian Legal Studies, pp. 218–236; R. Frowde, E. Dove and G. Laurie, 'Fail to Prepare and you Prepare to Fail: the Human Rights Consequences of the UK Government's Inaction during the COVID-19 Pandemic', (2020) 12(4), *Asian Bioethics Review*, pp. 459–480; T. Fish Hodgson and I. Seiderman, 'Covid-19 Responses and State Obligations Concerning the Right to Health (Part 2)', *Opinio Juris*, 01.04.2020, available at http://opiniojuris.org/2020/04/01/covid-19-symposium-covid-19-responses-and-state-obligations-concerning-the-right-to-health-part-2/, last accessed 05.06.2021; E. Stubbins Bates, 'Article 2 ECHR's Positive Obligations – How Can Human Rights Law Inform the Protection of Health Care Personnel and Vulnerable Patients in the COVID-19 Pandemic?', *Opinio Juris*, 01.04.2020, available at http://opiniojuris.org/2020/04/01/covid-19-symposium-article-2-echrs-positive-obligations-how-can-human-rights-law-inform-the-protection-of-health-care-personnel-and-vulnerable-patients-in-the-covid-19-pandemic/, last accessed 05.06.2021; H. Hasan, 'Is an Ineffective State Response to COVID-19 a Violation of Human Rights?', *Opinio Juris*, 16.06.2020, available at http://opiniojuris.org/2020/06/16/is-an-ineffective-state-response-to-covid-19-a-violation-of-human-rights, last accessed 05.06.2021.

4 V. P. Tzevelekos and K. Dzehtsiarou, 'Normal as Usual? Human Rights in Times of COVID-19', (2020) 1(2), *European Convention on Human Rights Law Review*, p. 147.

5 B. Toebes, L. Forman and G. Bartolini, 'Toward Human Rights-Consistent Responses to Health Emergencies: What Is the Overlap between Core Right to Health Obligations and Core International Health Regulation Capacities?' (2020) 22(2), *Health and Human Rights Journal*, p. 109.

6 The definitions of the phases adopted by the present chapter are those accompanying the Sendai Framework for Disaster Risk Reduction (2015). See UNGA, 'Report of the open-ended intergovernmental expert working group on indicators and terminology relating to disaster risk reduction', UN Doc A/71/644, 01.12.2016. For earlier works on protection of human rights in all emergency phases, see M. Hesselman, 'Establishing a Full "Cycle of Protection" for Disaster Victims: Preparedness, Response and Recovery according to Regional and International Human Rights Supervisory Bodies', (2013) 18(2), *Tilburg Law Review*, pp. 106–132.

7 F. Paddeu and F. Jephcott, 'COVID-19 and Defences in the Law of State Responsibility', *EJIL:Talk!*, 17.03.2020, available at https://www.ejiltalk.org/covid-19-and-defences-in-the-law-of-state-responsibility-part-ii/, last accessed 13.10.2021.

states' vertical duties (towards the persons under their jurisdiction), positive obligations under human rights law complement obligations enshrined in other areas of international law governing specific emergency situations that usually apply horizontally. Finally, delimiting the exact scope and content of the positive dimension of human rights law is important as references to the protection of human rights have been included in a plethora of international instruments directly applicable or relevant to emergency situations, such as in the field of international health law, international disaster law, nuclear disarmament and climate change.[8] It thus seems timely to clarify requirements under human rights law to ensure protection against emergency situations in terms of taking action.

This contribution aims at discussing the role of positive obligations in protecting against serious risks by focusing on all phases of the emergency management cycle, and specifically on duties relevant to the public health crisis, and at exploring to what extent positive obligations have been actually implemented against the current pandemic outbreak. In consideration of the still limited understanding of the scope and content of positive obligations applicable to emergencies, this contribution adopts a top-down approach as it presents relevant obligations as identified by international and regional authorities that are then applied to a specific case. The second section provides some introductory remarks on the positive dimension under human rights law (section 2.1), offers an overview of the practice of the United Nations (UN) human rights Treaty Monitoring Bodies and Charter-based mechanisms (section 2.2) and of the jurisprudence of the European Court of Human Rights (ECtHR), which has devoted particular attention to the development of positive obligations (section 2.3).[9] It also briefly discusses the interplay between positive obligations and other norms enshrined in relevant areas of international law (section 2.4). In the third section, the contribution applies positive obligations to the COVID-19 outbreak and assesses public health measures in Europe through these lenses. It identifies the main gaps in prevention and preparedness (section 3.1) and response and recovery (section 3.2). Some concluding remarks are offered on the role of positive obligations under human rights law to protect against emergency situations.

---

8 WHO, IHR, *supra* note 1, Articles 3 on Principles and 32 on Treatment of Travelers; UN, 'Sendai Framework for Disaster Risk Reduction (2015-2030)', UN Doc A/CONF.224/L.2, para. 19(c); Treaty on the Prohibition of Nuclear Weapons, adopted 7 July 2017, entered into force 22 January 2021, Article 7 on Victim assistance and environmental remediation; Paris Agreement, adopted 12 December 2015, entered into force 4 November 2016, preambular paragraph.

9 The focus on Europe is justified by the fact that the Strasbourg Court is the human rights supervising authority that has devoted more attention to identifying positive obligations applicable to emergency situations.

2. HUMAN RIGHTS LAW AND EMERGENCY SITUATIONS

This section provides some introductory remarks on the development of positive obligations under human rights law (section 2.1), offers an overview of positive obligations currently being identified by human rights supervising authorities at the universal (section 2.2) and European (section 2.3) levels and briefly discusses the interplay between positive obligations under human rights law and other norms enshrined in relevant areas of international law (section 2.4).

2.1. THE POSITIVE DIMENSION OF HUMAN RIGHTS LAW

More than a decade ago, Fredman noted that many steps have still to be taken to reach 'a full understanding of the implications of positive duties triggered by human rights, both from a theoretical and practical legal perspective'.[10] Important challenges in the identification and development of positive obligations include the possible arbitrariness of the negative/positive distinction and the difficulties in clearly framing a human rights violation as resulting from an omission; as well as the potentially open-ended scope of positive obligations and the difficulties in identifying what action is exactly required to protect rights and in adjudicating over resource-demanding obligations. While it is outside the scope of this contribution to discuss these challenges in detail, it is still important to bear them in mind. To partially mitigate these challenges, a working definition of positive obligations relevant to the present discussion is hereafter proposed and the legal basis for their development is clarified.[11]

Positive obligations investigated in the present contribution include those obligations to take active steps to protect human rights in all phases of the emergency management cycle, including prevention, preparedness, response and recovery. Obligations enshrined in this working definition are only those whose primary aim is to act to protect human rights against risks posed by third parties or by hazardous events, and not duties whose aim is to ensure that a

[10] S. Fredman, *Human Rights Transformed*, Oxford University Press, Oxford 2008, p. 3.

[11] On these challenges, see S. Besson, 'Les obligations positives de protection des droits fondamentaux – Un essai en dogmatique comparative', (2003) 1(49), *Revue de droit Suisse*, pp. 49–96 (discussing in particular the identification of the legal basis of positive obligations); D. Xenos, *The Positive Obligations of the State under the European Convention of Human Rights*, Routledge, London/New York 2012 (on their potential open-ended scope); L. Lavrysen, *Human Rights in a Positive State. Rethinking the Relationship between Positive and Negative Obligations under the European Convention on Human Rights*, Intersentia, Antwerp/Cambridge 2018 (on the negative/positive distinction).

specific measure complies with negative obligations.[12] Since this contribution is concerned with identifying positive obligations under human rights law applicable to emergency situations, particular attention is devoted to rights that are likely to be the most impacted in these contexts, including the right to life,[13] to health[14] and to private life.[15]

The focus on duties has the advantage that it emphasises what is required to implement rights, which usually demand a mix of abstention and action for their complete realisation. Different typologies of duties have been proposed, including the traditional dichotomy (negative/positive, used in particular by the authorities supervising civil and political rights); the tripartite typology (to respect, protect and fulfil); the quintuple typology (to respect, to create the institutional machinery essential to realise rights, to protect rights and prevent violations, to provide goods and services to satisfy rights and to promote rights); and even a continuum of duties.[16] Pisillo Mazzeschi, who looked at positive obligations through the lenses of the law of state responsibility, identified three types of obligations under human rights law, namely, of immediate result, of conduct or due diligence and of progressive realisation.[17] These range from the most definite and justiciable to those which are vaguer and which imply less strict responsibilities for states, but this categorisation is subject to changes over time, since positive obligations may assume more legal strength as our understanding of the role of the state in relation to human rights protection evolves.

The legal basis for positive duties is easy to identify for economic, cultural and social rights. An example is Article 2(1) of the International Covenant on Economic Social and Cultural Rights (ICESCR) which explicitly states that '[e]ach State Party to the present Covenant *undertakes to take steps*, individually and through international assistance and co-operation, especially economic and technical, to the maximum of its available resources, with a view to achieving

12 The difference between 'regular, freestanding positive obligations' and 'conditional positive obligations' based on negative obligations is discussed by L. Lavrysen, 'Protection by the Law: The Positive Obligation to Develop a Legal Framework to Adequately Protect ECHR Rights', in Y. Haeck and E. Brems (eds.), *Human rights and civil liberties in the 21st century*, Springer, Dordrecht 2014, pp. 79–82.

13 International Covenant on Civil and Political Rights, adopted 16 December 1966, entered into force 23 March 1976, 999 UNTS 171, Article 6 (ICCPR); European Convention on Human Rights (1951) Article 2 (ECHR).

14 International Covenant on Economic, Social and Cultural Rights, adopted 16 December 1966, entered into force 3 January 1976, 993 UNTS 3, Article 12 (ICESCR).

15 ECHR, *supra* note 13, Article 8.

16 For the quintuple typology, see H. Steiner and P. Alston, *International Human Rights in Context*, 2nd edition, Oxford University Press, Oxford 2000, p. 182. For the discussion of the continuum of duties, see I. E. Koch, 'Dichotomies, Trichotomies or Waves of Duties', (2005) 5(1), *Human Rights Law Review*, p. 81.

17 R. Pisillo Mazzeschi, 'Responsabilité de l'état pour violation des obligations positives relatives aux droits de l'homme', (2008) 333, *Collected Courses of the Hague Academy of International Law*, pp. 175–506.

progressively the full realization of the rights recognized in the present Covenant' (emphasis added). The two criteria of progressive realisation and maximum available resources are usually seen as somehow hampering the immediate realisation of economic, social and cultural rights, but a 'minimum core of obligations' exists that must be immediately implemented, such as the prohibition of discrimination, enshrined under Article 2(2) ICESCR. The legal basis for the development of positive obligations under civil and political rights is generally recognised in the provisions requiring states to 'ensure' or to 'secure' rights and in other standard-setting provisions.[18]

With reference to emergency situations, it may be also worth considering the phase to which a specific obligation pertains. The pre-disaster phase includes prevention and preparedness measures, while response refers to general obligations to face the emergency with due diligence. Recovery closes the loop of the emergency management cycle, as it is aimed at restoring the normal conditions and at building back better by implementing lessons learned in terms of Disaster Risk Reduction (DRR). As will be shown below, obligations of immediate result exist in the pre-disaster phase that may play a crucial role in mitigating the risk of an emergency or in mitigating its impacts should it occur. This suggests that the role of human rights law in these contexts is not limited to offering requirements to guide state actions *during* an emergency, when we are generally inclined to leave wide margins of discretion to public authorities. To fully comply with human rights law, states have to take specific measures to prevent, prepare and recover, as indicated by the practice analysed below.

2.2. THE PRACTICE OF THE UNITED NATIONS HUMAN RIGHTS SUPERVISING MECHANISMS

UN human rights treaty monitoring bodies have identified positive obligations as arising from different rights relevant to emergency situations and applicable to the different phases of the emergency management cycle. Within this practice, some recommendations are provided on addressing the specific implications of public health emergencies.

The Human Rights Committee (CCPR), the body responsible for supervising the implementation of the International Covenant on Civil and Political Rights (ICCPR), in 1982 asserted that a state has to take positive action to protect the right to life, including measures 'to reduce malnutrition and epidemics'.[19] The General Comment on the right to life recently adopted clarified that positive

---

18 See ICCPR, *supra* note 13, Article 2(1); ECHR, *supra* note 13, Article 1; for instance, the provision that the right to life shall be 'protected by law'.

19 HRC, *CCPR General Comment No. 6: Article 6 (Right to Life*, UN Doc HRI/GEN/1/Rev.6, 30.04.1982, para. 6.

obligations include to 'take appropriate measures to address the general conditions in society that may give rise to direct threats to life', including 'the prevalence of life-threatening diseases', and to:

> develop, when necessary, contingency plans and disaster management plans designed to increase preparedness and address natural and manmade disasters that may adversely affect enjoyment of the right to life.[20]

While the recommendation 'to take appropriate measures to address the general conditions in society' is very general, the advice to develop contingency plans 'designed to increase preparedness' refers to a more specific obligation of immediate result applicable to the pre-disaster phase. As discussed in the following paragraphs, this duty is confirmed and further clarified by other international and regional policy and legal instruments and the lack of adequate plans has been one of the main problems to face COVID-19. When commenting on States Parties' reactions in response to the COVID-19 pandemic, the CCPR emphasised the requirements not to derogate from the obligations to treat all persons without discrimination and to pay specific attention to the most vulnerable groups, such as persons deprived of their liberty, women victims of domestic violence or minorities and migrants.[21] As discussed below, similar requirements on non-discrimination and attention to vulnerable groups are supported by other treaty monitoring bodies.

Pursuant to Article 12(2)(c) ICESCR, the right to health enshrines the 'prevention, treatment and control of epidemic, endemic, occupational and other diseases'. As indicated by the CESCR, the term 'treatment' includes 'the creation of a system of urgent medical care in cases of accidents, epidemics and similar health hazards, and the provision of disaster relief and humanitarian assistance in emergency situations', while 'control' refers to:

> States' individual and joint efforts to, *inter alia*, make available relevant technologies, using and improving epidemiological surveillance and data collection on a disaggregated basis, the implementation or enhancement of immunization programmes and other strategies of infectious disease control.[22]

It is interesting to note that when discussing the 'core obligations' under the right of health, the CESCR refers to the need to identify these obligations reading them 'in conjunction with more contemporary instruments', therefore

---

20 HRC, *General Comment No. 36 (2018) on article 6 of the International Covenant on Civil and Political Rights, on the right to life*, UN Doc CCPR/C/GC/36, 30.04.2020, para. 26.

21 HRC, Statement on derogations from the Covenant in connection with the COVID-19 pandemic, UN Doc CCPR/C/128/2, 30.10.2018, para. 2(e).

22 CESCR, *General Comment No. 14: The Right to the Highest Attainable Standard of Health (Art. 12)*, UN Doc E/C.12/2000/4, 11.08.2000, para. 16.

suggesting that this category of obligations can be expanded over time.[23] Back in 2000, core obligations included the requirements to 'provide immunization against the major infectious diseases occurring in the community', to 'provide education and access to information concerning the main health problems in the community' and to 'provide appropriate training for health personnel'.[24] These are thus positive obligations of immediate result that shall be implemented before an emergency situation to protect the right to health.

The most detailed document on positive obligations under human rights law applicable to emergency situations has been recently issued by the Committee on the Elimination of Discrimination against Women (CEDAW). The General Recommendation No. 37 focused on DRR measures and discussed the general principles of the Convention applicable to disaster risk and climate change, as well as more specific measures and areas of concern.[25] DRR measures identified by the CEDAW include data collection and information sharing, policy coherence, extraterritorial obligations and international cooperation, as well as resource allocation, capacity development and access to technology. As far as international cooperation is concerned, as noted by Hesselmann in the practice of UN monitoring bodies, this duty 'seems to stretch equally to all phases of disaster management'.[26] States are thus under an obligation to get involved in international cooperation activities aimed at reducing the risk and being prepared to respond to disasters, as well as to seek and offer international assistance for response and recovery.

The practice of other UN treaty monitoring bodies, such as the Committee on the Right of the Child and the Committee on the Rights of Persons with Disabilities, confirms some of the duties mentioned above. Recurring themes in their Concluding Observations include taking into account, in the development of DRR plans, the views and needs of the most vulnerable groups in society (e.g. persons with disability, ethnic minorities, women and children) who are likely to be disproportionately affected by disasters, to collect data on disaster losses that should be disaggregated by factors of vulnerability, as well as to train emergency service personnel to the needs of these groups.[27] This practice will most likely further develop over time, along with the increase in disasters and the changing perception of positive obligations required to protect human rights, as recently acknowledged by the Human Rights Council resolution that encouraged the

---

23 Ibid., para. 43.

24 Ibid., para. 44.

25 CEDAW, 'General Recommendation No. 37 on Gender-Related Dimensions of Disaster Risk Reduction in the context of climate change', UN Doc CEDAW/C/GC/37, 07.02.2018.

26 M. Hesselman (2013), 'Establishing a Full "Cycle of Protection"', *supra* note 6, p. 114.

27 E. Sommario and S. Venier, 'Human Rights Law and Disaster Risk Reduction', (2018) 49, *QIL Zoom-in*, pp. 29–47.

UN monitoring bodies to keep on providing 'technical assistance to States' in these contexts.[28]

In addition to DRR, positive obligations have been identified with respect to response and recovery. In relation to the response to the Fukushima disaster, for instance, the CESCR commented on the lack of attention devoted to vulnerable groups 'during the evacuation and in the rehabilitation and reconstruction efforts' and requested Japan to provide comprehensive data disaggregated by factors of vulnerability, as well as information on how victims' right to justice has been guaranteed.[29] The Special Rapporteur on the right to health identified several aspects in which the response efforts of the Japanese government could have complied with human rights law, including in relation to the nuclear emergency response system, the availability of health management surveys, the decisions on dose limits of radiation and on evacuations and decontamination, access to accurate information on radiation and its health effects, transparency and accountability of the nuclear industry and of regulatory authorities and participation of affected communities and vulnerable groups in decision-making processes, including those related to recovery.[30] Procedural obligations including access to information, transparency and accountability in governance, access to remedies and participation of affected population in decision-making processes, were also identified as necessary to the enjoyment of the right to health.[31] In particular, it was observed that information 'should be made public immediately and in a coordinated manner' and should be 'useful, timely, truthful, consistent and appropriate'.[32]

During the Ebola outbreak that hit West Africa in 2014, UN monitoring bodies discussed human rights implications of public health emergencies for the first time, although this was not taken as an opportunity to propose a more coherent and detailed framework on the interplay between human rights law and public health emergencies. The Office of the High Commissioner for Human Rights (OHCHR) called for the adoption of a human-rights-based approach and identified the duties to ensure adequate working conditions for health workers and to ensure that information is provided in an accurate and timely manner, targeted to the needs of local audience, accessible from a wide variety of sources[33] and disseminated with the support of the local population and the press.

---

28 HRC Resolution 35/20, 'Human Rights and Climate Change', UN Doc A/HRC/35/L.32, 10.06.2017, para. 5.

29 CESCR, 'Concluding Observations on the third periodic report of Japan', UN Doc E/C.12/JPN/CO/3, 10.06.2013, para. 24.

30 HRC, 'Report of the Special Rapporteur on the right of everyone to the enjoyment of the highest attainable standard of physical and mental health. Mission to Japan', UN Doc A/HRC/23/41/Add, 03.05.2013.

31 Ibid., para. 13.

32 Ibid., para. 15.

33 OHCHR West Africa Regional Office, 'A human rights perspective into the Ebola outbreak', 2014, p. 3, available at http://www.globalhealth.org/wp-content/uploads/A-human-rights-perspective-into-the-Ebola-outbreak.pdf, last accessed 07.07.2021.

The COVID-19 outbreak may represent a turning point to clarify the role of positive obligations in relation to a public health crisis. UN monitoring bodies offered guidance notes, detailed advice and statements on how to respect positive obligations in preparedness, response and recovery. A compilation of documents and has issued guidance on COVID-19 was made available by the OHCHR.[34] Both documents put emphasis on a set of positive obligations related to the emergency response measures adopted by states, such as protection of the most vulnerable groups, adequate information and participation of all persons in the decision-making processes that affect their lives.[35] Interestingly for the present discussion, the OHCHR prepared a 'toolkit on treaty law perspectives and jurisprudence in the context of COVID-19', which aimed at contributing to strengthening the human rights compliance of the UN and states' responses to the COVID-19 pandemic.[36] Finally, the Special Rapporteur on toxic waste has discussed the duty to prevent exposure to COVID-19 as 'underscored by national and international recognition of the environmental and occupational rights to life, bodily integrity, safe and healthy working conditions and a healthy environment'.[37] The report identifies several areas in which the implementation of positive obligations would have ensured better prevention, preparedness and response to the pandemic, including measures to address environmental degradation, poor governance (in terms of responsiveness, the role of science and participation), inequalities and discrimination, lack of transparency and of adequate information, attacks on human rights defenders and weak international cooperation.

To sum up, UN treaty monitoring bodies are increasingly considering positive obligations as applicable to emergency situations, but further harmonisation and consolidation would be needed to clarify the specific role of positive obligations under human rights law to protect against emergency situations. Indeed, this effort remains rather ad-hoc and fragmented; for this reason, a special procedure or an independent expert could be envisaged at the UN level to shed further light on the interplay between human rights law and emergency situations and clarify relevant obligations. Should UN monitoring bodies be able to hear any

---

34 OHCHR, 'Compilation of statements by human rights treaty bodies in the context of COVID-19', 19.06.2020, available at https://www.ohchr.org/Documents/HRBodies/TB/COVID19/External_TB_statements_COVID-19_19jun20.pdf, last accessed 07.07.2021.

35 OHCHR, 'Covid Guidance', 2020, available at https://www.ohchr.org/EN/NewsEvents/Pages/COVID19Guidance.aspx, last accessed 07.07.2021.

36 OHCHR, 'Internal HRTB toolkit of treaty law perspectives and jurisprudence in the context of COVID-19', 2020.

37 HRC, 'Report of the Special Rapporteur on the implications for human rights of the environmentally sound management and disposal of hazardous substances and wastes, Duty to prevent exposure to the virus responsible for COVID-19', UN Doc A/HRC/45/12, 05.08.2020, para. 6.

individual complaints on negligence in protecting against emergency situations, this would also help in drawing attention on which omissions may amount to a human rights violation in these contexts.

2.3. THE JURISPRUDENCE OF THE EUROPEAN COURT OF HUMAN RIGHTS

The ECtHR is the human rights supervising authority that has devoted most attention to the development of positive obligations. Their imposition is inextricably linked with the effective application of the European Convention on Human Rights (ECHR), which 'is intended to guarantee not rights that are theoretical or illusory but rights that are practical and effective'.[38] A constant recalibration of the scope and content of positive obligations may be also required in light of the Court's interpretation of the Convention as a 'living instrument'.[39] Interestingly, the ECtHR has explicitly refused to propose a clear theoretical basis for the development of positive obligations under the ECHR.[40] The imposition of positive obligations is generally limited by the requirement not to impose an impossible or disproportionate burden upon public authorities.[41] The ECtHR has not yet decided cases related to public health emergencies in terms of positive obligations, but relevant issues have been discussed in the subset of cases dealing with medical negligence and with negligence in mitigating the risk of natural or man-made hazards (including counter-terrorism operations). Positive obligations emerge from the rights to life (Article 2) and to private and family life (Article 8) and cover all phases of the disaster management cycle.

In general, the primary duty imposed on public authorities is to establish a framework of laws and procedures that is adequate to protect life against any potential threats and risks, to ensure its correct implementation and independent supervision. The state also has to take preventive operational measures and ad-hoc preparedness measures targeted to the risk under consideration. In the most serious cases when the right to life is at stake, the predominant legal criterion regarding the duty to prevent harm is the so-called *Osman* test, that is based on the existence of a life-threatening risk (which has to be real and immediate and must concern an identifiable individual or group) and on the knowledge element (it must be established that the authorities knew or ought to have known about the risk and 'failed to take measures within the scope of their powers which,

[38] ECtHR, *Airey v Ireland*, no 6289/73, 09.10.1979, para. 24.

[39] ECtHR, *Tyrer v United Kingdom*, no 5856/72, 25.04.1978.

[40] ECtHR, *Plattform Ärzte für das Leben v Austria*, no 10126/82, 21.06.1988.

[41] ECtHR, *Lopes de Sousa Fernandes v Portugal* [GC], no 56080/13, 15.12.2015, para. 175.

judged reasonably, might have been expected to avoid that risk').[42] As pointed out by Stoyanova, responsibility for omissions can be established by comparing the actual state conduct with conduct that one can legitimately expect from a normally directed and diligent state.[43] Ex-post positive obligations include conducting impartial and timely investigations to establish the causes of death.

In the vast majority of medical negligence cases, the state's substantive positive obligations are limited to establishing a regulatory framework for professional standards. In two very exceptional circumstances, the responsibility of the state may be engaged in respect of the acts and omissions of health-care providers, namely, when life is 'knowingly put in danger by denial of access to life-saving treatment' and when a:

> systematic or structural dysfunction in hospital services results in a patient being deprived of access to life-saving emergency treatment, and the authorities knew or ought to have known about this risk and failed to undertake the necessary measures to prevent that risk materializing.[44]

In *Asiye Genc v Turkey* (concerning a newborn baby who was denied admission to a neonatal intensive care unit) and *Aydoğdu v Turkey* (concerning the death of a premature baby due to a structural dysfunction in the organisation of prenatal care), the ECtHR held that Turkey violated positive obligations under Article 2 since it had 'not taken sufficient care to ensure the smooth organisation and correct functioning of the public hospital service, and more generally of its system for health protection'.[45] In *Asiye Genc*, three distinct aspects where identified that amounted to structural dysfunction, including 'a lack of effective coordination between the hospitals, accompanied by a carelessness that was

---

42 ECtHR, *Osman v the United Kingdom* [GC], no 23452/94, 28.10.1998, para. 116. It has been suggested that the application of the Osman test to scenarios for which it was not originally conceived has given rise to conceptual confusion and that a more coherent doctrine of risk prevention is needed also in consideration that the importance of positive obligations is likely to increase in the near future, see F. C. Ebert and R. I. Sijniensky, 'Preventing Violations of the Right to Life in the European and Inter-American Systems: From the Osman test to a coherent doctrine of risk prevention?', (2015) 15(2), *Human Rights Law Review*, pp. 343–368.

43 V. Stoyanova, 'Fault, knowledge and risk within the framework of positive obligations under the European Convention on Human Rights', (2020) 33(3), *Leiden Journal of International Law*, pp. 601–620.

44 ECtHR, *Lopes de Sousa, supra* note 41, para. 192. However, in *Lopes de Sousa* the Court was not completely clear in providing guidance on how to distinguish the cases of mere medical negligence from the exceptional circumstances, see L. Lavrysen, 'Medical negligence after Lopes de Sousa Fernandes: a blank check to the Member States with respect to the substance of the right to life?', *Strasbourg Observers*, 08.02.2018, available at https://strasbourgobservers.com/2018/02/08/medical-negligence-after-lopes-de-sousa-fernandes-a-blank-check-to-the-member-states-with-respect-to-the-substance-of-the-right-to-life/, last accessed 04.07.2021.

45 ECtHR, *Asiye Genc v Turkey*, no 24109/07, 27.04.2015, para. 80; ECtHR, *Aydoğdu v Turkey*, no 40448/06, 30.08.2016, para. 76.

characterised by bureaucratic concerns; a shortage of equipment in the neonatal units of the hospitals in question, compounded by the fact that some incubators were out of order; a total lack of urgent medical examinations'.[46]

Looking at the second subset of cases on natural and technological hazards, positive obligations of immediate realisation and of due diligence were identified in all phases of the emergency management cycle. In *Öneryildiz* (involving the death of 39 people caused by a methane explosion at a municipal rubbish tip close to a slum area of Istanbul), the Court clarified the aspects that shall be covered by the legislative and administrative framework in the context of hazardous activities.[47] In *Budayeva* (where the deaths were caused by a mudslide in a Russian town), the authorities failed to comply with positive obligations under Article 2 as they omitted to implement land planning and emergency relief policies, despite the fact that that area was particularly vulnerable to mudslides.[48] Positive obligations thus include adopting ad-hoc risk mitigation measures, against mudslides in the present case. Furthermore, the Court found that states have 'a positive obligation to adequately inform the public about any life-threatening emergency' and that there was a 'causal link between the serious administrative flaws, including the lack of early warning, and the death of and injuries to the applicants'.[49] Similar requirements on warning and information sharing were confirmed and further clarified in recent case law.[50]

The crucial role of providing adequate information emerged from the subset of cases related to extensive environmental pollution under Article 8 on the right to private life, including the well-known cases of *Lopez Ostra* and *Guerra*, when the ECtHR found a violation of Article 8 in consideration of the lack of information that would have enabled citizens to assess risks, a duty that has been confirmed in recent case law.[51] It must be noted that Article 8 ECHR also recognises the right to safe working conditions, more explicitly spelled out in the European Social Charter (Article 3) and the European Union Charter of Fundamental Rights (Article 31).[52]

Finally, prevention and response requirements were revealed in two recent cases related to counter-terrorism operations. In *Finogenov* (concerning the

---

46 *Asiye Genc v Turkey*, *supra* note 45, para. 77.

47 ECtHR, *Öneryildiz v Turkey* [GC], no 48939/99, 30.11.2004, para. 89.

48 ECtHR, *Budayeva and others v Russia*, no 15339/02, 21166/02, 20058/02, 11673/02 and 15343/02, 20.03.2008, paras. 135–136.

49 Ibid., para. 182.

50 ECtHR, *Kolyadenko and others v Russia*, no 17423/05 and others, 28.02.2012; *M. Özel and others v Turkey*, no 14350/05 and 2 others, 02.05.2016.

51 ECtHR, *Lopez Ostra v. Spain*, no 16798/90, 09.12.1994, para. 58; ECtHR, *Guerra and others v. Italy*, no 116/1996/735/932, 19.02.1998, para. 60; ECtHR, *Fedayeva v Russia* no 55723/00, 30.11.2005; ECtHR, *Dubetska and others v Ukraine*, no 30499/03, 10.02.2011; ECtHR, *Tatar v Romania*, no 67021/ 01, 27.01.2009, para. 88.

52 See ECtHR, *Brincat and others v Malta*, no 60908/11 and others, 27.07.2014.

death of 130 hostages due to the adverse reactions to an anaesthetic gas used by Russian authorities when storming a theatre in Moscow where hundreds of civilians had been taken hostage by Chechen terrorists), the ECtHR clarified that 'it was not in a position to indicate to member States the best policy in dealing with a crisis of this kind',[53] but also affirmed that such a conclusion 'does not preclude the Court from examining whether the ensuing rescue operation was planned and implemented in compliance with the authorities' positive obligations under Article 2 of the Convention'.[54] A violation of positive obligations under Article 2 was found due to the inadequate planning and conduct of the operation, in consideration of 'the absence of any centralised coordination on the spot',[55] the inadequate information exchange on the type of gas used and the lack of appropriate medical treatment.[56] In *Tagayeva* (concerning a dramatic hostage taking that occurred in 2004 in a school of the town of Beslan, North Ossetia, which lasted three days and involved at least 1,100 persons, including more than 700 children, ending with the death of more than 300 persons), the Court found unanimously a violation of Article 2 because of the authorities' failure to prevent an event planned days before about which they had knowledge and because of the inadequacy of the response operation,[57] including in terms of lack of a high-level coordinating authority.[58]

The case law presented in this section suggests that the ECtHR is developing positive obligations to take active steps to prevent and being prepared to respond to serious threats to the rights to life and private life, to implement the emergency response plans with due diligence and to conduct impartial and timely investigations should any violation occur. As the criteria for establishing responsibility have never been made explicit by the Court, the key standards should be more openly clarified, such as knowledge of the risk or foreseeability of the event, seriousness of its impacts and the degree to which the hazard can be mitigated,[59] bearing in mind not imposing an impossible or disproportionate burden upon public authorities. Should any COVID-19-related case, dealing, for instance, with failed prevention and preparedness and poor emergency response, exhaust domestic remedies and be brought to Strasbourg, it can be expected that similar standards on public authorities' knowledge of risk and failure to act are applied. Before moving on to assess possible violations of positive duties in

---

53 ECtHR, *Finogenov and others v Russia*, no 18299/03 and 27311/03, 20.12.2011, para. 223.

54 Ibid., para 237.

55 Ibid., para. 247.

56 Ibid., paras. 250–251.

57 ECtHR, *Tagayeva and others v Russia*, no 26562/07 and 6 other applications, 18.09.2017.

58 Ibid., para. 491.

59 Foreseeability, gravity and mitigability have been identified as the key standards in the ECtHR case law by K. Cedervall Lauta and J. Elo Rytter, 'A Landslide on a Mudslide? Natural Hazards and the Right to Life under the European Convention on Human Rights', (2016) 7(1), *Journal of Human Rights and the Environment*, pp. 111–131.

relation to COVID-19 in section 3, the interplay between positive obligations and other norms specifically covering epidemic outbreaks is briefly discussed below.

2.4. THE INTERPLAY BETWEEN POSITIVE OBLIGATIONS AND OTHER NORMS APPLICABLE TO EPIDEMIC OUTBREAKS

As international law develops, it is to be expected that equivalent or similar norms enshrined under different sources interact, raising the questions of how to ensure coordination and consistency between separate but related legal frameworks. With reference to public health emergencies, human rights law interacts with international obligations enshrined in treaties specifically governing these contexts, including the IHR that govern epidemic outbreaks, or soft law instruments adopted in the DRR field such as the Sendai Framework. While there is a vast body of literature on human rights law impact on structural aspects and on specific areas of international law, its interplay with the branches of international law relevant to emergencies has not yet been studied in depth.[60]

Among the multiple novelties introduced by the revised version of the IHR, there are the references to human rights under Article 3(1) and Article 32 on travellers. Zidar emphasises that both provisions seem to 'allude to something that is "external" to Regulations' and that for this reason 'health and governmental officials may perceive the protection of human rights as ancillary during the implementation of health measures'.[61] Indeed, the references to human rights included in the revised IHR are usually read only in negative terms, that is, as requirements not to infringe upon human rights in a disproportionate or unnecessary manner when implementing public health measures. Through negative obligations, human rights law establishes that these measures shall be lawful, strictly necessary, limited in time, subject to review, not arbitrary or discriminatory, based on scientific evidence and information, respectful of human dignity and proportionate to achieving the objectives.

The interplay between human rights law and the IHR is more complex than that based only on negative obligations, however. For instance, a key requirement under the revised IHR is that states develop minimum core public health capacities for surveillance and response, which are essential for limiting the spread of epidemic outbreaks. As discussed above, similar requirements can be found under human rights law, namely, to develop capabilities to ensure the

---

60 An exception is D. Cubie, 'Promoting Dignity for All: Human Rights approaches in the post-2015 Climate Change, Disaster Risk Reduction and Sustainable Development Frameworks', (2014) 8(1), *Human Rights and International Legal Discourse*, pp. 36–51.

61 A. Zidar, 'WHO International Health Regulations and Human Rights: From Allusions to Inclusion', (2015) 19(4), *The International Journal of Human Rights*, pp. 505–526.

respect of minimum core obligations under the right to the highest attainable standard of health, or to take legislative and practical measures to protect the right to life. A recent contribution has discussed this interplay in detail, suggesting that 'there are considerable parallels between states' obligations to have core capacities under the IHR and their minimum core' and other obligations under the right to health and argued 'in favour of more cross-fertilization between these two regimes', which 'may enrich both frameworks from a normative perspective while also enhancing accountability, social justice, and public health outcomes'.[62]

More broadly, human rights law provides the fundamental principles for interpreting and implementing the IHR, including proportionality, prohibition of discrimination and attention to the most vulnerable groups, and establishes substantial and procedural obligations related to the steps to be taken to protect rights, while potentially offering stronger accountability mechanisms. On the other hand, more detailed requirements emerge in the IHR framework that 'provides considerable clarification of states' duty to prevent, treat, and control epidemic disease'.[63] For instance, the general positive obligation under human rights law to adopt adequate legislation is clarified by the requirements enshrined under the IHR which present what 'adequate' means in these particular contexts.[64]

Furthermore, in consideration that the defining element of human rights law is that it regulates the relationship between the state and its population, positive obligations under human rights law complement horizontal norms by clarifying similar vertical obligations. An example is the obligation to notify the WHO and the international community of an event that may constitute a PHEIC established under the IHR, which corresponds to early warning obligations towards the population potentially affected, as identified by the ECtHR in *Budayeva*. In this case, further requirements on what an adequate early warning mechanism looks like in specific circumstances can be found in other instruments, such as the Sendai Framework, which establishes that they should be people-centred and multi-hazard. In other cases, the similarities are not so manifestly evident, but nevertheless exist. For instance, under international environmental law the 'no-harm' principle requires states to take reasonable measures to prevent significant trans-boundary harm emanating from their territory or jurisdiction and affecting other states, with reasonable measures taken from the moment

62 B. Toebes, L. Forman and G. Bartolini (2020), 'Toward Human Rights-Consistent Responses to Health Emergencies', *supra* note 5, p. 106.

63 Ibid., p. 108.

64 This is recognised also by the CESCR when it refers to the 'implementation of health programmes developed by the World Health Organization (WHO)' as required for the realisation of the right to health, see CESCR (2000), 'General Comment no. 14', *supra* note 22, para. 1.

states know or should have known about the risk.[65] Under human rights law, similar parameters for establishing responsibility for harm (knowledge and significant risk) apply vertically between the state and persons under its jurisdiction, as emerging from the ECtHR case law discussed above.

3. ASSESSING THE LEVEL OF IMPLEMENTATION OF POSITIVE OBLIGATIONS UNDER HUMAN RIGHTS LAW IN RELATION TO THE COVID-19 PANDEMIC

After having proposed an overview of positive obligations as identified by international and regional actors, the level of implementation of positive obligations is discussed in relation to the current pandemic outbreak. The pre-disaster phase (section 3.1) and the acute response and recovery phases (section 3.2) are analysed in turn.

3.1. POSITIVE OBLIGATIONS APPLICABLE TO PREVENTION AND PREPAREDNESS

As indicated in the previous section, positive obligations under human rights law related to emergency prevention and preparedness primarily demand putting in place adequate legal, policy and administrative frameworks and taking measures for their implementation and independent supervision; performing accurate and regular risk assessments, possibly based on data on disaster losses in the past disaggregated by factors of vulnerability and considering the worst-case scenarios and potential implications on the wide variety of human rights that may be impacted; widely disseminating the outcomes of risk assessment, with particular attention paid to establishing mechanisms to keep the population informed of any life or health-threatening risk and warned of an imminent and actual risk in a timely manner; adopting ad-hoc risk mitigation measures targeted to different hazards; and producing and testing emergency response plans and other ad-hoc preparedness measures, including those aimed at protecting first responders (e.g. through personal protective equipment and training).

With reference to infectious diseases, ad-hoc prevention measures include reducing the risk of zoonoses (i.e. of new viruses jumping from animals to humans) and immunisation,[66] as well as measures aimed at reducing the risk of

65 ILC, 'Draft Articles on Prevention of Transboundary Harm from Hazardous Activities', 2001, Article 2.

66 Recent developments on this refer to the Resolution adopted in May 2020 by the 73rd World Health Assembly (WHA), which managed to reach wide consensus on the need of

international spread through the timely detection and notification of suspected cases.[67] The WHO Constitution and the revised IHR provide the basis for a 'stronger and more coordinated collective action' in global disease control,[68] while multiple guidance documents on epidemic preparedness and on the status of preparedness at the national level are available.[69] These requirements are reinforced at the regional level, for instance, in the scope of the European Union (EU) decision on cross-border threats to health and of guidance document prepared by the European Centre for Disease Control (ECDC).[70] The European Commission has recently presented a proposal for a Regulation in this field, which would provide 'for a stronger and more comprehensive legal framework within which the Union can react rapidly and trigger the implementation of preparedness and response measures to cross-border threats to health across the EU'.[71]

As discussed above, any prevention obligation enshrines the existence of the knowledge element, according to which states knew or should have known about the imminence of a significant risk. Furthermore, states should possibly be proactive in getting knowledge of serious risks and of potential impacts on

---

an investigation on the origins of the pandemic and on its final aims, i.e. to propose targeted interventions, a research agenda and guidelines aimed at reducing the risk of spill-over events in the future. WHA Resolution 73.1, 'COVID-19 response', A/73/CONF./1, 18.05.2020, para. 9(6); WHA Resolution 73.1 recognised 'the role of extensive immunization against COVID-19 as a global public good for health in preventing, containing and stopping transmission in order to bring the pandemic to an end, once safe, quality, efficacious, effective, accessible and affordable vaccines are available', see ibid., para. 6.

67 S. Negri, 'Communicable Disease Control', in G. Burci and B. Toebes (eds.), *Research Handbook on Global Health Law*, Edward Elgar, Cheltenham/Northampton 2018, p. 267.

68 Among the task assigned to the WHO, Article 2 lists '(g) to stimulate and advance work to *eradicate* epidemic, endemic and other diseases', while Article 21 establishes that the WHA 'shall have authority to adopt regulations concerning: (a) sanitary and quarantine requirements and other procedures designed to *prevent* the international spread of disease' (emphasis added). Pursuant to Article 22, WHO regulations automatically enter into force and are binding on all Member States that do not affirmatively opt out within a specified period of time. Constitution of the World Health Organization, adopted 1946, entered into force 1948, 2 *Official Records of the World Health Organization* 100; S. Negri (2018), 'Communicable Disease Control', *supra* note 67, p. 268.

69 An overview of international rules related to epidemic preparedness is provided by A. de Guttry, 'Is the International Community Ready for the Next Pandemic Wave? A Legal Analysis of the Preparedness Rules Codified in Universal Instruments and of their Impact in the Light of the COVID-19 Experience', (2020) 3, *Global Jurist*, pp. 30–67.

70 Decision No 1082/2013/EU of the European Parliament and of the Council of 22 October 2013 on serious cross-border threats to health, OJ L 293, Article 4 on Preparedness and Response Planning; European Centre for Disease Prevention and Control (ECDC), 'Guide to revision of national pandemic influenza preparedness plans: Lessons learned from the 2009 A(H1N1) pandemic', 2017, available at https://www.ecdc.europa.eu/sites/default/files/documents/Guide-to-pandemic-preparedness-revised.pdf, last accessed 05.06.2021.

71 European Commission, Proposal for a Regulation of the European Parliament and of the Council on serious cross-border threats to health and repealing Decision No 1082/2013/EU, COM(2020) 727 final 11.11.2020.

their own population and on vulnerable groups. In this regard, it is worth noting that international organisations and independent experts had been warning the international community that the risk of an epidemic outbreak with a pandemic potential was extremely high since at least 2005, when the links between climate change, environmental degradation and emerging infectious diseases were clearly demonstrated.[72] While early signals of this risk were offered by previous outbreaks such as SARS, MERS and Ebola, which also pointed out many lessons learned on how to strengthen national capacities and international coordination and cooperation mechanisms, the WHO, specialised agencies such as the ECDC and other actors repeatedly warned of the inevitability of a pandemic and of the need to increase preparedness at the domestic level.[73] As indicated by the Special Rapporteur on toxic waste, '[m]ost States did not take early warnings to heart, as deforestation, biodiversity collapse, climate change, illegal wildlife trade and other environmental conditions raised the risk of the emergence of a contagion such as the COVID-19 virus'.[74]

The question of to what extent legal and policy frameworks are relevant to the prevention of epidemic outbreaks in Europe is certainly very complex. It can be maintained that at the very least adequate legislation adopted at the national level shall integrate international obligations, such as those included within the IHR and EU instruments, and soft law guidance. A study commissioned in 2004 on zoonoses risks in Europe and on applicable legislative frameworks emphasised the need

> to integrate public and veterinary health systems […] to generate basic scientific knowledge on missing links, to integrate current knowledge and to develop new ways for early warning and outbreak control, to prepare as much as possible for new and currently unknown zoonoses, to develop new ways for early warning and outbreak control, to prepare as much as possible for new and currently unknown zoonoses.[75]

---

72 UNEP, 'Global environmental outlook Yearbook 2004/2005', 2005, p. 72, available at https://news.un.org/en/story/2005/02/129442-environmental-changes-are-spreading-infectious-diseases-un-study, last accessed 05.06.2021.

73 ECDC (2017), 'Guide to Revision', *supra* note 70; B. Gates, 'A Better Response to the Next Pandemic' blog post, 18.01.2010, available at https://www.gatesnotes.com/Health/A-Better-Response-to-the-Next-Pandemic, last accessed 05.06.2021; B. Gates, speech at the Munich Security Conference (2017), available at https://www.gatesfoundation.org/Media-Center/Speeches/2017/05/Bill-Gates-Munich-Security-Conference, last accessed 05.06.2021; Global Preparedness Monitoring Board (GPMB), 'A World at Risk: Annual Report on Global Preparedness for Health Emergencies', available at https://apps.who.int/gpmb/assets/annual_report/GPMB_Annual_Report_English.pdf, last accessed 05.06.2021.

74 HRC (2020), 'Report of the Special Rapporteur', *supra* note 37, para. 90.

75 J. W. B. van der Giessen, L. D. Isken and E. W. Tiemersma, 'Zoonoses in Europe: a risk to public health' (2004) Report by The National Institute for Public Health and the Environment in the Netherlands, available at https://www.rivm.nl/bibliotheek/rapporten/330200002.pdf, last accessed 05.06.2021.

The EU Directive on monitoring zoonoses adopted in 2003 represents a good starting basis as it lays down minimum requirements to be met in all EU countries, but the level of implementation by EU Member States is not completely clear and shall be more rigorously assessed. The potential risk of spill-over events from animal reservoirs shall be carried out at regular intervals, considering that zoonoses represent complex and evolving scenarios. It is essential that regional and national legislation and policies are updated not only to rigorously monitor the risk of zoonoses, but more generally to integrate the 'one health approach', which is based on increased coordination between different sectors that are relevant to public health. International guidance on elaborating adequate legislation that takes into consideration the one health approach has been offered.[76]

Turning our attention to preparedness, this is probably the most evident violation of positive obligations under human rights law (and of other international obligations) that has emerged during the COVID-19 crisis. Unprecedented as the pandemic may have been, it is particularly surprising that many states (including in Europe) had not adopted or updated adequate public health emergency response plans and had not scrupulously and promptly activated them, also in light of the repeated warnings mentioned above. Preparedness for the second and third waves would have also probably increased if accurate investigations into what went wrong during the first wave were carried out and had the adequacy of public health responses been assessed on the basis of available scientific evidence.[77]

In Italy, for instance, the existence of an out-dated anti-pandemic plan, dating back to 2006 and apparently never updated (even though it is required under, *inter alia*, EU legislation and WHO guidelines), represents a crucial element in the preliminary investigations of prosecutors in Bergamo, the Lombardy province hardest hit during the first wave.[78] The investigation aims at establishing the contours of possible criminal negligence by public authorities, in terms of the failure to update and activate the national pandemic response plan and of the lack of promptly imposing strict lockdown measures to minimise the spread of the virus in this area which holds the sad record of the highest

76 Food and Agriculture Organisation of the United Nations (FAO), 'One Health legislation: contributing to pandemic prevention through law', FAO Paper, 01.07.2020, available at http://www.fao.org/3/ca9729en/ca9729en.pdf, last accessed 07.07.2021.

77 As advocated for instance by V. Adeboale et al., 'Covid-19: Call for a rapid forward looking review of the UK's preparedness for a second wave – an open letter to the leaders of all UK political parties', (2020) 369, *British Medical Journal*, p. 1.

78 A. Giuffrida, 'WHO accused of conspiracy with Italy to remove damning Covid report', The Guardian, 11.12.2020, available at https://www.theguardian.com/world/2020/dec/11/who-accused-conspiring-italy-remove-damning-covid-report, last accessed 05.06.2021.

mortality rate in Europe due to COVID-19. The lack of a national anti-pandemic plan was identified as one of the main shortcomings in Italy's initial response to the coronavirus outbreak in a report prepared and released by the WHO Venice office on 13 May 2020 and then immediately removed from the website, which was funded by Kuwait's government with the objective of providing information to other countries.[79] A comprehensive and detailed anti-influenza pandemic plan was eventually released by the Italian Ministry of Health in January 2021, taking into account many lessons learned during the current outbreak.[80] Outdated, not comprehensive and not adequately implemented epidemic outbreaks response plans were a common problem in many other states.[81]

Finally, the COVID-19 outbreak demonstrates the enormous challenges for first responders and health care providers, with concerns raised not only in relation to their right to life, but also to the negative effects on their psychological condition both during and in the aftermath of the emergency and the potential for being stigmatised. Throughout Europe, preparedness was poor in terms of stockpiling essential equipment to protect first responders and of ensuring their adequate training. Indeed, the wearing of filtering facial respirators and masks and of isolation gowns is rather complex, and their use makes movements and communication with patients more difficult. One of the most common justifications for the failure to adopt adequate preparedness measures, such as stockpiling personal protective equipment, is that resources are limited. It has to be noted that to overcome the issue of having to allocate limited resources to increase preparedness states should rely more on international cooperation mechanisms.[82] Moreover, a study found that the shortage of personal protective equipment during the current pandemic depended not only on limited resources, but also on a set of market and government failures that could be addressed without particularly high costs.[83]

---

79 WHO, 'An Unprecedented Challenge: Italy's First Response to Covid-19', 2020, available at: available at https://www.dors.it/documentazione/testo/202005/COVID-19-Italy-response.pdf, last accessed 05.06.2021; The WHO was accused of conspiring with the Italian health ministry to remove this report, allegedly at the request of Ranieri Guerra, the WHO's assistant director general for strategic initiatives and former director general for preventive health at the Italian health ministry, between 2014 and late 2017 exactly when the preparedness plan would have needed to be updated. See A. Giuffrida (2020), 'WHO accused', *supra* note 78.

80 Italian Ministry of Health, 'Piano Strategico Operativo Nazionale di preparazione e risposta a una pandemia influenzale (Pan Flu) 2021-2023', 24.01.2021, available at http://www.salute.gov.it/imgs/C_17_pubblicazioni_3005_allegato.pdf, last accessed 05.06.2021.

81 For the UK, see R. Frowde, E. Dove and G. Laurie (2020), 'Fail to Prepare and you Prepare to Fail', *supra* note 3, p. 462.

82 As discussed in A. de Guttry (2020), 'Is the International Community Ready', *supra* note 69, pp. 30–36.

83 J. Cohen and Y. van der Meulen Rodgers, 'Contributing factors to personal protective equipment shortages during the COVID-19 pandemic', (2020), *Preventive Medicine*, pp. 1–7.

3.2. POSITIVE OBLIGATIONS APPLICABLE TO RESPONSE AND RECOVERY

While the negative dimension of human rights law provides a framework to assess if emergency response measures are necessary and proportionate, the positive dimension clarifies which actions have to be taken to protect rights in such difficult circumstances. In the response phase, these generally include to implement the contingency plan with due diligence, to ensure coordination among different authorities at the national and sub-national levels, to send early warning messages and keep the population regularly informed. The protection of vulnerable groups is particular important, as emergency situations and the related response measures usually have a disproportionate impact on these individuals, and specific support is thus required.

Positive obligations under human rights law were most likely violated during the early phases of the COVID-19 crisis when certain states did not promptly publicise the first suspected cases, as repeatedly denounced by the WHO.[84] This amounts to a violation of both the early warning requirement under human rights law and the IHR provisions which impose the requirement to notify within 24 hours the WHO and the international community of an event that may constitute a PHEIC.[85] Early warning messages are key to triggering protective actions by first responders and the population (such as the use of personal protective equipment or the installation of triage areas outside the hospitals where suspected cases can be investigated), contributing to protecting hospitals, limiting the spread of the virus and saving lives. Clear and detailed early warning messages are also crucial to countering panic, as during emergency situations persons are in need of as much information as possible.[86] Furthermore, considering that the increasing speed and volume of international travel and trade create the conditions for the rapid spread of diseases worldwide, promptly informing the international community is also paramount. The reluctance to notify the international community about potential disease outbreaks mainly derives from fear of economic and political repercussions, such as trade and travel restrictions, that were among the main problems that the revised IHR sought to address, apparently without much success.

In addition to failures in early warnings, a number of governments throughout the world failed to act promptly to control the spread of COVID-19, in some cases even denying for several critical weeks the seriousness of the emergency.

---

84 HRC (2020), 'Report of the Special Rapporteur', *supra* note 37, para. 62.

85 WHO, IHR, *supra* note 1, Article 6.

86 This was also a lesson learned for China from the SARS outbreak in 2002–2003, as described by D. Fidler, *SARS, Governance and Globalisation of Disease*, Palgrave MacMillan, London 2004, pp. 74–75.

On 11 March 2020, the Director-General of WHO expressed concern about the alarming levels of inaction, urging states to activate and scale-up emergency response mechanisms.[87] For instance, Coco and Da Souza Dias emphasise that 'in the United Kingdom, the government was initially hesitant to follow the WHO's advice to adopt more rigorous measures, wary as it was of their significant economic impact' and that 'it was only following serious criticism that the government started to gradually "recommend" more impactful measures, such as working from home, social distancing and restrictions on social gatherings'.[88] The delay in adopting strict control measures in consideration of the potential economic impacts was a common feature of response in many states. In the Netherlands, for instance, the main objective was not protecting public health, but 'preventing public concern so as to avoid economic disruption', and once this objective became politically untenable, the next objective was 'herd immunity'.[89] In some circumstances, when COVID-19 cases were identified and the seriousness of the situation acknowledged, some states failed to recommend even the most basic preventive measures, and then resisted declaring a national emergency and imposing stricter measures to prevent contagion. According to the Special Rapporteur on toxic waste, '[i]nstead of swift action, several leaders underestimated the risks, on the basis of unreasonable assumptions, such as that there would be a miraculous disappearance of the virus, and "herd immunity" theories, which, in practice, constitute death sentences for the most vulnerable'.[90] Some scholars have observed that:

> [a] common characteristic in all of the countries with low case levels and death tolls is that they all reacted quickly, decisively and robustly to the pandemic [... including] thorough pandemic planning (as well as implementation of recommendations from reports), adequate surge capacity and resources, rapid and well communicated responses such as implementation of stay home orders and comprehensive testing and tracing systems.[91]

When the seriousness of the outbreak was made evident in China in mid-January 2020, many countries in Europe were not able to perform adequate risk

---

87 HRC (2020), 'Report of the Special Rapporteur', *supra* note 37, para. 70. See also A. Coco and T. da Souza Dias (2020), 'Prevent, Respond, Cooperate', *supra* note 3, p. 228.

88 A. Coco and T. da Souza Dias (2020), 'Prevent, Respond, Cooperate', *supra* note 3, p. 234.

89 L. Bergkamp, 'State Liability for Failure to Control the COVID-19 Epidemic: International and Dutch Law', (2020) 11(2), *European Journal of Risk Regulation*, p. 346.

90 Ibid., para. 30. Herd immunity theories were referred to by, *inter alia*, the UK prime minister Boris Johnson at the outset of the crisis. See E. Yong, 'The UK's Coronavirus "Herd Immunity" Debacle', The Atlantic, 16.03.2020, available at https://www.theatlantic.com/health/archive/2020/03/coronavirus-pandemic-herd-immunity-uk-boris-johnson/608065/, last accessed 05.06.2021.

91 R. Frowde, E. Dove and G. Laurie (2020), 'Fail to Prepare and you Prepare to Fail', *supra* note 3, p. 467.

assessment and public health experts probably failed to adequately advise on immediately taking more stringent risk mitigation measures. In Italy, for instance, in a meeting held on 28 February 2020, the technical-scientific committee advising the Ministry of Health suggested that it was not necessary to extend the lockdown to the other areas where cases had been detected (including the province of Bergamo, which would then be one of the most impacted areas in Europe) and advised against the adoption of other measures such as temperature checks at airports.[92] It is worth emphasising – and public health experts who are advising governments are of course well aware of this aspect – that as epidemic outbreaks grow at an exponential rate, in these contexts 'every hour counts, as the window of opportunity for preventing deaths and further spread closes quickly'[93] and 'delayed recognition and response to emerging diseases may result in adverse consequences in terms of illness and death, spread to other countries, and disruption of trade and travel'.[94]

It has to be noted that the delayed declaration of a PHEIC (pursuant to IHR Article 12) on 30 January 2020 by the WHO may not have helped states to appreciate the new virus' contagiousness and lethality rate, which, however, were rather clear – as demonstrated by the impact the virus was having in China in terms of deaths and of overwhelming the capacities of hospitals. Under-resourced health care facilities, especially in terms of shortages of personal protective equipment for medical staff and of ventilators for affected patients, did not help in ensuring an adequate public health response. It then took some time to put in place test and tracing programmes, clear protocols in hospitals, adequate measures to isolate and protect vulnerable groups such as elderly persons, as well as increased coordination between national and regional or local governments.[95]

In relation to the protection of vulnerable groups, concerns have emerged for the situation of prisoners[96] and migrants,[97] the increase of domestic violence

---

92 Comitato Tecnico Scientifico, 'Verbale n.12', 28 February 2020, p. 4, available at https://github.com/pcm-dpc/COVID-19-Verbali-CTS/blob/master/elenco-verbali.md, last accessed 05.06.2021.

93 WHO, 'SARS: Status of the outbreak and lessons for the immediate future', 20.05.2003, pp. 1–2, available at https://www.who.int/csr/media/sars_wha.pdf?ua=1, last accessed 05.06.2021.

94 M. Baker and D. Fidler, 'Global Public Health Surveillance under New International Health Regulations', (2006) 12(7), *Emerging Infectious Diseases*, p. 1061.

95 HRC (2020), 'Report of the Special Rapporteur', *supra* note 37, para. 31.

96 International guidance produced by WHO/Europe relevant to the situation of prisoners is available at https://www.euro.who.int/en/health-topics/health-determinants/prisons-and-health/focus-areas/prevention-and-control-of-covid-19-in-prisons-and-other-places-of-detention, last accessed 05.06.2021.

97 See for instance the case of quarantine ships discussed in P. Petrucco, 'Ship-based quarantine: a Covid prevention measure for migrants only', CILD blog, 13.10.2020, available at https://cild.eu/en/2020/10/13/ship-based-quarantine-a-covid-prevention-measure-for-migrants-only/, last accessed 05.06.2021.

during lockdowns,[98] the difficulties experienced by children and students during school closure[99] and the impact of restrictions on movement and social life on elders.[100] To this author's knowledge, there were no specific plans to protect these groups against the impacts of a public health crisis and to take into consideration their views and needs when implementing emergency response measures. Psychological and emotional first aid is also of extreme importance during an emergency situation and should be integrated in any contingency plan.

Somehow related to this aspect was the fact that risk communication was also rather poor in some cases.[101] Inaccurate or inconsistent information regarding the spread of the virus and safety guidelines are a clear violation of positive obligations under the right to life and to health, which demand that information is provided in an accurate and timely manner, targeted to the needs of local audience, accessible from a wide variety of sources and disseminated with the support of the local population and the press. In the Netherlands, for instance, the communications from the National Institute for Public Health and the Environment 'caused much confusion, and some of them were incorrect, not supported by science or inconsistent with the WHO's recommendations'.[102] It has to be noted that WHO's somehow ambivalent approach did not help either. For instance, on one side the WHO praised the governments of China and Italy for their population-wide responses, including mass quarantines, on the other the WHO recommended only individualised quarantine and isolation.

During the response phase, the international community had the 'collective responsibility' to act,[103] based on the duty to cooperate that is enshrined both under human rights law and the IHR Article 44 on 'Collaboration and Assistance'.[104] Some experts and public health scholars recently sought to clarify what is required under the IHR in terms of international cooperation, while

98 For an overview, see UN, 'Impact of Covid-19 on violence against women and girls and service provisions: UN women rapid assessment and findings', 2020, available at https://www.unwomen.org/-/media/headquarters/attachments/sections/library/publications/2020/impact-of-covid-19-on-violence-against-women-and-girls-and-service-provision-en.pdf?la=en&vs=0, last accessed 05.06.2021.

99 G. Di Pietro et al., 'The likely impact of COVID-19 on education: Reflections based on the existing literature and recent international datasets', Joint Research Centre Technical Report, 2020, available at https://ec.europa.eu/jrc/en/publication/likely-impact-covid-19-education-reflections-based-existing-literature-and-recent-international, last accessed 05.06.2021.

100 K. O. Cathaoir and I. Gundersby Rognlien, 'The Rights of Elders in Ireland during COVID-19', (2021) 28(1), *European Journal of Health Law*, pp. 81–101.

101 F. Perraudin, '"It will cost lives": experts decry UK government's mixed Covid-19 messaging', The Guardian, 11.05.2020, available at https://www.theguardian.com/world/2020/may/11/it-will-cost-lives-experts-decry-uk-governments-mixed-covid-19-messaging, last accessed 05.06.2021.

102 L. Bergkamp (2020), 'State Liability', *supra* note 89, p. 345.

103 HRC (2020), 'Report of the Special Rapporteur', *supra* note 37, para. 40.

104 ICESCR, *supra* note 14, Article 2.1 and 12.2(c); WHO, IHR, *supra* note 1, Article 44.

back in 2000 the CESCR identified some requirements under the right to health related to international cooperation.[105] One of the most important tools at the disposal of the international community refers to sharing virus samples and genetic sequences, an activity that does not necessarily depend on a country's economic status and may significantly support other countries in improving their detection and treatment capacities.[106] Although this activity has been rather successful during the early phases of the COVID-19 crisis, the fact that it is governed only through soft law may represent a weakness that may be worth addressing.[107]

Looking at the post-COVID-19 phase, this will probably represent the most ambitious recovery effort in the recent history of humankind. As discussed above, positive obligations applicable to the recovery phase include to ensure genuine consultation and participation of victims in the design and implementation of all decisions affecting them and to guarantee that rights of the most marginalised groups are fully taken into account in recovery plans. With respect to this last point, a study has recently argued that the European Semester, which represents the basis of the EU recovery and resilience plan, does not sufficiently address inequalities and discrimination.[108] The EU recovery plan represents a historic opportunity to ensure the fulfilment of economic, social and cultural rights that have been significantly impacted by the COVID-19 outbreak and need long-term projects for their complete realisation. Finally, positive obligations under human rights law as well as recommendations under the Sendai Framework require public authorities to investigate gaps and to integrate lessons learned from previous emergencies in revised preparedness plans. In respect to this, Dagron has emphasised that two knowledge gaps exist that must be filled before a human rights based approach can be fully implemented in public health to ensure resilience, namely, clarifying the principles that must be applied to limit human rights during global public health emergencies and providing more detailed human rights-based guidance concerning states' longer-term preparations for

---

105 M. M. Cinà et al., 'The Stellenbosch Consensus on the International Legal Obligation to Collaborate and Assist in Addressing Pandemics. Clarifying Article 44 of the International Health Regulations', (2020), *International Organizations Law Review*, p. 1–30; CESCR (2000), 'General Comment no. 14', *supra* note 22, paras. 38 and 40.

106 G. L. Burci, 'Health and Infectious Diseases', in T. G. Weiss and S. Daws (eds.), *The Oxford Handbook on the United Nations*, 2nd edition, Oxford University Press, Oxford 2018, p. 689.

107 Soft law includes the Pandemic Influenza Preparedness Framework (PIP) that was produced under the WHO auspices to address concerns over the exorbitant prices of vaccines developed on the basis of the information provided by countries (sharing of virus sample in this case). WHO, 'Pandemic influenza preparedness Framework for the sharing of influenza viruses and access to vaccines and other benefits', 23.05.2011, available at https://www.who.int/publications/i/item/9789241503082, last accessed 05.06.2021.

108 L. Antonucci and F. Corti, 'Inequalities in the European Semester', FEPS Policy Paper, 07.10.2020, available at https://www.feps-europe.eu/attachments/publications/inequalities_in_the_european_semester%20online.pdf, last accessed 05.06.2021.

future public health emergencies.[109] It is hoped that this chapter has contributed to deepening the understanding of the latter aspect, that is, what actions are required to protect rights against the threats posed by public health crisis, in terms of prevention, preparedness, response and recovery.

4. CONCLUSIONS

This contribution has argued for the importance of looking at positive obligations under human rights law to understand what is required to protect against emergency situations. These refer to duties to take active steps in all phases of the emergency management cycle, from prevention and preparedness to response and recovery. The practice of the UN human rights supervising mechanisms and the jurisprudence of the ECtHR suggest that increasing attention is devoted to such obligations. Some standards and criteria for establishing responsibility in these contexts can be identified already, although this effort still remains rather fragmented. In particular, at the UN level a special procedure or an independent expert could be mandated to shed further light on the interplay between human rights law and emergency situations and relevant obligations. The ECtHR could more explicitly confirm the criteria for engaging the responsibility of public authorities, such as knowledge of the risk, the seriousness of its impacts and the degree to which the hazard could be mitigated, while keeping in mind that a constant recalibration of these criteria is possible in consideration of the ECHR being a living instrument.

The interaction between positive obligations and obligations enshrined in other branches of international law specifically covering epidemic outbreaks has been also briefly discussed. Positive obligations under human rights law both complement and are complemented by other norms applicable to specific risks, but their peculiarity is that they clarify vertical obligations (i.e. towards the population) and may offer further tools for ensuring accountability in case of violations. The added value of focusing on positive obligations is that these are more directly relevant to the emergency management cycle, while negative obligations are still seen as something external, whose main aim is to establish limits to emergency response measures.

In section 3, public health measures adopted against the current pandemic outbreak, or the lack thereof, have been assessed through the lenses of positive obligations, and some major gaps have been identified. In particular, there is a

---

[109] S. Dagron, 'Going Beyond the Rhetoric: Taking Human Rights Seriously in the Post-COVID-19 New Paradigm', *Verfassungsblog*, 27.03.2021, available at https://verfassungsblog.de/going-beyond-the-rhetoric-taking-human-rights-seriously-in-the-post-covid-19-new-paradigm/, last accessed 05.06.2021.

notable lack of preparedness – despite of several warnings in recent decades and recommendations and international obligations required to prepare and to take measures to protect health care workers, as well as failed early warnings and poor risk communication in the early phases of the outbreak. The COVID-19 emergency has exacerbated existing inequalities among vulnerable groups whose rights are even more impacted. Vulnerable groups are indeed likely to be disproportionately affected both by emergency situations and by the measures adopted to face them. While the human rights discourse aims at addressing the underlying patterns of discrimination and vulnerability that affect these groups, positive obligations applicable to emergency situations are important as they demand to ensure participation of these groups in the elaboration of DRR plans and of recovery programmes, as well as to adopt specific protection measures to reduce the impacts of disaster situations on them.

The world is currently facing an unprecedented global health crisis that is having deep societal and economic implications. Complex as it may be to understand the extent to which epidemic outbreaks can be prevented and their impacts minimised, this is exactly the moment when the opportunity emerges to investigate the main gaps and hopefully identify solutions – from the point of view of ensuring respect of the requirements enshrined in international law. It is hoped that shedding light on the role of positive obligations in these contexts can contribute to moving towards more positive, differentiated and sophisticated models of understanding the interaction between human rights law and emergencies. Bearing in mind the protection of human rights when planning and implementing emergency management measures is not only desirable, but legally required.

ELECTIONS IN TIMES OF COVID-19

A Human Rights Perspective

Christina BINDER and Adam DRNOVSKY*

ABSTRACT

The COVID-19 pandemic has undermined the capacity of states to hold elections. As a result, states are confronted with the following dilemma. While elections in accordance with international standards should be held at regular intervals, elections likewise pose a risk of spreading the disease due to the human-to-human contacts that occur especially during in-person voting on election day.

---

* This contribution is partly based on previous publications of the authors. See C. BINDER, 'Local and regional elections in major crisis situations', Council of Europe, Congress of Local and Regional Authorities, 2020, available at https://rm.coe.int/local-and-regional-elections-in-major-crisis-situations-monitoring-com/16809fa82f, last accessed 08.07.2021; C. BINDER and A. DRNOVSKY, 'To Vote or Not to Vote? An International Human Rights Perspective on Elections in Times of the COVID-19 Pandemic', *Verfassungsblog*, 07.07.2020, available at https://verfassungsblog.de/to-vote-or-not-to-vote/, last accessed 06.07.2021. C. BINDER and A. DRNOVSKY, 'Elections in Times of the COVID-19 Pandemic: An International Human Rights Perspective with a Specific Focus on Vulnerable Groups', (2020) 2(2–3), *Cross-Cultural Human Rights Review*, pp. 62–91.

There is thus a tension between states' duty to protect the rights to life and health of their citizens and their duty to respect the right to political participation and related political freedoms. To overcome this tension, various solutions have been introduced, such as sanitary measures mitigating the risk of contracting the virus during in-person voting, alternative voting methods allowing individuals to cast their ballot outside the polling station or postponement of elections to a later date when elections can be held safely. Still, it is difficult to tackle how to move forward with elections in times of pandemic and, most importantly, whether to hold or postpone elections. This contribution provides an international human rights perspective to assess the available options. It argues that while international human rights leave some leeway to states to decide what fits best for their domestic context, they also give guidance as to whether to hold or postpone elections. This contribution concludes that although certain limitations of electoral standards may be permissible in extraordinary times, international human rights, at the same time, set limits on state action and require that a minimum core of electoral principles be upheld at any time for elections to be meaningful and trustworthy to the public.

1. INTRODUCTION

The current COVID-19 pandemic has undermined states' capacities to hold elections. The danger of infection caused by participation in electoral procedures, most importantly in-person polling on election day, stands in tension with the necessity to conduct elections without any undue delay. Amplified by a high degree of uncertainty revolving around the virus especially during the first wave early in 2020, states have opted for different approaches. The magnitude of the crisis is evident from the fact that around eighty countries and territories across the world have decided to postpone national and subnational elections due to COVID-19. Over 120 states and territories have held national or subnational elections despite concerns related to COVID-19.[1] For example, some countries have decided in favour of in-person elections despite the health risks and practical difficulties, as was the case during the first round of local elections in France in March 2020.[2] Others have relied, at times even exclusively, on remote voting methods as postal voting, such as Bavaria (Germany) during

1 International Idea, 'Global overview of COVID-19: Impact on elections', 09.04.2021, available at https://www.idea.int/news-media/multimedia-reports/global-overview-covid-19-impact-elections, last accessed 09.04.2021.

2 R. Rambaud, 'Holding or Postponing Elections During a COVID-19 Outbreak: Constitutional, Legal and Political Challenges in France', *International IDEA*, 2020, available at https://www.idea.int/sites/default/files/publications/holding-or-postponing-elections-during-a-covid-19-outbreak-v2.pdf, last accessed 09.04.2021.

the second round of local elections held the same month.[3] Large-scale postal voting, complementing in-person voting at polls, was likewise used in the 2020 presidential elections in the United States, where voting by postal ballot became highly disputed during the heated election campaign and after the elections.[4] Among the elections which have been postponed as a result of the pandemic and held later than originally planned were the general elections in Bolivia, originally scheduled for May 2020, then moved to September and eventually held in October 2020 after another postponement.[5] Likewise, in the United Kingdom, local elections in England were postponed for a year to May 2021 due to the outbreak of pandemic.[6] Both holding and postponing elections in times of pandemic has implications for the political rights of individuals under states' jurisdictions.

There are different challenges for the authorities: On the one hand, a state has the obligation to protect the rights to life and health of the individuals under its jurisdiction. In doing so, states must limit the risks for their population: the spread of the disease needs to be contained by reducing human-to-human contact among voters and poll workers to avoid a situation similar to what happened during the local elections in France, where voters as well as poll-workers reportedly were infected during polling and ballot counting on election day.[7] States' duty to protect might thus call for risk-mitigation measures to secure the life and health of their population during the elections, as well as for a more widespread reliance on alternative voting methods. A state may also decide to postpone elections to a later date when risks can be expected to decrease.

At the same time, risk-mitigation measures, alternative voting methods or the postponement of elections encroach, to varying degrees, upon the right to political participation as well as upon the related freedoms of expression, assembly and movement. If an election is postponed indeterminately, the

3 R. Wagner, 'Responding to COVID-19 with 100 per cent Postal Voting: Local Elections in Bavaria, Germany', *International IDEA*, 2020, available at https://www.idea.int/sites/default/files/responding-to-covid-19-with-postal-voting-local-elections-in-bavaria.pdf, last accessed 09.04.2021.

4 L. Peeples, 'COVID and the US election: will the rise of mail-in voting affect the result?', *Nature*, 23.10.2020, available at https://www.nature.com/articles/d41586-020-02979-x, last accessed 09.04.2021.

5 France 24, 'Bolivian elections postponed again due to Covid-19, this time until October', 23.07.2020, available at https://www.france24.com/en/20200723-bolivian-elections-postponed-again-due-to-covid-19-this-time-until-october, last accessed 09.04.2021.

6 BBC News, 'Coronavirus: English local elections postponed for a year', 13.03.2020, available at https://www.bbc.com/news/uk-politics-51876269, last accessed 09.04.2021.

7 F. Magnenou, 'Elections municipales: à Saint-Ouen, un tiers des assesseurs ont déclaré des symptômes évocateurs du coronavirus', *France Info*, 23.04.2020, available at https://www.francetvinfo.fr/sante/maladie/coronavirus/elections-municipales-a-saint-ouen-un-tiers-des-assesseurs-ont-declare-des-symptomes-evocateurs-du-coronavirus_3928917.html, last accessed 09.04.2021.

criterion of periodic elections is at stake. Resorting to alternative voting methods (e.g. exclusive postal or Internet voting) or limitations during the election campaign interfere with the electoral principles of universal, equal, free and secret suffrage and the freedom of assembly and pose challenges, more generally, to the integrity of elections. Interferences with (some of) these principles and/or the integrity of an election may likewise occur if elections are held with mitigating measures in place to secure the health of voters (e.g. limiting the presence of observers). This illustrates the tension between a state's duty to protect (the rights to life and health) and its obligation to respect/not to interfere with the right to political participation and related political freedoms. What can states do to reconcile this tension? How can they deal with elections in times of COVID-19?

The existing literature has indeed approached some of these issues, yet due to the relative novelty of this problem, the extent of the multi-disciplinary research at its current stage is rather limited. Some authors have evaluated the impact of the pandemic from an electoral integrity and democratic theory perspective and arrived at a conclusion that, while justifiable at certain circumstances, postponements should be avoided due to their impact on institutional certainty.[8] Instead, available safeguards for electoral integrity and health safety should be implemented, such as early voting and strengthened risk management, as well as transparency and inclusivity in decision-making.[9] In this context, there is a growing body of literature on various alternative voting methods, such as Internet and postal voting, and their suitability for safeguarding democracy during pandemics.[10] Other authors have focused on impacts of the pandemic on various groups of electoral participants, such as vulnerable persons in general,[11] older voters in particular or election candidates,[12] analysing health risks and related obstacles to their participation in elections, with possible repercussions

---

8 T. S. James and S. Alihodzic, 'When Is It Democratic to Postpone an Election? Elections During Natural Disasters, COVID-19, and Emergency Situations', (2020) 19(3), *Election Law Journal*, pp. 344–362; T. S. James, 'New development: Running elections during a pandemic', (2021) 41(1), *Public Money & Management*, pp. 65–68; T. Landmann and L. Di Gennaro Splendore, 'Pandemic democracy: elections and COVID-19', (2020) 23(7–8), *Journal of Risk Research*, pp. 1060–1066.

9 T. S. James and S. Alihodzic, 'When Is It Democratic to Postpone an Election? Elections During Natural Disasters, COVID-19, and Emergency Situations' (2020), *supra* note 8.

10 R. Krimmer, D. Duenas-Cid and I. Krivonosova, 'Debate: safeguarding democracy during pandemics. Social distancing, postal, or internet voting – the good, the bad or the ugly?', (2020) *Public Money & Management*, pp. 8–10.

11 C. Binder and A. Drnovsky, 'Elections in Times of the COVID-19 Pandemic: An International Human Rights Perspective with a Specific Focus on Vulnerable Groups', (2020) 2(2–3), *Cross-Cultural Human Rights Review*, pp. 1–4.

12 P. Gronke, P. Manson, J. Lee et. at., 'How Elections Under COVID-19 May Change the Political Engagement of Older Voters', (2020) 30(4), *Public Policy & Aging Report*, pp. 147–153. L. Bach, A. Guillouzouic and C. Malgouyres, 'Does holding elections during a Covid-19 pandemic put the lives of politicians at risk?', (2021) 78, *Journal of Health Economics*, pp. 9–15.

on democracy and the rights of persons belonging to these groups.[13] However, no academic has approached this issue comprehensively from a human rights perspective in order to analyse the existing tension in international law between, on the one hand, the duty of states to protect the rights to health and life of their population and, on the other, the states' obligation to respect/not to interfere with the right to political participation and related political freedoms by the holding of periodic elections in line with international electoral standards.

This is the focus of this contribution which proposes a human rights and electoral standards perspective to assess the available options. It starts with states' general human rights obligations: their obligation to protect the rights to life and health of their population and the obligation not to interfere with the right to political participation and related political freedoms (section 2). It continues with possible ways how to approach elections in times of pandemic, namely: in-person elections with mitigation measures; alternative/remote voting; and the postponement of elections – drawing on relevant state practice (section 3). The possible implications of these options for the right to political participation and the principles of universal, equal, free and secret suffrage will be addressed in section 4. As will be shown, each country's situation is different, and the balance between the obligations to protect and respect is thus to be found in a case-/election-specific way. On that basis, we finally discuss parameters which should guide states in their decisions as to whether to hold or postpone elections (section 5). A brief evaluation concludes (section 6).

2. A GENERAL INTERNATIONAL HUMAN RIGHTS PERSPECTIVE ON ELECTIONS IN TIMES OF THE COVID-19 PANDEMIC: STATES' DUTIES TO PROTECT AND TO RESPECT

International human rights standards provide a framework of how to approach the dilemma faced by states in relation to elections in times of pandemic.[14] Challenges relate to all phases of the election process;[15] culminating on

---

13 C. Binder and A. Drnovsky, 'Elections in Times of the COVID-19 Pandemic: An International Human Rights Perspective with a Specific Focus on Vulnerable Groups' (2020), *supra note* 11. See also more generally T. Fernandez-Navia, E. Polo-Muro and D. Tercero-Lucas, 'Too afraid to vote? The effects of COVID-19 on voting behaviour', (2021) *European Journal of Political Economy*, pp. 8–11.

14 C. Binder and A. Drnovsky, 'To Vote or Not to Vote? An International Human Rights Perspective on Elections in Times of the COVID-19 Pandemic', *Verfassungsblog*, 07.07.2020, available at https://verfassungsblog.de/to-vote-or-not-to-vote, last accessed 09.04.2021.

15 See International IDEA, 'Global overview of COVID-19: Impact on elections', 09.04.2021, available at https://www.idea.int/news-media/multimedia-reports/global-overview-covid-19-impact-elections, last accessed 09.04.2021.

election day. This was shown in earlier health crises, such as during the Ebola outbreak in several Western African countries between 2014 and 2016.[16] It is most blatantly evidenced during the COVID-19 pandemic, as illustrated in this contribution. As will be shown, states have some leeway to mediate between their obligations to protect and to respect the rights at stake.

Starting with states' duty to protect, an obligation to contain the disease may first be found in a state's *duty to protect the life* of individuals under its jurisdiction as incorporated in Article 6 of the International Covenant on Civil and Political Rights (ICCPR) and Article 2 of the European Convention on Human Rights (ECHR). To draw on the right to life seems particularly plausible in severe cases where the further spread of the pandemic would put the life of persons at risk (e.g. when the capacities of hospitals are exhausted). This also finds a basis in human rights monitoring institutions' case law. For example, the European Court of Human Rights (ECtHR) has stated previously that a state may be responsible if it knows about life-threatening risks but fails to take the appropriate measures to prevent them. For example, the ECtHR found a violation of the right to life in *Brincat and others v Malta* since Maltese authorities knew about the dangers of asbestos but did not take appropriate measures to protect the health and life of exposed workers.[17]

Similar protection may be derived from the right to health as incorporated, *inter alia*, in Article 12 of the International Covenant of Economic, Social and Cultural Rights (ICESCR) (as well as from Article 11 of the (rev) European Social Charter) and the obligations following therefrom to limit the spread of a disease. Article 12(1) ICESCR recognises everyone's right to 'the enjoyment of the highest attainable standard of physical and mental health.' States also undertake measures for 'the … control of epidemic, endemic … and other diseases' in accordance with Article 12(2.c) ICESCR.[18] In the face of a pandemic, a state may thus be required to adopt a range of measures including individual

---

16 A. Banbury, 'Elections and COVID-19 – what we learned from Ebola', *IFES*, 08.04.2020, available at https://www.ifes.org/news/elections-and-covid-19-what-we-learned-ebola, last accessed 09.04.2021.

17 ECtHR, *Brincat and others v Malta*, nos 60908/11, 62110/11, 62129/11, 62312/11 and 62338/11, 24.07.2014. See also *Budayeva and others v Russia*, the failure of Russian authorities to implement land-use planning and emergency relief policies in the light of the foreseeable risk of a mudslide that led to loss of life was considered a violation of the substantive and procedural aspects of Article 2 ECHR by the ECtHR. ECtHR, *Budayeva and others v Russia*, nos 15339/02, 21166/02, 20058/02, 11673/02 and 15343/02, 20.03.2008. Likewise in *Öneryildiz v Turkey*, when the municipal authorities of Istanbul had failed to prevent a looming methane explosion that happened in a rubbish tip or at least warn the inhabitants who were living near the tip about the dangers, the ECtHR held that the Turkish authorities had not taken the necessary preventive measures to protect the inhabitants and found a violation of Article 2 ECHR, the right to life. ECtHR, *Öneryıldız v Turkey*, no 48939/99, 30.10.2004.

18 See also General Comment No 14 of the UN Committee on Economic, Social and Cultural Rights which establishes the duty to of states '[t]o take measures to prevent, treat and control epidemic and endemic diseases; …'. Postponing elections could be such measure.

quarantines and isolations and even community quarantines (so called '*cordons sanitaires*') to live up to its duty to protect.[19] Respectively, anti-contagion policies, social distancing and quarantines were viewed as most effective from a scientific/empirical viewpoint in the case of the COVID-19 pandemic and have been implemented by numerous countries.[20] On that basis, one may argue that in view of the foreseeable danger of a COVID-19 infection in the course of the electoral process (especially on election day), a state is required to protect the rights to life and health of people by adopting relevant mitigation measures and/or resorting to alternative voting methods or even by postponing elections.

To justify corresponding interferences with the right to political participation and related political freedoms, a state generally has two options. First, it can rely on the respective treaties' emergency clauses (Article 4 ICCPR; Article 15 ECHR) and derogate from pertinent human rights obligations. Especially at the height of the health crisis, when the death toll is high and infections are rising, a temporary derogation from political rights and related freedoms in reliance on the respective treaty's emergency clauses may be justified.[21] Indeed, in Europe, ten states have informed the Council of Europe Secretary General that they derogated from certain rights under the ECHR (although some have withdrawn the derogation since) in face of the COVID-19 pandemic;[22] 22 states

---

19 See respectively the possibility envisaged in Article 18 of the WHO's International Health Regulations: '1. Recommendations issued by WHO to States Parties with respect to persons may include the following advice: … – implement exit screening and/or restrictions on persons from affected areas.'; WHO, 'International Health Regulations', 2005, available at https://www.who.int/publications/i/item/9789241580496, last accessed 11.04.2021.

20 S. Hsiang, D. Allen, S. Annan-Phan et al., 'The effect of large-scale anti-contagion policies on the COVID-19 pandemic', *Nature*, 08.06.2020, available at https://www.nature.com/articles/s41586-020-2404-8, last accessed 09.04.2021. The list of countries changes. For constant updates, see the dynamic list in T. Hale, A. Petherick, T. Phillips et. al., 'Oxford COVID-19 Government Response Tracker', 2020, available at https://www.bsg.ox.ac.uk/research/research-projects/coronavirus-government-response-tracker, last accessed 11.04.2021.

21 The health crisis may be considered as a 'public emergency which threatens the life of the nation'. Likewise, the suspension of obligations may be 'required by the exigencies of the situation'. See the respective para. 1 of Article 4 ICCPR and Article 15 ECHR. As relevant country examples show, especially at the peak of the pandemic, social distancing/containment policies are necessary to flatten the curve of infections. This is amply documented and supported by medical evidence. See S. Hsiang, D. Allen, S. Annan-Phan et al. (2020), 'The effect of large-scale anti-contagion policies on the COVID-19 pandemic', *supra* note 20. See especially the experiences of some countries in R. M. Anderson, H. Heesterbeek, D. Klinkenberk et al., 'How Will Country-Based Mitigation Measures Influence the Course of the COVID-19 Epidemic?', *The Lancet*, 2020, p. 931, available at https://www.thelancet.com/journals/lancet/article/PIIS0140-6736(20)30567-5/fulltext?utm_campaign=tlcoronavirus20&utm_content=120403755&utm_medium=social&utm_source=twitter&hss_channel=tw-27013292, last accessed 11.04.2021.

22 A state is obliged to inform the other states parties (ICCPR) or the Secretary General of the Council of Europe (CoE) (ECHR) of the derogation which allows for some international scrutiny of a state's measures (paragraph 3). As of April 2021: Albania, Armenia, Estonia, Georgia, Latvia, Republic of Moldova, North Macedonia, Romania, San Marino and Serbia.

have done so under the ICCPR.[23] While not referring explicitly to the right to political participation, these derogations concerned related freedoms: for example, Latvia, North Macedonia, Moldova, Estonia, Georgia and Albania derogated, *inter alia*, from their obligations under Article 11 ECHR (freedom of assembly and association) as well as from the freedom of movement (Article 2 of Protocol No 4 to the ECHR). Romania, Armenia, San Marino and Serbia did not explicitly mention the articles affected by their derogation.[24] Under the ICCPR, most derogations were generally either related to the freedoms of movement and assembly (Articles 12, 21 ICCPR) or framed in rather broad terms.[25] Still, opinion is divided as to whether it is commendable that states derogate from their human rights obligations in times of pandemic. Arguments in favour are the increased transparency and international scrutiny in view of states' reporting obligations under the respective paragraphs 3 of Article 4 ICCPR and Article 15 ECHR.[26] Opponents argue that from an international human rights perspective, explicit derogations are not the best option since they limit the human rights monitoring institutions' (ECtHR, Human Rights Committee (HRC)) scrutiny of states' measures.[27]

Council of Europe Treaty Office, 'Reservations and Declarations for Treaty No. 005 – Convention for the Protection of Human Rights and Fundamental Freedoms', 2021, available at https://www.coe.int/en/web/conventions/full-list/-/conventions/treaty/005/declarations, last accessed 11.04.2021.

23 As of April 2021: Colombia, Dominican Republic, Kyrgyzstan, Peru, Argentina, Armenia, Chile, Ecuador, El Salvador, Estonia, Ethiopia, Georgia, Guatemala, Latvia, Republic of Moldova, Romania, San Marino, State of Palestine, Thailand, Namibia, Paraguay and Senegal. UN Treaty Collection, 'International Covenant on Civil and Political Rights', 2021, available at https://treaties.un.org/Pages/ViewDetails.aspx?src=TREATY&mtdsg_no=IV-4&chapter=4&clang=_en, last accessed 11.04.2021.

24 Some countries, such as Romania, have annexed laws which provide from derogation from similar rights. See for further details P. Zghibarta, 'The Whos, the Whats, and the Whys of the Derogations from the ECHR amid COVID-19', *EJIL Talk*, 11.04.2020, available at https://www.ejiltalk.org/the-whos-the-whats-and-the-whys-of-the-derogations-from-the-echr-amid-covid-19/, last accessed 09.04.2021.

25 UN Treaty Collection (2021), 'International Covenant on Civil and Political Rights', *supra* note 23.

26 See Venice Commission, 'Report – Respect for Democracy Human Rights and Rule of Law during States of Emergency: Reflections', CDL-AD(2020)014, 2020, para. 95. For details see K. Istrefi, 'Supervision of Derogations in the Wake of COVID-19: a litmus test for the Secretary General of the Council of Europe', *EJIL Talk*, 06.04.2020, available at https://www.ejiltalk.org/supervision-of-derogations-in-the-wake-of-covid-19-a-litmus-test-for-the-secretary-general-of-the-council-of-europe, last accessed 09.04.2021.

27 There are, however, divergent views: see for example A. Greene, 'States should declare a State of Emergency using Article 15 ECHR to confront the Coronavirus Pandemic', *Strasbourg Observer*, 01.04.2020, available at https://strasbourgobservers.com/2020/04/01/states-should-declare-a-state-of-emergency-using-article-15-echr-to-confront-the-coronavirus-pandemic, last accessed 09.04.2021. For an overview see S. Molloy, 'Covid-19 and Derogations Before the European Court of Human Rights', *Verfassungsblog*, 10.04.2020, available at https://verfassungsblog.de/covid-19-and-derogations-before-the-european-court-of-human-rights, last accessed 09.04.2021. See also M. Scheinin, 'COVID-19 Symposium: To Derogate or Not to Derogate?', *Opinio Juris*, 06.04.2020, available at https://opiniojuris.org/2020/04/06/covid-19-symposium-to-derogate-or-not-to-derogate, last accessed 09.04.2021.

In fact, an explicit derogation is not necessarily needed to justify interferences with the right to political participation and related freedoms.[28] A 'flexibilisation' is possible also in the framework of the respective provisions. All the aforementioned rights – the rights to political participation, expression, assembly and movement – are relative rights whose enjoyment can be restricted under certain conditions: restrictions must be based on law, pursue a legitimate aim and be necessary in a democratic society. Some provisions explicitly refer to these conditions, such as Article 21 ICCPR or Articles 10 and 11 para. 2 ECHR; others presuppose them implicitly, such as the right to political participation (Article 25 ICCPR; Article 3 of Protocol 1 to the ECHR) and the freedom of movement (Article 12 para. 1 ICCPR; Article 2 of Protocol No 4 to the ECHR). In light of a health crisis, to lawfully interfere with the respective political rights and freedoms, a state thus has to comply with the following conditions: the laws providing for the interference must be sufficiently clear and accessible to those concerned.[29] The measures (postponement of elections; restrictions of movement and assembly; mitigation measures on election day (see below, section 3)) must pursue a legitimate aim (including public health or the protection of the rights of others); and they have to be necessary in a democratic society – that is, they must be proportional.[30] On that basis, especially at the height of the pandemic, certain interferences with the right to political participation and related political freedoms are arguably permissible.

Thus, different approaches to elections in times of pandemic may be required and also justified in general human rights law which offers a framework of how to balance states' duties to protect and to respect. Let us now consider what concrete options states therefore have available.

3. THE CONDUCT OF ELECTIONS IN TIMES OF COVID-19: A VIEW FROM STATE PRACTICE

There are several options at the disposal of states how to conduct elections in times of COVID-19. In order to mitigate the existing risks while still

---

28 See for example K. Dzehtsiarou, 'COVID-19 and the European Convention on Human Rights', *Strasbourg Observer*, 27.03.2020, available at https://strasbourgobservers.com/2020/03/27/covid-19-and-the-european-convention-on-human-rights, last accessed 09.04.2021. See for a discussion also M. Scheinin (2020), 'COVID-19 Symposium: To Derogate or Not to Derogate?', *supra* note 27.

29 See, respectively, UN Sub-Commission on Prevention of Discrimination and Protection of Minorities 'Siracusa Principles on the Limitation and Derogation of Provisions in the International Covenant on Civil and Political Rights', 1984, paras. 15–18 (esp. para. 17: 'Legal rules limiting the exercise of human rights shall be clear and accessible to everyone').

30 For details on the balancing of rights and means, see O. De Schutter, *International Human Rights Law: Cases, Materials, Commentary*, Cambridge University Press, Cambridge 2010, pp. 293 et seq. See e.g. ECtHR where restrictions of movement were considered justified in

holding elections, social distancing and strict sanitary rules can be imposed.[31] Additionally, alternative/remote voting methods, such as postal voting, may be used to complement or even replace traditional voting in order to minimise the risk of human-to-human contact.[32] If none of these options are feasible or if the risk of infection is too high, authorities still may postpone elections.

3.1. MITIGATING MEASURES

In the midst of the COVID-19 pandemic, states may adopt different mitigating measures to ensure the health of all participants during in-person elections.[33]

Various countries have implemented according measures to avoid or reduce crowding during the electoral process. South Korea is often presented as a showcase example of a country implementing strict mitigating measures at the beginning of the pandemic during parliamentary elections in April 2020, when a comprehensive approach was adopted by the authorities to reduce human-to-human contact on election day: South Korean voters were encouraged to make use of in-person early voting options which were provided at any of the 3,500 polling stations nationwide. Along with early postal voting (see below), this helped to ensure that more than one-fourth of all registered voters voted ahead of election day.[34] Many of the measures implemented in South Korea have since been replicated in other countries holding elections during the pandemic.[35]

---

light of a health emergency: Directly interpreting restrictions of movement in the context of infectious diseases. ECtHR, *Enhorn v Sweden*, no 56529/00, 25.01.2005, paras. 43–45.

31 J. Hollingsworth and J. Kwon, 'South Korea sees the largest turnout in almost 30 years in election held during coronavirus outbreak', *CNN World*, 16.04.2020, available at https://edition.cnn.com/2020/04/15/asia/south-korea-election-intl-hnk/index.html, last accessed 09.04.2021.

32 Euronews, 'Germany: Bavaria's municipal elections go ahead despite coronavirus concerns', 15.03.2020, available at https://www.euronews.com/2020/03/15/germany-bavaria-s-municipal-elections-go-ahead-despite-coronavirus-concerns, last accessed 09.04.2021.

33 In particular, this includes crowding and human-to-human contact, which constitute a high risk of transmission of respiratory droplets among the crowd and/or people queuing. That can occur throughout different phases of the electoral process, such as campaign rallies, voter registration procedures, the training of electoral staff and observers and the administrative preparation of elections. However, the most critical phase is the polling procedures on election day. See C. D. Cotti, B. Engelhardt, J. Foster et al., 'The Relationship between In-Person Voting and Covid-19: Evidence from the Wisconsin Primary', NBER Working Paper No. w27187, 2020, available at https://papers.ssrn.com/sol3/papers.cfm?abstract_id=3603818, last accessed 09.04.2021.

34 A. Spinelli, 'Managing Elections under the COVID-19 Pandemic: The Republic of Korea's Crucial Test', *International IDEA*, 2020, available at https://www.idea.int/sites/default/files/publications/managing-elections-during-pandemic-republic-korea-crucial-test.pdf last accessed 09.04.2021.

35 E. Asplund, L. Heuver, F. Ahmed et al., 'Elections and Covid-19: Health and safety in polling stations', *International IDEA*, 2021, available at https://www.idea.int/news-media/news/elections-and-covid-19-health-and-safety-polling-stations, last accessed 09.04.2021.

Additional mitigating measures have been employed as well, such as extending the hours of voting or spreading out the turnout over more days, as was the case in the November 2020 general elections in Jordan as well as during the national referendum in Italy in September 2020,[36] respectively.[37] Likewise, establishing polling stations in bigger venues and raising the overall number of polling stations have contributed to reduced crowding in and around polling stations on election day. This played a role in the November 2020 US presidential elections during which voters could vote in large sports stadiums.[38] Drive-in voting proved to be a useful option to avoid contact between voters and poll worker in the polling station, especially when it came to vulnerable voters or those who are or might be infected, as was the case in the October 2020 elections in Lithuania.[39] Inside polling stations, markings and signs have been made to instruct voters to keep at least one meter apart (preferably up to two meters) from each other (this was used e.g. during the first round of local elections in France).[40]

Apart from polling procedures, restrictions were imposed on campaign activities with regard to implementing the required social distancing measures and/or banning public gatherings. For instance, in France, only campaign rallies with no more than 1,000 persons attending were allowed.[41] Before the July 2020 parliamentary elections in Singapore, all public gatherings were banned as permits for election rallies were simply not granted.[42] In South Korea, most in-person election campaign activities were suspended and moved online,

---

36 L. Al-Junaidi, 'Jordan: Elections see low turnout amid virus spread', *Anadolu Agency*, 11.11.2020, available at https://www.aa.com.tr/en/middle-east/jordan-elections-see-low-turnout-amid-virus-spread/2040736, last accessed 09.04.2021.

37 Il Fatto Quotidiano, 'Elezioni e referendum 2020, come e quando si vota: le regole di sicurezza anti-covid', 18.09.2020, available at https://www.ilfattoquotidiano.it/2020/09/18/elezioni-e-referendum-2020-come-e-quando-si-vota-le-regole-di-sicurezza-anti-covid/5936001, last accessed 09.04.2021.

38 E. Pilkington, 'Sports teams tackle voting crisis with plan to turn arenas into polling stations', *The Guardian*, 18.08.2020, available at https://www.theguardian.com/us-news/2020/aug/18/us-voting-mail-sports-arenas-football-basketball-hockey-baseball, last accessed 09.04.2021.

39 AP News, 'Lithuanians with COVID-19, self-isolating vote in drive-ins', 19.10.2020, available at https://apnews.com/article/virus-outbreak-national-elections-lithuania-elections-europe-75bef74b7e8985e81908345ead6bb8d8, last accessed 10.04.2021.

40 Note, however, that the example of France has shown, that recommended (social distancing) measures may not always be sufficient to avoid transmission. F. Magnenou (2020), 'Elections municipales: à Saint-Ouen, un tiers des assesseurs ont déclaré des symptômes évocateurs du coronavirus', *supra* note 7.

41 The Economist, 'France suspends local elections because of covid-19', 21.03.2020, available at https://www.economist.com/europe/2020/03/19/france-suspends-local-elections-because-of-covid-19, last accessed 10.04.2021.

42 Y. Tan, 'Coronavirus in Singapore: Election campaigning without the handshakes', *BBC News*, 06.06.2020, available at https://www.bbc.com/news/world-asia-53216390, last accessed 10.04.2021.

while campaigning on television and radio was used more extensively to reach out to voters preferring more traditional channels.[43]

Further measures for elections during a pandemic relate to the procedures of in-person voter registration and candidate nomination. For the former, this is the case especially in countries where active voter registration is in place or where voters' physical presence is necessary for certain registration procedures (e.g. verification or correction of data entries in voter registers). Mitigation measures to reduce crowding at the registration office may include the assignation of scheduled timeslots for registration. The process of candidate nomination can be regulated in a similar manner. Ultimately, both procedures may, to a certain degree, be conducted remotely.[44]

From the perspective of hygienic and sanitary measures, good practice indicates that wearing face masks and plastic gloves help contain the transmission of the disease among those participating in elections. This was made mandatory during elections in a number of countries, such as in Bolivia, Czech Republic, Jordan and others.[45] In addition, South Korea implemented widespread provisions for the disinfection of voters' hands and polling station premises as well as objects frequently touched by voters. Furthermore, voters in South Korea had their temperature checked, and those with a higher temperature were sent to specially designated polling stations to be allowed to vote, which helped to ensure that the principle of universal suffrage was respected.[46] Observance of social distancing, hygienic/cough etiquette and hand-washing among voters and poll workers can be encouraged with publicly displayed banners in and around polling stations and be accompanied by a code of conduct providing detailed instructions.[47] Voters may also be asked to bring their own pens to avoid transmission when signing the voter register, as was the case in France.[48]

Also for the protection of poll workers, a number of countries implemented strict measures, including personal protective equipment like face masks and plastic gloves which were made mandatory for polling staff, as well as instructions

---

43 A. Spinelli (2020), 'Managing Elections under the COVID-19 Pandemic: The Republic of Korea's Crucial Test', *supra* note 34.

44 See example of Iceland where presidential candidates collect electronic signatures to support their nomination. L. Kyzer. 'Six Candidates Running for President', *Icelandic Review*, 16.05.2020, available at https://www.icelandreview.com/politics/six-candidates-running-for-president/, last accessed 10.04.2021.

45 E. Asplund, L. Heuver, F. Ahmed et al. (2021), 'Elections and Covid-19: Health and safety in polling stations', *supra* note 35.

46 A. Spinelli (2020), 'Managing Elections under the COVID-19 Pandemic: The Republic of Korea's Crucial Test', *supra* note 34.

47 E. Asplund, L. Heuver, F. Ahmed et al. (2021), 'Elections and Covid-19: Health and safety in polling stations', *supra* note 35.

48 Euronews, 'Record low turnout in French municipal elections amidst coronavirus fears', 16.03.2020, available at https://www.euronews.com/2020/03/15/france-voters-take-to-the-polls-amid-coronavirus-fears, last accessed 10.04.2021.

on how to avoid touching the election materials (like voter identity documents) and regular disinfections of places where voters go. However, compliance has often been an issue; for example in Serbia, international observers noted that personal protective equipment was readily available but not used consistently.[49] Regarding the training of electoral staff and election observers, virtual training has been developed and used as an alternative to in-person activities. For instance, this was the case in the 2020 local elections in Ukraine, where online courses were made widely available, although were not mandatory for electoral staff to attend.[50]

Lastly, specific measures are necessary for vulnerable groups (the elderly, people with health conditions and/or hospitalised persons etc.) through the provision of adequate options for polling and voter information. To reduce the risk of infection, persons from these groups should be allowed and encouraged to vote through alternative voting methods even if the general population votes in-person. For example, in Italy, older people, pregnant women and other vulnerable persons were allowed to skip the lines at polling stations.[51] In South Korea, home voting provisions for hospitalised people were extended which guaranteed the enfranchisement of vulnerable citizens. Hence, polling stations could be relocated from areas close to independent or assisted living facilities, retirement communities and care centres to decrease the risk of transmission.[52] Alternatively, separate polling stations only for voters from vulnerable groups could be established.

3.2. ALTERNATIVE VOTING METHODS

The current COVID-19 pandemic has especially drawn attention to alternative methods to complement (or even replace) traditional in-person voting in order to avoid human-to-human contact amongst voters and poll workers on election day, while also maintaining voter turnout. Alternative voting methods include

---

49 See OSCE/ODIHR, 'Republic of Serbia – Parliamentary Elections, 21 June 2020', Statement of Preliminary Findings and Conclusions, 2020, p. 4, available at https://www.osce.org/files/f/documents/8/e/455155.pdf, last accessed 10.04.2021. See also Reuters, 'Masked and gloved: Israelis in quarantine from coronavirus vote in election', 02.03.2020, available at https://www.reuters.com/article/us-israel-election-health-coronavirus/masked-and-gloved-israelis-in-quarantine-from-coronavirus-vote-in-election-idUSKBN20P1BZ, last accessed 10.04.2021.

50 OSCE/ODIHR, 'Ukraine – Local Elections, 25 October 2020', Final Report, 2020, available at https://www.osce.org/files/f/documents/3/e/476974_1.pdf, last accessed 10.04.2021.

51 Il Fatto Quotidiano (2020), 'Elezioni e referendum 2020, come e quando si vota: le regole di sicurezza anti-covid', *supra* note 37.

52 Centers for Disease Control and Prevention, 'Polling Locations and Voters Interim guidance to prevent spread of coronavirus disease 2019 (COVID-19)', 01.04.2021, available at https://www.cdc.gov/coronavirus/2019-ncov/community/election-polling-locations.html, last accessed 10.04.2021.

sending a ballot by post (also called postal voting, mail-in ballot), casting a vote online through a computer or mobile phone application (also referred to as electronic voting, e-voting, Internet voting, online voting) or by means of voting by proxy or by mobile ballot box. These methods allow voters to cast their ballots either remotely or by involving other persons; some of them can be utilised to expand early voting provisions. A growing number of states have provided for alternative/remote voting or are considering doing so in upcoming elections.

Postal voting has become one of the most discussed, and indeed most widely used, options to replace/complement in-person voting during the COVID-19 pandemic. In some states, postal voting has been introduced for this purpose, mostly where such provision had already been provided for in the legal framework, for example for out-of-country voters (an option used recently in Romania),[53] for voters with disabilities (in use recently in Poland)[54] or those voters of a certain age considered vulnerable (e.g. voters in the Netherlands over the age of 70),[55] for voters in hospitals and prisons (recently used in Lithuania)[56] or as a general option of voting when certain conditions are met (e.g. early registration or provision of a specific reason, as is the option in Austria for those unable to vote in person).[57] Postal voting was successfully used in South Korea and in the United States where widespread provisions were made for early voting by postal ballot.[58] In the German Federal State of Bavaria, in March 2020, voters were free to decide to vote either in-person or by post in the first round and then provided with an all-postal voting ballot in the second round when the sanitary situation had further deteriorated.[59] The considerable success, demonstrated by

53 OSCE/ODIHR, 'Romania – Parliamentary Elections, 6 December 2020', Statement of Preliminary Findings and Conclusions, 2020, available at https://www.osce.org/files/f/documents/4/9/472812_0.pdf, last accessed 10.04.2021.

54 OSCE/ODIHR, 'Poland – Presidential Elections, 28 June and 12 July 2020', Final Report, 2020, available at https://www.osce.org/files/f/documents/6/2/464601.pdf, last accessed 10.04.2021.

55 OSCE/ODIHR, 'The Netherlands – Parliamentary Elections, 17 March 2021', Needs Assessment Mission Report, 2021, available at https://www.osce.org/files/f/documents/4/0/478501_0.pdf, last accessed 10.04.2021.

56 OSCE/ODIHR, 'Republic of Lithuania – Parliamentary Elections, 11 and 25 October 2020', Election Expert Team Report, 2021, available at https://www.osce.org/files/f/documents/e/a/477730_0.pdf, last accessed 10.04.2021.

57 OSCE/ODIHR, 'Republic of Austria – Early Parliamentary Elections, 29 September 2019', Needs Assessment Mission Report, 2019, available at https://www.osce.org/files/f/documents/1/a/429095.pdf, last accessed 10.04.2021.

58 For an overview of states' practices and their compatibility with international standards see Venice Commission, 'Report on the Compatibility of Remote Voting and Electronic Voting with the Standards of the Council of Europe', CDL-AD(2004)012, 2004, available at https://www.venice.coe.int/webforms/documents/default.aspx?pdffile=CDL-AD(2004)012-e, last accessed 10.04.2021.

59 R. Wagner (2020), 'Responding to COVID-19 with 100 per cent Postal Voting: Local Elections in Bavaria, Germany', *supra* note 3.

high electoral turnout, is also due to Bavaria's previous long-standing experience with postal voting which is considered trustworthy amongst voters, many of whom have grown accustomed to voting in this manner. Likewise, the option to vote by postal ballot boosted voter turnout in South Korea and in the US,[60] though in the latter this method of voting became highly politicised, and the overall results of elections were disputed on this ground, despite a lack of evidence of widespread fraud.[61]

Unlike traditional paper-based methods, new voting technologies (NVTs) provide electronic means to cast and count votes, using information and communications technologies. Perhaps the most commonly known NVT which regained prominence in debates especially during the COVID-19 pandemic is Internet voting. However, contrary to postal voting, Internet voting is much more difficult to set up. In fact, only a handful of countries in the world regularly rely on Internet voting, while several others have tested this method but later returned to traditional voting methods.[62] Due to the high levels of planning, preparation and testing needed, it is unlikely that countries which do not already have the systems in place would be able to introduce NVTs, and in particular Internet voting, as an immediate response to a pandemic. For instance, the Lithuanian government adopted new legal amendments to provide for Internet voting three months before the 2020 general elections. However, it was estimated that up to two years would be needed to develop and test such a system. The government was thus forced to back away from the planned introduction of Internet voting for the upcoming elections.[63]

Two more traditional methods have been considered or used in times of pandemic: proxy voting and voting by mobile ballot box. Proxy voting is a form of voting whereby a registered voter may delegate his or her voting power to a representative, to enable a vote in absence. Proxy voting can, under certain conditions preventing fraud,[64] offer a further option available to a limited number of voters, especially vulnerable groups, to participate in an election without being required to visit a polling station. For instance, proxy voting is in use in France where voters normally have to apply for permission personally,

[60] D. Desilver, 'Turnout soared in 2020 as nearly two-thirds of eligible U.S. voters cast ballots for president', *Pew Research Center*, 28.01.2021, available at https://www.pewresearch.org/fact-tank/2021/01/28/turnout-soared-in-2020-as-nearly-two-thirds-of-eligible-u-s-voters-cast-ballots-for-president, last accessed 10.04.2021.

[61] OSCE/ODIHR, 'United States of America – General Elections, 3 November 2020', Final Report, 2021, available at https://www.osce.org/files/f/documents/7/7/477823_2.pdf, last accessed 10.04.2021.

[62] Estonia, some cantons in Switzerland, tested e.g. in Norway.

[63] LRT English, 'Lithuanian government backs online voting, but with caveats', 22.06.2020, available at https://www.lrt.lt/en/news-in-english/19/1190786/lithuanian-government-backs-online-voting-but-with-caveats, last accessed 10.04.2021.

[64] See Venice Commission, 'Code of Good Practice in Electoral Matters', CDL-AD(2002)23, 2002, I.3.2.v, available at https://rm.coe.int/090000168092af01, last accessed 10.04.2021.

but due to the COVID-19 crisis certain groups of voters could request that a policeman come to their home to assess the application in advance. The exception was granted to persons in quarantine or confined due to illness, to those who could not move due to a disease or disability and to persons living in retirement facilities.[65] Likewise, this option was made available to these categories of voters during the pandemic in such countries as Croatia,[66] Poland and Switzerland.[67] In general terms, voting by proxy during a pandemic is possible in countries where this option is provided by law.

Voting by mobile ballot, on the contrary, entails poll workers bringing the ballot box to a voter's address. This method is often used in elections to allow those voters to cast their ballot who cannot come to the polling station due to their impaired mobility. In times of a pandemic, the use of mobile ballot boxes has been expanded to a wider group of voters. For example, voters infected with COVID-19 or in quarantine were allowed to vote by mobile ballot box during elections in Georgia and Croatia.[68] In addition, this provision was extended to voters from vulnerable groups, such as in Lithuania where voters over 70 years could request to vote this way.[69] In any case, high standards of protection must be applied when poll workers deliver the mobile ballot box to the voter.

To conclude, alternative/remote voting methods broaden the range of options a state has when holding elections in times of pandemic.[70]

---

65 IFES, 'Featured Elections Held and Mitigating Measures Taken During COVID-19', 2020, available at https://www.ifes.org/sites/default/files/elections_held_and_mitigating_measures_taken_during_covid-19.pdf, last accessed 10.04.2021.

66 Total Croatia News, 'DIP: People Infected with COVID-19 Allowed to Vote by Proxy', 03.06.2020, available at https://www.total-croatia-news.com/politics/44756-dip-people-infected-with-covid-19-allowed-to-vote-by-proxy, last accessed 10.04.2021.

67 OSCE/ODIHR (2020), 'Poland – Presidential Elections, 28 June and 12 July 2020', *supra* note 54. The Swiss Authorities Online, 'Abstimmungs- und Wahlhilfen für ältere Menschen, Menschen mit Behinderung und Kranke', 2021, available at https://www.ch.ch/de/demokratie/abstimmungen/abstimmungs-und-wahlhilfen-fur-altere-menschen-menschen-mit, last accessed 10.04.2021.

68 Election Administration of Georgia, 'The CEC Approved Special Lists of Voters in Isolation', 30.10.2020, available at https://cesko.ge/eng/list/show/122173-tseskom-izolatsiashi-mkofi-amomrchevlebis-spetsialuri-siebi-daamtkitsa-, last accessed 10.04.2021. OSCE/ODIHR, 'Republic of Croatia – Parliamentary Elections, 5 July 2020', Final Report, 2020, available at https://www.osce.org/files/f/documents/b/4/465120_0.pdf, last accessed 10.04.2021.

69 OSCE/ODIHR (2021), 'Republic of Lithuania – Parliamentary Elections, 11 and 25 October 2020', *supra* note 56.

70 In any case, alternative voting methods seem suitable to complement rather than replace traditional voting, during pandemics. It was held that, in light of international good practice, in-person voting should always be possible and available to voters when they preferred. Venice Commission (2002), 'Code of Good Practice in Electoral Matters', II.2.b., *supra* note 64.

3.3. POSTPONEMENT OF ELECTIONS

Nevertheless, both mitigating measures as well as alternative voting methods come at a price from the perspective of compliance with international electoral standards. At times, they are also difficult to implement from the practical point of view, such as when they require amendments of the legal framework governing the elections which need to be made sufficiently in advance. Issues of funding and human resources, *inter alia*, represent additional challenges. Therefore, authorities may eventually opt for the third available option at their disposal and decide to postpone elections. Although in some countries, such as the US, legal deadlines for holding of elections cannot be easily changed, election postponements are also often allowed, or at least not ruled out, by constitutions or electoral legal frameworks, *inter alia*, in times of state of emergency.[71] In some countries, postponement is even obligatory, for example, by a constitutional clause, when a state of emergency was declared, such as in Poland where, however, in May 2020 no state of emergency was declared in order for elections to take place – notwithstanding the pandemic.[72]

As a result, numerous elections worldwide have been postponed since the outbreak of the pandemic, most of which were moved to a later date and eventually held under conditions aiming to ensure their safer conduct. Sometimes, this was not without controversies, as was the case in Poland where postponement and determination of the new date of elections were both highly politicised.[73] In some countries, governments have been criticised for abusing election postponements for political aims, such as undermining a united opposition, as was the case after the postponed general elections in Serbia.[74] While most regularly scheduled elections have been postponed for a maximum of several months,[75] local elections in the United Kingdom originally planned for May 2020 were postponed for a year to May 2021 – and not without criticism for such a lengthy postponement.[76]

---

71 Many countries have relied on such clauses to postpone elections or referendums due to COVID-19: for example, Chile, France, Serbia, Sri Lanka and the United Kingdom. K. Ellena and C. Vickery, 'The Legal Quagmire of Postponing or Modifying Elections', IFES, 14 April 2020, available at https://www.ifes.org/news/legal-quagmire-postponing-or-modifying-elections, last accessed 09.06.2021.

72 V. Vashchanka, 'Political, legal and organizational lessons from elections in the time of a pandemic – Republic of Poland', *International IDEA*, 09.07.2020, available at https://www.idea.int/news-media/news/political-legal-and-organizational-lessons-elections-time-pandemic-republic-poland, last accessed 10.04.2021.

73 Ibid.

74 OSCE/ODIHR, 'Republic of Serbia – Parliamentary Elections, 21 June 2020', Final Report, 2020, available at https://www.osce.org/files/f/documents/a/3/466026.pdf, last accessed 10.04.2021.

75 International Idea (2021), 'Global overview of COVID-19: Impact on elections', *supra* note 15.

76 BBC News (2020), 'Coronavirus: English local elections postponed for a year', *supra* note 6.

Respectively, different situations need to be distinguished in terms of the postponement's implications. Elections can be cancelled, meaning that electoral processes like voter and candidate registration are discontinued and a new process is launched from scratch for the new election. Alternatively, elections can be delayed/postponed, meaning that the ongoing electoral processes and their timeframes are suspended and restored once the postponed election is held.[77] The difference is however not always clear, like, for example, in the 2020 postponed presidential elections in Poland, where the elections were held only *de jure*, but no voting took place on the election day until new elections were announced and held almost two months later.[78] Generally, the shorter the gap between the originally scheduled and the postponed election, the less impact may be expected due to the discontinuation of the electoral processes. When only the second round is postponed, typically, no issues should arise in terms of voter or candidate registration, except for regular situations like updating the voter register between rounds in terms of deleting deceased voters, adding voters who reached voting age and reflecting changes in residency of voters where relevant.[79]

Consequently, states have very different options when it comes to elections in times of pandemics, depending on the circumstances at stake. This brings us to the issue of the implications of these options from an electoral standards perspective.

4. AN ELECTORAL STANDARDS PERSPECTIVE ON ELECTIONS IN TIMES OF COVID-19

The right to political participation, in principle, requires the holding of periodic elections based on universal, equal, free and secret suffrage (Article 25 ICCPR, Article 3 of Protocol 1 to the ECHR).[80] It has been concretised and complemented

---

77 K. Ellena, 'Legal Considerations When Delaying or Adapting Elections', *IFES*, 2020, available at https://www.ifes.org/sites/default/files/ifes_covid-19_briefing_series_legal_considerations_when_delaying_or_adapting_elections_june_2020.pdf, last accessed 10.04.2021.

78 OSCE/ODIHR (2020), 'Poland – Presidential Elections, 28 June and 12 July 2020', *supra* note 54.

79 Venice Commission (2002), 'Code of Good Practice in Electoral Matters', I.1.2.vi., *supra* note 64.

80 See for relevant case law on the right to political participation in Article 25 ICCPR, e.g. M. Nowak, *UN Covenant on Civil and Political Rights. CCPR Commentary*, N. P. Engel, Kehl 2005, pp. 563 et seq. S. Joseph and M. Castan, *The International Covenant on Civil and Political Rights. Cases, Materials and Commentary*, Oxford University Press, Oxford 2013, pp. 738–750. In addition, on the right to free elections in Article 3 of Prot. 1 ECHR and relevant case law see W. Schabas, *The European Convention on Human Rights. A Commentary*, Oxford University Press, Oxford 2015, p. 1011 et seq. C. Grabenwarter, *The European Convention on Human Rights. Commentary*, Beck-Hart-Nomos, 2014, pp. 399 et seq.

by best practices/soft law standards in the context of international organisations such as in the Venice Commission's Code of Good Practice in Electoral Matters.[81] Therewith, electoral standards and best practices allow for a focused consideration of the above approaches (in-person voting with mitigating measures, alternative voting or postponement).

First of all, elections have to be held at regular intervals, as established by the principle of the periodicity of elections. While periodicity may be seen as a relatively vague term, relevant best practices imply a maximum of five years intervals between elections for the legislature (parliament) and seven years for the executive (president).[82] These limits generally have to be kept in mind when it comes to a postponement of elections.

The remaining principles apply to the practical realisation of the right to political participation. The principle of universal suffrage concerns the overall eligibility and the access of the general public to the electoral process. In essence, it requires the most widespread participation in the elections. In other words, elections must be as inclusive as possible, both in the positive and negative dimension of the right. This relates to voter (and candidate) registration and spans to the casting of the ballot on election day.[83] In times of COVID-19, from the perspective of the principle of universal suffrage, it matters whether mitigating measures entail the direct or indirect exclusion of certain groups of normally eligible persons. Direct exclusion may occur, for instance, when those infected with the virus are in home isolation or in hospital without being provided an alternative to casting the ballot in-person.[84] Indirect exclusion may affect certain groups of eligible voters who are technically not prevented from going to the polls but are considered COVID-19 risk groups, such as those aged over 65 and/or with underlying health conditions, who are as such less likely to vote for fear of contracting the virus. The principle of universal suffrage is also at stake in the case of active voter registration, when voter registers risk being incomplete due to pandemic-related restrictions; and for candidate registration, such as when the collection of signatures for (independent) candidates to qualify to run for election is encroached upon under conditions of limited freedom of movement and assembly.

---

81 Venice Commission (2002), 'Code of Good Practice in Electoral Matters', *supra* note 64. Additional protection/affirmative measures are required to facilitating the political participation of marginalised/disadvantaged groups as women or persons with disabilities etc. (Article 7 CEDAW, Article 5.c CERD, Article 29 CRPD). See generally also the prohibition of discrimination, Article 14 ECHR, Article 2, 26 ICCPR.

82 Venice Commission (2002), 'Code of Good Practice in Electoral Matters', I.6., *supra* note 64.

83 Ibid., I.1.

84 Likewise, out-of-country voters may not be able to cast the ballot by post from abroad or at their embassy/consulate due to limitations on freedom of movement within the country of their residence.

Relatedly, the principle of equal suffrage requires that the eligible population access the electoral process on equal footing and without distinctions based on obstacles of direct or indirect nature as described above. Should certain groups have reduced access, arguably, such a situation may amount to indirect discrimination on grounds of belonging to a particular group, be it older persons, out-of-country voters, independent candidates or others. Further, equal suffrage entails equality of opportunity – which in practice means an equal playing field for candidates and parties in the areas of election campaign and media coverage.[85] In times of COVID-19, with limitations imposed on freedoms of movement, expression and assembly, traditional campaign strategies that require human-to-human contact are limited, such as political rallies and door-to-door canvassing. As a result, campaign activities may rely to a greater degree than usual on other means, such as displaying campaign banners and billboards. Increased reliance on these methods entails greater risks as regards the misuse of administrative resources by incumbents, for example by taking advantage of public spaces for displaying banners. This applies even more to the media, as a vast majority of campaigning moves to the TV and radio, as well as to new media such as online advertisement and social media platforms. By that, the importance of equal coverage in the media during election campaigns grows even bigger. This is likely to give an advantage to the incumbents enjoying more media attention, both in private and public media.

In a related manner, the principle of free suffrage requires that voters be able to witness an electoral campaign where they have the opportunity to freely choose their elected representatives. Additionally, free suffrage entails freedom of voters to express their wishes at polls and combat electoral fraud.[86] In times of COVID-19, the principle of free suffrage is at risk when the freedom of voters to form an opinion based on the widest possible choice of parties/candidates is limited. This occurs in situations when traditional ways of campaigning are limited, giving an undue advantage to incumbents due to such malpractices as the misuse of administrative resources or unequal media coverage. Likewise, if mitigating measures are not (or not sufficiently) in place, voters may feel afraid of going to the polls due to a lack of confidence in the effectiveness of the implemented risk-mitigating measures aimed at preventing the spread of the virus. The element of free suffrage is also at risk when alternative voting methods are widely used, allowing voters to cast their ballots safely, such as remotely or outside the polling station, but falling short of some of the safeguards that normally ensure the integrity of the ballot. Postal voting may be insecure, that is, susceptible to intentional interference, and/or unreliable when postal services

---

85 Venice Commission (2002), 'Code of Good Practice in Electoral Matters', I.2., *supra* note 64.

86 Ibid., I.3.

cannot be trusted to deliver the ballots. In principle, the same applies to electronic voting, which is additionally more likely to lack transparency and thus limit the confidence of electoral stakeholders and confuse some voters. Finally, voting by proxy opens the door for voter impersonation, whereas voting by mobile ballot box exposes voters to possible interferences. Free suffrage can be then affected by intimidation and pressure on voters, such as in the case of family voting.

Indeed, the integrity of the ballot is inherently linked to the principle of secret suffrage, which entails that each voter casts the ballot individually without disclosing for whom she or he voted.[87] Secrecy of the vote must always be taken as a priority when introducing new voting methods or expanding the existing provisions for alternative voting. The secrecy must apply not only during the process of casting the ballot, be it physically outside the polling station or by remote means, but also when votes are counted. This again becomes a risk during pandemics when alternative voting methods are used. The voting procedures taking place outside the controlled environment of a polling station are generally more susceptible to violations of the secrecy of the vote.[88]

Moreover, practical realisation of the electoral principles is not possible without conditions guaranteeing respect for the political freedoms of expression, assembly and movement (Articles 19, 21, 22 and 12 ICCPR; Articles 10, 11 ECHR and Article 2 of Protocol 4 to the ECHR).[89] However, in times of a pandemic, these rights are significantly restricted. Most importantly, freedom of movement is limited for the purpose of reducing human-to-human contact, which proved to be a common policy of containment. As has been shown, this may affect, most fundamentally, voters' ability to travel to the polling station to cast their ballot. The freedom of assembly, conversely, is encroached upon when containment measures prevent parties and candidates from holding campaign rallies and other political events, both due to the limited movement of people as well as the unavoidable human-to-human contacts that occurs in such settings. Finally, freedom of expression is impacted by restrictions imposed on the former two freedoms, with journalists unable to freely travel and report on matters of relevance for voters during campaigns, or candidates banned from convening campaign rallies to inform voters about their platforms.

Conditions for implementing the electoral principles also relate to the regulatory levels and the stability of electoral law. Good electoral practice advises against adopting fundamental changes of the electoral law, in particular the electoral system itself, membership of electoral commissions and the drawing of constituency boundaries, less than a year before elections and without a broad consensus.[90] This may pose a challenge during a pandemic, when late

87 Ibid., I.4.
88 Ibid., I.3.2.
89 Ibid., II.1.
90 Ibid., II.2.

amendments to electoral legislation are needed in order to introduce/expand alternative voting methods, for example.

Furthermore, conditions for the implementation of electoral principles require certain procedural safeguards ensuring, first, the impartial and effective administration of elections.[91] In times of COVID-19, election management bodies may be paralysed, however, by the pandemic, lacking personnel to administer the elections (on the level of polling stations as well as on higher levels of management) and encounter limitations concerning the training of poll workers. These two challenges, possibly coupled with a lack of protective equipment against the virus and insufficient funding, can put the election administration in such a position that management of elections becomes unfeasible.

Moreover, the right to an effective remedy (Article 2.3 ICCPR, Article 13 ECHR)[92] calls for complaint mechanisms before election management bodies and a possible appeal to court at all stages of the electoral process.[93] This applies to challenges of the election results, decisions taken before the elections in connection to electoral registers and candidate registration, compliance with the rules governing the electoral campaign and access to the media and political party funding.[94] Functioning complaints and appeals mechanisms become even more crucial for elections held during a pandemic, when new voting modalities are used and compliance with various regulations may be at risk, for example, with regard to equal opportunities during the campaign, voter registration and nomination of candidates, among others. Lacking or limited access to remedies due to the pandemic may put the procedural guarantees for the integrity of elections at risk.

Finally, from the point of view of procedural safeguards, a sufficient and meaningful presence of election observers is considered an important element of transparency of the electoral process.[95] Pandemic-related restrictions are, however, likely to significantly limit the capacity of domestic as well as international actors to observe elections. The physical presence of an election

---

91 Ibid., II.3.1.

92 The ECtHR has pointed out that the existence of a domestic system for effective examination of individual complaints and appeals in matters concerning electoral rights is one of the essential guarantees of democratic elections. See ECtHR, *Uspaskich v Lithuania*, no 14737/08, 20.01.2017, para. 93. Further, in its case law, the ECtHR has pointed out that in electoral matters only those remedies that are capable of ensuring the proper functioning of the democratic process may be regarded as effective. See ECtHR, *Petkov and others v Bulgaria*, nos 77568/01, 178/02 and 505/02, 11.09.2009, para. 79. Finally, the ECtHR has also stressed the significance of judicial remedies for violations of electoral rights. See ECtHR, *Grosaru v Romania*, no 78039/01, 02.03.2010, paras. 55–56.

93 Venice Commission (2002), 'Code of Good Practice in Electoral Matters', II.3.3., *supra* note 64.

94 Ibid., II.3.3.

95 Ibid., II.3.2.

observation mission is conditioned by various factors. In the first place, states may put travel restrictions in place that do not allow international observers to come into or travel within a country.[96] Second, international observers may be required to quarantine or take a test upon arrival, as the pandemic is ongoing, which can significantly prolong the time needed for the deployment of the mission. Indeed, the protection of the life and health of observers is a priority which needs to be likewise taken into consideration, even when personal protection equipment and compliance with sanitary rules are in place.[97] All this may obviously limit a meaningful and thorough observation of the electoral process and reduce the beneficial role generally played by independent observers.

In sum, the implications for the right to political participation and related political freedoms and safeguards caused by pandemic-related restrictions may be considerable. They need to be assessed quantitatively (e.g. number/dimension of restrictions) as well as qualitatively (e.g. disproportionate impact on certain groups) in relation to a particular election to have an in-depth and profound view on the respective election scenario. Electoral standards and principles thus provide relevant and fine-tuned yardsticks for states' decisions as to whether – and how – to hold or postpone elections. Still, further (operational, financial, political, etc.) considerations may enter into play. What are the relevant parameters that are therefore at stake?

5. PARAMETERS ON WHETHER TO HOLD OR POSTPONE ELECTIONS

In line with the above, an international human rights and best practices perspective thus offers guidance as regards the decision of whether to hold (and if so how) or postpone elections; it also puts limits on state action – for example, an election cannot be postponed indeterminately. Within this frame set by international human rights law, it will be up to a state to decide in accordance with the domestic situation whether to hold an election notwithstanding the crisis situation and implement according mitigation measures (including increased/ exclusive reliance on alternative voting methods) or postpone the election. What parameters can be drawn upon for guidance in this difficult decision?

---

96 E. Asplund, L. Heuver, F. Ahmed et al., 'Elections and Covid-19: international electoral observation in 2020', *International IDEA*, 17.03.2021, available at https://www.idea.int/news-media/news/elections-and-covid-19-international-electoral-observation-2020, last accessed 10.04.2021.

97 EFOR, 'Planning election observation during the COVID-19 pandemic', Policy Brief no. 89, 2020, available at https://expertforum.ro/en/files/2020/08/PB-89-observation.pdf, last accessed 10.04.2021.

Among the most relevant parameters, as referred to above, is the human rights situation: in light of states' obligation to respect the right to political participation and related political freedoms, what is the probability of holding elections in accordance with international standards despite the health crisis or a pandemic in particular?[98] What are possible trade-offs? A state will have to consider whether and to what extent the principles of universal, equal, free and secret suffrage can be upheld notwithstanding measures to mitigate the risk of the spread of the disease. State authorities need to decide what restrictions and mitigating measures can ultimately be accepted as possible trade-offs. For example, to what extent does an election campaign which predominantly takes place on social media affect the level playing field among candidates? And does this imply an unfair advantage for the incumbent? Alternatively, is reliance on remote voting methods such as Internet or postal voting disproportionately affecting the right to universal or secret suffrage and, more generally, the integrity of the elections? Is a large number of voters excluded through mitigating measures and/or alternative voting methods; *a fortiori*, do they belong to specific vulnerable groups? In sum, an assessment will need to be made as to the extent to which the integrity of elections can be upheld in times of pandemic and elections be conducted in accordance with international standards.[99] A key component is always voters' trust in the integrity of elections, which can be also reflected in the voter turnout.

Moreover, there are further parameters. They include, perhaps most importantly, the extent of the health crisis and the spread/intensity of the pandemic. Relevant criteria can be the curve of infections, the reproduction factor (R below or over 1), the number of hospitalised persons, the number of persons in intensive care, the capacities of a state's hospitals and other factors. On the basis of these data, and in consultation with national health authorities, a state will have to assess the probability/extent to which the holding of elections (with according mitigation measures in place) may contribute to a further spread of the disease. Can the health risk for electoral officials and voters be reasonably reduced through the adoption of mitigation measures?[100] For example, the local elections in England were postponed for a year due to the outbreak of the pandemic.[101] On the contrary, authorities in Bulgaria decided to hold parliamentary elections in April 2021 despite the steep rise of COVID-19 cases in the country.[102] Likewise, is a meaningful election observation possible

---

98 See Venice Commission (2020), 'Report – Respect for Democracy Human Rights and Rule of Law during States of Emergency: Reflections', para. 95, *supra* note 26. In these circumstances, the fairness of the elections might be doubtful.

99 Ibid.

100 For possible mitigation measures, see above, Part 4.

101 BBC News (2020), 'Coronavirus: English local elections postponed for a year', *supra* note 6.

102 France 24, 'Bulgaria's centre-right PM seeking fourth term in Covid-hit elections', 04.04.2021, available at https://www.france24.com/en/europe/20210404-bulgaria-s-centre-right-pm-seeking-fourth-term-in-covid-hit-elections, last accessed 12.04.2021.

without incurring undue health risks for observers? If the remaining health risks for all electoral stakeholders are too high, this would warrant the postponement of the elections at hand.

In addition, financial and logistical considerations will play a role.[103] These include a state's means (financial and operational) to implement mitigation measures during the elections, such as additional/alternative polling stations and the allocation of disinfectants (see above, section 3). A state will have to assess whether it has the capacities and the manpower to implement what is required to reduce the risk of infection on election day. Another parameter is whether a state has the experience and the capacities to implement postal voting and/or rely on new voting technologies in addition to – or even instead of – in-person elections. Does the legal framework provide for these options? Are arrangements for alternative voting methods in place? Practically speaking, in case of postal voting, is the postal service reliable?[104]

Another important factor is the possible protection of vulnerable groups, especially of older persons and persons with certain underlying health conditions on election day.[105] Is a state able to make arrangements to protect these groups against infection, either through secure mobile voting, proxy voting or by making them vote remotely or in separate polling stations? Indeed, a state should assess on a more general basis whether elections in times of a pandemic disproportionally exclude certain groups of voters, such as the aforementioned risk groups, people in rural communities, the poor, members of minorities or illiterate persons who either do not dare to vote in view of related health risks or have – where remote voting is provided for – less access to and familiarity with Internet or postal voting.[106] The latter would raise issues in terms of non-discriminatory/equal participation.

More generally, turnout considerations may play a role for the decision whether to hold or postpone elections. A state should assess whether people will be willing to vote notwithstanding the pandemic and also whether they will be able to vote given the various obstacles that may have arisen as a result of the crisis: a very low turn-out risks de-legitimising the results, especially when members of the at-risk groups are disproportionately excluded. In France, for example, holding the first round of local elections by in-person voting amidst

---

[103] Venice Commission (2020), 'Report – Respect for Democracy Human Rights and Rule of Law during States of Emergency: Reflections', para. 114, *supra* note 26.

[104] For details on the possible measures see above, Part 4.

[105] Among health conditions classified as risk are lung or heart disease, diabetes or conditions that affect their immune system.

[106] Venice Commission (2020), 'Report – Respect for Democracy Human Rights and Rule of Law during States of Emergency: Reflections', para. 112, *supra* note 26. For a broader overview see C. Binder and A. Drnovsky, 'Elections in Times of the COVID-19 Pandemic: An International Human Rights Perspective with a Specific Focus on Vulnerable Groups', (2020) 2(2–3), *Cross-Cultural Human Rights Review*.

the COVID-19 pandemic resulted in a record-low turnout.[107] On the contrary, during the local elections in Bavaria (Germany) and in South Korea, the increased reliance on remote voting led to higher turnouts.[108]

Another factor is the legal/constitutional framework and whether there is a legal basis to postpone elections (or introduce alternative voting methods).[109] In times of pandemic, as was shown, an adaptation of voting modalities may become necessary, such as the increased reliance on remote voting. Even the postponement of an election may be warranted. Does the existing legal/constitutional framework provide for such options? Or are amendments necessary? The more the stability of a legal framework is at stake, the more complex will it be to alter the rules of the electoral process, for example, by postponing elections.[110] Even if one accepts a more flexible approach to the required stability of the election law in times of a crisis,[111] a lack of transparency and resulting insecurity will negatively impact on voters' trust and an election's legitimacy.[112]

---

107 The Economist, 'France Suspends Local Elections Because of Covid-19', 21.03.2020, available at https://www.economist.com/europe/2020/03/19/france-suspends-local-elections-because-of-covid-19, last accessed 10.04.2021.

108 Deutsche Welle, 'Coronavirus Affects Election Turnout in France, Bavaria', 15.03.2020, available at https://www.dw.com/en/coronavirus-affects-election-turnout-in-france-bavaria/a-52787502, last accessed 10.04.2021.

109 As regards the legal basis e.g. in times of emergency, this is different. See Venice Commission (2020), 'Report – Respect for Democracy Human Rights and Rule of Law during States of Emergency: Reflections', para. 97, *supra* note 26. '... Under several constitutions an extraordinary situation will postpone, or provide an opportunity to postpone upcoming elections, for example by extending the term of parliament (Croatia, Italy, Germany, Greece, Poland, Lithuania, Slovenia, Spain, Hungary and Canada). Similarly, a situation of emergency may prohibit the dissolution of parliament (Germany, Spain, Portugal, Poland, Hungary, Russia). In Turkey, a declared state of war causes elections to be postponed (Article 78 of the Constitution). In Estonia, the parliament, the President, and representative bodies of local authorities may not be elected, nor may their authority be terminated during a state of emergency or a state of war. If the term of office of the parliament, the President or representative bodies of local authorities should expire during a state of emergency or a state of war or within three months after the termination of a state of emergency or a state of war, that term is extended. In these cases, new elections are called within three months following the termination of the state of emergency or the state of war.'

110 Indeed, good electoral practice requires that the electoral law should generally not be changed/altered less than a year before the election, except in technical matters. Venice Commission (2002), 'Code of Good Practice in Electoral Matters', II.2.b., *supra* note 64.

111 Even if not foreseen, changes may indeed still be possible. As affirmed by the Venice Commission: during a pandemic it may not be possible to follow all principles governing elections as in normal times. Venice Commission (2020), 'Report – Respect for Democracy Human Rights and Rule of Law during States of Emergency: Reflections', para. 98, *supra* note 26. The stability of the legal framework might thus be relativised in times of pandemic, as possible trade off. See ibid., para. 110.

112 The consequences of a lack of transparency were shown by the negative example of the Polish presidential elections which were originally scheduled for beginning of May, should have been conducted entirely by postal voting to finally be postponed only a few days before the envisaged Election Day. See EPDE, 'Timeline of the Election Chaos', 2020, available at https://www.epde.org/en/news/details/timeline-of-the-election-chaos.html, last accessed 10.04.2021.

All these are relevant factors for a state to decide how to proceed.[113] In any case, utmost transparency towards all electoral stakeholders (parties, candidates, voters, observers, etc.) is required, and procedural safeguards (involvement of the parliament, not only the executive branch in case of amendments) must be maintained.[114]

A final parameter is the overall political situation. A state may face different scenarios, depending on local conditions: for example, there might be a risk of turbulence/civil unrest when deciding to hold elections. Certain groups of voters may feel excluded, or the trust of voters may be reduced in case of widespread/exclusive reliance on remote – mostly postal – voting methods. Conversely, there may likewise be unrest if voters fear a possible cementation of political power and abuse, for instance when elections are postponed for an indefinite period.[115] Indeed, especially in new and fragile democracies or in democracies under constraint, a careful balance needs to be struck with regards to decisions taken and measures implemented concerning elections during a pandemic. Although emergencies require a certain degree of flexibility and an ability to adapt existing rules, they should not serve as a means to destroy institutional certainty and bring about democratic breakdown.[116] As has been shown throughout this contribution, the risk is always present, be it with regards to postponement or holding of elections despite the pandemic. The decision is thus necessarily situation-specific. In any case, a process which is as inclusive as possible, should it lead to the holding of elections or to their postponement, seems necessary.

All these factors together should induce a state to opt either in favour of holding or postponing elections. A context-specific decision is to be taken accordingly on the basis of the domestic conditions in a particular state.

6. CONCLUDING REMARKS

The current COVID-19 pandemic shows that states may face the difficult decision of whether to hold or postpone elections in times of a health crisis. In the case of both possibilities, a state's obligation to protect the rights to life and health of

---

113 See also Venice Commission (2020), 'Report – Respect for Democracy Human Rights and Rule of Law during States of Emergency: Reflections', para. 118, *supra* note 26. 'A related question is who should decide on the postponement of elections: rules should be clear and competences well attributed/established.'

114 See above, section 4.

115 Venice Commission (2020), 'Report – Respect for Democracy Human Rights and Rule of Law during States of Emergency: Reflections', para. 101, *supra* note 26. See also ibid., para. 102 as regards the list of measures against such abuse, including judicial oversight, limitations in time as regards postponement, qualified majorities in parliament etc.

116 T. S. James and S. Alihodzic, 'When Is It Democratic to Postpone an Election? Elections During Natural Disasters, COVID-19, and Emergency Situations' (2020), *supra* note 8.

its population will require restrictions of the right to political participation and related political freedoms. Ultimately, situation-specific decisions are called for. International human rights law leaves leeway to states to decide in accordance with domestic conditions what is best for a particular situation. At the same time, human rights law gives guidance as to whether to go forward with or to postpone elections, and also sets limits to state action.

In any case, one thing is certain: pandemics make for extraordinary times. Not all electoral standards can be maintained in the face of such a health crisis.[117] Mitigation measures and also alternative/remote voting methods to reduce the risk of spreading the disease will imply certain limitations of the right to political participation and related freedoms. Still, a minimum core of electoral principles has to be upheld at any time for elections to be meaningful and to enjoy the trust of the public. Human rights law, electoral standards and best practices at least provide some guidance for this.

117 Ibid.

THE EFFECTS OF COVID-19 ON THE EU APPROACH ON THE RULE OF LAW

Implications for the Commission and European Parliament

Pietro DE PERINI, Paolo DE STEFANI and Marco MASCIA

ABSTRACT

The outbreak of COVID-19 in Europe has significantly affected European Union (EU, the Union) policy-making in a wealth of policy areas, partly altering the perception of policy priorities and the role of the EU in the scenario depicted by the crisis. This contribution aims to grasp the salience of COVID-19's effects in the context of the EU commitment to developing tools and procedures to address the ongoing rule of law crisis in some Member States and prevent future violations. Based on a content analysis of a wealth of public documents adopted by EU institutions from the beginning of the crisis, this contribution argues that the spread of COVID-19, namely, the unprecedented way in which the crisis has exposed the fragility of all EU values, has produced two specific consequences on the overall EU effort to uphold the rule of law (RoL). The first was urging all EU institutions and the majority of Member States to eventually converge to deliver without delay or obstructionism on pledged measures. The second was the beginning of a shift in the Commission's overall strategy to enhance European resilience vis-à-vis this crisis: from the primacy of the RoL as an 'umbrella principle' related to, but eventually subsuming other key EU values, to a more balanced, cooperative and comprehensive approach, where diverse monitoring and protection initiatives on the RoL, democracy and fundamental rights mutually complement each other. Despite these changes, however, the Commission's approach remains significantly distinct and distant from that proposed by the European Parliament (EP), weakening the potential of the newly adopted tools.

1. INTRODUCTION

The outbreak of COVID-19 in Europe has significantly affected the European Union (EU, the Union) policy-making in a wealth of policy areas (from the environment to health, from digitalisation to external action), partly altering the perception of policy priorities and the role of the EU in the scenario depicted by the crisis. The consequences of the COVID-19 pandemic have also regarded the overall EU commitment to developing more effective tools and procedures to face the rule of law (RoL) crisis in some EU Member States (MS) and prevent future violations. This is an objective that European institutions have been claiming to pursue since 2011 and has received an acceleration in the period underlying the passing of the baton between the Junker and the von der Leyen Commissions in 2019. The COVID-19 pandemic has, however, prompted emergency responses in all MS, putting further under stress the RoL principles and other EU values, including fundamental rights. In addition, countries like Hungary have adopted illiberal measures affecting, in particular, the separation of powers and freedom of expression and of the press, allegedly motivated under the COVID-19-based emergency. Hungary and Poland have also tried to undermine any attempt to make the allocation of financial anti-COVID-19 help to MS conditional to the respect of RoL standards. By the end of 2020, however, the EU has managed to take a number of much-anticipated initiatives to bolster the RoL and other fundamental values across the pillars of promotion, prevention and response.

This contribution aims to grasp the salience of COVID-19's effects in the context of the ongoing EU policy- and law-makers' commitment to protect the RoL. It focuses, in particular, on the response by the Commission and the European Parliament (EP), which are the institutions that have been shaping the initiative of the EU in this field since the early 2010s. How and to what extent has the pandemic affected the approach vis-à-vis the RoL enhancement tools developed by these EU institutions? Has the rationale behind EU proposed solutions to the RoL crisis changed following the outbreak of the pandemic? How has the European policy response to the consequences of the pandemic in other EU value-related policy areas, such as democracy and human rights, intersected and integrated planned RoL measures?

It is difficult to establish any direct causal connection between the COVID-19 crisis and the recently adopted measures. Most of what the EU established by the end of 2020 concerning RoL and other values had already been planned by the Commission in 2019. Nonetheless, this contribution argues that the spread of COVID-19 has produced two specific consequences on the overall EU approach to upholding the RoL. The first was urging all EU institutions and the majority of MS to eventually converge and deliver without delay or obstructionism on planned measures on the RoL, fulfilling, in addition, a number of other pledges related to the EU values set forth in Article 2 of the Treaty on European Union (TEU). The second consequence was the beginning of a shift in the overall Commission's strategy to enhance European resilience vis-a-vis this crisis: from the primacy of the RoL as an 'umbrella principle' related to, but eventually subsuming other values, to a more balanced and comprehensive approach, where diverse monitoring and promotion initiatives on the RoL, democracy and fundamental rights mutually complement each other in the perspective of a broader 'Article 2 toolbox'.

The second section of this contribution describes the methodology adopted. The third recapitulates the key developments in the definition of the EU RoL toolbox from the early concern by the EP to the presentation of Ursula von der Leyen's policy guidelines for her new Commission, highlighting progress and limits. The fourth section empirically analyses some observed challenges that COVID-19 brought to upholding the RoL and protecting fundamental rights in some MS. Finally, the fifth section analyses the response given by the Commission and the EP to observed challenges over the pandemic-marked year 2020, to assess how these values were eventually addressed in the approach of these European institutions.

2. METHODOLOGY

Overall, this contribution is based on a qualitative analysis of policy documents. In particular, the empirical work presented in section 5 was carried out on a wide range of official documents adopted by EU institutions in 2020, including communications, resolutions, regulations and their annexes, as well as speeches and interviews by European institutions' representatives. Specific attention was devoted to the Commission and the EP, the most enterprising and productive institutions in advancing efforts to uphold the RoL over time. The analysis was conducted through what Pashakhanlou defines as 'fully integrated content analysis'.[1] This approach distances itself from the positivistic, systematic and quantitative features traditionally associated with 'content analysis', especially when contrasted with the more interpretative and qualitative 'discourse analysis'.[2] Indeed, its 'fully integrated' feature promises to work in the considerable 'middle ground' between qualitative and quantitative approaches to the analysis of content and to combine the advantages of both methods.[3] From this perspective of broader 'discourse analytic methodology', all textual analysis eventually is an exercise in interpretation.[4] In particular, computer-assisted quantitative content analysis was employed to speed up efforts at reducing data – starting from policy documents which are often long, comprehensive and articulated – condensing communication to more relevant and manageable segments that could be explored more thoroughly.[5]

Documents were collected from the public online archives of the Commission, the EP and the Council/European Council, searching 'rule of law' in the body of text to filter among the large numbers of documents adopted by these institutions during the time frame in reference (30 March–31 December 2020). This effort was complemented by targeted desk research on search engines using the same entry. This process led to the collection and classification of 91 documents, 58% of which were produced in the context of the Commission's work.

Following Wesley,[6] a first open coding phase was then started on some documents which appeared to provide a broader frame (i.e. communications from the Commission, EP resolutions) to identify the main themes to be investigated in more detail. The recurrence of key-words outlining these themes was then searched numerically in all documents via computer software to assess their salience in the overall data set and identify the following codes: 'rule of law'; 'pandemic'; 'human rights/fundamental rights'; 'democracy'; 'interinstitutional cooperation'; and 'civil society engagement'. In the second phase, all documents were simultaneously consulted using a lexical search, and relevant segments of text were coded accordingly. The resulting reduced dataset was interrogated through different intersections of coded segments to retrieve those where key

1 A.H. Pashakhanlou, 'Fully Integrated Content Analysis in International Relations', (2017) 31(4), *International relations*, pp. 447–465.

2 K.A. Neuendorf, 'Content Analysis: A Contrast and Complement to Discourse Analysis', (2004), *Qualitative Methods*, pp. 33–36.

3 J.J. Wesley, 'The Qualitative Analysis of Policy Documents', in B. Kaal, I. Maks and A. van Elfrinkhof (eds.), *From Text to Political Positions. Text analysis across disciplines*, John Benjamin, Amsterdam 2014, p. 144.

4 C. Hardy, B. Harley and N. Phillips, 'Discourse Analysis and Content Analysis: Two Solitudes?' (2004), *Qualitative Method*, p. 20.

5 A. Bennet, 'Found in Translation: Combining Discourse Analysis with Computer Assisted Content Analysis', (2015) 43(3), *Millennium: Journal of International Studies*, p. 991; A.H. Pashakhanlou (2017), 'Fully Integrated Content Analysis', *supra* note 1, p. 449.

6 J.J. Wesley (2014), 'The Qualitative Analysis of Policy Documents', *supra* note 3, p. 149.

themes appear to be correlated (for instance, intersecting 'pandemic', 'rule of law' and 'interinstitutional cooperation' coded segments). The resulting pieces of text were ultimately analysed qualitatively with the aim of making more inferences to context and enhance interpretation.[7] Indeed, an underlying assumption of this contribution is that due to their strong political nature, the 'messages' related to EU values contained in institutions' policy documents, speeches and interviews cannot be taken at their face value. Accordingly, the aim of this analysis was not only the literal description of the content of the documents, but also seeking to 'illuminate patterns and trends that are not immediately observable'.[8] The qualitative analysis of this reduced quantity of text was therefore expected to allow for examination of what these messages convey, given their context and circumstances.[9] Finally, using both quantitative and qualitative forms of content analysis, this approach sought to enhance the validity and reliability of the study,[10] allowing some triangulation of findings.[11]

3. CONTEXT: EU INSTITUTIONS' COMMITMENTS TO UPHOLD THE RULE OF LAW

A European concern for possible breaches of the RoL by MS has emerged since 2011, as emphasised by the EP's early resolutions on the matter.[12] As the issue of MS compliance with the RoL gradually gained prominence in the broader European public debate, EU institutions – the Commission and the EP in particular – have increasingly been confronted with the need for actualising the existing toolbox provided in the treaties to protect the RoL and the other EU founding values set forth in Article 2 TEU. When this concern originated, the existing tools allowed for two types of response. One, of a judicial nature, was based on the recourse by the Commission (and potentially by MS under Article 259 of the Treaty in the Functioning of the European Union (TFEU))[13] to ad hoc infringement proceedings linked to a breach of EU law.

7 T.A. van Dijk, 'What is Political Discourse Analysis?' (1997), *Political Linguistics*, p. 14.

8 N. Green Saraisky, 'Analyzing Public Discourse: Using Media Content Analysis to Understand the Policy Process', (2015) 18(1), *Current Issues in Comparative Education*, p. 27.

9 M.G. Herman, 'Content Analysis', in A. Klotz and D. Prakash (eds.). *Qualitative Methods in International Relations. A Pluralist Guide*, Palgrave, Basingstoke 2008, pp. 155–156.

10 A.H. Pashakhanlou (2017), 'Fully Integrated Content Analysis', *supra* note 1, pp. 450–452.

11 F. Kohlbacher, 'The Use of Qualitative Content Analysis in Case Study Research', (2006) 7(1), *Forum: Qualitative Social Research*, p. 16; K.A. Neuendorf (2006), 'Content Analysis' *supra* note 2, p. 33.

12 See European Parliament (EP), 'Revised Hungarian constitution', P7_TA(2011)0315, 05.07.2011.

13 D. Kochenov, 'Biting Intergovernmentalism: The Case for the Reinvention of Article 259 TFEU to Make It a Viable Rule of Law Enforcement Tool', (2015) 7(2), *Hague Journal on the Rule of Law*, pp. 153–174.

However, this mechanism was not designed to deal with systematic violations of the RoL or other values in one MS.[14] The second type of response was represented by the 'nuclear option' laid out in Article 7 TEU, which might result in a number of sanctions, including the suspension of voting rights in the Council for the targeted country, an option which has proven difficult to trigger and impossible to seize in light of its political character and of the *de facto* possibility of vetoing the eventual Council's decision by any EU Member State, except for the one concerned. As the then-toolbox was evidently ill-designed to face the rising challenge of RoL backsliding within Europe,[15] new mechanisms and tools started to be developed at the EU level to complement and fill the existing gaps, while ordinary infringement actions under Articles 258 and 259 TFEU are also increasingly attracting the interest of those supporting a more active democratic stance of the EU.[16]

3.1. THE FIRST PHASE: EARLY STEPS AND EARLY CONTRADICTIONS (2014–2018)

Notably, the first phase in this endeavour developed from 2014, the year in which the Commission, based on the central imperative of its role as the 'guardian of the treaties',[17] established a 'Rule of Law Framework', marking the opening of a new chapter of EU efforts to defend EU values.[18] The Commission's Framework was conceived as an early warning mechanism and developed as a 'staged process of dialogue with a Member State, structured with opinions and recommendations from the Commission'.[19] It was described as a 'pre-article 7 mechanism' as it allowed the Commission to engage with a country considered to be in breach of

---

14 C. Hillion, 'Overseeing the Rule of Law in the EU: Legal Mandate and Means', in C. Closa and D. Kochenov (eds.), *Reinforcing Rule of Law Oversight in the European Union*, Cambridge University Press, Cambridge 2016, p. 73.

15 D. Kochenov and L. Pech, 'Monitoring and Enforcement of the Rule of Law in the EU: Rhetoric and Reality', (2015) 11(3), *European Constitutional Law Review*, p. 515.

16 K.L. Scheppele, D. Kochenov, and B. Grabowska-Moroz, 'EU Values Are Law, after All: Enforcing EU Values through Systemic Infringement Actions by the European Commission and the Member States of the European Union', (2020) 39, *Yearbook of European Law*, pp. 3–121.

17 European Commission, Communication from the Commission to the European Parliament, the European Council, the Council, The European Economic and Social Committee and the Committee of the Regions. Strengthening the rule of law within the Union. A blueprint for action, COM(2019) 343 final 17.07.2019, p. 1.

18 R.D. Kelemen and M. Blauberger, 'Introducing the debate: European Union safeguards against member states' democratic backsliding', (2017) 24(3), *Journal of European Public Policy*, p. 318.

19 European Commission, Communication from the Commission to the European Parliament, the European Council and he Council. Further strengthening the Rule of Law within the Union. State of play and possible next steps, COM(2019) 163 final 03.04.2019.

Article 2 TEU in the hope of avoiding the need to have recourse to (the threat of) sanctions.[20]

The Commission activated this Framework only once, in 2016, with a view to opening a dialogue with Polish authorities following concerns about the government's policies limiting the independence of the judiciary. However, the mechanism proved to be rather ineffective, as demonstrated by the ensuing decision by the Commission itself of triggering the Article 7 procedure in December 2017 in respect of laws impacting the whole judicial system, namely, the Constitutional Tribunal, the Supreme Court, ordinary courts, the National Council for the Judiciary, the prosecution service and the National School of Judiciary. Almost simultaneously, the Commission launched two (successful) Article 258 TFEU infringement procedures towards Poland focusing on the judges' status in ordinary tribunals and in the Supreme Court (a third, started in 2019, is still pending).[21]

The failure of the 'pre-article 7 procedure' was probably implicit in the conception of the 'Rule of Law Framework', due to the 'questionable presumption' by European policy-makers that 'a discursive approach between the Commission and a country possibly in breach of Article 2 TEU was bound to produce positive results'.[22] In addition, the Commission lacked support from the Council. The latter even sought to dismiss the initiative by both claiming, through its legal service, that the creation of a new monitoring mechanism for the respect of the RoL by MS in addition to the Article 7 TEU procedure was unlawful and establishing an alternative mechanism. The latter took the shape of a periodic intergovernmental 'rule of law dialogue' based on the principles of objectivity, non-discrimination and equal treatment of all MS, to be conducted on 'a non-partisan and evidence-based approach'.[23]

Therefore, this early phase exposed a fundamental feature characterising the broader EU approach to RoL challenges: the distinct and distant strategies pursued by single EU institutions on these matters. The Commission, as seen, favoured a preventive and discursive approach to avoid recurring to sanctions for RoL violations to be activated on an ad hoc basis. The Council's choice was, too, a soft mechanism – which, however, was designed to avoid putting additional blame on any MS. The structure of its RoL dialogue, indeed, recalls the rationale of EU

---

20 D. Kochenov and L. Pech, (2015), 'Monitoring and Enforcement of the Rule of Law in the EU', *supra* note 15, p. 539.

21 CJEU (GC), *Commission v Poland*, Case C-192/18, 05.11.2019, ECLI:EU:C:2019:924; CJEU (GC), *Commission v Poland*, Case C-619/18, 24.06.2019, ECLI:EU:C:2019:531; CJEU, *Commission v Poland*, Case 791/19 (pending).

22 D. Kochenov and L. Pech (2015), 'Monitoring and Enforcement of the Rule of Law in the EU', *supra* note 15, p. 532.

23 L. Pech, 'The Rule of Law in the EU: The Evolution of the Treaty Framework and Rule of Law Toolbox', Reconnect Working Paper No. 7, 2020, available at https://reconnect-europe.eu/wp-content/uploads/2020/03/RECONNECT-WP7-2.pdf, last accessed 30.06.2021.

external action 'dialogues' which,[24] especially when sensitive political issues are concerned, proved to be flexible, but ineffective and eventually serving as a pretext to avoid serious discussion on core matters.[25] Topics addressed in the first RoL dialogues sponsored by the Council included digitalisation, migrant integration and media pluralism in the digital age. They did not focus on the specific challenges to the independence of the judiciary, generalised corruption and restrictions to freedom of expression and other fundamental rights that measures adopted in some MS, namely in Hungary, Poland and Bulgaria, were raising. A third strategy was recommended by the EP, consistent with its role in monitoring EU values, to the Commission in a 2016 resolution. The EP envisaged the establishment of an EU mechanism on democracy, the rule of law and fundamental rights ('EU Pact for DRF') in the form of an inter-institutional agreement, which should integrate and complement existing mechanisms.[26] Besides the emphasis on the need to enforce a more formalised and substantially 'joined up' approach among EU institutions, the other key difference in the way forward proposed by the EP relates to the way of presenting the RoL in relation to other EU values.

While this last point will be discussed in-depth in section 5, with evidence from the COVID-19 phase, it is possible to claim that the weakness of the EU toolbox in the mid-2010s was in large part a symptom of these different views and, eventually, the lack of any clear consensus among European institutions on how to resolutely tackling RoL backsliding.[27] Rather than by EU powerlessness or a general lack of capabilities, therefore, the failure of these early-phase attempts seems to be more effectively explained by this 'institutional distance' and the overall fuzziness deriving from parallel positions held by different institutions and within them. Indeed, internal differences also matter, as demonstrated by, for instance, the proactive approach of some EU MS versus the Visegrad group's obstructionism to any progress within the Council, the controversial position within the EP of the European Popular Party, which for long has kept among its ranks representatives from RoL-violating parties (including, until early March 2021, Viktor Orbán's Fidesz), and the existence of selective attitudes among the members of the Commission.[28]

---

24 M. Mascia and P. de Perini, 'The EU's External Action "Dialogues": A Consistent Foreign Policy Strategy?', in L. Moccia (ed.), *Identity Issues and Intercultural Challenges: A European and Global perspective on Peace in the World*, Al Babhtein, Kwait City 2017, pp. 99–136.

25 P. de Perini, 'The Inconsistent Human Rights Agenda of EU Mediterranean Policy', (2020) 25(3) *European Foreign Affairs Review*, p. 451.

26 EP, 'EU mechanism on democracy, the rule of law and fundamental rights', P8_TA(2016)0409, 16.10. 2016.

27 D. Kochenov and P. Bárd, 'Rule of Law Crisis in the New Member States of the EU: The Pitfalls of Overemphasising Enforcement', Reconnect Working Paper No. 1, 2018, p. 8, available at https://reconnect-europe.eu/wp-content/uploads/2018/07/RECONNECT-KochenovBard-WP_27072018b.pdf, last accessed 20.06.2021.

28 D. Soyaltin-Colella, 'The EU's 'actions-without-sanctions'? The politics of the rule of law crisis in many Europes', (2020) *European Politics and Society*, p. 4.

The resulting fuzziness also favoured the effectiveness of the systematic misrepresentation of the EU's capacity by some MS,[29] which so far has been crucial to weakening any attempt at pressurising the state under monitoring to comply with EU values. Indeed, as was noted, 'political pressure for the EU is less likely to be effective, and EU tools to apply such pressure are less likely to be used unless there is grassroots support for European values'.[30] This consideration, among others, points out to another weakness of the broader EU's RoL toolbox developed during this first phase: the lack of any systematic effort by the EU at engaging and supporting civil society organisations. This problem was also raised by the EP in 2018 when it adopted a resolution to establish a 'European Values Instrument' to empower citizens, associations and NGOs committed to tackling RoL challenges locally and to educating the public as to the meaning and importance of European values to make the 'population more resilient to populist authoritarian attacks on the judiciary, fundamental rights and democracy'.[31] An additional weakness was identified in the sparse engagement of local governments which, especially through the EU Committee of the Regions, periodically stressed their centrality in applying from the bottom up the principle of subsidiarity from a multi-level governance perspective, also with reference to the promotion and protection of human rights,[32] a call which, incidentally, was reiterated just days before the outbreak of COVID-19.[33]

Characterised by these weaknesses, the resulting inconsistent, fuzzy and initially short-sighted response comprehensively given by EU institutions in the mid-2010s paradoxically ended up increasing public support for the accused governments instead of weakening them.[34] Threats to the RoL in MS intensify further, while the two attempts at advancing the Article 7 procedure – the one put forward by the Commission in 2017 in respect of Poland and that triggered by the EP in respect of Hungary in 2018 – were deadlocked by the impossibility of reaching an agreement in the Council.

---

29 D. Kochenov and P. Bárd (2018), 'Rule of Law Crisis', *supra* note 27, p. 8.

30 I. Butler, 'Two proposals to promote and protect European values through the Multiannual Financial Framework: Conditionality of EU funds and a financial instrument to support NGOs', 2018, available at https://dq4n3btxmr8c9.cloudfront.net/files/C6kowK/Liberties_MFF_Israel_20180302_ES.pdf, last accessed 30.06.2021.

31 EP, 'A European values instrument to support civil society organisations which promote democracy, rule of law and fundamental values within the European Union', P8_TA(2018)0184, 19.04.2018.

32 M. Mascia and P. de Perini, 'L'iniziativa della Commissione europea per il rafforzamento dello stato di diritto negli Stati membri: quali prospettive di governance multilivello?', (2018) 2, *La Cittadinanza Europea*, p. 42.

33 European Committee of the Regions, 'Strengthening the rule of law within the Union – A blueprint for action', Opinion (2020/C 141/04), 29.04.2020.

34 D. Soyaltin-Colella (2020), 'The EU's 'actions-without-sanctions'? *supra* note 28, p. 2.

3.2. THE SECOND PHASE (2018 ONWARD): BETWEEN CONTINUITY AND RE-ENERGISATION

Arguably in response to this wide and consolidated criticism, a second, more promising phase was begun just a few years later, in the period between the outgoing Junker Commission and the incumbent von der Leyen's mandate, that is, between the end of 2018 and early 2020. The Junker Commission launched for the first time the idea of linking EU structural funds under the new Multiannual Financial Framework (MFF) to RoL conditionality on the model of so-called 'human rights clauses' that the EU has included in all association and cooperation agreements with third countries since the 1990s.[35] The Junker Commission also presented a comprehensive blueprint for action to uphold the RoL, which followed an extensive consultation with all stakeholders, and elaborated on some of their key recommendations. As a candidate for President, Ursula von der Leyen stated a commitment to use the existing toolbox fully, supported the idea to make the RoL an integral part of the next MFF and tried to break new ground in this policy area as well.

Accordingly, on the one hand, the von der Leyen Commission moved in full continuity with the work undertaken by their predecessors, also in consideration that one of its three executive vice-presidents, Frans Timmermans, despite not having any more direct responsibility for advancing the RoL agenda, was the one leading the design of the Junker Commission' blueprint for action. Consistent with the proposals made in that document, the Commission also promised to engage the European public across many dimensions to raise awareness of the centrality of the RoL, to sponsor efforts by civil society actors and academia to support public understanding of this issue, and called on the EP, the Council and MS to bring complementary efforts to the promotion of this value, without, however, mentioning any commitment to establish formal inter-institutional cooperation.[36]

On the other hand, the new president of the Commission also promised to re-energise the European efforts to uphold the RoL while conciliating MS concerns. The key insight was to introduce within the existing toolbox an additional, comprehensive 'European Rule of Law Mechanism' (ERoLM), conceived as a 'review cycle' based on annual reporting by the Commission with an EU-wide scope, namely, monitoring all EU Member States at once on

---

35 European Commission, 'EU budget: Commission proposes a modern budget for a Union that protects, empowers and defends', Press Release, IP/18/3570, available at https://ec.europa.eu/commission/presscorner/detail/en/IP_18_3570, last accessed 30.06.2021.

36 A similar conclusion was reached by the Council, which saw the Commission's renewed toolbox as a possible basis for the annual Council RoL dialogue, but did not go further in terms of establishing forms of formal cooperation, see Council of the EU, 'Presidency conclusions – Evaluation of the annual rule of law dialogue', 14173/19, 19.11.2019.

an equal basis. The ERoLM was planned to be conducted in close dialogue with national authorities on the basis of law and aimed at bringing transparency, allowing early detection and offering targeted support to resolve issues at an early stage, without, however, 'ruling out an effective, proportionate and dissuasive response as a last resort'.[37] In parallel to this pledge, both Commissioners with responsibility for the RoL and other values voiced their intention to frame the envisaged RoL efforts within a broader commitment towards EU values, anticipating plans for upcoming strategies and blueprints on fundamental rights and democracy, although with a slight difference in their understanding: while the Commissioner-designate for values and transparency, Jourova, spoke about three (separate) 'strands of work', Commissioner-designate for Justice Reynders hinted at his commitment to 'build a process – with an interinstitutional discussion on the whole, comprehensive issue, of the rule of law, fundamental rights and democracy',[38] confirming the existence of multiple views on these matters within the current Commission, as well.

Some have stressed that the most mature answer to the problems at hand necessarily requires a long-term perspective and involves the reform of the Union as such, taking values out of the current instrumental use to play a central role in the day-to-day functioning of the EU.[39] Although less ambitious than this call for radical reform, the pledges on EU values made by the Commission in late 2019 presented promising plans to tackle some of the previously highlighted limits.[40]

These plans were almost immediately unsettled by the outbreak of COVID-19. The unprecedented challenges from the pandemic, however, do not seem to have particularly affected the ability of EU institutions to deliver on the pledges made. Quite the contrary: by the end of 2020, indeed, the Commission successfully implemented its newly proposed ERoLM with the adoption of the first annual report on the situation of the RoL in all 27 MS.[41] In addition, after a long and

---

37 U. von der Leyen, 'A Union That Strives For More. My Agenda For Europe. Political Guidelines For The Next European Commission 2019-2024', 2019, available at https://op.europa.eu/en/publication-detail/-/publication/43a17056-ebf1-11e9-9c4e-01aa75ed71a1, last accessed 30.06.2021.

38 Hearing Of Didier Reynders Commissioner-Designate (Justice), 02.10.2019 Brussels; Hearing Of Věra Jourová Commissioner-Designate (Values And Transparency), 07.10.2019, Brussels.

39 D. Kochenov and P. Bárd, (2018), 'Rule of Law Crisis in the New Member States of the EU', *supra* note 27, p. 4.

40 M. O'Neal, 'The European Commission's Enhanced Rule of Law Mechanism', SWP Comment, 05.12.2019, available at https://www.swp-berlin.org/10.18449/2019C48/, last accessed 02.07.2021.

41 European Commission, Communication from the Commission to the European Parliament, the Council, the European Economic and Social Committee and the Committee of the Regions. 2020 Rule of Law Report. The Rule Of Law Situation In The European Union, COM(2020) 580 final 30.09.2020.

contested confrontation and exhausting negotiations, the Council and the Parliament eventually adopted, on 17 December 2020, an ambitious MFF for 2021–2027 (which includes the unprecedented €750 million Next Generation EU recovery fund), together with a regulation establishing a mechanism which protects 'the Union budget against breaches of the principles of the rule of law affecting its sound financial management or the protection of the financial interests of the Union'.[42]

Although the final outcome might be seen as punching below the EU's weight,[43] the adoption of this mechanism added a new, probably more viable, form of sanction complementary to the Article 7 procedure, eventually giving teeth to the past 'action-without-sanctions' approach.[44] After all, in the 2014–2020 MFF programming period, nearly half of the MS used structural funds to support reforms strengthening the judiciary and public administration, or to help fight corruption.[45] In addition, the adopted MFF allocates a total of €377,768 million to the heading on cohesion, resilience and values, although only €47,533 million for the sub-heading on resilience and values. In turn, however, this sum is to be split among four programmes – EU4Health, Erasmus+, Creative Europe, Rights and Values – with the latter, which is devoted to supporting civil society and promoting a culture of EU values, receiving the smallest slice of this pie.[46]

By the end of 2020, the Commission also adopted a number of other strategies and plans on EU values, including the new strategy to strengthen the application of the Charter of Fundamental Rights (CFR Strategy) and the European Democracy Action Plan (EDAP), which was directly connected to EU efforts at resolutely countering COVID-19 disinformation and reinforce resilience in European societies. Although outside the scope of this contribution, this wave of value-protection initiatives also affected EU foreign policy, with the adoption of the updated EU Action Plan on Human Rights and Democracy (for 2020–2024)

---

42 Regulation (EU, Euratom) No 2020/2092 of the European Parliament and of the Council of 16 December 2020 on a general regime of conditionality for the protection of the Union budget, OJ LI 433.

43 K.L. Scheppele, L. Pech and S. Platon, 'Compromising the Rule of Law while Compromising on the Rule of Law', *Verfassungsblog*, 13.12.2020, available at https://verfassungsblog.de/compromising-the-rule-of-law-while-compromising-on-the-rule-of-law, last accessed 18.03.2021; see also, on a more optimistic tone, J. Bequiraj, 'The "Regulation on a general regime of conditionality for the protection of the Union budget" and its contested implementation', Reconnect blog, 12.01.2021, available at https://reconnect-europe.eu/blog/the-regulation-on-a-general-regime-of-conditionality-for-the-protection-of-the-union-budget-and-its-contested-implementation/, last accessed 18.03.2021.

44 D. Soyaltin-Colella, (2020), 'The EU's 'actions-without-sanctions', *supra* note 28.

45 European Commission, COM(2019) 163 final, *supra* note 19, p. 10.

46 Council Regulation (EU, Euratom) 2020/2093 of 17 December 2020 laying down the multiannual financial framework for the years 2021 to 2027, OJ LI 433.

and a new 'Global human rights sanction regime', which also aimed at enhancing coherence and breaking down silos between internal and external policy areas.[47]

It is not possible to establish a direct causal correlation between the pandemic and the adoption and implementation of the aforementioned policy initiatives and pieces of legislation, many of which, as mentioned, were considered or already in the pipeline before the COVID-19 epidemic broke out in Europe. At the same time, it appears difficult to claim that the pandemic has not had any meaningful consequences in shaping the EU's current response to uphold the RoL and other EU values. Having elaborated on the challenges to the RoL and EU values brought by the pandemic in EU MS, this contribution will inquire how EU policy-making on these matters was specifically affected.

4. THE ACTUAL EFFECTS OF THE PANDEMIC ON THE RoL AND OTHER EU VALUES

Since March – in some cases, February – 2020, governments worldwide have adopted stringent measures to combat the spread of COVID-19. EU MS have been among the most active in this field, as Europe was one of the geographic regions most quickly and intensely affected by the epidemic. Stringent measures include – based on a set of parameters produced by *Our World in Data* – policies on closing schools and workplaces (from remaining open to online-only activity),[48] cancelling of public events, restrictions on gatherings, reducing of public transport, more or less widespread and coordinated public information campaigns about the COVID-19 threat, stay-at-home orders, restrictions on internal movement and controls (up to border closures) on international travels, contact tracing, use of masks and vaccination policies involving increasingly larger segments of population.

Each of these measures and the combination of them have had an impact on the practical realisation of Article 2 TEU values. Different patterns, however, have characterised the response of any single MS. Overall, the pandemic has directly impacted virtually all fundamental rights. Individual rights and freedoms have been curtailed, economic and social rights have generally degraded for

---

47 See Council Regulation (EU) 2020/1998 of 7 December 2020 concerning restrictive measures against serious human rights violations and abuses, OJ LI 410. Council, Conclusions on the EU Action Plan on Human Rights and Democracy 2020-2024, 12848/20, 18.11.2020; Council Regulation (EU) 2020/1998 of 7 December 2020 concerning restrictive measures against serious human rights violations and abuses, OJ LI 410; European Commission, Joint Communication to the European Parliament and the Council, EU Action Plan on Human Rights and Democracy 2020-2024, JOIN(2020) 5 final 25.03.2020.

48 T. Hale, N. Angrist, R. Goldszmidt et al., (2021), 'A global panel database of pandemic policies (Oxford COVID-19 Government Response Tracker)', (2021) 5(4), *Nature Human Behaviour*, p. 531.

many categories, while lockdowns and social isolation have consolidated discriminatory patterns, including domestic violence.[49]

In addition, the 'procedural' dimensions of the EU values have been affected, including RoL features, constitutional checks-and-balances, rules governing the ordinary functioning of democratic processes (the regular holding of electoral consultations, for instance) and any forms of guarantees.

MS have responded to the unprecedented (but certainly not unexpected) health emergency with measures aimed at enhancing the resilience of individuals and communities. Indeed, some outcomes of the anti-pandemic measures – irrespective of whether they were intentionally pursued by policy-makers or were generated by spontaneous social dynamics – can be considered an *acquis* of post-COVID-19 societies. First of all, the relatively prompt (compared to other states) reaction by a majority of MS, which established stringent measures when evidence of an unknown infection was reported, has arguably saved lives and avoided the collapse of the health system.[50] A welcome outcome of the pandemic is the realisation of the vital importance of building and maintaining solid health preparedness capacities to face future epidemics in the light of the ongoing socio-economic megatrends.[51] Additionally, the rapid technological innovations and digitalisation in all sectors,[52] including education and public administration, may be seen as a permanent and arguably positive legacy of the coronavirus pandemic, especially as new technologies are increasingly perceived as part of a green economy strategy in line with the Sustainable Development Goals.

All in all, governments, medical and health care professionals, scientists, public servants, civil society organisations and individuals in all countries have made efforts and endured rights limitations for the sake of protecting the life and personal integrity of their family and community. In the pandemic, Europeans have felt that the 'EU values' of 'pluralism, non-discrimination, tolerance, justice, solidarity and equality between women and men' are actually worth being protected.

The negative side of state policies introduced to counter the pandemic has been much explored, however. Unintended and perhaps inevitable shortcomings have accompanied any measure adopted to this end. Since the inception of the crisis, the EU Fundamental Rights Agency (FRA) has systematically monitored

---

49 E. Mahase, 'Covid-19: EU states report 60% rise in emergency calls about domestic violence', (2020) 369, *BMJ: British Medical Journal* (Online).

50 E. Bertone, M.J. Luna Juncal, R.K, Prado Umeno et al., 'Effectiveness of the Early Response to COVID-19: Data Analysis and Modelling', (2020) 8(2), *Systems*, p. 21.

51 G. Tomson, S. Causevic, O.P. Ottersen et al., 'Solidarity and universal preparedness for health after covid-19', (2021) 372(59), *BMJ: British Medical Journal*, p. 1; E. Barrera-Algarín, F. Estepa-Maestre. J.L Sarasola-Sánchez-Serrano et al. 'COVID-19, neoliberalismo y sistemas sanitarios en 30 países de Europa: repercusiones en el número de fallecidos, (2020) 94, *Rev Esp Salud Pública*, pp. 1–4.

52 A. Brem, E. Viardot and P.A. Nylund, 'Implications of the coronavirus (COVID-19) outbreak for innovation: Which technologies will improve our lives?', (2021) 163(120451), *Technological Forecasting and Social Change*, pp. 4–5.

the impact of COVID-19-related policies on the daily life of individuals,[53] covering civil rights and freedoms and economic and social rights. Specific attention was paid to the predicament of the Roma and Traveller communities, and more generally to marginalised groups, which the pandemic-induced stress has rendered even more vulnerable. The FRA has also documented 'procedural' flaws brought about by anti-COVID-19 policies, although it never explicitly mentions the RoL (see below, section 5.2).

Almost all MS have operated in the framework of some form of state of emergency, although only three MS, during the 'first wave', formally derogated from their obligations under the European Convention on Human Rights and Fundamental Freedoms (ECHR).[54] On the opportunity of using the state of emergency clause enshrined in the ECHR, as well as in Article 4 of the International Covenant on Civil and Political Rights, observers have split. Many scholars found this course of action a perfectly legitimate and transparent form of self-restraint that states should adopt to address extraordinary threats, when they find it more appropriate to suspend certain human rights provisions altogether, instead of simply limiting their effects under the ordinary clauses – consistently respecting the principles of necessity and proportionality and the non-derogable nature of certain rights. Others feared that triggering the derogation clause might inevitably dramatise the emergency and pave the way for further restrictions which go beyond necessity and proportionality criteria.[55] Irrespective of this debate, most MS have operated under some forms of domestic emergency regime, either set forth in the constitution or based on statutory provisions – inevitably raising issues of legality. In many instances, the constitutional checks-and-balances system has been under stress. For example, the coordination between central/federal institutions and decentralised authorities (Länder, regions, etc.) have created some tensions and prompted adjudicative procedures, like in Germany and in Italy,[56] from the angle of accessibility and certainty of the law.[57]

---

53 Since April 2020 the FRA has published six bi-monthly bulletins on the Coronavirus pandemic in the EU, covering both the first and the second 'wave', available at https://fra.europa.eu/en/themes/covid-19, last accessed 13.10.2021.

54 ECHR, Article 15. The concerned MS are Estonia, Latvia, Romania (see https://www.coe.int/en/web/conventions/full-list/-/conventions/webContent/62111354, last accessed 13.10.2021). At the time of writing (March 2021), only Latvia has renovated the Article 15 declaration.

55 M. Scheinin, 'COVID-19 Symposium: To Derogate or Not to Derogate?', *Opinio Juris*, 06.04.2020, available at https://opiniojuris.org/2020/04/06/covid-19-symposium-to-derogate-or-not-to-derogate, last accessed 18.03.2021.

56 P. Thielbörger and B. Behlert, 'COVID-19 and the Basic Law: On the (Un)suitability of the German Constitutional "Immune System"' *Int'l J. Const. L. Blog*, 20.03.2020, available at http://www.iconnectblog.com/covid-19-and-the-basic-law-on-the-unsuitability-of-the-german-constitutional-immune-system, last accessed 18.03.2021.

57 D. Vese, 'Managing the Pandemic: The Italian Strategy for Fighting COVID-19 and the Challenge of Sharing Administrative Powers', (2020), *European Journal of Risk Regulation*, pp. 1–28.

RoL concerns were also raised in connection with the effective involvement of the parliaments in adopting and supervising emergency regulations, especially in countries where governments widely used in the past their exceptional legislative powers.[58] Equally problematic was in many countries the suspension of courts' regular functioning, potentially dealing a lethal blow to the RoL. Governments have managed the emergency with controversial measures, including extending the use of videoconferencing and other technological tools in courts,[59] as well as suspending the statutes of limitations.[60] The overall situation has sparked frustration among legal professionals, as the coronavirus crisis has exasperated long-standing structural problems, proving daunting for the work of the judiciary in many MS.[61]

Finally, and more importantly, some disruptive consequences of the epidemic on the preservation of EU values may have been intentionally engineered by public authorities. Indeed, many have observed that the pandemic has offered authoritarian regimes,[62] 'illiberal democracies' and 'populist' leaders a perfect opportunity to subvert constitutional rules, undermine the RoL, attack political opponents, and generally pursue their agenda based on 'dividing rhetoric, anti-science and securitization'.[63]

Hungarian Prime Minister Viktor Orbán has been blamed for cynically taking advantage of the pandemic-induced fear among his citizens, who have for years been exposed to the rhetoric that the nation must defend itself from threats that 'others' may bring from abroad. A national emergency was declared early in March, despite the then-very low level of epidemic risk, linking the potential outbreak of the disease to the inflow of 'foreigners' (the first people known to be infected with COVID-19 in Hungary were two Iranian students).[64]

58 Italy was a special case in this connection. Another reason for concern in Italy was the systematic use of executive decrees of the president of the council of ministers introducing rights-affecting measures. On Italy, *ex multis*: J. Beqiraj (2020) 'Italy's Coronavirus Legislative Response: Adjusting Along the Way', *Verfassungsblog*, 08.04.2020, available at https://verfassungsblog.de/italys-coronavirus-legislative-response-adjusting-along-the-way, last accessed 18.03.2021; F. Sorrentino, M. Luciani, S. Staiano et al., 'Liber Amicorum per Pasquale Costanzo. Diritto costituzionale in trasformazione', 2020, Consulta Online report, available at https://www.giurcost.org/COLLANA/2.pdf, last accessed 06.07.2021.

59 P. Gori and A. Pahladsingh, 'Fundamental rights under Covid-19: an European perspective on videoconferencing in court', (2021), *ERA Forum* 21, pp. 561–577.

60 Information on these trends are available on the European e-Justice Portal, available at https://beta.e-justice.europa.eu/37147/EN/impact_of_covid19_on_the_justice_field#tocHeader2.

61 An example is Case C-220/20 (ECLI:EU:C:2020:1022), a request for preliminary ruling rejected by the General Court as manifestly inadmissible.

62 See for instance K. Roth, 'How Authoritarians Are Exploiting the COVID-19 Crisis to Grab Power', 03.04.2020, available at https://www.hrw.org/news/2020/04/03/how-authoritarians-are-exploiting-covid-19-crisis-grab-power, last accessed 01.07.2021.

63 M. Scheinin and H. Molbæk-Steensig, 'Pandemics and Human Rights: Three perspectives on human rights assessment of strategies against COVID-19', (2021) (1), *EUI Law, EUI working papers*, p. 2.

64 N. Merkovity, M. Bene and X. Farkas, 'Hungary: The Illiberal Crisis Management', in R.M. Rodríguez and D.G. Lilleker (eds.), *Political Communication and COVID-19: Governance*

The 'Enabling Act' ratified on 30 March 2020 by the Hungarian Parliament gave the government full and unrestricted powers to fight the pandemic via executive orders, completely bypassing the parliament, and was therefore criticised for infringing the 2010 Constitution, the EU principles on the RoL and the ECHR. In addition, other international organisations, namely the Council of Europe, expressed their concern for the blatant disproportionality of the provisions.[65] The law was eventually repealed in June. In the meantime, by-elections were deferred, courts were closed and a law was adopted penalising the spreading of news that may interfere with the 'successful protection of the public'.[66] In fact, the only source of information and voice to be heard about the epidemic was the government's or, more precisely, that of Prime Minister Orbán himself.[67] In June 2020, the government proclaimed a 'medical emergency', while the parliament adopted complex constitutional reforms that introduced three different forms of state of exception ('state of war', 'state of emergency' and 'state of danger'), generally limiting the capabilities of the parliament and enhancing the role of the executive and of the military. The 'state of danger', in particular, is defined in extremely vague terms, so that any forms of confrontational opposition to the incumbent government may qualify as 'sabotage' and justify the adoption of exceptional measures.[68]

Finally, in autumn of 2020, with a second wave of the epidemic that proved to be much more lethal than the first, a 'state of danger' was proclaimed, alongside the 'medical emergency' and in addition to the 'mass migration emergency', which was declared in 2015 and never revoked. The 'state of danger', which entered into force on 10 November, has brought about an enhanced deployment of military personnel in the streets, to patrol the curfew imposed on the population, as well as in hospitals. In January 2021, a resurgence in the contagion sparked more severe confinement measures, including a total ban on any 'assembly', meaning 'a public gathering held with at least two persons to express an opinion in public affairs'.[69]

A 'RoL backsliding' may occur as an unintended consequence of some policies undertaken and carried out without the support of adequate data or reflection. But it can also be the effect of a political choice and affect a more or

---

and Rhetoric in Times of Crisis, Politics, Media and Political Communication, Routledge, Abingdon 2021, p. 273.

65 W. Benedek, 'Are the Tools of the Council of Europe Sufficient to Protect Human Rights, Democracy and the Rule of Law from Backsliding?' (2020) 1(2), *European Convention on Human Rights Law Review*, pp. 155–156.

66 K. Kovács, 'Hungary and the Pandemic: A Pretext for Expanding Power', *Verfassungsblog*, 11.03.2021, available at https://verfassungsblog.de/hungary-and-the-pandemic-a-pretext-for-expanding-power/, last accessed 18.03.2021.

67 N. Merkovity, M. Bene, and X. Farkas (2021), 'Hungary: The Illiberal Crisis Management', *supra* note 64, p. 275.

68 G. Halmai, G. Mészáros and K.L. Scheppele, 'So It Goes – Part I', *Verfassungsblog*, 19.11.2020, available at https://verfassungsblog.de/so-it-goes-part-i/, last accessed 18.03.2021.

69 K. Kovács (2021), 'Hungary and the Pandemic', *supra* note 66.

less wide spectrum of issues, well beyond the strict notion of the RoL. Orbán's Hungary is defying almost all dimensions of Article 2 values. Indeed, the case of Hungary seems to show quite clearly that, even within the EU, illiberal regimes may seize the opportunity of a natural disruptive event like a pandemic to challenge the RoL and the other core EU values.

Other governments may have had a more selective attitude. It may be recalled, for example, that on 7 April 2020, the Conte II Italian Government adopted a joint decree of the Ministers of Transport, Foreign Affairs, Interior and Health stipulating that all Italian ports were 'non-safe harbours' for non-Italian ships conducting rescue operations outside the Italian Search and Rescue (SAR) area, because of the risk of COVID-19. The ban is due to operate over the whole duration of the civil protection emergency which, proclaimed in February 2020, has been renewed three times and is still in force at the time of writing.[70]

5. ANALYSIS: HOW COVID-19 AFFECTED THE EU APPROACH TO THE ROL

After having outlined the concrete challenges that the heterogeneous responses to the pandemic brought to the respect of the RoL and other EU values, the following sections seek to investigate how these challenges have shaped the current EU approach to upholding the RoL. The analysis, in particular, focuses on the will and capability of EU institutions to converge and deliver on the pledges made, the diversity of institutions' views and strategies to uphold the RoL in relation to other values and the type of cooperation among European institutions on these matters.

5.1. URGING ACTION TO UPHOLD RESILIENCE

That the pandemic brought a significant challenge to the broader EU integration project is beyond a shadow of a doubt. The fact that 'RoL issues in one member state are actually European issues' was immediately acknowledged by all EU actors and discussed widely in Europe[71] by the academic community and society at large.[72] Another aspect which represents common wisdom is that in the wake

---

70 A.M. Pelliconi, 'Covid-19: Italy is not a "place of safety" anymore. Is the decision to close Italian ports compliant with human rights obligations?', *EJIL: Talk!*, 23.04.2020, available at https://www.ejiltalk.org/covid-19-italy-is-not-a-place-of-safety-anymore-is-the-decision-to-close-italian-ports-compliant-with-human-rights-obligations, last accessed 18.03.2021.

71 Speech by Věra Jourová on 'Equipping Europe with better tools to defend the rule of law and democratic values', Brussels, 08.07.2020.

72 EP, 'The impact of COVID-19 measures on democracy, the rule of law and fundamental rights', P9 TA(2020)0307, 13.11.2020.

of the COVID-19 outbreak, the EU managed to take decisions of historical significance, such as the agreement on the 'recovery package' during the Special European Council of 17–21 July 2020, which the president of the institution, Charles Michel, hailed as a renewal of marriage vows for EU MS for the next 30 years.[73]

Moving the focus onto the progress of the RoL, these considerations are substantially confirmed. All the selected documents for analysis also refer at least once to the challenges brought about by COVID-19. Generally speaking, however, the concrete challenge is not presented in detail. In the majority of documents, the reference to COVID-19 is 'contextual' rather than causally correlated to the pieces of initiative proposed in the analysed documents.

One of the findings which emerges from the qualitative analysis of retrieved segments of text is that when a significant bond is established between a proposed/decided action on the RoL and COVID-19, this is normally underlain by words connected to 'resilience'. This is a key term in EU jargon, which normally points to the ability of a community to 'withstand, cope, adapt, and quickly recover from stresses and shocks'.[74] This term, in particular, accompanies EU institutions' habit of referring to the pandemic as a 'stress test' for EU values, claiming for a rapid and adequate response. The EP, for instance, used the expression with reference to the 'resilience of national safeguards for the rule of law and fundamental rights' and linked the resulting scenario with a call for the activation of a number of initiatives by the Commission and the Council, including the support for the already referred 'Pact for DRF'.[75] The Commission also used the expression 'stress test' with reference to resilience in several documents, including when framing the scope of its first annual report on the RoL in all MS – the periodic outcome of the ERoLM – which was expected to provide a response to a COVID-19-induced 'wide variety of challenges for society, and more specifically for public administrations and legal and constitutional systems'.[76]

Although these specific terms are not employed, the same need for an urgent response also surfaced among MS. For instance, in a diplomatic statement adopted on 1 April 2020, a group of 19 countries linked their 'deep concern' for this 'unprecedented situation' about the risk of violations of the principles of the RoL, democracy and fundamental rights arising from the adoption of certain emergency measures, with the attribution of immediate support to

---

73 'This is historic. We renewed our marriage vows for 30 years. Europe is there, strong, standing tall'. Report by President Charles Michel at the European Parliament on the Special European Council of 17-21 July 2020 (SPEECH 517/20 23/07/2020).

74 European Commission, 'Building resilience – The EU's approach', Factsheet, 2016, available at https://ec.europa.eu/echo/files/aid/countries/factsheets/thematic/EU_building_resilience_en.pdf, last accessed 01.07.2021.

75 EP, P9 TA(2020)0307, *supra* note 72.

76 European Commission, COM(2020) 580 final, *supra* note 41.

the initiative, advanced by the Commission just the day before,[77] to monitor emergency measures and their application to ensure the fundamental values of the Union.[78] A similarly urgent action was requested to the Presidents of the Council and the Commission on 15 April when 80 among EP members and civil society groups published an open letter to stress the need for the two institutions to 'take swift and decisive actions to address the threats to the rule of law being carried out under the guise of emergency powers'.[79] Ultimately, the von der Leyen Commission's decision to act more assertively on the RoL was explained by Commissioner Jorouva precisely in terms of a responsible response to the instrumental use of the 'climate of permanent crisis' in Europe, which was compounded by COVID-19.[80]

Although the push by all concerned actors had slightly different priorities in sight, the way in which the correlation between the national responses to COVID-19 and the threats to the RoL was presented in analysed documents exposes a dual pattern. It shows both a strong EU awareness that the RoL was not the only value tested by the unprecedented stress brought about by the pandemic and a need to respond promptly and consistently so as not to risk dissipating the commendable European resilience in facing the crisis.

5.2. CHALLENGING THE COMMISSION'S APPROACH VIS-A-VIS EU VALUES PROTECTION

In the past, some scholars embraced a 'minimal approach' in criticising the EU conceptualisation of the RoL. Differently from what the EU put in practice, they claim, the RoL is not 'democracy, the protection of human rights, nor similar wonderful things, each of them definitely boosting its own sound claim to existence as a notion independent from the rule of law'.[81] In fact, the EU

---

77 See European Commission, 'Statement by President von der Leyen on emergency measures in Member States', Statement, 31.03.2020, available at https://ec.europa.eu/commission/presscorner/detail/it/statement_20_567, last accessed 06.07.2021.

78 Government of the Netherlands, 'Statement by Belgium, Bulgaria, Cyprus, Denmark, Estonia, Finland, France, Germany, Greece, Ireland, Italy, Latvia, Lithuania, Luxembourg, the Netherlands, Portugal, Romania, Spain, Sweden', diplomatic statement, 01.04.2020. available at https://www.government.nl/documents/diplomatic-statements/2020/04/01/statement-by-belgium-denmark-finland-france-germany-greece-ireland-italy-luxembourg-the-netherlands-portugal-spain-sweden, last accessed 06.07.2021.

79 ECPMF, 'Open letter: EU must not sit idly by while democracy is in jeopardy', open letter, 2020, available at https://www.ecpmf.eu/open-letter-eu-must-not-sit-idly-by-while-democracy-is-in-jeopardy/, last accessed 06.07.2021.

80 Speech by Věra Jourová on 'Equipping Europe with better tools to defend the rule of law and democratic values' Brussels, 08.07.2020.

81 D. Kochenov and P. Bárd, (2018), 'Rule of Law Crisis in the New Member States of the EU', *supra* note 27, p. 19.

treaties make references to the RoL but do not define it. It was the Commission that – on the occasion of the establishment of its Rule of Law Framework in 2014 – provided an initial comprehensive definition of what it meant by concept, a definition which has since been fine-tuned and consolidated in the ensuing communications on this matter.[82]

This definition substantially understands the RoL as a broader 'umbrella' principle which subsumes a number of other principles and values. In practice, although the definition provided by the Commission formally puts RoL at the same level as other EU fundamental values, 'under the RoL', it reads, 'powers always act within the constraints set out by law *in accordance* with the values of democracy and human rights' (*italics added*)[83] – the Commission made explicit on a number of occasions, that it intended the respect of the RoL as a prerequisite for the protection of all other fundamental values on which the EU is founded. For instance, in 2018, when the Commission first proposed to the EP and the Council to adopt a regulation on a 'rights and values' programmes to support civil society initiatives, the need for it was motivated as necessary to strengthen and uphold EU values and, specifically, the 'respect of the rule of law'.[84] Attempts at weakening other founding values on which the EU is built, including freedom of expression and information, media freedom and pluralism and pressuring civil society organisations – 'essential watchdogs in healthy democracies' – were first and foremost observed as an early warning sign concerning RoL deficiencies.[85] Additionally, the von der Leyen Commission embraced this conceptualisation of the RoL as an 'umbrella principle', claiming that the way to benefit rights-holders comes from the integration of the various RoL tools and mechanisms in the EU.[86] When she was a candidate for President, von der Leyen also stated that there could be no compromise when it comes to defending EU core values, but essentially framed her promised response to uphold these around the developments pledged for the RoL toolbox.[87]

If not technically hierarchical, therefore, there was a prioritisation of the RoL over other values, which has arguably pushed the Commission – as the guardian of the treaties – to face broader democratic backsliding in some MS primarily as a RoL crisis, although the contested measures in targeted countries

82 See European Commission, COM(2019) 343 final, *supra* note 17.

83 D. Kochenov and L. Pech, (2015), 'Monitoring and Enforcement of the Rule of Law in the EU', *supra* note 15, p. 53.

84 European Commission, Proposal for a regulation of the European Parliament and of the Council establishing the Rights and Values programme, COM(2018) 383 final/2 07.06.2018.

85 European Commission, COM(2019)163 final, *supra* note 19, pp. 8–9.

86 See OHCHR, 'The Case For A Human Rights Approach To The Rule Of Law In The European Union', 2020, p. 15, available at https://europe.ohchr.org/EN/Stories/Documents/Publication.pdf, last accessed 06.07.2021.

87 U. von der Leyen (2019), 'A Union That Strives For More', *supra* note 37.

had distinct and equally concerning consequences on other key values, as well.[88] Prioritising an all-encompassing conception of the RoL also allowed MS to commit to discussing value protection in the Council, touching upon more 'technical' aspects without addressing more controversial democracy and human rights-related political issues, as demonstrated by the practice of annual dialogues on the RoL.

The view held by the Commission and, with a different goal, by the Council, was not, however, the only EU opinion on this matter. For instance, although the FRA has increasingly been referred to by the Commission and EP as a key agent in collecting meaningful data for RoL monitoring in all MS under the EU-wide reporting mechanism proposed in 2019 – and despite the fact that it documented 'procedural' flaws in its reports – only one out of an additional set of 127 documents retrieved from the FRA's archives that also includes at least one reference to COVID-19 explicitly mentions RoL. More significantly, as already mentioned, the EP framed the RoL debate in the context of a broader and more equally balanced approach, emphasising the centrality of all values at once, as 'democracy, the rule of law and fundamental rights are mutually reinforcing values'.

In exposing the fragility of all EU values, the pandemic reinforced empirically the idea that approaching them primarily as a matter of RoL was not sufficiently effective. The EP, which reached this conclusion in 2016, took advantage of the COVID-19 crisis to further claim the need for the EU to acknowledge this limitation. In an ad hoc resolution, it made clear that 'government-led emergency measures that respect the RoL, fundamental rights and democratic accountability are needed to combat the pandemic and should be the cornerstone of all efforts to control the spread of COVID-19 since these measures have an impact on democracy, the rule of law and fundamental rights as they affect a wide range of individual rights and freedoms'.[89] This understanding, however, had to meet and compromise with that held by the Council, which maintained its view as well. Eventually, the regulation establishing the conditionality mechanism related to the MFF mixed both views, maintaining that 'the rule of law shall be understood having regard to the other Union values and principles enshrined in Article 2 TEU' and:

> while there is no hierarchy among Union values, respect for the rule of law is essential for the protection of the other fundamental values on which the Union is founded, such as freedom, democracy, equality and respect for human rights. Respect for the rule of law is intrinsically linked to respect for democracy and for fundamental rights. There can be no democracy and respect for fundamental rights without respect for the rule of law and vice versa.[90]

---

88 D. Soyaltin-Colella (2020), 'The EU's 'actions-without-sanctions', *supra* note 28, p 4.

89 EP, P9 TA(2020)0307, *supra* note 72.

90 EP and Council (2020), 'Regulation 2020/2092', *supra* note 42.

More significant were the consequences on the Commission's approach to these matters. In fact, in some cases, the Commission seemed to confirm its prevalent understanding of the RoL as a prerequisite which eventually subsumes the protection of other EU values concerned. In her 2020 'State of the Union' address, President von der Leyen reiterated that:

> the rule of law helps protect people from the rule of the powerful. It is the guarantor of our most basic of every day rights and freedoms. It allows us to give our opinion and be informed by a free press.[91]

Incidentally, the very consistency of this position was criticised by the EP, which complained that the first Commission monitoring report on the RoL failed to encompass the areas of democracy and fundamental rights, particularly freedom of association and the shrinking space for civil society.[92]

However, besides policy rhetoric and inconsistencies, the practice of the Commission during the pandemic also showed the consolidation of a parallel approach to EU values, which eventually sought to frame and not depart from RoL-related considerations. This 'broader endeavour' at the EU level to strengthen the values of democracy, equality and respect for human rights, including the rights of persons belonging to minorities,[93] gradually appears in a number of Commission's initiatives adopted by the end of 2020, including those related to the ERoLM and those devoted to other EU values: the EDAP; the Joint Communication by the Commission and High Representative on 'Tackling COVID-19 disinformation'; the CFR Strategy; and their preparatory documents.

As previously mentioned, plans to consolidate democracy and support a renewed monitoring of the CFR were mentioned among the pledges of Commissioner-designates Jourova and Reynders back in 2019. The claim here is that the COVID-19 emergency caused the Commission work ahead of schedule in relation to their planned design and adoption, and prompted it to place these pledges and RoL policy achievements at the core of its response to reinforce European resilience the facing the ongoing crisis, as magnified by the pandemic. As Commissioner Jourova put it, the concept was that 'by killing the virus, we cannot kill democracy!'[94] Therefore the Commission had to commit monitoring the emergency situation in MS, especially the impact on the RoL (to be assessed through the new ERoLM) and on fundamental rights, a reflection on which lay at the basis of the CFR Strategy.[95]

---

91 State of the Union Address by President von der Leyen at the European Parliament Plenary, Brussels, 16.09.2020.

92 EP, P9 TA(2020)0307, *supra* note 72.

93 European Commission, COM(2020) 580 final, *supra* note 41, p. 4.

94 Remarks by Vice-President Vera Jurova on 'Threats to Democracy during the Covid-19 Crisis', 11.05.2020 (SPEECH 20/861).

95 Ibid.

This led to the Commission explicitly integrating all new initiatives. By 'upholding freedom of expression and supporting media', the EDAP is expected to be used 'to draw the lessons and build resilience for the future', since 'our common values and democratic institutions, including free and plural media are keystones to the resilience of our societies to the challenges of the COVID-19 pandemic'.[96] The initiatives to counter COVID-19 disinformation, including the monitoring on emergency measures in all MS, are meant to inform the Commission's ERoLM (annual RoL report) as well as the CFR Strategy and the EDAP.[97] More specifically, the latter, taken together with the new ERoLM, the CFR Strategy and other measures seeking to promote and protect equality across the EU, is expected to act as a key driver for European democracy to face the challenges and reap the benefits of the digital age, which the pandemic made even clearer.[98] Eventually, the latest among the adopted blueprints, the CFR Strategy, confirmed this trend, as the Commission acknowledges that all these blueprints and strategies together illustrate 'its comprehensive approach to promoting and protecting the fundamental values on which the EU is founded'.[99]

5.3. TOWARDS AN EU-WIDE ARTICLE 2 MECHANISM?

Although it is in large part rhetorical, this move towards a comprehensive approach to European values is particularly significant in broader EU terms as it involves the institution with the most enterprising role for what concerns Article 2 TEU, due to its double role of 'executive arm' and 'guardian of the treaties'. Already before the COVID-19 outbreak, as shown, some within the Commission had envisaged to work on these strands and foster a more comprehensive and integrated discourse on EU values, although they did not necessarily take precedence in the institution plans. As the fragility of all EU values was equally exposed by the crisis, the pandemic contributed to enhancing and consolidating these views within the Commission, arguably starting a new pattern in the broader EU approach. Incidentally, the fact that textual segments

96 European Commission, Communication from the Commission to the European Parliament, the Council, the European Economic and Social Committee and the Committee of the Regions. Strategy to strengthen the application of the Charter of Fundamental Rights in the EU, COM(2020) 711 final 02.12.2020.

97 European Commission, Joint Communication to the European Parliament, the European Council, the Council, the European Economic and Social Committee and the Committee of the Regions. Tackling COVID-19 disinformation – Getting the facts right, Brussels, JOIN(2020) 8 final 10.06.2020.

98 European Commission, Communication from the Commission to the European Parliament, the Council, the European Economic and Social Committee and the Committee of the Regions. On the European democracy action plan, COM(2020) 790 final 03.12.2020, p. 25.

99 European Commission, COM(2020) 711 final, *supra* note 96. Emphasis added.

coded as 'rule of law', 'democracy' and 'human rights/fundamental rights' recur with a similar frequency in the documents selected for analysis (254, 202 and 244 times, respectively) confirms that in the period of analysis there has been, in general, almost equal attention to the three values by EU institutions.

At the same time, however, this pattern remains sketchy and inconsistent. The rationale behind the Commission's documents on 'single' EU values is functionally integrated, but the presented plans do not constitute pillars of a unique, consistent and interrelated approach, deeply involving all actors and equally covering all values. The relevance and visibility attributed by the Commission to its progress on the RoL toolbox, from the finalisation of the ERoLM to claiming success for the achievement of a RoL-conditioned MFF, remains significantly higher when compared to other values. After all, in spite of the move towards this comprehensive approach, according to the Commission, the COVID-19 pandemic:

> has highlighted the importance of ensuring that urgent and effective decision-making necessary of the protection of public health does not mean by-passing established checks and balances – including Parliaments – in particular when measures affect the fundamental freedoms and rights of the population as a whole.[100]

Additionally, the FRA has been represented by the Commission as a crucial source of information on the 'fundamental rights aspects of the rule of law' – that is,[101] again, a part of a whole which subsumes it. The broader endeavour vis-à-vis EU values displayed by the Commission since the end of 2020 cannot be labelled as a truly comprehensive approach. Nor can it be understood as a significant step towards reducing the well known distance between EU institutions' views on how to deal with EU values and fostering significant cooperation on these matters, a distance which eventually may reduce the prospect of success for the new set of tools. While the Commission stated that the ERoLM will help to streamline the discussion on the RoL at the EU level and strengthen inter-institutional cooperation, 'allowing for annual rhythm in the work of the EP and the Council and a structured and targeted follow-up',[102] this idea does not at all match the call for joining up forces advanced by other stakeholders. In particular, the analysis shows that while 'more cooperation' is occasionally referred to as an intended achievement in both the Council and Commission's documents, the need for formal and integrated cooperation, namely, the establishment of an inter-institutional agreement to govern these policy areas,

---

100 European Commission, COM(2020) 580 final, *supra* note 41, pp. 6–7.

101 FRA, 'Programming document 2021-2023', 2020, available at https://fra.europa.eu/sites/default/files/fra_uploads/fra-programming-document-2021-2023_en.pdf, last accessed 06.07.2021.

102 European Commission, COM(2020) 580 final, *supra* note 41, p. 4.

appears only in EP resolutions and working documents.[103] It is not surprising, therefore, that despite the commitment displayed by the Commission, the EP eventually expressed concern about 'the disjointed nature of the Union's toolkit in the field of EU values' and called for it to be streamlined and properly enforced.[104] The EP also stressed the need for an objective and evidence-based monitoring mechanism enshrined in a legal act binding the three institutions to a transparent and regularised process, with clearly defined responsibilities, so that the protection and promotion of all EU values becomes a permanent and visible part of the Union agenda.[105]

While the COVID-19 pandemic contributed to bridging different EU understandings on how to tackle the serious threats to all European values, since both the Commission and the EP currently support a broader and comprehensive approach to monitor and protect them, the path to implement such objective remains diametrically opposite. The Commission pursues a multiplication of the strands of work through a number of different but complementary plans, mechanisms and initiatives, which may eventually disperse existing efforts and lower the effectiveness and consistency of its response. The EP aims at consolidating and superseding existing instruments into a single monitoring mechanism where effective cooperation of EU institutions and MS is formally and legally established. A compromise is needed to meet the concerns of all MS within the Council and to put what is now an incipient and inconsistent approach to protecting European values at the core of the EU policy agenda for the years (and crises) to come.

6. CONCLUSION

This contribution sought to investigate how the COVID-19 emergency has affected the broader EU institutions' approach to upholding the RoL in consideration of parallel efforts at protecting other EU fundamental values. The analysis has not established any direct causal correlation between the pandemic (or the national response to tackle it) and the visible progress that the EU eventually made on this matter during 2020. However, investigating how a number of key themes were addressed in a wealth of EU institutions' and officials' public documents related to the RoL, this contribution discussed two aspects in which the effects of COVID-19 seemed particularly salient and to substantiate two conclusions. Both of these conclusions eventually conform to the goal of EU policy-makers,

---

103 EP, Report on the establishment of an EU Mechanism on Democracy, the Rule of Law and Fundamental Rights, 2020/2072(INL), 29.09.2020.

104 EP, 'The establishment of an EU Mechanism on Democracy, the Rule of Law and Fundamental Rights', P9_TA(2020)0251, 07.10. 2020.

105 EP, P9_TA(2020)0307, *supra* note 72.

whether it is truly felt or just instrumentally pursued, to strengthen European resilience towards this and possible future crises.

The first conclusion, as may be expected, is that the Commission, the EP and the majority of MS shared an urgency to provide a response to the now greatly exposed challenges to all EU values and ensure better protection of democracy, human rights and the RoL, which incidentally were recently indicated by European citizens as EU's 'most important asset'.[106] The second conclusion is that within the Commission, the acknowledgement has gradually taken root that to enhance resilience vis-à-vis the many challenges to EU values brought by current crises, prioritising the RoL over other EU values might not be the most promising response, if it ever was. If the move of the Commission towards this understanding of a more integrated and comprehensive approach, which has been championed by the EP since 2016, is in principle a significant step forward, since it provides more convergence between the two supranational institutions, the distance between the Commission and EP remains wide in a number of crucial aspects, including how inter-institutional cooperation is conceived. As a consequence, despite the progress made in framing the challenges, arguably prompted by the sense of urgency and the increased political and societal risks that the pandemic has brought about, the EU remains ill-equipped to face democratic, human rights and RoL backsliding.

---

[106] European Commission, Eurobarometer report on 'Rule of law in the European Union', 2019, available at https://europa.eu/eurobarometer/surveys/detail/2235, last accessed 12.07.2021.

CREATING A EUROPEAN HEALTH UNION IN TIMES OF COVID-19

A Trajectory Towards a Fundamental Right to Health Care?

Heidi Suorsa

ABSTRACT

COVID-19 appears to have provided the European Union (EU, the Union) with a window of opportunity to infiltrate the arena of policy-making in the field of health, which is evident in the proliferation of initiatives under the auspices of the creation of a European Health Union (EHU). To that effect, one of the first steps taken has been, *inter alia*, the Commission proposal for a regulation on serious cross-border health threats, which, if adopted, seeks to repeal an existing decision on the same issue. However, how influential can the EHU initiative be post-pandemic? This contribution seeks to discover what the role of COVID-19 has been for the materialisation of an EHU and what the implications are (if there are any) for the future of European health care. By combining an interest-based and structuralist narrative on the recognition of a right to health care, this contribution argues that COVID-19 has given the EU a marginal opportunity to prove its ability to act on health threats. Success in doing so may contribute towards resolving the joint-decision trap by providing the Member States with the confidence in the EU as a health actor.

1. INTRODUCTION

In 2017, the European Union (EU, the Union) and its Member States committed to ensuring that everyone has a 'right to timely access to affordable, preventive and curative health care of good quality' with the adoption of the European Pillar of Social Rights (EPSR).[1] This non-binding obligation echoes the treaty-based objective 'to promote [...] the well-being of its peoples' under Article 3(1) of the Treaty on European Union (TEU) and the obligation to ensure that 'everyone has the right of access to preventive health care and the right to benefit from medical treatment' under Article 35 of the Charter of Fundamental Rights of the European Union (CFREU).[2] Clearly, there is an EU-wide commitment towards the recognition of a right to health (and health care) – the practical materialisation of which, however, appears to still be lacking. European Commission President Ursula von der Leyen stated in March 2020 that 'we will stop at nothing to save lives', referring to the Commission's commitment to protecting European citizens from cross-border health threats and strengthening its role in European health.[3] Prompted by the novel COVID-19 pandemic, 2020 saw the first concrete steps being taken towards the creation of an EU-wide initiative for health protection in the form of a European Health Union (EHU).

This analysis sheds light on the extent to which the initiative for an EHU possibly could be able to deliver on some of these treaty-based health care-related objectives after the COVID-19 crisis and assumes that studying the Commission's vision for an EHU informs on its envisaged role in European health. According to the Commission, the three main targets of the EHU are to: '1) better protect the health of [its] citizens, 2) equip the EU and its Member States to better

---

1 European Commission, Commission Recommendation of 24 April 2017 on the European Pillar of Social Rights, C(2017) 2600 final 26.04.2017 (hereinafter EPSR).

2 Article 3(1) TEU; Article 35 CFREU.

3 G. Bazzan, 'Exploring Integration Trajectories for a European Health Union', (2020) 11, *European Journal of Risk Regulation*, p. 746.

prevent and address future pandemics, and 3) improve resilience of Europe's health systems'.[4] Though the context of COVID-19 can be read between the lines of all the aforementioned objectives, the first and third in particular would not strike as odd outside of a pandemic, either. This suggests that the EHU is not only intended to be influential under exceptional circumstances, such as the COVID-19 crisis, but also in a post-pandemic Europe.[5] The question which remains is: how can an EHU which has emerged in the context of COVID-19 contribute towards the recognition of a fundamental right to health care on the EU level?

This contribution seeks to analyse the potential influence of the EHU, and by extension COVID-19, on the recognition of a right to health care in the EU. As the title and research question suggests, it argues that a fundamental right to health care is absent in the current regulatory framework of the EU. However, the present contribution is based on observations of the EHU as it materialises and thereby constitutes an analysis of the Commission's vision thereof. It remains to be seen what the outcome of the legislative process will be in practice. The methodology is characterised by a combination of interest-based and structuralist considerations. The interest-based narrative on EU integration in the field of health emphasises the role of domestic political will and intergovernmental agency. The structuralist, or even federalist theories of integration, adopt a pessimistic outlook on the future of European-wide health care policy due to the asymmetry of EU integration which favours market liberalisation over social issues and social rights.[6]

The aim of the contribution is not to provide an in-depth analysis of the content of the proposed EHU. Such analyses, along with critiques on the extent to which it would contribute to the social *acquis*, have already been carried out. This contribution intends to uncover whether the EHU as proposed by the Commission may contribute with a possible trajectory towards recognising an EU-wide fundamental right to health care. In doing so, it provides guidance for the growing advocacy for 'more EU in health' on whether the context of COVID-19 is a favourable one for adopting health policy at the EU level.

---

4 European Commission, 'European Health Union', available at https://ec.europa.eu/info/strategy/priorities-2019-2024/promoting-our-european-way-life/european-health-union_en, last accessed 24.02.2021.

5 Disclaimer: At the time of writing the prospect of a 'post-pandemic Europe' seems unclear. The concept of a post-pandemic Europe in this contribution refers to a reality where COVID-19 may still be a widespread endemic disease but no longer a major cross-border health threat insofar as the number of infected people remains stable.

6 See for example: F.W. Scharpf, 'The Joint-Decision Trap Revisited', (2006) 44(4), *Journal of Common Market Studies*, pp. 845–864; F.W. Scharpf, 'The European Social Model: Coping with the Challenges of Diversity,' (2002) 40(4), *Journal of Common Market Studies*, pp. 645–670.

First, the contribution commences with an overview of the proposals put forward by the Commission concerning the initiative for an EHU, to identify opportunities and challenges connected to the context of COVID-19 in which the initiative is taking shape. Second, the state of play of the fundamental right to health care in the EU is discussed, focusing in particular on Article 35 of the CFREU and the pitfalls of an economic approach to health care rights. Following the interpretation by the CJEU on the legal differentiation between rights and principles enshrined in the CFREU, it is concluded that Article 35 CFREU is most likely to constitute a principle that must be given expression either in EU law or national law. Third, the legal and political challenges behind both avenues of recognising a fundamental right to health care across the EU are identified. Such challenges then constitute the backdrop against which the initiative for an EHU can be discussed to ultimately determine whether it might sufficiently address them. It is concluded that that the aim and contents of the current proposals fall short in view of the ambition to address trans-national health inequality, rendering it merely a short-term goal-oriented crisis management tool. However, by bringing European health onto domestic agendas, the window of opportunity for introducing more EU in health may open new doors later on.

2. WHAT EUROPEAN HEALTH UNION?

2.1. BACKGROUND

Lack of solidarity between the EU Member States has characterised the actions taken by governments in the face of the pandemic. During the first wave of COVID-19 infections in March 2020, the EU failed to converge the Member States' recommendations and policy responses in regards to protective face masks, teleworking, social distancing, cross-border mobility and more.[7] But more importantly for the purpose of this research, the health care systems of the Member States were unequally prepared and equipped to handle the sudden pressure on health care services. The premise of this contribution is therefore that COVID-19 has exacerbated and accentuated existing, spatial health inequalities between the EU Member States.

The present section seeks to evaluate the content of the proposed EHU in view of its social added value for the purpose of analysing the extent to which it has the potential of addressing the fragmented health care arrangements of EU Member States after the COVID-19 crisis. This section provides a textual interpretation of the Commission's communications that pave the way for an

[7] A. Alemanno, 'Towards a European Health Union: Time to Level Up', (2020) 11, *European Journal of Risk Regulation*, p. 724.

EHU. To that effect, it provides an overview of the ways that the Commission seeks to invigorate the role of the EU in European health. Such an overview can then be mirrored against the Union's treaty-based health targets as well as the ambitions of the growing advocacy for more EU in health and, perhaps ultimately, a fundamental right to health care.

In November 2020 the Commission published three legislative proposals as well as one communication, followed by another communication in May 2021, which collectively constituted the first official steps towards the formation of the EHU. These are:

- The Proposal for a Regulation of the European Parliament and of the Council on serious cross-border threats to health and repealing Decision No 1082/2013/EU;[8]
- The Proposal for a Regulation of the European Parliament and of the Council on a reinforced role for the European Medicines Agency in crisis preparedness and management for medicinal products and medical devices;[9]
- The Proposal for a Regulation of the European Parliament and of the Council amending Regulation (EC) No 851/2004 establishing a European Centre for disease prevention and control;[10]
- The Communication from the Commission to the European Parliament, the Council, The European Economic and Social Committee and the Committee of the Regions, Building a EHU: Reinforcing the EU's resilience for cross-border health threats;[11] and
- The Communication from the Commission to the European Parliament, the Council, the European Economic and Social Committee and the Committee of the Regions, EU Strategy on COVID-19 Therapeutics.[12]

The first communication provides an overview of the envisaged added value of the proposed legislation and expands upon the Commission's vision of an EHU.

---

8 European Commission, Proposal for a Regulation of the European Parliament and of the Council on serious cross-border threats to health and repealing Decision no 1082/2013/EU, COM(2020) 727 final 11.11.2020.

9 European Commission, Proposal for a Regulation of the European Parliament and of the Council on a reinforced role for the European Medicines Agency in crisis preparedness and management for medicinal products and medical devices, COM(2020) 725 final 11.11.2020.

10 European Commission, Proposal for a Regulation of the European Parliament and of the Council amending Regulation (EC) No 851/2004 establishing a European Centre for disease prevention and control, COM(2020) 726 final 11.11.2020.

11 European Commission, Communication from the Commission to the European Parliament, the Council, The European Economic and Social Committee and the Committee of the Regions Building a European Health Union: Reinforcing the EU's resilience for cross-border health threats, COM(2020) 724 final 11.11.2020.

12 European Commission, Communication from the Commission to the European Parliament, the Council, the European Economic and Social Committee and the Committee of the Regions EU Strategy on COVID-19 Therapeutics, COM(2021) 355 final/2 6.5.2021.

The second communication is more embedded in the context of COVID-19 and constitutes a first step towards a long-term strategy for the coordination of COVID-19 therapeutics. This contribution zooms in on the first communication as well as the proposal for a regulation on serious cross-border threats to health. This limitation is based on the rationale that the two other proposals do not address or inform on the perceived shortcomings in the coordination of health care in Europe, but merely seek to extend the mandate of two existing EU agencies and create a new one, and the second communication by definition does not seek to be applicable in a context outside of COVID-19. The first step is to provide an overview of the current plans for the EHU initiative in order to determine the extent to which it may be capable of addressing the political and legal landscape that enables the absence of fundamental rights-based protection of health care in Europe. The social added value thereof will be analysed from the perspectives of policy coordination and policy framing.

2.2. SOCIAL ADDED VALUE

2.2.1. Policy Framing

As an EHU materialises, so is a 'Manifesto for a European Health Union'.[13] The drafters of the Manifesto, together with the signatories thereof, maintain, *inter alia*, that the EU ought to have explicit competences in the field of health and that universal health coverage for all based on solidarity between the Member States ought to constitute one of the goals of the EHU. Therefore, it appears to constitute a call for an even stronger EU health mandate than what has been envisioned by the Commission. The main gap between the EHU called for by the Manifesto and the Commission's proposals for an EHU is the lack of collective commitment and EU involvement in health protection provoked by the latter. To that effect, the drafters of the Manifesto have expressed disappointment in the proposals from November 2020.[14] In their critique, they emphasise that the EHU as proposed by the Commission is short-term, goal-oriented and narrow in its scope of application. This is due to the EHU being created in the context of COVID-19. This line of reasoning suggests that the envisioned EHU is possibly only applicable in major health crises similar to COVID-19 in the future. This critique is relevant seeing as the Commission has explicitly confirmed that the

13 European Health Union, 'Manifesto for a European Health Union', available at https://europeanhealthunion.eu/#manifest, last accessed 23.02.2021.

14 See European Health Forum Gastein, 'Towards a European Health Union: A Vision for more EU in Health', Webinar delivered, 09.12.2020, available at https://www.ehfg.org/projects-events/side-events/towards-a-european-health-union-a-vision-for-more-eu-in-health, last accessed 11.04.2021.

regulation on cross-border health threats, as framed by the proposal, 'provides for an enhanced crisis management framework'.[15]

In the communication, the Commission commences by highlighting the need for increased coordination of European responses to cross-border health threats, as is evident from the ramifications of COVID-19.[16] This suggests that the EHU is intended to be future-proof not only in the face of another pandemic, but also any other foreseeable or unforeseeable cross-border health threats. Explicit examples are health threats emanating from climate change and antimicrobial resistance.[17] The role of crises is therefore central in the framing of the proposals, with a focus on future-proof policy beyond COVID-19. Consequently, it would appear that the EHU seeks to primarily be a crisis management tool rather than a long-term oriented health (care) policy measure, which also largely defines the policy frame.

Furthermore, in its communication, the Commission maintains that one of the most crucial interests at stake is the continued functioning of the internal market.[18] This is due to the unprecedented manners in which the pandemic has disrupted the free movement within the Union, which forms the backbone of the EU's activity, and the failure to coordinate a common reaction thereto.[19] The Commission emphasises that health is a precondition for the proper functioning of virtually all aspects of society.[20] This line of reasoning introduces a justification for EU involvement in health which is heavily rooted in economic considerations in particular. The Commission emphasises that failure to coordinate the national responses to COVID-19 has had far-reaching consequences to both human health and the internal market.[21] As will be shown later, in view of limited Union competences in the field of health, it makes sense that the Commission draws a link between saving lives and saving livelihoods by referring to internal market considerations.[22] For now, it is sufficient to note that as an aspirational commitment to health, the EHU appears to be an initiative that is justified based on economic freedoms rather than fundamental rights protection, contrary to what is called for in the Manifesto and this contribution.

It has been argued that the currently envisaged EHU does not contribute anything substantive to the landscape of the existing *acquis* of European health policy.[23] If this is the case, two ramifications are relevant for our analysis. First, it

15 European Commission, COM(2020) 727 final, *supra* note 8, p. 1.
16 European Commission, COM(2020) 724 final, *supra* note 11, p. 1.
17 Ibid., pp. 2–3.
18 Ibid., p. 1.
19 Ibid.
20 Ibid.
21 Ibid.
22 Ibid., p. 2.
23 A. Alemanno (2020), 'Towards a European Health Union', *supra* note 7, p. 724.

suggests that the EHU is not context-based, considering that in practice (though not in name) it already existed before COVID-19. Second, it suggests that the Union is efficient in policy framing, seeing as considerable attention has now been giving to the recently availed health policy *acquis* in the form of the EHU, even though substantively it may not introduce anything new.

It is relevant to observe that the currently envisaged and proposed EHU is not intended to address individual human health, or in other words, health care per se – not even within the context of COVID-19. However, that is where this present contribution comes into play. Should and could the EHU address individual health in terms of supporting the health care rights of individuals? Especially since it would appear that the proposed EHU also seeks to address health-related issues which transcend beyond COVID-19? What then should the EHU contribute with for it to constitute a contribution to the recognition of the right to health? Alemanno adds that ideally, an EHU is to set minimum health care standards, echoing the argument of Cucic that minimum quality standards are required if the EHU is to substantively address the trans-national health inequality and crisis preparedness fragmentation highlighted by COVID-19.[24] It will be evaluated in section 3 whether this is possible following the strengthened aspirational commitment towards the pooling of efforts in the field of health at the supranational level.

2.2.2. *Regulated Policy Coordination*

The Commission proposes that the regulation on cross-border health threats which would repeal an existing decision be based on Article 168(5) of the Treaty on the Functioning of the EU (TFEU), which would render it an incentive measure.[25] By definition, incentive measures adopted under Article 168(5) TFEU cannot harmonise national laws.[26] Coordination is thereby the leading concept and means of achieving policy convergence. To that effect, the main tools in the arsenal of the EU would be the EU Health Security Committee which constitutes the primary crisis response forum enabled by the Commission, the Early Warning and Response System (EWRS), and the EU Integrated Political Crisis Response (IPCR) managed at Council level not only for health crises.[27]

However, the existing decision on serious cross-border threats to health, which the proposed regulation seeks to repeal, already prescribes the exchanging of information similar to the new envisaged model, and a framework for coordination based on the EWRS.[28] The Commission maintains

---

24 Ibid. p. 725; S. Cucic, 'European Union Health Policy and its Implications for National Convergence', (2000) 12(3), *International Journal for Quality in Health*, p. 224.

25 European Commission, COM(2020) 727 final, *supra* note 8, p. 3.

26 Article 168(5) TFEU.

27 European Commission, COM(2020) 724 final, *supra* note 11, pp. 5–6.

28 A. Alemanno (2020), 'Towards a European Health Union', *supra* note 7, p. 724.

that the limited legal status of the instrument has proven insufficient in the face of COVID-19.[29] Therefore, it is relevant to briefly explore the significance of the proposed instrument being a regulation rather than a decision. Decisions constitute non-binding instruments of EU law. Consequently, Member States cannot be sanctioned by the CJEU for non-compliance. Regulations, however, do constitute legally binding instruments of EU law. And unlike directives, regulations do not need to be transposed into the domestic legislation of the Member States, but they automatically become the law of the land across the whole EU territory. By that token, the adoption of a regulation would in itself constitute a strengthening of the EU's foothold in the field of health, even if the regulation would be substantively comparable to the decision which currently is in force because it would render the Member States obliged to follow through on their coordination duties.

Although the creation of an EHU sounds like an ambitious endeavour, at least in terms of its name, it adds rather little to the existing framework of European health policy. A preliminary observation is therefore that the instrumental aim of the EHU is to create a binding coordination framework that *de facto* strengthens the position of the EHU in the field of European health. However, the extent to which the initiative may have a substantial impact on the European health care systems (and the convergence thereof in particular) remains questionable. However, as will be discussed, this is in line with the constraints of Union competences. A preliminary conclusion is that the main added value of the EHU for the purposes of this contribution is the envisaged strengthening of the commitment towards existing means of coordinating policy in times of health crises in particular.

2.3. CONCLUSION

The previous section has already demonstrated that the context in which the EHU has seen its humble beginnings can be read between the lines of the Commission proposals for the EHU, which raises the question of whether an EHU would have materialised at all in the absence of a pandemic. COVID-19 has successfully placed European health on the (domestic) agenda(s), which essentially proves that it has been a favourable context for those who wish to see the EU be more involved in health (care).[30] According to the proposal, the main imperative behind it is the fact that the existing framework for coordinating cross-border health threats in Europe is insufficient and 'has not ensured an

---

29 European Commission, COM(2020) 727 final, *supra* note 8, p. 1.

30 I. Kickbusch and A. de Ruijter, 'Commentary How a European Health Union Can Strengthen Global Health', (2021) 1, *The Lancet Regional Health – Europe*, p. 1.

optimal response at EU level to the COVID-19 pandemic'.[31] Furthermore, this appears to legitimise the EU's further involvement in the field of health. It appears from the foregoing that the EHU is intended to replace the existing framework on tackling cross-border health threats, and by that token, it constitutes a crisis aversion tool above anything else. At this point, it is relevant to consider the existing advocacy for further integration of health policy at the EU level.

3. THE 'RIGHT' TO HEALTH CARE IN THE EUROPEAN UNION

The right to health care has already been recognised at EU level, at least following a textual interpretation of EU law. The legal expression thereof is found in Article 35 of the CFREU, which maintains that 'Everyone has the right to benefit from medical treatment'.[32] However, the scope and the application of the provision are limited, first, by the provision itself which subjects health care rights to 'conditions established by national laws and practices'.[33] Second, under Article 51(1) of the CFREU, the application of the CFREU provisions is limited to circumstances where Member States are implementing EU law.[34] Following the entry into force of the treaties of Lisbon, the CFREU has the same legal status of the treaties, elevating the role of the CFREU into primary EU law.[35] Arguably, the right to health care has been constitutionalised at the Union level. However, a doctrinal analysis of the same provision, following the interpretation of 'rights' proclaimed by the CFREU in the Court of Justice of the European Union (CJEU), does not necessarily lend itself to the same conclusion. Consequently, a paradoxical question that arises is whether the right to health care under Article 35 CFREU constitutes a right that can be invoked before a European court. If not, are there alternative legal routes for accessing health care based on EU law?

3.1. ARTICLE 35 OF THE CHARTER OF FUNDAMENTAL RIGHTS OF THE EUROPEAN UNION

3.1.1. *Rights v. Principles*

Under Article 51(1) of the CFREU, the rights found therein are to be respected, whereas the principles it enshrines are to be observed.[36] Furthermore,

---

31 European Commission, COM(2020) 727 final, *supra* note 8, p. 1.

32 Article 35 CFREU.

33 Ibid.

34 Article 51(1) CFREU.

35 Article 6(1) TEU.

36 Article 51(1) CFREU.

Article 52(5) of the CFREU suggests that only rights are judicially enforceable, seeing as '[principles] shall be judicially cognisable only in the interpretation of such acts and in the ruling on their legality'.[37] Confusingly enough, the CFREU does not provide an explicit differentiation between the two categories. Three practical ramifications are relevant here. First, it suggests that not all 'rights' enshrined in the CFREU constitute rights in the sense that they can be invoked before a European court. Second, it raises the question of what constitutes a right vis-à-vis an obligation. And finally, it raises the question of what the degree of enforceability and practical use of those provisions that do not constitute rights for the private individual is (if any). Thus, where does the 'right' to health care under Article 35 CFREU fall in this amalgam of fundamental rights protection at the EU level?

The closest definition of a principle to be found in the CFREU is Article 52(5) CFREU, which reads:

> The provisions of this Charter which contain principles may be implemented by legislative and executive acts taken by institutions, bodies, offices and agencies of the Union, and by acts of Member States when they are implementing Union law, in the exercise of their respective powers. They shall be judicially cognisable only in the interpretation of such acts and in the ruling on legality.[38]

The material scope of Article 35 CFREU being subject to national laws and practices read in conjunction with Article 168(7) TFEU which states that the 'responsibilities of the Member States shall include the management of health services and medical care', the organisation and delivery of which must be respected by the Union, suggests that the right to health care is subject to domestic laws and practices to the extent that it would constitute a principle rather than a right.[39] However, it ought to be noted that the wording of Article 52(5) CFREU implies causality rather than correlation. The provision does not explicitly state that provisions requiring or prescribing implementation at either domestic or EU level constitute principles, but merely vice versa – principles may be implemented. It is therefore not a conclusive distinction in itself.

The formal Explanatory Notes of the CFREU include a non-exhaustive list with examples of principles.[40] These are Articles 25 (the rights of the elderly), 26 (integration of persons with disabilities) and 37 (environmental protection).[41]

---

37 Article 52(5) CFREU.

38 Ibid.

39 Article 168(7) TFEU; EU Network of Independent Experts on Fundamental Rights, coordinated by O. De Schutter, 'Commentary of the Charter of Fundamental Rights of the European Union', 2006, p. 308, available at https://sites.uclouvain.be/cridho/documents/Download.Rep/NetworkCommentaryFinal.pdf, last accessed 13.07.2021.

40 Explanations relating to the Charter of Fundamental Rights (2007/C 303/02), Official Journal of the European Union C 303, 14.12.2007.

41 Ibid.

It is relevant to note that not all provisions in this category contain an express reference to national laws or practices, confirming that the scepticism hinted towards above is not misdirected. The notes proceed to introduce provisions which share elements of both right and principles, which include Articles 23 (equality between women and men), 33 (family and professional life) and 34 (social security and social assistance), introducing the option that a provision does not necessarily fall in only one category.[42] The notes also clarify that '[principles] do not however give rise to direct claims for positive action by the Union's institutions or Member States authorities', echoing Article 52(5) of the CFREU.[43] In other words, principles enshrined in the CFREU lack direct effect by default. It is relevant here to apply the CJEU's interpretation on the distinction between rights and principles to Article 35 CFREU.

3.1.2. Direct Effect and Article 35 CFREU

Barnard has mapped alternative means of differentiating between rights and principles emanating from the CFREU, following jurisprudence of the CJEU and the rationale of advocates general (AG).[44] The present section closely follows the overview provided by Barnard, followed by an application of that rationale to Article 35 CFREU. The first option for differentiating between rights and principles as introduced by the AG in *AMS* suggests that the 'righthood' of a right found in the CFREU is attached to its ability to have direct effect.[45] The logic is that:

> [b]oth in the actual Charter and in the constitutional traditions of the Member States, it is common to regard as 'rights' or 'social rights' that substantive content relating to social policy which, because it cannot create legal situations directly enforceable by individuals, operates only following action or implementation by the public authorities. They are (social) 'rights' by virtue of their subject-matter, or even their identity, and 'principles' by virtue of their operation.[46]

This narrative implies that there is a distinction between rights and social rights, the latter of which lack direct effect and thereby adopts the legal value of principles as identified by the CFREU.[47] Therefore, one avenue of determining

---

42 Ibid.

43 Ibid.

44 C. Barnard, 'Are Social "Rights" Rights?', (2020) 11(4), *European Labor Law Journal*, pp. 351–363.

45 Ibid., pp. 352–353; *CJEU, Association de médiation sociale v Union locale des syndicats CGT and Others*, C-176/12, *Opinion of Advocate General Cruz Villalón*, 18.07.2013, ECLI:EU:C:2013:491.

46 Ibid., para. 45.

47 C. Barnard (2020), 'Are Social "Rights" Rights?', *supra* note 44, p. 352.

whether Article 35 CFREU is judicially cognisable would be by analysing whether it has direct effect.

In *AMS* the CJEU was called upon to decide on the direct effect of Article 27 of the CFREU and seemingly confirmed the narrative.[48] The Court maintained that in order for the provision to be effective, it must be implemented in a manner that is more specific than the provision itself dictates.[49] Therefore, the exercise of the right to information and consultation for workers is subjected to implementation by the Member States, rendering the resulting national legislation the relevant invokable instruments.

The conclusion drawn by Barnard is that the direct effect of social rights, as identified by the CJEU, is attached to the obligation of implementing said provision, which is expressly stated therein.[50] By extension, the 'righthood' of a social right would be linked to the express reference to national laws and practices in the provision itself. Such an understanding of what distinguishes a right from a principle would render the right to health care under Article 35 CFREU a principle rather than a right. Furthermore, a joint reading of the *AMS* judgment and the opinion of the AG in the same case would suggest that all provisions to be found under the solidarity title of the CFREU (the social rights) constitute principles by default.

However, Barnard has taken the analysis one step further. She proceeds to argue that even social rights can constitute rights in the strictest sense of the word, illustrated by the CJEU judgment in *Bauer*.[51] In *Bauer*, the Court concluded that the right to an annual period of paid leave under Article 31(2) CFREU constituted an invokable right.[52] In other words, the Court confirmed the direct effect of a social right enshrined in the CFREU. The conditions for direct effect introduced in *Bauer* are that a provision is mandatory and unconditional while falling within the scope of EU law.[53] The judgment is not clear on the definition of those concepts. However, following Barnard's interpretation of *Bauer* and *AMS*, the condition of unconditionality is connected to the express reference to national laws and practices, which in essence constitutes an additional limitation to the application of the CFREU provisions beyond the general limitations found in Article 52 CFREU. Insofar as this constitutes the relevant distinction between right and principles enshrined in the CFREU, Article 35 on the right to health care would constitute a principle due to the fact that it is

48 CJEU, *Association de médiation sociale v Union locale des syndicats CGT and Others (AMS)*, Case C-176/12, 15.01.2014, ECLI:EU:C:2014:2.

49 Ibid., para. 45.

50 C. Barnard (2020), 'Are Social "Rights" Rights?', *supra* note 44, p. 362.

51 Ibid.

52 CJEU, *Stadt Wuppertal and Volker Willmeroth als Inhaber der TWI Technische Wartung und Instadsetzung Volker Willmeroth e. K. v Maria Elisabeth Bauer and Martina Broßonn*, Joined Cases C-569/16 and C-570/16, 06.11.2018, ECLI:EU:C:2018:871.

53 Ibid., para. 85.

subjected to the provision-specific limitation based on national transposition. Consequently, Article 35 CFREU lacks direct effect and can therefore most likely not be invoked on its own before a European court. Instead, the right to health care must be transposed into EU law or national law.

3.2. ECONOMIC FREEDOMS AND HEALTH CARE

A fundamental right to health care may not be legally facilitated at the Union level; however, EU citizens invoking EU law in order to access health care does occur.[54] Directive 2011/24/EU (the Directive) on the application of patients' rights in cross-border health care facilitates cross-border patient mobility, together with Regulation (EC) No. 883/2004 on the coordination of social security systems (the Regulation).[55] The legal basis for the Directive is Article 48 TFEU (42 TEC) on social security for migrant workers, whereas the Regulation is based on Article 114 TFEU which is the general internal market legal basis. In sum, both provisions are primarily intended to facilitate intra-EU free movement.

It is not the aim of this contribution to provide a detailed overview of how the aforementioned legal instruments function in practice, but merely to observe the shortcomings in the existing approach to cross-border health care rights. However, to that effect, it is relevant to note that the Directive and the Regulation create two different approaches to cross-border mobility which exist next to each other.[56] This is likely to create concerns of legal certainty and normative clarity for the private individual who wishes to invoke EU law for the benefit of access to health care.[57] Second, and more generally, in order for the economic freedoms to apply, an inter-state element is required. In practice, this entails that either the recipient, the provider or the service itself must cross a state border within the Union. Hence, the instruments are irrelevant insofar as the recipient of the health care service resides in the same country in which they intend to receive said service. Third, seeing as the instruments are not rooted in human rights considerations, they are first and foremost intended to address impediments to the proper functioning of the internal market. This is a precondition for the

54 See C. M. Rieder, 'The Application and Interpretation of the EU Charter in the Context of Cross-Border Movement of Patients', (2017) 22(3), *Columbia Journal of European Law*, pp. 451–482.

55 Directive 2011/24/EU of the European Parliament and of the Council of 9 March 2011 on the application of patients' rights in cross-border, OJ L 88/45; Regulation (EC) No. 883/2004 of the European Parliament and of the Council of 29 April 2004 on the coordination of social security rights, OJ L 166/1.

56 G. Berki, 'Patient Mobility in the EU – A Playground for All of Us?', (2019) 1, *Revue Belgie de Securite Sociale*, p. 67.

57 Ibid.

instruments to be adopted under internal market legal bases. Consequently, they create considerable administrative burdens on the mobile patient.[58] The nature of the burden depends on which instrument is invoked. Finally, the fragmented health care systems may perpetuate further health inequality, seeing as patient mobility by default becomes more accessible with those who have the know-how and material resources to navigate the health care systems (and most commonly different language) of the host Member State.[59]

3.3. CONCLUSION

Observing the shortcomings of an internal market-based approach to EU health care law contributes to the advocacy for a fundamental right to health care by providing legitimising considerations. Furthermore, following the line of reasoning by the CJEU on the application of CFREU provisions as either rights or principles demonstrates that the explicit references to 'national laws and practises' constitute integral elements of making such a distinction. The direct effect of CFREU provisions appears to hinge on whether they contain limitations in the application beyond those found in Article 52 CFREU. Consequently, provisions such as the 'right' to health care under Article 35 CFREU are in fact principles rather than rights. This suggests that the invokable fundamental right to health care is yet to be recognised in the *acquis* of the EU. Considering that in order for the right to health care under Article 35 CFREU to be relevant for private individuals, it must be implemented at the national or EU level, the next step will be to evaluate the legal and political constraints that keep the adoption of more specific legislation on health care away from the EU level of governance.[60]

4. CHALLENGES OF EUROPEANISING HEALTH CARE RIGHTS

In view of the discussion carried out in section 2, it can be concluded that the initiative for an EHU is not at all intended to address individual human health or a corresponding right to health care, and therefore cannot be held accountable insofar as it falls short of those ambitions. However, seeing as the existing approach to health care rights at EU level have been proven to be insufficient in section 3, it is relevant to ask the question of whether perhaps the humble

58 Ibid.

59 Ibid., pp. 67–69.

60 CJEU, *Association de médiation sociale v Union locale des syndicats CGT and Others (AMS)*, *supra* note 45, para. 45.

beginnings of the EHU can facilitate the bridging of this gap between the current coordination-based framework and the ambitions behind the 'Manifesto for a European Health Union'.

The present section provides a brief overview of the explanations behind the EU having its hands tied when it comes to regulating health care while observing the limited influence it does wield in health care policy. The analysis of the legal, institutional landscape of EU health regulation is approached from two perspectives. First, the structuralist narrative of EU integrations highlights the tensions between economic and social aspects of EU integration and the corresponding competences. Second, the interest-based narrative focuses in particular on the collective political will of Member States (or lack thereof) to submit their health care systems to the oversight of the EU. The EHU is discussed against this backdrop for the purpose of determining whether the initiative for an EHU has the potential of addressing the identified challenges.

4.1. THE STRUCTURALIST NARRATIVE: SUPRANATIONAL COMPETENCES

In order for binding EU law to be adopted, the proposed legislation must have a legal basis that is to be found in the treaties. The EU's competences in the field of health have already been briefly touched upon in previous sections. This section seeks to provide a broader overview of the competences and their significance for integration.

Since the creation of the EU, its powers have consistently been strengthened and expanded upon, at the expense of Member States' competences.[61] However, harmonisation of domestic health care law and policy still remains outside of the EU's reach. In fact, 'health, at the heart of the welfare state, has been one of the slowest [sectors] to become Europeanized'.[62] One should not mistake this for absence of EU influence on health care systems. The EU has had great success in playing the legal basis game in order to regulate pharmaceuticals, social security, the training of health care professionals and so on, based on the legal bases for the internal market and competition law, *inter alia*.[63] The materialisation of these treaty provisions has been characterised by a curious ideological paradox. For some Member States, giving health policy a footing in the treaties

---

61 S. Cucic (2000), 'European Union Health Policy', *supra* note 24, p. 218.

62 J. Richardson, 'The Onward March of Europeanization: Tectonic Movement and Seismic Events', in J. Richardson, *Constructing a Policy-Making State? Policy Dynamics in the EU*, Oxford University Press, Oxford 2012, p. 337; A. de Ruijter, 'EU "Public Health" and "Health-care" Law and Policy', in A. de Ruijter, *EU Health Law & Policy: The Expansion of EU Power in Public Health and Health Care*, Oxford University Press, Oxford 2019, p. 59.

63 Ibid.

constitutes an effort to keep the Union in check by means of creating express legal limits to Union action. However, the very same development can also be viewed as a growing mandate for EU influence in the field of health.

Thus, the absence of health care-related ambitions in the regulatory framework of the Union can be explained by the lack of treaty-based Union competences to act in the field of health care. According to the treaty-based categorisation of EU competences, in particular Article 6 of the TFEU, the Union has been vested with the competence 'to carry out actions to support, coordinate or supplement the actions of the Member States' in the area of 'protection and improvement of human health'.[64] The exact legal basis for measures to be implemented to that effect is to be found in Article 168 TFEU. The treaty-based legal mandate of the EU to act in this field is limited to incentive measures, which according to Article 168(5) TFEU entails 'incentive measures designed to protect and improve human health and in particular to combat the major cross-border health scourges, measures concerning monitoring, early warning of and combating serious-cross border threats to health, and measures which have as their direct objective the protection of public health regarding tobacco and the use of alcohol'.[65] Most importantly, this competence excludes any harmonisation of national law.[66]

Embedding health care objectives within the EHU in the current legal institutional landscape is not without its problems, in particular regarding legitimacy. The issue with advancing health care rights and obligations under increasingly creative legal bases (in the absence of an existing one in the treaties) is the emergence of competence creep. In particular Article 114 TFEU has become the standard means of harmonising policy areas with even a marginal connection to the internal market. This consideration alone suggests that the only available avenue towards embedding health care objectives in the EHU is after treaty change. Such a change would ideally include minimum quality and accessibility standards for the provision of health care. Insofar as the right to health care under Article 35 CFREU must be given legal expression in either national or Union law constitutes a constitutional paradox seeing as the EU does not have many competences to that effect. In sum, an asymmetry arises where the responsibility more or less falls on the Member States by default. The diversity of preferences, which is described in the following section, is thereby also perpetuated by primary EU law. Assuming that treaty change would be necessary in order to offset this imbalance and to achieve a fundamental right to health care, how can the initiative for the EHU contribute towards this shift?

---

64 Article 6 TFEU.

65 Article 168(5) TFEU.

66 Ibid.

4.2. THE INTEREST-BASED NARRATIVE: POLITICAL WILL OF THE MEMBER STATES

The interest-based explanations for the lack of EU involvement in European health put intergovernmental drivers of EU integration at the fore by arguing, *inter alia,* that 'The EU's contribution to fighting COVID-19 was initially limited because the member states wanted it so'.[67] It is relevant to briefly discuss the law-making procedure of the EU and the role of Member States therein. Most legal bases found in the treaties of the EU prescribe the use of the ordinary legislative procedure (OLP).[68] Following Article 294 TFEU, the procedure commences with a legislative proposal from the Commission, which is then amended or approved by the European Parliament, followed by amendment or approval of the Council of Ministers (the Council) in up to three readings, respectively. Consequently, the Council gets the last word in the procedure, and legislation cannot be passed without intergovernmental consent. Although it constitutes common practice to adopt a decision in the Council by unanimity, formally, the standard practice is a decision by Qualified Majority Voting (QMV).[69] Consequently, the shadow of a vote by QMV, which requires the approval of 55% of the Member States representing at least 65% of the population of the EU, hangs heavy in the air.[70]

By virtue of the EU's decision-making procedure, which prescribes a fairly high intergovernmental consensus threshold, diversity of preferences among the Member States can constitute a significant impediment to EU integration. A natural implication is that as the EU has grown in membership, the consensus-building opportunities have become fewer. Partially due to the EU's lack of competence to harmonise the provision of health care across the continent, 27 health care systems, which can be more or less clustered into categories based on dominant features, still coexist within the Union.[71] In the context of COVID-19, this has given rise to fragmented policy responses prompted by the EU Member States unilaterally.[72] From the perspective of most nation-states, the legal structuring of health care systems is part of the core of state sovereignty and self-determinacy. Furthermore, patterns and means of state intervention

67 S. Greer and A. de Ruijter, 'Viewpoints EU Health Law and Policy in and after the COVID-19 Crisis,' (2020) 30(4), *The European Journal of Public Health*, p. 623.

68 Article 294 TFEU.

69 N. Nugent, *The Government and Politics of the European Union*, Palgrave, London 2017, pp. 176–177.

70 Ibid.

71 See for example C. Wendt, L. Frisina and H. Rothgang, 'Healthcare Systems Types: A Conceptual Framework for Comparison', (2009) 43, *Social Policy & Administration*, pp. 70–90; C. Wendt, 'Mapping European Healthcare Systems: A Comparative Analysis of Financing, Service Provision and Access to Health Care', (2009) 19(5), *Journal of European Social Policy*, pp. 5–18; I. Joumard, C. Andre and C. Nicq, 'Health Care Systems: Efficiency and Institutions', Economic Department Working Papers No. 769, OECD Publishing, Paris 2010.

72 G. Bazzan (2020), 'Exploring Integration Trajectories', *supra* note 3.

in the provision of health care are inextricably linked to various aspects of health regulation and beyond, such as social security and training of medical professionals. From the perspective of the private individual, accessibility of health care services is an indispensable necessity, the receiving of which can constitute a significant event in one's life.[73] Consequently, path dependency in health care systems and the reliance on the proper functioning thereof is high.

Various attempts have been made to categorise existing European health care systems into groupings based on different comparative parameters.[74] An underlying conclusion tends to be that few dominant features are shared by all EU Member States in the provision of health care. Consequently, European policy must accommodate this diversity of preferences, or initiate a shift of priorities. In order to overcome this problem-solving gap, the preferences of the Member States must be transformed in a common direction through a solidaristic shift of preferences, which necessitates that the Member States put their differences aside for the purpose of the benefits of a common policy approach.

The drafters of the 'Manifesto for a European Health Union' also emphasise the need for debate in the Member States themselves.[75] This strand of logic suggests that expansion of Union competence cannot come from within the Union, but is dependent on a call for integration from the Member States themselves. The context of the COVID-19 pandemic has been favourable, if not even the sole factor contributing to the creation of an EHU, and the Eurobarometer shows that in this context, EU citizens are increasingly expecting the EU to step in to tackle the economic and social ramifications of the pandemic.[76] This demonstrates the emergence of a bottom-up call for more EU in health, similar to that signified by the Manifesto for a EHU.

A plethora of health-related secondary legislation has been adopted by the EU, most commonly under legal bases related to the internal market. This alone renders the interest-based narrative on the lack of Union competence in the field of health unsatisfactory when discussing issues of Europeanised health care, even though the fundamental right to health care is yet to become operationalised within the framework of the Union. Section 2 demonstrated, *inter alia*, that the EHU appears to be an efficient tool for policy framing. By stressing the importance of saving both lives and livelihoods, the EHU erodes the boundaries between an economic and a social approach to health protection.

---

73 A. de Ruijter (2012), 'EU 'Public Health' and 'Health-care' Law and Policy', *supra* note 62, p. 58.

74 See for example *supra* note 71.

75 European Health Forum Gastein (2020), 'Towards a European Health Union: A Vision for more EU in Health', *supra* note 14.

76 European Parliament, 'Public Opinion in Times of COVID-19', A Public Opinion Survey Commissioned by the European Parliament, 14.07.2020, available at https://www.europarl.europa.eu/at-your-service/en/be-heard/eurobarometer/public-opinion-in-the-eu-in-time-of-coronavirus-crisis-2, last accessed 11.04.2020.

A similar approach for recognising the right to health care may be necessary in order to bring about a convergence of preferences among the Member States and ultimately a fundamental right to health care.

4.3. CONCLUSION

In view of the widespread ramifications of health inequality emanating from the fragmented policy responses in the context of COVID-19, the EU holds a disproportionally loose grip on the provision of health care in Europe. The recognition of a right to health care emanating from Article 35 CFREU would require treaty change, something which is unlikely to happen in the near future. Not only does the fragmentation in policy approaches to health care impede the right to health care under Article 35 CFREU from being recognised as a fundamental right within the EU, but it also appears to delegitimise the materialisation of an EU-wide right to health care which does not emanate from economic imperative. One could argue that such a development is reactionary, or even iterative.

However, the potential vesting of power in the field of health with the EU suggests an increasing confidence amongst the Member States in the EU as a health actor. By that token, the creation of an EHU which currently only has a rather limited mandate may act as the necessary impetus for intergovernmental shifting of priorities. Therefore, COVID-19 has constituted a favourable context of policy-making in the field of health for two reasons. First, it creates debate at the national level on the necessity to coordinate health at EU level which secondly may prompt a strategically coordinated transformation of domestic preferences. These two factors combined may contribute to a long-term convergence of priorities and agenda-setting on the domestic level, which ultimately are the factors which the EU-level recognition of a right to health care currently appears to hinge on.

5. CONCLUSION

The EU's role in addressing the social ramifications of the pandemic has given rise to mixed and paradoxical critiques. As observed by Delhomme, the lack of common responses prompted by the EU has been attributed to the lack of a treaty-based mandate to do so.[77] However, such an explanation proves

[77] V. Delhomme, 'Emancipating Health from the Internal Market: For a Stronger EU (Legislative) Competence in Public Health', (2020) 11, *European Journal of Risk Regulation*, p. 747.

unsatisfactory in view of the fact that the Union has acted in the field of health in the past.[78] Consequently, the role of the EU in addressing health inequality and coordinating policy to that effect remains somewhat ambiguous. This contribution has shown that the proposed EHU is an initiative which appears to add rather little substance to the *acquis* on European health beyond a binding policy coordination framework; that the EU lacks an enforceable right to health care; and that the existing health care provisions in EU secondary legislation do not sufficiently address human health.

The analysis carried out in this contribution has revealed the inconvenient truth that the EHU does not remove the necessity for treaty change if the EU is to provide a legitimate trajectory for the recognition of a fundamental right to health care, though that may currently look like an unrealistic prospect. However, the EHU presents a modest opportunity to invoke convergence towards common health objectives at the Member State level, which in turn may contribute to the development of an EU-wide right to health care.

A doctrinal analysis of the CJEU's distinction between rights and principles enshrined in the CFREU suggests that Article 35 on the right to health care is in fact a principle, insofar as the content of the provision is subject to national legislation and practices. The possible shift towards common national laws and practices perpetuated by the EHU in the context of COVID-19 may contribute to the recognition of an EU-wide standard of health care rights. Consequently, such a development is necessary for Article 35 to constitute an enforceable right within the current jurisprudential paradigm of the CJEU. However, for this to be possible, treaty change is still necessary because otherwise, the emanation of specific rights related to health care from EU law would constitute an infringement of Article 6(3) TEU when read in conjunction with Article 168(7) TFEU. Such a top-down narrative of the emergence of EU-wide health care rights feeds into the theories of the dynamic potential of EU law.[79] When it comes to the small prospect of treaty change which at the time of writing appears slim, a solidaristic shift of priorities within the Member States would be necessary for health care rights to be included. However, as suggested above, such a shift is likely to be perpetuated by the small policy steps taken by the EHU, thus facilitating intergovernmental consensus-building with a bottom-up approach.

In conclusion, COVID-19 did open up a window of opportunity for the EU to legitimise its role in the field of health care. However, the advocates for more EU in health are likely to be disappointed by what they see from it, considering that the Union has few options for how to make to most of the opportunity. But as the window closes, a door may open, and that is when the path paved

---

78 Ibid.

79 See T. Hervey and A. de Ruijter, 'The Dynamic Potential of European Union Health Law', Amsterdam Law School Legal Studies Research Paper No. 2020-44, available at https://ssrn.com?abstract=3675358, last accessed 26.02.2021.

by the EHU (and COVID-19 by extension) is most likely to prove itself useful. However, owing to the short-sighted policy framing which appears to be aimed at crisis management, and the unambitious substance of the EHU, it can hardly on its own be considered a reliable trajectory towards a fundamental right to health care.

THE RIGHT TO A HEALTHY ENVIRONMENT AS AN EU NORMATIVE RESPONSE TO COVID-19

A Theoretical Framework

Chiara Scissa*

ABSTRACT

The COVID-19 pandemic represents the umpteenth reason to establish a right to a healthy environment, still uncodified under EU law. Therefore, this contribution proposes an innovative theoretical framework that revolves mainly around the interpretative role of the European Court of Justice (CJEU) and Article 6.3 of the Treaty on European Union (TEU). Accordingly, an EU right to a healthy environment might be established on a threefold basis: first, this

* Many thanks to Giuseppe Martinico, whose comments and insightful suggestions significantly improved the consistency of the argument presented in this work.

fundamental right has been already embedded in the vast majority of EU Member States' constitutions or it has been ascertained by their constitutional courts. It is therefore argued that it constitutes a tradition common to the Member States. Second, it complies with the purposes, values and principles set out in the EU founding treaties, and it emerges as essential component to the fulfilling of the Union's secondary legislation on the environment. Third, its formulation is also supported by international and regional sources of law as required by the case law of the Court of Justice.

1. INTRODUCTION

In the attempt to give a rational explanation to the outbreak of the sudden, massively disruptive COVID-19 pandemic, numerous researchers linked its spreading to the level of air pollution, highlighting that highly polluted areas in Italy,[1] Spain[2] and in the United States correlate with the highest number of infection cases.[3] According to the literature, long-term exposure to fine particulate matter (PM) not only facilitates the diffusion of the virus but also increases its death rate.

Alas, the pandemic sheds light on states' failure in protecting both the environment and the health of their citizens. As regards the former, the Court of Justice of the European Union (CJEU, including also the former Court of the European Communities) found Italy,[4] one of the most severely coronavirus-affected countries, persistently and systematically violating the European Union (EU, the Union) rules against PM air pollution that, according to the World Health Organization (WHO), causes heightened mortality due to cardiovascular and respiratory diseases, such as COVID-19. As regards the latter, according to a study conducted by the University of Harvard, the exposition of African-Americans to the virus in the United States is three times higher than of white Americans, given their restricted access to the American health care system.[5]

---

1 L. Setti, F. Passarini, G. de Gennaro et al., 'Position Paper. Relazione circa l'Effetto dell'Inquinamento da Particolato Atmosferico e la Diffusione di Virus nella Popolazione', available at https://www.simaonlus.it/wpsima/wp-content/uploads/2020/03/COVID19_Position-Paper_Relazione-circa-l%E2%80%99effetto-dell%E2%80%99inquinamento-da-particolato-atmosferico-e-la-diffusione-di-virus-nella-popolazione.pdf, last accessed 22.03.2021.

2 M. Marquèsa, J. Roviraab, M. Nadala, et al., 'Effects of Air Pollution on the Potential Transmission and Mortality of COVID-19: A Preliminary Case-Study in Tarragona Province (Catalonia, Spain)', (2021) 192, *Environmental Research*.

3 X. Wu, R. C. Nethery, M. B. Sabath et al., 'Air pollution and COVID-19 Mortality in the United States: Strengths and Limitations of an Ecological Regression Analysis', (2020) 6(45), *ScienceAdvances*.

4 CJEU, *Commission v Italy*, Case C-644/18, 10.11.2020, ECLI:EU:C:2020:895.

5 X. Wu, R. C. Nethery, M. B. Sabath et al. (2020), 'Air pollution and COVID-19', *supra* note 3.

The pandemic, therefore, represents the latest reason to establish a European right to a healthy environment, as also recently reiterated by the United Nations (UN) High Commissioner for Human Rights,[6] the European Parliament[7] and the Council of Europe.[8] Despite the absence of an explicitly recognised right to a healthy environment in the European Convention on Human Rights (ECHR) and in the Charter of Fundamental Rights of the European Union (hereinafter, the EU Charter), judicial authorities have taken steps to protect people from environmental harm. For instance, the CJEU affirmed that environmental protection should be horizontally integrated into the definition and implementation of all EU policies to promote sustainable development pursuant to Article 11 of the Treaty on the Functioning of the European Union (TFEU),[9] while in nearly 300 cases, the European Court of Human Rights (ECtHR) has concluded that environmental harm may lead to violation of a broad range of hitherto guaranteed human rights – that is, the right to life, to health, to private and family life and to property. Finally, in two occasions the European Committee of Social Rights has interpreted Article 11 of the European Social Charter (ESC)[10] on the right to health as including the right to a healthy environment.[11]

Given the solid regional jurisprudence on the matter, the timely call for actions launched by EU institutions and the Council of Europe, as well as the urgent need to curb the dramatic effects that air pollution and COVID-19 have on the health and life of millions of people, this contribution is aimed at supporting the official recognition of an EU right to a healthy environment through a likely innovative theoretical framework, as a normative response to the pandemic.

To this end, this contribution is organised as follows: the second section substantiates the need to establish a right to a healthy environment at the EU level via Article 6.3 TEU, stressing the pivotal role of the CJEU for it to succeed. In taking the Court's case law on the general principles of EU law and the precise methodology set out by Advocate General (AG) Trstenjak in *Audiolux* as a

---

6 United Nations High Commissioner for Human Rights, 'Human Rights for the Planet – High-Level International Conference on Human Rights and Environmental Protection, Statement', 05.10.2020, available at https://www.ohchr.org/EN/NewsEvents/Pages/DisplayNews.aspx?NewsID=26343&LangID=E, last accessed 22.03.2021.

7 European Parliament, Draft Report on the Effects of Climate Change on Human Rights and the Role of Environmental Defenders on This Matter (2020/2134(INI)), 21.09.2020.

8 Georgian Presidency of the Committee of Ministers, Final Declaration, Environmental Protection and Human Rights, High-Level Conference organised under the aegis of the Georgian Presidency of the Committee of Ministers, 27.02.2020.

9 CJEU, *Commission of the European Communities v Republic of Austria*, Case C-320/03, 15.11.2005, ECLI:EU:C:2005:684.

10 European Committee on Social Rights, *Marangopoulos Foundation for Human Rights (MFHR) v Greece*, case 30/2005, 06.12.2006.

11 European Committee of Social Rights, *International Federation for Human Rights (FIDH) v Greece*, case 72/2011, 23.01.2013.

point of reference, the different sub-sections would seem to demonstrate the consistency of the right to a healthy environment with the set requirements. The third and last section contextualises the urgent need to recognise this fundamental right as a normative response to COVID-19, whose death rate has been found particularly severe in highly polluted areas. Against this scenario, an individual right to a healthy environment could provide a comprehensive and efficacious protection from environmental harm.

2. ESTABLISHING A RIGHT TO A HEALTHY ENVIRONMENT UNDER EU LAW: A THEORETICAL FRAMEWORK

The following paragraphs present some innovative suggestions for a new theoretical framework with the aim to contribute to the debate upon the formulation of a right to a healthy environment under EU law. The fundamental assumption is that several pieces composing the right to a healthy environment are already embedded in the EU founding treaties as well as in the Union's principles, values and aims. Consequently, it is also reflected in the secondary legislation adopted by EU institutions. For their part, the EU Member States and national courts are increasingly contributing to the emergence of the right to a healthy environment, set out in the majority of their constitutional charters or generated by case-laws. Moreover, both the Union and its Member States have adhered to international environmental treaties explicitly proclaiming a right to a healthy environment, which they are called to respect. In the author's view, these single, multilevel pieces could come together, flowing into Article 6.3 TEU, which recognises that fundamental rights, as guaranteed by the ECHR and as they result from the constitutional traditions common to the Member States, constitute general principles of EU law. Through this provision, the Court of Justice may extrapolate the main values underlining the right to a healthy environment declared under international, EU and national law and transpose a new, common reference to this right at the EU level.

2.1. THE GENERAL PRINCIPLES OF EU LAW

Although essential to the interpretation and validity of the law of the Union and its Member States, there is still no agreed definition concerning the general principles of EU law, mostly depending on the lack of any explicit reference in the treaties, except for Article 340 TFEU, which mentions, yet without defining them, the general principles common to the laws of the Member States in the field of contractual liability. Consequently, the genesis of the general principles has to be entirely attributed to the case law of the CJEU, which has over time *ex novo* created, or deduced, the existence of general principles of the Union which are not contemplated, or not expressly contemplated, by the treaties. Therefore, these principles result from a particular elaboration conducted by the Luxembourg judges, who have vested the EU legal order with principles common to the European legal culture, often present at the constitutional level or shared in the legislation of the Member States.

The Court led this operation, especially in cases where international or EU law was not sufficient to solve the dispute at stake, as well as to comply with its duty to ensure respect for the law in the interpretation and application of the treaties, as set out in Article 19 TEU. This task, therefore, justified, in the eyes of the judges, the creation of an unwritten source of law, superior to secondary legislation and binding to the Union and its Member States, that was functional to the achievement of EU objectives in general, and to the protection of fundamental rights, in particular.[12] Some of these new sources were introduced either in terms of principles, such as the principle of proportionality and of subsidiarity, or in terms of rights, such as the right to property[13] and the right to freedom of conscience and religion.[14] As emphasised by Sabino Cassese, two other implicit reasons underline the purposes of this clause: first, the establishment of pluralism as a common ground for the EU legal order, by recognising that national identities (expression of diversity) and the EU legal order (expression of uniformity) can go hand-in-hand; second, the rejection of the view that each legal system is necessarily and entirely peculiar to a nation-state, and therefore that legal systems cannot converge. In other terms, according to some scholars, the CJEU took this occasion to 'Europeanise' the different national concepts of fundamental rights.[15]

It is clear that the judiciary, by devising a new source of law not belonging to the treaties, has played the role of an active legislator,[16] giving rise to a so-called 'European jurisprudential law'[17] or, according to J. J. H. Weiler, to an 'integration through law scholarship'.[18] This action had also the effect of accelerating the process of cultural and legal integration of the legal systems of the Member States. In this sense, the Court 'has had an important task in integrating the legal

---

12 S. Cassese, 'The "Constitutional Traditions Common to the Member States" of the European Union', (2017) 4(1), *Rivista Trimestrale di Diritto Pubblico*, p. 942.

13 Among many others, CJEU, *Aquacultur*, C-20-64/00, 10.07.2003, ECLI:EU:C:2003:397.

14 Among many others, CJEU, *Achbita*, C-157/15, 14.03.2017, ECLI:EU:C:2017:203.

15 J. Jones, 'Common Constitutional Traditions: Can the Meaning of Human Dignity under German Law Guide the European Court of Justice?', (2004) 167(1), *Public Law*.

16 F. Wasserfallen, 'The Judiciary as Legislator? How the European Court of Justice Shapes Policy-making in the European Union', (2010) 17(8), *Journal of European Public Policy*.

17 G. Strozzi and R. Mastroianni, *Diritto dell'Unione Europea – Parte Istituzionale*, 2016, p. 220.

18 M. Cappelletti, M., Seccombe and J.J.H., Weiler, *Integration Through Law. Europe and the American Federal Experience*, WdeG, 1986.

systems, preferring to interpret Community law using the teleological method rather than the literal one, and thus pushing the national system towards interpenetration with the supranational one […]'.[19]

Thus, the emergence of general principles of law not only revealed the Court's protagonism through the production of a new positive source of law but also its contribution to standardise the different legal cultures of the Member States. In fact, it enhanced the internal coherence of the EU legal order by the means of '[…] a process of osmosis and spontaneous adjustment leading domestic legal systems to align themselves with those general principles of the Union'.[20]

As noted, and as we will see in the next paragraph, the Court has formulated a significant number of general principles, without bothering to assess how common these principles actually were.[21] Presumably, the constitutional traditions common to the Member States would require a constant exercise of comparative analysis to determine whether a fundamental right or principle were shared by all constitutional charters. Actually, the CJEU has been much more flexible,[22] as it included in the general principles of EU law not only those truly common to all the Member States, but even those present in a small minority of legal systems. Some commentators have acknowledged that 'the analysis of the CJEU case law reveals first of all a large group of judgments that appear to be stingy, if not silent, in terms of useful indications for the reconstruction of the methodological paths followed by judges to determine the cases of fundamental rights'.[23] At this point of the analysis, it is therefore relevant to note that the Court has not merely imported principles from the Member States and literally transposed them into EU law. Rather, it has developed them in such a way as to align them with the requirements and aims of the treaties.

2.2. FUNDAMENTAL RIGHTS AS GENERAL PRINCIPLES OF EU LAW

Fundamental rights were virtually absent at the origin of the European project, whose initial aim was to establish a common market and a functional type of economic integration. The issue of the protection of fundamental rights

19 A. Pin, *Precedente e Mutamento Giurisprudenziale, La Tradizione Angloamericana e il Diritto Sovranazionale Europeo*, Milano 2017, p. 193. Translation from Italian.

20 Ibid., p. 222.

21 S. Cassese, 'The "Constitutional Traditions Common to the Member States"', *supra* note 12, p. 942. See also, G. Balas, 'I Principi Generali dell'ordinamento Europeo nella Giurisprudenza della Corte di Giustizia dell'Unione Europea', (2019) 4, *Giuricivile*. Translation from Italian.

22 G. Martinico, 'Exploring the Platonic Heaven of Law: General Principles of EU Law from a Comparative Perspective', (2020) (1), *Nordic Journal of European Law*.

23 L. Cozzolino, 'Le tradizioni costituzionali comuni nella giurisprudenza della Corte di giustizia delle Comunità europee', in P. Falzea, A. Spadaro and L. Ventura (eds.), *La Corte Costituzionale e le Corti d'Europa*, Giappichelli 2003, p. 10. Translation from Italian.

was therefore mostly overcome through the exercises of judicial elaboration conducted by the CJEU.

After an initial rejection to take a position on the protection of fundamental rights by national authorities,[24] in *Stauder* the Court held,[25] for the very first time, that fundamental rights were a part of the general principles of Community law. In 1970, in the landmark *Internationale Handelsgesellschaft* case,[26] the CJEU not only confirmed its views, but added that the protection of fundamental rights '[...] albeit being informed by the constitutional traditions common to the Member States, is to be guaranteed within the structure and purposes of the Community'.[27] It is in this notorious decision that the Court mentions for the very first time the constitutional traditions common to the Member States, an expression that at that time was not used in the treaties and that, therefore, resulted from its judicial elaboration.[28] Despite reaching the conclusion that, in that case, the system of licences did not violate any right of a fundamental nature,[29] the CJEU examined whether any other fundamental right guaranteed in Community law had been disregarded, in light of the fact that: '[...] respect for fundamental rights forms an integral part of the general principles of law protected by the Court of Justice. The protection of such rights, whilst inspired by the constitutional traditions common to the Member States, must be ensured within the framework of the structure and objectives of the Community'.[30]

In this judgment, the clause was considered as a source of inspiration for European law, and not as an autonomous source of fundamental rights. Since *Costa v Enel*,[31] in fact, the CJEU declared the primacy of the EU legal order over the legislation of the Member States. In the context of the protection of fundamental rights, this implies that national, even constitutional, provisions do not have direct efficacy in the supranational order and cannot override EU law. Hence, the final rule applicable by the Court at the EU level could not be simply transposed from the legal order of a Member State – rather, it should derive from a re-elaboration of national provisions. In *Nold*,[32] the range of elements that the Court takes into account in protecting fundamental rights expands beyond the common constitutional tradition and includes the 'international Treaties on the protection of human rights that the Member States have signed or cooperated with'.[33]

---

24 CJEU, *Stork*, Case C-1/58, 04.02.1959, ECLI:EU:C:1959:4.

25 CJEU, *Stauder*, Case C-29/69, 12.11.1969, ECLI:EU:C:1969:57.

26 CJEU, *Internationale Handelsgesellschaft*, Case 11/70, 17.11.1970, ECLI:EU:C:1970:114.

27 Ibid., p. 1126.

28 For an in-depth analysis on the issue, please see G. Martinico (2020), 'Exploring the Platonic Heaven of Law', *supra* note 22.

29 Ibid.

30 Ibid., p. 1134.

31 CJEU, *Flaminio Costa v E.N.E.L.*, Case 6-64, 15.07.1964, ECLI:EU:C:1964:66.

32 CJEU, *Nold*, Case 4/73, 14.05.1974, ECLI:EU:C:1974:51.

33 Ibid., p. 507.

The Maastricht Treaty crystallised in Article 6.3 TEU the importance of, and the respect for, fundamental rights, then restated under the Amsterdam Treaty and, from 2009 onwards, also protected under the EU Charter. It is on this occasion that the reference to the common constitutional traditions acquired an autonomous position as well as the mention to the ECHR, therefore confirming that the protection of fundamental rights in the EU draws on both internal and external sources of law, as also repeatedly reiterated by the Court itself.[34] Emblematically, they are also present both in the Preamble and in Article 52.4 of the EU Charter.

Today, Article 6.3 TEU reads as follows: 'Fundamental rights, as guaranteed by the European Convention for the Protection of Human Rights and Fundamental Freedoms and as they result from the constitutional traditions common to the Member States, shall constitute general principles of the Union's law'. The term tradition implies two peculiar dimensions: that of culture and of time. According to Merryman,

> [a] legal tradition [...] is a set of deeply rooted, historically conditioned attitudes about the nature, about the role of law in the society and the polity, about the proper organization and operation of a legal system, and about the way law is or should be made, applied, studied, perfected and taught. The legal tradition relates the legal system to the culture of which it is a partial expression. It puts the legal system into cultural perspective.[35]

Similarly, Cassese affirmed that the term embraces not only states' constitutional provisions, but also their history and implementation, so as to make reference '[...] to the set of rules, but also to relevant customs, practices, beliefs, doctrines, as well as to their history', highlighting that this wording introduced 'a time dimension into European law: the newcomer (the EU) recognizes the older history of its seniors (the Member States' native institutions)'.[36]

Several experts have chronologically analysed the jurisprudence of the CJEU prior to the enactment of the EU Charter in the field of the constitutional traditions common to the Member States in order to understand how the Court usually determines that a certain principle derives from the common traditions of the Member States. For instance, how many constitutions must share a tradition for that to become common? What kind of comparative study shall the Court conduct in this regard? May the CJEU hold, and if so, under what circumstances, that a certain number of constitutional provisions, which

---

34 See, among others, CJEU, *P, X v Commission of the European Communities*, Case C-404/92, 05.10.1994, ECLI:EU:C:1994:361; CJEU, *Kremzow*, Case C-299/95, 29.05.1997, ECLI:EU:C:1997:254.

35 J.M. Merryman, *The Civil Law Tradition. An Introduction to the Legal Systems of Western Europe and Latin America*, Stanford University Press, Stanford 1969, p. 2.

36 S. Cassese (2017), 'The Constitutional Traditions', *supra* note 12, p. 3.

provide for a similar yet not identical tradition, could still be interpreted as shaping a shared tradition? As anticipated, the Court almost never conducted such an empirical examination, making it practically impossible to answer these questions. Conversely, as noted by Michele Graziadei, the jurisprudence shows that the CJEU upheld to a common tradition even provisions that can be found only in a marginal number of constitutions.[37]

In this sense, the *Hauer* case is particularly relevant because it represents almost the only ruling where the Court engages in a sort of comparative analysis on the issue.[38] Although it acknowledged that the right to property was protected in accordance with the principles common to the constitutions of the Member States and noted its transposition in the Additional Protocol to the ECHR, it also considered the latter insufficiently precise as to solve the issue raised by the German Administrative Court. Therefore, the judges decided to examine the constitutional texts of, at that time, nine Member States. However, the CJEU explicitly analysed only three constitutions (the German, Italian and Irish ones) and *a priori* concluded that the traditions of all the nine Member States allowed to regulate the use of private property in the general interest.

Conversely, in *Hoechst v Commission*,[39] the Court had to decide on the protection of the right to inviolability of the domicile to both natural and legal persons. The comparative analysis carried out by AG Kokott showed that, while both subjects were protected under the German, Danish, Spanish, French, English and Italian legal systems, it was not the case for Greece, Ireland and the Netherlands. In the remaining three countries (Belgium, Portugal and Luxembourg), the matter was deemed insufficiently clear. On these grounds, the CJEU concluded that the widest recognition of right to domicile was precluded, since 'the legal systems of the Member States show not inconsiderable differences as regards the nature and extent of the protection of business premises against intervention by the public authorities'.[40]

In *Mangold*,[41] the Court declared the prohibition of discrimination on grounds of age as pertaining to the common heritage of constitutional traditions of the Member States although, at the time, this principle was mentioned in the constitutions of two Member States only, namely, Finland and Portugal.[42] In this

---

37 M. Graziadei and R. De Caria, 'The "Constitutional Traditions Common to the Member States" in the Case-Law of the European Court of Justice: Judicial Dialogue at its Finest', (2017) 4, *Rivista Trimestrale di Diritto Pubblico*.

38 CJEU, *Liselotte Hauer v Land Rheinland-Pfalz*, Case 44/79, 13.12.1979, ECLI:EU:C:1979:290.

39 CJEU, *Hoechst AG v Commission of the European Communities*, Joined cases 46/87 and 227/88, 21.09.1989, ECLI:EU:C:1989:337.

40 Ibid., p. 2870.

41 CJEU, *Werner Mangold v Rüdiger Helm*, Case C-144/04, 22.11.2005, ECRI-9981.

42 The wide discretionality used by the Court in Mangold gave rise to wide criticism. Please see, A. Arnull, 'What is a General Principle of EU Law?' in S. Vogenauer (ed.), *Prohibition of Abuse of Law A New General Principle of EU Law?*, Hart, 2017; and M. Graziadei and R. De Caria (2017), 'The Constitutional Traditions Common to the Member States' *supra* note 37, p. 968.

respect, AG Mazàk supported the decision of the Court and justified the use of such a high level of flexibility on the grounds that:

> [b]y formulating general principles of Community law […] the Court has actually added flesh to the bones of Community law, which otherwise – being a legal order based on a framework treaty – would have remained a mere skeleton of rules, not quite constituting a proper legal 'order'. This source of law enabled the Court – often drawing inspiration from legal traditions common to the Member States, and international treaties – to guarantee and add content to legal principles in such important areas as the protection of fundamental rights and administrative law.[43]

The flexible attitude endorsed by the Court, along with its implicit evaluations, allegedly affecting the transparency of its legal reasoning,[44] does not seem to be replicated by the AGs, who, conversely, engaged in deep comparative exercises. For instance, AG Szpunar examined 25 constitutions to conclude that the principle of the retroactive application of a more lenient penal law was common to the constitutional traditions of the Member States, with the exception of the British and Irish ones.[45]

A final, significant point of this excursus on the general principles of EU law concerns the fact that the clause on common constitutional traditions, according to Cassese, cannot produce new sources of EU law, even if the Treaties and the EU Charter codified it in a standalone provision. In *X v Commission of the European Communities*,[46] the right to private life was included among the common traditions to the Member States because it was also embodied in Article 8 ECHR as well as, later in *Varec SA v Belgian State*,[47] in Article 7 EU Charter. This suggests therefore that the Court uses them in conjunction with other internal or external sources of law, probably with the aim 'to lend more authority to the latter'.[48] However, in *Council v Hautala*, AG Léger seemed to provide a different interpretation of the sources capable of generating general principles pertaining to two main issues. On the one hand, he stated that 'the convergence of the constitutional traditions of the Member States may suffice in order to establish the existence of one of those principles without the need to obtain confirmation

43 CJEU, *Félix Palacios de la Villa*, Case C-411/05, Opinion of Advocate General Mazàk, 16.10.2007, ECLI: EU:C:2007:106, paras. 83–86.

44 G. Martinico (2020), 'Exploring the Platonic Heaven of Law', *supra* note 22, p. 7.

45 CJEU, *Berlusconi et al.*, Case C-387-391-403/02, Opinion of Advocate General Kokott, 14.10.2004, ECLI:EU:C:2004:624.

46 CJEU, *X v Commission of the European Communities*, Case C-404/92 P, 05.10.1994, ECLI:EU:C:1994:361.

47 CJEU, *Varec SA v Belgian State*, Case C-450/06, 14.02.2008, ECLI:EU:C:2008:91.

48 S. Cassese (2017), 'The Constitutional Traditions', *supra* note 12, p. 6.

of its existence or content by referring to international rules'.[49] On the other hand, he found that, for the fundamental rights to be recognised at the EU level, the constitutional texts were not required to perfectly match, given the fact that, according to his view, it was sufficient to share a common conception.[50]

It is crucial to stress that a significant number of fundamental rights has been so far recognised as stemming from the traditions common to the Member States and from external law sources. The following non-exhaustive list of rights or principles has been acknowledged in approximately one hundred decisions of the CJEU that refer to common constitutional traditions:[51] the right to be heard;[52] the right to private life; the right to property; freedom of expression;[53] the right to workers' freedom of movement; the right to freedom of conscience and religion; the prohibition of discrimination;[54] the right to an effective remedy or to effective judicial protection;[55] the right to a fair trial;[56] the principle of retroactivity of more lenient criminal law;[57] and the principle of the legality of criminal offenses and of punishments.[58] Significantly, there is nothing in the treaties or in the jurisprudence of the CJEU contrary to a further expansion of this list in the future.[59]

In her opinion in *Audiolux*,[60] AG Trstenjak acknowledged that the Court, in approaching the matter with such wide flexibility, endorses a great margin of manoeuvre when it comes to deducing the existence of a general principle of EU law that, as recalled, led to 'scepticism about how conscientiously the Court of Justice has actually examined national and international law and expose it

---

49 CJEU, *Council of the European Union v Heidi Hautala*, Case C-353/99 P, Opinion of Mr Advocate General Léger delivered, 10.07.2001, para. 68.

50 Ibid., para. 68: '*Those national rules, although the content of their corresponding legal systems are not necessarily the same, demonstrate a common conception in most of the Member States […]*'.

51 M. Graziadei and R. De Caria (2017), 'The "Constitutional Traditions Common to the Member States"', *supra* note 37, p. 968.

52 CJEU, *Sopropé – Organizações de Calçado Lda v Fazenda Públic*, Case C-349/07, 18.12.2008, ECLI:EU:C:2008:746.

53 CJEU, *Herbert Karner Industrie-Auktionen*, Case C-71/02, 25.03.2004, ECLI:EU:C:2004:181.

54 CJEU, *Dansk Industri*, Case C-441/14, 19.04.2016, ECLI:EU:C:2016:278 on grounds of age; and CJEU, *Römer*, Case C-147/08, 10.05.2011, ECLI:EU:C:2011:286.

55 Among others, CJEU, *Agrokonsulting*, Case C-93/12, 27.06.2013, ECLI:EU:C:2013:432; and CJEU, *Unibet*, Case C-432/05, 13.03.2007, ECLI:EU:C:2007:163.

56 Among others, CJEU, *Trade Agency*, Case C-619/10, 06.09.2012, ECLI:EU:C:2012:531; CJEU, *Salzgitter Mannesmann*, Case C-411/04 P, 25.01.2007, ECLI:EU:C:2007:54.

57 Among others, CJEU, *Toshiba*, Case C-17/10, 14.02.2012, ECLI:EU:C:2012:72; and CJEU, *Campina*, Case C-45/06, 08.03.2007, ECLI:EU:C:2007:154.

58 Among others, CJEU, *Intertanko*, Case C-308/06, 03.06.2008, ECLI:EU:C:2008:312.

59 Ibid.

60 CJEU, *Audiolux SA e.a v Groupe Bruxelles Lambert SA (GBL) and Others and Bertelsmann AG and Others*, Case C-101/08, Opinion AG Trstenjak, 30.06.2009, ECLI:EU:C:2009:410.

to criticism that it is, in reality, pursuing an agenda of its own'.[61] To counteract these sources of criticism, and to fill the methodological gap left unresolved by the CJEU, AG Trstenjak outlined a precise methodology to be followed by the Luxembourg judges to evaluate the existence of a general principle. First, she distinguished between general principles in the narrow sense, such as the fundamental rights enlisted above, and those common to the legal and constitutional orders of the Member States:

> Whereas the first category of general principles can be derived directly from primary Community law, the Court essentially uses a critical legal comparison in order to determine the second category, which does not, however, amount to using the lowest common denominator method. Nor is it regarded as necessary for the legal principles developed in this way in their specific expression at Community level always to be present at the same time in all the legal orders under comparison.[62]

The proposed methodology therefore takes account of an analysis of the relevant sources of law (international guidelines, EU primary law and secondary legislation); the constitutional status of the norm at stake; and its general validity.

The *Audiolux* case concerned the feasibility to declare the existence of a general principle of equal treatment of stakeholders. In applying the aforementioned methodology to the case, the AG found that, on the one hand, neither international guidelines on company law nor international company law provided sufficient and clear elements to solve the issue. On the other hand, despite the considerable number of references to an equal treatment of stakeholders in secondary legislation acts, these were predominantly restricted to a specific branch of law, namely company law, thus lacking 'the general, comprehensive character which is otherwise naturally inherent in general principles'.[63] Apart from a lack of shared conviction in legal literature on the existence of such general principle and of a clear definition of the notion, the two main reasons that led AG Trstenjak to deny a general principle of equal treatment of stakeholders concerned therefore the lack of constitutional status and of general validity.

By contrast, by sustaining that the right to a healthy environment under EU law would have, among other features, both a constitutional status and general validity, this contribution attempts to support the recognition of the right to a healthy environment as stemming from Article 6.3 TEU.

Therefore, this work takes AG Trstenjak's methodology as point of reference, given that it structures in a comprehensive way the different elements progressively considered by the Court's jurisprudence and integrates the opinions of other

---

61 A. Arnull (2017), 'What is a General Principle of EU Law?', *supra* note 42, p. 10.

62 CJEU, *Audiolux*, Opinion AG Trstenjak, *supra* note 60, para. 69.

63 Ibid., para. 84.

AGs and legal scholars on the matter. For instance, AG Trstenjak excludes the use of a pure arithmetical approach in order to assess the existence of a tradition common to the Member States, as also highlighted by the legal literature as well as by AG Maduro[64] and Lagrange,[65] among others.[66]

It is therefore argued that the right to a healthy environment may be derived on three main grounds that are separately addressed in the following sections. First, it is expressly mentioned in external sources of law that reinforce its legitimation, such as Article 11 ESC as interpreted by the Committee on European Social Rights, and Article 1 of the 1998 Aarhus Convention, which both the Union and, singularly, all its Member States have adhered to. Moreover, there is wide institutional support to the establishment of this right at all levels of policy-making. Second, it is expressly endorsed in the constitutions of the majority of the EU Member States, while the constitutional Courts of several countries, whose Charter does not specifically contain this right, have nevertheless discerned its existence from other constitutional rights. Third, it is in line with the aims of the Treaties and of EU environmental policy, and it complies with the principle of sustainable development and of improvement of the quality of the environment as well as the protection of health, established both under the Treaties and under Article 37 EU Charter. It is reasonable therefore to consider the right to a healthy environment as an essential component to achieve transversal Union's objectives and principles, which in turn likely confirms its general validity.

2.3. THE RIGHT TO A HEALTHY ENVIRONMENT SUPPORTED BY EXTERNAL SOURCES OF LAW

The first remarkable steps taken by the EU in the field of the environment trace back to the post-Rio period, when it took the lead in the environmental policy-making process, becoming party or signatory to many international environmental agreements negotiated under the auspices of the United Nations.

Among these, the EU ratified the 1998 Aarhus Convention on Access to Information, Public Participation in Decision-making and Access to Justice in Environmental Matters (hereinafter, Aarhus Convention) in 2005 along with all its Member States. As mentioned before, the objective of the Convention

---

64 CJEU, *Fabbrica italiana accumulatori motocarri Montecchio SpA (FIAMM), Fabbrica italiana accumulatori motocarri Montecchio Technologies Inc. (FIAMM Technologies) v Council of the European Union, Commission of the European Communities and Giorgio Fedon & Figli SpA, Fedon America, Inc. v Council of the European Union*, Commission of the European Communities, Joined Cases C-120/06 P and C-121/06 P, Opinion AG Maduro, ECLI:EU:C:2008:98, para. 55.

65 CJEU, *Hoogovens v High Authority*, Case C-14/61, Opinion AG Lagrange, 04.06.1962, ECLI:EU:C:1962:19, para. 283–284.

66 For further analysis on the matter, please see G. Martinico (2020), 'Exploring the Platonic Heaven of Law', *supra* note 22.

is '[...] to contribute to the protection of the right of every person of present and future generations to live in an environment adequate to his or her health and well-being'. Hence, Article 1 correlates the right to health and wellbeing of present and future generations to an adequate environment. The Aarhus Convention also provides for a wide range of procedural rights in the field of environmental protection that enable citizens and environmental non-governmental organisations to request internal review of EU environmental acts.[67] Therefore, the Aarhus Convention represents the first international environmental agreement that recognises the indissoluble relationship between the protection of the environment and the protection of human rights, as stated in Article 1. Thus, according to AG Jääskinen, the Aarhus Convention is not a mere administrative environmental agreement, but rather, the expression of 'a human right to the environment in its most solemn form'.[68] The Union has transposed the procedural environmental rights enshrined in the Aarhus Convention into a vast number of secondary acts, such as Directive 2003/4/EC which provides for a wider application of the right to access information;[69] Regulation no. 1367/2006/EC ('Aarhus Regulation'),[70] which specifically refers to access to information held by EU institutions and bodies; Directive 2000/60/EC concerning public participation in water policy;[71] and Directive 2001/42/EC on participation in environmental plans and programmes, among others.[72]

Other international environmental Treaties that bind both the EU and its Member States are, to mention but a few, the UN Framework Convention on Climate Change (UNFCCC), which provides the fundamental international

---

67 For an in-depth analysis of the procedural rights in the field of environmental law enshrined in the Aarhus Convention, please see L. LANCEIRO, 'The Review of Compliance with the Aarhus Convention of the European Union', in E. CHITI and B.G. MATTARELLA, *Global Administrative Law and EU Administrative Law Relationships, Legal Issues and Comparison*, Springer 2011, pp. 359–383. For an analysis of the possible influence of the Aarhus Convention on the EU environmental policy, and in particular on the European Green Deal, see C. SCISSA, 'What room for the 1998 Aarhus Convention in the European Green Deal? An Analysis of the possible reluctance of the Court of Justice', (2021) 1, *Rivista Quadrimestrale di Diritto dell'Ambiente*, available at https://www.rqda.eu, last accessed 07.10.2021.

68 CJEU, *Council of the European Union and Others v Vereniging Milieudefensie and Stichting Stop Luchtverontreiniging Utrecht*, Case C-401/12 P, Opinion of Mr Advocate General Jääskinen, 08.05.2014, para. 89.

69 Directive 2003/4/EC of the European Parliament and of the Council of 28 January 2003 on public access to environmental information and repealing Council Directive 90/313/EEC, OJ L041.

70 Regulation (EC) No 1367/2006 of the European Parliament and of the Council of 6 September 2006 on the application of the provisions of the Aarhus Convention on Access to Information, Public Participation in Decision-making and Access to Justice in Environmental Matters to Community institutions and bodies, OJ L264.

71 Directive 2000/60/EC of the European Parliament and of the Council of 23 October 2000 establishing a framework for Community action in the field of water policy, OJ L327.

72 Directive 2001/42/EC of the European Parliament and of the Council of 27 June 2001 on the assessment of the effects of certain plans and programmes on the environment, OJ L197.

framework to address climate change issues; the 1997 Kyoto Protocol, with the aim to reduce greenhouse gas emissions through mitigation and reduction mechanisms; and the Paris Agreement, adopted in December 2015, which substitutes the Kyoto Protocol. Akin to the Aarhus Convention, the Preamble of the Paris Agreement acknowledges the relationship between the environment and human rights, especially the right to health and to development, both strictly related to the right to a healthy environment.[73] Despite its relevance, such reference was only included in its non-binding part, thus leading to some disappointment.[74] To date, 191 out of 197 parties to the UNFCCC are parties to the Paris Agreement, among which were the Union and all its EU Member States. Arguably, the right of people to live in a healthy environment could very well be considered as part of those human rights that states have to comply with, when tackling climate change.[75]

Most recently, the United Nations Human Rights Council passed a resolution requesting, *inter alia*, the Special Rapporteur to work on identifying challenges and obstacles to the full realisation of states' human rights obligations relating to the enjoyment of a safe, clean, healthy and sustainable environment and protection gaps thereto.[76] It also calls on states to conserve, protect and restore ecosystems, as well as to consider adopting and implementing national measures that respect and protect the rights of those who are particularly vulnerable to the loss of healthy ecosystems and biodiversity. Remarkably, during the council session, 15 UN entities delivered a joint statement expressing their support for the global recognition of the right to a healthy environment, seen as essential to guarantee present and future generation's human rights, to leave no one behind, and to ensure a just and equitable transition to a healthy world for all.[77]

The widespread importance of the right to a healthy environment is additionally confirmed at the regional level, where the majority of human rights conventions provide for a direct protection of human environmental rights, including a healthy environment, which is in fact explicitly proclaimed in regional treaties ratified by 126 states. In particular, 52 States are bound by Article 24

---

73 Adoption of the Paris Agreement, Decision 1/CP.21, in COP Report No. 21, Addendum, at 2, U.N. Doc. FCCC/CP/2015/10/Add.1, 12.12.2015, preambular para. 11.

74 R. Bratspies, 'Claimed not Granted: Finding a Human Right to a Healthy Environment', (2017) 26(2), *Transnational Law and Contemporary Problems*, p. 273.

75 In this regard, please see, among others, A. Savaresi, 'Human rights and the impacts of climate change: Revisiting the assumptions', (2021) 11(1), *Oñati Socio-Legal Series*, pp. 231–253; A. Savaresi and J. Setzer, 'Mapping the Whole of the Moon: An Analysis of the Role of Human Rights in Climate Litigation', in *Social Science Research Network* (SSRN) 2021.

76 Resolution 46/7 *Human rights and the environment*, adopted by the Human Rights Council on 23.03.2021, during the 46th session 22.02–24.03.2021, A/HRC/RES/46/7, para. 6.

77 Joint statement of United Nations entities on the right to healthy environment, Human Rights Council, 46th Session, General Debate, Item 3, available at https://www.unep.org/news-and-stories/statements/joint-statement-united-nations-entities-right-healthy-environment, last accessed 13.10.2021.

of the African Charter on Human and People's Rights (hereinafter, African Charter), which acknowledges the right of all people to a general satisfactory environment favourable to their development, and it was interpreted as the first binding international obligation relating to the right to the environment.[78] Additionally, Articles 18 and 19 of the 2003 Protocol to the African Charter on the Rights of Women in Africa guarantees to women the right to live in a healthy and sustainable environment. Both Article 38 of the 2004 Arab Charter on Human Rights and Article 11 of the additional protocol to the American Convention on Human Rights in the Area of Economic, Social and Cultural Rights (Protocol of San Salvador) declare the right to a healthy environment, respectively binding 16 state parties.[79] In the Asian continent, Article 28(f) of the Human Rights Declaration set out by the Association of South-East Asian Nations recognises the right to a safe, clean and sustainable environment as part of the right to an adequate standard of living, and has been adopted by ten states. Although not legally binding, the declaration succeeds in representing a shared vision towards higher levels of human environmental rights protection.

At the European level, the ECHR, as well as the ESC, both ratified by all the Member States, fail in recognising a right to a healthy environment and, according to Elisabeth Lamperts, this is 'what makes the European human rights instruments less satisfactory that all the other regional instruments'.[80] The Georgian Presidency of the Council of Europe has seen the healthy environment as a precondition for the very enjoyment of individuals' rights and liberties,[81] therefore encouraging, among other initiatives, both the ECtHR and the European Committee of Social Rights to further substantiate their case law and give priority consideration to complaints involving issues of environmental protection. In particular, experts have been advocating for the adoption of an additional protocol to the ECHR covering the so-called third-generation human rights – including those related to solidarity, the environment and peace, among others.[82] Most recently, the Parliamentary Assembly to the Council of Europe adopted, in September 2021, a draft resolution calling for an Additional Protocol to the ECHR in order to 'anchor' the right to a healthy environment to the Convention. The reason for this lies in the urgent need to secure a healthy, sustainable environment for present and future generations as well as to uphold

78 R. Zetter, 'Unlocking the Protracted Displacement of Refugees and Internally Displaced Persons: An Overview', (2011) 30(4), *Refugee Survey Quarterly*, p. 11.

79 For an excellent analysis of the right to a healthy environment in in the jurisprudence of the Inter-American Court of Human Rights, please see T. Zhunussova, 'Human Rights and the Environment before the IACtHR', in E. Chiti, A. di Martino and G. Palombella (eds.), *L'età della Interlegalità*, Il Mulino, 2021.

80 E. Lambert, 'The Environment and Human Rights, Introductory Report to the High-Level Conference Environmental Protection and Human Rights', 27.02.2020, p. 10, available at https://rm.coe.int/report-e-lambert-en/16809c827f, last accessed 13.07.2021.

81 Ibid.

82 Ibid., p. 11.

states and non-state actors' responsibilities towards the preservation of the environment and towards the protection of all people against environmental harm eventually caused by them. More specifically:

> The Assembly considers that an explicit recognition of a right to a healthy and viable environment would be an incentive for stronger domestic environmental laws and a more protection-focused approach by the Court. It would make it easier for victims to lodge applications for remedies and would also act as a preventive mechanism to supplement the currently rather reactive case law of the Court.
>
> Recognising an autonomous right to a healthy environment would have the benefit of allowing a violation to be found irrespective of whether another right had been breached and would therefore raise the profile of this right. [...][83]

However, the Court has so far refused to embark in this project.[84]

Nonetheless, as far as the ESC is concerned, in the only two complaints lodged on the right to a healthy environment, the European Committee of Social Rights introduced two novel elements: (i) It promoted a dynamic interpretation of the ESC, holding that for it to be a living instrument, its rights and freedoms should be interpreted in the light of the present-day conditions;[85] and (ii) it established a normative partnership between the ESC and the ECHR on the ground of human dignity, given that 'human dignity is the fundamental value and indeed the core of positive European human rights law – whether under the ESC or under the European Convention of Human Rights and [that] health care is a prerequisite for the preservation of human dignity'.[86] In its decision on *Marangopoulos Foundation for Human Rights v Greece*, it took account of 'the growing link that states party to the Charter and other international bodies [...] now make between the protection of health and a healthy environment [...]'.[87] The Committee found a complementarity between Article 11 ESC on right to the protection of health and Articles 2 and 3 ECHR,[88] by explicitly stating that the provisions contained in Article 11 ESC should be interpreted as to remove the causes of ill health also resulting from environmental threats. The Committee continued its legal reasoning by identifying environmental

83 Parliamentary Assembly to the Council of Europe, 'Anchoring the right to a healthy environment: need for enhanced action by the Council of Europe', draft resolution adopted on 1 September 2021, paras. 8–9, available at https://assembly.coe.int/LifeRay/SOC/Pdf/TextesProvisoires/2021/20210909-HealthyEnvironment-EN.pdf, last accessed 07.10.2021.

84 E. Lambert, 'The Environment and Human Rights', *supra* note 80, pp. 11–15 for a precise recollection of the grounds set out by the ECtHR in this regard.

85 European Committee of Social Rights, *Marangopoulos*, *supra* note 10, para. 194.

86 European Committee of Social Rights, 'Interpretative Statement on Article 11 of the Charter', para. 5, available at http://hudoc.esc.coe.int/eng/?i=2005_Ob_1-1/Ob/EN, last accessed 13.07.2021.

87 Ibid.

88 Article 11 ESC reads: '*Everyone has the right to benefit from any measures enabling him to enjoy the highest possible standard of health attainable*'.

protection as one of the key components of the right to health and concluded that states are responsible for harmful activities to the environment, whether carried out by public authorities or by private companies. Therefore, it ruled that Article 11 ESC had to be interpreted as to include the right to a healthy environment. In *International Federation for Human Rights (FIDH) v Greece*, the Committee went even further, by complementing the right to a healthy environment not only with Articles 2 and 3 ECHR, as previously ruled, but also with Article 8 ECHR on the right to private and family life, as far as severe environmental pollution may adversely affect individuals' well-being.[89]

By endorsing an extensive interpretation of the Convention's provisions, the ECtHR has repeatedly acknowledged the violation of the human rights enshrined therein owing to environmental factors. In so doing, the Court has recurrently found violations of the right to private and family life and,[90] in the most extreme cases, of the right to life owing to environmental threats.[91]

In particular, in *Lopez Ostra* and *Fadeyeva*,[92] the ECtHR held the respective states responsible for the violation of Article 8 ECHR due to industrial pollution,[93] the toxic emissions of which had impinged the applicants' right to private and family life, as well as to health and to property. In their joint dissenting opinion in *Hatton and others v the United Kingdom* Judgment, where conversely the Court denied the state's violation of Article 8 for presumed excessive acoustic pollution, the Judges Costa, Ress, Türmen, Zupančič and Steiner affirmed that 'the close connection between human rights protection and the urgent need for a decontamination of the environment leads us to perceive health as the most basic human need and as preeminent',[94] thus considering the healthy environment as a prerequisite for the enjoyment of other rights.

Interestingly, the recognition of a right to a healthy environment is particularly evident at the national level. According to the UN Special Rapporteur on the issue of human rights obligations relating to enjoyment of a safe, clean, healthy and sustainable environment,[95] there are 101 states where this right has been incorporated into national legislation, whereas more than 80% of UN States Members (156 out of 193) have legally recognised the right to a healthy

---

89 European Committee of Social Rights, *International Federation for Human Rights (FIDH) v Greece*, *supra* note 11.

90 Among others, ECtHR, *López Ostra v Spain*, no 303-C, 09.12.1994 and ECtHR, *Guerra and Others v Italy*, no 116/1996/735/932, 19.02.1998.

91 ECtHR, *Öneryıldız v Turkey*, no 48939/99, 30.11.2004.

92 ECtHR, *López Ostra v Spain*, no. 16798/90, 09.12.1994.

93 ECtHR, *Fadeyeva v Russia*, case no 55723/00, 09.06.2005.

94 Joint dissenting Opinion of Judges Costa, Ress, Türmen, Zupančič and Steiner in *Hatton and others v the United Kingdom* judgment, para. 1.

95 UN Human Rights Council, 'Right to a healthy environment: good practices. Report of the Special Rapporteur on the issue of human rights obligations relating to the enjoyment of a safe, clean, healthy and sustainable environment', UN Doc A/HRC/43/53, 30.12.2019.

environment. What's more, 100 national constitutions explicitly incorporate the right to a healthy environment, also with different terminology.[96] There are at least 12 additional countries where courts have ruled that the right to a healthy environment is an essential element of the right to life and therefore is an enforceable, constitutionally protected right. In total, at least 155 states are required, through Treaties, constitutions and legislation, to respect, protect and fulfil the right to a healthy environment.

One way to interpret these findings is that they encourage a global recognition of the right to a healthy and sustainable environment and could, as we will see, support the CJEU to move forward its establishment at the EU level.

In conclusion, it seems clear that the states parties to the EU and beyond have progressively increased their binding commitment to promote a healthy environment for the benefit of present and future generations, sharing common efforts towards the preservation of the planet in accordance with the principle of sustainable development. To this end, the number of treaties in the field of environmental protection has been also significantly rising, akin to the quantity of EU and national implementing measures and good practices to boost the quality of the environment.[97]

2.4. THE RIGHT TO A HEALTHY ENVIRONMENT AS A CONSTITUTIONAL TRADITION COMMON TO THE MEMBER STATES

Another essential requirement for the genesis of general principles according to AG Trstenjak's methodology is the constitutional status embodied by the provision at stake.

The previous analysis revealed that for the CJEU to extrapolate fundamental rights from the traditions common to the Member States was sufficient as a common underlining vision. Therefore, the Court put more emphasis on the alignment between that right and the spirit and the scopes of the EU treaties, rather than on the actual number of charters containing it.

Indeed, in order to overcome the normative gaps of the treaties in the field of the protection of fundamental rights, the Court has often extrapolated values and ideas shared by only a small minority of states and reproduced them so as to be accepted also by those members that originally did not enclose them in their

---

96 UN Human Rights Council, 'Issue of human rights obligations relating to the enjoyment of a safe, clean, healthy and sustainable environment', Report of the Special Rapporteur, UN Doc A/HRC/40/55, 08.01.2019, para. 13.

97 UN General Assembly, Special Rapporteur's Supplementary Report: Additional Good Practices in the Implementation of the Right to a Safe, Clean, Healthy and Sustainable Environment, UN Doc A/HRC/43/53/Annex III, 13.12.2019.

constitutions. As we have seen, the list of fundamental rights created by the case law increased over time and will continue to expand in the future according to the present-day conditions.

Today, 16 out of 27 Member States have expressly included the right to a healthy environment into their national constitutions: Portugal (1976); Spain (1978); the Netherlands (1983); Hungary (1989); Croatia (1990); Bulgaria and Slovenia (1991); Czech Republic along with Slovakia (1992); Belgium (1994); Finland (1995); Poland (1997); Latvia (1998); Greece (2002); Romania (2003); and France (2005).[98] More precisely, they all recognise the right to a healthy environment both in their constitutions and national legislation, and have also ratified international treaties covering the subject. This means that more than half of the Member States share a common view on the need to protect this right. What's more, 23 Member States have environmental provisions in their national constitutions. Beyond those already mentioned, these are: Italy (1948); Malta (1964); Austria (1984); Sweden (1987); Estonia and Lithuania (1992); Belgium and Germany (1994); Poland (1997); Romania (2003); and Luxembourg (2007).[99] The Supreme Courts of six other Member States (in Italy, the Netherlands, Poland,[100] Ireland, Estonia and Lithuania)[101] have ruled the implicit presence of this right into their constitutions and have discerned it from other constitutional provisions protecting fundamental rights, especially the right to health and to the protection of the environment. For instance, despite the absence of a specific provision setting out a right to a healthy environment, the Constitutional Court has repeatedly asserted that Article 32 of the Italian Constitution on the right to health provides for an adequate legal basis in order to recognise this right.[102] Interestingly, the Irish High Court based the existence of the right to a healthy environment on a different set of rights.[103] In affirming that the Constitution of the Republic of Ireland provided for the right to 'an environment that is consistent with the human dignity and well-being of citizens at large', it implied it from Articles 40.3.1 and 40.3.2 of the Irish Constitution, which respectively

98 A.G. González, 'The Right to a Clean and Healthy Environment: GMOs in Mexico and the European Union', (2019) 10(2), *Mexican Law Review*, p. 100.

99 Ibid.

100 There is no explicit right to a healthy environment in Poland's Constitution. However, in January 2019, in case VI C 1043/18, a Polish trial court found that such a right can be derived from Article 23 of the Polish Civil Code. This decision is currently under appeal.

101 UNGA Annex VIII, 'Recognition of the Right to a Healthy Environment in Constitutions, Legislation and Treaties: Western Europe and Others Region', 14.02.2020, UN Doc A/HRC/43/53/Annex VIII.

102 See, among others, Corte di Cassazione Sezioni Unite, Decision No. 5172/1989; Corte Costituzionale, Decision No. 210/1987; Corte Costituzionale, Decision No. 641/1987. For a recent reference in this regard, please see R. Luporini, 'The "Last Judgment": Early reflections on upcoming climate litigation in Italy', (2021) 8(1), *Questions of International Law*.

103 Irish High Court, *Merriman v Fingal County Council; Friends of the Irish Environment Clg v Fingal County Council* (2017) IEHC 695.

guarantee the personal rights of the citizen and the state vindication for the life, person, good name and property rights of every citizen. The Dutch courts have been particularly active in proclaiming a right to a healthy environment, even if not expressly provided. Some case laws have indicated that it is implicit in Article 21 of the Dutch Constitution, which states: 'It shall be the concern of the authorities to keep the country habitable and to protect and improve the environment'.[104] Most recently, in the landmark *Urgenda* case, the Supreme Court of the Netherlands found that Articles 2 and 8 ECHR gave rise to environmental rights to which all governments are bound.[105] Finally, it is significant to mention the case of Lithuania, whose Supreme Court ruled that 'a person's right to a healthy environment is a prerequisite for a dignified life and for the exercise of many other constitutional rights, and therefore, if actions (inaction) that violate this right are detected, the court must defend it'. The judges also found that 'The right to a safe and clean environment is a constitutional right guaranteed to all individuals [...]. Ensuring the right to a healthy and clean environment as one of the objectives of state activities is also a public interest'.[106]

In light of the foregoing, there might be evidence that the right to a healthy environment constitutes a common tradition among the vast majority of the Member States. A terminological analysis of the qualifications given by the 22 Member States where this right serves as a unifying principle that permeates legislation, regulations and policies, reveals that the adjective mostly used to describe the personal right to enjoy the environment is 'healthy' (in 15 cases out of 22).[107] Two constitutions, that of the Czech Republic and Slovakia, opt for the term 'favourable', while Latvia propended for a 'benevolent environment'. Two other Member States respectively acknowledged an individual right to a 'healthy and balanced' environment (France) and for a 'healthy and ecologically balanced living environment' (Portugal). The Spanish Constitution is the only one to provide for an 'adequate' environment, while Greece guarantees the protection of 'the natural and cultural environment' in the context of the principle of sustainable development.[108] From the comparative use of these

---

104 See, for example, Council of State, Administratieve beslissingen (Administrative decisions) 1991-591, 18.07.1991; Council of State, Administratieve beslissingen (Administrative decisions) 1991-592, 22.04.1991; Council of State, *Milieu en Recht* (Environment and Law) 1992, 29.05.1992, p. 477; Supreme Court, *Milieu en Recht* (Environment and Law) 1989, 14.04.1989, p. 258.

105 Dutch Supreme Court, *Urgenda Foundation v State of the Netherlands*, 22.12.2019, HAZA C/09/00456689.

106 Supreme Court of Lithuania, Case No. 3K-3-112/2013, 16.01.2013.

107 These are: Bulgaria, Croatia, Estonia, Hungary, Lithuania, Romania, Slovenia, Belgium, Finland, France, Ireland, Italy, the Netherlands, Norway, and Portugal. Poland's trial court also established a right to a 'healthy' environment in its case-law, however, this ruling is under appeal.

108 UNGA Annex VIII, 14.02.2020, *supra* note 101, pp. 1–50.

formulations, it could be inferred that there seems to be a common *fil rouge* that links the vast majority of the Member States in recognising and protecting the right to a healthy environment. The flourishing range of qualifications to describe the type of environment they ensure to their population is indicative of a '*comune sentire*', a common need towards the preservation of the environment. As seen, the Court may use these national provisions as a source of inspiration in order to extrapolate the ideas and values underlying them, to then identify the most adequate formulation to be transposed at the Union level. This solution should be the best suited to achieve the objectives of the treaties and must not collide with the legal order of the Member States. Given that all 27 Member States and the Union itself are bound to the 1998 Aarhus Convention, whose Article 1 proclaims the right to a healthy environment, it might be concluded that the transposition of this right at the Union level could hardly be contrary to any Member State's legal order.

2.5. THE RIGHT TO A HEALTHY ENVIRONMENT IN LINE WITH THE SCOPE OF THE TREATIES

According to AG Trstenjak, for a disposition to amount to general principle, it has to meet the specific objectives of the EU Treaties and the basic principles of EU law. As previously mentioned, the environmental component has been at the core of the objectives of the Union since the 1970s. At that time, and until the enactment of the Single European Act, the treaties did not provide the Union with a competence in the field of the environment. Still, to include environmental measures, the legislators relied upon a combination of provisions of the treaty establishing the European Economic Community, namely Articles 2 (standard of living and quality of life), 100 (approximation of laws, regulations or administrative provisions of the Member States) and 235 (the so-called flexibility clause). Consequently, the harmonisation of the legal orders of the Member States was already used not only to boost environmental acts, but also to overcome the normative gap of the treaties.

Today, environmental policy represents a shared competence by virtue of the principle of subsidiarity, according to Article 4.2 TFEU. The possibility given by the treaties to the EU and the Member States to implement environmental objectives is also affirmed in Article 191.4 TFEU, according to which both, within their respective spheres of competence, shall cooperate with third countries and competent international organisations to promote environmental protection. The EU environment policy is enshrined in Articles 11 and 191–193 TFEU. In particular, Article 191 TFEU contains a list of objectives to be pursued, which include: preserving, protecting and improving the quality of the environment; protecting human health; prudent and rational utilisation of natural resources; promoting measures at the international level to deal with regional or world-wide environmental problems – in particular, combating climate change. Arguably, providing Union law with the right to a healthy environment would considerably promote the achievement of each of these scopes, both in line with national legal orders and in compliance with environmental obligations undertaken at the international level.

The right to a healthy environment also seems perfectly in line with the values enshrined in Article 2 TEU, where the Union lies upon the respect for human rights. Article 3 TEU includes among the aims of the Union the 'sustainable development for Europe, based [...] on a high level of protection and improvement of the quality of the environment'. In promoting intergenerational solidarity (Article 3 TEU), the sustainable development of the Earth and the sustainable management of global natural resources (Article 21.2(f) TEU), as well as the protection of human rights and the strict observance and development of international law (Article 3.5 TEU), the EU Treaties appear to suggest to spontaneously embed the right to a healthy environment. Finally, the EU Charter states in its Article 37 that: 'A high level of environment protection and the improvement of the quality of the environment must be integrated into the policies of the Union and ensured in accordance with the principle of sustainable development'. The CJEU has repeatedly ruled that the protection of the environment constitutes one of the essential objectives of the Union.[109]

Finally, the Court has found that Article 11 TFEU, according to which environmental protection requirements must be integrated into the definition and implementation of the Union's policies and activities, emphasises the fundamental nature of the Union's aim to promote sustainable development and to protect the environment as well as its extension across the range of those policies and activities.[110]

Not only does the right to a healthy environment seem to perfectly align with the purposes and the values of the EU Treaties, but it also aligns with the current and future aspirations of the Union. Emblematically, Article 11 TFEU is at the core of the Commission's proposal for the 8th Environment Action Programme (2021–2030) presented in late 2020 and adopted in 2021. In particular, the Commission repeatedly emphasises the benefits that a healthy environment, a situation that the Commission strives to achieve by 2050, will bring to the wellbeing of citizens, biodiversity and natural capital.[111]

---

[109] Among others, CJEU, *Procureur de la République v Association de défense des brûleurs d'huiles usagées (ADBHU)*, Case 240/83, 07.02.1985, ECLI:EU:C:1985:59, para. 13; CJEU, *Commission v Denmark*, Case 302/86, 20.09.1988, ECLI:EU:C:1988:421, para. 8, CJEU, *Commission of the European Communities v Republic of Austria, supra* note 9, para. 71.

[110] CJEU, *Commission of the European Communities v Republic of Austria, supra* note 9, para. 73.

[111] European Commission, Proposal for a Decision of the European Parliament and of the Council on a General Union Environment Action Programme to 2030, COM(2020) 652 final, 14.10.2020, Article 2.1.

Furthermore, the European Green Deal demonstrates the core relevance that the EU is dedicating to the issue of environmental protection. It has been welcomed as a new growth strategy that aims to transform the EU into the first climate-neutral continent, with a modern, resource-efficient and competitive economy by 2050. Through its Communication, the Commission restates that it must put people first, recalling the principle to leave no one behind at the core of the 2030 Agenda on Sustainable Development. The Green Deal provides the guidelines for the development of a wide set of legislative proposals aimed at filling the current normative gaps, such as the proposal for the first-ever EU climate law, or at resetting the scopes of the EU environmental policy. From a zero-pollution ambition to the promotion of clean and circular economy, from renovating the energy sector to smart mobility, the Commission is pursuing the final aim of reaching a sustainable future for the present and future generation of EU citizens. In the author's view, this framework would inevitably suffer from the lack of an essential component such as the right to a healthy environment, which underlies all the proposals made by Commission. Arguably, tacking climate change and unsustainable policies without committing to upholding those fundamental rights associated with them could potentially frustrate the final outcomes. What otherwise would be the logic behind the attempt to improve Member States' industrial policies without equipping local populations with an explicit right to a healthy environment and clean air to claim in case of states' non-compliance?

Moreover, in the framework of the European Green Deal, the European Commission asserted that the achievement of the commitments undertaken under the EU Biodiversity Strategy 2030 are essential to the wellbeing and economic prosperity of present and future generations in a healthy environment.[112] In a recent resolution, the European Parliament shares the Commission's ambition by stressing that all people should be granted the fundamental right to a safe,[113] clean, healthy and sustainable environment and to a stable climate, without discrimination, and that this right must be delivered through ambitious policies and must be fully enforceable at all levels.[114]

3. THE RIGHT TO A HEALTHY ENVIRONMENT AS A NORMATIVE RESPONSE TO COVID-19

Air pollution poses a direct threat to the adequate enjoyment of numerous human rights, from the right to health, life, food and water to the intergenerational

---

112 European Commission, Communication from the Commission to the European Parliament, the European Council, the Council, the European Economic and Social Committee and the Committee of the Regions, The European Green Deal, COM(2020)0380, 11.12.2019.

113 European Parliament, Resolution on the effects of climate change on human rights, 21.09.2020, *supra* note 7.

114 Ibid., para. 6.

right to a healthy and sustainable environment. Fine particulate air pollution is the single largest environmental risk to health worldwide. More than 90% of the world's population lives in regions that exceed WHO guidelines for healthy ambient air quality.[115] In Europe, the major sources contributing to air pollution, which may expose individuals to risks to their health and wellbeing, are commonly known and relate to fossil fuel and biomass combustion, small- and large-scale emissions and industrial and agricultural productions. Similarly, assuming that air pollution is a vehicle for the spreading of respiratory diseases is far from being new or surprising. This connection has been verified by epidemiological findings and acknowledged both in the political arena and in judicial proceedings.

As a matter of fact, some epidemiological studies have demonstrated that the incidence and severity of COVID-19 depends on air pollution, therefore substantiating the existing association between highly polluted areas with the number of infection cases. Air pollution has been therefore interpreted as a boosting factor of the spreading of COVID-19, regardless of other socioeconomic, demographic, weather, behavioural, epidemic stage and health care-related confounders. Emblematically, the research conducted by the University of Harvard found that a small increase in PM produces a large increase (8%) in COVID-19 death rate. Similarly, research has found that the there is an occurrence of higher case rates in case of low-income families belonging to ethnic minorities, due to their precarious health status, potential higher exposures and reduced resilience to social, environmental and economic risks.[116]

At the political level, the European Environmental Agency (EEA) has frequently called the Union and its Member States for stronger commitment in avoiding exceeding the EU legal limits of air pollution levels for the protection of human health. Air pollution is, according to EEA, the primary cause of premature deaths from environmental factors in Europe, which takes around 400,000 lives every year.[117] In the framework of the European Green Deal, the EU has pledged to follow the revised WHO Air Quality Guidelines with the double aim to abate air pollution and decrease the risks to human health and

---

[115] World Health Organization, 'Don't Pollute my Future!: The Impact of the Environment on Children's Health', report, 2017, available at https://www.who.int/ceh/publications/don-t-pollute-my-future/en/, last accessed 10.05.2021.

[116] P. Fimiani, 'Inquinamento ambientale e Diritti Umani', Questione Giustizia, rubrica Diritti senza Confini, available at https://www.questionegiustizia.it/speciale/articolo/inquinamento-ambientale-e-diritti-umani_81.php, last accessed 13.07.2021.

[117] European Environmental Agency, 'Air Pollution: How It Affects Our Health', 14.12.2020, available at https://www.eea.europa.eu/themes/air/health-impacts-of-air-pollution#:~:text=In%202018%2C%20the%20EEA%20estimates,States%20and%20the%20United%20Kingdom, last accessed 24.03.2021.

the environment.[118] However, as several experts feared, the termination of national lockdowns has coincided with an immediate rise of air pollution levels.

In this regard, Italy, one of the most coronavirus-affected countries, has been repeatedly condemned for violation of the right to private and family life as well as of the right to effective remedy both under the ECHR and the EU Charter in the field of the environment.[119] Recently, the CJEU has held that Italy systematically exceeded the maximum limit values applicable to concentrations of PM10 laid down by the Air Quality Directive between 2008 and 2017,[120] thus infringing EU law on ambient air quality. These judgments not only reveal the Italian negligence towards clean air, but also corroborate the epidemiological thesis that COVID-19 spreads easily and more rapidly in highly polluted areas.

The multitude of scientific facts substantiating the impingement of human rights due to environmental factors, together with political and regulatory actions addressing air pollution as a coronavirus-counterstrategy substantiate the concrete and urgent need to a right to a healthy environment for all. The establishment of such a fundamental right is not merely a matter of legal theory. There is a real, concrete need for a right that both protects the environment and the human rights of those who live that environment, which can be appealed in case of violations and enforced. If the Court aims to be the guardian of the treaties as well as of the fundamental rights enshrined therein, the moment has come for it to step up and provide expressed protection from the current and future threats against them.

4. CONCLUSIONS

As I have attempted to illustrate above, the global health crisis caused by the COVID-19 pandemic has disrupted the life of millions of people along with their human rights. Some reliable epidemiological studies have suggested that the strength and incidence of this virus is associated with the level of air pollution, therefore giving a scientific explanation for the major occurrence of COVID-19

118 European Parliament, 'Air pollution and COVID-19', executive summary, 2021, available at https://www.europarl.europa.eu/RegData/etudes/STUD/2021/658216/IPOL_STU(2021)658216_EN.pdf, last accessed 22.03.2021.

119 For instance, in Di Sarno and others and Cordella and others, the Strasbourg judges found the Italian Republic responsible for having exposed the applicants to toxic and polluted emissions, hampering their fundamental rights. Please see, ECtHR, *Di Sarno and Others v Italy*, 10.01.2012 and ECtHR, *Cordella and Others v Italy*, Joined cases 54414/13 and 54264/15, 24.01.2019.

120 Directive 2008/50/EC of the European Parliament and of the Council of 21 May 2008 on ambient air quality and cleaner air for Europe, OJ L152.

cases and the related death rate in highly polluted areas of Italy, Spain and the United States.

The ongoing pandemic exacerbates therefore the already pressing urgency posed by environmental threats and climate change to expressly proclaim the right to a healthy environment under EU law.

This contribution intended to contribute to the discussion upon the establishment of this right by presenting a probable new theoretical framework, wherein the CJEU is called to play a paramount role. As a consequence, its feasibility depends on the interpretation of Article 6.3 TEU that the Court may or may not give, this representing a double-edged sword. According to some authors,[121] the CJEU already had the opportunity to derive the right to a healthy environment from its case law, but decided not to pursue it. Similarly, the Court may continue on the path already traced by its jurisprudence in the field of the environment – therefore ruling on the issue at stake without touching upon the right to a healthy environment – or, it could instead chart a new course. The reflections set out in this contribution depart from the second of these two possible choices.

In fact, by means of Article 6.3 TEU, it is suggested that the Court may establish a right to a healthy environment as stemming from the constitutional traditions common to the Member States. Following the methodology offered by AG Trstenjak, this contribution recalled some reliable international studies on the matter to note that the vast majority of them has already incorporated, with similar formulation, the right to a healthy environment into their national constitutions and in their national legislation, while in several other cases this right has been implicitly ascertained by other constitutionally protected rights. Moreover, the proclamation of the right to a healthy environment seems to be consistent with the aims, principles and values of the EU founding treaties. As recalled, the protection of human rights, the principle of sustainable development and the improvement of the quality of the environment guide the mandate of the Union. Finally, regional and international treaties that bind both the Union and its Member States – such as the 1998 Aarhus Convention on procedural environmental rights, the ESC and the ECHR – are external sources of law that explicitly provide for, or have been interpreted to include, a right to a healthy environment. These provisions therefore support the national movements in this direction. It has been concluded, therefore, that the CJEU may be considered as having all the elements to extrapolate from the national traditions the best suited formulation for a right to a healthy, favourable or adequate environment to be adapted at the EU level.

---

121 C. Feliziani, 'Il Diritto Fondamentale all'ambiente Salubre nella Recente Giurisprudenza della Corte di Giustizia e della Corte EDU in Materia di Rifiuti. Analisi di due Approcci Differenti', (2020) 6, *Rivista Italiana di Diritto Pubblico Comunitario*, p. 3. The author mentioned the CJEU case, *European Commission v Italy*, C-297/08, 04.03.2010, ECLI:EU:C:2010:115.

The active judicial role in deducing a binding source of EU law from the treaties is not new in the history of EU legal and cultural integration. The absence of fundamental rights in the first steps of the Community has led the Court to proclaim a wide range of fundamental rights as general principles of law in order to comply with its task and proceed swiftly towards a stronger 'Europeanisation'. Given the present-day conditions, the CJEU is called once again to shape a new course of EU law, rooted in the principle of sustainable development and of intergenerational solidarity.

THE EU SUSTAINABLE FINANCE AGENDA

A Strengthened Case for Human Rights in Times of COVID-19

Signe Andreasen Lysgaard and Jonas Grimheden*

ABSTRACT

Fuelled first by the climate crisis and since then by COVID-19, the European Union (EU, the Union) is actively pursuing an ambition of making the financial system sustainable for the planet as well as for people. An innovative policy instrument is that of a Sustainable Finance Taxonomy aiming to combat 'sustainability washing' and direct capital towards economic activities that contribute to sustainable development. Aside from a minimum safeguard clause in the current Taxonomy Regulation ((EU) 2020/852), international law and standards on human rights and respect for human rights by business have yet to feature as central components of the approach taken. This might change, however, as the European

* The two authors are members of the EU Platform on Sustainable Finance. Signe Andreasen Lysgaard is Strategic Adviser on Business and Human Rights at the Danish Institute for Human Rights, and Jonas Grimheden is Programme Manager for human rights systems at the European Union Agency for Fundamental Rights. The contribution is written in their personal capacities and does not express views of their respective institutions or the Platform on Sustainable Finance.

Commission considers extending the Taxonomy Regulation, currently focused on environmental sustainability, to social sustainability. This contribution examines the relationship between human rights and social sustainability, including in the context of EU regulation and policy. It identifies challenges and opportunities associated with incorporating human rights more firmly in the context of the taxonomy. Finally, it makes the case for human rights as key to ensuring policy coherence across EU level approaches to promoting responsible business conduct and private sector contributions to sustainable development.

1. INTRODUCTION

COVID-19 has exposed and exacerbated pre-existing fragilities and inequalities in business models, specific sectors and the financial system in its entirety. In addition to the health and social impacts of the pandemic, significant financial impacts have caused a shift in strategic priorities of public and private entities, sometimes with further negative consequences for human rights.[1] The crisis has, however, also caused businesses, financial institutions, Member States and the European Union (EU, the Union) itself to take renewed action to 'build back better' and ensure recovery plans that are both green and just.[2] A positive example is the EU's work on the green deal and sustainable finance, where a social dimension of sustainable development has been fast-tracked in part due to the underlining by COVID-19 of social vulnerabilities and impacts associated with our economies.

In a pre-COVID reality, the EU prioritised the development of a sustainable finance taxonomy as a key instrument to re-orient capital towards sustainable development. With a view to a subsequent extension of the taxonomy to cover more objectives, the EU in June 2020 initially adopted a taxonomy with six climate and environmental objectives.[3] Whereas the climate crisis has previously underlined the need and urgency of *greening* finance, the COVID-19 crisis demonstrates the need to broaden the understanding of sustainability, including in the context of a sustainable finance taxonomy, to also include a

---

1 See e.g. FRA, 'Coronavirus pandemic in the EU – Fundamental rights implications: focus on social rights', 2020, available at https://fra.europa.eu/sites/default/files/fra_uploads/fra-2020-coronavirus-pandemic-eu-bulletin-november_en.pdf, last accessed 31.03.2021; McKinsey & Company, 'COVID-19: Implications for Business', 2021, available at https://www.mckinsey.com/business-functions/risk/our-insights/covid-19-implications-for-business, last accessed 31.03.2021.

2 See e.g. European Commission, 'Recovery plan for Europe', available at https://ec.europa.eu/info/strategy/recovery-plan-europe_en, last accessed 31.03.2021.

3 Regulation (EU) No 2020/852 of the European Parliament and of the Council of 18 June 2020 on the establishment of a framework to facilitate sustainable investment, and amending Regulation (EU) 2019/2088, OJ L198 (hereinafter EU Taxonomy Regulation).

people-oriented, or social, dimension. In November 2020, EU Commissioner McGuinness, responsible for the Capital Markets Union and financial services thus highlighted that 'the COVID crisis reminds us that we cannot leave behind the social, the "S" of ESG.[4] We want to make the social element more important in our Strategy [on Sustainable Finance]. The public and private sector experts in the Platform on Sustainable Finance are assessing how a social taxonomy could work'.[5]

Similarly, in relation to the 2019 Sustainable Finance Disclosure Regulation – which provides rules on disclosures for the financial services, the European Supervisory Authorities decided to fast-track and tackle social, including human rights issues, at the same time as developing specific requirements and indicators related to environmental sustainability.[6] With such efforts, EU's approach to regulating finance will not only provide rules and offer incentives to financial market participants to 'go green', but also to 'go social'.[7] Such efforts resonate well with existing market practice, whereby many financial market participants including investors have committed to Environmental, Social and Governance (ESG) aligned investing. Whereas the EU taxonomy has provided direction for the environmental aspect, no uniform definition or classification system for the social and the governance aspects exists.

The ambition to include social sustainability in the EU's approach to sustainable finance is both timely and increasingly clear. At the same time, many questions remain around what this would look like in practice. Among these are how one could define 'social' in the context of sustainability and sustainable finance specifically, and what would be the interrelation between social sustainability and related paradigms, such as human rights.

This contribution makes the case for human rights in informing policy and legislative developments in the EU when it comes to sustainable finance, focusing in particular on the EU Taxonomy Regulation, which establishes a framework for assessment of the sustainability of investments. So far, the taxonomy includes environmental and climate-focused so called 'objectives' and criteria, but a

---

4 ESG: Environmental, Social and Governance.

5 European Commission, 'Keynote speech by Commissioner McGuinness at Climate Finance Week Ireland', 03.11.2020, available at https://ec.europa.eu/commission/commissioners/2019-2024/mcguinness/announcements/keynote-speech-commissioner-mcguinness-climate-finance-week-ireland_en, last accessed 31.03.2021.

6 See Joint Committee of the European Supervisory Authorities, 'Final report on draft Regulatory Technical Standards', 02.02.2021, available at https://www.eba.europa.eu/sites/default/documents/files/document_library/Publications/Draft Technical Standards/2021/962778/JC 2021 03 – Joint ESAs Final Report on RTS under SFDR.pdf, last accessed 31.03.2021.

7 For an overview of sustainable investments in the EU, see e.g. European Commission, 'Study on sustainability-related ratings, data and research', 2021, available at https://op.europa.eu/en/publication-detail/-/publication/d7d85036-509c-11eb-b59f-01aa75ed71a1/language-en/format-PDF/source-183474104, last accessed 31.03.2021.

'social taxonomy' – which would add social objectives to the existing green ones – has been proposed, and discussions are underway as to how such a taxonomy might be construed. Such discussions include identifying how human rights might best be included in a social taxonomy and thus how financial investors can chose to align their portfolios with EU-established environmental as well as social objectives – thereby delivering on globally agreed sustainability goals and aspirations.

Despite its environmental orientation, the EU Taxonomy Regulation, adopted in June 2020, already includes a minimum safeguard clause, with explicit references to international human rights law instruments and standards, including the 'International Bill of Human Rights', International Labour Organization (ILO) core labour standards and the United Nations (UN) Guiding Principles on Business and Human Rights. In addition, a Sustainable Finance Platform with representatives of EU bodies, industry and civil society is established under the regulation (Article 20), tasked with advising the EU on a range of issues, including the social taxonomy and the functioning of the minimum safeguards clause.

When analysed from a human rights perspective, the taxonomy provides an opportunity to become a lever for increased respect for human rights by business and financial institutions, along with an incentive for their positive impacts on human rights. However, it also raises fundamental questions around how the existing taxonomy framework can meaningfully be extended to cover the social dimension, including human rights and whether the taxonomy approach can be dovetailed with existing key frameworks on business and human rights, including the UN Guiding Principles on Business and Human Rights. In addition, the work is developing alongside other related policy initiatives from the EU, including potential mandatory human rights due diligence legislation and a review of the corporate sustainability reporting directive, which makes policy coherence another central concern.[8]

This contribution explores such key questions and considerations around aligning the EU's sustainable finance policy with human rights and outlines possible pathways for the future. The second of seven sections depicts the developments leading up to the understanding of sustainability and more specifically social sustainability in an EU context. The third section outlines key parts of the taxonomy regulation, while the fourth section looks at human rights as minimum safeguards. The fifth section explores why and how respect for human rights could be reflected in a social taxonomy, beyond minimum safeguards. The sixth section describes what the human rights framework might offer in the context of social goods and services, where included in the taxonomy.

---

8 European Commission, 'Sustainable corporate governance', available at https://ec.europa.eu/info/law/better-regulation/have-your-say/initiatives/12548-Sustainable-corporate-governance, last accessed 31.03.2021.

Finally, the seventh section argues that human rights might provide a pathway for policy coherence across the different regulatory files currently being explored at the EU level as it relates to ensuring responsible and sustainable markets.

2. THE PATH TOWARDS SOCIAL SUSTAINABILITY

The European Union has sustainability hardwired through Article 3(3) of the Treaty on European Union, which establishes that the internal market 'shall work for the sustainable development of Europe'. Article 3(3), in the same vein, describes several social and human rights-based features of such sustainable development. It envisages a Union that has 'a highly competitive social market economy, aiming at full employment and social progress', that:

> shall combat social exclusion and discrimination, and shall promote social justice and protection, equality between women and men, solidarity between generations and protection of the rights of the child. It shall promote economic, social and territorial cohesion, and solidarity among Member States. It shall respect its rich cultural and linguistic diversity and shall ensure that Europe's cultural heritage is safeguarded and enhanced.

Years later, the EU's Green Deal, launched in 2019, marks one of the EU's prominent attempts to turn sustainability commitments into action. As evident from the reform title, the initiative is environmentally oriented. At the same time, it includes a more holistic depiction of what sustainability includes: 'the EU has the collective ability to transform its economy and society to put it on a more sustainable path. It can build on its strengths as a global leader on climate and environmental measures, consumer protection, and workers' rights.'[9] Furthermore, in the Political Guidelines of the European Commission 2019–2024, 'an economy that works for people' – which includes several social and human rights-based political ambitions – is one six stated priorities.[10]

Sustainability, including in a form that moves beyond an environmental understanding of the term is, in other words, not a new phenomenon at the EU level. However, COVID-19 has underscored the urgency of emphasising social sustainability and has seemingly made the EU speed up efforts to ensure that sustainability as it relates to regulating our economy includes a social dimension. It is therefore clear that sustainability refers not only to a world that is not depleting the environmental resources, but a world which leaves no one behind.

---

9 European Commission, 'A European Green Deal', available at https://ec.europa.eu/info/strategy/priorities-2019-2024/european-green-deal_en, last accessed 31.03.2021.

10 European Commission, 'Political guidelines of the Commission 2019–2024', available at https://ec.europa.eu/info/strategy/priorities-2019-2024_en, last accessed 03.06.2021.

The holistic sustainability focus is following on from key global processes, including the 2030 Agenda and the Sustainable Development Goals (SDGs).[11] While the SDGs prominently are concerned with environment sustainability – albeit cross-cutting, with goals on clean water (Goal 6), clean energy (Goal 7), sustainable cities (Goal 11), responsible consumption and production (Goal 12), climate action (Goal 13) and life below water and on land (Goals 14 and 15) – there are also several goals aimed specifically at furthering social sustainability, including poverty (Goal 1), zero hunger (Goal 2), good health (Goal 3), quality education (Goal 4), gender equality (Goal 5), decent work (Goal 8), reduced inequalities (Goal 10) and peace and justice (Goal 16).

While human rights are not always at the forefront of SDG initiatives and calls to action, the UN and other human rights and development organisations have documented the strong anchorage of the SDGs in human rights and called for SDG efforts to focus on human rights.[12] Analysis by the Danish Institute for Human Rights concludes that more than 90% of the goals and their corresponding SDG targets (sub-goals) are linked to international human rights and labour rights instruments.[13] The Council of the EU has similarly stressed the importance of human rights in the context of the SDGs, requesting the European Commission to steer 'the EU policy framework to ensure that existing and new EU policies are in line with the SDGs and their targets; and by that contributing to equality for all, human rights and dignity, healthy and resilient planet, fair, inclusive, peaceful and resilient societies and sustainable economies'.[14] The Council also makes the link clear in the EU priorities in UN human rights fora, noting that '[t]he EU is making significant strides towards achieving the [SDGs and] will continue being at the forefront of a human rights-based approach to its full, effective and non-discriminatory implementation in all countries'.[15]

---

11 United Nations, 'Transforming our world: the 2030 agenda for sustainable development', UN Doc A/RES/70/1, 21.10.2015, available at https://sustainabledevelopment.un.org/content/documents/21252030 Agenda for Sustainable Development web.pdf, last accessed 31.03.2021.

12 See United Nations Human Rights Office of the High Commissioner, 'Transforming our world: human rights in the 2030 Agenda for Sustainable Development', available at https://www.ohchr.org/Documents/Issues/MDGs/Post2015/HRAndPost2015.pdf, last accessed 31.03.2021; UNDP, 'Human rights and the SDGs – two sides of the same coin', available at https://www.undp.org/content/undp/en/home/blog/2019/human-rights-and-the-sdgs---two-sides-of-the-same-coin.html, last accessed 31.03.2021.

13 Danish Institute for Human Rights, 'The Human Rights Guide to the Sustainable Development Goals', available at https://sdg.humanrights.dk/, last accessed 13.07.2021.

14 Council of the EU, 'Council Conclusions, A sustainable European future: The EU response to the 2030 Agenda for Sustainable Development', 20.06.2017, para. 18, available at https://data.consilium.europa.eu/doc/document/ST-10370-2017-INIT/en/pdf, last accessed 31.03.2021.

15 Council of the EU, 'Council Conclusions, EU Priorities in UN Human Rights Fora in 2020', 17.02.2020, para. 6, available at https://data.consilium.europa.eu/doc/document/ST-5982-2020-INIT/en/pdf, last accessed 31.03.2021.

The 2015 SDGs, due by 2030, are not the only global link for the EU to the sustainability agenda. The 2015 Paris Agreement on climate change is also a clear milestone for the EU,[16] being party to the agreement and the underlying UN Framework Convention on Climate Change.[17] The Framework Convention, in turn, dates from 1992, the year of the UN 'Earth Summit', in Rio de Janeiro.[18] The Rio Declaration also acknowledged the social dimension of sustainability.[19] Additionally, in contexts such as international financing of development projects, risk assessments have included a social and human rights-based dimension in addition to the environmental dimension for many years.[20]

Connected to the interrelation between (social) sustainability and human rights is also the relationship between the term 'social' and human rights as codified by international and regional instruments. In terms of the social dimension of human rights – social rights – this dimension is most explicitly included in the 1966 International Covenant on Economic, Social and Cultural Rights (ICESCR) and the 1961/1996 European Social Charter. In the European Union, the 2000 Charter of Fundamental Rights also includes a strong list of social rights in Title IV, Solidarity Rights, which constitute binding EU primary law since 2009.[21] The 2017 EU policy document, the Pillar of Social Rights, further provides new interpretations of what constitute 'social rights'.[22]

The half a century that the drafting of these documents span, and the nature of them, makes for quite a diverse reading in terms of length, level of detail and to some extent wording. However, the instruments have an extensive common core, related to rights associated with just working conditions, social security, health and non-discrimination. Interestingly, there are also some variations in

---

16 United Nations Treaty Collection, 'Paris Agreement', 12 December 2015, available at https://treaties.un.org/Pages/ViewDetails.aspx?src=TREATY&mtdsg_no=XXVII-7-d&chapter=27&clang=_en, last accessed 31.03.2021.

17 United Nations Treaty Collection, United Nations Framework Convention on Climate Change, 9 May 1992, available at https://treaties.un.org/Pages/ViewDetailsIII.aspx?src=TREATY&mtdsg_no=XXVII-7&chapter=27&Temp=mtdsg3&clang=_en last accessed 31.03.2021.

18 United Nations, 'Conference on Environment and Development', 1992, available at https://www.un.org/en/conferences/environment/rio1992, last accessed 31.03.2021.

19 United Nations, 'Report of the United Nations Conference on Environment and Development', 1992, UN Doc A/CONF.151.26/Rev.1, available at https://undocs.org/en/A/CONF.151/26/Rev.1(vol.I), last accessed 31.03.2021.

20 See e.g. International Finance Corporation (2012), Performance Standards on Environmental and Social Sustainability, available at https://www.ifc.org/wps/wcm/connect/24e6bfc3-5de3-444d-be9b-226188c95454/PS_English_2012_Full-Document.pdf?MOD=AJPERES&CVID=jkV-X6h, last accessed 27.05.2021.

21 See e.g. FRA, 'Charterpedia', available at https://fra.europa.eu/en/tags/charterpedia, last accessed 31.03.2021.

22 European Commission, 'The European Pillar of Social Rights in 20 principles', available at https://ec.europa.eu/info/european-pillar-social-rights/european-pillar-social-rights-20-principles_en, last accessed 31.03.2021.

scope across the instruments. The ICESCR refers to an adequate standard of living (Article 11(1)), which is also included in the Universal Declaration of Human Rights (Article 25(1)). The European Social Charter, apart from being the most detailed of the instruments, includes poverty and social exclusion (note that freedom from hunger is also included in ICESCR, Article 11(2)). The Charter of Fundamental Rights includes, under the solidarity title, references to environmental and consumer protection, and the EU's social pillar includes principles on minimum income, housing and assistance to homeless people.

The variation and breadth of issues covered illustrate that what is commonly understood as 'social' is wide-ranging, including in the context of human rights. Furthermore, whereas social rights formally are included in the ICESCR at the level of international human rights law, it is important to consider the interrelatedness of rights, for instance economic and social with civil and political, including in the context of working with social sustainability. While the language is often that of 'social', it is not intended to limit the human rights to social rights. Rather, social refers to social consequences or impact, which can affect rights across the full range, from worker's rights to freedom of expression and the right to life.

3. THE EU TAXONOMY REGULATION AND ASSOCIATED REGULATION: REGULATORY HOOKS FOR SOCIAL SUSTAINABILITY AND HUMAN RIGHTS

As illustrated above, there is a broad international consensus, well reflected in international and EU policy and law on the need for 'holistic' approaches to sustainability, including environmental, social and governance aspects. However, the conceptual overlaps between human rights and sustainable development are not always sufficiently pronounced or clear, and many initiatives fall short of an integrated or human rights-based approach to sustainable development. A promising example is the EU Taxonomy Regulation, which seeks to incentivise investments that support sustainability and make it harder to 'sustainability-wash' investments that do not align with sustainability objectives.

The regulation is addressed to EU and Member States (Article 4), to large companies required to submit non-financial information under the Non-Financial Reporting Directive (Article 8), as well as to financial market participants (Articles 5 to 7). The regulation, although focused on environmental sustainability, takes an active and strong stance on human rights by stating that:

> economic activities should only qualify as environmentally sustainable where they are carried out in alignment with the Guidelines for Multinational Enterprises of the Organisation for Economic Co-operation and Development (OECD) and UN

> Guiding Principles on Business and Human Rights, including the declaration on Fundamental Principles and Rights at Work[…] and the International Bill of Human Rights. […] Several of those international standards are enshrined in the Charter of Fundamental Rights of the European Union (Recital 35).

The regulation goes on to state that 'They should also be consistent with the principles enshrined in the European Pillar of Social Rights' (Recital 36).

Similar language is contained in Article 18:

> Minimum safeguards […] shall be procedures implemented by an undertaking that is carrying out an economic activity to ensure the alignment with the OECD Guidelines for Multinational Enterprises and the UN Guiding Principles on Business and Human Rights, including the principles and rights set out in the eight fundamental conventions identified in the Declaration of the International Labour Organisation on Fundamental Principles and Rights at Work and the International Bill of Human Rights.

The provision (Article 18(2)) also stipulates that complying with the minimum safeguards must not lead to any 'significant harm' to the objectives of the taxonomy.

The Taxonomy Regulation refers prominently to the 2030 Agenda and the Paris Agreement in Recitals 2 and 3 and notes that 'sustainability has long been central to the Union project, and [the EU treaties] reflect its social and environmental dimensions' (Recital 4). The instrument acknowledges that environmental objectives to guide economic actors is the first step, and that 'other sustainability objectives, including social objectives, might be developed at a later stage' (Recital 6, and similar reference in Recital 59). The regulation requires the European Commission to publish a report by the end of 2021 on how the taxonomy could be extended beyond environmental activities and how it could cover social objectives (Article 26(2)).

Article 9 onwards lays down the six environmental 'objectives' of the taxonomy, of which the first two should be detailed and ready for implementation as of 2022, and the remaining ones a year later:

1. Climate change mitigation
2. Climate change adaptation
3. Sustainable use and protection of water and marine resources
4. Transition to a circular economy
5. Pollution prevention and control
6. Protection and restoration of biodiversity and ecosystems

The extent of alignment of an investment with the taxonomy, and thus the level of environmental sustainability, is assessed based on these six objectives. An economic activity must contribute ('substantial contribution') to at least one of the six, 'do no significant harm' to any of the others and be in compliance with the minimum safeguards (Figure 1 provides an overview of these three elements of the instrument). Details on what substantial contribution and doing no significant harm to the objectives looks like are to be laid down through Technical Screening Criteria in delegated acts adopted by the European Commission (Article 3).[23]

Figure 1. The three levels of the taxonomy

Substantially contribute	At least to one of six environmental objectives
Do no significant harm	To any of the six environmental objectives
Minimum safeguards	International human rights law, including labour standards

Source: Produced by the authors.

Importantly, the taxonomy regulation provides for a rather innovative approach, with potential to influence investment decisions in addition to driving transparency and comparability in reporting.

Whereas the notion of a sustainable finance taxonomy is somewhat new, the element of utilising corporate reporting on sustainability issues is not. The outcome document of the RIO+20 conference, in 2012, entitled the 'Future we want', noted 'the importance of corporate sustainability reporting and encourage[d] companies [...] to consider integrating sustainability information into their reporting cycle'.[24] This was an important cue to engage more with companies to ensure sustainable development. The EU first addressed the area with its Non-Financial Reporting Directive from 2014.[25] This directive, currently being revised and renamed the 'Corporate Sustainability Reporting Directive',

[23] For discussions on how the taxonomy is expected to function, see e.g. Bloomberg Professional Services, 'Applying the EU Taxonomy to your investments, how to start?', 11.01.2021, available at https://www.bloomberg.com/professional/blog/applying-the-eu-taxonomy-to-your-investments-how-to-start/?utm_medium=LI_Elvt&utm_campaign=SustInvest&utm_source=Social-o&utm_content=SEB, last accessed 31.03.2021. Euractiv, 'How the EU taxonomy can be the tool for dynamic climate transition', 27.01.2021, available at https://www.euractiv.com/section/energy-environment/opinion/how-the-eu-taxonomy-can-be-the-tool-for-dynamic-climate-transition/, last accessed 31.03.2021.

[24] United Nations, 'United Nations Conference on Sustainable Development', 2012, para. 47, available at https://www.un.org/en/conferences/environment/rio2012, last accessed 31.03.2021.

[25] Directive (EU) 2014/95/EU of the European Parliament and of the Council of 22 October 2014 amending Directive 2013/34/EU as regards disclosure of non-financial and diversity information by certain large undertakings and groups, OJ L330.

advances the idea that it is essential to make publicly available a wider set of information than purely financial information.[26]

The non-financial aspects considered of relevance within the EU have included human rights aspects from the beginning. Already the 2014 instrument refers to 'information on the prevention of human rights abuses and/or on instruments in place to fight corruption and bribery' (Recital 7). The proposed Corporate Sustainability Reporting Directive includes numerous detailed references to international human rights law instruments, using wording very similar to the Taxonomy Regulation. For instance, the revised provision on sustainability reporting standards (Article 19b) specifies that companies have 'to disclose about social factors, including information about [...] equal opportunities'; 'working conditions'; and 'respect for the human rights, fundamental freedoms, democratic principles and standards established in the International Bill of Human Rights[[27]] and other core UN human rights conventions, the International Labour Organization's Declaration on Fundamental Principles and Rights at Work and the ILO fundamental conventions and the Charter of Fundamental Rights of the European Union'. A related instrument mentioned earlier, the Sustainable Finance Disclosure Regulation,[28] calls for 'sustainability indicators with regard to climate and other environment-related adverse impacts, to social and employee matters, to respect for human rights, and to anti-corruption and anti-bribery matters' (Recital 30).

The different regulatory files are jointly becoming a regulatory ecosystem, setting the direction for responsible business conduct and ESG investing. The 'S' in ESG and the social elements of reporting requirements are overlapping in large part with human rights, and hence human rights standards and the UN Guiding Principles on Business and Human Rights are key reference points to ensure robust regulation and ensure policy coherence.[29]

4. HUMAN RIGHTS AS MINIMUM SAFEGUARDS: PRINCIPLE AND PRACTICE

From a regulatory standpoint, Article 18 of the taxonomy is meant to ensure that negative human rights impacts associated with business activities are not

---

26 European Commission, Proposal for a Directive (EU) COM(2021) 189 final, 21.04.2021.

27 Typically, a concept referring to the three UN instruments: the 1948 Universal Declaration of Human Rights and the two 1966 covenants, that on civil and political rights and that on economic, social and cultural rights.

28 Regulation (EU) 2019/2088 of the European Parliament and of the Council of 27 November 2019 on sustainability-related disclosures in the financial services sector, OJ L317.

29 J. G. Ruggie, C. Rees, R. Davis, 'Ten Years After: From UN Guiding Principles to Multi-Fiduciary Obligations', 2021, available at https://corpgov.law.harvard.edu/2021/05/13/ten-years-after-from-the-un-guiding-principles-to-multi-fiduciary-obligations/, last accessed 04.06.2021.

overlooked, as the taxonomy regulation starts to be applied and expectedly result in channelling of investments into environmentally sustainable activities. This design feature is a recognition of how environmentally sustainable activities can have unsustainable social impacts which may sometimes amount to negative human rights impacts. For example, a 2021 analysis by the Transition Minerals Tracker identifies 276 allegations of human rights abuses against companies mining minerals central to renewable energy technologies (cobalt, copper, lithium, manganese, nickel and zinc).[30]

Not only mining is known for human rights challenges, but wind, hydro and other new energies have been associated with abuses including on the right to 'free prior and informed consent', right to land, labour rights and livelihood impacts on communities.[31] In a worker context, it is also increasingly recognised that the green transition might have unintended negative effects on workers, including related to job loss.[32] In short, environmental sustainability does not automatically imply social sustainability; in contrast, tensions between the two agendas have continued to demonstrate themselves as calls for a just transition have complemented calls for the green transition.

When developing the environmental taxonomy, the EU regulator rightly recognised the interplay between the environmental and the social agendas and reflected in the regulation that a safeguard clause around human rights was a necessary element of a robust taxonomy. The regulation itself, however, includes very limited detail around the functioning of Article 18.

The delegated acts, which will include technical screening criteria for the six objectives, will not include details or criteria around alignment with the minimum safeguards. In practice, this means that financial market participants have to start complying with a clause where no details exist around how such compliance should be ensured. Early stage experience sharing by financial market participants unsurprisingly indicates challenges in applying Article 18, including due to data gaps and raises questions about when and how compliance with Article 18 can simply be assumed due to legal compliance.[33] As the market waits for possible further specification of the functioning of the safeguards

30 Business & Human Rights, 'Transition Minerals Tracker', available at https://trackers.business-humanrights.org/transition-minerals/, last accessed 31.03.2021.

31 Business & Human Rights, 'Renewable Energy', available at https://www.business-humanrights.org/en/big-issues/natural-resources/renewable-energy/, last accessed 31.03.2021.

32 OECD, Just Transition Centre, 'Just transition', 2017, available at https://www.oecd.org/environment/cc/g20-climate/collapsecontents/Just-Transition-Centre-report-just-transition.pdf, last accessed 31.03.2021.

33 United Nations Environment Programme Finance Initiative and the European Banking Federation (EBF), 'Testing the application of the EU Taxonomy to core banking products: high level recommendations, 2021, pp. 34–36, available at https://www.unepfi.org/wordpress/wp-content/uploads/2021/01/Testing-the-application-of-the-EU-Taxonomy-to-core-banking-products-Final-v2.pdf, last accessed 31.03.2021.

clause, service providers have started to develop taxonomy services, some of which reveal disappointing examples of applying the safeguards clause. One rating company in February 2020 indicated that checking for compliance with the minimum safeguards clause would imply that: 'It must be verified that the company has not been subject to (allegations of) failing to meet minimum social safeguards in their operations'.[34] Rather than ensuring pro-active alignment with the minimum safeguard requirements, the provider seemingly suggests settling at an allegations check.

These examples of early adoption of the safeguards clause by the market are concerning reading when it comes to securing an impact of Article 18, or put differently, that the foreseen direction of capital towards green objectives rests on a solid foundation of respect for human rights as it relates to economic activities. If the recognition of the importance of human rights stops at the level of regulatory text and has little practical implication, then the environmental taxonomy does not effectively provide a push towards ensuring that the green transition avoids taking place at the expense of social sustainability. The Platform on Sustainable Finance has been asked to advise the European Commission on the functioning of Article 18 and hence, the Commission might act on these risks in the future. However, such potential action will likely come after the Commission develops its first report on extending the taxonomy to social objectives due by the end of December 2021. Against this backdrop, adequately capturing and reinforcing human rights directly in a potential social taxonomy becomes critical. This will also allow the Commission to include and address sectors and economic activities that might not be included in the existing taxonomy, given limited environmental footprint for instance, but which characteristics merit inclusion in a social taxonomy.

5. DOVETAILING RESPECT FOR HUMAN RIGHTS AND A SOCIAL TAXONOMY: CHALLENGES AND OPPORTUNITIES

The starting point for developing a social taxonomy is naturally the existing taxonomy with its environmental focus. Mirroring the environmental taxonomy in a social context involves identifying relevant social objectives and criteria for substantial contribution and doing no significant harm to such objectives.

If a potential social taxonomy is developed as a separate regulation, one scenario could be that future social objectives are complemented by

[34] Institutional Shareholder Services (ISS), 'EU Taxonomy in Focus Webinar', available at https://www.issgovernance.com/eu-taxonomy-in-focus-webinar/, last accessed 31.03.2021.

environmental safeguards, to mirror the use of social and governance oriented minimum safeguards in the environmental taxonomy. However, the social taxonomy may also become an evolution or expansion of the existing regulation, meaning that social objectives are added alongside the existing six environmental objectives and the existing minimum safeguards clause becomes applicable for environmental as well as social objectives. While there may be more, these two different scenarios for realising a social taxonomy carry varying challenges and opportunities when it comes to incorporating human rights. A shared pitfall of both will be the risk of undermining the importance of 'respect for human rights' by business, by a failure to incorporate the UN Guiding Principles on Business and Human Rights (UNGPs) in a meaningful and effective way.

Notably, the inclusion of human rights as minimum safeguards in the environmental taxonomy raises fundamental questions around the interplay between human rights and social sustainability. Importantly, key actors have made calls to put respect for human rights at the heart of business contributions to the global 2030 Agenda. The UN Working Group on Business and Human Rights have highlighted that: 'robust human rights due diligence enables and contributes to sustainable development ... For businesses, the most powerful contribution to sustainable development is to embed respect for human rights in their activities and across their value chains, addressing harm done to people and focusing on the potential and actual impacts.'[35]

Indeed, respect for human rights by business has the potential to transform lives of workers, consumers and communities and enable social sustainability rooted in internationally acknowledged principles and norms. In short, not doing harm to people is more than a mere minimum requirement that does not bring about positive change. Rather, when businesses proactively work to avoid and address potential and actual negative human rights impacts associated with its activities, it results in positive and potentially transformative social improvements for affected people. Take the example of workers who go from struggling to make ends meet to receiving a living wage; consumers who go from having inadequate information and insight into health and safety risks associated with products to getting full access to information; or communities that go from being negatively affected by noise and odour pollution associated with a local factory to receiving adequate compensation. The UNGPs importantly also recall that potential positive human rights impacts by business cannot compensate for negative impacts: 'Business enterprises may undertake other commitments or activities to support and promote human rights, which may contribute to the

35 United Nations Human Rights Office of the High Commissioner, '10 key recommendations to Governments and businesses from the UN Working Group on Business and Human Rights', 30.06.2017, available at https://www.ohchr.org/Documents/Issues/Business/Session18/InfoNoteWGBHR_SDGRecommendations.pdf, last accessed 31.03.2021.

enjoyment of rights. But this does not offset a failure to respect human rights throughout their operations.'[36]

The transformative potential and primacy of respect for human rights by business seem to suggest that it would be both critical and conceptually sound to capture this dimension directly in potential objectives of a social taxonomy, not just in the safeguards clause. The current examples of interpretation in the market of Article 18 further seem to suggest that the taxonomy in its current form might not be an instrument that supports – let alone secures – the uptake of respect for human rights by business. However, whereas there might be both principal and practical arguments in favour of this approach, doing so includes potential points of conflict with the basic approach and design features of the environmental taxonomy in several ways.

First, the environmental taxonomy has 'economic activities' as the unit, which may substantially contribute to one or more environmental objectives. Concretely, the environmental taxonomy makes use of so-called NACE codes to specify criteria for substantial contribution to environmental objectives as it relates to select economic activities, all covered by NACE codes.[37] In a NACE code context, an economic activity takes place when resources such as capital goods, labour, manufacturing techniques or intermediary products are combined to produce specific goods or services through processes. When considering 'respect for human rights' as a potential objective in a social taxonomy, it becomes clear, however, that such objective(s) would also need to address the economy entity as its unit, in addition to the economic activity. To take an example, the conditions under which workers labour are set at the company level and do not depend on the economic activity in which they are involved. To put it differently, whereas the environmental taxonomy, through use of NACE codes, covers some sectors and not others, objectives related to respect for human rights could potentially be sector-agnostic or relevant across all sectors. Interestingly, sector-agnostic objectives would widen the scope for inclusion of businesses as socially sustainable when it comes to respect for human rights and hence might expand the reach of a potential social taxonomy. Irrespective of what a certain business entity might be producing in terms of goods and services, it can take steps to respect workers' rights, for instance, which relate to social sustainability in the form of decent work (SDG goal 8). On the other hand, this also raises the question about whether some sectors should be excluded from being eligible for meeting criteria given the nature of their products or services. Examples demonstrating the paradoxical nature of

[36] United Nations Human Rights Office of the High Commissioner, Guiding Principles on Business and Human Rights, 2011, available at https://www.ohchr.org/documents/publications/guidingprinciplesbusinesshr_en.pdf, last accessed 31.03.2021 (hereinafter UN Guiding Principles).

[37] NACE is the acronym for '*Nomenclature statistique des activités économiques dans la Communauté européenne*'.

this approach could be tobacco or weapon producing companies, which, unless excluded, might otherwise become eligible for qualifying as socially sustainable due, for example, to strong standards related to workers' rights. Introducing one or more objectives that would require technical screening criteria to address the economic entity level in addition to the economic activity, although novel in the context of the taxonomy, would, however, resonate well with existing comparative regulations – for instance, the non-financial reporting directive and the sustainable finance reporting directive, both of which set conditions for business entities and require entity-level reporting.

Second, reflecting respect for human rights as one or more objectives in a social taxonomy raises some questions about the distinction between human rights policies and procedures and real-life human rights impacts. Whereas robust implementation of Article 18 would involve significant improvements for rights-holders currently affected negatively by business activities, the lack of current specificity around the implementation of Article 18 has led to some concern that the actual impact of the clause might not be in line with the intent. As a result, including respect for human rights, as defined by the UNGPs, in one or more objectives would allow the teething out of criteria for substantial contribution, some of which might relate to having in place adequate policies and processes that align with the UNGPs, and some of which might specify key human rights impact areas where it is possible to set criteria for what substantial contribution looks like in terms of ensuring certain rights are respected. Examples on rights where it might be possible to establish criteria for substantial contribution include freedom of association, where quantitative metrics around shares of workforces under collective bargaining agreements could be a useful indicator or freedom from non-discrimination based on gender, where the number of women in managerial positions might be a relevant metric to consider. It will likely not be possible or desirable to develop criteria for substantial contribution for all potential impacts on human rights, but it might be doable for some. Not including all human rights, but drawing out some, would, on the other hand, need to be carefully crafted so as not to undermine the expectation of the UNGPs for businesses to avoid negative impacts on all human rights.[38] However, the benefit of doing so includes steering attention of investors and businesses towards meeting 'performance objectives' on human rights, which would add to the focus on human rights policies and processes included in the UNGPs and already supported by existing reporting requirements.

Third, whereas the current taxonomy objectives set different criteria for substantial contribution and doing no significant harm, it remains to be seen whether that would be possible in relation to objectives related to respect for human rights. Indeed, it may only be possible to set 'pass or fail' type criteria

[38] UN Guiding Principles, principle 18.

for one or more objectives related to respect for human rights. Companies either provide decent working conditions – or they do not. In a scenario where objectives on respect for human rights contain only one set of criteria, companies that meet the criteria contribute to social sustainability, companies that do no significant harm, which would be different from how these criteria are being used in the current taxonomy regulation. This would involve departing from the current use of these concepts in the taxonomy, as in effect the 'substantial contribution' and 'do no significant harm' dimensions would collapse.

Fourth, and finally, introducing objectives related to respect for human rights includes the same data-related issues that were previously highlighted in relation to the current experiences with implementing Article 18 of the taxonomy regulation. The current revision of the non-financial reporting directive as well as the inclusion of human rights-related indicators and content in the regulatory technical standard of the sustainable finance disclosure regulation might, however, in and of themselves improve the existence and quality of available human rights-related information and data. Furthermore, a future social taxonomy would also create a needed push for improved data in this area. The Alliance for Corporate Transparency has highlighted a number of gaps in current reporting practices, highlighting how companies disclose general and vague information instead of comparable data. For example, in their analysis of reporting by 1,000 European companies, 22.2% of the companies provide some information on their human rights due diligence process, despite 82.8% reporting a human rights policy; 25.5% of the companies disclose specific human rights risks facing them (out of 56.6% that acknowledge the existence of such risks), yet only 14.6% report on the actual impacts; and merely 3.6% explain the outcomes of the management of the risks.[39] Against this backdrop, challenges associated with including respect for human rights as objectives include issues associated with relying on corporate self-reported data, on proxy indicators rather than outcome indicators and challenges in developing meaningful quantitative metrics related to human rights.

These different considerations highlight that whereas positioning respect for human rights by business as key to social sustainability might be relatively easy and non-controversial at the conceptual level, the practical implications for an instrument, such as potential social taxonomy, are much more complex and require careful analysis. The examples included here indicate that some form of adaptation of the current taxonomy design features is required given the different nature of environmental and social subject matter. The balancing

---

[39] Alliance for Corporate Transparency, 'Landmark research on 1000 European companies shows troubling poor quality of reporting on sustainability issues', 2020, available at https://allianceforcorporatetransparency.org/news/landmark-research.html, last accessed 31.03.2021.

act will therefore involve finding conceptually sound and implementable ways of extending the taxonomy to social objectives, without losing the strongpoints of the taxonomy as it was initially envisaged, including widespread interest and commitment by investors and financial market participants themselves.

6. A HUMAN RIGHTS LENS TO SOCIAL GOODS AND SERVICES

Aside from finding meaningful ways of incorporating respect for human rights in a social taxonomy, which would involve a focus on 'how business gets done', a social taxonomy might also meaningfully consider 'what business gets done' and what could make it socially sustainable including as seen from a human rights perspective. If a taxonomy will consider 'social goods and services' including housing, health, food, the question from a human rights perspective becomes whether the human rights framework can help qualify what substantial contribution and doing no significant harm looks like in this context. How could this be done in a constructive way so as to avoid mere publicity measures and 'social washing' and potentially even contribute to the fulfilment of select human rights?

Social goods and services, such as housing, food and education, are intimately linked to human rights – by being human rights (right to housing, right to food, and right to education) in themselves, but also as enablers for other rights. The right to education, for instance, supports many other rights, such as political participation and empowerment to prevent gender discrimination.[40]

Whereas there are authoritative definitions related to the corporate responsibility to 'respect' human rights, there is no equivalent when it comes to defining business 'support' for human rights. The 2005 United Nations Global Compact for corporations stresses, however, in its first of ten principles that '[b]usinesses should support and respect the protection of internationally proclaimed human rights'.[41] The social taxonomy provides a potential opportunity to mature the conceptualisation of business activities that not only respect but also 'support' human rights, for instance due to provision of social goods and services in a manner that supports the fulfilment of human rights.

---

40 United Nations, Committee on Economic, Social and Cultural Rights, *General Comment No. 13*, UN Doc E/C.12/1999/10, 08.12.1999. See also Right to Education, 'Understanding education as a right', available at https://www.right-to-education.org/page/understanding-education-right, last accessed 31.03.2021.

41 United Nations Global Compact, 'The Ten Principles of the UN Global Compact', available at https://www.unglobalcompact.org/what-is-gc/mission/principles, last accessed 31.03.2021 (hereinafter UN Global Compact).

Some United Nations human rights monitoring mechanisms have used a particular methodology to elaborate on the composition and measurability of social rights. The Treaty Body for the ICESCR, in its General Comment from 2000,[42] outlines the format of criteria setting around:

- Availability
- Accessibility
- Acceptability (culture, etc.)
- Quality

These are also known as AAAQ criteria to assess implementation of economic, social and cultural rights. The same or similar matrices have been used by mechanisms on the right to health,[43] right to housing[44] and right to education.[45] In the context of a social taxonomy, applying the AAAQ criteria in connection with economic activities such as housing or health care could enable ways of defining a role for business in supporting human rights in addition to respecting them. Rather than framing construction of housing as socially sustainable activity at face value, an AAAQ-based approach to including housing in a social taxonomy might establish benchmarks around, for example, accessibility of housing for people in situations of vulnerability.

Including the dimension of business support for human rights in a taxonomy context also includes some pitfalls and dilemmas, however. Notably, any objectives that incentivise support for human rights by business should come with some requirements on a meaningful link to a business' core activities in order to avoid 'social washing'.[46] Differently from some aspects of the green taxonomy where negative impacts can be offset by more positive measures in other areas, negative impacts on human rights cannot be offset by positive ones.[47]

Potential objectives that target social goods and services also raise questions around the social or human rights impacts of privatisation of government services, where companies are increasingly taking on the responsibility for

42 United Nations, Committee on Economic, Social and Cultural Rights, *General Comment No. 14*, UN Doc E/C.12/2000/4, 11.08.2000.

43 See e.g. United Nations, Economic and Social Council, 'The right of everyone to the enjoyment of the highest attainable standard of physical and mental health', UN Doc E/CN.4/2003/58, 13.02.2003.

44 See e.g. United Nations, Committee on Economic, Social and Cultural Rights, *General Comment No. 4*, UN Doc E/1992/23, 13 December 1991, referring to availability, affordability, habitability, accessibility, and cultural adequacy, in addition to other terms.

45 See e.g. United Nations, Special Rapporteur on the right to education, UN Doc E/CN.4/2000/6, 01.02.2000, referring to availability, accessibility, acceptability and adaptability.

46 Bloomberg, '"Social washing" a growing headache for ESG investors', available at https://www.pionline.com/esg/social-washing-growing-headache-esg-investors last accessed 31.03.2021.

47 See e.g. UN Global Compact, Principle 1, available at https://www.unglobalcompact.org/what-is-gc/mission/principles/principle-1, last accessed 31.03.2021.

social services. While government entities outsourcing such services maintain the obligation to provide the social rights, there is an inherent risk with the disconnect between the duty bearer and the service provider.[48] A carefully crafted social taxonomy could potentially contribute to bridging this gap, by driving capital towards social goods and services that are carried out in respect and support of human rights, including through application of AAAQ criteria.

7. THE FUTURE OF HUMAN RIGHTS IN THE EU'S SUSTAINABLE FINANCE AND BUSINESS EFFORTS: HUMAN RIGHTS AS KEY TO POLICY COHERENCE

The COVID-19 pandemic has underlined the importance of socially resilient and sustainable societies, including in the context of the European Union and its priorities. New efforts including to ensure positive contributions by business are needed. The global 2030 Agenda, with its Sustainable Development Goals, has so far successfully engaged business, but only some 40% of companies are believed to be on course to deliver on the goals by 2030.[49]

COVID-19 has underpinned a revitalised social sustainability agenda at the EU. The largest stimulus package in the history of the EU has a number of social components including the Just Transition Fund, a new health programme, EU4Health, as well as inherently social objectives such as ensuring gender equality when building back better.[50] At a time, where the climate crisis is as urgent as ever, the pandemic has forced populations and politicians not to forget about 'social' and not to think that protecting economic, social and cultural rights is a given, including in a European context. In March 2021 at the Porto Social Summit European Commission President, Ursula von der Leyen, reiterated the social emphasis: 'Europe's social targets must go hand in hand with its green and digital targets. We want to get closer to full employment, more Europeans to have access to the skills they need and ensure equal opportunities for all Europeans in a more digital and sustainable economy.'[51]

---

48 International Justice Resource Center, 'UN expert: privatization of government services undermines human rights protection', available at https://ijrcenter.org/2018/10/30/un-expert-privatization-of-government-services-undermines-human-rights-protections/, last accessed 31.03.2021.

49 UN News, 'Business sector still far from reaching sustainability goals', available at https://news.un.org/en/story/2020/07/1067662, last accessed 31.03.2021.

50 See European Commission, 'Recovery plan for Europe', available at https://ec.europa.eu/info/strategy/recovery-plan-europe_en, last accessed 31.03.2021.

51 Portuguese Presidency of the European Union, Press release, 07.05.2021, available at https://www.2021portugal.eu/en/porto-social-summit/news/porto-social-summit-all-partners-commit-to-2030-social-targets/, last accessed 03.06.2021.

In addition, the link between the environmental and the social crises have also become clearer. In January 2021 the Council of the EU acknowledged this connection and highlighted the potential threat to human rights associated with climate changes:

> The Council recognises that climate change and environmental degradation, including biodiversity and forest loss, are a threat to international stability and security, reinforcing disaster risks and pressures on ecosystems, posing challenges to food and water security, provoking local and regional conflicts while exacerbating the risk of the displacement of people, thereby constituting a major driver of humanitarian needs and threatening the effective enjoyment of human rights.[52]

Whereas the momentum for social sustainability and respect for human rights might currently have been reinforced by both the pandemic and the climate crisis, whether policy-makers succeed in harnessing this energy to drive real improvements for people remains to be seen. The development of a social taxonomy provides one such opportunity, but where the current taxonomy, focused on environmental objectives, was able to, for the most part, 'de-politicise' the design process through a science-based approach enabling broad support, the social taxonomy needs to find a different pathway to success. One suggested pathway to design social taxonomy that might enable broad consensus across countries and stakeholders is to ground it thoroughly in human rights instruments and methodologies thereby potentially rising above questions around differing social policy objectives across the Member States and potential criticism around the EU's competence in the context of social policy.

Human rights offer structure and content to the notion of 'social sustainability'. It offers standards and principles that will outlive the 2030 agenda, with its deadline fast approaching, and that have applicability beyond the EU – that is, it allows for discussion about the potential relevance of an EU taxonomy that includes social objectives beyond the internal market, for example, in the context of the International Platform on Sustainable Finance.[53]

Human rights might finally provide the EU with the key to ensuring policy coherence amongst the many files currently under development as it relates to

---

52 Council of the EU, Council Conclusions on Climate and Energy Diplomacy – Delivering on the external dimension of the European Green Deal, 5263/21, 25 January 2021, para. 4, available at https://www.consilium.europa.eu/media/48057/st05263-en21.pdf?utm_source=dsms-auto&utm_medium=email&utm_campaign=Council+adopts+conclusions+on+climate+and+energy+diplomacy, last accessed 31.03.2021.

53 European Commission, 'International Platform on sustainable finance', available at https://ec.europa.eu/info/business-economy-euro/banking-and-finance/sustainable-finance/international-platform-sustainable-finance_en, last accessed 31.03.2021.

making business and finance more sustainable, including in a social context.[54] In 2021 the Commission is expected to put forward a proposal for a sustainable corporate governance reform, which will include mandatory human rights due diligence obligation.[55] Further, in its February 2021 recommendations the European Financial Reporting Advisory Group (EFRAG) task force on non-financial reporting advised the Commission to base the inclusion of social in a revised non-financial reporting directive firmly on internationally recognised human rights.[56] Meaningful incorporation and alignment with human rights instruments and the UN Guiding Principles on Business and Human Rights in all such policy instruments that, through different regulatory approaches, are all meant to drive enhanced sustainability by business and financial market participant can help the EU navigate risks of patchwork policy developments, administrative burdens and a confused legislative audience.

This contribution has outlined the legal and policy developments in the EU when it comes to efforts to direct capital towards more sustainable business activities. It has provided considerations around what a human rights lens to these developments could entail, including when extending the sustainable finance taxonomy to social objectives. The authors have the privilege of participating in the European Sustainable Finance Platform established under the EU Taxonomy Regulation. However, the work in the platform on a social taxonomy was ongoing at the time of writing, and the final delivery of recommendations in that context may take a totally different route from what was alluded to in this contribution. Moreover, the European Commission may choose to propose legislation that departs from the approach eventually recommended by the platform. The discussions included in this contribution are therefore to be seen as an attempt to capture key questions and considerations around why and how the EU – and possibly actors beyond – could take a human rights-based approach to making finance sustainable.

---

54 Beyond the taxonomy, these include the sustainable finance reporting directive and the related regulatory technical standard, the sustainable corporate governance initiative and the review of the corporate sustainable reporting directive.

55 European Commission, 'Sustainable corporate governance', available at https://ec.europa.eu/info/law/better-regulation/have-your-say/initiatives/12548-Sustainable-corporate-governance, last accessed 31.03.2021.

56 European Financial Reporting Advisory Group, 'Proposal for a relevant and dynamic EU sustainability reporting standard-setting', 2021, pp. 7 and 20, available at https://www.efrag.org/Lab2, last accessed 31.03.2021.

HUMAN RIGHTS OF RESIDENTS IN LONG-TERM CARE FACILITIES DURING COVID-19

Saving Lives at the Cost of Deprivation of Rights?

Dragana Stöckel and Marina Pantelić*

ABSTRACT

The needs of vulnerable groups, such as the elderly and people with disabilities, are often overlooked in many societies, especially in the time of crisis, such as COVID-19. The ongoing epidemiological situation poses an increased risk of infection for these populations not only due to their health status and often pre-existing co-morbidities, but also because they often live in long-term care facilities (LTCFs). As early studies are documenting, the people living in the shared accommodation or in settings which require closer interpersonal interaction are at greater risk of acquiring COVID-19. Connected to these findings are the data showing that the majority of reported COVID-19 clusters and outbreaks are in health and social care settings, mainly in the LTCFs.[1] This result also corresponds with the confirmed COVID-19 deaths in LTCFs up to 5% and even 6% in some

* This contribution was supported by the Ministry of Education, Science and Technological Development of the Republic of Serbia (project's record no. 179076).

1 ECDC, 'Increase in fatal cases of COVID-19 among long-term care facility residents in the EU/EEA and the UK', 19.11.2020, p. 3, available at https://www.ecdc.europa.eu/sites/default/files/documents/Increase-fatal-cases-of-COVID-19-among-long-term-care-facility-residents.pdf, last accessed 18.03.2021.

countries of the European Union (EU, the Union) or of the European Economic Area (EEA) of all deceased LTCFs residents.[2] EU/EEA countries have been implementing different policies and measures to limit the spread of infections in LTCFs in order to prevent or minimise the high COVID-19 death rates. As the organisation and the operation of the LTCFs is the responsibility of various national authorities in EU/EEA countries, preparedness and response to the COVID-19 infections (the residents and the staff) is highly variable. While agencies like European Centre for Disease Prevention and Control are calling for 'addressing physical and mental wellbeing needs' in its recommended surveillance systems, the residents of LCTFs have been subjected to drastic isolation measures, compared not only to the general population but also to the same age groups living in the community. These restrictions, which are meant to protect the residents of LTCFs from the coronavirus, have also had severe negative impacts on their lives and family relations. By looking at the available national guidance for the LTCFs, the authors summarise the key strategies deployed, highlighting the main similarities and divergences between them. Through the lens of human rights and ethical principles, the authors examine the regulations in the LTCFs in EU/EEA countries, particularly concerning the impact of visiting bans, movement restrictions and social isolation on the human rights, dignity and quality of life of the LTC resident population.

1. INTRODUCTION

The long-term care (LTC) system is a highly fragmented policy field at the juncture of informal and formal care, health and social care services.[3] It is aimed at providing services to those with long-term care needs to ensure a life in accordance with fundamental human rights, freedoms and human dignity. Different actors are involved in the provision of LTC in EU/EEA countries, including public, private (profit and not-for-profit) and informal or unregistered providers. Therefore, the provision of LTC in the EU/EEA is very diverse in terms of organisation, funding mechanisms, access and availability. Furthermore, the LTC sector is often under the jurisdiction of different ministries, and depending on the type of facility, responsibilities are often distributed between national and sub-national authorities. Its complexity stems additionally from the combination of health and social care and the challenges in coordination between these two systems. Both LTC's organisational specificity and the long-standing problem of lack of public and political attention to LTC not only justifies its status as a 'Cinderella of the welfare state', but may also be rationales as to why in the early policy responses to the pandemic in many countries, LTC was left behind.

2 Ibid., p. 6.

3 K. Leichsenring, J. Bilings and H. Nies (eds.), *Long-term Care in Europe: Improving Policy and Practice*, Palgrave Macmillan, London 2013.

The pace of LTC services development across the member countries is highly varied. Although LTC in EU Member States has been subjected to several reforms over recent years, in most of the EU countries it is still under scrutiny.[4] The main directions of these reform processes have been made in areas of provision and enhancing of financial sustainability, improvement of access, availability and affordability of care, and transformation from residential towards community care which has involved the development of community-based services. Despite the identified trend towards prioritising both home care and community-based services, as well as highly present deinstitutionalisation processes in some countries (such as Nordic countries), residential care will indisputably remain the only option and reality for many European citizens.[5] Currently, in the EU/EEA countries and United Kingdom (UK), official data estimates that there are three and a half million residents in 62,000 of all LTCFs types,[6] representing approximately 0.7% of the total population.[7] A typical resident of LTCFs is in their eighth decade of life, their health status is characterised by multiple chronicle diseases and they requires support with their daily living activities.[8]

Although the COVID-19 pandemic has affected all areas of individuals' lives as well as all stages of their life cycle, the LTC sector has been put under additional pressure since the users of long-term care services were disproportionately impacted by the pandemic, particularly those living in the LTCFs. Accumulating evidence had documented this, showing that COVID-19-related deaths among residents of long-term care facilities account for 41% of all

---

4 S. Spasova, R. Baeten, S. Coster et al., 'Challenges in Long-term Care in Europe. A Study of National Policies', European Social Policy Network (ESPN) Report, 2018, available at https://ec.europa.eu/social/main.jsp?catId=738&langId=en&pubId=8128&furtherPubs=yes, last accessed 08.03.2021.

5 While Nordic countries report a decrease in the number of residential care institutions/beds due to an emphasis on the deinstitutionalisation process and priority on home- and community-based services, Southern and Eastern Europe, traditionally known as countries of informal care, shows a trend towards increasing number of LTC beds. See e.g. S. Spasova, R. Baeten, S. Coster et al. (2018), 'Challenges in long-term care in Europe', *supra* note 4.

6 Long-term care facilities include a variety of institutions such as nursing homes, skilled nursing facilities, assisted living facilities, residential facilities, and residential long-term care facilities. Long-term care facilities are a common name for all these institutions that focus on providing medical and assistive care to people who are unable to live independently in the community. In this contribution, the authors will not be dealing with home-based and community-based long-term care.

7 ECDC (2020), 'Increase in fatal cases of COVID-19 among long-term care facility residents in the EU/EEA and the UK', *supra* note 1, p. 3.

8 L-F. Low, K. Hinsliff-Smith, S. Sinha, et al., 'Safe visiting at care homes during COVID-19: A review of international guidelines and emerging practices during the COVID-19 pandemic', International Long-Term Care Policy Network Report, CPEC-LSE, 19.01.2021, available at https://ltccovid.org/wp-content/uploads/2021/01/Care-home-visiting-policies-international-report-19-January-2021-4.pdf, last accessed 25.05.2021.

COVID-19 related deaths, even though this subgroup represents less than 1% of the total population.[9]

Identifying and measuring the impact of COVID-19 on the residents of the LTCFs is important, since the COVID-19 pandemic seriously disrupted theorganisation and functioning of LTCFs. However, the severity of this impact was not the same in all countries. Even within particular regions like the EU/EEA there continue to be substantial differences between different countries depending on the availability and quality of data, as well as the operational definition of relevant concepts (such as 'long-term care facilities', how the data has been collected and what it covers).

Fully aware of the limitations of available data and the constraints for their direct comparison, the authors will focus on the specific policy responses in EU/EEA to protect the residents of LTCFs, and more specifically on the implications of COVID-19 related measures on the human rights of the residents in long-term care facilities. The objective is to identify the nature (timelines, 'severity', scope, etc.) of 'emergency measures' and their impact on the COVID-19-related mortality in LTCFs by identifying and evaluating diverse international experiences. The analysis included countries for which relevant data is already available, published by the European Centre for Disease Prevention and Control (ECDC), representing an official institution for gathering epidemiological data on COVID-19 in long-term care facilities for EU/EEA countries.

2. OUTBREAK OF COVID-19 IN LONG-TERM CARE FACILITIES

Since the spring of 2020, the EU has begun to record an increase in the number of deaths due to the COVID-19, comparing the average mortality rate of previous years in certain areas marked by high case numbers. According to the Eurostat, between January 2020 and March 2021, the EU experienced two complete cycles of excess mortality: the first between March and May 2020 (reaching a 25.1% excess rate in April); and the second between August 2020 and February 2021 (reaching a 40.6% excess rate in November 2020).[10] While the first wave of COVID-19 in the spring of 2020 mainly impacted older people, in the

9 A. Comas-Herrera, J. Zalakaín, E. Lemmon et al., 'Mortality associated with COVID-19 in care homes: international evidence', International Long-Term Care Policy Network Report, CPEC-LSE, 01.02.2021, available at https://ltccovid.org/wp-content/uploads/2021/02/LTC_COVID_19_international_report_January-1-February-1-2.pdf, last accessed 25.05.2021.

10 Eurostat Database, 'Excess mortality in 2020', statistics, 07.05.2021, available at https://ec.europa.eu/eurostat/statistics-explained/index.php?title=Excess_mortality_-_statistics, last accessed 25.05.2021.

second wave excess mortality was observed in other age groups, but this excess was primarily attributed to people aged 65 and older, especially those aged 75–84 years and 85 years and older.[11]

The ongoing health crisis poses an increased risk of infection and disease severity for certain population groups, in particular for those living in different health and social care settings.[12] It is not only demographic and epidemiological factors, like age, underlying health conditions and chronic comorbidities, that contribute to extreme vulnerability of this population – but the context where care is provided is also making this situation even more dramatic. In the context of the limited resilience of European healthcare systems to the pandemic, residents of long-term care facilities are often facing a higher risk of infection, lower preventive measures and inadequate resources to recover from COVID-19, as well as reduced access to essential health services.[13] LTCFs are high-risk environments due to several reasons, the most important being: (1) the virus can spread rapidly in enclosed environments where large numbers of people live and interact with each other; (2) the population of LTCFs is at higher risk than the general population because of their fragile and poorer health conditions and the existence of comorbidity; (3) older people are especially vulnerable to complications from the virus.

Evidence from numerous studies and national reports on the impact of COVID-19 on health and social care settings shows that this pandemic has disproportionally affected residents of long-term care facilities. Despite the significant differences between and within countries, almost half of the COVID-19-related deaths in Europe have been among residents of long-term care facilities,[14] with the death rate being higher than in the population of the same age living outside long-term care facilities.

---

11 Based on available data, the estimated mortality due to COVID-19 in people older than 76 years of age is reportedly 18%. See K. Dhama, S.K. Patel, R. Kumar et al., 'Geriatric Population During the COVID-19 Pandemic: Problems, Considerations, Exigencies, and Beyond', (2020) 8(574198), *Frontiers in Public Health*, p. 1. Available data from China differs slightly. Across all age groups an overall fatality rate of 2.3% has been reported, rising to 8.0% in patients aged 70–79 years old and even to 14.8% in those ≥ 80 years old. See Z. Wu and J. McGoogan, 'Characteristics of and Important Lessons From The Coronavirus Disease 2019 (COVID-19) Outbreak in China', (2020) 323(13), *JAMA*, pp. 1239–1242.

12 A. Comas-Herrera, J. Zalakaín, E. Lemmon et al. (2021), 'Mortality associated with COVID-19 in care homes: international evidence', *supra note* 9, p. 2.

13 WHO, 'Preventing and managing COVID-19 across long-term care services', Policy brief, 24.07.2020, p. 3, available at https://www.who.int/publications/i/item/WHO-2019-nCoV-Policy_Brief-Long-term_Care-2020.1, last accessed 18.03.2021.

14 Ibid., p. 2. According to available data on number of deaths associated with COVID-19 in 21 EU and non-EU countries, on average 46% are deaths of residents of care homes. See e.g. A. Comas-Herrera, J. Zalakaín, E. Lemmon, et al. (2021), 'Mortality associated with COVID-19 in care homes: international evidence', *supra note* 9.

One year after the World Health Organization (WHO) declared the COVID-19 pandemic, deaths among residents of LTCFs in several EU/EEA countries accounted for 4-57% of all COVID-19-related deaths (Table 1).[15] However, not all countries publish data on the number of COVID-19-related deaths among LTCF residents, which prevents a comprehensive comparison of data. The lack of available international statistics is further aggravated by differences between countries in terms of testing policies and procedures (especially in the first wave of the pandemic), criteria for recording deaths, an operating system for data collection (separate for data collection from hospitals and/or LTCFs or generic one) and the difference in the definition of the LTCFs.

Table 1. Surveillance data regarding COVID-19 cases and related deaths among long-term care facility residents in the EU/EEA, as of 31 March 2021

Country	Date of report	COVID-19 cases in LTCF residents	COVID-19-related deaths in LTCF residents	Total COVID-19-related deaths	% of total COVID-19-related deaths that were in LTCF residents
Austria	31/1/2021	18 589	3 380	7 653	44
Belgium	2/2/2021	–	12 055	21 135	57
Denmark	5/2/2021	3 654	892	2 216	40
Finland	8/2/2021	–	34% of 701	701	34
France	31/1/2021	153 219	31 795	76 057	42
Germany	8/2/2021	105 745	17 602	61 675	29
Greece	31/1/2021	1 512	228	5 796	4
Ireland	9/1/2021	9 113	1 172	2 344	50
Lithuania	5/2/2021	–	363	2 955	12
The Netherlands	7/2/ 2021	36 877	7 464	14 412	52
Slovenia	31/1/2021	12 035	1 978	3 752	53
Sweden	31/1/2021	15 534	4 961	11 773	42

Source: ECDC, March 2021 – https://www.ecdc.europa.eu/en/all-topics-z/coronavirus/threats-and-outbreaks/covid-19/prevention-and-control/LTCF-data.

The last available data for EU/EEA countries (Table 1) shows that Belgium had one of the highest reported rates of fatal COVID-19 cases among residents of LTCFs, with 12,055 COVID-19–related deaths, representing 57% of all COVID-19 deaths. Also, more than half of total COVID-19-related deaths were reported among residents of LTCFs in Slovenia (53%), the Netherlands (52%) and

15 ECDC, 'Surveillance data from public online national reports on COVID-19 in long-term care facilities', 2021, available at https://www.ecdc.europa.eu/en/all-topics-z/coronavirus/threats-and-outbreaks/covid-19/prevention-and-control/LTCF-data, last accessed 25.05.2021.

Ireland (50%). High incidence among LTCF residents was reported in Austria, Sweden, France, Denmark, Finland and Germany, accounting for 44-29% of total COVID-19-related deaths. In this period, the lowest numbers of reported fatal COVID-19 cases in the EU/EEA were in Lithuania and Greece, but available data for other EU/EEA countries is lacking.

To a significant extent, this data corresponds to that from the first wave of the pandemic, when the highest rates of COVID-19-related deaths among residents of LTCFs in EU/EEA countries were reported in Spain, Belgium, Ireland, France and Sweden.[16] As previous studies showed, the prevalence of fatal cases among the LTCFs population appears to correlate in the community, at the national and sub-national level;[17] hence, as long as there is community transmission of COVID-19, long-term care facilities will report a higher risk of infection among its residents and higher rates of COVID-19-related deaths.

3. MANAGING THE PANDEMIC IN LONG-TERM CARE FACILITIES

Despite such a high death toll in LTCFs, many national governments have been implementing the whole range of measures, from socio-economic and public-health measures aimed at limiting contacts, maintaining social distance restricting movement and even stricter lockdowns, to prevent or reduce the spread of infection. Those measures have been justified in order to maintain the functionality of health systems and the health of the population.

Looking at general movement restrictions/lockdown policies by epidemiological timeliness and stringency, Italy was classified as a country with a hard, but also late lockdown policy, while most other countries opted for moderate but also late lockdowns.[18] According to the same source, countries that applied a soft lockdown were Slovenia, Denmark, Latvia and Lithuania, while some countries – like Germany, Netherlands, Hungary and Romania – have adjusted their lockdown strategies from soft to moderate. Countries without lockdowns

---

16 ECDC Public Health Emergency Team, D. Kostas, L. Fonteneau et al., 'High impact of COVID-19 in long-term care facilities, suggestions for monitoring in EU/EEA, May 2020', (2020) 25(22), *Eurosurveillance*, p. 2.

17 ECDC (2020), 'Increase in fatal cases of COVID-19 among long-term care facility residents in the EU/EEA and the UK', *supra* note 1, p. 6.

18 According to Hale et al. (2020), soft lockdown is described in terms of a recommendation not to leave the house, moderate as a requirement not to leave the house, except essential grocery shopping, exercise and business and strict or hard lockdown represents not leaving the house with minimal exceptions such as an allowance to leave only once in a week or with special permissions, etc.; see T. Plümper and. E. Neumayer, 'Lockdown policies and the dynamics of the first wave of the Sars-CoV-2 pandemic in Europe', (2020), *Journal of European Public Policy*, p. 8.

were Norway, Sweden and Iceland, although they 'implemented a relatively strict anti-coronavirus regime, but avoided a formal lockdown'.[19]

Generally strict restrictions were even stricter in LTCFs in all member countries, justified under the veil of higher risk for virus transmission and more fatal consequences. In many countries, guidance on infection prevention and control for long-term care providers has been developed relatively late in the pandemic, covering only long-term care facilities, with no guidance available for providers of community-based care and family caregivers.[20] Additionally, the adoption of this guidance has not been followed by the development of mechanisms to ensure the implementation and monitoring of these guidelines. In the EU, the ECDC is the body responsible for setting this type of regulation. In May 2020, ECDC published a technical report regarding the surveillance of COVID-19 in the EU/EEA LTCFs.[21] This surveillance protocol has contained technical specifications for weekly reporting of aggregate national surveillance data on COVID-19 in long-term care facilities, covering mitigation action, infection rates and mortality.

The objectives of COVID-19 surveillance in LTCFs at the EU/EEA level are to detect COVID-19 cases among LTCF residents and staff early and to limit transmission through the appropriate implementation of infection prevention and control measures.The leading causes of an increased COVID-19 spread inside LTCFs are: (i) members of the staff working while contagious; (ii) under-qualified or inadequately trained staff; (iii) staff working in multiple facilities; (iv) shortage of personal protective equipment (PPE); and (v) limited testing. As it is stated in ECDC's guidance for infection prevention and control,[22] to infection prevention and control in all LTCFs administrative measures, physical distancing, hand hygiene and the appropriate use of PPE are central.

Although data is still emerging, evidence from different national reports on the impact of COVID-19 on LTCFs shows that most of the countries implemented a similar set of measures aiming to provide guidance, strengthen medical support, prevent the spread of the virus, minimise infection and support the long-term care sector by increasing working staff and funding.

As is well documented, one of the first protective measures adopted in almost all countries has been restricting visitors to long-term care facilities. As early as

---

19 Ibid., p. 8.

20 WHO (2020), 'Preventing and managing COVID-19 across long-term care services', *supra* note 13, p. 19.

21 ECDC, 'Surveillance of Covid-19 at long-term care facilities in the EU/EEA', 10.05.2020, available at https://www.ecdc.europa.eu/sites/default/files/documents/covid-19-long-term-care-facilities-surveillance-guidance.pdf, last accessed 23.06.2021.

22 ECDC, 'Infection prevention and control and preparedness for COVID-19 in healthcare settings', 09.02.2021, available at https://www.ecdc.europa.eu/sites/default/files/documents/Infection-prevention-and-control-in-healthcare-settings-COVID-19_6th_update_9_Feb_2021.pdf, last accessed 23.06.2021.

the first wave of the pandemic, residents of LTCFs were isolated in facilities for many weeks, on end, unable to socialise with other residents or receive visits from their family and friends, resulting in the severe restriction of social contact and change in their daily routines.[23]

After the first wave, many governments lifted some measures, and the populace became more relaxed and/or careless. The second wave, which started to roll over Europe during autumn 2020, along with travel restrictions, increased testing and quarantine regimes for incoming passengers, initiated a more moderate version of lockdowns across EU countries. Having acknowledged insufficient time distance and reliable data, it can be noted that measures implemented during this wave were to some extent milder. After a period of a strict ban on social contacts and restrictions on movement, with the recognition of the negative effects of these restrictive measures, the great majority of countries allowed visits to LTCFs, while respecting strict requirements regarding the number of visitors allowed, as well as the circumstances for the visits.[24] In many Member States (controlled) outdoor visits were available along with maintaining the physical distance and all necessary infection prevention measures (such as wearing masks, hand washing) or so-called 'window visitation', while in-door visits were still mostly prohibited. For example, LTCFs in Germany and the Netherlands have enabled their residents to see and speak with family members and relatives by using virus-proof containers, garden sheds, telephone boxes or other solutions.[25] Also, as the initial peak of the pandemic was subsiding in most Member States, LTCFs have introduced innovative solutions, such as technical tools that enable virtual contact with their families and friends. Although these new measures tended to be innovative and more humane, they did not prevent residents' distress. Furthermore, in some countries (such as France, Denmark, Sweden, etc.) public health authorities or directors of LTCFs could decide on a case-by-case basis, based on assessed health risk, national guidelines and recommendations.

Despite these measures, high COVID-19-related mortality rates among residents of LTCFs indicate that the LTC sector has largely failed to protect its beneficiaries.[26] The strategies for disease prevention are very often copied from

---

23 WHO (2020), 'Preventing and managing COVID-19 across long-term care services', *supra* note 13, p. 32.

24 These requirements included the number of visitors allowed, where the visit is going to be held (in or outdoors) and enforcement of additional infection prevention and control measures (usage of face masks).

25 M. Langins, N. Curry, K. Lorenz-Dant et al., 'The COVID-19 Pandemic and Long-Term Care: What Can We Learn From The First Wave About How To Protect Care Homes?' (2020) 26(2), *Eurohealth*, p. 80.

26 Measuring the impact of the pandemic by incident infection and mortality rates, as the most frequent way of measuring its impact, is affected by case definition, whether they are expressed as trends over time or cumulatively, but also depending on the extent of testing due to the country's willingness to test and/or their test availability.

one country to another, without sensitivity to local contexts and reflections on needs and threats. For instance, a closer look at visiting policies in LTCFs in Belgium and Denmark, the countries with the latest available data but with differences in the reported rates, can give us insight into applied strategies and their effects despite some limitations noted in their interpretations.

Table 2. Visiting policies in selected countries

Country	First COVID-19 wave	The period between the waves	Second COVID-19 wave
Belgium	Prohibited visits (from 10–13* March until 23 April – 18 May*)	Number of visitors per resident depending on the national measures in the populations (number of contacts allowed) and regional measures in LTCFs;	One visitor per resident, the same person for 15 days. Visit to be held at dedicated spaces Brussels: only essential visits are permitted.
Denmark	Prohibited visits, with exception only for essential visits (from 8 March – 10 June)	Primarily outdoor visits Visits to LTCFs allowed under specific conditions (only for 1–2 regular visitors)	Visits to LTCFs allowed under specific conditions

*depending on the region
Source: Authors' overview based on data published by the European Centre for Disease Prevention and Control (2020).

As can be noted in Table 2, both countries put visitors bans in place relatively early and almost simultaneously. Likewise, both countries had the most rigorous measures during the first wave. Although this ban lasted longer in Denmark, some exceptions, such as essential visits, were allowed. Policies following the onset of the first wave were very similar, and visits took place mostly outside the institution, with Denmark enabling visits in this phase. The second wave in terms of visiting policies – although very similar in both countries – was slightly more relaxed in Denmark, especially compared to the Belgian capital, where only essential visits were allowed. The Danish parliament went further and provided municipalities additional funds to develop solutions (like digital technologies or reconstructing the space so as to facilitate visits) which would enable residents of LTCFs to maintain social relations and quality of life in general.[27] Total COVID-19-related deaths in LTCF residents were 17% higher in Belgium than in Denmark (although strategies of the two countries did not significantly differ); moreover, Denmark had a somewhat milder approach. This implies that unselective visitor bans and social isolation jeopardised the human rights of the elderly in LTCFs without succeeding in saving lives, as initially intended and communicated. There were obviously some other factors

[27] M. Langins, N. Curry, K. Lorenz-Dant et al., 'The COVID-19 Pandemic and Long-Term Care: What Can We Learn from the First Wave about how to Protect Care Homes?', *supra* note 25, p. 77.

that contributed to such high death rates, such as a lack of personal protective equipment delays both in testing and diagnostic and implementation of protocols regarding isolation, *inter alia*.[28]

In most of the LTCFs across EU/EEA there are still some restrictions in place, but they are currently slightly milder compared to those in previous COVID-19 waves.

4. EMERGING COVID-19-RELATED HUMAN RIGHTS CHALLENGES: BETWEEN SAVING LIVES AND VIOLATING THE HUMAN RIGHTS OF LTCF RESIDENTS

As previously stated, the extent of measures taken as a response to the outbreak of COVID-19 in LTCFs has been considerably varying across the countries, with the most restrictive measures being implemented during the first wave. As a result of insufficient crisis preparedness for the pandemic, the lack of knowledge about the virus, and fear over outbreaks in LTCFs, many LTCFs across the EU/EEA put into force highly restrictive protocols. Although the adoption of restrictive measures has been justified by the states on the grounds of the protection of life and health, some of these 'emergency measures' significantly impacted fundamental human rights and democratic principles.

These rights and principles became even more fragile in times of crisis, such as COVID-19, especially when they have to be guaranteed to the most disadvantaged and vulnerable groups in the society, such as LTCF resident population. This situation is further aggravated by the fact that there is a lack of legally binding instruments and insufficient visibility, although all human rights standards can and should be indirectly applicable to the residents of LTCFs as well. For instance, even though all human rights conventions also apply to older people, they are not explicitly recognised under any current international human rights laws. Despite some of the existing commitments,[29] the lack of a

[28] Since the beginning of the pandemic, we have witnessed media reports on the causes for outbreaks in LTCFs, most often in institutions for the elderly, mostly as a result of lack of protective equipment, delays in test results and inadequate procedure for isolation of suspected COVID-19 cases – and even staff pleading for external control. See V. Cornette, 'ÜberallMängel: Corona-ProtokolleinesAltenheim-Mitarbeiter', *BR24*, 12.01.2021, available at https://www.br.de/nachrichten/bayern/ueberall-maengel-corona-protokoll-eines-altenheim-mitarbeiters,SLmryOM, last accessed 27.05.2021.

[29] An example of such commitments exclusively dedicated to older people, although it dates back to 2002, is the Madrid International Plan of Action on Ageing (MIPAA). Although it is advocating for integration of old people's needs and rights in national policies, it is relying only on governments' readiness for its implementation as it is not legally binding. Evaluation of its effects by the UN Independent Expert on the Enjoyment of all Human Rights by Older

legally binding obligation on governments to realise the rights of older persons increases their invisibility under international law and often leads to the violation of their rights. Restrictions of fundamental rights in such unregulated areas, like the LTC sector, have produced serious problems in their implementation, especially in the LTCFs. During the pandemic, problems caused by the lack of legislation has intensified and culminated,[30] pointing at the necessity of this area being more regulated.

Dispersion of the standards that protect older people's human rights makes it even more difficult to identify ones that are relevant to older people in LTCFs or people seeking LTC. At the same time, there are some standards, which are not referring directly to the elderly but still significantly relevant, as is the case with the United Nations Convention on the Rights of Persons with Disabilities (UNCRPD), which bear in mind the prevalence of people with disability in performing activities of daily living (ADL) and thus becoming itself a party to the CRPD.[31]

Moreover, the adoption of the UNCRPD was a breakthrough for the rights of persons with disabilities. It entered into force in the EU in 2010, being at the same time the first human rights convention that the EU concluded.[32] This legally binding human rights treaty in the EU found its operationalisation in the European disability strategy 2010–2020, and later in the Union of equality – Strategy for the rights of persons with disability 2021–2030.

The European disability strategy 2010–2020, as the policy framework for the implementation of UNCRPD at the EU level, reflected the main components

---

Persons pointed very weak application in national legislative and policies across almost all EU countries. National reports are available at https://digitallibrary.un.org/search?ln=en&as=0&p=subjectheading:[UN.+Human+Rights+Council.+Independent+Expert+on+the+Enjoyment+of+All+Human+Rights+by+Older+Persons+--+Recommendations].Those critiques were followed by AGE Platform Europe, a European network of non-profit organisations of and for people aged 50+, stressing 'a lost opportunity to trigger policy change in the field of aging and, ultimately, to improve the situation of older people on the ground. It had failed to address the full spectrum of civil, political, social, economic and cultural rights'. See Age Platform Europe, 'AGE Platform Europe Contribution to the 2017 Review of the Madrid International Plan of Action on Ageing (MIPAA)', Policy Statement, 2016, available at https://www.age-platform.eu/sites/default/files/AGE%20MIPAA%20Review%202016_0.pdf, last accessed 21.03.2021.

30 Human Rights Centre, 'The impacts of the coronavirus pandemic on the implementation of fundamental and human rights – Recommendations by the Human Rights Delegation', Recommendations, 2020, available at https://tbinternet.ohchr.org/Treaties/CCPR/Shared%20Documents/FIN/INT_CCPR_NHS_FIN_44416_E.pdf, last accessed 27.05.2021.

31 According to the newer studies, ADL disability and cognitive impairments are observed – depending on sex – in between 68.0% (for females) and 81.3% (for males) of residents in nursing homes. See G. Onder, I. Carpenter, H. Finne-Soveri et al., 'Assessment of Nursing Home Residents in Europe: The Services and Health for Elderly in Long-term Care (SHELTER) Study', (2012) 12(5), *BMC Health Services Research*, pp. 1–10.

32 All Member States ratified the Convention by 2018.

of this convention. Although the past decade(s) brought some progress, mostly in relation to the improved accessibility by developing solid legal framework in this field many areas are still not fully or sufficiently covered or are overlooked.[33] One of the key areas where the improvements had been necessary was social protection, aiming at the promotion of decent living conditions for persons with disability, equality (seen as combating discrimination on the grounds of disability) and health viewed as equal access to health services and related facilities. Despite the overall progress that was made in fulfilling some of the objectivesregarding the full participation, one of the key obstacles that still requires special attention is a 'limited data on collection on life conditions in residential institutions'.[34]

Using the results of the European disability strategy 2010–2020, the European Commission developed the new strategy – *Strategy for the Rights of Persons* with *Disabilities 2021–2030*, primarily aiming to protect the persons with disabilities from any form of discrimination and violence. Furthermore, it clearly recognises that 'the COVID-19 crisis revealed weak spots in health systems, in particular regarding persons with disabilities living in institutions with limited access to emergency and intensive care'.[35] Additionally, 'the Commission calls on Member States and all EU institutions and agencies to take needs of persons with disabilities into consideration when designing, implementing and monitoring policies, legislation and funding programmes through targeted action and mainstreaming'.[36] Combating discrimination based on different basis, among which are disability and age, has been already embedded in the Treaty on the Functioning of the European Union (TFEU) (Article 10), giving the power to the EU to take the action to address such discrimination (Article 19).

Despite all these commitments and obligations, it seems that the pandemic has additionally increased the discrimination against the elderly and persons with disability living in the residential institutions. Preventive and protective measures that were taken by governments against the coronavirus not only reinforced it and widened the abyss between them and rest of population, but they were also compared to the same population using LTC in home- or community-based settings. Therefore, increasingly frequent statements that the

---

33 For example, the European Accessibility Act, Directive 2016/2102 on the accessibility of the websites and mobile applications of public sector bodies, regulations on the rights for travellers with disabilities or reduced mobility, etc.

34 European Commission, 'Commission Staff Working Document Evaluation Of The European Disability Strategy 2010–2020', 27.11.2020, available at https://eur-lex.europa.eu/legal-content/EN/TXT/?uri=CELEX:52020SC0289, last accessed 23.06.2021.

35 European Commission, Union of Equality: Strategy of the Rights of Persons with Disabilities 2021–2030, COM(2021) 101 final 03.03.2021, p. 19.

36 Ibid., p. 25.

current 'health crisis has developed into a human rights crisis' point to the need to take stock of how LTCFs in the EU/EEA have fared in terms of the human rights of people living in these institutions.[37]

During the pandemic, most of the measures were developed and adopted in an *ad-hoc* manner: quickly and without serious consideration of the underlying human rights principles. The inviolability of human dignity (Article 1), freedoms such as respect for private and family life (Article 8), religion (Article 10) and equality in terms of prohibition of discrimination based on any ground, recognised in the EU Charter of Fundamental Rights, were particularly vulnerable to neglect when measures to prevent COVID-19 outbreaks in LTCFs were being conceived. Article 25 in particular sets out the rights for the elderly to lead a life of dignity and independence and to participate in social and cultural life. In addition, Article 26 recognises the right of persons with disabilities 'to benefit from measures designed to ensure their independence, social and occupational integration and participation in the life of the community'.[38]

Visiting and contact bans and/or restrictions, cancellation of joint meals and activities and relocations, *inter alia*, significantly restricted freedoms and human rights of the residents of LTCFs. One of the most restrictive measures in LTCFs, as well as the most disputable one from the perspective of human rights, was the visitors bans. This restriction was given the euphemistic term 'voluntary lockdowns' in many countries and LTCFs, although the residents who are affected by this measure were not consulted. Although such bans could have been reasonable, given that residents of LTCFs are at a greater risk of requiring hospitalisation or dying if diagnosed with COVID-19, especially given pre-existing co-morbidities, many fundamental rights and freedoms of this population were severely violated. Visiting bans led to restrictions on the right to family life and personal freedom, not only of the residents but also of their family members. The right to enjoy family and friendships through regular contacts was impossible to realise. While visits to elderly family members were only strongly discouraged in official regulations issued by the countries/relevant authorities, many LTCFs opted at the very beginning of the pandemic for complete visiting bans.

Furthermore, residents' participation in the decision-making process on the matters that affect them directly or indirectly is not only a desirable feature of care

---

37 Council of Europe Commissioner for Human Rights, 'Protecting the right to health through inclusive and resilient health care for old', Issue Paper, 2021, p. 5, available at https://rm.coe.int/protecting-the-right-to-health-through-inclusive-and-resilient-health-/1680a177ad, last accessed 28.05.2021.

38 European Union, *Charter of Fundamental Rights of the European Union*, 26 October 2012, 2012/C 326/02, available at https://eur-lex.europa.eu/legal-content/EN/TXT/?uri=CELEX:12012P/TXT, last accessed 01.06.2021.

and social services or one of its essential components, it is also an imperative and an obligation.[39] Regarding this issue, the UNCRPD states that '[...] State Parties shall closely consult with and actively involve persons with disabilities [...]'.[40] At the same time, family, relatives and friends were deprived of participation in their care, both planning and monitoring, and hence were unable to spot the insufficient or inadequate care. Those factors represented serious threats to the wellbeing of LTCF residents. Therefore, the residents of the LTCFs and/or the representative bodies such as family members/guardians had to be consulted in appropriate ways and should have participated in decision-making processes prior to introduction of measures.

Fundamental rights and principles are preconditions for a decent quality of life, making those policies in the LTCFs during the COVID-19 pandemic even more questionable. This is not only a matter of human rights, but also of ethics of care.

Extensive scientific literature confirms that both social isolation and loneliness are associated with increased mortality. However, the effects of social isolation are likely to be more relevant to mortality,[41] especially in the older population. The health effects of loneliness and social isolation extend even beyond mortality as they can significantly influence the risk of developing some health conditions and the overall quality of life. Many studies have already shown that residents of LTCFs developed different mental health problems during the pandemic such as depression, anxiety and worsening dementia, *inter alia*, while undergoing strict social isolation. It is suggested, thus, that social isolation should be applied only when a person is infected or has been in close contact with an infected person.[42]

Movement restrictions in general, regardless of whether they are in the form of social isolation or quarantine, can have adverse effects not only on mental but also on physical health. Procoagulant states, sarcopenia and functional impairment are only some of the health conditions connected to immobility and are associated with COVID-19.[43] Increased risk of cardiovascular disorders and morbidities is also documented as connected to poor social relations.[44]

---

39 P. Nykänen, 'Shared Decision Making in the Social Services? Reasons to Consider when Choosing Methods for Service User Participation', (2019) 26(2), *Journal of Evaluation in Clinical Practice*, pp. 1–6.

40 UN, Convention on the Rights of Persons with Disabilities, available at https://www.un.org/development/desa/disabilities/convention-on-the-rights-of-persons-with-disabilities.html, last accessed 26.05.2021.

41 A. Steptoe, A. Shankar, P. Demakakos et al., 'Social isolation, loneliness, and all-cause mortality in older men and women', (2013) 110(15), *PNAS*, pp. 5797–5801.

42 H. Blain, Y. Rolland, J.M.G.A. Schols et al., 'August 2020 Interim EuGMS guidance to prepare European Long-Term Care Facilities for COVID-19', (2020) 11, *European Geriatric Medicine*, pp. 899–913.

43 I. Aprahamian and M. Cesari, 'Geriatric Syndromes and SARS-COV-2: More Than Just Being Old', (2020) 9(3), *The Journal of Frailty and Aging*, pp. 127–129.

44 N.K. Valtorta, M. Kanaan, S. Gilbody et al, 'Loneliness and Social Isolation as Risk Factors for Coronary Heart Disease and Stroke: Systematic Review and Meta-Analysis of Longitudinal Observational Studies', (2016) 102(13), *Heart*, pp. 1009–1016.

Those shielding measures applied in LTCFs, especially during the first wave, have had an intense impact on the physical and cognitive status of particularly vulnerable groups of LTCF residents, such as people living with dementia, thereby rendering them even more vulnerable. Numerous studies confirmed the association between the increased risk of dementia and cognitive decline in older people, on the one hand, and high levels of loneliness,[45] low levels of social contacts with family and friends and participation in community groups on the other.[46] Given that 57% of residents from 3,052 general nursing homes, residential homes and mixed facilities in 24 countries in the EU/EEA and the UK in 2016–2017 had cognitive impairment,[47] adverse effects can be expected especially for this subgroup of LTCF residents. Even the easing of measures and introduction of some innovative concepts such as the use of technology for keeping in contact with family is counterproductive for many residents with dementia, who often found these interactions confusing and frustrating.

Besides implications on the health status of elderly individuals in LTCFs and the more vulnerable subgroups, such as old people with dementia, one further dimension which should be considered is the longitudinal – that is, the mid- and long-term impacts of such measures. As documented in some cohort studies,[48] older adults who report social isolation and loneliness show poorer cognitive function four years later. For some residents of LTCFs, prolonged isolation may even be deadly.[49]

In addition, the implied measures also affected family members of the LTCF residents who lived away from them. The staff of LTCFs reported decreased patience, increased complaints about the care provided and about being unable to supervise that care and available rehabilitation offers, *inter alia*. At the same time, the care workers in LTCFs have already been overburdened due to the rising care needs and shortage of care workers in facilities. The emphasis on priority to treating COVID-19 patients has led many countries to suspend non-urgent treatment and to limit access to certain health services and medical staff. This situation has significantly hampered elderly and persons with disabilities due to their underlying health conditions that require continuous medical treatment.

---

45 Even by 50%, according to Kuiper et al. (2015) cited in: National Academies of Sciences, Engineering, and Medicine, *Social Isolation and Loneliness in Older Adults: Opportunities for the Health Care System*, The National Academies Press, Washington DC 2020, p. 18.

46 Ibid., p. 18.

47 ECDC (2020), 'Increase in fatal cases of COVID-19 among long-term care facility residents in the EU/EEA and the UK', *supra* note 1, p. 8.

48 J.T. Cacioppo and S. Cacioppo, 'Older adults reporting social isolation or loneliness show poorer cognitive function 4 years later', (2014), 17(2), *Evidence Based Nursing*, pp. 59–60.

49 J. Abbasi, 'Social Isolation – The Other COVID-19 Threat in Nursing Homes', (2020), *JAMA*, pp. 1–2.

5. HOW TO FIND THE RIGHT 'MEASURE' OF MEASURES?

Although Europe (and the whole world) suffered and has still been suffering greatly, especially in the early pandemic stages, the impact varied among different countries. At the same time, almost all national governments opted for a wide range of very restrictive measures in many areas. These measures and restrictions have differed from one country to another depending on the wave of the COVID-19 pandemic as well as their implications and outcomes not only at macro-level but also on the level of certain groups of populations. One year on, although still far from over, it can be noted that some countries responded at least slightly better than others due to numerous underlying factors but any definitive assessment would be premature, especially now when a large part of European countries are at the start of a third coronavirus wave as of March 2021.

Nevertheless, the ongoing health crisis has brought to the fore ethical and legal debate on violations of human rights, especially its impact on the social distribution of justice and actualisation of fundamental rights of particular social groups.[50] The failures of policy and practice in ensuring human rights, among others right to life and health, were particularly evident when it comes to LTC resident population. The pandemic ignited the conflict between the responsibility to protect the people residing in the LTCFs and keeping their environment safe on the one hand, and professional, ethical and legal principles to respect autonomy, dignity, participation and freedom of the residents on the other.

The organisational specificity of the setting related to communal living and intensive interpersonal interaction in meeting care needs makes the spread of COVID-19 within LTCFs difficult to prevent and manage. Therefore, it was completely understandable that the LTCFs could not risk a virus outbreak, especially since the majority of the LTCF residents are under greater risk for a variety of severe physical and mental health conditions, including cognitive decline, such as people with dementia who are at a higher risk of contracting the virus and having higher mortality.[51] But, although the analyses show that 'the calendar date of the lockdown and the population-standardised number of known infections are positively correlated',[52] in case of lockdowns of LTCFs in

---

[50] For instance, only in Germany, although it has never been declared state of emergency since the beginning of the pandemic, as it was a case in some other Member States (such as Hungary, etc.) according to the German Association of Judges, German constitutional and administrative courts have received over 10,000 urgent applications and lawsuits related to the general restrictions during the pandemic.

[51] The proportion of fatal cases of residents of LTCFs with dementia ranges from an estimated 19% in Italy to 31% in the UK; See ECDC (2020), 'Increase in fatal cases of COVID-19 among long-term care facility residents in the EU/EEA and the UK', *supra* note 1, p. 8.

[52] T. Plümper and E. Neumayer (2020), 'Lockdown policies and the dynamics of the first wave of the Sars-CoV-2 pandemic in Europe', *supra* note 18, p. 7.

most of the EU countries and the introduction of very severe restrictions for their residents and visitors, it can be noted that the duration of social isolation did not positively affect the mortality rate.[53]

With acknowledgments of all limitations in data interpretation, such as the lack of cross-country comparable data, the lack of nationally representative empirical data and their uncertainty, as mass testing was still not possible and because of lack of precise rates' measures, the restrictions and measures enforced especially in first months of the pandemic were causing human rights violations of people living in the LTCFs across EU/EAA. The growing body of evidence shows that restrictive measures that EU/EEA states have introduced at the onset of the pandemic have had a disproportionately greater devastating effect on the elderly, endangering their autonomy and freedom of choice.

Not only was the right to participate in all decisions concerning their living conditions in the institution neglected but also one of the main principles in social welfare services, i.e. service user involvement/participation. Even governmental policies, emergency measures, and guidelines for infection prevention and control, adopted later on the pandemic, did not consider the participation and inclusion of older persons and their representatives in the discussion and decision-making process.

The COVID-19 crisis, unfortunately, showed a lack of respect for LTCF residents' private and family life and negligence of dignity. Even the basic right to freedom of movement and related to that, the obligation to only lawful, proportionate, and necessary restrictions has been constantly violated. At the same time, these restrictions have not only affected numerous rights but have also had significant negative consequences on human well-being, especially on this population who is living alone or away from their families and friends. It is widely recognised that movement restrictions have had an enormous impact on the well-being of both the residents of long-term care facilities and their families. Conducted measures taken to protect residents in LTCFs have led to their increased social isolation. Documented and potential health and psychological consequences, directly or indirectly brought on by COVID-19, are having devastating effects, not to mention dying in unfamiliar surroundings without seeing any family member for weeks or months before death. 'Collective decisions, such as the restriction of visits, have had a major impact on residents and caregivers' quality of life, causing much grief, especially at the end of life'.[54]

---

53 Sweden stands out because although it had some recommendations on maintaining interpersonal distancing, it rejected many restrictions imposed elsewhere by choosing a different strategy from which was expected, at least at the beginning, to achieve the goal of herd immunity.

54 M. Inzitari, E. Risco, M. Cesari et al., 'Nursing Homes and Long Term Care After COVID-19: A New Era?' (2020) 24(10), *The Journal of Nutrition, Health and Aging*, pp. 1042–1046.

Therefore, it would not be exaggerating to say that during the pandemic the residents in LTCFs did not have any choice and control over care and services which are adapted to their specific needs and health condition. In order to be able to conclude on all effects of measures implemented during the COVID-19 pandemic, follow up studies must be conducted in years to come as this would be the only way to have a coherent and comprehensive assessment on all the devastating effects of the pandemic on the status of human rights and health conditions on LTC resident population across the globe. The difficulties in developing a necessary balance between best practices for infection prevention/control in LTCFs and rights and autonomy of the people who live in them re-emphasised the need for authentic, human rights-based culture inside this institutional setting.[55]

Although the limitation of human rights and freedoms in the time of crisis may only be temporary, the inevitable question is how to justify the lockdowns of one subcategory of the population – residents of long-term care facilities, but at the same time not the same age group living in their homes? Moreover, it should be kept in mind that life in the institution (retirement or nursing home), even at an old age, although not often, can be out of choice because a person is not willing to live alone in the private household and not only because of need for intensive care. Can the concern for the public health as a common good and the severity of the danger be above the principles of non-discrimination? Movement restrictions, visitors' bans, and social isolation were merely based on the place of LTC provision (residential/home/community-based) across most of the EU/EEA countries wherefore it seems to be the only division criterion or put in other words, the basis for discrimination.

The representation of the COVID-19 outbreak as 'the problem of older adults' in the public discourse by portraying older people either as a threat, and a burden or as a vulnerable minority, has led to direct age division in societies and potential discrimination on the grounds of age.[56] As various documents reported, this was particularly evident in the policy-making process and discriminatory practices within the LTCFs, since some policy measures have been implemented exclusively using the chronological age criterion violating, in particular, the rights of the elderly.[57]

This health crisis showed that there is no one-size-fits-all solution, but rather privileges individual approach, not only at the state level, but also based on

---

55 H. Meenan, N. Rees and I. Doron (eds.), *Human Rights and Residential Care for Older Persons: International Perspectives on a Right's Culture*, Routledge, London 2016.

56 J. Ayalon, 'There is nothing new under the sun: Ageism and intergenerational tension in the age of the COVID-19 outbreak', (2020) 32(10), *International Psychogeriatrics*, pp. 1221–1224.

57 Age Platform Europe, 'COVID-19: Older Persons' Rights Must Be Equally Protected During the Pandemic', Press Release, 02.04.2020, available at https://www.age-platform.eu/coronavirus-covid-19, last accessed 21.05.2021.

the individual needs and characterises of the user groups and the social care institution itself. Acknowledging the necessity of fast response to the crisis, such an approach could be manoeuvred, followed by prior careful measures' analyses and questioning whether the particular measure is the only way of achieving the set goals, especially when they are aimed at the restriction of human rights. Therefore, it should be considered whether: (1) the measures are suitable for achieving the goal, (2) there are less drastic ones but with the same impact, and (3) the restrictions are not in balance with the intended goal (so-called appropriateness).[58] When restricting human rights, the individual's or groups' situation should be taken into account at all those three levels of proportionality to ensure that particular measures/decisions do not have discriminatory effects, as it is in the case of LTCFs residents.[59] Even when applied, restrictions must be the last resort and should be lifted as soon as possible. Too strong focus on the infection protection stood in the way of a comprehensive and differentiated design of new regulations.

At the implementation level and in terms of managing the COVID-19 crisis and preventing the outbreak in LTCFs, instead of the question of life or death, the main argument should be a comprehensive risk assessment which should include variables such as health status/condition of resident(s) and interrelating factors such as individual, environmental, social, cultural, etc. Furthermore, as available data shows,[60] a very strong correlation between the size and degree of occupancy of LTCFs and likelihood of having a COVID-19 positive resident, when designing the strategies those identified characteristics of LTCFs which are associated with COVID-19 incidence should be appraised. Also, the protocols have to be much more fine-tuned and context-dependent, representing the specific local, regional and national settings and institutional arrangements. At the same time, personal, societal and professional norms and views have to be incorporated when designing the measures which affect the quality of life of the users. It can be concluded that restrictiveness was not a significant predictor of the success of strategy against COVID-19 and that timeliness could be of higher importance. That coincides with some findings that there is no major advantage of the combination of early and hard lockdown over a similarly early but milder.[61]

---

58 See O. Lepsius, 'Vom Niedergang grundrechtlicher Denkkategorien in der Corona-Pandemie', *Verfassungsblog*, 06.04.2020, available at https://verfassungsblog.de/vom-niedergang-grundrechtlicher-denkkategorien-in-der-corona-pandemie/, last accessed 05.03.2021.

59 Deutsches Institut Für Menschenrechte, 'Menschenrechte Älterer auch in der Corona-Pandemie wirksam schützen', Stellungnahme, 2020, p. 4, available at https://www.institut-fuer-menschenrechte.de/fileadmin/Redaktion/Publikationen/Stellungnahme_Menschenrechte_AElterer_auch_in_der_Corona-Pandemie_wirksam_schuetzen.pdf, last accessed 11.03.2021.

60 H.R. Abrams, L. Loomer, A. Gandhi, et al., 'Characteristics of U.S. Nursing Homes With COVID-19 Cases', (2020) 68(8), *Journal of American Geriatrics Society*, pp. 1–10.

61 T. Plümper and E. Neumayer (2020), 'Lockdown policies and the dynamics of the first wave of the Sars-CoV-2 pandemic in Europe', *supra* note 18, p. 17.

Besides the above-mentioned factors, the strategies should be balanced with the critical need for the support provided by families or close others and regularly adjusted with the incidence rate in the area surrounding the LTCFs and the situation within the institution in terms of suspected or confirmed COVID-19 cases.[62] Therefore, timely testing and protocols for isolation after being in contact with another resident diagnosed with COVID-19 are imperative. Despite exceptional circumstances, such as the coronavirus pandemic, this current health crisis has brought up and intensified already existing problems in the LTC sector in general and particularly in LTC residential institutions, such as lack of staff.[63] One of the regulations issued by German Robert-Koch Institute was stating that in emergency cases even the infected staff can still look after also infected residents using FFP2 masks at special wards.[64]

At the same time there is a hope that this crisis could also have positive impact and open up the opportunity to tackle the existing problems, prevent present mistakes and improve the preparedness of LTC for coming times. The discourse on structural and financial solutions should incorporate also human rights dimension for people living in LTCFs not only in their everyday life but also in crisis or unpredictable situations and their equal treatment as for people living in the community. The central goal of care should not only be a maintenance of physical/mental health but also protection of the autonomy of the people who must never be just the objects of care, no matter on their health conditions and/or limitations.

Given that this will probably not be the last pandemic and the duration of the current one, it is important to address all those issues because of the implications on the policy. So far, national governments have not had clear and well tailored strategies in combating the pandemic but rather ones that arise from panic. Hence going forward well informed, evidence-based and well-planned measures are required to assure that the implemented policies and measures are sensitive to the various and individual needs and rights of different population groups to ensure that no one is neglected.

---

62 See H. Blain, Y. Rolland, J.M.G.A. Schols et al. (2020) 'August 2020 Interim EuGMS guidance to prepare European Long-Term Care Facilities for COVID-19', *supra* note 42, pp. 899–913.

63 The formal care sector seems not to be too attractive to potential workers as its image is eroded by the negative perception of working conditions, primarily described in terms of a stressful working environment, a lack of clearly defined carrier paths, high rates of turnover, limited career mobility and the lack of opportunities for personal and professional development and lifelong learning. See e.g. EU Skills Panorama, 'Skills for Social Care', Analytical Highlight', 2014, available at https://skillspanorama.cedefop.europa.eu/sites/default/files/EUSP_AH_SocialCare_0.pdf, last accessed 10.03.2021.

64 In German media, the controversial document issued by Robert Koch InstituteIt has been frequently stressed. See e.g. RKI, 'Optionen zum Management von Kontaktpersonen unter Personal der kritischen Infrastruktur bei Personalmangel', Recommendation, 30.04.2021, available at https://www.rki.de/DE/Content/InfAZ/N/Neuartiges_Coronavirus/Personal_KritIs.html, last accessed 02.06.2021.

Finally, the COVID-19 health crisis provides an opportunity to address and choose the appropriate and right LTC reform direction as it shows that one's home despite all real and anticipated difficulties in meeting complex needs is still the safest environment for older people. A pandemic could give the needed impetus for further developing community-based services and the deinstitutionalisation process, although existing but rather underdeveloped in many EU/EEA countries.

THE TRANSITION FROM INSTITUTIONAL CARE TO COMMUNITY LIVING IN THE EU

Lessons Learned in the Shadows of the COVID-19 Pandemic

Andrea Broderick and Silvia Favalli*

* On the whole, this contribution is the product of joint reflection. However, (sub-)sections 1, 2, 3.2, 3.3 and 4.2.1 were written by Andrea Broderick. Sub-sections 3.1, 4.1 and 4.2.2 were written by Silvia Favalli, while (sub-)sections 4.3.1, 4.3.2 and 5 were written by Andrea Broderick and Silvia Favalli together.

Time and again it has been demonstrated that people who were deemed too 'disabled' to benefit from community inclusion thrive in an environment where they are valued, where they partake in the everyday life of their surrounding community, where their autonomy is nurtured and they are given choices.[1]

ABSTRACT

The COVID-19 pandemic has brought to the fore the many inequalities encountered by persons with disabilities in all spheres of life. In institutional settings, the pandemic has not only resulted in increased risks of isolation and exploitation, but it has also caused a disproportionate number of deaths among inhabitants of residential institutions and group homes. This has underlined the increased urgency to promote the transition from institutional care to community living globally and at the European Union (EU, the Union) level. Following the conclusion by the EU, in 2010, of the 2006 United Nations (UN) Convention on the Rights of Persons with Disabilities (CRPD) – which has since been ratified by all EU Member States – the Union adopted several legal and policy instruments promoting the transition away from institutional care. Those instruments sought to ensure compliance with Article 19 CRPD (on living independently and being included in the community). Arguably the most prominent example of the EU's commitment to deinstitutionalisation is embodied in the European Structural and Investment Funds (ESIF, or Funds) 2014–2020, which have very recently been replaced by new measures for the programming period 2021–2027. However, concerns about the use of the ESIF have been raised by the Council of Europe's Human Rights Commissioner and the UN Committee on the Rights of Persons with Disabilities, among others. UN Special Rapporteurs have also drawn attention to the fact that the European Commission has authorised national projects whereby the ESIF have been used to continue practices of institutionalisation and segregation. Furthermore, the European Ombudsman has invited the European Commission to address the lack of an appropriate legal basis to ensure that the spending of EU Funds complies with the CRPD. The COVID-19 crisis has not only highlighted the structural challenges pertaining to institutional and social care systems in the EU, but it has also exacerbated the difficulty in monitoring the use of EU Funds, particularly in emergency situations. Against this background, this contribution critically analyses the response of the EU institutions to the pandemic, including the two key Coronavirus Response Investment Initiatives (CRII and CRII+), and the Strategy for the Rights of Persons with Disabilities 2021–2030. Moreover, this contribution reflects on the potential of the EU crisis recovery initiatives to represent either an extraordinary occasion or a missed opportunity to accelerate the transition to community living, depending on the implementation and monitoring mechanisms put in place in respect of post-2020 EU policies.

---

1 Council of Europe, 'The Right of People with Disabilities to Live Independently and be Included in the Community', 2012, p. 9, available at https://rm.coe.int/the-right-of-people-with-disabilities-to-live-independently-and-be-inc/16806da8a9, last accessed 26.08.2021.

1. INTRODUCTION

The COVID-19 pandemic has shone a glaring light on the persisting inequalities faced by persons with disabilities.[2] In residential institutions, the crisis has greatly increased the vulnerability of individuals with intellectual and psychosocial disabilities, as well as that of older people and children with disabilities. Not only have there been amplified risks of isolation and exploitation in institutional settings, but there has also been a disproportionate mortality rate among inhabitants of institutions.[3] In light of the fact that institutional settings have become 'COVID-19 hotspots', urgent calls have been made to 'accelerate' measures of deinstitutionalisation.[4] The pandemic has therefore precipitated the exigent need to foster the transition to community living globally and at European Union (EU, the Union) level.

In December 2010, the EU concluded the UN Convention on the Rights of Persons with Disabilities (CRPD, or Convention), which came into force for the EU in January 2011.[5] The Convention represents the global

---

2 CRPD Committee, 'Statement on COVID-19 and the Human Rights of Persons with Disabilities', 09.06.2020, available at https://www.ohchr.org/EN/NewsEvents/Pages/DisplayNews.aspx?NewsID=25942&LangID=E, last accessed 26.08.2021. The term 'persons with disabilities' has been used in this contribution in order to align with the person-first language used in the UN Convention on the Rights of Persons with Disabilities and to ensure consistency throughout this contribution. However, the authors fully acknowledge and respect the fact that certain individuals with disabilities have a strong preference for the term 'disabled people'.

3 FRA, 'Coronavirus Pandemic in the EU – Fundamental Rights Implications: With a Focus on Older People', 30.06.2020, p. 28, available at https://fra.europa.eu/en/publication/2020/covid19-rights-impact-june-1, last accessed 26.08.2021.

4 A. Guterres, 'Policy Brief on Persons with Disabilities and COVID-19', 06.05.2020, available at https://www.un.org/en/coronavirus/un-secretary-general, last accessed 26.08.2021. See further the calls for 'emergency deinstitutionalization': https://validity.ngo/2020/07/20/covid-19-disability-rights-monitor-drm%E2%80%AFcalls-for-an-emergency-response-to-the-catastrophic-abuse-of-the-human%E2%80%AFrights-of-persons-with-disabilities-in-institutions%E2%80%AF/, last accessed 15.03.2021. See also the subsequent establishment of a working group on deinstitutionalisation by the CRPD Committee in September 2020; and the Statement of the Chair of the CRPD Committee on behalf of the CRPD Committee and the Special Envoy of the UNSG on Disability and Accessibility, 'Persons with Disabilities and COVID-19', 01.04.2020, available at https://www.ohchr.org/EN/HRBodies/CRPD/Pages/CRPDStatements.aspx, last accessed 26.08.2021. While a consideration of the deinstitutionalisation agenda within the Council of Europe is outside the scope of this contribution, it is noteworthy that deinstitutionalisation has also become a priority issue in that sphere: see, for instance, the most recent hearing on deinstitutionalisation of persons with disabilities organised on 16 March 2021 by the Committee on Social Affairs, Health and Sustainable Development of the Parliamentary Assembly and the on-line speech by Dunja Mijatovic (Council of Europe Commissioner for Human Rights): https://rm.coe.int/hearing-on-deinstitutionalisation-of-persons-with-disabilities-organis/1680a1c779, last accessed 26.08.2021.

5 The UN Convention on the Rights of Persons with Disabilities, UNGA res. 61/106, 24 January 2007, UN Doc A/RES/61/106 was concluded by the EU by means of Council decision of 26 November 2009 concerning the conclusion, by the European Community, of the United Nations Convention on the Rights of Persons with Disabilities (2010/48/EC), OJ L 23/35.

normative standard concerning the rights of individuals with disabilities, and it has been ratified by all EU Member States. One of the core provisions binding the Union and its Member States, which are jointly responsible for fulfilling CRPD obligations, is Article 19 CRPD, requiring the transition to independent living in the community. Since concluding the Convention, the EU institutions have adopted several legal and policy instruments designed to implement Article 19 CRPD, including the European Structural and Investment Funds (ESIF, or Funds), as well as the accompanying Regulations governing the Funds. Nonetheless, there is a long road ahead in the implementation of Article 19. In addition to the inappropriate use of the ESIF to maintain or expand existing institutions, concerns have been raised about the use of the Funds to develop services that do not truly promote community living.[6] Moreover, the COVID-19 crisis has highlighted the difficulty in monitoring the ESIF, particularly in emergency situations; and the pandemic has underlined deficiencies in the social care sector, which is essential to community living.

Against the foregoing background and informed by doctrinal legal methodology, including the Vienna Convention on the Law of Treaties of 1986,[7] this contribution critically analyses the global and EU legal and policy framework promoting the transition to community living in sections 2 and 3, respectively. Section 4 evaluates the lessons that can be distilled from the pandemic and the response of the EU institutions thereto, including the Coronavirus Response Investment Initiative (CRII),[8] the CRII Plus (CRII+)[9] and the Strategy for the Rights of Persons with Disabilities 2021–2030 (European Disability Strategy 2021–2030).[10] In addition, section 4 examines

6 J. Šiška and J. Beadle-Brown, 'Transition from Institutional Care to Community-Based Services in 27 EU Member States: Final Report. Research Report for the European Expert Group on Transition from Institutional to Community-based Care', 2020, p. 14, available at https://deinstitutionalisationdotcom.files.wordpress.com/2020/05/eeg-di-report-2020-1.pdf, last accessed 26.08.2021.

7 Vienna Convention on the Law of Treaties between States and International Organizations or between International Organizations 1986.

8 Regulation (EU) 2020/460 of the European Parliament and of the Council of 30 March 2020 amending Regulations (EU) No 1301/2013, (EU) No 1303/2013 and (EU) No 508/2014 as regards specific measures to mobilise investments in the health care systems of Member States and in other sectors of their economies in response to the COVID-19 outbreak, OJ L99/5 (hereinafter CRII).

9 Regulation (EU) 2020/558 of the European Parliament and of the Council of 23 April 2020 amending Regulations (EU) No 1301/2013 and (EU) No 1303/2013 as regards specific measures to provide exceptional flexibility for the use of the European Structural and Investments Funds in response to the COVID-19 outbreak, OJ L130/1 (hereinafter CRII+).

10 European Commission, Communication from the Commission to the European Parliament, the Council, the European Economic and Social Committee and the Committee of the Regions, 'Union of Equality: Strategy for the Rights of Persons with Disabilities 2021–2030', COM(2021) 101 final 26.08.2021 (hereinafter European Disability Strategy 2021–2030).

the systemic challenges inherent to monitoring deinstitutionalisation and reflects on ways forward in implementing post-2020 EU policies with a view to fulfilling the key obligation of deinstitutionalisation embedded in the CRPD. Finally, section 5 sets forth concluding remarks.

2. THE GLOBAL FRAMEWORK ON DEINSTITUTIONALISATION

Article 11 CRPD – which 'applies throughout the continuum' of emergency situations, according to the Office of the High Commissioner for Human Rights (OHCHR),[11] and from which no derogations are permitted –[12] mandates the adoption of 'all necessary measures to ensure the protection and safety of persons with disabilities in situations of risk'.[13] In the context of the COVID-19 pandemic, Article 11 applies to the right to live independently and be included in the community enshrined in Article 19 CRPD. The latter Article is 'hybrid' in that it 'guarantees civil rights such as freedom and independence', as well as 'the socio-economic right to resources and social support to make it a reality'.[14]

While Article 19 CRPD does not refer explicitly to deinstitutionalisation, according to the text of Article 19 read in conjunction with General Comment No. 5 of the Committee on the Rights of Persons with Disabilities (CRPD Committee), all individuals with disabilities should benefit from three inter-related guarantees:

(i) The choice as to where to live and with whom (an immediately applicable obligation in Article 19(a));
(ii) The right to personalised services (a progressively realisable duty under Article 19(b)); and

---

11 OHCHR, 'Thematic Study on the Rights of Persons with Disabilities under Article 11 of the Convention on the Rights of Persons with Disabilities, on Situations of Risk and Humanitarian Emergencies', UN Doc A/HRC/31/30, 30.11.2015, para. 14.

12 CRPD Committee, 'Statement of the CRPD Committee on Disability Inclusion for the World Humanitarian Summit', 2015, available at https://www.ohchr.org/EN/HRBodies/CRPD/Pages/CRPDStatements.aspx, last accessed 26.08.2021.

13 Article 11, CRPD.

14 K. Wilson, 'The COVID-19 Pandemic and the Human Rights of Persons with Mental and Cognitive Impairments Subject to Coercive Powers in Australia', (2020) 73, *International Journal of Law and Psychiatry*, p. 80. See further O. Lewis and G. Richardson, 'The Right to Live Independently and be Included in the Community', (2020) 69, *International Journal of Law and Psychiatry*; C. Parker and L. Clements, 'The UN Convention on the Rights of Persons with Disabilities: A New Right to Independent Living?', (2008) 4, *European Human Rights Law Review*, p. 508; and CRPD Committee, *General Comment No. 5 on Living Independently and Being Included in the Community*, UN Doc CRPD/C/GC/5, 27.10.2017, para. 7.

(iii) The right to have disability-specific in-home, residential and other community support services, including personal assistance and accessible mainstream community services (a progressively realisable obligation in Article 19(c)).[15]

Article 19 CRPD is linked to the recognition of legal capacity in Article 12 and the prohibition of disability-based detention in Article 14 of the Convention.[16] Palmisano asserts that Article 19 'turns into normative terms and legal obligations' a fundamental principle enshrined in Article 3(c) CRPD, that of full inclusion and effective participation in society of persons with disabilities.[17] Together with the principle of respect for the individual's inherent dignity, autonomy and independence in Article 3(a) CRPD, it is deemed to be 'the foundation of the right to live independently and be included in the community'.[18] These two principles are mirrored in the CRPD's purpose, outlined in Article 1, and in the non-discrimination norm in Article 5, described as the CRPD's 'leitmotif'.[19] The latter norm lies at the heart of the deinstitutionalisation mandate, since institutionalisation is viewed as a discriminatory practice.[20]

The web of principles and duties underpinning Article 19 CRPD reflect the Convention's theoretical framework. Specifically, the CRPD embodies the shift from the individual model of disability – which views functional limitations as a consequence flowing from impairment – to the social-contextual model

---

15 CRPD Committee (2017), *General Comment No. 5, supra* note 14, para. 39. See generally P. M. Gooding, 'The Right to Independent Living and Being Included in the Community: Lessons from the United Nations', (2018) 24, *International Journal of Mental Health and Capacity Law*.

16 CRPD Committee (2017), *General Comment No. 5, supra* note 14, para. 27.

17 G. Palmisano, 'Article 19', in V. Della Fina, R. Cera and G. Palmisano (eds.), *The United Nations Convention on the Rights of Persons with Disabilities: A Commentary*, Springer, Cham 2017, p. 354.

18 CRPD Committee (2017), *General Comment No. 5, supra* note 14, para. 3.

19 O.M. Arnardóttir, 'A Future of Multidimensional Disadvantage Equality', in O.M. Arnardóttir and G. Quinn, *The UN Convention on the Rights of Persons with Disabilities: European and Scandinavian Perspectives*, Martinus Nijhoff, The Hague-New York 2009, p. 41.

20 See the 'Mandates of the Special Rapporteur on the Rights of Persons with Disabilities and the Special Rapporteur on Adequate Housing as a Component of the Right to an Adequate Standard of Living, and on the Right to Non-discrimination in this Context', 18.05.2020, available at https://spcommreports.ohchr.org/TMResultsBase/DownLoadPublicCommunicationFile?gId=25267, last accessed 26.08.2021 (hereinafter Mandates of the Special Rapporteurs).

of disability –[21] acknowledging that 'disability results from the *interaction* between persons with impairments and attitudinal and environmental barriers that hinder their full and effective participation in society on an equal basis with others'.[22] In that connection, the CRPD's accessibility duty, contained in Article 9, requires parties to the Convention to take generalised and anticipatory measures to guarantee that people with disabilities have equal access to life in the community.[23] The accessibility norm complements the duty in Article 5(3) CRPD to provide individualised reasonable accommodations – necessary and appropriate modifications which do not impose a disproportionate or undue burden on the duty-bearer.[24]

While the social-contextual model explains how disability arises, the human rights model of disability underpins the provisions of the CRPD, taking into account human difference and addressing intersectional disadvantages.[25] Reflecting the human rights model, services provided in the context of Article 19(c) CRPD must be gender- and age-sensitive,[26] including in 'disaster risk management activities'.[27] Moreover, a human rights-based approach to disability has been deemed 'critical to response and recovery efforts' related to the ongoing pandemic.[28]

The human rights model of disability is intertwined with the CRPD's overarching model of inclusive equality, which mandates that parties to the Convention accommodate people with disabilities, address socio-economic disadvantages and combat stereotyping regarding the right to live independently

---

21 A. Broderick, *The Long and Winding Road to Equality and Inclusion for Persons with Disabilities: The United Nations Convention on the Rights of Persons with Disabilities*, Intersentia, Cambridge/Antwerp 2015, p. 77. The social-contextual model addresses criticisms of the 'pure' social model, which neglects the role of impairment in disablement, see T. Shakespeare and N. Watson, 'The Social Model of Disability: An Outdated Ideology?', (2001) 2, *Research in Social Science and Disability*, pp. 9–28.

22 Preamble (e) CRPD. Emphasis added. The Preamble must be read in conjunction with the 'non-definition of disability' in Article 1 CRPD: see A. Broderick and D. Ferri, *International and European Disability Law and Policy: Text, Cases and Materials*, Cambridge University Press, Cambridge 2019, pp. 65–67.

23 European Commission, 'Disability Law and the Duty to Reasonably Accommodate Beyond Employment: A Legal Analysis of the Situation in EU Member States', written by L. Waddington and A. Broderick with the assistance of A. Poulos, 2016, p. 45, available at http://edz.bib.uni-mannheim.de/daten/edz-k/gdj/16/reasonable_accomodation_beyond_employment_final.pdf, last accessed 26.08.2021.

24 See also Article 2, CRPD.

25 CRPD Committee, *General Comment No. 6 on Equality and Non-discrimination*, UN Doc CRPD/C/GC/6, 26.04.2018, para. 11.

26 CRPD Committee, Sixth session, 19–23 September 2011, UN Doc CRPD/C/ESP/CO/1, para. 37.

27 CRPD Committee (2017), *General Comment No. 5*, *supra* note 14, para. 79.

28 CRPD Committee (2020), 'Statement on COVID-19', *supra* note 2.

in the community.[29] Ensuring inclusive equality also requires facilitating, in accordance with Article 4(3) CRPD and the Convention's *travaux préparatoires*,[30] the active involvement of individuals with disabilities – through representative organisations of persons with disabilities (DPOs) – in the 'adoption of all plans and strategies as well as for follow-up and monitoring when implementing the right to independent living in the community'.[31] The duty to ensure close consultation with, and active involvement of, DPOs also applies to the national frameworks set up under Article 33 CRPD to monitor the Convention domestically, complementing the focal points that must be established to implement the CRPD.

Notably, the margin of appreciation that applies in the implementation of Article 19 relates to 'programmatic implementation, but not to the question of replacement' of institutions.[32] In that regard, the general obligation in Article 4(d) CRPD to refrain from any act or practice inconsistent with the Convention prohibits the construction of new institutions. This is confirmed by the CRPD Committee, which asserts that no new institutions may be built, 'nor may old institutions be renovated beyond the most urgent measures necessary to safeguard residents' physical safety',[33] including in the wake of situations of disaster.[34] Furthermore, according to Quinn and Doyle, the prohibition in Article 4(d) CRPD applies to silence on the ESIF Regulations that could be interpreted 'as permissive toward the construction of new institutions'.[35]

Foreshadowing potential economic crises following emergency situations, the CRPD Committee has warned that retrogressive measures cannot be introduced with respect to the minimum core obligations of Article 19 CRPD.[36] These include the requirement to collect consistent quantitative and qualitative data on people with disabilities living in institutions, and to use available funding to develop inclusive and accessible independent living services.[37] In that regard,

---

29 CRPD Committee (2018), *General Comment No. 6*, *supra* note 25, para. 11.

30 Inclusion International, 4th Session of the Ad Hoc Committee, Volume 5, 27.08.2004.

31 CRPD Committee (2018), *General Comment No. 6*, *supra* note 25, para. 11; CRPD Committee (2017), *General Comment No. 5*, *supra* note 14, para. 70.

32 CRPD Committee (2017), *General Comment No. 5*, *supra* note 14, para. 42.

33 Ibid., para. 49.

34 Ibid., paras. 65 and 79.

35 OHCHR (written by G. Quinn and S. Doyle), 'Getting a Life – Living Independently and Being Included in the Community. A Legal Study of the Current Use and Future Potential of the EU Structural Funds to Contribute to the Achievement of Article 19 of the United Nations Convention on the Rights of Persons with Disabilities', 2012, p. 8, available at https://europe.ohchr.org/Documents/Publications/Getting_a_Life.pdf, last accessed 26.08.2021.

36 CRPD Committee (2017), *General Comment No. 5*, *supra* note 14, para. 43.

37 Ibid., para. 38. See generally I. Bulic-Cojocariu, 'Advocating for Independent Living in the European Union', in K. Soldatic and K. Johnson (eds.), *Global Perspectives on Disability Activism and Advocacy*, Routledge, Oxfordshire 2019.

the CRPD Committee has recommended that the EU 'strengthen the monitoring of the use of the ESIF' to ensure that they are 'used strictly for the development of support services for persons with disabilities'.[38] Additionally, the Committee has urged the Union to 'suspend, withdraw and recover payments if the obligation to respect fundamental rights is breached'.[39]

3. EU LAW AND THE TRANSITION TO COMMUNITY LIVING

3.1. THE EU LAW FRAMEWORK ON DEINSTITUTIONALISATION

The EU institutions have developed a significant body of disability discrimination law and policy over the last twenty years under Article 19 of the Treaty on the Function of the European Union (TFEU).[40] However, deinstitutionalisation only became a priority in EU policy-making following the conclusion by the EU of the CRPD in 2010.

The CRPD constitutes a mixed agreement under EU law, in that the Union and its Member States are required to work together to fulfil the obligations laid down in the Convention in situations of mixed competence.[41] In the context of Article 19 CRPD, the EU has limited competences.[42] In that field, the EU action is largely confined to supporting implementation in the Member States of Article 19 CRPD, primarily through the ESIF and soft law measures.

The ESIF are among the primary tools of EU Cohesion Policy, having their legal basis in Articles 174 and 175 TFEU, which support a large range of measures devoted, *inter alia*, to promoting the social inclusion of persons with disabilities. It is paramount that EU Member States implement the ESIF in line with the Charter of Fundamental Rights of the EU (CFREU, or Charter),[43] while taking into account the guiding principles in the European Pillar of Social

---

38 CRPD Committee, Concluding Observations on the Initial Report of the European Union, UN Doc CRPD/C/EU/CO/1, 02.10.2015, para. 51.

39 Ibid.

40 See generally D. Ferri and S. Favalli, 'Defining Disability in the EU Non-Discrimination Legislation: Judicial Activism and Legislative Restraints', (2016) 22(3), *European Public Law*, p. 552.

41 Council Decision 2010/48/EC, *supra* note 5, para. 7; and CJEU, *Parliament v Council*, Case C-316/91, 02.03.94, ECLI:EU:C:1994:76, paras. 24–35.

42 The Commission has described it as an area of competences that is 'shared' between the EU and its Member States: European Commission, 'Report on the Implementation of the UN Convention on the Rights of Persons with Disabilities by the European Union', SWD(2014) 182 final 05.06.2014, para. 93.

43 Charter of Fundamental Rights of the European Union, OJ C 326/391.

Rights (EPSR)[44] and its accompanying Action Plan.[45] The provisions of the Charter relevant to deinstitutionalisation and independent living are Article 21 CFREU, prohibiting discrimination on any ground, including disability; and Article 26 CFREU, providing for the integration of persons with disabilities in community life.[46] Notably, the European Commission has issued guidance on the use of the ESIF, whereby it considers housing segregation as falling within the prohibition in Article 21 CFREU.[47] Moreover, the European Ombudsman confirms that 'the Commission is obliged to respect the Charter in its entirety, in all its activities', including in the distribution and monitoring of the Funds.[48] In turn, the Commission has published a 'fundamental rights checklist' for EU Member States, with the aim of ensuring respect for the Charter when they make use of the ESIF.[49] Complementing the Charter's provisions, the EPSR is an inter-institutional proclamation that sets out guiding principles to ensure, *inter alia*, social inclusion. Of particular note is principle 17, enshrining the right of persons with disabilities to income support that ensures living in dignity and services that enable them to participate in society. If implemented in line with CRPD obligations and in coordination with DPOs, it has 'the potential to positively contribute to the transition to community and family-based care beyond the closure of institutions'.[50]

The principles of the EPSR are reflected in the goals of the European Semester of economic policy coordination, which synchronises Member States' national

---

44 Interinstitutional Proclamation 2017/C 428/09 on the European Pillar of Social Rights, OJ C428/10. See generally S. Sabato and F. Corti, 'The Times they are a-changin'?: The European Pillar of Social Rights from Debates to Reality Check', in B. Vanhercke, D. Ghailini and S. Sabato (eds.), *Social Policy in the European Union: State of the Play 2018*, European Social Observatory and European Trade Union Institute (2019), pp. 51–70.

45 European Commission, Communication from the Commission to the European Parliament, the Council, the European Economic and Social Committee and the Committee of the Regions, 'The European Pillar of Social Rights Action Plan', COM(2021) 102 final 04.03.2021.

46 See generally D. Ferri, 'Disability in the EU Charter of Fundamental Rights', in D. Ferri and A. Broderick (eds.), *Research Handbook on EU Disability Law*, Edward Elgar Publishing, Cheltenham 2020, pp. 29–51.

47 European Commission, 'Guidance for Member States on the Use of European Structural and Investment Funds in Tackling Educational and Spatial Segregation', 11.11.2015, p. 5, available at https://ec.europa.eu/regional_policy/sources/docgener/informat/2014/thematic_guidance_fiche_segregation_en.pdf, last accessed 08.03.2021.

48 European Ombudsman, Decision of the European Ombudsman OI/8/2014/AN, para. 42.

49 European Commission, Commission Notice – Guidance on Ensuring the Respect for the Charter of Fundamental Rights of the European Union when Implementing the European Structural and Investment Funds ('ESI Funds'), C(2016) 4384, OJ C 269.

50 European Expert Group on Transition from Institutional to Community-Based Care (EEG), 'The European Pillar of Social Rights and its Potential to Build an Inclusive Europe for All', p. 2, available at https://deinstitutionalisationdotcom.files.wordpress.com/2017/10/eeg-position-on-the-european-pillar-of-social-rights-and-its-potential.pdf, last accessed 26.08.2021.

reform priorities, including the deinstitutionalisation process, and monitors their implementation through the measures set out in the ESIF. Member States' progress in that regard is detected through the Social Scoreboard – a monitoring tool that forms the basis for the Commission's Country Specific Recommendations (CSR) – providing guidance to EU Member States on how to realise the goals identified in the European Semester.

3.2. THE EUROPEAN STRUCTURAL AND INVESTMENT FUNDS 2014–2020

The ESIF constitute the primary financial instruments supporting implementation of the EPSR and enhancing deinstitutionalisation, as reiterated in the European Disability Strategy 2010–2020.[51] The ESIF are implemented through multi-annual, seven-year programmes agreed upon between the Member States and the European Commission,[52] and they have been described by McEvoy as 'one of the key instruments to implement the rights of persons with disabilities across the EU'.[53] Significantly, the ESIF Regulations for the period 2014–2020, which sought to implement the Europe 2020 Strategy – designed to develop smart, sustainable and inclusive growth in the Union – refer to the CRPD and CFREU for the first time.[54]

The 2014–2020 ESIF were governed by the Common Provisions Regulation (CPR),[55] which incorporates the European Regional Development Fund (ERDF) Regulation[56]

---

51 European Commission, Communication from the Commission to the European Parliament, the Council, the European Economic and Social Committee and the Committee of the Regions, 'European Disability Strategy 2010–2020: A Renewed Commitment to a Barrier-Free Europe', COM(2010) 0636 final 15.11.2010.

52 For a detailed analysis of the use of the ESIF in the context of deinstitutionalisation, see Open Society Foundations, 'Community not Confinement: The Role of the European Union in Promoting and Protecting the Right of People with Disabilities to live in the Community', Open Society Foundations, New York 2015. See generally C. Parker and I. Bulic Cojocariu, 'European Structural and Investment Funds and People with Disabilities in the European Union', 2016, available at https://www.europarl.europa.eu/RegData/etudes/STUD/2016/571386/IPOL_STU(2016)571386_EN.pdf, last accessed 26.08.2021.

53 E. McEvoy, 'EU Structural and Investment Funds and Disability', in D. Ferri and A. Broderick (eds.), *Research Handbook on EU Disability Law*, Edward Elgar Publishing, Cheltenham 2020, p. 321.

54 European Commission, 'Europe 2020: A Strategy for Smart, Sustainable and Inclusive Growth', COM(2010) 2020 final 03.03.2010.

55 Regulation (EU) No 1303/2013 laying down common provisions on the ERDF, the ESF, the CF, the EARFD and the EMFF and laying down general provisions on the ERDF, the ESF, the CF and the EMFF, OJ L347/320 (hereinafter 2014–2020 Common Provisions Regulation (CPR)).

56 Regulation (EU) No 1301/2013 on the European Regional Development Fund and on specific provisions concerning the Investment for growth and jobs goal, OJ L 347/289 (hereinafter 2014–2020 ERDF).

and the European Social Fund (ESF) Regulation.[57] The ESIF have immense potential to facilitate the transition to community living. Specifically, the ERDF can be used to finance investments in health and social care infrastructure, such as accessible housing. In a complementary fashion, the ESF is intended to support the training of staff providing community-based services to people with disabilities.

Influenced in part by the CRPD, the 2014–2020 framework addressed concerns regarding national ESIF implementation.[58] First, it increased the onus on EU Member States to monitor the impact of the Funds by requiring them to compile a Partnership Agreement, setting out their plans for implementation of the ESIF in line with the Europe 2020 Strategy and the CSR.[59] Additionally, a Delegated Regulation on a European Code of Conduct on Partnership was promulgated, Article 7 of which requires EU Member States to provide information on the actions taken to ensure the active participation of relevant partners, including accessibility measures.[60] In that connection, Article 5 of the 2014–2020 CPR strengthened the role of DPOs in monitoring the national implementation of funded projects.

Most importantly, the 2014–2020 CPR incorporated general and thematic '*ex-ante* conditionalities',[61] which established pre-conditions to be satisfied before funding could be granted.[62] Failure to comply with those conditionalities constituted a ground for the European Commission to suspend interim payments.[63] General *ex-ante* conditionalities on anti-discrimination and disability,[64] as well as the thematic *ex-ante* conditionality 9 on promoting social inclusion, combating poverty and discrimination,[65] in addition to the horizontal principles of accessibility and non-discrimination (including on the ground of gender) served to embed an intersectional approach to disability within the Union's funding framework.[66] Notably, the European Union Agency for Fundamental Rights (FRA) views the *ex-ante* conditionalities as constituting

---

57 Regulation (EU) No 1304/2013 of the European Parliament and of the Council of 17 December 2013 on the European Social Fund and repealing Council Regulation (EC) No 1081/2006, OJ L 347/470 (hereinafter 2014–2020 ESF).

58 L. Polverari, 'The New Ambitions for 2014–2020 European Structural and Investment Funds Evaluation: Pouring Water in a Leaking Container?', (2016) 4(2), *European Structural and Investment Funds Journal*, p. 59.

59 Articles 14–16 2014–2020 CPR.

60 Article 7(b), Commission Delegated Regulation (EU) No 240/2014 of 7 January 2014 on the European code of conduct on partnership in the framework of the European Structural and Investment Funds, OJ L 74/1, 14.03.2014.

61 Annex XI, 2014–2020 CPR.

62 Article 19 and Annex XI, 2014–2020 CPR.

63 Articles 19 and 142, 2014–2020 CPR.

64 General *ex-ante* conditionalities 1 and 3, 2014–2020 CPR.

65 Annex XI, Part 1, 2014–2020 CPR.

66 Article 7, 2014–2020 CPR.

'a major step towards supporting deinstitutionalisation',[67] and a Commission report acknowledged that they enhanced socially inclusive investments.[68]

In spite of these innovations and certain promising practices throughout the Member States,[69] the existing body of literature demonstrates the extent to which the ESIF have been used to construct and maintain institutions for persons with disabilities.[70] In this regard, concerns have been raised about the spending of EU Funds on institutional living in Bulgaria, Hungary and Latvia, among several other Member States –[71] where the Funds have been used to replace large institutions with smaller ones, referred to as 'group homes', 'sheltered housing' or 'independent living centres'.[72] Instead of promoting community-based alternatives, these facilities perpetuate segregation,[73] and they arguably constitute a retrogressive measure in the realisation of Article 19 CRPD.[74]

Acknowledging these issues implicitly and underlining the increasing urgency to transition to community living, the European Parliament stressed, in a 2017 Resolution, that the ESIF 'must, particularly in the [2021–2027] programming period, adhere to the [CRPD] and should continue to foster deinstitutionalisation as a matter of priority'.[75]

---

67 FRA, 'From Institutions to Community Living for Persons with Disabilities: Perspectives from the Ground', 23.11.2018, p. 26, available at https://fra.europa.eu/en/publication/2018/institutions-community-living-persons-disabilities-perspectives-ground, last accessed 26.08.2021.

68 European Commission, 'The Value Added of Ex-ante Conditionalities in the European Structural and Investment Funds', SWD(2017) 127 final 31.3.2017, p. 6.

69 Community Living for Europe: Structural Funds Watch, 'Inclusion for All: Achievements and Challenges in Using EU Funds to Support Community Living', 2018, pp. 22–24, available at https://communitylivingforeurope.org/, last accessed 26.08.2021.

70 C. Parker, 'Forgotten Europeans, Forgotten Rights – The Human Rights of Persons Placed in Institutions', *OHCHR*, 2011, available at http://www.holdingouthope.co.uk/wp-content/uploads/forgotten-europeans-forgotten-rights.pdf, last accessed 08.03.2021. See generally https://www.disability-europe.net/theme/independent-living, last accessed 26.08.2021.

71 See FRA, 'From Institutions to Community Living, Part II: Funding and Budgeting', 08.12.2017, p. 11, available at https://fra.europa.eu/en/publication/2017/institutions-community-living-part-ii-funding-and-budgeting, last accessed 26.08.2021.

72 I. Bulić-Cojocariu and N. Kokić, 'Lost in Interpretation. The Use of ESI Funds during 2014–2020 and the Impact on the Right of Persons with Disabilities to Independent Living', European Network on Independent Living (ENIL), 2020, p. 25, available at https://enil.eu/wp-content/uploads/2020/12/Study_EP_EN_09122020.pdf, last accessed 26.08.2021.

73 Ibid. See also G. Quinn, L. Waddington, G. de Búrca et al., 'Legal Memo. Segregation and Segregated Facilities as a Prima Facie Form of Discrimination. The Impermissibility of Using the ESIF to Invest Monies in Long Term Care Residential Institutions for Persons with Disabilities', 17.03.2018, available at https://enil.eu/news/segregation-and-segregated-facilities-as-a-prima-facie-form-of-discrimination/, last accessed 26.08.2021.

74 See the 'Mandates of the Special Rapporteurs' (2020), *supra* note 20.

75 European Parliament, European Parliament Resolution of 30 November 2017 on implementation of the European Disability Strategy (2017/2127(INI)), P8_TA(2017) 0474 30.11.2017.

3.3 THE EUROPEAN STRUCTURAL AND INVESTMENT FUNDS 2021–2027

In June 2021, the framework CPR that will govern the 2021–2027 ESIF, Regulation 2021/1060,[76] was formally adopted by the EU institutions and was published in the Official Journal of the European Union, along with the Regulations on the 2021–2027 European Social Fund Plus (ESF+)[77] and the 2021–2027 ERDF.[78] The 2021–2027 regulatory framework contains a few important changes to the Funds' management that have relevance for CRPD implementation.

In the first instance, the 'partnership principle' is stated in paragraph 14 of the Preamble of the 2021–2027 CPR to be a

> key feature in the implementation of the Funds, building on the multi-level governance approach and ensuring the involvement of regional, local, urban and other public authorities, civil society, economic and social partners and, where appropriate, research organisations and universities.

Article 8 of Regulation 2021/1060 further elaborates on the 'partnership principle', requiring Member States to organise and implement 'a comprehensive partnership' that should include, *inter alia*, the competent regional and local authorities, as well as relevant bodies representing civil society and bodies responsible for promoting the rights of people with disabilities. Together with a simplification of the administrative burden in the 2021–2027 funding rules, this clearly facilitates the participation of DPOs and is an important provision given the role that civil society can play in monitoring ESIF use.[79] Second, the *ex-ante* conditionalities were replaced in the 2021–2027 CPR with horizontal 'enabling conditions' that apply across all thematic objectives and are designed to support implementation of the EPSR. Those enabling conditions are deemed to be 'more focused and aligned with EU priorities and policy objectives' than the previous *ex-ante* conditionalities.[80] It is noteworthy that the enabling

---

76 Regulation (EU) No 2021/1060 of the European Parliament and of the Council of 24 June 2021 laying down common provisions on the European Regional Development Fund, the European Social Fund Plus, the Cohesion Fund, the Just Transition Fund and the European Maritime, Fisheries and Aquaculture Fund and financial rules for those and for the Asylum, Migration and Integration Fund, the Internal Security Fund and the Instrument for Financial Support for Border Management and Visa Policy, OJ L 231 (hereinafter 2021–2027 CPR).

77 Regulation (EU) No 2021/1057 of the European Parliament and of the Council of 24 June 2021 establishing the European Social Fund Plus (ESF+) and repealing Regulation (EU) No 1296/2013, OJ L 231 (hereinafter 2021–2027 ESF+).

78 Regulation (EU) No 2021/1058 of the European Parliament and of the Council of 24 June 2021 on the European Regional Development Fund and on the Cohesion Fund, OJ L 231 (hereinafter 2021–2027 ERDF).

79 See also FRA (2017), 'From Institutions to Community Living, Part II: Funding and Budgeting', p. 12, *supra* note 71.

80 FRA (2018), 'From Institutions to Community Living for Persons with Disabilities', *supra* note 67, p. 27.

conditions do not serve as a precondition at the onset of the 2021–2027 funding period; rather, they are intended to be applied and fulfilled throughout the entire implementation period.[81] While there is no longer an *ex-ante* conditionality on disability in the 2021–2027 ESIF regulatory framework, the spirit of Article 19 CRPD has been incorporated directly into the text of the 2021–2027 CPR via the horizontal enabling condition in Article 15 and Annex III to the 2021–2027 CPR, on implementation and application of the CRPD. Notably, the fulfilment criteria listed in the Annex refer to a national framework to ensure CRPD implementation that includes: (i) Objectives with measurable goals, data collection and monitoring mechanisms; (ii) Arrangements to ensure that the accessibility policy, legislation and standards are properly reflected in the preparation and implementation of the programmes; and (iii) Reporting arrangements to the monitoring committee that each Member State is obliged to set up regarding cases of non-compliance of operations supported by the Funds with the CRPD.

This embedding of the CRPD in the EU funding framework is also evidenced in Article 6 of the ESF+ governing the period 2021–2027. That provision requires the Member States and the Commission to support targeted actions for ensuring accessibility for persons with disabilities, and promoting the transition from residential or institutional care to family and community-based care. In a similar vein, Preamble paragraph 6 of the 2021–2027 CPR urges the Member States to 'ensure accessibility in line with Article 9 [CRPD] and in accordance with Union law harmonising accessibility requirements for products and services'. In that context, the Preamble states that the 'Funds should be implemented in a way that promotes the transition from institutional to family-based and community-based care'.

While these positive developments in the 2021–2027 EU funding framework certainly seek to ensure respect for CRPD obligations in the use and monitoring of the Funds, they have been overshadowed by the COVID-19 pandemic, which has shed a cold light on the obstacles that still persist regarding the implementation and monitoring of Article 19 CRPD.

4. LESSONS LEARNED FROM THE COVID-19 PANDEMIC: PAVING PATHWAYS AHEAD

4.1. YAWNING GAPS IN LIGHT OF COVID-19

Before the pandemic, the CRPD Committee observed gaps 'between the goals and spirit of [A]rticle 19 and the scope of its implementation'.[82] Those gaps

81 Article 15(6) 2021–2027 CPR.

82 CRPD Committee (2017), *General Comment No. 5*, *supra* note 14, para. 15.

included the inadequacy of social support schemes, stereotypes preventing persons with disabilities from being included in the community, and a lack of adequate monitoring mechanisms and participation of DPOs. Moreover, inappropriate decentralisation, resulting in disparities between regional and local authorities largely responsible for the management of institutions, was a growing concern.[83] In that respect, there has been 'a widespread transfer of responsibility from the national to the local level, not always accompanied by funding', leading to 'potential issues in terms of coordination [and] consistency' of services.[84] That gap was amplified by a lack of national deinstitutionalisation strategies, meaning that the transition to community living risks being limited to single local projects funded by the ESIF, without 'scaling up of results beyond EU funding'.[85]

The COVID-19 outbreak has unveiled further deficiencies regarding the implementation of Article 19 CRPD. In fact, the UN Special Rapporteur on the rights of persons with disabilities and the UN Special Rapporteur on adequate housing have noted that the pandemic has highlighted 'systemic challenges' in institutions.[86] As emerged from the COVID-19 Disability Rights Monitor,[87] the crisis measures adopted worldwide exacerbated an existing lack of access to health care for residents of institutions. In a similar vein, the European Disability Forum (EDF) reported limited access to health care and information for persons with disabilities in institutions.[88]

Furthermore, the pandemic has magnified large-scale deficiencies in service provision. Not only have persons with disabilities living in the community who rely on support for daily living found themselves without essential services due to physical distancing measures,[89] but the European Association of Service Providers for Persons with Disabilities (EASPD) remarks on the challenges encountered in securing the continuity of services providing choice

---

83 See also FRA (2017), 'From Institutions to Community Living, Part II: Funding and Budgeting', p. 8, *supra* note 71.

84 J. Šiška and J. Beadle-Brown (2020), 'Transition from Institutional Care', *supra* note 6, p. 4.

85 Ibid.

86 See the 'Mandates of the Special Rapporteurs' (2020), *supra* note 20.

87 COVID-19 DRM, 'Disability Rights During the Pandemic – A Global Report on Findings of the COVID-19 Disability Rights Monitor', 2020, pp. 22–27, available at https://covid-drm.org/assets/documents/Disability-Rights-During-the-Pandemic-report-web.pdf, last accessed 26.08.2021.

88 EDF, 'Impact of COVID-19 on Persons with Disabilities. European Leaders Must Act Now. Extract from the Human Rights Report 2020', 2020, p. 8, available at https://www.edf-feph.org/publications/human-rights-report-impact-of-covid-19-on-persons-with-disabilities/, last accessed 26.08.2021.

89 FRA, 'Coronavirus Pandemic in the EU – Fundamental Rights Implications: Focus on Social Rights', 27.11.2020, p. 10, available at https://fra.europa.eu/en/themes/covid-19, last accessed 26.08.2021.

and control to people with disabilities.[90] This stems from the fact that national governments have primarily focused on addressing the health and economic aspects of the crisis, and the social care sector has been 'left behind' at certain junctures,[91] even though many service providers have shown flexibility and innovativeness during the pandemic.[92]

In addition, numerous barriers relating to ESIF implementation and monitoring have been amplified during the COVID-19 crisis. In the first instance, the pandemic has had negative impacts on DPO involvement in planning the 2021–2027 programming period, raising concerns about the content and participatory nature of the projects to be implemented at Member State level.[93] Additionally, it has become increasingly difficult to monitor the situation prevailing in institutions, as many Member States have failed to collate data on the health and social consequences of the pandemic.[94] According to EDF, the approach to disability at EU and Member State levels has been *ad hoc* during the pandemic, and the widespread lack of data is 'a stark example of this lack of a systematic approach across governments'.[95]

A further issue of grave concern that has been magnified in the shadows of the COVID-19 pandemic concerns the extent to which the EU institutions truly support the implementation of Article 19 CRPD. In fact, apprehensions have recently been raised in that regard by UN Special Rapporteurs.[96] On this issue, it is noteworthy that the European Commission has authorised national projects in which the 2014–2020 ESIF were employed to continue practices of institutionalisation, raising serious concerns in relation to fundamental rights' protection for persons with disabilities throughout the Union.[97] In July 2020, the European Ombudsman took a strong stance when deciding on the use of

---

90 EASPD, 'The Impact of COVID-19 on Disability Services in Europe', 2020, p. 3, available at https://www.easpd.eu/sites/default/files/sites/default/files/COVID19/second_report_impact_of_covid-19_on_disability_services_in_europe.pdf, last accessed 26.08.2021.

91 EEG, 'Joint Statement, "COVID-19 Crisis: People Living in Institutions Must not be Written Off"', 24.04.2021, available at https://deinstitutionalisation.com/2020/04/24/covid-19-crisis-people-living-in-institutions-must-not-be-written-off/, last accessed 28.06.2021.

92 EASPD, 'Social Services Call on EU to Uphold the Rights and Health of Staff and Users in Next Phase of COVID-19 Response', available at https://www.easpd.eu/de/content/social-services-call-eu-uphold-rights-and-health-staff-and-users-next-phase-covid-19, last accessed 26.08.2021.

93 I. Bulić-Cojocariu and N. Kokić (2020), 'Lost in Interpretation', *supra* note 72, p. 34.

94 See generally N. Reed, L. Meeks and B. K. Swenor, 'Disability and COVID-19: Who Counts Depends on Who is Counted', (2020) 5(5), *The Lancet Public Health*.

95 EDF (2020), 'Impact of COVID-19 on Persons with Disabilities', *supra* note 88, p. 18.

96 See the 'Mandates of the Special Rapporteurs' (2020), *supra* note 20.

97 Ibid. See further the actions of non-governmental organisations in that regard: available at https://validity.ngo/2020/11/25/hungary-validity-takes-legal-action-against-the-european-commission-for-refusing-to-release-information-on-its-funding-of-human-rights-abuses/, last accessed 26.08.2021.

the Funds to construct institutions for persons with disabilities in Hungary and Portugal, and responded to the Commission's assertion that ESIF use supporting long-stay residential institutions is not prohibited by the EU legal framework.[98] Administering a stringent rebuke, the European Ombudsman affirmed that the Commission's standpoint was 'difficult to comprehend'.[99] Separately, the Ombudsman recommended that the Commission verify from the outset projects that receive EU funding, in order to prevent institutionalisation.[100] Moreover, in February 2021, against the background of the COVID-19 pandemic, the Ombudsman opened an inquiry into the Commission's role in monitoring the use of EU funds by the Member States to promote independent living.[101]

4.2. THE EU RECOVERY PLAN

4.2.1. The Coronavirus Response Investment Initiatives and Amendments to EU Cohesion Policy

In light of the systemic gaps in implementation of Article 19 CRPD that were augmented during the COVID-19 crisis, the future trajectory of the deinstitutionalisation process hinges partly on the ongoing response of the EU institutions and national authorities to the pandemic.

Even though the EU institutions were initially criticised in certain quarters for their lack of action,[102] they eventually responded to the pandemic with a wide-ranging package of financial measures.[103] On 10 November 2020, political agreement was reached on NextGenerationEU – the temporary instrument designed to boost recovery efforts – and on the 2021–2027 Cohesion Policy.[104]

98 I. Bulic-Cojocariu and N. Kokić (2020), 'Lost in Interpretation', *supra* note 72, p. 17.

99 European Ombudsman, *Case 1233/2019/MMO*, para. 31.

100 Ibid.

101 European Ombudsman, Strategic Inquiry OI/2/2021/MMO.

102 T. Tesche, 'The European Union's Response to the Coronavirus Emergency: An Early Assessment', (2020) 157, *LSE 'Europe in Question' Discussion Paper Series*, p. 1.

103 See generally E. Castellarin, 'The European Union's Financial Contribution to the Response to the COVID-19 Crisis: An Overview of Existing Mechanisms, Proposals Under Discussion and Open Issues', (2020) 5(2), *European Papers*.

104 European Commission, Communication from the Commission to the European Parliament, the European Council, the Council, the European Economic and Social Committee and the Committee of the Regions, Europe's moment: Repair and Prepare for the Next Generation, COM/2020/456 final (NextGenerationEU). More generally, see European Commission, 'Recovery Plan for Europe', 2020, available at https://ec.europa.eu/info/strategy/recovery-plan-europe_en#nextgenerationeu, last accessed 26.08.2021.

The Recovery and Resilience Facility (RRF) lies at the heart of Next Generation EU, comprising €672.5 billion in loans and grants to support reforms undertaken by EU Member States. NextGenerationEU also includes a sum of €47.5 billion for REACT-EU (Recovery Assistance for Cohesion and the Territories of Europe), which complements the recovery measures delivered through the CRII and CRII+.[105]

The CRII focused on the immediate mobilisation of EU Funds, allowing for a prompt response to the pandemic. Moreover, it provided for flexibility in applying EU spending rules and extended the scope of the EU Solidarity Fund,[106] which furnished additional assistance of up to €800 million in 2020 to the worst affected countries. In April 2020, the CRII+ bolstered the existing EU support package by introducing 'extraordinary flexibility' in the use of the ESIF, enabling all non-utilised, uncommitted Funds to be mobilised to the 'fullest' extent.[107] Significantly, the CRII+ is designed to provide assistance to vulnerable groups by amending the Regulation on the Fund for European Aid to the Most Deprived (FEAD),[108] thereby introducing further flexibility and liquidity for the Member States to address the evolving needs related to the pandemic.[109]

Following the COVID-19 outbreak, the European Commission also proposed amendments to the 2021–2027 Cohesion Policy package,[110] which were mirrored in the legislative text that was finally adopted (Regulation 2021/1060). The proposed modifications do not substantially alter the 'architecture and cornerstones' of the initially proposed package, outlined above, but are targeted towards bringing 'limited improvements and adjustments on the basis of lessons learnt in the context of the COVID-19 pandemic'.[111] Essentially, the amendments

---

105 European Commission, 'EU Budget for Recovery: Questions and Answers on REACT-EU, Cohesion Policy Post-2020 and the European Social Fund+', *Press Corner*, 28.05.2020, available at https://ec.europa.eu/commission/presscorner/detail/en/QANDA_20_948, last accessed 26.08.2021.

106 European Council, Regulation (EC) No 2012/2002 of 11 November 2002 establishing the European Union Solidarity Fund, 14.11.2002, OJ L 311/3.

107 See https://ec.europa.eu/regional_policy/en/newsroom/news/2020/04/04-02-2020-coronavirus-response-investment-initiative-plus-new-actions-to-mobilise-essential-investments-and-resources, last accessed 26.08.2021.

108 Regulation (EU) No 223/2014 of the European Parliament and of the Council of 11 March 2014 on the Fund for European Aid to the Most Deprived, OJ L 72/1.

109 Regulation (EU) 2020/559 of the European Parliament and of the Council of 23 April 2020 amending Regulation (EU) No 223/2014 as regards the introduction of specific measures for addressing the outbreak of COVID-19, OJ L 130/7.

110 European Commission, 'Amended Proposal for a Regulation of the European Parliament and of the Council laying down common provisions on the European Regional Development Fund, the European Social Fund Plus, the Cohesion Fund, the Just Transition Fund and the European Maritime and Fisheries Fund and financial rules for those and for the Asylum and Migration Fund, the Internal Security Fund and the Border Management and Visa Instrument', COM(2020) 450 final 28.05.2020.

111 Ibid., p. 4.

focus on guaranteeing 'exceptional flexibility' in spending, and empower the Commission to adopt implementing acts allowing for temporary measures to be adopted for the use of the Funds in 'exceptional and unusual' circumstances.[112] Concomitantly, the Commission published amended proposals for the Regulation on the ERDF and the Cohesion Fund,[113] as well as for the Regulation on the ESF+,[114] which are reflected in the legislative measures finally adopted in June 2021 and mentioned above.[115]

On the whole, the financial response of the EU institutions has been described as 'ambitious', and the increased funding for EU Cohesion Policy was 'welcomed by [national] programme authorities and regional interest groups'.[116] It is noteworthy, however, that there is no specific reference to supporting the transition from institutional living to community care in the originally proposed 2021–2027 ERDF Regulation. This was described as a 'missed opportunity' by McEvoy, since the previous thematic *ex ante* conditionality 9 on social inclusion in the 2014–2020 funding framework 'laid out specific conditions for the ERDF to invest in health and social infrastructure, to support the transition from institutional to community-based services'.[117] Nevertheless, the newly adopted Regulation on the ERDF explicitly mentions the promotion of the transition from institutional to family-based and community-based care among the specific objectives to be achieved by spending under the ERDF and the Cohesion Fund. Given that many EU Member States 'are still at an early phase of reform', explicit reference to the transition to community-based care in the newly adopted Regulation on the ERDF serves to embed this mandate in the EU law framework.[118]

4.2.2. *The Strategy for the Rights of Persons with Disabilities 2021–2030*

In addition to the robust financial response of the EU institutions, the rights violations experienced by persons with disabilities during the COVID-19 pandemic also left their mark on the development of the European Disability

---

112 Ibid.

113 European Commission, 'Amended Proposal for a Regulation of the European Parliament and of the Council on the European Regional Development Fund and on the Cohesion Fund', COM(2020) 452 final 28.05.2020.

114 European Commission, 'Amended Proposal for a Regulation of the European Parliament and of the Council on the European Social Fund Plus', COM(2020) 447 final, 28.05.2020.

115 See section 3.3 above, *supra* notes 77 and 78.

116 European Regional Policy Research Consortium, 'The Recovery Plan for Europe and Cohesion Policy: An Initial Assessment', Consortium Paper 20/1, 03.07.2020, available at https://www.eprc-strath.eu/public/dam/jcr:0bde4db2-61d4-4cc6-b463-d7de1d3c049e/THE%20RECOVERY%20PLAN%20FOR%20EUROPE%20AND%20COHESION%20POLICY:%20AN%20INITIAL%20ASSESSMENT.pdf, last accessed 26.08.2021.

117 E. McEvoy (2020), 'EU Structural and Investment Funds and Disability', *supra* note 53, p. 341.

118 Community Living for Europe: Structural Funds Watch (2018), 'Inclusion for All', *supra* note 69, p. 34.

Strategy 2021–2030.[119] In fact, the need to address the inequalities amplified by the pandemic permeates certain parts of the new strategy, which revolves around three key themes: enjoying EU rights, a decent quality of life and independent living, as well as equal access and non-discrimination. The new strategy also innovates when compared to its predecessor by including independent living as a distinct pillar of post-2020 EU disability policy, in explicit acknowledgement of the fact that the pandemic 'intensified the challenges faced by persons living in institutions'.[120]

Notwithstanding this renewed commitment in the new strategy to reinforcing deinstitutionalisation policies, Ferri maintains that the Commission envisages that 'only soft law measures will be implemented', given the limited competence of the EU in this field.[121] In that connection, the Commission vows to support Member States' actions. Along with providing EU Funds to foster deinstitutionalisation, the Commission outlines two 'flagship initiatives'. Under the umbrella of those initiatives, the Commission intends to issue guidance to the Member States by 2023 in the form of recommendations designed to 'enable persons with disabilities to live in accessible, supported housing in the community or to continue living at home (including personal assistance schemes)'.[122] Moreover, by 2024, the Commission intends to put in place a framework for Social Services of Excellence for persons with disabilities. This is a noteworthy development in that the EU institutions appear to have acknowledged the deficiencies in the social care sector laid bare by the pandemic and seem committed to remedying those fragilities within the limits of their competences. Nonetheless, the strategy does not go so far as to ensure the establishment of an Emergency Fund for Social Services, as called for by DPOs.[123]

Markedly, the European Disability Strategy 2021–2030 pays substantial attention to the development of implementation and monitoring mechanisms aimed at 'efficiently delivering' the strategy with a view to supporting Member States' use of the Funds in compliance with the CRPD, including the accessibility norm, thereby ensuring that the Funds 'do not support actions that contribute to segregation or exclusion'.[124] In that respect, the Commission

119 See also the various Resolutions adopted by the European Parliament, such as Resolution of 8 July 2020 on the rights of persons with intellectual disabilities and their families in the COVID-19 crisis (2020/2680(RSP)).

120 European Commission (2021), 'European Disability Strategy 2021–2030', *supra* note 10, p. 11.

121 D. Ferri, 'The New Strategy for the Rights of Persons with Disabilities 2021–2030: A Step Forward in Realising the Human Rights Model of Disability', *EU Law Live*, 05.03.2021, available at https://eulawlive.com/, last accessed 26.08.2021.

122 European Commission (2021), 'European Disability Strategy 2021–2030', *supra* note 10, p. 12.

123 See EASPD, 'Social Services Call on EU to Uphold the Rights and Health of Staff and Users in Next Phase of COVID-19 Response', *supra* note 92.

124 European Commission (2021), 'European Disability Strategy 2021–2030', *supra* note 10, pp. 25 and 28.

will reinforce data collection to monitor implementation of the new strategy in areas where gaps have been identified, including data on those living in institutions.[125] This is pivotal, since data gaps on the use of the ESIF impede a thorough understanding of the costs and timeframe required to make effective transitions to community living, according to FRA.[126]

Ferri asserts that while the new strategy 'seems to represent a step forward in the protection of the rights of persons with disabilities, and its values and core tenets are in line with the CRPD', it nonetheless 'places a strong emphasis on soft law measures, the effect of which will have to be [closely evaluated]'.[127] Although the Commission avows to support national, regional and local authorities in deinstitutionalisation processes by means of 'coordinated action', including through the 2021–2027 ESIF and the RRF, one cannot underestimate the significance of the 'strong commitment' required from national authorities to deliver on the actions proposed by the Commission.[128]

4.3. DISTILLING LESSONS AND PAVING PATHWAYS AHEAD

4.3.1. *Implementation of Post-2020 Policies*

From the collective response of the EU institutions to the COVID-19 crisis, assessed against the normative standards in the CRPD, several lessons can be distilled with regard to the implementation of post-2020 policies.

First, the failure to explicitly mention the social care sector – part of the frontline of the crisis – in the financial package adopted by the EU in response to the pandemic is a real missed opportunity.[129] While the EU's 'limited' support for disability services during the pandemic can mainly be explained by the fact that health and social care competences lie at the national level,[130] EASPD maintains that the EU institutions 'should do more to guarantee the continuity and sustainability of a sector which is essential to its social policies and to respect[ing] its human rights obligations'.[131] This would entail adaptations to policies affecting social services, such as EU public procurement policies, given

[125] Ibid., p. 31.

[126] FRA (2018), 'From Institutions to Community Living for Persons with Disabilities', *supra* note 67, p. 24.

[127] D. Ferri (2021), 'The New Strategy for the Rights of Persons with Disabilities 2021–2030' *supra* note 121.

[128] European Commission (2021), 'European Disability Strategy 2021–2030', *supra* note 10, p. 5.

[129] EASPD, 'Social Services Call on EU to Uphold the Rights and Health of Staff and Users in Next Phase of COVID-19 Response', *supra* note 92.

[130] EASPD (2020), 'The Impact of COVID-19 on Disability Services in Europe', *supra* note 90, p. 17.

[131] Ibid.

that 'authorities showed little flexibility' with regard to their contracts with national social service providers during the pandemic.[132] In this connection, it is noteworthy that the EPSR Action Plan envisages the publication of a Commission Guidance Notice on Public Procurement of Innovation and on Socially Responsible Public Procurement by the end of 2021.[133] Such an initiative would contribute to fostering access to essential support services in post-2020 recovery efforts.

Furthermore, given the cross-cutting effects of the pandemic across a range of EU policies, the deinstitutionalisation agenda should be adequately mainstreamed across all relevant domains. It is therefore of concern that none of the CSR published in spring 2020 address the need to transition to community living,[134] which appears to indicate that this topic has been accorded low priority in the European Semester to date during the pandemic. This worrying trend is repeated in the Annual Sustainable Growth Strategy (ASGS) for 2021,[135] published in September 2020 to guide the European Semester process. While the ASGS 2021 focuses on setting out strategic guidance for the implementation of the RRF, since it does not set out a protection mechanism by which to avoid investments in institutional facilities there is a real danger that the RRF will be used to reinforce institutional care, as highlighted by Cojocariu and Kokić.[136] In this connection, the increased flexibility accorded to EU Member States under the CRII and CRII+ raises grave concerns about a potentially increased misuse of the Funds. There are particular concerns that the ESIF could be used to 'provide conditions for social distancing in institutions, to build new facilities for isolation of COVID-19 positive residents or to further medicalise the provision of care in these settings'.[137] A related concern expressed by the European Court of Auditors is that 'the extraordinary relaxation of key rules, even if temporary', may challenge the capacity of the EU 'to coordinate national economic policy responses during the crisis'.[138] With 'major flows'[139]

---

132 Ibid., p. 4.

133 European Commission (2021), 'The European Pillar of Social Rights Action Plan', *supra* note 45, p. 23.

134 EEG, 'One Step Forward, Two Steps Back?', 29.05.2020, available at https://deinstitutionalisation.com/2020/05/29/one-step-forward-two-steps-back/, last accessed 26.08.2021.

135 European Commission, Communication from the Commission to the European Parliament, the European Council, the Council, the European Central Bank, the European Economic and Social Committee, the Committee of the Regions and the European Investment Bank, Annual Sustainable Growth Strategy 2021, COM/2020/575 final 17.09.2020.

136 I. Bulic Cojocariu and N. Kokić (2020), 'Lost in Interpretation', *supra* note 72, p. 37.

137 Ibid.

138 European Court Of Auditors, 'Risks, Challenges and Opportunities in the EU's Economic Policy Response to the COVID-19 Crisis', 2020, p. 51, available at https://www.eca.europa.eu/Lists/ECADocuments/RW20_06/RW_Economic_response_to_Covid19_EN.pdf, last accessed 26.08.2021.

139 European Regional Policy Research Consortium (2020), 'The Recovery Plan for Europe and Cohesion Policy: An Initial Assessment', *supra* note 116.

of REACT-EU being allocated to Southern European countries like Romania, where the institutionalisation of persons with disabilities is rife,[140] considerable attention must be paid to mobilising the EU budget in all Member States in such a manner as to guarantee continuity of care and support in the community, including the adoption of emergency social security measures for carers and preventative measures to avoid increases in institutionalisation.[141]

Above all, it is crucial to facilitate the participation of DPOs representing individuals with varied impairments in ESIF implementation, considering the negative impact that the pandemic has had on the involvement of DPOs in planning the 2021–2027 programming period. Implementing post-2020 EU policies in line with the CPR's so-called 'partnership principle' implies regular and transparent dialogue with DPOs at EU level. This could be operationalised through the designation of disability coordinators in EU institutions, bodies and agencies, as well as in high-level meetings between EU institutions, as envisaged in the European Disability Strategy 2021–2030.[142] Likewise, the active participation of DPOs should be guaranteed through adequate resource allocation within the ESIF managing authorities, given the increasing concerns regarding decentralisation of the Funds at national level. Moreover, each entity benefitting from EU Funds 'should report on how persons with disabilities were included', and indicators to that effect should be incorporated into each implementation programme, according to EDF.[143] Particular attention must be paid to ensuring accessibility for persons with disabilities in the implementation of Member States' operational programmes, in line with the 2021–2027 CPR.

4.3.2. Monitoring of Post-2020 Policies

Accountability for Member States' use of the Funds is essential, especially in times of crisis. To that end, it is paramount to ensure the involvement of a range of institutional and non-institutional actors at EU and national levels in monitoring post-2020 policies.

The European Commission must keep a close eye on Member States' activities under the CRII and CRII+. In view of the fact that monitoring

140 See M. Šveřepa, 'Deinstitutionalisation essentially is a Struggle for Independence', *Inclusion Europe*, 03.05.2019, available at https://www.inclusion-europe.eu/deinstitutionalisation-essentially-is-a-struggle-for-independence/, last accessed 26.08.2021.

141 EASPD (2020), 'The Impact of COVID-19 on Disability Services in Europe', *supra* note 91, p. 17.

142 European Commission (2021), 'European Disability Strategy 2021–2030', *supra* note 10, p. 26.

143 EDF, 'EU Budget Post-2020. A Budget that Should Leave No-one Behind', available at https://www.edf-feph.org/eu-budget-post-2020/, last accessed 26.08.2021.

by national human rights institutions (NHRIs) and non-governmental organisations has been severely restricted during the pandemic,[144] the Commission should enhance its cooperation with NHRIs and national ombudsmen to ensure oversight of deinstitutionalisation activities. In line with the shared management principle to which the ESIF are subject, the Commission has an overarching responsibility to ensure that Member States' operational programmes comply with EU law, including the CRPD; and that their national strategies are in line with relevant EU strategies and policies, including the European Disability Strategy 2021–2030.[145] According to Waddington and Broderick, monitoring should focus on whether the ESIF are 'properly targeted towards achieving the overall goals' of the new strategy and 'are distributed in a CRPD-compliant way'.[146]

The activities of the Commission are complemented by the EU CRPD Monitoring Framework, which has been established under Article 33 of the Convention.[147] That Framework consists of the European Parliament, the European Ombudsman, FRA and EDF. The European Parliament, in particular, has a clear role to play, according to Priestley, who asserts that the Parliament's Committee on Petitions can aid in implementing Article 19 CRPD at EU level where petitioners identify breaches, 'whether or not the planning and organisation of long-term care systems lies within the responsibility of national authorities'.[148] Given the existence of specific EU law relating to the ESIF and public procurement, Priestley is of the view that this is 'conceivably [...] an issue where Commission infringement proceedings could be invoked as [a] consequence of a well-substantiated petition'.[149]

In addition, it is fundamental to the effectiveness of post-2020 EU policies that monitoring activities at the EU level are complemented by those in place at the national level. In that regard, the European Disability Strategy 2021–2030 draws attention to the 'important role' that domestic focal points established under Article 33 CRPD can play in supporting the fulfilment of the CPR's

144 ENIL (2020), 'Lost in Interpretation', *supra* note 72, p. 37.

145 European Commission (2014), 'Report on the Implementation of the UN Convention', *supra* note 42, para. 99.

146 L. Waddington and A. Broderick, 'The Post-2020 European Disability Strategy', 2020, p. 140, available at https://www.europarl.europa.eu/RegData/etudes/STUD/2020/656398/IPOL_STU(2020)656398_EN.pdf, last accessed 26.08.2021.

147 The activities of the EU CRPD framework during the COVID-19 crisis are outlined at https://fra.europa.eu/sites/default/files/fra_uploads/eu-crpd-framework-activities-during-covid-19-pandemic_en.docx, last accessed 26.08.2021.

148 M. Priestley, 'The Protection Role of the Committee on Petitions in the Context of the Implementation of the UN Convention on the Rights of Persons with Disabilities', study for the PETI Committee, 2016, p. 41, available at https://euagenda.eu/upload/publications/untitled-70600-ea.pdf, last accessed 26.08.2021.

149 Ibid.

enabling conditions throughout the programming period.[150] According to the European Expert Group on Transition from Institutional to Community-based Care (EEG), 'national leadership is essential in making widespread changes' comprising 'multi-level and cross-sectoral coordination'.[151] In that connection, national (emergency) strategies on deinstitutionalisation should cut across all sectors affected by the pandemic, such as health, education, employment and social services – ensuring that concrete monitoring mechanisms are in place as well as the requisite legislative amendments to operationalise the effective transition to community living.[152] In this regard, the optional coordination mechanisms that States should give 'due consideration' to establishing under Article 33 CRPD can facilitate action in different sectors and at different levels of Member State governments.

Furthermore, it is of utmost importance that people with disabilities – including those living in institutions – have access, through their representative organisations, to relevant complaint mechanisms, and that they are involved in all matters related to monitoring Article 19 CRPD in compliance with the CRPD's model of inclusive equality. To that end, capacity-building of DPOs is of vital importance given that the pandemic has hindered the participation of such organisations in relevant planning processes. In a similar vein, training should be provided to officials in the ESIF managing authorities on the requirements of the CRPD and on the importance of the enabling conditions attached to the Funds, thereby seeking to eliminate stereotyping regarding the right to live independently and be included in the community.[153]

Scholars have warned that the monitoring of Member States' activities related to deinstitutionalisation will be complicated by a lack of data in the wake of the pandemic and that the Commission 'will not have easy access to reliable information on the [use of] funding under the ESIF'.[154] Accordingly, strengthened data collection is vital at both national and EU levels. In line with the CRPD's human rights model of disability, data should be disaggregated by age, gender and disability. It should also recount the lived experience of persons with disabilities regarding implementation to date of Article 19 CRPD. Interestingly, the European Disability Strategy 2021–2030 provides that, by 2023, new disability indicators will be developed related

---

150 European Commission (2021), 'European Disability Strategy 2021–2030,' *supra* note 10, p. 27.

151 J. Šiška and J. Beadle-Brown (2020), 'Transition from Institutional Care', *supra* note 6, p. 4.

152 Community Living for Europe: Structural Funds Watch, 'Inclusion for All', *supra* note 69, p. 28.

153 CRPD Committee, *General Comment No. 6*, *supra* note 25, para. 11.

154 A. Le Piece and E. Mertens de Wilmer, 'Coronavirus Crisis: More Flexibility for European Structural and Investment Funds', 06.05.2020, available at https://www.lexgo.be/en/papers/tax-law/european-law/coronavirus-crisis-more-flexibility-for-european-structural-and-investment-funds,136323.html, last accessed 26.08.2021.

to, *inter alia*, social protection and social exclusion, living conditions and health; and the indicators are expected to provide input for the European Semester.[155] In that regard, it is vital that progress on deinstitutionalisation is linked to the Social Scoreboard, thereby strengthening the links between the CRPD and the EPSR.

Finally, appropriate follow-up remedies must be put in place in case of misuse of the Funds. Under the 2021–2027 CPR, EU Member States are supposed to make suitable arrangements in order to ensure that an effective mechanism is in place for examining complaints connected to the Funds, without prejudice to the general possibility for citizens and relevant stakeholders to submit complaints to the Commission.[156] However, at the time of writing, several reports have been submitted to the Commission relating to the misuse of the ESIF,[157] raising doubts about the effectiveness of domestic complaints procedures.[158] Compounding this issue are the concerns of the European Ombudsman regarding the absence of an appropriate legal basis enabling the Commission to recover misused Funds.[159] This lacuna must urgently be addressed in line with the CRPD Committee's recommendation to the EU institutions to suspend, withdraw and recover spending of the Funds that violates Article 19 CRPD.

5. CONCLUDING REMARKS

On account of the pervasive effects of the COVID-19 crisis, deinstitutionalisation has become a 'pressing' human rights' issue.[160] Thus, the transition from institutional to community care must be accorded sustained priority at the EU level in order to meet key CRPD obligations. In that vein, Quinn and Doyle assert that the 'failure to take the CRPD seriously will needlessly expose the EU – and its [M]ember [S]tates – to international legal liability if the Funds are used to build new institutions'.[161]

---

155 European Commission (2021), 'European Disability Strategy 2021–2030', *supra* note 10, p. 32.

156 Article 69(7) 2021–2027 CPR (Regulation 2021/1060).

157 See Validity, available at https://validity.ngo/tag/european-structural-and-investment-funds/, last accessed 26.08.2021.

158 In circumstances where there is inaction on the part of both the Member States and Commission, no remedy is available, and the European General Court recently clarified that an action for annulment under Article 263 TFEU was inadmissible: Case T-613/19, *ENIL Brussels Office and Others v Commission* [2019] OJ C413/1.

159 European Ombudsman, *Case 417/2018/JN*, para. 19.

160 European Commission (2021), 'European Disability Strategy 2021–2030', *supra* note 10, p. 23.

161 G. Quinn and S. Doyle, 'Marrying Principle with Power in the EU-test case of the structural funds negotiations: update', (2013) 11, *The Equal Rights Review*, p. 61; see further European Coalition for Community Living (ECCL), 'Wasted Time, Wasted Money,

As highlighted throughout this contribution, the ESIF play a pivotal role in facilitating the transition away from institutional care facilities and in ensuring adequate support services in the community. However, the existing body of literature elaborates on the 'well-attested history' of the ESIF being used to construct segregated institutions for persons with disabilities.[162] The recovery initiatives adopted by the EU to fight the COVID-19 crisis have the potential to represent either an extraordinary opportunity to accelerate deinstitutionalisation or a sorely missed opportunity. Whichever of these scenarios transpires depends largely on the implementation and monitoring mechanisms put in place in respect of post-2020 EU policies.

Domestic and EU institutions have a vital role to play in deinstitutionalisation processes going forward. Most importantly, the urgency in responding to the ongoing pandemic should not impede the involvement of persons with disabilities, through their representative organisations, in decision-making processes, as well as in the implementation and monitoring of relevant policies. This is essential to guaranteeing that the transition to community living is conducted in line with the 'partnership principle' underpinning the EU regulatory framework.

The Commissioner for Cohesion and Reforms, Elisa Ferreira, asserts that while EU Cohesion Policy 'remains the beating heart of European solidarity', it needs to be filled 'with content' in the form of investments that will result in 'real change'.[163] This assertion rings true in the context of disability, whereby the protection of fundamental rights is vital to ensuring meaningful reforms in transitioning to independent community living. There is no doubt that the common values of equality, respect for human dignity and human rights upon which the Union is built take on increased significance in times of crisis. These values also form the bedrock of the CRPD. Indeed, the human rights model of disability and model of inclusive equality underpinning the Convention urge parties to guarantee that the right of individuals with disabilities to live independently in the community is not further compromised by the ongoing COVID-19 pandemic and recovery efforts.

Wasted Lives – A Wasted Opportunity?: A Focus Report on How the Current Use of Structural Funds Perpetuates the Social Exclusion of Disabled People in Central and Eastern Europe by Failing to Support the Transition from Institutional Care to Community-Based Services', 2010, available at http://community-living.info/wp-content/uploads/2014/02/ECCL-StructuralFundsReport-final-WEB.pdf, last accessed 26.08.2021.

162 OHCHR (written by G. Quinn and S. Doyle) (2012), 'Getting a Life – Living Independently and Being Included in the Community', *supra* note 35, p. 8.

163 See European Commission, 'Commissioner Ferreira welcomes the political agreement on the EU Cohesion policy legislative package 2021–2027', 16.12.2020, available at https://ec.europa.eu/regional_policy/en/newsroom/news/2020/12/16-12-2020-commissioner-ferreira-welcomes-the-political-agreement-on-the-eu-cohesion-policy-legislative-package-2021-2027, last accessed 26.08.2021.

MIGRANTS AT SEA AMID THE CORONAVIRUS PANDEMIC

The Perfect Pretext for Endorsing *à la carte* Respect for Human Rights

Aphrodite Papachristodoulou

ABSTRACT

Over the past decade, the Mediterranean maritime space has become increasingly securitised, as the humanitarian objective of saving lives of those in distress at sea has been subordinated to the objective of protecting European borders. Amid the coronavirus outbreak in 2020, states (like Italy and Malta) have introduced 'quarantine ships' for the transfer of rescued migrants at sea upon declaring that their ports were no longer 'safe' for migrant arrivals. In this regard, the right to liberty and security, as found in Article 5 of the European Convention on Human

Rights (ECHR), allows under paragraph 1(e) the deprivation of liberty and the lawful detention of persons by virtue of preventing the spread of infectious diseases. Accordingly, the European Court of Human Rights (ECtHR, the Court) will often assess the manner and method of execution of the detention in conjunction with Article 3 of the ECHR in order to provide adequate safeguards against the risk of ill-treatment during such deprivation. This contribution aims to critically assess the impact and lawfulness of the measures adopted during the COVID-19 pandemic against the human rights of migrants rescued at sea. Against this background, it ponders the following question: are the 'special' quarantine measures – the use of quarantine ships – adopted by Italy and Malta in respect of migrants rescued at sea in accordance with existing criteria for the lawful deprivation of liberty? It is posited that the answer lies in evaluating these practices in light of human rights principles at stake as well as examining the jurisprudence of the ECtHR in light of similar issues concerning the prevention of the spread of infectious diseases. In this way, the pandemic angle becomes central to this analysis, underlining the need to advance human rights principles together with the rule of law. The contribution maintains that from a human rights perspective, quarantining migrants offshore is problematic, as the practice involves detaining persons at sea, precisely after a traumatic and perilous sea journey, without considering that a large number of them have escaped persecution, violence and other atrocious conditions. In conclusion, these practices might give rise to other potential human rights violations, including Article 2 and Article 3 of the ECHR.

1. INTRODUCTION

The sheer volume of migrants crossing the Mediterranean Sea from the Middle East and North Africa in the last decade denotes a cardinal humanitarian crisis at Europe's shores, with little signs of receding. The aftermath of the Arab Spring has caused the 'biggest transformation of the Middle East since decolonization' and produced a revolutionary migration wave across the North African regions, forcing millions of people to flee in the face of horrendous violence and atrocities.[1] Prior to the COVID-19 outbreak, attention on saving lives at sea and preventing deaths that occur once people embark on dangerous sea journeys has been deflected to stem the flow of migrants reaching European shores. In this regard, there has been alarming evidence of human rights violations at sea manifested through instances where states might ignore distress calls or fail to coordinate rescue operations that lead to the loss of

[1] L. Bacon, 'To What Extent Can the Right to Asylum Be Limited by a State's Sovereign Right to Control Its Borders? A Comparative Assessment of the Lawfulness of European National Asylum Law and Procedure', (2016) 22, *Auckland University Law Review*, p. 70.

thousands of lives.[2] Consequently, the Central Mediterranean route – migrant crossings, largely from Libya and other North African countries to Italian or Maltese coasts – presents the world's deadliest migrant route, with per capita death rate rising each year.[3]

Undoubtedly, the phenomenon of irregular migration by sea is considered, fundamentally, a state sovereignty challenge. Accordingly, the governments of the Central Mediterranean, especially those most affected by migratory flows in virtue of geographic proximity to the issue (Italy and Malta in this case), have strengthened their border controls and adopted migration policies that project an extra-territorialisation of European borders.[4] Such practices have stretched the concept of state sovereignty even beyond the territorial limits of a state to countries of origin and transit, hence creating a 'foreign border', which will keep migrants as far from European shores as possible and subjected to dire consequences.[5] On top of this humanitarian crisis, the COVID-19 outbreak had substantial implications on the access to asylum procedures, as Europe was no longer considered a 'safe' haven. In turn, this made the right of irregular migrants to seek international protection elusive. Understandingly, most (if not *all*) nations' legal orders were unprepared to respond effectively and at the appropriate scale. Hence, containing the rapid transmission of the virus in the community still presents an ongoing challenge and a priority for all governments. In this vein, it is generally accepted that states have the right to protect their citizens against the spread of infectious diseases, such that protection may require some *legitimate* intrusion into the individual rights of the person. Accordingly, quarantine provides an integral strategy to halt the spread of the virus and a potent tool for protecting the public's health and safety.

Notwithstanding the above concerns, in an ever more populist political climate characterised by a 'moral hysteria' at the prospect of migrant arrivals, the Italian and Maltese governments have introduced 'quarantine ships' as a response to COVID-19, where migrants rescued at sea arguably face indefinite

---

2 In particular, see the most recent decision by the HRC in the context of SAR operations, where the Committee found Italy to have failed to carry out its positive obligations to protect the lives of persons in distress at sea by virtue of its negligent acts and omissions in cooperating the rescue operation, which had fatal consequences; CCPR, *A.S. and others v Italy*, UN Doc CCPR/C/130/D/3042/2017, 27.01.2021; See also, C. Heller and L. Pezzani, 'Case: "Left-to-die boat"', 2014, available at https://www.forensic-architecture.org/case/left-die-boat/, last accessed 20.05.2021.

3 A. Papachristodoulou and R. Collins, 'Pulling Back Navies and Pushing Back Migrants: Questioning the EU's Legal Responsibility in the Mediterranean Sea', (2018), *UCD Working Papers in Law, Criminology & Socio-Legal Studies*, Research Paper No. 01/2020, pp. 13–15.

4 V. Moreno-Lax, 'The EU Humanitarian Border and The Securitization of Human Rights: The "Rescue-Through-Interdiction/Rescue-Without-Protection" Paradigm', (2018) 56(1), *Journal of Common Market Studies*, pp. 124–125.

5 M. Den Heijer, *Europe and Extraterritorial Asylum*, Hart, Oxford 2012, p. 5.

forced detention or forced quarantine on board of state-chartered ships. At the same time, the right to liberty in the European Convention on Human Rights (ECHR or Convention) permits the deprivation of liberty, including the lawful detention of persons, in order to prevent the spread of infectious diseases. While the grounds appear, *prima facie*, to be legitimate for adopting such extraordinary measures, the manner of implementation, as well as the conditions and length of quarantine, might seem inappropriate to provide proper safeguards for the health and life of rescued migrants. In this vein, such practices might also risk violating the right to life and the freedom from ill-treatment. For Cathryn Costello, crises may sometimes stimulate deep change, 'prompting a "never again" impulse', or 'they can distract from structural problems or even generate policy paralyses'.[6] I concur with this view, and I will add that concurrent crises (the migration and health crises in this instance) might even *amplify*, rather than 'distract' from existing structural problems, in the absence of legal oversight.

The structure of my argument is four-pronged. Section 2 sets the scene by introducing the measures adopted for migrants rescued at sea in the Central Mediterranean during the pandemic. The study focuses solely on the actions taken by Italy and Malta, which are Europe's frontline states in that region. Section 3 gives an overview of the international law of the sea rules, governing the state's duty to render assistance to persons in distress at sea and deliver them to a place of safety as well as the state's sovereign right to control access to its ports. This will be examined in light of the 'closed-ports' policy, which raises strong implications for the human rights of migrants. In turn, this will allow the assessment of the subsequent measures, namely, the introduction of state-owned quarantine ships for the transfer of those persons that are rescued at sea. Section 4 provides the legal framework on the right to liberty as well as the grounds for permissible deprivations of liberty. In doing so, it proceeds through an exploration of the relevant case law in order to elucidate the factors taken into account by courts when assessing the legality of such deprivations, with a particular focus on the European Court of Human Rights (ECtHR, the Court, or Strasbourg court) jurisprudence. A caveat necessary to be mentioned is that there are only a limited number of cases decided in the context of containing the spread of an infectious disease. Having provided the grounds in which an individual's liberty can be lawfully deprived, the last two sections scrutinise the legality of the migration measures – quarantine ships – providing also contemporary material as the situation is (still) evolving.

6 C. Costello, 'Overcoming Refugee Containment and Crisis', (2020) 21, *German Law Journal*, p. 21.

2. MEASURES ADOPTED FOR MIGRANTS RESCUED AT SEA IN THE COVID-19 ERA

The protection of public health is widely recognised as a core governmental function.[7] Border closures (including seaports and airports), internal border controls, travel bans and quarantine restrictions upon entry to a country are some of the broader measures adopted by governments, either to internally protect their resident population or to prevent third-country nationals from entering their territory, with the primary aim being to flatten out the growth in the rate of infections. For persons seeking international protection overseas, this necessarily translates into a practical suspension of the asylum system, effectively hindering the right to seek protection.[8] In this vein, the European Commission, in its recommendations with regards to temporary travel restrictions, has stressed that these bans do not apply to persons in need of international protection or for other humanitarian reasons.[9] Nevertheless, Europe's frontline states in the Central Mediterranean migration route have taken extreme measures during the coronavirus-pandemic that primarily challenge well-established customary norms and international human rights obligations, which states seem to be increasingly deconstructing by invoking reasons of national security and sovereignty.[10]

Both the Italian and Maltese governments have closed their seaports during the coronavirus pandemic. In particular, the Italian government adopted a 'Ports Closed Decree' on 7 April 2020, clarifying that the Italian ports are no longer classified as a 'place of safety' for migrant arrivals 'for the entire duration of the national health emergency'.[11] A similar approach was followed by the Maltese

---

7 WHO, 'Chapter 4: Building blocks for effective public health laws', (2016) available at https://www.who.int/healthsystems/topics/health-law/chapter4.pdf, last accessed 03.02.2021.

8 The Dublin III regulation establishes that the responsibility for dealing with an asylum seeker's application falls on the country of first entry; see Regulation (EU) No 604/2013 of the European Parliament and of the Council of 26 June 2013 establishing the criteria and mechanisms for determining the Member State responsible for examining an application for international protection lodged in one of the Member States by a third-country national or a stateless person (recast), OJ L180 (hereinafter Dublin III Regulation).

9 European Commission, 'Communication From The Commission: Covid-19: Temporary Restriction on Non-Essential Travel to the EU', COM(2020) 115 final, 16.03.2020.

10 For example, similar aggravated measures have been taken by Greece, Cyprus, Croatia and other EU Member States towards migrants who attempted to arrive by sea or in an irregular manner. However, the study focuses solely on Italy and Malta.

11 Interministerial Decree no.150 adopted on 07.04.2020, available at https://www.avvenire.it/c/attualita/Documents/M_INFR.GABINETTO.REG_DECRETI(R).0000150.07-04-2020%20(3).pdf?fbclid=IwAR1ND4AFGVqsfnO7pzXcIdlG2NlPGcPKUgT1Mjjg6lYqsU-3cEsfPu3ovU4, last accessed 21.06.2021; V.M. Keller, F. Schöler and M. Goldoni, 'Not a Safe Place?', *Verfassungsblog*, 14.04.2020, available at https://verfassungsblog.de/not-a-safe-place/, last accessed 21.06.2021.

government, which issued a declaration stipulating that 'the Maltese authorities are not in a position to guarantee the rescue of prohibited immigrants on board of any boats, ships or other vessels, nor to ensure the availability of a "safe place" on the Maltese territory to any persons rescued at sea'.[12] These measures *a priori* appear to be legally justified as they are based on the premise of safeguarding the functionality of national health structures and containing the spread of the virus in light of a state of emergency. Respectively, a few days after, both governments implemented further extraordinary measures, namely the use of 'quarantine ships' for migrants who are rescued at sea 'for whom it is not possible to indicate the "Place of Safety"'.[13] In essence, this required the transfer of migrants onto state-chartered ships for 'quarantine' purposes in order to prevent and contain the spread of COVID-19. Accordingly, the Civil Liberties Immigration Department of the Italian Ministry of Interior, in cooperation with the Italian Red Cross, were tasked with administering procedures relating to the implementation of the quarantine and health care monitoring aboard ships.[14] It must be noted that these decisions were adopted unilaterally and not with the European Commission's coordination,[15] amid a climate of growing hostility towards migrants attempting to reach Europe. In this context, the United Nations High Commissioner for Refugees (UNHCR) stressed that the Member States of the European Union (EU, the Union), who adopted border closures or entry bans, should not preclude persons from seeking international protection under the principle of *non-refoulement*.[16] In those cases, 'an explicit exemption for asylum-seekers should be considered'.[17]

---

12 Declaration by the Government of Malta, 09.04.2020, available at https://www.gov.mt/en/Government/DOI/Press%20Releases/Pages/2020/April/09/pr200648.aspx, last accessed 20.03.2021; see also, Reuters Staff, 'Malta says it can no longer rescue, accept migrants', Reuters, 09.04.2020, available at https://www.reuters.com/article/us-health-coronavirus-malta-migrants/malta-says-it-can-no-longer-rescue-accept-migrants-idUSKCN21R3DO, last accessed 20.03.2021.

13 Article 1 of the Interministerial Decree no. 1287 adopted on 12.04.2020, available at https://www.protezionecivile.gov.it/en/normativa/decreto-del-capo-dipartimento-n--1287-del-12-aprile-2020--nomina-del-soggetto-attuatore-per-le-attivit--emergenziali-connesse-all-assistenza-e-alla-so., last accessed 10.07.2021.

14 D. Loprieno and C. Di Maio, 'The "quarantine ships" experience: a practice to isolate migrants', 29.10.2020, available at https://www.glimer.eu/the-quarantine-ships-experience-a-practice-to-isolate-migrants/, last accessed 20.03.2021.

15 See also S. Montaldo, 'The COVID-19 Emergency and the Reintroduction of Internal Border Controls in the Schengen Area: Never Let a Serious Crisis Go to Waste', (2020) 5(1), *European Papers*, p. 526.

16 UNHCR, 'Practical Recommendations and Good Practice to Address Protection Concerns in the Context of the Covid-19 Pandemic', 15.04.2020, p. 2, available at https://data2.unhcr.org/en/documents/details/75453, last accessed 14.02.2021.

17 Ibid.

3. RIGHTS AND OBLIGATIONS UNDER THE INTERNATIONAL LAW OF THE SEA

This section will briefly present the obligations of states with regards to persons in distress at sea and, accordingly, the rights of states to control their borders in light of the above measures.

3.1. DUTY TO RENDER ASSISTANCE AND 'PLACE OF SAFETY'

The principle of saving the lives of those in distress at sea is not only a long-standing and fundamental tradition of seafaring, but is also incorporated as a legal obligation of the search and rescue (SAR) system under international law of the sea.[18] Commercial vessels when conducting SAR activities are operating under the duty to render assistance to persons in distress at sea, as enshrined in Article 98 of the United Nations Convention on the Law of the Sea 1982 (UNCLOS).[19] In this regard, the International Convention for the Safety of Life at Sea 1974 (SOLAS)[20] and the International Convention on Maritime Search and Rescue 1979 (SAR Convention)[21] specify that in providing such assistance, masters of ships need to disembark the rescued persons in a 'place of safety'. The general principles that regulate disembarkation derive from the sovereign right of states to grant or refuse access to vessels in their territory and from the *non-refoulement* principle. In particular, Chapter 1 of the SAR Convention provides that 'rescue' is 'an operation to retrieve persons in distress, provide for their initial medical or other needs, and deliver them to a place of safety'.[22] Among various scholars, Violeta Moreno-Lax treats this provision as creating an obligation of result; for the SAR operation to be considered completed the persons

---

18 A. Papachristodoulou, 'The Principle of Saving Lives at Sea: Just a Fool's Hope', *International Law Blog*, 27.06.2019, available at https://internationallaw.blog/2019/06/27/the-principle-of-saving-lives-at-sea-just-a-fools-hope/, last accessed 25.03.2021; See, *inter alia*, S. Cacciaguidi-Fahy, 'The Law of the Sea and Human Rights', (2007) 2(9), *Panóptica*, p. 4; I. Papanicolopulu, *International Law and the Protection of People at Sea*, Oxford University Press, Oxford 2018.

19 United Nations Convention on the Law of the Sea, 1982, 183 UNTS 397, 21 ILM 1261, 10.12.1982.

20 International Convention for the Safety of Life at Sea, 1974, as amended, 1184 UNTS, 01.11.1974.

21 International Convention on Maritime Search and Rescue, 1979, with annexes, 1405 UNTS 97, 27.04.1979.

22 IMO, Resolution MSC. 70 (69), *Adoption of Amendments to the International Convention on Maritime Search and Rescue, 1979*, 18.05.1998, paras. 1.3.3 and 1.3.4.

need to be effectively disembarked.[23] This is supported by the SAR Convention, which requires the disembarkation of people to a place where the safety of their life is 'no longer threatened and where their basic human needs (such as food, shelter and medical needs) can be met'.[24] As such, the obligation stemming from the law of the sea framework is not only an obligation of cooperation and conduct, but it legally denotes the disembarkation of rescued persons to a place of safety.[25] Accordingly, the coastal state is responsible for ensuring that such a place is afforded but is not required to accept the rescued persons in its territory. In this vein, the International Maritime Organization's (IMO) 2004 amendments to the SOLAS and SAR Convention refrain from elaborating any normative criteria of a place of safety, allowing for such interpretation to be varying in practice and allowing for ad hoc arrangements.[26]

Accordingly, the question of disembarkation to a 'place of safety' has always been perceived as a grey area, whereby controversial tactics by governments sketch the fate of seaborne migrants.[27] Most importantly, in complying with this duty, states should refrain from returning migrants to a place where their life or liberty could be at risk.[28] As such, the prohibition of *refoulement* under international refugee law ties into the disembarkation of persons to a 'place of safety' in order for a rescue operation to be marked as completed.[29] Given the ongoing migration crisis at Europe's shores, it is evident that the paramount

---

23 V. Moreno-Lax and E. Papastavridis, 'Tracing the Bases of an Integrated Paradigm for Maritime Security and Human Rights at Sea' in V. Moreno-Lax and E. Papastavridis (eds.), *'Boat refugees' and Migrants at sea: A comprehensive approach, Integrating Maritime Security with Human Rights*, Brill Nijhoff Publishers, Leiden 2016, p. 196; see also S. Trevisanut and S. Nicolosi, 'Saving Lives in the Mediterranean – A Legal Analysis of Aquarius-like Incidents', (2019) *Ars Aequi* 121, pp. 122–123.

24 IMO, Resolution MSC. 167 (78), Annex 34, *Guidelines on the Treatment of Persons Rescued at Sea*, 20.05.2004, para. 3.

25 See also E. Papastavridis, 'Rescuing "Boat People" in the Mediterranean Sea: The Responsibility of States under the Law of the Sea', *EJIL: Talk!*, 31.05.2011, available at https://www.ejiltalk.org/rescuing-boat-people-in-the-mediterranean-sea-the-responsibility-of-states-under-the-law-of-the-sea/, last accessed 10.06.2021.

26 IMO Resolutions MSC.155 (78) and MSC 153 (78), 20.05.2004.

27 A. Papachristodoulou, 'Mediterranean Maritime Migration: The Legal Framework of Saving Lives at Sea', (2020) 20, *University College Dublin Law Review*, p. 107.

28 Article 33 of the Refugee Convention; The interpretation of the term 'place of safety' has channelled through the debates on disembarkation and received much scholarly attention, see, *inter alia*, V. Moreno-Lax, D. Ghezelbash and N. Klein, 'Between life, security and rights: Framing the interdiction of "boat migrants" in the Central Mediterranean and Australia', (2019) 32(4), *Leiden Journal of International Law*, pp. 715–740; K.S. O'Brien, 'Refugees on the High Seas: International Refugee Law Solutions to a Law of the Sea Problem', (2001) 3(2), *Goettingen Journal of International Law*, pp. 715–732; P. Mallia, 'The MV Salamis and the State of Disembarkation at International Law: The Undefinable Goal', (2014) 18 (11), *American Society of International Law*.

29 Article 33 Convention Relating to the Status of Refugees (Refugee Convention), 189 U.N.T.S. 150, 28.07.1951; K. Wouters and M. Den Heijer, 'The *Marine I* Case: A Comment', (2009) 22(1), *International Journal of Refugee Law*, p. 6.

principle of *non-refoulement* in application to persons rescued at sea is a point of contention, as states are more than ever unwilling to allow the disembarkation of migrants to their territory, who will subsequently claim rights of asylum.[30] This alone stands to be among the underlying reasons why governments have increasingly limited SAR capacity in the Mediterranean and have adopted a 'closed-ports' approach even before the outbreak of COVID-19.[31] Undoubtedly, the pandemic has aggravated the existing gaps in migrant protection at sea.

3.2. SOVEREIGN RIGHT TO CONTROL ACCESS TO PORTS

As expounded, international law does not impose an unequivocal duty on any state to take rescued persons into its territory.[32] The international law of the sea allows a state to control its ports as they are found in its internal waters, where a state enjoys a sovereign right to control entry to vessels in its territory. This power is enshrined in Article 8 of UNCLOS, where it clarifies the meaning of 'internal waters', and subsequently, Article 25 confers 'rights of protection of the coastal state'. In particular, Article 25(3) states that:

> The Coastal State may, *without discrimination* in form or in fact among foreign ships, *suspend temporarily* specified areas of its territorial sea the innocent passage of foreign ships if such suspension is essential for the protection of its security [...] (emphasis added).[33]

Accordingly, the innocent passage can be suspended if there is a perceived security threat to the coastal state, as Article 19(1) of UNCLOS clarifies that 'passage is innocent so long as it is not prejudicial to the peace, good order or security of the coastal state'. Subsequently, Article 19(2) makes available a list of activities that

---

[30] Arguably, this is the outcome of a dysfunctional Dublin system which plays a catalyst role to the heavy strain on the asylum systems of Europe's frontline states in the Mediterranean, see Dublin III Regulation; A. Papachristodoulou (2020), 'Mediterranean Maritime Migration', *supra* note 27, p. 104; See also A. Lauterpacht and D. Bethlehem, 'The Scope and Content of the Principle of Non-Refoulement: Opinion' in E. Feller, V. Türk and F. Nicholson (eds.), *Refugee Protection in International Law: UNHCR's Global Consultations on International Protection*, Cambridge University Press, Cambridge 2003; R. Barnes, 'The International Law of the Sea and Migration Control', in B. Ryan and V. Mitsilegas (eds.), *Extraterritorial Immigration Control: Legal Challenges*, Martinus Nijhoff, Leiden 2010, p. 100.

[31] The closure of ports to vessels transporting migrants was first introduced on 24.09.2018 by the then Minister of the Interior, Matteo Salvini, available at https://www.gazzettaufficiale.it/eli/id/2018/10/04/18G00140/s, last accessed 02.06.2021.

[32] P. Mallia (2014), 'The MV Salamis and the State of Disembarkation at International Law', *supra* note 28.

[33] Article 25(3) UNCLOS.

will render the passage non-innocent, and in this context, the relevant activity is 'the loading or unloading of any commodity, currency or person contrary to the customs, fiscal, immigration or sanitary laws and regulations of the coastal state'.[34] From this perspective, states have lawful grounds for restricting access into their territories in light of health and safety reasons during the pandemic. On the one hand, this can be sustained by the argument that the 'loading' or 'unloading' of people who are susceptible to becoming infected with a novel virus or are suspected to be already infected are grounds to consider the passage as not innocent. On the other hand, one cannot simply presume that the rescued people will pose a threat to the health systems if they are automatically rejected without any medical checks.[35] It is posited that the disembarkation of migrants on land or their admission to the territory might not have deteriorated the functionality of the health system, given that this was not a period of large-scale influx.[36] In this vein, Andrea Maria Pelliconi posits that '[i]t cannot be excluded *a priori* that the safest place is Italy, only by virtue of proclamation of state of emergency'.[37] Accordingly, states should not derelict further their law of the sea obligations, particularly the obligation to preserve the safety of life at sea.[38] Thereby, choosing to declare ports as 'unsafe' for asylum seekers by virtue of the public health emergency remains highly dubious.[39]

On top of this, what becomes particularly problematic, and the point of departure of this analysis, is whether the use of 'quarantine ships' for the purpose of transferring migrants rescued at sea can be considered a lawful measure in light of human rights principles and the objectives laid out in the decrees (to control new infections; to protect the national health system; and to protect migrants' health).[40]

---

34 Article 19(2) UNCLOS.

35 A.M. Pelliconi, 'Covid-19: Italy is not a "place of safety" anymore. Is the decision to close Italian ports compliant with human rights obligations?', *EJIL: Talk!* 23.04.2020, available at https://www.ejiltalk.org/covid-19-italy-is-not-a-place-of-safety-anymore-is-the-decision-to-close-italian-ports-compliant-with-human-rights-obligations/, last accessed 12.06.2020.

36 S. Nicolosi, 'Non Refoulement During a Health Emergency', *EJIL: Talk!*, 14.03.2020, available at https://www.ejiltalk.org/non-refoulement-during-a-health-emergency/, last accessed 11.06.2020.

37 A.M. Pelliconi (2020), 'Covid-19: Italy is not a "place of safety" anymore', *supra* note 35.

38 S. Galani, 'Persons at Sea, International Law, and Covid-19', *EJIL Talk!*, 24.11.2020, available at https://www.ejiltalk.org/persons-at-sea-international-law-and-covid-19/, last accessed 02.01.2021; S. Trevisanut, 'Is there a right to be rescued at sea? A constructive view', 2014, *available at* http://www.qil-qdi.org/is-there-a-right-to-be-rescued-at-sea-a-constructive-view/, last accessed 24.11.2020; For example, the ITLOS coined the topic of human rights at sea by reiterating the concept of 'considerations of humanity' first used in the *Corfu Channel* judgment by the ICJ, in its *M/V Saiga (No. 2)* case concerning enforcement activities at sea, *The M/V 'Saiga' (No. 2) (Saint Vincent and the Grenadines v Guinea)*, 01.07.1999, ITLOS Case No. 2, ITLOS Reports 1999, 10.

39 For a detailed analysis of the closed-ports policy see the recent article by S. Galani, 'Port Closures and Persons at Sea in International Law', (2021) 70(3), *International and Comparative Law Quarterly*, pp. 605–633.

40 A.M. Pelliconi (2020), 'Covid-19: Italy is not a "place of safety" anymore', *supra* note 35.

4. THE LEGAL FRAMEWORK FOR DEPRIVATION OF LIBERTY UNDER THE ECHR

Against this backdrop, migrants who are rescued at sea and transferred aboard state-owned ships come under the authority of the saving state, which exercises *de facto* or *de jure* control over them.[41] Hence, the duties under the ECHR to safeguard the human rights of those persons are triggered for both Italy and Malta from the moment migrants are transferred to their state-owned ships. In this vein, the right to liberty and security of the person is a fundamental human right, which is firmly established in international law and regulates the grounds of any deprivation of liberty.

4.1. THE SCOPE OF THE RIGHT TO LIBERTY AND SECURITY

The right to liberty and security of the person is enshrined in Article 5 of the ECHR. According to paragraph 1, the Convention provides an exhaustive list of specific grounds upon which any deprivation of liberty taken in accordance with a procedure prescribed by law will be justified.[42] The most relevant for this analysis is found in Article 5(1)(e), stipulating, *inter alia*: 'the lawful detention of persons for the prevention of the spreading of infectious diseases'. Ergo, quarantine measures that lead to the compulsory confinement of people to a certain place, for example, in a hotel, or as exemplified herein, aboard a ship, will *de facto* fall into the category of detention, in the absence of valid consent to the confinement in question.[43] Importantly, in the only case considered by the ECtHR with reference to quarantine measures, *Kuimov v Russia*,[44] the Court clarified that restrictions should be 'a temporary measure, to be discontinued as soon as circumstances permit' and noted that the fact that they may last for a long duration indicates their disproportionality.[45] Relatedly, where the lawfulness of detention (quarantine) is in issue, in addition to conformity with national law, the ECHR requires that any deprivation of liberty should be in line with the purpose of protecting the individual against arbitrariness.[46] In this regard, the ECtHR's vast case law on the notion of arbitrariness in the context of

41 ECtHR, *Hirsi Jamaa and others v Italy*, no 27765/09, 23.02.2012, para. 81; ECtHR, *Medvedyev and others v France*, no 3394/03, 29.03.2021, para. 67.

42 Article 5(1) ECHR.

43 ECtHR, *Storck v Germany*, no 61603/00, 16.06.2005, paras. 73–74.

44 ECtHR, *Kuimov v Russia*, no 32147/04, 08.01.2009; The case is relevant as it is the only one concerning quarantine measures, yet it must be noted that it concerned the impact of influenza quarantine in the family life related to a parent-child contact, considered under Article 8 ECHR.

45 Ibid., para. 96.

46 ECtHR, *Saadi v the United Kingdom*, no 13229/03 [GC] 29.01.2008, para. 67; See also ECtHR, *Khlaifia v Italy*, no 16483/12, 15.12.2016, paras. 106–107.

Article 5 focuses, *inter alia*, on the type of detention involved.[47] More pertinent to this analysis is that there must be some connection between the ground of permitted deprivation of liberty asserted – to halt the spread of the virus – and the place and conditions of detention – quarantine ships.[48]

In conjunction with Article 5(1)(e), Article 5(1)(f) becomes concurrently relevant to this assessment. It provides: '[t]he lawful arrest or detention of a person to prevent his effecting an unauthorised entry into the country or of a person again who action is being taken with a view to deportation or extradition'. As a matter of clarity, before continuing the analysis, one remark is in order. It should be noted that the measures adopted will be scrutinised under the exception of paragraph (e) as long as there exists a danger of the spreading of an infectious disease. Accordingly, if this purpose ceases to exist and quarantine ships are used instead as immigration control facilities, then the examination will fall under paragraph (f). Notwithstanding, paragraph (f) is overall considered pertinent to this analysis, as it provides vast jurisprudential guidance on the detention of asylum seekers. In this regard, the Court, in its case law, has often taken into account the vulnerability intrinsic in an asylum seeker's situation when scrutinising the detention conditions.[49] Ergo, given that these measures are solely employed towards migrants rescued at sea,[50] it is useful to shed light on the Court's interpretation of lawfulness in those cases.

4.2. RELEVANT CASE LAW

The case law of the Strasbourg court has so far interpreted the permitted exceptions listed in Article 5(1)(a)–(f) narrowly.[51] In light of Article 5(1)(f), the Court has clarified in *Saadi v the United Kingdom*[52] that such detention must be consistent with the overall purpose of Article 5, which is to protect the right to liberty and ensure that any deprivation of liberty is not disposed of in an arbitrary fashion. This is in line with Article 5(1)(e), which makes it a justified ground to limit one's liberty based on the prevention of an infectious disease, given that the prescribed form and manner of detention is lawful and is not arbitrary. Notably, the ECtHR dealt with an alleged violation of deprivation

47 ECtHR, *James, Wells and Lee v the United Kingdom*, nos 25119/09, 57715/09 and 57877/09, 18.09.2021, paras. 190–196.

48 Ibid., para. 194; ECtHR, *Enhorn v Sweden*, no 56529/00, 22.01.2005, para. 42.

49 See ECtHR, *M.S.S. v Belgium and Greece*, no 30696/09 [GC] 21.01.2011, para. 233.

50 Persons crossing the Mediterranean Sea are migrants, refugees and asylum seekers; it is understood that they travel in the same boats; hence, there is a 'mixed migration phenomenon'. See International Organization for Migration, 'International Migration Law No 34, Glossary on Migration' (IOM, 2019), available at https://publications.iom.int/system/files/pdf/iml_34_glossary.pdf, last accessed 10.09.2021.

51 D. Cline, 'Deprivation of Liberty: Has the European Court of Human Rights Recognised a "Public Safety" Exception?', (2013) 29(76), *Merkourios*, p. 44.

52 ECtHR, *Saadi v the United Kingdom*, no 13229/03 [GC], 29.01.2008, paras. 64–66.

of liberty under Article 5(1)(e) in the famous case of *Enhorn v Sweden*,[53] which concerned controlling of the spread of HIV. *In casu*, the Court acknowledged the scarcity of comparable cases in its jurisprudence by specifying that it 'has only to a very limited extent decided cases where a person has been detained for the prevention of spreading infectious diseases'.[54] It further noted that an essential element of the lawfulness of a detention within the meaning of Article 5(1)(e) is the absence of arbitrariness.[55] Accordingly, it found a violation of Article 5(1) as the detention of the individual did not constitute a *proportionate* response nor a last resort in order to prevent the spread of infectious disease as permitted under paragraph (e). The Court took the opportunity to illustrate the criteria necessary to assess whether public health powers will comply with the Convention's rights, and provided that compulsory isolation needs to comply not only with the principle of proportionality, but also it needs to be non-arbitrary, such that other, less severe measures have been considered and found to be insufficient to safeguard the public interest.[56]

In order to scrutinise the necessity of the detention measures, there needs to be a proportionality assessment. This involves a consideration of whether, in the specific circumstances, the detention scheme is fit for the purported aim and whether there is a less invasive method of achieving that aim.[57] In the case that an individual's detention would lead to a violation of another human right, it may be considered arbitrary.[58] Moreover, a detention that is *bona fide* (legitimate) at the outset may become arbitrary over time. This is the case because the rationale for detention may cease to be relevant or exist.[59] In this context, the mandatory quarantine ships were introduced, *inter alia*, for the purpose of screening individuals in order to inform an assessment of whether they present or could present a risk of infecting others. Thereby, if it becomes no longer reasonable to assume that a person poses a risk, then the detention reason will cease to exist, and states will need to disembark those rescued to a place of safety. Analogously, the ECtHR in expounding the meaning of 'freedom from arbitrariness' in the context of detention under Article 5(1)(f), makes clear that the place and conditions of detention should be appropriate, especially since this measure 'is applicable not to those who have committed criminal offences but to *aliens who, often fearing for their lives, have fled from own country*' (emphasis added).[60]

---

53 ECtHR, *Enhorn case, supra* note 48, para. 44.

54 Ibid., para. 41.

55 Ibid., para. 36.

56 Ibid., paras. 41, 55.

57 D. Moeckli, S. Shah and S. Sivakumaran (eds.), *International Human Rights Law*, 3rd edition, Oxford University Press, Oxford 2017, p. 257.

58 Ibid., p. 257.

59 Ibid., p. 264.

60 Council of Europe, 'ECtHR: Guide on Article 5 of the European Convention on Human Rights', 31.12.2020, p. 28, available at https://www.echr.coe.int/documents/guide_art_8_eng.pdf, last accessed 10.07.2021.

At this juncture, it is worth noting that unlike Article 10 of the International Covenant on Civil and Political Rights (ICCPR), which provides a right to 'humane treatment' to all persons deprived of their liberty,[61] the ECHR does not expressly provide for this right under the deprivation of liberty. Notwithstanding, it can be submitted that the Court will consider any inhumane treatment in conjunction with the absolute right under Article 3 of the Convention, that is, freedom from torture, or inhuman and degrading treatment or punishment. Relatedly, the Court will find 'inhuman treatment' in the circumstances where the treatment reached a minimum level of severity, and it caused 'either actual bodily harm or intense mental suffering'.[62] For example, the ECtHR, in its recent case *R.R. and others v Hungary*,[63] in examining the conditions of asylum seekers' detention in a transit zone, found a violation of Article 3 of the ECHR. Notably, the Court took into account the inherent vulnerability of the applicants and reasoned that the duration of nearly four months where asylum seekers and vulnerable pregnant women and children were kept inside transit zones while awaiting the outcome of their asylum applications exceeded the threshold of severity and amounted to degrading treatment.[64] Accordingly, the Court dealt separately with the alleged violation of deprivation of liberty and distinguished it from cases of a mere restriction on liberty of movement.[65] In particular, it confirmed that the lack of any domestic legal provisions setting the maximum duration of the applicants' stay, the excessive duration of that stay and the conditions in which they were held amounted to a *de facto* deprivation of liberty; hence Article 5(1) was applicable.[66] The Court ruled that the detention was unlawful as the applicants were deprived of their liberty without any formal reasoned decision issued by the authorities.[67]

At the time of writing, the ECtHR delivered its first judgment on a pandemic-related case, *Feilazoo v Malta*,[68] whereby the applicant, a migrant, has been exposed to a health risk through his unnecessary placement with new arrivals in COVID-19 quarantine. In the same vein as above, the complaint concerned alleged violations of Article 5(1) and Article 3 of the ECHR. *In casu*, the migrant complained, *inter alia*, of the 'hazardous situation' and a 'total disregard to his health' during his quarantine period.[69] The Court argued that on the facts before it, the conditions of detention, that is, his placement in quarantine with

61 The ICCPR provides specific conditions for the standard of treatment of persons in the case of a deprivation of liberty, in particular Article 10(1) prescribes the right to humane treatment in those cases; International Covenant on Civil and Political Rights 1966, 999 UNTS 171.

62 ECtHR, *Ireland v The United Kingdom*, no 5310/71, 13.12.1997.

63 ECtHR, *R.R. and others v Hungary*, no 36037/17, 02.03.2021.

64 Ibid., paras. 57, 65.

65 The latter is governed by Article 2 of Protocol No. 4 ECHR.

66 ECtHR, *R.R. and others v Hungary*, *supra* note 63, paras. 82–83.

67 Ibid., para. 91.

68 ECtHR, *Feilazoo v Malta*, no 6865/19, 11.03.2021.

69 Ibid., para. 73.

others could not be considered as complying with basic sanitary requirements and was unjustified; therefore, it determined a violation of Article 3.[70] In reaching this conclusion, the Court reiterated that the measures adopted by the state must ensure:

> that a person is detained in conditions which are compatible with respect for his human dignity and that the manner and method of the execution of the measure do not subject the individual to distress or hardship of an intensity exceeding the unavoidable level of suffering inherent in detention.[71]

In turn, in considering whether the deprivation of liberty was arbitrary under Article 5(1)(f), the Court specified the criteria it will take into account:

> To avoid being branded as arbitrary, detention under Article 5 §1 (f) must be carried out in *good faith*; it must be *closely connected* to the ground of detention relied on by the Government; the *place* and *conditions* of detention should be appropriate; and the *length* of the detention should not exceed that reasonably required for the purpose pursued (emphasis added).[72]

Accordingly, the Court ruled that the applicant's detention had not remained lawful throughout the whole period of his detention, and therefore it was treated as unlawful under Article 5(1) of the ECHR. The case (though dry-grounded) is a paradigmatic example of the dire conditions and the treatment migrants are constantly subjected to, which signal violations of their fundamental rights. In a similar line, the European Commission has made clear that its Member States need to ensure that mandatory quarantine arrangements, even though not covered by the EU asylum legislation, 'may also be imposed on asylum seekers in accordance with national legislation, *if necessary, proportionate and non-discriminatory*' (emphasis added).[73] Moreover, the Committee for the Prevention of Torture issued a statement of principles relating to the treatment of persons deprived of their liberty during the COVID-19 pandemic, and it particularly illustrated that any protective measures adopted 'must never' result in inhuman or degrading treatment.[74]

---

70 Ibid., para. 92.

71 Ibid., paras. 81–82; See also ECtHR, *Khlaifia case, supra* note 46, para. 159 (c); ECtHR, *Rahimi v Greece*, no 8687/08, 05.04.2011, para. 60.

72 Ibid., para. 104.

73 European Commission, Communication from the Commission. COVID-19: Guidance on the implementation of relevant EU provisions in the area of asylum and return procedures and on resettlement, 2020/C 126/02, 17.04.2020, available at https://eur-lex.europa.eu/legal-content/EN/TXT/HTML/?uri=CELEX:52020XC0417(07)&from=EN, last accessed 10.06.2021; See also D. Loprieno and C. Di Maio (2020), 'The "quarantine ships" experience', *supra* note 14.

74 CPT, 'Statement of principles relating to the treatment of persons deprived of their liberty in the context of the coronavirus disease (Covid-19) pandemic', CPT/Inf (2020)13, 20.04.2020, available at https://rm.coe.int/16809cfa4b, last accessed 05.03.2021.

5. ASSESSING THE LEGALITY OF THE 'SPECIAL' QUARANTINE MEASURES UNDER ARTICLE 5 OF THE ECHR

The quarantine measures adopted for migrants rescued at sea by the Italian and Maltese governments – the transfer of rescued persons on quarantine ships – appear to be, *a priori*, legally justified under the permissible exception in Article 5(1)(e) of the ECHR. However, as per the International Health Regulations, it is understood that the use of quarantine ships will have to be justified in a manner that shows that it is 'not more invasive or intrusive to persons than reasonably available alternatives that would achieve the appropriate level of health protection'.[75] Accordingly, this examination begs the following troubling questions: is holding persons rescued at sea aboard quarantine ships a proportionate measure to address a nation's concern to prevent the spread of an infectious disease? Does it align with the principles of non-discrimination and non-arbitrariness such that other, less severe measures have been considered to safeguard migrants and the public? Is the differential treatment at issue suitable for, and effective in, advancing the aim sought to be achieved? What other potential allegations might arise in conjunction with Article 5?

Undoubtedly, quarantine is one of the most aggressive measures that public health officials have at their disposal in order to control a disease outbreak. Civil society organisations, experts and academics have repeatedly expressed concerns over the use of quarantine ships during the pandemic emergency and have highlighted the overcrowding on those facilities as well as concerns of the ratio of medical staff to migrants.[76] It is interesting to note here that Malta's declaration makes clear that they are not in a position to guarantee rescue of 'prohibited immigrants' – already a word containing an implicit negative value judgment, which signifies a lack of *bona fide* interest in complying more generally with its international law obligations. Accordingly, in order to not infringe one's right to liberty, the measures adopted should comply with the principles for the protection of persons deprived of their liberty in the context of COVID-19 pandemic and, specifically, should guarantee on-ship medical isolation that is proportionate, non-arbitrary, and non-discriminatory.[77]

---

75 International Health Regulations, 2509 UNTS 79, 23.05.2005, Article 43(1)(b).

76 FRA, 'Migration: Key Fundamental Rights Concerns', Quarterly Bulletin, 2020, available at https://fra.europa.eu/sites/default/files/fra_uploads/fra-2021-migration-bulletin_en.pdf, last accessed 15.02.2021; See also, A. Petroni, 'Italy Is Using the Pandemic to Keep More Migrants From Its Shores', 05.10.2020, available at https://www.worldpoliticsreview.com/articles/29108/italy-is-using-the-pandemic-to-keep-more-migrants-from-its-shores, last accessed 20.01.2021.

77 UNHCR (2020), 'Practical Recommendations and Good Practice', *supra* note 16, p. 2.

5.1. PROPORTIONALITY

The ships chartered in order for migrants to quarantine post-rescue are either former passenger vessels or commercial ships. To begin with, it is questionable whether quarantining people on ships is a proportionate or even a fair measure to adopt, following a period where people have been struggling for days to survive at sea. In this regard, the narrow spaces inside the ships (sleeping berths, the few metres of available space, lack of appropriate ventilation) might not align with the health and safety measures for preventing the spread of the virus. In this regard, the reasoning of the ECtHR in *Rooman v Belgium*[78] concerning deprivation of liberty under Article 5(1)(e) – for persons of unsound mind – provides important insights into the interpretation of the term 'lawfulness'. *In casu*, the Court stressed that the 'mere fact' that the individual was not placed in an appropriate facility 'did not automatically render' his detention unlawful under Article 5(1).[79] Consequently, the Court was of the view that sometimes a delay in admission to a clinic, if it is related to 'disparity between the available and required capacity' of mental institutions, is acceptable.[80] To alleviate the strictness of this assertion, the Court reiterated that a significant delay in the transfer to an appropriate institution (and thus in the treatment necessary for that person) might entail a breach of Article 5. Importantly, it emphasised that there is an intrinsic link between the lawfulness of a deprivation of liberty and its condition of execution.[81] Applying this reasoning by analogy to the transfer of rescued migrants to quarantine aboard ships for the purpose of preventing the spread of COVID-19, it is debatable whether: (i) quarantine ships will be considered appropriate to guarantee long-term protection of all persons' health amidst the inherent conditions aboard ships and the risk of conducting the virus; and (ii) whether a significant delay in disembarking persons (more than the quarantine incubation period) will be in contravention with the purpose of containing the spread of an infectious disease. Ergo, the interference with the liberty of persons must be proportionate to the legitimate aim pursued.[82]

Interestingly, in the *Oxford Dictionary*, quarantine means 'a period, instance, or state of detention, isolation, seclusion, or prohibition comparable with that *necessitated by disease*' (emphasis added).[83] In this vein, the word 'necessitated' points to an assessment between what is actually necessary in light of the

78 ECtHR, *Rooman v Belgium*, no 18052/11, 31.01.2019.

79 Ibid., para. 198.

80 Ibid.

81 Ibid.

82 ECtHR, *Kuimov* case, *supra* note 44, para. 96.

83 Oxford English Dictionary, 'Quarantine', available at https://www-oed-com.ucd.idm.oclc.org/view/Entry/155959?isAdvanced=false&result=1&rskey=h7F1H5&, last accessed 02.02.2021.

disease and the period for which a person is detained. In light of the COVID-19 pandemic, the World Health Organization (WHO) has provided that the standard quarantine involves normally 14 days. Arguably, for migrants rescued at sea, the balancing exercise appears to be evaded, as the 14-day rule is sometimes not followed. For instance, it has been reported that in some instances, migrants were kept aboard quarantine ships indefinitely and for longer periods than the prescribed medical isolation period (even longer than a month).[84] In this regard, the length of the detention could act as an aggravating factor in the assessment of the proportionality of this measure, as it should not go beyond the required period to satisfy the aim of controlling the spread of the virus. In fact, in cases where quarantine is unreasonably prolonged, the lawful rationale for a deprivation of liberty will cease to be justified.[85]

5.2. NON-ARBITRARINESS

In assessing whether the deprivation of liberty is non-arbitrary, courts take into consideration 'inappropriateness, injustice, and lack of predictability and due process of law' as well as 'elements of reasonableness, necessity and proportionality'.[86] It should be reminded that states have also made available facilities on land (like hotels) to accommodate persons who return from travel abroad for quarantine purposes. Manifestly, this highlights the inconsistency between the migration measures adopted to control the spread of the virus, especially when comparing the onerous facilities provided for rescued migrants and the more humane measures adopted for the rest of the people. Adding to that, the United Nations (UN) Network on Migration condemned these practices and described quarantine ships as 'inadequate locations … rather than using human rights-respecting quarantine measures'.[87] Accordingly, for quarantine ships to escape a characterisation of arbitrariness, not only should the detention not continue beyond the appropriate quarantine period, but governments also need to demonstrate that less invasive means of achieving the same ends have been considered and that there is a sufficiently strong connection between controlling the spread of COVID-19 and the use of quarantine ships (place of detention).

---

84 InfoMigrants, 'Were migrant rights infringed in Italy because of the coronavirus pandemic?', 07.08.2020, available at https://www.infomigrants.net/en/post/26493/were-migrant-rights-infringed-in-italy-because-of-the-coronavirus-pandemic, last accessed 03.01.2021.

85 See ECtHR, *Weeks v the United Kingdom*, no 9787/82, 02.03.1987.

86 D. Moeckli, S. Shah and S. Sivakumaran (2017), *International Human Rights Law, supra* note 57, p. 257.

87 United Nations Network on Migration, 'Annex to Policy Brief, COVID-19 & Immigration Detention: What Can Governments and Other Stakeholders Do?', 2021, available at https://migrationnetwork.un.org/sites/default/files/docs/annex_to_policy_brief_on_atd_and_covid-19.pdf, last accessed 03.03.2021.

In this vein, migrants have the right to bring *habeas corpus* proceedings under Article 5(4), which provides fundamental safeguards against unlawful detention.[88] This will translate that the rescued persons should have the opportunity to challenge the legality of their prescribed method of detention, as there are specific remedies to be afforded in those cases. Relatedly, the Italian national guarantor for prisoners' rights noted that there is a lack of reliable information and support given to those rescued,[89] which will be in direct breach of the guarantees provided by the WHO for quarantine measures and by international human rights law more generally, under the provisions for the deprivation of liberty. It is questionable in this case if effective procedural guarantees were made available in order to enable the termination of quarantine, where it was no longer necessary nor proportionate.

5.3. NON-DISCRIMINATION

Central to all non-discrimination norms is the formal equality requirement that likes should be treated alike as found in Aristotle's classical works.[90] The principle of non-discrimination is enshrined in international law, national constitutions and has been recognised to all human beings universally. Yet, equality has always been at the heart of political struggle. In this vein, the UN Human Rights Committee (HRC) has defined discrimination as:

> any distinction, exclusion, restriction or preference which is based on any ground such as race, colour, sex, language, religion, political or other opinion, national or social origin, property, birth or other status, and which has the purpose or effect of nullifying or impairing the recognition, enjoyment or exercise by all persons on an equal footing of all rights and freedom.[91]

It further added that 'not every differentiation of treatment will constitute discrimination, if the criteria for such differentiation are reasonable and objective and if the aim is to achieve a purpose which is legitimate under the Covenant'.[92]

---

88 See for instance ECtHR, *Mooren v Germany*, no 11364/03, 09.07.2009, para. 106.

89 National Guarantor for the Rights of Persons Detained or Deprived of Liberty, 'The National Guarantor in the context of Covid-19 outbreak', 28.04.2020, available at https://www.garantenazionaleprivatiliberta.it/gnpl/resources/cms/documents/5dc95b2b5e67707b64a2fc66b880a231.pdf, last accessed 12.06.2021.

90 D. Moeckli, S. Shah and S. Sivakumaran (2017), *International Human Rights Law, supra* note 57, p. 197.

91 UN HRC, *CCPR General Comment No. 18: Non-discrimination*, 10.11.1989, para. 7.

92 Ibid., para. 13.

Arguably, one of the aggravating factors, which will challenge the legality of these restrictive measures, is that the use of quarantine ships, specifically applicable to a specific group of vulnerable people – migrants – can be deemed to be discrimination based on race, ethnicity or nationality,[93] in the absence of providing an alternative solution (on land) that takes into consideration the circumstances of these people and that is more humane. Accordingly, it has been argued that these measures have been adopted, *inter alia*, to anticipate for other Member States to step in and commit to relocating those persons *ipso facto* in an attempt to avoid processing their asylum applications.[94] Thus, such actions have arguably made safe disembarkation on land 'dependent on other member states'.[95]

On the one hand, it will not be difficult for states to satisfy *a priori* the legitimate aim requirement, as it is within their public health powers to enforce quarantine as well as a recognised permitted exception under the ECHR. On the other hand, such measures will not likely satisfy the principles of non-discrimination, non-arbitrariness and proportionality. What is at stake is whether states have considered other, less severe measures,[96] rather than the use of quarantine aboard a vessel in order to satisfy that the deprivation of liberty was necessary to be adopted in that prescribed manner. As such, it is hard to comprehend how the governments, after a reasonable period of time, have not found less invasive means of achieving the same ends that will ensure humane treatment (needless to mention that chartering a ship for a month costs governments approximately €1 million).[97] Intriguingly, the Italian Coalition for Civil Liberties and Rights (CILD), a civil society organisation, in its recent report for the treatment of migrants during COVID-19 stressed that '[b]y depriving its ports of safe places, arbitrarily and without providing alternatives, Italy was and is accused of not guaranteeing human rights and neglecting its responsibilities; the Government should have and must allow landings during the health emergency'.[98]

---

93 See for instance ECtHR, *Saidoun v Greece*, no 40083/07, 28.10.2010.

94 Commissioner for Human Rights, 'Statement: Immediate action needed to disembark migrants held on ships off Malta's coast', 04.06.2020, available at https://www.coe.int/en/web/commissioner/news-2020/-/asset_publisher/Arb4fRK3o8Cf/content/immediate-action-needed-to-disembark-migrants-held-on-ships-off-malta-s-coast?inheritRedirect=false, last accessed 10.06.2021.

95 Ibid.

96 See, for example, UNHCR (2020), 'Practical Recommendations and Good Practice', *supra* note 16, p. 2.

97 See InfoMigrants, 'Migrant rights in Italy', *supra* note 84.

98 CILD, 'Migrant detention in Covid-19 times', 2020, available at https://cild.eu/en/wp-content/uploads/sites/2/2020/08/Dossier_MigrantiCovid-_Eng_rev3.pdf, last accessed 03.03.2021; at the time of writing (May 2021), the latest report online suggested that Italy still uses quarantine ships (in particular it has chartered nine cruise vessels) for the same purposes, see InsideHook, 'The Red Cross is Using Cruise Ships for Pandemic Quarantine in Italy', 10.05.2021, available at https://www.insidehook.com/daily_brief/news-opinion/red-cross-italy-cruise-ships-pandemic-quarantine, last accessed 10.07.2021.

Moreover, the practice of international judicial institutions suggests that even consistent treatment can constitute discrimination if it has disproportionate effects on a particular group.[99] This is otherwise known as 'indirect discrimination', which is prohibited in the same way as direct discrimination and will be triggered if a seemingly equal treatment – quarantine measure – has the effect of disproportionately disadvantaging a particular group of persons.[100] Hence, even if the governments have no intention *prima facie* to discriminate against migrants, this would be immaterial for the purposes of assessing the measures in question. To justify this, an instructive case to recall is *Jew Ho v Williamson* from 1900,[101] where a federal court struck down a quarantine measure imposed in San Francisco as a response to an outbreak of bubonic plague, as it reasoned it was racially motivated and ill-suited to stop the outbreak. Accordingly, the court affirmed that measures cannot be imposed in a racially unfair manner. Applying this reasoning by analogy to the situation in the Mediterranean and the pandemic, it would have to be assessed whether quarantining people aboard vessels is a reasonable measure to accomplish the purposes sought, and particularly if there is an objective justification for the prolonged difference in treatment.

In summarising, while courts have usually upheld quarantine measures in respect to the state's wide-ranging powers to protect public health, this would not always be the case when the measures adopted are unreasonable or when the necessary procedures have not been followed.[102] Accordingly, it can be contended that the citizens of Italy and Malta have been treated more favourably with regards to quarantine protocols, as they do not share the same nationality or status with the asylum seeker, the refugee and/or the migrant because the former are citizens (and nationals) of the state. As the UN Network on Migration pointed out, 'discriminatory measures targeting migrants that purport to protect public health but in fact amount to de facto immigration detention are not legal'.[103] The measures could have been accepted as lawful in the first days, or even the first few months of the coronavirus outbreak, as all governments were in a state of emergency; however, the measures are no longer a temporary practice and have rather become entrenched in the governments' migration policies. In fact, quarantine ships from an exceptional (short-term) measure have rather become the rule – floating immigration facilities that

99 D. Moeckli, 'The Human Right to Non-discrimination' in D. Moeckli, *Human Rights and Non-discrimination in the 'War on Terror'*, Oxford Scholarship Online, Oxford 2008, p. 74.

100 CCPR, *Althammer et al. v Austria*, UN Doc CCPR/C/78/D/998/2001, 22.09.2003, para. 10.2.

101 103 Fed. Rep. 10, 1900 U.S.

102 W.E. Parmet and M.S. Sinha, 'Covid-19 – The Law and Limits of Quarantine', (2020) *The New England Journal of Medicine*, p. e28(1).

103 United Nations Network on Migration (2021), 'Annex to Policy Brief', *supra* note 87.

isolate thousands of migrants, effectively hindering their human rights.[104] To be sure, we are currently witnessing the normalisation of practices that entail gross human rights violations.[105] It is my submission that the choice of quarantine ships, specifically adopted for migrants rescued at sea, is increasingly discriminatory, amounts to an arbitrary deprivation of liberty and completely disregards those persons' experiences and vulnerabilities.

6. OTHER POTENTIAL HUMAN RIGHTS VIOLATIONS

6.1. THE RIGHT TO LIFE

The lawfulness of the quarantine measures adopted during the pandemic may also be assessed in light of the right to life under Article 2 ECHR. From the Strasbourg court's jurisprudence, it is evident that the right to life prescribes a duty to prevent a violation from occurring in circumstances where it is reasonably foreseeable or known that life is exposed to danger.[106] Accordingly, state authorities are required to adopt preventive measures that, in a reasonable manner, aim to avoid risks from materialising. In this regard, the transfer of rescued persons on quarantine ships might increase the risks to one's health or create a situation of distress. Importantly, in the case that states do not provide access to adequate medical treatment or they do not provide the necessary medical care on board, or in the case that they cause rescued migrants to live under a protracted situation in distress at sea that endangers their health (and life), this might lead to a violation of the right to life. In this vein, the ECtHR, in *Makaratzis v Greece*,[107] highlighted that on several occasions, Article 2 of the Convention might apply even if a person whose right to life was allegedly breached has not lost her life.[108] In its reasoning, the Court illustrated that in certain circumstances, a merely 'potential' or 'virtual' victim of a violation of the right to life could take action under the ECHR.[109] In this vein, the HRC in its most recent *General Comment No. 36* on the right to life under the ICCPR, provided that:

> State parties also have a heightened duty of care to take any necessary measure to protect the lives of individuals deprived of their liberty by the State, since by arresting,

---

104 S. D'Ignoti, 'Pressure grows on Italy to abolish migrant quarantine ships', 07.01.2021, available at https://www.politico.eu/article/italy-migrants-offshore-quarantine-incidents-deaths/, last accessed 20.01.2021.

105 C. Costello (2020), 'Overcoming Refugee Containment', *supra* note 6, p. 20.

106 For example, see the CCPR, *A.S. case, supra* note 2, para. 7.8.

107 ECtHR, *Makaratzis v Greece*, no 50385/99, 20.12.2004.

108 Ibid., para. 55.

109 Ibid., paras. 43 and 45.

> detaining, imprisoning or otherwise depriving individuals of their liberty, State parties assume the responsibility to care for their life and bodily integrity, and they may not rely on lack of financial resources or other logistical problems to reduce this responsibility.[110]

For example, on one occasion last year (though not an isolated case in 2020), it has been reported that upon the transfer of rescued persons in an Italian quarantine ship, one of the individuals jumped off the ship in an effort to escape to reach land – but subsequently drowned.[111] As expounded above, the duty to render assistance at sea, which legally denotes the delivery of rescued persons to a place of safety, where their basic human needs can be met, is perceived as the operational obligation deriving from the application of the right to life at sea.[112] Hence, the act of transferring rescued persons to a place where their safety would be at risk might result in a violation of the right to life.[113] Importantly, in a recent case, *Rackete/Sea-Watch 3*, the Italian Supreme Court confirmed the illegality of keeping people aboard ships instead of promptly providing a place of disembarkation.[114] The incident arose amidst a rescue operation conducted by a non-governmental organisation (NGO) vessel, Sea-Watch 3, which – after keeping the rescued migrants on board for 17 days – entered the Italian port of Lampedusa in defiance of the 'closed-ports' decree that was then in place (a year prior to the pandemic). The Court articulated that a ship *cannot* be considered a place of safety for disembarkation purposes, since 'not only it is at the mercy of adverse weather events, but also it does not ensure respect from fundamental human rights of rescued people', and this includes applying for international protection.[115] This judgment could have significant ramifications for rendering quarantine ships contrary to domestic

---

110 UN HRC, *General comment no. 36, Article 6 (Right to Life)*, CCPR/C/GC/35, 03.09.2019, para. 25.

111 See InfoMigrants, 'Migrant drowns after jumping off quarantine ship', 22.05.2020, available at https://www.infomigrants.net/en/post/24913/migrant-drowns-after-jumping-off-quarantine-ship, last accessed 02.09.2021; further distress incidents have been reported, see DW, 'Ocean Viking: Italy to transfer migrants to quarantine ship after suicide attempts', 05.07.2020, available at https://www.dw.com/en/ocean-viking-italy-to-transfer-migrants-to-quarantine-ship-after-suicide-attempts/a-54056662, last accessed 05.06.2021.

112 Annex 34 (2004), 'Guidelines on the Treatment of Persons', *supra* note 24, para. 3; See also, S. Galani (2020), 'Persons at Sea, International Law, and Covid-19', *supra* note 38; S. Trevisanut (2014), 'Is there a right to be rescued at sea? A constructive view', *supra* note 38; A similar conclusion is reached by F.G. Attard, *The Duty of the Shipmaster to Render Assistance at Sea under International Law*, Queen Mary Studies in International Law, 2020, pp. 41, 193.

113 See also ECtHR, *Cyprus v Turkey*, no 25781/94, 12.05.2014, para. 219.

114 Available in Italian: http://www.lacostituzione.info/wp-content/uploads/2020/03/Corte-di-Cassazione.pdf, last accessed 10.07.2021.

115 Ibid.

and international laws (law of the sea, human rights law and refugee law).[116] In particular, the situation for quarantine ships is very similar to the *Rackete* case, as it is understood that these ships are not docked in port but remain in the open sea.[117] I elaborate further on this below.

6.2. THE FREEDOM FROM ILL-TREATMENT

The conditions and place of quarantine may also be assessed in conjunction with Article 3 of the ECHR, on further grounds of unfair sufferance provoked by the possibility of being contaminated by an unknown virus in light of the ambiguous quarantine circumstances. Notably, the Court in *M.S.S. v Belgium and Greece*,[118] in finding a violation of Article 3 by virtue of the detention conditions *in casu*, stressed that 'the applicant's distress was accentuated by the vulnerability inherent in his situation as an asylum seeker'.[119] Hence, the vulnerability of the victim together with physical or emotional suffering are factors that courts may take into account when assessing the level of ill-treatment.[120]

Moreover, in a prison-related case, *Ghavtadze v Georgia*, the Court highlighted that 'the lack of appropriate care and, more generally, the detention of a sick person in inadequate conditions may in principle constitute treatment contrary to Article 3'.[121] For instance, this could be *de facto* the case for a migrant aboard a quarantine ship who tests positive for COVID-19 and develops severe respiratory symptoms, requiring immediate hospitalisation. This scenario begs the following question: are the conditions aboard quarantine ships adequate for sick persons to guarantee the protection of their health? Given that these ships are not located close to ports and will thus need a certain amount of time to reach the port, should an emergency arise, it is difficult to see how this measure provides proper safeguards for one's medical care and needs. Therefore, it is likely to be *a priori* contrary to treatment compatible with Article 3.

---

116 For instance, Italian constitutional law requires emergency decrees to be adopted only in 'extraordinary cases of necessity and urgency' and in accordance with the principles of proportionality, reasonableness and adequacy; for further analysis see, A.M. Pelliconi (2020), 'Covid-19: Italy is not a "place of safety" anymore', *supra* note 35.

117 See InfoMigrants, 'Italy: Quarantines on board ships are "discriminatory towards migrants"', 09.04.2021, available at https://www.infomigrants.net/en/post/31351/italy-quarantines-on-board-ships-are-discriminatory-towards-migrants, last accessed 10.06.2021.

118 ECtHR, *M.S.S. v Belgium and Greece, supra* note 49.

119 Ibid., para. 233.

120 See also for example CAT, *Besim Osmani v Republic of Serbia*, UN Doc CAT/C/42/D/261/2005, 08.05.2009, paras. 3.3 and 10.4.

121 ECtHR, *Ghavtadze v Georgia*, no 23204/07, 03.03.2009, para. 76.

Interestingly, in the *Khlaifia* case (explained above), three people were placed in a reception facility and later aboard a ship. In challenging the lawfulness of the conditions in these places, the Court considered, *inter alia*, the short period of detention along with the mass influx of migrants during the time (amidst the Arab Spring) and found no violation of Article 3. From this rationale, it appears that the courts will give leeway to states in the way they handle migration arrivals in such a way that allows detention to take place in 'otherwise substandard conditions'.[122] Notwithstanding, this ruling must be distinguished from the pandemic period as it was a time when migrant arrivals had fallen sharply. As such, the 'mass-influx' consideration is not likely to be applicable as a justification ground for opting to use quarantine ships. Concluding, it is posited that the place of quarantine, coupled with the (likely) inadequate health and safety standards, as well as the exacerbation of inherent vulnerability of those persons through the dangerous and uncertain situation aboard quarantine ships, might as well amount to inhuman or degrading treatment within the meaning of Article 3 of the ECHR.

7. CONCLUSION

While the pandemic has to some extent disrupted the migrant flows in the Mediterranean, it did not bring them to an end, as people keep trying to reach Europe on barely functional boats in a daring attempt to seek international protection. Some of the more 'fortunate' migrants who have managed to be rescued have faced indefinite forced quarantine aboard state-chartered ships in dubious conditions that are nullifying their liberty. Unlike the asymmetrical impact of the migration crisis, COVID-19 has affected all nations, bar none, as the virus knows no borders. Yet again, the virus' impact on the migration crisis, in terms of the impugned migration measures, is still asymmetric, as people face horrendous human rights violations on a daily basis committed on supposedly lawful grounds.

Whilst the points raised above with regards to quarantine ships are by their very nature somewhat speculative, it might be the case that a legal challenge is brought against a Member State that will scrutinise the legality of the measures adopted for rescued migrants during the period of COVID-19. As Mann elucidates, 'if these rights abuses are not usually prevented and implicitly accepted by powerful actors as normal', then we have a *de facto*

---

122 J.I. Goldenziel, 'Khlaifia and Others v. Italy', (2018) 112(2), *American Journal of International Law*, p. 279.

situation of rightlessness.[123] One should not forget that the ECtHR's role is to protect the inalienable rights of *all* human beings. For migrants to be no longer marginalised, arbitrary practices such as this should not be left unchallenged.[124] Accordingly, it is my belief that international judges present one powerful source of international law to effectively address this dire situation and try to remedy its systemic deficiencies, with the hope that an *á la carte* respect for human rights is no longer entertained.[125]

123 I. Mann, 'Maritime Legal Black Holes: Migration and Rightlessness in International Law', (2018) 29(2), *The European Journal of International Law*, p. 364.

124 M. Dembour, *When Humans Become Migrants: Study of the European Court of Human Rights with an Inter-American Counterpoint*, Oxford University Press, Oxford 2015, p. 480.

125 The use of the language 'á la carte respect' is inspired from the Concurring Opinion of Judge Bonello in ECtHR, *Al-Skeini and Others v United Kingdom*, no 55721/07, 07.07.2011.

THE EUROPEAN APPROACH TO IRREGULAR MIGRATION IN PANDEMIC TIMES

The More Things Change, the More they Stay the Same?

Alan Desmond*

* Lecturer, Leicester Law School and member of the Migration, Mobility and Citizenship Network (MMCN), University of Leicester. I am grateful to the two anonymous reviewers for their invaluable feedback on the first draft of this contribution, and to Philip Czech for his help in readying the contribution for publication. I am also indebted to Ed Bates, Ronan Desmond, Mimi Mitsue, Bernard Ryan and Katja Ziegler for fruitful conversations on a number of topics addressed in the contribution. Any errors are solely my responsibility.

ABSTRACT

In this contribution, I examine the European Union's (EU, the Union) response to irregular migration and irregular migrants' rights during the ongoing pandemic. By analysing efforts to prevent unwanted arrivals, entrench pre-removal detention and increase expulsion, I highlight a consistency in the EU treatment of irregular migrants over the past decade and note an intensification of the rights-restrictive and control-expansive thrust of EU policy on irregular migration since the 2015 migration and refugee 'crisis'. I show how this trend is reflected in the New Pact on Migration and Asylum and is increasingly being facilitated and endorsed by the European Court of Human Rights (ECtHR) and the Court of Justice of the EU (CJEU). At the same time, however, I argue that there is scope for a more rights-respecting European approach to irregular migrants, one of the most vulnerable categories of migrant present in Europe today. In particular, I argue that serious consideration needs to be given to regularisation, the conferral of a right to remain on irregular migrants, as an alternative to, or in conjunction with, the current focus on expulsion. I suggest that the pause for thought provided by the pandemic may allow for meaningful discussion of ambitious measures, such as an EU regularisation mechanism, that would previously have been dismissed out of hand. I also show how the pandemic itself, and the need for an effective response to it, provides compelling arguments for regularisation.

1. INTRODUCTION

The COVID-19 pandemic has impacted the lives of people in almost every country around the world, and nearly two years after the emergence of the disease it continues to play havoc with the lives and livelihoods of individuals and the economies of nations. The large and growing body of academic and expert legal commentary and literature on the pandemic has included analysis of travel restrictions and the implications of the pandemic for the protection of migrants' rights.[1] Migrants, especially those in an irregular situation, are

[1] For an early overview of the role of international law in dealing with the pandemic, see A. von Bogdandy and P.A. Villareal, 'International Law on Pandemic Response: A First Stocktaking in Light of the Coronavirus Crisis', (2020) 7, *MPIL Research Paper Series*, pp. 1–25; for a useful global overview of the travel restrictions and border closures adopted in response to COVID-19, see M. Benton, J. Batalova, S. Davidoff-Gore and T. Schmidt, *COVID-19 and the State of Global Mobility in 2020*, MPI and IOM, Washington D.C. and Geneva 2021.

particularly vulnerable to the ramifications of the pandemic. This is most obviously true in states in the Global South where resource constraints mean that such countries often struggle to secure even the basic needs of their own citizens and where the deterioration in the human rights situation as a result of the pandemic is having a particularly adverse effect on migrants.[2] Even in Europe, however, one of the richest regions of the world that can claim the most complex and highly developed system of human rights protection, the pandemic has unleashed significant challenges to the protection of migrants' rights.

This contribution adds to the emerging literature on the impact of the novel coronavirus on migrants' rights by highlighting how the pandemic has provided cover for an intensification of the business-as-usual approach to irregular migration in Europe whereby migration control efforts eclipse human rights obligations vis-à-vis irregular migrants. In sections 2–4, I zoom in on the issues of (preventing) arrival, pre-removal detention and expulsion of irregular migrants to highlight the consistency and intensification of the EU's approach to irregular migration. Within the highly politicised and combustible field of immigration,[3] these issues are particularly controversial because they go to the heart of states' sovereign power to control their borders, articulated by the ECtHR as the well-established international law principle that states have the right to control the entry, residence and expulsion of non-citizens.[4] It has long been argued that the tension between the international legal principle of state sovereignty and the human rights of migrants is more often resolved in favour of the former.[5] In this contribution I argue by reference to irregular migration that this continues to be the case, and that the emergency generated by the pandemic is being instrumentalised to further buttress states' sovereign exclusionary powers.[6] In section 2, I provide a broad overview of developments concerning irregular

---

2 The Global State of Democracy Indices, 'Global monitor of COVID-19's impact on democracy and human rights', *International Institute for Democracy and Electoral Assistance*, available at https://www.idea.int/gsod-indices/about-covid19, last accessed 28.06.2021; UN, 'Sustainable Development Goals Report 2020', UN report, 2020, pp. 15 and 58, available at https://unstats.un.org/sdgs/report/2020/, last accessed 12.07.2021.

3 See M. Krzyżanowski, A. Triandafyllidou and R. Wodak, 'The Mediatization and the Politicization of the "Refugee Crisis" in Europe', (2018) 16 *Journal of Immigrant & Refugee Studies*, pp. 1–14; A. Desmond, 'Who's Afraid of the UN Global Compact for Migration?', 11.12.2018, *RTE Brainstorm*, available at https://www.rte.ie/brainstorm/2018/1210/1016278-whos-afraid-of-the-un-global-compact-for-migration/, last accessed 28.06.2021; H. Motomura, 'The New Migration Law: Migrants, Refugees, and Citizens in an Anxious Age', (2020) 105, *Cornell Law Review*, pp. 484–485 and 534–536.

4 E.g., ECtHR, *Moustaquim v Belgium*, no 12313/86, 18.02.1991, para. 43.

5 E.g., L. Bosniak, 'Human Rights, State Sovereignty and the Protection of Undocumented Migrants under the International Migrant Workers Convention', (1991) 25, *The International Migration Review*, pp. 737–770; M.B. Dembour, *When Humans Become Migrants*, OUP, Oxford 2015.

6 For the analogous argument that the pandemic has precipitated trends towards elimination of the right to seek asylum in the Global North, see D. Ghezelbash and N.F. Tan, 'The End of the Right to Seek Asylum? COVID-19 and the Future of Refugee Protection', (2020)

migration in European human rights law over the past decade. In section 3, I illustrate how the New Pact on Migration and Asylum,[7] unveiled in September 2020, sets the scene for further entrenchment of long-standing and ongoing restrictionist and rights-restrictive tendencies in the immigration law field. In section 4, I discuss Europe's pandemic-related responses to irregular migration.

In section 5, however, I argue that there is scope for a more rights-respecting European approach to migrants, specifically, irregular third-country nationals (TCNs), one of the most vulnerable categories of migrants present in Europe today. In particular, I argue that serious consideration needs to be given to regularisation, the conferral of a right to remain on irregular migrants, as an alternative to or in conjunction with the current focus on expulsion. I also propose the urgent operationalisation of firewalls as a way of protecting the rights of irregular migrants in the absence of regularisation. Throughout the contribution I thread an awareness of and an appeal to the vulnerability to rights denial experienced by irregular migrants. This is with the aim of strengthening the argument made in section 5 for what some might initially dismiss as an unrealistic and politically unfeasible EU approach to regularisation.

I am concerned in this contribution primarily with the EU's treatment of migrants who are unlawfully present in the EU. The law relating to such migrants overlaps, however, with the legal framework governing individuals seeking international protection. Although people in this latter category often migrate irregularly, they are lawfully present in the host EU Member State while their applications are being examined,[8] and they are protected under international law against penalisation for unauthorised entry or stay.[9] Before having an opportunity to make an international protection claim, however, and following a definitive rejection of a protection application, they are in a similar situation to unlawfully present migrants and vulnerable to the same risks of abuse and rights violation. I therefore refer at various points in the contribution to the Common European Asylum System (CEAS) that the EU has been developing since it gained law-making powers in the field of asylum and immigration with the

32(4), *International Journal of Refugee Law*, pp. 668–679; for the argument that states have conflated the 'war' on the virus with the 'war' on migrants, see C. Heller, 'De-confine Borders: Towards a Politics of Freedom of Movement in the Time of the Pandemic', Centre on Migration, Policy and Society (COMPAS) Working Paper No. 147, 2020, available at https://www.compas.ox.ac.uk/wp-content/uploads/WP-2020-147-Heller_De-confine_Borders_Towards_Politics_Freedom_Movement_Time_Pandemic.pdf, last accessed 28.06.2021.

7 European Commission, Communication from the Commission to the European Parliament, the Council, the European Economic and Social Committee and the Committee of the Regions on a New Pact on Migration and Asylum, COM(2020) 609 final 23.09.2020.

8 Directive 2013/32/EU of the European Parliament and of the Council of 26 June 2013 on common procedures for granting and withdrawing international protection, OJ L 180, pp. 60–95, Article 9.

9 Convention relating to the Status of Refugees, adopted 28 July 1951, entered into force 22 April 1954, 189 UNTS 137, Article 31(1).

entry into force of the Treaty of Amsterdam in 1999. In particular, the difficulties both created and faced by the Dublin system,[10] the cornerstone of the CEAS that determines which Member State is responsible for examining an application for international protection, have generated a flurry of migration control activities and related judicial decision-making affecting individuals seeking to reach and remain in Europe.

To be properly understood, developments in the CEAS itself, and the wider common migration system of which it is a central part, must be viewed against the background of the 2015 migration and refugee 'crisis' during which over a million migrants arrived at Europe's borders in mixed flows.[11] The fact that the EU's return and asylum policies are inextricably intertwined, with unsuccessful applicants for international protection often becoming automatically liable for deportation, means that the EU's zeal for 'fighting' irregular migration adversely affects individuals with legitimate international protection claims. Indeed, the New Pact on Migration and Asylum articulates the objective of integrating asylum and return policy so as to close the loopholes between asylum and return procedures,[12] and carries risks of rights dilution and denial discussed in section 3. Throughout this contribution, the EU's preferred euphemism, return, is used interchangeably with the terms removal, expulsion and deportation.

2. SETTING THE SCENE: PRE-PANDEMIC DEVELOPMENTS IN EUROPEAN HUMAN RIGHTS LAW CONCERNING IRREGULAR MIGRANTS

The primary response of the EU to the issue of irregular migration has been to try to prevent the arrival of irregular migrants and to deport those who have

---

10 Regulation (EU) No. 604/2013 of the European Parliament and of the Council of 26 June 2013 establishing the criteria and mechanisms for determining the member state responsible for examining an application for international protection lodged in one of the member states by a third-country national or a stateless person, OJ L 180, pp. 31–59 (hereinafter Dublin Regulation).

11 UNHCR, 'Over one million sea arrivals reach Europe in 2015', 30.12.2015, available at http://www.unhcr.org/afr/news/latest/2015/12/5683d0b56/million-sea-arrivals-reacheurope-2015.html, last accessed 28.06.2021. The Mixed Migration Centre provides a working definition of mixed migration: 'Mixed migration refers to cross-border movements of people including refugees fleeing persecution and conflict, victims of trafficking and people seeking better lives and opportunities. Motivated to move by a multiplicity of factors, people in mixed flows have different legal statuses as well as a variety of vulnerabilities. Although entitled to protection under international human rights law, they are exposed to multiple rights violations along their journey. Those in mixed migration flows travel along similar routes, using similar means of travel – often travelling irregularly and wholly or partially assisted by migrant smugglers.' Available at http://www.mixedmigration.org/about/, last accessed 28.06.2021.

12 European Commission, COM(2020) 609 final, *supra* note 7, pp. 3–4.

managed to enter or remain unlawfully in the EU, prioritising migration control over protection of migrants' rights.[13] The EU's emphasis on the detention and expulsion elements of migration control is exemplified by the 2008 Return Directive,[14] arguably the most consequential piece of legislation adopted in the area of irregular migration, which sets out common standards and procedures in EU Member States for returning irregular migrants.[15] Against the background of the 2015 refugee and migration 'crisis', the ECtHR and the CJEU appear increasingly deferential to states' migration control endeavours, while the European Commission has doubled down on the need to beef up EU return policy.[16]

2.1. ARRIVALS

The well-documented efforts of the EU and its Member States to deter the arrival of unwanted migrants are increasingly being complemented by rulings from the CJEU in Luxembourg and the ECtHR in Strasbourg which,[17] delivered

---

13 R. Cholewinski, 'European Union Policy on Irregular Migration: Human Rights Lost?', in B. Bogusz, R. Cholewinski, A. Cygan and E. Szyszczak (eds.), *Irregular Migration and Human Rights: Theoretical, European and International Perspectives*, Nijhoff, Leiden 2004, pp. 159–192.

14 Directive 2008/115/EC of the European Parliament and of the Council of 16 December 2008 on common standards and procedures in Member States for returning illegally staying third-country nationals, OJ L348/98 (hereinafter Return Directive).

15 The directive is binding on all EU Member States, except for Ireland and Denmark, and also binds four Schengen states outside the EU, namely, Iceland, Liechtenstein, Norway and Switzerland. For a recent overview of the directive see e.g., I. Majcher, *The European Union Returns Directive and Its Compatibility with International Human Rights Law: Analysis of Return Decision, Entry Ban, Detention, and Removal*, Brill Nijhoff, Leiden 2020.

16 European Commission, Communication from the Commission to the European Parliament, the Council, the European Economic and Social Committee and the Committee of the Regions, A European Agenda on Migration, COM(2015) 240 final 13.05.2015; European Commission, Communication from the Commission to the European Parliament and the Council On A More Effective Return Policy in the European Union – A Renewed Action Plan, COM(2017) 200 final 02.03.2017; European Commission, Commission Recommendation of 07.03.2017 on making returns more effective when implementing the Directive 2008/115/EC of the European Parliament and of the Council, C(2017) 1600 final 07.03.2017; European Commission, Annex to the Commission Recommendation establishing a common 'Return Handbook' to be used by Member States' competent authorities when carrying out return related tasks, C(2017) 6505 Annex 1 27.09.2017.

17 E.g., T. Gammeltoft-Hansen and N. F. Tan, 'The End of the Deterrence Paradigm? Future Directions for Global Refugee Policy', (2017) 5(1), *Journal on Migration and Human Security*, pp. 28–56; A. Pijnenburg, 'Containment Instead of Refoulement: Shifting State Responsibility in the Age of Cooperative Migration Control?', (2020) 20(2), *Human Rights Law Review*, pp. 306–332.

in the shadow of the migration crisis, have failed to unlock the full protective potential of the law for migrants seeking to reach Europe. This is illustrated by the reluctance of the CJEU and the ECtHR to impose any obligation on states to issue humanitarian visas at diplomatic posts outside the EU to migrants facing persecution. In two cases bearing remarkable similarities, *X and X v Belgium* and *M.N. v Belgium*,[18] both courts failed to find any obligation on a state under EU law or the European Convention on Human Rights (ECHR) to issue a visa that would allow a family to travel to Belgium in order to make an application for asylum.

It is noteworthy here that the 2017 CJEU ruling had been preceded by an Opinion from AG Mengozzi who, taking a strict approach to the prohibition on torture and inhuman and degrading treatment,[19] argued that Belgium was obliged to issue a short-term visa under the EU Visa Code. This obligation arose because there were serious grounds to believe that refusal would directly result in the applicants being subjected to treatment prohibited by Article 4 of the EU Charter of Fundamental Rights and would prevent them from their only legal route to enjoy their right to apply for international protection. The rulings in both of these cases betray a clear judicial sensitivity to the practical and political difficulties states would have faced in the event of a finding for the applicants.[20]

The supranational courts in *X and X* and *M.N.* employed contestable legal reasoning to relieve states of what many might consider to be a moral obligation to assist persons facing a real risk of persecution or ill-treatment by allowing their entry to Europe to lodge a claim for international protection. The rulings in these cases, along with the judgments in *Khlaifia* and *N.D. and N.T.* discussed below in section 2.3, create the impression that the supranational judiciaries are reluctant to interfere with efforts at the Member State and EU levels to fortify the walls of 'fortress Europe'. These judicial endorsements of migration control efforts reflect and feed into a wider and long-standing deterrence paradigm whereby policies are deployed to frustrate the arrival of asylum seekers and migrants and to make host countries less attractive for those who do arrive.[21]

---

18 CJEU, *X and X v Belgium*, Case C-638/16 PPU, 07.03.2017; ECtHR, *M.N. and Others v Belgium*, no 3599/18 [GC] 05.05.2020.

19 The Opinion of AG Mengozzi concerning the irrelevance of policy considerations for the issue of torture or inhuman or degrading treatment bears similarities to the dissenting judgment in the well-known ECtHR, *N. v The United Kingdom*, no 26565/05 [GC] 27.05.2008.

20 Insightful analysis of the CJEU ruling in *X and X* is provided in L. Heschl and A. Stankovic, 'The Decline of Fundamental Rights in CJEU Jurisprudence after the 2015 "Refugee Crisis"', in W. Benedek, P. Czech, L. Heschl, K. Lukas and M. Nowak (eds.), *European Yearbook on Human Rights*, Intersentia, Cambridge 2018, pp. 103–135.

21 T. Gammeltoft-Hansen and N. F. Tan (2017), 'The End of the Deterrence Paradigm?' *supra* note 17.

2.2. DETENTION

The EU has long cast the 'fight' against irregular migration as a law enforcement and security issue,[22] essentially criminalising such migration.[23] Criminalisation of irregular migration in the EU is exemplified by the Return Directive, which devotes four of its 23 articles to the issue of detention of TCNs for the purposes of removal. The broad powers the directive gives states to detain TCNs who are the subject of return procedures have facilitated the adoption of detention as a key element of migration management across the EU.[24] It bears emphasis that TCNs subject to return procedures under the directive have been neither charged with nor convicted of a criminal offence, but may nonetheless be deprived of their liberty for an initial period of up to six months, and a subsequent period of up to 12 months. This latter extension of detention may be ordered where there are delays in obtaining the necessary documentation from third countries. The end result is that an individual may be detained for up to 18 months due to difficulties in effecting expulsion which are beyond the control of the individual concerned. The directive's detention provisions provide a striking example of the capacity for common EU measures in the field of migration to result in a reduction in human rights standards. Following adoption of this piece of EU legislation some states whose detention period for TCNs subject to return procedures were shorter than that sanctioned by the directive went on to extend such periods.[25] This also attests to the punitive, securitised approach taken at the EU level to irregular migration.

---

22 E.g., European Commission, Communication from the Commission to the European Parliament, the Council, the European Economic and Social Committee and the Committee of the Regions: a Common Immigration Policy for Europe: Principles, Actions and Tools, COM(2008) 359 final, p. 3; European Commission, Commission Staff Working Document accompanying the Communication on a Common Immigration Policy for Europe: Principles, actions and tools, ibid.; and Impact Assessment, SEC (2008) 2026 final at 24; European Commission, Commission Staff Working Document on the fulfilment of the 29 measures for reinforcing the protection of the external borders and combating illegal immigration adopted at the Justice and Home Affairs Council meeting, held in Brussels on 25 and 26 February 2010, SEC (2010) 1480 final.

23 Criminalisation of irregular migration, part of the wider deterrence paradigm discussed in *supra* note 17, is a broad concept that involves both the application of criminal law sanctions to immigration law breaches such as irregular entry and stay, as well as deployment against irregular migrants of administrative measures which mimic criminal ones, such as detention; see M. Grange, 'The Migrant Workers Convention: A legal tool to safeguard migrants against arbitrary detention', in A. Desmond (ed.), *Shining New Light on the UN Migrant Workers Convention*, Pretoria University Law Press, Pretoria 2017, pp. 75–76; E. Guild, *Criminalisation of Migration in Europe: Human Rights Implications*, Council of Europe, Strasbourg 2009, p. 5.

24 PICUM, *Position Paper on EU Return Directive*, PICUM, Brussels 2015, available at https://picum.org/Documents/Publi/2015/ReturnDirective_EN.pdf, last accessed 13.07.2021.

25 Ibid.; European Commission, Communication from the Commission to the Council and the European Parliament on EU Return Policy, COM(2014) 199 final, p. 17. For examples, on the other hand, of the beneficent effects of the directive on, *inter alia*, detention periods for TCNs facing expulsion, see M. Moraru, G. Cornelisse and P. de Bruycker (eds.), *Law and Judicial Dialogue on the Return of Irregular Migrants from the European Union*, Hart, London 2020.

States' recourse to immigration detention has long been endorsed by the ECtHR. While Article 5 ECHR provides that everyone has a right to liberty that may be abridged only if strictly necessary, when it comes to Article 5(1)(f) on lawful detention either to prevent unauthorised entry into a country or to effect deportation or extradition, detention does not have to be strictly necessary. In the seminal case of *Chahal v the UK*,[26] the Grand Chamber of the ECtHR found a quarter century ago that states are entitled to detain migrants with a view to deporting them even when, for example, they do not pose a flight risk and detention is therefore not necessary to ensure that the deportation takes place. The Court would have been hard-pushed to interpret Article 5(1)(f) in such a way as to give any more discretion to the state in this field or to more effectively remove migrants facing deportation from the protection potential of Article 5.[27] Somewhat more recently, the Grand Chamber held in *Saadi v the UK* that routine short-term detention of asylum seekers for administrative purposes does not have to meet a necessity requirement because such detention aims to prevent unauthorised entry in line with Article 5(1)(f).[28] It is difficult therefore to dispute the diagnosis that the Strasbourg case law on migration detention is infected with 'overblown statism'.[29]

2.3. EXPULSION

At the time of its adoption, the Return Directive was widely criticised for codifying a rights-deficient expulsion regime.[30] The main body of the directive is devoted to setting out the formalities, procedures and safeguards for enforced removal. The directive imposes a general obligation on states to issue TCNs who are not granted, or do not avail of, the possibility of voluntary return with an entry ban of up to five years, or longer in the case of a serious threat to public

---

26 ECtHR, *Chahal v The United Kingdom*, no 22414/93[GC] 15.11.1996.

27 G. Cornelisse, *Immigration Detention and Human Rights: Rethinking Territorial Sovereignty*, Martinus Nijhoff, The Hague 2010, p. 295.

28 ECtHR, *Saadi v The United Kingdom*, no 13229/03 [GC] 29.01.2008; see the analysis in H. O'Nions, 'Exposing flaws in the detention of asylum seekers: a critique of *Saadi*', (2008) 17(2), *Nottingham Law Journal*, pp. 34–51.

29 C. Costello, *The Human Rights of Migrants and Refugees in European Law*, OUP, Oxford 2016, p. 313.

30 D. Acosta, *Latin American Responses to the Adoption of the Returns Directive*, CEPS, Brussels 2009; A. Baldaccini, 'The Return and Removal of Irregular Migrants under EU Law: An Analysis of the Returns Directive', (2009) 11(1), *European Journal of Migration and Law*, pp. 1–17; OHCHR, 'UN Experts Express Concern about Proposed EU Return Directive', 18.07.2008, available at https://newsarchive.ohchr.org/EN/NewsEvents/Pages/DisplayNews.aspx?NewsID=8440&LangID=E, last accessed 28.06.2021; UNHCR, 'Position on the Proposal for a Directive on Common Standards and Procedures in Member States for Returning Illegally Staying Third-Country Nationals', 16.06.2008, available at https://www.unhcr.org/4d948a1f9.pdf, last accessed 28.06.2021.

policy, public security or national security.[31] In recent years the Commission has repeatedly prioritised the need to enhance the effectiveness of EU return policy.[32] As part of its efforts, and against the background of the 2015 migration 'crisis', the Commission in 2018 proposed significant amendments to the Return Directive that,[33] if adopted, will make the directive even more punitive and less rights-friendly than its original incarnation.

The 2018 proposal, still a key priority for the Commission,[34] is premised on the belief that return policy would be improved and the duration of return procedures shortened by addressing some key flaws in the current implementation of the directive, such as inconsistent use of detention across states and inconsistent interpretation of a risk of absconding. The Commission has therefore proposed that the legislation be revised to increase the grounds for detention of TCNs subject to a return procedure. Furthermore, the proposal to define a 'risk of absconding' would facilitate refusal of voluntary departure and use of detention, simultaneously increasing the number of persons subject to an entry ban. The revised directive would also require states, where necessary, to change their national laws to ensure TCNs facing expulsion may be detained for a minimum of three months. The Commission's proposal is objectionable not only for the adverse impacts on irregular migrants' rights that its adoption would entail. A recent report for the European Parliament also found that it would generate substantial costs for Member States and the EU without any clear evidence that it would lead to a more effective return policy.[35]

The EU's expulsion focus efforts appear to meet minimal resistance from the ECtHR. Despite the Court's repeated insistence that the challenges posed by migration flows cannot justify practices that are incompatible with states' ECHR obligations,[36] it seems increasingly willing to interpret and apply those obligations in a way that relieves states of onerous potential duties. The Grand Chamber in *Khlaifia*, for example, held that failure to provide irregular migrants with an individual interview prior to deportation from Italy did

---

31 Article 11(1) and (2) Return Directive, *supra* note 14. Article 11(3) sets out exceptions to the mandatory nature of entry bans.

32 European Commission, COM(2015) 240 final, *supra* note 16; European Commission, COM(2017) 200 final, *supra* note 16; European Commission, C(2017) 1600 final, *supra* note 16; European Commission, Annex to the Commission Recommendation establishing a common 'Return Handbook', C(2017) 6505, *supra* note 16.

33 European Commission, COM(2015) 240 final, *supra* note 16; European Commission, COM(2017) 200 final, *supra* note 16; European Commission, C(2017) 1600 final, *supra* note 16; European Commission, Annex to the Commission Recommendation establishing a common 'Return Handbook', C(2017) 6505, *supra* note 16.

34 European Commission, COM(2020) 609 final, *supra* note 7, p. 3.

35 European Parliamentary Research Service, *The Proposed Return Directive (Recast) Substitute Impact Assessment*, European Parliament, Brussels 2019.

36 E.g., ECtHR, *Hirsi Jamaa and Others v Italy*, no 27765/09 [GC] 23.02.2012, paras. 122, 176 and 179; ECtHR, *Khlaifia and Others v Italy*, no 16483/12 [GC] 15.12.2016, para. 241.

not violate the prohibition of collective expulsion codified in Article 4 of Protocol 4. An individual interview is not necessarily entailed by the Article 4 requirement that migrants must have a genuine and effective possibility of submitting and having examined in an appropriate manner arguments against expulsion.[37] In the same case, in an unfortunate setback for migrants' rights,[38] the ECtHR also held that the detention conditions endured by the irregular migrant applicants did not constitute inhuman or degrading treatment for the purposes of Article 3 ECHR, essentially reaching this conclusion because of the 'situation of extreme difficulty facing the Italian authorities at the relevant time.'[39]

More recently, the Grand Chamber revealed 'a paradigmatic shift' in approaches to border control and migrants' fundamental rights by again overturning an earlier Chamber decision to find no violation of Article 4 of Protocol 4 in the case of two applicants from Mali and the Ivory Coast who had been amongst 600 people who attempted to scale the fences separating Spain's North African enclave of Melilla from Morocco in August 2014.[40] While the Court accepted that the applicants, having been forcibly transferred from Spanish territory to Morocco in handcuffs, had been expelled for the purposes of Article 4 Protocol 4, it held that the expulsions did not violate the prohibition on collective expulsion. This is because the applicants had placed themselves in an unlawful situation by deliberately attempting to enter Spain as part of a large group and at an unauthorised location, thereby creating a disruptive situation endangering public safety. It had been open to the applicants to avail of the legal procedures which existed in order to enter Spanish territory lawfully, procedures which would have provided a genuine and effective possibility of submitting arguments against expulsion.[41] The lack of individual removal decisions in the case of the applicants was attributable to their own conduct.[42] *N.D. and N. T.* was the first time the ECtHR addressed the applicability of Article 4 Protocol 4 to the forcible return of migrants from a land border in the context of a large-scale unauthorised attempt at entry. Having endorsed pushbacks at sea borders

---

37 Ibid., para. 248.

38 P. Pinto de Albuquerque, 'The Rights of Migrants and Refugees under the European Convention on Human Rights: Where are we now?', (2018) 13, *The Irish Yearbook of International Law*, pp. 5–22.

39 ECtHR, *Khlaifia*, *supra* note 36, para. 185.

40 I. Barbero and A. López-Sala, 'The Spanish Borders on the Cusp of the New European Pact on Migration and Asylum', in S. Carrera and A. Geddes (eds.), *The EU Pact on Migration and Asylum in light of the United Nations Global Compact on Refugees: International Experiences on Containment and Mobility and their Impacts on Trust and Rights*, EUI, Florence 2021, pp. 91–92; ECtHR, *N.D. and N.T. v Spain*, nos 8675/15 and 8697/15 [GC] 13.02.2020, paras. 24–27.

41 Ibid., paras. 201 and 231.

42 Ibid., para. 231.

in *Khlaifia*, the Court used the opportunity presented by *N.D. and N.T.* to give its imprimatur to violent pushbacks at Europe's land borders.[43]

3. THE PACT: FURTHER FORTIFICATION OF FORTRESS EUROPE

The most recent comprehensive EU statement on its plans for developing European law and policy around migration and asylum is the long-awaited New Pact on Migration and Asylum, unveiled on 23 September 2020, which includes five legislative proposals and a number of recommendations.[44] The New Pact is presented as a 'fresh start' for EU efforts to manage migration for the achievement of growth and innovation in a manner that complies with human rights law.[45] Like much of the EU agenda-setting literature in the field of asylum and migration,[46] it strikes a number of positive notes about the benefits of migration and observes that migration has been a constant feature of human history.[47] It has been likened by Commissioner Schinas to a three-storey house with EU partnership with third countries, the external dimension, being the first floor.[48] The second floor focuses on tightening borders, articulated as 'robust management of external borders', capped off with a third floor of rules ensuring support for Member States under migration pressure.

It is important to view the New Pact, and its focus on further fortifying Europe's borders, in the broader context of EU efforts to develop the CEAS.

---

43 S. Jones, 'European Court under Fire for Backing Spain's Express Deportations: ECHR Accused of "Ignoring Reality" in Ruling on Men Who Entered North African Enclave', *The Guardian*, 13.02.2020, available at https://www.theguardian.com/world/2020/feb/13/european-court-under-fire-backing-spain-express-deportations, last accessed 28.06.2021. A detailed and nuanced analysis of the ruling is provided by S. Carrera, *The Strasbourg Court Judgement N.D. and N.T. v Spain: A Carte Blanche to Push Backs at EU External Borders?*, EUI Working Paper RSCAS, Florence 2020.

44 For detailed discussion of different elements of the Pact, see the excellent series of blogposts coordinated and edited by Daniel Thym for the Odysseus Network, available at https://eumigrationlawblog.eu/series-on-the-migration-pact-published-under-the-supervision-of-daniel-thym/, last accessed 28.06.2021.

45 European Commission, COM(2020) 609 final, *supra* note 7, p. 1.

46 E.g., European Council, Presidency Conclusions, Tampere European Council, 15–16 October 1999, Bulletin EU 10–1999.

47 In this regard, the New Pact chimes with the UN Global Compact for Safe, Orderly and Regular Migration. For an examination of the New Pact in light of the two UN compacts adopted in 2018, see the contributions to S. Carrera and A. Geddes (eds.), *The EU Pact on Migration and Asylum in light of the United Nations Global Compact on Refugees: International Experiences on Containment and Mobility and their Impacts on Trust and Rights*, EUI, Florence 2021.

48 See European Commission, 'Speech by Vice-President Schinas on the New Pact on Migration and Asylum', 23.09.2020, available at https://ec.europa.eu/commission/presscorner/detail/en/SPEECH_20_1736, last accessed 28.06.2021.

Of particular contextual relevance is the aforementioned 2015 'crisis' during which over a million migrants arrived in the EU. From the perspective of the CEAS, this was a traumatic event that exacerbated and deepened the existing fault lines in EU asylum policy whereby states at the coalface of migrant arrivals chafed against the lack of solidarity shown to them in the face of the disproportionate burden they had to shoulder by virtue of the combination of their geographical location and the operation of the Dublin system.[49] The default position under Dublin is that responsibility for examining asylum applications lies with the first EU state of entry. Prior to the 2015 'crisis' the Dublin system had been severely weakened by a number of debilitating blows inflicted by the ECtHR in Strasbourg and the CJEU in Luxembourg.[50] The 2015 crisis therefore brought it to the brink of collapse, forcing the EU to administer a number of emergency stomach pumps in an effort to prevent the Dublin system's demise.[51] The New Pact must be partly viewed as a post-traumatic symptom of the 2015 crisis as well as yet another attempt to preserve the general structure of the Dublin system, nomenclatural niceties notwithstanding, and the CEAS more broadly.

3.1. ARRIVALS

When it comes to irregular migration, the Pact represents a business-as-usual approach. Its proposal of new procedures to 'swiftly' establish the status of those arriving at the EU's external borders in an irregular manner entails the closure of 'the gaps between external border controls and asylum and return procedures' so as to reduce 'the possibilities to circumvent the asylum system'.[52] Thus the proposed new procedures will essentially seek to identify as quickly as possible whether a TCN may have a legitimate claim for international protection that should be examined or, conversely, is an irregular migrant to be summarily removed. In the following two sub-sections, I illustrate how these proposed procedures are rich with risks of rights reduction and violation.

---

49 See *infra* note 83 and related text for examples of the dissatisfaction of frontline states with the Dublin system.

50 E.g., ECtHR, *M.S.S. v Belgium and Greece*, no 30696/09 [GC] 21.01.2011; e.g., CJEU, *N.S. v SSHD* and *M.E. v Refugee Applications Commissioner*, Cases C-411/10 and C-493/10, 21.12.2011.

51 E.g., Council Decision (EU) 2015/1601 of 22 September 2015 establishing provisional measures in the area of international protection for the benefit of Italy and Greece, OJ L 248, pp. 80–94.

52 European Commission, COM(2020) 609 final, *supra* note 7, pp. 4 and 8.

In addition to fears that the Pact disregards the protection needs of arriving migrants as part of an ongoing EU strategy of discouraging arrivals,[53] it is also likely that the Pact will entrench efforts to frustrate arrival through further use of externalisation and containment policies such as the 2016 EU-Turkey Statement.[54] The Pact's identification of, *inter alia*, assistance to refugees in third countries and addressing the root causes of irregular migration as 'valuable objectives'[55] clearly signposts an intention to foster the immobility of prospective migrants to Europe. Indeed, in relation to Africa, Loren Landau and Iriann Freemantle make a compelling case for the proposition that the framework furthered in the Pact, particularly Commissioner Schinas's 'first floor', will result in 'a regulatory regime that intercepts and prevents mobility while coding even the most coercive means as necessary to "protect" Africans and foster their continent's development.'[56]

3.2. ENTRENCHING DETENTION

The Pact provides the tools to turbo-charge pre-removal detention. The Screening Regulation proposed in the Pact would introduce a pre-entry screening procedure for TCNs crossing the EU's external borders without authorisation, with the aim of facilitating the swift execution of return procedures where international protection is not applicable.[57] While the Screening Regulation is aimed mainly at border arrivals and appears to mandate detention for up to five days to determine whether a TCN should be referred to asylum authorities or

---

53 E. Easton-Calabria, 'The Global Compact on Refugees and the EU's New Pact on Migration and Asylum: The Ripples of Responsibility-Sharing', in S. Carrera and A. Geddes (eds.), *The EU Pact on Migration and Asylum in light of the United Nations Global Compact on Refugees: International Experiences on Containment and Mobility and their Impacts on Trust and Rights*, EUI, Florence 2021, p. 127.

54 M. Ineli-Ciger and O. Ulusoy, 'A Short Sighted and One Side Deal: Why The EU-Turkey Statement Should Never Serve As a Blueprint', in S. Carrera and A. Geddes (eds.), *The EU Pact on Migration and Asylum in light of the United Nations Global Compact on Refugees: International Experiences on Containment and Mobility and their Impacts on Trust and Rights*, EUI, Florence 2021, p. 112.

55 European Commission, COM(2020) 609 final, *supra* note 7, p. 2.

56 L. B. Landau and I. Freemantle, 'Containment Development and Africa's Time-Space Trap', in S. Carrera and A. Geddes (eds.), *The EU Pact on Migration and Asylum in light of the United Nations Global Compact on Refugees: International Experiences on Containment and Mobility and their Impacts on Trust and Rights*, EUI, Florence 2021, p. 275.

57 European Commission, Proposal for a Regulation of the European Parliament and of the Council introducing a screening of third country nationals at the external borders and amending Regulations (EC) No 767/2008, (EU) 2017/2226, (EU) 2018/1240 and (EU) 2019/817, COM(2020) 612 final 23.09.2020, 2020/0278 (COD).

return procedures,[58] it also applies to irregular migrants already in the territory of the EU, regardless of their length of residence, where those individuals have unlawfully entered the EU.[59] The regulation entails a draconian detention regime for such territorially present TCNs. The screening procedure could result in their detention for up to three days. While the proposed procedure will include verification of identity, and preliminary health and vulnerability checks, it is silent on individuals' rights to contact their families, to access legal assistance and to appeal their detention. Instead, where an unlawfully present TCN has not applied for international protection and has no legal grounds for remaining in the EU, he or she will be subjected to return procedures in accordance with the Return Directive.[60]

While states will be obliged to establish an independent monitoring mechanism to ensure compliance with human rights standards during the screening and to guarantee investigation of allegations of non-respect for fundamental rights in relation to the screening,[61] the Screening Regulation in its current incarnation raises serious concerns vis-à-vis safeguards and procedural fairness for irregular TCNs facing expulsion from the EU. In particular, detention for screening purposes for up to three days upon apprehension within the territory of an EU state,[62] without the right to inform legal representatives or family members, may conflict with migrants' right to respect for private and family life as enshrined in Article 8 ECHR and Article 7 of the EU Charter, the principle of the best interests of the child codified in Article 24 of the Charter and the principle that immigration detention should be used only as a measure of last resort.[63] Furthermore, the possibility of subjecting territorially present TCNs to such screening procedures raises the spectre of racial profiling and discriminatory policing.

---

58 Ibid., Article 6(3), pp. 27–28. Exceptionally, where a disproportionate number of TCNs needs to be screened at the same time, making it impossible in practice to conclude the screening within that time-limit, the period of five days may be extended by a maximum of an additional five days.

59 Ibid., pp. 2, 6 and 27. The proposed Screening Regulation would not, however, apply to irregular TCNs whose unlawful stay is the consequence of expiry of valid documents such as tourist visas or work permits, as such persons will have been subject to border checks upon arrival. Screening would be triggered by an inability on the part of TCNs to credibly show they had lawfully crossed an external border, e.g., by failure to provide a relevant travel document or an entry stamp in a travel document.

60 Ibid., Articles 5, 6 and 14, pp. 27–28 and 33.

61 Ibid., Article 7, p. 28.

62 For detailed discussion of detention at the external borders, see G. Cornelisse, 'The Pact and Detention: An Empty Promise of certainty, clarity and decent conditions', *Special Collection on the 'New' Migration and Asylum Pact*, 06.01.2021, available at https://eumigrationlawblog.eu/the-pact-and-detention-an-empty-promise-of-certainty-clarity-and-decent-conditions/, last accessed 28.06.2021.

63 E.g., Return Directive, *supra* note 14, Article 15.

3.3. EXPANDING EXPULSION EFFORTS

Two aspects of the Pact concerning expulsion merit mention, as illustrations of what might be legitimately characterised as an EU fixation on return. Firstly, it puts forward a Regulation on Migration and Asylum Management (RAMM) to replace the Dublin Regulation,[64] the central pillar of the CEAS which sets out the criteria for establishing which state will be responsible for examining an asylum application. While RAMM generally preserves the Dublin criteria for determining responsibility,[65] it sets out a framework to dilute the burden imposed by irregular arrivals on individual states by enforcing support for those states. As part of the reform of the CEAS, RAMM proposes a new compulsory but flexible solidarity mechanism for the benefit of states facing migratory pressure,[66] to be coordinated by the Commission. One option for states to show solidarity under the new mechanism would be to strengthen the return capacity of countries facing migratory pressure. In particular, a state could undertake 'return sponsorship' whereby it would carry out the necessary activities to return individually identified irregular TCNs from the territory of a state benefitting from a compulsory solidarity measure.[67] If, after eight months, return efforts have not succeeded, the sponsoring state would transfer the persons concerned to its own territory and continue its efforts to return them in accordance with the Return Directive.[68]

Return sponsorship is a tool that may have a number of arguably adverse consequences for migrants. First, it may concentrate EU returns in the hands of a small number of states with the necessary capacity for and interest in undertaking expulsion. This may result in migrants being expelled to third countries with which the expelling state has ties, without necessarily any similar connection between the expelled migrants and the receiving state.[69] Second, the

---

64 Dublin Regulation, *supra* note 10.

65 European Commission, Proposal for a Regulation of the European Parliament and of the Council on asylum and migration management and amending Council Directive (EC) 2003/109 and the proposed Regulation (EU) XXX/XXX [Asylum and Migration Fund], COM(2020) 610 final 23.09.2020, 2020/0279 (COD), p. 16.

66 It is important to note that the Pact also envisages voluntary solidarity measures, including in the form of return sponsorship. See European Commission, COM(2020) 610 final, *supra* note 65, Recital 32 on p. 32.

67 Ibid., pp. 18–19 and 22. The sponsoring state could, e.g., provide counselling on return and reintegration to illegally TCNs, assist voluntary return and reintegration using its programme and resources, lead dialogue with third countries for facilitating readmission and ensure the delivery of a valid travel document.

68 Ibid.

69 This risk arises because under Article 3 of the Return Directive return means the process of a TCN going back to her country of origin; or a country of transit in accordance with EU or bilateral readmission agreements or other arrangements; or another third country, to which the TCN voluntarily decides to return and in which she will be accepted. For further discussion of the return sponsorship tool, see M. Moraru, 'The New Design of the EU's

transfer of migrants following the aforementioned eight months' time limit may result in migrants who have been *de facto* long-term resident in one EU country being moved to another EU Member State with which they have no connection. This may clearly give rise to violations of the right to respect for private and family life, as well as the principle of the best interests of the child.[70]

A second feature of the New Pact that makes clear the centrality of its objective to enhance EU return policy is its focus on readmission cooperation with third countries. One of the many obstacles to expulsion is the reluctance or refusal of some countries to accept prospective deportees.[71] The Pact therefore calls for a full-blooded implementation of the 24 existing EU readmission agreements, completion of ongoing readmission negotiations and practical cooperative solutions to increase the number of effective returns.[72] The Pact emphasises the need to incentivise third countries to receive migrants through, for example, linking EU visa policy and readmission policy whereby poor cooperation from a third country on readmission of TCNs would lead to application of restrictive visa measures for that country's citizens and, conversely, good cooperation would trigger favourable visa measures.[73] This approach to readmission also increases the aforementioned risk that migrants will be expelled to third countries with which they do not necessarily have any connection.

The New Pact, which pledges continued commitment to a preference for voluntary return,[74] clearly signals plans for greater EU involvement in return policy and practice. For example, the Commission will coordinate the operational aspects of return sponsorship and the Pact calls for conclusion of further EU readmission agreements where appropriate. Of particular significance is the

---

Return System under the Pact on Asylum and Migration', *Special Collection on the 'New' Migration and Asylum Pact*, 14.01.2021, available at https://eumigrationlawblog.eu/the-new-design-of-the-eus-return-system-under-the-pact-on-asylum-and-migration/, last accessed 28.06.2021; see also N. Nielsen, 'Internal Paper Lays Out EU Splits on "Returning" Migrants', *EU Observer*, 17.05.2021, available at https://euobserver.com/migration/151816?utm_source=euobs&utm_medium=email, last accessed 28.06.2021.

70 For a more exhaustive critique of return sponsorship see L. Vosyliūtė, 'When Principles Are Compromised: EU Return Sponsorship in Light of the UN Global Compacts', in S. Carrera and A. Geddes (eds.), *The EU Pact on Migration and Asylum in light of the United Nations Global Compact on Refugees: International Experiences on Containment and Mobility and their Impacts on Trust and Rights*, EUI, Florence 2021, pp. 291–313.

71 Tacitly admitted in European Commission, COM(2020) 609 final, *supra* note 7, p. 21.

72 Ibid.

73 Ibid. See also, E. Guild, 'Negotiating with Third Countries under the New Pact: Carrots and Sticks?', *Special Collection on the 'New' Migration and Asylum Pact*, 27.11.2020, available at https://eumigrationlawblog.eu/negotiating-with-third-countries-under-the-new-pact-carrots-and-sticks/#more-3368, last accessed 28.06.2021.

74 European Commission, COM(2020) 609 final, *supra* note 7, pp. 8–9. In April 2021 the Commission published its first strategy on voluntary return and reintegration. See European Commission, Communication from the Commission to the European Parliament and the Council: The EU strategy on voluntary return and reintegration, COM(2021) 120 final, 27.04.2021.

introduction of an EU Return Coordinator, inside the European Commission, and the creation of the post of Deputy Executive Director for Return within Frontex. The Return Coordinator will coordinate national approaches to returns and ensure consistency across the EU, contributing to a common strategic approach on return and readmission across states and EU institutions and agencies.[75] It seems, therefore, that greater EU involvement has been identified as the life support technique for the CEAS.

4. THE EUROPEAN RESPONSE TO MIGRATION AND MIGRANTS' RIGHTS DURING THE PANDEMIC

4.1. DISCOURAGING ARRIVAL

Broadly speaking, there is evidence that the EU and its Member States have instrumentalised the pandemic to continue the tightening of Europe's borders and the transformation of Europe into a hostile environment for 'unwanted' migrants such as asylum seekers and unlawfully present TCNs. At the Member State level, for example, Malta and Italy were quick to invoke the global health emergency to justify the adoption of non-disembarkation policies.[76] These pandemic-related port closures by Italy and Malta arguably fell foul of international human rights and maritime law and international health regulations.[77] They resulted in migrants being stranded at sea,[78] potentially putting lives at risk.[79] While these actions must be understood as a practical

[75] New Pact on Migration and Asylum: Questions and Answers, available at https://ec.europa.eu/commission/presscorner/detail/en/qanda_20_1707, last accessed 28.06.2021; European Commission, COM(2020) 609 final, *supra* note 7, pp. 8–9; European Commission, COM(2020) 610 final, *supra* note 65, p. 2.

[76] Human Rights Watch, 'Port Closures Cut Migrant and Refugee Lifeline', 09.04.2020, available at https://www.hrw.org/news/2020/04/09/eu/italy-port-closures-cut-migrant-and-refugee-lifeline, last accessed 28.06.2021.

[77] See A. Farahat and N. Markard, *Closed Ports, Dubious Partners: The European Policy of Outsourcing Responsibility Study Update*, Heinrich-Böll-Stiftung European Union, Brussels 2021. For the view that the closure of the Italian ports was 'not illegal under maritime, human rights and European law' see E. Cusumano and K. Gombeer, 'In Deep Waters: The Legal, Humanitarian and Political Implications of Closing Italian Ports to Migrant Rescuers', (2020) 25(2), *Mediterranean Politics*, pp. 245–253.

[78] E.g., L. Tondo, M. Stierl and M. Blackall, 'UN refugee agency calls on EU nations to let in migrants rescued in Mediterranean', *The Guardian*, 29.08.2020, available at https://www.theguardian.com/world/2020/aug/29/banksy-european-authorities-ignoring-pleas-crew-migrant-rescue-vessel, last accessed 28.06.2021.

[79] UNHCR, 'News comment on search and rescue in the Central Mediterranean by the Assistant High Commissioner for Protection at UNHCR, the UN Refugee Agency, Gillian Triggs', 01.05.2020, available at https://www.unhcr.org/mt/13871-news-comment-on-search-and-rescue-in-the-central-mediterranean-bythe-assistant-high-commissioner-for-protection-at-unhcr-the-un-refugee-agency-gillian-triggs.html, last accessed 28.06.2021.

manifestation of the dissatisfaction of EU states at the frontline of migrant arrivals with the operation of the CEAS and its Dublin system,[80] they are also an extension of a deterrence practice that can be traced at least as far back as the push-back campaign initiated by Italy in 2009 that sought to return migrants to Libya before they could reach European territorial waters.[81]

At the EU level, the initial response to the pandemic was to discourage travel to and from the EU. On 16 March 2020, with the EU the centre of the global health emergency, the European Commission issued a short Communication calling for a sharp reduction in arrivals at the external borders through the imposition of a temporary restriction on all non-essential travel from third countries.[82] This would effectively deploy the capacity for common action facilitated by the EU external border regime as a tool to limit the spread of the virus. The Commission did, however, foresee exceptions to the proposed travel restrictions for persons travelling for essential purposes, including international protection or 'other humanitarian reasons'.[83] More detailed Guidance on the implementation of EU law on asylum and return procedures in the context of the travel restrictions was issued by the Communication one month later, on 16 April 2020.[84] The guidance, prepared with the support of the European Asylum Support Office (EASO) and the European Border and Coast Guard Agency (Frontex), advises that the operation of travel restrictions in the field of asylum and return must be proportionate, consistent with international

80 Italy and Malta had engaged in the practice of closing their ports to private rescue vessels with migrants on board in 2018, before the pandemic. See Amnesty International, 'Italy/Malta: Stop playing with refugee and migrants' lives by closing ports', 14.08.2018, available at https://www.amnesty.org/en/latest/news/2018/08/italy-malta-stop-playing-with-refugee-and-migrants-lives-by-closing-ports/, last accessed 28.06.2021. This practice was successful in that it yielded a declaration from a number of EU Member States to accept on a voluntary basis migrants disembarked following SAR operations in the high seas, and falling under the responsibility of Italy and Malta. See Joint Declaration of Intent on a Controlled Emergency Procedure – Voluntary Commitments by Member States for a Predictable Temporary Solidarity Mechanism, 23.09.2019. For discussion of the joint declaration, see S. Carrera and R. Cortinovis, *The Malta declaration on SAR and relocation: A predictable EU solidarity mechanism*?, CEPS Policy Insights No. 14, Brussels 2019.

81 M. Giuffre, *The Readmission of Asylum Seekers under International Law*, Hart, Oxford 2020, p. 244.

82 European Commission, Communication from the Commission to the European Parliament, the European Council and the Council, COVID-19: Temporary Restriction on Non-Essential Travel to the EU Brussels, COM(2020) 115 final 16.3.2020. The Commission's proposal for a coordinated temporary travel restriction was immediately endorsed by the Heads of State or Government: European Council, Conclusions by the President of the European Council following the video conference with members of the European Council on COVID-19, 17.03.2020.

83 European Commission, COM(2020) 115 final, *supra* note 82, p. 2.

84 European Commission, Communication from the Commission, COVID-19: Guidance on the implementation of relevant EU provisions in the area of asylum and return procedures and on resettlement Brussels, C(2020) 2516 final 16.04.2020.

law obligations, and take account of states' health protection measures to fight the spread of COVID. The Commission's emphasis on ensuring continuity of procedures as far as possible in the face of the pandemic is commendable from the perspective of access to international protection in Europe. It is, however, inconsistent with a preference for travel restrictions to call for continuation of expulsions and pre-removal detention where possible and necessary. Such an approach illustrates how pursuit of a hostile European environment for irregular migrants is in tension with efforts to combat the pandemic.

4.2. DETENTION DESPITE THE PANDEMIC

As indicated in section 2.2, immigration detention, a key pillar of the contemporary phenomenon of criminalising migration, is a central feature of the EU's return regime. This is reflected in the Return Directive, which, despite its stated preference for voluntary return, devotes four of its 23 articles to detention of TCNs for the purposes of removal. Article 15 provides that when no other, less coercive measures would be effective, states may detain irregular migrants for as short a period as possible where removal arrangements are in progress, in particular but not only where there is a risk of absconding or the TCN is hampering the removal process. Detention must be ordered in writing by administrative or judicial authorities, for an initial maximum period of six months and an absolute maximum period of 18 months.

The CJEU has taken a clear and strict approach to the Article 15(4) provision that once a reasonable prospect of removal no longer exists, detention ceases to be justified and the person concerned shall be released immediately.[85] The Commission has been equally emphatic in its view that the measures adopted by states to combat the spread of COVID-19 do not automatically lead to the conclusion that a reasonable prospect of removal no longer exists in all cases.[86] The health risks posed to individuals as a result of being held in detention are not, therefore, a justification for recourse to alternatives to detention. Instead, Member States are advised to consider various factors to determine whether, in each individual case, a reasonable prospect of removal continues to exist. In the event of a conclusion that there is no longer any such reasonable prospect, states should use measures less coercive than detention, such as the obligation to stay at certain place or to submit documents to the authorities.[87]

---

85 E.g., CJEU, *Said Shamilovich Kadzoev (Huchbarov)*, Case C-357/09 PPU, 30.11.2009; CJEU, *Bashir Mohamed Ali Mahdi*, Case C-146/14 PPU, 05.06.2014.

86 European Commission, C(2020) 2516 final, *supra* note 84, p. 23.

87 Ibid.

The CJEU has interpreted strictly the Article 16(1) obligation on states to detain irregular TCNs facing removal in specialised detention facilities,[88] and the accompanying exception to keep TCNs separated from ordinary prisoners where accommodation cannot be provided in a specialised detention facility.[89] Pandemic-related precautionary measures such as social distancing will reduce the effective maximum capacity of specialised detention facilities, leading the Commission to take the view that this excuses states from being unable to provide accommodation in specialised detention facilities, and justifies the use of other appropriate facilities in line with Article 16(1). It is important to point out that the Commission's guidance does stress the need to take measures to reduce the spread of COVID-19,[90] and the propriety of providing irregular TCNs with medical screening. The Commission refers states, for example, to guidance of the World Health Organization (WHO) on how to prevent and address a potential disease outbreak in a place of detention.[91] The message that emerges most clearly from the April 2020 guidance, however, is that EU efforts in the realm of detention and return should be impeded as little as possible by the ongoing global health emergency.

This approach to pre-removal detention is in tension with the view of the guardians and interpreters of human rights standards. The Council of Europe Commissioner for Human Rights, for example, has called for the release of irregular migrants in immigration detention to the maximum extent possible, noting that expulsion is currently clearly not feasible in many cases and that immigration detention facilities are generally conducive environments for the spread of COVID-19.[92] The Commissioner's reference to feasibility of return is a clear acknowledgment of the risk that failure to release migrant detainees in the context of the pandemic may result in arbitrary detention, as prohibited by international human rights law. As mentioned above, Article 15(4) of the Return Directive provides that when a reasonable prospect of removal no longer exists, detention ceases to be justified. Similarly, although the right to liberty enshrined in Article 5 ECHR has famously been interpreted to relieve states of

---

88 CJEU, *Adala Bero v Regierungspräsidium Kassel and Ettayebi Bouzalmate v Kreisverwaltung Kleve*, Case C-473/13 and Case C-514/13, 17.07.2014.

89 CJEU, *Thi Ly Pham v Stadt Schweinfurt, Amt für Meldewesen und Statistik*, Case C-474/13, 17.07. 2014.

90 European Commission, C(2020) 2516 final, *supra* note 84, pp. 23–24.

91 WHO/Europe, 'Preparedness, prevention and control of COVID-19 in prisons and other places of detention: interim guidance', 15.03.2020, available at https://apps.who.int/iris/bitstream/handle/10665/336525/WHO-EURO-2020-1405-41155-55954-eng.pdf?sequence=1&isAllowed=y, last accessed 28.06.2021.

92 Council of Europe, 'Commissioner calls for release of immigration detainees while Covid-19 crisis continues', 26.03.2020, available at https://www.coe.int/en/web/commissioner/-/commissioner-calls-for-release-of-immigration-detainees-while-covid-19-crisis-continues, last accessed 28.06.2021.

a necessity requirement when detaining migrants with a view to expulsion,[93] it has nonetheless been applied by the European Court of Human Rights to mean that detention for removal becomes unlawful if there is no realistic prospect of expulsion.[94]

The United Nations (UN) Committee on Migrant Workers and the UN Special Rapporteur on the human rights of migrants, however, have stopped short of characterising ongoing detention of irregular migrants during the pandemic as unlawful or arbitrary. In keeping with the relatively deferential tone they evince in relation to expulsion during the pandemic, they only go so far as to call for a reduction of detained migrant populations to the lowest possible level, and immediate release from immigration detention facilities of families with children and unaccompanied or separated children.[95]

The reality on the ground concerning pre-removal detention in Europe is something of a mixed bag. Despite the call from the European Commission to continue detention of TCNs facing return where possible and necessary, it appears that at least some states acted in line with the recommendations of actors such as the Council of Europe Commissioner for Human Rights and the European Council for Refugees and Exiles (ECRE)[96] by ceasing returns and releasing irregular TCNs from detention.[97] At the same time, however, some countries continue to detain such migrants despite an official or *de facto* suspension of removals owing to the pandemic.[98]

---

93 ECtHR, *Chahal*, *supra* note 26; G. Cornelisse (2010), *Immigration Detention and Human Rights*, *supra* note 27.

94 E.g., ECtHR, *Al Husin v Bosnia and Herzegovina* (*No. 2*), no 10112/16, 25.06.2019, para. 107.

95 UN Committee on Migrant Workers and UN Special Rapporteur on the Human Rights of Migrants, 'Joint Guidance Note on the Impacts of the COVID-19 Pandemic on the Human Rights of Migrants UN Committee on the Protection of the Rights of All Migrant Workers and Members of their Families and UN Special Rapporteur on the human rights of migrants', 26.05.2020, p. 3, available at https://www.ohchr.org/Documents/Issues/Migration/CMWSPMJointGuidanceNoteCOVID-19Migrants.pdf, last accessed 28.06.2021.

96 This is not to suggest that such action was taken by states as a direct result of the positions articulated by the actors in question.

97 PICUM, 'Non-exhaustive overview of European government measures impacting undocumented migrants taken in the context of COVID-19', 2020, pp. 15–16, available at https://picum.org/wp-content/uploads/2020/10/Non-exhaustive-overview-of-European-government-measures-impacting-undocumented-migrants-taken-in-the-context-of-COVID-19.pdf, last accessed 28.06.2021.

98 Although Slovakia suspended removals in 2020, it did not view this as a reason for abstaining from detention. See Global Detention Project, 'Slovakia COVID-19 update', 19.08.2020, available at https://bit.ly/36A6Oy4, last accessed 28.06.2021. Similarly, by the end of 2020, France had begun to increase pre-removal detention in spite of a dearth of flights. See FRA, 'Migration Quarterly Bulletin', 05.11.2020, available at https://bit.ly/3otjcpy, last accessed 28.06.2021.

4.3. CONTINUED FOCUS ON RETURN DURING THE PANDEMIC

Efforts to expel irregular migrants from the EU, already largely ineffective,[99] have been further hampered by the global health emergency. A worldwide tightening of borders, a dearth of flights, redeployment of state officials to deal with public health measures and the reduction in human contact essential to combatting a communicable infectious disease all combined to make deportation less feasible than ever before. Despite this, the COVID-19 pandemic has not dented the EU's enthusiasm for deportation as the central plank in its response to unlawfully present TCNs. In its April 2020 guidance, the Commission advised that return procedures should continue as far as possible and that any backlog caused by the pandemic should be addressed as soon as circumstances permit.[100]

The Return Directive explicitly favours allowing irregular TCNs to voluntarily leave the EU, in preference to undertaking a forced return.[101] This preference has been underscored by the Commission in the context of the pandemic. It calls for the promotion and prioritisation of voluntary returns because they 'lower the health and safety risks of return operations, including by minimising the risks for irregular migrants and the accompanying staff involved.'[102] Voluntary return and reintegration activities should therefore, in the view of the Commission, continue as much as possible, using tools that reduce or remove physical proximity such as videoconferencing, written exchanges and other types of electronic and remote communication.[103]

The preference for voluntary return codified in the directive entails an obligation on states issuing a return decision to provide, as per Article 7, for an appropriate period for voluntary departure of between seven and 30 days. In light of the legitimate difficulties that TCNs may face in complying with the timeline for voluntary departure in the midst of a global health emergency, the Commission has recommended that states comply with their Article 7(2) obligation to extend, where necessary, the period for voluntary departure 'by an appropriate period, taking into account the specific circumstances of the individual case'.[104] Such an extension will save TCNs and Member States from

---

[99] European Parliamentary Research Service, *Data on Returns of Irregular Migrants*, European Parliament, Brussels 2019; F. Lutz, 'Non-removable returnees under Union law: status quo and possible developments', (2018) 20(1), *European Journal of Migration and Law*, pp. 28–52.

[100] European Commission, C(2020) 2516 final, *supra* note 84, pp. 2 and 17–18.

[101] Return Directive, *supra* note 14, Recital 10 of the Preamble.

[102] European Commission, C(2020) 2516 final, *supra* note 84, p. 18.

[103] Ibid., p. 19.

[104] Ibid., p. 20.

the consequences of failure to meet the deadline for voluntary departure, namely, the Article 8 obligation on states to enforce the return decision and the automatic imposition, as per Article 11, of an entry ban.

The Commission's focus on voluntary returns diverges with the position adopted by civil society. ECRE, for example, has called for an official moratorium on returns which would, it argues, reflect the principles of effectiveness and fundamental rights underpinning EU return policy, and demonstrate solidarity with third countries.[105] The Commission's position is, however, more in line with the recommendations of the key custodians of migrants' rights in the international system for human rights protection. The UN Committee on Migrant Workers,[106] the dedicated treaty body for the UN Migrant Workers Convention, and the UN Special Rapporteur on the human rights of migrants have called on states to 'consider' the temporary suspension of enforced returns during the pandemic and to ensure that returns are carried out on a voluntary basis.[107] The practice on the ground in European states reflects the EU level desire for return to continue where possible. By the end of 2020, at least seven EU states had carried out either forced or voluntary removals.[108]

4.4. ACCESS TO VACCINES FOR UNDOCUMENTED MIGRANTS IN EUROPE

The need for all migrants, regardless of status, to be included in states' vaccine rollout programmes is self-evident: in the case of a communicable disease like COVID-19, the failure to vaccinate a discrete portion of a state's population will mean that the rest of society continues to remain at risk. The widely recited maxim that no one is safe until everyone is safe must be the guiding

105 ECRE, 'Return as "Non-essential Travel" in the Time of Pandemic: ECRE's Position on Return and Detention during Covid-19', 2020, p. 2, available at https://www.ecre.org/wp-content/uploads/2020/06/PN_26.pdf, last accessed 28.06.2021.

106 See OHCHR, Committee on Migrant Workers, available at https://www.ohchr.org/EN/HRBodies/CMW/Pages/CMWIndex.aspx, last accessed 28.06.2021.

107 See OHCHR, Special Rapporteur on the human rights of migrants, available at https://www.ohchr.org/EN/Issues/Migration/SRMigrants/Pages/SRMigrantsIndex.aspx, last accessed 28.06.2021; UN (2020), 'Joint Guidance Note on the Impacts of the COVID-19 Pandemic on the Human Rights of Migrants', *supra* note 95, p. 3.

108 ECRE, 'Information Sheet: Covid-19 Measures and Updates Related to Asylum and Migration across Europe', 07.12.2020, available at https://www.ecre.org/wp-content/uploads/2020/12/ECRE-COVID-information-sheet-Dec-2020.pdf, last accessed 28.06.2021; D. Pelz, 'Germany presses on with deportations despite COVID pandemic', *Deutsche Welle*, 21.03.2021, available at https://www.dw.com/en/germany-presses-on-with-deportations-despite-covid-pandemic/a-57011088, last accessed 28.06.2021.

principle underpinning any vaccination programme.[109] This principle entails the assumption that particular efforts need to be made in order to ensure that undocumented migrants have access to vaccination programmes not only as a matter of policy, but also as a matter of practice. A number of factors, including their (lack of) immigration status, mean that irregular migrants are likely be disproportionately susceptible to, and impacted by, COVID-19: often residing in over-crowded, confined spaces and informally employed in low-skilled jobs, irregular migrants are especially vulnerable to being forced to live and work in situations and conditions conducive to the spread of the virus.[110] In some countries, irregular migrants who lose their jobs are excluded from unemployment benefit and other financial support schemes introduced to protect individuals left without work as a result of the pandemic.[111] Often already experiencing substandard living and working conditions, irregular migrants are likely to have experienced an intensification of exclusion and deprivation as a result of the global health emergency and related lockdown measures.

I discuss the centrality of irregular TCNs' migration status to their treatment in and by the EU, and its potential impact on vaccine uptake, in section 5, along with a proposal to effectively address that status and the manifold ills to which it gives rise. In the specific context of vaccination programmes, however, it is important to note the broad consensus across regional and international organisations about the need not only to include irregular migrants in vaccine deployment campaigns,[112] but for migrants to be one of the target groups in such

---

109 E.g., Gavi the Vaccine Alliance, 'Why is no one safe until everyone is safe during a pandemic?', 14.09.2020, available at https://www.gavi.org/vaccineswork/why-no-one-safe-until-everyone-safe-during-pandemic, last accessed 28.06.2021; UN DESA, 'No one is safe, until everyone is', 02.08.2020, available at https://www.un.org/development/desa/en/news/sustainable/no-one-is-safe-until-everyone-is.html, last accessed 28.06.2021.

110 Labour Behind the Label, *Boohoo & COVID-19*, Labour Behind the Label, Bristol 2020; EMN/OECD, *EU and OECD Member States responses to managing residence permits and migrant unemployment during the COVID-19 pandemic*, European Migration Network, Brussels 2020, p. 2. This latter report related to lawfully present TCNs, but its findings apply *a fortiori* in the context of irregular TCNs.

111 FLEX, *No Worker Left Behind: Protecting Vulnerable Workers from Exploitation during and after the Coronavirus (Covid-19) Pandemic*, Focus on Labour Exploitation, London 2020, pp. 3–4.

112 Council of Europe Committee on Bioethics, 'Covid-19 and Vaccines: Ensuring Equitable Access to Vaccination During the Current and Future Pandemics', 22.01.2021, available at https://www.coe.int/en/web/bioethics/-/covid-19-and-vaccines-equitable-access-to-vaccination-must-be-ensured, last accessed 28.06.2021; WHO, 'A virus that respects no borders: protecting refugees and migrants during COVID-19', 25.03.2021, available at https://www.who.int/news-room/feature-stories/detail/a-virus-that-respects-no-borders-protecting-refugees-and-migrants-during-covid-19, last accessed 28.06.2021; J. Weekers, 'To be effective, COVID-19 vaccination plans must include migrants', IOM, 18.12.2020, available at https://www.gavi.org/vaccineswork/be-effective-covid-19-vaccination-plans-must-include-migrants, last accessed 28.06.2021.

campaigns.[113] Many irregular migrants will fall within some of the potential target groups for the vaccine identified by the European Commission in 2020 such as communities and workers unable to physically distance and vulnerable socioeconomic groups and other groups at higher risk.[114] The EU institutions so far, however, appear to have failed to explicitly articulate the urgency of ensuring irregular migrants are included in vaccination programmes.[115]

The picture on the ground in Europe is mixed.[116] Poland, for example, appears to limit vaccinations to lawfully present migrants.[117] Even where countries like France, Finland, Portugal and Spain explicitly include irregular migrants in their vaccination strategies, promising availability of the vaccine to them, there are serious concerns about the ability of irregular TCNs to access the vaccine as a matter of practice. Concerns amongst migrants about fees, and difficulties faced by public authorities in reaching undocumented migrant populations, are some of the obstacles to effective inclusion of irregular migrants in vaccination programmes. Irregular migrants' very lack of a right to be lawfully present in a state is arguably the root cause of most obstacles to their participation in the vaccine rollout across Europe.[118] I will return to this issue in section 5 where I sketch a solution for addressing irregular migration status that eradicates this root cause and, amongst other beneficent effects, widens the possibilities for uptake of the vaccine by such migrants.

---

113 European Centre for Disease Prevention and Control, 'Key aspects regarding the introduction and prioritisation of COVID-19 vaccination in the EU/EEA and the UK', 26.10.2020, available at https://www.ecdc.europa.eu/sites/default/files/documents/Key-aspects-regarding-introduction-and-prioritisation-of-COVID-19-vaccination.pdf, last accessed 28.06.2021.

114 European Commission, Communication from the Commission to the European Parliament and the Council, Preparedness for COVID-19 vaccination strategies and vaccine deployment, COM(2020) 680 final 15.10.2020, p. 12.

115 A. Vallianatou, E. Venturi and S. Zinser, 'Brussels silent on vaccinating undocumented migrants', *EU Observer*, 15.03.2021, available at https://euobserver.com/opinion/151219, last accessed 28.06.2021.

116 The information in this paragraph is drawn from PICUM, 'The COVID-19 Vaccines and Undocumented Migrants: What Are European Countries Doing?', 11.02.2021, available at https://picum.org/covid-19-vaccines-undocumented-migrants-europe/, last accessed 28.06.2021. These findings are largely consistent with the information reported in the slightly more recent bulletin of the EU Fundamental Rights Agency. See FRA, 'Coronavirus Pandemic in the EU – Fundamental Rights Implications: Vaccine Rollout and Equality of Access in the EU', 16.06.2021, available at https://s3.eu-central-1.amazonaws.com/euobs-media/9e963f6a0c43b7d92add444b4c30565f.pdf, last accessed 28.06.2021.

117 The Polish government's FAQ on vaccines provides: 'Cudzoziemcy z prawem pobytu podlegają szczepieniom na takich samych zasadach jak obywatele RP.' See Szczepienie przeciwko COVID-19: Pytania i odpowiedzi, available at https://www.gov.pl/web/szczepimysie/pytania-i-odpowiedzi, last accessed 28.06.2021.

118 Fear of arrest/deportation is created by some states' requirement for health workers to inform immigration authorities of irregular migrants' attempts to access health services. See IOM, *Migrant Inclusion in Covid-19 Vaccination Campaigns*, IOM, Geneva 2021.

5. SCOPE FOR CHANGING TACK? CHARTING A COURSE TOWARDS A MORE PROTECTIVE EUROPEAN SPACE FOR IRREGULAR MIGRANTS' RIGHTS

5.1. A ROUTE TO BETTER PROTECTION OF IRREGULAR MIGRANTS' RIGHTS IN EUROPE

Despite the relatively sombre tone of much of the foregoing from the perspective of migrants' rights, it is important to emphasise that the EU legal order contains much raw material out of which a more rights-respecting migration policy may be fashioned.[119] This is evident not just in EU policy acknowledgments of the need for migration control measures to comply with human rights standards,[120] but also in the far-reaching rulings delivered by the CJEU and the ECtHR that have imposed obligations on states vis-à-vis migrants within their jurisdiction, notwithstanding those migrants' unlawful presence. In the context of expulsion, for example, the ECtHR in recent years has made it easier for seriously ill migrants to resist deportation by reference to Article 3 ECHR,[121] while the CJEU has delivered a series of rulings on the Return Directive that significantly reined in the more exuberant Member States whose efforts to detain and expel irregular migrants ran roughshod over their rights.[122]

Despite, however, the increasing volume of case law confirming the application of human rights to irregular migrants in the EU, and the scope of those rights, such migrants continue to be amongst the most vulnerable people in Europe, and therefore most urgently in need of protection. Their very presence puts them at constant risk of deportation. This has many deleterious consequences. Ultimately, it means that irregular migrants will often avoid enforcing their rights because they fear being reported to immigration authorities and expelled from

---

119 See e.g., A. Desmond, 'The Development of a Common EU Migration Policy and the Rights of Irregular Migrants: A Progress Narrative?' (2016) 16(2), *Human Rights Law Review*, pp. 247–272.

120 E.g., European Commission, Communication from the Commission on policy priorities in the fight against illegal immigration of third-country nationals, COM(2006) 402 final 19.07.2006, para. 8, p. 3; European Commission, Communication from the Commission to the European Parliament, the Council, the European Economic and Social Committee and the Committee of the Regions: A Common Immigration Policy for Europe, COM(2008) 359 final 17.06.2008, pp. 3–4; European Commission, Report from the Commission to the European Parliament and the Council: First Annual Report on Immigration and Asylum, COM(2010) 214 final 06.05.2010, p. 5.

121 ECtHR, *Paposhvili v Belgium*, no 41738/10 [GC] 13.12.2016.

122 See, e.g., A. Desmond, 'The Return Directive: Clarifying the Scope and Substance of the Rights of Migrants facing Expulsion from the EU', in R. King and K. Kuschminder (eds.), *Handbook of Return Migration*, Edward Elgar, Cheltenham 2021; V. Mitsilegas, *The Criminalisation of Migration in Europe: Challenges for Human Rights and the Rule of Law*, Springer, London 2015.

the host state. Of particular relevance in light of the global health emergency, they may defer accessing health care services until an illness becomes acute, creating a health risk not just for themselves, but for the wider community. Furthermore, in spite of any formal entitlements, they may avoid participating in national vaccination programmes.

The presence of irregular migrants in a state therefore creates, *inter alia*, a situation where the health of the community at large is put at risk. The outbreak of the COVID-19 pandemic highlighted how states' failure to adequately respond to the presence of irregular migrants works to the detriment of both migrants themselves as well as the host state, as illustrated by reports from countries such as the UK and Italy.[123] To address this unsatisfactory situation, I make the case in section 5.2 for the regularisation of irregular migrants in the EU. Broadly, regularisation is a process whereby non-citizens who are illegally present in a host state are granted a legal status.[124] Calls for regularisation as a response to the pandemic have already been made by international human rights bodies.[125] Despite official opposition from Member States and EU institutions,[126] regularisation has been a frequently employed tool in the migration realm. In light of the ongoing pandemic, I argue that it should be put on an EU legislative footing.

5.2. THE CASE FOR REGULARISATION OF IRREGULAR MIGRANTS IN A TIME OF PANDEMIC

Sections 2–4 have shown how the default EU approach to irregular migrants consists largely in seeking to make the EU return policy more effective.

---

123 E.g., M. Bulman, 'Undocumented migrants dying of coronavirus because they're too afraid to seek help, MPs and charities warn', *The Independent*, 18.04.2020, available at https://www.independent.co.uk/news/uk/home-news/coronavirus-undocumented-migrants-deaths-cases-nhs-matt-hancock-a9470581.html#comments, last accessed 28.06.2021; M. Bulman, 'The pro-migrant support you're seeing from the public is under threat – and this is what could turn things sour', *The Independent*, 06.06.2020, available at https://www.independent.co.uk/voices/coronavirus-immigration-hostile-environment-windrush-mujinga-alien-nation-a9550386.html, last accessed 28.06.2021; L. Tondo and M. Bellingreri, 'Brutal deaths of exploited migrants shine a spotlight on Italy's farms', *The Guardian*, 13.07.2020, available at https://www.theguardian.com/global-development/2020/jul/13/brutal-deaths-of-exploited-migrants-shine-a-spotlight-on-italys-farms, last accessed 28.06.2021.

124 M. Baldwin-Edwards and A. Kraler (eds.), *REGINE: Regularisations in Europe*, European Commission/Amsterdam University Press, Amsterdam 2009, p. 9.

125 E.g., UN (2020), 'Joint Guidance Note on the Impacts of the COVID-19 Pandemic on the Human Rights of Migrants', *supra* note 95.

126 M. Baldwin-Edwards and A. Kraler (2009), *REGINE*, *supra* note 124, p. 286; European Commission, Communication from the Commission to the Council, the European Parliament, the European Economic and Social Committee and the Committee of the Regions – Study on the links between legal and illegal migration, COM(2004) 412 final 4.06.2004, pp. 10 and 17; C. Costello, *The Human Rights of Migrants and Refugees in European Law*, OUP, Oxford 2016.

An alternative response to irregular migration is to allow unlawfully present migrants to remain lawfully. The case for this course of action has been strengthened by the pandemic.[127] Migrant workers have been disproportionately impacted by the fallout from the global health emergency.[128] Irregular migrants, often informally employed in low-skilled jobs, are especially vulnerable to being forced to work in situations and conditions conducive to the spread of the virus.[129] In some countries, irregular migrants are excluded from unemployment benefit and other financial support schemes introduced to protect individuals left without work as a result of the pandemic.[130] Even though many EU Member States allowed unlawfully staying migrants to access all emergency health care services on an equal footing with citizens,[131] fear of deportation will have prevented many such migrants from doing so. There have been reports of irregular migrants dying from COVID-19 because they were too afraid to access the necessary health care.[132] In the case of a transmissible infectious disease like COVID-19, reluctance to access health care poses a risk not just to the health of individual irregular migrants, but also to the wider community.[133]

It is therefore perhaps not surprising that the current crisis has led a number of EU countries such as Italy and Portugal,[134] and states further

---

127 A. Desmond, *Out of Crisis Comes Opportunity: Reconsidering Regularisation of Irregular Migrants in the EU in light of COVID-19*, UNESCO Chair on International Migration Policy Brief Series, 2020.

128 J. Gelatt, *Immigrant workers: Vital to the U.S. COVID-19 response, disproportionately vulnerable*, MPI, Washington DC 2020; L. Guadagno, *Migrants and the COVID-19 pandemic: An initial analysis*, IOM, Geneva 2020; M. Morris, 'Migrant workers and coronavirus: risks and responses', *Institute for Public Policy Research*, 2020, available at https://www.ippr.org/blog/migrant-workers-and-coronavirus, last accessed 28.06.2021.

129 Labour Behind the Label (2020), *Boohoo & COVID-19, supra* note 110; EMN/OECD (2020), *Responses to managing residence permits and migrant unemployment during the COVID-19 pandemic, supra* note 110, p. 2; M. Mallet-Garcia and N. Delvino, 'Migrants with irregular status during the COVID-19 pandemic: Lessons for local authorities in Europe', City Initiative on Migrants with Irregular Status in Europe (C-MISE) Working Paper, 2020, available at https://www.compas.ox.ac.uk/wp-content/uploads/CMISE-Impact-of-COVID-on-access-to-services-for-irregular-migrants.pdf, last accessed 28.06.2021.

130 FLEX (2020), *No Worker Left Behind: supra* note 111, pp. 3–4.

131 EMN/OECD (2020), *Responses to managing residence permits and migrant unemployment during the COVID-19 pandemic, supra* note 110, p. 8.

132 M. Bulman, 'Undocumented migrants dying of coronavirus because they're too afraid to seek help, MPs and charities warn', *The Independent*, 18.04.2020, available at https://www.independent.co.uk/news/uk/home-news/coronavirus-undocumented-migrants-deaths-cases-nhs-matt-hancock-a9470581.html#comments, last accessed 28.06.2021.

133 D. Vincent, 'Coronavirus: Undocumented workers an "invisible public health risk"', *BBC*, 24.06.2020, available at https://www.bbc.co.uk/news/uk-england-london-52919418, last accessed 28.06.2021.

134 P. Chesnet, 'Régularisation de sans-papiers: le Portugal et l'Italie font les premiers pas …', *La Nouvelle Vie ouvrière (NVO)*, 25.05.2020, available at https://nvo.fr/regularisation-de-sans-papiers-le-portugal-et-litalie-font-les-premiers-pas/, last accessed 28.06.2021.

afield,[135] to create pathways out of irregularity for migrants. These schemes, however, miss the opportunity to meaningfully address the presence of irregular migrants. They repeat the mistakes that have undermined past efforts at regularisation by, for example, including eligibility criteria which preclude applications from a large number of irregular migrants.[136] For a regularisation scheme to be effective it needs, firstly, to be open to as large a number of the irregular migrant population as would be politically and practically feasible and, secondly, to provide regularised migrants with a migration status that even if initially temporary is easily renewable and reckonable towards long-term resident status.[137]

Given the large number and wide range of regularisation schemes that have been used by EU Member States,[138] and their evident failure to appreciably reduce Europe's irregular migrant population, it is worth considering an EU wide approach to regularisation. The European Commission has displayed an appetite for discussion of the need for a common legal framework on regularisation at EU level and has called for the consideration of establishing common standards for taking charge of non-deportable irregular migrants.[139] The legal basis for a common EU framework for regularisation is to be found in Article 79(2) of the Treaty on the Functioning of the EU which requires, as part of the development of a common migration policy, the adoption of measures concerning the entry and residence of TCNs, irregular migration

---

135 World Bank, 'Potential Responses to the COVID-19 Outbreak in Support of Migrant Workers', 2020, pp. 22 and 35, available at http://documents1.worldbank.org/curated/en/428451587390154689/pdf/Potential-Responses-to-the-COVID-19-Outbreak-in-Support-of-Migrant-Workers-June-19-2020.pdf, last accessed 28.06.2021.

136 L. Palumbo, 'The Italian Plan for Regularisation: Real progress for migrants' rights?', *EUI Migration Policy Centre Blog*, 08.06.2020, available at https://blogs.eui.eu/migrationpolicycentre/italian-plan-regularisation-real-progress-migrants-rights/#:~:text=To%20apply%2C%20migrants%20must%20have,residence%20permit%20for%20work%20reasons, last accessed 28.06.2021; L. Tondo and M. Bellingreri, 'Brutal deaths of exploited migrants shine a spotlight on Italy's farms', *The Guardian*, 13.07.2020, available at https://www.theguardian.com/global-development/2020/jul/13/brutal-deaths-of-exploited-migrants-shine-a-spotlight-on-italys-farms, last accessed 28.06.2021.

137 A broad outline of the elements necessary for an effective regularisation scheme is provided in, e.g., A. Desmond (2020), *Out of Crisis Comes Opportunity*, *supra* note 127; and A. Desmond, 'The Possibility for Regularisation in the UK in Light of the New Plan for Immigration', *RLI Blog on Refugee Law and Forced Migration*, 28.05.2021, available at https://rli.blogs.sas.ac.uk/2021/05/28/the-possibility-for-regularisation-in-the-uk-in-light-of-the-new-plan-for-immigration/, last accessed 28.06.2021.

138 It is estimated that between 1996 and 2007 over six million migrants may have been involved in transitions from irregularity to a legal status in the EU alone. See M. Baldwin-Edwards and A. Kraler (2009), *REGINE*, *supra* note 124, pp. 35–36.

139 European Commission, COM(2006) 402 final, *supra* note 120, para. 35; European Commission, Communication from the Commission to the European Parliament and the Council: An area of freedom, security and justice serving the citizen, COM(2009) 262 final 10.06.2009, para. 5.1.4, pp. 26–27.

and unauthorised residence. EU legislation on regularisation would have to satisfy the requirements of subsidiarity and proportionality that apply to any EU legislative initiative.[140] A common EU approach to regularisation would bring a degree of clarity, certainty and consistency compatible with the rule of law, one of the fundamental values of the EU, as enshrined in Article 2 the Treaty on European Union.

Furthermore, the European Commission has long noted the need for legislation concerning irregular migration to comply with the human rights obligations set out in the European Convention on Human Rights and the Charter of Fundamental Rights of the EU.[141] This creates space for discussion of regularisation of unlawfully resident migrants on the basis of strong attachments to their host state, including family ties.[142] Indeed, the ECtHR has found in a number of cases that states' expulsion of long-term resident undocumented migrants would violate their Article 8 ECHR right to respect for private life and family life.[143] The Return Directive is also, despite its title and general thrust, relevant to any argument for regularisation in the EU. Article 6(4) provides that, instead of expulsion, states may at any time grant an irregular TCN a right to remain for compassionate, humanitarian or other reasons. Clear guidance is offered as to what may ground a right to remain, with Article 5 providing that implementation of the directive entails due account being taken of, *inter alia*, family life, the health of the TCN in question and the best interests of the child. Similarly, the Preamble to the directive identifies the primary considerations of states when implementing the directive as being the child's best interests, in line with the UN Convention on the Rights of the Child, and the respect for family life, in line with the ECHR. Irregular migrants who are, to all practical intents and purposes, non-removable, present a particularly compelling argument for regularisation.[144]

Given the EU's preference for dealing with irregular migration through tightening its borders and seeking the return of undocumented TCNs, as well as the difficulty of achieving consensus on contentious issues in an organisation of 27 sovereign states and multiple institutional actors, the call for an EU wide approach to regularisation may seem unrealistic. We are now, however, in a

---

140 K.F. Hinterberger, 'An EU Regularization Directive. An effective solution to the enforcement deficit in returning irregularly staying migrants', (2019) 26(6), *Maastricht Journal of European and Comparative Law*, pp. 736–769.

141 See *supra* note 120.

142 A. Desmond, 'Regularization in the European Union and the United States: The Frequent Use of an Exceptional Measure', in D. Acosta and A. Wiesbrock (eds.), *Global Migration: Old Assumptions, New Dynamics*, Praeger, Santa Barbara 2015, pp. 69–99.

143 E.g., ECtHR, *Rodrigues da Silva and Hoogkamer v the Netherlands*, no 50435/99, 31.01.2006; ECtHR, *Jeunesse v the Netherlands*, no 12738/10 [GC] 03.10.2014.

144 G. Eckert, 'Caught in limbo: the precarious (legal) situation of non-removable migrants stranded in Europe', (2021) 35(3), *Journal of Immigration, Asylum and Nationality Law*, pp. 252–277.

moment where significant change is possible, where we can 'step back from the fray and rethink basic premises'.[145] The global health emergency has created space for the consideration and advancement of ideas that before now would have had little public or political purchase. There is anecdotal evidence that the pandemic has fostered a more favourable public opinion of migrants.[146] Low-skilled workers have become key frontline workers and migration status has become a matter of life or death. The time is therefore ripe for regularisation to be fashioned as a central feature of an overall EU strategy for addressing the phenomenon of irregular migration.

5.3. PROTECTIVE MEASURES SHORT OF REGULARISATION: THE CASE FOR FIREWALLS

In the absence of regularisation, the use of 'firewalls' is one of the most effective measures available to states to encourage irregular migrants to access health care when ill and to participate in vaccination programmes. Use of a firewall in the context of irregular migration entails a guarantee that information concerning the immigration status of persons accessing public or social services will not be shared with those responsible for immigration law enforcement.[147] The aim here, of course, is to avoid situations where irregular migrants are in practice prevented from accessing rights and services to which they are formally entitled through fear that contact with public authorities or service providers may ultimately lead to their expulsion. Meaningful implementation of firewalls between public services and immigration enforcement would, *inter alia*, allow irregular migrants to access health care without fear of detention and deportation. It is noteworthy, if unsurprising, that the International Organization for Migration (IOM) has recently found in the context of vaccination campaigns that fear of arrest and deportation is created by some states' requirement for health workers to inform immigration authorities of irregular migrants' attempts to access health services.[148]

---

145 H. Motomura (2020), 'The New Migration Law', *supra* note 3, p. 547. See also the call to re-think the politics of mobility in the context of the pandemic as part of the process of creating a more just and sustainable world in C. Heller, 'De-confine Borders', *supra* note 6.

146 M. Bulman, 'The pro-migrant support you're seeing from the public is under threat – and this is what could turn things sour', *The Independent*, 06.06.2020, available at https://www.independent.co.uk/voices/coronavirus-immigration-hostile-environment-windrush-mujinga-alien-nation-a9550386.html, last accessed 28.06.2021; R. Carter, 'The corona crisis has made us value migrants: here's how to build on that', *Open Democracy*, 25.04.2020, available at https://www.opendemocracy.net/en/opendemocracyuk/the-corona-crisis-has-made-us-value-migrants-heres-how-to-build-on-that/, last accessed 28.06.2021.

147 See, e.g., J. Carens, *The Ethics of Immigration*, OUP, Oxford 2013, pp. 132–135; PICUM, *Data Protection and the Firewall: Advancing Safe Reporting for People in an Irregular Situation*, PICUM, Brussels 2020.

148 IOM (2021), *Migrant Inclusion in Covid-19 Vaccination Campaigns, supra* note 118.

Recent years have seen increasing support for and promotion of firewalls amongst UN human rights treaty bodies and special rapporteurs,[149] as well as other regional and international actors concerned with human rights and labour standards.[150] The existence of a global health emergency provides a compelling motivation to translate this support into practice. While regularisation may encounter strong opposition from certain political quarters, the use of firewalls does not entail a change of migration status and may therefore be less likely to generate the same level of impassioned, high profile hostility from anti-immigrant constituencies. *Faute de mieux*, firewalls should be energetically pursued as a means of facilitating generally the enjoyment of rights by irregular migrants and, specifically, as a way of ensuring as effective as possible a response to the continuing pandemic.

6. CONCLUSION

This contribution has illustrated a large degree of consistency in the approach of the EU and its Member States to irregular migration since the Treaty of Amsterdam conferred law-making powers on the EU in the field of migration and asylum in 1999. The rights-restrictive and control-expansive thrust of much EU law and policy concerning irregular migration has been bolstered by rulings from the CJEU and ECtHR that endorse states' sovereign powers of exclusion of irregular migrants both within and without EU borders. This trend has become even more pronounced following the 2015 migration and refugee 'crisis'. Given the recently unveiled New Pact on Migration and Asylum, and the ongoing global pandemic, it is a trend that looks unlikely to be susceptible to any sudden shift in emphasis, much less a reversal of course.

At the same time, however, I have shown that there is plentiful raw material out of which a more rights-respecting common EU migration and asylum system may be fashioned. The evidence for this lies not only in EU policy statements stretching back over the past two decades, but also in important rulings delivered by the region's two supranational courts that have set limits to states' freedom to control migration and have had far-reaching consequences for the protection of the rights of irregular migrants in Europe. I have suggested

149 E.g., CMW, *General Comment 2 on the rights of migrant workers in an irregular situation and members of their families*, UN Doc CMW/C/CG/2, 28.08.2013, paras. 63, 74 and 77; UN Special Rapporteur on adequate housing as a component of the right to an adequate standard of living and on the right to non-discrimination in this context, *Visit to France*, UN Doc A/HRC/43/43/Add.2, 03.03.2020, paras. 70 and 93(f).

150 E.g., ECRI, General Policy Recommendation 16 on Safeguarding Irregularly Present Migrants from Discrimination, ECRI, Strasbourg 2016, pp. 7, 13, 15 and 19; ILO, *Promoting Fair Migration*, ILO, Geneva 2016, paras. 481–482.

that regularisation is the most effective way of ensuring that migrants are in a position to enjoy in practice the rights to which they are entitled on paper. The case for regularisation has been brought into sharp relief by the global health emergency where we are all at risk until no one is at risk. The EU therefore should do more to develop common rules around regularisation for the benefit of everyone in Europe, citizens and non-citizens alike.

IMPLEMENTING THE UN GLOBAL COMPACTS FOR REFUGEES AND MIGRANTS IN TIMES OF PANDEMIC

A View from the EUMS

Elspeth Guild, Kathryn Allinson and Nicolette Busuttil*

* This contribution is part of 'PROTECT. The Right to International Protection: A Pendulum between Globalization and Nativization?', available at www.protect-project.eu, last accessed 12.07.2021; a research and innovation project which is funded by the European Union's Horizon 2020 Framework Programme and coordinated by the University of Bergen (Grant Agreement No 870761). The authors would like to thank Dr Madeline Garlick, UNHCR, Mr Alexander Sorel, EASO, and Ms Catherine Woollard, ECRE, for their presentations at the PROTECT Expert Forum on 13-14 November 2020 which provided us with much inspiration for this contribution. All errors or omissions are our exclusive responsibility.

Elspeth Guild, Kathryn Allinson and Nicolette Busuttil

ABSTRACT

This contribution explores the impact of the COVID-19 pandemic on refugees' and migrants' access to human rights protection in the European Union (EU, the Union), in light of its Member States' commitments in the UN Global Compacts on Refugees and Migrants (Compacts). It holds that those in precarious and vulnerable positions vis-à-vis the state were among the first to experience a loss of access to rights in the face of the pandemic. Through analysis of the commitments made in the Global Compacts and their relationship to existing legal frameworks, as expressed in the Common European Asylum System (CEAS) and European Human Rights treaties, we assess implementation and policy in response to COVID-19. We contend that both the CEAS and the Compacts balance the human rights protections of refugees and migrants against the observance of state sovereign control over borders. A focus on three areas of contention in EU law and policy – access to migration procedures, use of immigration detention and access to health care – demonstrates that there was a fragmented response to the pandemic based upon differing accounts of this balance. The contribution concludes that, in line with the Global Compacts' call for respect for the human rights of refugees and migrants, states are obliged by their Global Compact commitments to extend basic health care and social service provisions to all migrants and refugees as well as to release those detained under immigration powers. This would go a long way to preserve *their* basic rights in the face of COVID-19 and ensure EU policy is in line with the commitments made within the Global Compacts.

1. INTRODUCTION

There has been much discussion of rights restrictions in response to the COVID-19 pandemic – movement, education, health care – and the list goes on. This contribution highlights the effect of COVID-19 measures on those whose access to rights is precarious. During the pandemic, some European Union Member States (EUMSs) differentiated among groups of persons based on their immigration status to limit their obligations towards certain 'categories' of individuals found on their territory. This rights limitation is in stark contrast to the commitments EUMSs (and the European Union (EU, the Union)) made by voting for two Compacts that are founded on existing refugee and human rights obligations.[1] We propose that there is a balance in the two Global Compacts (Compacts) and the Common European Asylum System (CEAS) between human rights protections for refugees and migrants and the observance of state

[1] Global Compact on Refugees, UN Doc A/73/12 (Part II), 02.08.2018 (hereinafter GCR) paras. 5, 9, 56, and 85; Global Compact for Safe, Orderly and Regular Migration, UN Doc A/RES/73/195, 19.12.2018 (hereinafter MC) paras. 2, 11, 12, and 15(f) MC.

sovereign control over borders. Yet, the discriminatory practices of some EUMSs in response to COVID-19 undermines this balance.

The Compacts were affirmed by the United Nations General Assembly (UNGA) in December 2018 following two years of inter-governmental negotiations.[2] Our study considers the relationship between *both* the Global Compact on Refugees (GCR) and the Marrakesh Compact (MC) with the CEAS for two reasons. First, the CEAS provides the rules for recognition of refugees, the determination of applications for international protection and the treatment of these persons while their applications are under consideration.[3] There is an artificiality in dividing people into refugees and migrants when all refugees are also migrants, and migrants are often future asylum-seekers and unrecognised refugees.[4] Second, the Compacts converge and provide for complementary treatment of all third-country nationals (TCNs). The Refugee Convention sets out the rights of refugees as reaffirmed in the GCR, including refugees who not yet been recognised.[5] Comparably, migrants have no widely

---

2 UNGA, 'The New York Declaration for Refugees and Migrants', UN Doc A/RES/71/1, 19.09.2016 (hereinafter NY Declaration).

3 The CEAS comprises Directive 2013/32/EU of the European Parliament and of the Council of 26 June 2013 on common procedures for granting and withdrawing international protection (recast), OJ L 180, 29.06.2013 (hereinafter Asylum Procedures Directive or APD); Directive 2013/33/EU of the European Parliament and of the Council of 26 June 2013 laying down standards for the reception of applicants for international protection (recast) L 180/96 (hereinafter the Reception Conditions Directive or RCD) establishes the applicable entitlements in terms of access to social rights for all persons who have a pending application for international protection (including refugees); Regulation (EU) No 604/2013 of the European Parliament and of the Council of 26 June 2013 establishing the criteria and mechanisms for determining the Member State responsible for examining an application for international protection lodged in one of the Member States by a third-country national or a stateless person (recast), OJ L 180, 29.06.2013 (hereinafter Dublin III Regulation); and Directive 2011/95/EU of the European Parliament and of the Council of 13 December 2011 on standards for the qualification of third-country nationals or stateless persons as beneficiaries of international protection, for a uniform status for refugees or for persons eligible for subsidiary protection, and for the content of the protection granted (recast), OJ L337 (hereinafter Qualification Directive or QD). It includes Regulation 603/2013 (the Eurodac Regulation) which is not considered further.

4 Under the UN Convention Relating to the Status of Refugees, a person is a refugee from the time they fulfil the elements of the refugee definition contained therein, with this recognised by a state when it grants asylum to the refugee. This position is affirmed under EU law. CJEU, *A & S*, Case C-550/16, 12.04.2018, ECLI:EU:C:2018:248, para. 54; International Organisation for Migration (hereinafter IOM), *Glossary on Migration*, IOM, Geneva 2019, pp. 132-133, defines a migrant as 'a person who moves away from his or her place of usual residence, whether within a country or across an international border, temporarily or permanently, and for a variety of reasons'. Since a refugee has to be 'outside his or her country of origin' to meet the refugee definition under Article 1A(2) Refugee Convention, they must be a migrant as well as a refugee.

5 See GCR, *supra* note 1, para. 5 which presents the instrument as 'grounded in the international refugee protection regime, centred on the cardinal principle of *non-refoulement*, and at the core of which is the 1951 Convention and its 1967 Protocol'; MC, *supra* note 1, para. 4

ratified equivalent convention,[6] so their rights arise from general international human rights conventions where such rights apply to everyone and, on this basis, are included in the MC.[7] However, the Achilles heel of refugee status is national procedures which may, or may not, result in recognition of refugee status, the allocation of a subsidiary status, or, in the EU context, recognition as a person entitled to international protection.[8] Consequently, many people who are classified under national law as 'not refugees' but receive some protection, or are treated as irregular migrants, might well, should their claim be considered in another country, be recognised as refugees.[9] To fully explore the alignment of the CEAS with the commitments to refugees in the Compacts, we must consider refugees, asylum seekers and migrants as three administrative categories that substantially overlap.

Our research analyses the implementation of the Compacts in EUMSs throughout the COVID-19 pandemic. During drafting there was extensive debate concerning the legal status of a 'Compact' but the final versions confirm that they are non-legally binding at the international level.[10] However, they are still internationally negotiated agreements, signed and committed to by states that are founded on existing international human rights law.[11] Through the adoption of the Compacts, states have acknowledged that existing international human rights obligations apply to migrants as well as refugees

---

outlines how '[o]nly refugees are entitled to the specific international protection defined by international refugee law.'

6 The UN Migrant Workers Convention still has only 56 parties and 12 additional signatories at the time of writing. See further at https://indicators.ohchr.org/.

7 See para. 15(f) MC, *supra* note 1, see also E. Guild and T. Basaran (eds.), 'Analysis on the Final Draft for the UN Global Compact on Safe, Orderly and Regular Migration', *RLI Research Series, 2019*, available at https://rli.sas.ac.uk/sites/default/files/files/Global%20Compact%20for%20Migration_RLI%20blog%20series.pdf, last accessed 09.04.2021.

8 Qualification Directive, *supra* note 3, Article 15(b) and (c).

9 See UNHCR, 'Statistical Yearbooks: Eurostat', available at https://ec.europa.eu/eurostat/statistics-explained/index.php?title=File:Table6_-_First_instance_decisions_by_citizenship_and_outcome,_selected_Member_States,_3rd_quarter_2020.png, last accessed 09.04.2021.

10 Para. 7 MC, *supra* note 1; Para. 4 GCR, *supra* note 1; See E. Guild and S. Grant, '*Migration Governance in the UN: What is the Compact and What does it mean?*', (2017) 252, *Queen Mary School of Law Legal Studies Research Paper*; T. Gammeltoft-Hansen, E. Guild, V. Moreno-Lax, M. Panizzon and I. Roele, *What is a Compact? Migrants' Rights and State Responsibilities Regarding the Design of the UN Compact for Safe, Orderly and Regular Migration*, Raoul Wallenberg Institute of Human Rights and Humanitarian Law, Lund 11.10.2017.

11 See para. 15 MC, *supra* note 1: Guiding Principle – Human Rights 'The Global Compact is based on international human rights law and upholds the principles of non-regression and non-discrimination. By implementing the Global Compact, we ensure effective respect, protection and fulfilment of the human rights of all migrants, regardless of their migration status, across all stages of the migration cycle; para. 5 GCR, *supra* note 1: 'the global compact is guided by relevant international human rights instruments.'

and committed to implement the Compacts in line with these.[12] In examining the implementation of the Compacts, we are looking to whether states have upheld the commitment they made when signing them, and in particular, in respect of their existing human rights obligations under international law as applicable to refugees and migrants.

This contribution begins by presenting the analytical framework from which our discussion will build. Section 2 positions the Compacts within the existing human rights framework and the CEAS. It examines the tensions between the legal and political commitments to respect human rights and the rule of law with the preservation of EU borders and asylum procedures. It proposes that both the CEAS and the Compacts are constructed to reconcile these competing obligations. However, the COVID-19 pandemic has cast the implementation of human rights into stark relief in the European context. Sections 3 to 5 analyse this tension through three examples of EUMSs' practice in response to the pandemic: access to asylum procedures, continued use of immigration detention and access to health care. This discussion demonstrates how, despite the commitments in the Compacts, EUMS' delivery of their CEAS obligations is often discriminatory and invariably fragmented.

Our conclusions bring together the analysis to propose that the balancing of sovereign border control and respect of human rights is evident in both the Compacts and the CEAS. In practice, even prior to COVID-19, states frequently limited access to human rights for TCNs and justified this as a permissible exercise of their sovereign right to control who enters their territory. COVID-19 shattered any illusions that these policies were non-discriminatory. Thus, the balancing between sovereignty and human rights, which the Compacts and CEAS purport to do, is too often confounded in practice. This tension has merely been rendered more visible during the COVID-19 pandemic.

2. THE UN COMPACTS, HUMAN RIGHTS AND STATE SOVEREIGNTY

This section compares the extent to which the Compacts' and CEAS' structural frameworks are embedded in human rights protection, with a focus on those elements that maintain the preservation of state sovereign control over borders. This will set the backdrop against which COVID-19 pandemic-related measures came to exacerbate tensions evident in the Compacts and the CEAS between commitments to the human rights of refugees, asylum seekers, and migrants and states' focus on fighting the pandemic through border and asylum/immigration procedures.

---

12 See paras. 40-47 MC, *supra* note 1; paras. 101-106 GCR, *supra* note 1.

2.1. THE COMPACTS' HUMAN RIGHTS FRAMEWORK

The Compacts add value to the existing EU framework on refugees, asylum seekers and migrants. They articulate their rights in considerable detail and populate, in concrete terms, the substantive scope and content of pre-existing obligations.[13] In their role as states-negotiated agreements, they express states' concerns and commitments.[14] They are a manifestation of state sovereignty, and as non-legally binding instruments can facilitate the implementation of pre-existing obligations into (national and) EU legal orders.[15] As will be explored, the gap between EUMS' human rights commitments vis-à-vis refugees and asylum seekers and their implementation emanates from an absence of political will and limited European institutional mandates and capacity to translate binding obligations into the enjoyment of rights in practice.

From the international and European perspectives, the Compacts' commitment to end discrimination,[16] together with the MC-expressed duty to avoid discrimination based on migratory status, fit well with pre-existing international and regional obligations.[17] While the United Nations (UN) Convention on the Elimination of all forms of Racial Discrimination (CERD) sets the international standards as regards the prohibition of discrimination, Articles 1(1) and (2) limit its application as regards the treatment of citizens and non-citizens. Within Europe, the Council of Europe's European Convention on Human Rights (ECHR) allows for discrimination between migrants and

---

13 See para. 2 MC, *supra* note 1; See E. Guild, T. Basaran, and K. Allinson, 'From Zero to Hero? An Analysis of the Human Rights Protections with the Global Compact for Safe, Orderly and Regular Migration (GCM)', (2019) 57, *International Migration*, p. 43; V. Turk, 'The Promise and Potential of the Global Compact on Refugees', (2019) 30, *International Journal of Refugee Law*, p. 575; See also E. Guild and T. Basaran (2019), 'Analysis on the Final Draft for the UN Global Compact on Safe, Orderly and Regular Migration' *supra* note 7.

14 See J. McAdam, 'The Global Compacts on Refugees and Migration: A New Era for International Protection', (2019) 30, *International Journal of Refugee Law*, p. 571.

15 E. Guild and R. Weiland, 'The UN Global Compact for Safe, Orderly and Regular Migration: What does it mean in International Law?', (2020) 10(1), *Global Community: Yearbook of International Law and Jurisprudence*.

16 In para. 9 GCR, *supra* note 1, all states are called on 'to end exploitation and abuse, as well as discrimination of any kind on the basis of race, colour, sex, language, religion, political or other opinion, national or social origin, property, birth, disability, age, or other status ...'; para. 84 GCR calls for programmes and projects to 'be designed in ways that combat all forms of discrimination and promote peaceful coexistence between refugee and host communities'. Para. 15(f) MC, *supra* note 1, noted that it 'is based on [IHRL] and upholds the principles of non-regression and non-discrimination'; Objective 17 seeks to 'Eliminate all forms of discrimination'.

17 Para. 4 MC, *supra* note 1 recalls the universality of human rights means '[r]efugees and migrants are entitled to the same universal human rights and fundamental freedoms', with para. 11 outlining 'an overarching obligation to respect, protect and fulfil the human rights of all migrants, regardless of their migration status'.

citizens, albeit within specified and limited circumstances.[18] EU primary law similarly prohibits discrimination on a number of protected grounds, including race, ethnic or social origin and differential treatment is tightly circumscribed.[19] Discrimination on the basis of (EUMS) nationality is prohibited, even if the differential treatment of TCNs is permitted, unless tainted by one of the protected grounds.[20] The Compacts reiterate these commitments, providing clear guidelines on how refugees and migrants should be treated and place human rights at their core, ensuring that refugees and migrants are entitled to the same human rights protections as everyone else.[21]

2.2. EU LAW'S RECONCILIATION OF BORDER CONTROL WITH RESPECT FOR FUNDAMENTAL RIGHTS: THE EXPRESSION OF STATE SOVEREIGNTY

EU law reflects international law's acceptance that state sovereignty entails the corresponding power and responsibility to determine the entry, stay, and expulsion of non-citizens.[22] A sophisticated legal and policy framework dedicated to migration control distinguishes between EU citizens and TCNs and addresses its various dimensions,[23] including through measures that regulate TCNs' entry,

---

18 Article 14 ECHR outlines the prohibition of discrimination for 'sex, race, colour, language, religion, political or other opinion, national or social origin, association with a national minority, property, birth or other status', however, Article 5(1)(f) permits 'the lawful arrest or detention of a person to prevent his effecting an unauthorised entry into the country or of a person against whom action is being taken with a view to deportation or extradition …'; Article(1) of Protocol 7 outlines the procedural safeguards relating to expulsion of aliens and Article 16 ECHR permits Contracting States placing restrictions on political activity of aliens.

19 EU Charter of Fundamental Rights of the European Union (hereinafter 'the Charter' or CFREU). Article 21 CFREU prohibits any discrimination based on any ground such as sex, race, colour, ethnic or social origin, genetic features, language, religion or belief, political or any other opinion, membership of a national minority, property, birth, disability, age or sexual orientation. Article 51(1) CFREU sets out the limitations of Charter rights. See also Article 19 TFEU.

20 Articles 18 and 19 TFEU; See, for example, CJEU, *Servet Kamberaj v Istituto per l'Edilizia Sociale della Provincia Autonoma di Bolzano (IPES) and others*, Case C-571/10, 24.04.2012, ECLI:EU:C:2012:233.

21 See McAdam, 'The Global Compacts on Refugees and Migration: A New Era for International Protection', *supra* note 14; see also para. 5 GCR, *supra* note 1, 'The global compact is guided by relevant [IHRL] instruments,' and para. 9 commits all States to 'to promote, respect, protect and fulfil human rights and fundamental freedoms for all …'

22 J.A.R. Nafziger, 'The General Admission of Aliens under International Law', (1983) 77(4), *American Journal of International Law*, p. 804.

23 See generally, S. Peers, V. Moreno-Lax, M. Garlick and E. Guild (eds.), *EU Immigration and Asylum Law (Text and Commentary)*, Brill/Nijhoff, Leiden 2015.

stay and removal.[24] Like international law, EU law accepts that immigration control can only be exercised in line with fundamental rights obligations, which are embedded at the apex of the EU legal order. The Charter of Fundamental Rights (CFREU) enumerates the rights which bind EUMSs when they act within the scope of EU law, including their treatment of migrants and refugees.[25] In the field of asylum, this consists of the Common European Asylum System (CEAS), which flows from the Treaty of the Functioning of the European Union's (TFEU) obligation for the EU to create a common asylum policy in full compliance with the 1951 Refugee Convention, the obligation of *non-refoulement*,[26] and 'other relevant treaties', like the ECHR.[27] Respect for fundamental rights, which include international human rights law (IHRL) obligations,[28] frame the CEAS which establishes common standards in relation to eligibility for international protection and the content of such protection,[29] the reception conditions for applicants for international protection,[30] the allocation of responsibility among the EUMSs for examining their applications[31] and the procedures to be followed in their determination.[32] Its implementation is subordinated to fundamental rights considerations, particularly *non-refoulement*, since CEAS provisions

24 For e.g., Regulation (EU) 2016/399 of the European Parliament and of the Council of 9 March 2016 on a Union Code on the rules governing the movement of persons across borders (Schengen Borders Code), OJ L 77; Regulation (EC) No 810/2009 of the European Parliament and of the Council of 13 July 2009 establishing a Community Code on Visas (Visa Code), OJ L243, as amended by multiple instruments, most recently, Regulation (EU) 2019/1155 of the European Parliament and of the Council of 20 June 2019 amending Regulation (EC) No 810/2009 establishing a Community Code on Visas (Visa Code), OJ L188; Directive 2011/98/EU of the European Parliament and of the Council of 13 December 2011 on a single application procedure for a single permit for third-country nationals to reside and work in the territory of a Member State and on a common set of rights for third-country workers legally residing in a Member State, OJ L343.

25 Article 51 CFREU; CJEU, Case C-617/10, *Åklagaren v Hans Åkerberg Fransson*, 26.02.2013, ECLI:EU:C:2013:105, para. 19.

26 In international refugee law and IHRL, *non-refoulement* outlines the prohibition on returning a person to a state where they have a well-founded fear of persecution on the grounds set out in the Refugee Convention or where there is a real risk that he or she will be subject to torture contrary to the UN Convention against Torture, enforced disappearance under the UN Convention against Enforced Disappearances, or cruel, inhuman or degrading treatment, as under the ECHR. See generally, K. Wouters, *International Legal Standards for the Protection from Refoulement*, Intersentia, Mortsel 2009.

27 Article 78 TFEU.

28 See Article 6 TEU. See generally V. Moreno-Lax, *Accessing Asylum in Europe*, Oxford University Press, Oxford 2017.

29 Qualification Directive, *supra* note 3.

30 RCD, *supra* note 3.

31 Dublin III Regulation, *supra* note 3.

32 Asylum Procedures Directive, *supra* note 3.

'must be interpreted and applied in a manner consistent with the fundamental rights guaranteed by the Charter [...]'.[33]

Accordingly, the EU legal framework – itself an expression of EUMS' sovereignty – reconciles the existence of border control with the obligation to uphold migrants' and refugees' fundamental rights. The emphasis on fundamental rights protection in the exercise of border control commits the EU and its MSs and reflects the commitments states made in adopting both Compacts.

2.3. THE COMPACTS AND STATE SOVEREIGNTY

The Compacts recognise the importance of state sovereignty in respect of border controls yet emphasise that borders are a shared responsibility among states. They further acknowledge that states' claim to sovereignty is constrained by the application of their human rights obligations. Paragraph 33 GCR echoes how '[w]hile recognising the primary responsibility and sovereignty of States, a multistakeholder and partnership approach will be pursued, in line with relevant legal frameworks and in close coordination with national institutions ...'.[34] The GCR's provisions are contingent upon the primary responsibility and sovereignty of each state (as are all protection of human rights and rule of law). The GCR's focus on responsibility and burden-sharing reflects the voluntary nature of the commitments undertaken which respect each state's sovereignty.[35] Similarly, the MC places national sovereignty as a guiding principle that: 'reaffirms the sovereign right of States to determine their national migration policy'.[36] This position, and the provisions on state cooperation, places the protections and the commitments to non-discrimination secondary to each state's sovereign ability to define its own national laws. There are tensions at play between upholding the rights of refugees and migrants and the sovereignty of States who want control over border and migration policies.

---

[33] For example, Recitals 9 and 20 RCD; CJEU, *C.K. and others*, Case C-578/16, 16.02.2017, ECLI:EU:C:2017:127, para. 59; CJEU, *N.S. v Secretary of State for the Home Department and M.E. and Others v Refugee Applications Commissioner and Minister for Justice, Equality and Law Reform*, Joined Cases C-411/10 and C-493/10, 21.12.2011, paras. 77, 99.

[34] Emphasis added.

[35] See for example, section 3 of the GCR, *supra* note 1, on '3. Key tools for effecting burden- and responsibility-sharing; Para. 4 further highlights the voluntary nature of State's commitments thereunder and continued respect for national policies ... voluntary contributions to achieve collective outcomes and progress towards its objectives ... These contributions will be determined by each State and relevant stakeholder, taking into account their national realities, capacities and levels of development, and respecting national policies and priorities ...'.

[36] Para. 15(c) MC, *supra* note 1, a sentiment that is echoed under Objective 11 in relation to border management that respects national sovereignty, see para. 27.

The CEAS and both Compacts maintain the balance between the preservation of state sovereign control over borders and the human rights of refugees and migrants, yet the protection of migrants' and refugees' fundamental rights remains beholden to EUMS' penchant to prioritise border control over their fundamental rights commitments. The CEAS's implementation gap preceded COVID-19 and the Compacts' adoption and while the CEAS purports to implement *common* standards, its disparate implementation by EUMSs challenges its designation as a harmonised system.[37] Thus, the tension between the two facets of sovereignty is not due to an absence of law; indeed, the Compacts equip EUMSs with a blueprint for a sovereignty-preserving, rights-conforming implementation of their pre-existing obligations, including in times of crisis. Yet, as will become apparent, EUMS' fragmented response to COVID-19 indicates their reliance on their state sovereignty, as expressed through border control, to justify exceptional measures in response to a crisis. Nowhere is this more evident than in March 2020 when several EUMSs reacted to COVID-19's arrival in Europe through border closures, territorial limitations on movement, including enhanced detention and the closure of processing centres for asylum seekers and migrants. While the CEAS *is* sufficiently flexible to be implemented consistently with the two Compacts and human rights obligations – as was the case in some EUMSs (most notably Portugal)[38] – others relied on discretionary provisions or simply disregarded aspects of the CEAS in their treatment of asylum seekers, refugees and undocumented migrants who may need international protection and departed from the commitments they made when embracing the two Compacts. This highlights the extent to which voluntary state cooperation, which preserves state sovereignty, is instrumentalised in the European context despite legal frameworks that seek to place refugee and asylum seeker protection at their centre.

---

37 The need for reform is accepted across the board. See, European Commission, Communication from the Commission to the European Parliament, the Council, the European Economic and Social Committee and the Committee of the Regions on a New Pact on Migration and Asylum, COM(2020) 609 final 23.90.2020. On the CEAS, see generally V. Chetail, 'A Common European Asylum System: Bric-à-brac or System?', in V. Chetail, P. De Bruycker and F. Maini, *Reforming the Common European Asylum System. The New European Refugee Law*, Brill/Nijhoff, Leiden/Boston 2016, pp. 3-38; M. Den Heijer, J. Rijpma and T. Spijkerboer, 'Coercion, Prohibition, and Great Expectations: The Continuing Failure of the Common European Asylum System', (2016) 53, *Common Market Law Review*, p. 4.

38 Some EUMSs have been exemplary in ensuring that refugees, asylum seekers and migrants have not suffered discrimination as a result of pandemic related measures. In particular, from the commencement of the pandemic in Europe, Portugal implemented measures to ensure all persons were entitled to equal treatment with nationals as regards health care, socio-economic rights and civil rights other than those protected for citizens. See IOM, 'Portugal's Contribution to the IOM Regional Review', 19.10.2020, p. 5, available at https://migrationnetwork.un.org/sites/default/files/docs/oim-portugal-contribution_global_compact_migration-nv_400-2020.pdf, last accessed 21.03.2021.

3. ACCESSING ASYLUM PROCEDURES IN THE EU DURING THE COVID-19 PANDEMIC

Among the foundations of both Compacts is states' commitment to the rule of law and due process through which they undertake to ensure access to justice in all aspects of refugee protection and migration governance.[39] The Compacts specify that state, public and private institutions and entities are accountable to laws that are publicly promulgated, equally enforced, independently adjudicated and consistent with all relevant international law.[40] For our purposes here, the reference to international law is primarily international and regional human rights commitments.

In respect of asylum procedures, this commitment is reiterated in the GCR where states undertake to ensure the establishment of mechanisms for identification, screening and referral of those with specific needs to appropriate and accessible processes and procedure.[41] This commitment to fair and efficient procedures is extended to a particular sensitive category of procedures: simplified or accelerated procedures for cases likely to be manifestly founded or unfounded.[42] This classification is important for the intersection of the GCR and the MC as an insufficiently rigorous application of these procedures can result in people who should be recognised as refugees being rejected or otherwise categorised.

In the MC, this foundation is developed through a commitment to strengthen certainty and predictability in migration procedures for appropriate screening, assessment and referral.[43] This is to be achieved, as stated in the MC, by developing and strengthening effective and human rights-based mechanisms for an adequate and timely screening and individual assessment of all migrants.[44] The five measures which are set out to achieve this objective in the MC are also relevant to the correct implementation of the GCR in light of the intersection of the two Compacts and the multiple legal identities of refugees. The measures are to: increase transparency and accessibility of migration procedures; develop and conduct regional specialised human rights and trauma-informed training for officials; establish gender-responsive and child sensitive assessments at borders and places of first arrival through standardised operating procedures; ensure that migrant children are promptly identified and swiftly referred to child protection authorises; and ensure that relevant information on rights and

[39] See GCR, *supra* note 1, para. 9; MC, *supra* note 1, para. 15(d).
[40] GCR, *supra* note 1, para. 9; MC, *supra* note 1, para. 7.
[41] GCR, *supra* note 1, para. 60.
[42] GCR, *supra* note 1, para. 61.
[43] MC, *supra* note 1, objective 12.
[44] MC, *supra* note 1, para. 28.

obligations under national laws and procedures is appropriately, promptly and effectively communicated and accessible.[45]

Among those most affected by the changing administrative frameworks of EUMSs in the face of the COVID-19 pandemic were those seeking international protection. The rule of law foundation of border-crossing and the entitlement of those in need of international protection to a fair and effective procedure are central elements of EU law. In this section, we look at the problems which have occurred in this field under the following subheadings: access to the territory to seek international protection, access to registration procedures, access to reception conditions and access to the substantive procedure for applicants for international protection. As will become apparent, not only did the EUMSs fall short of their Compact commitments as regards the treatment of refugees and migrants during the pandemic, but they also failed to live up to their commitments to the rule of law and their international human rights obligations reaffirmed so recently in 2018 in the Compacts.

3.1. ACCESS TO THE TERRITORY

Through the Schengen Borders Code, EU law provides for a common set of rules for the admission of TCNs at the external borders of (most) EUMSs.[46] Article 3 of the Code states that it is without prejudice to the rights of refugees and persons requesting international protection, in particular as regards *non-refoulement*.[47] This obligation means that where someone arrives at an EU border and claims international protection, the state is required to consider that application and to allow the person to remain until an assessment of their case is completed and a decision taken.

One of the first impacts of COVID-19's arrival in the EU in February 2020 was the abandonment of coordination through the EU institutions to protect EU law in light of the new circumstances, which was particularly evident in national decisions to close external borders with third countries. It was not until 30 March 2020 that the European Commission (EC) issued guidance to the EUMSs on how to apply their restrictions on access to territory in light of the pandemic.[48] Provision was made in those guidelines calling on EUMSs to permit admission to those carrying out essential travel who were described by

45 MC, *supra* note 1, para. 28(a–e).

46 Schengen Borders Code, *supra* note 24. Those EUMSs outside the common Schengen area are Bulgaria, Croatia, Cyprus, Ireland, and Romania. No further mention will be made to these states in particular hereafter.

47 See *supra* note 26.

48 European Commission, Guidance on the implementation of the temporary restriction on non-essential travel to the EU, on the facilitation of transit arrangements for the repatriation of EU citizens, and on the effects on visa policy, COM(2020) 2050 30.03.2020.

profession, personal situation and economic activity. Those seeking international protection were not included.[49] Rather, in the last indent of a section headed 'Other [TCNs] who can be authorised to enter the EU despite the closure of the EU external borders', the Commission suggests that EUMSs should allow access to the territory to 'persons in need of international protection or for other humanitarian reasons respecting the principle of *non-refoulement*'.[50] It is rather unedifying that the European Commission (EC) should consider people fleeing persecution and torture as undertaking non-essential travel.

An immediate result of the closure of EU external borders was the exclusion of people in need of international protection from access to the territory. This was recognised by the EU institution, the European Asylum Support Office (EASO), which has been issuing regular updates on national practices.[51] It noted a 31% decrease in asylum applications between 2019 and 2020, which it attributed to COVID-19-related emergency travel restrictions (and obstacles).[52] This appears to confirm that EUMSs failed to take the necessary measures to ensure that those fleeing persecution and torture had access to the EU territory. Travel restrictions covered a wide range of measures, including limitations on flights from certain destinations (which started with China) to the closure of ports for the duration of the national public health emergency. These measures particularly affected people seeking international protection. This was the case in Italy.[53] According to Human Rights Watch (HRW), the day before the adoption of the Italian decree, the German government advised their non-governmental organisations (NGOs) engaged in saving lives in the Mediterranean that neither Italy nor Malta would permit them to disembark the people they saved at their ports and so the NGOs should cease this activity.[54] Challenges to the EU obligation of *non-refoulement* through practices to prevent people, including those who are likely to be seeking international protection, from arriving at EU points of entry intensified under the cover of COVID-19 measures.[55]

---

49 Ibid.

50 Ibid.

51 EASO, 'COVID-19 emergency measures in asylum and reception systems – Issue 2', 07.12.2020, available at https://www.easo.europa.eu/sites/default/files/publications/COVID-19%20emergency%20measures%20in%20asylum%20and%20reception%20systems-December-2020_new.pdf, last accessed 02.03.2021.

52 Ibid.

53 Italian Decree, 07.04.2020, available at https://www.avvenire.it/c/attualita/Documents/M_INFR.GABINETTO.REG_DECRETI(R).0000150.07-04-2020%20(3).pdf, last accessed 03.03.2021.

54 HRW, 'EU/Italy: Port Closures Cut Migrant and Refugee Lifeline', 09.04.2020, available at www.hrw.org/news/2020/04/09/eu/italy-port-closures-cut-migrant-and-refugee-lifeline, last accessed 09.04.2021.

55 UNHCR, 'UNHCR warns asylum under attack at Europe's borders, urges end to pushbacks and violence against refugees', 28.01.2021, available at https://www.unhcr.org/news/press/2021/1/601121344/unhcr-warns-asylum-under-attack-europes-borders-urges-end-pushbacks-violence.html, last accessed 03.03.2021; M. Stevis-Gridneff, EU Border Agency

3.2. ACCESS TO REGISTRATION PROCEDURES

Once a refugee has arrived at an EU border or entered the territory, it is necessary for them to apply for asylum. Accordingly, the Asylum Procedures Directive defines an asylum application as an 'application for international protection … "application" means a request made by a [TCN] or a stateless person for protection from a [EUMS], who can be understood to seek refugee status or subsidiary protection status …'.[56] When a refugee makes an asylum application it is obligatory for state authorities to ensure that the individual is registered as an asylum seeker and provided with a document establishing their status. From the commencement of the COVID-19 pandemic in Europe, many EUMSs suspended their registration procedures for asylum seekers.[57] This ranged from complete suspension as in Belgium, Greece or Poland, to almost complete suspension with some exceptions (in particular for the most vulnerable) in France and elsewhere.[58] These suspensions were often accompanied by closure of application centres, changes of hours at short notice or without notice, cancellation of appointments and failure to issue documents.[59] If a refugee is unable to register their asylum application in an EUMS, their status remains ambiguous. If they have arrived irregularly in the EU, they remain an irregularly present migrant in the EU, subject to the EU and EUMS' coercive measures against such migrants in an irregular situation (including, severe limitations on access to housing, health care, food and other essential assistance, prohibition of working and vulnerability to summary expulsion).[60]

3.3. ACCESS TO RECEPTION CONDITIONS

The Reception Conditions Directive requires all EUMSs to provide reception conditions for asylum seekers registered on their territory.[61] This includes

Accused of Covering Up Migrant Pushback in Greece, *New York Times*, 26.11.2020, available at https://www.nytimes.com/2020/11/26/world/europe/frontex-migrants-pushback-greece.html, last accessed 03.03.2021.

56 APD, *supra* note 3, Article 2.

57 EASO, 'Special Report: Asylum Trends and COVID-19', 11.06.2020, available at https://www.easo.europa.eu/sites/default/files/easo-special-report-asylum-COVID-june-2020.pdf, last accessed 03.03.2021.

58 Ibid.

59 Ibid.

60 EU Agency for Fundamental Rights (FRA), 'Fundamental Rights of Migrants in an Irregular Situation in the European Union', 2011, available at https://fra.europa.eu/en/publication/2012/fundamental-rights-migrants-irregular-situation-european-union, last accessed 11.04.2021. See generally, FRA, 'Asylum, Migration and Borders', available at https://fra.europa.eu/en/themes/asylum-migration-and-borders, last accessed 11.04.2021.

61 RCD, *supra* note 3, Article 3(1).

refugees who make their application at the borders, in the territorial waters, or in the transit zones of an EUMS. EUMSs are required to ensure that material reception conditions provide an adequate standard of living for applicants, which guarantees their subsistence and protects their physical and mental health.[62] It is access to reception conditions which enables destitute asylum seekers to be housed, fed and cared for while their asylum claim is under consideration. Registration is central to ensuring that asylum seekers are not reduced to conditions which are inhuman and degrading treatment, which is condemned by the European Court of Human Rights (ECtHR) as vulnerability created by EUMS' own inaction.[63] Yet on the basis of COVID-19 related measures, it is this access to registration which was diminished or extinguished in many EUMSs.

3.4. ACCESS TO A SUBSTANTIVE PROCEDURE

The Asylum Procedures Directive sets out the requirements of an asylum procedure in the EU which includes a personal interview so that the applicant can explain the reasons for their flight and need for international protection.[64] So long as state authorities are still processing asylum applications, the asylum seeker *only* has access to reception conditions. Once the asylum seeker is recognised as a refugee or beneficiary of international protection, they can start a new life in the EUMS: work, take up education and enjoy equal treatment with nationals in a series of fields.[65]

COVID-19 measures in several EUMSs have resulted in the suspension or cancelling of personal interviews with asylum seekers.[66] Further, not all EUMSs have made accommodation for COVID-19 restrictions as regards the application of time limits for applying for asylum and lodging full applications.[67] This has resulted in asylum seekers being unable to comply with the conditions of their status. In addition, some EUMSs have failed to put in place systems whereby asylum seekers can renew the validity of their registration documents in order to lawfully remain.[68] Many asylum seekers have become vulnerable to expulsion decisions as a result of the failure of state authorities to process their asylum applications in a timely manner.[69]

62 Ibid., Article 17.

63 ECtHR, *M.S.S. v Belgium and Greece*, no 30696/09 [GC] 21.01.2011, para. 263.

64 Asylum Procedures Directive, *supra* note 3.

65 Qualification Directive, *supra* note 3.

66 EASO (2020), Special Report, *supra* note 57.

67 Ibid.

68 Ibid.

69 See for example, in Germany where the courts required authorities to reconsider over 5,500 applications: S. Sanderson, 'German courts repeal more than 5,600 Afghan asylum rejections', 07.12.2020, available at https://www.infomigrants.net/en/post/28966/german-courts-repeal-more-than-5-600-afghan-asylum-rejections, last accessed 03.03.2021.

As set out in detail above, many EUMSs have failed to comply with EU law regarding the treatment of refugees and asylum seekers in the implementation of their COVID-19 measures. This is contrary to the Compacts undertaking to respect rule of law. In the MC, states committed themselves to ensuring certainty and predictability in migration procedures.[70] As a result of COVID-19 measures, many EUMSs have fallen short of this obligation. They have failed to take into account their duties towards migrants, refugees and asylum seekers to ensure certainty and predictability in the processing of their applications. Access to the territory, procedures, reception conditions and substantive determination of their applications has been made fragile by COVID-19 measures, and in some cases frustrated entirely. Times of pandemic place increased pressures on public administrations to deliver services to everyone on their territory. But these increased demands cannot justify the failure to comply with internationally accepted and EU binding obligations to migrants, refugees and asylum seekers.

4. CONTINUED USE OF IMMIGRATION DETENTION DURING A PANDEMIC

Immigration detention is only lawful when it has a lawful objective – expulsion or whilst procedures are being undertaken.[71] As the COVID-19 pandemic tightened its grip on states, many refugees, asylum seekers, and migrants continued to be detained in reception and detention centres, without any prospect of release. The tensions evident in the continued use of detention during a pandemic will be examined from two perspectives. The first is the arbitrary nature of the detention, and the second is the breach of human rights caused by the poor conditions within detention centres.

4.1. IMMIGRATION DETENTION AS A FIRST RESORT?

The ECHR protects all people from arbitrary detention and protects their freedom of movement.[72] However, the CEAS permits detention in specific circumstances, including for purposes of identification, to determine admission

70 MC, *supra* note 1, para. 28.

71 See ECHR, *supra* note 18, Article 5(1)(f).

72 Article 5 ECHR states '1. Everyone has the right to liberty and security of person. No one shall be deprived of his liberty save in the following cases and in accordance with a procedure prescribed by law'; Article 2 of Protocol 4 to the ECHR provides 'Everyone lawfully within the territory of a State shall, within that territory, have the right to liberty of movement and freedom to choose his residence'.

and to enforce transfer, as well as enforcing returns of migrants.[73] This leaves broad discretion to authorities to regularly detain asylum-seekers during the whole asylum determination procedure.[74] However, immigration detention must be in line with Article 5(1)(f) ECHR such that it can only be utilised to prevent TCNs unauthorised entry into the country or during deportation proceedings.[75] This preserves the sovereign control over borders whilst providing clear protections from arbitrariness for TCNs.

Despite the framework prohibiting arbitrary and prolonged detention, as well as guidance that detention should only be used in immigration situations as a last resort, state practice demonstrates that it has been frequently utilised as a matter of course, even prior to the COVID-19 pandemic. The UN Working Group on Immigration Detention reported in 2016 that immigration detention was utilised routinely and systematically in Malta,[76] and in 2015 found that Germany made wide use of its prison system to hold foreigners in administrative detention despite CJEU cases holding this was incompatible with the Returns Directive.[77] In *Khlaifia v Italy*, the ECtHR Grand Chamber found a violation of Articles 5 and 4 ECHR for the use of early detention centres in Lampedusa.[78] Furthermore, conditions within immigration detention centres have been frequently called into question before courts and by human rights organisations.[79] Despite commitments to human rights within the CEAS's framework, in practice, immigration detention has been used as a first, rather than the last, resort.

However, very recently EUMSs reaffirmed their political commitment to ensuring freedom of movement for refugees, asylum seekers, and migrants. These human rights protections are evident in the GCR which commits states to using

---

73 RCD, *supra* note 3, Article 8(3); Directive 2008/115/EC of the European Parliament and of the Council of 16 December 2008 on common standards and procedures in Member States for returning illegally staying third-country nationals, OJ L348, Article 15 (hereinafter Returns Directive); See for further discussion I. Majcher, 'Creeping Crimmigration in CEAS Reform: Detention of Asylum-Seekers and Restrictions on Their Movement under EU Law', (2020) *Refugee Survey Quarterly*, p. 2.

74 See M. Bosworth and S. Turnbull, 'Immigration Detention, Punishment, and the Criminalization of Migration', in S. Pickering and J. Ham (eds.), *The Routledge Handbook on Crime and International Migration*, Routledge, New York 2015, pp. 91–106.

75 Article 5(1)(f) ECHR; Article 6(4) Returns Directive, *supra* note 73, holds that detention ceases to be justified where there is no longer a reasonable prospect of removal. See also, CJEU, *K. v Staatssecretaris van Veiligheid En Justitie*, Case C-18/16, 14.09.2017, ECLI:EU:C:2017:680, paras. 36 and 39, where the CJEU discusses compatibility with Article 5 ECHR.

76 UN Working Group on Arbitrary Detention (WGAD), 'Report of the Working Group on Arbitrary Detention on its follow-up mission to Malta', UN Doc A/HRC/33/50/Add.1, 23.06.2016, p. 2.

77 WGAD, 'Report of the Working Group on Arbitrary Detention on its follow-up mission to Germany', UN Doc A/HRC/30/36/Add.1, 10.07.2015, p. 7; see also CJEU, *Bero and Bouzalmate*, Joined Cases C-473/13 and C-514/13, 17.07.2014, ECLI:EU:C:2014:2095.

78 ECtHR, *Khlaifia and Others v Italy*, no 16483/12, 15.12.2016, para. 106.

79 Ibid., paras. 158-211.

detention only where community-based alternatives are not possible.[80] Further, the MC specifically provides that detention must be used only as a last resort after all alternatives have been found to be unsuitable.[81] When EUMSs signed the Compacts, they committed to uphold these protections and work towards their realisation. Despite this, with the spread of COVID-19 and EUMSs efforts to curb the pandemic, measures taken in relation to immigration detention demonstrated that refugees, asylum seekers and migrants were the first to suffer a degradation of human rights protection justified as exercise of sovereign power.

4.2. ARBITRARY DETENTION

The GCR makes clear that all alternatives to detention must be sought and the MC commits to ensuring any immigration detention is 'non-arbitrary, is based on law, necessity, proportionality and individual assessments, is carried out by authorised officials and is for the shortest possible period of time'.[82] The tension between the CEAS powers to detain individuals who are awaiting asylum procedures or expulsion,[83] and the commitments under the Compacts were put into stark contrast during the pandemic because, with asylum processing at a standstill and returns to countries of origin on hold, the detention of these individuals became arbitrary.

First, failed asylum-seekers and migrants who were in detention awaiting expulsion were no longer being held in accordance with IHRL as the purpose of the detention – to achieve expulsion was no longer possible because of border closures. In Greece, HRW reported that the government implemented a policy of detaining asylum seekers arriving at its borders whilst simultaneously suspending the procedures and removals.[84] Similar policies were reported in Italy and France.[85] The detention of asylum seekers and migrants where there

---

80 Para. 60 GCR, *supra* note 1.

81 Para. 29 MC, *supra* note 1, see E. Guild and T. Basaran (2019), 'Analysis on the Final Draft for the UN Global Compact on Safe, Orderly and Regular Migration' *supra* note 7. *supra* note 7, Objective 13.

82 Para. 60 GCR; Objective 13, para. 29 MC, *supra* note 1.

83 Article 8(3) RCD; See also Article 28(2) Dublin Regulation, where EUMS states may detain the person concerned pending transfer to the responsible EUMS if there is a 'significant' risk of absconding.

84 HRW, 'Curb Immigration Detention Amid Pandemic', Report, 2020, available at https://www.hrw.org/news/2020/03/27/europe-curb-immigration-detention-amid-pandemic, last accessed 04.04.2021.

85 ASGI, 'COVID-19, l'impatto sui diritti delle cittadine e cittadini stranieri e le misure di tutela necessarie', 2020, available at: https://www.asgi.it/asilo-e-protezione-internazionale/COVID-stranieri-proposte/, last accessed 05.09.2021; Le Monde, 'Coronavirus: "Let's safeguard fundamental rights during the health crisis"', 2020, available at https://www.lemonde.fr/idees/article/2020/03/20/coronavirus-sauvegardons-les-droits-fondamentaux-pendant-la-crise-sanitaire_6033892_3232.html, last accessed 06.09.2021.

is no possibility of pursuing expulsion is no longer justified by a legitimate objective.[86] While processes are suspended for effectuating removals, detention becomes increasingly arbitrary.

In March 2020, the Council of Europe's Commissioner for Human Rights called for the release of all immigration detainees because detention can only be lawful 'as long as it is feasible that return can indeed take place ... This prospect is clearly not in sight in many cases at the moment ...'.[87] As a result, some EUMSs recognised that, under COVID-19, detention risked becoming arbitrary. In Spain, following an official declaration, all people in detention centres were released, and no new detentions orders were permitted.[88] In Belgium many detainees were released in practice, albeit on a case-by-case basis.[89] In some EUMSs, moves were made to avoid continued immigration detention being rendered arbitrary by COVID-19 measures.

Second, reception centres which had been open closed their doors in response to the pandemic, preventing asylum seekers from leaving at all. Liberty of movement is a human right that has been severely curtailed since the outbreak of the COVID-19 pandemic. Under Article 7 of the Reception Conditions Directive (RCD), states may restrict asylum applicants' freedom of movement to an assigned area or an actual residence of the applicant. However, rather than this simply being a matter of interference with the right of freedom of movement, the policies taken towards asylum seekers in reception centres became tantamount to detention.[90] Without a clear end in sight, as asylum procedures were often suspended, this also became arbitrary detention.[91]

---

86 See UNGA, 'Report of the Working Group on Arbitrary Detention – United Nations Basic Principles and Guidelines on Remedies and Procedures on the Right of Anyone Deprived of Their Liberty to Bring Proceedings Before a Court', UN Doc A/HRC/30/37, 06.07.2015, para. 45; UNGA, 'Report of the Working Group on Arbitrary Detention', UN Doc A/HRC/10/21, 16.02.2009, para. 75.

87 CoE, 'Commissioner calls for release of immigration detainees while COVID-19 crisis continues,' 2020, available at https://www.coe.int/en/web/commissioner/-/commissioner-calls-for-release-of-immigration-detainees-while-COVID-19-crisis-continues, last accessed 09.04.2021.

88 JRS-Europe, 'COVID-19 and Immigration detention: Lessons Not Learned, Report, February 2021', p. 5, available at https://jrseurope.org/wp-content/uploads/sites/19/2021/02/Report-Covid-19-and-immigration-detention.pdf, last accessed 09.04.2021.

89 See Belgian Federal Centre for Migration, 'Visites de Myria dans les centres fermés de Merksplas, Bruges et Vottem entre le 10 avril et le 14 mai 2020 dans le cadre de la pandémie de COVID-19', Report, 2020, p. 6, available at: https://www.myria.be/files/Rapport_visites_aux_centres_fermes_-_COVID-19.pdf, last accessed 09.04.2021.

90 Border Criminologies, 'Confine to Protect: Greek Hotspots and the Hygienic-Sanitary Borders of COVID-19', Report, 2020, available at https://www.law.ox.ac.uk/research-subject-groups/centre-criminology/centreborder-criminologies/blog/2020/09/confine-protect, last access 09.04.2021.

91 See for further discussion of the lack of procedural safeguards for people in immigration detention in the UK: BiD, 'Immigration bail hearings during the COVID-19 Pandemic', 2020, available at https://hubble-live-assets.s3.amazonaws.com/biduk/redactor2_assets/files/1263/201214_v6_Immigration_bail_monitoring.pdf, last accessed 09.04.2021.

Numerous cases were brought before national courts to challenge the measures taken to curb the spread of COVID-19 as a breach of human rights. The Romanian Supreme Court held the isolation and quarantine measures violated Article 5 ECHR.[92] This case held that for ongoing measures to be legal, the state must declare a state of emergency under Article 15 ECHR limiting the application of human rights.[93] In relation to the specific situation of the ongoing and arbitrary detention of individuals, two cases in France held that the risk generated by the extension of the administrative detention was disproportionate to the prospect of return, since most countries had closed their borders.[94] Further, a report by Bail for Immigration Detainees (BID) in 2020 on applications for bail of immigration detainees demonstrates the dubious claims by states that immigration detention remained necessary during COVID-19 due to the 'risk of harm' the detainees represented.[95] Immigration detention during the COVID-19 pandemic was rendered arbitrary because there was no prospect of asylum procedures being completed or of return.

4.3. IMMIGRATION DETENTION CONDITIONS

The GCR outlines the importance to access to health care for refugees and asylum seekers and reaffirms the commitments in the New York Declaration to provide access to health care and adequate conditions upon arrival.[96] Additional obligations accrue towards those in immigration detention, who are wholly dependent on the EUMSs for fulfilment of their right.[97] The MC commits to 'safeguard[ing] physical and mental integrity, and that, at a minimum, access to food, basic health care … as well as adequate accommodation is granted, in accordance with [IHRL]' for those in detention.[98] These commitments are not discordant with the CEAS which

92 Decision of the Romanian Constitutional Court no. 458 of 25.06.2020 published in the Official Gazette, part I, no. 581 of 02.07.2020; see L. Stefan, 'Rule of Law in Tough Times–A Case Study on the Romanian Sanctioning Policy During the COVID-19 Pandemic', (2020) *Transylvanian Review of Administrative Sciences*, pp. 121–148.

93 R. Duminica, 'Some Reflections about the Activation of Article 15 of the European Convention on Human Rights by Romania in the Context of the COVID-19 Pandemic', (2020) 13, *JL & Admin Sci*, p. 78.

94 France – Lille Judicial Tribunal, n° 20/00633, 17.03.2020; France – Judiciary Tribunal of Perpignan, No RG20/00356, 18.03.2020.

95 BiD, 'COVID-19 Detention Research', Report, 2020, available at https://hubble-live-assets.s3.amazonaws.com/biduk/redactor2_assets/files/1203/BID_COVID-19_Detention_research_report.pdf, last accessed 06.04.2021.

96 GCR, *supra* note 1, para. 72-73; NY Declaration, *supra* note 1, para. 5(c).

97 See, Article 11 RCD, *supra* note 3; Article 16 Returns Directive, *supra* note 73.

98 MC, *supra* note1, para. 29(f).

commits to adequate reception conditions for all refugees and asylum seekers.[99] However, often access to these basic human rights are undermined during detention, and this was made particularly clear during the pandemic.

Several cases went before the ECtHR to challenge the conditions people were placed in during detention because of COVID-19. In *Feilazoo v Malta*, the applicant was detained in a part of the detention facility that was reserved for COVID-19 quarantine breaching Article 3 ECHR.[100] In France, the domestic court held that an Egyptian national with a serious health condition, held in an administrative detention centre in a room with three other persons without masks available or social distancing possible, must be immediately released.[101] A German case similarly found that where compliance with the distancing rules in an asylum seeker accommodation centre was not possible, they should be able to seek alternative accommodation.[102] Further, legal proceedings in the UK were brought against the government challenging the use of detention during a pandemic as it presents ideal incubation conditions for the spread of COVID-19.[103] It became clear that the detention that individuals were being forced into due to their migratory status was not only arbitrary, but also threatened their wider access to rights to health and life.[104] While many interior ministries seemed unable or unwilling to implement their Compact obligations as set out in the CEAS during COVID-19, their courts took a much more robust approach ordering them to do so.

What happened in many countries with the slippage from open reception facilities to detention because of COVID-19 is inconsistent with human rights and states' commitments in the Compacts. The CEAS provisions relating to detention are intended to protect the state's ability to enforce and maintain control over borders. During the pandemic this has been pursued at the expense of human rights provisions, resulting in detention becoming arbitrary and threatening human rights to health, life and free movement.

99 RCD, *supra* note 3, Article 3(1).

100 ECtHR, *Feilazoo v Malta*, no 6865/19, 11.03.2021, paras. 73, 92.

101 France Tribunal Administratif de Montpellier, *X v Le Prefet des Pyrenees Orientales*, N 2020-213, 19.03.20.

102 Germany Administrative Court Leipzig (VG), *Decision 3 L 204/20.A*, 22.04.20.

103 Detention Action, 'High Court Orders Government to Respond Urgently To COVID-19 Immigration Detention Legal Challenge', 2020, available at https://detentionaction.org.uk/2020/03/20/high-court-orders-government-to-respond-urgently-to-COVID-19-immigration-detention-legal-challenge/, last accessed 09.04.2021.

104 See 'Human Mobility and Human Rights in the COVID-19 Pandemic: Principles of Protection for Migrants, Refugees, and Other Displaced Persons', (2020) 32(3), *International Journal of Refugee Law*, p. 549–558; See JRS-Europe, *supra* note 88, p. 11.

5. ACCESS TO ESSENTIAL HEALTH CARE DURING THE COVID-19 PANDEMIC

COVID-19 highlighted the extent to which access to good quality health care is a precursor to the enjoyment of all other fundamental rights.[105] It strengthened the case for universal health coverage, which refers to the effective possibility for individuals and communities to receive the health services they require, includes 'access to quality essential health-care services and access to safe, effective, quality and affordable essential medicines' and which states had committed to achieve through Agenda 2030.[106] COVID-19 illustrated how the application of an individualistic lens to health collapses in the face of a highly transmissible disease, which does not distinguish by migration status, since a response which safeguards public health needs to consider the health of all its members, including migrants, refugees and host communities.[107]

This section assesses EUMS' practices towards migrants' and refugees' access to appropriate health care in the COVID-19 response against their commitments under the two Compacts, which reaffirm pre-existing IHRL and EU law obligations. It shows how effective enjoyment of the right to health during the pandemic was prejudiced by pre-existing barriers which limited access, particularly to appropriate health care. As will become apparent, some EUMSs realigned their frameworks with pre-existing fundamental rights obligations, to extend basic health care to those hitherto excluded in practice and drew on the skills of migrants and refugees to strengthen their COVID-19 response. Yet, the effectiveness of these measures was prejudiced by the longstanding limitations placed on migrants' and refugees' practical access to health care.

5.1. A RIGHT TO ACCESS HEALTH CARE OF GOOD QUALITY

Both Compacts frame the right to health of migrants and refugees alongside that of the host community and commit to providing *both* migrant and refugee populations with appropriate health care. States need to 'promote the physical

105 See, for example, the UN Committee on Economic, Social and Cultural Rights (hereinafter ICESCR-Committee), General Comment no 14 on the right to the highest attainable standard of physical and mental health ICESCR-Committee, UN Doc E/C.12/2000/4 (2001) (hereinafter GC 14), para. 1.

106 UNGA, 'Transforming Our World: The 2030 Agenda for Sustainable Development', UN Doc A/RES/70/1, 25.09.2015, Target 3.8.

107 WHO, 'ApartTogether Survey: Preliminary Overview of Refugees and Migrants Self-reported Impact of COVID-19', 18.12.2020, p. VI, available at https://www.who.int/publications/i/item/9789240017924, last accessed 09.04.2021.

and mental health of migrants and communities overall',[108] and 'expand and enhance the quality of national health systems [within host countries] to facilitate access by refugees and host communities'.[109] States' commitments are grounded in the fulfilment of pre-existing IHRL obligations which prescribe the equal entitlement of migrants and refugees to the enjoyment of the highest attainable standard of physical and mental health, which includes access to health care that is acceptable and of good quality, and is to be realised without distinction on the basis of migration status.[110] Accordingly, states commit that 'all migrants, regardless of their basic status, can exercise their human rights through safe access to basic services', and acknowledge the relationship between non-discrimination and service provision.[111] The GCR contemplates state cooperation and input by relevant stakeholders, such as the World Health Organization (WHO), to 'facilitate access by refugees and host communities' to 'national health systems'.[112] Like the UN core IHRL treaties which articulate a right to health adapted to specific categories, such as women, children, migrant workers, and persons with disabilities,[113] both Compacts commit states to tailor health care provision to migrants' and refugees' specific experience and their intersecting identities, including an age and gender dimension.[114]

Under EU law, the Charter asserts that everyone has 'the right of access to preventive health care and the right to benefit from medical treatment'.[115] The CEAS concretises migrants' and refugees' right to access health care within EUMSs. Although these prescribe varying entitlements at different stages of their (legal) journey, they all outline a minimum entitlement to emergency and primary health care, which includes treatment for COVID-19.[116] Like the

---

108 MC, *supra* note 1, para. 31(e).

109 GCR, *supra* note 1, para. 72.

110 Article 12 of the International Covenant on Economic, Social and Cultural Rights (ICESCR) provides 'States Parties *must* take steps to prevent, treat and control epidemic [...] diseases whilst taking the necessary steps to create conditions that would assure medical service and attention to all in the event of sickness.' While the right to health is broader than the right to health care, for health care to be IHRL-compliant, it must meet the principles of availability, accessibility, acceptability, and quality (AAAQ). See ICESCR-Committee, *supra* note 105, para. 12.

111 MC, *supra* note 1, para. 31. See also Objectives 1, 2, 6, 7, and 13.

112 GCR, *supra* note 1, para. 72.

113 For an overview, P. Pace, 'Migration and the Right to Health: A Review of International Law', IOM, 2009, available at https://publications.iom.int/system/files/pdf/iml_19.pdf, last accessed 11.04.2021.

114 See, NY Declaration, *supra* note 1, para. 30. For example, for women and girls and children, see GCR, *supra* note 1, paras. 75-76. The MC, *supra* note 1, para. 31 recognises that 'nationals and regular migrants may be entitled to more comprehensive service provision'.

115 Article 35 CFREU. This is subject to national rules given the limited EU competence in the area, even if these cannot obviate the provision of meaningful content.

116 See RCD, *supra* note 3, Article 19(1); QD, *supra* note 3, Articles 31 and 32; Returns Directive, *supra* note 73, Article 14. See also, CJEU, *Centre public d'action social d'Ottignies-Louvain-La-Neuve v Moussa Abdida*, Case C-562/13, 18.12.2014, ECLI:EU:C:2014:2453.

Compacts' acknowledgment that specific groups require additional support, the CEAS includes a heightened obligation to secure health care for those designated as vulnerable populations, including children, persons with serious health care needs, survivors of torture and persons with disabilities.[117]

5.2. ACCESS TO HEALTH CARE DURING COVID-19

Notwithstanding the comprehensive legal framework, in March 2020, it was amply clear that, compared to EUMS citizens, migrants and refugees were at a disadvantage in their enjoyment of the right to health,[118] with 'many … at heightened risk [of COVID-19 infection]'.[119] While health care needs are 'a complex combination of biological and socioeconomic factors developed over [migrants' and refugees'] lives', migration is also a social determinant of health which affects individual health status.[120] Discrimination, inequalities and exclusion from health and welfare services constitute negative health influences yet are the lived experience of a significant number of migrants and refugees across EUMSs.[121] Through the Compacts, in an attempt to address these barriers to effective access, states committed to incorporate migrants' health needs 'into national and local health-care policies and plans, such as by strengthening capacities for service provision, facilitating affordable and non-discriminatory access, reducing communication barriers and training health-care providers on culturally sensitive service delivery'.[122]

Against this framework, the EC's March 2020 Guidance reminded EUMSs that, notwithstanding the challenges posed by the pandemic, 'emergency and essential treatment of illness, including for COVID-19 must be ensured'.[123] EUMS' responses varied significantly, not least according to the migrant's

117 For example, Articles 19(2) and 21 RCD, *supra* note 3; Article 30 QD, *supra* note 3, Article 14 Returns Directive, *supra* note 73.

118 H.H.P. Kluge et al., 'Refugee and Migrant Health in the COVID-19 Response', (2020) 395, *The Lancet*, p. 1237.

119 OHCHR, IOM, UNHCR and WHO, 'The Rights and Health of Refugees, Migrants and Stateless must be protected in COVID-19 response', Joint Press Release, 31.03.2020, available at https://www.unhcr.org/uk/news/press/2020/3/5e836f164/rights-health-refugees-migrants-stateless-must-protected-covid-19-response.html, last accessed 09.04.2021.

120 I. Abubaker, R. Aldridge, D. Devakumar et al., 'The UCL–Lancet Commission on Migration and Health: The Health of a World on the Move', (2018) 392 *The Lancet*, p. 2634.

121 Ibid.; S.P. Juárez et al., 'Effects of Non-health-targeted Policies on Migrant health: A Systematic Review and Meta-analysis', (2019) 7 *Lancet Global Health*, p. 435.

122 MC, *supra* note 1, para. 31(e). See WHO, 'Global Action Plan 2019-2023, Promoting the Health of Refugees and Migrants', Doc. A72/25 Rev.1, 02.05.2019, paras. 12 and 26, which seeks 'to assert health as an essential component of refugee assistance and good migration governance' in view of the large number of migrants and refugees who lack access to health care services and the need for international cooperation.

123 EC (2020), COVID-19 Guidance, *supra* note 48.

legal status which attracts different levels of entitlement, although an emphasis was retained on access to emergency COVID-19 care. The European Migration Network (EMN) and Organisation for Economic Co-operation and Development (OECD) report that in several EUMS, irregularly present migrants were entitled to access COVID-19-related emergency health care across a spectrum which included free health care, subsidised health care or health care against payment.[124] Most EUMSs continued to provide emergency health care and essential treatment to all migrants, including those facing removal.[125] In some cases, authorities relaxed administrative rules to encourage irregularly staying migrants to get tested and provided COVID-related emergency health care for free.[126] Yet, as PICUM reports highlight, the trend to extend emergency health care to all migrants, including irregularly staying ones is best contextualised against restrictive pre-COVID-19 policies; in Luxembourg, the 'provision of free COVID-related emergency [care] is more striking', given the previous 'extremely limited access to all forms of care, even emergency care'.[127] Despite the welcome extension of EUMS' health care services to all migrants and refugees, it bears noting that the provision of emergency medical care, as is treatment for COVID-19, is a long-standing obligation under the CEAS for *all* migrants.

Among the EUMSs, Portugal recognised early on that ensuring access to health care for all 'is consistent with a rights-based approach and is also logical from a public health perspective ... [since] restricting access to health care not only puts individuals at risk but also threatens the health and safety of members of their community'.[128] The initiative to extend state support, including health care, to all refugees, applicants for international protection, and those awaiting decisions on residence applications prioritised the health of citizens and non-citizens alike and recognised the symbiotic relationship between the two.[129] Similarly, the inclusion of migrants and refugees, regardless

---

124 The EMN/OECD, 'EU and OECD Member States Responses to Managing Residence Permits and Migrant Unemployment During the COVID-19 Pandemic', 2020, p. 8, available at https://ec.europa.eu/home-affairs/sites/default/files/oo_eu_inform1_residence_permits_and_unemployment_en_updated_final.pdf, last accessed 09.04.2021; refers to Belgium, Estonia, Greece, Finland, Lithuania, Luxembourg, Spain, Poland and Slovakia as extending free health care. See further PICUM, 'Non-exhaustive overview of European government measures impacting undocumented migrants taken in the context of COVID-19', 2020, p. 12, available at https://picum.org/wp-content/uploads/2020/10/Non-exhaustive-overview-of-European-government-measures-impacting-undocumented-migrants-taken-in-the-context-of-COVID-19.pdf, last accessed 09.04.2021.

125 EMN, 'Impact of COVID-19 Pandemic on Voluntary and Forced Return Procedures and Policy Responses', EMN-OECD Inform, 2021, p. 7, available at https://ec.europa.eu/home-affairs/sites/default/files/00_eu_inform5_return_en.pdf, last accessed 11.04.2021.

126 Ibid.

127 PICUM, 'Non-exhaustive Overview', *supra* note 124, p. 12.

128 A. Moore and P. Kortsaris, 'Adaptable Asylum Systems in Portugal in the Context of COVID-19', (2020) *Forced Migration Review*, p. 51.

129 See IOM, 'Portugal's Contribution to the IOM Regional Review', *supra* note 38.

of migration status, in several EUMSs' national vaccination strategies reflect their obligations to respect, promote and fulfil the right to health of all those within their jurisdiction and aligns with both Compacts' commitments to non-discrimination on the basis of migration status in access to basic services, even if their concrete implementation remains to be seen.[130]

Health care provision during COVID-19 is contextualised against pre-existing inequalities which prejudiced migrants' and refugees' access to health care, placing them at heightened risk of infection and, as members of the community, having a concomitant impact on public health. The pandemic affected the continuity of health care services, including routine testing and treatment of other illnesses, which disproportionately affected migrants.[131] The European Centre for Disease Prevention and Control (ECDC)'s Guidance outlines how, in the absence of evidence of higher rates of transmission amongst migrants and refugees, 'environmental factors such as overcrowding in reception and detention centres may increase their exposure to the disease', with pre-existing restricted access to social security systems, to the labour market, and the absence of appropriate accommodation 'exacerbat[ing] the vulnerabilities of migrants and refugees living in reception and detention centres.'[132] The EC acknowledges this heightened risk and includes those in refugee camps among the groups to be prioritised for vaccine delivery.[133]

Yet, entitlement does not equate to effective access. Research highlights migrants feared accessing available health care services due to the potential impact on their rights of residence or exposure to removal action.[134]

---

130 For e.g., PICUM noted Belgium, Finland, France, and the Netherlands made vaccination available to all, including undocumented migrants, although it is not always clear how authorities will reach out to these populations. In contrast, Poland explicitly limits vaccine entitlement to those with a residence permit. See, PICUM, 'The COVID-19 Vaccines and Undocumented Migrants: What Are European Countries Doing?', 11.02.2021, available at https://picum.org/covid-19-vaccines-undocumented-migrants-europe/, last accessed 11.04.2021.

131 T. Burton, 'Tackling TB amidst a Global Crisis' (*UNDP*)', available at https://www.undp.org/content/undp/en/home/blog/2021/tackling-tb-amidst-a-global-crisis.html, last accessed 06.04.2021.

132 ECDC, 'Guidance on Infection Prevention and Control of Coronavirus Disease (COVID-19) in Migrant and Refugee Reception and Detention Centres in the EU/EEA and the United Kingdom', 15.06.2020, available at https://www.ecdc.europa.eu/sites/default/files/documents/COVID-19-guidance-refugee-asylum-seekers-migrants-EU.pdf, last accessed 11.04.2021. See also JRS-Europe, 'From Bad to Worse: COVID-19 Aggravates Existing Gaps in the Reception of Asylum Seekers', 2021, available at https://jrseurope.org/en/resource/from-bad-to-worse/, last accessed 09.04.2021.

133 EC, Communication from the Commission to the European Parliament and the Council Preparedness for COVID-19 vaccination strategies and vaccine deployment, COM(2020) 680 final 15.10.2020.

134 In the WHO, ApartTogether report, *supra* note 107, migrants and refugees shared that their residence status had a significant bearing on their willingness to seek medical care, even when having COVID-symptoms, p. 27.

While the MC stops short of establishing a 'firewall' between service providers and immigration enforcement,[135] States commit not to compromise migrants' 'safe access to basic services or unlawfully infringing upon the human rights to privacy, liberty and security of the person at places of basic service delivery'.[136] Irish authorities recognised the importance of firewall protection in encouraging migrants and refugees with COVID-19 symptoms to come forward and confirmed that health care providers would not share these migrants' data with immigration officers.[137]

5.3. REFUGEES AND MIGRANTS AS CONTRIBUTORS

Simultaneously, some EUMSs harnessed the potential contribution of migrants and refugees to national health care systems. This aligns with the GCR's presentation thereof as contributors to host communities[138] and foresees that states and relevant stakeholders contribute to the capacity development of national health systems, including through opportunities for 'refugees and members of host communities who are or could be engaged as health care workers'.[139] While pre-COVID-19, TCNs formed a sizeable group of workers within several EUMS' health systems, migrants and refugees faced barriers such as administrative hurdles related to the recognition of qualifications.[140] Throughout the pandemic, German medical authorities endorsed initiatives which encouraged migrant and refugee health care professionals to join the COVID-response.[141] The Spanish government fast-tracked the migration status applications of foreign-born doctors and nurses to allow their participation in the health care system.[142] French authorities allowed the recruitment of refugees

135 See E. Guild and T. Basaran (2019), 'Analysis on the Final Draft for the UN Global Compact on Safe, Orderly and Regular Migration' *supra* note 7, objective 15.

136 MC, *supra* note 1, para. 30.

137 Parliamentary Debate (Ireland) on the Health (Preservation and Protection and other Emergency Measures in the Public Interest) Bill 2020: Committee and Remaining Stages, 20.03.2020, p. 390, available at https://data.oireachtas.ie/ie/oireachtas/debateRecord/seanad/2020-03-20/debate/mul@/main.pdf, last accessed 12.07.2021.

138 GCR, *supra* note 1, para. 13 speaks of a programme of action which 'is underpinned by a strong partnership and participatory approach, involving refugees and host communities'.

139 GCR, *supra* note 1, para. 73.

140 UNHCR, 'Council of Europe and UNHCR Support Member States in Bringing Refugee Health Workers Into the COVID-19 Response', 14.04.2020, available at https://www.unhcr.org/uk/news/press/2020/4/5e957e9611/council-europe-unhcr-support-member-states-bringing-refugee-health-workers.html, last accessed 11.04.2021.

141 K. Connelly, 'Germany calls on migrant medics to help tackle coronavirus', *The Guardian*, 14.04.2020, available at https://www.theguardian.com/world/2020/apr/14/germany-calls-on-migrant-medics-to-help-tackle-coronavirus, last accessed 09.04.2021.

142 La Moncloa, 'El Gobierno impulsa la contratación de cerca de 200 profesionales extranjeros en situación regular del sector sanitario ante la crisis del COVID-19', 27.03.2020, available at https://www.lamoncloa.gob.es/serviciosdeprensa/notasprensa/sanidad14/Paginas/2020/270320-contratacion.aspx, last accessed 09.04.2021.

who had previously qualified as health care workers in their countries of nationality but who lacked the documentation usually required for registration purposes.[143] These examples highlight EUMS' incorporation of migrants and refugees within the national COVID-19 effort, as crucial actors in the implementation of the right to health for the entire community.

6. CONCLUSION

The COVID-19 pandemic shed light on the continued practice of some EUMSs to differentiate access to human rights based upon migration status, despite, first, their commitments in the Compacts and, second, the exigencies of the global COVID-19 pandemic. In outlining a framework for the treatment of refugees and migrants, the balancing of human rights protections, on the one hand, and preservation of state sovereign control over borders on the other is evident in both the CEAS and the Compacts. When put under pressure, this balancing of obligations rarely survives implementation, with States resorting to their sovereign powers to justify preventing access to human rights. This policy of discrimination was rendered visible in the EU's treatment of refugees and migrants in the response to COVID-19, which exposed existing fault lines between sovereign border control and respect for human rights in refugee and migrant protection. An examination of the migrant's journey into the EU from arrival (or prevention) to detention and to health care belies the difference in treatment between those seeking access to EU territory, whom EUMSs shut out, as opposed to those already within the territory, whom EUMSs were compelled to treat as one of their own, not least because of the nature of a virus which does not discriminate by migration status.

The treatment of migrants and refugees in the EU during the pandemic varied significantly and, in the absence of a coordinated EU response, largely depended on individual EUMSs. COVID-19 exposed the extent to which EUMS' practice was inconsistent with their existing CEAS obligations and highlighted the existing gap between EU law and its implementation. In some respects, it mirrored pre-existing trends and approaches which, irrespective of COVID-19, already sought to minimise TCNs' access to the territory for the purpose of seeking international protection, as reflected in the closure of borders at pandemic's outset, which EUMSs instrumentalised to negate migrants' and refugees' right

143 Ministiere de L'Interieur, 'Citizen Mobilization: Refugees with Diplomas from Outside the EU can Contribute to the Public Health Service', 14.04.2020, available at https://accueil-integration-refugies.fr/2020/04/14/les-refugies-peuvent-contribuer-au-service-public-de-sante/, last accessed 09.04.2021.

to seek asylum. It is evident in those EUMS' reluctance to treat migrants and refugees as one of their own, by continuing to detain them and expanding the use of immigration detention by reference to COVID-19. In others, it signalled a (cautious) shift away from restrictive laws and policies which limit migrants' effective access to socio-economic rights, with some EUMSs relaxing earlier restrictive measures concerning migrants' access to health care and actively encouraging their access thereto, albeit for the purposes of COVID-19 testing and treatment. Nonetheless, structural inadequacies which continued to fail to adapt services to the specific needs of migrant populations were exacerbated during the pandemic, with a concomitant risk to the health of migrants and host communities.

Moreover, unlike most other human rights obligations which admit of limitation, the prohibition of *refoulement* and the right to seek asylum are absolute obligations under both international and EU law. In addition to affirming states' pre-existing human rights obligations, including *non-refoulement*, the Compacts illustrate how in times of crisis – such as the COVID-19 situation – states committed to seek collaborative ways of working to address migratory movements, in full compliance with human rights obligations. The instrumentalisation of COVID-19 to justify the closure of ports to possible new arrivals by reference to the potential strain on their health care systems belies the collaborative approach under the GCR, through which states can call upon UNHCR and other relevant stakeholders for support in times of crisis and provides a template which eases pressures on EUMSs and benefits both refugees and the wider community. The fragmentation of EUMS' approaches towards migrants and refugees within their pandemic response reneges on their commitments – asserted in 2018 as a contemporary state-led, migrant-specific articulation of rights – to address crises collectively. These fragmented responses belied the existence of a *Common* European Asylum System, despite the Compacts articulating a blueprint ready for deployment in crisis settings.

TECHNOLOGY COMPANIES' DUE DILIGENCE AND THE RESPONSIBILITY TO RESPECT AMID COVID-19

What are Proportionate Means where there is Power and Reliance?

Sabrina RAU*

* Sabrina Rau is a Senior Research Officer in the Human Rights, Big Data and Technology Project, based at the University of Essex. This work was supported by the Economic, Social and Research Council [grant number ES/M010236/1]. The author would like to thank the anonymous reviewers for their helpful comments.

ABSTRACT

Technology companies have played a central role worldwide during the COVID-19 pandemic by assisting states, individuals, businesses and other entities to get through not only a public health crisis but also a socio-economic one. Through an investigation of reliance and corporate power over human rights in the context of COVID-19, this contribution investigates whether current understandings of 'proportionate means' of meeting the responsibility to respect are sufficient and whether considerations of 'enhanced due diligence' are appropriate in this context. Following an exploration of the reliance on, and power of, tech companies during the pandemic, this contribution investigates changes in the factors that determine what proportionate means of meeting the responsibility to respect under Principles 14 and 15 of the United Nations Guiding Principles on Business and Human Rights (UNGPs) look like, including through a power lens. Finally, based on the concept of 'enhanced due diligence' for businesses operating in conflict affected regions, this contribution scopes out similarities to the COVID-19 context and explores the opportunity of employing heightened human rights due diligence in contexts such as COVID-19. Ultimately, this contribution tackles the understudied notion of 'proportionate means', probes the influence that power has on the corporate responsibility to respect, and suggests the need for enhanced due diligence where there is significant change, power and reliance. This does not only bear significance during the pandemic, but can also help develop an enhanced understanding of corporate responsibility and due diligence requirements post-pandemic.

1. INTRODUCTION

COVID-19 was declared a global pandemic by the World Health Organization (WHO) on 11 March 2020. While primarily threatening the right to life and health, the pandemic, and responses to it, have brought about a wide range of effects that negatively impact people's lives and livelihoods.[1] Due to restrictions of the freedom of movement and association in the form of lock downs and quarantine measures, individuals and communities around the world have depended on digital technologies to stay in touch, work and have access to education, information and even health services.[2] Using digital technologies in diverse areas of everyday life is not completely new. The Internet, search engines, social media, video conferencing and cloud computing platforms existed before the pandemic and will continue to play a major role in society after the crisis.

1 United Nations, 'COVID-19 and Human Rights: We are all in this together', 01.04.2020, p. 2, available at https://www.un.org/victimsofterrorism/sites/www.un.org.victimsofterrorism/files/un_-_human_rights_and_Covid_april_2020.pdf, last accessed 21.06.2021.

2 United Nations, 'Shared Responsibility, Global Solidarity: Responding to the Socio-Economic Impacts of COVID-19', 01.03.2020, p. 6, available at https://www.un.org/sites/un2.un.org/files/sg_report_socio-economic_impact_of_Covid19.pdf., last accessed 14.04.2021.

There is one clear difference, however: it used to be a supplement – a choice – at least to some extent. For example, when it comes to access to education, while online learning supplements were increasingly already available before the pandemic, with global investment in education technology (EdTech) reaching US $18.66 billion in 2019. They were a useful supplement rather than an indispensable tool to replace face-to-face learning in schools.[3] Since the start of the pandemic, as many schools were required to close, online and distance learning often appeared to be the only option through which the right to education was enabled.[4] This shift from an optional education enhancement tool to an instrument on which individuals, educational institutions and states rely on for the fulfilment of the right to education makes a distinct difference on the value and influence of the tool and the power and responsibility of those that create it, namely, private companies.

The reliance that states, individuals and business entities have on technology, and tech companies, especially during the pandemic, shows the tremendous opportunities that technology presents not only in contributing to fighting the pandemic, but also in enabling the fulfilment of human rights that would otherwise not be possible, such as the right to education via learning platforms, right to assembly via social media platforms, right to information via social media and online news outlets and the right to work via cloud computing, among others. This reliance on tech companies for the facilitation of rights that cannot be fulfilled in any other way is also associated with the power that companies developing and deploying such influential technology have, namely, 'Big Tech'. While there is no singular, uniform definition of what 'Big Tech' is, acronyms such as GAFAM, referring to Google, Amazon, Facebook, Apple and Microsoft, are commonly used to refer to dominant tech companies in the media and by civil society. They also come under the notion of 'gatekeepers' under the new European Union (EU, the Union) Digital Markets Act proposal, which refers to a company with one or more 'core platform services' and that: (i) 'has a strong economic position, significant impact on the internal market and is active in multiple EU countries'; (ii) 'has a strong intermediation position,' and (iii) 'has (or is about to have) an entrenched and durable position in the market'.[5] For the purposes of this contribution, the term 'Big Tech' will be used to refer to these types of businesses.

---

3 C. Li and F. Lalani, 'The COVID-19 Pandemic has Changed Education Forever. This is How', World Economic Forum, 29.04.2020, available at https://www.weforum.org/agenda/2020/04/coronavirus-education-global-covid19-online-digital-learning/, last accessed 21.06.2021.

4 L. Bicker, 'Coronavirus: How South Korea is Teaching Empty Classrooms', BBC News, 10.04.2020, available at https://www.bbc.com/news/world-asia-52230371, last accessed 21.06.2021.

5 European Commission, 'The Digital Markets Act: ensuring fair and open digital markets', 2020, available at https://ec.europa.eu/info/strategy/priorities-2019-2024/europe-fit-digital-age/digital-markets-act-ensuring-fair-and-open-digital-markets_en, last accessed 21.06.2021.

Alongside reliance on Big Tech for the opportunities that enable human rights, there are, however, also negative impacts on human rights. Human rights harms associated with technology generally fall within two broad categories: (i) harms associated with the use and deployment of these tech products and services; and (ii) harms resulting from a lack of access to these services, as will be discussed in the following section. In regard to potential harms through use, the deployment of artificial intelligence (AI) and diverse data processing practices can pose significant risks to human rights due to a lack of safeguards built into these technologies and a lack of regulation in the sector. The right to privacy, non-discrimination and freedom of expression are most commonly associated with human rights risks of technology.[6] These rights are, however, often referred to as 'gatekeepers' to other rights.[7] Digital technologies, data processing and AI therefore present risks to all human rights. The universality, indivisibility, interdependence and interrelatedness of human rights, as stated in the Vienna Declaration, further highlight this.[8] In the context of COVID-19, for example, data collection and processing of personal data and location data in the interest of stopping the spread of the virus have led to surveillance on entire populations, risking chilling effects and also putting individuals in vulnerable positions at risk.[9] The contact tracing app in South Korea, for example, collected and distributed various kinds of data which was shared not only with health authorities and the government, but also publicly with other citizens, resulting in privacy concerns, as their sexual preferences or activities were exposed, leading to online harassment, loss of business and loss of the right to work.[10] This case exemplifies not only how privacy can be a gateway right to other human rights violations, but also how questions of necessity and proportionality of responses,

---

6 L. McGregor, V. Ng, A. Shaheed et al., 'The Universal Declaration of Human Rights at 70: Putting Human Rights at the Heart of the Design, Development and Deployment of Artificial Intelligence', Human Rights, Big Data and Technology Project, 20.12.2018, pp. 11–14, available at https://www.hrbdt.ac.uk/the-universal-declaration-of-human-rights-at-70-putting-human-rights-at-the-heart-of-the-design-development-and-deployment-of-artificial-intelligence/, last accessed 21.06.2021.

7 Ibid., pp. 11–14.

8 UN General Assembly, 'Vienna Declaration and Programme of Action', 12.07.1993, A/CONF.157/23, para. 5, available at: https://www.refworld.org/docid/3ae6b39ec.html, last accessed 21.06.2021.

9 A. Toh and D. Brown, 'How Digital Contact Tracing for COVID-19 Could Worsen Inequality', Human Rights Watch, 04.06.2020, available at https://www.hrw.org/news/2020/06/04/how-digital-contact-tracing-covid-19-could-worsen-inequality, last accessed 21.06.2021; for further information on chilling effect please see D. Murray and P. Fussey, 'Bulk Surveillance In The Digital Age: Rethinking The Human Rights Law Approach To Bulk Monitoring Of Communications Data', (2019) 52(1), *Israel Law Review*, pp. 43–47.

10 BSR, 'Decisions, Decisions, Decisions', 01.12.2020, pp. 37–38, available at https://www.bsr.org/reports/BSR-Decisions-Rights-Based-Approach-Tech-Data-Public-Health-Emergencies.pdf, last accessed 21.06.2021.

particularly including technology, have not been thoroughly considered in terms of the impacts on human rights.

Although many tech companies were relied on more heavily than ever for their products and services by individuals as well as governments and other businesses, increasing their power at an economic and political level, the changes seen in their policies and attention to human rights has been minimal. According to the UNGPs, every business has a responsibility to respect human rights.[11] The means by which they must know and show they are respecting rights depend, however, on the size, structure, ownership, operational context and severity of harm. Various UN bodies have emphasised the importance of due diligence for companies during the pandemic, with UNDP and UNICEF, for example, providing guidance on due diligence related to a company's work force and supply chain in their 'Rapid Self-Assessment for Business' Guidance. Still, the due diligence we should expect from companies in terms of their products and services has received far less attention. Some scholars, practitioners and civil society groups have called for greater transparency and accountability from tech companies developing and deploying technology.[12]

Mozilla Foundation reported that companies have only been superficially forthcoming about harms or their policies.[13] This is significant as the policies of tech companies and the impact of their products and services can have profound implications on the human rights of millions of people who use the technologies or are subjected to them by state deployment. Pre-COVID-19, the UN special advisory group on digital cooperation already noted that companies have often reacted 'slowly and inadequately to learning that their technologies are being deployed in ways that undermine human rights'.[14] The situation is no different now. Ranking Digital Rights (RDR) reported that in 2020 'none of the 26 companies [RDR] rank[s] – which collectively provide information and communications services to billions of people around the world – came even close to earning a passing grade on [RDRs]

---

11 United Nations, 'Guiding Principles of Business and Human Rights: Implementing the United Nations "Protect, Respect and Remedy" framework', UN Doc HR/PUB/11/04, 2011, available at https://www.ohchr.org/documents/publications/guidingprinciplesbusinesshr_en.pdf, last accessed 21.06.2021.

12 S. Windwehr and J. York, 'Thank You for Your Transparency Report, Here's Everything That's Missing', Electronic Frontier Foundation, 13.10.2020, available at https://www.eff.org/deeplinks/2020/10/thank-you-your-transparency-report-heres-everything-thats-missing, last accessed 21.06.2021.

13 Mozzilla Foundation, 'Internet Health Report 2020', 2021, available at https://2020.internethealthreport.org/, last accessed 21.06.2021.

14 UN Secretary-General's High-level Panel on Digital Cooperation, 'The age of digital interdependence', 26.09.2019, available at https://www.un.org/en/pdfs/DigitalCooperation-report-for%20web.pdf, last accessed 21.06.2021.

international human rights-based standards of transparency and accountability'.[15] While transparency is the key to empowering rights holders and a step towards meeting their business responsibility to respect, accountability can only be achieved if responsibilities are clearly defined.

Given the reliance on Big Tech for the facilitation of rights and their respective power, this contribution argues that power and reliance, in combination with significant and rapid changes in the factors determining proportionate means of meeting the responsibility to respect, point to heightened due diligence requirements for companies in positions of power. This will be demonstrated by first illustrating how Big Tech is relied upon during the pandemic for the facilitation of rights and the power they hold over human rights. Second, the background for corporate responsibility to respect will be provided with a detailed analysis of the underexamined notion of change in the factors that constitute what appropriate 'proportionate means' of meeting the responsibility to respect entail. Finally, using the approach taken by the UN Working Group on Business and Human Rights of 'enhanced human rights due diligence' for businesses in conflict affected regions, the final section will consider similarities of factors and argue for a heightened due diligence responsibility for tech companies where there is significant change, power and reliance, such as during COVID-19, and implications thereof beyond the pandemic.[16]

2. RELIANCE ON, AND POWER OF, TECH COMPANIES

While a wide range of businesses have seen changes due to the pandemic in the way in which they must, and can, operate, the technology sector has had to adapt, too, but in perhaps a different way. While many companies have been struggling to stay afloat during COVID-19, attempting to continue their business in one way or another, tech companies have been thriving, with increased users and profits.[17] The reliance on tech companies in particular

---

15 A. Brouillette, 'Key findings: Companies are improving in principle, but failing in practice', Ranking Digital Rights, available at https://rankingdigitalrights.org/index2020/key-findings, last accessed 21.06.2021.

16 The scope of this contribution will be limited to corporate responsibility as understood by the United Nations Guiding Principles on Business and Human Rights (UNGPs) with a focus exclusively on the responsibility of 'Big Tech' companies.

17 C. Thorbecke, 'The winners in a pandemic economy: Big tech and lockdown essentials soar', abc News, 26.08.2020, available at https://abcnews.go.com/Business/winners-pandemic-economy-big-tech-lockdown-essentials-soar/story?id=72495436, last accessed 21.06.2021; D. Wakabayashi, J. Nicas, S. Lohr et. al., 'Big Tech Could Emerge From Coronavirus Crisis Stronger Than Ever', 23.03.2020, The New York Times, available at https://www.nytimes.com/2020/03/23/technology/coronavirus-facebook-amazon-youtube.html, last accessed 21.06.2021.

has increased tremendously by enabling rights that would not be possible any other way. This reliance that most actors have on these companies comes with great power over human rights in a variety of ways. This section explores these two aspects of reliance and power before considering how they factor into assessments of proportionate means of meeting the responsibility to respect.

2.1. RELIANCE ON BIG TECH

The reliance on technology and Big Tech can be evidenced by (i) the high demand from various actors for tech and corresponding challenges for companies and (ii) the harm that results from having a lack of access to such technologies. Facebook reported that in the first month of the pandemic, total Messenger use increased by over 50% compared to previous months and that 'in those places hit hardest by the virus', the demand for voice and video calling doubled on Facebook Messenger and WhatsApp.[18] While not strictly 'Big Tech', Zoom faced challenges in rapidly scaling up their operations to accommodate millions of new, and diverse users. CEO, Eric Yuan, disclosed that the maximum daily participants up to December 2019 had been 10 million, but that three months later, with the announcement of the global pandemic, the daily participant count was over 200 million.[19] Additionally, not only did the number of participants change dramatically, but so did the type of user of the service. Yuan noted that Zoom was primarily built for 'enterprise customers – large institutions with full IT support', but that since the beginning of COVID-19 the user demographics include several other groups, like children for example, with over 90,000 schools across 20 countries using Zoom to facilitate the continuation of education.[20]

At an individual level, as stated in the introduction, the use of digital products and services allowed for the fulfilment of individual rights that would otherwise not be possible, such as freedom of association, right to education, right to work, access to health care and many more. Additionally, to foster social cohesion, the usual social media platforms remained functional, such as Facebook, Twitter, Instagram, TikTok and many others, however, COVID-specific tech was also integrated into these existing platforms. Community help apps, for example, played a significant role in allowing individuals to create supportive communications and volunteer their time. Facebook's 'community help' feature

---

18 A. Schultz, 'Keeping Our Services Stable and Reliable During the COVID-19 Outbreak', Facebook, 24.04.2020, available at https://about.fb.com/news/2020/03/keeping-our-apps-stable-during-Covid-19/, last accessed 21.06.2021.

19 E. Yuan, 'A Message to Our Users', Zoom Blog, 01.04.2020, available at https://blog.zoom.us/a-message-to-our-users/, last accessed 21.06.2021.

20 Ibid.

for example allows individuals to request and offer assistance during the COVID-19 pandemic.[21]

Governments and international organisations additionally relied on social media and messaging services in particular for disseminating information about the pandemic and to counter misinformation and disinformation about the virus.[22] Content moderation by Facebook, Alphabet (Google) and Twitter were particularly engaged.[23] Keeping at bay conspiracy theories and mis- and disinformation that threaten the right to life are truly essential services that tech companies have been providing in this time. While these companies are working hard at this, there is, however, little known about how they make such decisions.[24] While some companies refer to their community standards, they are not based on international human rights law and create definitions in their own judgement.[25] Furthermore governments relied on Big Tech for COVID-19 response mechanisms through a range of products and services.[26] Contact tracing apps were a key technology for which governments relied on Big Tech, as a new tool that promised to slow the spread of COVID-19, but in reality this

---

21 J. Porter, 'Facebook has a new way for communities to help each other through COVID-19', The Verge, 01.04.2020, available at https://www.theverge.com/2020/4/1/21202580/facebook-community-help-coronavirus-Covid-19-request-offer-help-neighbors, last accessed 21.06.2021.

22 E. Abrusci, S. Dubberley, and L. McGregor, 'An "Infodemic" in the Pandemic: Human Rights and Covid-19 Misinformation', in C. Ferstman and A. Fagan (eds.), *Covid-19, Law and Human Rights: Essex Dialogues. A Project of the School of Law and Human Rights Centre*, University of Essex, Essex 2020.

23 G. Rosen, 'An Update on Our Work to Keep People Informed and Limit Misinformation About COVID-19', Facebook, 16.04.2020, available at https://about.fb.com/news/2020/04/Covid-19-misinfo-update/ last accessed 21.06.2021; K. Jin, 'Keeping People Safe and Informed About the Coronavirus', Facebook, 18.12.2020, available at https://about.fb.com/news/2020/12/coronavirus/#Community-Help, last accessed 21.06.2021.

24 E. Abrusci, S. Dubberley, and L. McGregor (2020), 'Infodemic', *supra* note 22, p. 293; D. Kaye, 'A Conversation with UN Special Rapporteur David Kaye: COVID-19 and Freedom of Expression', Just Security, 21.05.2020, available at https://www.justsecurity.org/70288/a-conversation-with-u-n-special-rapporteur-david-kaye-covid-19-and-freedom-of-expression/, last accessed 21.06.2021.

25 R. Jorgensen, 'What Platforms Mean When They Talk about Human Rights', Policy and Internet, 29.05.2017, pp. 289–292, available at https://onlinelibrary.wiley.com/doi/abs/10.1002/poi3.152, last accessed 21.06.2021; see specific community standards of individual tech companies for more details.

26 The World Economic Forum, in collaboration with the Boston Consulting Group, put forward a white paper on 'leveraging technology to combat Covid-19' in which seven categories were created to organise the types of actions, or 'solutions' as they call it, covering 232 use cases in which technology has been used for COVID-19 response. These categories are information management, detection and containments, health care provider enablement, treatment acceleration, economic resilience, social cohesion, and cyber security. Within these categories are products and services such as contact tracing apps, educational platforms, interactive mapping technologies, Covid-specific content moderation algorithms, communication and knowledge sharing platforms; World Economic Forum, 'Critical Frontier: Leveraging Technology to Combat COVID-19', 01.07.2020, pp. 9–29, available at http://www3.weforum.org/docs/WEF_Critical_Frontier_Leveraging_Technology_Combat_COVID_19_2020.pdf, last accessed 21.06.2021.

technology came with a wide variety of questions and concerns over privacy, surveillance and 'mission creep'.[27]

The fact that that only a few companies control much of the digital infrastructure that is currently used by most entities illustrates their tremendous power in shaping the boundaries of what is acceptable and possible online. The Mozilla Internet Health Report of 2020 found that seven companies control the Internet and its infrastructure and that these are also in the top ten largest companies in the world.[28] This, for example, gives these few big tech companies disproportionate control over the types of apps and solutions that are available, while being subjected to minimal oversight and regulation.[29] To support other actors aiding the COVID-19 response, some companies also offered data-sharing and free access to their intellectual property. A range of tech companies including Amazon, Facebook, International Business Machines Corporation (IBM), Intel and Microsoft, signed the Open Covid Pledge, which makes their 'intellectual property available free of charge for use in the ending of the COVID-19 pandemic and minimising the impact of the disease'.[30] On Apple's website, Apple stated in the context of contact tracing apps in April 2020 that: 'In this spirit of collaboration, Google and Apple are announcing a joint effort to enable the use of Bluetooth technology to help governments and health agencies reduce the spread of the virus, with user privacy and security central to the design.'[31] These various examples demonstrate the reliance that individuals, states and other businesses and organisations had on Big Tech.

While this contribution is focused primarily on the human rights harms associated through the use of technology, the lack of access to technology – and the digital divide specifically – exemplify the flip side of the coin in which the lack of access to technology blocked gateways to the fulfilment of rights that

---

27 Amnesty International, 'Bahrain, Kuwait and Norway contact tracing apps among most dangerous for privacy', 16.06.2020, available at https://www.amnesty.org/en/latest/news/2020/06/bahrain-kuwait-norway-contact-tracing-apps-danger-for-privacy/, last accessed 21.06.2021; Human Rights Watch, 'Covid-19 Apps Pose Serious Human Rights Risks', 13.05.2020, available at https://www.hrw.org/news/2020/05/13/Covid-19-apps-pose-serious-human-rights-risks, last accessed at 21.06.2021; see also Ada Lovelace Institute, 'Exit through the App Store, COVID-19 Rapid Evidence Review', 19.04.2020, available at https://www.adalovelaceinstitute.org/evidence-review/Covid-19-rapid-evidence-review-exit-through-the-app-store/, last accessed 21.06.2021; Article 19, 'UK: Human rights organisations warn that coronavirus measures risk drift to surveillance state', 21.06.2021, available at https://www.article19.org/resources/uk-human-rights-organisations-warn-that-coronavirus-measures-risk-drift-to-surveillance-state/, last accessed 21.06.2021.

28 Mozzilla Foundation (2020), 'Internet Health Report 2020', *supra* note 13.

29 BSR (2020) 'Decisions', *supra* note 10, pp. 19, 40.

30 Open Covid Pledge, 'Make the pledge to share your intellectual property in the fight against COVID-19', available at https://openCovidpledge.org/, last accessed 21.06.2021.

31 Apple, 'Apple and Google partner on COVID-19 contact tracing technology', 10.04.2020, available at https://www.apple.com/ae/newsroom/2020/04/apple-and-google-partner-on-Covid-19-contact-tracing-technology/, last accessed 21.06.2021.

could otherwise not be fulfilled. The digital divide exemplifies harms associated with the lack of access to certain technologies, intensifying the reliance that exists on technologies to facilitate the fulfilment of rights.

The digital divide has demonstrated the extent to which technologies are needed for the fulfilment of rights during COVID-19 specifically. Challenges of accessibility to the Internet and technologies such as mobile devices and computers have highlighted the digital divide and have made evident how a lack of access to the Internet and technology can result in human rights harms. This is apparent around the world, where individuals and communities most at risk lack access to education, work, health and information as a result.[32] The Executive Director of the UN Children's Emergency Fund (UNICEF) stated that 'so many children and young people having no internet at home is more than a digital gap –it is a digital canyon.'[33] Not only are children and economically vulnerable individuals at risk, but also elderly people, refugees and asylum seekers. Additionally, the gender digital divide has put more women at risk, isolating them in situations of domestic violence.[34] The digital divide has also affected the effectiveness of novel contact tracing apps that were developed in response to the pandemic, such as causing false positives or negatives, in omitting large parts of communities in vulnerable positions and further entrenching risks to their human rights.[35] As the Council of Europe Commissioner for human rights said, 'We were not equal before the pandemic, and we have not been equal in the face of it. Those who were poor before it have become poorer; those who were disadvantaged now face even greater disadvantages.'[36] Human rights harm as a result of lack of access to technology therefore demonstrates the reliance on technology for the fulfilment of rights and the unique role of Big Tech.[37]

---

32 L. McGregor and A. Shaheed, 'The Covid-19 Pandemic: Five Urgent Principles for Leaving No One Behind Through Technology', Universal Rights Group, 19.05.2020, available at https://www.universal-rights.org/blog/the-Covid-19-pandemic-five-urgent-principles-for-leaving-no-one-behind-through-technology/, last accessed 21.06.2021.

33 UNICEF, 'Two Thirds of The World's School-Age Children Have No Internet Access at Home, New UNICEF-ITU Report Says', 02.12.2020, available at https://www.unicef.org/romania/press-releases/two-thirds-worlds-school-age-children-have-no-internet-access-home-new-unicef-itu#:~:text=%E2%80%9CThat%20so%20many%20children%20and,Henrietta%20-Fore%2C%20UNICEF%20Executive%20Director, last accessed 21.06.2021.

34 Human Rights, Big Data and Technology Project, 'Bridging the Gender Digital Divide from a Human Rights Perspective', available at https://www.hrbdt.ac.uk/bridging-the-gender-digital-divide-from-a-human-rights-perspective/, last accessed 21.06.2021.

35 Ada Lovelace Institute (2020), 'Exit through the App Store, *supra* note 27, p.30.

36 D. Mijatovic, 'The impact of COVID-19 on human rights and how to move forward', Council of Europe, 10.12.2020, available at https://www.coe.int/en/web/commissioner/-/the-impact-of-covid-19-on-human-rights-and-how-to-move-forward, last accessed 21.06.2021.

37 While understanding harm through questions of accessibility are crucial, they require treatment of respective state responsibility which lies outside the scope of this contribution and will therefore not be covered here.

Understanding reliance in these two ways puts tech companies in a unique position of power that must also be assessed before trying to understand their respective responsibility.

2.2. CORPORATE POWER OVER HUMAN RIGHTS

The reliance of various actors on technology and Big Tech has resulted in their increasing power. While Big Tech was already considered powerful prior to COVID-19, the pandemic has shone a spotlight on the central role and power they exert over human rights. Using David Birchalls' approach of understanding corporate power over human rights, this section demonstrates how Big Tech exerts power over human rights in order to consider the implications thereof in the proportionality assessment of corporate responsibility to respect human rights later in the contribution.

The definition of power used here is one produced by Birchall in the context of power over human rights, which he defines as 'the production, by business enterprises, in and through social relations, of effects that shape the capacities of individuals to enjoy their human rights'.[38] This definition is built on an understanding of power in the fields of political science and international relations and definitions built by Strange and Barnett and Duvall.[39] It moves away from a Weberian understanding of power as the ability to achieve desired outcomes to one that captures the ability of an enterprise 'to shape individuals' human rights realisation, retrogression or possibilities'.[40] Understanding power in this manner is to understand responsibilities not only defined by law, but within a wider socio-economic setting in which laws and norms are created and enforced. Birchalls' approach to power over human rights is significant here as it can help shape a comprehensive understanding of potential human rights impacts both within business operations and relationships, as well as harms as an externality to it.[41] Birchall puts forward a framework of four sites of corporate power over human rights: the power over individuals; the power of materialities; the power over institutions; and the power over knowledge. These four sites of power have the intension of better signifying how a business can have power and influence over the realisation or retrogression of human rights, such as in the context of COVID-19.

---

38 D. Birchall, 'Corporate Power over Human Rights: An Analytical Framework', (2021) 6(1), *Business and Human Rights Journal*, p. 43.

39 Ibid., p. 43.

40 Ibid., p. 43.

41 Ibid., p. 43.

This broader conception of power and potential harm, beyond control that is typically discussed in the business and human rights space, allows for an analysis of responsibilities and means to respect human rights that reaches beyond the cause, contribute, linked relationship to potential and actual human rights harm in the UNGPs. It allows for a more comprehensive understanding of a corporations' position within society among other actors in that system. Taking this understanding of power to influence, the unique position of Big Tech during the pandemic as economically thriving entities upon which other actors are dependent for the realisation of rights gives them power that must be taken into consideration when assessing how they meet that responsibility to respect. The following will be a first attempt to apply Birchall's framework to tech companies during COVID-19 to assess how power, when understood in these ways, might give a better understanding of where 'reliance' and power sit in relation to corporate responsibility and whether these factors need extra consideration in an assessment of proportionate means of meeting the responsibility to respect during the pandemic.[42]

'Power over individuals', based on notions of compulsory power developed by Barnett and Duval, is the power to directly impact individuals' human rights.[43] This may be the most direct form of power applicable in the traditional sphere of business and human rights in the relations that an employer has with employees, a parent company has on a subsidiary and '*de facto* direct power over individuals such as through supply chain intermediaries'.[44] In the context of Big Tech companies during COVID-19 this applies to the thousands of workers employed by companies such as Facebook, Amazon and Google and direct human rights impact on employees both in a physical sense in the way warehouses are managed, but also through policies adopted by a company that inadvertently have effects on human rights, such as digital surveillance of employees through video surveillance, attention tracking and social media monitoring to understand and predict their work habits and productivity.[45] It also, however, covers the 'discursive power' that businesses have in incentivising harmful choices such as through marketing. In the online digital context, an

---

42 'Power of materialities' will be omitted from this analysis as it does not closely fit the analysis of factors nor does it explain the unique power of tech companies during COVID-19.

43 D. Birchall (2021), 'Corporate Power', *supra* note 38, p. 50.

44 Ibid.

45 O. Solon, 'Big Brother Isn't Just Watching: Workplace Surveillance Can Track Your Every Move', The Guardian, 06.11.2017, available at https://www.theguardian.com/world/2017/nov/06/workplace-surveillance-big-brother-technology, last accessed 21.06.2021; D. West, 'How Employers Use Technology to Surveil Employees', Brookings, 05.01.2021, available at https://www.brookings.edu/blog/techtank/2021/01/05/how-employers-use-technology-to-surveil-employees/ last accessed 21.06.2021; K. Rodriguez and S. Windwehr, 'Workplace Surveillance in Times of Corona', Electronic Frontier Foundation, 10.09.2020, available at https://www.eff.org/deeplinks/2020/09/workplace-surveillance-times-corona, last accessed 21.06.2021.

example of this may be nudging and dark patterns related to consent, in which rights holders are 'nudged' to agree to 'community standards' dictated by digital platforms and opt into data processing and personalisation practices that waive, to some extent, an individual's right to privacy in the first instance but can have detrimental impacts on a whole range of rights.[46] While autonomy and choice are central to this conversation, the practices by businesses to shape the choices in the interest of profit prompts the question as to their responsibility in respecting human rights. Questions pertaining to limitations of choice, particularly in the COVID-19 context where various actors rely on certain companies and technologies, must be considered as part of the consideration of their corporate responsibility.

'Power over Institutions' include, for Birchall, lobbying, 'structural power of free-moving capital's advantage over jurisdictionally bounded states' and privatisation.[47] When it comes to lobbying particularly, the Big Tech companies, Amazon, Apple, Facebook, Google and Microsoft, cumulatively spent US $61.09 million in the US in 2020 on a range of issues including privacy, content moderation, advertising models and antitrust issues, as well as COVID-19 legislation.[48] Similarly, while spending on lobbying in the EU context was lower than in the US, the cumulative sum of €19 million invested in lobbying in Brussels was unlike any lobbying efforts seen by private actors in the European space.[49] While Big Tech has been in the hot seat throughout 2020 with antitrust cases, in the European context there has been little success of such efforts to date, as European leaders continue to see Big Tech companies as 'threats to democracy and anticompetitive' feeling a need to rein them in.[50] The Digital Service Act and Digital Markets Act exemplify the emergence of regulation to rein in these powers.[51] The unprecedented and increasing influence that Big Tech companies are seeking in this area of law enforcement can have serious consequences on future regulation on data processing, AI and new tech, weighing in the interest of profit and private actors over the protection of human

---

46 S. Leader and S. Rau, 'Background Paper on Consent Online', Human Rights, Big Data and Technology Project, available at https://www.hrbdt.ac.uk/download/background-paper-on-consent/, last accessed 21.06.2021; see also S. Deva, *Regulating Corporate Human Rights Violations: Humanizing Business*, Routledge, London 2012.

47 D. Birchall (2021), 'Corporate Power', *supra* note 38, p. 58.

48 J. Chung, 'Big Tech, Big Cash: Washington's New Power Players', PublicCitizen, 24.03.2021, available at https://www.citizen.org/article/big-tech-lobbying-update/, last accessed 21.06.2021.

49 A. Satariano and M. Stevis-Grindness, 'Big Tech Turns Its Lobbyists Loose on Europe, Alarming Regulators', The New York Times, 14.12.2020, available at https://www.nytimes.com/2020/12/14/technology/big-tech-lobbying-europe.html, last accessed 21.06.2021.

50 Ibid.

51 European Commission, 'The Digital Service Act package', 2020, available at https://digital-strategy.ec.europa.eu/en/policies/digital-services-act-package, last accessed 21.06.2021.

rights by states and respect for human rights by businesses. The tremendous power over institutions that companies are wielding in the tech space and the increasing spending in lobbying also on COVID-19 legislation illustrate the power and influence these companies have in shaping the environment in which decisions are made on red lines, safeguards and permissible interferences with human rights. This is, of course, true not only in the context of COVID-19 and will become increasingly important even after the pandemic. An additional consideration in power over institutions is how the fulfilment of private actors, like social media companies, of public functions like online policing in content moderation can constitute power over institutions, given the power the social media companies have in shaping what content is permissible on their platform and how hate speech is defined, for example. Such setting of standards also wields tremendous power normatively in what is perceived as acceptable by a wider audience. In the context of COVID-19, as mentioned earlier, it was governments that heavily relied on social media giants to counter mis- and disinformation to protect the right to life of millions of individuals present online. This also related to power over knowledge, as will be discussed below.

'Power over knowledge and norms in human rights' is a unique form of power that Birchall describes which 'cannot be linked to any outcome that could be termed a human rights impact or any other form of breach'.[52] Aspects of this power include the power for a business to define its own scope of responsibilities and to legitimise its own authority as a human rights actor as well as defining the scope of individual rights. The example Birchall gives of this is the allegation that Facebook's content moderation algorithm helped stoke anti-Rohingya sentiments in Myanmar, leading to the normalisation of hateful views and facilitating actors of violence against Rohingya and other Muslim communities in Myanmar.[53] In the first aspect of power over knowledge, companies define how to address human rights. Flexibility is given within the UNGPs for companies on how to prevent, mitigate and remedy actual and potential human rights impact, but how they are translated into the internal functioning of a business is unique and individual to each business itself. This, however, also means that in multi-stakeholder dialogues where businesses engage with civil society and academics, for example, flow of information occurs in two ways: first from human rights practitioners and academics to businesses on the promotion and protection of human rights, and second from business to civil society on information and educating about how business views respect to human rights and approaches taken to prevent, mitigate and remedy harm.[54] In such dialogues,

---

52 D. Birchall (2021), 'Corporate Power', *supra* note 38, p. 61.

53 C. Fink, 'Dangerous Speech, Anti-Muslim Violence, and Facebook in Myanmar', (2018) 71(1.5), *Journal of International Affairs*, pp. 43–52.

54 D. Birchall (2021), 'Corporate Power', *supra* note 38, p. 62; C. Scheper, 'From Naming and Shaming to Knowing and Showing': Human Rights and the Power of Corporate Practice', (2015) 19(6), *The International Journal of Human Rights*, pp. 737, 738.

due to the unique knowledge that the business has over its internal processing and challenges, the business gives authority to its own role of practising human rights due diligence and may normalise aspects of this within the sector.

Furthermore, the 'managerialism of human rights' allows companies to set own priorities and exclusion of their work including along 'social purpose lines'.[55] This may be seen in voluntary donations made to certain causes or campaigns advocating for human rights and social and environmental causes that are important for the progressive realisation of rights, but not central to the business operations of a particular company. An example of this is Facebook's donations to bridging the digital divide and supporting small businesses through its grants.[56] While such applaudable efforts can lead directly to the fulfilment and protection of human rights, they do not 'offset' or 'balance out' shortcomings within a company itself for actual and potential human rights harm it may cause, contribute to or be linked to. As Birchall states, 'Progressive agendas can be conceived as an attempt to build political capital that can be used to stultify critique over other issues more directly connected to profits. Human rights responsibilities are proving acceptable insofar as they do not hurt the share price.'[57] Such measures can have an influence on public perception of a firm and help their 'trustworthiness'.[58] The pandemic in this way has been used as an opportunity by some tech companies to place themselves as trustworthy partners and helpers in times of crisis by providing tools individuals, business and states need to continue to have some normalcy of life.

Having considered how tech companies hold power over human rights in Birchall's framework and how they are relied on for the fulfilment of rights during COVID-19, their particular role in the context of COVID-19 can be described as powerful and significantly influential. Beyond power over

---

55 D. Birchall (2021), 'Corporate Power', *supra* note 38, p. 62; S. Green, 'Going Beyond Ethics and Compliance: The Growing Corporate Movement to Embrace Social Value Creation', 2018 49(3), *Loyola University Chicago Law Journal*, p. 573; F. Wettstein and D. Baur, '"Why Should We Care about Marriage Equality?": Political Advocacy as a Part of Corporate Responsibility', (2016) 138, *Journal of Business Ethics*, p. 208.

56 Facebook, 'Partnering with ITDRC and NetHope to Address the Digital Divide', 22.04.2020, available at https://about.fb.com/news/2020/12/coronavirus/#Community-Help, last accessed at 21.06.2021; Nethope, 'Nethope Partners With Facebook Connectivity To Increase Internet Access During Covid-19', 22.04.2020, available at https://nethope.org/2020/04/22/nethope-partners-with-facebook-connectivity-to-increase-internet-access-during-Covid-19/, last accessed 21.06.2021; Facebook, 'Helping Small Businesses', 02.04.2020, available at https://about.fb.com/news/2020/12/coronavirus/#small-business-investment, last accessed 21.06.2021.

57 D. Birchall (2021), 'Corporate Power', *supra* note 38, p. 63.

58 H. Sareen, 'An Economy of Trust: How Transparency Is Changing the Tech Industry', Wired, 2015, available at https://www.wired.com/insights/2015/03/economy-trust-transparency-changing-tech-industry/, last accessed 21.06.2021.

individual rights, power and reliance in these three categories should factor into current considerations of what should be expected from tech companies during COVID-19 and what proportionate means of meeting the responsibility to respect should entail in this context.

3. 'PROPORTIONATE MEANS' OF MEETING THE RESPONSIBILITY TO RESPECT

Assessing corporate responsibility includes understanding what proportionate means of meeting the responsibility to respect entail. Following some background on corporate responsibility under the UNGPs, this section investigates changes in the factors determining what appropriate 'proportionate means' involve in the context of COVID-19. By incorporating findings from the previous section on the role of reliance and power, the key arguments put forward here are that (i) the factors in the UNGP's determination means of respect should not be seen as stagnant, but rather in a state of change, and that (ii) power and reliance must be factored into assessments of proportionality. This will raise the question of whether rapid or significant change in any of these factors can or should trigger heightened due diligence obligations.

3.1. RESPONSIBILITY OF BUSINESSES UNDER THE UNGPs

The UNGPs were developed by the Special Representative of the Secretary-General on the issue of 'human rights and transnational corporations and other business enterprises'.[59] They were endorsed by the Human Rights Council in 2011 and thereby have been affirmed by UN Member States. The UNGPs do not create new substantive human rights obligations, but rather, enshrine states' obligations to protect human rights from third-party harm and articulate businesses' responsibilities to respect human rights and provide effective remedy.[60] The UNGPs do not impose new obligations on actors, but instead reinforce existing obligations found under international human rights law. The UNGPs are divided into three pillars: (i) the state duty to protect human rights; (ii) the corporate responsibility to respect human rights; and (iii) access to remedy.[61] Additionally, the UN Working Group of Business and Human Rights was established to promote and support the implementation of the UN Guiding

[59] UN (2011), 'Guiding Principles', *supra* note 11.

[60] J. Ruggie, 'The Social Construction of the UN Guiding Principles on Business & Human Rights', HKS Working Paper Series, Harvard University, 12.06.2017, p. 1, available at https://papers.ssrn.com/sol3/papers.cfm?abstract_id=2984901, last accessed 14.04.2021.

[61] UN (2011), 'Guiding Principles', *supra* note 11.

Principles. Taking stock at the decennial anniversary of the UNGPs this year, remarkable developments included the increase in uptake by states of mandatory human rights due diligence measures such as in France and Germany.[62]

Under the UNGPs all businesses have a responsibility to respect human rights. This means that they should prevent, mitigate and address any actual or potential adverse human rights impact they may have caused, contributed to or are linked to.[63] This includes human rights impacts within their business operations, supply chains and business relationships, as well as impacts on individuals and communities that may be adversely affected by their products and services. In this way, the UNGPs provide an accountability framework based on prevention, oversight, monitoring and remedies for victims.

Businesses respect human rights by conducting human rights due diligence, which is the ongoing process whereby a company assesses its human rights impacts, acts upon the findings, transparently reports on its prevention and mitigation efforts and provides effective remedies to affected rights-holders.[64] Respecting human rights is not only good for rights-holders, but can also support businesses in building consumer trust and mitigating future legal liability.[65] As confirmed by the UN Working Group on Business and Human Rights in its COVID-19 statement: 'human rights due diligence is key to ensuring that any risks to people are identified and mitigated'.[66] The notion of due diligence as found in the UNGPs can also be found at regional level in new and upcoming regulations such as the EU Digital Service Act and Digital Markets Act proposals, which suggest 'asymmetric due diligence obligations on different types of digital service providers'.[67]

While the responsibility to respect human rights applies to all businesses regardless of the sector, size, operational context, ownership and structure, these factors, in combination with severity of harm, do determine the 'scale and

62 D. Sharma and F. Kaps, 'Human Rights Due Diligence Legislation in Europe – Implications for Supply Chains to India and South Asia', DLA Piper, 26.03.2021, available at https://www.dlapiper.com/en/southafrica/insights/publications/2021/03/human-rights-due-diligence-legislation-in-europe/, last accessed 21.06.2021.

63 UN (2011), 'Guiding Principles', *supra* note 11, principle 13.

64 UN (2011), 'Guiding Principles', *supra* note 11, principle 17.

65 G. Kangeson, 'Arguing the Business Case for Respecting Human Rights', DLA Piper, 04.11.2016, available at https://www.dlapiper.com/en/australia/insights/publications/2016/11/arguing-the-business-case-for-human-rights/, last accessed 21.06.2021.

66 United Nations Working Group on Business and Human Rights, 'Ensuring that Business Respects Human Rights during the Covid-19 Crisis and Beyond: The Relevance of the UN Guiding Principles on Business and Human Rights', available at https://www.ohchr.org/EN/NewsEvents/Pages/DisplayNews.aspx?NewsID=25837&LangID=E, last accessed 21.06.2021.

67 European Commission, Proposal for a Regulation of the European Parliament and of the Council on a Single Market For Digital Services (Digital Services Act) and amending Directive 2000/31/EC, COM(2020) 825 final 15.12.2020, p. 6.

complexity of the means' through which a business meets that responsibility.[68] This means that companies must have measures in place that are proportionate and appropriate to the factors listed above.

UNGP Principle 14:

> The responsibility of business enterprises to respect human rights applies to all enterprises regardless of their size, sector, operational context, ownership and structure. Nevertheless, the scale and complexity of the means through which enterprises meet that responsibility may vary according to these factors and with the severity of the enterprise's adverse human rights impacts.[69]

UNGP Principle 15:

> In order to meet their responsibility to respect human rights, business enterprises should have in place policies and processes appropriate to their size and circumstances, including:
>
> (a) A policy commitment to meet their responsibility to respect human rights;
> (b) A human rights due diligence process to identify, prevent, mitigate and account for how they address their impacts on human rights;
> (c) Processes to enable the remediation of any adverse human rights impacts they cause or to which they contribute.[70]

The working group has noted that due diligence 'is commensurate with risk' and 'is appropriate to an enterprise's circumstances'.[71] Various National Action Plans (NAP), have also directly addressed Principle 14, such as those of Belgium and Norway, Sweden and Switzerland, which reiterate that the responsibility to respect applies to all businesses, although the criteria of how they do so vary.[72]

While the UNGPs are high-level, responding to the needs of all actors and giving sufficient flexibility for actors to adopt the principles into their practice, clear challenges have been identified by companies in adopting them and putting these to practice.[73] Questions around what sufficient and

---

68 UN (2011), 'Guiding Principles', *supra* note 11, principle 14.

69 UN (2011), 'Guiding Principles', *supra* note 11, principle 14.

70 UN (2011), 'Guiding Principles', *supra* note 11, principle 15.

71 United Nations Working Group on Business and Human Rights, 'Companion note I to the Working Group's 2018 report to the General Assembly', UN Doc A/73/163, 16.10.2018, p. 7, available at https://www.ohchr.org/Documents/Issues/Business/Session18/CompanionNote1DiligenceReport.pdf, last accessed 21.06.2021.

72 National Action Plans on Business and Human Rights, 'Guiding Principle 14', available at https://globalnaps.org/ungp/guiding-principle-14/, last accessed 21.06.2021.

73 D. Allison-Hope, 'Human Rights Assessments in the Decisive Decade: Applying UNGPs in the Technology Sector', BSR, 11.02.2020, available at https://www.bsr.org/en/our-insights/blog-view/human-rights-assessments-in-the-decisive-decade-ungp-challenges-technology, last accessed 21.06.2021.

appropriate safeguards might mean are often grey areas. Most often when proportionate means of meeting the responsibility to respect are addressed in the business and human rights context, it is in the context of small and medium enterprises (SMEs) as opposed to corporations that fall on the larger side of transnational actors.[74] While the responsibility to respect applies to all businesses, the means of how a business meets its responsibility can differ dramatically according to a change in the factors. It is interesting therefore in this context, and specifically with powerful tech companies that are heavily relied on for the fulfilment of some human rights, to investigate how the factors determining what proportionate means of meeting their responsibility to respect human rights can look like given their unique position amid the pandemic. This is useful not only during COVID-19, but also beyond, in a global environment where change is constant both within businesses and in their operational contexts.

3.2. CHANGES IN FACTORS DETERMINING WHAT CONSTITUTE 'PROPORTIONATE MEANS'

Understanding that the size, sector, operational context, ownership, structure and severity of harm of an enterprise's adverse human rights impact affects the means by which a company is expected to meet its responsibility to respect, this section investigates change in these factors as a result of the pandemic to determine whether a heightened human rights due diligence requirement may be appropriate. The reason these factors are essential to assess is to demonstrate that businesses, and especially Big Tech companies, are not static but constantly evolving in various ways that change the actual and potential adverse human rights impacts they may cause, contribute or be linked to. In the context of a state of emergency, public health crisis or this pandemic specifically, this is crucial to understand in order to assess the responsibility that businesses have and their capacity to deal with expected and unexpected changes within their operations and business relationships in the future. The following details the factors for which a significant change can be observed in Big Tech during COVID-19.[75]

---

74 For example, European Union, 'SMEs and the Responsibility to Respect Human Rights', 2019, available at https://shiftproject.org/wp-content/uploads/2020/01/index.pdf, last accessed 21.06.2021.

75 Ownership and structure have been omitted from this list as there has been no observable difference according to publicly available information. Observable changes may occur internally at companies, but due to lack of transparency and reporting, it is currently not feasible to see changes.

3.2.1. Size

The size of a business will often influence the kinds of approaches it can take to meet its responsibility.[76] The UNGP Interpretive Guidance gives the example of the difference of small enterprises versus large enterprises, where large enterprises are more likely to have complex systems and procedures in place for communication, decision-making, control and oversight. Their value chain relationships are more complex, as opposed to smaller businesses which have less capacity and more informal processes.[77] This does not always have to be the case, however, as the severity of impact plays a significant role in determining the types of processes a company must have in place to respect human rights, as will be discussed later in this section.

It is interesting to note here that while size is noted as a factor determining process and procedure, it does not account for responsibility associated with change in size. In the example of Zoom given earlier in this contribution, the company experienced massive growth within a very short time frame, and questions of capacity in meeting consumer demands of services were quickly addressed as was reported publicly. However, information about their due diligence process or new or renewed human rights impact assessment seemed to lack transparency. While many of the Big Tech companies discussed in this contribution already had millions of users or customers, the pandemic nevertheless further increased the use of these services. A summary report by WeAreSocial and Hootsuite showed that from January 2020 to January 2021, the number of Internet users worldwide increased by 7%, and active social media users increased by 9.2%.[78] This rise in users coincided with many companies increasing the number of employees and high profits allowing for growth.[79] These changes in size should be seen in the context of growing power and potentially increased responsibility. A change in size should constitute a trigger for renewed evaluation of whether the company is meeting its responsibility to respect, particularly if it is a significant change over a short amount of time.

3.2.2. Sector and Operational Context

The interpretive guidance to the UNGPs states that the sector and operational context in which a business operates will typically determine which human

---

[76] UN, 'The Corporate Responsibility to Respect Human Rights: An Interpretive Guide', UN Doc HR/PUB/12/02, 2012, p. 19, available at https://www.ohchr.org/Documents/Issues/Business/RtRInterpretativeGuide.pdf, last accessed 21.06.2021.

[77] Ibid., pp. 19–20.

[78] S. Kemp, 'Digital 2020: 3.8 Billion People Use Social Media', WeAreSocial, 30.01.2020, available at https://wearesocial.com/digital-2020, last accessed 21.06.2021.

[79] E. Dwoskin, 'Tech giants are profiting – and getting more powerful – even as the global economy tanks', The Washington Post, 27.04.2020, available at https://www.washingtonpost.com/technology/2020/04/27/big-tech-coronavirus-winners/, last accessed 20.06.2021.

rights it is at greatest risk of having an impact on.[80] The sector in which the business operates determines the types of activities it conducts and associated risks. In the context of the technology sector, as stated earlier in this contribution, the harms typically associated are related to the right to privacy, non-discrimination and freedom of expression – but reach much further.[81] It is also important to consider the sectors in which the businesses' products and services are used. In the context of COVID-19, for example, while the sector of Big Tech itself has not changed, the use of tech products and services has expanded to numerous new sectors and to different scales. Digitalisation of government services was already a factor before COVID-19, yet the uptake of digitalised solutions supported by tech companies was unprecedented.[82] Communication and social media platforms uptake by a range of other sectors and industries to promote social cohesion and allow continuation of work in a wide range of fields allowed some sense of normalcy in a time when it was not possible another way.

The context factor is perhaps one of the most significant in determining what proportionate means of meeting the responsibility to respect looks like in the context of the pandemic, due to serious changes to operational context in a variety of ways. The operational context includes the environment in which companies work and the nature of the relationship in which they are involved. This includes environmental, social, economic, political and legal factors that determine how a business functions within this operational context and the potential impact it has. As many places of work, education and social life were closed for safety measures, companies faced three challenges: (i) navigating their own businesses operations and adapting to most of their employees working from home while ensuring all services were running; (ii) meeting new demands for the products and services in a context where virtually all industries and sectors depend on their functioning; and (iii) operating in a context with little state regulation or even environments where states derogate from certain human rights in declaring a state of emergency.[83]

In regard to the first element of navigating changes within their own business operations, COVID-19 has brought about major shifts in operational context not only for Big Tech, but for most businesses worldwide, especially in the way the expectations of day-to-day business moved away from office

---

80 UN (2012), 'Interpretive guidance', *supra* note 76, p. 20.

81 L. McGregor, V. Ng, A. Shaheed et al. (2018), 'UDHR at 70', *supra* note 6, pp. 11–14.

82 The Economist, 'Covid-19 is Spurring the Digitisation of Government', 05.09.2020, available at https://www.economist.com/international/2020/09/01/covid-19-is-spurring-the-digitisation-of-government, last accessed 21.06.2021.

83 A. Greene, 'State of emergency: how different countries are invoking extra powers to stop the coronavirus', The Conversation, 31.03.2020, available at https://theconversation.com/state-of-emergency-how-different-countries-are-invoking-extra-powers-to-stop-the-coronavirus-134495, last accessed 20.06.2021.

settings and face-to-face meetings to working and communicating through digital technologies. This aspect has been no different for tech companies, who have had to overcome numerous challenges that come with a workforce working from home rather than an office space, such as content moderators. Second, as individuals, states and other businesses increasingly rely on tech companies to fulfil rights that are otherwise impossible to fulfil as a result of the pandemic, as was demonstrated in the section on reliance on Big Tech, the context and the central role the companies played should be significant in determining proportionate means related to context.

Third, the operational context also includes the regulatory and political context in which it operates. While many tech companies already face challenges pre-pandemic with the lack of regulation, such as lacking data protection regulations in many states in which they operate, the pandemic and the move to tech solutionism without adequate legal protection in place placed a greater burden on tech companies to understand their responsibility to respect human rights and potential adverse impacts that the technology could cause in this unprecedented context. Additionally, with some states derogating from certain rights, declaring a state of emergency and/or resorting to the use of emergency powers, human rights protections provided by a state are lowered significantly, affecting the context in which the business operates.[84] A state of public emergency is defined as 'an exceptional situation of crisis or public danger, actual or imminent, which affects the whole population or the whole population of the area to which the declaration applies and constitutes a threat to the organised life of the community of which the state is composed'.[85] As associated emergency powers often run the risk of being abused, in the case of state business relationships, business must take special care that they continue to respect international human rights conventions, even if the state in which they operate does not.[86] This puts businesses in a challenging position in using their knowledge and leverage to ensure that the technology they create and share or sell does not cause human rights violations down the line. In the case of contact tracing apps for example, many concerns arose not only about privacy, but about the disproportionate and unnecessary use of these technologies in the first place which had not been tested, nor had sufficient safeguards in place to ensure human rights were protected if used by governments.[87]

---

84 A. Lebret, 'COVID-19 pandemic and derogations to human rights', (2020) 7(1), *Journal of Law and the Biosciences*, pp. 1–15; M. Scheinin, 'COVID-19 Symposium: To Derogate or Not to Derogate', *Opinio Juris*, 06.04.2020, available at http://opiniojuris.org/2020/04/06/Covid-19-symposium-to-derogate-or-not-to-derogate/, last accessed 21.06.2021.

85 BSR (2020), 'Decisions' *supra* note 10, p. 22.

86 A. Radjenovic and G. Eckert, 'Upholding Human Rights in Europe during the Pandemic', European Parliament, 2020, available at https://www.europarl.europa.eu/thinktank/en/document.html?reference=EPRS_BRI(2020)652085, last accessed 21.06.2021.

87 See Ada Lovelace Institute (2020), 'Exist through the app, *supra* note 27.

The rapid and unprecedented change in operational context thus requires companies to consider their role and power and how the impact of existing products and services might have changed in relation to that context, as well as new risks for end use of products and services. All these changes in sector and operational context point to an elevated need for companies to careful conduct their due diligence and assess the actual and potential impact in this rapidly changing context to ensure they respect human rights throughout their business operations and relationships.

3.2.3. *Severity and Probability of Harm*

Perhaps the most important of factors in determining the appropriate means of meeting the responsibility of tech companies to respect human rights is severity of harm. The UNGPs define severity of harm as being judged by their 'scale, scope and irremediable character'.[88] Here the scale refers to 'the gravity of the impact', while the scope refers to 'the number of individuals that are or will be affected'.[89] The irremediable character refers to 'the ability to restore those affected to a situation at least the same as, or equivalent to, their situation before the adverse impact'.[90] There is a range of factors that can also affect the 'remediability' of a particular harm. This can include the timeframe in which an action can be reversed or remedied.

Because not only actual but also potential human rights impacts must be considered, probability of the harm occurring should also be included in the question of severity, as not necessarily all harms are immediately known – but actors should try to be foresee such harms so they can be prevented.[91] Understanding the severity and probability of harm is significant to determining how a company might need to prioritise efforts to prevent, mitigate and address adverse human rights impacts, as well as the types of structures it must have in place to show that it is respecting human rights.

Interestingly, the interpretive guidance for the UNGPs states that severity 'should not be seen as an absolute concept, but as relative to the other human rights impacts the enterprise has identified'.[92] While this is important mostly when it comes to questions of prioritisation within a business, this factor should also be considered in a wider context. Questions pertaining, for example, to the cumulative impact beyond individual right harms that the use

---

88 UN (2011), 'Guiding principles', *supra* note 11, p. 15; UN (2012), 'Interpretive guide', *supra* note 76, p. 19.

89 UN (2012), 'Interpretive guide', *supra* note 76, p. 19.

90 UN (2012), 'Interpretive guide', *supra* note 76, p. 19.

91 OHCHR, 'Identifying and Assessing Human Rights Risks related to End-Use; a B-Tech Foundational Paper', B-Tech Project, pp. 1–8, available at https://www.ohchr.org/Documents/Issues/Business/B-Tech/identifying-human-rights-risks.pdf, last accessed 21.06.2021.

92 UN (2012), 'Interpretive guide', *supra* note 76, p. 26.

of a product and service can have on society as a whole must be considered. In the context of targeted advertising, for example, a business can have direct impact on an individual's right to privacy and non-discrimination, but can have a cumulative effect on a whole community or society.[93] Harms here can occur not only through the practice of the business model allowing such targeted advertising, but also through responses in trying to solve this problem, such as with excessive content moderation strategies that consequently affect freedom of expression and which may have in a chilling effect.[94] In the context of the deployment of AI in targeted political advertising, it can have an effect not only on an individual's right to privacy, freedom of expression and the right to take part in the conduct of public affairs, but also on society as a whole.[95]

When it comes to 'remediability' of harms, content moderation provided a great example of the far-reaching and diverse impacts that mis- and disinformation, as well as policies to counter mis- and disinformation, can have on human rights and its remediability. In the context of content moderation, the remediability of harm often is associated with the timeframe in which something can either be removed or appealed and reactivated. Mis- and disinformation regarding public health have resulted in severe human rights harm, such as in Iran, for example, where as a result of misinformation about injecting methanol and alcohol based sanitisers to protect against the virus, over 300 people died and over 1,000 people became sick, directly affecting the right to life.[96] When it comes to 'remediability' due to the absolute and finite nature on the right to life, and the irremediability to return the individual to a position in which they were prior to the harm, this type of harm can be considered severe.

---

93 Ranking Digital Rights, 'Human Rights Risk Scenarios: Targeted Advertising', 2019, available at https://rankingdigitalrights.org/wp-content/uploads/2019/02/Human-Rights-Risk-Scenarios-targeted-advertising.pdf, last accessed 21.06.2021; N. Marechal, 'Targeted Advertising Is Ruining the Internet and Breaking the World', VICE, 16.11.2018, available at https://www.vice.com/en/article/xwjden/targeted-advertising-is-ruining-the-internet-and-breaking-the-world, last accessed 21.06.2021.

94 Article 19, 'European Court of Human Rights: the use of government hacking "represents one of the greatest threats to fundamental rights in the digital age"', 19.09.2019, available at https://www.article19.org/resources/european-court-of-human-rights-the-use-of-government-hacking-represents-one-of-the-greatest-threats-to-fundamental-rights-in-the-digital-age/#:~:text=The%20use%20of%20government%20surveillance,organising%20or%20supporting%20protests%20online, last accessed 21.06.2021.

95 For an example see, M. Saccaro, 'The Secret Experiment Behind Facebook's "I voted' Sticker"', Mic, 04.11.2014, available at https://www.mic.com/articles/103350/the-secret-experiment-behind-facebook-s-i-voted-sticker#.aEtJHDbgT, last accessed 21.06.2021.

96 C. Roger, 'Media Misinformation that Led to 300 Deaths in Iran Claimed that Drinking Methanol was a Cure for COVID-19', Tech Times, 29.03.2020, available at https://www.techtimes.com/articles/248428/20200329/social-media-misinformation-that-led-to-300-deaths-in-iran-claimed-drinking-methanol-was-a-cure-for-Covid-19.htm, last accessed 21.06.2021; see also A. Coleman, '"Hundreds dead" because of Covid-19 misinformation', BBC News, 12.08.2020, available at https://www.bbc.com/news/world-53755067, last accessed 21.06.2021.

A good example in terms of harm through policies to respond to mis- and disinformation is through responses to human moderators being required to stay home during the pandemic. As a result, thereof, some companies increasingly deployed algorithms more extensively to review content. A difference in Facebook's and YouTube's approaches, for example, was that Facebook 'shut off' its appeals option while YouTube kept it enabled and put further resources into reviewing appeals and restoring content.[97] In this scenario, Facebook turning off its appeals process made it impossible for millions of users who increasingly flocked to Facebook to appeal moderation decisions at all.[98] In comparison, although the same change of sending human content moderators home affected YouTube's content moderation policies, when it came to the appeals process due to the employment of AI and an anticipation that it might lead to more wrongful removals and therefore appeals from users, YouTube was able to restore many of the videos on which there were appeals.[99] This demonstrates how the type of business response can change the severity of impact.

When looking specifically at the scale and scope of actual and potential human rights harm, due to the increasing number of users of digital platforms and products, one might reach the conclusion that the probability of potential harm increases as increasing and diverse individuals use and are dependent on a particular product or service. Investigating closely the criteria of severity of harm thus suggests that the types of harm associated with the use of tech is not completely new, but that the scale of the potentially affected rights-holder has drastically and rapidly increased, along with an increased scope of harm due to technologies being used for new purposes, by new users and in new sectors. Therefore the probability of potential human rights harm is increased and must be taken into consideration when considering what appropriate means of meeting the responsibility to respect entail.

3.3. CONTEXTUALISING POWER AND RELIANCE AMONG PROPORTIONALITY FACTORS

Having considered the factors as they appear in the UNGPs, it might seem that power is an implied component of several of the factors considering there appears to be a direct correlation between increase in any of these factors with what would be expected of a company in order to meet the responsibility to respect. The power over human rights, however, exceeds this. The UNGPs to some extent consider influence that a company has through the notion of leverage: 'Leverage

97 J. Rydzak and E. Renieris, 'Context before code: Protecting human rights in a state of emergency', Ranking Digital Rights, available at https://rankingdigitalrights.org/index2020/spotlights/context-before-code, last accessed 21.06.2021.

98 Ibid.

99 Ibid.

is considered to exist where the enterprise has the ability to effect change in the wrongful practices of an entity that causes a harm.'[100] The UNGPs, however, talk about leverage in relation to the influence a company can exert primarily in its business relationships rather than onto its own increased responsibility.[101] Understanding of a company's power over human rights and reliance from various actors on a company appear outside of the current understanding of power and leverage in business relationships under the UNGPs.

Broader considerations of power and implications on influence and harm might have to be factored into questions and considerations of proportionate means of meeting the responsibility to respect outside of business relationships. Is using leverage in business relationships sufficient to meeting their responsibility to respect? There are different kinds of leverage a company can exert within its business relationships; however, these are typically limited to its value chain relationships either in contracts and relationships with suppliers or purchasers.[102] These can also include states. Questions regarding companies exerting leverage over states also calls into question the role that companies are fulfilling in calling for states to uphold their responsibility to protect human rights.[103] With many data protection laws and AI regulations lacking in most countries, it is important that even if states do not have adequate protection in place, that companies continue to uphold and respect international human rights law. However, the power of corporations must also be understood in the context of the role of leverage to determine whether there is something specific about this context and position that might affect what proportionate means of meeting the responsibility to respect entail. These types of considerations call into question whether in unique contexts – in which companies are heavily relied on by all actors and exert power over human rights – rapid changes in the factors determining appropriate means should trigger a heightened due diligence requirement.

What constitutes proportionate means therefore must include an encompassing understanding of both change in factors, as determined in the UNGPs, as well as implications of power and reliance when it comes to appropriate means of meeting the responsibility to respect. The following section proposes how we might understand what proportionate means of meeting the responsibility to respect may look like in the form of heightened due diligence and draw comparisons to the area of business and human rights in conflict-affected areas.

---

100 UN (2011), 'Guiding principles', *supra* note 11, p.21.

101 Shift, 'Using Leverage in Business Relationships to Reduce Human Rights Risks', 2013, available at https://shiftproject.org/resource/using-leverage-in-business-relationships-to-reduce-human-rights-risks/, last accessed 21.06.2021.

102 Ibid., pp. 3–4.

103 Ibid., pp. 10–11.

4. TRIGGERS OF HEIGTENED DUE DILIGENCE

Having considered the variety of factors that affect what proportionate means of meeting the responsibility to respect might entail for Big Tech companies, this contribution has illustrated how significant or rapid change to factors determining proportionate means, particularly operational context and severity of harm, in parallel with Big Techs' position of power, elevates their responsibility in knowing and showing how they respect human rights in their business operations, relationships and more generally in the socio-economic context in which they function. While the responsibility to respect human rights is applicable to all businesses in all sectors and of all sizes, appropriate means must be proportionate, meaning that heightened risk equates to higher expectations of human rights due diligence. An area in which enhanced human rights due diligence is discussed is in the context of business and human rights in conflict-affected areas. The first part of this section will investigate what enhanced human rights due diligence means in conflict-affected contexts, and the second section proposes what heightened human rights due diligence might look like during COVID-19.

4.1. THE NOTION OF 'ENHANCED DUE DILIGENCE' IN CONFLICT-AFFECTED REGIONS

The similarities between the pandemic and conflict settings, are interesting to briefly investigate here as a commonality between the two is the sudden change of operational context. In the report by the Working Group (WG) on issues of human rights and transnational corporations and other business enterprises on business and human rights in conflict-affected regions in 2020, the WG reaffirms that despite a different operational context, a specific due diligence processes for conflict-affected contexts is not envisioned.[104] Rather, the due diligence requirement is built on the concept of proportionality, and therefore the WG explains that 'because the risk of gross human rights abuses is heightened in conflict-affected areas, action by states and due diligence by business should be heightened accordingly'.[105] Interestingly, other forms of instability beyond armed conflict are considered as part of potential triggers for heightened due diligence, including 'volatility in economic or social affairs caused by acute

---

104 UN General Assembly, *Report of the UN Working Group on the Issue of Human Rights and Transnational Corporations and other Business Enterprises. Business, Human Rights and Conflict-Affected Regions: Towards Heightened Action*, UN Doc A/75/212, 21.07.2020, para. 13.

105 Ibid., para. 13.

poverty, mass unemployment or deep horizontal inequalities'.[106] A question might be raised as to whether states of emergency and public health crises in which human rights are limited and the right to life is at stake as a result of a global pandemic could constitute conditions of similar instability that would trigger a heightened due diligence obligation.

Another factor of interest in this comparison is the emphasis put on the level of stress a state is under in situations of armed conflict and being prone to serious human rights violations.[107] Might the use of emergency power such as that seen in the pandemic constitute such levels of stress, as well? Considering the risks that states are taking in limiting human rights and conducting broad surveillance activities in the name of mitigating the spread of the virus, considerations must be taken by businesses about the context in which their business operations take place and with whom they have business relationships. Providing surveillance technologies to states with limited human rights protection can easily cause a business to contribute to human rights harm as a result of increased surveillance.

The UN Working Group on Business and Human Rights reaffirms the need for human rights due diligence to assess, avoid and mitigate adverse human rights impacts, and adds the need for an additional element as part of human rights due diligence that takes note of the conflict-sensitive approach.[108] This involves getting 'a sound understanding of the two-way interaction between activities and context and acting to minimise negative impacts.'[109] In conflict settings, they also have conflict analysis integrated into human rights impact assessments (HRIAs) and have standalone and issue-specific impact assessments as necessary due to complexity of the context. This is what is needed for tech companies, particularly Big Tech, which are relied on and exert power over human rights while experiencing rapid and significant changes in the unprecedented COVID-19 context.

4.2. HEIGHTENED DUE DILIGENCE IN TIMES OF COVID-19

Based on an assessment of individual factors determining the nature of appropriate proportionate means during the pandemic and an exploration of the power of and reliance on tech companies during COVID-19, this contribution

---

106 Ibid., para. 16.

107 Ibid., para. 13.

108 A. Graf, and A. Iff, 'Respecting Human Rights in Conflict Regions: How to Avoid the "Conflict Spiral"', (2017) 2(1), *Business and Human Rights Journal*, pp. 109–133.

109 UN General Assembly (2020), UN Working Group 'Towards heightened action', *supra* note 103, para. 44.

argues that similar conditions are met and heightened due diligence is required. Taking into special consideration the significant or rapid changes in factors determining proportionate means alongside wider contextual factors, such as power over human rights and reliance, allows for a more comprehensive understanding of corporate responsibility, required impact assessments and ultimately effective grievance mechanisms for rights-holders.

An approach to enhanced due diligence could entail context- and power-specific impact assessments for both existing and new products and services, as well as business relationships.[110] While ideally baseline assessments and human rights policies would already be in place for companies, these should become a priority for companies especially in positions of power. Understanding enhanced due diligence not only in assessing harm but also in better understanding the position they are in for providing effective remedies if a harm occurs would be an advantageous aspect of an enhanced due diligence approach.

Communicating their human rights commitment and policies in an accessible, transparent manner externally and reporting on findings of impact assessments and means of mitigating and remedying these should be a priority, particularly in volatile contexts such as the pandemic. While these components of human rights due diligence are already required of companies, the urgency to enhance performance and transparency of knowing and showing how a tech company meets its responsibility to respect cannot be highlighted better than in the context of COVID-19. Given Big Tech's power over human rights in the context of COVID-19, particular emphasis must also be placed on operational level grievance mechanisms that a business can provide to ensure rapid effective remedies are guaranteed for rights-holders who experience harm as a result of a business (in-)activity or through a related business relationship.

Further exploration is required into what heightened due diligence might look like for Big Tech, as well as a closer investigation to obstacles and challenges of achieving heightened due diligence. It must be acknowledged that conducting due diligence, particularly when it comes to stakeholder engagement and consultations, will bring about unique challenges, as will internal governance mechanisms and situations that may also be affected by the change in operational context – such as is the case with employees working outside the office setting during COVID-19. This exploration of heightened due diligence is, however, not only applicable in COVID-19, but may have implications in the future depending on how factors of proportionality affect the position of a business, not necessarily even in the tech sector. As proposals at the EU level have come out for the Digital Services Act and Digital Markets Act,

---

110 S. Rau, 'With Great Reliance Comes Great Responsibility: The Role of Technology Companies during Covid-19', in C. Ferstman and A. Fagan (eds.), *Covid-19, Law and Human Rights: Essex Dialogues*, University of Essex, Essex 2020, pp. 277–286.

with considerations of 'asymmetric' due diligence, the UNGPs in combination could – with findings from this research – point to effective, more concrete obligations for companies and shape regulations that ensure that human rights are fully protected and respected.[111]

5. CONCLUSION

The COVID-19 pandemic has shone a spotlight on the unique role of tech companies and the opportunities they present in terms of supporting the progressive realisation of rights, but also the adverse human rights impact that can result from the use of, or lack of access to, digital products and services. This contribution has investigated several issues to answer the question of what proportionate means for meeting the responsibility to respect for Big Tech companies entail during COVID-19 and whether an obligation of enhanced due diligence is triggered in that context. The initial assessment of the role of Big Tech during COVID-19 focused on reliance and power. Reliance on technology was demonstrated through the increasing demands from various actors for the products offered by Big Tech companies in order to enable rights that could not be fulfilled in other ways during the pandemic, and the harm that results from a lack of access to these products and technologies. Using Birchall's framework of corporate power over human rights, this contribution also closely investigated how *power over individuals, power over institutions* and *power over knowledge* can have a broadening, more encompassing effect on how harm is perceived, and how responsibilities of businesses towards such harm are understood. Considering the significance of reliance and power, this initial section argued that reliance and power must be accounted for in considerations of what proportionate means of meeting the responsibility to respect entail.

Keeping in mind these factors, this contribution continued to investigate change in the factors that determine proportionate means of meeting the responsibility to respect under Principles 14 and 15 of the UNGPs. Findings in this section suggested that first, changes particular in size, sector, operational context and severity of harm in the context of COVID-19 raise the expectations of means required by Big Tech to meet their responsibility to respect. Second, beyond the factors established under the UNGPs, this contribution considered how reliance and different notions of power may coincide with the other factors and influence how proportionate means are determined. Third, the section concluded by illustrating that the factors determining means of respect cannot

111 European Commission (2020), 'The Digital Service Act package', *supra* note 51.

be seen as stagnant, but rather as changing, and that rapid or significant change in any of these factors should trigger a heightened, or enhanced, due diligence obligation.

Finally, based on this broader understanding of factors that shape businesses' responsibility to respect, the contribution concluded with a comparative look at 'enhanced human rights due diligence' as found and promoted for businesses operating in conflict-affected regions. Lessons learned from this comparison illustrate some similarities of concepts such as stress on states and notions of instability, suggesting that heightened human rights due diligence requirements may also be appropriate in the context of tech companies during COVID-19. While some suggestions were made on what enhanced due diligence could look like for tech companies in this context, more research is needed into what such an enhanced due diligence processes and obligations might entail specific to the COVID-19 context, but also more generally for businesses with significant power over human rights.

SERBIA'S COMPLIANCE WITH ARTICLE 2(1) OF THE INTERNATIONAL COVENANT ON ECONOMIC, SOCIAL AND CULTURAL RIGHTS IN TIMES OF THE COVID-19 PANDEMIC

Pandemic or Endemic?

Danilo Ćurčić and Vlada Šahović

ABSTRACT

As the COVID-19 pandemic spread to Serbia, the government took measures in order to mitigate its effects and protect the population from infection. However, some of those measures have had a detrimental impact on the enjoyment of economic, social and other human rights. Measures related to access to the right to education and social security of the most vulnerable have exhibited a lack of consideration and understanding of obligations under the International Covenant on Economic, Social and Cultural Rights (ICESCR, the Covenant) to which Serbia is party, particularly in relation to the obligations stemming from Article 2(1) and 2(2). Many children belonging to particularly vulnerable groups, especially to the Roma national minority, were effectively left without access to education as a result of the introduction of distance learning, while those most vulnerable members of society were not targeted by financial social measures, but rather were precluded from accessing additional financial aid that was made available to the general population. Having in mind the particular obligations incumbent upon Serbia stemming from the above-mentioned articles, the analysis below will illustrate the non-alignment of measures taken with those obligations.

1. INTRODUCTION

As the American historian, professor Frank Snowden pointed out at the beginning of the COVID-19 crisis, epidemics hold up the mirror to the social, cultural and political conditions in which they arise.[1] Similarly, the state responses to the COVID-19 pandemic are the images in that mirror. These images show us the key values that guide the societies we live in and who is considered as a priority in times of the unprecedented global crisis. The COVID-19 infectious disease caused by the SARS-CoV-2 virus has claimed over three million lives and infected more than 140 million people.[2] Since the virus first spread from China outwards,[3] was declared a public health emergency of international concern and then characterised as a pandemic,[4] the majority of countries introduced measures limiting or derogating from human rights. Certain limitations to and derogations from human rights obligations being permissible in international human rights law and under certain treaties when the exigencies of a certain

1 Yale News, 'Historian Frank Snowden: May we be "forever changed" by coronavirus', 08.04.2020, available at https://news.yale.edu/2020/04/08/historian-frank-snowden-may-we-be-forever-changed-coronavirus, last accessed 19.04.2021.

2 WHO, 'Weekly operational update on COVID-19 – 19 April 2021', 2021, available at https://www.who.int/publications/m/item/weekly-operational-update-on-covid-19---19-april-2021, last accessed 20.04.2021.

3 WHO, 'WHO statement on novel coronavirus in Thailand', 13.01.2020, available at https://www.who.int/news-room/detail/13-01-2020-who-statement-on-novel-coronavirus-in-thailand, last accessed 15.04.2021.

4 WHO, 'WHO Director-General's statement on IHR Emergency Committee on Novel Coronavirus (2019-nCoV)', 30.01.2020, available at https://www.who.int/director-general/speeches/detail/who-director-general-s-statement-on-ihr-emergency-committee-on-novel-coronavirus-(2019-ncov), last accessed 17.04.2021; WHO, 'Twitter status of 11 March 2020', 2020, available at https://twitter.com/WHO/status/1237777021742338049, last accessed 17.04.2021.

situation require it or are such that they threaten the life of a nation,[5] states were quick to use that opportunity. For example, already by June 2020, almost 190 countries had introduced some form of measures mandating the closure of schools.[6]

The International Covenant on Economic, Social and Cultural Rights (ICESCR, the Covenant) contains a limitation clause in Article 4,[7] and while the issue of the measures introduced in light of the COVID-19 pandemic can be observed from a limitations perspective, this contribution will focus on the positive obligations of the Republic of Serbia as a State Party to ICESCR, introduced via virtue of Article 2(1) of the ICESCR – which requires States Parties to '[undertake] to take steps, individually and through international assistance and co-operation, especially economic and technical, to the maximum of [their] available resources, with a view to achieving progressively the full realization of the rights recognized in the present Covenant by all appropriate means, including particularly the adoption of legislative measures' – and evaluate whether the measures taken by this State Party were aligned with the obligations of the outlined Article. Particular attention will be given to the obligation to use the maximum of available resources in the protection of Covenant rights. In the context of the COVID-19 pandemic, this perspective is particularly important as it challenges dominant approaches of the states in relation to resource allocation and the use of the maximum available resources.

---

5 For example, treaties such as the International Covenant on Civil and Political Rights (ICCPR), the American Convention on Human Rights (ACHR), the European Convention on Human Rights (ECHR) and the European Social Charter (Revised) (ESC(Rev)) contain derogation clauses (Article 4 ICCPR, Article 27 ACHR, Article 15 ECHR and Article F), while those treaties and a number of other core human rights treaties also contain general limitations clauses and limitation clauses pertaining to specific rights. Seeing as the issue of limitation and derogation of human rights far exceeds the scope of this paper, for more information, see: J. Fitzpatrick, *Human Rights in Crisis: the International System for Protecting Human Rights during States of Emergency*, University of Pennsylvania Press, Pennsylvania 1994; D. McGoldrick, 'The Interface between Public Emergency Powers and International Law', (2004) 2(2), *International Journal of Constitutional Law*, pp. 380–429; J.F. Hartman, 'Derogation from Human Rights Treaties in Public Emergencies-A Critique of Implementation by the European Commission and Court of Human Rights and the Human Rights Committee of the United Nations', (1981) 22, *Harvard International Law Journal*, pp. 1–16.

6 Organization for Economic Co-operation and Development (OECD), 'Education and COVID-19: Focusing on the long-term impact of school closures', 29.06.2020, available at https://www.oecd.org/coronavirus/policy-responses/education-and-covid-19-focusing-on-the-long-term-impact-of-school-closures-2cea926e/, last accessed 17.04.2021.

7 Article 4 – 'The States Parties to the present Covenant recognize that, in the enjoyment of those rights provided by the State in conformity with the present Covenant, the State may subject such rights only to such limitations as are determined by law only in so far as this may be compatible with the nature of these rights and solely for the purpose of promoting the general welfare in a democratic society.' United Nations General Assembly (UNGA), 'International Covenant on Economic, Social and Cultural Rights', UN Doc 993 U.N.T.S. 3 (hereinafter ICESCR), opened for signature: 16.12.1966, entry into force: 03.01.1976.

As noted by the Committee on Economic, Social and Cultural Rights, 'States must make every effort to mobilize the necessary resources to combat COVID-19 in the most equitable manner, in order to avoid imposing a further economic burden on these marginalized groups'.[8]

The human rights community have been relatively successful in advocating for the adoption of the human rights-based approaches (HRBA) to the right to health,[9] education,[10] poverty reduction[11] and other 'development' aspects of our lives, as well as the state's responses to its obligation to protect, respect and fulfil its human rights responsibilities. On the other hand, one of the key principles the rights-based approach introduces is similar to the non-discrimination provision of ICESCR contained in Article 2(2) – it prescribes that all types of discrimination should be prohibited, prevented and eliminated.[12] Having this in mind, it could be said that both the legal (obligations stemming from ICESCR) and the policy and development responses (based on the HRBA) of the state should be driven by the non-discrimination requirement when designing, implementing and evaluating its COVID-19 responses. The importance of these obligations is even more emphasised during the pandemic, as the spread of the virus and the measures for its containment have 'profoundly negative impacts on the enjoyment of economic, social and cultural rights'.[13] In the situation of stark pre-existing inequalities in the country,[14] the importance of these obligations is even more underlined.

In this contribution, the Republic of Serbia's responses to the COVID-19 pandemic will be illustrated and analysed from two different angles. The first is related to the right to education, while the other deals with the issue of financial support programmes for vulnerable groups and individuals. These two issues

8 Committee on Economic, Social and Cultural Rights (CESCR), Statement on the coronavirus disease (COVID-19) pandemic and economic, social and cultural rights, UN Doc E/C.12/2020/12020, para. 14.

9 For the discussion about the human rights-based approach to health, please see P. Hunt, 'Interpreting the International Right to Health in a Human Rights-Based Approach to Health', (2016) 18(2), *Health and Human Rights*, pp. 109–130.

10 UNICEF and UNESCO, 'A Human Rights-based Approach to Education for All: A Framework for the Realization of Children's Right to Education and Rights within Education', 2007, available at https://www.right-to-education.org/sites/right-to-education.org/files/resource-attachments/A%20Human%20Rights-based%20Approach%20to%20Education%20for%20All_0.pdf, last accessed 12.07.2021.

11 Office of the United Nations High Commissioner for Human Rights (OHCHR), *Principles and guidelines for a human rights approach to poverty reduction strategies*, UN Doc HR/PUB/06/12, 2006.

12 See, e.g. European Network of National Human Rights Institutions, 'Respect My Rights, An ENNHRI Toolkit on Applying a Human Rights-Based Approach to Long-term Care for Older Persons', 2017, available at http://ennhri.org/wp-content/uploads/2019/10/ennhri_17_005_toolkit_for_care_providers-03a-page.pdf, last accessed 17.04.2021.

13 ICESCR, *supra* note 7.

14 For additional reference, see section 3.

will be in the spotlight of this contribution because of their crucial importance for the achievement of social and economic rights and for addressing social inequalities vulnerable groups experience in the country.

As the United Nations (UN) Committee on Economic, Social and Cultural Rights (CESCR) noted: '[A]s an empowerment right, education is the primary vehicle by which economically and socially marginalized adults and children can lift themselves out of poverty and obtain the means to participate fully in their communities'.[15] While education should be considered as a long-term commitment, and both the obligation of the means and of the result, specific measures adopted for *immediate protection* of the most vulnerable in times of the pandemic were equally important, especially at the beginning of the pandemic.[16] For example, 'providing social relief and income-support programmes to ensure food and income security to all those in need' or 'taking specially tailored measures to protect the health and livelihoods of vulnerable minority groups, such as the Roma' are some of the recommendations the Committee mentioned in its statement on the COVID-19 pandemic and economic, social and cultural rights, adopted in April 2020.[17] One-off financial support for all adult citizens, introduced by the government of Serbia in 2020 should be perceived as one such measure, and in this contribution, we will use it to demonstrate the state's short-term commitments to the protection of economic and social rights of the most vulnerable population.

2. THE USE OF MAXIMUM AVAILABLE RESOURCES

As highlighted by the CESCR, Article 2(1) of the ICESCR is 'of particular importance to a full understanding of the Covenant and must be seen as having a dynamic relationship with all of the other provisions of the Covenant'.[18] Although 'the principal obligation of result reflected in Article 2(1) is to take steps "with a view of achieving progressively the full realization of rights recognized" in the Covenant,'[19] the maximum amount of resources available need to be employed to that end in order to ensure compliance with said treaty obligations.

---

15 CESCR, *General Comment No. 13: The Right to Education (Article 13 of the Covenant)*, UN Doc E/C.12/1999/10, 08.12.1999, para. 1.

16 Probably the best illustration for this could be found in the Joint statement issued by 60 UN special rapporteurs and mandate holders, OHCHR, 'No exceptions with COVID-19: "Everyone has the right to life-saving interventions" – UN experts say', 26.03.2020, available at https://www.ohchr.org/EN/NewsEvents/Pages/DisplayNews.aspx?NewsID=25746&LangID=E, last accessed 17.04.2021.

17 CESCR, Statement on the coronavirus disease (COVID-19), *supra* note 8.

18 CESCR, *General Comment No. 3: The Nature of States Parties' Obligations (Art. 2, Para 1, of the Covenant)*, UN Doc E/1991/23, 14.12.1990, para. 1.

19 Ibid., para. 9.

Indeed, a failure to do so when ensuring the discharge of at least the minimum core obligations requires extensive justification on part of the State Party in order not to be considered a violation of the treaty.[20]

This obligation does not only apply to resources that are readily available, but also to those that can be attained through international cooperation,[21] much like it is prescribed by the Universal Declaration on Human Rights or the UN Charter.[22] Both public and private sector measures should be applied to that end, as well as policy initiatives and legislative and administrative measures.[23] What is more, and relevant to the current global crisis, 'in times of severe resources constraints whether caused by a process of adjustment, economic recession, or by other factors the vulnerable members of society can and indeed must be protected by the adoption of relatively low cost targeted programs'.[24] The Committee is particularly adamant about this, repeatedly stressing that in times of particular hardship this obligation assumes even greater importance, rather than diminishing in importance.[25] This also means that the states should give particular attention to the rights-holders that are coming from vulnerable groups or communities.

Although the term seems as though shrouded in a form of 'vagueness',[26] the various literature and expert guidelines are sufficient to enable States Parties to give effect to this obligation. For example, 'steps' in the wording of Article 2(1) can be understood as referring to 'specific actions', while '"resources" represent that upon which the satisfaction of the rights is dependent'.[27] According to different authors, resources can be understood to encompass a number of things, including 'human, technological, organizational, natural, informational

20 Ibid., paras. 10 and 11. This has been additionally iterated by the Committee in its other general comments, such as, for example CESCR, *General Comment No. 19: The right to social security (art. 9)*, UN Doc E/C.12/GC/19, 04.02.2008, paras. 59–60, or CESCR, *General Comment No. 12: The Right to Adequate Food (Art. 11)*, UN Doc E/C.12/1999/5, 12.05.1999, para. 17.

21 CESCR, *General Comment No. 3, supra*, note 18, para. 13.

22 UNGA, *Universal Declaration of Human Rights*, UN Doc 217 A (III), 10.12.1948; UN, *Charter of the United Nations*, UN Doc 1 UNTS XVI, 24.10.1945, Article 22s.

23 CESCR, *General Comment No. 4: The Right to Adequate Housing (Art. 11 (1) of the Covenant)*, UN Doc E/1992/23, 13.12.1991, paras. 14 and 15.

24 CESCR, *General Comment No. 3, supra*, note 18, para. 12.

25 CESCR, *General Comment No. 8: The relationship between economic sanctions and respect for economic, social and cultural rights*, UN Doc E/C.12/1997/8, 12.12.1997, para. 10.

26 Term borrowed from Magdalena Sepúlveda in M. Sepúlveda, *The Nature of the Obligations under the International Covenant on Economic, Social and Cultural Rights*, Intersentia, Cambridge 2003, pp. 131–133.

27 R.E. Robertson, 'Measuring State Compliance with the Obligation to Devote the "Maximum Available Resources" to Realizing Economic, Social, and Cultural Rights', (1994) 16(4), *Human Rights Quarterly*, p. 695.

and financial resources, both public and private'.[28] And although it might be difficult for the Committee to supervise whether the States Parties' use of said resources is such that it is in compliance with the ICESCR requirements to use the maximum of resources available, it has through its practice established certain indicators. Namely, the Committee can assess whether States have allocated sufficient portions of their budgets to issues pertaining to housing, agriculture or health as opposed to military defence;[29] examine whether 'budget items earmarked for [Covenant related] expenditure in the State's overall budget' are utilised and 'used for the purposes for which they were budgeted', that is, whether they are misspent as a result of poor administration/corruption;[30] or when a state's expenditure for an ICESCR-related issue is proportionally less than in other developed counterpart countries.[31]

Additionally, the Committee has also expressly outlined that when assessing the compliance of measures taken by States Parties with the obligation to use the maximum of resources available, it will examine whether they are 'adequate' and 'reasonable' – which involves assessing, among other things: 'the extent to which the measures taken were deliberate, concrete and targeted [...]'; whether they were arbitrary or discriminatory; '[w]hether the State party's decision (not) to allocate available resources was in accordance with international human rights standard'; whether they are legitimate, proportionate and timely; and '[w]hether the steps had taken into account the precarious situation of disadvantaged and marginalized individuals or groups [...]' in a non-discriminatory manner, *accordingly prioritising those in situations of risk*.[32] Considering the current

28 D. Elson, R. Balakrishnan and J. Heintz, 'Public Finance, Maximum Available Resources and Human Rights', in A. Nolan, R. O'Connel and C. Harvey (eds.), *Human Rights and Public Finance, Budgets and the Promotion of Economic and Social Rights*, Hart Publishing, Oxford 2013, p. 14; R.E. Robertson outlines five resources in 'Measuring State Compliance with the Obligation to Devote the "Maximum Available Resources" to Realizing Economic, Social, and Cultural Rights', *supra* note 27, p. 697, while Himes outlines three in J.R. Himes, *Implementing the Convention on the Rights of the Child: Resources Mobilization in Low-Income Countries*, UNICEF, Martinus Nijhoff Publishers, Leiden 1995, p. 5.

29 See for example, CESCR, *Concluding observations of the Committee on Economic, Social and Cultural Rights on the second periodic report of Korea*, UN Doc E/C.12/Add.59, para. 9, or CESCR, *Concluding observations of the Committee on Economic, Social and Cultural Rights on the initial report of the Philippines*, UN Doc E/C.1/1995/7, 07.06.1995, para. 21.

30 See, for example, CESCR, *Concluding observations of the Committee on Economic, Social and Cultural Rights on the third periodic report of Colombia*, UN Doc E/C.12/1995/12, para. 28(b), or CESCR Concluding observations on the third periodic report of Mexico, UN Doc E/2000/22, para. 381.

31 See, for example, Economic and Social Council (ECOSOC), *Official Records 1997, Supplement No. 2 – Concluding observations of the Committee on Economic, Social and Cultural Rights on the second periodic report of the Dominican Republic* UN Doc E/1997/22, para. 228; informed by M. Sepúlveda, *The Nature of the Obligations under the International Covenant on Economic, Social and Cultural Rights*, *supra* note 26, pp. 315–319.

32 CESCR, *An Evaluation of the Obligation to take Steps to the 'Maximum of Available Resources' under an Optional Protocol to the Covenant*, UN Doc E/C.12/2007/1, para. 8. Emphasis added.

situation in Serbia, caused by the COVID-19 pandemic, and the way in which the government has chosen to combat it, the following segments of this contribution will attempt to analyse the measures taken towards the realisation of the rights to education and social assistance/financial support through the prism of 'maximum available resources' and 'progressive realization'. Before doing so, it is pertinent to emphasise that although there may be a margin of discretion in the allocation of rights related resources, this discretion cannot such as to abolish 'the existence of any real obligation'.[33]

In the context of the pandemic, it is pertinent to recall that minimum core obligations relevant for each economic and social right are 'non-derogable' and that they 'continue to exist in situations of conflict,[34] emergency and natural disaster'.[35] However, albeit non-derogable, the minimum core obligation is not easy to determine. As Young finds, 'it is unlikely that the concept will ever offer the relative determinacy'.[36] Bearing in mind the lack of consistent approach from the CESCR on the issue of minimum core obligations,[37] and the challenges caused by the lack of the consistency, in the analysis we will use Sepúlveda's standpoint that 'all provisions contained in Part II [Articles 2 to 5] of the Covenant apply to all the substantive rights of the Covenant'.[38] Similarly to what was happening during the introduction of the austerity measures after the global financial crisis, the central challenge in the discussion about the state compliance with the Covenant in times of COVID-19 pandemic lies in the question of prioritisation, which – when governments deal with resource constraints – cannot be completely solved either by the human rights framework, or by the principles of (re-)distributive justice.[39]

---

33 P. Alston and G. Quinn, 'The Nature and Scope of States Parties' Obligations under the International Covenant on Economic, Social and Cultural Rights', (1987) 9(2), *Human Rights Quarterly*, p. 177.

34 For a valuable discussion about the nature of minimum core obligation, see K. Young, 'The Minimum Core of Economic and Social Rights: A Concept in Search of Content' (2008) 33, *Yale Journal of International Law*.

35 CESCR, *Statement on Substantive Issues Arising in the Implementation of the International Covenant on Economic, Social and Cultural Rights: Poverty and the International Covenant on Economic, Social and Cultural Rights*, UN Doc E/C.12/2001/10, 10.05.2001, para. 18.

36 See K. Young, 'The Minimum Core of Economic and Social Rights', *supra* note 34, p. 116.

37 The lack of consistency could be seen when comparing the Committee's standpoints about the minimum core obligation in different General Comments. For example, in General Comment No. 3, the Committee found that States should 'demonstrate that every effort has been made to use all resources that are at its disposition in an effort to satisfy, as a matter of priority, those minimum obligations', while in General Comment No. 14 Committee finds that 'State party cannot, *under any circumstances whatsoever* [emphasis added], justify its noncompliance with [...] core obligations [...] which are non-derogable'.

38 M. Sepúlveda, *The Nature of the Obligations under the International Covenant on Economic Social and Cultural Rights*, Intersentia, Cambridge 2003, p. 313.

39 For the discussion about the creation of winners and losers by the decision makers in situations when resources are limited, and the proposals for addressing this issue, see S. Gruskin and N. Daniels, 'Process Is the Point, Justice and Human Rights: Priority Setting and Fair Deliberative Process', (2008) 98(9), *American Journal of Public Health*.

Because of that, this contribution focuses on the question of who is affected by the measures imposed for stopping the spread of the coronavirus, and addresses particularly the situation of disadvantaged and marginalised individuals and groups.[40]

3. THE ROMA NATIONAL MINORITY IN SERBIA

Although this contribution focuses on the measures implemented by the Serbian government, or lack thereof, in relation to the most vulnerable members of the Serbian population, the majority of the analysis will focus on the Roma national minority, considering their vulnerability and marginalisation. According to the last census implemented in Serbia, there are 147,604 members of the Roma national minority in Serbia,[41] making them formally second only to the Hungarian national minority.[42] However, other data suggests that there are up to 500,000 members of this national minority,[43] which – if correct – would constitute the largest national minority in Serbia. Treaty bodies and the European Commission have pointed out on numerous occasions the particularly difficult position the Roma minority finds itself in, pertaining to issues such as employment, education, women's rights, inclusion and general discrimination, and the need for the government of Serbia to take measures to align itself

40 For Committee on Economic, Social and Cultural Rights' position on the protection of the most vulnerable individuals and groups in times of the austerity measures, please see: CESCR, *Concluding observations on the second periodic report of Greece*, UN Doc E/C.12/GRC/CO/2, 27.10.2015, paras. 7 and 20; CESCR, *Concluding observations on the fourth periodic report of Portugal*, UN Doc E/C.12/PRT/CO/4, 08.12.2014, para. 6; CESCR, *Consideration of reports submitted by States parties under articles 16 and 17 of the Covenant, Concluding observations of the Committee on Economic, Social and Cultural Rights on Spain*, UN Doc E/C.12/ESP/CO/5, 06.06.2012, paras. 8 and 17; CESCR, *Concluding observations on the third periodic report of Ireland*, UN Doc E/C.12/IRL/CO/3, 08.07.2015, para. 11; CESCR, *Concluding observations on the sixth periodic report of the United Kingdom of Great Britain and Northern Ireland*, UN Doc E/C.12/GBR/CO/6, 14.07.2016, paras. 16 and 18.

41 S. Radovanović and A. Knežević, *2011 Census of Population, Households and Dwellings in the Republic of Serbia – Roma in Serbia*, Statistical Office of the Republic of Serbia, 2014, p. 8, available in Serbian at https://pod2.stat.gov.rs/ObjavljenePublikacije/Popis2011/Romi.pdf last accessed 18.04.2021.

42 Which stands at 253,899 individuals – Statistical Office of the Republic of Serbia, *2011 Census of Population, Households and Dwellings in the Republic of Serbia/Ethnicity data by municipalities and cities*, 2012, p. 14, available at https://pod2.stat.gov.rs/ObjavljenePublikacije/Popis2011/Nacionalna%20pripadnost-Ethnicity.pdf, last accessed 18.04.2021.

43 Ministry of Human and Minority Rights of the Republic of Serbia, *Strategy for the Improvement of the Status of Roma in Serbia*, 2010, p. 9, available at https://www.google.com/url?sa=t&rct=j&q=&esrc=s&source=web&cd=&cad=rja&uact=8&ved=2ahUKEwi639Sjqq7wAhXsN-wKHcklCskQFjASegQIIRAD&url=https%3A%2F%2Fwww.undp.org%2Fcontent%2Fdam%2Fserbia%2FPublications%2520and%2520reports%2FEnglish%2FUNDP_SRB_Strategy_for_the_Improvement_of_the_Status_of_Roma_in_the_Republic_of_Serbia.pdf&usg=AOvVaw1_kMwa30k11XjiUkQo9wyr, last accessed 18.04.2021.

with the requirements of international treaties in relation to the respect for, protection and fulfilment of human rights of this group.[44]

According to a recent mapping study, there are 167,975 Roma living in 702 mapped substandard Roma settlements throughout Serbia.[45] The study found that almost 20% of these individuals lack access or have irregular access to water; more than 55% have no access or have irregular access to the sewage network; more than 14% lack access to or have irregular access to electricity; while more than 6% lack access to or have irregular access to all of the above.[46] Considering that such a vast number of Roma live in these conditions, even if the estimated size of this national minority is correct, it is clear that this is the most disenfranchised group in Serbia. Their integration still remains a distant goal, as '[t]he institutional structure dealing with Roma integration remains ineffective and complicated, without a clear distribution of tasks'.[47] With all this in mind, the COVID-19 pandemic measures taken by Serbia should have clearly targeted members of this community, considering their exposure to risk.[48]

In addition, the last Multiple Indicator Cluster Survey published by the United Nations Children's Emergency Fund (UNICEF) in October 2020 shows significant disparity between Roma and non-Roma communities in Serbia. For example, the UN Inter-agency Group for Child Mortality Estimation shows that the under-five child mortality in general population of Serbia is 5.32 per 1,000 live births,[49] while the Multiple Indicator Cluster Survey (MICS) demonstrated

---

44 CESCR, *Concluding observations of the Committee on Economic, Social and Cultural Rights on the second periodic report of the Republic of Serbia*, UN Doc E/C.12/SRB/CO/2, 10.07.2014, paras. 12–13, 17, 28, 30–31, 35; CRC, *Concluding observation of the Committee on the Rights of the Child on the combined second and third periodic reports of the Republic of Serbia*, UN Doc CRC/C/SRB/CO/2-3, 07.03.2017; CCPR, *Concluding observations of the Human Rights Committee on the third periodic report of the Republic of Serbia*, UN Doc CCPR/C/SRB/CO/3, 10.04.2017, paras. 11, 14–15 and 40–41; CEDAW, *Concluding observation of the Committee on Elimination of All Forms of Discrimination against Women on the fourth periodic review of the Republic of Serbia*, UN Doc CEDAW/C/SRB/CO/4, 14.03.2019.; annual progress reports of the European Commission for Serbia from 2005 and onwards, available at https://www.mei.gov.rs/eng/documents/eu-documents/annual-progress-reports-of-the-european-commision-for-serbia, last accessed 18.04.2021.

45 Social Inclusion and Poverty Reduction Unit of the Republic of Serbia (SIPRU) and the UN Human Rights Team in Serbia, *Mapping of Substandard Roma Settlements according to Risks and Access to Rights in the Republic of Serbia with Particular Attention to the COVID-19 Epidemic*, 30.11.2020, available at https://serbia.un.org/sites/default/files/2020-12/web-mapiranje_podstandardnih_romskih_naselja-27-11-eng%20%28002%29.pdf, last accessed 18.04.2021.

46 Ibid., pp. 10–17.

47 European Commission, *Serbia 2020 Report*, SWD(2020) 352 final, Brussels 06.10.2020, p. 39.

48 See section 2: The use of maximum available resources.

49 UN Inter-agency Group for Child Mortality Estimation, available at https://childmortality.org/data/Serbia, last accessed 20.04.2021.

that number is 8 per 1,000 live births among Roma children.[50] Furthermore, only 7% of Roma children aged 36–59 months are included in Early Childhood Education (ECE), compared to 61% of their non-Roma peers included in the ECE.[51] This survey also demonstrated that '[i]n Serbia as a whole, 82% of households rely on clean fuels and technologies for cooking', while this number drops to 42% in Roma settlements.[52] MICS also indicated that in comparison to only 3% of non-Roma households receiving financial social assistance, 53% of Roma households receive this type of financial support.[53] The Government of the Republic of Serbia in its Strategy for Roma Inclusion noted that 'there are no precise data on the unemployment rate among members of the Roma national minority in Serbia',[54] but that there is 'low participation of the Roma minority in the formal labour market'.[55]

CESCR in its last review of Serbia's compliance with its obligations under ICESCR urged the State Party to '[i]ntensify its efforts to promote equality and combat discrimination against members of ethnic minorities, [...] including Roma, [...] and other marginalized persons and groups with regard to access to employment, social security, housing, health and education'.[56] The same Committee also recommended the state to '[i]ncrease the social assistance benefits, taking into account the Committee's general comment No. 19 (2007)' and to '[p]revent any unjustified interruptions in the allocation of social security benefits, [...] which are recognized only for a period of up to nine months per calendar year'.[57]

4. ACCESS TO EDUCATION IN SERBIA DURING THE COVID-19 PANDEMIC

4.1. ACCESS TO EDUCATION AND THE CONTEXT IN SERBIA

As the Committee for Economic, Social and Cultural Rights aptly stresses, '[e]ducation is both a human right in itself and an indispensable means of realizing

50 UNICEF Belgrade, Serbia, *Multiple indicator cluster survey 2019 and Serbia Roma settlements Multiple indicator cluster survey 2019*, October 2020, p. 9, available at https://www.unicef.org/serbia/en/MICS6-Multiple-Indicator-Cluster-Survey-for-2019, last accessed 20.04.2021.

51 Ibid., p. 35.

52 Ibid., p. ix.

53 Ibid., p. xxvi.

54 Government of the Republic of Serbia, *Strategy for Social Inclusion of Roma in the Republic of Serbia 2016–2025*, p. 41, Belgrade, 2016.

55 Ibid.

56 CESCR, *Concluding observations of the Committee on Economic, Social and Cultural Rights on the second periodic report of the Republic of Serbia*, UN Doc E/C.12/SRB/CO/2, 10.7.2014, para. 11.

57 Ibid., para. 24.

other human rights', and, as previously mentioned, a vehicle through which the marginalised can lift themselves from poverty and participate in their community.[58] Education has been shown to be widely beneficial – from an economic perspective in the sense of the impact on the state's gross domestic product (GDP),[59] as well as in relation to increased labour market earnings for individuals and lower poverty rates.[60] It has also been shown to have a positive impact on social areas and health.[61] Regarding the latter, a strong correlation has been established between infant mortality rates and levels of education of women,[62] which is particularly important in relation to the data outlined above on live birth mortality rates among the Roma population and the general population in Serbia, as well as the discrepancies in inclusion to education among these two groups. While almost 100% of children from the general population complete primary school education and 95% transitions to secondary education, these numbers are far different among the Roma population living in settlements, where 64% complete primary education and the effective transition rate is 55%.[63] The European Commission noted the high drop-out rates among the Roma population, particularly of Roma girls, and that segregation in education is still a looming issue.[64] The differences in access to and participation in education were therefore stark before the onset of the COVID-19 crisis, and they have only been exacerbated since.

4.2. SCHOOL CLOSURES IN SERBIA AND THE POSITION IN RELATION TO EDUCATION OF THE MOST VULNERABLE

Since 17 March 2020, the Government of the Republic of Serbia has instituted measures that would support the continuation of education of all children during the COVID-19 pandemic, which essentially entail a transfer to distance learning via television and the Internet.[65] Furthermore, the format of the lessons has been

---

58 CESCR, *General Comment No. 13, supra* note 15, para. 1.

59 For an overview of studies that indicate the connection, see Table 1 in: United Nations Children's Fund, *The Investment Case for Education and Equity*, UNICEF, 2015, p 7, available at www.unicef.org/publications/files/Investment_Case_for_Education_and_Equity_FINAL.pdf, last accessed 19.04.2021.

60 Ibid., pp. 8–9.

61 Ibid., p. 10.

62 E. Gakidou, K. Cowling, R. Lozano and C.J.L. Murray, 'Increased Educational Attainment and Its Effect on Child Mortality in 175 Countries between 1970 and 2009: A systematic analysis', (2019) 376(9745), *Lancet*, pp. 959–974.

63 UNICEF, *Multiple indicator cluster survey 2019, supra* note 50, p. xviii.

64 European Commission, *Serbia 2020 Report, supra* note 47, p. 40.

65 Republic of Serbia, Ministry of Education, Science and Technological Development, 'Realization of educational activities via distance learning for elementary and high school students', No. 601-00-9/2020-01, 16.03.2020, available in Serbian at http://www.mpn.gov.rs/wp-content/uploads/2020/03/Nastava-na-daljinu-u-vanrednom-stanju.pdf, last accessed 12.04.2021.

adapted in such a way that the lessons have been shortened from 45 minutes per class to 30 minutes per class,[66] while the schools themselves have been charged with deciding whether they will be implementing in-person classes or distance learning.[67] They were so charged by the Crisis Headquarters for the Suppression of the COVID-19 Infectious Disease, a body formed at the onset of the epidemic in Serbia in order to monitor and prevent the spread of COVID-19 and mitigate its effects, by providing the government with recommendations on actions to take in that avail.[68]

In response to the latest discontinuation of in-person learning as a result of the epidemiological situation, the Minister of Education, Science and Technological Development issued an instruction to education institutions providing guidelines on how to address the problems with access to education of those children that are socioeconomically disadvantaged, tasking those institutions to find alternative ways to provide support in education 'to children of lower socioeconomic status, as well as to other students that lack access to the necessary technology' and to ensure accessibility to information important for realising the right to education to parents and their children.[69] As highlighted by the A11 – Initiative for Economic and Social Rights: '[a]lthough schools are also part of the State apparatus, this approach seems to neglect the difference in budgeting and resources of schools in various local self-government units throughout Serbia, and therefore their capacity to individually address this problem'.[70]

---

66 *Rulebook on a Special Format of Education*, 'Official Gazette of the RS' No. 110/2020-3 – relevant segment: Recommendations for the realization of classes during emergency situations.

67 Mondo, *Danas odluka o nastavi! Kon kaže: Svaka škola sama odlučuje, a o maskama kaže ovo …*, 05.08.2019, available in Serbian at https://mondo.rs/Info/Drustvo/a1357571/Nastava-od-septembra-skole-same-odlucuju-o-modelu-nastave-Predrag-Kon.html, last accessed 14.04.2021.

68 The Crisis Headquarters were apparently formed via a government conclusion on the formation of said body, dated 13 March 2020, which the government claims was adopted, but cannot be accessed via regular research methods. However, a decision came into force on 31 October 2020 which outlined that the precise mission of said body is to 'monitor the situation, direct and coordinate the actions and activities of all competent bodies, organizations and services, as well as all other entities in controlling and preventing the spread of COVID-19, give proposals and recommendations for measures and activities to control the spread of COVID-19, monitor and coordinate the actions of crisis headquarters of local self-government units in controlling ad preventing the spread of the COVID-19 infectious disease, recommend the Government and competent bodies, organizations, services and other entities to take measures within their competence, as well as implement other tasks in controlling and preventing of the spread and protecting the population from the COVID-19 infectious disease.' *Decision on the Formation of the Crisis Headquarters for the Suppression of the COVID-19 Infectious Disease*, "Official Gazette of the RS" No. 132/2020-1, Article 2.

69 *Letter of the Minister of Education, Science and Technological Development on the realization of educational activities via distance learning for elementary and secondary school students*, No. 601-00-9/2020-1, 16.03.2021.

70 A 11 – Initiative for Economic and Social Rights, *Written contribution to the 2021 Annual Report for Serbia on Political Criteria and chapters 23 and 24*, 15.04.2021, available at https://www.a11initiative.org/en/publications/comments/, last accessed on 15.04.2021.

Although the government of Serbia and the responsible ministry have taken measures related to the procurement of necessary equipment for children that lack access thereto,[71] they do not satisfy its obligations under the ICESCR to ensure equal access to education to all, particularly considering that only 28.8% of households in Roma settlements have computers, laptops or tablets, as opposed to 64.4% of general households in Serbia,[72] which clearly implies that a procurement of that size cannot account for the needs of all the household the mapped 167,975 residents of 'substandard' Roma settlements occupy.[73] Furthermore, considering the previously described socioeconomic status of the members of the Roma national minority, the measures introduced do not seem to satisfy the ICESCR obligations in relation to education, outlined in the following section.

4.3. ICESCR AND ACCESS TO EDUCATION IN SERBIA DURING COVID-19

The right to education as enshrined in the ICESCR imposes an obligation on States Parties to 'recognize the right of everyone to education', as well as to make primary education 'compulsory and available free to all', and secondary education 'generally available and accessible to all by every appropriate means'.[74] In view of the Committee, 'compulsory' highlights 'the fact that neither parents, nor guardians, nor the State are entitled to treat as optional the decision as to whether the child should have access to primary education', and further underlines the requirements related to prohibition of discrimination outlined in Articles 2 and 3 of the Covenant. 'Available free to all', or 'free of charge', as phrased in Article 14 of the ICESCR, means exactly what it states – that the enjoyment of the right to primary education must not be contingent upon fees.[75] However, distance learning incurs direct costs, in the form of technical equipment such

---

71 In the form of 2,400 tablets and 2,450 Internet cards. Ministry of Education, Science and Technological Development, *Ружић: Ради се на унапређењу постојећих мера подршке образовању ромске заједнице*, 22.03.2021, available in Serbian at http://www.mpn.gov.rs/ruzic-radi-se-na-unapredjenju-postojecih-mera-podrske-obrazovanju-romske-zajednice/, last accessed 14.04.2021; and Ministry of Education, Science and Technological Development, *Почела дистрибуција лаптопова и таблета у оквиру пројекта „Премошћавање дигиталног јаза у Србији за најугроженију децу"*, 13.04.2021, available in Serbian at http://www.mpn.gov.rs/pocela-distribucija-laptopova-i-tableta-u-okviru-projekta-premoscavanje-digitalnog-jaza-u-srbiji-za-najugrozeniju-decu/, last accessed 14.04.2021.

72 UNICEF, *Multiple indicator cluster survey 2019*, *supra* note 50, pp. 21–24.

73 See section 3 – The Roma national minority in Serbia.

74 UNGA, *International Covenant on Economic, Social and Cultural Rights*, *supra* note 7, Articles 13(1), 13(2)(a) and 13(2)(b).

75 CESCR, *General Comment No. 11: Plan of Action for Primary Education (Article 14 of the Covenant)*, UN Doc E/1992/23, 10.05.1999, paras. 6–7.

as television, computers or tablets, as well as Internet bills, which – considering that 23.2% of the population in Serbia is in risk of poverty[76] – are significant.

Four features of education have been identified by the Committee as being of central importance: (i) *availability* – requiring that '[f]unctioning educational institutions and programmes have to be available in sufficient quantity within the jurisdiction of the State party'; (ii) *accessibility* – meaning that educational institutions must be accessible to all, in a manner that is not discriminatory, that ensures the physical accessibility of the institutions or accessibility via modern technologies, as well as their economic accessibility, that is, that education is affordable to all; (iii) *acceptability* – pertaining to the acceptability of the substance of education, namely, its quality and cultural adequacy; and (iv) *adaptability* – pertaining to the flexibility of education and its ability to adapt to changing societies and communities.[77] Therefore, considering that any measures introduced on part of a State Party must be such to be sufficiently available, accessible to all, of quality and adaptable while, with particular reference to COVID-19, 'learning must be implemented keeping in mind the [said] framework in order to avoid widening rather than narrowing inequalities',[78] the distance learning as introduced in Serbia can hardly be said to satisfy these requirements.

Although Article 2(1) of the Covenant introduces the concept of progressive realisation of the rights enshrined in the treaty, certain obligations are of an immediate nature, such as the prohibition of discrimination, which 'encompasses all internationally prohibited grounds of discrimination.'[79] The Committee highlighted that States Parties have a 'minimum core obligation to ensure the satisfaction of, at the very least, minimum essential levels of each of the rights',[80] while in relation to Article 13, it made clear that a minimum core obligation includes the obligation of States Parties 'to ensure the right of access to public educational institutions and programmes on a non-discriminatory basis'.[81] Any reading of the ICESCR that does not establish a minimum core obligation 'would largely deprive it of its *raison d'être*'.[82]

Furthermore, if any retrogressive measures are taken in relation to the enjoyment of this right, they require consideration of *all alternatives* prior to the

---

76 Statistical Office of the Republic of Serbia, *Poverty and Social Inequality 2019*, 15.10.2020, available at https://www.stat.gov.rs/en-US/vesti/20201015-siromastvo-i-socijalna-nejednakost-2019/?s=0102, last accessed 20.04.2021.

77 Ibid., para. 6.

78 Human Rights Council (HRC), Report of the Special Rapporteur on the right to education, *Right to education: impact of the coronavirus disease crisis on the right to education – concerns, challenges and opportunities*, UN Doc A/HRC/44/39, 2020, para. 15.

79 Ibid., para. 31.

80 CESCR, *General Comment No. 3, supra* note 18, para. 10.

81 CESCR, *General Comment No. 13, supra* note 15, para. 57.

82 CESCR, *General Comment No. 3, supra* note 18, para. 10.

implementation of such measures, introduce a burden of justification on States Parties for taking said measures and require the application of a state's maximum available resources in view of those alternatives in order for said state not to be in violation of its treaty obligations.[83] Considering that the measures of distance learning are such that they prevent children from Roma households located in informal Roma settlements that lack access to the necessary technology,[84] and even electricity, to participate in education, they hardly comply with the aforementioned requirements.[85] There is no indication that alternative measures have been considered as they were introduced at the very onset of the COVID-19 crisis in Serbia, nor that those measures accordingly prioritise those in situation of risk, as per the guidance of the CESCR.[86] And although Article 4 of the ICESCR provides States Parties with the possibility to limit those rights enshrined in Article 13 as long as they are determined by law, compatible with the nature of the right and introduced 'solely for the purpose of promoting general welfare in a democratic society',[87] the introduction of distance learning was such that its effects have a disproportionate impact on a particular national minority, directly contradicting an immediate Covenant obligation, and in fact depriving it of its *raison d'être*.[88] As previously noted, 'a State party cannot, *under any circumstances whatsoever* [emphasis added], justify its noncompliance with [...] core obligations [...] which are non-derogable'.[89] Bearing in mind that the introduction of distance learning precluded Roma children living in informal settlements from the minimum core obligation of accessing public educational institutions and programmes on a non-discriminatory basis,[90] it could be argued that the situation reached the level of constituting a material breach of the Covenant, as envisaged by Article 60 para. 3(b) of the Vienna Convention on the Law of Treaties.[91]

Furthermore, States Parties to the ICESCR, in this case Serbia, have an obligation to respect, protect and fulfil the rights enshrined by said treaty, and '[the] obligation to respect requires states to refrain from interfering with the enjoyment of economic, social and cultural rights', while '[t]he obligation to protect requires States to prevent violations of rights by third parties', and the

---

83 CESCR, *General Comment No. 13*, *supra* note 15, para. 45.

84 UNICEF, *Multiple indicator cluster survey 2019*, *supra* note 50, pp. 21–24.

85 Social Inclusion and Poverty Reduction Unit of the Republic of Serbia and the UN Human Rights Team in Serbia, *Mapping of Substandard Roma Settlements*, *supra* note 45.

86 See section 2: The use of maximum available resources.

87 UNGA, *International Covenant on Economic, Social and Cultural Rights*, *supra* note 7, Article 4.

88 For more on the views of the Committee on the justifiability of non-compliance with the minimum core obligations of rights, see section 2 and note 37.

89 CESCR, *General Comment No. 14: The Right to the Highest Attainable Standard of Health (Art. 12)*, UN Doc E/C.12/2000/4, para. 47.

90 CESCR, *General Comment No. 11*, *supra* note 75.

91 Vienna Convention on the law of treaties (with annex), Concluded at Vienna on 23 May 1969.

'obligation to fulfill requires States to take appropriate legislative, administrative, budgetary, judicial and other measures towards the full realization of such rights'.[92] A failure to do so may amount to a violation. In relation to education, the obligation to fulfil additionally includes the obligation to facilitate, meaning that states have an obligation to 'take positive measures that enable and assist individuals and communities to enjoy the right to education', as well as the obligation to provide, that is, provide access to the right to education,[93] neither of which seem to have been fulfilled by Serbia. Moreover, it appears as though Serbia left behind the most vulnerable Roma children as a result of the measures necessary to combat the pandemic.[94] Additionally, whether through acts of commission, such as the introduction of distance learning, a policy which is 'manifestly incompatible with pre-existing legal obligations relating to the right to education, considering its disproportionate impact on the Roma population';[95] or omission, such as the failure of the Republic of Serbia to utilise the maximum of its available resources towards the realisation of a Covenant right; or '[t]he failure to implement without delay a right which it is required by the Covenant to provide immediately', such as assuring non-discriminatory access to education to all,[96] the way in which access to the right to education was addressed by Serbia in light of COVID-19 seems to engage the issue of justifiability of said measures.

Additionally, the Convention on the Rights of the Child, to which Serbia is also party, includes an obligation to States Parties to ensure that they take measures to the maximum of their available resources towards undertaking 'all appropriate legislative, administrative, and other measures for the implementation of the rights recognized' therein.[97] The Committee on the Rights of the Child in fact recognises the similarity of this provision to Article 2 of the ICESCR[98] and points out that States Parties need to demonstrate that they have sought to use the maximum of their available resources in the progressive realisation of rights that require resource allocation,[99] reiterating the point on progressive realisation

---

92 International Commission of Jurists (ICJ), *Maastricht Guidelines on Violations of Economic, Social and Cultural Rights*, UN Doc E/C.12/2000/13, 02.10.2000, para. 6.

93 CESCR, *General Comment No. 13*, *supra* note 15, paras. 46–47.

94 CESCR, 'Statement on the coronavirus disease', *supra* note 8, para. 2.

95 Which according to the Committee can amount to discrimination under Article 2(2). See CESCR, *General comment No. 20: Non-discrimination in economic, social and cultural rights (art. 2, para. 2, of the International Covenant on Economic, Social and Cultural Rights)*, UN Doc E/C.12/GC/20, 02.07.2009, para. 10(b).

96 ICJ, *Maastricht Guidelines on Violations of Economic, Social and Cultural Rights*, *supra* note 92, paras. 14–15.

97 UNGA, *Convention on the Rights of the Child*, UNTS vol. 1577, 20.11.1989, Article 4.

98 Committee on the Rights of the Child (CRC), *General Comment No. 5: General measures of implementation of the Convention on the Rights of the Child (arts. 4, 42 and 44, para. 6)*, UN Doc CRC/GC/2003/5, 27.11.2003, para. 5.

99 Ibid., para. 7.

of economic, social and cultural rights via wording of Article 4 in its General Comment 19,[100] thereby intentionally reading progressivity into said Article.[101] Considering this and various other overlaps in relation to rights enshrined in both the ICESCR and said Convention,[102] it is prudent to note that the Committee also clearly outlines that obligations introduced by Article 4 require States Parties to refrain from taking deliberately retrogressive measures related to economic, social and cultural rights, and if doing so they must consider all other options 'ensuring that children are last to be affected, especially children in vulnerable situations'.[103] Furthermore, the Committee stresses that '[t]he immediate and minimum core obligations imposed by children's rights shall not be compromised by any retrogressive measures, even in times of economic crisis', expressly recalling the general comments of the CESCR, with particular reference to General Comment No. 13 on the right to education.[104] Therefore, the way in which distance learning was implemented in Serbia clearly requires, in reference to the views of two treaty bodies and everything outlined above, thorough justification on part of the State Party before both Committees, should it not be considered a violation of treaties' obligations, and in particular the requirements of Article 2(1) and Article 13 of the ICESCR.

5. ONE-TIME FINANCIAL SUPPORT TO ALL ADULT CITIZENS OF SERBIA

On 10 April 2020, the Government of the Republic of Serbia introduced a set of economic measures aimed at providing support to the business sector and individuals. With the idea of mitigating the effects of the coronavirus in the country, the government introduced an economic stimulus package worth €5.1 billion.[105] Economic measures consisted of three different segments: (i) tax policy measures (postponement of payroll tax and social security contributions payments for private sector during the state of emergency, with a subsequent repayment in instalments beginning at the earliest from 2021, payments of

100 CRC, *General Comment No. 19 (2016) on public budgeting for the realization of children's rights*, UN Doc CRC/C/GC/19, 20.07.2016, para. 25.

101 A. Nolan, 'Children's economic and social rights', in U. Kilkelly and T. Liefaard (eds.), *International Human Rights of Children*, Springer, 2020, pp. 239–258.

102 Such as the right to education, the right to social security, the right to an adequate standard of living, the right enjoyment of the highest attainable standard of physical and mental health.

103 CRC, *General Comment No. 19*, *supra* note 100, para. 31.

104 Ibid.

105 Propisi.net, 'Program ekonomskih mera za podršku privredi Srbije pogođenoj posledicama epidemije (korona virus – COVID-19)', 31.03.2020, available at https://www.propisi.net/program-mera-za-pomoc-privredi-srbije-pogodjenoj-posledicama-epidemije-korona-virus-covid-19/, last accessed 23.04.2021.

advances on corporate income tax in second-quarter earnings of 2020 were postponed, donation contributors exemptions from the value-added tax payment obligation, etc.); (ii) direct support to the private sector included direct financial assistance to flat-rate entrepreneurs and those who pay real income tax, small and medium enterprises (SMEs) in the form of payment of minimum wage for 900,000 employees during the state of emergency; and (iii) direct assistance to large private sector companies with payment of 50% of the net minimum wage for employees whose work has been terminated by a resolution in accordance with the labour law. Other measures included the moratorium on dividend payment until the end of 2020, except for public enterprises, and the support of the Development Fund for entrepreneurs, micro, SMEs, agricultural holdings and cooperatives through subsidised working capital loans valued at €200 million.

5.1. CRITERIA FOR ACCESSING ONE-TIME FINANCIAL SUPPORT

Most importantly, along with the aforementioned measures, the government introduced the one-time cash transfer in the amount of €100 per each citizen of legal age with the valid identity document (ID) card.[106] It was reported that this measure amounted to €615 million, and that 6,145,529 citizens received this financial support.[107] At the time when this measure was adopted, Serbia was the only European and 'one of only five countries in the world that introduced a kind of emergency universal basic income (EUBI), alongside Hong Kong, Singapore, Japan and South Korea'.[108] The Rulebook on the Application and the Payment Procedures of One-time Financial Assistance prescribed that pensioners and social assistance beneficiaries were exempted from this application: their payments were immediately processed.[109] Under the provision of Article 4 of the Rulebook, all other individuals needed to submit their citizens unique personal numbers (JMBG) and the numbers of their valid ID cards. This means that citizens without personal documents were precluded from accessing this kind of assistance.

---

106 *Decree on fiscal incentives and direct grants to private companies and citizens aimed at reducing the economic effects caused by the COVID-19 illness* ('Uredba o fiskalnim pogodnostima i direktnim davanjima privrednim subjektima u privatnom sektoru i novčanoj pomoći građanima u cilju ublažavanja ekonomskih posledica nastalih usled bolesti COVID-19'), 'Official Gazette of the RS' Nos. 54 and 60/2020.

107 Ministarstvo finansija, 'Mali: Završava se isplata 100 evra, ispunili smo dato obećanje', 2020, available in Serbian at https://mfin.gov.rs/aktivnosti/mali-zavrsava-se-isplata-100-evra-ispunili-smo-dato-obecanje, last accessed 28.04.2021.

108 G. Matković and P. Stubbs, *Social Protection in the Western Balkans, Responding to the COVID-19 Crisis*, Fridrih Ebert Stiftung, July 2020, p. 8, online available at http://library.fes.de/pdf-files/bueros/sarajevo/16380.pdf, last accessed 29.04.2021.

109 'Official Gazette of the RS' Nos. 73/2020, 76/2020 and 78/2020.

Even more importantly, those who are precluded from getting one-time financial assistance are by far the most vulnerable individuals in Serbia – legally invisible Roma.[110] The number of legally invisible Roma is still unclear, but it is estimated that there are at least a couple thousand. The Committee on the Rights of the Child expressed its concern at the fact that 'approximately 8,500 persons are not registered at birth, with the vast majority declaring themselves as Roma'.[111] On the other hand, the UNHCR survey conducted in 2015 showed that there was 3.9% of Roma without basic identity documents, 1% of Roma from informal settlements who are not registered in birth registries and 5.2% of Roma from informal settlements who have no ID cards.[112] Although the criteria of the possession of valid ID cards may seem neutral, they need to be viewed from the perspective of the situation of Roma in Serbia – 'the requirement of the possession of an identity card has a disproportionately negative effect on persons who, in addition to not having documents, have in common that they are members of a specific ethnic minority'.[113] This specific ethnic minority is the most disadvantaged social group in Serbia, as already noted.[114]

5.2. PROHIBITION OF DISCRIMINATION AND THE ONE-TIME FINANCIAL SUPPORT

Bearing in mind the fact that the criteria for accessing the abovementioned one-time financial assistance, it is worth discussing whether such criteria

---

110 Generally speaking, those are Roma without registration in birth registry books, without determined citizenship, residence or ID cards. For more information about the situation of legally invisible Roma, see Praxis, *Persons at risk of Statelessness in Serbia, Case studies*, Belgrade, 2011, available at http://praxis.org.rs/images/praxis_downloads/praxis-persons-at-risk-of-statelessness-in-serbia.pdf, last accessed 28.04.2021, and UNHCR, 'Lica u riziku od apatridije u Srbiji: Pregled trenutnog stanja i preporuke za budućnost', 2020, online available at https://www.unhcr.org/rs/wp-content/uploads/sites/40/2021/04/01-Lica-u-riziku-od-apatridije-u-Srbiji-CeSid-UNHCR-2020-SRB.pdf, last accessed 05.07.2021.

111 CRC, *Concluding Observations on the Combined Second and Third Periodic Reports of Serbia*, UN Doc CRC/C/SRB/CO/2-3, 07.03.2017 para. 30.

112 S. Cvejić, *Persons at Risk of Statelessness, Progress Report 2020–2015*, UNHCR, 2016, available at http://www.unhcr.rs/media/docs/UNHCR_Brosura_Apatridi_ENGLESKI.pdf, last accessed 30.04.2021.

113 M. Trifković, *Kako identično postupanje prema grupama u znatno različitoj situaciji produbljuje nejednakosti – primer jednokrtatne novčane pomoći za ublažavanje ekonomskih posledica epidemije COVID-19 u Srbiji*, research paper, University of Belgrade, Faculty of Law, Belgrade 2021, p. 3. See also M. Trifković, 'Human Rights in Serbia during the First Wave of Coronavirus: from denial of danger to state of emergency', A 11 – Initiative for Economic and Social Rights, 2020, available at https://www.a11initiative.org/wp-content/uploads/2020/10/Human-Rights-in-Serbia-during-the-First-Wave-of-Coronavirus-1.pdf, last accessed 28.04.2021.

114 Please see section 3 of the contribution for more information about the Roma national minority in Serbia.

constitute the violation of the anti-discrimination provisions of the Covenant. The CESCR in its interpretative standards stressed that the prohibition of discrimination is both a fundamental component of the Covenant, as in Article 2(2), and a specific provision guaranteed with respect to some individual rights.[115] The right to social security, if we see the right to receive one-time financial support as the emanation of the right to social security in times of the pandemic, does not explicitly prohibit discrimination in that regard. However, as already pointed out, 'all provisions contained in Part II of the Covenant apply to all the substantive rights of the Covenant', and therefore this right should be perceived from the perspective of Article 2(2) of the Covenant.[116]

In General Comment 20 on non-discrimination in economic, social and cultural rights, the Committee emphasised that the states are obliged to eliminate both formal and substantive discrimination.[117] In eliminating substantive discrimination, states should pay 'sufficient attention to groups of individuals which suffer historical or persistent prejudice instead of merely comparing the formal treatment of individuals in similar situations'.[118] This means that the state was obliged to pay at least *some attention* to the situation of Roma without access to personal documents. Even if the state was not aware of the fact that some Roma are still facing challenges in their access to personal documents, some non-governmental organisations reminded the state officials about this problem, giving the state enough time and space to rectify the situation.[119] Bearing in mind that Serbia is the only country in the region and one of the rare countries in Europe that failed to introduce specifically targeted measures for socially excluded individuals in times of the COVID-19 pandemic,[120] the fact that one-time financial support was inaccessible for the most vulnerable individuals and communities needs to be included in the analysis of whether the state paid 'sufficient attention to groups of individuals which suffer historical or persistent prejudice'. Mere sameness in treatment in this regard cannot address inequalities in access to economic, social and other human rights, or basic services provided by the state. In order to assess whether this omission

---

115 CESCR, *General comment No. 20: Non-discrimination in economic, social and cultural rights*, *supra* note 95, paras. 3–4.

116 M. Sepúlveda, *supra* note 38, p. 313.

117 Ibid., para. 8.

118 Ibid.

119 Belgrade Center for Human Rights, 'Država neodložno da omogući građanima bez ličnih dokumenata ostvarivanje prava na jednokratnu novčanu pomoć', 21.05.2020, available at http://www.bgcentar.org.rs/2020/page/6/?cat=2, last accessed 28.04.2021.

120 G. Matković, 'Social Safety Nets in Times of the COVID-19 Crisis', Social Inclusion and Poverty Reduction Unit of the Government of the Republic of Serbia, 28.08.2020, available at http://socijalnoukljucivanje.gov.rs/en/social-safety-nets-in-times-of-the-covid-19-crisis-2/, last accessed 29.04.2021.

can be justified as reasonable and objective, further discussion about the aim and the effects of this measure is needed.

5.3. ASSESSMENT OF THE EFFECTS OF THE ONE-TIME FINANCIAL SUPPORT

The one-time financial assistance was introduced with the aim to support the citizens to overcome economic consequences of the COVID-19 pandemic, and the relevant Ministry of Finance justified these measures as 'financial social assistance'.[121] Even though this measure was also explained as 'helicopter money', its main goal was to ease the financial burden individuals faced due to the COVID-19 pandemic, and as such it is, by some researchers, even considered as a clear example of universal basic income.[122]

The economists are not of a unanimous opinion about the economic and fiscal effects of this measure. The research conducted by the International Labour Organization (ILO) demonstrated that the employment retention measure in the combination with the one-time financial support produced a remarkably strong effect as it reduced the relative poverty rate to 22.9% and brought down the Gini coefficient by one full point.[123] On the other hand, the Fiscal Council of the Republic of Serbia commented on this report and found that there is no justification for measuring the effects of the one-time financial assistance on long-term improvement of the poverty rates and the inequalities. It also stressed that the findings in this report were mathematically inaccurate and that the study failed to provide alternatives to the models the government introduced in its first package of economic stimulus.[124] At the conclusion of its comment, the Fiscal Council found that the one-time financial assistance was 'irresponsible fiscal policy that will hamper the future implementation of systemic measures for the reduction of inequalities and poverty'.[125]

---

121 Ministarstvo finansija, 'Mali: Završava se isplata 100 evra', *supra* note 107.

122 International Labour Organization, European Bank for Reconstruction and Development, 'COVID-19 and the World of Work, Rapid Assessment of the Employment Impact and Policy Responses', 2020, available at https://www.ilo.org/wcmsp5/groups/public/---europe/---ro-geneva/---sro-budapest/documents/publication/wcms_754624.pdf, last accessed 29.04.2021.

123 Ibid., pp. 8–9.

124 Fiscal Council of Serbia, 'Efekti mere "100 evra punoletnim građanima na nejednakost i siromaštvo, Komentar studije Međunarodne organizacije rad ai Evropske banke za obnovu i razvoj', p. 1, available at http://fiskalnisavet.rs/doc/analize-stavovi-predlozi/2020/FS_Efekti_mere_100_evra_na_siromastvo_i_nejednakost.pdf, last accessed 29.04.2021.

125 Ibid., p. 5.

Most importantly, from the perspective of the state obligation to use the maximum of available resources, it is important to note that this measure was financed through additional borrowing on international financial market. Because of this, the state was obliged to conduct human rights impact assessments prior to engaging with the borrowing of funds from other states or international financial institutions.[126] Guiding principles on human rights impact assessment of economic reforms adds to this point, especially in the course of the preparation of preventive function of the economic reform policies, such as the mitigation of economic consequences of the COVID-19 pandemic.[127] As noted in Principle 7 of the Guiding Principles, 'directly and indirectly discriminatory impact of economic reform policies on the most disenfranchised or marginalised individuals has to be assessed, and alternative measures evaluated'.[128] However, no such assessment was conducted before the introduction of the measure, similar to the case when the government started introducing the set of austerity measures in 2014.[129]

6. CONCLUSION

As has been demonstrated, the sameness in treatment adopted as a key guiding principle for government's measures in times of the COVID-19 pandemic was not sufficient to address the challenges most vulnerable groups experience in accessing their economic, social and other human rights. Considering that the state is well aware of the situation of Roma in the country, and that it already adopted other pre-COVID-19 measures for the improvement of their situation, such as the ones prescribed by the National Roma Strategy, it remains unclear whether this sameness in treatment was the consequence of the urgent situation Serbia was in, at the beginning of the pandemic, or the failure of the state to implement human rights impact assessments and adopt the least limiting measures in the area of education and social security, as well as ensure the respect for and fulfilment of those rights, or at least their

---

126 CESCR, *Public Debt, Austerity Measures and the International Covenant on Economic, Social and Cultural Rights, Statement*, UN Doc E/C.12/2016/1, 22.07.2016, para. 11.

127 Independent Expert on the effects of foreign debt and other related international financial obligations of States on the full enjoyment of human rights, particularly economic, social and cultural rights, *Guiding principles on human rights impact assessments of economic reforms*, UN Doc A/HRC/40/57, 19.12.2018.

128 Ibid.

129 For more information about this, see: A 11 – Initiative for Economic and Social Rights, Second-Class Rights, Social Rights in the Light of Austerity Measures, Serbia, 2012–2020, 2020, available at https://www.a11initiative.org/wp-content/uploads/2020/06/Second-Class-Rights_Social-Rights-in-the-Light-of-Austerity-Measures-SERBIA-2012-%E2%80%93-2020.pdf, last accessed 29.04.2021.

minimum core components. This situation had a detrimental effect on the particularly vulnerable members of the Roma national minority, since their situation was not even considered when the measures were designed, adopted and implemented. Furthermore, not only did the state fail to take into account the situation of this group, but it also failed to prioritise those in situations of risk, as prescribed by the obligation to take steps to the maximum of available resources in order to progressively realise economic, social and cultural rights. Maximum utilisation of the available administrative, technical, legislative and other resources the state had at its disposal would have require the introduction of measures that are participatory, transparent, deliberate, concrete, targeted and non-discriminatory in their effect.

Bearing in mind the well known vulnerability of the Roma in Serbia, this omission reached the limit of discrimination, as it is understood by the CESCR. This discrimination was both formal and substantive, in both areas, and it demonstrates that the failure is of a systemic nature – it was the result of both short-term and long-term measures, and it affected both measures that demanded significant financial resources and the resources that are of a lesser amount. The state failed to devote sufficient and adequate attention to groups of individuals who suffer historical or persistent prejudice and challenges in accessing economic, social and other human rights. Because of this act of omission, the most disadvantaged groups were precluded from accessing their right to education and the right to social security. Furthermore, this omission proved not to be reasonable and objective. This is the case because the proclaimed aim of the measures was to mitigate the challenges citizens experience due to the COVID-19 pandemic, and yet they entirely 'missed' those that should have been targeted by them. Not only did the state fail to take positive measures to ensure the realisation of rights of the most vulnerable and its Covenant obligations, but the measures introduced in effect had a detrimental impact on the rights of the most vulnerable groups. With that in mind, it could be expected that the state would have to exhaustively justify these measures, and exhibit that, in their adoption and implementation, it was guided by its obligations under the ICESCR, particularly in keeping with the obligation to ensure access to rights to all.

PART II
HUMAN RIGHTS IN EUROPE AND BEYOND

BUSINESS AND HUMAN RIGHTS IN EUROPE 2011–2021

A Decade in Review

Claire Methven O'Brien*

* The author extends thanks to two anonymous reviewers, and to Prof. Andrea Ross and Prof. Alice Belcher, for helpful comments on an earlier draft of this contribution and to Lukas Bogner for research assistance.

ABSTRACT

Business-related human rights abuses remain endemic in Europe and globally. European actors have implemented measures to address business-related human rights abuses both prior and subsequent to the United Nations (UN) 2011 Guiding Principles on Business and Human Rights, a central reference point of the emerging field of business and human rights. This contribution reviews steps taken in Europe towards preventing and redressing business-related human rights abuses in the European Union (EU, the Union), Council of Europe and nationally. Its analysis discloses a decade of conceptual change, legislative and policy innovations that encompass some concrete advances in the regulation of specific value chains, technologies and forms of abuse. It shows a downwards cascade from international to regional norms, but also endogenous and regionally-specific European initiatives, and the lack of uniform or linear transposition of the UN Guiding Principles on Business and Human Rights (UNGPs) across European states, sectors and institutions. It also demonstrates the complex goals and diverse regulatory approaches applied to secure respect for human rights in Europe's market sphere, and their reliance on the capacities and involvement of a multiplicity of public, private, local and transnational actors. Highlighting challenges to the normative, doctrinal and institutional coherence of human rights law and policy attendant on the transmission of human rights norms and standards into the market sphere, it identifies conflicts and dilemmas for human rights scholars, practitioners and policy-makers. Ten observations are advanced on a decade of business and human rights in Europe relating to: the extension of human rights' normative horizon; concomitant doctrinal challenges; the role of hard and soft law; impacts of the business and human rights field for Europe's regional human rights systems; divergencies between intra-EU and 'global' business and human rights agendas; the financialisation of business and human rights accountability; remediation of business-related violations and abuses; implications for a UN business and human rights treaty; and business and human rights knowledge and research.

1. INTRODUCTION

In 2021, rights-holders in Europe experience business-related human rights abuses, from forced labour, unsafe working conditions, denials of collective and individual labour rights and discrimination, to environmental pollution, breaches of privacy, freedom of expression and harassment via the Internet. Beyond the continent, European companies and governments are implicated in abuses including forcible relocations, human trafficking and attacks on trade unionists and human rights defenders via activities of subsidiaries, supply chain and investment relationships.

Business-related threats to human rights are increasingly acknowledged by social, economic, political and legal actors. While such recognition is rooted in longer-range discursive and doctrinal developments, it has accelerated over recent decades alongside globalisation and associated patterns of transnational production, trade and investment, financialisation and social dislocation. Re-constituting corporate goals and aligning corporate forms and conduct to support universal human dignity, basic needs and freedoms while respecting planetary boundaries is now an urgent mission. Failing to answer this challenge jeopardises the political relevance and future popular legitimacy of the human rights concept, in Europe and abroad.

The United Nations (UN) 'Protect, Respect, Remedy' Framework and Guiding Principles on Business and Human Rights (UNGPs) are central reference points of the emerging field of business and human rights.[1] Albeit a soft law instrument, the UNGPs have prompted normative developments inside the

[1] UN Human Rights Council, Report of the Special Representative of the Secretary-General on the Issue of Human Rights and Transnational Corporations and Other Business Enterprises: Protect, Respect, Remedy: A Framework for Business and Human Rights, UN Doc A/HRC/8/5, 07.04.2008; UN Human Rights Council, Report of the Special Representative of the Secretary-General on the Issue of Human Rights and Transnational Corporations and Other Business Enterprises: Guiding Principles on Business and Human Rights: Implementing the United Nations 'Protect, Respect and Remedy' Framework, UN Doc A/HRC/17/31, 21.03.2011, Annex, adopted by the UN Human Rights Council; UN Human Rights Council, Human Rights and Transnational Corporations and Other Business Enterprises, UN Doc A/HRC/RES/17/4, 06.07.2011 (hereafter UNGPs); see UN Human Rights Council, Report of the Special Representative of the Secretary-General on the Issue of Human Rights and Transnational Corporations and Other Business Enterprises: Protect, Respect, Remedy: A Framework for Business, UN Doc A/HRC/17/31, 21.03.2011.

UN human rights system,[2] by bodies such as the International Labour Organization (ILO) and Organisation for Economic Cooperation and Development (OECD),[3] by regional human rights organisations and human rights entities at national level and by businesses themselves.[4] The UN Framework and UNGPs reaffirm states' duties to respect, protect and fulfil human rights in the sphere of business activities, and the right to access to effective remedies for business-related human rights abuses. In addition, they identify a 'corporate responsibility to respect human rights' as an implication of human rights treaties as well as a 'social expectation' that requires businesses to comply with all applicable laws and perform 'human rights due diligence'.[5]

European human rights law contributed to the conceptual and doctrinal antecedents as well as the specific concerns of the UN Framework and UNGPs.[6] Since 2011, legal and policy innovations across Europe's multi-jurisdictional space have responded to the UNGPs but also advanced their normative horizon. Ten years after the UNGPs' adoption, it is timely to review steps taken in Europe towards preventing and redressing business-related human rights abuses.

This contribution combines analysis of European Union, Council of Europe and national business and human rights measures in Europe. It discloses a decade of conceptual change, legislative and policy innovations that encompass concrete advances in the regulation of specific value chains, technologies and forms of abuse. Human rights standards are now penetrating, albeit in many areas still superficially, domains of business regulation and activity where their language was not observable previously. New measures have been applied with reference to the UNGPs, exhibiting a cascade effect from international to regional level. Yet some European initiatives are endogenous and reflect regional specificities. There is no uniform or linear transposition of the UNGPs across European states and institutions. Further, this analysis demonstrates the complex goals and diverse regulatory

2 E.g. UN Committee on the Rights of the Child (CRC), *General comment No. 16 (2013) on State obligations regarding the impact of the business sector on children's rights*, UN Doc CRC/C/GC/16, 17.04.2013; UN Committee on Economic, Social and Cultural Rights (CESCR), *General comment No. 24 (2017) on State obligations under the International Covenant on Economic, Social and Cultural Rights in the context of business activities*, UN Doc E/C.12/GC/24, 10.08.2017.

3 OECD, OECD Guidelines for Multinational Enterprises, OECD Publishing, Paris 2011; ILO, 'Tripartite Declaration of Principles concerning Multinational Enterprises and Social Policy, Fifth edition', International Labour Office, Geneva 2017.

4 C. Methven O'Brien, 'Business and Human Rights and Regional Systems of Human Rights Protection: A Governance Analysis', in A. Marx, G. van Calster and J. Wouters (eds.), *Research Handbook on Business and Human Rights*, Edward Elgar, Cheltenham (forthcoming 2022); C. Methven O'Brien and J. Ford, 'Business and Human Rights: From Domestic Institutionalisation to Transnational Governance and Back Again', (2019) 37(3), *Nordic Journal of Human Rights*, pp. 216–233.

5 UNHRC, UNGPs, *supra* note 1.

6 A. Clapham, *Human Rights in the Private Sphere*, Clarendon, New York 1996; C. Methven O'Brien, 'The State Duty to Protect against Business-related Human Rights Abuses' in C. Methven O'Brien (ed.), *Business and Human Rights. A Handbook for Legal Practitioners*, Council of Europe, Strasbourg 2018.

approaches applied to secure respect for human rights in Europe's market sphere, and their reliance on the capacities and involvement of a multiplicity of public, private, local and transnational actors. Also revealed are challenges to the normative, doctrinal and institutional coherence of human rights law and policy attendant on their transmission into the market sphere. The resulting conflicts and dilemmas warrant attention by business and human rights specialists but also present conundrums for general human rights scholars, practitioners and policy-makers.

The contribution proceeds as follows. Section 2 considers ten years of business and human rights regulation in the European Union (EU, the Union). First it analyses shifts in the underlying conceptual framework of EU policy.[7] It then examines how company human rights impacts are indirectly regulated through non-financial reporting and sustainable finance rules, and considers their prospective direct regulation via EU-level corporate human rights due diligence legislation. Next it reviews measures taken in the areas of public procurement; human trafficking; tech and Internet-related abuses; and in relation to remedy for business-related human rights abuses.

Section 3 addresses the Council of Europe, examining the contribution of the general system of human rights protection as well as post-2011 measures prompted by the UNGPs. Section 4 reviews developments in national regulation, focusing on National Action Plans on business and human rights and corporate human rights due diligence laws. Based on the foregoing analysis, section 5 advances ten observations on a decade of business and human rights in Europe, relating to: the extension of human rights' normative horizon; concomitant doctrinal challenges; the respective roles of hard and soft law; impacts of the business and human rights field for Europe's regional human rights systems; divergencies between intra-EU and 'global' business and human rights agendas; the financialisation of business and human rights accountability; remediation of business-related human rights violations and abuses; implications of European business and human rights developments for a UN business and human rights treaty; and also for business and human rights knowledge and research. Section 6 concludes.

2. BUSINESS AND HUMAN RIGHTS IN THE EUROPEAN UNION

2.1. CONCEPTS AND DEFINITIONS

For decades, in support of market integration, EU laws and policies have sought, without as such saying so, to regulate areas where businesses can pose risks for

[7] The approach here, given space constraints, is selective and trade and investments-related measures, notably, while relevant, are excluded. For an alternative account, see M. Footer, 'The EU's Engagement with Business on Human Rights', in J. Wouters, M. Nowak, A.L. Chané et al. (eds.), *The European Union and Human Rights: Law and Policy*, Oxford University Press, Oxford 2020.

human rights, including: discrimination in employment and access to services,[8] health and safety at work,[9] working hours,[10] environmental pollution,[11] consumer protection,[12] privacy and data protection,[13] and human trafficking.[14] Since the Lisbon treaty, the EU's foundational instruments have also embodied commitments to human rights, dignity and non-discrimination, social justice and social protection with inward and external dimensions,[15] alongside the goals of free and fair trade.[16]

8 E.g. Council Directive 2000/43/EC of 29 June 2000 implementing the principle of equal treatment between persons irrespective of racial or ethnic origin, OJ L180, pp. 22–26 (prohibits discrimination based on racial or ethnic origin in employment, social protection (including social security and health care, education and access to goods and services)); Directive 2006/54/EC of the European Parliament and of the Council of 5 July 2006 on the implementation of the principle of equal opportunities and equal treatment of men and women in matters of employment and occupation, OJ L204 (prohibits discrimination on grounds of religion or belief, disability, age or sexual orientation in employment and occupation).

9 Consolidated text: Council Directive of 12 June 1989 on the introduction of measures to encourage improvements in the safety and health of workers at work, 89/391/EEC.

10 Directive 2003/88/EC of the European Parliament and of the Council of 4 November 2003 concerning certain aspects of the organisation of working time, OJ L299, pp. 9–19; Council Directive 2001/23/EC of 12 March 2001 on the approximation of the laws of the Member States relating to the safeguarding of employees' rights in the event of transfers of undertakings, businesses or parts of undertakings or businesses.

11 European Commission, 'Environment and Climate Change', available at https://eur lex.europa.eu/summary/chapter/environment.html?root_default=SUM_1_CODED%3D20%2CSUM_2_CODED%3D2001&locale=en, last accessed 03.04.2021.

12 Directive 2011/83/EU of the European Parliament and of the Council of 25 October 2011 on consumer rights, amending Council Directive 93/13/EEC and Directive 1999/44/EC of the European Parliament and of the Council and repealing Council Directive 85/577/EEC and Directive 97/7/EC of the European Parliament and of the Council Text with EEA relevance OJ L304, 22.11.2011, pp. 64–88.

13 Consolidated text: Regulation (EU) 2016/679 of the European Parliament and of the Council of 27 April 2016 on the protection of natural persons with regard to the processing of personal data and on the free movement of such data, and repealing Directive 95/46/EC (hereinafter General Data Protection Regulation, GDPR).

14 Directive 2011/36/EU of the European Parliament and of the Council of 5 April 2011 on preventing and combating trafficking in human beings and protecting its victims and replacing Council Framework Decision 2002/629/JHA.

15 Consolidated version of the Treaty on European Union (TEU) OJ C236, e.g. Articles 2, 3, 5, 6, 21; Consolidated version of the Treaty on the Functioning of the European Union (TFEU) [2016] OJ C202/47, e.g. Article 10; Charter of Fundamental Rights of the European Union (ECFR) OJ C326, pp. 391–407. ECFR refers, *inter alia*, to the rights of the child (Article 24); prohibition of child labour, protection of young people at work (Article 32), fair and just working conditions (Article 31), the prohibition of slavery, trafficking in human beings and forced labour (Article 5); Article 47 provides the right to an effective remedy and to a fair trial, which guarantees judicial protection against violations of any EU or national rule which grants rights to people.

16 Treaty of Lisbon amending the Treaty on European Union and the Treaty establishing the European Community, signed at Lisbon, OJ C306, 17.12.2007, pp. 1–271, Article 2. See further C. Altafin, K. Lukas and M. Nowak, 'The Normative Framework of the EU's Commitment to Human Rights: The Treaties, the Charter, Member States' Constitutional Traditions, and International Law', in J. Wouters, M. Nowak, A.L. Chané et al. (eds.), *The European Union and Human Rights, supra* note 7.

Post-2011, EU policies have repeatedly indicated that businesses, as well as governments and EU actors, should uphold the UN Framework and UNGPs. A 2011 European Commission (EC) Communication exhorted enterprises 'To identify, prevent and mitigate their possible adverse impacts' on human rights as well as environmental and social concerns. 'Large enterprises and enterprises at particular risk of having such impacts', it continued, 'are encouraged to carry out risk-based due diligence, including through their supply chains'.[17]

This and ensuing statements marked a gradual shift in the EU's concept of corporate responsibility for human rights. Earlier, EU policy revolved around 'corporate social responsibility' (CSR). This the EC defined in 2001 as 'a concept whereby companies integrate social and environmental concerns in their business operations and in their interaction with their stakeholders on a voluntary basis'.[18] According to this idea of CSR, companies might themselves define what action, if any, to take in response to subjectively-assessed social and environmental 'impacts'.

Ten years later, the new EC CSR Strategy of 2001 defined 'corporate responsibility' as 'the responsibility of enterprises for their impacts on society', without qualifications linked to voluntariness or otherwise.[19] To meet their responsibility, companies 'should have in place a process to integrate social, environmental, ethical, human rights and consumer concerns into their business operations and core strategy in close collaboration with their stakeholders, with the aim of maximising the creation of shared value for their owners/shareholders and civil society at large and identifying, preventing and mitigating possible adverse impacts'.[20] Further, according to the White Paper, 'Respect for applicable legislation, and for collective agreements between social partners' was now prerequisite to businesses' fulfillment of their responsibility, while 'preventing and remedying abuses or toleration of abuses by businesses' became 'a joint responsibility of the private sector and public authorities'.[21]

Perhaps seeming slight, these revised formulations represented a conceptual transition in EU policy. The EC's 2001 definition suggested faith in the corporation as an autopoietic form,[22] capable of harmonising its operations with its social and physical environment autonomously. Its 2011

---

17 European Commission, A renewed EU strategy 2011–14 for Corporate Social Responsibility, COM(2011) 681 final 25.10.2011, p. 6.

18 European Commission, *Green Paper Promoting a European framework for Corporate Social Responsibility*, UN Doc OC/01/9, 18.07.2001 [emphasis added]. On the EU legal and policy landscape in the CSR era, see further: J. Wouters and L. Chanet, 'Corporate Human Rights Responsibility: A European Perspective', (2008) 6(2), *Northwestern Journal of International Human Rights*, pp. 261–303.

19 European Commission, COM(2011) 681 final 25.10.2011, *supra* note 17, p. 6.

20 Ibid., emphasis added.

21 Ibid., emphasis added.

22 G. Teubner, *Law as an Autopoietic System*, Blackwell, Oxford 1993.

iteration rather embodies a reflexive or de-centred orientation.[23] Discerning and deciding how to react to impacts on society is no longer in companies' unlimited discretion or knowledge. On the other hand, neither does EC policy define the content of company responsibility for human rights directly. Rather, it establishes specific legal benchmarks (applicable laws and collective agreements, selected international human rights standards) and the steps of a process (corporate human rights due diligence) by which company self-assessment and self-regulation are to be conducted.[24]

Putting more flesh on this skeleton, subsequently the EC linked 'corporate responsibility' to the terminology of 'Responsible Business Conduct' (RBC) latterly adopted by the OECD. By 2019, the EC referred to the latter as an 'alternative term' for 'corporate responsibility', which entails for businesses '(a) making a positive contribution to economic, environmental and social progress with a view to achieving sustainable development and (b) avoiding and addressing adverse impacts related to an enterprise's direct and indirect operations, products or services'.[25] Since 2011, the OECD's Guidelines for Multinational Enterprises have assimilated the corporate responsibility to respect human rights and due diligence.[26] The EC's overlaying of its own revised 'corporate responsibility' concept and RBC, then, imports the OECD's more granular definition of expected due diligence practice.[27] Yet, at the same time, this move risks regression, and confusion, by situating human rights in a broader matrix of elements that lack the legal, indeed constitutional,[28] status afforded to human rights in the EU and Council of Europe legal orders.[29]

---

23 J. Black, 'Decentring Regulation: Understanding the Role of Regulation and Self-Regulation in a 'Post-Regulatory' World', (2001) 54(1), *Current Legal Problems*, pp. 103–146.

24 E.g. European Commission, Implementing the UN Guiding Principles on Business and Human Rights – State of Play, Staff Working Document, SWD (2015) 144 final 14.07.2015; Council of the European Union, EU Strategic Framework on Human Rights and Democracy, 11855/12, 25.06.2012; European Commission, Communication Next steps for a sustainable European future European action for sustainability, COM(2016) 739 final 22.11.2016; Council of the European Union, EU Action Plan on Human Rights and Democracy 2015–2019, 10897/15, 20.07.2015. In a 2016 EC Communication 'Next steps for a sustainable European future: European action for sustainability', with CSR/RBC featuring as a contributory set of actions under SDG 8. The Communication stated that: 'The Commission will intensify its work on Responsible Business Conduct, focusing on concrete actions to meet current and future social, environmental and governance challenges, building upon the main principles and policy approach identified in the Commission's 2011 EU Corporate Social Responsibility Strategy'.

25 European Commission, Staff Working Document Corporate Social Responsibility, Responsible Business Conduct, and Business & Human Rights: Overview of Progress, SWD(2019) 143 final 20.03.2019.

26 OECD Guidelines for MNEs (2011), *supra* note 3; OECD, 'OECD Due Diligence Guidance for Responsible Business Conduct', OECD Publishing, Paris 2018.

27 Ibid.

28 The OECD Guidelines also refer, for instance, to transparency, taxation, technology transfer and consumer protection.

29 Lisbon Treaty, Article 2, *supra* note 16; ECtHR, *Norwegian Confederation of Trade Unions (LO) and Norwegian Transport Workers' Union (NTF) v Norway*, no 45487/17, 10.06.2021;

This risk has been exacerbated by the EU's articulation of corporate responsibility and RBC with the 2030 Agenda and UN Sustainable Development Goals.[30] 'Given the overlaps between CSR/RBC, the SDGs and UNGPs,' the EC has recently stated, it 'has taken a holistic and integrated approach focused on practical action, irrespective of whether it is labelled 'CSR', 'RBC', 'Business and Human Rights', 'SDG' or all four together while at the same time recognising the differences in focus between those agendas'.[31]

'Policy coherence' is preferable to policy-making 'in silos'. Yet total holism is impossible.[32] An intertextual mesh may weaken, rather than strengthen, accountability, by clouding the actual content of corporate responsibility for human rights. How should corporations be held to account for their human rights 'impacts', where this comprises just one aspect of a corporate 'responsibility' that also extends to 'maximising shared value' and contributing to 'economic progress'? Assumptions (such as, for instance, that economic growth or increased business activity entail or are associated with increasing respect for human rights) lying behind the full interchangeability of terms as asserted by the EC remain unsupported by evidence.[33]

If recent EU policies have consolidated the integration of respect for human rights into 'corporate social responsibility', and the expectation of operationalisation via due diligence, this advance hence appears unstable and at risk from rear-guard blending with the pre-UNGPs concept of CSR. Still, as seen in the next sections, the significance of unclarity at the level of the general CSR/RBC concept may diminish with the emergence of specific legislative due diligence requirements; on the other hand, some current legislative proposals seem set instead to reproduce it.

---

cf. International Transport Workers' Federation and Finnish Seamen's Union v Viking Line ABP and OÜ Viking Line Ee and Laval un Partneri Ltd v Svenska Byggnadsarbetareförbundet, Svenska Byggnadsarbetareförbundets avdelning 1, Byggettan and Svenska Elektrikerförbundet.

30 UN General Assembly, UN General Assembly Res. 70/1, Transforming our world: the 2030 Agenda for Sustainable Development, UN Doc A/RES/70/1, 21.10.2015. See further: N. Jagers, 'Sustainable Development Goals & the Business and Human Rights Discourse: Ships Passing in the Night?', (2020) 42(1), *Human Rights Quarterly*, pp. 145–173.

31 European Commission, SWD(2019) 143 final, *supra* note 25, p. 5.

32 Integrating corporate 'environmental and social responsibility' into corporate missions, for instance, cannot secure competitive advantage for all companies at once, as a matter of logic: European Commission, 'Reflection Paper: Towards a Sustainable Europe by 2030', COM(2019) 22 final 30.01.2019.

33 It thus seems premature, for instance, to account actions under the heading of CSR/RBC as automatically contributing to realisation of SDG 8: European Commission, Next steps for a sustainable European future European action for sustainability, COM(2016) 0739 final 22.11.2016: '*The Commission will intensify its work on Responsible Business Conduct, focusing on concrete actions to meet current and future social, environmental and governance challenges, building upon the main principles and policy approach identified in the Commission's 2011 EU Corporate Social Responsibility Strategy*.'

2.2. INDIRECT REGULATION: NON-FINANCIAL REPORTING AND SUSTAINABLE INVESTMENT RULES

Initially, EU measures sought to encourage the adoption of human rights due diligence by companies indirectly. The 2014 EU Directive on disclosure of non-financial information (Non-Financial Reporting Directive, NFR) foresaw public disclosures of company impacts on human rights.[34] The directive required about 6,000 of the largest EU companies ('public interest entities') with more than 500 employees listed on EU markets to disclose their business model; their policies (including due diligence processes); outcomes, principal risks and risk management arrangements; and Key Performance Indicators (KPIs) relevant to the particular business, in four areas, being environment, social and employee matters, respect for human rights, and anti-corruption and bribery. The directive was supplemented by non-binding EC Guidelines for reporting of non-financial and climate-related information.[35]

The efficacy of a disclosure-based approach to encouraging businesses to respect human rights turns on two clusters of assumptions. The first of these holds that fixing companies with obligations to report publicly about their human rights impacts and risk management systems will gradually institutionalise respect for human rights inside corporations. Whether responsibility for preparing and signing off company reports sits with compliance officers or corporate boards, disclosure duties should, on this hypothesis, trigger measurement of human rights 'performance', according to standard metrics, such as the Global Reporting Initiative. Gradually, the disciplines of measurement and reporting should have the effect of engendering respect for human rights by the business, for instance, via revisions to standing operating procedures and contractual terms, role descriptions, education and capacity building initiatives, and so on. The second cluster of assumptions holds that human rights 'performance', made visible in a company's non-financial reports, will be observed by investors and other stakeholders. While weak 'performance' may trigger sanctions, such as disinvestment and hence a falling share-price, ethically motivated companies may also compete *inter se* as a result of reputational 'race to the top' dynamics.

Definitive assessments of whether sustainability or, more specifically, human rights disclosure requirements actually do operate via these mechanisms

34 Directive 2014/95/EU of the European Parliament and of the Council of 22 October 2014 amending Directive 2013/34/EU as regards disclosure of non-financial and diversity information by certain large undertakings and groups.

35 European Commission, Guidelines on Non-financial Reporting (Methodology for Reporting Non-financial Information), C(2017) 4234 final 05.07.2017; European Commission, Guidelines on reporting climate-related information, C(2019) 4490 final 17.06.2019. This introduced the concept of 'double materiality', according to which companies should report on material risks to company value as well as risks to people and the environment.

to influence companies to respect human rights in practice are difficult. Scholarly studies point in different directions.[36] Still, early studies suggested the inadequacy of company reporting under the NFR, including on human rights.[37] In tandem, the uptake and performance of human rights due diligence by large European companies, in spite of the exhortations of the UNGPs and 2011 White Paper, were demonstrated to be poor.[38]

By 2020, the EU had made high-profile commitments to a European New Green Deal,[39] and the goal of a systemic redirection of capital towards sustainably operating companies.[40] In this context, reinforcing the mechanisms needed to facilitate what might be termed 'transparency-driven multi-polar investor and social control', the hypothesis of the second cluster of assumptions above, became politically imperative.[41] Consequently, EU bodies have taken additional steps to extend transparency, standardisation and accountability in relation to 'green' and 'social' investments.[42]

---

36 K. Macphail and C. Adams, 'Corporate Respect for Human Rights: Meaning, Scope, and the Shifting Order of Discourse', (2016) 29(4), *Accounting Auditing and Accountability Journal*, pp. 650–678; S. Parsa, I. Roper, M. Muller-Camen et al., 'Have Labour Practices and Human Rights Disclosures Enhanced Corporate Accountability? The Case of the GRI Framework', (2018) 42(1), *Accounting Forum*, pp. 47–64; M. Doan and R. Sassen, 'The Relationship Between Environmental Performance and Environmental Disclosure: A Meta-Analysis' (2020) 24(5), *Journal of Industrial Ecology*, pp. 1140–1157; Corporate Human Rights Benchmark, 'Corporate Human Rights Benchmark: 2019 Key Findings', Report, 2019, available at https://www.corporatebenchmark.org/sites/default/files/2019-11/CHRB2019KeyFindingsReport.pdf, last accessed 19.07.2021.

37 Alliance for Corporate Transparency, 'An Analysis of the Sustainability Reports of 1000 Companies Pursuant to the EU Non-financial Reporting Directive', Report, 2019, available at: https://allianceforcorporatetransparency.org/assets/2019_Research_Report%20_Alliance_for_Corporate_Transparency-7d9802a0c18c9f13017d686481bd2d6c6886fea6d9e9c7a5c3cfafea8a48b1c7.pdf, last accessed 19.07.2021.

38 C. Methven O'Brien and O. Martin-Ortega, 'EU Human Rights Due Diligence Legislation. Monitoring, Enforcement and Access to Justice for Victims', European Parliament Briefings, 2020, available at https://www.europarl.europa.eu/RegData/etudes/BRIE/2020/603495/EXPO_BRI(2020)603495_EN.pdf, last accessed 19.07.2021; NYU Stern Center for Business and Human Rights, 'Assessing Legislation on Human Rights in Supply Chains: Varied Designs but Limited Compliance', 19.06.2019, available at https://issuu.com/nyusterncenterforbusinessandhumanri/docs/nyu_jaco_research_brief_june14_final, last accessed 19.07.2021; Corporate Human Rights Benchmark, 'Total Ranking – Europe and Central Asia', Website, 2020, available at https://www.worldbenchmarkingalliance.org/publication/chrb/rankings/type/ungp/, last accessed 19.07.2021.

39 European Commission, The European Green Deal, COM(2019) 640 final 11.12.2019.

40 European Commission, Capital Markets Union – Accelerating Reform, COM(2016) 0601 final 14.09.2016; European Commission, Action Plan: Financing Sustainable Growth, COM(2018) 97 final 08.03.2018.

41 See also European Parliament, Resolution of 29 May 2018 on Sustainable Finance, 2018/2007(INI).

42 European Commission, Taxonomy, Corporate Sustainability Reporting, Sustainability Preferences and Fiduciary Duties: Directing finance towards the European Green Deal, COM(2021) 188 final 21.04.2021.

Foremost amongst these has been the 2020 Taxonomy Regulation. This instrument seeks to establish 'appropriate definitions for companies, investors and financial market participants on which economic activities can be considered environmentally sustainable': in other words, to establish an EU-wide classification for 'sustainable' or 'ESG' financial products. Hence the EC is to provide, via delegated acts, technical screening criteria for determining whether an economic activity can be considered as contributing substantially to environmental objectives,[43] and thus marketed and sold as an 'ESG' financial product. Though not part of the initial package, 'social' screening criteria, to address human rights, are likely to be adopted soon.[44]

Second, the Sustainable Finance Disclosure Regulation (SFDR)[45] aims to establish harmonised transparency rules for financial market participants, such as pension funds, insurers and fund managers as well as financial advisers on how they integrate sustainability risks in internal processes.[46] A 'sustainable investment' in this context is 'an investment in an economic activity that contributes to an environmental objective … or … that contributes to a social objective, in particular an investment that contributes to tackling inequality or that fosters social cohesion, social integration and labour relations, or an investment in human capital or economically or socially disadvantaged communities, provided that such investments do not significantly harm any of those objectives and that the investee companies follow good governance practices, in particular with respect to sound management structures, employee relations, remuneration of staff and tax compliance'.[47] Together with the Taxonomy Regulation, SFDR is intended to improve, if not perfect, the market for ESG investment products which, relevantly for present purposes, should be investments in companies and business activities or projects that promote and do not harm human rights.

---

43 Regulation (EU) 2020/852 of 18 June 2020 on the establishment of a framework to facilitate sustainable investment, and amending Regulation (EU) 2019/2088 PE/20/2020/INIT, OJ L198, pp. 13–43.

44 The Sustainable Finance Platform has a Social Working Group which will consider extension of the Taxonomy; See European Commission, 'The Platform on Sustainable Finance', 2021, available at https://ec.europa.eu/info/business-economy-euro/banking-and-finance/sustainable-finance/overview-sustainable-finance/platform-sustainable-finance_en, last accessed 19.07.2021.

45 Regulation (EU) 2019/2088 of the European Parliament and of the Council of 27 November 2019 on sustainability-related disclosures in the financial services sector, OJ L317, 09.12.2019, p. 1.

46 European Commission, 'Sustainability-related disclosure in the financial services sector', 2021, available at https://ec.europa.eu/info/business-economy-euro/banking-and-finance/sustainable-finance/sustainability-related-disclosure-financial-services-sector_en, last accessed 19.07.2021.

47 Regulation (EU) 2019/2088, *supra* note 43, Article 2(17).

Third, a new Corporate Sustainability Reporting Directive (CSRD) was proposed in 2021 to supersede the 2014 NFRD discussed above.[48] The new CSRD aims to provide 'the foundation of a consistent flow of sustainability information through the financial value chain', from companies undertaking business activities to 'analysts in banks, insurance companies, asset management companies or credit rating agencies, for end investors and for non-governmental organisations and other stakeholders that wish to better hold companies to account for their social and environmental impacts'.[49]

The CSRD would apply to all large companies (approximately 49,000), compared to (by now) around 11,000 covered by the earlier NFR Directive. Reporting required by companies should extend to 'the full range of environmental, social and governance issues relevant to a company's business', including 'information on companies' global supply chains regarding issues such as forced and child labour'. Instead of non-binding guidance, as under the NFR, mandatory EU sustainability reporting standards will be provided for in later delegated acts, following consultation with technical, financial and stakeholder bodies, including the European Agency on Fundamental Rights (FRA).[50]

With these measures, the EU has renewed its efforts to create a conducive environment for the internalisation of respect for human rights by businesses. On the upside, this aligns with a recent trend towards the nominal espousal by financial actors of 'ESG' values and policies. Yet, at the same time the above measures have so far failed to determine the exact role of respect for human rights and due diligence in relation to 'sustainable' products, investment practices and disclosures. Moreover, sustainability disclosures and investor action are, at best, insufficient mechanisms for guaranteeing corporate respect for human rights.[51] Indeed, it has arguably been the increasing influence of investment actors and the overall financialisation of the broader economy and public sphere that have been if not the principal driver of business-related

---

48 European Commission, Proposal for a directive amending Directive 2013/34/EU, Directive 2004/109/EC, Directive 2006/43/EC and Regulation (EU) No 537/2014, as regards sustainable corporate, COM (2021) 189 final 21.04.2021.

49 European Commission, EU Taxonomy, Corporate Sustainability Reporting, Sustainability Preferences and Fiduciary Duties: Directing finance towards the European Green Deal, COM(2021) 188 final, 21.04.2021.

50 To be developed by the sustainability reporting standards. The draft standards would be developed by the European Financial Reporting Advisory Group (EFRAG), whose membership includes FRA. Information reported by companies under CSRD is to be audited but also 'digitally tagged' so that it can feed into the European Single Access Point envisaged under the Capital Markets Union Action Plan'.

51 See references at n.36 above; also C. Methven O'Brien and S. Dhanarajan, 'The Corporate Responsibility to Respect Human Rights: A Status Review', (2016) 29(4), *Accounting Auditing & Accountability*, Journal, pp. 542–567.

human rights abuses, one of them.[52] The increasing role afforded in EC policy to disclosure- and investor-driven corporate reform thus constitutes a high-risk if not a paradoxical strategy. It is also one that makes crucial the supplementary adoption of measures directly to regulate business-related human rights abuses. As related next, besides continuing to set substantive standards in the spheres of employment, social and environmental matters, over the last decade the EU has also innovated new due diligence measures across specific global value chains and 'horizontally'.

2.3. DIRECT MEASURES: DUE DILIGENCE LEGISLATION

2.3.1. Conflict Minerals

'Conflict minerals' refers to various high-value metal ores whose production and trade is linked to human rights abuses, whether perpetrated directly by armed groups or that result from their wider consequences in terms of perpetuating hostilities and corruption. In 2010, the United States (US) was the first jurisdiction to enact legislation intended to stem trade in conflict minerals: Section 1502 of the Dodd Frank Act required US-listed companies to carry out due diligence on minerals sourced from the Democratic Republic of Congo and neighbouring countries.[53] In 2017, the EU adopted a Conflict Minerals Regulation establishing a regime centred on the elements of due diligence, traceability and disclosure,[54] with reference to OECD conflict minerals guidance.[55] Effective from 2021, this regulation establishes requirements on approximately 600–1,000 EU importers of tin, tantalum, tungsten and gold from conflict-affected and high-risk areas.

Specifically, such importers are required to establish a management system that comprises a 'chain of custody or supply chain traceability system' that evidences, for imported minerals and metals, their country of origin, date of extraction, supplier, and additional data specified for the substance in question in OECD guidance.[56] EU importers are further required to undertake

52 S. Hiss, 'The Politics of the Financialization of Sustainability', (2013) 17(3), *Competition and Change*, pp. 234–47; M. Dowell-Jones and D. Kinley, 'Minding the Gap: Global Finance and Human Rights', (2011) 25(2), *Ethics & International Affairs*, pp. 183–210.

53 Dodd-Frank Wall Street Reform and Consumer Protection Act s1502, available at https://www.govinfo.gov/content/pkg/COMPS-9515/pdf/COMPS-9515.pdf, last accessed 19.07.2021.

54 Regulation (EU) 2017/821 of the European Parliament and of the Council of 17 May 2017 laying down supply chain due diligence obligations for Union importers of tin, tantalum and tungsten, their ores, and gold originating from conflict-affected and high-risk areas.

55 OECD, 'OECD Due Diligence Guidance for Responsible Supply Chains of Minerals from Conflict-Affected and High-Risk Areas,' OECD Publishing, Paris 2016.

56 Regulation (EU) 2017/821 on supply chain due diligence obligations, *supra* note 54, Article 4.

third-party audit of their conflict-minerals supply chain due diligence;[57] to disclose audit reports to Member State authorities and suppliers; and to report on these publicly on an annual basis.[58] They must also apply overall risk management measures intended gradually to 'weed out' non-compliant smelters and refiners, wherever in the world located, from EU supply chains. Such measures should include grievance mechanisms.[59] Other elements of the overall regime include duties on Member States to appoint competent national oversight authorities;[60] to publish lists of companies subject to due diligence requirements; and undertake checks on company compliance;[61] as well as publication by the EC of a list of global 'responsible smelters and refiners'.[62]

The regulation is supplemented, *inter alia*, by guidelines for importers on how to identify conflict-affected and high-risk areas;[63] for Member States on how to carry out *ex post* checks on importers; and a delegated regulation on recognition of supply chain due diligence schemes.[64] 'Accompanying measures' to support the achievement of the regulation's ultimate objectives include financial support to OECD's Due Diligence for responsible sourcing of minerals programme and other projects intended to bring 'legal, conflict-free, and traceable gold from artisanal mines to the international market'; a European Partnership on Responsible Minerals that involves public, private and civil society actors along the supply chain; and a programme to support EU small and medium-sized enterprises (SMEs) who 'want to develop and implement due diligence of mineral supply chains, irrespective of whether they have obligations under the Regulation', with particular attention paid to the competitiveness aspects of SMEs applying due diligence.[65]

---

57 Ibid., Article 6.

58 Ibid., Article 7, 7(3). See further, OECD, Trends in Stakeholder Reporting: Mineral Supply Chains (2021), available at https://mneguidelines.oecd.org/trendsinstakeholderreporting mineralsupplychains.htm, last accessed 14.10.2021.

59 Ibid., Article 5.

60 Ibid., Article 10.

61 Ibid., Article 11.

62 Ibid., Article 9.

63 Commission Recommendation (EU) 2018/1149 of 10 August 2018 on non-binding guidelines for the identification of conflict-affected and high-risk areas and other supply chain risks under Regulation (EU) 2017/821 of the European Parliament and of the Council, OJ L208, pp. 94–106.

64 Supplementing Regulation (EU) 2017/821 of the European Parliament and of the Council as regards the methodology and criteria for the assessment and recognition of supply chain due diligence schemes concerning tin, tantalum, tungsten and gold.

65 K. Nowrot, 'The 2017 EU Conflict Minerals Regulation: An Effective European Instrument to Globally Promote Good Raw Materials Governance?', Rechtswissenschaftliche Beiträge der Hamburger Sozialökonomie, 2008, available at https://www.wiso.uni-hamburg.de/fachbereich-sozoek/professuren/nowrot/archiv/heft-20-nowrot-conflict-minerals.pdf, last accessed 19.07.2021.

Early evaluations indicate that in combination, EU, US and OECD measures are contributing to alleviating at least some human rights abuses linked to conflict minerals.[66] The pursuit of an 'integrated approach' encompassing hard rules and more loosely suasive measures draws tentative support from scholars.[67] At the same time, surging global demand for minerals and ores central to 'green' technologies are bringing a new wave of often similar threats to human rights,[68] which appear set to trigger further EU-level supply chain due diligence requirements in future.[69] Overall, however, the conflict minerals case clearly demonstrates the extensive, dynamic, cross-jurisdictional and multi-actor character of governance activity required to give effect to the norm of business respect for human rights in specific value chain contexts. This is a salutary insight for the EU's initiative to establish cross-sectoral due diligence requirements, considered next.

2.3.2. *'Horizontal' EU Corporate Human Rights Due Diligence Legislation*

European Council Conclusions adopted in 2016 'encourage[d] the Commission to enhance the implementation of due diligence … and to implement policy measures aimed at promoting … human rights due diligence at company level'.[70] In 2020, following the adoption in France of a national due

---

66 IPIS, Project on Resources and Governance (PRG), Sub-Saharan Field Research and Consultancies (SFR) and ULULA, 'Evaluating Due Diligence Programs for Conflict Minerals: A Matched Analysis of 3T Mines in Eastern DRC', 29.03.2021, available at https://ipisresearch.be/wp-content/uploads/2021/03/eval-ddp-20210217.pdf, last accessed 19.07.2021.

67 M. Taka, 'A Critical Analysis of Human Rights Due Diligence Frameworks for Conflict Minerals. Challenges for the Electronics Industries.' in B.A. Andreassen and V. Khanh Vinh (eds.), *Duties Across Borders. Advancing Human Rights in Transnational Business*, Intersentia, Cambridge 2016. See also V. Grado, 'EU Approaches on 'Conflict Minerals': Are they Consistent with the UN/OECD Supply Chain Due Diligence Standards', in A. Bonfanti (ed.), *Business and Human Rights in Europe: International Law Challenges*, Routledge, Milton Park 2020.

68 C. Xu, D. Qiang, L. Gaines et al., 'Future Material Demand for Automotive Lithium-based Batteries', (2020) 1(1), *Communications Materials*, pp. 1–10.

69 European Commission, Proposal for a Regulation of the European Parliament and of the Council concerning batteries and waste batteries, repealing Directive 2006/66/EC and amending Regulation (EU) No 2019/1020, 10 December 2020; see further European Commission, 'Batteries and Accumulators', 2021, available at https://ec.europa.eu/environment/topics/waste-and-recycling/batteries-and-accumulators_en, last accessed 19.07.2021.

70 Council of the European Union, 'The EU and Responsible Global Value Chains – Council conclusions', 12.05.2016, available at https://data.consilium.europa.eu/doc/document/ST-8833-2016-INIT/en/pdf, last accessed 19.07.2021. See also Council of the European Union, 'Council Conclusions on Business and Human Rights', 20.06.2016, available at https://ec.europa.eu/anti-trafficking/sites/antitrafficking/files/council_conclusions_on_business_and_human_rights_foreign_affairs_council.pdf last accessed 19.07.2021. The EC subsequently commissioned a study on due diligence: L. Smit, C. Bright, R. McCorquodale et al., 'Study on Due Diligence Requirements through the

diligence law,[71] the EU Commissioner for Justice made a political commitment to present draft legislation on mandatory human rights and environmental due diligence obligations for EU companies in 2021.[72] Though details are not public at time of writing, a Commission proposal was tabled for regulatory impact assessment in 2021. In parallel, the European Parliament (EP) presented a legislative proposal for corporate due diligence on its own initiative in early 2021.[73]

Hence the EU appears on track to enact cross-sectoral or 'horizontal' corporate human rights due diligence legislation. Key questions regarding such a law include: whether it will encompass all companies or, like the NFR/CSRD, only larger companies meeting certain characteristics in terms of size and value; whether it will extend to environmental as well as human rights harms, and how such 'harm' may be defined;[74] how far due diligence duties will extend through chains of contractual or other business relationships between companies; whether it will seek to establish civil liability for harm caused by breaches of companies' due diligence obligations,[75] besides exposure to administrative enforcement action by authorities in Member States;[76] and whether, as in the conflict minerals scenario, companies will be able to fulfil their due diligence duties via participation in multi-stakeholder or other supply chain initiatives.

Whatever its eventual scheme, such a law will inevitably raise difficult and as yet scarcely acknowledged questions as to how, particularly in the contexts of enforcement and adjudication, the scope and content of 'human rights' should be interpreted and applied given, *inter alia*, the term's specific meaning

---

Supply Chain for the European Commission', 01.01.2020, available at https://op.europa.eu/en/publication-detail/-/publication/8ba0a8fd-4c83-11ea-b8b7-01aa75ed71a1/language-en, last accessed 19.07.2021.

71 LOI n° 2017-399 du 27 mars 2017 relative au devoir de vigilance des sociétés mères et des entreprises donneuses d'ordre, 27.03.2017, available at https://www.legifrance.gouv.fr/loda/id/JORFTEXT000034290626/, last accessed 19.07.2021.

72 European Coalition for Corporate Justice, 'Commissioner Reynders Announces EU Corporate Due Diligence Legislation', 30.04.2020, available at https://corporatejustice.org/news/commissioner-reynders-announces-eu-corporate-due-diligence-legislation/, last accessed 19.07.2021.

73 European Parliament, 'Corporate due diligence and corporate accountability: European Parliament resolution of 10 March 2021 with recommendations to the Commission on corporate due diligence and corporate accountability (2020/2129(INL))', 11.03.2021. Prior to this, the EP commissioned studies: M Krajewski, B. Faracik, C. Methven O'Brien et al., 'Human Rights Due Diligence Legislation – Options for the EU: Briefing', 24.04.2020.

74 See further C. Mackie, 'Due diligence in global value chains: Conceptualizing 'adverse environmental impact'. *RECIEL*. 2021; 00: 1–16.

75 See e.g. N. Bueno and C. Bright, 'Implementing Human Rights Due Diligence Through Corporate Civil Liability' (2020) 69, *International and Comparative Law Quarterly* 789.

76 C. Methven O'Brien and O. Martin-Ortega (2020), 'EU Human Rights Due Diligence Legislation', *supra* note 38; R. Chambers and A.Y. Vastardis, 'Human Rights Disclosure and Due Diligence Laws: The Role of Regulatory Oversight in Ensuring Corporate Accountability', (2021) 21(4), *Chicago Journal of International Law*, pp. 323–366.

within the EU's legal order, with reference to the Charter of Fundamental Rights of the European Union (ECFR) and the European Convention on Human Rights (ECHR), as well as national constitutions and human rights treaty obligations in EU Member States and third countries; and broader issues under public international law relating to causation, attribution and shared responsibility.

2.4. PUBLIC PROCUREMENT

EU governments spend around 14% of gross domestic product (GDP) on public procurement of services, works and supplies.[77] As 'megaconsumers' they should be able to leverage their buying power to induce businesses to revise or adopt new practices, a point long recognised by EU procurement policy, more recently by the UN Framework and UNGPs and other actors.[78] Albeit the exact scope of their liability across global value chains is still unclear, governments are not exculpated by human rights laws in relation to abuses in the public procurement context.[79] Public authorities however remain implicated in human rights abuses linked to suppliers, while reforms remain scant.[80] As national governments and the EU legislator prepare to enact statutory due diligence duties for companies, the exclusion of public authorities from such laws makes for a striking paradox: why should businesses, as non-state actors shoulder heavier human rights

[77] European Commission, 'Public Procurement', 2021, available at https://ec.europa.eu/growth/single-market/publicprocurement, last accessed 19.07.2021.

[78] UN General Assembly, The 2030 Agenda for Sustainable Development, *supra* note 30; CESCR, *General comment No. 24 (2017) on State obligations under the International Covenant on Economic, Social and Cultural Rights in the context of business activities*, UN Doc E/C.12/GC/24, 10.08.2017; CRC, *General comment No. 16 (2013) on State obligations regarding the impact of the business sector on children's rights*, UN Doc CRC/C/GC/16, 17.04.2013; OECD, *Integrating Responsible Business Conduct in Public Procurement*, OECD Publishing, Paris 2020. For almost a century, the ILO has highlighted the importance that governments lead by example and applied minimum labour standards to public contracts: International Labour Organization, 'Report III (Part 1B). General Survey concerning the labour clauses (public contracts) convention, 1949 (No. 94) and recommendation (No. 84) (Report of the Committee of Experts on the Application of conventions and Recommendations)', International Labour Office, Geneva 2008. See further: O. Martin-Ortega and C. Methven O'Brien, 'Advancing Respect for Labour Rights Globally through Public Procurement', (2017) 5(4), *Politics and Governance*, pp. 69–79.

[79] O. Martin-Ortega and C. Methven O'Brien, 'Advancing Respect for Labour Rights Globally through Public Procurement', (2017) 5(4), *Politics and Governance*, pp. 69–79; C. Methven O'Brien and O. Martin-Ortega, 'Public procurement', in S. Deva (ed.), *Research Handbook on Human Rights and Business*, Edward Elgar, Cheltenham 2020.

[80] C. Methven O'Brien, A. Mehra, and N.V. Meulen, 'Public Procurement and Human Rights: A Survey of Twenty Jurisdictions', International Learning Lab on Public Procurement and Human Rights, DIHR/ICAR, 2016, available at http://www.hrprocurementlab.org/resources/reports/, last accessed 19.07.2021.

burdens in the supply chain scenario than the governments who are actually parties to human rights treaties?[81]

The explanation for the diverging duc diligence duties of private and public buyers lies partly in the lexical priority afforded to market integration over human rights concerns within the EU legal order.[82] Historically, this had a 'chilling effect' on the application of 'social' considerations in EU procurements by public authorities.[83] Notwithstanding the constitutional status afforded human and fundamental rights by the Lisbon Treaty,[84] this orientation has continued to condition EC interventions in the procurement arena. Many EU public buyers and suppliers who would otherwise apply progressive human rights terms to public contracts indeed struggle to navigate tendering rules so intent on promoting cross-border tendering that they often deter businesses from bidding for public contracts at all.[85]

The EC's 2011 Communication alluded to public procurement under the banner of 'enhancing market reward for CSR'. Stating that sustainability criteria must remain subordinate to the 'due process' rights of potential tenderers and should never create 'additional administrative burdens for contracting authorities or enterprises',[86] the Strategy omitted any actual legal or policy measures on public procurement. Unsurprisingly, given this, the 2014 EU Procurement Directives, and their transposing legislation in Member States, did not establish human rights-related supply chain duties for public buyers either. The Directives did marginally extend the scope for the temporary exclusion of suppliers from eligibility for public contracts and for public buyers to require that their

---

81 C. Methven O'Brien and O. Martin-Ortega, 'Public procurement and human rights: Discretion, divergence, paradox', in S. Bogojevic, X. Groussot and J. Hettne (eds.), *Discretion in EU Procurement Law*, Hart Publishing, Oxford 2019.

82 *Transport Workers' Federation v Viking and Laval, supra* note 29; cf. ECtHR, *Norwegian Confederation of Trade Unions (LO) and Norwegian Transport Workers' Union (NTF) v Norway, supra* note 29. see further C. Methven O'Brien and O. Martin-Ortega (2020), 'EU Human Rights Due Diligence Legislation', *supra* note 38.

83 C. Methven O'Brien and O. Martin-Ortega, 'Public Procurement and the Erosion of the EU Social Model: Outline of a Polanyian Perspective and the Emerging Regulatory Role of Human Rights?', in L.M. Hinojosa Martínez and P.J. Martín (eds.), *International Markets Regulation and the Erosion of the European Political and Social Model*, Thomson/Reuters, Toronto 2019; A. Sanchez Graells (ed.), *Smart Public Procurement and Labour Standards Pushing the Discussion after RegioPost*, Hart, Oxford 2018.

84 C. Methven O'Brien and O. Martin-Ortega (2019), 'Public Procurement and the Erosion of the EU Social Model: Outline of a Polanyian Perspective and the Emerging Regulatory Role of Human Rights?', *supra* note 83.

85 European Committee of the Regions, 'Next European Commission should avoid introducing new public-procurement legislation', 08.10.2019, available at https://cor.europa.eu/en/news/Pages/next-european-commission-should-avoid-introducing-new-public-procurement-legislation.aspx, last accessed 19.07.2021.

86 European Commission, COM(2011) 681 final 25.10.2011, *supra* note 17, pp. 2–3.

suppliers qualify for 'social labels'.[87] Yet the legality and practical applicability of even such minor measures continue to be contested: procurement lawyers maintain that their market distorting potential is a greater problem for EU law than the market distortion caused by actual human rights abuses, such as human trafficking and child labour.[88] The OECD's recent engagement in this area,[89] and by actors at national level, thus appear to proceed more in spite, than because of, EU procurement law and policy.

2.5. READY-MADE CLOTHES

Exploitative working conditions in the garment and footwear sectors were one of the original triggers for the business and human rights movement in the early 1990s.[90] The catastrophic human toll of the 2013 Rana Plaza disaster prompted renewed public and policy focus on the persistence in clothes production of working conditions amounting to human rights abuses.[91] Besides 'fast fashion' patterns of consumption, cross-disciplinary scholarship has indicated that such conditions result from market dynamics that squeeze the profit margins of local producers competing for contracts from global brands;[92] contexts of weak collective labour rights, gender discrimination and other governance deficits in production locations;[93] as well as ineffectual 'social auditing' regimes.[94]

---

87 A. Marx, 'Public Procurement and Human Rights: Current Role and Potential of Voluntary Sustainability Standards', in O. Martin-Ortega and C. Methven O'Brien (eds.), *Public Procurement and Human Rights*, Edward Elgar, Cheltenham 2018.

88 A. Sanchez-Graells, 'Public Procurement and "Core" Human Rights: A Sketch of the EU Legal Framework', in O. Martin-Ortega and C. Methven O'Brien (eds.), *Public Procurement and Human Rights*, Edward Elgar, Cheltenham 2018.

89 OECD (2020), 'Integrating Responsible Business Conduct in Public Procurement', *supra* note 78.

90 See e.g. L. A. Compa and T. Hinchcliffe Darricarrere, 'Enforcing Labor Rights through Corporate Codes of Conduct', (1995) 33(1), *Columbia Journal of Transnational Law*, pp. 663–673.

91 ILO, 'The Rana Plaza Accident and its Aftermath', 2021, available at https://www.ilo.org/global/topics/geip/WCMS_614394/lang--en/index.htm, last accessed 27.03.2021.

92 K. Marslev, *The Political Economy of Social Upgrading: A Class-relational Analysis of Social and Economic Trajectories of the Garment Industries of Cambodia and Vietnam*, PhD Thesis, Roskilde Universitet 2019.

93 Ibid., S. Barrientos, 'Gender Dynamics in Global Value Chains', in S. Ponte, G. Gereffi and G. Raj-Reichert (eds.), *Handbook on Global Value Chains*, Edward Elgar, Cheltenham 2019.

94 G. LeBaron, J. Lister and P. Dauvergne, 'Governing Global Supply Chain Sustainability through the Ethical Audit Regime', (2017) 14(6), *Globalizations*, pp. 958–975; L. Fransen and G. LeBaron, 'Big Audit Firms as Regulatory Intermediaries in Transnational Labor Governance', (2019) 13(1), *Regulation & Governance*, pp. 260–279.

For various reasons, the regulatory approach applied in the conflict minerals setting is not fully replicable in the garment sector: a traceability regime linked to centralised lists of 'safe' production sites, for example, is less viable where some clothes can be sewn anywhere, without industrial infrastructure.[95] This partly explains the preponderance, and continuing importance, of 'supply side' EU measures, such as financial and political support for international partnerships and development action,[96] on one hand, and on the other, trade-related instruments or sanctions in response to government involvement in violations of collective labour and other human rights in textile producing countries.[97]

2.6. HUMAN TRAFFICKING AND SEVERE LABOUR EXPLOITATION

Human trafficking and severe labour exploitation such as wage theft, excessive working hours and occupational hazards are common across European business sectors including construction, agriculture, manufacturing, catering, care services, cleaning services and domestic work, entertainment, fishing, hospitality, retail and transportation.[98] EU responses to human trafficking pre-date the UNGPs, while they have in places become intermeshed with UNGPs-triggered initiatives as well as standards and processes of the Council of Europe.[99]

---

95 Council of the European Union, *Sustainable Garment Value Chains – Council conclusions*, 19.05.2017, available at https://www.consilium.europa.eu/media/24008/garment-value-chains-st09381en17.pdf, last accessed 19.07.2021.

96 European Commission, Sustainable garment value chains through EU development action Brussels, SDW(2017) 147 final 24.04.2017; J. Kenner and K. Peake, 'The Bangladesh Sustainability Compact: An Effective Exercise of Global Experimentalist EU Governance', (2017) 19(1), *Cambridge Yearbook of European Legal Studies*, pp. 86–115; A. Trebilcock, 'The Rana Plaza Disaster Seven Years on: Transnational Experiments and Perhaps a New Treaty?', (2020) 159(4), *International Labour Review*, pp. 545–568.

97 European Commission, Commission Implementing Decision of 11 February 2019 on the initiation of the procedure for temporary withdrawal of the tariff preferences provided to the Kingdom of Cambodia under Article 19 of Regulation (EU) No 978/2012, 2019/C 55/07; European Council, Council Implementing Regulation (EU) 2021/478 of 22 March 2021 implementing Regulation (EU) 2020/1998 concerning restrictive measures against serious human rights violations and abuses, OJ LI 99.

98 European Union Agency for Fundamental Rights, 'Protecting Migrant Workers from Exploitation in the EU: Workers' Perspectives', Publications Office of the European Union, Luxembourg 2019.

99 A. Lietonen, A. Jokinen and A. Pekkarinen, 'Normative Framework Guide Responsibility of Businesses Concerning Human Rights, Labour Exploitation and Human Trafficking', HEUNI Publication Series No. 94, 2020, https://administrativeapproach.eu/sites/default/files/publication/files/HEUNI_Publication_series_94_FLOW_Normative_framework_Web_11052020.pdf, last accessed 19.07.2021.

Relevant EU rules include those establishing minimum requirements for annual leave, breaks and maximum weekly working time applicable to all workers, including undocumented migrant workers and seasonal workers.[100] The Single Permit Directive provides for common rights to third-country workers legally residing in a Member State, irrespective of the purpose for which they were initially admitted, based on equal treatment with Member State nationals.[101] Under the Anti-Trafficking Directive, Member States should provide for liability of legal persons for trafficking-related offences committed for their benefit,[102] which is important given the lack of a unified framework on labour exploitation and varying definitions of offences of trafficking as such under national criminal laws.[103]

A 2012 EC anti-trafficking strategy introduced programmatic measures to support the Anti-Trafficking Directive.[104] Likewise the Posted Workers Directive,[105] and Enforcement Directive[106] address fraud, inspections and

---

100 Directive 2011/98/EU of the European Parliament and of the Council of 13 December 2011 on a single application procedure for a single permit for third-country nationals to reside and work in the territory of a Member State and on a common set of rights for third-country workers legally residing in a Member State, OJ L343, Article 12(1)(a) (third-country nationals in an irregular situation employed on EU territory); seasonal workers have the right to equal treatment concerning terms of employment including minimum working age, pay and working conditions including dismissal, working hours, leave, and health and safety requirements (Article 23 of the Seasonal Workers Directive 2014/36/EU).

101 Directive 2011/98/EU of the European Parliament and of the Council of 13 December 2011 on a single application procedure for a single permit for third-country nationals to reside and work in the territory of a Member State and on a common set of rights for third-country workers legally residing in a Member State, OJ L343.

102 Directive 2011/36/EU of the European Parliament and of the Council of 5 April 2011 on preventing and combating trafficking in human beings and protecting its victims, and replacing Council Framework Decision 2002/629/JHA, OJ L101, Article 5. The latter applies unless the contractor can prove that it has fulfilled 'due diligence obligations' as defined by national legislation, which might require e.g. informing the subcontractor about the illegality of employment of illegally staying third-country nationals and its consequences.

103 A. Jokinen and N. Ollus (eds.), 'Shady Business: Uncovering the Business Model of Labour Exploitation', HEUNI Publication Series No. 92a, 2020, available at https://www.heuni.fi/en/index/researchareas/humantrafficking/flow_thb.html, last accessed 19.07.2021.

104 European Commission, 'The EU Strategy Towards the Eradication of Trafficking in Human Beings 2012–2016', 07.11.2012, available at https://ec.europa.eu/anti-trafficking/sites/antitrafficking/files/eu_strategy_towards_the_eradication_of_trafficking_in_human_beings_2012-2016_1.pdf, last accessed 19.07.2021; EU Strategy towards the Eradication of Trafficking in Human Beings 2012–2016. This highlights a European Court of Human Rights decision, clarifying states' duties in connection with trafficking prevention: ECtHR, *Rantsev v Cyprus and Russia*, no 25965/04, 10.05.2010.

105 Posting of Directive 96/71/EC of the European Parliament and of the Council of 16 December 1996 concerning the posting of workers in the framework of the provision of services, OJ L18.

106 Directive 2014/67/EU of the European Parliament and of the Council of 15 May 2014 on the enforcement of Directive 96/71/EC concerning the posting of workers in the framework of the provision of services and amending Regulation (EU) No 1024/2012 on administrative cooperation through the Internal Market Information System, OJ L159 (hereinafter the IMI Regulation).

monitoring, joint liability in subcontracting chains and information exchange between Member States.[107] The Employers' Sanctions Directive provides for minimum standards and sanctions on employers of illegally staying third-country nationals,[108] as well as joint liability of contractors and subcontractors.[109] It also requires the establishment of measures to protect undocumented non-EU workers' rights, such as recuperation of outstanding wages, complaint mechanisms, information about rights and access to residence permits. Guidance for companies on due diligence to combat forced labour was published in 2021.[110] Despite an apparently comprehensive regulatory package, trafficking and exploitative practices do not appear to be abating, however, demonstrating the resilience of underlying drivers and the difficulties of policing cross-sectoral forms of abuse, by comparison with those embedded in unique value-chain or technological settings. Besides further enhancement of commitment, powers and resources for enforcement, this also points to the persistent role of and need for further measures to address systemic factors such as weak labour rights and low pay.[111]

2.7. TECH GIANTS AND THE INTERNET

Despite a relationship between the virtual realm and formal human rights jurisdiction that remains hazy in some respects, human rights abuses linked to Internet-based platforms and services, mostly operated by tech giants,[112] have attracted several EU-level responses. Most prominently, in 2016, the EU

[107] Amending Directive to the PWD (2018/957). This addresses challenges faced by posted workers and unclear subcontracting rules. With this amendment, all the mandatory elements of remuneration (until now it was only pay) as well as the rules of the receiving Member State on workers' accommodation and the reimbursement of expenses will be applied to posted workers.

[108] Directive 2009/52/EC of the European Parliament and of the Council of 18 June 2009 providing for minimum standards on sanctions and measures against employers of illegally staying third-country nationals, OJ L168. The directive, for instance, establishes the employer's duty to verify the legal status of workers (Article 4(1)); such as exclusion from entitlement to public benefits; exclusion from participation in a public contract for up to five years; closure of establishments used to commit violations (see Article 7(1)).

[109] Directive 2009/52/EC of the European Parliament and of the Council of 18 June 2009 providing for minimum standards on sanctions and measures against employers of illegally staying third-country nationals, OJ L168.

[110] European Commission, 'Guidance on Due Diligence for EU Businesses to Address the Risk of Forced Labour in their Operations and Supply Chains', 12.07.2021, available at https://trade.ec.europa.eu/doclib/docs/2021/july/tradoc_159709.pdf.

[111] G. Lebaron, 'Wages: An Overlooked Dimension of Business and Human Rights in Global Supply Chains', (2021) 6(1), *Business and Human Rights Journal*, pp. 1–20.

[112] C. Methven O'Brien, R. Jørgensen and B. F. Hogan, 'Tech Giants: Human Rights Risks and Frameworks', 15.12.2020, available at https://ssrn.com/abstract=3768813 or http://dx.doi.org/10.2139/ssrn.3768813, last accessed 19.07.2021. 'Tech giants' refers to technology

adopted its General Data Protection Regulation (GDPR). GDPR requirements protecting the human rights to privacy and data protection apply to all processing of personal data and include data minimisation, purpose limitation, informed consent and access to data.[113] They include 'data protection by design', which requires businesses to assume a proactive approach to data protection and to respect individuals' human right to privacy throughout product development. Under 'privacy by design', no action may be required by an individual user to protect privacy: the highest standards must be applied by default.[114]

Besides the GDPR, many EU measures on tech-related abuses have remained hortatory, in part reflecting their incidence on a transnational, virtual plane. In 2014, the Council adopted compendious *EU Human Rights Guidelines on Freedom of Expression Online and Offline* which cross-refer to EU, Council of Europe, business and human rights and tech-specific standards.[115] A 2017 communication and later recommendation provide extensive guidance to platforms, but lack obvious mechanisms for enforcement.[116] The E-Commerce Directive encouraged companies to adopt codes of conduct and initiated multi-stakeholder voluntary efforts against specific types of illegal online content.[117] In 2015, an EU Internet Forum comprising 'EU Home Affairs Ministers, the Internet industry and other stakeholders' was launched to address misuse of the Internet by terrorist groups. Another non-binding measure, in 2016 the Commission agreed with Facebook, Microsoft, Twitter and YouTube a 'Code of conduct on countering illegal hate speech online' which, by 2020, Instagram, Snapchat, Dailymotion, Jeuxvideo.com and TikTok had also joined.[118]

---

companies that have a dominant position in markets. Alphabet, Amazon, Apple, Facebook and Microsoft are usually referred to as tech giants as to technology companies whose business activities, size and market position raise human rights issues that are qualitatively different to those of other businesses.

113 Regulation (EU) 2016/679 of 27 April 2016 on the protection of natural persons with regard to the processing of personal data and on the free movement of such data and repealing Directive 95/46/EC (General Data Protection Regulation), OJ L119.

114 See further A. Bonfanti, 'ICT Companies' Responsibility to Respect Human Rights: Remarks in the Light of the EU General Data Protection Regulation', in A. Bonfanti (ed.), *Business and Human Rights in Europe: International Law Challenges*, Routledge, Milton Park 2020.

115 Council of the EU, 'EU Human Rights Guidelines on Freedom of Expression Online and Offline', Foreign Affairs Council meeting Brussels, 12.05.2014, available at https://www.consilium.europa.eu/media/28348/142549.pdf, last accessed 19.07.2021.

116 European Commission, Tackling Illegal Content Online Towards an enhanced responsibility of online platforms, COM(2017) 555 final, 28.09.2017; European Commission, Commission recommendation of 1.3.2018 on measures to effectively tackle illegal content online, C(2018) 1177 final, 01.03.2018.

117 Directive 2000/31/EC of the European Parliament and of the Council of 8 June 2000 on certain legal aspects of information society services, in particular electronic commerce, in the Internal Market ('Directive on electronic commerce'), OJ L178.

118 European Commission, 'The EU Code of Conduct on Countering Illegal Hate Speech Online', available at https://ec.europa.eu/info/policies/justice-and-fundamental-rights/combatting-discrimination/racism-and-xenophobia/eu-code-conduct-countering-illegal-hate-speech-online_en, last accessed 19.07.2021.

Performance under the code is subject to periodic monitoring and evaluation.[119] EU multi-stakeholder initiatives likewise address child sexual abuse material, and online disinformation, with a Communication on the latter published in 2018.[120]

2.8. REMEDY FOR BUSINESS-RELATED HUMAN RIGHTS ABUSES

Enhancing access to effective remedies for business-related abuses is the third main focus or 'pillar' of the UN Framework and UNGPs.[121] Victims of business-related abuses both inside and outside Europe continue to face legal and practical obstacles to remedy. These include lack of access to legal representation, information and evidence; attacks on human rights defenders; the risk of counter-litigation; as well as the limits of representative and collective redress mechanisms. Parent company liability for human rights abuses remains restricted.[122]

Over past decades, without close connections to the UN business and human rights agenda, the EU extended access to remedy for victims of business-related abuses in various respects, for instance, concerning discrimination in employment and access to services and environmental liability.[123] More recent measures have sought to counter human trafficking and intra-EU labour exploitation, as considered above. Others have included EU rules on collective redress mechanisms,[124] victims' rights and whistle-blower

119 Ibid.

120 European Commission, Communication from the Commission to the European Parliament, the Council, the European Economic and Social Committee and the Committee of the Regions: Tackling online disinformation: a European Approach, COM(20218) 236 final 26.04.2018.

121 OHCHR Accountability and Remedy Project, 'Improving accountability and access to remedy in cases of business involvement in human rights abuses', 2020, available at https://www.ohchr.org/EN/Issues/Business/Pages/OHCHRaccountabilityandremedyproject.aspx, last accessed 19.07.2021.

122 European Union Agency for Fundamental Rights, 'Business-related human rights abuse reported in the EU and available remedies', 2019, available at https://fra.europa.eu/sites/default/files/fra_uploads/fra-2019-business-and-human-rights-focus_en.pdf, last accessed 19.07.2021.

123 Under the Race Discrimination Directive persons who consider themselves victims of discrimination are entitled to bring their case before competent national authorities, including courts; Directive 2004/35/EC on environmental liability with regard to the prevention and remedying of environmental damage, OJ L143.

124 Commission Recommendation of 11 June 2013 on common principles for injunctive and compensatory collective redress mechanisms in the Member States concerning violations of rights granted under Union Law, OJ L201; This recommendation establishes principles for the establishment by Member States of collective redress mechanisms.

protections.[125] A 2020 Communication sought to enhance access to justice in environmental matters,[126] building on the Union's initial implementation of the Aarhus Convention.[127] EU development aid has been applied to support the development of non-judicial remediation via, for instance, OECD National Contact Points and National Human Rights Institutions. Business and human rights scholarly and policy discussions have however focused, in terms of remedy, mainly on the goal of facilitating civil remedies for extra-EU claimants against EU-based parent companies or EU lead companies purchasing from foreign suppliers.[128] Whether EU diligence legislation will ultimately amend relevant private international law conventions to facilitate such claims remains to be seen.[129] In any event, this goal needs to be situated in the wider framework of remedies alluded to above and via Council of Europe mechanisms, considered next.

---

[125] Directive 2012/29/EU of the European Parliament and of the Council of 25 October 2012 establishing minimum standards on the rights, support and protection of victims of crime, and replacing Council Framework Decision 2001/220/JHA, OJ L315; this directive lays down rights to information, support and protection according to victims' individual needs. Concerning victims of corporate crimes, the directive applies if the act constitutes a crime under national law, unless a crime is defined at EU level (e.g. environmental crimes; European Commission, Proposal for a Directive of the European Parliament and of the Council on the protection of persons reporting on breaches of Union law, COM(2018) 218 final, 23.04.2018.

[126] European Commission, Improving access to justice in environmental matters in the EU and its Member States Brussels, COM(2020) 643 final, 14.10.2020.

[127] Directive 2003/4/EC of the European Parliament and of the Council of 28 January 2003 on public access to environmental information and repealing Council Directive 90/313/EEC, OJ L41; Directive 2003/35/EC of the European Parliament and of the Council of 26 May 2003 providing for public participation in respect of the drawing up of certain plans and programmes relating to the environment and amending with regard to public participation and access to justice Council Directives 85/337/EEC and 96/61/EC, OJ L 156.

[128] E.g. J. Rubio and K. Yannibas (eds.), *Human Rights in Business. Removal of Barriers to Access to Justice in the European Union*, Routledge, Milton Park 2017; A. Bonfanti (ed.), *Business and Human Rights in Europe. International Law Challenges*, Routledge, Milton Park 2019. European Parliament, Resolution of 25 October 2016 on Corporate Liability for Serious Human Rights Abuses in Third Countries, 2015/2315(INI), 25.10.2016; A. Marx et al., *Access to legal remedies for victims of corporate human rights abuses in third countries, European Parliament Study*, 2019, available at https://www.europarl.europa.eu/RegData/etudes/STUD/2019/603475/EXPO_STU(2019)603475_EN.pdf, last accessed on 18.10.2021. European Union Agency for Fundamental Rights, 'Business and human rights – Access to Remedy', Report, 2020, available at https://fra.europa.eu/en/publication/2020/business-human-rights-remedies, last accessed 19.07.2021.

[129] The Brussels I, Rome I and II Regulations define rules on the jurisdiction of Member State courts to adjudicate cross-border private litigation and on applicable law. The Brussels I Regulation (recast) permits claimants to pursue EU-domiciled companies in European courts for damages caused or arising outside the EU; while the Rome II Regulation establishes the applicable law for tort cases, including those concerning human rights infringements.

3. BUSINESS AND HUMAN RIGHTS IN THE COUNCIL OF EUROPE

3.1. BUSINESS AND HUMAN RIGHTS IN THE GENERAL SYSTEM OF PROTECTION

Though not explicitly, the Council of Europe's general system of protection has slowly extended its reach over the corporate domain, even before the 'business and human rights' era.[130] To illustrate, in 2005 the ECtHR identified a state 'duty to regulate' private businesses in environmental cases that has since been applied in other contexts,[131] including human trafficking.[132] ECHR rights have been applied to protect activists against corporations.[133] State-owned enterprises are the subject of a relatively elaborated jurisprudence.[134] ECHR rights to a fair trial and effective remediation have been marshalled in business-related cases,[135] while protection of the right to freedom of association generally impinges

---

130 See generally C. Methven O'Brien, *Business and Human Rights: A Handbook for Legal Practitioners*, Council of Europe, Strasbourg 2018; C. Methven O'Brien, 'Business and Human Rights and Regional Systems of Human Rights Protection: A Governance Analysis', in A. Marx, G. van Calster and J. Wouters, *supra* note 4.

131 ECtHR, *Fadeyeva v Russia*, no 557323/00, 09.06.2005; ECtHR, 'Environment and the European Convention on Human Rights', Factsheet, 01.04.2021, available at https://echr.coe.int/Documents/FS_Environment_ENG.pdf, last accessed 19.07.2021.

132 In ECtHR, *Siliadin v France*, no 73316/01, 26.07.2005, the ECtHR found a specific positive obligation on member States to penalise and prosecute effectively any act aimed at maintaining a person in a situation of slavery, servitude or forced or compulsory labour. In *Rantsev v Cyprus and Russia*, 2010, the ECtHR held that to comply with these positive obligations under Article 4 ECHR, states must put in place a legislative and administrative framework to prohibit and punish trafficking (paragraph 89,112). Further, 'the spectrum of safeguards set out in national legislation must be adequate to ensure the practical and effective protection of the rights of victims or potential victims of trafficking. Accordingly, in addition to criminal law measures to punish traffickers, Article 4 requires Member States to put in place adequate measures regulating businesses often used as a cover for human trafficking.' (Judgment, paragraph 284). See further: ECtHR, 'Factsheet on Slavery, Servitude and Forced Labour and on Trafficking', Factsheet, 01.02.2021, available at https://www.echr.coe.int/Documents/FS_Forced_labour_ENG.pdf, last accessed 19.07.2021.

133 ECtHR, *Steel & Morris v the United Kingdom*, no 68416/01, 15.02.2005; ECtHR, *Steel and others v the United Kingdom*, no 67/1997/851/1058, 23.09.1998.

134 C. Methven O'Brien (2018), *Business and Human Rights. A Handbook for Legal Practitioners, supra* note 6, pp. 33–39; see further C. Wee, 'Regulating the Human Rights Impact of State-owned Enterprises: Tendencies of Corporate Accountability and State Responsibility', ICJ, Denmark, 2008; UNHRC, 'Report of the Working Group on the issue of human rights and transnational corporations and other business enterprises', UN Doc A/HRC/32/45, 04.05.2016.

135 On Article 13, see recently ECtHR, *Cordella et al. v Italy*, joint applications nos. 54414/13 and 54264/15, 24.06.2019.

on business.[136] Collective rights under the 1961 European Social Charter (ESC)/Revised ESC are subject to remediation via a non-judicial collective complaints mechanism.[137] Such rights include the right to work, to organise and collective bargaining; to social security; social assistance; the right of the family to social, legal and economic protection; and certain rights of migrant workers.[138] Attempts to engage the Court in adjudicating business-related abuses occurring beyond the territorial jurisdiction of states parties to CoE legal instruments have not however so far succeeded.[139]

Still, the CoE has concluded specialised instruments on threats to human rights where businesses are particularly implicated, with a growing focus on technology-related issues. Initially these addressed processing of personal data.[140] More recently, the CoE has adopted a Convention on Cybercrime addressing private and public 'service providers';[141] and a 2014 Recommendation on the human rights of Internet users.[142] Instruments on women's and children's rights encompass the private sector,[143] which is also strongly in focus in the Convention on Action against Trafficking in Human

---

136 Most recently, see ECtHR, *Norwegian Confederation of Trade Unions (LO) and Norwegian Transport Workers' Union (NTF) v Norway*, no 45487/17, 20.06.2021.

137 Additional Protocol to the European Social Charter Providing for a System of Collective Complaints (ETS No. 158), 1995.

138 See C. Altafin, K. Lukas and M. Nowak, 'The Normative Framework of the EU's Commitment to Human Rights', *supra* note 16.

139 ECCHR, 'Nestlé precedent case: Murder of trade unionist Romero in Colombia', available at https://www.ecchr.eu/en/case/nestle-precedent-case-murder-of-trade-unionist-romero-in-colombia/, last accessed 19.07.2021; see further C. Methven O'Brien, 'The Home State Duty to Regulate the Human Rights Impacts of TNCs Abroad: A Rebuttal', (2018) 31(1), *Business and Human Rights Journal*, pp. 47–73; M. Fasciglione, 'Enforcing the State Duty to Protect under the UN Guiding Principles on Business and Human Rights: Strasbourg Views', in A. Bonfanti (ed.), *Business and Human Rights in Europe: International Law Challenges*, Routledge, Oxford 2018.

140 Convention for the Protection of Individuals with regard to Automatic Processing of Personal Data (ETS No. 108), 1981, Article 3.

141 Convention on Cybercrime (ETS No. 185), 2001.

142 Recommendation CM/Rec(2014)6 of the Committee of Ministers to member States on a Guide to human rights for Internet users.

143 Convention on Preventing and Combating Violence against Women and Domestic Violence (CETS No. 210), 2011; Recommendation CM/Rec(2018)7 of the Committee of Ministers to member States on guidelines for the respect, protection and fulfilment of the rights of the child in the digital environment, provides guidance on measures to be taken with regard to all stakeholders, including businesses; recommend that governments 'require companies to take responsibility and enforcement measures to respect children's rights in the digital environment and encourage them to cooperate with state stakeholders, civil society organizations and children, taking into account relevant international and European standards and guidelines'; an annex outlines measures for member States in relation to business; Convention on the Exercise of Children's Rights (ETS No. 160), 1996; Convention on the Protection of Children against Sexual Exploitation and Sexual Abuse (CETS No. 201), 2007.

Beings and the Criminal Law Convention on Corruption.[144] Newer mandates on environment and climate change,[145] and cloning of human beings, human organs and tissue transplants and genetic testing foresee and aim to counter business-related abuses.[146]

3.2. RESPONSE TO UNGPs

The UNGPs have not served as an organising cross-institutional framework or motor for innovation in the CoE as they have in the EU setting. An initial CoE declaration in support of the UNGPs was followed by a non-binding recommendation.[147] Mirroring the overall approach of the UNGPs, though introducing some specific regional concerns, the recommendation calls for governments to implement the UNGPs and periodically to review their adherence across areas such as company regulation, state-owned enterprises and public procurement, trade agreements, investment promotion and access to justice for victims of business-related abuses.[148] It also provides for embryonic regional arrangements for state reporting on business and human rights.[149] Until now, however, these commitments have not been well honoured in practice.[150] There is little trace either of a discrete influence on states, businesses or other actors owing to the CoE's UNGPs-specific measures. The CoE's marginal contribution in advancing international business and human rights norms thus appears curiously out of kilter with its potential, judged by its impact on national law, policy and the effectiveness of human rights in other areas.[151]

---

144 Council of Europe Convention on Action against Trafficking in Human Beings (CETS No. 197), 2005; Criminal Law Convention on Corruption (ETS No. 173), 1999, Articles 7, 8.

145 Drafting Group on Human Rights and the Environment (CDDH-ENV) is preparing non-binding instruments of the Committee of Ministers on Human Rights and the Environment.

146 Convention on Human Rights and Biomedicine (ETS No. 164), 1997 and its additional protocols.

147 Recommendation CM/Rec(2016)3 of the Committee of Ministers to member States on human rights and business.

148 Appendix, paragraph 1.

149 Via a public 'shared information system, created and managed by the [CoE]', to incorporate CoE Member States' National Action Plans and 'good practices': Council of Europe, 'Online Platform for Human Rights and Business', 2021, available at https://www.coe.int/en/web/human-rights-intergovernmental-cooperation/online-platform-for-human-rights-and-business, last accessed 11.07.2021.

150 A questionnaire was issued and responded to by only 14 of 47 member States: CDDH(2016)06; document CDDH(2019)01 and in June 2020; specific questionnaire on access to remedies sent to the relevant Council of Europe steering and convention-based committees (document CDDH(2020)26, also in June 2020).

151 See further C. Methven O'Brien, 'Business and Human Rights and Regional Systems of Human Rights Protection: A Governance Analysis', in A. Marx, G. van Calster and J. Wouters, *supra*, note 4.

4. THE NATIONAL LEVEL: BUSINESS AND HUMAN RIGHTS IN EUROPEAN STATES

Capturing aggregate changes across all areas where businesses jeopardise enjoyment of human rights, and both in the public and private sectors, in a single state is hard. Doing so across the European continent would be an invaluable exercise but is not possible in the constraints of the current contribution, if at all. Here, accordingly, the approach is selective, focusing on business and human rights national action plans and national laws requiring due diligence, as two elements emblematically associated with business and human rights in the post-2011 era of the UNGPs.

4.1. NATIONAL ACTION PLANS ON BUSINESS AND HUMAN RIGHTS

Since 2011, the EU has repeatedly encouraged states to develop NAPs as a vector to support implementation of the UNGPs, convening various regional meetings to foster this goal.[152] As mentioned above, the CoE's Recommendation likewise exhorts states to produce NAPs. Guidance has been concluded by international bodies on how such NAPs should be developed and on matters they should address.[153] Of 26 NAPs produced to date, 19 are European.[154]

How to evaluate business and human rights NAPs is a question that has attracted interest from scholars.[155] Self-evidently, NAPs are not a substitute for business regulation. At least on some theoretical accounts, however, NAPs may be have a governance potential in relation to in relation to complex, multi-level business and human rights problems.[156] In support of this hypothesis, at

---

152 European Commission, COM(2011) 681 final, *supra* note 17, pp. 2–3; European Commission, SWD(2019) 143, section 8, *supra* note 25.

153 UN Working Group on Business and Human Rights, 'Report of the Working Group on the Issue of Human Rights and Transnational Corporations and Other Business Enterprises', UN Doc A/HRC/20/29, 10.04.2012.

154 DIHR, 'National Action Plans on Business and Human Rights', 2020, available at https://globalnaps.org, last accessed 19.07.2021.

155 E.g. C. Methven O'Brien, A. Mehra, S. Blackwell et al., 'National Action Plans: Current Status and Future Prospects for a New Business and Human Rights Governance Tool', (2016) 1(1), *Business and Human Rights Journal*, pp. 117–126; M. Bordignon, 'National Action Plans. A Pathway to Effective Implementation of the UNGPs?', in A. Bonfanti (ed.), *Business and Human Rights in Europe: International Law Challenges*, Routledge, Milton Park 2020; H. Cantú Rivera, 'National Action Plans on Business and Human rights: Progress or Mirage?', (2019) 4(2), *Business and Human Rights Journal*, pp. 213–237.

156 C. Methven O'Brien, J. Ferguson and M. Mcvey, 'National Action Plans on Business and Human Rights: An Experimentalist Governance Analysis', (2021) *Human Rights Review*, https://doi.org/10.1007/s12142-021-00637-x.

least some NAPs have stimulated sector-based dialogues, networks, analyses, and commitments albeit it remains premature to evaluate their ultimate consequences.[157] Such hybrid mechanisms may be crucial where the wider legal framework may constrain hard law interventions,[158] or where knowledge and capacities needed to define regulatory modalities and give effect to them in practice are widely dispersed amongst actors, as illustrated above in the conflict minerals scenario, to take but one example. Though seldom, NAPs have also paved the way for new business and human rights legislation. Germany's NAP, for instance, pegged a promise to take further action to a target for uptake by companies of human rights due diligence.[159] When the target was missed, a process was set in train that culminated in adoption of a new national due diligence law.[160] Viewed as devices that exert governance effects through coordination, dialogue and, potentially, linkages to sectoral, regional and international reporting and oversight mechanisms, European NAPs seem to deserve an initially positive if still tentative assessment.

4.2. CORPORATE HUMAN RIGHTS DUE DILIGENCE LAWS

National laws that directly require the performance of human rights due diligence by companies have emerged in a small number of European states. France's *Loi sur le devoir de vigilance* was the first to establish such a duty.[161] To fulfil their

---

157 H. Huyse and B. Verbrugge, 'Belgium and the Sustainable Supply Chain Agenda: Leader or Laggard? – Review of human right due diligence initiatives in the Netherlands, Germany, France and EU, and implications for policy work by Belgian civil society', Report, 2018, available at https://limo.libis.be/primo-explore/fulldisplay?docid=LIRIAS1899399&context=L&vid=Lirias&search_scope=Lirias&tab=default_tab&lang=en_US&fromSitemap=1, last accessed 19.07.2021.

158 A. Ansong, 'SDG 8 and Elimination of Child Labour in the Cocoa Industry in Ghana: Can WTO Law and Private Sector Responsible Business Initiatives Help?', (2020) 47(2), *Forum for Development Studies*, pp. 261–281; A. Sanchez-Graells (2018), 'Public Procurement and "Core" Human Rights: A Sketch of the EU Legal Framework', *supra* note 88.

159 The target was that 50% of enterprises with more than 500 employees should adopt due diligence by 2020: German Federal Foreign Office, 'National Action Plan: Implementation of the UN Guiding Principles on Business and Human Rights 2016–2020' National Action Plan, 16.12.2016, available at https://globalnaps.org/wp-content/uploads/2018/04/16uropa16-national-action-plan-business-and-human-rights.pdf, last accessed 19.07.2021.

160 German Federal Ministry of Labour and Social Affairs, 'Commitment of the Federal Government: Monitoring', Website, 2021, available at https://www.csr-in-deutschland.de/EN/Business-Human-Rights/Commitment-of-the-Federal-Government/Monitoring/monitoring.html, last accessed 02.04.2021.

161 LOI n° 2017-399 du 27 mars 2017 relative au devoir de vigilance des sociétés mères et des entreprises donneuses d'ordre, 27.03.2017. This duty applies to companies incorporated or

obligations under this law, companies must develop, disclose and implement a 'vigilance plan' that should comprise 'reasonable vigilance measures adequately to identify risks and prevent serious violations of human rights and fundamental freedoms, risks and serious harms to health and safety and the environment'. Liability under the French Civil Code may follow a failure to comply with this duty where it can be linked to actual harm to fundamental freedoms, health and safety or the environment. Several sets of proceedings are underway against companies in French courts, though none has yet issued in a final positive result for victims.[162]

In the Netherlands, a 2019 law requires companies selling goods on the Dutch market to investigate whether there is reasonable suspicion of the use of child labour in their supply chains. Where there is, the company needs to adopt and implement an action plan to combat it. Companies must certify that they exercise due diligence to prevent goods or services from being produced using child labour.[163] Failure to comply with requirements under the Act may, in principle, result in administrative orders or fines.

As mentioned above, a German due diligence law (Act on Corporate Due Diligence in Supply Chains) was passed in 2021, to enter into force in 2023.[164] Companies covered by the law must identify risks of human rights violations and environmental destruction by direct suppliers and,[165] where relevant, indirect suppliers.[166] In line with the elements of due diligence signalled by the

registered in France and employing at least 5,000 people including through their French subsidiaries, or employing at least 10,000 people including through their subsidiaries located in France and abroad.

162 S. Cossart, J. Chaplier, and T. Beau De Lomenie, 'The French Law on Duty of Care: A Historic Step Towards Making Globalization Work for All', (2017) 2(2), *Business and Human Rights Journal*, pp. 317–323; E. Savourey and S. Brabant, 'The French Law on the Duty of Vigilance: Theoretical and Practical Challenges Since its Adoption', (2021) 6(1), *Business and Human Rights Journal*, pp. 141–152.

163 Ministerie Van Buitenlandse Zaken, Wet van 24 oktober 2019 houdende de invoering van én zorgplicht ter voorkoming van de levering van goederen en diensten die met behulp van kinderarbeid tot stand zijn gekomen (Wet zorgplicht kinderarbeid), 13.11.2019, available at https://zoek.officielebekendmakingen.nl/stb-2019-401.html, last accessed 19.07.2021.

164 Deutscher Bundestag, 'Gesetzesentwurf der Bundesregierung: Entwurf eines Gesetzes über die Unternehmerischen Sorgfaltspflichten in Lieferketten', Drucksache 19/28649, 19.04.2021, available at https://dserver.bundestag.de/btd/19/286/1928649.pdf, last accessed 19.07.2021; see further: Bundesministerium für Arbeit und Soziales, 'Sorgfaltspflichtengesetz – Gesetz über die unternehmerischen Sorgfaltspflichten zur Vermeidung von Menschenrechtsverletzungen in Lieferketten', 2021, available at https://www.bmas.de/DE/Service/Gesetze-und-Gesetzesvorhaben/gesetz-unternehmerische-sorgfaltspflichten-lieferketten.html, last accessed 19.07.2021; for the taking effect of the law, see Article 4.

165 The Act will initially cover companies with 3,000 or more employees, and from 2024 onwards companies with 1,000 or more employees; ibid., Articles 1, 3.

166 Ibid., Article 2(7) and (8).

UNGPs, the German law specifically requires of companies a policy statement on respect for human rights;[167] human rights risk analysis;[168] a human rights risk management system;[169] to include remedial measures;[170] a grievance mechanism for reporting of human rights abuses which must be investigated by the company;[171] and documentation and transparent public reporting.[172]

In terms of penalties, the Act provides for fines by the German Federal Office of Economics and Export Control (Bundesamt für Wirtschaft und Ausfuhrkontrolle);[173] and exclusion from public tenders for up to three years in serious cases.[174] Victims of adverse human rights impacts can seek remediation through German civil courts via a representative action for damages.[175] However, under German tort law, companies will only be vicariously liable for a supplier's abuses, restricting this element's practical application, and demonstrating how due diligence laws are being fashioned to fit with the specificities of national laws as well as institutions.[176]

A new Norwegian law mandates due diligence on human rights and labour covering approximately 9,000 larger enterprises.[177] This also guarantees public access to information on how companies respond to impacts on human rights

---

167 Ibid., Article 6(2).

168 Ibid., Article 5.

169 Ibid., Article 4(1).

170 Ibid., Article 7(1), (2) and (3).

171 Ibid., Article 8.

172 Ibid., Article 10(1) and (2).

173 The Act sets out that the exact amount will be determined by reference to the company's annual turnover; see ibid., Article 24(3).

174 Ibid., Article 24(1).

175 Ibid., Article 11(1): 'Anyone who is violated in an important legal position from section 2(1) can authorize a domestic trade union or non-governmental organization to conduct legal proceedings in order to assert their rights in court' (own translation).

176 In the commentary to Article 9, the law anchors the due diligence of a company with regard to the risks at the indirect supplier (own translation), ibid., p. 50.

177 In their preface to the proposed law, the Norwegian Ministry for Children and Families estimates 8830 enterprises to be affected; See Det Kongelige Barne- Og Familiedepartmenet, 'Lov om Virksomheters Åpenhet og Arbeid med Grunnleggende Menneskerettigheter og Anstendige Arbeidsforhold (Åpenhedsloven)' (Prop. 150 L), 09.03.2021, p. 93. The law expects (a) the anchoring of accountability in the company's guidelines; (b) the identification and assessment of actual and potential consequences for fundamental human rights and decent working conditions that the company has either caused or contributed to, or that are directly linked to the company's business activities, products or services through supply chains or business partners; (c) the implementation of appropriate measures to stop, prevent or limit negative consequences based on the company's priorities and assessments set out in letter (b); (d) monitoring of implementation and results of the measures implemented; (e) communicating with affected stakeholders and licensees about how negative consequences have been handled in accordance with letters (c) and (d); (f) arrange for or cooperate on recovery and compensation where this is required (own translation; Article 4). If companies fail to comply, they face the risk of injunction or fines, which can be imposed on both companies and responsible individuals within a company (own translation; Article 9).

and decent work.[178] Proposals for further due diligence laws are, with various degrees of political support, under discussion in other European states, including Belgium,[179] Finland,[180] Austria[181] and the Netherlands.[182]

European due diligence laws, then, exhibit diversity in the scope and extent of duties articulated as well as their specific anchoring in national civil, criminal and administrative law. Such divergences, it should be expected, will also characterise approaches to implementation of any European regional norms on mandatory due diligence, and more so in the context of an international business and human rights treaty. Such variation should not be viewed as surprising from a comparative law standpoint[183] or past experiences of market integration legislation in the European Union setting.[184]

5. A DECADE OF BUSINESS AND HUMAN RIGHTS IN EUROPE: TEN OBSERVATIONS

Building on the foregoing analysis, this section offers ten observations regarding emerging characteristics, advances, trends, contradictions, biases and gaps manifesting across a decade of European business and human rights developments.

---

178 Ibid., Article 6, 7.

179 In Belgium, the Federal Parliament voted in favour of a due diligence bill proposal to strengthen the obligations of companies throughout their supply chains in 2021; available at https://www.cncd.be/Pour-une-loi-belge-sur-le-devoir, last accessed 19.07.2021.

180 The Finnish Ministry of Economic Affairs and Employment published an analysis to outline the obligations that could be imposed on companies within the Finnish legislative framework; see Ministry of Economic Affairs and Employment of Finland, 'Judicial Analysis Specifies the Planned Corporate Social Responsibility Act in Finland', Press Release, 30.06.2020, available at https://tem.fi/en/-/judicial-analysis-specifies-the-planned-corporate-social-responsibility-act-in-finland, last accessed 19.07.2021.

181 The Austrian Social Democrats, at the time opposition party, suggested a mandatory human rights due diligence law in March 2021; see Entschließungsantrag der Abgeordneten Julia Herr, Petra Bayr, MA MLS, betreffend ein Lieferkettengesetz for eine soziale, menschenrechtskonforme und nachhaltige Produktionsweise (1454/A(E) XXVII. GP), 25.03.2021, available at https://www.parlament.gv.at/PAKT/VHG/XXVII/A/A_01454/index.shtml, last accessed 19.07.2021.

182 A new Bill for Responsible and Sustainable International Business Conduct 2021 would impose a duty of care to prevent negative impacts on human rights and the environment anywhere within the value chain on all companies registered in the Netherlands or that sell products or services on the Dutch market: Mvoplatform, 'Translation of the Bill for Responsible and Sustainable International Business Conduct', 22.03.2021, available at https://www.mvoplatform.nl/en/translation-of-the-bill-for-responsible-and-sustainable-international-business-conduct/, last accessed 19.07.2021.

183 J.S. Bell, 'Comparative Administrative Law' in M. Reimann and R Zimmermann (eds.), *The Oxford Handbook of Comparative Law*, OUP, Oxford 2006, p. 1260.

184 O. Lando, 'Principles of European Contract Law: An Alternative to or a Precursor of European Legislation?', (1992) 40(3), *The American Journal of Comparative Law*, pp. 573–585; F. De Elizalde (ed.), *Uniform Rules for European Contract Law? A Critical Assessment*, Hart, Oxford 2020.

5.1. EXTENDING HUMAN RIGHTS' NORMATIVE HORIZON

In Europe, human rights norms are now being applied regularly, directly and explicitly, to confront the business sphere and the workings of individual corporations, not just rhetorically, but also through an increasing systematic integration into business-related legal and policy instruments. Previously, markets were disciplined only sporadically and superficially by human rights standards through the operation of general doctrinal devices and substantive rules. Since 2011, any presumption that business activity as such and corporations should remain beyond the reach of human rights has lapsed. At the level of principle, this should be recognised as a significant and positive change, perhaps even signalling a paradigmatic shift, which has potential to extend the emancipatory possibilities associated with human rights principles and practice.

5.2. NEW DOCTRINAL CHALLENGES

While an ethical and political victory, the new application of human rights principles, and their substantive content, to the sphere of business actors, activities and relations carries consequences for human rights as a field of *law*. The substantive and procedural rules of human rights law generally presuppose a sovereign, territorially delimited state as duty bearer for whom human rights should ultimately supplant almost all other considerations. Businesses, on the other hand, are legally constituted to perform 'specialised' social functions, with a broad licence to prioritise the interests of shareholders. They also lack the competence and legitimacy to adjudicate conflicting human rights or public interests. Not all the content of human rights norms, or even much of it, transposes readily to the corporate context.

European human rights jurisprudence comprises an extensive and intricate normative architecture, embodying the careful weighing over decades of competing ethical, political, cultural, institutional and inter-jurisdictional considerations, many regionally- or nationally-specific. Textual references to 'human rights' in business and human rights laws or policies in Europe cannot be isolated from and will inevitably be interpreted within this context. Juridification of business and human rights principles, where Europe is currently leading the way, hence carries challenges of coherence that do not appear to have been fully recognised by policy-makers or jurists up to this point. These will arise, for instance, in the context of mandatory due diligence legislation, particularly where this envisages related civil liabilities; with reference to the status and effects of the ECFR; as regards EU extraterritoriality of the CoE and EU instruments;[185] and in context of EU accession to the ECHR, amongst many others.

5.3. A FIELD OF MULTI-LEVEL GOVERNANCE

Business and human rights in Europe is a field of multi-level governance.[186] Its rules and regimes originate from international, regional and national levels, but also from hybrid public-private and transnational regimes. These multiple 'jurisdictions' are interconnected, rather than autonomous, increasingly technical and often competing. Their rules are often overlapping but are not organised according to neat hierarchies, and they display multiple legal 'transplants', borrowings and re-purposings. New international standards have triggered regional and state-level initiatives, but initiatives at subordinate levels give them concrete effect and pull them into new directions.

The entire field is dynamic, complex and dense. The intricacies of non-financial reporting and due diligence, as well as sector or thematic regimes (for example, on conflict minerals, trafficking, procurement and the Internet) are highly esoteric. Understanding their goals and mechanisms requires knowledge and resources that will often exceed those of the rights-holders they are intended to benefit, and even represents a challenge for legislators and scholars. The multiple 'peripheries' of business and human rights have already escaped the view of national and regional 'centres': the business and human rights field, like economy and society, is truly polycentric. General rules, accordingly, will not produce identical or even similar effects horizontally and continuing heterogeneity amongst regulatory approaches and outcomes is a certainty.

5.4. BUSINESS AND HUMAN RIGHTS LAW: A COMPOSITE OF HARD AND SOFT

A common critique of the UNGPs has centred on their soft law character, and the lack of 'binding' measures to enforce them. In some areas such observations remain valid. Still, the above analysis shows the picture to be more complex. Even without direct 'corporate' human rights duties under international

185 Cf. J. Scott, 'The New EU Extraterritoriality', (2014) 51(5), *Common Market Law Review*, pp. 1343–1380.

186 C. Methven O'Brien, 'Governance, Business and Human Rights: From State to Market and Back Again', in B.A. Andreassen, *Research Handbook on Politics of International Human Rights Law: Governance, Distributive Justice and International Politics* (forthcoming 2022); C. Methven O'Brien and J. Ford (2019), 'Business and Human Rights', *supra* note 4, pp. 216–233.

human rights law, and prior to the UNGPs, human rights were protected against corporate activity via regional and national norms and mechanisms across multiple domains. Looking at measures tracing their origins to the UNGPs, there is evidence in Europe, moreover, of a trajectory from soft to hard law. Mandatory human rights due diligence laws were not called for by or widely anticipated prior to the UNGPs.[187] Yet they are providing a vector for 'hardening' of the corporate responsibility to respect human rights at an accelerating pace. On the other hand, some more mature European regimes (for example, concerning conflict minerals) demonstrate the likelihood of a continuing role for soft laws, especially those linked to technical standards, in supplementing higher-level legal rules.

5.5. RE-CONFIGURING REGIONAL AS WELL AS NATIONAL HUMAN RIGHTS SYSTEMS

Business and human rights has re-drawn the perimeter of 'national human rights systems', pulling existing national human rights actors into new mandates and activities; enrolling new public and private entities into domestic human rights implementation efforts; and via national components of associational or hybrid governance mechanisms.[188] Similar dynamics are in play at regional level. Through the business and human rights agenda, EU actors (including the EC, EU External Action Service, EP and FRA) have acquired new objectives, policies, activities and resource allocations.[189] Businesses, business associations, financial sector actors, civil society entities, domestic regulators, courts and legal professionals now join human rights policy debate and dialogues at the EU level, as well as implementation and oversight of corporate human rights performance, domestically and transnationally (e.g. third party monitoring of supply chain audits under EU Conflict Minerals Regulation). In the CoE setting, such changes have remained marginal, beyond long-standing thematic mandates (human trafficking, Internet), striking a curious contrast with the EU.

---

187 J. Wouters and L. Chanet (2008), 'Corporate Human Rights Responsibility' *supra* note 18, pp. 261–303.

188 C. Methven O'Brien and J. Ford (2019), 'Business and Human Rights', *supra* note 4, pp. 216–233.

189 The Communication on Smart Regulation introduced an assessment of the impact of any future legislation and policies on fundamental rights. For this purpose, in 2011, the Commission developed Operational Guidance on taking account of Fundamental Rights in Commission Impact Assessments. Based on these guidelines, depending on the policy context, it is necessary to take international human rights conventions into account when interpreting the rights set out in the Charter. All Commission legislative proposals and their implementation at Member States level have to respect the Charter of Fundamental Rights: Commission Better Regulation Guidelines: 'Where relevant, the impact assessments should examine the impact of the different options on fundamental rights and the potential exposure to fraud in the context of spending programmes'.

5.6. SILOED INTRA-EU AND 'GLOBAL' BUSINESS AND HUMAN RIGHTS AGENDAS

The publication of the UN Framework in 2008 coincided with a global financial crisis whose fallout was deleterious for the human rights of many millions of people in Europe. Even before COVID-19, post-2008 'recovery' measures led to an unprecedented enrichment of financial players, engorged with government-backed debt and cheap public assets, and the siphoning of wealth to tech companies via global monopoly positions and exploitative working arrangements. The very real consequences for rights-holders in Europe of this scenario, in which businesses, investors, business models and, increasingly, foreign companies operating in the EU are implicated, include a calculated corporate erosion of labour rights and a correlate extension of precarious employment and labour exploitation; deepening child poverty, carrying life-long consequences; diminished access to essential public services and effective access to justice; and other widespread denials of basic civil, political, social and economic rights, particularly for vulnerable and discriminated groups.

This business and human rights history of the last ten years is rarely represented in European business and human rights materials, which typically focus on abuses outside Europe to which European companies are connected via global value chains. Vice versa, business and human rights standards have not been integrated into European economic and social rights agendas and initiatives such as the EU Social Pillar.[190] Neither have they been activated in the context of recent European conflicts between freedom of establishment and freedom of association, for example.[191]

Such disconnects are damaging. Threats from business to rights-holders inside Europe in many cases share root causes with those in transnational supply chains. Foreign factory collapses or land grabs are often blamed on the weak capacity of local actors or bad animus of individual European lead companies or investors. While attribution of blame in specific cases is prerequisite to certain forms of remedy, greater recognition of the widespread and persistent character of business-related abuses also inside Europe would highlight common

[190] In 2017, the European Pillar of Social Rights was proclaimed comprising 20 key principles and rights to support fair and well-functioning labour markets and welfare systems structured around three categories: equal opportunities and access to the labour market, fair working conditions and social protection and inclusion. It is intended to 'provide … a compass for EU and Member States' social and economic governance with the objective to improve upward convergence in the EU'; Council of the European Union, Commission Staff Working Document Corporate Social Responsibility, Responsible Business Conduct, and Business & Human Rights: Overview of Progress, SWD(2019) 143 final 20.03.2019, p. 34; See also: EPR, 'European Pillar of Social Rights', 2019, available at https://www.epr.eu/what-we-do/policy-analysis/european-pillar-of-social-rights/, last accessed 19.07.2021.

[191] S. Sciarra, 'Viking and Laval: Collective Labour Rights and Market Freedoms in the Enlarged EU', (2008) 10(1), *Cambridge Yearbook of European Legal Studies*, pp. 563–580.

structural causes and the need for systemic transformation. It might also help to give business and human rights policies stronger anchoring with Europe's national governments. An emphasis on extra-EU business and human rights impacts is associated with the allocation of responsibility for NAPs to foreign ministries, for instance, which does not appear to have supported their overall impact or credibility.

5.7. THE FINANCIALISATION OF BUSINESS AND HUMAN RIGHTS

Amongst likely structural causes of business and human rights abuses, as just alluded to, is the financialisation of the European as well as global economy. Of concern, then, is the increasing financialisation of the business and human rights field itself via an increasingly predominant focus on investor-driven accountability mechanisms for corporate accountability to human rights and broader social and environmental standards. Though sustainable reporting and ESG investment are ascendant in policy terms and corporate practice, scholarship counsels scepticism about overreliance on this approach, which at minimum requires hedging via direct regulation; and measures to empower to a greater extent other accountability principals, particularly organised labour as well as citizens, regulators and legislators. 'Big data' solutions, which the RBCD and Taxonomy rules aim to facilitate, may mitigate but ultimately appear unlikely to transcend underlying weaknesses in the reliability of corporate sustainability reports and accountability mechanisms built on them. The scope for mystification and regulatory capture attendant on such characteristics are a particular challenge for human rights as an emancipatory discourse and discipline that relies for its legitimacy on universal relevance and accessibility. A further concern is the tendency in EU measures (Taxonomy, NFRD, procurement) to prioritise 'green' over social objectives, the former to be given 'harder' effect first, with human rights protections, under the umbrella of 'social' considerations, following later, if at all. Though, technically, this may make sense, given the greater ease of quantifying company contributions to carbon emissions, such an approach jars with the Union's foundational human rights commitments and may not prove politically durable in the longer run.

5.8. REMEDIATION

The range of European business and human rights regulations above illustrate the context-dependency of effective remediation, and why it is appropriate that remedies should encompass prosecution and punishment of perpetrators, for instance, in the context of trafficking or other serious exploitative labour practices, as well as compensation for economically assessable damage, orders for restitution; changes in company policies, guarantees of non-repetition; or disciplinary action against responsible personnel and public apologies.[192] Though tort liability may be the best route to remedy in certain cases, it would be misleading to present it as the only route or even the most appropriate in all instances. An EU due diligence law should hence include a broad duty on Member States to establish penalties for non-compliance which are effective, proportionate and dissuasive; create national enforcement bodies (or provide specific competences to existing national bodies to exercise this function); and establish clear and specific roles for interested parties in enforcement procedures, while Member States should also report periodically on national enforcement actions.[193] Regional oversight and supervisory mechanisms will also remain essential in highlighting weaknesses and deficits in remediation across European jurisdictions. The CoE should assume a greater and more proactive role in this context. National human rights bodies and non-judicial grievance mechanisms, that seem far from fulfilling their potential, likewise require further activation.[194]

5.9. IMPLICATIONS FOR UN BUSINESS AND HUMAN RIGHTS TREATY PROCESS

As seen here, European regulatory interventions address business conduct directly through new substantive standards, due diligence duties, criminal and administrative sanctions; and indirect mechanisms, such as transparency requirements for companies and financial sector actors. According to context, to be effective regulation needs to address both 'push' and 'pull' factors, including framework conditions set by trade and investment regimes; social

192 European Union Agency for Fundamental Rights, 'Business-related human rights abuse reported in the EU and available remedies', 2019, available at https://fra.europa.eu/sites/default/files/fra_uploads/fra-2019-business-and-human-rights-focus_en.pdf, last accessed 19.07.2021; International Labour Organization, 'Time to Act for SDG 8: Integrating Decent Work, Sustained Growth and Environmental Integrity', 2019, available at https://www.ilo.org/wcmsp5/groups/public/---dgreports/---inst/documents/publication/wcms_712685.pdf, last accessed 19.07.2021.

193 C. Methven O'Brien and O. Martin-Ortega (2020), 'EU Human Rights Due Diligence Legislation', *supra* note 38.

194 R. Wolfsteller, 'The Unrealized Potential of National Human Rights Institutions in Business and Human Rights Regulation: Conditions for Effective Engagement and Proposal for Reform', (forthcoming 2022) 23(1), *Human Rights Review*; UN Human Rights Council, Report of the Working Group on the Issue of Human Rights and Transnational Corporations and Other Business Enterprises. Role of national human rights institutions in facilitating access to remedy for business-related human rights abuses. UN Doc A/HRC/47/39/Add.3, 22.06.2021.

rights, economic position and bargaining power of workers and work-seekers; capacities of government, business and other actors including rights-holders or victims; and consumer rights, information and awareness.

There is hence no single set of measures that can solve business-related harms across all value-chains, geographies, products, services, technologies or types of business perpetrator. Abuses of privacy by tech giants will never be amenable to the same solutions as abuses of female workers in garment production, of abattoir or call-centre workers, discrimination against women and ethnic minorities in white-collar professional settings, or tenants of private or public landlords bought out by private equity or vulture funds. Corporate due diligence practices may be built on the same basic template, but beyond this their geometry must remain variable, if it is to perform its function. Such diverse measures further entail heterogenous and dispersed legal, administrative and social institutions.

State duties to protect, corporate responsibility to respect and the right to remedy, as articulated via the UN Framework and UNGPs, are purposive, dynamic and broad enough to embrace these spectra. Likewise, regional due diligence laws, and an international instrument at the level of the UN, should be framed to do so. Front-loading such a UN treaty with narrowly prescriptive rules not only lessens the chances of its adoption, but would also diminish its longer-term relevance. Further, central UN oversight and review mechanisms will never be able to reach all peripheries of the business and human rights constellation, entailing the need for global standards to articulate with other regulatory 'centres' frameworks and institutions. As argued elsewhere, this suggests the relevance of a business and human rights treaty adopting a framework instrument approach in the UN setting.[195]

5.10. BUSINESS AND HUMAN RIGHTS: KNOWLEDGE AND RESEARCH

Have the measures undertaken in Europe discussed here been effective? Recent data and policy studies point towards a negative answer.[196] Still, from

[195] C. Methven O'Brien, 'Transcending the Binary: Linking Hard and Soft Law Through a UNGPS-Based Framework Convention', (2020) 114, *AJIL Unbound*, p. 186.

[196] Corporate Human Rights Benchmark, 'Corporate Human Rights Benchmark: 2019 Key Findings', Report, 2019, available at https://www.corporatebenchmark.org/sites/default/files/2019-11/CHRB2019KeyFindingsReport.pdf, last accessed 19.07.2021; Alliance for Corporate Transparency, 'Research Report 2019: An analysis of the sustainability reports of companies pursuant to the EU Non-Financial Reporting Directive', 2019, available at https://allianceforcorporatetransparency.org/assets/2019_Research_Report%20_Alliance_for_Corporate_Transparency.pdf, last accessed 19.07.2021; L. Smit, C. Bright, R. McCorquodale et al. (2020), 'European Commission Due Diligence Study', *supra* note 70; NYU Stern Center for Business and Human Rights (2019), 'Assessing Legislation on Human Rights in Supply Chains', *supra* note 38.

a scholarly standpoint, we should ask: how should the impacts of new business and human rights norms be measured – according to what baseline, metrics, comparators or counterfactual scenarios? What research methods should be deployed? Charting changes in legal doctrine, in isolation, is clearly not an adequate approach for business and human rights research. Based on the observation above of a multiplicity of standards and regimes, it should be recognised that comprehensive or binary reckonings are unlikely to be possible. Such considerations make critical the pursuit of synthetic, systematic and longitudinal regional as well as national surveys, baseline studies and appropriate markers. In an until now predominantly legal field, scholars must also be ready to address the need for cross- and inter-disciplinary work and the application of new and unfamiliar social-scientific research methods.

6. CONCLUSION

This contribution has provided an account and analysis of the last ten years of business and human rights regulation across Europe's multi-level and multi-jurisdictional space. Arguably, the emergence of the business and human rights field has been crucial for the continuing relevance and legitimacy of human rights, in an era characterised by increasing anxiety worldwide over economic, social and sustainability challenges in which corporate actors are deeply implicated. Still, this contribution has highlighted new challenges attendant on the transposition of human rights norms into the private sphere. If of growing interest amongst commercial law professionals, business and human rights, however, remain a niche concern, whose conceptual intricacies, practices and rapid development are still mostly unknown amongst wider communities of human rights and public international law scholars and practitioners. Until now, tensions between business and human rights norms, and wider international, transnational and domestic legal frameworks have escaped broad notice. With EU and national due diligence laws on the horizon, this is soon set to change. Sustained reflection is therefore needed to promote the coherent resolution of theoretical, doctrinal and policy dilemmas and lacunae highlighted here, on which continuing progress in business and human rights prevention, protection and remediation will depend, for rights-holders inside Europe and beyond.

TOWARDS MANDATORY HUMAN RIGHTS DUE DILIGENCE IN THE EUROPEAN UNION?

Opportunities and Challenges for Corporate Accountability

Virginie Rouas

ABSTRACT

In 2011, the United Nations Guiding Principles on Business and Human Rights (UNGPs) established that business enterprises should exercise human rights due diligence (HRDD) as part of their responsibility to respect human rights. HRDD requires companies to undertake processes to identify, prevent, mitigate and account for how they address potential and actual impacts on human rights. Following the adoption of the UNGPs, corporate HRDD has become a norm of expected conduct. In Europe, an increasing number of countries have adopted or taken steps to adopt legislation imposing mandatory HRDD on businesses. In this context, Didier Reynders, the Commissioner for Justice, recently announced that the European Commission would introduce legislation to impose mandatory HRDD on companies by 2021. This announcement was a turning point in the field of business and human rights. If adopted, this European Union (EU) instrument would be the first regional legislation to translate HRDD from a concept into hard law. Given the economic and political leverage of the EU, such an instrument could have a significant impact on respect of human rights by companies around the world. It would also be a fundamental change in the way the EU sees its role in ensuring corporate accountability for human rights. In addition, an EU mandatory HRDD instrument could encourage countries in other parts of the world to adopt similar standards. This contribution discusses how a mandatory EU HRDD instrument could effectively improve corporate accountability for human rights. First, it considers the legal value-added of a mandatory EU HRDD instrument. It maps the current EU legislative and policy framework on business and human rights and identifies the gaps that justify the adoption of HRDD norms at EU level. Second, this contribution examines potential options to ensure that the EU mandatory HRDD instrument fills these gaps. Provisions on scope of application, enforcement mechanisms, business due diligence obligations and access to justice and remedies will have a significant impact on this instrument's effectiveness in protecting human rights. Nevertheless, they will be the most difficult to negotiate. Ultimately, this contribution argues that a number of substantive and political barriers, such as business lobbying against strong mandatory HRDD standards, risks undermining the potential value-added of the EU mandatory HRDD instrument.

1. INTRODUCTION

In 2011, the United Nations (UN) Human Rights Council (HRC) adopted the UN Guiding Principles on Business and Human Rights (UNGPs).[1] This policy instrument contains a set of principles implementing the UN Protect, Respect and Remedy: A Framework for Business and Human Rights (UN Framework).[2] Both the UN Framework and the UNGPs recognise three 'pillars': (i) the state duty to protect against human rights abuse committed by third parties, including business enterprises; (ii) the corporate responsibility to respect human rights; and (iii) the need for effective access to remedy. The UNGPs provide that in order to meet their responsibility to respect human rights, business enterprises should have in place a human rights due diligence (HRDD) process to identify, prevent, mitigate and account for how they address their impacts on human rights.[3] In particular, the HRDD process should include 'assessing actual and potential human rights impacts, integrating and acting upon the findings, tracking responses, and communicating how impacts are addressed'.[4]

1 HRC, 'Guiding Principles on Business and Human Rights: Implementing the United Nations "Protect, Respect and Remedy" Framework', UN Doc A/HRC/17/31, 21.03.2011.

2 HRC, 'Protect, Respect and Remedy: A Framework for Business and Human Rights', UN Doc A/HRC/8/5, 07.04.2008.

3 HRC (2011), UNGPs, *supra* note 1, GP 15(b).

4 Ibid., GP 17.

Following the adoption of the UNGPs, business HRDD has become a norm of expected conduct, prompting some commentators to refer to 'the beginning of a paradigm shift'[5] in how companies are required to interact with human rights. In Europe, a growing number of countries have enacted or are in the process of enacting legislation requiring mandatory HRDD for businesses. For example, in 2017, France passed pioneering legislation imposing a general 'duty of vigilance' on parent and controlling companies of multinational enterprises (MNEs) for the human rights and environmental impacts of their global operations (Act on the Duty of Vigilance).[6] The European Union (EU) has committed to mandatory HRDD as well. In April 2020, Didier Reynders, the EU Commissioner for Justice, announced that by 2021, the European Commission (EC) would introduce legislation to impose mandatory HRDD on companies. This legislation would be part of the EU's COVID-19 recovery package.[7] The adoption of a legally binding EU instrument on HRDD (EU Instrument) would mark a watershed moment in business and human rights (BHR). It would be the first regional legislation to translate the HRDD concept into hard law. Given the EU's economic and political leverage, such an instrument could have a significant impact on respect of human rights by companies around the world. It could encourage, if not compel, companies in third countries to establish and implement HRDD in their operations, as well as prompt countries around the world to follow the EU's lead by enacting similar legislation. A legally binding EU instrument would also mark a fundamental shift in the EU's approach to corporate responsibility for human rights. To date, the EU has been primarily interested in encouraging businesses to respect human rights through voluntary initiatives rather than legally binding rules. The EC's announcement of this instrument sparked a great deal of interest and commentary from various actors in the BHR sector, including non-governmental organisations (NGOs), companies and governments.[8] Some of the EU institutions have also shown a strong interest in the future instrument. In March 2021, the European Parliament (EP) adopted a resolution requesting the EC to submit a legislative proposal on

---

5 UNWG, 'Corporate human rights due diligence – emerging practices, challenges and ways forward', UN Doc A/73/163, 16.07.2018, para. 20.

6 LOI n° 2017-399 du 27 mars 2017 relative au devoir de vigilance des sociétés mères et des entreprises donneuses d'ordre, 27.03.2017.

7 RBC, 'European Commission Promises Mandatory Due Diligence Legislation in 2021', 30.04.2020, available at https://responsiblebusinessconduct.eu/wp/2020/04/30/european-commission-promises-mandatory-due-diligence-legislation-in-2021/, last accessed 31.03.2021.

8 See BHRRC, 'Towards EU Mandatory Due Diligence Legislation: Perspectives from Business, Public Sector, Academic and Civil Society', 11.11.2020, available at https://www.business-humanrights.org/en/from-us/briefings/towards-eu-mandatory-due-diligence-legislation/, last accessed 31.03.2021.

mandatory supply chain due diligence without undue delay.[9] This resolution also includes non-binding recommendations for the future instrument (EP Proposal). For the coming years, the legislative process leading to the EU Instrument will take centre stage in the European BHR sector.

In this context, this contribution discusses how a legally binding EU instrument on mandatory HRDD could improve corporate respect for human rights,[10] as well as the opportunities and challenges that are likely to arise. It examines the need for such an instrument before delving into what the EU Instrument should include to effectively achieve corporate respect for human rights. This contribution examines whether those suggestions are already reflected in the EP Proposal.

2. THE NEED FOR AN EU HUMAN RIGHTS DUE DILIGENCE INSTRUMENT

This section considers the legal value-added of an EU mandatory HRDD instrument. It summarises some persistent BHR issues, maps the current EU legislative and policy framework on BHR and identifies the gaps that justify the adoption of HRDD norms at EU level.

2.1. OVERVIEW OF BUSINESS-RELATED HUMAN RIGHTS ISSUES

Business enterprises can contribute to the economic and social development of the countries in which they operate. However, their activities may also cause, or benefit from, harm to humans and the environment, either directly or indirectly.[11] Companies can impact the full range of human rights, including civil and political rights, economic, social and cultural rights and labour rights.[12] Business activities, particularly in the extractive sector, can also cause pollution and other significant environmental damage that can significantly impact a number of rights, including the right to health or the right to food.[13]

---

9 European Parliament, Resolution of 10 March 2021 with recommendations to the Commission on corporate due diligence and corporate accountability (2020/2129(INL)), 10.03.2021.

10 This contribution focuses solely on human rights due diligence and excludes environmental due diligence.

11 See K.E. Bravo, J. Martin and T. Van Ho, *When Business Harms Human Rights: Affected Communities That Are Dying to Be Heard*, Anthem Press, London and New York 2020.

12 For an overview of corporate-related human rights abuse, see SRSG, 'Corporations and Human Rights: A Survey of the Scope and Patterns of Alleged Corporate-Related Human Rights Abuse', UN Doc A/HRC/8/5/Add.2., 23.05.2008.

13 Ibid.

As economic globalisation has increased over recent decades, the risk of business-related human rights violations has become particularly acute in the context of MNE activities. MNEs usually comprise companies or other entities established in more than one country and are linked in such a way that they may coordinate their operations in various manners.[14] MNEs are more likely to operate in sectors where human rights abuses are common, such as the garment industry where labour rights violations are prevalent in supply chains,[15] and the extractive sector where environmental pollution and conflicts with local communities are frequent issues.[16] Furthermore, the way MNEs are structured may reduce the incentive for these enterprises to consider the risk of human rights abuses in their operations. For instance, the application of separate legal personality and limited liability, two important principles of modern company law, has often shielded the parent company from liability for human rights violations and environmental damage committed by its subsidiary.[17] Such factors enable parent companies to engage in hazardous or polluting activities through their subsidiaries without fear of legal repercussions. Company liability for damage caused by human rights violations committed by third parties is a critical issue in BHR. According to the UN Special Representative of the Secretary-General on the issue of human rights and transnational corporations and other business enterprises (SRSG), 40% of cases alleging business-related human rights abuses involved indirect forms of company involvement.[18] In those cases, companies were generally alleged to have contributed to or benefited from the abuses committed by third parties, including individuals, public authorities and other business enterprises. Indirect company involvement in particular stood out in the context of human rights abuses occurring in supply chains.[19] The global COVID-19 pandemic and its resulting economic crisis have recently highlighted the complex relationship between businesses and human rights.[20]

---

14 OECD, 'OECD Guidelines for Multinational Enterprises: 2011 Edition', 2011, p. 17, available at https://www.oecd.org/corporate/mne/1922428.pdf, last accessed 26.06.2021.

15 See BHRRC, 'Labour violations & abuses rampant among suppliers of large international garment brands', 13.04.2015, available at https://www.business-humanrights.org/en/latest-news/labour-violations-abuses-rampant-among-suppliers-of-large-international-garment-brands/, last accessed 31.03.2021.

16 See P. Muchlinski, 'Research Notes: Social and Human Rights Implications of TNC Activities in the Extractive Industries', (2010) 18(1), *Transnational Corporations*.

17 See P. Muchlinski, 'Limited Liability and Multinational Enterprises: A Case for Reform?', (2010) 34(5), *Cambridge Journal of Economics*.

18 SRSG (2008), Corporations and Human Rights, *supra* note 12, para. 65.

19 Ibid., paras. 40–42. See KnowTheChain, 'The 2021 Apparel and Footwear Benchmark Report', Report, 2021, available at https://www.business-humanrights.org/en/from-us/briefings/2021-knowthechain-apparel-footwear-benchmark/, last accessed 26.06.2021.

20 See S. Tripathi, 'Companies, COVID-19 and Respect for Human Rights', (2020) 5(2), *Business and Human Rights Journal*, pp. 252–260.

A significant issue that arises when companies commit or are involved in human rights violations is the difficulty victims face in seeking and obtaining redress. Limited access to justice has been a major issue in litigation against MNEs. Over the last two decades, victims have lodged legal claims against MNEs in the country where they are headquartered or have their main business activity (home country) for human rights violations and environmental damage committed in foreign countries (host countries). This type of transnational litigation against MNEs has been significant in the United States (US) and in Europe, with proceedings initiated in numerous countries such as the United Kingdom (UK), France, the Netherlands, Germany, Italy, Sweden and Belgium.[21] However, the existence of procedural, practical and substantive barriers has limited victims' access to an effective remedy. In the US, the Alien Tort Statute (ATS) appeared to be a promising instrument for holding companies liable for alleged human rights violations in their foreign operations.[22] However, the US Supreme Court has rejected the idea that the ATS could apply when violations take place outside the US and be used to hold foreign companies liable.[23] In Europe, plaintiffs have struggled to establish the jurisdiction of national courts to hold parent companies and their foreign subsidiaries liable.[24] Furthermore, the Rome II Regulation,[25] which governs the national substantive law applicable to non-contractual obligations in cross-border disputes, prevents the application of the EU home state's law, even if it is more protective of victims. In addition, liability regimes are often inadequate to deal with the complexities of human rights violations committed by MNEs and to compensate victims of those violations.[26] They usually require plaintiffs to demonstrate that the parent company breached a duty of care or was involved in the human rights violation. However, MNEs are generally in possession of evidence needed to establish such a breach. As such, victims are often unable to prove their case in the absence of adequate

---

21 See G. Skinner, R. McCorquodale, O. De Schutter et al., 'The Third Pillar: Access to Judicial Remedies for Human Rights Violations by Transnational Business', ICAR, CORE and ECCJ Report, 2013, available at https://corporatejustice.org/documents/publications/eccj/the_third_pillar_-access_to_judicial_remedies_for_human_rights_violation.-1-2.pdf, last accessed 31.03.2021.

22 28 USC §1350 (1789) Alien's Action for Tort.

23 US Supreme Court, *Kiobel v Royal Dutch Petroleum Co.*, 133 S. Ct. 1659 (2013); US Supreme Court, *Jesner v Arab Bank*, 138 S. Ct. 1386 (2018).

24 A. Marx, C. Bright, J. Wouters et al., 'Access to legal remedies for victims of corporate human rights abuses in third countries', Study of the European Parliament, 01.02.2019, pp. 15–16.

25 Regulation (EC) No 864/2007 of the European Parliament and of the Council of 11 July 2007 on the law applicable to non-contractual obligations, OJ L199 (hereinafter Rome II Regulation).

26 See R. Mares, 'Liability within Corporate Groups: Parent Company's Accountability for Subsidiary Human Rights Abuses', in S. Deva and D. Birchall (eds.), *Research Handbook on Human Rights and Business*, Edward Elgar Publishing, Cheltenham and Northampton 2020.

disclosure and/or burden of proof rules. The imbalance in access to evidence between victims and businesses is just one example of the general asymmetry between the parties in business-related human rights claims.

2.2. EXISTING EU FRAMEWORK ON BUSINESS AND HUMAN RIGHTS

The EU has described itself as a 'strong supporter' of the UNGPs, which it considers to be 'the authoritative policy framework' in the BHR field.[27] However, the EU has never adopted a formal BHR strategy to implement the UNGPs. Instead, it has included a limited number of specific actions on BHR and the UNGPs in the EU Action Plan on Human Rights and Democracy 2015–2019 and, to some extent, in the EU Action Plan on Human Rights and Democracy 2020–2024.[28] The lack of a general EU strategy on the UNGPs was criticised by the Responsible Business Conduct Working Group (RBC WG), an informal and cross-party group of Members of the EP, which responded by adopting the *Shadow EU Action Plan on the Implementation of the UNGPs within the EU*.[29] EU institutions have, nonetheless, adopted separate policy documents that touch upon BHR and the implementation of the UNGPs. Shortly after the adoption of the UNGPs in 2011, the EC described its intended actions to implement the UNGPs in its corporate social responsibility (CSR) strategy (this strategy is discussed in more detail below).[30] However, this CSR strategy has not been updated since its publication in 2011. The EC has also published two Staff Working Documents outlining past and ongoing implementation and streamlining of the UNGPs in EU activities.[31] In 2016, the

[27] EU Permanent Delegation to the UN Office and Other International Organisations in Geneva, 'Contribution of the EU before the first session of the UN Working Group on Human Rights and Transnational Corporations and Other Business Enterprises', D(2012)703034, 06.01.2012.

[28] European Commission, Joint Communication to the European Parliament and the Council – EU Action Plan on Human Rights and Democracy 2020–2024, JOIN(2020) 5 final, 25.03.2020; Council of the European Union, Council Conclusions on the Action Plan on Human Rights and Democracy 2015–2019, 10897/15, 20.07.2015.

[29] RBC, 'Shadow EU Action Plan on the Implementation of the UN Guiding Principles on Business and Human Rights within the EU', 19.03.2019, available at https://responsiblebusinessconduct.eu/wp/wp-content/uploads/2019/03/SHADOW-EU-Action-Plan-on-Business-and-Human-Rights.pdf, last accessed 31.03.2021.

[30] European Commission, A renewed EU strategy 2011–14 for Corporate Social Responsibility, COM(2011) 681 final, 25.10.2011.

[31] European Commission, Commission Staff Working Document on Implementing the UN Guiding Principles on Business and Human Rights – State of Play, SWD(2015) 144 final, 14.07.2015; European Commission, Commission Staff Working Document – Corporate Social Responsibility, Responsible Business Conduct, and Business & Human Rights: Overview of Progress, SWD(2019) 143 final, 20.03.2019.

Council of the EU also adopted its *Conclusions on Business and Human Rights*, in which it provided direction on the manner in which the UNGPs should be implemented.[32] While the EP has not adopted a resolution specifically on the UNGPs, it has passed a number of resolutions on BHR-related issues.[33] In addition, the EU has, to some extent, considered the implementation of Pillar III of the UNGPs on access to remedy. Following a request of the Council of the EU, in 2017 the EU Agency for Fundamental Rights (EU FRA) published an opinion on improving access to remedy in the area of BHR at the EU level.[34] The EU FRA suggested that 'more could be done to ensure effective access to remedy for business-related human rights abuse within the EU'.[35]

In general, the EU has supported the implementation of the UNGPs through several legal and policy initiatives addressing BHR issues both directly and indirectly. For example, as early as 2011, the EC has encouraged its Member States to develop National Action Plans (NAPs) on BHR and has produced guidance documents on BHR for small and medium-sized enterprises (SMEs). The EU has also promoted adherence to the UNGPs in its internal and external policies and programmes.[36] Furthermore, the EU has addressed BHR-related issues indirectly in sectoral policy and legal instruments. For instance, the EU has adopted a number of legislative instruments governing the employment of third-country migrants, which provide such migrants with labour rights protection in the context of business activities.

In relation to Pillar II of the UNGPs, the EU has favoured a voluntary approach to encourage companies to respect human rights. In this regard, the concept of CSR has played a significant role. In its 2001 Green Paper *Promoting a European framework for Corporate Social Responsibility*, the EC defined CSR as 'a concept whereby companies integrate social and environmental concerns in their business operations and in their interaction with their stakeholders on a voluntary basis'.[37] CSR was seen as voluntary in nature. Following the adoption of the UNGPs, the EC adopted a new CSR policy called *Renewed EU*

---

32 Council of the European Union, Council Conclusions on Business and Human Rights, 10254/16, 20.06.2021.

33 See European Parliament, Resolution of 25 October 2016 on corporate liability for serious human rights abuses in third countries, (2015/2315(INI)), 25.10.2016.

34 EU FRA, Improving access to remedy in the area of business and human rights at the EU level, FRA Opinion – 1/2017 [B&HR], 10.04.2017.

35 Ibid.

36 European Commission, COM(2011) 681 final, *supra* note 30; see European Commission, Commission Staff Working Document – Corporate Social Responsibility, Responsible Business Conduct, and Business & Human Rights: Overview of Progress Brussels, SWD(2019) 143 final, 20.03.2019; European Commission, Commission Staff Working Document on Implementing the UN Guiding Principles on Business and Human Rights – State of Play Brussels, SWD(2015) 144 final, 14.07.2015.

37 Commission of the European Communities, Green Paper – Promoting a European framework for Corporate Social Responsibility, COM/2001/0366 final, 18.07.2001.

Strategy 2011–2014 for Corporate Social Responsibility (2011 CSR Strategy).[38] In this document, the EC revised its CSR policy to reflect various aspects of the UNGPs, including the corporate responsibility of respect and the concept of due diligence. First, the EC provided a new definition of CSR as 'the responsibility of enterprises for their impacts on society'. To fully meet their CSR, 'enterprises should have in place a process to integrate social, environmental, ethical, human rights and consumer concerns into their business operations and core strategy in close collaboration with their stakeholders', with the aim of 'maximising the creation of shared value for their owners/shareholders and civil society at large' and 'identifying, preventing and mitigating their possible adverse impacts'. The EC has removed explicit references to the voluntary nature of CSR in this definition. However, a closer look at the 2011 CSR Strategy reveals that CSR continues to be achieved through voluntary processes. For instance, the 2011 CSR Strategy emphasises that '[t]he development of CSR should be led by enterprises themselves'. Furthermore, '[p]ublic authorities should play a supporting role through a smart mix of voluntary policy measures and, where necessary, complementary regulation, for example to promote transparency, create market incentives for responsible business conduct, and ensure corporate accountability'. The 2011 CSR Strategy echoes the UNGPs, which recommend states to consider 'a smart mix of measures – national and international, mandatory and voluntary – to foster business respect for human rights'.[39] However, unlike the UNGPs, which do not focus on a specific type of instrument, the 2011 CSR Strategy emphasises voluntary state measures, with regulation serving as a complement to voluntary measures if deemed necessary. Second, the 2011 CSR Strategy provides that '[t]o identify, prevent and mitigate their possible adverse impacts, large enterprises, and enterprises at particular risk of having such impacts, are encouraged to carry out risk-based due diligence, including through their supply chains'. Therefore, in the 2011 CSR Strategy, due diligence is first and foremost a voluntary process to meet CSR.

Having said that, in recent years the EU has adopted a number of legal instruments imposing some due diligence obligations for human rights and environmental impacts. In 2010, it adopted Regulation 995/2010 (Timber Regulation), which aims to combat illegal logging by prohibiting the importing and placing on the EU market of illegally harvested timber and timber products derived from such timber.[40] The Timber Regulation requires operators to

---

38 European Commission, COM(2011) 681 final, *supra* note 30.

39 HRC (2011), UNGPs, *supra* note 1, Commentary to GP3.

40 Regulation (EU) No 995/2010 of the European Parliament and of the Council of 20 October 2010 laying down the obligations of operators who place timber and timber products on the market, OJ L295.

exercise due diligence when placing timber or timber products on the market. In particular, they must set up a 'due diligence system' – namely, a framework of procedures and measures to minimise the risk that illegally harvested timber and timber products derived from such timber are placed on the internal market.[41] This due diligence system includes three elements inherent to risk management: access to information, risk assessment and risk mitigation. Recently, the EU adopted Regulation 2017/821 (Conflict Minerals Regulation), which imposes due diligence requirements on EU-based importers of certain minerals and metals.[42] This instrument establishes an EU system for supply chain due diligence to curtail opportunities for armed groups and security forces to trade in tin, tantalum and tungsten, their ores and gold. This system is designed 'to provide transparency and certainty regarding the supply practices of Union importers, and of smelters and refiners sourcing from conflict-affected and high-risk areas'.[43] EU importers of specific minerals and metals must comply with 'supply chain due diligence obligations,'[44] which involve 'their management systems, risk management, independent third-party audits and disclosure of information with a view to identifying and addressing actual and potential risks linked to conflict-affected and high-risk areas to prevent or mitigate adverse impacts associated with their sourcing activities.'[45]

The Timber Regulation and the Conflict Minerals Regulation are important instruments because they impose due diligence obligations on business actors across their value chain (or a significant part thereof). In this way, they are likely to have an extraterritorial reach since timber and minerals are often imported from third countries into the EU. However, the potential of those instruments to improve corporate responsibility for human rights (and the environment) remains limited. First, the EU legislature has neglected the enforcement dimension of the EU Conflict Minerals Regulation. While the Timber Regulation requires Member States to punish operators, traders and monitoring organisations who violate its provisions, the Conflict Minerals Regulation does not require Member States to punish EU importers for non-compliance. As a result of this lack of sanctions, there is a risk of non-compliance, rendering the Conflict Minerals Regulation a toothless instrument. While Member States are not prohibited from punishing those who infringe on this regulation, they may be reluctant to do so if other states do not provide for similar sanctions. Second, both instruments fail to provide effective access to redress when damage occurs as a

41 Ibid., Article 4.

42 Regulation (EU) 2017/821 of the European Parliament and of the Council of 17 May 2017 laying down supply chain due diligence obligations for Union importers of tin, tantalum and tungsten, their ores, and gold originating from conflict-affected and high-risk areas, OJ L130/1.

43 Ibid., Article 1(1).

44 Ibid., Article 3.

45 Ibid., Article 2(d).

result of non-compliance with due diligence obligations. The Timber Regulation makes no mention of the possibility for third parties, whether EU consumers or local communities where the timber was illegally harvested, to seek redress for any damage they may have suffered. Similarly, the Conflict Minerals Regulation does not provide for the possibility for third parties to seek redress if importers fail to comply with their due diligence obligations, resulting in damage. Finally, the scope of both instruments is sector-specific (e.g. timber, certain minerals), which means that no EU instrument currently imposes a general due diligence obligation on companies.

In parallel to these regulations, the EU has also attempted to improve transparency by requiring certain companies to disclose information on human rights and environmental risks. It adopted Directive 2014/95/EU (NFRD),[46] which amends Directive 2013/34/EU (Accounting Directive) on reporting standards of companies' financial statements.[47] In general, the NFRD seeks to improve the consistency and comparability of non-financial information disclosed by certain large undertakings and groups throughout the EU to provide a more complete picture of their development and performance, as well as the impact of their activities on humans and the environment. It requires large public-interest companies (primarily listed companies, banks, insurance companies and designated public-interest entities) to include a non-financial statement in their management report. This statement must contain 'information to the extent necessary for an understanding of the undertaking's development, performance, position and impact of its activity, relating to, as a minimum, environmental, social and employee matters, respect for human rights, anti-corruption and bribery matters'.[48] However, so far, the implementation of the NFRD has failed to achieve this goal. According to a 2020 NGO study, only a small percentage of companies provide comprehensive and reliable sustainability-related information.[49] Furthermore, the quality and comparability of companies' sustainability reporting are insufficient to understand their impacts, risks or even their plans.[50] This view was also expressed in a 2020 public consultation conducted by the EC, where a majority

---

46 Directive 2014/95/EU of the European Parliament and of the Council of 22 October 2014 amending Directive 2013/34/EU as regards disclosure of non-financial and diversity information by certain large undertakings and groups, OJ L330/1.

47 Directive 2013/34/EU of the European Parliament and of the Council of 26 June 2013 on the annual financial statements, consolidated financial statements and related reports of certain types of undertakings, amending Directive 2006/43/EC of the European Parliament and of the Council and repealing Council Directives 78/660/EEC and 83/349/EEC, OJ L 182/19.

48 Article 1 NFRD.

49 Alliance for Corporate Transparency, '2019 Research Report: An analysis of the sustainability reports of 1000 companies pursuant to the EU Non-Financial Reporting Directive', 2020, available at https://corporatejusticecoalition.org/resources/alliance-corporate-transparency-2019-research-report/, last accessed 29.06.2021.

50 Ibid., p. 10.

of users of non-financial information believed that non-financial information reported by companies was deficient in terms of comparability, reliability and relevance.[51] This situation probably results from broad discretion granted to Member States and companies by the directive. Moreover, the NFRD applies to a limited number of companies. Furthermore, it does not require statutory auditors to review the information contained in the non-financial statement. Finally, companies are unlikely to be punished for including irrelevant or inaccurate information in their non-financial statements. Following a review of the NFRD, in April 2021, the EC published a proposal for a Corporate Sustainability Reporting Directive (CSRD), which aims to amend the NFRD's reporting requirements and fix some of the mentioned gaps.[52]

2.3. VALUE-ADDED OF AN EU HUMAN RIGHTS DUE DILIGENCE INSTRUMENT

To date, the EU has largely encouraged businesses to respect human rights through voluntary initiatives. When it has passed binding legislation requiring corporate due diligence and transparency, the narrow scope and inadequate design of these instruments have limited their ability to incentivise business respect for human rights. Meanwhile, business-related human rights abuses involving European companies continue to be reported in the media and by civil society organisations (CSOs). Moreover, the absence of substantive standards on corporate obligations vis-à-vis human rights impedes victims, especially foreign individuals, from seeking redress in the EU. The EC itself recently acknowledged that regulatory failure has been a driving force behind corporate short-termism and a lack of consideration for environmental, social and human rights interests. The current legal framework – in particular, corporate legislation – fails to foster accountability towards stakeholders and 'lags behind the development of global value chains and corporate structures when it comes to the responsibility of a limited liability company for identifying and preventing harm in its group-wide operations and production channels.'[53] As a result, a number of actors, including

51 European Commission, Summary Report of the Public Consultation on the Review of the Non-Financial Reporting Directive 20 February 2020–11 June 2020, Ref. Ares(2020)3997889, 29.07.2020.

52 European Commission, Proposal for a Directive of the European Parliament and of the Council amending Directive 2013/34/EU, Directive 2004/109/EC, Directive 2006/43/EC and Regulation (EU) No 537/2014, as regards corporate sustainability reporting, COM(2021) 189 final, 21.04.2021. The legislative process for adopting the CSRD was still ongoing at the time of writing.

53 European Commission, Inception Impact Assessment – Sustainable corporate governance, Ref. Ares(2020)4034032, 30.07.2020.

CSOs, academics and business actors, have called for the adoption of more stringent corporate accountability standards.[54]

An EU instrument on mandatory HRDD would have several advantages. First, it would ensure that HRDD standards are in place throughout the EU internal market. Some Member States have already enacted HRDD legislation (e.g. France, Germany, the Netherlands), while others are considering doing so (e.g. Finland). However, most Member States still continue to lack HRDD requirements, placing companies in Member States with standards at a disadvantage. Furthermore, as more EU Member States adopt HRDD legislation, the risk of fragmentation increases, resulting in legal uncertainty and the need for harmonisation at EU level.[55] The adoption of the EU Instrument would ensure the application of common HRDD requirements across Member States, thereby creating a level playing field, because businesses in all Member States would have to comply with similar rules. Furthermore, establishing mandatory HRDD rules at the EU level would reduce regulatory and compliance burdens for companies operating in different Member States, while also providing greater legal certainty for businesses. Finally, effective due diligence standards could help strengthen access to remedy[56] and address some of the barriers that hinder victims' ability to gain access to justice (e.g. the attribution of liability to parent companies in corporate groups).[57]

3. DESIGNING AN EFFECTIVE EU HUMAN RIGHTS DUE DILIGENCE INSTRUMENT

In the context of the UNGPs, HRDD is viewed as a process that business enterprises should have in place to meet their responsibility to respect human rights. This responsibility entails that '[b]usiness enterprises should respect human rights', that is, 'they should avoid infringing on the human rights of others and should address adverse human rights impacts with which they are involved'.[58] As a result, the objective of HRDD is presumably to prevent businesses from committing or being involved in human rights abuses and to ensure businesses respond to such abuses when they occur.

Legal regimes that incorporate HRDD may be articulated in several ways. First, in terms of scope, an HRDD regime may require businesses to respect human rights in general or to address specific human rights challenges, such

---

54 BHRRC (2020), 'Towards EU Mandatory Due Diligence Legislation', *supra* note 8.

55 A. Marx, C. Bright, J. Wouters et al. (2019), 'Access to legal remedies', *supra* note 24.

56 EU FRA (2017), Improving access to remedy, *supra* note 34, Opinion 21.

57 A. Marx, C. Bright, J. Wouters et al. (2019), 'Access to legal remedies', *supra* note 24, pp. 107–110.

58 HRC (2011), UNGPs, *supra* note 1, GP 11.

as child labour or slavery. It may also create obligations for all companies or specific groups of companies, or differentiated obligations that take into account the size and structure of companies. In addition, it may require companies to conduct due diligence in the context of their own direct activities, the activities of companies they own and/or control or the activities of companies with which they have a business relationship (e.g. suppliers, subcontractors). Second, in terms of substantive due diligence, an HRDD regime can impose different obligations on companies. For instance, the UNGPs provide that business enterprises should carry out HRDD 'to identify, prevent, mitigate and account for how they address their adverse human rights impacts'.[59] This process should include 'assessing actual and potential human rights impacts, integrating and acting upon the findings, tracking responses, and communicating how impacts are addressed'.[60] Third, an HRDD regime may impose sanctions on businesses that fail to meet their HRDD obligations. Under certain circumstances, it may also require companies to provide remedies when human rights abuses occur in the course of their operations.

This section discusses how the EU Instrument should be designed to achieve the twofold objective of HRDD, namely, prevention and mitigation of business-related human rights abuses, based on the current business-related human rights issues and gaps in the EU legal and policy framework on BHR identified earlier in this contribution. It focuses on four key elements: scope, HRDD obligations, enforcement and access to justice and remedy. The analysis considers non-binding recommendations for the future instrument contained in the EP's resolution of March 2021. The EU Instrument should at the very least be aligned with the UNGPs to ensure consistency with the current international BHR framework. However, the future instrument should be tailored to the European context and should not refrain from going beyond the UNGPs.

3.1. SCOPE

Several questions arise as to the scope of the future instrument. First, which human rights should companies be required to respect as part of their due diligence obligations? This is a complex but critical issue, because the smaller the scope of human rights covered, the less effective the future instrument will be. As mentioned earlier, businesses can impact on the full range of human rights.[61] Therefore, to be effective, an EU Instrument should apply to all human rights. However, this approach faces significant practical challenges. The list of existing human rights is extensive, and one right may be expressed differently

59 Ibid., GP 17.

60 Ibid.

61 SRSG (2008), Corporations and Human Rights, *supra* note 12, para. 65.

in various instruments or even across national contexts. This aspect is critical for HRDD obligations applicable to MNEs, which, by definition, operate in multiple countries and may find themselves in legal systems with varying human rights standards. An approach requiring companies to exercise due diligence towards a wide range of human rights is likely to require significant financial and technical resources. In this context, without delineating the human rights scope of the EU Instrument, it may be challenging for companies to consider impacts on all human rights enshrined in international, regional and national instruments. This approach may also be counterproductive, as companies may overlook human rights impacts that are most relevant to their activities. At the same time, an instrument with an overly narrow list of human rights may lead companies to ignore less obvious business-related abuses and being of no assistance to rights-holders affected by corporate activities.

The EU Instrument should require companies to focus on the human rights that may be impacted in their operations. Identifying potential and actual human rights impacts, which is a component of conducting HRDD (and is discussed further below), is critical in determining the most relevant human rights. This exercise should be 'ongoing' as 'human rights risks may change over time'.[62] More broadly, the EU Instrument should specify the human rights instruments that companies must respect. To ensure consistency with international standards and practice, the EU Instrument should, at the very least, reflect the internationally recognised human rights reflected in the UNGPs. GP 12 refers to the International Bill of Human Rights and the principles concerning fundamental rights outlined in the International Labour Organization's Declaration on Fundamental Principles and Rights at Work. The EU Instrument should probably go a step further and require companies to respect rights enshrined in European instruments, that is, the EU Charter and the ECHR. When HRDD applies to activities in other countries, the EU Instrument should also require companies to exercise a HRDD tailored to the local context, taking into account the applicable national and regional human rights instruments. Furthermore, it should also require businesses to pay special attention to the human rights of vulnerable groups, such as women, children, indigenous peoples, migrant workers and people with disabilities.

Article 1 of the EP Proposal refers to 'human rights, the environment and good governance' without defining their scope. However, its recital states that the EC should include an annex outlining 'a list of types of business-related adverse impacts on human rights' as expressed in various human rights instruments, including 'the international human rights conventions that are binding upon the Union or the Member States,' the International Bill of Human Rights, international humanitarian law, UN instruments on the rights of vulnerable

62 HRC (2011), UNGPs, *supra* note 1, GP 17(c).

persons or groups and the ILO Declaration on Fundamental Principles and Rights at Work and various ILO conventions.[63] It also suggests that regional and national human rights instruments be included. Given the potentially large number of instruments, the EP Proposal attempts to strike a balance by stating that 'the Commission should ensure that those types of impacts listed are reasonable and achievable'.[64] It does not, however, explain how the Commission should strike such a balance. The EP Proposal also refers to additional similar annexes listing the types of business-related adverse impacts on the environment and good governance that fall within its scope.[65]

The second issue concerns the type of companies, or 'undertakings', that should conduct HRDD. This raises several questions. Should the EU Instrument apply to all companies, regardless of size (whether SMEs or large corporate groups)? Should it apply to companies headquartered in EU Member States, that operate in those states or that place products on the internal market? In general, the UNGPs apply to 'all business enterprises, both transnational and others, regardless of their size, sector, location, ownership and structure'.[66] More specifically, the responsibility of business enterprises to respect human rights applies 'fully and equally' to all enterprises 'regardless of their size, sector, operational context, ownership and structure'.[67] On this basis, it is reasonable to assume that all business enterprises should engage in HRDD. However, the UNGPs stress that 'the scale and complexity of the means through which enterprises meet [their] responsibility may vary according to these factors and with the severity of the enterprise's adverse human rights impacts'.[68] This means two things. First, '[t]he means though which a business enterprise meets its responsibility to respect human rights will be proportional to, among other factors, its size'.[69] For instance, SMEs are expected to meet their responsibility to respect human rights through policies and processes that are proportional to their size. At the same time, some SMEs 'can have severe human rights, which will require corresponding measures regardless of their size'.[70] Furthermore, the UNGPs provide that HRDD will 'vary in complexity with the size of the business enterprise, the risk of severe human rights impacts, and the nature and context of its operations'.[71] As a result, all business enterprises should establish an HRDD process that is proportional to their size, unless they have severe human rights impacts, in which case corresponding measures to the impacts must be adopted.

63 Recital 21 EP Proposal.
64 Ibid.
65 Ibid., Recitals 22 and 25.
66 HRC (2011), UNGPs, *supra* note 1.
67 Ibid., GP 14.
68 Ibid.
69 Ibid., Commentary to GP 14.
70 Ibid.
71 Ibid., GP 17(b).

Until now, only large companies have been subject to the few domestic statutes imposing HRDD obligations (e.g. France). Legislators are wary of due diligence requirements that are perceived to be burdensome for small businesses.[72] However, a similar approach in the context of the EU Instrument could be detrimental to meeting the objective of HRDD because SMEs account for the vast majority of enterprises in the EU.[73] The fact that small EU businesses can be involved in human rights abuses should not be overlooked. Scholars have suggested that the EU Instrument should require all companies operating in the EU to carry out HRDD that is proportionate to their size and/or supply chain leverage, and commensurate with the nature of the adverse human rights impact. It should, in particular, address the specific challenges that SMEs face when carrying out HRDD.[74] To some extent, the EP Proposal follows this approach. It addresses large undertakings governed by the law of the Member States or established in the EU,[75] publicly listed SMEs and SMEs operating in high-risk sectors presumably established in the EU or,[76] in some circumstances, established outside of the EU 'when they operate in the internal market selling goods or providing services'.[77] The EP Proposal covers SMEs in a restrictive manner, which is problematic since it excludes a significant number of SMEs from the scope of HRDD obligations. One of the EP Proposal's strengths is that it would require undertakings to 'carry out value chain due diligence which is proportionate and commensurate to the likelihood and severity of their potential or actual adverse impacts and their specific circumstances, particularly their sector of activity, the size and length of their value chain, the size of the undertaking, its capacity, resources and leverage'. Technical assistance would be provided to the obliged undertakings. The EC would be required to publish non-binding guidelines for undertakings on 'how best to fulfil the due diligence obligations', which would provide 'practical guidance on how proportionality and prioritization' may be applied to HRDD obligations 'depending on the size and sector of the undertaking'.[78] Furthermore, the EP Proposal would include support for SMEs, such as financial assistance.[79]

Another question regards whether companies should conduct HRDD solely for their own activities or also for the activities of subsidiaries, contractors and subcontractors, and suppliers. This question is especially pertinent in the context of MNE activities. It also raises the potential for extraterritorial reach

---

72 M. Krajewski and B. Faracik, 'Briefing 1 – Substantive elements of potential legislation on human rights due diligence', European Parliament, 24.04.2020, p. 8.

73 Ibid., p. 9.

74 Ibid.

75 Article 2(1) EP Proposal.

76 Ibid., Article 2(2).

77 Ibid., Article 2(3).

78 Ibid., Article 14.

79 Ibid., Article 15.

of HRDD obligations. Given that the EU is home to one of the world's largest numbers of MNEs,[80] HRDD rules imposed in a broad manner (i.e. companies must exercise HRDD for their activities, as well as the activities of the companies they own or control, and/or with which they have a business relationship, whether in the EU or outside the EU) could have far-reaching consequences and ensure that businesses respect human rights beyond the EU. At the same time, the complexity of today's global value chains is likely to create practical and resource issues for businesses when conducting HRDD, potentially affecting the quality and efficacy of HRDD.

GP 13 provides that the responsibility to respect human rights requires that business enterprises avoid causing or contributing to adverse human rights 'impacts through their own activities and seek to prevent or mitigate adverse human rights impacts that are directly linked to their operations, products or services by their business relationships', even if they have not contributed to those impacts. The Commentary to GP 13 explains that 'a business enterprise's "activities" are understood to include both actions and omissions; and its "business relationships" are understood to include relationships with business partners, entities in its value chain, and any other non-State or State entity directly linked to its business operations, products or services.' The UN Working Group on the issue of human rights and transnational corporations and other business enterprises (UNWG) has clarified that the HRDD of a business enterprise 'extends not only to its relationships with first-tier suppliers, but to business relationships along the whole of its value chain, including business connections in the extended supply chain, business relations using products and services, joint venture partners, corporate lenders, project financers, investors, and governments'.[81] It has recommended that HRDD not be limited to an enterprise's own activities and first-tier suppliers.[82] Similarly, CSOs have suggested that businesses should conduct HRDD in their own operations, in their global value chains, and within their business relationships.[83] The EP Proposal also adopts a broad approach. Obliged undertakings would 'fulfil their duty to respect human rights, the environment and good governance' and 'not cause or contribute to potential or actual adverse impacts on human rights, the

---

80 According to the EuroGroups Register, 213,146 MNE groups were registered in the EU in 2018, 150 541 of which were from the EU-27. See Eurostat, 'Structure of multinational enterprise groups in the EU', 2020, available at https://ec.europa.eu/eurostat/statistics-explained/index.php/Structure_of_multinational_enterprise_groups_in_the_EU#:~:text=The%20EGR%20defines%20an%20MNE,in%20the%20EU%20Member%20States), last accessed 31.03.2021.

81 UNWG (2020), Letter to European Commissioner for Justice Didier Reynders, Ref SPB/SHD//NF/GF/ff, 22.10.2020.

82 Ibid.

83 Action Aid, Amnesty International, Anti-Slavery et al., 'Joint open letter: An EU mandatory due diligence legislation to promote businesses' respect for human rights and the environment', 01.09.2020.

environment and good governance through their own activities or those directly linked to their operations, products or services by a business relationship or in their value chains, and that they prevent and mitigate those adverse impacts'.[84] Therefore, businesses would exercise HRDD for their own activities as well as for activities directly related to their operations, products or services through a business relationship or through their value chains. In practice, this means that undertakings should respect, avoid causing or contributing to, prevent and mitigate human rights abuses in a large number of situations (i.e. direct activities and activities of a business relationship or in its value chains directly linked to its operations, products or services).

3.2. BUSINESS HRDD OBLIGATIONS

The UNGPs provide that business enterprises should have an HRDD process in place 'to identify, prevent, mitigate and account for how they address their impacts on human rights'.[85] In practice, the EU Instrument should require businesses to conduct an assessment to identify actual and potential human rights abuses. This assessment should involve meaningful consultation with potentially affected groups and other relevant stakeholders.[86] Businesses should also be required to take 'appropriate action' to prevent potential human rights abuses and mitigate existing abuses.[87] They should track the effectiveness of their response.[88] Lastly, businesses should communicate their approach to addressing human rights impacts.[89]

The EU Instrument should go beyond reporting requirements, which already exist under the NFRD. Furthermore, the UNWG has clarified that 'a "comply or explain" approach is not a sufficient [mandatory HRDD] regime' under the UNGPs.[90] The EU should adopt a substantive due diligence model,[91] where 'covered businesses meet the regime's requirements regarding meaningful HRDD processes and outcomes, including creative uses of leverage to address root causes and systemic challenges'.[92] In general, the EP Proposal adopts a substantive due diligence model. It provides that the exercise of due diligence should require undertakings 'to identify, assess, prevent, cease, mitigate, monitor, communicate, account for, address and remediate the potential and/or actual

84 Article 1(1) EP Proposal.
85 HRC (2011), UNGPs, *supra* note 1, GP 15(b).
86 Ibid., GP 18.
87 Ibid., GP 19.
88 Ibid., GP 19, 20.
89 Ibid., GP 21.
90 UNWG (2020), Letter to European Commissioner, *supra* note 81.
91 M. Krajewski and B. Faracik (2020), 'Briefing 1', *supra* note 72, p. 14.
92 UNWG (2020), Letter to European Commissioner, *supra* note 81.

adverse impacts on human rights, the environment and good governance that their own activities and those of their value chains and business relationships may pose.'[93] More specifically, undertakings would have to conduct a 'risk based monitoring methodology' to identify and assess potential or actual impacts on human rights, the environment, and good governance.[94] In addition, they would have to establish and implement 'a due diligence strategy', which would specify potential actual adverse impacts, map the value chain of the undertaking, adopt and indicate 'all proportionate and commensurate policies and measures with a view to ceasing, preventing or mitigating potential or actual adverse impacts'. In their due diligence strategy, undertakings would be required to set up 'a prioritisation strategy' where they are unable to deal with all the potential or actual adverse impacts at the same time.[95] Importantly, undertakings would be required to engage with relevant stakeholders when establishing and implementing their due diligence strategy and to publish and communicate their due diligence strategy.[96] The EP Proposal would also require undertakings to provide a grievance mechanism 'both as an early-warning mechanism for risk-awareness and as a mediation system'.[97] Where an adverse impact occurs, the undertaking would be required to provide for or cooperate with the remediation process depending on whether it has caused or contributed to the adverse impact, or whether it is directly linked to the adverse impact.[98]

3.3. ENFORCEMENT

The French experience with the implementation of the Act on the Duty of Vigilance demonstrates the importance of having monitoring and enforcement mechanisms in place.[99] Businesses are unlikely to meet their HRDD obligations without such mechanisms. The EU Instrument should establish monitoring mechanisms to ensure that all obliged undertakings have an HRDD process in place and that they effectively comply with the EU Instrument's requirements. A crucial question here is whether such monitoring mechanisms should be established at EU or national level. An EU monitoring mechanism would offer the advantages of ensuring harmonised application of the EU Instrument among Member States while centralising resources in a single monitoring mechanism. However, there is a risk that such a mechanism would be overwhelmed by the

93 Article 1(2) EP Proposal.
94 Ibid., Article 4(2).
95 Ibid., Article 4(4).
96 Ibid., Article 6.
97 Ibid., Article 9.
98 Ibid., Article 10(1).
99 See E. Savourey and S. Brabant, 'The French Law on the Duty of Vigilance: Theoretical and Practical Challenges Since its Adoption', (2021) 6(1), *Business and Human Rights Journal*.

sheer volume of monitoring required in 27 Member States. Therefore, a hybrid approach, where national and EU authorities are involved in monitoring, appears to be preferable. Furthermore, the UNWG has recommended the creation of a 'central registry of covered companies' annual reporting'.[100] However, to be a useful tool, such a registry should be accompanied by the mandatory publication of a list of obliged undertakings falling within the scope of the EU Instrument by each Member State. Finally, companies that fail to comply with their HRDD obligations should face sanctions under the EU Instrument. The EU Instrument should go beyond the wording 'effective, proportionate and dissuasive penalties' and provide a list of adapted penalties that ensure deterrence.

The EP Proposal includes both monitoring and sanctions. According to Article 13, competent authorities in Member States would have 'the power to carry out investigations' to ensure that undertakings comply with their due diligence obligations. They should be empowered to conduct checks on undertakings, such as an examination of their due diligence strategy and the operation of the grievance mechanism, on-the-spot checks, and interviews with affected stakeholders.[101] Additionally, Member States would be required to impose effective, proportionate and dissuasive sanctions that take into account 'the severity of the infringements committed and whether or not the infringement has taken place repeatedly'.[102] They could 'impose proportionate fines calculated on the basis of an undertaking's turnover, temporarily or indefinitely exclude undertakings from public procurement, from state aid, from public support schemes including schemes relying on Export Credit Agencies and loans, resort to the seizure of commodities and other appropriate administrative sanctions.'[103]

3.4. ACCESS TO JUSTICE AND REMEDY

A significant BHR issue is the difficulty for victims of business-related human rights violations to hold companies accountable and obtain reparation for the harm they have suffered. The absence of substantive standards on corporate human rights obligations has been particularly problematic for claimants suing MNEs in EU Member States, thereby limiting their ability to obtain remedies. Therefore, the EU Instrument should facilitate access to effective justice and remedy.

The EU Instrument should guarantee effective access to remedy by allowing victims to choose from several remediation mechanisms. Member States

[100] UNWG (2020), Letter to European Commissioner, *supra* note 81.

[101] Article 13(1) EP Proposal.

[102] Ibid., Article 18(1).

[103] Ibid., Article 18(2).

should be required to provide adequate remedy mechanisms, whether judicial or non-judicial in nature. Member States could be given the option to decide whether civil, criminal or administrative mechanisms are best suited to their domestic circumstances. In any case, such mechanisms should be low-cost (or made affordable through legal aid), expeditious and effective for victims.[104] Furthermore, the EU Instrument should require companies to engage actively in remedying any adverse impacts on human rights resulting from their activities or connected to them in their business relations.[105] They could do so by setting up corporate grievance mechanisms as part of their HRDD procedures. Another solution could be to promote access to remedies through the use of alternative dispute resolution (ADR) mechanisms outside of the corporate sphere, such as mediation, conciliation or arbitration. However, the existence of non-judicial mechanisms, such as corporate grievance and ADR mechanisms, should not preclude victims from bringing their claims to courts. The EP Proposal includes access to remedy through corporate grievance mechanisms and civil courts. However, the emphasis is on corporate grievance mechanisms.

Companies should be held liable under the EU Instrument. However, two main scenarios are possible in this situation. First, companies may be held liable if they fail to meet their due diligence obligations. For example, a company would potentially be liable if it did not conduct HRDD, or if it did so in an insufficient or inadequate manner. This liability would subject the company to the previously mentioned sanctions. CSOs have advocated for corporate liability based on the failure to carry out due diligence.[106] The UNWG has also recommended that the EU Instrument should establish 'grounds for liability when a covered company fails to engage in meaningful HRDD and when and how this might give rise to a cause of action and/or access to remedy by rights-holders'.[107] Second, a company may be held liable for harm caused by its own activities and, in certain cases, the activities of other companies. For instance, the UNWG and CSOs have called for covered companies to 'be liable for harms that they, or a company they control or have the ability to control, have caused or contributed to through acts or omissions'.[108] The second type of liability appears to address a significant barrier to suing parent or controlling companies for harm caused by group activities. However, it is unclear whether this liability should be based on the company's violation of the

---

104 M. Krajewski and B. Faracik (2020), 'Briefing 1', *supra* note 72, p. 15.

105 Ibid., pp. 14–15.

106 Actionaid, Aefjn, Amnesty International et al., 'Civil society statement on the adoption of European Parliament – Due Diligence & Corporate Accountability Legislative Report', 11.03.2021, available at https://www.amnesty.eu/news/due-diligence-corporate-accountability-legislative-report/, last accessed 29.06.2021.

107 UNWG (2020), Letter to European Commissioner, *supra* note 81.

108 Ibid.

EU Instrument's requirements or on another legal basis, such as a tortious duty of care. In France, the Act on the Duty of Vigilance states that failure to comply with due diligence obligations triggers liability of the company, and along with it the requirement to compensate victims, for damage that would have been avoided if they had met their obligations. In this regime, liability arises from the company's failure to meet its due diligence obligations. Finally, provisions on liability may be of no help to victims if the EU Instrument does not address barriers that may impede the ability of victims, in particular foreign victims, to hold companies liable, such as the exclusion of EU Member State law as a result of the application of the Rome II Regulation or evidentiary rules that place the burden of proof on victims without ensuring access to evidence in the hands of companies.

While a number of BHR actors have called for liability to be included in the EU Instrument, this will undoubtedly be a major sticking point in the legislative process. Businesses have expressed concern about the increased risk of litigation as a result of undertaking HRDD processes.[109] Furthermore, the question of liability raises a number of issues for victims. First, businesses could hide behind HRDD, using it as a defence when harm occurs despite having undertaken a proper due diligence process. This approach would be consistent with the notion that due diligence imposes an obligation of conduct and would provide an incentive for companies to comply with the EU Instrument. However, the use of due diligence as a defence could create a potential obstacle for victims to hold companies to account, particularly if it is unclear what companies should have done to conduct sufficient and appropriate due diligence. Litigators have suggested that such a defence should not be available 'in case of control over the entity that caused the harm because victims should not bear the consequences of internal corporate structure decisions'.[110] The use of due diligence as a defence against liability also raises the issue of the burden of proof. Should victims demonstrate that the harm is the result of the company's acts or omissions in relation to its HRDD obligations? Or should the company prove that it carried out sufficient and appropriate due diligence to ensure that no human rights violations occur in its value chain? The question of the burden of proof is critical because companies usually have the evidence needed by victims to establish corporate liability. In the French context, the inclusion of a provision placing the burden of proof on companies was met with resistance.

---

109 Amfori, 'Human Rights Due Diligence's Journey: Are You Ready to Be on Board?' in BHRRC (2020), 'Towards EU Mandatory Due Diligence Legislation', *supra* note 8, pp. 63–65.

110 L. Chatelain, 'Corporate Due Diligence and Civil Liability: Comment from multi-stakeholders', *NOVA BHRE*, 03.03.2021, available at https://novabhre.novalaw.unl.pt/corporate-due-diligence-civil-liability-comment-from-multi-stakeholders/, last accessed 31.03.2021.

Civil liability provisions are likely to be included in the EU Instrument. Commissioner Reynders has stated on several occasions that civil liability should be included in the EU instrument.[111] The EP Proposal also has provisions on civil liability.[112] Inclusion of civil liability in the EU Instrument would significantly improve access to justice. Nevertheless, the EP Proposal includes several provisions which, if included in the EU Instrument, may limit the civil liability regime's applicability. It provides for a reversal of the burden of proof on the undertaking in certain circumstances. For instance, the burden of proof 'would be shifted from a victim to an undertaking to prove that an undertaking did not have control over a business entity involved in the human rights abuse'.[113] However, victims would still have to demonstrate causation between the acts or omissions of the undertaking, or those under its control, and the harm arising out of potential or actual adverse impacts, which is likely to be difficult without the guarantee of adequate disclosure rules. Furthermore, the EP Proposal's provisions would be regarded as overriding mandatory provisions in line with Article 16 Rome II Regulation.[114] This would ensure that the law of the Member State implementing the EU Instrument, rather than the law of a third country, applies to claims involving corporate liability in the context of transnational claims. However, the EP Proposal is ambiguous on whether HRDD should provide undertakings with a defence against liability claims. On the one hand, it provides that an undertaking which respects its due diligence obligations shall not be absolved of any liability which it may incur pursuant to national law.[115] On the other hand, Member States would have an obligation to ensure that their liability regime is such that 'undertakings that prove that they took all due care in line with this Directive to avoid the harm in question, or that the harm would have occurred even if all due care had been taken, are not held liable for that harm'.[116] Here, it would be important to clarify the situations in which an undertaking is considered to have failed to comply with its obligations under the future instrument and how such situations may lead to its liability.

Another crucial issue is the availability of appropriate remedies. Victims should have access to a wide range of remedies. While the award of damages, or financial compensation, should always be guaranteed, other remedies, such as injunctive relief, rehabilitation or account of profits, should also be available options for courts and non-judicial bodies to consider. The EP Proposal includes a variety of remedies, including 'financial or non-financial compensation, reinstatement, public apologies, restitution, rehabilitation or a contribution to

---

111 RBC, 'European Commission Promises Mandatory Due Diligence Legislation in 2021', *supra* note 7.

112 Article 19 EP Proposal.

113 Ibid., Recital 53.

114 Ibid., Article 20.

115 Ibid., Article 19(1).

116 Ibid., Article 19(3).

an investigation'.[117] However, this reference to remedies is made in the context of extra-judicial remedies, and it is unclear whether such remedies could be used in the context of judicial proceedings.

4. CONCLUSION

The adoption of an EU instrument on mandatory HRDD would be a powerful catalyst in the normative development of BHR law. However, for such an instrument to have an effective value-added, it must be appropriately designed to address recurring BHR issues and close the current regulatory loopholes that allow businesses to ignore human rights and rights-holders with near-complete impunity. Despite the EU's considerable competence in company law and the primary legal value of fundamental rights, the current EU legal framework lacks binding legislation establishing corporate human rights obligations. Its rules on due diligence and corporate disclosure of non-financial information are too few, fragmented and inadequate to capture the complexity of global value chains. They also overlook the significance of monitoring and enforcement, as well as the ability for victims to seek and obtain redress, as mechanisms for ensuring compliance, deterrence and accountability. In the EU Instrument, provisions pertaining to scope, substantive business HRDD obligations, enforcement mechanisms and access to justice and remedy will have a significant impact on the effectiveness of this instrument from a human rights standpoint. Yet, they will be the most difficult to negotiate. Furthermore, the diversity of corporate actors, which include SMEs, corporate groups and MNEs, will require the EU to strike a delicate balance between appropriate HRDD and the resources requested from companies to exercise this diligence. In addition to technical challenges, more political issues will emerge during the legislative process. The outpouring of support for Commissioner Reynders' announcement should not obscure the political tensions in a field where businesses have staunchly opposed binding norms for decades. While some businesses have welcomed the initiative, they do not represent the majority of business actors. It is likely that business representatives will vigorously lobby for weak HRDD standards, putting the EU initiative at risk. Another potential issue is how Member States that have passed or intend to pass HRDD legislation prior the adoption of the EU Instrument will interfere with the legislative negotiations. Ultimately, there is a risk for substantive and political barriers to erode the EU Instrument's potential impact in the BHR field. As a result, the value-added of the first European mandatory HRDD instrument could undoubtedly be diminished, which would represent a missed opportunity for the EU to ensure businesses effectively respect human rights.

---

117 Ibid., Article 10(3).

THE EUROPEAN UNION'S GLOBAL HUMAN RIGHTS SANCTIONS REGIME AND THE 'ROLE RESPONSIBILITY' OF INTERNATIONAL ORGANISATIONS

Carmelo Danisi*

ABSTRACT

In 2020 the European Union (EU, the Union) adopted the Global Human Rights Sanctions Regime which, similarly to some national efforts, allows the EU to intervene against serious human rights abuses occurring beyond the Union's borders by adopting targeted sanctions. This contribution aims to critically assess the new regime's essential elements, also drawing on existing EU sanctions regimes' relevant practice. It explores the potential pitfalls that may prevent the new regime to achieve the desired results, as well as the innovative features that may contribute to the development of international law in this field. In this respect, attention is brought onto the theoretical concept of 'role responsibility' and on the examination of possible (international and/or internal) legal grounds for EU action in this field. The contribution closes by looking at the first implementation of the Global Human Rights Sanctions Regime in light of the critical aspects raised in the overall analysis.

* University of Bologna, Italy. The author wishes to thank the anonymous referees, prof. M. Balboni and dr. N. Bergamaschi for their comments on earlier versions of this contribution.

1. INTRODUCTION

According to the consolidated version of the Treaty on European Union (TEU),[1] the European Union (EU, the Union) shall contribute to the protection of human rights as well as to the strict observance and the development of international law in its relations with the wider world. In doing so, the Union shall seek to advance values such as democracy, the rule of law, respect for human dignity and respect for the principles of the United Nations (UN) Charter and international law across the world. Whether this post-Lisbon framework implies a positive duty for the EU – where this is reasonably possible within the exercise of its powers – to set the conditions for a fairer and more effective enjoyment of human rights worldwide is debatable.[2] Despite its rather unclear content, such a general duty has nonetheless facilitated more resolute action against (some) violations of human rights taking place worldwide.

In 2020, taking stock of the Union's autonomous role in adopting restrictive measures[3] based, *inter alia*, on human rights considerations against third countries and non-state actors or on thematic grounds,[4] the EU adopted its 'Global Human Rights Sanctions Regime' (GHRSR).[5] This move on the part of the EU reflects the general evolution of sanctions,[6] which favours individualised

---

1 See consolidated version of the Treaty on European Union, OJ C 326, 26.10.2012, Articles 3(5) and 21.

2 On how human rights are embedded horizontally in the EU post-Lisbon external policy, see M. Balboni and C. Danisi (eds.), *Human Rights as a Horizontal Issue in EU External Policy*, Editoriale Scientifica, Napoli 2021.

3 Although the common term for these measures in EU law is 'restrictive measures', in this contribution we will interchangeably use the terms 'sanctions' and 'restrictive measures'. In this respect, it is worth noting that there is no single, clear international definition of 'sanction'. It could nonetheless be read as a measure (not only of economic nature) adopted against a subject (not only a state) in order to induce it to comply with international law or to punish it in the event of such a violation. See T. Ruys, 'Sanctions, Retortions and Countermeasures: Concepts and International Legal Framework', in L. van den Herik (ed.), *Research Handbook on UN Sanctions and International Law*, Elgar, Cheltenham 2017, pp. 19–51.

4 *Ex multis*, C. Eckes, 'EU Restrictive Measures against Natural and Legal Persons: From Counterterrorist to Third Country Sanctions', (2014) 51(3), *Common Market Law Review*, pp. 869–906; M. Brzoska, 'International Sanctions before and beyond UN Sanctions', (2015) 9(6), *International Affairs*, pp. 1339–1349. The GHRSR joins the already existing thematic regimes, set up respectively against chemical weapons, cyber-attacks and terrorism, along 29 autonomous sanctions regimes with a geographical scope (as of 31 March 2021): see the useful map summarising all regimes at https://sanctionsmap.eu.

5 Council Decision (CFSP) 2020/1999 of 7 December 2020 concerning restrictive measures against serious human rights violations and abuses, OJ L 410 I (hereinafter Council Decision 2020/1999); Council Regulation (EU) 2020/1998 of 7 December 2020, OJ L 410 I (hereinafter Council Regulation).

6 As a key document for this evolution, see UN Security Council, Non-paper on the humanitarian impact of sanctions, attached to the Letter from the Permanent Representatives of China, France, the Russian Federation, the United States and the United Kingdom to the United Nations addressed to the President of the Security Council, S/1995/300, 13.04.1995.

measures in place of generalised restrictions against third countries to avoid, as far as possible, collateral effects on entire populations.[7] Indeed, through the new legal framework, the EU aims to prevent relevant – or to avoid further – violations by imposing a range of specific restrictive measures against actual or potential perpetrators.[8] Similarly to some national efforts, such as the famous 'Magnitsky Act' of the United States of America,[9] this regime establishes the key elements that enable the relevant EU institutions to target individuals and entities as well as identify the human rights abuses that justify the adoption of restrictive measures. The first implementation of the GHRSR has already been controversial within and beyond the Union, although mostly in international political terms rather than legal ones. The Council's adoption of restrictive measures against specific Chinese nationals for the treatment of the Uyghur minority and China's 'sanctions' in response clearly demonstrate the difficulties associated with implementing the new regime without the EU being accused of unjustified interference in the internal affairs of a sovereign state in contrast to international law key principles.[10] Although the GHRSR emphasises individual responsibility by de-linking human rights from a specific country and targeting non-state actors as well, sanctions are perceived as directed against a country.

See also Council of the European Union, Basic Principles on the Use of Restrictive Measures (Sanctions), 10198/1/04 REV 1, 07.06.2004.

7 For a general analysis on EU, C. Portela, *European Union Sanctions and Foreign Policy: When and Why Do They Work?*, Routledge, London 2010; C. Portela, *Targeted Sanctions against Individuals on Grounds of Grave Human Rights Violations – Impact, Trends and Prospects at EU Level*, Study requested by the European Parliament, Brussels 2018; M. Gestri, 'Sanctions Imposed by the European Union: Legal and Institutional Aspects', in N. Ronzitti (ed.), *Coercive Diplomacy, Sanctions and International Law*, Brill, Leiden 2016, pp. 70–102.

8 The preventive role of such restrictive measures in general is underlined in Council of the European Union, Guidelines on Implementation and Evaluation of Restrictive Measures (Sanctions) in the Framework of the EU CFSP, 11205/12, 15.06.2012. Yet, from the initial implementation of the new regime, one may wonder whether the EU aims also 'to punish', at least indirectly, perpetrators of human rights abuses (see section 4, below).

9 The 'Global Magnitsky Human Rights Accountability Act' was adopted on 18 April 2016 and followed the 2012 Magnitsky Act focused on sanctions against the death of the Russian whistle-blower S. Magnitsky. The Act is available on the United States Congress website at www.congress.gov/bill/114th-congress/senate-bill/284/text. Unlike the EU GHRSR, it covers also acts of significant corruption. For a comment, M. Smoler, 'The Global Magnitsky Act Represents New Era of Smart Sanctions', *Human Rights First*, 20.09.2017, available at www.humanrightsfirst.org/blog/global-magnitsky-act-represents-new-era-smart-sanctions, last accessed 15.02.2021.

10 See Annex of the Council Implementing Regulation (EU) 2021/478 of 22 March 2021 implementing Regulation (EU) 2020/1998 concerning restrictive measures against serious human rights violations and abuses, OJ L 99 I (hereinafter Council Implementing Regulation 2021/478). The human rights violations suffered by this minority is also reflected in the European Court of Human Rights' (ECtHR) case law: see ECtHR, *M.A. and others v Bulgaria*, no 5115/18, 20.02.2020, and the wide documentation mentioned therein. See also China's reaction at www.euronews.com/2021/03/22/eu-foreign-ministers-to-discuss-sanctions-on-china-and-myanmar, last accessed 23.03.2021.

As we explore here, the focus on 'key political figures' signals a denunciation of violations led or sponsored by third states against their own population or minority groups, something that echoes at least implicitly the rationale beyond the so-called 'responsibility to protect' (RtP).[11] The resulting impact on EU international affairs risks having a negative influence on the development of the GHRSR.

This contribution aims to provide one of the first comprehensive analyses of the Union's new global regime in order to verify whether such an EU move actually is the key international human rights achievement that some initial commentators have claimed.[12] To this end, its essential elements will be critically assessed to identify any potential legal and/or practical difficulties that may prevent the new regime from achieving the desired results. Given that targeted sanctions have been a cornerstone of the European Common Foreign and Security Policy (CFSP), the analysis will also draw on other existing EU sanctions regimes. In particular, the principles that have emerged in connection with such regimes in the case law of the Court of Justice of the EU (CJEU)[13] will help us to determine if the GHRSR is, or could be implemented in such a way that is, in compliance with the rights of targeted individuals and entities under EU and international law. Pending implementation issues around the potentially wide scope of the new regime are not our sole concern. Indeed, a more substantive point should be addressed here: all things being equal, when will the EU resort to restrictive measures for serious human rights abuses? It is unrealistic to expect that every perpetrator of human rights abuses will be subject to EU sanctions. Whereas discretion in foreign affairs will certainly play

---

11 UN General Assembly, 2005 World Summit Outcome, A/RES/60/1 24.10.2005, p. 30. On the RtP, *ex multis* J. Hoffmann and A. Nolikaemper, *Responsibility to Protect: From Principle to Practice*, Amsterdam University Press, Amsterdam 2012; R. Thakur and W. Maley, *Theorising the Responsibility to Protect*, Cambridge University Press, Cambridge 2015. At least formally, the EU endorsed the RtP (see Council of the EU, Conclusions – UN World Summit, 07.11.2005), although it has been reticent to implement it as analysed by C. De Franco, C. O'Meyer and K.E. Smith, '"Living by Example?" The European Union and the Implementation of the Responsibility to Protect (R2P)', (2015) *Journal of Common Market Studies*, p. 996 et seqq.

12 To the author's knowledge, at the time of writing there is still a lack of literature on the new regime, apart from some short comments: F. Finelli, 'A New EU Sanctions Regime against Human Rights Violations', (2020) *European Papers*, pp. 1569–1571; Y. Miadzvetskaya, 'Habemus a European Magnitsky Act', *European Law Blog*, 13.01.2021, available at https://europeanlawblog.eu/2021/01/13/habemus-a-european-magnitsky-act; R. Youngs, 'The New EU Global Human Rights Sanctions Regime: Breakthrough or Distraction', *Carnegie Europe*, 14.12.2020, available at https://carnegieeurope.eu/2020/12/14/new-eu-global-human-rights-sanctions-regime-breakthrough-or-distraction-pub-83415; T. Ruys, 'Introductory Note to the European Union Global Human Rights Sanctions Regime (EUGHRSR)', *The American Society of International Law*, 7.12.2020, all last accessed 20.03.2021.

13 C. Cellerino, 'Human Rights, Court of Justice and External Action', in M. Balboni and C. Danisi (eds.), *supra* note 2, pp. 73–96.

a role, an examination of possible (international and/or internal) legal grounds for EU action in this field is essential to clarify if and, in the positive, when such measures should necessarily be adopted. An investigation into international organisations' responsibility regime under international law as well as of the theoretical concept of 'role responsibility' could provide some answers in this respect.

For these reasons, this contribution is structured as follows. The next section analyses the framework of the GHRSR by focusing on the nature of abuses and the categories of individuals and entities covered by the regime, as well as the expected protection against restrictive measures (section 2). After a discussion on the legality/legitimacy of the EU's role in imposing restrictive measures (section 3), the GHRSR will be tested in light of its first implementation and the subsequent reactions within the international community, the significance of which cannot be overlooked (section 4). The contribution ends with some final remarks (section 5). In summary, whereas the GHRSR certainly provides an additional tool for implementing existing EU policies designed to protect human rights globally, the idea of 'acting by sanctions' in itself is called into question given, *inter alia*, the legal pitfalls that will be identified in this contribution.

2. THE NEW EU GLOBAL SANCTIONS REGIME

Acting upon a proposal by the Commission and the High Representative for Foreign Affairs (HRVP) and supported by the European Parliament,[14] in 2020 the Council established the first EU-wide horizontal mechanism for freezing funds and economic resources as well as imposing travel bans in the case of serious human rights abuses occurring outside the EU.[15] Among the Council's intentions, as reported in the relevant Decision (see whereas four and five),[16] the new regime 'enhance[s] the Union's capacity to promote respect for human rights'

---

14 European Parliament, Resolution on a European Human Rights Violations Sanctions Regime, 2019/2580(RSP) 14.03.2019. On the need for individualised restrictive measures, already European Parliament, Recommendation to the Council on a consistent policy towards regimes against which the EU applies restrictive measures, when their leaders exercise their personal and commercial interests within EU borders, 2011/2187(INI) 02.02.2012. An account of the first phase of the elaboration process can be found in N. van der Have, 'The Proposed EU Human Rights Sanctions Regime', (2019) *Security and Human Rights*, pp. 56–71.

15 The relevant Decision is based on Article 29 TEU, whereas the Council Regulation is based on Article 215 of the Treaty on the Functioning of the European Union. On the need for a 'two-steps procedure' given the EU current framework, see C. Portela, *Targeted Sanctions against Individuals*, *supra* note 7, p. 11.

16 Across the contribution reference is made to the relevant 'Decision' (agreed in the framework of the CFSP), although its content is overall equal to the parallel Council Regulation (EU). Where needed, direct reference to the relevant 'Regulation' will be made.

worldwide and contributes to the common foreign and security objectives set out in Article 21 TEU. It also complements existing third-country sanctions[17] that cannot horizontally address human rights violations in light of their specific and limited geographical scope. Other than its global dimension,[18] three elements of the GHRSR would appear to be essential in order to pursue these aims and need to be briefly explored here: the nature of abuses; the individuals and the entities targeted; and the (expected) protection against such restrictive measures.

2.1. THE SERIOUSNESS AND NATURE OF ABUSES

The GHRSR covers a range of human rights abuses. In fact, according to Article 1 of the relevant Decision, the new regime applies in relation to: genocide; crimes against humanity; torture and other cruel, inhuman or degrading treatment or punishment; slavery; extrajudicial, summary or arbitrary executions and killings; enforced disappearance of persons; and arbitrary arrests or detentions. The gravity that such violations need to reach in order to justify the adoption of restrictive measures – and whether, for example, a single case of torture or arbitrary execution would suffice – remains unclear. For example, a broad reading of these abuses would allow the EU to impose sanctions against the individuals who are accused of having arbitrarily detained and killed the Saudi dissent journalist Khashoggi, even though this may be considered an isolated case, in order to prevent similar human rights violations.[19] Yet, the nature of the 'other human rights violations' that, according to the GHRSR founding acts, could trigger restrictive measures supports the view that it is mostly 'widespread' and 'systematic' abuses or those that entail a 'serious concern as regards the objectives of the common foreign and security policy' that would be likely to reach the required threshold of seriousness to fall within the new sanctions regime. For the GHRSR, such 'other' human rights violations consist of trafficking in human beings, abuses of human rights by migrant smugglers, sexual and gender-based violence and abuses of the freedoms of peaceful assembly and of association,

17 Among others, see Council Regulation (EU) 2016/44 concerning restrictive measures in view of the situation in Libya, OJ L 12, Article 6(2).

18 The Commission's Guidance Note on the connected Council Regulation specifies that 'EU sanctions are expected to produce effects in third countries through pressure on the listed persons. However, they do not apply *extra-territorially*' (emphasis added). In fact, non-EU operators do not have the same obligations as EU operators, 'unless the business is conducted at least partly within the EU' (something that may still be problematic, however). See Council Regulation 2020/1998, *supra* note 5, Article 19 and European Commission, Guidance Note on the Implementation of certain Provisions of Council Regulation (EU) 2020/1998, C(2020) 9432 final 17.12.2020 (hereinafter, Commission Guidance).

19 For the international and human rights law implications of this case, see M. Milanovic, 'The Murder of Jamal Khashoggi: Immunities, Inviolability and the Human Right to Life', (2020) *Human Rights Law Review*, pp. 1–49.

of opinion and expression and of freedom of religion or belief. Importantly, no specific limitations are set out in relation to the victims of any of the violations covered by the GHRSR for it to be activated.

In order to define such a broad range of human rights, the relevant Decision emphasises the importance of international human rights law as well as its interaction with international humanitarian law (whereas 4 and Article 1(2)). Reference is made to customary international law and 'widely' accepted international treaties, such as the two international covenants, the Rome Statute of the International Criminal Court and the UN Protocol to Prevent, Supress and Punish Trafficking in Persons. Whereas the reference to the International Criminal Court (ICC) may prove essential as the EU could use its activity for raising the necessary grounds for listing when relevant human rights abuses are involved,[20] it is curious that no consideration is afforded to the International Convention on the Protection of the Rights of All Migrant Workers and Members of their Families. Interestingly, the European Convention on Human Rights (ECHR) is instead expressly mentioned among relevant key international treaties despite its 'narrow' regional scope. In terms of 'European' material focus, the lack of reference to the EU Charter of Fundamental Rights (CFR) is, arguably, more understandable, even though the Charter, by virtue of its scope, would nonetheless apply to sanctions imposed via the GHRSR (see Article 51 CFR) thus enhancing the protection which targeted subjects could enjoy under EU law (see section 2.3, below).[21]

As a result, and especially in comparison with other previous national frameworks, the GHRSR has a potentially wide scope of application in spite of the possible interpretative restraints in the relevant Decision. First, as anticipated, the new sanctions mechanism marks a fundamental difference from other relevant international law frameworks that primarily aim to deal with gross human rights violations.[22] Second, and as a consequence, it could lead the EU to act in situations that would usually evade sanctioning powers. Third, owing to this broad range of violations, EU partners in key external policy areas could also be directly or indirectly subject to sanctions, which is something that could test the credibility and impartiality of the new regime.

To name an example, there are currently two situations that could be covered by what is perhaps the most innovative aspect of the new GHRSR: widespread and systematic sexual and gender-based violence that is not associated with

20 See discussion in N. van der Have, 'The Proposed EU Human Rights Sanctions Regime', *supra* note 14, p. 65.

21 See also Council Regulation 2020/1998, *supra* note 5, whereas 2, that, in affirming the application of the Charter, refers in particular to the right to an effective remedy, the right to defence, and the right to the protection of personal data.

22 An example can be the RtP, as explained in section 3 below.

specific situations such as conflicts or wars. First, according to institutional and non-governmental sources,[23] gender-based violence in Turkey has reached the very high threshold required to be defined as systematic and widespread human rights abuse. The latest decision of Turkey to withdraw from the Council of Europe Convention on preventing and combating violence against women and domestic violence (Istanbul Convention) appears to confirm that these are structural issues, rather than signalling, as the Turkish government has claimed, that the Convention offers unnecessary added value for Turkey's legal order.[24] It remains to be seen if, despite the cooperation with Turkey in fields such as migration control, the EU is prepared to target Turkish individuals and entities under the GHRSR to facilitate a significant policy change in the contrast to gender and sexual-based violation. Second, a similar argument can apply to Russia, which is already subject to restrictive measures in view of its actions destabilising the situation in Ukraine.[25] If the interpretation of sexual and gender-based violence is really based on the International Covenant on Civil and Political Rights and the ECHR,[26] the widespread and systematic character of abuses against sexual and gender minorities in Russia should trigger sanctions under the GHRSR.[27] This would apply especially if such abuses are considered in combination with the connected violations of freedoms of peaceful assembly, association, opinion and expression, which are remarkably also covered by the new regime. The fact that – according to Russia – the legislation giving rise to such abuses aims to protect internal 'traditional values' would be irrelevant in the face of international human rights law.[28] Yet, other than the EU's willingness to push the boundaries of the new thematic regime, it remains to be seen which individuals and entities can actually be targeted with restrictive measures in light of the tension between sanctions and internal state sovereignty.

23 See the sources considered in one of the latest cases on domestic violence at the ECtHR, *M.G. v Turkey*, no 646/10, 22.03.2016.

24 B. Çali, 'Withdrawal from the Istanbul Convention by Turkey: A Testing Problem for the Council of Europe', *EJILTalk!*, 22.03.2021, available at www.ejiltalk.org/withdrawal-from-the-istanbul-convention-by-turkey-a-testing-problem-for-the-council-of-europe, last accessed 25.03.2021.

25 Council Regulation (EU) No 833/2014 of 31 July 2014 concerning restrictive measures in view of Russia's actions destabilising the situation in Ukraine, OJ L 229.

26 For example, ECtHR, *Bayev and Others v Russia*, nos 67667/09, 44092/12 and 56717/12, 20.06.2017. For more, C. Danisi, *Tutela dei diritti umani, non discriminazione e orientamento sessuale*, Editoriale Scientifica, Napoli 2015.

27 Human Rights Council, Discrimination and Violence against Individuals Based on Their Sexual Orientation and Gender Identity, A/HRC/29/23 4.05.2015, para. 48.

28 See M. Balboni and C. Danisi, 'Reframing Human Rights in Russia and China', in S. Bianchini and A. Fiori (eds.), *Rekindling the Strong State in Russia and China*, Brill, Leiden 2020, pp. 61–78.

2.2. TARGETS OF SANCTIONS

The new GHRSR provides for restrictive measures to apply to three broad categories of natural or legal persons, entities or bodies. According to Article 1(3) of the relevant Decision, these consist of state actors, other actors exercising effective control or authority over a territory and other non-state actors. Perhaps most importantly, Articles 2 and 3 specify that the GHRSR targets not only the perpetrators of the above violations, but also persons 'who provide financial, technical, or material support for, or are otherwise involved in' those abuses and persons associated with them. As such, the new regime has the potential for a very wide global reach. This can be seen in Article 2(1)(b), which includes 'planning, directing, ordering, assisting, preparing, facilitating, or encouraging' relevant abuses among the actions that could qualify a person as a potential target of sanctions.[29] While such an approach is certainly welcome when compared to some international regimes,[30] it affords the EU considerable discretion in selecting potential targets of sanctions despite the principles developed by the CJEU to protect concerned people, as analysed below.

The possibility of granting exemptions is nonetheless available. For instance, in relation to travel and transit bans, Member States hosting an international governmental organisation or an international conference convened under the auspices of the UN or that are bound by multilateral agreements conferring privileges and immunities can avoid the application of restrictive measures (see Article 2 of the relevant Decision). As for the freezing of funds and the availability of economic resources, a derogation allows Member States as they deem appropriate to, for example, release the funds and economic resources if they are needed to satisfy the basic needs of the targeted natural or legal persons, entities or bodies or for humanitarian reasons (Articles 3 and 4 of the relevant Decision).

---

29 It may follow that the implementation of the GHRSR is based on criteria that seem far more flexible and broader than the usual rules on the attribution of an act or omission to a state or an international organisation under the law of international responsibility: see INTERNATIONAL LAW COMMISSION (ILC), 'Draft Articles on Responsibility of States for Internationally Wrongful Acts', (2001) 2, *Yearbook of the International Law Commission*, and ILC, 'Draft Articles on Responsibility of International Organisations for Internationally Wrongful Acts', (2011) 2, *Yearbook of the International Law Commission*. This is true especially in light of the International Court of Justice (ICJ)'s test for attribution: e.g. ICJ, *Case concerning the Military and Paramilitary Activities in and against Nicaragua (Nicaragua v United States of America)*, 27.06.1986, section VII.

30 See the well documented difficulties associated with satisfying the key elements of attribution in the law of international responsibility of States for wrongful acts in cases involving serious human rights violations: ICJ, *Case concerning Application of the Convention on the Prevention and Punishment of the Crime of Genocide* (*Bosnia and Herzegovina v Serbia and Montenegro*), 26.02.2007, section VII.

As the Commission's guide clarifies, the result is that EU operators cannot put any funds or economic resources at the disposal of listed persons, either directly or indirectly. For example, once a person is listed, no services or products can be provided by an EU business, and no donations can be received, even from a third country national, from the territory of a Member State.[31] Of course, restrictive measures apply equally to entities owned or controlled by the listed persons, giving rise to the same obligations on the part of EU operators.[32] Member States should grant the enforcement of these sanctions laying down appropriate penalties in the event of non-compliance.

The importance of focusing on specific perpetrators, rather than adopting measures of general scope, is certainly commendable. It is in line with a wider international trend toward smart sanctions that avoid any unnecessary negative impact on an entire population or group of people, as is often the case with economic embargoes.[33] All of these sanctions share the same preventive character, being primarily aimed at producing a change in the policy of a country or in the actions of natural or legal persons, entities or bodies responsible for, involved in or supporting serious human rights abuses – rather than primarily seeking to punish. Yet, the lack of well defined criteria for identifying the possible targets of EU sanctions, as pointed out above, gives rise to the risk of erroneous listings and could hamper appropriate de-listings. Considering the impact on the addressees' right to property at least, the new regime overall needs strong procedural guarantees which, as we show now, can avoid giving rise itself to new human rights violations.

2.3. THE REQUIRED PROTECTION AGAINST RESTRICTIVE MEASURES

The Decision establishing the GHRSR provides for some guarantees to the benefit of the target of the sanction (Articles 5 and 6),[34] as supported initially by its proponents and requested by the European Parliament.[35] First, it requires that the Council's relevant decision is communicated to the concerned natural or legal person, entity or body. Second, it ensures that the addressee is given an opportunity to present observations. Third, in the event that such observations or relevant evidence are submitted, the Council is required to review its decision

---

31 See Commission Guidance, *supra* note 18, p. 4.

32 To understand when it is possible to say that a listed person owns or controls an entity, see ibid., pp. 6–7.

33 For such an evolution, see L. van den Herik (ed.), *Research Handbook on UN Sanctions and International Law*, *supra* note 3.

34 See also Council Regulation 2020/1998, *supra* note 5, Articles 14 and 15.

35 European Parliament, Resolution on a European Human Rights Violations Sanctions Regime, *supra* note 14, para. 11.

accordingly and to provide information about the outcome. Fourth, and perhaps most importantly, not only shall the Council provide the person or entity concerned with the grounds for listing, but these grounds shall also be included in the relevant amended Annex, where all identification details are provided. Finally, the Council should carry out a periodic review of the list of designated targets.

These guarantees can be briefly assessed, and integrated, in light of the principles already developed by the CJEU in connection with other restrictive measures frameworks.[36] Indeed, in that the new measures are based on the competences provided for in Article 215 of the Treaty on the Functioning of the European Union (TFEU), the targets of sanctions may thus see the legality of the relevant restrictive measures undergo review by the EU courts.[37] Although the principles established by the CJEU in this field relate to other scenarios,[38] including also the relationship between the Security Council's anti-terrorism sanctions and their implementation within the EU legal order, they define minimum standards of protection, the applicability of which is not called into question by the nature of the human rights abuses or other elements featuring in the GHRSR.[39] The outcomes of the well-known *Kadi* saga are certainly relevant here.[40] According to the CJEU, the listing of individuals for the imposition of restrictive measures must comply with their right to effective judicial review as protected by the EU legal order.[41] This implies that the concerned person should, as a minimum, be able to receive the reasons for and be granted (limited, if need be) access to the evidence supporting the listing, to have the case properly reviewed and to obtain the reasons for any delisting refusal.[42]

---

36 For reasons of space, we cannot refer to all issues at play. Nor can we explore the relevant principles established by the ECtHR in its case law (as for Article 13 – right to an effective remedy) that might reasonably apply as well to restrictive measures imposed under the GHRSR: see ECtHR, *Nada v Switzerland*, no 10593/08, 12.09.2012; ECtHR, *Al-Dulimi and Montana Management Inc v Switzerland*, no 5809/08 [GC], 21.06.2016.

37 Having regard to Article 275(2) TFEU, it is the individual nature of restrictive measures that permits access to EU courts, as the CJEU confirmed in CJEU, *Laurent Gbagbo et al. v Council*, Joined cases C-478-482/11 P, 23.04.2013, ECLI:EU:C:2013:258, para. 57. Where this review is not possible, relevant measures remain nonetheless challengeable before national courts: see, in relation to travel bans implemented by Member States, CJEU, *Council v Manufacturing Support & Procurement Kala Naft*, Case C-348/12 P, 28.11.2013, ECLI:EU:C:2013:776.

38 M. Sossai, 'UN Sanctions and Regional Organizations: An Analytical Framework', in L. van den Herik (ed.), *supra* note 3, pp. 395–417.

39 Even the fact that terrorist listings is adopted under Article 75 TFEU and is part of the area of Justice, Freedom and Security rather than the CFSP, like the other sanctions regimes, does not justify a different view.

40 CJEU (GC), *European Commission and Others v Yassin Abdullah Kadi (Kadi II)*, Joined Cases C-584/10 P, C-593/10 P and C-595/10 P, 18.07.2013, ECLI:EU:C:2013:518; CJEU (GC), *Yassin Abdullah Kadi and Al Barakaat International Foundation v Council and Commission (Kadi I)*, Joined cases C-402/05 P and C-415/05 P, 03.09.2008, ECLI:EU:C:2008:461.

41 E.g. CJEU, *Kadi II*, *supra* note 40, para. 97.

42 CJEU, *Kadi I*, *supra* note 40, para. 324 et seqq.

The standard of proof has been a central aspect of the cases brought before the EU courts, especially in relation to limited access to the reasons for listings. As the *OMPI/PMOI* cases showed and *Kadi II* confirmed, the absence of information or evidence supporting the imposition of restrictive measures under the new regime could easily lead to their annulment.[43] In relation to the new regime, however, this aspect may be less problematic than in previous cases.[44] First, as anticipated, the wording of the GHRSR provides for the communication of the grounds for listing. Second, most human rights violations covered by the GHRSR are generally known, as often they are well documented by international organisations and NGOs. As a result, the EU courts will be able to access relevant information, which, given that listing under the GHRSR is autonomous and will not depend on external bodies like the UN Security Council, could make de-listing easier.

One factor could nonetheless hamper this: under the new regime, some doubts remain as to how a sufficient link can be established between (the different kinds of) targets and the relevant human rights violations. If restrictive measures are to be truly preventive in nature,[45] the ability of the targets to contribute to preventing, or to ending, the relevant abuses should be central and would need to always be verified. There would be no justification for a lower standard of review in light of previous case law. In this respect, it would also be useful to clarify whether a de-listing is dependent either on a change in behaviour on the part of the perpetrator or on an improvement in the human rights of (actual or potential) victims, or both. In the absence of clear criteria for determining and assessing the aforementioned link as well as the desired change, including the possibility of requiring a different standard of proof if restrictive sanctions are to be maintained for extended periods, there is a risk of sanctions continuing indefinitely with limited practical effect on the ground. Without further guidance, for example, the Council's periodic review could not lead to adjust sanctions in response to target behaviour. Furthermore, given the discretion to be enjoyed by the Council in this field,[46] the Court's assessment may result in a formal review exercise (potentially) in conflict with applicable human rights (e.g. Article 47 CFR). As has been argued elsewhere in relation to the CJEU's 'new take on country sanctions',[47] there is a risk that the minimum standards of legality established so far in connection with anti-terrorist sanctions may be 'renegotiated' in order to meet the Council's discretion in expanding

---

43 CJEU (GC), *Organisation des Modjahedines du people d'Iran v Council and UK (PMOI I)*, Case T-228/02, 12.12.2006, ECLI:EU:T:2006:384, para. 160 et seqq.

44 E.g. CJEU (GC), *Fulmen*, Joined Cases T-439-440/10, 21.03.2012, ECLI:EU:T:2012:142, para. 100.

45 For instance, see CJEU, *Kadi II*, *supra* note 40, para. 130.

46 E.g. CJEU, *PMOI I*, *supra* note 43, para. 159.

47 C. Beaucillon, 'Opening up the Horizon: The ECJ's New Take on Country Sanctions', (2018) *Common Market Law Review*, pp. 387–416.

listing criteria, including under the GHRSR. This evolution may not be excluded in the future implementation of the new regime if, for example, in relation to the category of 'state actors' the CJEU will not be able to distinguish the legal personality of the real targets of the sanctions from the legal personality of the state to which they belong even in order to assess the need to maintain restrictive measures.

In short, the guarantees provided for targeted individuals and entities in the GHRSR Decision and associated Regulation seem to reflect overall the principles established in EU courts' case law. Whereas an administrative challenge before the Council is granted to all targets, they will also be able to challenge their listing before the EU courts, which are likely to apply the standards established so far. Inasmuch as targeted entities can avoid restrictive measures by relying solely on formal legal arguments, there may be some truth to the argument that there is a sort of 'procedural fetishism' in the EU courts' approach.[48] Nevertheless, the enjoyment of such procedural guarantees hardly ensures an immediate delisting or award of damages, even in the event of a successful judicial outcome. The risk of being relisted is also very real. Yet, the possibility of having one's case fully reviewed in terms of compatibility with EU fundamental rights has – at a minimum – the effect of providing (more) legitimacy to the GHRSR. Such a legitimacy, as well as the legality, of the EU's role in imposing sanctions on human rights grounds could be investigated further from an international law perspective, before turning to an assessment of the very first implementation of the GHRSR.

3. A 'RIGHT' OR A 'DUTY' TO PREVENT ABUSES? THE 'ROLE RESPONSIBILITY' OF INTERNATIONAL ORGANISATIONS

Even if the new EU sanctions regime is implemented in compliance with the principles analysed above to ensure that procedural guarantees are respected, the setting up of the GHRSR as an autonomous sanctions framework – that is, not dependant on a previous UN decision – entails a more fundamental question: is the EU acting based on a 'right' to adopt restrictive measures against human rights abusers worldwide? Or, conversely, is the EU under an obligation to prevent or punish such violations? If so, does such a right or obligation exist, either under international law or EU 'internal' law? Clarifying this aspect is more than a theoretical necessity; it could also have practical consequences, as

[48] This expression is used by P. Nevill, 'Interpretation and Review of UN Sanctions by European Court: Comity and Conflict', in L. van den Herik (ed.), *supra* note 3, p. 438, where she provides an example of such a scenario by referring to the *Al-Dulimi* case of the ECtHR.

we will see in relation to (the (il)legality of) possible reactions from countries whose citizens are targeted. More broadly, it also throws into question the international role of the EU as a global human rights actor in comparison with other international organisations.

To start with, it is difficult to say that international organisations have either a right or an obligation to prevent human rights abuses under international law. For example, neither the United Nations nor the EU are parties to international treaties containing such rules and, apart from an exception on the part of the EU,[49] they have yet to ratify any human rights treaties. In short, any obligations under such treaties to prevent or punish bind only their Member States if they have ratified or accessed such treaties. Moreover, unless these treaty obligations apply extraterritorially, the current prevailing understanding of human rights law does not call on parties to prevent or punish human rights abuses anywhere in the world.

A more limited rule, which does not even entail these extraterritorial issues, can be derived from a situation where an obligation arising under a peremptory norm of general international law is breached, according to the responsibility of states and international organisations alike under international law.[50] As such, in case a peremptory norm has a human rights content, Article 42 of the Draft Articles on the Responsibility of International Organisations (DARIO) calls upon international organisations to cooperate to bring to an end any serious breach of such a human rights obligation. Moreover, the international organisation at stake must also not recognise as lawful the situation created by such a serious human rights breach and must avoid providing any aid or assistance in maintaining that situation. For our purposes, two observations are useful. First, Article 42 of DARIO specifies that the duty to cooperate should be carried out 'through lawful means'. In terms of 'sanctions', this means that restrictive measures are allowed only to the extent that they do not entail a breach of international law. Second, any attempt to identify peremptory norms having a human rights content would not do much to address the absence of clear obligations for international organisations concerning a general right or duty to prevent (or punish) human rights violations.

If we consider the EU's move in light of these rules, a range of problems arises. A preliminary issue concerns the reasons for the GHRSR. Other than a commitment to protect the values on which it is founded (see the initial part of the new regime's relevant Decision), it is unclear whether the EU sees itself as an 'injured'[51] subject to respond to breaches of the international Community's

49 The EU ratified the Convention on the Rights of Persons with Disabilities. See Council Decision of 26 November 2009 concerning the Conclusion, by the European Community, of the United Nations Convention on the Rights of Persons with Disabilities, OJ 2010 L 23/35.

50 For international organisations, see ILC, DARIO, *supra* note 29.

51 Yet, in the DARIO commentary, the ILC included the example of the EU's reaction against serious human rights violations in Burma/Myanmar in the section related to 'non-injured' international organisations: see ibid., p. 89.

collective interests, as underlined by Article 42 DARIO, or for other – unrelated – reasons.[52] Second, the aforementioned rules on the responsibility of international organisations for breaches of peremptory norms would nonetheless be relevant only for some human rights abuses covered by the GHRSR – for example, the prohibition of genocide. However, the DARIO rules would certainly not cover many of the violations falling within the scope of the new sanctions regime (see section 2.1, above). For example, a serious breach of the 'other' human rights specified in the GHRSR would not justify an EU (re)action as a member of the international Community under those rules. Yet, clarifying these issues would shed light on the nature of EU sanctions as part of the general framework of international responsibility. Indeed, it is disputable if EU restrictive measures can be considered 'retortions' (i.e. unfriendly actions) or 'countermeasures' (i.e. proportional self-help measures that would otherwise constitute wrongful acts themselves if not seeking to react against relevant prior breaches of international law).[53] But even if we accept that EU sanctions in relation to human rights abuses could be generally conceived of as retortions, especially in light of the punitive character of some measures adopted under the GHRSR, states that are directly or indirectly targeted could nonetheless perceive those measures as violations of the principle of non-interference in internal affairs.[54] Concerned states would therefore see their reaction as being justified under international law. In short, the right or obligation of the EU to act against human rights abuses, as it is framed in the GHRSR, cannot be easily found in international treaties or derived from the rules on the responsibility of international organisations.

Yet, for the sake of completeness, it is worth remembering the potential role that the RtP framework could play in providing an international legal ground for the EU's action in this field. As it is known, in affirming a primary responsibility of states to protect their populations from genocide, war crimes, ethnic cleansing and crimes against humanity, the RtP calls the entire international community – of which regional organisations like the EU are a part – to 'encourage, as

---

52 According the DARIO commentary, the lack of practice in this field does not even allow confirmation of the existence of a general entitlement of international organisations to invoke responsibility and, if so, whether they would invoke such a responsibility on their own or by implementing rights that are owed to Member States: see ibid. and bibliography mentioned in fn. 317.

53 Interestingly, the ILC does not refer often to 'sanctions' in its Drafts Articles on Responsibility, while legal doctrine resorts to this term mainly when acts of international organisations are at stake. Yet, sanctions are not a separate group of measures but may fall within one of the categories mentioned in the text.

54 Although the scope of this principle is still debatable: see ICJ, *Military and Paramilitary Activities in and against Nicaragua*, *supra* note, 29, para. 205 et seqq. For an in-depth discussion of these aspects, T. Ruys, 'Sanctions, Retortions and Countermeasures', *supra* note 3, p. 24 et seqq. See also the discussions in the General Assembly on the legality and legitimacy of sanctions analysed in M. Brzoska, *supra* note 4, p. 1345 et seqq.

appropriate' and to 'help States to exercise this responsibility'.[55] The responsibility to prevent and react against such human rights abuses through 'peaceful means' are key pillars of the RtP. It can be therefore argued that, to the extent that the measures adopted through the GHRSR pursue these aims and could qualify as 'peaceful' means following the reasoning explained above, the new EU regime is – at least implicitly – implementing such a responsibility as far as their respective material scope coincides (section 2.1). Even in this case, however, the RtP would nonetheless provide legal grounds for *some* EU 'sanctions' only.

In the face of such ambiguity, perhaps a more comprehensive explanation for the right or duty to adopt restrictive measures against human rights abuses committed abroad could lie in the concept of 'role responsibility',[56] which delves into omissions of international organisations. To use J. Klabbers' words, the answer cannot be found 'by the simple deontological exercise of pointing to a positive obligation'.[57] As such, he argues that 'some obligation flows directly from the function that has been delegated to the international organisation (its mandate), without the need to identify a separate legal obligation contained in some primary obligation or other'.[58] If this is true, then the organisation at issue can be held responsible for not carrying out its mandate, in terms of its general function within the international community and not simply of attributed powers. Some conditions will nonetheless apply: the concerned international organisation should have knowledge of the situation that requires action and it should be in a position to act.[59]

If its mandate is key, then the EU's right or duty to act against human rights violations worldwide can be found in its founding treaties. Although the Council Regulation on the GHRSR refers to Article 215 TFEU, this part of the founding

---

55 The role of international organisations, which should act in compliance with the UN taking into account Chapter VIII of the UN Charter, was given attention more recently: e.g. UN Secretary-General, The Role of Regional and Subregional Arrangements in Implementing the Responsibility to Protect, A/65/877 28.06.2011. On the potential role and limits of the EU vis-à-vis the RtP, J. Wouters and P. De Man, 'The Responsibility to Protect and Regional Organisations: The Example of the European Union', (2013) *Leuven Centre for Global Governance Studies Working Paper*; Report of the 2005 World Summit Outcome, *supra* note 11, para. 138. See also UN Secretary-General, Implementing the Responsibility to Protect, A/63/677 12.01.2009. For a specific application of the RtP to EU foreign policy taking Myanmar as a case-study, see E. Staunton and J. Ralph, 'The Responsibility to Protect Norm Cluster and the Challenge of Atrocity Prevention: An Analysis of the European Union's Strategy in Myanmar', (2020) *European Journal of International Relations*, pp. 660–686.

56 J. Klabbers, 'Reflections on Role Responsibility: The Responsibility of International Organizations for Failing to Act', (2018) *European Journal of International Law*, pp. 1133–1161.

57 Ibid., p. 1134.

58 Ibid., p. 1135. In developing his argument, most analysis is based on responsibility for state omissions. In this respect, for example, it is worth noting that Albania's responsibility in *Corfu Channel* was not based on clear legal rules alone but, in part, on the basis of 'elementary considerations of humanity' (ibid., p. 1149).

59 Ibid., p. 1150 et seqq.

treaties cannot offer guidance to the Council, the HRVP and the Commission in this field. It provides only, in paragraph 2, for the power of the Council to adopt restrictive measures against natural or legal persons and groups or non-state entities. Hence, we need to look elsewhere and, especially, at Articles 3(5) and 21 TEU, which appear central in relation to the grounds for adoption and guidance for the implementation of the new regime. They respectively call upon the EU to 'contribute [...] to the protection of human rights' and to '[seek] to advance globally values like [...] respect for human dignity', while respecting and contributing to the development of international law. Although one could be argued that this general guidance does not actually add much in comparison to the past, it has clarified the EU global 'role' towards human rights. Similarly, whereas the respect of international law reminds the EU to abide by principles such as the non-interference in others' affairs, the founding treaties themselves requires the EU to contribute to the evolution of international law. This means, for example, that the EU is accomplishing this part of its mandate in deciding to go well beyond what customary international law allows in connection with breaches of international peremptory norms *when* these entail human rights violations as explained above. Moreover, the same provisions offer some guidance as to when this 'role' should be played. Indeed, the protection of human rights *is not defined in* geographical terms or political alliances. It follows that such a framework seems to call upon EU Member States to activate – through the Council – the GHRSR whenever sanctions may prevent, in the context of a given documented situation, additional human rights violations irrespective of political considerations and in spite of immediate consequences. It may even call into question, in terms of responsibility, their option to block EU institutions from carrying out the Union's mandate or, alternatively, may support the call for a reform of the regime's institutional framework in order to overcome the unanimity rule.

The importance of this potential role of the EU can be fully appreciated if compared with what the UN and, specifically, the Security Council are able to achieve in this field. The object and the purpose of UN sanctions is – and will probably only ever be – based on the Security Council's essential task: the maintenance or restoration of international peace. As such, unless human rights violations fall within the broad situations in which the Security Council is called upon to act (Article 39 of the UN Charter), no action will follow.[60] Thanks to the GHRSR, the EU finds itself in a unique position to react against a broader range of human rights abuses worldwide because it does not need to connect sanctions to specific situations or the specific aim of maintaining international peace. It follows that the EU could potentially even fill the gap left by the inaction of the

60 M. Happold, 'UN Sanctions as Human Rights and Humanitarian Law Devices', in L. van den Herik (ed.), *supra* note 3, pp. 125–145.

UN or other international organisations in the event of serious human rights abuses, when it has *the knowledge* and *the capacity* to act.

In brief, more than acting in compliance with a right or an obligation under international law, the EU appears to be carrying out its 'role responsibility' worldwide which, despite some discretion in relation to the means to be used, is firmly required by its mandate. In doing so, the EU is contributing to the development of international law. Indeed, the GHRSR strengthens the growing practice of some states to react against human rights violations worldwide, even beyond those human rights that have acquired the status of peremptory norms of international law or those covered by specific frameworks like the RtP. It also enables the EU to reaffirm its role as a responsible international actor with a capacity even beyond that of the UN this field. Yet, to be genuinely significant in respect to both these aspects, the way in which the new sanctions regime is implemented will be key, as the unilateral character of EU restrictive measures risks raising questions of legitimacy (e.g. Western powers v. the rest of the world) and accusations of double standards (e.g. sanctions against specific states only). For this reason, we now turn to the first implementation of the GHRSR and the reactions that this generated across the world.

4. TESTING THE IMPLEMENTATION OF THE GHRSR: MATTERS OF DISCRETION, TARGETED INDIVIDUALS AND 'COUNTERSANCTIONS'

In light of the key elements of the GHRSR as analysed above and the (potential) duty to act grounded in the EU's own mandate, this section assesses the first implementation of the new regime.

Our analysis has already shown that there are no objective criteria that would necessarily trigger the activation of the new regime. The adoption of new restrictive measures is left to the Council's discretion. In this respect, in accordance with Article 5 of Council Decision (CFSP) 2020/1999, the 'Council, acting by unanimity upon a proposal from a Member State or from the [HRVP], shall establish and amend the list' of targeted natural or legal persons, entities or bodies. The unanimity requirement constitutes a very high threshold for the adoption of the restrictive measures at stake. The risk is that, even if serious human rights abuses occur beyond the EU's borders, the EU will not be able to prevent further violations by sanctioning the categories of perpetrators covered by the GHRSR. Conversely, if the unanimity among EU Member States is motivated by other political goals, this could lead to the adoption of restrictive measures against human rights abuses that may not otherwise be serious enough to warrant international sanctions, which could have implications in terms of the overall effectiveness and neutrality of the new EU mechanism.

There is, then, a further risk that if the exercise of such discretion gives rise to inconsistent practice, this could limit the relevance of the EU's contribution to the development of international law in this field.

The Council exercised this discretion for the first time in March 2021, on two different occasions, to target human rights violations occurring in Russia, China, North Korea, Libya, South Sudan and Eritrea.[61] In total, 15 individuals and four entities were included in the list set out in Annex I to Regulation (EU) 2020/1998. According to the Council, those listed were involved in a wide range of abuses. These include arbitrary arrests and detentions; torture; extrajudicial killings; enforced disappearances; systematic use of forced labour; widespread and systematic repression of freedom of peaceful assembly and of association, of freedom of opinion and expression as well as freedom of religion. While this move already shows a determination to use the GHRSR to sanction a variety of violations, the official status of the individuals who are now subject to EU restrictive measures demonstrates a willingness to target key state actors in third countries, such as the Minister of State Security and the Minister of Social Security of the Democratic People's Republic of Korea, who have both been in charge of implementing the repressive security policies against political dissidents. In relation to human rights abuses in China, the EU listed individuals belonging to the governing elite of the Xinjiang Uyghur Autonomous Region. According to the Council, Zhu Hailun, for example, is subject to restrictive measures because he was in 'charge of overseeing and implementing a large-scale surveillance, detention and indoctrination programme targeting Uyghurs and people from other Muslim ethnic minorities'.[62] Interestingly, although Mr Hailun has not held this position since 2019, the grounds for listing take into account the fact that, until February 2021, he 'continued to exercise a decisive influence'[63] in the implementation of such a programme. As such, the link between targeted individuals and violations appears to be quite loose, if a 'key political position' connected with the planning of systematic human rights violations is enough to be subject to EU restrictive measures. Although no specific evidence is provided

61 In addition to the aforementioned Council Implementing Regulation (EU) 2021/478, *supra* note 10, see: Council Decision (CFSP) 2021/372 of 2 March 2021 amending Decision (CFSP) 2020/1999 concerning restrictive measures against serious human rights violations and abuses, OJ L 71 I; Council Implementing Regulation (EU) 2021/371 of 2 March 2021 implementing Regulation (EU) 2020/1998 concerning restrictive measures against serious human rights violations and abuses, OJ L 71 I, 2 March 2021; Council Decision (CFSP) 2021/481 of 22 March 2021 amending Decision (CFSP) 2020/1999 concerning restrictive measures against serious human rights violations and abuses, OJ L 99 I, 22 March 2021. On 22 March 2021, giving the existence of a third country sanction regime addressing Myanmar, the Council also adopted further restrictive measures against key political figures for the serious human rights violations taking place after the 2021 military coup (see the same OJ), thus showing the strong interaction between the different sanctions frameworks.

62 Council Regulation (EU) 2020/1998, *supra* note 5, Annex, A(5).

63 Ibid.

in the Council's relevant acts, it is worth also noting the gender and sexual dimension of the human rights abuses involved. In connection with human rights abuses occurring in Chechnya, the EU targeted individuals that have been involved, since 2017, in widespread and systematic persecution of lesbian, gay, bisexual, transgender and intersex (LGBTI) persons or of those presumed to belong to LGBTI groups. As anticipated – and although restrictive measures do not cover the more general situation of these minorities in Russia – the willingness of the EU to take action in this field cannot be overlooked because it signals a firm position on the protection against discrimination based on these grounds in line with the *internal* clash with Poland and Hungary. Finally, the EU appears to be willing to punish (rather than simply to prevent) non-state actors for *past* human rights abuses. This can be seen in the case of the Kaniyat Militia, a Libyan armed militia now subject to restrictive measures in EU. It exercised control in the Libyan town of Tarhuna between 2015 and June 2020, where mass graves were found.

The first implementation of the GHRSR also allows a brief analysis of the reactions of concerned states. In particular, China denied the existence of the human rights abuses to which EU restrictive measures refer and responded by imposing its own 'countersanctions' on ten European individuals and four entities.[64] These individuals seem now prevented from travelling to China, whereas the companies are not permitted to operate in China or with Chinese operators. According to the only available sources, China acted in protest against the EU for interfering in its internal affairs and thus violating basic rules of international law. In China's view, the imposition of 'countersanctions' was therefore a legitimate action under international law in response to what it viewed as a wrongful act. China is therefore refuting – at least indirectly – that the EU is acting to protect collective interests, and adopted restrictive measures against EU targets in terms of countermeasures under international law. Given China's position within the international Community, this reaction could ultimately hamper the rise of new international law rules in this field, and it signals a dissatisfaction with the EU's view of its role as a global human rights actor. Whether or not the EU will be intimidated by China's moves remains to be seen, but it certainly gives the EU cause to reflect on whether sanctions are indeed an effective tool for achieving a change in the actions of concerned countries, or whether they simply fuel international tensions, with other, more innovative strategies required instead.

---

64 According to media reports, these mainly include EU and national politicians, the Political and Security Committee of the Council of the EU and the Subcommittee on Human Rights of the European Parliament: see Euronews, 'EU agrees first sanctions on China in more than 30 years', *Euronews*, 22.03.2021, available at www.euronews.com/2021/03/22/eu-foreign-ministers-to-discuss-sanctions-on-china-and-myanmar, last accessed 25.03.2021.

5. CONCLUDING OBSERVATIONS

Regarding its content and initial implementation, the EU GHRSR is a step forward in the EU's efforts to prevent and react (if not punish?) against serious human rights violations abroad. It indicates an increasing willingness on the part of the EU to act as a responsible global power in promoting its founding values, if not also in ensuring the protection of the international Community's collective interests. It adds a fundamental tool to respond quickly to extra-territorial human rights violations without the need to establish a country-based regime and, for this reason, avoids a situation in which human rights protection is conflated with other sanctions-related goals. On paper, it sends a strong message both to state and non-state human rights abusers and their supporters worldwide, who risk falling foul of new restrictive measures within the EU. It avoids collateral effects by targeting specific individuals rather than entire countries, in line with the general evolution of international sanctions. Furthermore, targeting individuals could also avoid pointing the finger at a state for violating widely accepted international human rights norms, although it may be difficult not to stigmatise a state if the GHRSR targets the governmental elite and its supporters or associated entities of that country. China is a case in point in this respect.

From an international law perspective, the EU's adoption of the GHRSR pushes the boundaries of the human rights violations to be prevented and/or punished by non(directly)-injured international actors and models a relevant practice for the scope of international organisations to take action towards violations committed in their own non-Member States. Despite the lack of clarity on whether the EU restrictive measures and, more generally, unilateral/non-UN sanctions could be qualified as retortions or (third-party) countermeasures, the EU's move confirms an increasing trend in states' practice toward strong reactions against a broad range of human rights violations outside their boundaries. In this respect, in order to contribute to the development of international law in this field, the future GHRSR-related acts could clarify or make more explicit the – either international or internal – grounds on which the EU effectively bases its action, thus providing in turn appropriate evidence to further develop the 'role responsibility' framework here applied.

That having been said, this analysis has shown that its implementation could prove to be more difficult than expected owing to a broad range aspects which remain unclear. First, there is no certainty that the EU will be able to activate the targeted sanctions given the procedural requirement for the adoption of necessary decisions by the Council. Unanimity is a high threshold that may not be reached when close allies of EU Member States are at risk of being identified as human rights abusers. The example of Morocco's violations in Western Sahara could be a good tester for the EU's willingness to ensure a consistent application of the new sanctions regime.[65] A non-arbitrary and consistent listing practice would also be key to granting international legitimacy and significance to the EU's role in the development of international rules in this field. Second, from a substantive perspective, given the extent of human rights violations demanding sanctions, it could be difficulty to verify a direct causal relationship between future restrictive measures and the change that the EU will pursue worldwide. As a result, the listing could easily remain unaltered for a long time. This aspect calls into question who should be targeted, what the EU will be really willing to achieve and even the nature of the new restrictive measures, in that they are also punitive rather than simply preventive, as we have seen so far even in the CJEU's case law.[66] Third, there are issues with the effectiveness of individual sanctions more generally. Despite the stigmatisation and deterrent effect (if any) that may be generated, there is no clear indication that these restrictive measures work. For instance, it is unclear whether and how the restrictive measures adopted in the past, via the third-country sanction regime, in relation to serious human rights violations in Iran, have brought about an improvement in the human rights enjoyment in that country.[67] What is more, the unintended negative effects in terms of such an enjoyment on the individuals that depend on the subjects that are targeted, as well as the impacts on the victims, have not been given the attention they deserve. Fourth, given the financial dimension of most sanctions and despite the EU's economic power, doubts can be raised on the effect of Brexit which could hamper the achievement of the desired effects. An agreement with the UK on a common strategy in this field seems needed in the near future to achieve common positions on the identification of the relevant targets. Finally, protests by third countries against the EU for the imposition of restrictive measures on human rights grounds could prevent relevant EU institutions and Member States from implementing the GHRSR. The risk of generating unwanted international tensions is already evident from the restrictive measures targeting China.

---

65 M. Balboni and G. Laschi (eds.), *The EU Approach Towards Western Sahara*, Peter Lang, Brussels 2017; C. Danisi, 'Self-Determination as a Peremptory Norm of International Law and Human Rights in Non-Self-Governing Western Sahara: A Test for the European Union', in M. Balboni and C. Danisi (eds.), *supra* note 2, pp. 231–275.

66 CJEU, *Kadi II*, *supra* note 40, para. 130.

67 According to the EU sanctions map, these were introduced in 2011 in the form of travel restrictions and asset freezes against 'persons complicit in or responsible for directing or implementing grave human rights violations in the repression of peaceful demonstrators, journalists, human rights defenders, students or other persons who speak up in defence of their legitimate rights': see Council Decision 2011/235/CFSP of 12 April 2011 concerning restrictive measures directed against certain persons and entities in view of the situation in Iran, OJ L 100. A similar study was carried out in relation to other sanctions regimes, for example as far as sanctions against Russia are concerned: see V. Veebel, 'Lessons from the EU-Russia Sanctions 2014–2015', (2015) 8(1), *Baltic Journal of Law and Politics*, pp. 165–194.

To conclude, the fact that sanctions are imposed by the EU, rather than individual Member States, appears to grant them greater legitimacy. Yet, given the existing doubts on the effectiveness of sanctions as a game changer, for the GHRSR to truly be successful, the EU needs to learn from past restrictive measures and be willing to implement the new regime objectively, irrespective of political or other unrelated factors. If the EU's mandate is the key in line with the Union's 'role responsibility', it is also fundamental that the new sanctions regime operates hand-in-hand with a more proactive approach to human rights protection when the EU exercises its powers in relations with third countries in order to support real change in the situations covered by the GHRSR.

NATIONAL HUMAN RIGHTS INSTITUTIONS

An Emerging Human Rights Actor in the European Union

Cristina Pugnale and Mathilde Bénard*

* The views expressed within this contribution are those of the authors only and do not represent the views of the UNHCR.

ABSTRACT

National Human Rights Institutions (NHRIs) enjoy a *sui generis* standing in society, being state bodies, yet independent of their governments. With their strong mandates, they provide an institutional space for the promotion and protection of human rights within their domestic orders. Over the last two decades, the crucial role played by NHRIs in upholding human rights in the European Union (EU) has been increasingly recognised. 2020 marked a milestone year for the EU-NHRI cooperation, with a number of policy developments opening windows of opportunity for a stronger partnership. This contribution aims at further exploring the unique potential of European NHRIs as emerging human rights actors in the EU. After providing an overview of European NHRIs' mandates, functions and status, the contribution will investigate promising practices and areas of closer NHRI cooperation with the EU in the fields of rule of law and migration, including in the COVID-19 context, for the better protection and promotion of human rights in the region.

1. INTRODUCTION

The unprecedented COVID-19 crisis highlighted the need for strong, independent and effective national actors to ensure that human rights are promoted and protected, including in times of emergency. The existence of such national entities is as old as the idea of international human rights,[1] yet today's concept of National Human Rights Institutions (NHRIs) was formalised in 1991 with the adoption of the so-called Paris Principles, setting out high standards of independence and effectiveness for the functioning of these institutions.

As of today, wider Europe hosts 47 NHRIs.[2] Within the remits of their mandates, these institutions have increasingly engaged with regional actors, such as the Council of Europe (CoE), the Organization for Security and Co-operation in Europe (OSCE) and the European Union (EU, the Union). Nevertheless, the level of NHRIs' regional engagement, notably with the EU, is yet to be fully explored. In the last decade, EU-NHRI cooperation has increasingly expanded,[3] boosted by the creation of the European Network of National Human Rights Institutions (ENNHRI) in 2013. Several EU policy instruments and processes have already explicitly recognised NHRIs' significant role in the protection and promotion of fundamental rights both at national and regional levels.[4] At the same time, however, scope for further recognition and stronger strategic

---

1 M. Nowak, 'National Human Rights Institutions in Europe. Comparative, European and International Perspectives', in J. Wouters and K. Meuwissen (eds.), *National Human Rights Institutions in Europe. Comparative, European and International Perspectives*, Intersentia, Cambridge/Antwerp/Portland 2013, p. 14.

2 This number also includes institutions that are still seeking an accreditation status and, therefore, are not formally NHRIs. For an overview on NHRIs in Europe, see section below 'NHRIs in the EU: an overview'.

3 FRA, 'Strong and Effective National Human Rights Institutions – Challenges, Promising Practices and Opportunities', Report, 03.09.2020, pp. 26–27, available at https://fra.europa.eu/en/publication/2020/strong-effective-nhris, last accessed 04.03.2021.

4 For instance see: European Commission, Communication from the Commission to the European Parliament, the Council, the European Economic And Social Committee And The Committee Of The Regions 2020 Rule of Law Report – The Rule of Law Situation in the European Union, COM(2020) 580 final 30.09.2020; European Commission, Annex to the Joint Communication to the European Parliament and the Council, EU Action Plan on Human Rights and Democracy 2020–2024, JOIN(2020) 5 final, 25.03.2020; Report on the establishment of an EU Mechanism on Democracy, the Rule of Law and Fundamental Rights (2020/2072(INL)), Committee on Civil Liberties, Justice and Home Affairs Rapporteur: Michal Šimečka, 29.09.2020; Council of the European Union, Council Conclusions on the Charter of Fundamental Rights after 10 Years: State of Play and Future Work 12357/19, 20.09.2019.

engagement remain.[5] For instance, unlike other human rights bodies, NHRIs are not included in any EU secondary law.[6]

In this context, 2020 has marked a turning point for the EU-NHRI engagement, with different policy instruments opening windows of opportunity for a stronger partnership. This contribution aims at examining the scope for further cooperation between European NHRIs and the EU, in light of these recent developments. Previous literature had fostered discussions on the interaction between European NHRIs and regional frameworks, as well as the integration of NHRIs in the European human rights working culture.[7] This contribution intends to inform such debate, tacking stock of most recent achievements and lessons learned, while cautioning about possible backlashes. Due to space constraints, the contribution will mostly focus on the EU internal dimension.[8] Similarly, it will target only key thematic areas that are indicative of the progress made in EU-NHRI engagement, and relevant to explore the scope for better cooperation.

In order to understand the specificity of these actors, the contribution will first provide a brief overview on European NHRIs' status, functions and mandates. It will then underline and discuss the growing EU-NHRI relationship, focusing on the areas of rule of law and of asylum and migration. The COVID-19 pandemic features in the analysis as a cross-cutting issue. In this context, NHRIs have exploited their special standing within domestic institutional orders, in the

---

5 The 2020 FRA report underlined that, while 'ENNHRI has played an important role in improving NHRIs' connection to regional policies and processes, including at the EU level, (…) [o]verall exchanges between NHRIs and the EU could be increased significantly – both in EU processes and in Member States' involvement in EU procedures.', in FRA (2020), 'Strong and Effective NHRIs', *supra* note 3, p. 14.

6 By contrast, the EU has legislated on equality bodies through a number of tools. See e.g. Directive (EU) 2019/1158 of the European Parliament and of the Council of 20 June 2019 on work-life balance for parents and carers and repealing Council Directive 2010/18/EU, OJ L 188, Article 15; Directive 2010/41/EU of the European Parliament and of the Council of 7 July 2010 on the application of the principle of equal treatment between men and women engaged in an activity in a self-employed capacity and repealing Council Directive 86/613/EEC, OJ L 180, Article 11; Directive 2006/54/EC of the European Parliament and of the Council of 5 July 2006 on the implementation of the principle of equal opportunities and equal treatment of men and women in matters of employment and occupation (recast), Article 20; Council Directive 2000/43/EC of 29 June 2000 implementing the principle of equal treatment between persons irrespective of racial or ethnic origin, OJ L 180, Article 13; for further info see Equinet, 'EU Legislative Framework', available at https://equineteurope.org/equality-in-europe/eu-legislative-framework/, last accessed 07.02.2021.

7 J. Wouters and K. Meuwissen (eds.) (2013), *National Human Rights Institutions in Europe*, *supra* note 1.

8 Albeit outside of the scope of this contribution, progress made in the recognition of NHRIs within the EU external action can certainly be acknowledged. For instance, through the recently adopted European Union Action Plan on Human Rights and Democracy 2020–2024,

effort to counterbalance and exercise oversight over national executive powers. This chapter will showcase examples of NHRI good practices during times of crisis.

2. NATIONAL HUMAN RIGHTS INSTITUTIONS: A PECULIAR ACTOR AT THE NATIONAL AND REGIONAL LEVEL

2.1. DEFINITION AND PARIS PRINCIPLES

2.1.1. Definition

NHRIs are relatively new actors in the human rights landscape. While some form of national institutions for the promotion and protection of human rights was already conceptualised in 1946,[9] NHRIs in their present form only emerged in 1991,[10] when the Centre for Human Rights held in Paris the first 'International Workshop on National Institutions for the Promotion and Protection of Human Rights'.[11] As a result, a set of standards for NHRIs to qualify as such was drafted:[12] the so-called 'Paris Principles'.[13] They are now internationally recognised benchmark, setting out NHRIs' responsibilities, composition and working methods as follows:

- *Broad human rights mandate*: NHRIs shall be vested with a broad remit to promote and protect human rights. NHRIs shall freely address any human rights issue, including through submitting recommendations to the government, reviewing draft legislation, engaging in human rights

the EU encouraged third countries to support and engage with Paris Principles-compliant NHRIs. A serious commitment to coherence and consistency inevitably calls upon the EU to take similar commitments within its territory, too. See Council of the European Union, EU Action Plan on Human Rights and Democracy 2020–2024, 12848/20, 18.11.2020.

9 OHCHR, 'National Human Rights Institutions. History, Principles, Roles and Responsibilities', 2010, available at https://www.ohchr.org/Documents/Publications/PTS-4Rev1-NHRI_en.pdf, last accessed 07.02.2021.

10 For a brief historical account of the conceptualisation of NHRIs, see M. Nowak (2013), 'National Human Rights Institutions in Europe', *supra* note 1, p. 14.

11 The Center for Human Rights was then the Geneva-based UN division for human rights.

12 UN Commission on Human Rights, Report of the International Workshop on National Institutions for the Promotion and Protection of Human Rights, E/CN.4/1992/43, 16.12.1991.

13 UN General Assembly, Principles relating to the Status of National Institutions (The Paris Principles), Resolution adopted on 20 December 1993, UN Doc AS/RES/48/143, 04.03.1994 (hereinafter The Paris Principles).

education, conducting monitoring activities and, if conferred quasi-judicial competences, examining individual complaints or seeking amicable settlements;

- *Strong legal basis*: NHRIs must be established by a constitutional or legislative text, clearly specifying NHRI mandate, composition and methods of work;
- *Independence*: NHRIs must meet high requirements of independence (formal and functional) from the executive power and other actors;
- *Pluralism*: NHRI composition shall ensure a sufficient level of pluralism through representation of, or/and cooperation with, different groups comprising the national society;
- *Adequate funding*: governments hold the primary responsibility to adequately resource their NHRI(s), without any undue interference with NHRI independence;
- *Cooperation*: NHRIs must cooperate with relevant national and international human rights actors, such as local NGOs or the UN;
- *Accountability*: NHRIs have to ensure transparency and accountability, including through their internal procedures and annual reporting to national authorities. Many NHRI establishing laws envisage parliamentary debates for annual reports, which may in turn promote better follow-up by the legislative and executive powers.[14]

Paris Principles-compliant NHRIs can therefore be defined as: state-mandated bodies, independent of governments, with a broad constitutional or legal mandate to protect and promote human rights at the national level. Paris Principles-compliant NHRIs were defined as *sui generis* actors occupying a 'fourth space' within the international human rights framework, being neither state representatives, nor NGOs, nor international organisations.[15] The very added value of NHRIs lies in 'their ability to navigate this unique place and be able to leverage their embeddedness within the administration while retaining the necessary independence'.[16]

In March 1992, the United Nations (UN) Commission on Human Rights formally recognised the Paris Principles.[17] Furthermore, the 1993 Vienna World

14 FRA (2020), 'Strong and Effective NHRIs', *supra* note 3, p. 56.

15 K. Roberts, 'The Role and Functioning of the International Coordinating Committee of National Human Rights Institutions in International Human Rights Bodies', in J. Wouters and K. Meuwissen (eds.) (2013), *National Human Rights Institutions in Europe*, *supra* note 1, p. 227.

16 S. Jensen, S. Lagoutte, and S. Lorion, 'The Domestic Institutionalisation of Human Rights: An Introduction', (2019) 37(3), *Nordic Journal of Human Rights*, p. 168. For an insightful analysis of the relationship NHRI-State see K. Meuwissen, 'NHRIs *and* The State: New and Independent Actors in The Multi-layered Human Rights System', (2015) 15(3), *Human Rights Law Review*, pp. 441–484.

17 UN Commission on Human Rights, National institutions for the promotion and protection of human rights, Resolution adopted on 3 March 1992, UN Doc 199/54.

Conference on Human Rights encouraged states to establish and strengthen 'national institutions, having regard to the "Principles relating to the status of national institutions"',[18] which were endorsed by the UN General Assembly shortly after. Since then, the Paris Principles have been increasingly recognised as universal criteria to assess NHRIs' independence and trustworthiness, beyond regional and national specificities. In May 2013, 'General Observations'[19] were issued to provide stakeholders better guidance on the interpretation of the Paris Principles.

2.1.2. The Accreditation Process

NHRIs worldwide are periodically reviewed against their compliance with the Paris Principles. Only those institutions which are fully or partially compliant with these standards are accredited as NHRIs. The NHRI accreditation is a peer-review process carried out by the Sub-Committee on Accreditation (SCA) of the Global Alliance of NHRIs (GANHRI), with the support of the Geneva-based Office of the UN High Commissioner for Human Rights. The SCA is formed by four Paris Principles-fully compliant NHRIs, each representing a regional NHRI grouping (Africa, the Americas, Asia-Pacific and Europe).[20] As a result of this process, NHRIs are accredited with:

- A status,[21] when they are fully compliant with the Paris Principles. A-status NHRIs enjoy independent participation rights in international and regional mechanisms.[22] and Treaty Bodies.[23] In Europe, A-status NHRIs have

18 UN General Assembly, Vienna Declaration and Programme of Action, UN Doc A/CONF.157/23, 12.07.1993, para. 36.

19 International Coordinating Committee of National Institutions for the Promotion and Protection of Human Rights, 'ICC Sub-Committee on Accreditation General Observations as adopted in May 2013', 2013.

20 GANHRI, Rules of procedure for the GANHRI Sub-Committee on Accreditation, amended version adopted on 4 March 2019, para. 3.1.

21 For instance, they have voting rights in regional NHRI coordinating bodies, such as the European Network of National Human Rights Institutions (ENNHRI), governance functions in the GANHRI bureau, or membership in the SCA. See: ENNHRI, 'Constitution', 20.06.2013, Article 6, available at http://ennhri.org/wp-content/uploads/2019/09/ENNHRI-statutes.pdf, last accessed 21.02.2021; GANHRI, Statute, version adopted at the General Assembly on 5 March 2019; GANHRI, SCA Rules of Procedure, *supra* note 20, para. 3.1.

22 The UN HRC Resolution 16/21 on the review of the work and functioning of the Human Rights Council of 12 April 2011 regulates the participation of NHRIs that are 'consistent with the principles relating to the status of national institutions for the promotion and protection of human rights annexed to the General Assembly resolution 48/134 (the Paris Principles)' in the UPR and the Special Procedures.

23 The Paris Principles provide that NHRIs shall 'contribute to the reports which States are required to submit to the United Nations bodies and committees (…) pursuant to their treaty obligations'. Today, the NHRI engagement with UN Human Rights Treaty Bodies is a quite well established practice. For more information on the matter, see GANHRI, 'National Human Rights Institutions and United Nations Treaty Bodies: Background Paper', 2016, available at https://

become credible interlocutors and info-providers for co-legislators and policy makers.[24]
- *B status*, if they are only partially compliant with the Paris Principles.[25]
- NHRIs may be given *no status* if they are found not to be compliant with the Paris Principles.[26]

A-status NHRIs are reviewed by the SCA every five years,[27] while B-status and no-status institutions can apply for accreditation at any time.[28] Following its assessment, the NHRI under review is issued recommendations to better comply with the Paris Principles and the General Observations.[29]

It can be argued that peer-review dynamics may create constraints and raise conflicts of interest.[30] Being accredited by peer NHRIs, however, may allow

nhri.ohchr.org/EN/IHRS/TreatyBodies/Annual%20Meeting%20of%20Chairpersons%20of%20 Human%20Rights%20Tre/GANHRI%20background%20paper%20FINAL.pdf, last accessed 21.02.2021; and D. Zipoli, 'NHRI Engagement with UN Human Rights Treaty Bodies: A Goal-based Approach', (2019) 37(3), *Nordic Journal of Human Rights*, pp. 259–280.

24 For more information, see section 3 of this contribution 'The Potential of European NHRIs as Emergining Human Rights Actors in the European Union' which especially focuses on the EU-NHRI collaboration in the fields of rule of law and migration.

25 B-status NHRIs cannot vote in regional fora and are not eligible for governance functions in the GANHRI bureau. While B-status NHRIs do not enjoy speaking rights before the Human Rights Council, they can attend its sessions, as well as submit parallel reports to UN Treaty Bodies and to the Universal Periodic Review (UPR). See: ENNHRI, Commission National Consultative des Droits de L'homme (CNCDH), 'The Accreditation of National Human Rights Institutions: Practical Guide', 29.10.2018, p. 9, available at http://ennhri.org/news-and-blog/new-ennhri-cncdh-practical-guide-on-the-accreditation-of-nhris-released/, last accessed 21.02.2021.

26 'No status', however, is not a formal outcome of the accreditation process. While institutions with no status may still engage with regional NHRI coordinating bodies, they do not enjoy any participation right in international or regional human rights mechanisms. While GANHRI does not allow no-status institutions to become its members, regional NHRI networks of Europe, Asia-Pacific, Africa and the Americas grant associate membership to institutions who do not yet have a status.

27 In exceptional circumstances, when an NHRI is deemed to undergo any changes potentially affecting its compliance with the Paris Principles, the SCA may initiate a special review. See GANHRI, Statute, *supra* note 21, Article 16.1.

28 This may partially address concerns with regards to the Paris Principles' adequacy to periodically assess NHRI performance and effectiveness in practice, beyond their institutional design. See G. De Beco, 'Compliance with The Paris Principles and The ICC Sub-Committee on Accreditation', in J. Wouters and K. Meuwissen (eds.) (2013), *National Human Rights Institutions in Europe*, *supra* note 1, p. 473.

29 In Europe, SCA's most frequent concerns pertain to the decision-making bodies' selection and appointment process (often considered insufficiently transparent or participative), the lack of appropriate funding, or the mandate's limited scope. See FRA (2020), 'Strong and Effective NHRIs', *supra* note 3, p. 33.

30 In his analysis, Gauthier de Beco stated that the interest of GANHRI, formerly known as International Coordinating Committee of national institutions for the promotion and

for more aware assessments, while reinforcing mutual trust and ownership of results. NHRIs have an interest in keeping the accreditation standards high to safeguard their own credibility. Also, the absence of political actors from the accreditation process is positive.[31] The ability of NHRIs to carry out their work in an effective and independent manner can be easily affected by the actions of national governments and the lack of a conducive environment. As it was noted, '[t]he recommendations of the SCA, although addressed to NHRIs, are in reality issues which the state must often rectify'.[32] Overall, however, the participation of actors other than governments can foster transparency and contribute to get more realistic pictures from the ground. While representatives from GANHRI, OHCHR and NHRI regional networks participate in accreditation sessions as permanent observers, third parties, like experts or civil society, may submit information relevant to the assessment of the NHRI under review.[33]

2.1.3. *Types of NHRIs*

Depending on the national political context and legal tradition, NHRIs take different forms on the ground. The European landscape reflects a wide diversity of institutions, from which this contribution considers three main categories:

1. *Commissions*: collegiate bodies comprised of commissioners acting as board or as members of the institution. Commissions may act as mere advisory bodies – with a stronger promotional mandate, or may be conferred quasi-judicial competences – enabling them to examine individual complaints.
2. *Ombuds-institutions*: single-person bodies appointed by the national parliaments and supported by an office. These institutions often have a constitutional basis, which entrusts them with a strong mandate, including complaints handling.
3. *Institutes*: research bodies or documentation centres, delivering evidence-based advice to governments.

---

protection of human rights (ICC), may be overrepresented during the accreditation process. See G. de Beco (2013), 'Compliance with The Paris Principles', *supra* note 28, p. 254. In this regard, however, the SCA Rules of Procedures stipulate that a member 'is expected to remove themselves from deliberation where they have a real or perceived conflict of interest', while empowering NHRIs under review to raise the issue before the SCA Secretariat (Article 4.7).

31 G. de Beco (2013), 'Compliance with The Paris Principles', *supra* note 28, p. 254.

32 K. Roberts, 'The Role and Functioning of the ICC', *supra* note 15, P. 235.

33 GANHRI, 'SCA Rules of Procedure', *supra* note 20, Article 5–6. In this regard, De Beco remains critical towards the accreditation process. In his opinion, the participation of third parties and especially civil society is too limited. See G. de Beco (2013), 'Compliance with The Paris Principles', *supra* note 28, p. 261.

The Paris Principles, however, do not indicate which of these types of institutions is most fit-for-purpose.

2.2. NHRIS IN EUROPE

2.2.1. The European Network of NHRIs (ENNHRI)

Since the Paris Principles were endorsed by the international community, the number of accredited NHRIs has significantly grown worldwide. In Europe, the need for a regional body mandated to coordinate the cooperation and engagement of European NHRIs gradually became more pressing and, in 2013, a permanent secretariat for European NHRIs was created: the European Network of National Human Rights Institutions (ENNHRI).[34]

Today, ENNHRI brings together over 40 NHRIs from wider Europe. Through providing advice and facilitating peer exchanges, it works to strengthen and support NHRIs, including during their establishment/accreditation process, or when they come under threat. ENNHRI unifies its members' voices before regional mechanisms, while it promotes NHRI strategic engagement with key actors like the CoE or the EU institutions.

In 2020, ENNHRI fostered a stronger NHRI partnership with the European Commission and EU co-legislators, notably in the areas of rule of law, asylum and migration, as well as economic and social rights.[35]

2.2.2. NHRIs in the EU: An Overview

As of today, 47 NHRIs operate in wider Europe: 31 institutions are accredited with an A status, nine with a B status and seven are seeking accreditation. All EU countries except two (Italy, Malta), and all CoE countries except seven (Andorra, Iceland, Italy, Malta, Monaco, San Marino, Switzerland), have an accredited NHRI. In some countries, more than one institution with complementary mandates coexist (Bulgaria, Belgium).

---

34 For a detailed overview of the NHRI regional coordination prior to the establishment of ENNHRI, see B. Adamson, 'NHRI and Their European Counterparts: Scope for Strengthened Cooperation and Performance Towards European Human Rights Institutions', in J. Wouters and K. Meuwissen (eds.) (2013), *National Human Rights Institutions in Europe*, *supra* note 1, pp. 128–132.

35 For more information, on ENNHRI's role in fostering the engagement of European NHRIs at the regional level, see section 3 of this contribution 'The Potential of European NHRIs as Emergining Human Rights Actors in the European Union'.

Figure 1. Accreditation Status

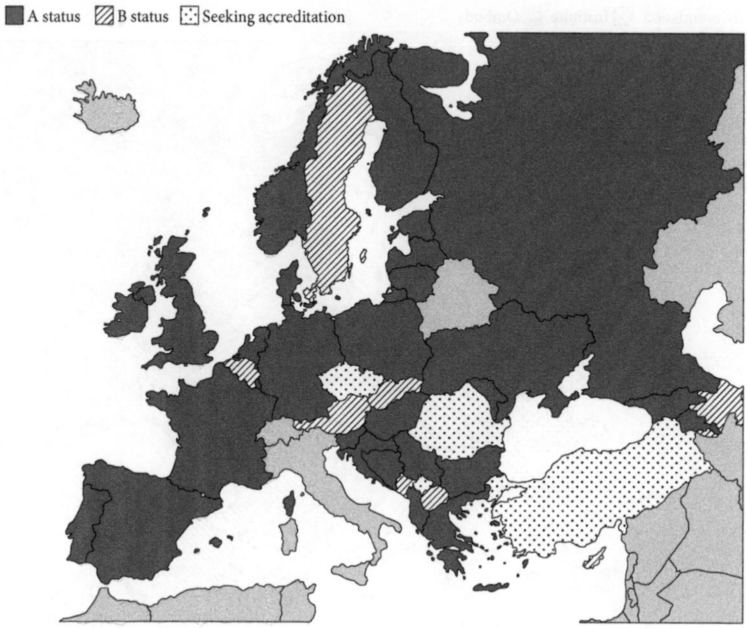

Source: Produced by the authors based on ENNHRI data, 2021.

Out of the 47 NHRIs from wider Europe, 27 are Ombud-type institutions, 22 are institutes and eight are commissions. Beyond this three-fold classification, due to their capacity, areas of expertise, and mandates, NHRIs may operate in diversified ways. A single institution can therefore cumulate several mandates, the most notable ones being:

- *Equality bodies* are established to 'promote equality and tackle discrimination on grounds of gender, race, age, sexual orientation, religion and belief, disability or other grounds'.[36]
- *National Preventive Mechanisms* support the implementation the UN Optional Protocol to the Convention against Torture.[37]
- *National Monitoring Mechanisms* support the implementation of the UN Convention on the Rights of Persons with Disabilities.[38]

---

[36] Equinet, 'Equality Bodies And Equinet', available at https://equineteurope.org/2019/equality-bodies-and-equinet-promoting-equality-in-europe/, last accessed 20.05.2021.

[37] OHCHR, 'Preventing Torture: The Role of National Preventive Mechanisms', Practical Guide, 2018, available at https://www.ohchr.org/Documents/HRBodies/OPCAT/NPM/NPM_Guide.pdf, last accessed 18.03.2021.

[38] United Nations, 'Monitoring of the implementation of the Convention', available at https://www.un.org/development/desa/disabilities/convention-on-the-rights-of-persons-with-disabilities/monitoring-of-the-implementation-of-the-convention.html, last accessed 20.05.2021.

Figure 2. Types of Institution

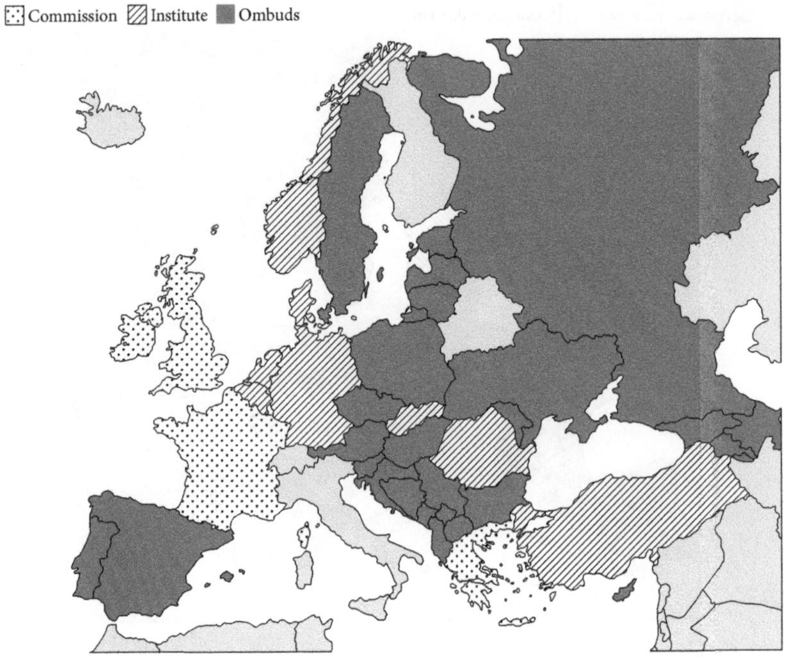

Source: Produced by the authors based on ENNHRI data, 2021.

3. THE POTENTIAL OF EUROPEAN NHRIS AS EMERGING HUMAN RIGHTS ACTORS IN THE EUROPEAN UNION

3.1. NHRIS IN THE DEVELOPING EUROPEAN RULE OF LAW FRAMEWORK

Rule of law, human rights and democracy are mutually reinforcing and interlinked principles.[39] Human rights can only be fully enjoyed and protected in a strong regime of rule of law. NHRIs must therefore indisputably defend such a regime to fulfil their mandates to promote and protect human rights. European NHRIs identified this as a clear priority, including within the ENNHRI's framework.[40] As state-mandated bodies independent from governments, NHRIs are an

39 United Nations, Declaration of the High-level Meeting of the General Assembly on the Rule of Law at the National and International Levels, Un Doc A/67/L.1, 19.09.2012, para. 5.

40 ENNHRI, 'Strategic Plan 2018-21', available at http://ennhri.org/wp-content/uploads/2019/07/ennhri__strategicplan_2018-21-1.pdf, last accessed 10.02.2021.

integral part of national checks and balances systems and hold a unique position to act on these issues.

In the last decade, the EU faced a growing democracy and rule of law crisis.[41] While the emphasis is often placed on the worrying autocratisation in Hungary and Poland, this crisis is in fact regional.[42] To address the situation, the EU has recently intensified its efforts to better promote and protect the rule of law, human rights and democracy within its borders. European NHRIs seized this opportunity and cooperated through their ENNHRI to support the EU initiatives, which resulted in a greater recognition of their added value on these matters.

This section aims at further scrutinising the potential of European NHRIs in EU rule of law processes, to better advance human rights and rule of law on the ground. It will explore the added value of their engagement while analysing how this was reflected in EU's recent policy initiatives. The section will underline the role of NHRI in times of crisis, such as the current COVID-19 pandemic, and explore ways forward for their engagement.

3.1.1. *NHRIs and the Rule of Law*

Safeguarding a solid rule of law environment naturally flows from NHRIs' mandate. At the national level, this is done, *inter alia*, by monitoring the situation on the ground, sending recommendations to public authorities, alerting institutions or the media on worrying issues, handling complaints or intervening before the courts.[43] At the regional level, NHRIs' engagement in EU rule of law processes can be threefold.

3.1.1.1. NHRIs as Rule of Law Indicators

Information on a given NHRI's ability to perform its mandate independently, effectively and with sufficient resources is in itself an indicator of the respect for the rule of law in its country.[44] Such information includes mainly the national regulatory framework applicable to the NHRI as well as the enabling space for the NHRI to carry out its work. This includes information on the level of consultation during the follow-up on NHRI's recommendations,

---

41 D. Kochenov and P. Bárd, 'The Last Soldier Standing? Courts Versus Politicians and the Rule of Law Crisis in the New Member States of the EU', in E. Hirsch Ballin, G. van der Schyff and M. Stremler (eds.), *European Yearbook of Constitutional Law 2019. European Yearbook of Constitutional Law*, vol 1. T.M.C. Asser Press, The Hague 2020.

42 Ibid.

43 Paris Principles, *supra* note 13.

44 FRA (2020), 'Strong and Effective NHRIs', *supra* note 3, p. 77.

potential obstacles for the institution to perform its mandate and its ability to counter them.[45]

3.1.1.2. NHRIs as Information Providers

Human rights monitoring and reporting are core elements of NHRIs' mandate.[46] NHRIs can perform these tasks from a comprehensive perspective, deriving from their central position bridging civil society, citizens and public institutions on the one hand, and bridging national, regional and international levels, on the other.[47] This unique place in society allows for a better understanding of the national human rights situation compared to other relevant actors. Besides, NHRIs' broad mandate enables them to gather information on a variety of issues relevant for an accurate picture of the national rule of law environment. In its submissions to the European Commission (EC) Rule of law monitoring cycle in 2020 and 2021 (cf. section 3.1.2.1), ENNHRI identified areas NHRI can particularly report on:[48]

- *NHRIs' independence and effectiveness.* NHRIs themselves are indeed best placed for this assessment, which may then serve as a rule of law indicator (cf. section 3.1.1.1)
- *Human rights defenders (HRDs) and civil society space.* These topics are at the core of activities led by NHRIs, which have a unique role in promoting and safeguarding them, as outlined by the GANHRI 2018 Marrakesh Declaration and ENNHRI 2019 Regional Action Plan to promote and protect HRDs and enable democratic space.[49] NHRIs are mandated to monitor the free exercise of the right to freedom of assembly and expression, alert on abuses, handle complaints and support those in danger.[50] Being HRDs themselves, NHRIs

45 ENNHRI, 'The rule of law in the European Union: Reports from National Human Rights Institutions', 11.05.2020, available at http://ennhri.org/wp-content/uploads/2020/06/The-rule-of-law-in-the-European-Union-Reports-from-NHRIs_11-May-2020.pdf, last accessed 26.03.2021.

46 Paris Principles, *supra* note 13.

47 ENNHRI, 'About NHRIs', available at http://ennhri.org/about-nhris/, last accessed 22.02.2021.

48 ENNHRI, 'State of the Rule of Law in Europe: Reports from National Human Rights Institutions', 2020, available at http://ennhri.org/rule-of-law-report/, last accessed 20.05.2021; ENNHRI, 'State of the rule of law in the European Union: Reports from National Human Rights Institutions', 2021, available at http://ennhri.org/wp-content/uploads/2021/03/EU-RoL-Report-2021.pdf, last accessed 26.03.2021.

49 GANHRI, Marrakesh Declaration, available at https://nhri.ohchr.org/EN/ICC/International Conference/13IC/Background%20Information/Marrakech%20Declaration_EN_%20 12102018%20-%20FINAL.pdf, last accessed 20.03.2021.

50 ENNHRI, 'Regional Action Plan on GANHRI Marrakesh Declaration', 2019, available at http://ennhri.org/wp-content/uploads/2019/09/Regional-Action-Plan-on-GANHRI-Marrakesh-Declaration.pdf, last accessed 22.02.2021.

face challenges and threats, and are well placed to understand and report on them.[51]

- *Checks and balances.* NHRIs' peculiar status as independent state-mandated bodies provides them with a privileged perspective on public powers' dynamics. Furthermore, as directly questioning and advising on public laws and practices,[52] NHRIs are not only observer but also part of the national system of checks and balances and, as such, well placed to inform on its (dis)functioning.
- *Justice system.* NHRIs monitor and alert on the content of national legislation and on its application, and some institutions also have the ability to intervene in courts proceedings.[53] They are therefore aware of many specificities and deficiencies of their national justice apparatus. NHRIs are a privileged interlocutor for citizens on these issues, and they sometimes play an alleviating part in dispute resolution, alongside judicial processes.[54]
- *Media pluralism.* As a bridge between civil society and the state, NHRIs have an overview of the interactions between different society sectors, and their mandate includes public awareness-raising activities 'by making use of all press organs'.[55] Media freedom and pluralism are therefore crucial for NHRIs to correctly function, and they often follow potential threats to their realisation. Furthermore, they have a role in supporting and defending journalists subjects to attacks or intimidation.[56]
- *Corruption.* NHRIs' work on corruption is not their more natural focus, as it requires a total impartiality, resulting from financial and legal autonomy,[57] and a technical expertise which is not widely spread in the

---

51 ENNHRI, 'NHRIs and Human rights Defenders: Enabling democratic space in Europe', 2019, available at http://ennhri.org/wp-content/uploads/2019/09/Publication-NHRIs-and-Human-Rights-Defenders-Enabling-Human-Rights-and-Democratic-Space-in-Europe.pdf, last accessed 22.02.2021.

52 Paris Principles, *supra* note 13.

53 Ibid.

54 L. McGregor, R. Muray and S. Shipman, 'The Role of National Human Rights Institutions In Access to Justice and Dispute Resolution', Research Project, 2014, available at https://www.essex.ac.uk/research-projects/the-role-of-national-human-rights-institutions-in-access-to-justice-and-dispute-resolution, last accessed 24.02.2021.

55 Paris Principles, *supra* note 13.

56 J. Barata Mir, 'How To Strengthen Soft Powers For Press Freedom: National Human Rights Institutions', Report, 2016, available at https://rm.coe.int/CoERMPublicCommonSearchServices/DisplayDCTMContent?documentId=090000168066d07a, last accessed 24.02.2021.

57 International Council on Human Rights Policy, 'Corruption and Human Rights: Making the Connection', 2009, available at https://reliefweb.int/sites/reliefweb.int/files/resources/9B49DD6CB2609631492575BB001B821D-Corruption_HRts.pdf, last accessed 24.02.2020.

human rights field. However, NHRIs are increasingly addressing corruption issues, and several of them provide securised channels or support for whistleblowers.[58]

Therefore, NHRIs have a legitimacy to report on these core elements impacting the rule of law environment in each country. Many civil society organisations (CSOs) have also experience and expertise on some of these matters, however the added value of NHRIs' reporting comes, on the one hand, from their comprehensive understanding of these issues combined and, on the other hand, from the fact that they are institutionalised actors internationally accredited, therefore providing information that can be considered as reliable and objective.

Both 2020 and 2021 ENNHRI submissions also included a section on COVID-19 impacts, which in fact often concentrated most of the NHRIs' reporting. Indeed, all aforementioned topics were impacted by the pandemic and related public measures. NHRIs, due to their mandate(s), were at the front position to be aware of new human rights and rule of law challenges, and to provide precise and up-to-date information to the EC.[59]

3.1.1.3. NHRIs as Privileged National Interlocutors for Follow-Up

The role of NHRIs in engaging in EU rule of law initiatives can go beyond their input, including after this information has been processed by the EU institutions. Their central role, combined to their specific mandate and status, make them natural and effective relays to follow-up on the implementation of the given EU recommendations or objectives at national level.[60]

3.1.2. Growing NHRI Recognition by the EU in the Area of Rule of Law

The previous section highlighted NHRIs' added value to address rule of law issues and related European processes. However for a long time this potential has neither been fully exploited by NHRIs, nor acknowledged by the EU institutions. This contribution focuses on these problematics precisely because the dynamics recently started to change. In particular, 2020 has seen numerous European initiatives to monitor and improve the rule of law situation in the region, in which NHRIs have systematically engaged through ENNHRI. This increasing engagement led in turn to a stronger recognition of these actors as

---

58 ENNHRI, 'The rule of law in the European Union', Report, 2020, available at http://ennhri.org/wp-content/uploads/2020/06/The-rule-of-law-in-the-European-Union-Reports-from-NHRIs_11-May-2020.pdf, last accessed 26.03.2021.

59 More information on NHRIs' role in the COVID-19 crisis below.

60 FRA (2020), 'Strong and Effective NHRIs', *supra* note 3, p. 77.

reliable counterparts to enhance human rights, rule of law and democracy on the ground. This section will go over key EU policy developments of the past year related to rule of law matters, to better analyse these recent dynamics.

3.1.2.1. European Commission Rule of Law Report (September 2020)

The EC announced in 2019 its commitment to urgently act upon the regional rule of law crisis, and to take measures addressing related challenges.[61] As the guardian of treaties, the EC has a duty to guarantee the respect of EU values including the rule law as set out in Article 2 TEU.[62] This commitment follows three branches: 'promoting a rule of law culture, preventing rule of law problems, and responding effectively to breaches of the rule of law'.[63] In order to pursue the second objective (although all three pillars and connected actions are interlinked), the EC set up a Rule of Law Review Cycle, including an annual rule of law report covering all EU MS to help detecting emerging rule of law problems. The report is aimed at collating key information on the situation in each country, while provoking debates at national levels within governments and parliaments on its findings.[64]

On both aims, NHRIs can have roles to play (cf. section 3.1.1), and they indeed organised through ENNHRI to do so. As a network, they developed a collective strategic engagement in 2020 to submit a unique report to feed into the EC process.[65] They engaged directly with the EC DG JUST to tailor their submission to the needs of the process and produced a report including information on the rule of law situation in every EUMS, based on the national reporting of NHRIs, and an overview of regional trends.[66] Considering that the reporting exercise was new both for ENNHRI and the EC, and considering the challenging timelines to collate reports from over 20 different institutions, this first submission was a trial effort.

---

61 European Commission, Further strengthening the Rule of Law within the Union State of play and possible next steps, COM(2019) 163 final 03.04.2019.

62 Consolidated version of the Treaty on European Union, OJ C 236/1.

63 European Commission, 'Strengthening the rule of law through increased awareness, an annual monitoring cycle and more effective enforcement', Press release, IP/19/4169, 17.07.2019, available at https://ec.europa.eu/commission/presscorner/detail/en/IP_19_4169, last accessed 20.03.2021.

64 European Commission, '2020 Rule df Law Report – Questions and Answers', Question and answers, QANDA/20/1757, 30.09.2020, available at https://ec.europa.eu/commission/presscorner/detail/en/qanda_20_1757, last accessed 20.03.2021.

65 ENNHRI, 'ENNHRI High-level Consultation – Council of Europe Recommendation on NHRIs and EU Rule of Law Mechanism', 2020, available at http://ennhri.org/news-and-blog/event/ennhri-high-level-consultation-council-of-europe-recommendation-on-nhris-and-eu-rule-of-law-mechanism/, last accessed 20.03.2021.

66 ENNHRI (2020), 'Rule of law Report', *supra* note 48.

Nevertheless, the EC 2020 Rule of Law Report expressly acknowledged the value of NHRIs both in the process and on the ground, stating that NHRIs 'play an important role as rule of law safeguard and can provide an independent check on the system in a rule of law crisis'[67] and emphasising that 'checks and balances rely on (...) effective independent authorities such as ombudsperson institutions or national human rights institutions'.[68] The report cites ENNHRI as one of the stakeholders that provided 'valuable horizontal and country-specific contributions'[69] and includes in all country chapters information on the establishment and accreditation status of NHRIs.[70] These elements demonstrate EU recognition of both NHRIs' role regarding rule of law at the national level and the added value of their collective reporting at the regional level. Drawing on the success of the exercise, ENNHRI recently submitted an updated report to the EC 2021 rule of law consultation, this time also including recommendations addressed to the EU.[71] Both submissions were produced at the invitation of the EC, marking the beginning of an annual cooperation with European NHRIs through ENNHRI on this major EU process. A gap in this cooperation, however, remains in the lack of precise role for NHRIs in the follow-up of the implementation of the EC Report, in respect of which they would be well placed.[72]

3.1.2.2. Revised EU Charter Strategy (December 2020)

The EC also consulted NHRIs in the framework of their revised strategy on the implementation of the EU Charter of fundamental rights in 2020, launched to improve awareness and impact of the Charter in the EU.[73] Through ENNHRI, NHRIs shared a submission highlighting recommendations based on their experience.[74] While NHRIs' role had already been recognised as 'play[ing] a crucial role in the protection and promotion of fundamental rights and ensuring compliance with the Charter' in 2019 Council Conclusions,[75] the EC went further in its 2020 revised strategy. It dedicated a section to NHRIs, underlining their

---

67 European Commission, '2020 Rule of Law Report The rule of law situation in the European Union', COM(2020) 580 final 30.09.2020, p. 23.

68 Ibid., p. 20.

69 Ibid., p. 5.

70 European Commission, '2020 Rule of Law Report – Communication and country chapters', 30.09.2020, available at https://ec.europa.eu/info/publications/2020-rule-law-report-communication-and-country-chapters_en, last accessed 13.07.2021.

71 ENNHRI (2021), 'Rule of law Report', supra note 48.

72 FRA (2020), 'Strong and Effective NHRIs', *supra* note 3, p. 77.

73 European Commission, New Strategy for the Implementation of the Charter of Fundamental Rights: Roadmap, Ares(2020)1655297, 19.03.2020.

74 ENNHRI, 'New European Commission Strategy on the Effective Application of the Charter of Fundamental Rights in the EU: ENNHRI Submission', 20.05.2020, available at http://ennhri.org/wp-content/uploads/2020/05/ENNHRI-Submission_Charter-Strategy.pdf, last accessed 20.03.2021.

75 Council of the European Union, 12357/19, *supra* note 4.

role to 'monitor the application, implementation and promotion of the Charter on the ground, provide information and support to victims of fundamental rights violations and cooperate with the national institutions to improve their use and awareness of the Charter',[76] and provided recommendations to Member States to either establish an independent NHRI or to 'ensure they are given the tools and means to comply with the Paris Principles and refer to the Charter in their mandate'.[77] These elements reflects ENNHRI's submission by providing NHRIs with the legitimacy and push for the resources necessary for them to better uphold their role as national guardians of the EU Charter,[78] a role many already strived to undertake in their daily work.[79]

3.1.2.3. EP Resolution on the EU DRF Mechanism (October 2020)

The European Parliament (EP), notably the Committee on Civil Liberties, Justice and Home Affairs (LIBE), has also been drawing attention to the necessity of updating the EU toolbox to guarantee and defend rule of law, human rights and democracy in the region. In 2018, the LIBE Committee has set up a working group on rule of law issues, which catalised important rule of law EP resolutions, for example, on Poland and Hungary,[80] and on the establishment of an EU Mechanism on Democracy,[81] the Rule of Law and Fundamental Rights.[82] This latter resolution is the result of a process initiated in 2016 by the LIBE Committee. The discussion is still ongoing, and the Committee invited representatives of national parliaments to exchange on 'The first Annual Rule of Law Report by the Commission and the role of national Parliaments'.[83]

---

76 European Commission, 'Strategy to strengthen the application of the Charter of Fundamental Rights in the EU', COM(2020) 711 final 20.12.2020, p. 11.

77 Ibid., p. 11.

78 Ibid.

79 ENNHRI, 'Implementation of the EU Charter of Fundamental Rights: Activities of National Human Rights Institutions', Report, 2019, available at http://ennhri.org/wp-content/uploads/2019/11/Implementation-of-the-EU-Charter-of-Fundamental-Rights-Activities-of-NHRIs.pdf, last accessed 27.03.2021.

80 European Parliament, Resolution on the proposal for a Council decision on the determination of a clear risk of a serious breach by the Republic of Poland of the rule of law, COM(2017) 0835, 17.09.2017.

81 European Parliament Committee on Civil Liberties, Justice and Home Affairs, Report on a proposal calling on the Council to determine, pursuant to Article 7(1) of the Treaty on European Union, the existence of a clear risk of a serious breach by Hungary of the values on which the Union is founded, A8-0250/2018, 04.07.2018.

82 European Parliament, Resolution of 7 October 2020 on the establishment of an EU Mechanism on Democracy, the Rule of Law and Fundamental Rights, (2020/2072(INI)), 07.10.2020.

83 European Parliament Committee on Civil Liberties, Justice and Home Affairs, 'Chairman invitation to Members of national Parliaments to an inter-parliamentary committee meeting on "The first Annual Rule of Law Report by the Commission and the role of national Parliament"', IPOL-COM-LIBE D (2020)2982.

As a bridge between the European and national levels, NHRIs can play an important role in bringing this debate to domestic public institutions – even more so considering ENNHRI's engagement in the EC rule of law cycle. Following up on ENNHRI's input,[84] the resolution includes multiple references to the role of NHRIs, recognising them as indicators (cf. section 3.1.1.1)[85] and highlighting their 'indispensable role […] in all stages of the Annual Monitoring Cycle, from providing input to facilitating implementation and monitoring',[86] opening an avenue for future cooperation. The resolution furthermore cites the ENNHRI submission to the EC 2020 Rule of law cycle as a reference document, proving the legitimacy and trust placed in NHRIs' reporting and views.[87]

3.1.2.4. EU FRA Study (September 2020)

Another element further showcasing the EU's growing interest and recognition of NHRIs potential is the 2020 EU Agency for Fundamental Rights (FRA) Study on NHRIs. While FRA is an independent centre of reference from the Union,[88] its choices of research naturally reflect developments relevant regarding both the promotion and protection of human rights in the region, and the EU's functioning. For years already, FRA has supported the work of NHRIs in the EU, and its recent research further explores how to use their potential at best.[89] NHRIs have engaged closely with FRA on this study,[90] which identifies recommendations to the EU to better support and benefit from the institutions' work.

The study recalls the need to guarantee independent, effective and well funded NHRIs and dedicates a section to the potential of such institutions at the EU level on, *inter alia*, rule of law issues.[91] FRA highlighted elements developed in the previous section (cf. section 3.1.1), and further suggested ways to improve NHRI-EU engagement, notably through a more systematic cooperation, building on NHRIs' national monitoring and on their privileged place to support the rule of law and the use of the EU Charter.[92]

---

84 ENNHRI, 'NHRIs' engagement in EU action to promote and protect rule of law, human rights and democracy: taking stock and looking ahead', Policy Paper, 2020, available at http://ennhri.org/wp-content/uploads/2021/02/NHRIs-engagement-in-EU-action-to-promote-and-protect-rule-of-law-human-rights-and-democracy-November-2020.pdf, last accessed 27.03.2021.

85 European Parliament, Resolution on DRF Mechanism, 2020, *supra* note 82, para. 10.

86 Ibid.

87 ENNHRI, 'Rule of law Report', 2020, *supra* note 48.

88 FRA, 'About FRA', available at https://fra.europa.eu/en/about-fra, last accessed 27.03.2021.

89 FRA (2020), 'Strong and Effective NHRIs', *supra* note 3.

90 ENNHRI (2020), 'NHRIs' engagement in EU action', *supra* note 84.

91 FRA (2020), 'Strong and Effective NHRIs', *supra* note 3, p. 77.

92 Ibid.

3.1.2.5. EU Action Plan on Human Rights and Democracy (March 2020)

Since the adoption of the Strategic Framework on Human Rights and Democracy,[93] the EU regularly develops action plans to implement its objectives. ENNHRI produced a submission to the public consultation on the third action plan,[94] looking at the 2020-2024 period.[95] The submission called for a greater recognition of NHRIs' role and urged the EC to ensure synergies with ongoing EU rule of law processes,[96] such as the ones evoked above. The 2020–2024 action plan indeed stressed the need to 'support independent NHRIs and commissions, ombudspersons and equality bodies, in line with the Paris and Venice Principles,[97] and engage with them including in the context of human rights dialogues',[98] to achieve the objectives set out in the plan.[99]

3.1.2.6. Beyond the EU: Council of Europe Recommendation on NHRIs (March 2021)

While this contribution focuses on the EU scale, the aforementioned developments go beyond this scope. A European policy initiative of relevance for this section must be mentioned: the updated Council of Europe (CoE) Recommendation on National Human Rights Institutions. European NHRIs submitted through ENNHRI several recommendations to ensure that the text would support at best NHRIs' impact,[100] and through them human rights and the rule of law in Europe. ENNHRI engaged closely with the CoE in the process, and the draft text which followed was already acknowledged by NHRIs as a 'pivotal step for further recognition and strengthening of European NHRIs and their cooperation with the Council of Europe,[101] helping to realise

[93] Council of the European Union, EU Strategic Framework and Action Plan on Human Rights and Democracy 11855/12, 25.06.2012.

[94] ENNHRI, 'European Democracy Action Plan: ENNHRI Submission', 2020, available at http://ennhri.org/wp-content/uploads/2020/09/ENNHRI-submission_Democracy-Action-Plan.pdf, last accessed 27.03.2021.

[95] European Commission, JOIN(2020) 5 final, *supra* note 4.

[96] ENNHRI (2020), 'European Democracy Action Plan: ENNHRI Submission', *supra* note 94.

[97] The Venice Principles represent the first, independent, international set of standards for the Ombudsman institution. They are the equivalent of the Paris Principles to NHRIs. See Council of Europe Venice Commission, 'Principles on the protection and promotion of te Omudsman Institutions (the Venice principles)', CDL-AD(2019)005, 2019.

[98] Council of the European Union, 12848/20, *supra* note 8, pp. 26–27.

[99] Ibid., pp. 6–7.

[100] ENNHRI, 'Submission to CDDH INST on the revision of the Council of Europe Committee of Ministers Recommendation on NHRIs', 2020, available at http://ennhri.org/wp-content/uploads/2020/02/ENNHRI-submission-to-CDDH-INST-on-the-review-of-CoE-CoM-Recommendation-on-NHRIs.pdf, last accessed 27.03.2021.

[101] Council of Europe, Drafting Group On Civil Society And National Human Rights Institutions (Cddh-Inst) 6th Meeting Report, CDDH-INST (2019)R6, 19.03.2020.

human rights across the region'.[102] The recommendation's text was adopted on 31 March 2021.[103]

3.1.3. NHRIs in Rule of Law Crisis: Focus on the COVID-19 Context

The NHRIs' role analysed in this section has been recently tested in times of rule of law crisis, on the one hand regarding the general democratic backsliding observed in the EU for several years, and on the other hand regarding the impacts of the COVID-19 pandemic. When democratic safeguards are jeopardised, NHRIs have many roles to play both on the ground (monitoring laws and practices, receiving complaint and support citizens, exchanging with the authorities) and at the EU level (early warning, reporting, recommending, following up at national level).

The failure of the state to effectively protect and support NHRIs is in itself an indicator of the rule of law situation in the country (cf. section 3.1.1.1), as can be witnessed in Poland where the NHRI has faced repeated attacks and intimidation from politicians and media.[104] The Polish institution has received the support of many European institutional actors,[105] highlighting the importance of NHRIs to prevent and combat autocratical drifts.

The COVID-19 pandemic and related restrictions have impacted a wide range of fundamental rights and worryingly 'justified' infringements to core pillars of the rule of law, such as: extended executive powers, fast-track legislation, lack of parliamentary and judicial oversight, lack of consultation (e.g. by NHRIs), lack of transparency, insufficient efforts to maintain a working justice system and restriction to freedom of assembly, among others. European NHRIs have acted at national and regional levels to alert and react to these serious developments. At the national level, they swiftly adapted to ensure a continuity of service, monitored emergency measures, advised governments, underlined needs of vulnerable groups and informed and supported citizens,[106] including by stepping up to fill in the gaps in public action. As part of the national

---

102 ENNHRI, 'Council Of Europe Drafting Group Proposes Text For Updated Recommendation On The Development And Strengthening Of Effective, Pluralistic And Independent NHRIs', 26.03.2020, available at http://ennhri.org/news-and-blog/council-of-europe-drafting-group-proposes-text-for-updated-recommendation-on-the-development-and-strengthening-of-effective-pluralistic-and-independent-nhris/, last accessed 27.03.2021.

103 Council of Europe, Draft Recommendation of the Committee of Ministers to member States on the development and strengthening of effective, pluralist and independent NHRIs, CM (2021)22-add1, 31.03.2021.

104 OHCHR Europe, GANHRI, ENNHRI et al., 'Joint Statement in Support of the Polish Commissioner for Human Rights', 26.06.2019, available at http://ennhri.org/wp-content/uploads/2019/09/Joint-Statement-in-Support-of-the-Polish-Commissioner-for-Human-Rights.pdf, last accessed 15.03.2021.

105 *Inter alia* from OHCHR Europe, Council of Europe, OSCE.

106 FRA (2020), 'Strong and Effective NHRIs', *supra* note 3, pp. 93–94.

system of checks and balances, particularly undermined in many countries, NHRIs were well placed to do so. They could, moreover, provide a space for dialogue for CSOs and other actors, which the public authorities often failed to allow in these emergency times, crucial to keep ensuring consultation and transparency.[107] At the European level, NHRIs provided a valuable insight on the COVID-19 situation in their country: for instance, as mentioned above, the impact of COVID-19 featured centrally in the NHRI reporting to the EC rule of law cycle.[108] In the context of this sudden, unprecedented crisis that keeps evolving and impacting a wider range of issues, such informed country-specific information from reliable sources like NHRIs can enable EU actors to reach a comprehensive understanding of the situation and priorities to address in the region. NHRIs through ENNHRI also collaborated in 2020 with the OSCE Office for Democratic Institutions and Human Rights (ODIHR) for a report on 'NHRIs in a Public Emergency',[109] looking at their role during the COVID-19 pandemic and beyond.

NHRIs' work to monitor, alert and react to the effects of the COVID-19 crisis has been recognised by many actors, at international and regional level. The UN OHCHR dedicated a page to NHRIs' actions during the pandemic, showcasing their good practices worldwide,[110] the OSCE ODIHR underlined the 'crucial role NHRIs have in times of public emergency',[111] while FRA stressed the importance to ensure 'strong and independent NHRIs to champion people's fundamental rights during and after COVID-19'.[112] Indeed, NHRIs' role goes beyond the support already provided during the pandemic. It also is important to prepare and face its consequences. The crisis already started to deepen inequalities and worsen structural disfunctionings (e.g regarding the justice system), however such issues are still often overshadowed by more striking issues.

Such institutional recognition at EU level is indispensable for the establishment and strengthening of fully independent and effective NHRIs in the region,[113] in turn major assets to support and alert on the state of rule of law

---

107 OSCE ODIHR, 'National Human Rights Institutions in times of emergency', available at https://www.osce.org/files/f/documents/8/0/465906.pdf, last accessed 20.05.2021.

108 ENNHRI (2020), Rule of law Report, *supra* note 48, pp. 26–27.
ENNHRI (2021), Rule of law Report, *supra* note 48, pp. 36–39.

109 OSCE ODIHR, available at https://www.osce.org/files/f/documents/8/0/465906.pdf, last accessed 20.05.2021.

110 OHCHR, 'NHRIs responses to the COVID-19 pandemic', available at https://www.ohchr.org/EN/Countries/NHRI/Pages/NHRIS-and-Covid-19.aspx, last accessed 20.05.2021.

111 OSCE ODIHR, 'National Human Rights Institutions in times of emergency', *supra* note 107.

112 EU FRA, 'National human rights institutions: guaranteeing fundamental rights compliance during COVID-19 and beyond', available at https://fra.europa.eu/en/news/2020/national-human-rights-institutions-guaranteeing-fundamental-rights-compliance-during-covid, last accessed 20.05.2021.

113 ENNHRI (2020),'NHRIs engagement in EU action', *supra* note 84.

on the ground. While the recent developments at the EU level are encouraging, there is still significant room for progress in order to maximise NHRI's impact on these issues. The main necessary steps include a more formal recognition of NHRIs' role by the EU, instituting a regular exchange with NHRIs (including through ENNHRI) taking place in a clear framework and collaborating with NHRIs as privileged interlocutors to monitor and support follow-up of EU initiatives and recommendations on the ground.

3.2. NHRIS WITHIN THE CHANGING EUROPEAN MIGRATION LANDSCAPE

Asylum and migration (A&M) is a long-standing thematic priority for European NHRIs.[114] NHRIs have used their mandates to advance migrants' rights in different ways, from advising governments to monitoring places of detention. Since 2008, a Working Group on Asylum and Migration has brought together migration experts from NHRIs across Europe.[115] The creation of a permanent secretariat for European NHRIs in 2013 boosted the participation and cooperation within the A&M Working Group, whose members grew from 23 in 2015, to 32 in 2020.[116] Building on NHRIs' work, the working group has increasingly advocated for the better protection and promotion of migrants' human rights in Europe, including through regular exchanges, common position contributions and awareness-raising activities.

While the NHRI-EU cooperation on A&M has remained limited, NHRIs have continuously engaged with regional human rights actors, such as the CoE and OSCE, including through the ENNHRI Working Group.[117] However, 2020

---

114 A, Kampf, 'National Human Rights Institutions and their work on migrants' human rights. Results of a survey among NHRIs', Analysis, German Institute for Human Rights and GANHRI, 2019, available at https://www.institut-fuer-menschenrechte.de/fileadmin/user_upload/Publikationen/ANALYSE/Analysis_NHRI_and_their_work_on_migrants__human_rights.pdf, last accessed 22.03.2021.

115 B. Adamson (2013), 'NHRI and Their European Counterparts', *supra* note 34, pp. 135–136.

116 See ENNHRI, Annual Reports 2014, 2015, 2016, 2017, 2018 and 2019, which are available at http://ennhri.org/about-us/annual-reports/, last accessed 22.03.2021.

117 For instance, in March 2019, the ENNHRI A&M Working Group coordinated the submission of NHRI inputs to the Council of Europe's draft 'Practical Guidance on Alternatives to Immigration Detention', see ENNHRI, 'ENNHRI's Asylum and Migration Working Group submission to the Council of Europe's Drafting Group on Migration and Human Rights (CDDH-MIG) – consultation on the draft "Practical Guidance on Alternatives to Immigration Detention"', 12.03.2019, available at http://ennhri.org/news-and-blog/ennhri-comments-on-council-of-europes-draft-practical-guidance-on-alternatives-to-immigration-detention/, last accessed 22.03.2021; see also ENNHRI, 'Submission to the Council of Europe consultation on the Draft European Rules on the Conditions for the Administrative Detention of Migrants', 04.07.2017, available at http://ennhri.org/news-and-blog/ennhri-calls-for-alternatives-to-detention-in-its-submission-to-the-open-consultation-of-the-draft-european-rules/, last accessed 22.03.2021.

was a crucial year to advance a more strategic engagement between the EU and NHRIs in the field of migration.

First, the flagrant pushback allegations at the EU external borders put existing mechanisms for reporting and redressing violations in the spotlight. Also, the release of the new pact on migration and asylum, notably the proposal for a screening regulation, offered policymakers an opportunity to better consider the work of monitors and defenders at borders, such as NHRIs. In the meantime, the implementation of a project on human rights monitoring at borders run by the ENNHRI A&M Working Group contributed to place NHRIs strategically within regional discussions on A&M.[118] Finally, COVID-19 underlined the need for policies that truly leave nobody behind, to which NHRIs can make important contributions.[119]

This section aims at exploring the scope for a strengthened NHRI-EU cooperation in the area of A&M in light of recent developments. The potential role of NHRIs in the new pact will be scrutinised, while NHRIs' added value in other related areas will be also considered. The analysis will draw from the established relationship between NHRIs and other human rights systems as a possible blueprint for stronger engagement with the EU.[120] Finally, good NHRI practices in the defence and promotion of migrants' rights during the COVID-19 pandemic will be showcased.

---

118 Among others, the project sought to give further visibility to NHRIs' work at borders in light of the regional discussions on fundamental rights border monitoring, including in the context of the pact. For instance, in February 2020, ENNHRI contributed to a briefing on fundamental rights violations at borders, which was jointly organised by the Open Society European Policy Institute and MEP Tineke Strik. For further information see ENNHRI, 'ENNHRI contributes to discussion at the European Parliament on violations of human rights of migrants at the borders', 21.02.2020, available at http://ennhri.org/news-and-blog/ennhri-contributes-to-discussion-at-the-european-parliament-on-violations-of-human-rights-of-migrants-at-the-borders/, last accessed 25.03.2021. Thereafter, ENNHRI published two statements providing a good insight on the role of European NHRIs in the context of independent fundamental rights border monitoring. See: ENNHRI, 'Stronger human rights monitoring at Europe's borders – why NHRIs are part of the solution', 27.05.2020, available at http://ennhri.org/our-work/topics/asylum-and-migration/stronger-human-rights-monitoring-at-europes-borders-why-nhris-are-part-of-the-solution/, last accessed 25.03.2021; ENNHRI, 'ENNHRI's Opinion on Independent Human Rights Monitoring Mechanisms at Borders under the EU Pact on Migration and Asylum', 10.03.2021, available at http://ennhri.org/our-work/topics/asylum-and-migration/opinion-on-independent-human-rights-monitoring-mechanisms-at-borders-under-the-eu-pact-on-migration-and-asylum/, last accessed 25.03.2021. Further information is available at http://ennhri.org/our-work/topics/asylum-and-migration/, last accessed 24.03.2021.

119 See ENNHRI, 'Now is the time for solidarity on human rights. The need for human rights in COVID-19 responses in Europe', 23.04.2020, available at http://ennhri.org/statement-on-covid-19/, last accessed 28.03.2021.

120 FRA (2020), 'Strong and Effective NHRIs', *supra* note 3, pp. 68–71.

3.2.1. *Setting the Context: The New Proposal for a Screening Regulation*

In September 2020, the EC presented its long-awaited pact on migration and asylum, in the effort to overcome the deadlock on the 2016 reform of the common European asylum system (CEAS).[121] Among others, the pact included a proposal for a new regulation setting up a pre-entry screening phase for irregular third country nationals at the EU external borders.[122] The screening envisaged the identification, registration, as well as health, security and vulnerability checks, of third country nationals in order to channel them to the appropriate border procedure (i.e. asylum or return) on the basis of a 'debriefing form'.[123] In this context, MS were left wide discretion as to the screening's accommodation solutions and detention rules. Finally, Recital 23 of the regulation stated that '[i]n order to ensure compliance with EU and international law, including the Charter of Fundamental Rights, during the screening, each Member State should establish a monitoring mechanism and put in place adequate safeguards for the independence thereof'.[124]

Overall, the proposal for an independent national monitoring mechanism at borders can be understood as the Commission's reaction to the increasing allegations of systematic pushbacks, as well as the growing sentiment of impunity and lack of accountability at EU external borders.[125] While unlawful border practices have been regularly reported since 2016, in 2020 the situation escalated.[126] In March 2020, prompted by Turkey's border opening, the European Border and Coast Guard Agency (Frontex) launched two rapid interventions at Greece's external borders.[127] Soon thereafter, the agency was accused of covering up illegal pushbacks in the Aegean Sea, and multiple investigations

---

121 European Commission, 'Migration and Asylum Package: New Pact on Migration and Asylum documents adopted on 23 September 2020', 23.09.2020, available at https://ec.europa.eu/info/publications/migration-and-asylum-package-new-pact-migration-and-asylum-documents-adopted-23-september-2020_en, last accessed 24.03.2021.

122 European Commission, Proposal for a regulation of the European parliament and of the council introducing a screening of third country nationals at the external borders and amending Regulations (EC) No 767/2008, (EU) 2017/2226, (EU) 2018/1240 and (EU) 2019/817, COM/2020/612 final 23.09.2020.

123 Ibid., Article 6.

124 Ibid., Recital 23.

125 Border Violence Monitoring Network, 'The Black Book of Pushbacks', 18.12.2020, available at https://www.guengl.eu/issues/publications/black-book-of-pushbacks-volumes-i-ii/, last accessed 24.03.2021.

126 FRA, 'Migration: Fundamental rights issues at land borders', 08.12.2020, available at https://fra.europa.eu/en/publication/2020/migration-fundamental-rights-issues-land-borders, last accessed 24.03.2021.

127 Frontex, 'Frontex launches rapid border intervention on Greek land border', Press Release, 13.02.2020, available at https://frontex.europa.eu/media-centre/news/news-release/frontex-launches-rapid-border-intervention-on-greek-land-border-J7k21h, last accessed 24.03.2021.

were opened.[128] This exacerbated the existing concerns with regards to the lack of accountability and an independent oversight on the work of the agency.[129]

Against this backdrop, many have criticised the proposed independent national monitoring mechanism's scope and nature, due to its lack of clarity and strong legal safeguards.[130] In the present proposal, the establishment of such a mechanism takes the form of a side saving clause. However, strong fundamental rights safeguards should feature centrally in the proposal's text to prevent the monitoring mechanism from becoming just a fig leaf, which is neither independent, nor effective.

3.2.2. *The Pact's Screening Proposal and Independent National Monitoring Mechanisms at Borders: What Role for NHRIs?*

The Commission's proposal opened a window of opportunity for the EU and European NHRIs to enhance their partnership in the area of A&M. At the same time, recent regional policy developments contributed to the increase of the EU awareness and recognition of NHRIs' work at borders.

To begin with, in September 2020, the updated FRA study on European NHRIs encouraged the EU to 'draw more consistently on NHRIs as crucial actors for the implementation of fundamental rights, including by ensuring independent and effective fundamental rights monitoring' of key areas governed by EU law, 'such as asylum and migration, data protection and criminal justice'.[131]

Moreover, in December 2020, the EP adopted a resolution on the implementation of the Return Directive, which, among others, raised concerns on the limited procedural safeguards in return and entry-ban decisions, as

---

128 ECRE, 'Frontex: One Investigation Closes as Another Begins and the Agency's Role in Return and Ability to Purchase Firearms Under Scrutiny', 05.03.2021, available at https://www.ecre.org/frontex-one-investigation-closes-as-another-begins-and-the-agencys-role-in-return-and-ability-to-purchase-firearms-under-scrutiny/, last accessed 24.03.2021.

129 M. Fink, 'Why it is so Hard to Hold Frontex Accountable: On Blame-Shifting and an Outdated Remedies System', *EJIL:Talk! Blog of the European Journal of International Law*, 26.11.2020, available at https://www.ejiltalk.org/why-it-is-so-hard-to-hold-frontex-accountable-on-blame-shifting-and-an-outdated-remedies-system/, last accessed 24.03.2021.

130 See, for instance: R. Lanneau, 'The Commission's proposal for a new Independent Monitoring Mechanism at the external border of the EU: a necessary but limited mechanism', *Odysseus Academic Network Blog*, 22.02.2021, available at https://eumigrationlawblog.eu/the-commissions-proposal-for-a-new-independent-monitoring-mechanism-at-the-external-border-of-the-eu-a-necessary-but-limited-mechanism/, last accessed 24.03.2021; ECRE, 'Joint Statement: Turning rhetoric into reality: New monitoring mechanism at European borders should ensure fundamental rights and accountability', 10.11.2020, available at https://www.ecre.org/turning-rhetoric-into-reality-new-monitoring-mechanism-at-european-borders-should-ensure-fundamental-rights-and-accountability/, last accessed 24.03.2021.

131 FRA (2020), 'Strong and Effective NHRIs', *supra* note 3, p. 13.

well as on the widespread use and conditions of detention in the pre-return phase.[132] Accordingly, the European Parliament encouraged MS to respect the mandate of 'relevant and competent national and international bodies, such as National Human Rights Institutions, (…) which conduct independent oversight of conditions of detention'.[133] Moreover, the resolution stressed that 'return monitoring should encompass all phases of return operations', while calling 'on the Commission and Member States to make use of existing independent monitoring bodies, such as (…) National Human Rights Institutions, by cooperating with or designating them as forced return monitoring systems'.[134]

Finally, in early 2021, the EP adopted another resolution on the implementation of Article 43 of the Asylum Procedures Directive.[135] In this context, the EP stressed the importance to establish an independent monitoring mechanism with 'unimpeded access to border facilities' to protect fundamental rights, report violations, as well as oversight the decision-making process, detention conditions and compliance with procedural safeguards. The resolution clearly stated that independent and competent NHRIs and NGOs, EU agencies such as the FRA, and international organisations such as UNHCR should be part of the monitoring bodies.'[136]

The EU's acknowledgement of the role of NHRIs as independent and credible fundamental rights border monitors is surely a good achievement. Yet key questions arise: to which extent may NHRIs contribute to an independent monitoring mechanism at borders? How can this be envisaged under the current pact's proposals, and beyond?

The following section will examine European NHRIs' roles as fundamental rights monitors at borders, in relation to the main features of the pact's screening proposal. It is noteworthy that, as underlined by the previous section, not all

---

132 European Parliament Resolution of 17 December 2020 on the implementation of the Return Directive (2019/2208(INI)), (hereinafter European Parliament Resolution on the Return Directive).

133 Ibid., para. 33. In July 2020, ENNHRI submitted to LIBE its inputs on a draft report on the implementation of the return directive, calling for stronger recognition of NHRIs' role as independent fundamental rights monitoring at borders and places of deprivation of liberty. See: Report on the implementation of the Return Directive (2019/2208(INI)), Committee on Civil Liberties, Justice and Home Affairs, Rapporteur: Tineke Strik, 09.06.2020, para. 19; ENNHRI, 'European Parliament recognises NHRIs' key role in monitoring human rights in forced returns of migrants', 09.02.2021, available at http://ennhri.org/news-and-blog/european-parliament-recognises-nhris-key-role-in-monitoring-human-rights-in-forced-returns-of-migrants/, last accessed 25.03.2021.

134 European Parliament Resolution on the Return Directive, *supra* note 132, para. 35.

135 This Article, in certain specific circumstances, gives MS the possibility to apply fast-track border procedures to decide on the admissibility and/or the merits of an application.

136 European Parliament resolution of 10 February 2021 on the implementation of Article 43 of Directive 2013/32/EU of the European Parliament and of the Council of 26 June 2013 on common procedures for granting and withdrawing international protection (2020/2047(INI)), para. 16.

NHRIs in the EU are fully compliant with the Paris Principles. Qualified institutional relationships envisaged below ought to be reserved to A status NHRIs.

3.2.2.1. Establishment

The wording of the screening proposal suggests the need to 'establish', rather than 'strengthen' or 'designate' existing national monitoring bodies.

NHRIs, alongside other national actors such as NGOs, NPMs and Ombudsmen,[137] already conduct monitoring activities under their various mandates. As recently underlined by FRA, most NHRIs in the EU conduct monitoring activities, either as an explicit obligation and possibility, or based on established practices.[138] Monitoring can take different forms: individual complaints handling, access to documentation, draft legislation review, collection of data, as well as on-site visits to places of detention, reception facilities, green borders or police stations.[139] In March 2020, drawing from NHRIs' mandates and functions, ENNHRI drafted a guidance for monitoring fundamental rights at borders, identifying a set of key human rights issues to scrutinise.[140]

Entrusting existing bodies, such as NHRIs, with the screening's monitoring tasks would allow MS to comply with their obligations in a cost-efficient manner, while building on existing expertise and high standards of independence and pluralism.

3.2.2.2. Domestic Legislation

The purpose of the monitoring is ensuring 'compliance with EU and international law, including the Charter of Fundamental Rights, during the screening'. However, a separate provision mandates the monitoring 'to ensure compliance with *national* rules of detention [emphasis added]', disregarding higher standards guaranteed by regional and international frameworks in the field of detention.[141]

The Paris Principles establishes that NHRIs shall 'promote and ensure the harmonization of national legislation, regulations and practices with the

---

[137] Where they are not the NHRIs.

[138] FRA (2020), 'Strong and Effective NHRIs', *supra* note 3, p. 17.

[139] ENNHRI, 'Protecting human rights of migrants at the borders. Evidence and work of European National Human Rights Institutions', 28.01.2020, available at http://ennhri.org/news-and-blog/new-paper-outlines-how-european-nhris-promote-and-protect-human-rights-of-migrants-at-borders/, last accessed 26.03.2021.

[140] ENNHRI, 'Guidance. Monitoring human rights of migrants at the borders. Building on the mandate and functions of National Human Rights Institutions', 26.03.2020, available at http://ennhri.org/news-and-blog/ennhri-launches-new-guidance-for-stronger-monitoring-of-migrants-rights-at-borders/, last accessed 26.03.2021.

[141] European Commission, COM/2020/612 final, *supra* note 122, Article 7(2).

international human rights instruments to which the State is a party, and their effective implementation'. In this context, many NHRIs report to international mechanisms, with participation rights at the UN and the Council of Europe.

The involvement of NHRIs in the monitoring mechanism would allow national human rights concerns to be raised at the regional and international levels, while encouraging the compliance with higher supranational standards, including in relation to detention conditions.

3.2.2.3. Independence

The screening proposal gives particular emphasis to the independent functioning of the national monitoring mechanism, providing that MS 'shall put in place adequate safeguards to guarantee the independence of the mechanism', while remaining silent on its specific requirements for independence. Rather, the provision invites MS to seek FRA's guidance on the mechanism's methodology, independence safeguards and training schemes.

Independence is the overriding hallmark of NHRIs. The SCA periodic accreditation process guarantees that NHRIs carry out their mandate without any undue interference, notably by the executive power, both in law and in practice. In this sense, the Paris Principles offer a good benchmark for EU policymakers and national authorities with regards to independence *lato sensu* – encompassing, therefore, pluralism, composition, funding and legal foundation. Nonetheless, the Paris Principles have not enjoyed much consideration within the EU policies so far, notably in the area of A&M.[142]

The situation is different at the international level. Relevant UN human rights treaties required MS to use the Paris Principles as a key reference when designating and/or establishing 'non-judicial domestic bodies with specific implementation and monitoring tasks.'[143] For instance, Article 18(4) of the optional protocol of the convention against torture and other cruel, inhuman or degrading treatment or punishment (OPCAT) states that:

> [w]hen establishing national preventive mechanisms, States Parties shall give due consideration to the Principles relating to the status of national institutions for the promotion and protection of human rights.[144]

---

142 As this contribution wishes to argue, NHRIs and the Paris Principles have featured more prominently within EU policies only recently, with a significant consideration given in the area of rule of law. See section 3.1. 'NHRIs in the Developing European Rule of Law Framework' for further information on the EU-NHRI engagement in the field of rule of law.

143 M. Nowak (2013), 'National Human Rights Institutions in Europe', *supra* note 1, p. 22.

144 UN General Assembly, Optional Protocol to the Convention Against Torture and other Cruel, Inhuman and Degrading Treatment or Punishment, Resolution adopted on 18 December 2002, UN Doc A/RES/57/199, 09.01.2003, Article 18(4).

Similarly, Article 33(2) of the CRPD provides that:

> State Parties shall (...) maintain, strengthen, designate or establish within the State Party, a framework, including one or more independent mechanisms, as appropriate, to promote, protect and monitor implementation of the present Convention. When designating or establishing such a mechanism, States Parties shall take into account the principles relating to the status and functioning of national institutions for protection and promotion of human rights.[145]

The UN reliance on the Paris Principles when establishing and/or designating national fundamental rights monitoring bodies can surely be a blueprint for EU legislators in the context of the screening proposal. According to the FRA study, as of today, 12 EU NHRIs are designated as NPMs, while 17 NHRIs operate as NMM under the CRPD.[146]

Finally, the envisaged FRA's advisory role on independence safeguards is strategic for NHRIs. Since FRA's establishment in 2007, European NHRIs have actively engaged with the agency.[147] FRA's founding regulation obliges the agency to cooperate with NHRIs and include a representative from 'an independent national human rights institution or other public or private sector organisation' in its management board.[148] Today, the FRA-NHRI cooperation encompasses a variety of activities, including in relation to the agency's annual planning.[149] It is noteworthy that, in its recent study, FRA clearly called for a strong engagement between the EU and NHRIs, including in the context of fundamental rights monitoring.[150] Recently, a FRA representative publicly valued the involvement of national actors in the screening, which arguably 'allows for adjustments on realities on the ground, and to build on the work of National Human Rights Institutions and National Preventive Mechanisms'.[151]

3.2.2.4. Other Bodies

The screening proposal establishes that MS can invite national, international and non-governmental organisations and bodies to take part in the monitoring.

---

145 UN General Assembly, Convention on the Rights of Persons with Disabilities, Resolution adopted on 13 December 2006, UN Doc A/RES/61/106, 24.01.2007, Article 33(2).

146 FRA (2020), 'Strong and Effective NHRIs', *supra* note 3, p. 31.

147 B. Adamson (2013), 'NHRI and Their European Counterparts', *supra* note 34, pp. 150–152.

148 Council Regulation (EC) No 168/2007 of 15 February 2007 establishing a European Union Agency for Fundamental Rights, OJ L 53, 22.2.2007, Article 8(2) and Article 12(1), respectively.

149 Further information can be found on the ENNHRI website, available at http://ennhri.org/about-us/partners/#eu, last accessed 26.03.2021.

150 FRA (2020), 'Strong and Effective NHRIs', *supra* note 3, p. 13.

151 The speaker made this declaration during a public event entitled 'After five years of EU refugee response on the Greek islands, what does the future hold?', organised by Oxfam on 18 March 2021. More information is available at https://www.eventbrite.com/e/five-years-of-eu-refugee-response-on-the-greek-islands-tickets-145672790237, last accessed 26.03.2021.

While its optional nature is regrettable, this provision seems to point to the added value of cooperating with existing monitors, such as NHRIs.

The Paris Principles oblige NHRIs to cooperate with local NGOs, as well as 'other bodies, whether jurisdictional or otherwise, responsible for the promotion and protection of human rights'. NGOs and grassroots are valuable partners for NHRIs. Due to their field presence in remote geographical areas, these actors are best placed to detect pushback practises, which often occur away from official border crossing points. By contrast, most European NHRIs are present at the capital level and few also have regional representations.[152] Moreover, in some cases, the accredited NHRI may not be given as a strong mandate as to effectively investigate and redress human rights violations.[153] Consequently, different mandates may jeopardise a coherent approach to the monitoring at borders.

Therefore, only the close collaboration among all relevant stakeholders can guarantee the effectiveness of a national monitoring mechanism. As it was stated, 'NHRIs do not replace other stakeholders in the field of human rights and will not always be the most appropriate partner for the EU'.[154] NHRIs, however, may use their special standing to act as bridge builders between grassroots and national authorities, as well as between national and regional actors. Finally, regional networks comprising actors from wider Europe, such as ENNHRI, may facilitate cooperation with non-EU NHRIs or other relevant bodies, to address violations that occur beyond the EU geographical boundaries.[155]

3.2.3. *Towards More Accountability and Effectiveness at Borders: Beyond the Pact's Proposals*

The above analysis explored NHRIs' added value in relation to the screening regulation. However, additional considerations can go beyond the pact's proposals.

Independence of human rights monitors is certainly a crucial feature. However, a monitoring exercise should also be effective.[156] The effectiveness of NHRIs' work, including at borders, is highly dependent on the environment in which they operate. A recent ENNHRI opinion outlined that an enabling and

---

152 The ENNHRI website provides an overview of its members, which includes information on NHRIs' regional offices, available at http://ennhri.org/our-members/, last accessed 27.03.2021.

153 Complaint handling is only an optional function under the Paris Principles.

154 J. Wouters, K. Meuwissen and A.S. Barros, 'The European Union and National Human Rights Institutions', in J. Wouters and K. Meuwissen (eds.) (2013), *National Human Rights Institutions in Europe*, *supra* note 1, p. 220.

155 ENNHRI (2021), 'Opinion on Independent Human Rights Monitoring Mechanisms', *supra* note 118, pp. 10–11.

156 Effectiveness is understood here by the institution's ability to attain its goals, while achieving a tangible impact.

conducive environment, where monitors are granted strong mandates, adequate funding, as well as unhindered access to relevant information, border areas and facilities by competent authorities, is an essential prerequisite for the effectiveness of any monitoring activity.[157] Therefore, obstacles to the monitoring mechanism's proper functioning must be properly addressed by the EU through any available means to enforce compliance with EU law. The 'necessity of safeguarding an enabling environment for independent national human rights institutions' was also underlined by the Council of the European Union in its 2019 conclusions on the implementation of the Charter of Fundamental Rights.[158]

One of the most tangible impacts of an effective border monitoring is accountability. Human rights monitoring is not an end. Rather, it should be a mean to enforce more compliant behaviours, within a functioning system of checks and balances. While individuals must be ensured access to justice and legal redress, findings and recommendations arising from the monitoring must be adequately addressed and followed up. NHRIs' practices can offer good examples in this regard. According to FRA, 29 NHRIs in the EU can investigate systematic human rights violations and make recommendations for redress, while 23 are also able to examine individual complaints.[159] For instance, the Cypriot NHRI, through mediatory interventions before the competent authorities, has facilitated migrants' release from detention, access to basic services, removal from 'stop lists', and the expenditure of other administrative procedures.[160] Another way to ensure better accountability and follow-up by authorities is through parliamentary debates of NHRIs' reporting. The Paris Principles set out a clear responsibility for NHRIs to submit to parliaments their 'opinions, recommendations, proposals and reports on any matters concerning the promotion and protection of human rights'. FRA's findings show that most NHRIs address their annual reports to national parliaments, but only in 12 MS these reports are subject to an obligatory parliamentary discussion.[161] FRA also observed that, to some extent, all NHRIs monitor the follow up on their recommendations, including by making public relevant data and information. Building on these findings, FRA encouraged MS to 'ensure that there is a systematic tracking and public reporting of the follow-up and implementation of NHRIs' recommendations'.[162]

NHRIs can also contribute to hold EU Home Affairs Agencies more accountable. EU agencies, such as Frontex, have increasingly engaged

---

[157] ENNHRI (2021), 'Opinion on Independent Human Rights Monitoring Mechanisms', *supra* note 118.

[158] Council of the European Union, 12357/19, *supra* note 4, para. 22.

[159] FRA (2020), 'Strong and Effective NHRIs', *supra* note 3, pp. 61–62.

[160] Ibid., p. 62.

[161] Ibid., p. 56.

[162] Ibid., p. 15.

in migration and border management, including through inter-agency cooperation.[163] Accordingly, the screening regulation foresees that national authorities can be supported by teams, experts and liaisons officers deployed by Frontex, among others.[164] Yet the long-standing concerns over the lack of accountability of Frontex call for stronger fundamental rights safeguards.[165] The 2019 Frontex Regulation leaves space for further engagement with NHRIs towards better fundamental rights compliance and accountability.

- *Complaint mechanism*: the Frontex regulation establishes that any person may submit a written complaint to the agency, if they consider their fundamental rights to have been affected by staff deployed by Frontex. The Frontex fundamental rights officer (FRO), who is responsible for handling complaints, shall 'forward complaints concerning members of the teams to the home Member State, including the relevant authority or body competent for fundamental rights in a Member State for further action in accordance with their mandate'.[166] The involvement of NHRIs in this process, as well as other internal reporting mechanisms, can guarantee that such complaints are handled with the necessary degree of independence from the executive power and law enforcement authorities.
- *National parliaments*: a novelty introduced by Regulation 2019/1896 is the interparliamentary cooperation between the EP and national parliaments

163 D. Vitiello, 'Agencification as A Key Component of the EU Externalisation Toolkit. Observations on a Silent Escape from the Rule of Law', in S. Carrera, A.P. Leonhard den Hertog, M. Panizzon et al. (eds.), *EU External Migration Policies in an Era of Global Mobilities: Intersecting Policy Universes*, Brill Nijhoff, Leiden 2018, pp. 125–152.

164 C. Dumbrava, 'Screening of third-country nationals at the EU's external borders', European Parliamentary Research Service, Briefing, 17.11.2020, p. 6, available at https://www.europarl.europa.eu/RegData/etudes/BRIE/2020/659346/EPRS_BRI(2020)659346_EN.pdf, last accessed 27.03.2021.

165 Concerns with regards to the effective functioning of Frontex's internal reporting lines for alleged fundamental rights violations have been raised by a multitude of actors: *inter alia*, the Frontex Consultative Forum on Fundamental Rights and the Frontex Management Board itself. See: Frontex Consultative Forum on Fundamental Rights, 'Seventh Annual Report', 2019, available at https://frontex.europa.eu/assets/Partners/Consultative_Forum_files/Frontex_Consultative_Forum_annual_report_2019.pdf, last accessed 27.03.2021; Frontex Management Board Working Group, 'Fundamental Rights and Legal Operational Aspects of Operations in the Aegean Sea', final report, 01.03.2021, available at https://frontex.europa.eu/assets/Key_Documents/MB_Documents/Agenda_Point_WG_FRaLO_final_report.pdf, last accessed 27.03.2021. Moreover, holding Frontex accountable can be particularly difficult due to other factors too, such as the composite multi-actor nature of its operations decision-making processes. See S. Tas, 'Frontex actions: out of control? The complexity of composite decision-making procedures', TARN Working Paper 03/2020, 2020, available at https://cadmus.eui.eu/bitstream/handle/1814/69417/TAS_2020.pdf?sequence=1&isAllowed=y, last accessed 27.03.2021.

166 Regulation (EU) 2019/1896 of the European Parliament and of the Council of 13 November 2019 on the European Border and Coast Guard and repealing Regulations (EU) No 1052/2013 and (EU) 2016/1624, OJ L 295, Article 111(4) (hereinafter 2019 Frontex Regulation).

in ensuring their effective scrutiny functions over the agency and national authorities, respectively.[167] According to the regulation, the Frontex Executive Director (ED) and the Chairperson of the Management Board shall participate in such interparliamentary meetings, while Frontex must transmit its annual activity reports to national parliaments. NHRIs may exploit their close legal and political relationships with national parliaments to raise any fundamental rights concerns arising from Frontex's activities. For instance, NHRIs may report their concerns to national parliaments and invite them to further escalate alleged fundamental rights violations to the EP and Frontex management.

- *Forced-return operations*: EU law prescribes that forced-return operations of illegally staying third country nationals have to be effectively monitored.[168] To this purpose, Frontex has established a pool of forced-return monitors from competent national authorities.[169] However, different actors, such as FRA, noted that several designated monitoring bodies do not enjoy a sufficient level of independence.[170] As of today, only four Member States entrusted accredited NHRIs with forced-return monitoring functions (Bulgaria, Cyprus, Latvia, Spain).[171] While guaranteeing higher standards, a stronger involvement of Paris Principles-compliant NHRIs in the monitoring of forced-return operations would also align with the recent EP calls.[172]
- *Suspension or termination of an activity*: Article 46 of Regulation 2019/1896 provides that the Frontex ED shall terminate, suspend, or prevent from launching any activity if they consider 'that there are violations of fundamental rights or international protection obligations related to the activity concerned that are of a serious nature or are likely to persist'.[173] To this purpose, the

---

167 Ibid., Article 112.

168 See: Directive 2008/115/EC of the European Parliament and of the Council of 16 December 2008 on common standards and procedures in Member States for returning illegally staying third-country nationals, OJ L 348, Article 8(6); 2019 Frontex Regulation, Article 51.

169 A good overview on the human rights implications of Frontex return operations see M. Gkliati, 'Frontex Return Operations and their Human Rights Implications', in S. Ibrahim and N. Mihaela (eds.), *Deportation of Foreigners: EU instruments, Nation- State practices and social actors' involvement*, Peter Lang Editions, Bern Forthcoming, 10.01.2020.

170 For instance, the monitoring entities of Germany and Sweden are closely connected with national return authorities. In other countries, the forced-return monitoring functions are held by the public prosecutor's office.

171 FRA, 'Forced return monitoring systems – 2020 update', 03.07.2020, available at https://fra.europa.eu/en/publication/2020/forced-return-monitoring-systems-2020-update, last accessed 27.03.2021.

172 In its resolution on the implementation of the return directive, the European Parliament called 'on the Commission to ensure that Member States and Frontex have monitoring bodies in place that are supported by a proper mandate, capacity and competence, a high level of independence and expertise, and transparent procedures'. See European Parliament Resolution on the Return Directive, *supra* note 132, para. 35.

173 This provision was triggered by the first time in January 2021 when, following a judgment from the Court of Justice of the European Union finding the Hungarian asylum law in breach

ED shall take into account a variety of sources, which includes complaints unresolved by a 'national competent authority'. In this context, information provided by NHRIs can contribute to producing credible fundamental rights assessments.[174]

3.2.4. *NHRIs' Responses to COVID-19 in the Field of Asylum and Migration*

Times of emergency often lead to significant restrictions to fundamental freedoms. People at the margins of society, like refugees and migrants, are amongst those mostly affected by liberty-threatening measures. Since the COVID-19 pandemic outbroke, NHRIs have promoted and protected the rights of migrants in different manners. As set out by the Paris Principles, a number of NHRIs have addressed their advice on emergency draft laws to governments towards better human rights compliance.[175] Others have been consulted on national recovery plans.[176] For instance, the Slovenian NHRI questioned the proportionality of the government's attempt to increase capacity at borders through the military, despite the reduced migratory inflows.[177] This advisory role was acknowledged by FRA which encouraged MS to invite NHRIs 'to make recommendations on the fundamental rights implications of draft legislation and policies to improve fundamental rights compliance, including during the state of emergency as recently declared in the context of the COVID-19 pandemic.'[178] NHRIs have also resorted to remote methods of work, such as mobile hotlines, or info-sharing with grassroots and authorities, to continue performing their monitoring functions.[179] Moreover, NHRIs have actively engaged in advocacy and awareness-raising activities. For instance, the Greek NHRI invited the government to promptly tackle the increase in migrant stigmatisation and discrimination through

---

with EU law and fundamental rights, Frontex suspended its operational activities in Hungary. See N. Nielsen, 'Frontex suspends operations in Hungary', *euobserver*, 27.01.2021, available at https://euobserver.com/migration/150744, last accessed 28.03.2021.

174 Recently, MEPs involved in the newly established EP Frontex Scrutiny Working Group questioned the sources used by Frontex to assess the fundamental rights situation on the ground during operations. See European Parliament, 'First meeting of the Frontex Scrutiny Group with Leggeri and Johansson', Press Release, rif.: 20210303IPR99105, 03.03.2021, available at https://www.europarl.europa.eu/news/it/press-room/20210303IPR99105/first-meeting-of-the-frontex-scrutiny-group-with-leggeri-and-johansson, last accessed 28.03.2021.

175 FRA (2020), 'Strong and Effective NHRIs', *supra* note 3, p. 94.

176 Myria, the Belgian Federal Migration Center provided inputs on migrant integration, economic migrants, labour exploitation during government consultations on the national recovery plan. See Myria, 'Fiche de relance', 27.07.2020, available at https://www.myria.be/fr/publications/fiche-de-relance, last accessed 30.03.2021.

177 ENNHRI, 'Protecting the rights of migrants during the pandemic: How have NHRIs responded?', 19.10.2020, available at http://ennhri.org/news-and-blog/protecting-the-rights-of-migrants-during-the-pandemic-how-have-nhris-responded/, last accessed 30.03.2021.

178 FRA (2020), 'Strong and Effective NHRIs', *supra* note 3, p. 15.

179 ENNHRI, 'Protecting the rights of migrants', *supra* note 177.

tailored information campaigns.[180] Finally, worth of note are some successful actions undertaken by the Spanish NHRI during the pandemic. In early 2020, further to the NHRI's calls,[181] all immigration detention centers across Spain were completely evacuated within few months.[182] This extraordinary result was made possible by the joint efforts of the Spanish Ministry of Interior, the Spanish NHRI, local municipalities, the judiciary, detention centres, as well as organisations arranging alternative accommodations for detainees. Further to the issuance of judicial orders, the end of custodial periods, and in due consideration of the lack of reasonable deportation prospects, migrants were released from detention and placed in reception facilities, former places of domicile, or other alternative accommodation solutions. In this context, the NHRI has especially monitored the early releases, while facilitating the allocation of migrants within the national reception system, with special attention to those intending to apply for asylum.[183] The Spanish NHRI's voice proved to carry particular weight in other circumstances too. For instance, in April 2021, following an unannounced visit by the NHRI, the Spanish authorities shut down a quarantine ship due to its inadequate reception and living conditions.[184] Only a day after this decision, 22 women and three kids were already transferred outside of the facility.[185]

In October 2020, ENNHRI launched guidance on fundamental rights border monitoring during a pandemic which drew from European NHRIs' good practices and experiences.[186]

---

180 ENNHRI, 'Protecting the rights of migrants', *supra* note 177.

181 Defensor del Pueblo, 'El defensor traslada a las administraciones las preocupaciones de los ciudadanos en la crisis del coronavirus', 03.04.2020, available at https://www.defensordelpueblo.es/noticias/mas-millar-quejas-covid-19/, last accessed 22.05.2021.

182 M. Majkowska-Tomkin, 'Countries are suspending immigration detention due to coronavirus. Let's keep it that way | View', euronews, 29.04.2020, available at https://www.euronews.com/2020/04/29/countries-suspending-immigration-detention-due-to-coronavirus-let-s-keep-it-that-way-view, last accessed 22.05.2021.

183 Defensor del Pueblo, 'Informe anual 2020 Volumen l. Informe de gestión', Annual Report, Madrid, 2021, pp. 231–232, available at https://www.defensordelpueblo.es/wp-content/uploads/2021/05/Informe_anual_2020-1.pdf, last accessed 22.05.2021.

184 Eldiario, 'Migraciones ordena desalojar la nave para cuarentenas de Fuerteventura tras una denuncia del Defensor del Pueblo sobre sus malas condiciones', 24.04.2021, available at https://www.eldiario.es/canariasahora/migraciones/migraciones-ordena-desalojar-nave-cuarentena-fuerteventura-denuncia-defensor-pueblo-malas-condiciones_1_7855264.html, last accessed 22.05.2021.

185 Eldiario, 'Salen de la nave para cuarentenas de Fuerteventura 22 mujeres y tres niños tras la orden de desalojo de Migraciones', 24.04.2021, available at https://www.eldiario.es/canariasahora/migraciones/salen-nave-cuarentenas-fuerteventura-22-mujeres-tres-ninos-orden-desalojo-migraciones_1_7856081.html, last accessed 22.05.2021.

186 ENNHRI, 'Complementary Guidance – Monitoring human rights of migrants at borders during the COVID-19 pandemic', 13.10.2020, available at http://ennhri.org/news-and-blog/new-resource-for-monitoring-rights-of-migrants-at-borders-during-covid-19/, last accessed 30.03.2021.

4. CONCLUDING REMARKS

European NHRIs operate in one of the most advanced human rights systems worldwide; nevertheless, their potential has not yet been fully exploited by regional actors. This contribution explored the role of these peculiar actors and pointed to some areas where scope for further EU-NHRI cooperation can be identified, to achieve better protection and promotion of human rights in the region.

Recent major EU policy processes in the rule of law field opened a promising, more structured channel for the EU-NHRI cooperation. The past year has seen a rise of EU initiatives aiming at addressing the problematic democratic drifts in the region, and European NHRIs collectively engaged through their regional network ENNHRI on the most impactful ones. This allowed a greater visibility of NHRIs' potential and willingness to be further involved in this area. Their efforts led to the explicit recognition of their possible role in advancing and informing on rule of law issues on the ground, by several EU entities, including the European Commission (DG JUST) and the European Parliament (LIBE Committee), with which ENNHRI has opened a direct channel for cooperation. These EU institutions acknowledged NHRIs' role as a rule of law indicator, their added value on the ground, and solicited their reporting. A trust-based relationship is the first step towards more developed cooperation, *inter alia*, by establishing a more formalised exchange with NHRIs at the regional level, and more systematic collaboration for follow-up at the national level. A specific role for NHRIs as national guardians of the Charter is also a promising avenue for progress.

The new pact on migration and asylum, notably its screening regulation, offered a great opportunity for the EU to better consider the role of NHRIs in promoting and protecting the rights of migrants, including at borders. Through a better involvement in fundamental rights monitoring activities, NHRIs can contribute to bring up higher human rights standards across Europe, while filling the gaps left by the Commission's proposals. For instance, while the screening regulation does not explicitly foresee any access to remedy, NHRIs may guarantee individual access to justice due to their investigative powers and broad mandates. NHRIs may also contribute to the EU agencies' accountability through facilitating their officers' legal scrutiny by the competent authorities. To this purpose, the EU may encourage its JHA agencies to engage more with NHRIs on the ground, including out of the EU territory. This analysis, however, would like to go beyond the pact's proposals. For instance, NHRIs may also serve as a credible info-provider when assessing country-specific fundamental rights situations. In this regard, NHRIs' findings and recommendations can well feed into broader assessment exercises on MS compliance with the Schengen or the asylum *acquis*.

Any additional functions, however, should be assigned to NHRIs with caution. As recommended by FRA and ENNHRI, additional tasks need to come with adequate funding and safeguards. In some MS, the relationship between NHRIs and their governments is grounded on a delicate balance. While performing their functions, NHRIs may raise concerns over their governments' actions or inquiry into national authorities' behaviours. Without adequate safeguards in place, NHRIs may face their governments' disregard, retaliation, or lack of cooperation. This can be a disincentive for NHRIs to take on additional responsibilities, notably when these arise from new regional or international instruments.

Despite the recent considerable progress in the EU-NHRI cooperation, the EU has not yet formalised the recognition of NHRIs and the Paris Principles within its legal and policy frameworks. This gap may be filled in different manners. An EC directive under Article 288 TFEU would seal the highest foundation for a structured EU-NHRI cooperation. The binding nature of such act would guarantee a consistent commitment to effective and independent NHRIs across the EU, while leaving MS a margin to adapt to national contexts. Similarly, the EP may adopt a dedicated resolution on NHRIs. Both acts should encourage MS to strengthen and establish Paris Principles-compliant NHRIs, while formalising their role in areas such as A&M or rule of law. The Council of the EU has already called on MS, the Commission, FRA, as well as other Union institutions, bodies and agencies to enhance cooperation with NHRIs and support their independent mandates.[187]

A closer EU-NHRI engagement may give NHRIs' findings and recommendations more weight and encourage MS to better consider and follow up on these, for improved fundamental rights situations at the national level. By interacting with NHRIs, the EU can get credible human rights insights from the ground and inform its actions and policies accordingly. At the same time, NHRIs can become a driving force for human rights in wider Europe, bringing up European standards when working on A&M, rule of law, among other areas. Through NHRIs, the 'nationalisation' of EU standards and the 'Europeanisation' of national issues can advance hand in hand.

Finally, the COVID-19 context further demonstrated the importance of supporting and guaranteeing independent, strong and effective institutions. The crisis caused by the pandemic and the often securitarian governmental responses already impacted a wide range of human rights and announce worrying long-term effects. In this context, NHRIs proved to be central actors to inform, alert, advise and report on these new challenges, a role which was recognised by EU institutions.

[187] Council of the European Union, 12357/19, para. 22, *supra* note 4.

PART III

JURISPRUDENCE BY THE COURTS

THE RIGHT TO AN EFFECTIVE (AND JUDICIAL) EXAMINATION OF ELECTION COMPLAINTS

Eirik HOLMØYVIK

ABSTRACT

In its case law the European Court of Human Rights (ECtHR, the Court) holds the effective examination of election complaints as one of the essential guarantees of free and fair elections. For just over a decade, the Court has adopted an institutional approach to election disputes by interpreting Article 3 of Protocol No. 1 to the European Convention of Human Rights (ECHR) to contain a positive obligation for states to maintain a domestic system for effective examination of individual complaints and appeals concerning electoral rights. This contribution endeavours to provide an overview of the procedural requirements for effective examination as developed in the case law and what it means for existing election dispute resolution systems in the Member States. In particular, this contribution argues that the seminal Grand Chamber decision in *Mugemangango v Belgium* from 2020 will require fundamental changes in all Member States where parliament is the judge of its own elections. On a more general level, the contribution argues that this decision may herald a shift in the Court's traditionally state deferent approach to Article 3 of Protocol No. 1 in favour of a more substantive approach to democracy.

1. INTRODUCTION

Democracy lies at the heart of the European Convention of Human Rights (ECHR).[1] Its preamble maintains that fundamental freedoms 'are best maintained by an effective political democracy'. In its case law, the European Court of Human Rights (ECtHR) has also underscored that '[d]emocracy is without doubt a fundamental feature of the European public order.'[2] Articles 10 on freedom of expression and 11 on the right to assembly are key prerequisites for a well-functioning democracy, and clauses in other convention rights require interferences to be necessary in a democratic society. Whilst these concepts are well known from the ECtHR's case law, Article 3 of Protocol No. 1 of the ECHR also protects the fundamental element of democracy itself, which underpins the other Convention rights. This is the right to 'free elections at reasonable intervals by secret ballot, under conditions which will ensure the free expression of the opinion of the people in the choice of the legislature'.

As of 2020, the ECtHR and the Commission before it had found violations of Article 3 of Protocol No. 1 in 102 cases, with 54 of them in the last ten years.[3] While violations of Article 3 of Protocol 1 only make up a tiny fraction (0.5%) of the total number of violations found by the ECtHR, the number of complaints is increasing, and a number of important decisions in recent years suggests that the ECtHR has added new emphasis on the right to free elections for the Convention system.[4]

Commentators have previously remarked that Article 3 of Protocol No. 1 is an 'unsatisfactory text, which is the result of a compromise, and which continues to give rise to problems of interpretation.'[5] Unlike the other articles of

---

1 On the concept of democracy in the ECHR, see H.-M. Ten Napel, 'The European Court of Human Rights and political rights: the need for more guidance', (2009) 5(3), *E.C.L. Review*, pp. 464–480.

2 ECtHR, *United Communist Party of Turkey v Turkey*, no 19392/92, 30.01.1998, para. 45; ECtHR, *Refah Partisi (The Welfare Party) and Others v Turkey*, nos 41340/98, 41342/98, 41343/98 and 41344/98 [GC] 13.02.2003, para. 86.

3 European Court of Human Rights, 'Overview 1959–2020 ECHR', February 2021, available at https://www.echr.coe.int/Documents/Overview_19592020_ENG.pdf, pp. 8–9, last accessed 02.07.2021.

4 B. Rainey, P. McCormick and C. Ovey, *Jacobs, White, and Ovey: The European Convention on Human Rights*, 8th edition, Oxford University Press, Oxford 2020, p. 611.

5 See B. Rainey, P. McCormick and C. Ovey (2020), *Jacobs, White, and Ovey: The European Convention on Human Rights*, *supra* note 4, p. 610. In a similar vein, see M. O'Boyle, 'Electoral

the ECHR, the text of Article 3 of Protocol No. 1 does not refer to an individual right, nor does it contain explicit limitations to such a right. Both the individual right and its implied limitations inferred by the Commission were confirmed by the ECtHR in the first case where it had to apply Article 3 of Protocol No. 1, *Mathieu-Mohin and Clerfayt v Belgium* in 1987.[6]

One issue that has long been unclear is whether and to what extent the right to free elections in Article 3 of Protocol No. 1 also requires a judicial remedy and procedural guarantees for electoral disputes. The terse text offers little guidance other than the concept of 'free elections' with the aim to 'ensure the free expression of the opinion of the people'. Indeed, since its early case law, the ECtHR has drawn a sharp distinction between, on the one hand, civil rights and obligations and criminal charges, enjoying access to court and the procedural guarantees of a fair trial according to Article 6, and the so-called 'political rights' enshrined in Article 3 of Protocol No. 1, to which Article 6 does not apply.[7] In contrast, General Comment No. 25 to the International Covenant on Civil of Political Rights (ICCPR) makes it clear that the equivalent Article 25 of that instrument also includes an access to judicial review.[8]

However, in recent years the ECtHR has recognised a positive obligation flowing from Article 3 of Protocol No. 1 for the Member States to provide an effective examination of electoral disputes. Such minimum procedural requirements for election dispute resolution have long been recognised by non-binding Council of Europe 'soft law' documents. In the wider Council of Europe system, too, there has been a growing emphasis on election dispute resolution.[9]

---

disputes and the ECHR: an overview', in *The Cancellation of Election Results, Science and Technique of Democracy No. 46*, Council of Europe Publishing, Strasbourg 2010, pp. 39–55.

6 ECtHR, *Mathieu-Mohin and Clerfayt v Belgium*, no 9267/81, 02.03.1987, paras. 48–52. From the Commission's case law, see ECtHR, *W., X., Y. et Z. c. Belgique*, nos 6745/74, 6746/74, 30.05.197. On the development, see A. Ruiz Robledo, 'The Construction of the Right to Free Elections by the European Court of Human Rights', (2018) 7(2), *Cambridge International Law Journal*, pp. 225–240; S. Golubok, 'The Right to Free Elections: Emerging Guarantees or Two Layers of Protection?', (2009) 27(3), *Netherlands Quarterly of Human Rights*, pp. 361–390.

7 ECtHR, *Pierre Bloch v France*, no 24194/94, 21.10.1997, paras. 50–51; ECtHR, *Cheminade v France*, no 31599/96, 26.01.1999. This interpretation had previously been made by the Commission, see EComHR, *Priorello v Italy*, no 11068/84, 06.05.1985; EComHR, *I. Z. v Greece*, no 18997/91, 28.02.1994.

8 CCPR General Comment No. 25, para. 20: 'There should be independent scrutiny of the voting and counting process and access to judicial review or other equivalent process so that electors have confidence in the security of the ballot and the counting of the votes.'

9 Election dispute resolution was the topic for the 16th European Conference for Electoral Management Bodies in 2019. In 2020 the Venice Commission published a report on election dispute resolution, containing an extensive overview of national approaches and regulations of key elements of election dispute resolution, such as competent bodies, grounds for complaints, standing, time limits, procedural issues, and decision-making power. See Venice Commission, 'CDL-AD(2020)025, Report on election dispute resolution', 08.10.2020, available at https://www.venice.coe.int/webforms/documents/?pdf=CDL-AD(2020)025-e, last accessed 06.07.2021.

This development culminated in the seminal ECtHR Grand Chamber judgment *Mugemangango v Belgium* on 10 July 2020, which may herald an end to the long-established Western European model of parliament being the judge of its own election.

This development raises the question as to what effective examination of election disputes implies as a positive obligation for Member States. To answer this question, I will perform a legal-dogmatic analysis of the ECtHR's case law leading up to and including *Mugemangango v Belgium*. The aim in section 3 is to provide an overview of the procedural requirements for effective examination flowing from Article 3 of Protocol No. 1 based on the case law. However, since effective examination has long been a requirement in the Venice Commission's Code of Good Practice in Electoral Matters, I will first in section 2 discuss what elements of effective examination can be deduced from this document and the Commission's country-specific opinions on electoral law. The purpose of doing this is two-fold. First, the notion of effective examination in a key Council of Europe standard on electoral law serves as a relevant backdrop and point of reference to the subsequent development of an effective examination requirement by the ECtHR. Second, certain reservations in the Grand Chamber's reasoning in *Mugemangango v Belgium* may bring it at odds with the Venice Commission's understanding of effective examination of election complaints. Indeed, while the Grand Chamber concluded in the specific case that the Belgian model of Parliament being the judge of its own election did not provide sufficient guarantees for an effective examination of election disputes, it is not clear from the decision whether this model is in itself incompatible with Article 3 of Protocol No. 1. In section 4 I therefore discuss whether and how the right to effective examination of election disputes can be considered a structural right that would require Belgium and other Member States where parliament is the judge of its own election to change their election dispute resolution systems.

2. EFFECTIVE EXAMINATION ACCORDING TO COUNCIL OF EUROPE 'SOFT LAW' STANDARDS

Within the Council of Europe system, the arguably most important and well established standard for electoral legislation is the Venice Commission's Code of Good Practice in Electoral Matters, adopted in 2002.[10] This document has

[10] Venice Commission, 'CDL-AD(2002)23, Code of Good Practice in Electoral Matters', 30.10.2002, available at https://www.venice.coe.int/webforms/documents/default.aspx?pdffile=CDL-AD(2002)023rev2-cor-e, last accessed 02.07.2021.

been the mainstay of the Venice Commission's more than 130 opinions on electoral law in its Member States and more than 60 texts of general character on elections, referendums, and political parties.[11]

Unlike Article 3 of Protocol No. 1 of the ECHR, the Code of Good Practice in Electoral Matters lists an efficient system of appeal as one of several procedural guarantees for implementing the principles considered as Europe's electoral heritage: 'universal, equal, free, secret and direct suffrage.'[12]

3.3. An effective system of appeal

A. The appeal body in electoral matters should be either an electoral commission or a court. For elections to parliament, an appeal to parliament may be provided for in first instance. In any case, final appeal to a court must be possible.

B. The procedure must be simple and devoid of formalism, in particular concerning the admissibility of appeals.

C. The appeal procedure and, in particular, the powers and responsibilities of the various bodies should be clearly regulated by law, so as to avoid conflicts of jurisdiction (whether positive or negative). Neither the appellants nor the authorities should be able to choose the appeal body.

D. The appeal body must have authority in particular over such matters as the right to vote – including electoral registers – and eligibility, the validity of candidatures, proper observance of election campaign rules and the outcome of the elections.

E. The appeal body must have authority to annul elections where irregularities may have affected the outcome. It must be possible to annul the entire election or merely the results for one constituency or one polling station. In the event of annulment, a new election must be called in the area concerned.

F. All candidates and all voters registered in the constituency concerned must be entitled to appeal. A reasonable quorum may be imposed for appeals by voters on the results of elections.

G. Time-limits for lodging and deciding appeals must be short (three to five days for each at first instance).

H. The applicant's right to a hearing involving both parties must be protected.

I. Where the appeal body is a higher electoral commission, it must be able ex officio to rectify or set aside decisions taken by lower electoral commissions.

---

11 See P. Craig, 'Transnational Constitution-Making: The Contribution of the Venice Commission on Law and Democracy', (2017) 2, *UC Irvine Journal of International, Transnational, and Comparative Law*, p. 63. On the statistics, see Venice Commission, 'Election and referendums, political parties', 2021, available at https://www.venice.coe.int/WebForms/pages/?p=01_Elections_and_Referendums, last accessed 02.07.2021.

12 Venice Commission (2002), 'Code of Good Practice in Electoral Matters', *supra* note 10, Guideline II.3.3.

From this list, five requirements for an effective examination of election complaints can be outlined.

First, an independence and impartiality requirement can be identified. The appeal body should be either an electoral commission or a court, which implies that the appeal body must be independent and impartial.[13] Due to this requirement, the Code does not accept parliament as the final appeal body in parliamentary elections. While the Code requires a final appeal to a 'court', this wording should not be taken literally. The explanatory report to the Code refers to 'a judicial appeal', which implies a functional approach comprising also bodies formally not designated as courts, but which offer the same guarantees of independence and impartiality as well as a judicial procedure.[14] In its 2010 opinion on the electoral law of Norway, the Venice Commission found that the Norwegian model of parliament being the sole and final judge of its own election was incompatible with European standards and that complaints on the election result should be ultimately decided by a 'high judicial body, such as the Supreme Court'.[15] As mentioned above and to be discussed in section 4 below, ten years later the ECtHR arrived at the same conclusion in the case of *Mugemangango v Belgium* concerning the similar Belgian model. However, it is not clear whether the ECtHR shares the Venice Commission's firm position that an appeal to a judicial body must always be possible.

Second, we can identify an access to justice requirement, by demanding simple and effective complaints procedures and standing for all candidates and voters in the constituency. Any violation of electoral law should be considered legitimate for grounds for appeal.[16] In its country-specific opinions, the Venice Commission has criticised excessive costs and opaque formal requirements that result in a high inadmissibility rate.[17]

Third, there is a legality requirement, meaning that the appeal procedure and the powers of the various must be clearly regulated by law.

Fourth, there is an effective remedy requirement. States must ensure that the appeal body has the necessary powers to rectify the whole spectrum of

---

13 See Venice Commission (2002), 'Code of Good Practice in Electoral Matters', *supra* note 10, Guideline II.3.1, which requires electoral commissions to be independent and impartial.

14 Venice Commission (2002), 'Code of Good Practice in Electoral Matters', *supra* note 10, para. 94.

15 Venice Commission, 'CDL-AD(2010)046, Joint Opinion on the Electoral Legislation of Norway', 22.12.2010, para. 44, available at https://www.venice.coe.int/webforms/documents/default.aspx?pdffile=CDL-AD(2010)046-e, last accessed 06.07.2021.

16 Venice Commission (2002), 'Code of Good Practice in Electoral Matters', *supra* note 10, para. 92. See also more specifically in Venice Commission (2020), 'Report on Election Dispute Resolution', *supra* note 9, paras. 49–52.

17 Venice Commission, 'CDL-AD(2009)001, Joint Opinion on the Election Code of Georgia as revised up to July 2008', 09.01.2009, paras. 109, 115, and 117, available at https://www.venice.coe.int/webforms/documents/default.aspx?pdffile=CDL-AD(2009)001-e, last accessed 06.07.2021.

errors, from correcting errors in the voter lists to annulling the elections where irregularities have affected the outcome. Moreover, an effective remedy in the electoral context requires short time limits for lodging and deciding appeals. In electoral procedures, the time element is highly important, which makes violation of rights impossible to rectify after certain deadlines, for example, the exercise of voting rights after election day.

Finally, the Code requires a fair hearing of election complaints. In the explanatory report, the Venice Commission states that the 'appeal procedure should be of a judicial nature'.[18] In its country-specific opinions on electoral legislation, the Venice Commission has interpreted the fair hearing requirement to include the right to present evidence in support of the complaint after it is filed (a contradictory procedure), the right to a fair, public, and transparent hearing of the complaint, and the right to appeal the decision on the complaint to a court.[19]

In *Mungemangango v Belgium*, the Grand Chamber invited the Venice Commission to submit an *amicus curiae* opinion. In that opinion, the Venice Commission summarised the Code's procedural requirements for an effective examination of election complaints as 'similar to those of Article 6 of the ECHR, but account must be taken of the specific context of elections. For example, a balance must be struck between the length and scope of hearings and the need to resolve electoral disputes promptly.'[20]

While the Code of Good Practice in Electoral Matters is not legally binding for the Venice Commission's 62 Member States,[21] it may nonetheless be considered as the Council of Europe's minimum standard for electoral law and has since its adoption in 2002 been the basis of the Commission's country specific recommendations. The Code is also frequently referred to by the ECtHR in cases concerning Article 3 of Protocol No. 1 and appears to have been

---

18 Venice Commission (2002), 'Code of Good Practice in Electoral Matters', *supra* note 10, para. 100.

19 See e.g. Venice Commission, 'CDL-AD(2006)013, Joint Recommendations on the Laws on Parliamentary, Presidential and Local Elections, and Electoral Administration in the Republic of Serbia', 23.03.2006, para. 65, available at https://www.venice.coe.int/webforms/documents/?pdf=CDL-AD(2006)013-e, last accessed 06.07.2021.

20 Venice Commission, 'CDL-AD(2019)021, Amicus Curiae Brief for the European Court of Human Rights in the Case of *Mugemangango v Belgium* on Procedural Safeguards which a State Must Ensure in Procedures Challenging the Result of an Election or the Distribution of Seats', 19.12.2019, para. 49, available at https://www.venice.coe.int/webforms/documents/?pdf=CDL-AD(2019)021-e, last accessed 06.07.2021.

21 On the impact of Venice Commission soft law standards, see W. Hoffmann-Riem, 'The Venice Commission of the Council of Europe – Standards and Impact', (2014) 25(2), *The European Journal of International Law*, pp. 579–597, and P. Craig (2017), 'Transnational Constitution-Making: The Contribution of the Venice Commission on Law and Democracy', *supra* note 11, pp. 80–85.

influential on the interpretation of the ECHR in some cases.[22] As we shall see below, the ECtHR has developed its effective examination requirement largely consistent with that of the Code, yet it does not prove a normative influence of the latter. It might be more correct, as suggested by Hoffmann-Riem, to say that the Code and other Venice Commission standards and opinions serve as sources of information and inspiration to the ECtHR.[23] Notably in *Petkov and Others v Bulgaria* from 2009, explicit reference was made to the Code in what is possibly the first decision where the ECtHR referred to effectiveness as a standard for assessing post-electoral rights, in this case the failure of complying with court decisions allowing candidates to stand for election. Here:

> the Court observes that an effective system of electoral appeals, as described in the Venice Commission's Code of Good Practice in Electoral Matters (see paragraph 52 above), is an important safeguard against arbitrariness in the electoral process. Failure to abide by final decisions given in response to such appeals undoubtedly undermines the effectiveness of such a system.[24]

However, soft law documents are only advisory to the Member States and have never been considered decisive by the ECtHR.[25] Indeed, in *Mugemangango v Belgium*, the Grand Chamber noted that it 'will have regard, where necessary, to the standards developed and the recommendations issued by other European and international bodies, without, however, treating them as decisive […]'.[26]

---

22 See e.g. ECtHR, *Davydov and Others v Russia*, no 75947/11, 30.05.2017, paras. 283–288; ECtHR, *Riza and Others v Bulgaria*, nos 48555/10 and 48377/10, 13.10.2015, paras. 177–179; *Karimov v Azerbaijan*, no 12535/06, 25.09.2014, para. 39; *Grosaru v Romania*, no 78039/01, 02.03.2010, paras. 56–57; ECtHR, *Petkov and Others v Bulgaria*, nos 77568/01, 178/02, and 505/02, 11.06.2009. An explicit example concerning guidelines for the financing of political parties, see ECtHR, *Parti nationaliste basque – Organisation régionale d'Iparralde v France*, no 71251/01, 07.06.2007, para. 47. On the influence of the Venice Commission on the ECtHR's interpretation of Article 3 of Protocol No. 1, see S. Golubok (2009), 'The Right to Free Elections: Emerging Guarantees or Two Layers of Protection?', *supra* note 6, pp. 386–389 and L. Bode-Kirchhoff, 'Why the Road from Luxembourg to Strasbourg Leads Through Venice', in K. Dzehtsiarou et al. (eds.), *Human Rights Law in Europe: The Influence, Overlaps and Contradictions of the EU and ECHR*, Routledge, London and New York 2014, pp. 55–72, on p. 59. On the interaction between the ECtHR and the Venice Commission in general, see G. Buquicchio and S. Granata-Menghini, 'The interaction between the Venice Commission and the European Court of Human Rights: Anticipation, Consolidation, Coordination of Human Rights Protection in Europe', in L-A. Sicilianos, I. A. Motoc and R. Chenal (eds.), *Regards Croisés sur la Protection Nationale et Internationale des Droits de L'homme / Intersecting Views on National and International Human Rights Protection: Liber Amicorum Guido Raimondi*, Wolf Legal Publishers, Tilburg 2019, pp. 35–50.

23 W. Hoffmann-Riem, 'The Venice Commission of the Council of Europe – Standards and Impact', *supra* note 21, p. 587.

24 ECtHR, *Petkov and Others v Bulgaria, supra* note 22, para. 63.

25 See ECtHR, *Partei die Friesen v Germany*, no 65480/10, 28.01.2016, para. 43; ECtHR, *Muršić v Croatia*, no 7334/13 [GC] 20.10.2016, para. 111.

26 ECtHR, *Mugemangango v Belgium*, no 310/15 [GC] 10.07.2020, para. 99.

This approach to non-binding soft law documents is necessary since the ECHR is legally binding for the Member States. While the ECHR is the 'primary yardstick' in the Venice Commission's work,[27] it would certainly be problematic for the Commission and the legitimacy of its and other Council of Europe standards if the ECtHR without convincing reasons explicitly departed from long-held general principles in the Code of Good Practice in Electoral Matters. In my view, it would be wrong to consider *Mugemangango v Belgium* as a departure from the Venice Commission's requirements for effective examination in the Code of Good Practice in Electoral Matters. Yet, as will be discussed in more detail in section 4 below, the decision can be read as taking a more nuanced approach to the independence and impartiality requirement.

3. EFFECTIVE EXAMINATION ACCORDING TO ARTICLE 3 OF PROTOCOL NO. 1 TO THE ECHR

3.1. A TWO-STEP TEST

In its earlier case law, the ECtHR as well as the Commission before it limited its scrutiny of decisions of election complaint bodies to testing for arbitrariness in the outcome in the specific case.[28] While the ECtHR still assesses arbitrariness in relation to the electoral process including election complaints,[29] the Court has in recent years also adopted a more institutional approach, by interpreting Article 3 of Protocol No. 1 to contain a positive obligation for states to maintain a domestic system for effective examination of individual complaints and appeals concerning electoral rights.

In *Namat Aliyev v Azerbaijan* from 2010, and reiterated in several subsequent decisions, the ECtHR held that such a system 'is one of the essential guarantees of free and fair elections' and 'an important device at the State's disposal in achieving the fulfilment of its positive duty under Article 3 of Protocol No. 1'.[30] The state would therefore have a positive obligation under Article 3 of Protocol No. 1 to establish and maintain a legislative framework that provides effective

---

[27] See L. Bode-Kirchhoff, 'Why the Road from Luxembourg to Strasbourg Leads Through Venice', *supra* note 22, p. 57–58.

[28] See ECtHR, *Babenko v Ukraine*, 43476/98, 04.05.1999, and see EComHR, *I.Z. v Greece*, no 18997/91, 28.02.1994.

[29] See e.g. ECtHR, *Kovach v Ukraine*, no 39424/02, 07.02.2008.

[30] See ECtHR, *Namat Aliyev v Azerbaijan*, no 18705/06, 08.04.2010, para. 81. See similarly in ECtHR, *Gahramanli and Others v Azerbaijan*, no 36503/11, 08.10.2015, para. 69. Similarly in the 2009 decision *Petkov and Others v Bulgaria*, the ECtHR referring to the Code of Good Practice in Electoral Matters stated that an effective system of electoral appeals was an important safeguard against arbitrariness in the electoral process, see ECtHR, *Petkov and Others v Bulgaria, supra* note 22, para. 63.

examination of election disputes.[31] As a systemic obligation, the effective examination approach is typically applied where there are shortcomings of the electoral complaint system which considered individually may not violate Article 3 of Protocol No. 1, but which taken together risks arbitrariness and thus undermining individual electoral rights, the general confidence in the election administration, and the integrity of the election result. In *Gahramanli and Others v Azerbaijan* from 2015 for example, the ECtHR shied away from concluding that the composition of electoral commissions was in itself incompatible with an impartiality requirement under Article 3 of Protocol No. 1. Instead, the Court noted that 'the method in question was one of the systemic factors contributing to the ineffectiveness of the examination'.[32]

Being a systemic obligation, the effective examination test does not require the applicant to prove or the ECtHR to find specific breaches of the national electoral law that affected the election result. In line with its subsidiary role and similar to its approach to Article 13, the ECtHR applies the effective examination test in two steps.[33] First, the applicant must put forward 'a very serious and arguable claim disclosing an appearance of a failure to hold free and fair elections in his constituency'.[34] In doing so, the ECtHR appears to rely on evidence provided by the applicant as well as election observation reports from international observers. Second, the ECtHR will then consider whether the election complaints system in the state concerned provided an effective examination of the applicant's complaint. While the effective examination test is clearly inspired by the right to an effective remedy in Article 13, the ECtHR has emphasised that it is a distinct positive obligation under Article 3 of Protocol No. 1. As such, it can be regarded as containing procedural requirements specific for election complaints. The ECtHR will only find a separate violation of Article 13 if the electoral complaint has not been subject to review by a domestic court and the examination by other state bodies has not been effective.[35]

3.2. PROCEDURAL REQUIREMENTS FOR EFFECTIVE EXAMINATION

Unlike the Venice Commission, the ECtHR has not detailed the basic requirements for a domestic system of effective examination of electoral

31 See ECtHR, *Paunović and Milivojević v Serbia*, no 41683/06, 24.05.2016, para. 61.

32 ECtHR, *Gahramanli and Others v Azerbaijan*, *supra* note 30, para. 79.

33 See e.g. *Mugemangango v Belgium*, *supra* note 26, para. 79. Compare the approach to Article 13 in ECtHR, *Ilhan v Turkey*, no 22277/93 [GC] 27.06.2000, para. 97.

34 ECtHR, *Namat Aliyev*, *supra* note 30, para. 79; ECtHR, *Davydov and Others v Russia*, *supra* note 22, paras. 289 and 312.

35 See e.g. *Riza and Others v Bulgaria*, *supra* note 22, paras. 94–95; ECtHR, *Grosaru v Romania*, *supra* note 22, paras. 55–56, and 62.

disputes according to Article 3 of Protocol No. 1 or Article 13. However, the same procedural requirements have been applied in and can be inferred from the case law.

Considering access to justice, the ECtHR, referring to the Venice Commission's Code of Good Practice in Electoral Matters, found in *Namat Aliyev* that a rigid and formalistic approach, which denied the applicants judicial review of election complaints on procedural grounds, was incompatible with Article 3 of Protocol No. 1.[36]

As for effective remedy, the ECtHR has found this to be a positive obligation also under Article 3 of Protocol No. 1. The ECtHR has emphasised the importance of a timely decision of the election dispute bodies to allow the applicants to exercise their rights – for example due to registration deadlines, election day or the finalisation of the election result. For the same reason, short deadlines for launching election complaints are acceptable.[37] In *Gahramanli and Others*, an effective remedy was denied the applicants since the Constitutional Court finalised the election result before the election complaints had been decided in the appeal system.[38] In *Abdalov and Others v Azerbaijan*, the Supreme Court corrected erroneous decisions by lower courts which had prevented the applicants to register as a candidate, but at that time the applicants had irretrievably lost much time for campaigning.[39]

For a domestic system of election complaints to provide an effective remedy under Article 3 of Protocol No. 1, the competent bodies must also have jurisdiction to consider election complaints and the necessary powers to remedy irregularities, for example by annulling the election or by restoring a mandate unlawfully deprived from a candidate. In case the domestic electoral dispute resolution system does not allow for the complaint to be examined by a court and left the complaint to be decided by an administrative or parliamentary body, the ECtHR has found a violation of Article 13 in conjunction with Article 3 of Protocol No. 1. In *Grosaru v Romania* from 2010 and *Mugemangango v Belgium* from 2020, the courts simply didn't have jurisdiction to consider complaints on the decisions of Parliament finalising the election result.[40] In *Paunović and Milivojević v Serbia* from 2016, courts had jurisdiction to consider the applicant's electoral complaint, but due to domestic procedural law, the

---

36 See ECtHR, *Namat Aliyev*, *supra* note 30, para. 85.

37 See ECtHR, *Etxeberria and Others v Spain*, nos 35579/03, 35613/03, 35626/03 and 35634/03, 30.06.2009, paras. 78–82.

38 ECtHR, *Gahramanli and Others v Azerbaijan*, *supra* note 30, para. 86. See also ECtHR, *Namat Aliyev*, *supra* note 30, para. 84.

39 See ECtHR, *Abdalov and Others v Azerbaijan*, nos 28508/11, 37602/11 and 43776/11, 11.07.2019, para. 100.

40 See ECtHR, *Grosaru v Romania*, *supra* note 22, paras. 54–56 and 58–62; ECtHR, *Mugemangango v Belgium*, *supra* note 26, paras. 135–139. See also ECtHR, *Ofensiva tinerilor v Roumania*, no 16732/05, 15.12.2015, para. 60.

competent courts lacked the powers to restore the applicant's mandate.[41] In *Petkov and Others v Bulgaria* from 2009, the problem was that while courts might have had the necessary powers, domestic rules on standing precluded the applicants from initiating court procedures directly.[42]

However, the positive obligation for the state is not limited to offer judicial review of election complaints if the competent judicial bodies do not engage in an effective examination in the specific case. In *Davydov and Others v Russia* from 2017, the problem was that courts competent to perform an independent and effective review refrained from doing so despite serious and arguable claims of serious irregularities in the counting and tabulation of votes that could impact the election result.[43] The ECtHR accepted that the right of individual voters to appeal against the election result may be subject to reasonable limitations in domestic law. Yet the ECtHR found that the state had failed to set up a system of effective examination, since no court would go into the substance of the allegations of serious irregularities.[44] In a number of cases involving Azerbaijan, the ECtHR has found that the whole election dispute resolution system is failed in the sense that despite formal guarantees, courts and electoral commission has shown no genuine concern for upholding the rule of law and protecting the integrity of the election.[45]

Considering legality, although Article 3 of Protocol No. 1 – unlike other convention rights – does not explicitly contain a legality requirement, it is nonetheless considered an implied limitation of the states' discretion in order to prevent arbitrary interferences in electoral rights.[46] As a result, the ECtHR has found violations when decisions on electoral rights were not based on rules set out clearly and foreseeably in domestic law.[47] Obviously, this also applies to the appeals procedure in deciding election complaints. In *Mugemangango v Belgium*, the ECtHR framed the legality requirement as preventing excessive discretion of the body deciding on the election complaint, which may otherwise

---

41 ECtHR, *Paunović and Milivojević v Serbia, supra* note 31, paras. 46–48.

42 See ECtHR, *Petkov and Others v Bulgaria, supra* note 22, para. 82. See also ECtHR, *Russian Conservative Party of Entrepreneurs and Others v Russia*, no 55066/00 and 55638/00, 11.01.2007, paras. 88–89.

43 See ECtHR, *Davydov and Others v Russia, supra* note 22.

44 See similarly in ECtHR, *Political Party 'Patria' and Others v the Republic of Moldova*, no 5113/15 and 14 others, 04.08.2020.

45 See ECtHR, *Namat Aliyev, supra* note 30, para. 90; ECtHR, *Kerimli and Alibeyli v Azerbaijan*, nos 18475/06 and 22444/06, 10.01.2012, para. 41; ECtHR, *Karimov v Azerbaijan, supra* note 22, para. 49; ECtHR, *Mammadov v Azerbaijan (No 2)*, no 4641/06, 10.01.2012, paras. 58–59; ECtHR, *Gahramanli and Others v Azerbaijan, supra* note 30, para. 87; ECtHR, *Tahirov v Azerbaijan*, no 31953/11, 11.06.2015, para. 70. The systemic problem in Azerbaijan with arbitrary refusals of candidate registration has led the ECtHR to finding a violation in numerous Committee decisions following the *Tahirov* decision, see ECtHR, *Abdalov and Others v Azerbaijan, supra* note 39, para. 98.

46 See ECtHR, *Ždanoka v Latvia*, no 58278/00, 16.03.2006, para. 108.

47 See ECtHR, *Riza and Others v Bulgaria, supra* note 22, para. 176.

lead to arbitrary decisions.[48] In that case, the ECtHR found that the powers of the Walloon Parliament were not circumscribed with sufficient precision, as no established procedural rules existed, and the election complaint was decided according to ad hoc rules.

As for fair hearing, the ECtHR in several cases has addressed procedural guarantees – such as adversarial proceedings, equality of arms and transparency through reasoned proceedings – as elements in an effective examination. In *Namat Aliyev v Azerbaijan*, the ECtHR noted that states might find it hard to abide by strict procedural safeguards and to deliver very detailed decisions within the short time-limits necessary to avoid delaying the electoral process.[49] Yet the Court did not accept that such considerations undermined the effectiveness of the appeal procedure. In that that case, for example, the competent electoral commission had relied exclusively on the statements of election officials, and in the subsequent judicial procedure, the courts did not allow the applicant to submit additional evidence. Likewise, in *Gahramanli and Others v Azerbaijan* and in *G.K. v Belgium*, the applicants were not allowed to defend their interests before the body deciding their complaints, and the decisions lacked reasoning.[50] In *Uspaskich v Lithuania* on the other hand, the ECtHR found no violation and noted that the applicant was represented by a lawyer before both the Central Electoral Commission and the courts, and the applicant's complaints were dismissed in reasoned decisions.[51] Indeed, in its earlier case law, and reiterated in *Mugemangango v Belgium* in 2020, the ECtHR found that a judicial procedure in which the applicant has been allowed to defend his interests in adversarial proceedings and where arguments have been duly considered by a court, would normally satisfy the requirements of Article 3 of Protocol No. 1.[52]

Finally, as for the independence and impartiality requirement, the ECtHR has in general placed significant emphasis on impartiality for election administration bodies.[53] Naturally, the impartiality requirement has also been extended to bodies deciding election complaints. In *Mugemangango v Belgium* from 2020, the Grand Chamber clarified the impartiality requirement in

---

48 ECtHR, *Mugemangango v Belgium*, *supra* note 26, paras. 109–114. See however the objections in the concurring opinion of Judges Lemmens and Sabato.

49 ECtHR, *Namat Aliyev v Azerbaijan*, *supra* note 30, para. 90.

50 ECtHR, *Gahramanli and Others v Azerbaijan*, *supra* note 30, paras. 85–87; ECtHR, *G.K. v Belgium*, no 58302/10, 21.05.2019, paras. 60–61.

51 ECtHR, *Uspaskich v Lithuania*, no 14737/08, 20.12.2016, para. 94.

52 See ECtHR, *Babenko v Ukraine*, *supra* note 28; ECtHR, *Mugemangango v Belgium*, *supra* note 26, para. 139.

53 Article 3 of Protocol No. 1 requires the body 'in charge of electoral administration to function in a transparent manner and to maintain impartiality and independence from political manipulation', see ECtHR, *Georgian Labour Party v Georgia*, no 9103/04, 08.07.2008, para. 101. See also ECtHR, *Podkolzina v Latvia*, no 46726/99, 09.04.2002, para. 35; ECtHR, *Riza and Others v Bulgaria*, *supra* note 22, para. 143.

Article 3 of Protocol No. 1 by interpreting it in light of the corresponding requirement in Article 6.[54] In doing so, the Grand Chamber at least partly departed from the old maxim that the so-called political rights according to Article 3 of Protocol No. 1 do not fall under and enjoy the procedural guarantees offered by Article 6. Consistent with the case law under Article 6, we should therefore consider impartiality has having both a subjective and objective component also in relation to Article 3 of Protocol No. 1.

While the ECtHR has not as a general rule dismissed that bodies composed of politicians can be considered impartial, a collegial body in which a majority are politicians is clearly problematic. The ECtHR has previously held that members of parliament cannot be considered neutral in an electoral context.[55] In *Grosaru v Romania* from 2010, the ECtHR found guarantees for impartiality lacking, since the applicant's complaint on the election result was decided first by the Central Election Office and then in the final instance by the chamber of deputies in Parliament. The latter – being a solely political body – was clearly not impartial, but the ECtHR also found that the Central Election Office could not be considered impartial despite the fact that seven of its members were judges, since a majority of 16 members were representatives of the political parties.[56] In line with this reasoning, the Grand Chamber found a violation in *Mugemangango v Belgium*, where only parliament itself was competent to pronounce on election complaints. Here, the Grand Chamber noted that the plenary in the Walloon Parliament deciding the election complaint included all newly elected members, including those that had yet to have their credentials approved, as well as the members elected from the applicant's constituency, and who were his direct opponents.[57] Following this reasoning, a guiding principle for assessing the impartiality of a body deciding election disputes, should be whether or not the majority of its members represent political parties.

However, in *Mugemangango v Belgium*, the Grand Chamber refrained from explicitly requiring appeals on the election result to be decided by a judicial body. Recall here the position of the Venice Commission in the Code of Good Practice in Electoral Matters, which requires such decision to be made by a judicial body. On the face of it, it appears that the Grand Chamber has taken a more nuanced position, as it does not rule out that parliament may be the judge of its own election provided sufficient procedural safeguards and guarantees for impartiality. This position brings the scope of the Grand Chamber decision into

---

54 ECtHR, *Mugemangango v Belgium*, *supra* note 26, para. 96.

55 In general terms, the ECtHR has held that '[t]he criterion of "political neutrality" cannot be applied to members of parliament in the same way as it pertains to other State officials, given that the former cannot be "politically neutral" by definition', see ECtHR, *Ždanoka v Latvia*, *supra* note 46, para. 117.

56 ECtHR, *Grosaru v Romania*, *supra* note 22, paras. 54 and 34. See also ECtHR, *Ofensiva tinerilor v Roumania*, *supra* note 40, para. 60.

57 ECtHR, *Mugemangango v Belgium*, *supra* note 26, paras. 105–106.

question, and I will therefore discuss that decision and its consequences in more detail in the following.

4. CAN PARLIAMENT OFFER AN EFFECTIVE EXAMINATION OF COMPLAINTS ON ITS OWN ELECTION?

4.1. CONTEXT

The issue the Grand Chamber was invited to consider in *Mugemangango v Belgium* was the election dispute resolution model where parliament is the judge of its own election. According to this model, courts have no jurisdiction in deciding complaints on the election result. By 'election result', I mean the transfer of votes into mandates, and thus disputes concerning which candidates won a specific mandate. Formally, the election result is decided by the newly elected Parliament when validating the credentials of its members. This decision is final and not appealable to a court.

Historically, the model of parliament being the judge of its own election was considered as a safeguard for the separation of powers and parliament's autonomy vis-à-vis the executive. As a result, the model was found in the English constitution following the 1689 Glorious Revolution, the US Constitution of 1787 and the French Constitution of 1791, as well as in many 19th-century monarchical constitutions in Europe with elected legislative assemblies. However, following several cases of corruption in parliament's validation of the election result, the United Kingdom in 1868 abolished the model of parliament being the judge of its own election. With the aptly named Election Petitions and Corrupt Practices Act 1868, complaints on the election result could be brought before the courts.[58] In the 20th century, the model of parliament being the judge of its own elections was steadily abolished in European constitutions in favour of judicial review either in the ordinary courts or special courts. An early example of a special election court is the Wahlprüfungsgericht of the 1919 Weimar Constitution, composed of three members appointed by parliament and two Supreme Court judges appointed by the president.[59] In 1920, the new Austrian Constitution assigned election disputes to a specialised constitutional court, which today is common in countries with constitutional courts.[60]

---

58 See C. Morris, *Parliamentary Elections, Representation and the Law*, Hart Publishing, Oxford 2012, pp. 83–85.

59 See the Constitution of Germany 1919, Article 31. A special election court was also set up in Czechoslovakia in 1920, see the Constitution of the Czechoslovak Republic 1920, Article 19.

60 See the Constitution of Austria 1920, Article 141.

Throughout the 20th century and up to today, we can observe a clear trend among European states to consider disputes on the election result as legal disputes to be adjudicated by a judicial body. According to a recent comparative overview by the Venice Commission, 31 of its Member States confer the adjudication of disputes on the election result to the highest court or a specialised election court, while nine states confer that power to a lower court.[61] Only nine Member States allow Parliament to validate its own election, and two of those states allow for judicial review of that decision. This leaves seven states in Europe where Parliament is still the judge of its own election without the possibility of appeal to a judicial body. In addition to Belgium these are Denmark, Iceland, Italy, Luxembourg, Norway, and the Netherlands.[62] All of them, save for Italy, have constitutions with roots in the 19th century, and all of them are frequently ranked highly in democracy indexes.[63]

The fact that seven European states maintain the model of parliament being its own election adds to the significance of the Grand Chamber's decision in *Mugemangango v Belgium*. Yet does this decision require those states to introduce a judicial appeal for parliament's decision to validate the election?

4.2. THE GRAND CHAMBER'S REASONING IN *MUGEMANGANGO v BELGIUM*

The case originated from the 2015 elections to the Walloon Parliament in Belgium, where the applicant stood but failed to win a seat by a mere 14 votes. Since more than 20,000 ballot papers were declared blank, void or disputed in his constituency, the applicant demanded a recount. When his request was denied by the election authorities, the applicant lodged a formal complaint to the Walloon Parliament, which is the only and final authority on election complaints. The Credentials Committee hearing the case recommended that

---

61 See Venice Commission (2020), 'Report on election dispute resolution', *supra* note 9, para. 45. The comparative overview is based on the 62 Member States of the Venice Commission, some of which are non-European and not members of the Council of Europe.

62 Access to judicial review may vary in other electoral disputes such as voting rights. In Denmark, disputes on the requirements for the right to vote can be appealed to a court, but not Parliament's validation of the election result, cf. Articles 30 and 33 in the Constitution of Denmark. See J.P. Christensen, J. Albæk Jensen and M. Hansen Jensen, *Dansk statsret*, 3rd edition, Jurist og Økonomiforbundets forlag, København 2020, p. 112. By contrast in Norway, Parliament has exclusive jurisdiction in all electoral disputes, including voting rights, cf. Articles 55 and 64 in the Constitution of Norway. See E. Holmøyvik, 'Den norske klageordninga ved stortingsval og europeisk rett', in I. Nguyen Duy et al. (eds.), *Uten sammenligning. Festskrift til Eivind Smith 70 år*, Universitetsforlaget, Bergen 2020, pp. 307–321.

63 See e.g., V-dem, 'Democracy Report 2021', March 2021, pp. 32–35, available at https://www.v-dem.net/media/filer_public/c9/3f/c93f8e74-a3fd-4bac-adfd-ee2cfbc0a375/dr_2021.pdf, last accessed 02.07.2021.

the ballots in the applicant's constituency be recounted. However, the plenary, which included the newly elected members from the applicant's constituency, voted to approve the credentials of all the elected representatives, and thus dismissed the applicant's demand for a recount.

Before the Grand Chamber of the ECtHR, the case was more or less framed as a matter of principle: can parliament be the judge of its own elections without any recourse to a court or another judicial body? The applicant argued that the Walloon Parliament had acted as both judge and party in the examination of his complaint, and that this had infringed on his right according to Article 3 of Protocol No. 1 to stand as candidate in free elections. The Belgian government, on the other hand, argued that the Walloon Parliament's decision to deny a recount was correct, and that the Belgian system of parliament being the judge of its own election was part of the country's constitutional heritage, in which parliamentary autonomy was rooted in the principle of separation of powers.

As mentioned above, and in line with the reasoning in *Grosaru v Romania* from 2010, the Grand Chamber found a violation of both Article 3 of Protocol No. 1 and Article 13 ECHR for not providing an effective examination of the election complaint. In its reasoning, the Grand Chamber noted that the Walloon Parliament adjudicating in its own election could not be considered impartial, did not have its powers circumscribed with sufficient precision in the law, and did not offer procedural guarantees against an arbitrary decision.

As for the consequences of the Grand Chamber's decision, the crucial point is the impartiality requirement. While laws can be written more precisely and procedural safeguards can be introduced in the proceedings before parliamentary bodies, it is much harder if not impossible to fundamentally alter the composition of parliament to make it impartial. Considering the potential for a decision on principle, the Grand Chamber's decision was disappointing since important parts of the reasoning were quite narrow and did not as a matter of principle rule out that Parliament could be impartial in deciding complaints on the election result.

As the basis for its conclusion, the Grand Chamber carefully noted that the members elected in the applicant's constituency, and who were his direct opponents, participated in voting on the applicant's complaint in the plenary. In its conclusion on the impartiality requirement, the Grand Chamber further noted that the risks of political decisions were not averted in the present case by the applicable voting rules:

> The decision on the applicant's complaint was taken by a simple majority. A voting regulation of that kind allowed the prospective majority to impose its own view, even though there would also be a significant minority. Thus, contrary to the Venice Commission's recommendations (see paragraph 64 above), the rule on voting by simple majority that was applied without any adjustment in this particular case was incapable of protecting the applicant – a candidate from a political party not

represented in the Walloon Parliament prior to the elections of 25 May 2014 – from a partisan decision.[64]

From this reasoning, the Grand Chamber appears to suggest that if voting rules in parliament can prevent partisan decisions on the election result, then the effective examination principle does not bar parliament from being the judge of its own election. Whilst there is a certain functional logic in this reasoning, it does not pass a reality test.

Given that parliaments are usually organised according to political parties voting according to political lines, it is very hard to see how voting rules can prevent partisan decisions. Even if parliamentary voting rules exclude those directly affected by the vote, in this case the members elected from the disputed constituency, their party colleagues would on behalf of the political parties have a direct interest in the outcome of the vote. Nor would a qualified majority requirement eliminate the risk of partisan decisions, either. While a qualified majority requirement might mitigate the risk of partisan decisions, that safeguard will only extend to candidates representing the parties forming a qualified majority. Candidates representing smaller parties whose members are not required to form a qualified majority would find themselves defenceless against partisan decisions by the qualified majority. A qualified majority requirement would therefore be particularly disadvantageous for candidates representing smaller parties, minorities or holding unpopular views.

I will add, as did Judge Wojtyczek in a concurring opinion, that the Grand Chamber is incorrect in referring to the Venice Commission and implying that it recommended and thus approved of a model where the Walloon Parliament decided complaints on the election result by a qualified majority.[65] In fact, the Venice Commission in its *amicus curiae* before the Grand Chamber reiterated its position in the Code of Good Conduct in Electoral Matters that parliament's validation of the election result must be subject to a judicial appeal.[66] Its recommendations on voting rules related more generally to electoral commissions, which often have a political composition, and were therefore cited out of context by the Grand Chamber.

The Grand Chamber's reasoning on impartiality in *Mugemangango v Belgium* does not sit well with its own long-held doctrine of considering impartiality as an objective criterion.[67] Democratic elections are fragile processes where even appearances of political influence on the election result can undermine

---

64 ECtHR, *Mugemangango v Belgium*, *supra* note 26, para. 107.

65 ECtHR, *Mugemangango v Belgium*, *supra* note 26, concurring opinion of Judge Wojtyczek, para. 8.

66 See Venice Commission, 'Amicus Curiae Brief for the European Court of Human Rights in the Case of Mugemangango v Belgium', *supra* note 20, paras. 30 and 32.

67 See e.g. ECtHR, *Micallef v Malta*, no 17056/06 [GC] 15.10.2009, paras. 93–97.

public confidence in the electoral system.[68] As mentioned above, the ECtHR has previously stressed the importance of impartiality and independence of electoral administration bodies. Therefore, it is all the more surprising that the Grand Chamber leaves the door open for a political body to make a final decision on the election result, which is the very essence of the right to free elections enshrined in Article 3 of Protocol No. 1. It should be recalled that in *Ždanoka v Latvia* from 2006, the Grand Chamber held that '[t]he criterion of "political neutrality" cannot be applied to members of parliament in the same way as it pertains to other State officials, given that the former cannot be "politically neutral"'.[69] In my view, the Grand Chamber's reasoning on impartiality in *Mugemangango v Belgium* is therefore flawed both in relation to the facts and its own case law. However, the fact that three judges wrote concurring opinions arguing in vain that parliament should never be considered impartial in disputes on the election result, suggests that the Grand Chamber's failure to do so was no failure from its part.[70]

4.3. THE RIGHT TO EFFECTIVE EXAMINATION AS A STRUCTURAL RIGHT

While the Grand Chamber in *Mugemangango v Belgium* did not rule out that parliament can in principle adjudicate in its own election, and thus took a more nuanced position than the Venice Commission, it did not accept the Belgian model either. Accordingly, the similar model for the validation of the election result by parliament found in Denmark, Iceland, Italy, Luxembourg,

---

68 There is a wealth of social science scholarship on perceptions of electoral integrity for which independent and impartial institutions is an important element, see e.g. J. Elklit and A. Reynolds, 'Analysing the impact of election administration on democratic politics', (2001) 38(1), *Representation*, pp. 3–10, who on p. 5 state: 'Perceptions about EMB independence are in any case almost as important as the actual, but indiscernible, level of independence, for perceptions might also be the basis for actions and counteractions of political actors at all levels.'; See also F.E. Lehoucq, 'Can parties police themselves? Electoral governance and democratization', (2002) 23(1), *International Political Science Review*, pp. 29–46, and P. Norris, 'Do perceptions of electoral malpractice undermine democratic satisfaction? The US in comparative perspective', (2019) 40(1), *International Political Science Review*, pp. 5–22, in particular on p. 19. See also with further references to scholarship S. Birch, 'Electoral institutions and popular confidence in electoral processes: A cross-national analysis', 2008 27(2), *Electoral Studies*, pp. 305–320, who fails to find a correlation between formal independence and public confidence but suggests that the yardstick should be the institutions' real independence.

69 In general terms, the ECtHR has held that '[t]he criterion of "political neutrality" cannot be applied to members of parliament in the same way as it pertains to other State officials, given that the former cannot be "politically neutral" by definition', ECtHR, *Ždanoka v Latvia*, *supra* note 46, para. 117.

70 The Judges Turković and Lemmens, and Wojtyczek.

the Netherlands and Norway, is most likely not compatible with Article 3 of Protocol No. 1, either.

The decision should also have consequences for Sweden and other countries where the body validating the election result has a majority of politicians. In Sweden, complaints on parliamentary elections are decided by an Election Review Board appointed by parliament for each ordinary election.[71] The decisions of the Election Review Board are final and cannot be appealed to a court. The Election Review Board is composed of seven members, of which the chair must be a permanent judge and is elected separately. The remaining six members are elected by parliament and all current members are members of parliament, although this is not a legal requirement. Whilst the Swedish Election Review Board may fulfil the procedural requirements for an effective examination even with a majority being lay members, it is hard to see how it can be considered impartial unless guarantees against political members are introduced in the law.

The wide-ranging consequences of the Grand Chamber's decision in *Mugemangango v Belgium* are due to the fact that the ECtHR has since *Namat Aliyev v Azerbaijan* in 2010 framed effective examination as a positive obligation incumbent on all Member States. Flowing from this case law is what recent scholarship has coined a structural human right inherent in Article 3 of Protocol No. 1 and which requires changes to a state's governmental structure or institutions.[72]

The structural element of the effective examination principle is accentuated by the Grand Chamber's rejection of the subsidiarity arguments advanced by Belgium and Denmark. Both states argued that the model of parliament being the judge of its own election was an integral part of their 'constitutional heritage and was founded on the constitutional principle of the separation of powers.'[73] Denmark in particular explicitly argued that 'neither Article 3 of Protocol No. 1 nor Article 13 of the Convention could require States to abolish long-established electoral systems in which parliaments validated their members' credentials'.[74] Moreover, both states called on the Grand Chamber to take into account 'the specific context and the democratic tradition of the State in question'.[75]

---

71 See the Swedish Instrument of Government, Chapter 3, Article 12, and the Swedish Election Act 2005, Chapter 15.

72 M. Leloup, 'The Concept of Structural Human Rights in the European Convention on Human Rights', (2020) 20(3), *Human Rights Law Review*, pp. 480–501, on p. 493 in relation to Articles 13 and on 496 in relation to Article 3 of Protocol No. 1. On the concept of structural rights in general, see O. Varol, 'Structural Rights', (2017) 105(4), *Georgetown Law Journal*, pp. 1001–1054.

73 ECtHR, *Mugemangango v Belgium*, *supra* note 26, paras. 58 (Belgium) and 65 (Denmark).

74 ECtHR, *Mugemangango v Belgium*, *supra* note 26, para. 66.

75 ECtHR, *Mugemangango v Belgium*, *supra* note 26, paras. 66 (Denmark) and 58 (Belgium, 'the application of one of the basic principles of the democratic edifice').

The Belgian and Danish arguments played on the political evolution doctrine adopted by the ECtHR in the first case on Article 3 of Protocol No. 1, *Mathieu-Mohin and Clerfayt v Belgium*. Here, the Court held:

> For the purposes of Article 3 of Protocol No. 1 (P1-3), any electoral system must be assessed in the light of the political evolution of the country concerned; features that would be unacceptable in the context of one system may accordingly be justified in the context of another, at least so long as the chosen system provides for conditions which will ensure the 'free expression of the opinion of the people in the choice of the legislature'.[76]

In light of this traditional deference to the Member States' organisation of their electoral systems and institutions, it is therefore significant that the Grand Chamber rejected Belgium and Denmark's argument that their well-entrenched democratic tradition provided a certain safeguard for the right to free elections. The ECtHR has within the context of Article 3 of Protocol No. 1 accepted that historical considerations and the specific political context of a state can for a certain time justify restrictions intended to protect the integrity of the democratic process.[77] Not so in *Mugemengango v Belgium*. Moreover, the Grand Chamber also dismissed Belgium's argument based on parliamentary autonomy, encompassing the validation of its members, being a well-established constitutional principle in Europe and therefore requiring a wide margin of appreciation for the Member States. The principle of parliamentary autonomy was recognised in the Grand Chamber decision *Karácsony and Others v Hungary* from 2016 concerning Article 10.[78] However, with reference to that decision, the Grand Chamber in *Mugemangango v Belgium* noted that parliamentary autonomy is not absolute and that 'discretion enjoyed by the national authorities should nevertheless be compatible with the concepts of "effective political democracy" and "the rule of law" to which the Preamble to the Convention refers (ibid.). It follows that parliamentary autonomy can only be validly exercised in accordance with the rule of law.'[79]

In my view, this apparent departure from the political evolution doctrine in favour of a more substantive approach to democracy through the effective examination principle is well founded and timely. The historical context and democratic traditions in a state should not be relevant where restrictions may

---

[76] ECtHR, *Mathieu-Mohin and Clerfayt v Belgium*, *supra* note 6, para. 54. From the Commission's case law, see ECtHR, *W., X., Y. et Z. c. Belgique*, *supra* note 6.

[77] See ECtHR, *Yumak and Sadak v Turkey*, no 10226/03 [GC] 08.07.2008; see ECtHR, *Ždanoka v Latvia*, supra note 46, paras. 119–135; ECtHR, *Tănase v Moldova*, no 7/08, 27.04.2010, para. 159; *Ādamsons v Latvia*, no 3669/03, 24.06.2008, paras. 123–128.

[78] See ECtHR, *Karácsony and Others v Hungary*, nos 42461/13 and 44357/13 [GC] 17.05.2016, paras. 142–147.

[79] ECtHR, *Mugemangango v Belgium*, *supra* note 26, para. 88.

threaten the fundamental aim of the democratic process, as in the case of a parliament deciding on its own election. Member states may indeed have a wide margin of appreciation as to the choice of electoral system and how they organise it, but the margin of appreciation should be narrower when the output of that electoral system is concerned.[80] The ECtHR has repeatedly reiterated that states must 'maintain the integrity and effectiveness of an electoral procedure aimed at identifying the will of the people through universal suffrage'.[81] For the election result to reflect the will of the people, which is the very core of the right in Article 3 of Protocol No. 1, there must be in place a system for effective examination of election complaints.

Indeed, the importance of the ECtHR to enforce the core of the right to free elections was noted by Judge Wojtyczek in his concurring opinion: 'blind spots in the system of rule-of-law guarantees do not belong to the core of the common constitutional heritage, even if they are deeply rooted in a national constitutional tradition.'[82] Such a 'core-periphery approach' to the states' margin of appreciation would bring the application of Article 3 of Protocol No. 1 more in line with the case law on other rights aimed at ensuring an effective political democracy, namely freedom of expression and freedom of assembly.[83] In recent scholarship this dis-analogy between the ECtHR's democracy-enhancing approach to Article 10 and its traditional state deferent approach to Article 3 of Protocol No. 1 has been emphasised in particular by Zysset, who makes a convincing argument for a more coherent approach to the concept of democracy in the ECHR.[84] Recall here the link between free elections and freedom of expression made by the ECtHR in *Bowman v The United Kingdom*:

> Free elections and freedom of expression, particularly freedom of political debate, together form the bedrock of any democratic system [...] The two rights are

---

80 This approach would correspond to what Letsas has coined a common value-based interpretation of the ECHR compared to the consensualist interpretation applied by the ECtHR in *Mathieu-Mohin and Clerfayt v Belgium* and predominant in older case law, see notably G. Letsas, *A Theory of Interpretation of the European Convention of Human Rights*, Oxford University Press, Oxford 2007, pp. 80–98, and G. Letsas, 'The ECHR as a Living Instrument: Its Meaning and Legitimacy', in A. Føllesdal, B. Peters and G. Ulfstein (eds.), *Constituting Europe: The European Court of Human Rights in a National, European and Global Context*, Cambridge University Press, Cambridge 2013, pp. 106–141.

81 See e.g. ECtHR, *Hirst v United Kingdom (No. 2)*, no 74025/01 [GC] 06.10.2005, para. 62.

82 ECtHR, *Mugemangango v Belgium*, *supra* note 26, concurring opinion of Judge Wojtyczek, para. 3.

83 See e.g. ECtHR, *Lingens v Austria* [Plenary], no 9815/82, 08.07.1986, para. 42; ECtHR, *Sørensen and Rasmussen v Denmark*, nos 52562/99 and 52620/99 [GC] 11.01.2006, para 58; ECtHR, *Animal Defenders International v The United Kingdom*, no 48876/08 [GC] 22.04.2013, para. 102. On the 'core-periphery approach' to the margin of appreciation and further references to ECtHR case law, see J. Gerards, 'Pluralism, Deference and the Margin of Appreciation Doctrine', (2010) 17(1), *European Law Journal*, pp. 80–120, on p. 112.

84 See A. Zysset, 'Freedom of expression, the right to vote, and proportionality at the European Court of Human Rights: An internal critique', (2019) 17(1), *International*

inter-related and operate to reinforce each other: for example, as the Court has observed in the past, freedom of expression is one of the 'conditions' necessary to 'ensure the free expression of the opinion of the people in the choice of the legislature'.[85]

The more substantive approach to 'effective political democracy' in *Mugemengango v Belgium*, which mirrors that in *Karácsony and Others v Hungary* concerning Article 10, may signal a more coherent approach from the ECtHR. In my view, it would be consistent with the fundamental aim of the ECHR 'to promote and maintain the ideals and values of a democratic society'[86] for the ECtHR to narrow the states' margin of appreciation in cases concerning the core of the right to free elections in Article 3 of Protocol No. 1.

It is true that the ECtHR in *Davydov v Russia* stated that it would perform an even less stringent scrutiny on what it called the more technical stage of vote counting and tabulation.[87] Yet it is important to recall that the wide margin of appreciation in the post-electoral stage was conditioned by the ECtHR 'if the general principles of equality, transparency, impartiality and independence of the electoral administration were complied with.'[88] Considering that the ECtHR in *Namat Aliyev v Azerbaijan*, cited in section 3.1 above and reiterated in several subsequent decisions, views the effective examination of election disputes as 'one of the essential guarantees of free and fair elections', states should not be afforded a wide margin appreciation in this specific part of the post-electoral stage.

In conclusion, as to the positive obligation of effective examination of election complaints, which forms a structural part of Article 3 of Protocol No. 1, national models rooted in tradition and history but not complying with the minimum requirements for effective examination, must yield to a European convergence of electoral law.

Journal of Constitutional Law, pp. 230–251. Zysset's argument draws on the case law on disenfranchisement of voting rights, but his observation on the dis-analogy of the ECtHR's interpretative approach to Article 10 and Article 3 of Protocol No. 1 and his argument for a more teleological approach to the interpretation of the latter, is equally persuasive for the electoral process. See also M. O'Boyle, 'Electoral disputes and the ECHR: an overview', *supra* note 5, 53.

85 ECtHR, *Bowman v The United Kingdom*, no 24839/94 [GC] 19.02.1998, para. 42.

86 The aim of maintaining a democratic society is invoked by the ECtHR both in relation to Article 11 and Article 3 of Protocol No. 1, see e.g. ECtHR, *Russian Conservative Party of Entrepreneurs, supra* note 42, para. 47; ECtHR, *Bączkowski and Others v Poland*, no 1543/06, 03.05.2007, para. 61 with references to further case law.

87 Such a threshold test, requiring that the breach of law relates to a fundamental rule for the values the law is to guarantee and not technical rules for which a breach do not have such an effect, has been established also in other areas, see in relation to 'tribunal established by law' in Article 6; see ECtHR, *Guðmundur Andri Ástráðsson v Iceland*, no 26374/18 [GC] 01.12.2020, para. 246.

88 See ECtHR, *Davydov and Others v Russia, supra* note 22, para. 287.

4.4. WHAT ELECTION COMPLAINT RESOLUTION SYSTEM?

A loyal implementation of the Grand Chamber's decision in *Mugemangango v Belgium* should lead to changes in the election complaint resolution system not only in Belgium, but also in Denmark, Iceland, Italy, Luxembourg, the Netherlands, Norway and possibly Sweden. Since such rules are often entrenched in the constitution and parliament's autonomy over its election is deeply rooted in history, change may not come easy. The Danish intervention before the Grand Chamber can be explained by the fact that amending the Danish constitution is politically very complicated. According to Article 88 of the Danish constitution, a constitutional amendment requires both the dissolution of parliament and a referendum in which a majority and at least 40% of the total electorate votes in favour of the amendment. Whether compliance with *Mugemangango v Belgium* can be achieved through interpretation and legislation is uncertain. Article 33 of the Danish constitution provides parliament with an exclusive competence to 'itself determine the validity of the election of any Member'. The Danish Supreme Court has so far declared complaints on the validity of parliamentary elections as inadmissible.[89] The same view is taken in Danish legal doctrine, though it argued that the courts may admit complaints on the election result in exceptional cases where there is evidence of abuse of power by the parliamentary majority.[90] Not surprisingly, the Grand Chamber's decision has raised considerable political concerns in Denmark.[91]

It falls within the states' margin of appreciation to decide on how to organise their election dispute resolution system as long as it fulfils the criteria for an effective examination. The Grand Chamber stated in *Mugemangango v Belgium* that 'a judicial or judicial-type remedy, whether at first instance or following a decision by a non-judicial body, is in principle such as to satisfy the requirements of Article 3 of Protocol No. 1'.[92] States are therefore not required to place disputes on the election result within the jurisdiction of ordinary courts or a constitutional court. A permanent or ad hoc election court or even a tribunal formally part of the election administration would be acceptable, so long as its powers, procedure, and composition fulfil the criteria for an effective examination of election disputes.

89 See the Danish Supreme Court's decision in U 1933.373 Ø concerning the parliamentary elections in 1932.

90 See J. P. Christensen, J. Albæk Hansen and M. Hansen Jensen. *Dansk Statsret,* 3rd edition, Jurist og Økonomiforbundets forlag, København 2020, p. 112; P. Germer. *Statsforfatningsret,* 3rd edition, Jurist og Økonomiforbundets forlag, København 2007, pp. 67–68.

91 See M. Skærbæk, 'Eksperter: Ny menneskeretsdom udfordrer grundloven', *Politiken,* 21.08.2020, available at https://politiken.dk/indland/art7890162/Eksperter-Ny-menneskeretsdom-udfordrer-grundloven, last accessed at 02.07.2021.

92 ECtHR, *Mugemangango v Belgium, supra* note 26, para. 139.

In two countries, change was already underway before the Grand Chamber's decision in *Mugemangango v Belgium*. In Luxembourg, the 2019 proposal for a new constitution introduces the possibility to appeal the Parliament's verification of credentials to the Constitutional Court.[93]

In Norway, a mixed judicial-parliamentary model of election dispute resolution was proposed in 2020 by a joint expert and political commission drafting a new electoral law.[94] The new Norwegian model may be considered a compromise between formal parliamentary autonomy and judicial review of election disputes. A new judicial body, the National Electoral Committee (*Riksvalgstyret*), will be established to decide on all election disputes. This body is formally an independent tribunal outside the ordinary court system. However, the tribunal is judicial in the sense that it offers full procedural guarantees and has full powers to remedy errors of electoral law and criminal law violations relevant to the electoral process. The tribunal can restore voting rights, order corrections to the electoral process and order a new election if the errors are likely to have influenced the election result. The five members are appointed by parliament for four years, but crucially a majority of three members including the leader will be selected from permanent judges. The remaining two are lay members, but cannot be elected representatives at any level, members of the government or political advisors to the government or parliamentary factions.

After the National Electoral Committee has decided all individual election complaints, parliament will proceed to verify the credentials of its newly elected members. In other words, the formal validation of the election result will still be done by parliament, which will still have the power to invalidate the election of its members. It is expected that since all election disputes are expected to have been settled by the National Electoral Committee before parliament's verification of the credentials, its validation will be purely formal. However, to prevent any possibility of political abuse of the verification power, the draft law allows parties and candidates running for election to appeal parliament's decision to the Supreme Court sitting in the plenary. The proposed Norwegian election dispute resolution system will effectively transfer the final decision on the election result from the parliament to the Supreme Court but maintains parliament's formal and public role in validating the credentials of its members.

If reverence of tradition is important, it may also be possible to maintain parliament as a purely formal and final validator of the election result. For this to be in accordance with the effective examination principle, I would argue that parliament's powers must be circumscribed so narrowly in the law that no

93 See Venice Commission, 'CDL-AD(2019)003, Luxembourg, Avis sur la proposition de revision de la constitution', 18.03.2019, para. 82.

94 Official Norwegian Reports, 'NOU 2020: 6, Frie og hemmelige valg', available at https://www.regjeringen.no/contentassets/0516829ddd434b86880c80e9ceec0281/no/pdfs/nou202020200006000dddpdfs.pdf, last accessed 02.07.2021.

discretion is left that could be abused for political gains. The ECtHR accepted a similar approach in terms of limiting prisoners' voting rights in *Scoppola v Italy (No. 3)*.[95] However, like proposed in Norway, this approach would require a proper judicial remedy before the formal validation by parliament. This is because the effective examination of an election complaint would require at some stage the application of discretion in the interpretation of the law and the weighing of evidence.

5. CONCLUSIONS

Just over ten years after the ECtHR in *Namat Aliyev v Azerbaijan* introduced effective examination of election disputes as a distinct positive obligation flowing from Article 3 of Protocol No. 1, the case law of the ECtHR provides an increasingly nuanced set of procedural requirements for the Member States' election dispute resolution systems. While the case law is piecemeal, the analysis above shows that effective examination of election disputes according to Article 3 of Protocol No. 1 requires minimum safeguards for the independence and impartiality as well as the legality concerning the election dispute resolution bodies, and access to justice, effective remedy, and fair hearing for the voters or candidates involved.

Today, I would argue that the essential elements of effective examination according to the Venice Commission's Code of Good Practice in Electoral Matters have been interpreted by the ECtHR to follow from Article 3 of Protocol No. 1 and thus being binding legal obligations for the Member States. For the Venice Commission the developments in ECtHR case law on election dispute resolution would be welcome as analogies to this case law will bolster its advisory opinions on electoral law reforms in the Member States.

In 2009, Ten Napel argued that the different wording of Article 3 of Protocol No. 1 could be used, more than in the past, to emphasise the positive obligations of the Member States.[96] Such a positive application of Article 3 of Protocol No. 1 would recognise it as a structural human right which requires a certain degree of convergence of national electoral systems. More than a decade later, and culminating with *Mugemangango v Belgium* in 2020, it appears that the ECtHR has let go of the deference to the states' unique political evolution leading to different electoral systems which dominated the early case law. By defining effective examination of election disputes as an essential guarantee for free and fair elections, and letting this fundamental aim prevail over the

95 ECtHR, *Scoppola v Italy (No. 3)*, no 126/05 [GC] 22.05.2012, paras. 105–109.

96 H.-M. Ten Napel (2009), 'The European Court of Human Rights and political rights: the need for more guidance', *supra* note 1, p. 479.

affected states' specific historical and democratic context, the ECtHR may have shed its traditional state deference in relation to Article 3 of Protocol No. 1 in favour of a more substantive approach to democracy comparable to that of Articles 10 and 11. According to one of the standard reference works on the ECHR, 'there has been considerable narrowing of the wide margin of appreciation referred to in the earlier cases now that the Court seems to be adopting a more robust test for interferences which States impose.'[97] Time will tell if the ECtHR continues this approach in future cases.

In my view, the shift in the ECtHR's approach to Article 3 of Protocol No. 1 is significant and timely. Elections are inherently legal in the meaning that every step of the electoral cycle is governed by law. It is therefore wrong to consider the application of electoral law and electoral rights as belonging to the political domain and thus not subject to equal safeguards for a fair examination as civil rights and obligations. The effective examination principle is a significant development in the ECtHR case law, because it effectively does away with the old distinction between the so-called political rights in Article 3 of Protocol No. 1 and other civil rights and obligations according to Article 6. This development is timely in a Europe where democracy is under increasing pressure, even within the European Union. By requiring some of the most well developed democracies in the world to introduce additional formal safeguards to prevent political manipulation of the election result, the ECtHR is sending a clear message that democracy and human rights cannot be separated.

---

97 See B. Rainey, P. McCormick and C. Ovey (2020), *Jacobs, White, and Ovey: The European Convention on Human Rights*, *supra* note 4, p. 627.

THE CASE LAW OF THE ECtHR IN 2020 IN THE LIGHT OF THE PRINCIPLE OF SYSTEMIC HARMONISATION

Lorenzo Acconciamessa

ABSTRACT

This contribution provides an overview of relevant developments in the case law of the European Court of Human Rights (ECtHR, the Court) in 2020. Priority will be given to Grand Chamber (GC) judgments and decisions and those of the chambers deemed to be highly relevant from a substantial and procedural viewpoint. Given that in 2020 the Council of Europe's Steering Committee for Human Rights published its report on 'The Place of the European Convention of Human Rights in the International and European Legal Order', the case law will be selected and examined from the viewpoint of the principle of systemic harmonisation. The aim is highlighting positive and negative examples of application of general international law by the ECtHR, of cross-fertilisation between the ECtHR and other international courts and tribunals, as well as of interpretation of the European Convention on Human Rights (ECHR) in the light of international human rights instruments.

1. INTRODUCTION

Due to the COVID-19 pandemic, 2020 has been a challenging year for the protection of human rights in Europe and worldwide. Indeed, some Member States of the European Convention on Human Rights (ECHR, or the Convention) notified derogations pursuant to Article 15 ECHR to the Secretary-General of the Council of Europe (CoE).[1] In any case, it has been pointed out that in the protection of human rights, a 'normal-as-usual' approach should be adopted even in times of a pandemic, given that 'the extraordinary nature of states of emergencies cannot and should not prevent human rights from performing their normal role in society'.[2]

Moreover, the measures that have been adopted in order to contain the spread of the virus – namely, strict lockdowns – also affected the capacity of national and international justice systems to function, therefore affecting the capacity of victims of (past) human rights violations to obtain justice and reparation. However, except for a temporary suspension of procedural time limits,[3] during the pandemic the European Court of Human Rights (ECtHR, the Court)

---

1 Notifications of derogations are published on the CoE website and are available at https://www.coe.int/it/web/conventions/notifications. The author's opinion is that states should have resorted to their right to derogate in order to deal with the pandemic, L. Acconciamessa, 'COVID-19 e diritti umani: le misure di contenimento alla luce della CEDU', *Ius in Itinere*, 28.03.2020, available at https://www.iusinitinere.it/covid-19-e-diritti-umani-le-misure-di-contenimento-alla-luce-della-cedu-26455, last accessed 31.05.2021. *Contra*, A. Spadaro, 'COVID-19: Testing the Limits of Human Rights', (2020) 11(2), *European Journal of Risk Regulation*, p. 317. There has been an intense debate on this issue: A. Greene, 'Derogating from the European Convention on Human Rights in Response to the Coronavirus Pandemic: If not Now, When?', (2020) (3), *European Human Rights Law Review*, p. 262, highlighted, in the light of Schmitt's theory, the risk of emergency power becoming ordinary powers, and the role of Article 15 derogation in preventing such risk; K. Dzehtsiarou, 'Article 15 Derogations: Are They Really Necessary during the COVID-19 Pandemic?', (2020) (4), *European Human Rights Law Review*, p. 359, by contrast, considered that limitations sufficed; see also A. Greene, 'On the Value of Derogations from the European Convention on Human Rights in Response to the COVID-19 Pandemic: A Rejoinder', (2020) (5), *European Human Rights Law Review*, p. 526; T. Hickman, 'The Coronavirus Pandemic and Derogation from the European Convention on Human Rights', (2020) (6), *European Human Rights Law Review*, p. 593.

2 V.P. Tzevelekos and K. Dzehtsiarou, 'Normal as Usual? Human Rights in Times of COVID-19', (2020) 1(2), *European Convention on Human Rights Law Review*, p. 49.

3 A. Saccucci, 'La sospensione dei termini processuali da parte della Corte europea per l'emergenza COVID-19', *SIDIBlog*, 27.03.2020, available at http://www.sidiblog.org/2020/03/27/la-sospensione-dei-termini-processuali-da-parte-della-corte-europea-per-lemergenza-covid-19/, last accessed 31.05.2021.

continued to handle its caseloads as usual. And indeed, throughout the year the Court issued a significant number of interesting judgments and decisions. Therefore, leaving aside issues concerning human rights in times of pandemics,[4] the present contribution deals with the developments in the ECHR systems and in the ECtHR's case law in 2020,[5] in the light of the principle of systemic integration. That is to say, the Court's case law will be selected for – and examined in the light of – its relationships with general international law, other international human rights instruments as well as other international courts and tribunals' case law.

Indeed, given that it would be impossible to deal with the whole of the ECtHR's 2020 case law, the cases have been selected in the light of a very specific criterion. Due to the publication, in November 2020, of the Steering Committee for Human Rights' (*Comité directeur pour les droits de l'homme*, CDDH) report on 'The Place of the European Convention on Human Rights in the European and International Legal Order' (CDDH's 2020 Report),[6] which had been adopted at the 92nd meeting in Strasbourg (26–29 November 2019), those selected are cases that, in addition to clarifying and developing the interpretation of substantive and procedural ECHR dispositions, also concern the role and place of the ECHR in the European and international legal order. In most of the selected cases, indeed, the Court engaged in the application of general international law; in the harmonisation of the Convention with other human rights and international instruments; or, lastly, in the jurisprudential cross-fertilisation with other international courts and tribunals.[7] The said report

4 Because of the admissibility condition concerning the exhaustion of domestic remedies, it is quite unlikely that the ECtHR will rule soon (with some exceptions) on the merits of COVID-19-related issues. See ECtHR, *Ranaud Le Mailloux v France*, no 18108/20, 05.11.2020. The application complained about state's omissions in the context of the COVID-19 crisis, but the applicant did not claim to be a victim of the alleged violations. Therefore, the Court declared the application inadmissible, for the Convention does not allow an *actio popularis*.

5 See also ECtHR, 'Annual Report 2020 of the European Court of Human Rights, Council of Europe', annual report, 2020, available at https://www.echr.coe.int/Pages/home.aspx?p=court/annualreports&c=, last accessed 06.07.2021.

6 CoE, CDDH, *The Place of the European Convention on Human Rights in the European and International Legal Order*, Report of the Steering Committee for Human Rights (CDDH) adopted at its 92nd meeting in Strasbourg 26–29.11.2019, Strasbourg, para. 440: 'In the light of significant differences between the regional and the universal systems of human rights protection, achieving absolute harmony in international human rights law is not a probability. In order to avoid a risk of fragmentation of the international legal order, the ECtHR, just as all other systems making up the European architecture of human rights protection, should, however, strive to develop its practice while being aware of the other systems. It would be desirable if the international and regional human rights organs, be they judicial or monitoring proceed, to the extent possible, in the direction of a harmonisation of their practice. To that end, dialogue between the different organs is one of the most powerful tools to enhance consistency in the case-aw and practice of these different organs and should be further encouraged.'

7 See C. Brown, *A Common Law of International Adjudication*, Oxford University Press, Oxford 2007. Sometimes, especially when dealing with procedural issues, cross-fertilisation is seen as part of the inherent powers of an international court or tribunal, ECtHR included.

examined the interaction between the ECHR and other branches of international law, other human rights instruments and other regional organisations as a challenge to solve. In the present contribution, however, such interactions are seen as an opportunity for the development of the ECtHR's case law and of its coherence with, and contribution to the further expansion of, international law. In some of the selected cases it will be argued that the Court could have reached a different conclusion had it engaged in systematic interpretation and/or in cross-fertilisation techniques.[8]

In short, this contribution deals with (part of) the ECtHR's 2020 case law 'in its normative environment' and in the light of the principle of systemic integration or harmonisation, which is (mostly, although not exclusively) based on Article 31(3)(c) of the 1969 Vienna Convention on the Law of Treaties (VCLT), according to which treaties must be interpreted by taking into account 'any relevant rules of international law applicable in the relations between the parties', as also clarified by the International Law Commission (ILC).[9]

The contribution will be structured as follows. Section 2 deals with Article 1 ECHR, notably, states' jurisdiction in extra-territorial situations. Section 3 concerns cases dealing with the interpretation and application of the dispositions concerning rights and liberties protected under the ECHR; cases relating to the core rights and those relating to the evolutive and systematic interpretation of other rights will be preferred. Section 4 deals with developments concerning procedural and admissibility issues. Some conclusions concerning the relationship between the ECHR and international law and other human rights instruments, as well as between the ECtHR and other international courts and tribunals, will be drawn.

2. STATES' EXTRATERRITORIAL JURISDICTION

In the case *M.N. and others v Belgium*, the Grand Chamber ruled on (the absence of) extraterritorial jurisdiction under Article 1 ECHR in diplomatic premises.[10]

---

8 The importance of jurisprudential cross-fertilisation cannot be overlooked: it has been one of the main subjects that have been discussed at the 2021 Human Rights Forum which has been held (virtually) between judges of the three regional human rights courts. See Second International Human Rights Forum (Regional Courts), 25.03.2021, video available at https://vodmanager.coe.int/cedh/webcast/cedh/2021-03-25-1/lang, last accessed 31.05.2021.

9 ILC, *Fragmentation of International Law: Difficulties Arising from the Diversification and Expansion of International Law*, Report of the Study Group finalised by Martti Koskenniemi, UN Doc A/CN.4/L.682, 13.04.2006, para. 426. See also C. Pitea, 'Interpreting the ECHR in the Light of "Other" International Instruments: Systemic Integration or Fragmentation of Rules on Treaty Interpretation?', in N. Boschiero, T. Scovazzi, C. Pitea and C. Ragni (eds.), *International Courts and the Development of International Law*, Springer, The Hague 2013, pp. 545–599.

10 ECtHR, *M.N. and others v Belgium*, no 3599/18 [GC] 05.05.2020. The Chamber had relinquished jurisdiction to the Grand Chamber; M. Milanovic, *Extraterritorial Application of Human Rights Treaties. Law, Principles, and Policy*, Oxford University Press, Oxford 2011.

The applicants were a Syrian family (a couple and their two minor children) from Aleppo who requested the Belgian Embassy in Beirut to grant them short-term visas in order to enter Belgian territory and claim protection as refugees there. The Alien Office in Belgium rejected their application. Therefore, they appealed, unsuccessfully, before the Belgian courts. In their application to the ECtHR, they argued that Belgium, by refusing the visas, violated their right not to be subjected to inhuman and degrading treatments (*non-refoulement*), under Article 3 ECHR, as well as their right to an effective remedy, pursuant to Article 13 ECHR.

First of all, the Grand Chamber assessed whether, in processing the visa application, Belgium was exercising authority and control abroad and, therefore, jurisdiction.[11] The Grand Chamber recognised that the Belgian authorities took a 'decision concerning the conditions for entry to Belgian "territory" and, in doing so, exercised a public power'.[12] However, in the Court's view it cannot be accepted that decisions taken at a national level affecting people abroad suffice in order to create a jurisdictional link, without any other connection. In particular, the applicants were not Belgian nationals and had never been under the *de facto* control of Belgian diplomatic agents (for the latter did not exercise physical authority over them). They had entered the Belgian embassy freely, and they had freely walked away after presenting their visa application. In short, the Court considered that exercise of 'public authority' abroad can create a jurisdictional link only when state officials exercise effective control over buildings, aircrafts or ships; physical control over persons (personal model of jurisdiction); or when a state exercises effective control over a territory (spatial model of jurisdiction), while 'administrative control' over the diplomatic premises does not suffice.[13] However, in previous cases, the Court stated that the decision not to admit aliens and to accept their asylum applications (although at the state's borders) falls within states' jurisdiction.[14]

Secondly, the Court considered whether the appeals lodged with the Belgian courts could have created the otherwise missing jurisdictional link.[15] It found that the applicants had freely and unilaterally initiated administrative proceedings without having any other connection with the respondent state and,[16] in the

---

11 ECtHR, *Al-Skeini and others v the United Kingdom*, no 55721/07 [GC] 07.07.2011, para. 135.

12 ECtHR, *M.N. and others v Belgium, supra* note 10, para. 112.

13 Ibid., para. 119.

14 ECtHR, *M.A. and others v Lithuania*, no 59793/17, 11.12.2018, para. 70.

15 On jurisdiction triggered by 'procedural control', see ECtHR, *Güzelyurtlu and others v Cyprus and Turkey*, no 36925/07, 29.01.2019, para. 188. See also, S. Kieber, 'The Jurisprudence of the European Court of Human Rights in 2019', in P. Czech, L. Heschl, K. Lukas, M. Nowak and G. Oberleitner (eds.), *European Yearbook on Human Rights 2020*, Intersentia, Cambridge-Antwerp-Chicago 2020, pp. 593–620, 594.

16 ECtHR, *Abdul Wahab Khan v the United Kingdom*, no 11987/11, 28.01.2014, para. 28: '[t]he mere fact that the applicant availed himself of his right to appeal against the decision to cancel his leave to remain has no direct bearing on whether his complaints [...] fall within the jurisdiction of the United Kingdom'.

Court's view, it would not be acceptable to give individuals the possibility of universally extending jurisdiction by merely lodging an application with the courts of a Member State.[17]

The Court once again justified its restrictive approach by invoking the states' right, under international law, to control entry, residence, and expulsion of aliens.[18] It also stated that the decision does not prejudice endeavours made by states to facilitate access to asylum procedures through their embassies and/or consular representations.[19] In the *N.D. and N.T. v Spain* case, indeed, the Grand Chamber found that border areas fall within the state's jurisdiction.[20] However, it also found that there was no violation of Article 4 of Protocol No. 4 to the ECHR (the prohibition of collective expulsion) given that, *inter alia*, the applicants could have applied for international protection at embassies and consulates.[21] However, the Court intentionally did not rule on whether resorting to such means would have brought the applicants within the state's jurisdiction.[22]

While the case is disappointing – at least from a moral viewpoint – commentators' opinions were divided. According to some authors, the Court's reasoning was 'formally convincing and politically unsurprising'.[23] Moreover, it has been argued that it correctly recognised that the creation of legal pathways to asylum is a political issue 'which cannot currently be found in European

---

17 ECtHR, *M.N. and others v Belgium, supra* note 10, para. 123: '[t]he Court made clear […] that the mere fact that an applicant brings proceedings in a State Party with which he has no connecting tie cannot suffice to establish that State's jurisdiction over him […]. The Court considered that to find otherwise would amount to enshrining a near-universal application of the Convention on the basis of the unilateral choices of any individual, irrespective of where in the world they find themselves, and therefore to create an unlimited obligation on the Contracting States to allow entry to an individual who might be at risk of ill-treatment contrary to the Convention outside their jurisdiction'.

18 Ibid., para. 124. The Court invoked the 'well-established principle of public international law, […] according to which the State Parties, subject to their treaty obligations, including the Convention, have the right to control the entry, residence and expulsion of aliens'.

19 ECtHR, *M.N. and others v Belgium, supra* note 10, para. 126.

20 ECtHR, *N.D. and N.T. v Spain*, nos 8675/15 and 8697/15 [GC] 13.02.2020, para. 110. The Grand Chamber considered that Spain exercised *territorial* jurisdiction, while the Chamber had considered that jurisdiction was established by means of the 'continuous and exclusive control, at least *de facto*' that Spanish official had exercised over the applicants.

21 *Infra*, section 3.5.

22 ECtHR, *N.D. and N.T. v Spain, supra* note 20, para. 222: '[a]s the Court has already found that the respondent State provided a genuine and effective access to Spanish territory […] it is not required to take a position in the present case on whether and to what extent such embassies and consulates would have brought the applicants within the jurisdiction of Spain, if they had sought international protection there, and whether these embassies and consulates would thus also have been capable of providing them with the required level of access'.

23 V. Stoyanova, 'M.N. and Others v Belgium: no ECHR protection from refoulment by issuing visas', *EJIL:Talk!*, 12.05.2020, available at https://www.ejiltalk.org/m-n-and-others-v-belgium-no-echr-protection-from-refoulement-by-issuing-visas/, last accessed 31.05.2021. However, '[i]f the author is juxtaposed against the reality characterised with massive loss of life since […] there are no legal channels for asylum-seekers to travel and enter countries of protection, a disappointment appears inevitable'.

human rights law'.[24] In others' view, however, the Court could have followed some United Nations (UN) treaty-bodies' approaches to the extraterritorial application of human rights treaties,[25] thereby adopting a 'non-formalistic approach' which emphasises 'the obligations that States Parties have undertaken under the ECHR, also in terms of positive obligations to protect and prevent against harm caused by external sources, when they exercise authority in denying entry to aliens'.[26] In particular, Danisi mentioned the UN Human Rights Committee's General Comment on the right to life,[27] which developed a jurisdictional model based on the state's 'direct and reasonably foreseeable impact' on such a right. This *functional approach*, which has been also proposed by Judge Bonello in the ECtHR's *Al-Skeini* case,[28] has been recently adopted by the Human Rights Committee in finding Italy in violation of the International Covenant on Civil and Political Right for its failure to save migrants' lives in the high sea, therefore outside Italy's territorial sea and outside its search and rescue area, as established under the relevant international instruments.[29] But it can also be noted that the UN Committee on the Rights of the Child stated that

---

24 M. Baumgärtel, 'Reaching the Dead-End: M.N. and others and the question of humanitarian visa', *Strasbourg Observers*, 07.05.2020, available at https://strasbourgobservers.com/2020/05/07/reaching-the-dead-end-m-n-and-others-and-the-question-of-humanitarian-visas/, last accessed 31.05.2021.

25 Many of these decisions are commented in S. Besson, 'Due Diligence and Extraterritorial Human Rights Obligations – Mind the Gap!', ESIL Reflections, 28.04.2020, available at https://esil-sedi.eu/wp-content/uploads/2020/04/ESIL-Reflection-Besson-S.-3.pdf, last accessed 31.05.2021.

26 C. Danisi, 'A "Formalistic" Approach to Jurisdiction in the European Court of Human Rights' Decision on Humanitarian Visa: Was Another Interpretation Possible?', *SIDIBlog*, 27.05.2020, available at http://www.sidiblog.org/2020/05/27/a-formalistic-approach-to-jurisdiction-in-the-european-court-of-human-rights-decision-on-humanitarian-visas-was-another-interpretation-possible/, last accessed 31.05.2021.

27 UN Human Rights Committee, *General Comment No. 36 (2018) on Article 6 of the International Covenant on Civil and Political Rights, on the right to life*, 30.10.2018, Un Doc CCPR/C/GC/36, para. 22.

28 ECtHR, *Al-Skeini and others v the United Kingdom*, no 55721/07 [GC] 07.07.2011, Concurring Opinion of Judge Bonello, paras. 10–11: 'States ensure the observance of human rights in five primordial ways: firstly, by not violating (through their agents) human rights; secondly, by having in place systems which prevent breaches of human rights; thirdly, by investigating complaints of human rights abuses; fourthly, by scourging those of their agents who infringe human rights; and, finally, by compensating the victims of breaches of human rights. […] A "functional" test would see a State affectively exercising "jurisdiction" whenever it falls within its power to perform, or not to perform, any of these five functions. Very simply put, a State had jurisdiction for the purposes of Article 1 whenever the observance or the breach of any of these functions is within its authority and control'.

29 UN Human Rights Committee, *A.S., D.I., O.I and G.D. v Italy*, no 3042/2017, 27.01.2021, UN Doc CCPR/C/130/D/3042/2017, para. 7.8: 'in the particular circumstances of the case, a special relationship of dependency had been established between the individuals on the vessel in distress and Italy. This relationship comprised of factual elements – in particular, the initial contact made by the vessel in distress with the MRCC, the close proximity of ITS Libra to the vessel in distress and the ongoing involvement of the MRCC in the rescue operation and – as well as relevant legal obligations incurred by Italy under the international law of

states' obligations under the UN Convention on the Rights of the Child (CRC) apply even 'with respect to those children who *came under the State's jurisdiction* when attempting to enter the country's territory'.[30] Said approach has been applied in the *D.D. v Spain* case,[31] although this case differs from the *M.N.* case. In the *D.D.* case, indeed, the applicants had tried to enter the state's territory through its land border.

The decision at hand, therefore, is one example of those cases in which cross-fertilisation techniques could have led the Court to a more liberal approach. However, one should also consider that the political pressure the ECtHR faces when dealing with mass migration and asylum does not affect, to the same extent, the UN treaty bodies. And indeed, given its regional character, a significant number of ECHR Member States are receiving countries of the 21st-century mass migration phenomenon. In the European human rights system, due to the 'migration crisis' which currently affects CoE and European Union (EU) Member States, the latter invoke a wide margin of appreciation in the area of immigration control. According to Lingaas, the ECtHR case law which treats migrants as 'others' is the result of states' political pressure, as has been also highlighted in several dissenting and concurring opinions attached to the Court's judgments and decisions.[32] In particular, Judge Pinto de Albuquerque took note of 'the present adverse political climate in respect of asylum-seekers and migrants in general and towards African migrants arriving in Europe in particular, and of the attendant mounting pressure on the Court on the part of some Governments'.[33] Additionally, other scholars noted that recently, in the migration-asylum field as well as in others, the Court tends to adjust to the expectations and perceptions of their constituency.[34]

---

the sea, including a duty to respond in a reasonable manner to calls of distress pursuant to SOLAS Regulations and a duty to appropriately cooperate with other states undertaking rescue operations pursuant to the International Convention on Maritime Search and Rescue. As a result, the Committee considers that the individuals on the vessel in distress were directly affected by the decisions taken by the Italian authorities in a manner that was reasonably foreseeable in light of the relevant legal obligations of Italy, and that they were thus subject to Italy's jurisdiction for the purposes of the Covenant, notwithstanding the fact that they were within the Maltese search and rescue region and thus also subject concurrently to the jurisdiction of Malta'.

30 UN Committee on the Rights of the Child, *General Comment No. 6, Treatment of Unaccompanied and Separated Children Outside their Country of Origin*, 01.09.2005, UN Doc CRC/GC/2005/6, para. 12, emphasis added.

31 UN Committee on the Rights of the Child, *D.D. v Spain*, no 4/2016, 15.05.2019, UN Doc CRC/80/d/4/2016, para. 14.3.

32 C. Lingaas, 'Judicial Responses to the Migration Crisis: The Role of Courts in the Creation of a European Identity', in G.B. Bruno, F.M. Palombino and A. Di Stefano (eds.), *Migration Issues before International Courts and Tribunals*, CRD Edizioni, Rome 2019, pp. 1–24, p. 24.

33 ECtHR, *M.A. and others v Lithuania*, no 59793/17, 11.12.2018, Concurring Opinion of Judge Pinto de Albuquerque, para. 16.

34 B. Çali, 'Coping with Crisis: Whither the Variable Geometry in the Jurisprudence of the European Court of Human Rights', (2018) 35(1), *Wisconsin International Law Journal*, p. 22.

With regard, more generally, to issues of jurisdiction under Article 1 ECHR, states' pressure is even more evident. And indeed, in the 2018 Copenhagen Declaration, states welcomed 'the Court's continued *strict* and consistent application of the criteria concerning admissibility and jurisdiction'.[35] The same restrictive approach has been adopted in the CDDH's 2020 Report which criticises to some extent the Court's case law on extraterritorial jurisdiction, by observing that:

> This development [of the extraterritorial application of the Convention] [...], entails to a certain extent a lack of foreseeability for the States of the exact obligations under Article 1. Such uncertainty may compromise the States' willingness, in particular, to participate in certain forms of international cooperation, including peacekeeping missions, governed by international law. [...] For this reason, an evolutive interpretation in this area could reduce the ability of States to reliably predict the likely approach of the Court and thus to meet their legal obligations under the Convention.[36]

The report confirms that there is a significant consensus among states according to which the interpretation of Article 1 should remain strict and essentially territorial.[37] The same Court, recently, seems 'worried' about the alleged 'chilling effect' that the exterritorial application of the Convention could have on states' willingness to participate to forms of international cooperation.[38] However, different approaches are legally possible, and the Court should at least consider drawing inspiration from the aforementioned UN treaty bodies' case law.

3. DEVELOPMENTS CONCERNING SUBSTANTIAL ISSUES

The following cases concerning *substantial* issues are selected as they are relevant both from an intra-systemic and an inter-systemic viewpoint. The term substantial here refers to issues concerning the merits of the cases and, therefore,

35 High Level Conference of the CoE Member States, *Copenhagen Declaration on the Reform of the European Convention on Human Rights System*, 13.4.2018, para. 32, available at https://rm.coe.int/copenhagen-declaration/16807b915c, last accessed 31.05.2021, emphasis added.

36 CoE, CDDH (2019), *The Place of the European Convention on Human Rights, supra* note 6, paras. 150–151.

37 Ibid., para. 2. The same report recognises that it 'sets out in broad terms the views of States parties [...] on these questions concerning the interaction of Convention obligations with obligations that they owe under other bodies of law'.

38 ECtHR, *Hanan v Germany*, no 4871/16 [GC] 16.02.2021, para. 135: 'establishing a jurisdictional link merely on the basis of the institution of an investigation may have a chilling effect on instituting investigations at the domestic level into deaths occurring in extraterritorial military operations and result in an inconsistent application of the Convention in respect of Contracting States participating in the same operation'.

the interpretation and application of the individuals' rights and liberties guaranteed by the ECHR, both in their substantial and procedural limbs.

3.1. ATTRIBUTION OF CONDUCTS IN VIOLATION OF THE RIGHT TO LIFE AND STATES' PROCEDURAL DUTIES

Moving from jurisdiction to attribution, the case *Makuchyan and Minasyan v Azerbaijan and Hungary* involved issues of general international law concerning state responsibility.[39] It is well known that the ECHR does not stipulate any *lex specialis* concerning the attribution of conducts. Therefore, as the CDDH's 2020 Report acknowledged, the Court has on a number of occasions referred to the ILC Draft Articles on the Responsibility of States for Internationally Wrongful Acts (ARSIWA) under the heading of the 'applicable law'.[40] However, the Report highlights that the Court 'does not explicitly refer to these rules when deciding at the merits stage whether an impugned act can be attributed to the respondent State'.[41] Nevertheless, in the case at hand, the Court was forced to do so, because the ARSIWA had been expressly invoked by the applicants.

The facts can be summarised as follows. R.S., an Azerbaijani officer taking part in a course in Budapest sponsored by the North Atlantic Treaty Organization (NATO), murdered (by decapitation) an Armenian officer and attempted to kill another Armenian soldier. He was sentenced to life imprisonment in Hungary, but a number of years later, Azerbaijan asked him to be transferred, under the CoE Transfer Convention, to serve the rest of the sentence in his home country. Upon his return he was released, pardoned, promoted in the army and celebrated as a national hero. The applicants – the surviving soldier and a relative of the one who had been killed – complained about a violation of Article 2 ECHR. They considered the violation to be attributable to the Azerbaijani state and,[42] as a consequence, they argued that there was a violation of the substantial

39 ECtHR, *Makuchyan and Minasyan v Azerbaijan and Hungary*, no 17247/13, 20.05.2020.

40 CoE, CDDH (2019), *The Place of the European Convention on Human Rights, supra* note 6, para. 155.

41 Ibid., para. 189.

42 They argued that R.S. had been in Budapest in his official capacity as a member of the State's Army. Secondly, they invoked Article 11 ARSIWA, according to which '[c]onduct which is not attributable to a State under the preceding articles shall nevertheless be considered an act of that State under international law if and to the extent that the State acknowledges and adopts the conduct in question as its own'. They also invoked the judgment in the case *United States Diplomatic and Consular Staff in Teheran* where the International Court of Justice (ICJ) considered that 'the approval given by the Ayatollah Khomeni and other organs of the Iranian State [to the occupation of the US embassy and detention of its staff], and the decision to perpetuate them, translated continuing occupation of the Embassy and detention of the hostages to an act of that State'.

limb of said provision. Moreover, they argued that Azerbaijan also violated its procedural limb, in having pardoned the author of the murder.

In order to rule on the substantial limb of Article 2 ECHR, the Court had to deal with the *attribution* of R.S.'s conduct to Azerbaijan. It considered that the conduct could not be directly attributed to the state given that,[43] although R.S. was a member the army, he was not exercising his duties when he committed the crimes, and his conduct could not have been foreseen by the state. Then the Court considered that Article 11 ARSIWA, as clarified by its commentary and as interpreted and applied by the International Court of Justice (ICJ) and the International Criminal Tribunal for the Former Yugoslavia, sets a 'very high threshold for State responsibility for an act otherwise not attributable to a State at the time of its commission'. The acknowledgement or adoption threshold, in the Court's view, is not triggered when the state limits itself to 'approve and endorse' an individual's conduct,[44] as Azerbaijan's conduct (although 'particularly disturbing') was qualified by the Court.[45] For these reasons, the conduct was not attributable to the state and, therefore, there was no violation of the substantial limb of Article 2 ECHR. The Court's approach has been criticised by Ryngaert and Istrefi, who highlighted that the international practice (although rare) does not confirm the Court distinction between 'approval and endorsement', on the one hand, and 'acknowledgment and adoption', on the other.[46] Moreover, in his partly dissenting opinion, Judge Pinto de Albuquerque considered that, notwithstanding the absence of express acknowledgment and adoption, 'it is clear from the facts that [Azerbaijan] behaved in a manner from which such acknowledgment and adoption can be inferred'.[47] However, according to Milanovic, 'the Court's analysis is in line with the approaches of the ILC and the ICJ' and is not particularly disturbing.[48]

---

43 ECtHR, *Makuchyan and Minasyan, supra* note 39, para. 111. But see M. Milanovic and T. Papic, 'Case Note on Makuchyan and Minasyan v Azerbaijan and Hungary', (2021) 115 (2), *American Journal of International Law*, p. 299: 'the Court's conclusion [...] is sound, though its reasoning is problematic'.

44 ECtHR, *Makuchyan and Minasyan, supra* note 39, para. 112. In the Court's view, for Article 11 to be applied the state should have approved and endorsed the conduct as its own (that is to say, as perpetrated by the State of Azerbaijan) in a clear and unequivocal way, in the form of words or conduct able to show a direct and categorical assumption of responsibility for the conduct.

45 Ibid., para. 115.

46 C. Ryngaert and K. Istrefi, 'An Azeri Kills an Armenian Soldier at a NATO Training in Budapest: The ECtHR Decides a Case of State Responsibility and Presidential Pardon' *Strasbourg Observers*, 29.06.2020, available at https://strasbourgobservers.com/2020/06/29/an-azeri-kills-an-armenian-soldier-at-a-nato-training-in-budapest-the-ecthr-decides-a-rare-case-of-state-responsibility-and-presidential-pardon/, last accessed 31.05.2021.

47 ECtHR, *Makuchyan and Minasyan v Azerbaijan and Hungary*, no 17247/13, 20.05.2020, Partly Dissenting Opinion of Judge Pinto de Albuquerque, para. 10.

48 M. Milanovic, 'Attribution, Jurisdiction, Discrimination, Decapitation: A Comment on Makuchyan and Minasyan v Azerbaijan and Hungary', *EJIL Talk!*, 10.07.2020, available at

Turning to the procedural limb of Article 2, the Court assessed whether, although a large portion of the procedural obligations had been carried out by Hungary (where R.S. was prosecuted), Azerbaijan had an obligation of effectively enforcing the life-prison sentence after the transfer. It considered that while Article 12 of the Transfer Convention allows amnesties and pardoning, the CoE Parliamentary Assembly stated that it was not designed for the immediate release of prisoners upon their return to their home countries, while Resolution 2022 (2014) of the Parliamentary Assembly expressly qualified Azerbaijan's conduct in the case at hand as being in violation of the principle of good faith and of the rule of law.[49] Moreover, in the Court's view, the reasons Azerbaijan had given for the release (humanitarian concerns related to R.S.'s state of health and the alleged unfairness of the proceedings in Hungary) were not acceptable. The Court found that upon his return R.S. 'was treated as an innocent or wrongfully convicted person and bestowed benefits that appear not to have had any legal basis under domestic law'[50] and granted impunity, in violation of the procedural obligations enshrined in Article 2 ECHR.[51] Moreover, the Court concluded that Azerbaijan had also violated Article 14 ECHR, in conjunction with Article 2, because R.S.'s release was racially motivated.[52]

Lastly, in the applicants' view, Hungary was in violation of the procedural obligations under Article 2 ECHR, too. They argued that it had a positive obligation to ensure the enforcement of its judges' sentences and, therefore, to require adequate binding assurance from Azerbaijan before the transfer. They argued, in short, that 'the Hungarian authorities know or ought to have known that the Azerbaijani authorities would release R.S.'.[53] The Court was therefore 'called upon to determine whether and to what extent a transferring State might be responsible for the protection of the right of the victims of a crime or their next-of-kin'.[54] In its view, however, Hungary observed the procedure under the Transfer Convention, and – albeit incomplete and worded in general terms – Azerbaijan had given assurances.[55] The Court was satisfied by a very low standard of due diligence imposed on the Hungarian authorities and considered that such assurances sufficed for excluding the violation.

The case at hands is relevant for at least three reasons. First, by applying Article 11 of the ARSIWA, the Court (indirectly) contributed to the consolidation of the said provision (in its restrictive version, as codified by the ILC and

https://www.ejiltalk.org/attribution-jurisdiction-discrimination-decapitation-a-comment-on-makuchyan-and-minasyan-v-azerbaijan-and-hungary/, last accessed 31.05.2021.

49 ECtHR, *Makuchyan and Minasyan*, *supra* note 39, para. 162.

50 Ibid., para. 170.

51 Ibid., para. 172.

52 Ibid., para. 218.

53 Ibid., para. 181.

54 Ibid., para. 195

55 Ibid., para. 196.

interpreted by the ICJ) as a rule of customary international law.[56] In this regard, the case highlights an omission in the CDDH's 2020 Report. The latter focuses on the relevance of international law as applicable law in ECtHR proceedings, but it does not engage with the ECtHR role in further developing (or modifying) international law as such, by endorsing an emerging rule and generating subsequent state practice. What is striking is that, usually, the Court (implicitly) departs from the international rules on state's responsibility and, instead, applies its own methods, in the light of the 'Convention's special character as a human rights treaty', as the CDDH's 2020 Report pointed out.[57] The report criticises the Court on this point, arguing that the general rules on attribution should be applied 'in order to preserve the effectiveness of the Convention system against risks of fragmentation of the European and international legal space in the field of human rights protection'.[58] In the case at hand, by contrast, the Court rigidly applied (what it considered to be established) general international law. However, one could argue that, given the scarcity of state practice, Article 11 was to be intended not as codifying existing customary law, but as aiming at its progressive development. Therefore, the Court could have tried to reverse this trend by adopting a more liberal approach.

Second, the Court for the first time considered (although implicitly) that presidential pardoning might constitute a violation of the procedural obligations arising from Article 2.[59] The Court considered that procedural obligations do not exclusively bind the state responsible for investigation and prosecution of the (material) author of a violation of the right to life, but also his national state when the author is transferred to its territory. Such a conclusion is extremely relevant. Indeed, as Judge Pinto de Albuquerque highlighted, international law does not prohibit as such the issuance of a pardon.[60] Some commentators considered that in the case at hand, the Court has 'judicially reviewed a presidential pardon' and

---

56 C. Ryngaert and K. Istrefi (2020), 'An Azeri Kills an Armenian Soldier', *supra* note 46. See also M. Milanovic, T. Papic (2021), 'Case Note on Makuchyan and Minasyan', *supra* note 43, p. 299: 'The relatively strict approach of the ICJ and the ILC now also has the imprimatur of a human rights court which otherwise tends to employ more expansive standards'.

57 CoE, CDDH (2019), *The Place of the European Convention on Human Rights, supra* note 6, paras. 191–192. For example, the report highlighted that in the *Ilascu* case the Court applied a lower threshold than the one imposed under Article 8 ARSIWA (as interpreted by the ILC and the ICJ) in order to attribute the conduct of a group of persons to a state.

58 CoE, CDDH (2019), *The Place of the European Convention on Human Rights, supra* note 6, para. 198.

59 M. Milanovic and T. Papic (2021), 'Case Note on Makuchyan and Minasyan', *supra* note 43, p. 299: 'Domestic (let alone international) judicial review of pardons and clemency is extremely limited [...]. The Court attempted to avoid these difficulties by assessing whether Azerbaijan violated Article 2 by *releasing* R.S., not by *pardoning* him. Yet the former was formally conditioned on the latter [...]'.

60 ECtHR, *Makuchyan and Minasyan*, Opinion of Judge Pinto de Albuquerque, *supra* note 47, para. 11.

'enlarged the scope of procedural obligations under the right to life provision'.[61] Actually, the Court decided not to directly assess whether the issuance of the pardon was at odds with the Convention. It rather considered that its effects and consequences – the grant of impunity to the author of a serious crime – were at odds with the state's procedural obligations under Article 2 ECHR.

Third, the Court recognised that states have to ensure respect for ECHR procedural obligations when transferring the author of a crime to his/her home country. However, the Court's application of said principle was rather disappointing. It applied a very low standard of *due diligence* to the transferring state and considered that '[it] does not see how the competent Hungarian bodies could have done anything more than respect the procedure and the spirit of the Transfer Convention'.[62] However, there is no presumption according to which the fulfilment of an international obligation guarantees respect of the substantive and procedural obligations under the ECHR. By contrast, in its case law, the Court made it clear that Member States must abide by their obligations under the ECHR, irrespective of whether the act or omission in question was a consequence of the necessity to comply with other international obligations, whether bilateral or multilateral.[63]

3.2. POSITIVE OBLIGATIONS UNDER ARTICLE 3 ECHR: THE RELATIONSHIP BETWEEN DOMESTIC VIOLENCE AND CYBERVIOLENCE

In the case *Buturugă v Romania* the Court recognised that cyberviolence is related to violence against women and domestic violence.[64] It interpreted the meaning of such crimes in an evolutive way, by taking into account other international conventions as well as non-binding reports.

The applicant, Ms Buturugă, lodged a complaint before the Romanian authorities alleging that she had been the victim of domestic abuse – physical

61 C. Ryngaert and K. Istrefi (2020), 'An Azeri Kills an Armenian Soldier', *supra* note 46.

62 ECtHR, *Makuchyan and Minasyan*, *supra* note 39, para. 196.

63 See, *ex multis*, ECtHR, *Soering v the United Kingdom*, no 14038/88 [GC] 07.07.1989, para. 91 and ECtHR, *Al-Saadoon and Mufdhi v the United Kingdom*, no 61498/08, 02.03.2010, paras. 126–128, concerning the relationship between the ECHR and extradition treaties; ECtHR, *Bosphorus Hava Yollari Turizm ve Ticaret Anonim Sirketi v Ireland*, no 45036/98 [GC] 20.06.2005, para. 153 and, *mutatis mutandis*, ECtHR, *M.S.S. v Belgium and Greece*, no 30696/09 [GC] 21.01.2011, para. 338, concerning the relationship between the ECHR and EU obligations; ECtHR, *Hirsi Jamaa and others v Italy*, no 27765/09 [GC] 23.02.2012, para. 129, concerning the relationship between the ECHR and bilateral agreements concerning the control of migration flows; recently, see ECtHR, *Bivolaru and Moldovan v France*, nos 40324/16 and 12623/17, 25.03.2021, concerning the violation of the ECHR arising from the enforcement of a European Arrest Warrant.

64 ECtHR, *Buturugă v Romania*, no 56867/15, 11.02.2020.

violence and death threats – by M.V., her former husband. One month later, she lodged a new complaint concerning the threats she had received from M.V. with the aim of inducing her to withdraw the allegations. She also requested an electronic search of the family computer, alleging that M.V. had accessed her private accounts and copied her conversations and documents and, later, she filed a new complaint for breach of correspondence. However, the prosecutor dismissed both the complaints arguing that the former, concerning domestic violence, was not sufficiently serious, while the latter, involving the breach of confidentiality, had been filed outside of the requested time period. Therefore, Ms Buturugă lodged an application with the ECtHR, which was examined under Articles 3 and 8 ECHR.[65]

As for the complaints concerning domestic violence, the Court highlighted that such cases must be treated (by domestic authorities) differently from 'normal' cases, given that they involve vulnerable individuals' protection against physical harm,[66] psychological violence and harassment. In these cases, as the Court stipulated in the past,[67] national authorities must fulfil their positive obligations of protection (under Articles 3 and 8 of the Convention) in the light of the 'due diligence' standards (of investigation) established under the Convention on preventing and combating violence against women and domestic violence ('Istanbul Convention'). The domestic authorities had not respected this standard. While the existence and severity of the physical violence suffered by the applicant were acknowledged due to a forensic report, no steps had been taken to identify the perpetrator and protect the applicant.[68] Although domestic authorities had (belatedly) adopted a protective order in the applicant's favour, it proved ineffective in remedying the violations.[69]

The Court then considered the claims regarding the violation of confidentiality which, in the applicant's view, were strictly connected with those concerning domestic violence.[70] According to the Court, the same standard should have been adopted by the domestic authorities because violence against women as well as domestic violence include forms of cyberviolence. The latter manifests itself in different forms, such as access to private laptops and personal data.[71] However, in the case at hand the authorities did not address the applicant's complaints as a case involving domestic violence because they

65 Ibid., para. 44.
66 Ibid., para. 60.
67 ECtHR, *M.G. v Turkey*, no 646/10, 22.03.2016, para. 93.
68 ECtHR, *Buturugă v Romania*, *supra* note 64, para. 67, paras. 69–71.
69 Ibid., para. 72.
70 Ibid., para. 74.
71 Ibid.

failed to consider cyberviolence as a manifestation of that crime.[72] The Court reached this conclusion by merely mentioning some international instruments and reports:[73]

> The Court notes that, both in domestic and international law, the phenomenon of domestic violence [...] includes, among others, psychological violence and harassment. Moreover, cyberviolence is currently recognised as an aspect of violence against women and girls and can manifest itself in different forms, including informatic violations of private life, the intrusion in the victim's laptop and the taking and manipulation of data and images. (Translated by the author.)

Its reasoning seems to be the following: a definition of the notion of cyberviolence has been provided by the Cybercrime Convention Committee (instituted under the 2001 CoE Convention on Cybercrime) in its report concerning 'Mapping study on cyberviolence', according to which:

> Cyberviolence is the use of computer systems to cause, facilitate, or threaten violence against individuals that results in, or is likely to result in, sexual, psychological or economic harm or suffering and may include the exploitation of the individual's circumstances, characteristics or vulnerabilities.[74]

According to the same report, illegal access to intimate personal data, the destruction of data and blocking access to a computer system or data are forms of cyberviolence.[75] Lastly, the Cyber Crime Convention Committee considered that the Convention on Cybercrime is complementary to, and should be implemented in accordance with, the Istanbul Convention.[76]

The Istanbul Convention does not explicitly deal with cyberviolence. However, according to the latter, the notion of 'violence against women' includes 'all acts of gender-based violence that result in, or are likely to result in, [...]

72 Ibid., para. 67.

73 It is well known that 'in searching for a common ground among the norms of international law [the Court] has never distinguished between sources of law according to whether or not they have been signed or ratified by the respondent State' (ECtHR, *Demir and Bayakara v Turkey*, no 34504/91, 12.11.2008, para. 44), although binding instruments usually have more relevance. See A. Nußberger, 'Hard Law or Soft Law – Does it Matter? Distinction Between Different Sources of International Law in the Jurisprudence of the ECtHR', in A. van Aaken, and I. Motoc (eds.), *The European Convention on Human Rights and General International Law*, Oxford University Press, Oxford 2018, pp. 41–58. A different issue is whether the ECtHR's approach is in line with customary international law, as codified in Article 31(3)(c) of the VCLT, and with the practice of other international courts and tribunals.

74 CoE, Cybercrime Convention Committee (T-CY), Working Group on cyberbullying and other forms of online violence, especially against women and children, *Mapping study on cyberviolence* no. T-CY(2017)10, 09.07.2018, p. 5.

75 Ibid., p. 14.

76 Ibid., p. 25.

psychological […] harm or suffering to women' (Article 3(a)), while the notion of 'domestic violence' includes 'all acts of […] psychological […] violence that occur within the family or domestic unit or between former or current spouses or partners' (Article 3(b)). Articles 33 and 40 define, respectively, psychological violence as 'any intentional conduct of seriously impairing a person psychological integrity through coercion or threat' and stalking as 'intentional conduct repeatedly engaging in threatening conduct directed at another person, causing her or him fear for her or his safety'. As the Cybercrime Convention Committee explained, such crimes can be perpetrated through (and in) the cyberspace. In this regard, the Court also mentioned the UN Broadband Commission for Digital Development Working Group on Broadband and Gender's report on 'Cyberviolence Against Women', which acknowledged that the term 'cyber' refers to different ways through which the Internet exacerbates or broadcasts forms of violence against women by taking different forms such as hacking, impersonation, surveillance and harassment in the cyberspace.[77]

If allegations of cyberviolence fall within the definition of violence against women and domestic violence, the *same* standard of due diligence which the ECHR requires, when interpreted in the light of the Istanbul Convention, applies to such allegations. The domestic authorities, by contrast, had unduly excluded the connection between the claims concerning domestic violence and those related to the breach of confidentiality. They did not examine the applicant's claims because of a procedural bar, applying a 'formalisme excessif' which is incompatible with the due diligence standard required under the Istanbul Convention and, consequently, under the ECHR.[78]

For these reasons, the Court concluded that the domestic authorities failed in carrying out an effective investigation concerning domestic violence. Therefore, the Respondent State was found in violation of the positive obligations arising from Articles 3 and 8 of the Convention, as interpreted under the international (binding and not binding) instruments concerning domestic violence and cybercrimes (although Article 31(3)(c) VCLT was not explicitly invoked). In this regard, one should consider that the Court's approach to systemic interpretation widens the approach endorsed in the VCLT (and customary international law), given that in the Court's view even non-binding reports of international monitoring bodies and experts commissions might endorse an evolutive and extensive interpretation of the ECHR.

In any case, while the judgment at hand should be welcomed as it developed ECHR positive obligations and included cyberviolence within the scope of

---

[77] UN Broadband Commission for Digital Development, 'Cyberviolence Against Women and Girls. A World-Wide Wake Up Call', report, 23.10.2015, p.22, available at https://www.broadbandcommission.org/publication/cyber-violence-against-women/, last accessed 06.07.2021.

[78] ECtHR, *Buturugă v Romania, supra* note 64, para. 75. See also para. 78.

domestic violence, one aspect of the Court's approach has been criticised. In particular, it seems that the Court stipulated that while domestic violence falls under the scope of Article 3 ECHR, cyberviolence falls (exclusively) under Article 8 ECHR, although being *closely linked* to the complaint of violence.[79] In van Leeuwen's view, moreover, although the applicant did not invoke Article 14 ECHR, the Court should have assessed the case in the light of gender discrimination, as well.[80]

3.3. CONTEMPORARY FORMS OF SLAVERY

In 2020 the Grand Chamber ruled for the first time on the interpretation of Article 4 ECHR in relation to contemporary forms of slavery and servitude, such as human trafficking and forced prostitution, clarifying (some of the) issues that had emerged in *Rantsev v Cyprus and Russia* and in subsequent judgments.[81]

The case *S.M. v Croatia* concerned a woman who lodged a criminal complaint, alleging that a former policeman,[82] T.M., had (physically and psychologically) forced her into prostitution. Although the domestic authorities ascertained that T.M. had recruited the applicant, they concluded that there was no evidence that she had been forced. Therefore, since T.M. had been charged for the aggravated offence (forcing into prostitution), the criminal court considered that he could not be convicted for the minor offence (procuring prostitution) and acquitted him. S.M. lodged an application with the ECtHR, claiming that she had been subjected to forced prostitution, in violation of Articles 3 and 8 ECHR.

79 F. van Leeuwen, 'Cyberviolence, Domestic Abuse and Lack of Gender-Sensitive Approach – Reflection on Buturugă versus Romania' *Strasbourg Observers*, 11.03.2020, available at https://strasbourgobservers.com/2020/03/11/cyberviolence-domestic-abuse-and-lack-of-a-gender-sensitive-approach-reflections-on-buturuga-versus-romania/, last accessed 31.05.2021.

80 Ibid.

81 It is well known that the ECtHR adopted an evolutive interpretation of Article 4 ECHR, by considering that human trafficking falls within the scope of Article 4 ECHR, although it did not clarify whether it was considered as slavery or servitude. See ECtHR, *Rantsev v Cyprus and Russia*, no 25965/04, 07.01.2010, paras. 280–281: 'The Court considers that trafficking in human beings, by its very nature and aim of exploitation, is based on the exercise of powers attaching to the right of ownership. It treats human beings as commodities to be bought and sold and put to forced labour, often for little or no payment, usually in the sex industry but also elsewhere […]. It implies close surveillance of the activities of victims, whose movements are often circumscribed […]. It involves the use of violence and threats against victims, who live and work under poor conditions. […] There can be no doubt that trafficking threatens the human dignity and fundamental freedoms of its victims and cannot be considered compatible with democratic societies and the values expounded by the Convention. In view of its obligation to interpret the Convention in light of present-day conditions, the Court considers it unnecessary to identify whether the treatment about which the applicant complains constitutes "slavery", "servitude" or "forced and compulsory labour"'; ECtHR, *Chowdury and others v Greece*, no 21884/15, 30.03.2017.

82 ECtHR, *S.M. v Croatia*, no 60561/14 [GC] 25.06.2020.

The chamber, in the light of the *iura novit curia* principle, considered that the fact raised issues under Article 4 given that 'trafficking in itself as well as exploitation of prostitution fall within the scope of Article 4 of the Convention'.[83] While according to the international definition of human trafficking (Article 3 of the Palermo Protocol to Prevent, Suppress and Punishing Trafficking in Persons, supplementing the United Nations Convention against Transnational Organized Crime (Palermo Protocol) and Article 4(a) of the CoE Convention against Human Trafficking (Anti-Trafficking Convention)), sexual exploitation is one of the possible purposes of human trafficking, the chamber reached a different conclusion: it considered that human trafficking and sexual exploitation are different offences, which both fall within the scope of Article 4 ECHR.[84] However, the government requested and obtained the referral to the Grand Chamber.

In line with the *Rantsev* precedent and by expressly relying on the principle of harmonious interpretation of the Convention and other instruments of international law (therefore, implicitly relying on Article 31(3)(c) VCLT), the Grand Chamber considered that when the constituent elements (action, means, purpose)[85] of the crime of human trafficking (as defined under other international instruments) exist, Article 4 ECHR is applicable.[86] However, given the different scope of application of the Palermo Protocol and the Anti-Trafficking Convention, the Court preferred the latter's approach, according to which human trafficking does not require the crime to be transnational and/or organised.[87] But why would human trafficking fall within the scope of Article 4

83 ECtHR, *S.M. v Croatia*, no 60561/14 [GC] 25.06.2020, Concurring opinion of Judges O'Leary and Ravarani. In their opinion, the Court unduly resorted to the *jura novit curia* principle in order to alter the factual and legal arguments on which the original application was grounded. The original application complained about the domestic authorities' failure in prosecuting forced prostitution, while only in her written submissions S.M. complained of the failure to charge and convict T.M. for human trafficking. ECtHR, *S.M. v Croatia*, no 60561/14, 19.07.2018.

84 Ibid., para. 54.

85 In particular, under Article 3(a) of the Palermo Protocol, the said elements are: (1) the *action* (what is done), consisting in 'the recruitment, transportation, transfer, harbouring of persons'; (2) the *means* (how it is done), namely 'the threat or use of force or other forms of coercion, of abduction, of fraud, of deception, of abuse of power or of a position of vulnerability or of the giving or receiving payments or benefits to achieve the consent of a person having control over another person'; (3) the *aim of exploitation* (why it is done), which shall include 'at a minimum, the exploitation of the prostitution of others or other forms of sexual exploitation, forced labour or services, slavery or practices similar to slavery, servitude or the removal or organs [...]'.

86 ECtHR, *S.M. v Croatia*, *supra* note 82, para. 290.

87 However, the Court did not clarify why the case was comparable to previous cases of *international* human trafficking; see F. Tammone, 'L'interpretazione evolutiva della CEDU sulle forme contemporanee di schiavismo: tratta di esseri umani e sfruttamento della prostituzione nel caso *S.M. c Croazia*', (2020) 15(1), *Diritti Umani e Diritto Internazionale*, pp. 221 et seq.

ECHR? The Grand Chamber considered that the constitutive elements of human trafficking 'cut across the three categories set out under Article 4' and that 'trafficking runs counter to the spirit and purpose of Article 4'.[88] Moreover, the International Labour Organization (ILO) considered that human trafficking falls within the definition of forced labour.[89] Furthermore, international law and all CoE Member State criminalise human trafficking.[90]

As for the exploitation of prostitution, the Grand Chamber confirmed the assumption that it is prohibited under Article 4 as such, and not as a manifestation of human trafficking. However, it considered that only forced prostitution falls within its scope of application.[91] The Court then recalled that given that the said offences are usually perpetrated by private actors, states have positive obligations in this regard,[92] including:

> (i) the duty to put in place a legislative and administrative framework to prohibit and punish trafficking; (ii) the duty, in certain circumstances, to take operational measures to protect victims [...]; and (iii) a procedural obligation to investigate situations of potential trafficking. In general, the first two aspects of the positive obligations can be denoted as substantive, whereas the third aspect designates the States' (positive) procedural obligations.[93]

The Court also highlighted that these obligations must be interpreted and applied in the light of the principles established in relation to positive obligations under Articles 2 and 3 ECHR.[94] Therefore, domestic authorities have

88 ECtHR, *S.M. v Croatia*, *supra* note 82, para. 291 et seq.

89 Ibid., para. 293. The Court adopted a similar approach in *Chowdury and others v Greece*. However, according to some authors, the ILO definition would be erroneous; see V. Stoyanova, 'The Grand Chamber Judgment in S.M. v Croatia: Human Trafficking and the Definitional Scope of Article 4 ECHR' *Strasbourg Observers*, 03.07.2020, available at https://strasbourgobservers.com/2020/07/03/the-grand-chamber-judgment-in-s-m-v-croatia-human-trafficking-prostitution-and-the-definitional-scope-of-article-4-echr/, last accessed 31.05.2021.

90 Ibid.

91 The Court clarified that the term 'force' must be interpreted as encompassing also subtle forms of coercive conduct. But see ECtHR, *S.M. v Croatia*, no 60561/14 [GC] 25.06.2020, Concurring opinion of Judge Pastor Vilanova, paras. 3–5: 'the Court has [...] required the presence of a threat, but also the absence of genuine consent. [...] Nevertheless, the time has come to address the question whether exploitation of prostitution, as such, remains compatible with the European Convention on Human Rights. As a general rule, I do not believe so'. The judge invoked, *inter alia*, Rule 70 of the International Criminal Court's (ICC) Rules of Procedure and Evidence in order to show that consent to prostitution cannot be presumed, unless it is express and explicit, and, in any case, it can be vitiated for many reasons. ECtHR, *S.M. v Croatia*, *supra* note 82, para. 300.

92 Ibid., para. 290.

93 Ibid., para. 306. The Court also considered that, 'given the conceptual proximity of human trafficking and forced prostitution [...] the relevant principles relating to human trafficking are accordingly applicable in cases concerning forced prostitution'.

94 Ibid., para. 311. See also ECtHR, *S.M. v Croatia*, no 60561/14 [GC] 25.06.2020, Concurring opinion of Judge Turković: 'the criteria for an effective investigation [...] should be the same

an obligation of (on their own motion) initiating an effective investigation,[95] 'capable of leading to the establishment of the facts and of identifying and – if appropriate – punishing those responsible'.[96] In the case at hand, those obligations had not been fulfilled. Indeed, once they had knowledge of the situation, the authorities should have taken into account the vulnerability of the victim and should have immediately initiated a careful investigation.[97] The existence of an arguable claim of having been subjected to treatment contrary to the Convention indeed triggers such procedural obligations.[98] In the case at hand, however, the police merely questioned the victim, the accused and one of his friends, and searched his premises and car (where they found condoms, rifles, ammunition and mobile phones). Despite these elements, and notwithstanding the fact that he had been previously convicted for procuring prostitution through coercion and rape, he was acquitted. In the Court's view, such 'significant flaws' in the authorities' investigation involved a violation of Article 4 ECHR.

The *S.M.* case (and the Court's approach to the interpretation of Article 4 ECHR, in general) is a positive example of interpretation of the ECHR in the light of other international instruments. And indeed, Article 4 ECHR does not define the notions of slavery, servitude and forced or compulsory labour. Therefore, as the same Grand Chamber recognised, 'in determining the material scope of Article 4, the Court has sought guidance in various instruments of international law dealing with these concepts'.[99] In particular, the Court defined the term 'slavery', in the light of the 1927 Convention to Suppress Slave Trade and Slavery, as 'the status or condition of a person over whom any or all the powers attaching to the right of ownership are exercised'.[100] Similarly, the notion of 'servitude' had been defined, by recalling the 1956 Convention to Suppress Slave Trade and Slavery, as a 'particularly serious form of denial of freedom' which includes 'in addition to the obligation to perform certain services for others […] the obligation for the "serf" to live on another person's property and the impossibility of altering his condition'. Lastly, the notion of forced or compulsory labour has been determined in the light of the 1930 ILO Forced Labour Convention (No. 29), according to which it includes 'all work or service which is exacted from any person under the menace of any penalty and for

---

across all the Articles of the Convention'. But see ECtHR, *S.M. v Croatia*, Concurring opinion of Judges O'Leary and Ravarani, *supra* note 83: 'There is a risk that the technique of blanket transposition fails to take into account the specificity of the type of investigation which the authorities would have to initiate when confronted with an "arguable claim" or prima facie evidence under Article 2 as distinct from Articles 3 and 4'.

95 ECtHR, *S.M. v Croatia*, *supra* note 82, para. 314.

96 Ibid., para. 313.

97 Ibid., para. 329.

98 Ibid., para. 324.

99 Ibid., para. 279.

100 ECtHR, *Siliadin v France*, no 73316/01, 27.07.2005, para. 122.

which the said person has not offered him or herself voluntarily'. In doing so, the Court recognised that ILO Conventions 'are binding on almost all of the Council of Europe member States', therefore implicitly admitting that the conditions provided for in Article 31(3)(c) VCLT were satisfied.[101] Other international instruments, therefore, were resorted to for clarifying the meaning of the ECHR, under the systematic interpretation technique, but also as an element for identifying an international and/or European consensus which justifies the evolutive interpretation of the Convention. In the case at hand, said evolutionary approach has been further extended. While human trafficking had already been included in the scope of Article 4 in the *Rantsev* case, in *S.M.*, by relying on the Anti-Trafficking Convention, the Court stated that human trafficking does not necessarily need to be the result of organised and/or transnational crime. Moreover, it clarified that also forced prostitution falls within the notion of human trafficking and is prohibited under Article 4.

3.4. INCLUSIVE EDUCATION FOR CHILDREN WITH DISABILITIES

The chamber judgment in the case *G.L. v Italy* is relevant from the viewpoint of the right to inclusive education for children with disabilities,[102] as well as for the due relevance it gave to the United Nations Convention on the Rights of Persons with Disabilities (CRPD).

The applicant was an Italian young girl, G.L., suffering from nonverbal autism who, during the first two years of her primary education, had not received specialised learning support at school. Although Italian law expressly provides for it, the authorities argued that they lacked financial resources. As a consequence, G.L. had to repeat one year of school, and her parents had to provide her with specialised assistance, at their own cost. Consequently, they applied to the Regional Administrative Tribunal, claiming compensation. Both the Tribunal and the Council of State rejected their applications. Before the ECtHR, the applicant claimed a violation of the prohibition of discrimination

---

101 ECtHR, *Stummer v Austria*, no 37452/02 [GC] 07.07.2011, para. 117.

102 ECtHR, *G.L. v Italy*, no 59751/15, 10.09.2020; see, in this regard, A. Arnadóttir, 'The Right to Inclusive Education for Children with Disabilities – Innovations in the CRPD', in A. Eide, J.T. Möller and I. Ziemele (eds.), *Making Peoples Heard. Essays on Human Rights in Honour of Godmundur Alfredsson*, Martinus Nijhoff, Leiden–Boston 2011, pp. 197–227. In CRPD Committee, *General Comment No. 4 (2016) on the right to inclusive education*, UN Doc CRPD/C/GC/4, 02.09.2016, para. 11, inclusive education has been defined as 'a process that transforms culture, policy and practice in all educational environments to accommodate the differing needs of individual students, together with a commitment to remove the barriers that impede that possibility. An inclusive approach involves strengthening the capacity of an education system to reach out all learners'; ECtHR, *Çam v Turkey*, no 51500/08, 13.02.2016, para. 64.

(Article 14) in conjunction with the right to education (Article 2 of Protocol No. 1).

In line with some previous judgments,[103] the Court stated that the right to education must be interpreted in the light of the right to respect for private life,[104] as well as of other international instruments.[105] Moreover, the Court stipulated that the prohibition of discrimination is informed by the evolution of international and European law,[106] according to which inclusive education is a means for promoting equal opportunities to everyone.

Therefore, the Court examined whether, in the case at hand and under the ECHR, the state had an obligation to adopt a 'reasonable accommodation' in the applicant's favour. It observed that the Italian legislator, in the exercise of its margin of appreciation, recognised that children with disabilities have the right to inclusive education within mainstream schools.[107] However, in assessing the measures the state should have adopted, the Court considered that Article 14 must be read in the light of the CRPD.[108] Article 24(2)(c) of said Convention requires, while guaranteeing the right to education, the adoption of reasonable accommodations which are defined in Article 2 as:

> necessary and appropriate modification[s] and adjustment[s] not imposing a disproportionate or undue burden, where needed in a particular case, to ensure to persons with disabilities the enjoyment or exercise on an equal basis with others of all human rights and fundamental freedoms.

Although the determination of the measures required by the circumstances of a case falls within the states' margin of appreciation, failure in adopting them amounts to discrimination on the ground of disability.[109] Moreover, in

---

103 ECtHR, *Timichev v Russia*, nos 55762/00 and 55974/00, 13.12.2005, para. 64: 'This right [to education] is also to be found in similar terms in other international instruments such as the Universal Declaration of Human Rights (Article 26), the International Covenant on Economic, Social and Cultural Rights (Article 13), the International Convention on the Elimination of All Forms of Racial Discrimination (Article 5(e)(v)), and the Convention on the Rights of the Child (Article 28)'.

104 ECtHR, *G.L. v Italy, supra* note 102, para. 50.

105 Ibid., para. 51.

106 Ibid., para. 53.

107 Ibid., para. 60. But see M. Vrancken, 'Substantive Equality as the Driving Force Behind Reasonable Accommodations for Pupils with Disabilities: The Case of G.L. v. Italy', *Strasbourg Observers*, 01.10.2020, available at https://strasbourgobservers.com/2020/10/01/substantive-equality-as-the-driving-force-behind-reasonable-accommodations-for-pupils-with-disabilities-the-case-of-g-l-v-italy/, last accessed 06.07.2021: 'In stating this, the Court seems to disregard relevant obligations stemming from the CRPD [...]'.

108 See also ECtHR, *Çam v Turkey, supra* note 102, para. 65: 'la Cour considère que l'Article 14 de la Convention doit être lu a la lumière des exigences [...] des aménagements raisonnables [...] que les personnes en situation de handicap sont en droit d'attendre [...]'.

109 ECtHR, *G.L. v Italy, supra* note 102, para. 62.

the exercise of that discretion they must take into consideration the extreme vulnerability of disabled children.[110]

The Court found that the applicant had not been able to attend school in conditions equivalent to non-disabled students and that this interference was due to her disability.[111] It considered that the authorities should have attempted to strike a fair balance between the competing interests (the right to education in conditions of equality and the financial interests of the administration) and should have put in place a reduction of the overall educational provision, in order to distribute the lack of financial resources between students with and without disabilities.[112] To this end, the Court invoked Article 15 of the Revised European Social Charter, which stipulates that states must 'promote [the] full social integration and participation in the life of the community [of persons with disabilities] in particular through measures aimed to overcome barriers to communication and mobility', as well as Articles 24(2)(c) and (d) and 24(3) of the CRPD, concerning the right to inclusive education.[113] The respondent state's authorities had not considered the adoption of measures aimed at ensuring equal access to education, and the discrimination was aggravated because it was realised during a fundamental stage of the development of the applicant's social integration.[114] For these reasons, the authorities had not respected the due diligence standard the Convention requires, thereby violating Article 14, in combination with Article 2 of Protocol No. 1.

In Judge Wojtyczek's opinion, however, the Court unduly extended states' obligations under the CRPD by requiring a more demanding standard (attending mainstream schools in conditions of equality). In his opinion, while inclusive education is the more appropriate solution for many (but not all) children with disabilities, the Court should not have presented it as the best and mandatory solution.[115] However, Article 24 CRPD, as interpreted by the UN Committee on

---

110 Ibid., para. 63. In general, when the applicant is a 'vulnerable' individual, States' margin of appreciation is narrower and only particularly weighty reasons might justify the complained measure. See, *ex multis*, ECtHR, *Kozak v Poland*, no 13102/02, 02.03.2010, para. 94 (in relation to discrimination on the basis of sexual orientation); ECtHR, *Z.H. v Hungary*, no 28973/11, 08.11.2012, para. 29 (in relation to individuals with mental disorders).

111 ECtHR, *G.L. v Italy, supra* note 102, para. 66.

112 Ibid., para. 68.

113 Ibid., para. 69. The Court also mentioned the CoE Committee of Ministers' Recommendation Rec(2006)5, Action Plan to promote the rights and full participation of people with disabilities in society: improving the quality of life of people with disabilities in Europe in 2006–2015, 05.04.2006, p. 16, available at https://rm.coe.int/1680595206, last accessed 06.07.2020: 'The creation of opportunities for disabled people to participate in mainstream education if not only important for disabled people but will also benefit non-disabled people's understanding of human diversity'.

114 ECtHR, *G.L. v Italy, supra* note 102, para. 70.

115 ECtHR, *G.L. v Italy*, no 59751/15, 10.09.2020, Concurring opinion of Judge Wojtyczek, para. 5.

the Rights of Persons with Disabilities, clearly requests states to provide children with disabilities with the possibility of accessing mainstream education.

Therefore, the Court's approach should be welcomed – both for the solution it reached in the specific case, and for the interpretative value it recognised to the relevant international legal framework.[116] The CRPD has triggered, in particular, an incredible development in the interpretation of Article 14 ECHR.[117] The Court stated that disability is one of the 'other' grounds of discrimination under the said provision in the case *Glor v Switzerland*,[118] by directly referring to the CRPD which had recently entered into force. The CRPD then was invoked by the ECtHR in order to justify its evolutive interpretation of the ECHR: in 2016 the ECtHR ruled, in the cases *Guberina v Croatia* and *Çam v Turkey*,[119] that Article 14 also requires the adoption of 'reasonable accommodations' and that a failure in adopting them amounts to indirect discrimination. As far as 'inclusive education' is concerned, the case *Enver Şahin v Turkey* must be mentioned: by implicitly relying on Article 31(3)(c) VCLT, the Court considered that Article 2 of Protocol No. 1 to the ECHR must be interpreted by taking into account 'any relevant rules and principles of international law applicable in the relations between the parties', such as the European Social Charter and the CRPD,[120] as well as 'the fundamental principles of universality and non-discrimination in the exercise of the right to education, which are enshrined in many international texts'.[121] Therefore, the Court concluded that states have, under the Convention, a due diligence obligation to ensure that persons with disabilities can exercise the right to education on an equal footing with other students, and to strike a fair balance between the competing interests at stake.[122]

The development of the ECtHR case law concerning disability, in general, and inclusive education, in particular, has been oriented by the CRPD and its

---

116 M. Marchegiani, '"La disabilità è negli occhi di chi guarda" (e resta a guardare): tra previsioni normative e attuazione concreta in tema di educazione inclusiva nella prospettiva della Corte europea. Considerazioni a margine del caso G.L. c. Italia', *SIDIBlog*, 06.10.2020, available at http://www.sidiblog.org/2020/10/05/la-disabilita-e-negli-occhi-di-chi-guarda-e-resta-a-guardare-lo-iato-tra-previsioni-normative-e-attuazione-concreta-in-tema-di-educazione-inclusiva-nella-prospettiva-della-corte-e/, last accessed 31.05.2021.

117 D. Ferri, 'L'accomodamento ragionevole per le persone con disabilità in Europa: Da Transatlantic Borrowing alla Cross-Fertilization', (2017) 19(2), *Diritto Pubblico Comparato ed Europeo*, p. 381; D. Ferri, 'Reasonable Accommodations as a Gateway to the Equal Enjoyment of Human Rights: From New York to Strasbourg', (2018) 6(1), *Social Inclusion*, p. 40.

118 ECtHR, *Glor v Switzerland*, no 13444/04, 30.04.2009, para. 53. The Court invoked the CRPD in order to conclude that 'there is a European and worldwide consensus on the need to protect people with disabilities from discriminatory treatment'.

119 ECtHR, *Guberina v Croatia*, no 23682/12, 23.03.2016, para. 98; ECtHR, *Çam v Turkey*, *supra* note 102, para. 65.

120 ECtHR, *Enver Şahin v Turkey*, no 23065/12, 30.01.2018, para. 53.

121 Ibid., para. 55.

122 Ibid., para. 68.

reception in the European legal order.[123] However, the Court's approach is not always consistent.[124] For example, the CDDH's 2020 Report acknowledges a significant divergence between the case law of the ECtHR and the opinion of the UN Committee on the Rights of Persons with Disabilities concerning the right to vote of persons with disability.[125] And indeed, in the recent judgment *Støbye and Rosenlind v Denmark*, the Court concluded that the applicants' disenfranchisement pursued the legitimate aim of ensuring that voters had the required level of mental skills and was proportionate to that aim.[126] A request for referral to the Grand Chamber is currently pending. The applicant argues that, *inter alia*, the judgment is at odds with Article 29 CRPD. That case shows that the Court should more consistently rely on other international human rights instruments, especially those relating to very specialised issues, when interpreting the Convention. In this regard, while the CDDH's 2020 Report highlights the Court's approach towards systematic and harmonious interpretation, an additional emphasis could have been put on the need to address specific issues in the light of more specific rules and principles.

3.5. THE 'OWN'S CULPABLE CONDUCT' TEST IN COLLECTIVE EXPULSION CASES

On 13 February 2020 the Grand Chamber ruled in the case *N.D. and N.T. v Spain* and found that the Spanish practice of pushbacks at the Spanish-Moroccan border of Melilla was not at odds with the prohibition of collective expulsions of aliens under Article 4 of Protocol No. 4 to the ECHR.[127]

The applicants, a Malian and an Ivorian citizen, attempted to access Spanish territory by overcoming the three fences at the border of Melilla. After climbing the inner fence, they were immediately handcuffed and handed over by the Spanish *guardia civil* to Moroccan officials in Morocco. Therefore, N.D. and N.T.

---

123 S. Favalli, 'The United Nations Convention on the Rights of Persons with Disabilities in the Case Law of the European Court of Human Rights and in the Council of Europe Disability Strategy 2017–2023: "From Zero to Hero"', in (2018) 18(2), *Human Rights Law Review*, pp. 517 et seq.

124 In ECtHR, *Dupin v France*, no 2282/17, (dec.) 18.12.2018 the Court made no reference to the CRPD and considered that there was no violation of Article 2, Protocol No 1 to the ECHR; see also ECtHR, *Stoian v Romania*, no 289/14, 15.06.2019. See M. Spinoy and K. Willems, 'Inclusive Education in Strasbourg: Still Learning?', in P. Czech, L. Heschl, K. Lukas, M. Nowak and G. Oberleitner (eds.), *European Yearbook on Human Rights 2020*, Intersentia, Cambridge-Antwerp-Chicago 2020, pp. 281–319.

125 CoE, CDDH (2019), *The Place of the European Convention on Human Rights*, *supra* note 6, paras. 273.

126 ECtHR, *Strøbye and Rosenlind v Denmark*, nos 15802/18 and 27338/18, 02.02.2021, paras. 121 and 130.

127 ECtHR, *N.D. and N.T. v Spain*, *supra* note 20.

applied to the Court, arguing that they had been expelled without an individual assessment of their case and identity, and in the absence of any procedure and legal assistance.[128] By introducing the so-called 'one's culpable conduct' test, the Grand Chamber reversed the Chamber judgment,[129] which had been described as a possible 'new Hirsi'.[130]

The Grand Chamber rejected the government's arguments on the (in) applicability of Article 4 of Protocol No. 4,[131] and found that the applicants had been subjected to an *expulsion*, given that 'it [was] […] beyond dispute that the applicants were [apprehended in and] removed from Spanish territory and forcibly returned to Morocco'.[132] In reaching this conclusion, the Grand Chamber relied on Article 2 of the ILC Draft Articles on the Expulsion of Aliens,[133] as well as on EU law, and concluded that the term must be interpreted in its common sense ('to drive away from a place') and that the protection from *refoulment* 'cannot be dependent on formal considerations such as whether the persons to be protected were admitted to the territory in conformity with a particular provision of national or European law'.[134] In the Court's view, the term also encompasses forcible removals of aliens (from the territory or at a border) in the context of attempts to access a territory by sea or by land.[135]

---

128 They also claimed a violation of the principle of *non-refoulement* under Article 3 ECHR, as well as a violation of the right to an effective remedy under Article 13 (alone and in combination with Articles 3 ECHR and 4 Protocol 4). These parts of the applications regarding to Article 3 alone and read together with Article 13 had been declared inadmissible by the Chamber in a separate decision: ECtHR, *N.D. and N.T. v Spain*, nos 8675/15 and 8697/15 (dec.) 07.07.2015.

129 ECtHR, *N.D. and N.T. v Spain*, nos 8675/15 and 8697/15, 03.10.2017. The Chamber concluded that the applicants had been expelled without any procedure and without any assessment of the circumstances of the case. Therefore, the expulsion was collective and at odds with Article 4 Protocol 4 and with the right to effective remedy, under Article 13.

130 A. Pijnenburg, 'Is N.D. and N.T. v Spain the New Hirsi?', *EJIL Talk!*, 17.10.2017, available at https://www.ejiltalk.org/is-n-d-and-n-t-v-spain-the-new-hirsi/, last accessed 31.05.2021.

131 The government argued that the applicants were subjected to refusal to admission to the Spanish territory and not to an expulsion.

132 ECtHR, *N.D. and N.T. v Spain*, *supra* note 20, para. 191.

133 ILC, *Draft Articles on the Expulsion of Aliens*, Yearbook of the International Law Commission, 2014, Vol. II, Part Two, Article 2: '[expulsion is] a formal act or conduct attributable to a State, by which an alien is compelled to leave the territory of that State; it does not include […] the non-admission of an alien to that State'. However, the Commentary explains that the term expulsion has to be understood broadly (including 'exclusion of an alien') while Article 6 of the Commentary stipulates that 'the present draft articles are without prejudice to the rules of international law relating to refugees, as well as to any more favorable rules or practice on refugee protection […]'.

134 ECtHR, *N.D. and N.T. v Spain*, *supra* note 20, para. 183. Expulsion refers to 'any forcible removal of an alien from a State's territory, irrespective of the lawfulness of the person's stay, the length of time he or she has spent in the territory, the location in which he or she was apprehended, his or her status as a migrant or an asylum seeker and his or her conduct when crossing the border'.

135 But see ECtHR, *N.D. and N.T. v Spain* [GC] nos 8675/15 and 8697/15, 13.02.2020, Partly dissenting opinion of Judge Koskelo, para. 1: 'the position taken by the majority […] makes the scope of application of this provision wider than is justified'. In Koskelo's view, while the

What the Court excluded is that the expulsion was collective. It recognised that there had been no reasonable and objective examination of the circumstances of each applicant's case,[136] while the Convention requires that individuals must have 'a genuine and effective possibility of submitting arguments against their expulsion and [to have] those arguments [...] examined in an appropriate manner'.[137] However, the Court considered that in the light of its previous case law, 'the applicant's own conduct is a relevant factor in assessing the protection to be afforded under Article 4 of Protocol 4'.[138] In the case at hand, such 'own conduct' included, in the Court's view, an attempt to cross a land border in an unauthorised manner, taking advantage of large number [of persons] and use of force in order to create a situation which is difficult to control and endangers public safety.[139] By contrast, the applicants could have resorted to the available and effective means of legal entry in Spanish territory and

> where such arrangements exist and secure the right to request protection under the Convention, and in particular under Article 3, in a genuine and effective manner, the Convention does not prevent States, in the fulfilment of their obligation to control borders, from requiring applications for such protection to be submitted at the existing border crossing points [...]. Consequently, they may refuse entry to their territory to aliens, including potential asylum seekers, who have failed, without cogent reason [...] to comply with these arrangements by seeking to cross the border at a different location [...].[140]

The Court assessed the availability of such arrangements (requesting visas or applying for international protection at border crossing points, or diplomatic and consular representations)[141] and held that the applicants failed in demonstrating why there had been no possibility of lodging applications for international protection through these means.[142] Actually, the Court did not assess whether such means were effectively accessible for the applicants. It only assessed whether the applicants had 'cogent reasons' not to resort to these arrangements and observed that racial profiling and other impediments at borders were not attributable to Spain,[143] but rather to Moroccan officials. Therefore, the Court

---

obligation of *non-refoulement* (under Article 3 ECHR) is absolute [...], it applies only to those aliens seeking for international protection. In her view, however, the majority's approach extends the applicability of Article 4 of Protocol No 4 'even in the absence of any indication that [aliens] are seeking international protection, and even in the presence of circumstances indicating other motives for entry into the jurisdiction' (para. 23).

136 ECtHR, *N.D. and N.T. v Spain*, *supra* note 20, paras. 203 and 207.

137 Ibid., para. 198.

138 Ibid., para. 200.

139 Ibid., para. 201.

140 Ibid., para. 210.

141 Ibid., para. 212.

142 Ibid., para. 214.

143 Ibid., para. 221.

concluded that, although the Convention is meant to ensure rights that are practical and effective, this 'does not […] imply a general duty for a Contracting State under Article 4 of Protocol No. 4 to bring persons who are under the jurisdiction of another State within its own jurisdiction'.[144]

The Grand Chamber presented the 'own's culpable test' as part of 'its settled case law'.[145] Nevertheless, it can be (at least) doubted that the two mentioned cases (*Berisha and Haljiti v the Former Yugoslav Republic of Macedonia* and *Dritsas and others v Italy*)[146] are 'settled' case law. Moreover, in these cases the applicants' conduct (producing the same allegations for two spouses' asylum application, in the former, and refusing to communicate their names, in the latter) had an impact on the authorities' capacity to give individualised motivations,[147] while, in any case, 'there was at least an attempt of the authorities to assess the applicants' circumstances'.[148] It seems that in the *N.D. and N.T.* case, the Court did not actually apply the exclusionary principle established in the abovementioned precedents, but it rather 'invented'[149] or 'developed a new exception to the prohibition of collective expulsion',[150] in the light of a two-pronged test: (i) the assessment of the existence of genuine and effective means of legal entry; and (ii) the absence of cogent reasons which could justify the applicants for not having resorted to such means. However, as it has been argued, the Court failed to explain why the 'means of legal access' were genuine and effective and reasonably accessible for the applicants, and it established a very high threshold for satisfying the second phase of the test.[151]

---

144 Ibid., para. 221.

145 Ibid., para. 231: 'in accordance with its settled case-law, the Court considers that the lack of individual removal decision can be attributed to the fact that the applicants, if they indeed wished to assert rights under the Convention, did not make use of the official entry procedures existing for that purpose, and was thus a consequence of their own conduct […]. Accordingly, there has been no violation of Article 4 of Protocol No. 4'. Moreover, given that the applicant had placed themselves in an unlawful situation, the Court considered that Spain had no obligation to provide effective remedies under Article 13 ECHR.

146 ECHR, *Berisha and Haljiti v Former Yugoslav Republic of Macedonia*, no 18670/03, 10.04.2007; ECHR, *Dritsas and others v Italy*, no 2344/02, 01.02.2011.

147 G. Ciliberto, 'A Brand-New Exclusionary Clause to the Prohibition of Collective Expulsion of Aliens: The Applicant's Own Conduct in *N.D. and N.T. v Spain*', (2021) 21(1), *Human Rights Law Review*, p. 8.

148 J. Hakiki, 'N.D. and N.T. v Spain: Defining Strasbourg's Position on Push Backs Land Borders?', *Strasbourg Observer*, 26.03.2020, available at https://strasbourgobservers.com/2020/03/26/n-d-and-n-t-v-spain-defining-strasbourgs-position-on-push-backs-at-land-borders/, last accessed 31.05.2021.

149 M. Pichl and D. Schmalz, '"Unlawful" May Not Mean Rightless. The Shocking ECtHR Grand Chamber Judgment in Case N.D. and N.T.', *Verfassungsblog*, 14.02.2020, available at https://verfassungsblog.de/unlawful-may-not-mean-rightless/, last accessed 31.05.2021.

150 G. Ciliberto (2021), 'A Brand-New Exclusionary Clause', *supra* note 147, p. 9 and p. 11. The author explained the test in the light of the exhaustion of domestic remedies clause.

151 Ibid., pp. 11–15.

The Court's approach has been found very problematic, not only because it has restricted the level of protection under Article 4, Protocol No. 4, but also since it 'sets a very dangerous precedent' that impacts the effective guarantee of the principle of *non-refoulment*,[152] while also being at odds with EU law and international law concerning the protection of unaccompanied children.[153] And indeed, in the aforementioned *D.D. v Spain* case, where the facts were identical, the UN Committee on the Rights of the Child concluded that

> in accordance with article 37 [CRC] and the principle of *non-refoulement*, the State has an obligation to carry out a prior assessment of the risk, if any, of irreparable harm to the child and serious violations of his or her rights in the country to which he or she will be transferred or returned.[154]

The Court's ruling has been criticised as at least 'questionable'[155] or even 'shocking'.[156] Thym, in particular, observed that the case at hand, together with the abovementioned *M.N.* decision, was influenced by the politicisation of migration in the European context[157] and that they 'may mark a symbolic endpoint of 30 years of dynamic ECtHR jurisprudence which considerably expanded the human rights of migrants and refugees without, however, negating countervailing claims to migration control'.[158] Others, however, have doubted that the judgment will likely have an impact in cases concerning similar

---

152 M. Pichl and D. Schmalz (2020), '"Unlawful" May Not Mean Rightless', *supra* note 149; See also A. Lübbe, 'The Elephant in the Room. Effective Guarantee of Non-Refoulement after ECtHR N.D. and N.T.?', *Verfassungsblog*, 19.02.2020, available at https://verfassungsblog.de/the-elephant-in-the-room/, last accessed 31.05.2021.

153 D. Thym, 'A Restrictionist Revolution? A Counter-Intuitive Reading of the ECtHR's N.D. & N.T. Judgment on "Hot Expulsion" at the Spanish-Moroccan Border', *Verfassungsblog*, 17.02.2020, available at https://verfassungsblog.de/a-restrictionist-revolution/, last accessed 31.05.2021; C. Oviedo Moreno, 'A Painful Slap from the ECtHR and an Urgent Opportunity for Spain', *Verfassungsblog*, 14.02.2020, available at https://verfassungsblog.de/a-painful-slap-from-the-ecthr-and-an-urgent-opportunity-for-spain/, last accessed 31.05.2021.

154 UN Committee on the Rights of the Child, *D.D. v Spain*, *supra* note 31, para. 14.4. See also para. 14.6: 'the Committee reiterates that the State party has an obligation not to return a child "to a country where there are substantial grounds for believing that there is a real risk of irreparable harm to the child". The Committee also notes that, before returning the author to Morocco, the State party did not ascertain his identity, did not ask about his personal circumstances and did not conduct a prior assessment of the risk, if any, of persecution and/or irreparable harm in the country to which he was to be returned. The Committee considers that, given the violence faced by migrants in the Moroccan border area and the ill-treatment to which the author was subjected, the failure to assess the risk of irreparable harm to the author prior to his deportation or to take into account his best interests constitutes a violation of articles 3 and 37 of the [CRC]'.

155 G. Ciliberto (2021), 'A Brand-New Exclusionary Clause', *supra* note 147, 18.

156 M. Pichl and D. Schmalz (2020), '"Unlawful" May Not Mean Rightless', *supra* note 149.

157 Ibid., section 2.

158 D. Thym, 'The End of Human Rights Dynamism? Judgment of the ECtHR on "Hot Returns" and Humanitarian Visas as a Focal Point of Contemporary European Asylum Law and Policy', (2021) 32(4), *International Journal of Refugee Law*, pp. 569–596.

practices at the EU external borders and considered that its true impact will be 'less dramatic and more nuanced'.[159]

An intermediate position has been adopted by Di Filippo, who identified some 'ways ahead'. He pleaded a restrictive reading of the newly established exception and argued that the Court could have, in already pending cases, taken the occasion to do so.[160] And indeed, a few months later the First Chamber of the Court tried to adjust the Grand Chamber's approach – in the case *M.K. v Poland.* That ruling confirmed that in order to determine whether an expulsion has been collective, the applicants' conduct in resorting to legal means of entry must be assessed.[161] However, while in the *N.D. and N.T.* case such legal means were hardly effective, the *M.K.* case makes it clear that such means must be genuine and effective for the said exception to apply.[162]

While the *M.K.* judgment engenders some hope, it remains to be seen whether CoE states will actually implement the Court's request to provide asylum-seekers with effective means of legal entry to their territory, or whether they will try to shield their growing practice of pushbacks and externalisation of borders behind the *N.D. and N.T.* judgment.

4. DEVELOPMENTS CONCERNING PROCEDURAL ISSUES

This section deals with those cases in which the Court clarified some procedural issues concerning both individual and inter-state applications. In these cases, cross-fertilisation and systemic integration are of fundamental importance as well.

---

159 R. Wissing, 'Push Backs of "Badly Behaving" Migrants at Spanish Border Are Not Collective Expulsions (But Might Still Be Illegal Refoulements)', *Strasbourg Observer*, 25.02.2020, available at https://strasbourgobservers.com/2020/02/25/push-backs-of-badly-behaving-migrants-at-spanish-border-are-not-collective-expulsions-but-might-still-be-illegal-refoulements/, last accessed 31.05.2021.

160 M. Di Filippo, 'Walking the (Barbed) Wire of the Prohibition of Collective Expulsion: An Assessment of the Strasbourg Case Law', (2020) 14(2), *Diritti Umani e Diritto Internazionale,* p. 508.

161 ECtHR, *M.K. v Poland*, nos 40503/17, 42902/17 and 43643/17, 23.07.2020, para. 207: '[…] the applicants in the present case were to make use of the procedure of accepting applications for international protection that should have been available to them under domestic law. They attempted to cross a border in a legal manner, using an official checkpoint and subjecting themselves to border checks as required by the relevant law. Hence, the fact that the State refused entertain their arguments concerning justification for their applications for international protection cannot be attributed to their own conduct'.

162 U. Brandl and P. Czech, 'A Human Right to Seek Refuge at Europe's Borders: The ECtHR Adjusts its Case-Law in *M.K. vs Poland*', *EU Immigration and Asylum Law Policy*, 11.09.2020, available at https://eumigrationlawblog.eu/a-human-right-to-seek-refuge-at-europes-external-borders-the-ecthr-adjusts-its-case-law-in-m-k-vs-poland/, last accessed 31.05.2021; see also F.L. Gatta, 'Systematic Push Back of "Well-Behaving" Asylum Seekers at the Polish

4.1. THE COURT'S JURISDICTION CONCERNING INTER-STATE APPLICATIONS

In 2020 the Court issued its (in-)admissibility decision in the *Slovenia v Croatia* case, the first inter-state dispute in which both parties were EU Member States.[163] In the decision, the Court clarified the scope of its jurisdiction concerning inter-state applications under Article 33 ECHR and the grounds of inadmissibility which apply to such applications.

The Slovenian Government had lodged an application against Croatia, concerning the alleged violations of the Ljubljana Bank's rights. Notwithstanding its existence as a separate entity, the bank had been nationalised, and in a previous (individual) application the ECtHR had concluded that it did not enjoy sufficient institutional and operational independence from the State to be regarded as a 'non-governmental organisation' for the purposes of Article 34 ECHR.[164]

In the decision at hand the Court assessed, first of all, whether it may examine a preliminary objection concerning lack of jurisdiction in the admissibility phase. It clarified that, in principle, 'the only reasons for which inter-State applications can be rejected at the admissibility stage, on the basis of Article 35 ECHR, are the non-exhaustion of domestic remedies and the failure to comply with the six month time-limit'.[165] However, in the Court's view, as any other international tribunal, nothing prevents it from assessing at this stage whether it has jurisdiction to deal with the case which, as the Court clarified, is a separate issue from that concerning the admissibility of an application.[166]

Border: M.K. and Others v. Poland', *Strasbourg Observers*, 07.10.2020, available at https://strasbourgobservers.com/2020/10/07/systematic-push-back-of-well-behaving-asylum-seekers-at-the-polish-border-m-k-and-others-v-poland/#:~:text=Poland,-October%207%2C%202020&text=On%2023%20July%202020%2C%20the,case%20M.K.%20and%20Others%20v.&text=With%20an%20encouraging%20decision%2C%20the,borders%20between%20Poland%20and%20Belarus, last accessed 31.05.2021.

163 ECtHR, *Slovenia v Croatia*, no 54155/16 [GC] 18.11.2020.

164 ECtHR, *Ljubljanska Banka D.D. v Croatia*, no 29003/07, 12.05.2015. See also ECtHR, *Democratic Republic of the Congo v Belgium*, no 16554/19, 06.10.2020. The application was lodged by the Democratic Republic of the Congo in its quality of a minority shareholder in a mining company incorporated under Zairean law.

165 ECtHR, *Slovenia v Croatia, supra* note 163, para. 40. Except where the applicant state complains about an administrative practice as such, with the aim of preventing its continuation or recurrence (see, *inter alia*, ECtHR, *Georgia v Russia (II)*, no 38263/08, 13.12.2011, para. 85).

166 Ibid., para. 69. That admissibility conditions concerning procedural requirements (Article 35 (2) ECHR) and the merits (non-manifest ill-founded cases) do not apply in inter-State cases is clear. See ECommHR, *France, Norway, Denmark, Sweden and the Netherlands v Turkey*, nos 9940/82, 9941/82, 9942/82, 8843/82 and 9944/82, 07.12.1985, para. 9. States under Article 33 ECHR have an 'unqualified right [...] to bring any alleged breaches of the Convention to the Court', given the 'quality of the inter-State procedure as an expression of the system of the collective guarantee of the Convention' (CoE, CDDH, *Drafting Group on Effective Processing and Resolution of Cases relating to Inter-State Disputes*, DH-SYSC-IV (2020)04, 08.07.2020, paras. 3 and 28).

The Court considered that in the admissibility stage, it can also assess whether it has 'any competence at all to deal with the matter laid before it', in accordance with general principles concerning the exercise of jurisdiction of international tribunals and with the principle of procedural economy.[167] Therefore, it has the possibility of declaring an inter-state application inadmissible if it is 'wholly unsubstantiated, or otherwise lacking the requirements of a genuine application in the sense of Article 33 of the Convention'.[168] The Court also gave some examples of the preliminary issues which can be assessed in the admissibility stage of an inter-state dispute, which basically relate to the *prima facie* existence of the four jurisdictional grounds,[169] such as: the lack of *locus standi* of the applicant governmental entity as the legitimate representative of the respective state and the *prima facie* (in-)existence of the jurisdiction of the respondent state; the jurisdiction *ratione loci* of the Convention institutions; the lack of a *prima facie* evidence of a breach of the Convention; the existence of a special agreement between the parties within the meaning of Article 55 ECHR; and the manifest abuse of the right to inter-state application.

Given said distinction between jurisdiction and admissibility, the Grand Chamber's view is that the relevant issue – whether it may examine an inter-state application concerning rights of a legal entity which does not appear 'non-governmental' – is not an admissibility issue.[170] It concerns the same existence of the Court's *jurisdiction* pursuant to Article 32 ECHR:

> In fact, the question whether the Convention as a human rights treaty can create fundamental rights for State-owned and State-run entities goes beyond the boundaries of the Convention mechanism and touches upon a general issue of international law, especially in the light of the universally recognised specific nature of human rights treaties.[171]

Therefore, the Court assessed whether the violation of the rights of an entity that itself could not lodge an application can be claimed by the state. It observed that the absence of legal standing of a governmental organisation to lodge an individual application is aimed at preventing a contracting party from 'acting as an applicant and a respondent'.[172] Recalling the principles of harmonious

---

167 ECtHR, *Slovenia v Croatia*, *supra* note 163, para. 41.

168 Ibid., para. 41

169 Ibid., para. 42.

170 Ibid., para. 43.

171 Ibid., para. 44.

172 Ibid., para. 61. The term encompasses 'legal entities which participate in the exercise of governmental power or run a public service under government control', such as central organs of the State but also decentralised authorities that exercise public functions, regional and local authorities. The qualification must be assessed in the light of the organisation 'legal status and, where appropriate, the rights that status gives it, the nature of the activity it carries out, the context in which it is carried out, and the degree of its independence from the

and consistent interpretation, the Court rejected the applicant government's arguments, according to which the term 'governmental organisation' should be interpreted differently in individual and inter-state cases: 'the internal coherence of the Convention is an important principle that applies to the substantive rights [...] but equally to the jurisdictional and procedural provisions [...]'.[173] As a consequence, the meaning of the term 'non-governmental organisation' must be the same. Secondly, in the Court's view the specific nature of the ECHR as a human right treaty must be taken into account. It therefore mentioned the 1951 ICJ Advisory Opinion on reservations to the Genocide Convention,[174] as well as some precedents of the Inter-American Court of Human Rights (IACtHR)[175] and the UN Human Rights Committee (HRC),[176] stipulating the objective and *erga omnes* nature of human rights treaty obligations.[177] Therefore, inter-state applications under the ECHR cannot aim at protecting states' interests. By contrast, 'according to the very nature of the Convention, even in an inter-state case *it is always the individual*, and not the State, who is directly or indirectly harmed and primarily "injured" by a violation'.[178] Given that states do not bear rights under the Convention, they cannot lodge inter-state applications alleging the violations of rights pertaining to states' entities.[179]

In the light of the classic distinction between inter-state cases aimed at 'protecting the public order of Europe' and those that are substantially similar to both individual applications and diplomatic protection claims, the Court qualified the application at issue in the latter sense. However, even in such cases the 'injured' is the individual, and not the state, as demonstrated by the fact that just satisfaction is directed at the benefit of individual victims.[180] For all these

---

political authorities'. However, all the factual and legal circumstances must be assessed, such as the historical and legal context.

[173] Ibid., para. 65.

[174] ICJ, *Reservations to the Convention on the Prevention and Punishment of the Crime of Genocide (Advisory Opinion)*, 28.05.1951, ICJ Rep. 1951, pp. 15 et seq., p. 23.

[175] IACtHR, *Effect of Reservations on the Entry into Force of the American Convention on Human Rights (Articles 74 and 75)*, Advisory Opinion OC-2/82, 24.09.1982, para. 29.

[176] UN Human Rights Committee, *General Comment No. 24 on the Issues Relating to Reservations Made upon Ratification of Accession to the International Covenant on Civil and Political Rights or the Optional Protocol thereto, or in Relation to Declarations under Article 41 of the Covenant*, adopted at the 52th session on 04.11.1994, UN Doc CCPR/C/21/Rev.1/Add.6, para. 17.

[177] ECommHR, *Austria v Italy*, no 788/60, (dec.) 11.01.1961: 'the obligations undertaken by the High Contracting Parties are essentially of an objective character, being designed rather to protect the fundamental rights of individual human beings from infringement by any of the High Contracting Parties than to create subjective and reciprocal rights for the High Contracting Parties themselves'. See also E.W. Vierdag, 'Some Remarks about Special Features of Human Rights Treaties', (1994) 25, *Netherlands Yearbook of International Law*, p. 125: 'The axiom [...] will be that breaches of human rights treaties are breaches vis-à-vis individuals, not vis-à-vis states'.

[178] ECtHR, *Slovenia v Croatia*, *supra* note 163, para. 66.

[179] Ibid., para. 66.

[180] ECtHR, *Cyprus v Turkey*, no 25781, 12.05.2014.

reasons, the Court considered that it had no jurisdiction to examine an inter-state claim lodged under Article 33 ECHR to vindicate rights of a 'governmental organisation'. Since the Court found no reasons for departing from its precedent, where it ascertained that the Ljubljana Bank is a governmental organisation, it concluded that Article 33 ECHR does not empower the Court to examine an inter-state application alleging a violation of any Convention right in respect of that entity.

In the decision at hand, the Court finally drew a clear distinction between, on the one hand, its jurisdiction (concerning the very existence of its power to deal with a case) and, on the other hand, the admissibility of an application which concerns procedural issues allowing (or not) the Court to deal with the merits of an inter-state application. It is now clear that in the 'admissibility phase' the Court has the power to examine: (i) the existence of an issue on which the Court has jurisdiction under Article 32 ECHR, which includes the – at least – *prima facie* existence of the four jurisdictional grounds (*ratione materiae, personae, temporis* and *loci*) covered by Article 33 ECHR, as indicated above; and (ii) the existence of the conditions of admissibility which expressly apply to inter-state disputes, namely those enumerated in Article 35, para. 1, of the Convention.[181] Moreover, the Court clarified that the admissibility conditions established by Article 34 ECHR cannot be circumvented through inter-state applications, and that the latter, in any case, are aimed at protecting individuals' rights and not states' own interests.

The Court solved one of the main issues – whether it can rule on its own jurisdiction in the admissibility phase – in the light of the general principles governing the exercise of jurisdiction by international tribunals. And indeed, the prejudicial resolution of jurisdictional issues is imposed not only by interests of judicial economy, by also by the principle of the consent of the state parties to the dispute.

One should also note that several recent disputes brought before the ICJ are grounded on the compromissory clauses included in the UN human rights treaties (in particular, the UN Convention on the Prevention and Repression of the Crime of Genocide, and the UN Convention on the Elimination of All Forms of Racial Discrimination). In those cases, applicant states are seen as vindicating their own right to demand respect of the (*erga omnes partes*) human rights obligations enshrined in the relevant treaty, although a close connection between states' rights and duties and individuals' rights is recognised.[182]

---

181 See M. Stavridi, 'Slovenia v Croatia: A New Admissibility Criterion for Inter-State Applications under the ECHR?', *EJIL:Talk!*, 06.01.2021, available at https://www.ejiltalk.org/slovenia-v-croatia-a-new-admissibility-criterion-for-inter-state-applications-under-the-echr/, last accessed 31.05.2021.

182 E.g. ICJ, *Application of the International Convention on the Elimination of All Forms of Racial Discrimination (Georgia v Russian Federation)*, Order on the Request for the Indication of

However, the ECtHR's clarification (according to which inter-state applications under the ECHR are, in any case, aimed at protecting the individuals) might indeed trigger a discussion on whether applicant states before the ICJ pursuant to human rights treaties should be considered as acting *on behalf* of the individuals (or groups) which are victims of human rights violations, and not as claiming their own rights.

4.2. ADMISSIBILITY *RATIONE PERSONAE* CONCERNING INDIVIDUAL APPLICATIONS: THE '*DE FACTO* REPRESENTATION'

In two relevant chamber judgments of 2020, the Court followed, and partially extended, its *Câmpeanu* jurisprudence on '*de facto* representation' of extremely vulnerable individuals.[183] According to that case law, when certain conditions are fulfilled, a third party – namely, a non-governmental organisation (NGO)[184] – can apply to the Court on behalf of individuals who, because of *de jure* or

Provisional Measures, 15.10.2008, para. 126: 'Whereas the Court notes that Articles 2 and 5 of the CERD are intended to protect individuals from racial discrimination by obliging State parties to undertake certain measures specified therein; [...] whereas States parties to the CERD have the right to demand compliance by a State party with specific obligations incumbent upon it under Articles 2 and 5 of the Convention; whereas there is a correlation between respect for individual rights, the obligations of the States parties under CERD and the right of State parties to seek compliance therein; whereas in the view of the Court the rights which Georgia invokes in, and seeks to protect by, its Request for the indication of provisional measures have a sufficient connection with the merits of the case it brings for the purposes of the current proceedings'; ICJ, *Application of the Convention on the Prevention and Punishment of the Crime of Genocide (The Gambia v Myanmar)*, Order of the Request for the Indication of Provisional Measures, 23.01.2020, para. 45: 'The Court further observers that the provisions of the Convention are intended to protect the members of a national, ethnical, racial or religious group from acts of genocide or any other punishable acts enumerated in Article III. The Court also considers that there is a correlation between the rights of the members of groups protected under the Genocide Convention, the obligations incumbent on States parties thereto, and the rights of any State party to seek compliance therewith by any other State party'.

183 ECtHR, *Centre for Legal Resources on Behalf of Valentin Câmpeanu v Romania*, no 47848/08 [GC] 17.07.2014; ECtHR, *Association for the Defence of Human Rights in Romania – Helsinki Committee on Behalf of Ionel Garcea v Romania*, no 2959/11, 24.03.2015. The Court identified the *exceptional circumstances* that must be considered when a third party claims to be a *de facto* representative of a victim who is unable to apply her/himself: (1) the victim's vulnerability; (2) the nature and gravity of the alleged violations; (3) the absence of next-of-kin or legal guardians likely to lodge an application; (4) the existence of direct contacts between the victim and the representative; and (5) the involvement of the alleged representative in the domestic proceedings and the recognition of *locus standi* in these proceedings.

184 In 2020 the Court also ruled that an application is admissible when the domestic remedies have been exhausted, in the victims' interest, by an NGO, but then the application with the Court is lodged by the victims themselves (ECtHR, *Beizaras and Levickas v Lithuania*, no 41288/15, 14.01.2020).

de facto incapacity, are not able to apply themselves or to confer power of attorney (under Rules 36(1) and 45(3) of the Rules of Court) or issue specific and explicit instructions. However, the Court's precedents left some questions unanswered. In particular, it seemed that: (i) quite paradoxically, *de facto* representation was allowed only when the victim had lost his/her life;[185] (ii) the element of the direct contact between the victim and the representative was extremely difficult to meet in some cases; (iii) moreover, the Court considered that the third party claiming itself as a *de facto* representative must have been recognised as representative in the domestic proceedings;[186] and (iv) lastly, the Court considered that *de facto* representation was possible when the victims had no parents or relatives, but did not clarify whether it was also possible when parents and relatives are the actual or alleged material authors of the violations.

The Court clarified the first three issues in *L.R. v North Macedonia* and the last one in *Association Innocence en Danger and Association Enfance et Partage v France*.[187] The former concerned an eight-year-old disabled child who had been put by his guardian (a public authority) in a state-run institution unable to provide him with the necessary care. He had been subjected to inhuman and degrading treatments – notably, he had been kept tied to his bed for more than one year. The latter case concerned M., also an eight-year-old child, who had been subjected to ill-treatment from his own parents that led to the child's death in 2009. The abuses had been communicated from the child's teachers to the authorities a year before. In both cases, domestic investigations, although initiated, were discontinued. The applications to the ECtHR were lodged by NGOs that, in principle, are not allowed to apply on behalf of victims without a power of attorney or direct and specific instructions. However, this condition was impossible to fulfil in these cases: while L.R. was a mentally disabled child, M. had died. The governments in both cases objected to the applications' admissibility.

---

185 C. Cojocariu, 'Hit and Miss: Procedural Accommodations Ensuring the Effective Access of Applicants with Mental Disabilities to the European Court of Human Rights', in P. Blanck and E. Flynn (eds.), *Routledge Handbook on Disability Law and Human Rights*, Routledge, London and New York 2016, pp. 105–117, p. 114.

186 ECtHR, *Bulgarian Helsinki Committee v Bulgaria*, nos 35653/12 and 66172/12, 28.06.2016, para. 58.

187 ECtHR, *L.R. v North Macedonia*, no 38067/15, 23.01.2020. See also L. Acconciamessa, 'Legittimazione ad agire e rappresentanza dei minori nei giudizi a Strasburgo: la sentenza L.R. c. Macedonia del Nord del 23 gennaio 2020', (2020) (2), *Ordine Internazionale e Diritti Umani*, p. 407; L. Acconciamessa, 'Bringing the Child's Procedural Rights before the ECtHR through Interpretative Tools: Access to Justice, Participation and Representation', in P. Czech, L. Heschl, K. Lukas, M. Nowak and G. Oberleitner (eds.), *European Yearbook on Human Rights 2020*, Intersentia, Cambridge-Antwerp-Chicago 2020, pp. 50–77, 58; ECtHR, *Association Innocence en Danger and Association Enfance et Partage v France*, nos 15343/15 and 16806/15, 04.06.2020.

The Court clarified the issues mentioned above. First, it made clear that, when the conditions established in the *Câmpeanu* case are fulfilled, a *de facto* representative may apply also on behalf of victims who are still alive. Second, the Court considered that the absence of direct contacts between the victim and the representative might be compensated by other elements which can create a sufficient link and demonstrate a direct interest of the representative in pursuing the case.[188] Third, the ECtHR admitted that the *locus standi* in domestic proceedings is not an essential condition, provided that the representative exercises any faculty it retains under domestic law to pursue the victim's claims.[189] Lastly, it considered that the fact that the (extremely vulnerable) victim has living parents, next-of-kin or a state-appointed guardian does not exclude *de facto* representation. The Court will consider their willingness and likelihood to apply on behalf of the victim, which can be excluded when they are the alleged or actual authors of the violation,[190] when they have no effective relationship with the victim or no legal capacity to act,[191] and, in any case, when there is an actual or potential conflict of interests.[192]

---

188 ECtHR, *L.R. v North Macedonia, supra* note 187, para. 51: 'the Court takes note of the fact that only shortly after the applicant's case had been revealed in public […] the HCHR visited […] and contacted different competent authorities about his situation, with a view to elucidating the relevant circumstances and attributing responsibility. Similarly, it submitted the criminal complaint to the competent public prosecutor without delay and pursued the matter […].'; ECtHR, *Association Innocence en Danger, supra* note 187, para. 130: 'the Court notes that the associations, which certainly did not have contacts with M. before her death, have demonstrated their "attempt of raising the issues before the national authorities before bringing them before the Court" […]' (translated by the author).

189 ECtHR, *L.R. v North Macedonia, supra* note 187, para. 52.

190 Ibid., para. 50: 'the Court attaches particular importance to the fact that the applicant's guardian was accused, both before the domestic authorities and before the Court, of having failed in its responsibility to protect the applicant's interests'; ECtHR, *Association Innocence en Danger, supra* note 187, para. 126: 'M. is dead […] as a consequence of the abuse perpetrated on her by her parents. Therefore, the latter cannot represent the direct victim in their quality of legal representatives' (translated by the author).

191 ECtHR, *L.R. v North Macedonia, supra* note 187, para. 49: 'There is nothing to suggest that the applicant's parents, who also suffer from a mental disability, or any other relative, contacted or visited him or showed any interest in his situation […]'; ECtHR, *Association Innocence en Danger, supra* note 187, para. 129: '[…] taking note of the fact that, throughout the proceedings, the paternal aunt was not heir or representative of the child, the Court considers, on the basis of the available information, that she cannot be considered as a close relative that can potentially lodge an application with the Court' (translated by the author). ECtHR, *Association Innocence en Danger, supra* note 187, para. 127: 'M's brothers and sister were minors at the moment of M.'s death […] and they still were at the moment when the present application was lodged' (translated by the author).

192 Ibid., para. 127: '[…] irrespective of the young age of M's brothers and sister, the latters' proximity with both the victim and the authors of the violence – their parents – made it extremely difficult, or impossible, that they would have introduced an application against the State with the aim of invoking the violation, by the latter, of its positive obligations towards their sister' (translated by the author).

The consolidation of the case law concerning *de facto* representation is extremely relevant from an access to (international) justice perspective.[193] Moreover, in adopting such an approach, the Court is progressively (albeit slowly) harmonising its procedural rules with those of other human rights courts and monitoring bodies. In particular, it is a positive, albeit implicit, example of procedural cross-fertilisation, given that the procedural framework of other international bodies – such as the UN Committee for the Rights of the Child and the African Committee on the Rights and Welfare of the Child,[194] the UN Committee for the Rights of Persons with Disabilities,[195] the UN Human Rights Committee and the African Commission on Human and Peoples' Rights – expressly allow third party representatives to apply on behalf of children, persons with disabilities and, in general, those who are unable to lodge applications or communications for themselves.[196] The harmonisation of procedural rules, and the adoption of uniform admissibility criteria 'as far as allowed by the respective treaties and without curtailing individuals rights', is one of the proposals that have been made in the CDDH's 2020 Report.[197] However, while the example provided in this contribution concerned the *extension* of the ECHR's admissibility criteria, in the light of other procedural instruments, the 2020 report instead suggests the introduction, within the UN treaty bodies' procedural framework, of 'stricter time-limits for filing communication', in conformity with the ECHR, in order to avoid overlapping jurisdictions and forum-shopping.[198] In this regard, one should also consider that on 1 August 2021, Protocol No. 15 to the ECHR entered into force. According to Article 4 of the Protocol, the time limit for lodging applications with the Court will be reduced from six to four months starting from, pursuant to Article 8(3) of the Protocol, 1 February 2022. The time limits for introducing communications to the UN treaty bodies are much longer (e.g. five years for the UN Human Rights Committee) and a reduction of such limits is far from desirable. In the light of the principle of the effective protection

[193] M. Scheinin, 'Access to Justice before International Human Rights Bodies: Reflections of the Practice of the UN Human Rights Committee and the European Court of Human Rights', in F. Francioni (ed.), *Access to Justice as a Human Right*, Oxford University Press, Oxford 2007, pp. 135 et seq.

[194] UN Committee on the Rights of the Child, *Rules of Procedure under the Optional Protocol to the Convention on the Rights of the Child on a communication procedure*, CRC/C/62/, 06.04.2013, Rule 13, para. 3; African Committee for the Rights and Welfare of the Child, *Revised Guidelines for the Consideration of Communications*, section I, para. 3.

[195] UN Committee on the Rights of Persons with Disabilities, *Fact sheet on the procedure for submitting communications to the Committee on the Rights of Persons with Disabilities under the Optional Protocol to the Convention*, CRPD/C/5/2/Rev.1, 12.04.2012, para. 7.

[196] UN Human Rights Committee, *Rules of procedure of the Human Rights Committee*, CCPR/C/3/Rev.11, 09.01.2019, Article 99 (b); African Commission on Human and Peoples' Rights, *Information sheet no. 2. Guidelines on the Submission of Communication*, p. 5.

[197] CoE, CDDH (2019), *The Place of the European Convention on Human Rights, supra* note 6, para. 353.

[198] Ibid.

of human rights, indeed, such protection must not be made contingent upon concerns of judicial economy.

4.3. EVIDENCE AND STANDARD OF PROOF

On 16 December 2020 (although it was read at a public hearing on 14 January 2021), the Grand Chamber adopted its admissibility decision in the case *Ukraine v Russia (re Crimea)*.[199] The decision raises several interesting issues concerning effective control under Article 1 ECHR, and the existence of an administrative practice of human rights violations, which cannot be dealt with in this article,[200] which merely deals with the Court's approach concerning the issue of *evidence* in proceedings before it. The same approach has been followed in the Grand Chamber judgment on the merits of the case *Georgia v Russia (II)*.[201] It clarified some assumptions which are already part of the well-established case law of the ECtHR, but which had never been object of a clear and exhaustive analysis. The Court's clarification deals with inter-state cases, but they can in part be translated to individual ones.[202]

First, it clarified that the evidentiary materials include those submitted by the parties and those which are in the public domain, notably national legislation, relevant bilateral agreements, instruments of the CoE and other international bodies, reports issued by international governmental organisations (especially UN organs but also documents of other international courts and tribunals, such as the International Criminal Court (ICC)),[203] NGOs' reports, official governmental documents and statements, witness evidence and media articles.[204] The Court added that, in principle, there are no procedural barriers to the admissibility of evidence, nor predetermined *formulae* for its assessment and that, in any case, it can obtain *proprio motu* the necessary material.[205] International instruments and reports are relevant, in particular, for the assessment of facts.[206]

---

199 ECtHR, *Ukraine v Russia (re Crimea)*, nos 20958/14 and 38334/18 [GC] 16.12.2020.

200 M. Milanovic, 'ECtHR Grand Chamber Declares Admissible the Case of Ukraine v Russia re Crimea', in *EJIL Talk!*, 15.01.2021, available at https://www.ejiltalk.org/ecthr-grand-chamber-declares-admissible-the-case-of-ukraine-v-russia-re-crimea/, last accessed 31.05.2021.

201 ECtHR, *Georgia v Russia (II)*, no 38263/08 [GC] 21.01.2021.

202 CoE, CDDH, Drafting Group on the Effective Processing and Resolution of Inter-State Disputes, DH-SYSC-IV(2021)R3, 16.04.2021, pp. 44: 'As regards the assessment of the evidence and the application of Article 38 [fact-finding], the Court does not distinguish principles that apply specifically or exclusively to inter-State applications or to individual applications. Instead, the principles developed regarding individuals applications are applied *mutatis mutandis* to inter-State applications and vice-versa'.

203 Ibid., para. 67.

204 Ibid., para. 74; ECtHR, *Ukraine v Russia (re Crimea), supra* note 199, paras. 250–251.

205 Ibid., para. 257.

206 ECtHR, *Georgia v Russia (II), supra* note 201, para. 61.

Second, it specified the principles on the assessment on evidence, both in relation to the burden of proof and the standard of proof. As for the former, it recalled the general principle of law *affirmanti incumbit probatio*, according to which 'the initial burden of proof in relation to an allegation is borne by the party which makes the allegation in question'.[207] However, when the relevant events lie wholly or in large part within the exclusive knowledge of the respondent, 'the burden of proof may be regarded as falling on the respondent Government to provide sufficient and convincing explanation'; in the absence of explanations, the Court can draw inferences in disfavour of the respondent government.[208] As for the standard of proof, it has to be borne in mind that the case was dealt with at the admissibility stage. The Court then recalled its previous statements in the judgments *Georgia v Russia (I)* and *(II)*, where it declared that the existence of an administrative practice in violation of human rights, at the admissibility stage, require a 'prima facie [or substantial] evidence', namely allegations which are 'sufficiently substantiated, considered as a whole and in the light of the submissions of both the applicant and the respondent Party'.[209] As for the existence of the state's jurisdiction under Article 1, by contrast, the Court stated that it has to be assessed under the beyond reasonable doubt standard of proof 'it being understood that such proof [...] may follow from the coexistence of sufficiently strong, clear and concordant inferences or of similar unrebutted presumptions of fact'.[210] The same standard (usually) applies for assessing violations of the rights and freedoms protected under the Convention.

The Court's clarification of evidentiary issues should be welcomed, especially in the light of the huge number of inter-state cases which are currently pending.[211] Such proceedings are often related to armed conflicts between CoE Member States, and the correct ascertainment of the facts is of crucial importance, given that such activity can also be relevant for the huge number of individual applications related to the same facts.[212] Processing and solving inter-state disputes therefore requires, on the one hand, significant fact-finding efforts which the Court can and should order *proprio motu* and, on the other hand, the careful assessment of the evidence submitted by the parties.

---

207 ECtHR, *Ukraine v Russia (re Crimea)*, *supra* note 199, para. 255.

208 Ibid., para. 256.

209 ECtHR, *Georgia v Russia (I)*, no 13255/07, 20.06.2009, para. 41; ECtHR, *Georgia v Russia (II)*, *supra* note 201, para. 86.

210 ECtHR, *Ukraine v Russia (re Crimea)*, *supra* note 199, para. 265.

211 Detailed information on inter-State application are published on the Court's website and available at https://echr.coe.int/Documents/InterState_applications_ENG.pdf, last accessed 31.05.2021.

212 See the discussion on the relationship between inter-state and individual applications, also in relation to evidence and fact-finding, in the Symposium: 'Inter-State Cases under the ECHR', *Völkerrechtsblog*, 26.04.2021, available at https://voelkerrechtsblog.org/symposium/inter-state-cases/, last accessed 31.05.2021.

While neither the Convention nor the Rules of Court regulate how evidence is to be admitted and assessed, and while the issue has not attracted significant attention in scholarship,[213] the relevant rules and principles can be deducted from the Court's case law concerning both inter-state and individual applications, but also, as the CDDH highlighted in the 2021 Report on inter-state proceedings, from the procedural framework and practice of the ICJ and the IACtHR.[214]

4.4. THE SCOPE OF ADVISORY PROCEEDINGS UNDER PROTOCOL NO. 16

On 29 May 2020 the Court issued its second Advisory Opinion pursuant to Protocol No. 16 to the ECHR.[215] The substantive issues are not dealt with in this contribution. However, the Court also clarified some issues concerning the admissibility and scope of advisory requests.

It is well known that Article 1 of Protocol No. 16 stipulates that (the highest) domestic courts and tribunals may seek advisory opinions 'on questions of principle relating to the interpretation or application of the rights and freedoms defined in the Convention or the protocols thereto'; however, pursuant to paragraph 2 such questions have to be relevant in the context of pending cases before the requesting court. The Explanatory Report to the Protocol clarifies that '[t]he procedure is not indented, for example, to allow for abstract review of legislation which is not to be applied in that pending case'.[216]

The ECtHR did not answer the first two questions submitted by the Armenian Constitutional Court because it considered that there was *no direct link* with the pending domestic proceeding.[217] However, while stating that it will not, in

---

213 But see T. Thienel, 'The Burden and Standard of Proof in the European Court of Human Rights', (2007) 50, *German Yearbook of International Law*, pp. 543 et seq.; M. Ambrus, 'The European Court of Human Rights and Standards of Proof. An Evidentiary Approach towards the Margin of Appreciation', in L. Gruszcynski and W. Werner (eds.), *Deference in International Courts and Tribunals: Standards of Review and Margin of Appreciation*, Oxford University Press, Oxford 2014, pp. 235–253, who considers that the ECtHR's towards evidentiary issues is opaque and not always consistent, and changes in the light of the substantive issues the Court has to deal with; C. Heri, 'Evidence: European Court of Human Rights (ECtHR)', (2018) *Max Planck Encyclopedia of International Procedural Law*.

214 CoE, CDDH, Drafting Group on the Effective Processing and Resolution of Inter-State Disputes, *supra* note 202, pp. 56–59.

215 ECtHR, Advisory Opinion No. 2, concerning the use of the 'blanket reference' or 'legislation by reference' technique in the definition of an offence and the standard of comparison between the criminal law in force at the time of the offence and the amended criminal law, no. P16-2019-001, 29.05.2020. So far Protocol No. 16 has been ratified by fifteen states.

216 CoE, Explanatory Report to Protocol No. 16 to the Convention for the Protection of Human Rights and Fundamental Freedoms, CETS No. 214, 02.10.2013, para. 10.

217 ECtHR, Advisory Opinion No. 2, *supra* note 215, para. 206: 'The Court's answer to the Constitutional Court's first and second questions would be of an abstract and general nature, thus going beyond the scope of an advisory opinion as envisaged by Protocol No. 16.

the future, accept *too abstract* questions, the Grand Chamber specified that *too concrete* questions are not allowed neither, given that '[t]he aim of the procedure if not to transfer the dispute to the Court'.[218]

However, the request had been accepted by the five-judge panel, pursuant to Article 1, paragraph 2, of the Protocol. Paragraph 2 stipulates that '[i]f the panel accepts the request, the Grand Chamber shall deliver the advisory opinion'.[219] In this regard, the Grand Chamber considered that it has the power of reformulating and combining the submitted questions.[220] Secondly, it clarified that the acceptance of the request by the five-judge panel does not 'preclude the Grand Chamber from assessing whether each of the questions composing the request fulfils the requirements of Article 1 of Protocol No. 16'. Therefore, the Grand Chamber is not bound by the Panel's acceptance. In the light of its powers under Articles 19 and 32 ECHR it can decide not to examine issues that are irrelevant for the pending domestic proceedings.[221]

Moreover, the Advisory Opinion was requested by a constitutional court, in the context of a proceeding concerning the constitutional legitimacy of a domestic statute. These proceedings, in Armenia as in many other ECHR Member States, are incidental and, therefore, there is the possibility of a 'double referral' (from the judge of the principal proceeding to its national constitutional court, and from the latter to the ECtHR). Consequently, the Court clarified the scope of the last sentence of Article 1, paragraph 3, of the Protocol, according to which the requesting court or tribunal 'shall provide the relevant legal and factual background of the pending case'.[222] It stipulated that, in cases of double referral, it has to 'proceed on the basis of the facts as provided by the Constitutional Court, albeit those facts may be subject to subsequent review by the first instance court'.[223]

The Court's approach on the scope of advisory requests has been criticised by Lavrysen, who considers that it is 'unlikely to spark a lot of enthusiasm among

---

In particular, it does not appear possible to reformulate the questions so as to allow the Court to confine its advisory opinion "to points that are directly connected to the proceedings pending at domestic level"'.

218 Ibid., para. 43.

219 The Explanatory Report merely states that the panel accepts the request if it satisfies the requirements stipulated in Article 1 of the Protocol.

220 ECtHR, Advisory Opinion No. 2, *supra* note 215, para. 45: '[the Court has] the power to reformulate questions asked by the requesting Court having regard to the specific factual and legal circumstances at issue in the domestic proceedings'; 'similarly, it may also combine certain questions asked by the requesting court'.

221 Ibid., para. 47: 'Should it come to the conclusion, taking due account of the factual and legal context of the case, that certain questions do not fulfil these requirements, it shall not examine these questions […]'.

222 CoE (2013), Explanatory Report to Protocol No. 16, *supra* note 216, para. 12.

223 ECtHR, Advisory Opinion No. 2, *supra* note 215, para. 49.

domestic courts'.[224] In his opinion, in the light of the subsidiarity principle and the purposes of the Protocol, the Grand Chamber should not reject too abstract questions, but rather answer them and leave to the domestic judges the assessment of the relevance for the pending proceedings. And indeed, while the Explanatory Report excludes abstract assessment of domestic legislation, it does not exclude questions of principle concerning the interpretation of the Convention. There is a significant distinction between asking the Court to assess the abstract compatibility of a piece of domestic legislation with the ECHR (which, in proceedings originating from an individual application would be qualified as an inadmissible *actio popularis*) or giving abstract answers to abstract questions (where there is no relevant domestic proceeding or where the question is unclear), and asking the Court to interpret the provisions of the ECHR which should be applied in a domestic proceeding.

In this regard, although several procedural differences exist,[225] the Court might draw some inspiration by the IACtHR advisory practice, which has solved issues of general interest concerning the protection of human rights and further advanced the IACtHR case law. In particular, Article 64 of the Inter-American Convention on Human Rights (IACHR) allows Member States, as well as the organs of the Organization of American States, to consult the Court 'regarding the interpretation of [the IACHR] or of other treaties concerning the protection of human rights in the American States' (para. 1). Moreover, Member States can also ask the Court to render an opinion 'regarding the compatibility of any of its domestic laws with the aforesaid international instruments' (para. 2). The IACtHR's (advisory) competence *ratione materiae*, therefore, is much wider than that of the ECHR and extends to general questions. It basically aims at *preventing* violations of the IACHR and has been used to deal with general issues concerning the protection of human rights also in the light of other international human rights instruments, in a system where the judicial/contentious function of the Court established by the treaty is not as solid as in the European system.[226]

---

224 L. Lavrysen, 'Advisory Opinion No. 2: A Slightly Bigger Rodent', *Strasbourg Observers*, 05.06.2020, available at https://strasbourgobservers.com/2020/06/05/advisory-opinion-no-2-a-slightly-bigger-rodent/, last accessed 31.05.2021.

225 N. Posenato, 'New Opinions ex Protocol No. 16 to the ECHR and the Inter-American Advisory Practice: Some Comparative Remarks', in (2020) 4, *Eurojus*, pp. 353 et seq.

226 The IACHR has also the competence to assess the abstract compatibility with the IACHR of states' projects of constitutionals reforms (e.g. IACtHR, *Propuesta de modificación de la Constitución política de Costa Rica relacionada con la naturalización*, advisory opinion no. OC-4/84, 19.04.1984) and legislative reforms (e.g. IACtHR, *Compatibilidad de un Proyecto de ley con el artículo 8.2.h de la Convención Americana sovre Derechos Humanos*, advisory opinion no. OC-12/91, 06.12.1991); consider, for example, IACtHR, *Condición juridica y derechos de los migrantes indocumentados*, advisory opinion no. OC-18/03, 17.09.2003, on the right of undocumented migrants and where the Court considered the principle of equality and non-discrimination as not derogable; IACtHR, *Garantías judiciales en estados de emergencia (arts. 27(2), 25 y 8 Convención Americana sobre Derechos Humanos)*, advisory opinion no. OC-9/87, 06.10.1987, on the protection of human rights in situations of emergency.

For these reasons, the IACtHR expressly considered that 'owing to the general interests of its advisory opinions, their scope should not be restricted to specific States'.[227]

Notwithstanding the aforesaid differences, the ECtHR might draw some important lessons from the IACtHR.[228] In particular, without overcoming the limits established in Article 1 of Protocol No. 16 to the ECHR, the Court should develop its advisory function in order to exploit its preventive function. And indeed, allowing domestic highest courts to request, within pending proceedings, answers to questions concerning the interpretation of the Convention *in general* would be in line with the principle of subsidiarity.[229] Such an approach would allow the advisory function to work as an instrument aimed at further expanding the protection of human rights in the domestic legal orders. A practical consequence could be the reduction of Court's caseload.

5. CONCLUSION

This contribution examined some developments in the Court's case law in 2020 in light of its normative environment. The analysis confirms the assumption that the ECHR does not, and cannot, exist in splendid isolation.[230]

On one hand, it is an instrument which is capable of developing general international law or consolidating its rules and principles by endorsing its trends (*Makuchyan and Minasyan v Azerbaijan and Hungary*),[231] and whose

227 IACtHR, *The Environment and Human Rights (State Obligations in Relation to the Environment in the Context of the Protection and Guarantee of the Rights to Life and to Personal Integrity: Interpretation and Scope of Article 4(1) and 5(1) in relation to Articles 1(1) and 2 of the American Convention on Human Rights)*, advisory opinion no. OC-23/17, 15.11.2017, para. 35.

228 For some interesting observations in this regard, see P. De Sena, 'Caratteri e prospettive del Protocollo 16 nel prisma dell'esperienza del sistema interamericano dei diritti dell'uomo', (2014) 8(3), *Diritti Umani e Diritto Internazionale*, pp. 593 et seq.

229 CoE, Protocol No. 15 amending the Convention for the Protection of Human Rights and Fundamental Freedoms, Strasbourg, ETS no. 5, 24.06.2013, entry into force 01.08.2021.

230 C.L. Rozakis, 'The European Judge as a Comparatist', (2005) 1, *Tulane Law Review*, p. 278: 'the European Court of Human Rights and its judges do not operate in the splendid isolation of an ivory tower built with materials originating solely from the ECHR's interpretative inventions or those of the States party to the Convention. The nature of the ECHR as an international court – working in a regional environment and aiming simultaneously to protect, provide for and integrate human rights in Europe – is undoubtedly the main reasons reason behind its cosmopolitan tendencies, which are gradually becoming a solid feature of its way of functioning and which seem to be influenced by a more general evolution of the protection of human rights around the world'.

231 The said case also shows that the Court does not always resort to a clear and precise methodology for ascertaining customary international law. It usually applies customary law by endorsing the findings of the ICJ and the ILC, without engaging in the assessment of State practice and *opinio juris*. See I. Ziemele, 'Customary International Law in the Case-Law of the European Court of Human Rights', in CoE Conference Proceedings, *The Judge and International Custom*,

substantive content is expanded in the light of the developments in international and European human rights law (*S.M. v Croatia* and *G.L. v Italy*). As for systematic interpretation, the analysis confirms that the Court's approach goes beyond the rule of general international law codified in Article 31(3)(c) VCLT, for it also considers non-binding instruments as a source of interpretation of the Convention (*Buturugă v Romania*).

On the other hand, the Court's approach in some cases might not reflect developments and trends that are already taking place in other systems or may even have a chilling effect on the progressive expansion of human rights law (*M.N. v Belgium*). Alternatively, it might itself appear as being at odds with other international human rights instruments or principles (*N.D. and N.T. v Spain*).

International law has also played an important role in the clarification of procedural issues. The Court, indeed, distinguished between jurisdiction and admissibility in inter-state applications in the light of the 'general principles governing the exercise of jurisdiction by international tribunals' (*Slovenia v Croatia*). In some cases, the procedural developments realised, even if not expressly, a cross-fertilisation between the ECtHR and other human rights bodies' procedural framework and practice (*L.R. v North Macedonia* and *Association Enfant en Danger v France*). Other international instruments, as well as the case law of other international courts, might also play an important role for the establishment of facts and the assessment of evidence (*Ukraine v Russia (re Crimea)* and *Georgia v Russia (II)*). Relevant differences might exist, however, between the ECtHR and other human rights courts, as the procedural framework and the case law concerning the advisory function show (*Advisory Opinion No. 2*).

In light of the proliferation of international courts, tribunals and monitoring bodies, as well as international human rights instruments, the Court will have to rely more frequently on the principle of systemic integration or harmonisation while interpreting and applying the Convention. Of course, the specific features of the system, as well as the regional values which underpin the Convention, justify and perhaps impose some differences. The CoE, however, is conscious of the need to integrate the ECHR in its normative environment, as the report which was commissioned to the CDDH by the Committee of Ministers makes clear. The same report, while excluding in its conclusions 'any realistic aspiration of absolute uniformity' in international human rights law, makes some proposals to 'contain divergence'.[232] As for the relationship with general international law,

20.03.2013, pp. 75–86, available at https://www.coe.int/en/web/cahdi/publication-the-judge-and-international-custom-pdf/-/asset_publisher/7xs6VSV36P9P/content/conference-proceedings-the-judge-and-international-custom, last accessed 13.06.2021.

232 CoE, CDDH (2019), *The Place of the European Convention on Human Rights, supra* note 6, paras. 346 and 355.

the report pleads for the adoption of a more coherent approach by the Court, which should more clearly rely on general international law and in a more consistent way.

As this contribution showed, the principle of systemic integration can expand the rights and liberties protected under the Convention. At the same time, the Court's engagement with general international law can improve the perceived legitimacy of the ECtHR's judgments and decisions, and trigger its development towards a more humanised international legal order. In this regard, the Court should follow its already established trend and should more explicitly rely on general international law, other human rights instruments and other international courts' and tribunals' case law.

THE COURT OF JUSTICE OF THE EUROPEAN UNION AND HUMAN RIGHTS IN 2020

Christian Breitler and Martin Traussnigg*

* The present contribution was finalised in April 2021. It is to be emphasised that the views expressed are those of the authors and may not be attributed to their employers or any other entity or institution with which the authors are or have been affiliated.

ABSTRACT

In 2020, the Court of Justice of the European Union (CJEU) delivered a number of important judgments in the field of fundamental and human rights law. The purpose of the present contribution is to provide a succinct overview of this jurisprudence. It considers judgments in areas such as the rule of law, right to asylum, the protection of personal data, freedom of religion, academic freedom and non-discrimination. Following a brief summary of each case discussed, selected aspects of the case law are accentuated. In conclusion, the Court's jurisprudence in 2020 reveals a certain trend towards emancipation from the jurisprudence of the European Court of Human Rights (ECtHR), without, however, compromising the afforded level of protection.

1. INTRODUCTION

Despite the effects that the COVID-19 crisis had on the conduct of proceedings before the Court of Justice of the European Union (CJEU),[1] the Court again delivered a number of important judgments in the field of the European Union (EU, the Union) fundamental and human rights law in 2020.

---

1 See C. Popostas, 'COVID-19 and the Courts. The Case of the CJEU', (2020) 2/3(7), *Access to Justice in Eastern Europe*, pp. 160–171.

In order to provide a succinct overview of this jurisprudence, the contribution at hand presents and discusses seven judgments the authors consider to be of particular interest and relevance. The contribution's foremost aim is to provide the reader with a representative summary of the most important cases in such different fields as the rule of law, right to asylum, the protection of personal data, freedom of religion, academic freedom and non-discrimination. All of the cases – one review proceeding, one infringement proceeding and five preliminary reference proceedings – were Grand Chamber (GC) judgments delivered by the European Court of Justice (ECJ, the Court). The selection of cases to be included in this contribution is based on subjective criteria.

Each case note consists of four sections: (i) a brief introduction; (ii) a summary of the facts and background to the case; (iii) a summary of the judgment; and (iv) a short comment. It is not intended to provide an exhaustive analysis of the Court's case law, but rather to highlight noteworthy trends, developments and/or peculiarities.

2. THE RULE OF LAW

2.1. DEFECTIVE APPOINTMENT PROCEDURES FOR JUDGES: *RÉEXAMEN SIMPSON v COUNCIL*[2]

2.1.1. *Introduction*

In last year's contribution, it was predicted that the rule of law would likely remain the central issue of the CJEU's human rights jurisprudence in the years to come.[3] There is definitely no reason to retreat from this statement. What is interesting though is that the rule of law theme popped up in a rather unexpected context in 2020: a staff case. *Réexamen Simpson* adds an important piece of constitutional significance to the Court's 'rule of law mosaic' and will most likely have repercussions in the future that go far beyond the proceedings at issue.

2.1.2. *Facts of the Case*

In March 2016, the Council appointed three new judges to the (no longer existing[4]) Civil Service Tribunal (CST). The appointees were taken from a

[2] CJEU (ECJ), *Réexamen Simpson v Council*, Joined Cases C-542/18 RX-II and C-543/18 RX-II, 16.03.2020, ECLI:EU:C:2020:232.

[3] C. Breitler and M. Traussnigg, 'The Court of Justice of the European Union and Human Rights in 2019', in P. Czech, L. Heschl, K. Lukas et al. (eds.), *European Yearbook on Human Rights 2020*, Intersentia/NWV, Cambridge/Vienna 2020, p. 592.

[4] Regulation (EU, Euratom) No 2015/2422 of the European Parliament and of the Council of 16 December 2015 amending Protocol No 3 on the Statute of the Court of Justice of the

list previously drawn up by a selection committee following a public call for applications. However, that call only encompassed the filling of vacant posts for two judges whose terms of office were about to expire, while the Council filled also a third vacant post with a candidate from the list.[5]

In 2018, the European General Court (EGC) set aside a judgment of the CST because the chamber that had delivered it was not correctly composed, as it included the candidate for the third vacant post, for which there was no public call, thus violating Article 47 of the Charter of Fundamental Rights (CFR).[6] Contrary to the recommendation of the First Advocate General (AG), the ECJ decided not to review the EGC's judgment in this case.[7]

Soon after, however, the issue arose again. The EGC set aside an order and a judgment in two other staff cases on the grounds that the procedure to fill the third vacant post suffered from an irregularity.[8] This time, the ECJ followed the recommendation by the First AG to review the EGC's judgments.[9] The review extends to the question whether the EGC's judgments affect the unity or consistency of EU law and whether the appointment of a judge may form the subject matter of a review of indirect legality.[10]

2.1.3. Judgment

The Court first establishes that the EGC did not err in law by examining the regularity of the composition of the panel of the judges of its own motion. The right to an effective remedy before an independent and impartial tribunal previously established by law pursuant to Article 47 para. 2 CFR constitutes a central aspect of the right to a fair trial. Thus, not only must everyone be able to invoke an infringement of that right, but is it a question of public policy that must be examined of the court's own motion.[11]

With regard to the appointment procedure, the Court finds no error in law in terms of the EGC's assessment that the Council had failed to comply with the specifications set by the call for applications to fill the vacant post. However,

European Union, OJ L 341/14; Regulation (EU, Euratom) No 2016/1192 of the European Parliament and of the Council of 6 July 2016 on the transfer to the General Court of jurisdiction at first instance in disputes between the European Union and its servants, OJ L 200/137.

5 CJEU, *Réexamen Simpson*, *supra* note 2, paras. 13–19.

6 CJEU (GC), *FV v Council*, Case T-639/16 P, 23.01.2018, ECLI:EU:T:2018:22.

7 CJEU (ECJ), *Réexamen FV v Council*, Case C-141/18 RX, 19.03.2018, ECLI:EU:C:2018:218.

8 CJEU (GC), *Simpson v Council*, Case T-646/16 P, 19.07.2018, ECLI:EU:T:2018:493; CJEU (GC), *HG v Commission*, Case T-693/16 P, 19.07.2018, ECLI:EU:T:2018:492.

9 CJEU (ECJ), *Réexamen Simpson v Council*, Case C-542/18 RX, 17.09.2018, ECLI:EU:C:2018:763; CJEU (ECJ), *Réexamen HG v Commission*, Case C-543/18 RX, 17.09.2018, ECLI:EU:C:2018:764.

10 CJEU, *Réexamen Simpson*, *supra* note 2, paras. 49–52.

11 Ibid., paras. 53–58.

besides the fact that there was no call for applications for the filling of the third post, the appointment procedure for judges to the CST was observed.[12]

The Court further elaborates that the independence and impartiality of courts is essential for the right to effective judicial protection and the fundamental right to a fair trial. In order to safeguard independence and impartiality, rules – specifically with regard to appointment procedures – are required to ensure that in the minds of individuals the neutrality and insusceptibility to external influence of a court is beyond reasonable doubt.[13]

In accordance with Article 52 para. 3 CFR, Article 47 para. 2 of the Charter corresponds to Article 6 para. 1 of the European Convention on Human Rights (ECHR). By reference to the jurisprudence of the European Court of Human Rights (ECtHR), the ECJ states that the 'established by law' criterion is to guarantee that the organisation of the judicial system is determined by law deriving from the legislature and is not dependent on the discretion of the executive. Therefore, irregularities in an appointment procedure may constitute a violation of Article 47 CFR.[14]

In the present case, however, the only irregularity occurred from the Council's disregard of the call for applications. The Court finds that this irregularity does not suffice to establish the violation of a fundamental rule in the appointment procedure giving rise to an infringement of the first sentence of Article 47 para. 2 CFR.[15]

The Court eventually finds that this error in law by the EGC affected the unity and consistency of EU law.[16] Therefore, the ECJ sets aside the judgments under review and refers the two cases back to the EGC.[17]

2.1.4. *Comment*

In the Court's recent case law in the context of the rule of law, the substantive guarantee of Article 47 para. 2 CFR concerning 'an independent and impartial tribunal previously established by law' was primarily an issue due to concerns regarding the independence and impartiality of Member States' courts and tribunals.[18] Particularly in the case of

12 Ibid., paras. 59–68.
13 Ibid., paras. 69–71.
14 Ibid., paras. 72–75.
15 Ibid., paras. 76–83.
16 Ibid., paras. 84–87.
17 Ibid., paras. 88–90.
18 See e.g. CJEU (ECJ), *Minister for Justice and Equality (Défaillances du système judiciaire)*, Case C-216/18 PPU, 25.07.2018, ECLI:EU:C:2018:586; CJEU (ECJ), *A.K. and Others (Indépendance de la chambre disciplinaire de la Cour suprême)*, Joined Cases C-585/18, C-624/18 and C-625/18, 19.11.2019, ECLI:EU:C:2019:982.

A.K. and Others,[19] deficits in appointment procedures have been linked to the requirement of independence, rather than the proper establishment by law.[20]

With the case at hand, however, the focus of interest is shifted on the 'previously established by law' criterion. Although the ECJ ultimately found no violation of Article 47 para. 2 CFR in the present case as the necessary threshold to that effect was not reached, it did not disagree with the EGC's general proposition that irregularities in appointment procedures are capable of calling into question the character of a tribunal as 'established by law'. The Court's approach thus generally aligns with the reasoning applied by the ECtHR in *Ástráðsson v Iceland*, in which the ECtHR held that a series of flaws in the appointment procedure for the Icelandic Court of Appeals amounted to a breach of Article 6 para. 1 ECHR.[21]

While dealing with the appointment procedure for the CST, the judgment in *Réexamen Simpson* will most likely have further ramifications for more 'typical' rule of law cases concerning the courts and tribunals in the Member States.[22] The pending cases *W. Ż.* and *Prokurator Generalny* might provide the ECJ with the opportunity to apply the 'established by law' test to appointment procedures for the national judiciary.[23]

---

19 CJEU, *A.K. and Others*, *supra* note 18. See further C. Breitler and M. Traussnigg (2020) 'The Court of Justice of the European Union and Human Rights in 2019', *supra* note 3, pp. 553–558; M. Leloup, 'An Uncertain First Step in the Field of Judicial Self-government. ECJ 19 November 2019, Joined Cases C-585/18, C-624/18 and C-625/18, A.K., CP and DO', (2020) 16(1), *European Constitutional Law Review*, pp. 145–169.

20 See P. Filipek, 'Only a Court Established by Law Can Be an Independent Court: The ECJ's Independence Test as an Incomplete Tool to Assess the Lawfulness of Domestic Courts', *Verfassungsblog*, 23.01.2020, available at https://verfassungsblog.de/only-a-court-established-by-law-can-be-an-independent-court, last accessed 20.04.2021.

21 ECtHR, *Ástráðsson v Iceland*, no 26374/18 [GC] 01.12.2020.

22 For an analysis see M. Leloup, 'The Appointment of Judges and the Right to a Tribunal established by Law: The ECJ Tightens Its Grip on Issues of Domestic Judicial Organization', (2020) 57(4), *Common Market Law Review*, pp. 1139–1162; L. Pech, 'Dealing With "Fake Judges" under EU Law: Poland as a Case Study in light of the Court of Justice's Ruling of 26 March 2020 in Simpson and HG', *RECONNECT*, Working Paper No 8, 2020, available at https://reconnect-europe.eu/wp-content/uploads/2020/05/RECONNECT-WP8.pdf, last accessed 20.04.2021.

23 See P. Filipek (2020), 'Only a Court Established by Law Can Be an Independent Court', *supra* note 20. In his opinions in the two cases, AG Tanchev relied heavily on the precedent set in *Réexamen Simpson*; see CJEU (ECJ), *W. Ż. (Chambre de contrôle extraordinaire et des affaires publiques de la Cour suprême – nomination)*, Case C-487/19, Opinion of AG Tanchev, 15.04.2021, ECLI:EU:C:2021:289; CJEU (ECJ), *Prokurator Generalny (Chambre disciplinaire de la Cour suprême – Nomination)*, Case C-508/19, Opinion of AG Tanchev, 15.04.2021, ECLI:EU:C:2021:290.

2.2. INDEPENDENCE OF THE JUDICIARY IN POLAND AND THE EUROPEAN ARREST WARRANT: *OPENBAAR MINISTERIE*[24]

2.2.1. *Introduction*

Last year's prediction concerning the continuing relevance of the rule of law in the Court's jurisprudence particularly holds true for the situation in Poland.[25] In the *Openbaar Ministerie* case, a follow-up to the prominent *Minister for Justice and Equality* case,[26] the ECJ reaffirmed its standing case law on the European Arrest Warrant (EAW) in the light of the ongoing Polish rule of law backslidings. The judgment concerned the interpretation of the EAW Framework Decision,[27] essentially raising the delicate question of whether the established two-step systemic deficiency test that the executing judicial authorities must perform before declining to execute a EAW issued by another Member State's court ought (still) be kept up where the independence of the judiciary and, as a result, the rule of law is not only notoriously but increasingly endangered.

2.2.2. *Facts of the Case*

The proceedings before the referring court (District Court Amsterdam, the Netherlands) concerned the execution of EAWs issued by two Polish regional courts in connection with criminal proceedings as well as a custodial sentence imposed on Polish nationals, respectively.[28] In its preliminary references, the referring court brought up recent developments in the light of which it had doubts as to the independence of the judiciary in Poland, in particular the preceding ECJ judgments in *A.K. and Others* and *Miasto Łowicz* alongside the pending infringement proceedings initiated by the European Commission.[29]

---

24 CJEU (ECJ), *Openbaar Ministerie (Indépendance de l'autorité judiciaire d'émission)*, Case C-354/20 PPU, 17.12.2020, ECLI:EU:C:2020:1033.

25 See section 2.1.1 above and, again, C. Breitler and M. Traussnigg (2020), 'The Court of Justice of the European Union and Human Rights in 2019', *supra* note 3, p. 592.

26 CJEU, *Minister for Justice and Equality*, *supra* note 18. See also CJEU (ECJ), *Aranyosi and Căldăraru*, Joined Cases C-404/15 and C-659/15 PPU, 05.04.2016, ECLI:EU:C:2016:198.

27 Council Framework Decision 2002/584/JHA of 13 June 2002 on the European arrest warrant and the surrender procedures between Member States, OJ L 190/1, as amended by Council Framework Decision 2009/299/JHA of 26 February 2009, OJ L 81/24 (the Framework Decision).

28 CJEU, *Openbaar Ministerie*, *supra* note 24, paras. 2, 9–10, 22–23.

29 Ibid., paras. 14–20, 24. See CJEU, *A.K. and Others*, *supra* note 18, and C. Breitler and M. Traussnigg (2020), 'The Court of Justice of the European Union and Human Rights in 2019', *supra* note 3, pp. 553–558; CJEU (ECJ), *Miasto Łowicz (Régime disciplinaire concernant les magistrats)*, Joined Cases C-558/18 and C-563/18, 26.03.2020, ECLI:EU:C:2020:234; CJEU (ECJ), *Commission v Poland*, Case C-791/19 (pending); CJEU (ECJ), *Commission v Poland*, Case C-204/21 (pending).

Eventually, the referring court wanted to know whether Article 6 para. 1 and Article 1 para. 3 of the Framework Decision must be interpreted to the extent that, where the executing judicial authority has evidence of systemic or generalised deficiencies concerning the independence of the issuing Member State's judiciary, that authority may deny the status of 'issuing judicial authority' to the respective Member State's court and may presume that there are substantial grounds for believing that the individual concerned will, if surrendered to that Member State, run a real risk of breach of his/her fundamental right to a fair trial as laid down in Article 47 para. 2 CFR. The referring court questioned whether, in that case, the executing judicial authority may abstain from carrying out a specific and precise verification taking into account the personal situation of the individual, the nature of the offence in question and the factual context in which the EAW was issued.[30] In other words, it essentially 'argue[d] the second step of the [...] case law regarding the specifics of the individual concerned might be abandoned in the light of such further deterioration of the rule of law in Poland since [the *Minister for Justice and Equality* case]'.[31]

2.2.3. *Judgment*

The Court, however, acting under the urgent preliminary ruling procedure,[32] was not convinced. First of all, it holds that systemic or generalised deficiencies affecting the independence of the issuing Member State's judiciary, 'however serious',[33] are not sufficient on their own to enable the executing judicial authority to consider that all of that Member State's courts fail to fall within the status of 'issuing judicial authority' pursuant to Article 6 para. 1 of the Framework Decision. After all, such deficiencies do not affect every decision that those courts may be led to adopt.[34] Although limitations may in 'exceptional circumstances' be placed on the principles of mutual trust and mutual recognition which underpin the operation of the EAW mechanism, that cannot lead to a 'general exclusion' of the application of these principles in the context of EAWs issued by those courts. Moreover, such an approach would have other significant consequences since it would also imply that those courts could no longer be regarded as courts or tribunals within the meaning of Article 267 of the Treaty

---

30 Ibid., paras. 21, 25, 33.

31 T. Vandamme, '"The two-step can't be the quick step": The CJEU reaffirms its case law on the European Arrest Warrant and the rule of law backsliding', *European Law Blog*, 10.02.2021, available at https://europeanlawblog.eu/2021/02/10/the-two-step-cant-be-the-quick-step-the-cjeu-reaffirms-its-case-law-on-the-european-arrest-warrant-and-the-rule-of-law-backsliding/, last accessed 20.04.2021.

32 CJEU, *Openbaar Ministerie*, *supra* note 24, paras. 26–30. See Article 107 of the Rules of Procedure of the Court of Justice, OJ L 265/1.

33 Ibid., paras. 50, 59.

34 Ibid., paras. 34 et seqq., 41–42.

on the Functioning of the European Union (TFEU).[35] The preceding judgment in *OG and PI* on the independence of public prosecutors in Germany, as mentioned by the referring court, cannot call these considerations into question either.[36]

Furthermore, the Court states that existing (or increasing) systemic or generalised deficiencies affecting the independence of the issuing Member State's judiciary which are indicative of a risk of breach of the right to a fair trial do not permit a presumption that the individual concerned will actually run such a risk if surrendered to that Member State. Thus, the Court maintains the requirements of the 'two-step examination' set out in the *Minister for Justice and Equality* case and stresses that the finding of such deficiencies cannot dispense from conducting the second step of that examination – namely, a specific and precise assessment of the risk in question.[37] In particular, that assessment must take into account the personal situation of the individual, the nature of the offence in question and the factual context in which the EAW was issued, such as statements by public authorities which are liable to interfere with the way in which the individual case is handled.[38] But a general suspension of the EAW mechanism with regard to a Member State which would make it permissible to refrain from carrying out such an assessment and to automatically refuse to execute EAWs issued by that Member State's courts remains possible only if the European Council formally declares that said Member State has failed to respect the Union's values laid down in Article 2 of the Treaty on European Union (TEU) according to Article 7 paras. 2 (and 3) TEU.[39]

2.2.4. Comment

The Court, in accordance with the AG's opinion,[40] reiterates that the sensitive issue in question is and shall (still) remain a political decision. In the absence

---

35 Ibid., paras. 43–44.

36 Ibid., paras. 45–50. See CJEU (ECJ), *OG and PI (Public Prosecutor's Offices in Lübeck and Zwickau)*, Joined Cases C-508/18 and C-82/19 PPU, 27.05.2019, ECLI:EU:C:2019:456. For an analysis see M. Böse, 'The European arrest warrant and the independence of public prosecutors: *OG & PI, PF, JR & YC*', (2020) 57(4), *Common Market Law Review*, pp. 1259–1282.

37 Ibid., paras. 51 et seqq. See CJEU, *Minister for Justice and Equality*, *supra* note 18, paras. 61 et seqq., 79. For an analysis see e.g. P. Bárd and W. van Ballegooij, 'Judicial Independence as a Precondition for Mutual Trust? The CJEU in Minister for Justice and Equality v. LM', (2018) 9(3), *New Journal of European Criminal Law*, pp. 353–365; M. Wendel, 'Rechtsstaatlichkeitsaufsicht und gegenseitiges Vertrauen – Anmerkung zum Urteil des EuGH v. 25.7.2018, Rs. C-216/18 PPU (Minister for Justice and Equality gegen LM)', (2019) 54(1), *Europarecht*, pp. 111–131.

38 Ibid., paras. 55, 69.

39 Ibid., paras. 57–59. See also Recital 10 of the Framework Decision. Article 1 para. 3, therefore, is not considered a part of the exceptions in Articles 3 to 5 of the Framework Decision unless Article 7 TEU has successfully been triggered.

40 CJEU (ECJ), *Openbaar Ministerie (Indépendance de l'autorité judiciaire d'émission)*, Joined Cases C-354/20 PPU and C-412/20 PPU, Opinion of AG Campos Sánchez-Bordona, 12.11.2020, ECLI:EU:C:2020:925.

of such a decision, notorious (or increasing) threats to the independence of the judiciary in a Member State and, as a result, the rule of law as protected by Article 19 para. 1 TEU and Article 47 para. 2 CFR should indeed 'prompt [the executing judicial] authority to exercise vigilance', but it cannot rely on such indications alone[41] – even if, one may add, these indications were after all confirmed by no less than the ECJ itself in infringement proceedings. The political approach, deadlocked by the unanimity quorum, however, must not be bypassed. In scholarly literature, the judgment thus did not draw much praise. Some 'minor improvements such as the new emphasis on the need to 'exercise vigilance' were acknowledged, but besides that the ECJ's refusal 'to accept that "in a situation of systemic attacks *targeting the whole judicial system*, there is, by definition, *already* a "real risk" of a breach of the fundamental rights to an independent tribunal and to a fair trial in *every single case*"' was strongly criticised.[42]

Notably, the Court explicitly emphasises the close interconnection of the issue in question with the preliminary reference procedure: indeed, independence of the judiciary is also a requirement under that procedure, whose crucial role within a Union based on the rule of law cannot be stressed enough.[43] Therefore, potentially, the consequence of a general suspension of the EAW mechanism would have literally resulted in 'punishing Polish judges twice', as was noted in this context earlier: with targeting their judicial independence by a power-hungry executive on one side and with depriving them of their (remaining) external access to and support from Luxembourg under Article 267 TFEU on the other.[44]

3. PLACING OF ASYLUM SEEKERS IN TRANSIT ZONES: *FMS AND OTHERS*[45]

3.1. INTRODUCTION

From a human rights perspective, in *FMS and Others*, the ECJ delivered a tremendously important judgment in references from the Administrative and Labour Court, Szeged, Hungary. It concerned the interpretation of certain

41 CJEU, *Openbaar Ministerie*, *supra* note 24, para. 60.

42 L. Pech, P. Wachowiec and D. Mazur, '1825 Days Later: The End of the Rule of Law in Poland (Part II)', *Verfassungsblog*, 18.01.2021, available at https://verfassungsblog.de/1825-days-later-the-end-of-the-rule-of-law-in-poland-part-ii/, last accessed 20.04.2021.

43 See in general K. Lenaerts, I. Maselis and K. Gutman, *EU Procedural Law*, Pb. Edition, Oxford University Press, Oxford 2015, pp. 48 et seqq.

44 T. Vandamme (2021), '"The two-step can't be the quick step"', *supra* note 31.

45 CJEU (ECJ), *Országos Idegenrendeszeti Főigazgatóság Dél-alföldi Regionális Igazgatóság* (*FMS and Others*), Joined Cases C-924/19 PPU and C-925/19 PPU, 14.05.2020, ECLI:EU:C:2020:367.

provisions of the Returns Directive, the Procedures Directive and the Reception Conditions Directive,[46] as well as the CFR vis-à-vis the Hungarian legislation on the right to asylum and the return of illegally resident third-country nationals. Essentially, the Court ruled that the placing of asylum seekers or third-country nationals who are subject to a return decision in the infamous Röszke transit zone at the Serbian-Hungarian border must be classified as 'detention'.[47]

3.2. FACTS OF THE CASE

The applicants in the two sets of proceedings before the referring court were, on the one hand, FMS and FNZ, a married couple of Afghan nationality, and on the other hand, SA and SA junior, an Iranian national with his infant child. They applied for asylum to the asylum authority in the Röszke transit zone in February 2019 and December 2018, respectively.[48] Pursuant to the Hungarian legislation, their applications were dismissed as inadmissible since they arrived in Hungary via a country classified as a 'safe transit country' (Serbia), and return decisions to that country were adopted. However, Serbia refused to readmit them into its territory since the conditions set out in the agreement on readmission concluded between the EU and Serbia were allegedly not met.[49]

Following that, the asylum authority did not examine the applications for asylum in substance, but amended the countries of destination stated in the return decisions, replacing them with the applicants' respective countries of origin. The applicants lodged objections against those amending decisions which were rejected. They then took legal action before the referring court

---

46 Directive 2008/115/EC of the European Parliament and of the Council of 16 December 2008 on common standards and procedures in Member States for returning illegally staying third country nationals, OJ L 348/98 (the Returns Directive); Directive 2013/32/EU of the European Parliament and of the Council of 26 June 2013 on common procedures for granting and withdrawing international protection, OJ L 180/60 (the Procedures Directive); Directive 2013/33/EU of the European Parliament and of the Council of 26 June 2013 laying down standards for the reception of applicants for international protection, OJ L 180/96 (the Reception Conditions Directive).

47 For an analysis of the judgment see P. Dumas, 'L'arrêt FMZ, FNZ, SA, SA junior : l'harmonisation à la hausse du standard de protection des droits fondamentaux et le renforcement du contrôle juridictionnel en matière d'asile et d'immigration', (2020) 2, *Revue des affaires européennes*, pp. 499–513; B. Nagy, 'A – pyrrhic? – victory concerning detention in transit zones and procedural rights: FMS & FMZ and the legislation adopted by Hungary in its wake', *Odysseus Blog*, 15.06.2020, available at https://eumigrationlawblog.eu/a-pyrrhic-victory-concerning-detention-in-transit-zones-and-procedural-rights-fms-fmz-and-the-legislation-adopted-by-hungary-in-its-wake/, last accessed 20.04.2021.

48 CJEU, *FMS and Others*, *supra* note 45, paras. 48–50, 80–83.

49 Ibid., paras. 51–55, 84–88. See Agreement between the European Community and the Republic of Serbia on the readmission of persons residing without authorisation, annexed to the Council Decision of 8 November 2007, OJ L 334/45.

for annulment of those rejecting decisions and to have the asylum authority ordered to conduct new asylum procedures, though no provision is made for such a remedy under Hungarian law. Also, they brought actions for failure to act relating to their detention and continuing presence in the Röszke transit zone.[50] The referring court, under Article 267 TFEU, submitted a number of questions to the ECJ, essentially touching upon the following issues: validity of the ground of inadmissibility; requirement to conduct asylum procedures (in substance); transit zone as a place of detention in the context of asylum procedures/of Alien Police; and effective judicial protection with regard to the decisions amending the countries of destination.[51]

3.3. JUDGMENT

The Court, acting under the urgent preliminary ruling procedure,[52] foremost holds that the placing of the applicants in the Röszke transit zone must be classified as 'detention'. It emphasises that the concept of detention refers to a coercive measure which presupposes the deprivation of the freedom of movement of the individual concerned and isolates that individual from the rest of the population, by requiring him/her to remain at all times within a limited and closed area.[53] Consequently, the conditions prevailing in the Röszke transit zone amount to a deprivation of liberty, because individuals such as the applicants cannot lawfully leave that zone of their own free will in any direction whatsoever. In fact, they may not leave that zone for Serbia, since such an attempt would be considered unlawful by the Serbian authorities and would expose them to penalties which might result in their losing any (remaining) chance of obtaining refugee status in Hungary.[54]

As regards the legal requirements related to detention, the Court holds that under Articles 8 and 9 of the Receptions Conditions Directive and Article 15 of the Returns Directive, respectively, neither an applicant for asylum nor a third-country national who is subject to a return decision may be detained solely on the ground that they cannot meet their own needs.[55] As to the duration of detention, the Member States are not required to lay down a maximum period for continuing to detain applicants for international protection, but they must ensure, in that case, that the detention lasts only for as long as the ground

50 Ibid., paras. 56–60, 89–92. The applicants were first obliged to stay in the sector of the transit zone reserved for applicants for asylum before being required, later, to stay in the sector reserved for third-country nationals whose asylum applications have been rejected.

51 Ibid., paras. 62–79, 93.

52 Ibid., paras. 94–107. See again Article 107 of the Rules of Procedure of the Court of Justice.

53 Ibid., paras. 215–225.

54 Ibid., paras. 226–231.

55 Ibid., paras. 249–281.

for detention remains applicable and that the administrative procedures are executed diligently. Otherwise, their right to liberty pursuant to Article 6 CFR would be violated. By contrast, in the case of third-country nationals who are subject to a return decision, their detention may not exceed 18 months and may be maintained only as long as removal arrangements are ongoing and are executed with due diligence.[56]

Generally, the Court holds that the lawfulness of a detention measure must be amenable to judicial review. Therefore, in the absence of national legislation providing for such a review, the principle of primacy of EU law and the right to effective judicial protection require the national court hearing the case to declare that it has jurisdiction to rule on that matter. Moreover, if, following its review, the national court considers the detention measure at issue as contrary to EU law, it must be able to substitute its decision for that of the administrative authority which adopted the measure and order the immediate release of the individual concerned or possibly an alternative measure to detention.[57]

In particular, the Court rules on the jurisdiction of the referring court to hear an action for annulment brought by the applicants against the decisions rejecting their objections to the decisions amending the countries of destination in their initial return decisions. In that regard, the Court considers such amending decisions so substantial that they must be regarded as new return decisions. Under Article 13 of the Returns Directive, the addressee of such a decision must then have an effective remedy against it which is consistent with the right to effective judicial protection guaranteed by Article 47 CFR.[58]

Lastly, the Court examines the ground of inadmissibility laid down in the Hungarian legislation used to justify the rejection of the applications for asylum. That legislation allows such a rejection where the applicant has arrived in Hungary via a country classified as a 'safe transit country' – namely, Serbia. Recalling its preceding case law, the Court states that such a ground is contrary to Article 33 of the Procedures Directive,[59] before specifying the consequences thereof for the asylum procedure in so far as in cases as those at issue before the referring court the rejection of the applications which were based on that unlawful ground have already been confirmed by final and binding judicial decisions (*res iudicata*).[60]

---

56 Ibid., paras. 263–264, 279–280. Furthermore, as regards the detention of applicants for international protection in the particular context of a transit zone, it is necessary to take account of Article 43 of the Procedures Directive which imposes a time limit of four weeks; ibid., paras. 232–248.

57 Ibid., paras. 289–301. To that extent see also CJEU, *Mahdi*, Case C-146/14 PPU, 05.06.2014, ECLI:EU:C:2014:1320.

58 Ibid., paras. 109–147.

59 Ibid., paras. 148–165. See CJEU, *Bevándorlási és Menekültügyi Hivatal (Tompa)*, Case C-564/18, 19.03.2020, ECLI:EU:C:2020:218.

60 Ibid., paras. 175–203.

3.4. COMMENT

In reaction to the present judgment of the ECJ, Hungary ultimately closed down its transit zones in Röszke and Tompa – so far, so good. However, since then, applications for international protection in Hungary have only been possible by visiting the Hungarian embassies in Belgrade (Serbia) or Kiev (Ukraine) in order to lodge a so-called 'statement of intent'. Depending on the approval of that statement, the would-be applicants for international protection are issued with a special travel permit for Hungary, allowing them to submit an application there. In response to this new requirement, an infringement procedure was initiated by the European Commission.[61] In the meantime, in another landmark infringement case, Hungary was formally declared to have (previously) failed to comply with EU law by restricting access to asylum procedures, unlawfully detaining applicants in transit zones and illegally removing them to Serbia.[62] Explicitly, the Court acknowledged 'the virtual impossibility of making an application for international protection in Hungary'.[63]

Most interestingly for human rights doctrine, the ECJ's present judgment is not fully consistent with the ECtHR's preceding case law in so far as, in fact, Luxembourg claims a higher human rights standard on the particular issue of detention in the Röszke transit zone than Strasbourg (at first) did. In *Ilias and Ahmed*, for that matter, the ECtHR did precisely not classify the placing of asylum seekers in the Röszke transit zone as 'detention', since it was (supposedly) possible for the applicants in that case to return at any time to Serbia, from where they had entered Hungary.[64] Just recently, however, in *R.R. and Others*,

---

61 European Commission, 'October infringements package: key decisions', Press Release, INF/20/1687, 30.10.2020, available at https://ec.europa.eu/commission/presscorner/detail/en/inf_20_1687, last accessed 20.04.2021. On a related issue see also CJEU (ECJ), *Commission v Hungary (Incrimination de l'aide aux demandeurs d'asile)*, Case C-821/19 (pending).

62 CJEU (ECJ), *Commission v Hungary (Accueil des demandeurs de protection internationale)*, Case C-808/18, 17.12.2020, ECLI:EU:C:2020:1029; on the particular issue of detention in the Röszke and Tompa transit zones see paras. 157 et seqq. For a brief contextual analysis see A. Léderer and M. Pardavi, 'Still Waters Run Deep. The CJEU finds pushbacks in Hungary illegal', *Verfassungsblog*, 21.12.2020, available at https://verfassungsblog.de/still-waters-run-deep/, last accessed 20.04.2021.

63 Ibid., para. 118.

64 ECtHR, *Ilias and Ahmed v Hungary*, no 47287/15 [GC] 21.11.2019. For an analysis see U. Brandl, 'Anhaltung von Aslywerbern in Transitzentren: Zum Urteil der Großen Kammer im Fall Ilias und Ahmed gg. Ungarn', (2020) 2, *Newsletter Menschenrechte*, pp. 85–91. The referring court, in *FMS and Others*, brought up the related ECtHR case, but while the AG did briefly discuss it, the Court does not; see CJEU, *FMS and Others*, *supra* note 45, para. 71; CJEU (ECJ), *Országos Idegenrendeszeti Főigazgatóság Dél-alföldi Regionális Igazgatóság (FMS and Others)*, Joined Cases C-924/19 PPU and C-925/19 PPU, Opinion of AG Pikamäe, 23.04.2020, ECLI:EU:C:2020:294, para. 48.

the ECtHR eventually seems to have changed its mind, as that court now also finds that the applicants' stay in the Röszke transit zone in that case amounted to a *de facto* deprivation of liberty within the meaning of Article 5 ECHR.[65]

4. PROTECTION OF PERSONAL DATA: *SCHREMS II*[66]

4.1. INTRODUCTION

Although it is sometimes asserted that the CJEU is not a human rights court,[67] there is no denying the fact that in the field of data protection, the Court serves as a model for fundamental rights protection and has established itself as a weighty bulwark against unwarranted intrusions into the privacy of EU citizens.[68] Landmark cases such as *Digital Rights Ireland, Tele2 Sverige, Google Spain* and *Schrems I* have significantly contributed to the Court's reputation as a 'key player in privacy and data protection'.[69] The latter case is particularly noteworthy as it addresses the relationship between the individual on the one side and private corporations and public authorities on the other side.[70] In 2020, almost five years after the judgment in *Schrems I*, the ECJ was called upon to decide on the follow-up case.

---

65 ECtHR, *R.R. and Others v Hungary*, no 36037/17, 02.03.2021.

66 CJEU (ECJ), *Facebook Ireland and Schrems (Schrems II)*, Case C-311/18, 16.07.2020, ECLI:EU:C:2020:559.

67 For the classical debate see J. Coppel and A. O'Neill, 'The European Court of Justice: Taking Rights Seriously?', (1992) 29(4), *Common Market Law Review*, pp. 669–692; J.H.H. Weiler and N.J.S. Lockart, '"Taking Rights Seriously" Seriously: The European Court and Its Fundamental Rights Jurisprudence – Part I', (1995) 32(1), *Common Market Law Review*, pp. 51–94; J.H.H. Weiler and N.J.S. Lockart, '"Taking Rights Seriously" Seriously: The European Court and Its Fundamental Rights Jurisprudence – Part II', (1995) 32(2) *Common Market Law Review*, pp. 579–627.

68 See H.-P. Folz, 'Artikel 8 GR-Charta', in C. Vedder and W. Heintschel v. Heinegg (eds.), *Europäisches Unionsrecht. EUV | AEUV | GRCh | EAGV. Handkommentar*, 2nd edn., Nomos, Baden-Baden 2018, p. 1333, para. 9.

69 CJEU (ECJ), *Digital Rights Ireland*, Joined Cases C-293/12 and C-594/12, 08.04.2014, ECLI:EU:C:2014:238; CJEU (ECJ), *Tele2 Sverige*, Joined Cases C-203/15 and C-698/15, 21.12.2016, ECLI:EU:C:2016:970; CJEU (ECJ), *Google Spain and Google*, Case C-131/12, 13.05.2014, ECLI:EU:C:2014:317; CJEU (ECJ), *Schrems (Schrems I)*, Case C-362/14, 06.10.2015, ECLI:EU:C:2015:650. See C. Docksey and H. Hijmans, 'The Court of Justice as a Key Player in Privacy and Data Protection: An Overview of Recent Trends in Case Law at the Start of a New Era of Data Protection Law', (2019) 5(3), *European Data Protection Law Review*, pp. 300–316.

70 See L. Azoulai and M. van der Sluis, 'Institutionalizing Personal Data Protection in Times of Global Institutional Distrust: Schrems', (2016) 53(5), *Common Market Law Review*, p. 1356.

4.2. FACTS OF THE CASE

Under the General Data Protection Regulation (GDPR),[71] there are three possible grounds on which the transfer of personal data to a third state may be permissible: an adequacy decision adopted by the European Commission by which it is certified that the third state in questions offers an adequate level of protection of personal data (Article 45 GDPR); appropriate safeguards such as Standard Contractual Clauses (SCCs) (Articles 46 and 47 GDPR); or in cases of situations for specific derogations (Article 49 GDPR).

In October 2015, in *Schrems I*, the ECJ invalidated the 'Safe Harbour Decision' by which the Commission found that the United States of America (US) offers an adequate level of protection of personal data.[72] The judgment was delivered following a request for a preliminary reference made by the Irish High Court ruling on a complaint made by the Facebook user Mr Schrems who demanded that the Irish Data Protection Commissioner would prohibit the transfer of his personal data to the US by Facebook Ireland, as no adequate level of protection was ensured due to the surveillance activities of US authorities.[73] Following the judgment, the question arose of whether such data transfers could legitimately be based on SCCs. Following a reformulated complaint by Mr Schrems, the Irish High Court again referred the matter to the ECJ. The Irish High Court, in essence, sought clarification whether the SCC Decision was valid in the light of Articles 7, 8, and 47 CFR.[74] Meanwhile, however, a new adequacy decision, the so-called 'Privacy Shield Decision',[75] was adopted by the Commission, trying to address the shortcomings of the Safe Harbour Decision.[76]

---

71 Regulation (EU) 2016/679 of the European Parliament and of the Council of 27 April 2016 on the protection of natural persons with regard to the processing of personal data and on the free movement of such data, and repealing Directive 95/46/EC (General Data Protection Regulation), OJ L 119/1.

72 CJEU, *Schrems (Schrems I), supra* note 69; 2000/520/EC: Commission Decision of 26 July 2000 pursuant to Directive 95/46/EC of the European Parliament and of the Council on the adequacy of the protection provided by the safe harbour privacy principles and related frequently asked questions issued by the US Department of Commerce (notified under document number C(2000) 2441), OJ L 215/7.

73 CJEU (ECJ), *Facebook Ireland and Schrems*, *supra* note 66, paras. 50–53.

74 Ibid., paras. 54–68.

75 Commission Implementing Decision (EU) 2016/1250 of 12 July 2016 pursuant to Directive 95/46/EC of the European Parliament and of the Council on the adequacy of the protection provided by the EU-U.S. Privacy Shield (notified under document C(2016) 4176), OJ L 207/1.

76 For an analysis of the 'Privacy Shield' see S. Monteleone and L. Puccio, 'From Safe Harbour to Privacy Shield. Advances and shortcomings of the new EU-US data transfer rules', European Parliamentary Research Service In-Depth Analysis, 2017, available at https://www.europarl.europa.eu/RegData/etudes/IDAN/2017/595892/EPRS_IDA(2017)595892_EN.pdf, last accessed 20.04.2021.

4.3. JUDGMENT

The Court answers the request for a preliminary ruling first by clarifying that the GDPR applies to the case at hand irrespective of whether the transferred data is being processed by third countries' authorities for the purposes of public security, defence or state security.[77] The Court further elaborates that when data is being transferred to a third country based on SCCs, it must be guaranteed that the level of protection is 'essentially equivalent' to the degree of protection ensured within the EU provided by the GDPR, read in light of the CFR.[78] Although a valid adequacy decision prevents national supervisory authorities from finding that the third country in question lacks an adequate protection level, the competent supervisory authority must still perform its tasks by examining complaints lodged by individuals and potentially bringing actions before national courts.[79]

The ECJ then proceeds to examine the validity of the SCC Decision in the light of Articles 7, 8 and 47 CFR. The Court states that the very fact that the decision does not have binding effect on the authorities in third states does not render it invalid. According to the Court, the validity of the SCC Decision depends on effective mechanisms that guarantee observance of the required level of protection under EU law and the possibility to suspend or prohibit data transfers in case of non-compliance with the SCCs.[80] In this context, the Court points out that under the SCC Decision both the recipient and the processor of personal data are under the obligation to respect applicable data protection law – that is, in the EU the GDPR read in light of the Charter – and to ascertain themselves prior to any transfer of data that the legislation in a third country allows the recipient compliance with the SCCs.[81] Further, if the third country's legislation does not allow for such compliance, there is a duty to return data that has been transferred and a right to compensation for the person concerned. In case of a change in the relevant legislation in the third country which might severely affect the ability to comply with the SCCs, the controller established in the EU is required to forward a notification of such a change in legislation to the competent supervisory authority, which then may decide whether any further transfer of data must be suspended or prohibited.[82] Therefore, the Court concludes that the SCC Decision provides for effective mechanisms to ensure that data transfers are suspended or prohibited in case of non-compliance with the SCCs and upholds the validity of the decision.[83]

---

77 CJEU (ECJ), *Facebook Ireland and Schrems*, *supra* note 66, paras. 80–89.
78 Ibid., paras. 90–105.
79 Ibid., paras. 106–121.
80 Ibid., paras. 122–137.
81 Ibid., paras. 138–139.
82 Ibid., paras. 140–147.
83 Ibid., para. 148.

Lastly, the Court examines – against the recommendation of AG Saugmandsgaard Øe – the validity of the Privacy Shield Decision in the light of Articles 7, 8 and 47 of the Charter.[84] Although the main proceedings only deal with the validity of the SCC Decision, the Court considers the examination of the validity of the Privacy Shield Decision necessary in order to clarify the responsibilities of the controller and recipient of personal data under the SCCs, as well as the obligations of the competent supervisory authority.[85] The ECJ holds that the processing of personal data falls within the scope of Articles 7 and 8 CFR and that the transmission of personal data to a third party constitutes a limitation of these rights.[86] However, none of these rights are absolute rights and therefore may be restricted in accordance with Article 52 para. 1 CFR, meaning that any limitation must be provided for by law, respect the essence of the rights and freedoms concerned, pursue an objective of general interest and be proportionate.[87] The proportionality of the measure has been challenged due to the fact that the inferences arising from US surveillance programs do not comply with the requirements of an essentially equivalent level of protection as guaranteed by Article 52 para. 1 CFR. In that context, the Court notes that the US surveillance programmes for the purpose of foreign intelligence gathering are neither subject to any limitations, nor are there any guarantees for non-US persons potentially affected by those programmes available. In particular, no actionable rights are given that could be enforced against US authorities. In addition, the possibility of bulk collection of data in transit to the US without the option of judicial protection does not adequately delimit the scope of bulk collection of personal data. The Court therefore concludes that the afforded level of protection may not be considered to be essentially equivalent to the guarantees pursuant to Article 52 para. 1 CFR.[88] As far as Article 47 CFR is concerned, the Court recalls its finding in *Schrems I* that legislation not providing for any effective judicial review regarding access, correction or erasure of personal data does not respect the essence of that provision of the Charter. The Court stresses that the existence of such mechanisms for judicial review is particularly important in the context of transfer of personal data to a third country, since the Member States' authorities do not have the power to effectively handle complaints concerning the processing of data in third countries. The Court finds that since data subjects do not have actionable rights against US authorities before US courts, there is no effective judicial remedy available. The existence of an Ombudsperson cannot alter this conclusion either, as the Ombudsperson is not afforded the guarantees of an independent and impartial court and also may not adopt decisions that are

[84] See CJEU (ECJ), *Facebook Ireland and Schrems (Schrems II)*, Case C-311/18, Opinion of AG Saugmandsgaard Øe, 19.12.2019, ECLI:EU:C:2019:1145.

[85] CJEU (ECJ), *Facebook Ireland and Schrems*, *supra* note 66, paras. 150–161.

[86] Ibid., paras. 169–171.

[87] Ibid., paras. 172–177.

[88] Ibid., paras. 178–185.

binding on intelligence services.[89] The Court thus declares the Privacy Shield Decision invalid.[90]

4.4. COMMENT

As early as 2016, Mr Schrems stated that the Privacy Shield Decision constituted only 'a soft update of Safe Harbor, which does not address any of the material issues identified by the court'.[91] In that sense, after the *Schrems II* ruling, several commentators stated that the outcome was not surprising after all.[92] And yet, the ruling includes a number of novel aspects, such as the strengthened role for supervisory authorities or the fact that the transfer of personal data based on SCCs must also guarantee an essentially equivalent level of protection, as is the case with an adequacy decision.[93]

Moreover, it is interesting to compare the reasoning which led to the conclusion that the respective adequacy decision is invalid in *Schrems I* and *Schrems II*. As is well known, in *Schrems I*, the ECJ for the first time invoked the 'essence' of two Charter rights to declare a legal act invalid, namely, the essence of Articles 7 and 47 CFR.[94] In *Schrems I*, the Court found the Safe Harbour Decision to compromise the essence of Article 7 CFR due to the possibility of 'blanket access' to personal data transferred to the US.[95] In *Schrems II*, the Court did not invoke the essence of Article 7 CFR to conclude that the Privacy Shield Decision was invalid. Rather, the Court offered a refined test consisting of four steps for the assessment of foreign surveillance programmes and their (non-)compliance with Articles 7 and 8 CFR.[96] By contrast, concerning

89 Ibid., paras. 186–197.

90 Ibid., paras. 198–201.

91 M. Schrems, 'The Privacy Shield is a Soft Update of the Safe Harbor', (2016) 2(2), *European Data Protection Law Review*, p. 148.

92 See R.Á. Costello, 'Schrems II: Everything is Illuminated?', (2020) 5(2), *European Papers*, p. 1052; C. Kuner, 'The Schrems II judgment of the Court of Justice and the future of data transfer regulation', *European Law Blog*, 17.07.2020, available at https://europeanlawblog.eu/2020/07/17/the-schrems-ii-judgment-of-the-court-of-justice-and-the-future-of-data-transfer-regulation, last accessed 20.04.2021; T. Christiakis, 'After Schrems II: Uncertainties on the Legal Basis for Data Transfers and Constitutional Implications in Europe', *European Law Blog*, 21.07.2020, available at https://europeanlawblog.eu/2020/07/21/after-schrems-ii-uncertainties-on-the-legal-basis-for-data-transfers-and-constitutional-implications-for-europe, last accessed 20.04.2021.

93 See generally R.Á. Costello (2020), 'Everything is Illuminated?', *supra* note 92.

94 CJEU, *Schrems (Schrems I)*, *supra* note 69, paras. 94 and 95. Interestingly, however, not (expressly) the essence of Article 8 CFR. See on this point C. Kuner, 'Reality and Illusion in EU Data Transfer Regulation Post Schrems', (2017) 18(4), *German Law Journal*, p. 892.

95 CJEU, *Schrems (Schrems I)*, *supra* note 69, para. 94.

96 See M. Tzanou, 'Schrems I and Schrems II: Assessing the Case for the Extraterritoriality of EU Fundamental Rights', in F. Fabbrini, E. Celeste, and J. Quinn (eds.), *Data Protection*

Article 47 CFR and the right to an effective remedy enshrined therein, the Court again found the lack of effective redress mechanisms in the US to disregard the very essence of that right. Therefore, as long as the question of individual redress is not resolved,[97] the adoption of a new adequacy decision would suffer the same fate as its two predecessors, as any measure that encroaches upon the essence of a Charter right cannot be justified whatsoever.[98] The Court thus makes it clear that despite the necessity to interact with other parts of the world,[99] the rule of law must not be compromised.

5. RITUAL SLAUGHTER BETWEEN RELIGIOUS FREEDOM AND ANIMAL WELFARE: *CENTRAAL ISRAËLITISCH CONSISTORIE VAN BELGIË AND OTHERS*[100]

5.1. INTRODUCTION

The question how to deal with matters of religion or belief in the context of EU law has become a recurring theme in the ECJ's case law in recent years.[101] The EU's unprecedented powers to regulate in an ever-increasing number of policy fields also enhances the risk of potential clashes between religious practices, on the one hand, and EU law, on the other. One particular religious practice that repeatedly has been at the centre of legal disputes before the ECJ is the ritual slaughter of animals in accordance with Islamic and Jewish rite.

Beyond Borders. Transatlantic Perspectives on Extraterritoriality and Sovereignty, Hart Publishing, Oxford 2021, pp. 111–114.

97 For possible solutions to this conundrum see K. Propp and P. Swire, 'After Schrems II: A Proposal to Meet the Individual Redress Challenge', *Lawfare Blog*, 13.08.2020, available at https://www.lawfareblog.com/after-schrems-ii-proposal-meet-individual-redress-challenge, last accessed 20.04.2021; C. Docksey, 'Schrems II and Individual Redress – Where There's a Will, There's a Way', *Lawfare Blog*, 12.10.2020, available at https://www.lawfareblog.com/schrems-ii-and-individual-redress-where-theres-will-theres-way, last accessed 20.04.2021.

98 See K. Lenaerts, 'Limits on Limitations: The Essence of Fundamental Rights in the EU', (2019) 20(6) *German Law Journal*, p. 782.

99 CJEU, *Facebook Ireland and Schrems*, Opinion of AG Saugmandsgaard Øe, *supra* note 84, referencing former Data Protection Supervisor Peter Hustinx.

100 CJEU (ECJ), *Centraal Israëlitisch Consistorie van België and Others*, Case C-336/19, 17.12.2020, ECLI:EU:C:2020:1031.

101 See e.g. CJEU (ECJ), *G4S Secure Solutions*, Case C-157/15, 14.03.2017, ECLI:EU:C:2017:203; CJEU (ECJ), *Bougnaoui and ADDH*, Case C-188/15, 14.03.2017, ECLI:EU:C:2017:204; CJEU (ECJ), *Egenberger*, Case C-414/16, 17.04.2018, ECLI:EU:C:2018:257; CJEU (ECJ), *IR*, Case C-68/17, 11.09.2018, ECLI:EU:C:2018:696; CJEU (ECJ), *Jehovan todistajat*, Case C-25/17, 10.07.2018, ECLI:EU:C:2018:551; CJEU (ECJ), *Cresco Investigation*, Case C-193/17, 22.01.2019, ECLI:EU:C:2019:43.

In *Liga van Moskeeën en Islamitische Organisaties Provincie Antwerpen and Others,*[102] the Court had to decide whether the obligation to conduct ritual slaughter in a prior authorised slaughterhouse violates Article 10 CFR. In *Oeuvre d'assistance aux bêtes d'abattoirs,*[103] the Court was confronted with the question of whether the EU's organic production logo may also certify products originating from animals which have been slaughtered in accordance with religious rites without prior stunning. *Centraal Israëlitisch Consistorie van België and Others* now adds to this line of cases by raising the question of whether Member States are allowed to outlaw the slaughter of animals without prior stunning as required by Jewish and Muslim rite altogether.

5.2. FACTS OF THE CASE

In 2019, a decree took effect in the Flemish region of Belgium banning the slaughtering of animals in accordance with Jewish and Muslim rite and to require the previous reversible stunning of these animals in order to alleviate their suffering. Several Jewish and Muslim associations brought the matter before the Belgian Constitutional Court, seeking the annulment of the decree, as it allegedly interferes with an essential element of their religious practices and beliefs.[104]

The EU legal framework for the protection of animals at the time of killing is provided by Regulation 1099/2009.[105] Article 4 para. 1 of that regulation lays down the general rule that animals may only be killed after stunning. Article 4 para. 4 of the regulation, however, stipulates an exception to this for religious slaughter, provided that it takes place in slaughterhouse. Article 26 para. 2 subpara. 1 point c of the regulation in turn allows for higher standards of animal welfare protection in the context of ritual slaughter.[106]

The Belgian Constitutional Court decided to refer the matter to the ECJ. The Constitutional Court wanted to know if Article 26 para. 2 subpara. 1 point c of the regulation allows Member States to derogate from Article 4 para. 4 of that regulation to enact rules as the decree in question in order to achieve a higher level of animal welfare.

---

102 CJEU (ECJ), *Liga van Moskeeën en Islamitische Organisaties Provincie Antwerpen and Others,* Case C-426/16, 29.05.2018, ECLI:EU:C:2018:335.

103 CJEU (ECJ), *Oeuvre d'assistance aux bêtes d'abattoirs,* Case C-497/17, 26.02.2019, ECLI:EU:C:2019:137.

104 CJEU, *Centraal Israëlitisch Consistorie van België and Others, supra* note 100, paras. 14 and 26–28.

105 Council Regulation (EC) No 1099/2009 of 24 September 2009 on the protection of animals at the time of killing, OJ L 303/1.

106 CJEU, *Centraal Israëlitisch Consistorie van België and Others, supra* note 100, paras. 15–23.

5.3. JUDGMENT

The Court stresses that the main objective of Regulation 1099/2009 is the protection of animal welfare.[107] Further, the derogation allowing for ritual slaughter is based on the requirement to show consideration for certain conventions of the Member States concerning culture and religion and reflects a pledge to guarantee effective observance of freedom of religion and the right to manifest religion or beliefs.[108] At the same time, a certain discretion is left to the Member States to maintain higher standards of animal welfare, as long as these do not obstruct the putting into circulation of animal products from other Member States derived from animals slaughtered without prior stunning in accordance with religious rites.[109]

The Court states that the regulation does not in itself create a balance between the protection of animal welfare and the freedom to manifest religion, as guaranteed by Article 10 para. 1 CFR, but rather, provides a framework for the Member States to attain this balance. The fact that Article 26 para. 2 subpara. 1 point c of the regulation authorises the adoption of higher standards, such as an obligation to stun animals prior to killing, cannot lead to the conclusion that the freedom to manifest religion is not sufficiently considered. However, Member States must respect the fundamental rights enshrined in the Charter when adopting such higher standards.[110]

The Court finds that domestic legislation that requires reversible stunning in the context of ritual slaughter falls within the scope of Article 10 para. 1 CFR and that the Flemish decree limits the right to the freedom to manifest one's religion in the case of Muslim and Jewish believers.[111]

The Court then proceeds to emphasise that pursuant to Article 52 para. 3 CFR, Article 10 para. 1 of the Charter corresponds to Article 9 ECHR and stresses that any restriction of Article 10 para. 1 CFR must be provided for by law and respect the essence of the right, pursue a legitimate aim or the protection of rights and freedoms of others and observe the principle of proportionality.[112]

The ECJ holds that the limitation is provided for by law as it is based on a decree and that it does not touch upon the essence of Article 10 para. 1 CFR either. Further, pursuant to Article 13 TFEU and the case law of the Court, the protection of animal welfare constitutes a legitimate aim recognised by the Union.[113]

---

107 Ibid., paras. 39–42.

108 Ibid., paras. 43–44.

109 Ibid., paras. 45–46.

110 Ibid., paras. 47–49.

111 Ibid., paras. 50–55.

112 Ibid., paras. 56–59.

113 Ibid., paras. 60–63.

Examining the proportionality, the Court first considers the decree to be appropriate for the attainment of the aim of protecting animal welfare.[114] The ECJ then stresses – with reference to the concept of the margin of appreciation doctrine developed by the ECtHR – that in the absence of a consensus on ritual slaughter, there is a legislative discretion afforded to the Member States by Regulation 1099/2009.[115] Concerning the necessity of the limitation, the Court holds that a scientific consensus exists that was taken into account that prior stunning is the best way to lessen the animal's suffering when being slaughtered.[116] Examining the proportionality *strictu sensu*, the ECJ emphasises that the decree is based on scientific evidence. More importantly, the Court stresses that the Charter, much like the ECHR, is a living instrument, meaning that it is to be interpreted dynamically and thus needs to take into consideration prevailing ideas and developments in society. The ECJ notes that animal welfare is a value of increasing importance in democratic societies and consequently, this change of perception is capable of justifying restrictions on ritual slaughter. Eventually, the Court notes that the decree does not affect the putting into circulation of ritual slaughter products from other Member States.[117]

5.4. COMMENT

The judgment of the Court is noteworthy. First, it contrasts with the opinion of AG Hogan, who considered that Article 4 para. 4 of Regulation 1099/2009 constitutes a deliberative decision by the EU legislature to grant a higher level of protection of religious freedom than required by virtue of Article 9 ECHR. The AG therefore reached the conclusion that the Flemish decree was incompatible with EU law.[118]

Second, while arriving at the same result as the ECtHR when dealing with ritual slaughter, the reasoning applied by the ECJ deserves further attention. To recall, the ECtHR in *Cha'are Shalom Ve Tsedek v France* decided that a ban on ritual slaughter only constitutes an interference with Article 9 ECHR '[...] if the illegality of performing ritual slaughter made it impossible [...] to eat meat from animals slaughtered in accordance with the religious prescriptions [...].'[119] Thus, the ECtHR does not consider a ban on ritual slaughter to constitute a limitation of Article 9 ECHR as long as there are other ways of ensuring that

114 Ibid., paras. 64–66.

115 Ibid., paras. 67–71.

116 Ibid., paras. 72–74.

117 Ibid., paras. 75–78.

118 See CJEU (ECJ), *Centraal Israëlitisch Consistorie van België and Others*, Case C-336/19, Opinion of AG Hogan, 10.09.2020, ECLI:EU:C:2020:695.

119 ECtHR, *Cha'are Shalom Ve Tsedek v France*, no 27417/95, 27.06.2000, para. 80.

animal products derived from ritual slaughter can be obtained. The ECJ could easily have adopted this reasoning. The Court, however, applied a different approach. Unlike the ECtHR, the ECJ affirmed the existence of an interference with Article 10 para. 1 CFR. Instead of denying the existence of a limitation, the Court relied on two concepts developed by the ECtHR – the margin of appreciation and the living instrument doctrines – in order to establish the proportionality of the interference. In particular, the first-ever invocation of the CFR as a 'living instrument' by the Court is significant insofar as the doctrine is not relied upon to expand the scope of protection, but to allow for its restriction. In the context of the ECHR, there is a lively scholarly debate whether the living instrument doctrine may also serve as a justification for lowering the level of protection afforded by Convention rights or whether there is a non-regression principle inherent to the doctrine.[120] The ECJ has now answered the question for the purposes of the Charter: the nature of the CFR as a living instrument implies that an interpretation of Charter rights 'in the light of present-day conditions' allows for considering aspects such as the protection of animal welfare in order to further restrict the right to manifest one's religion. It remains to be seen whether the invocation of the Charter as a living instrument – in particular with the intention to allow for a further restriction of fundamental rights – will resurface in the ECJ's fundamental rights jurisprudence in the future.

6. RIGHT TO ACADEMIC FREEDOM AND FREEDOM TO FOUND EDUCATIONAL ESTABLISHMENTS: *COMMISSION V HUNGARY*[121]

6.1. INTRODUCTION

In the autumn of 2020, in a highly anticipated infringement judgment, the ECJ ruled on the Hungarian legislation on higher education as amended in 2017 which required foreign higher education institutions from states outside the European Economic Area, in order to commence or continue their activities in Hungary, to prove the conclusion of an international agreement between Hungary and their state of origin. Additionally, those institutions were required to offer higher education services also in their state of origin. That legislation was commonly referred to as 'lex CEU', since it had the sole aim of ceasing the operation of the renowned Central European University (CEU) which has a

---

120 For an overview of the discussion see L.R. Helfer and E. Voeten, 'Walking Back Human Rights in Europe?', (2020) 31(3), *European Journal of International Law*, pp. 802–805.

121 CJEU (ECJ), *Commission v Hungary (Enseignement supérieur)*, Case C-66/18, 06.10.2020, ECLI:EU:C:2020:792.

reputation of promoting liberal values. Ultimately, since the CEU was unable to fulfil the new requirements, it had to relocate (most of) its Budapest campus to Vienna, Austria, in November 2019.[122]

6.2. FACTS OF THE CASE

The European Commission considered the Hungarian legislation at issue as failure to fulfil obligations: (i) under Article XVII of the General Agreement on Trade in Services (GATS);[123] (ii) under Article 16 of the Services Directive as well as Articles 49 and 56 TFEU;[124] and (iii) under Article 13, Article 14 para. 3 and Article 16 CFR. Therefore, after completing the pre-litigation procedure, in February 2018, it brought an infringement action under Article 258 TFEU.[125]

6.3. JUDGMENT

The Court essentially shares those doubts, holding that Hungary has failed to fulfil its obligations under Article XVII of the GATS and under Article 49 TFEU, as well as Article 16 of the Services Directive since the new requirements – without plausible justification – modified the conditions of competition to the benefit of like Hungarian providers.[126] More interestingly from a fundamental

---

122 For some more general information see the AG's opinion: CJEU (ECJ), *Commission v Hungary (Enseignement supérieur)*, Case C-66/18, Opinion of AG Kokott, 05.03.2020, ECLI:EU:C:2020:172, paras. 1-4; for a contextual personal account see R. Uitz, 'What Being Left Behind by the Rule of Law Feels Like, Part I', *Verfassungsblog*, 29.10.2018, available at https://verfassungsblog.de/what-being-left-behind-by-the-rule-of-law-feels-like-part-i/, last accessed 20.04.2021; R. Uitz, 'What Being Left Behind by the Rule of Law Feels Like, Part II', *Verfassungsblog*, 31.10.2018, available at https://verfassungsblog.de/what-being-left-behind-by-the-rule-of-law-feels-like-part-ii/, last accessed 20.04.2021.

123 General Agreement on Trade in Services (GATS) in Annex 1B to the Agreement establishing the World Trade Organisation, approved by Council Decision 94/800/EC of 22 December 1994 concerning the conclusion on behalf of the European Community, as regards matters within its competence, of the agreements reached in the Uruguay Round multilateral negotiations (1986-1994), OJ L 336/1.

124 Directive 2006/123/EC of the European Parliament and of the Council of 12 December 2006 on services in the internal market, OJ L 376/36 (the Services Directive).

125 CJEU, *Commission v Hungary*, *supra* note 121, paras. 1, 26–38.

126 Ibid., paras. 94 et seqq., 156, 190, 207. For an analysis see C.I. Nagy, 'The Commission's Al Capone Tricks. Using GATS to protect academic freedom in the European Union', *Verfassungsblog*, 20.11.2020, available at https://verfassungsblog.de/the-commissions-al-capone-tricks/, last accessed 20.04.2021; J. Bornemann, 'Academic freedom in illiberal times – A bittersweet victory for the Central European University', *European Law Blog*, 21.10.2020, available at https://europeanlawblog.eu/2020/10/21/academic-freedom-in-illiberal-times-a-bittersweet-victory-for-the-central-european-university/, last accessed 20.04.2021.

rights point of view, of course, the ECJ holds that Hungary has also violated the aforementioned provisions of the Charter, which was unsurprisingly considered applicable.[127]

Conducting a textbook fundamental rights test, the Court emphasises that according to Article 13 CFR 'academic freedom shall be respected'. Referring to Article 10 ECHR, the case law of the ECtHR as well as Council of Europe and United Nations recommendations on university autonomy, it holds that the concept of academic freedom must be understood more broadly since it also incorporates an institutional and organisational dimension, 'a link to an organisational structure being an essential prerequisite for teaching and research activities'.[128] In that light, the Court consideres the measures at issue capable of endangering the academic activities of foreign higher education institutions in Hungary and, therefore, of depriving those institutions of the autonomous organisational structure that is necessary for conducting their academic tasks.[129]

Turning to Article 14 para. 3 and Article 16 CFR, the Court stresses that the freedom to found educational establishments with due respect for democratic principles shall be respected in accordance with the national laws governing the exercise of such freedom. Moreover, the freedom to conduct a business in accordance with EU law and national laws and practices must be recognised.[130] In that regard, the Court notes that the measures at issue are, depending on the circumstances, such as to render uncertain or to exclude the very possibility of founding or continuing to operate higher education institutions in Hungary. Consequently, those measures must be regarded as limiting both the freedom to found educational establishments and the freedom to conduct a business.[131]

On the question of justification as governed by the proportionality clause in Article 52 para. 1 CFR, the Court concludes that the limiting measures at issue are not justified by any of the objectives of general interest recognised by the Union upon which Hungary relied and did not adequately substantiate, namely, the maintaining of public order, the prevention of deceptive practices and the need to ensure the good quality of higher education. Therefore, the ECJ

---

127 Ibid., paras. 212–216.

128 Ibid., paras. 222–227. See ECtHR, *Mustafa Erdoğan and Others v Turkey*, nos 346/04 and 39779/04, 27.05.2014; ECtHR, *Hasan Yazıcı v Turkey*, no 40877/07, 15.04.2014; Recommendation 1762 (2006) of the Parliamentary Assembly of the Council of Europe of 30 June 2006, available at https://pace.coe.int/en/files/17469, last accessed 20.04.2021; Recommendation of the General Conference of the United Nations Educational, Scientific and Cultural Organisation of 11 November 1997, available at http://portal.unesco.org/en/ev.php-URL_ID=13144&URL_DO=DO_TOPIC&URL_SECTION=201.html, last accessed 20.04.2021. See also the convergence clause in Article 52 para. 3 CFR and the comments on Article 13 CFR in the Explanations relating to the Charter, OJ C 303/17.

129 Ibid., para. 228.

130 Ibid., paras. 229–232.

131 Ibid., paras. 233–234.

ultimately states that by adopting those measures Hungary has (also) failed to fulfil its obligations under Article 13, Article 14 para. 3 and Article 16 CFR.[132]

6.4. COMMENT

The 'lex CEU' allowed the Court, for the first time, to rule on the institutional dimension of the fundamental right to academic freedom as deduced primarily from the right to freedom of thought and expression in Article 10 ECHR and laid down in the second sentence of Article 13 CFR. The Court thereby draws lines which were previously not covered by ECtHR case law. In accordance with the AG's opinion,[133] echoing the European Commission's initial concerns and referring to the aforementioned soft law instruments, the Court convincingly emphasises the criterion of institutional autonomy being a fundamental prerequisite for the functioning of academia in an open society and, for that matter, democracy.[134] Therefore, the ECJ's judgment not least is a prime example of the effectiveness of infringement action against illiberal policies stigmatising persons or institutions which eventually undermine a Union based on the rule of law.[135]

7. NON-DISCRIMINATION: *ASSOCIAZIONE AVVOCATURA PER I DIRITTI LGBTI*[136]

7.1. INTRODUCTION

There is no doubt that the principles of non-discrimination and equal treatment form cornerstones of the EU legal order.[137] This is not only reflected in a number of provisions of EU primary law,[138] but also in a bundle of

---

132 Ibid., paras. 239–242; see also paras. 132, 138, 154–155, 189.

133 CJEU, *Commission v Hungary*, Opinion of AG Kokott, *supra* note 122, paras. 130 et seqq., 181–188.

134 For a detailed analysis of the Hungarian legislation concerned which the Court, however, did not refer to, see Venice Commission, Opinion 891/2017 on Act XXV of 4 April 2017 on the amendment of Act CCIV of 2011 on national tertiary education, 09.10.2017, available at https://www.venice.coe.int/webforms/documents/default.aspx?pdffile=CDL-AD(2017)022-e, last accessed 20.04.2021.

135 See R. Uitz, 'Finally: The CJEU Defends Academic Freedom', *Verfassungsblog*, 08.10.2020, available at https://verfassungsblog.de/finally-the-cjeu-defends-academic-freedom/, last accessed 20.04.2021.

136 CJEU (ECJ), *Associazione Avvocatura per i diritti LGBTI*, Case C-507/18, 23.04.2020, ECLI:EU:C:2020:289.

137 See on this point also last year's contribution, C. Breitler and M. Traussnigg (2020) 'The Court of Justice of the European Union and Human Rights in 2019', *supra* note 3, p. 579.

138 See e.g. Articles 8, 10, 18, 19, 36, 45, 65 and 157 TFEU as well as Title III of the Charter.

anti-discrimination directives adopted pursuant to what is now Article 19 TFEU.[139] These directives address equal treatment based on racial and ethnic origin, equal treatment concerning matters of employment and occupation and equal treatment between men and women in the access to and supply of goods and services.[140] As a common feature, all of these directives are aimed at eliminating inequalities. Moreover, in the context of employment matters, it is a declared objective to attain a high level of employment and social protection.[141] Typically, there is a specific victim seeking justice and redress by relying on the guarantees provided by one of the directives. However, how should a situation be qualified, in which general discriminatory remarks are made with no specific victim directly affected?

7.2. FACTS OF THE CASE

During a radio interview, NH, a senior lawyer in an Italian law firm, made derogatory remarks about homosexuals and stated he would never hire a homosexual person. At the time of this statement, however, no recruitment procedure was taking place at his law firm.[142]

Following the broadcast of this interview, the Associazione Avvocatura per i diritti LGBTI – Rete Lenford, an association of lawyers dedicated to the protection of the rights of the lesbian, gay, bisexual, transgender and intersexual (LGBTI) community, took legal action against NH. NH lost the case at first instance and was ordered to pay 10,000 EUR in damages to the association and to publish extracts of the verdict in a newspaper.[143]

After having unsuccessfully appealed against the order, NH turned to the Supreme Court of Cassation, which decided to refer two questions about the interpretation of Directive 2000/78.[144] First, the court wanted to know whether the association is to be considered a 'body representing collective interests' within the meaning of Article 9 para. 2 of the directive.[145] Second, the court was wondering if the statements in question concern 'employment' and therefore

139 Ex-Article 13 of the Treaty establishing the European Community.

140 Council Directive 2000/43/EC of 29 June 2000 implementing the principle of equal treatment between persons irrespective of racial or ethnic origin, OJ L 180/22; Council Directive 2000/78/EC of 27 November 2000 establishing a general framework for equal treatment in employment and occupation, OJ L 303/16; Council Directive 2004/113/EC of 13 December 2004 implementing the principle of equal treatment between men and women in the access to and supply of goods and services, OJ L 373/37.

141 See Recital 11 of Directive 2000/78.

142 CJEU, *Associazione Avvocatura*, *supra* note 136, paras. 18 and 21.

143 Ibid., paras. 16–18.

144 Ibid., paras. 19–20.

145 Ibid., paras. 22–24 and 27.

come under the scope of the directive or if they constitute merely expressions of opinion not amounting to discrimination.[146]

7.3. JUDGMENT

The Court, answering the questions in reversed order, first assesses whether the statements made by NH fall within the material scope of Directive 2000/78. Article 3 para. 1 letter a of the directive lays down that its scope applies 'to all persons in relation to conditions for access to employment, to self-employment or to occupation, including selection criteria and recruitment conditions'. The Court clarifies that the norm has an autonomous meaning under EU law and that Directive 2000/78 – as a specific manifestation of Article 21 CFR – must not be interpreted restrictively.[147]

The Court proceeds to clarify that the term 'conditions for access to employment […] or to occupation, including recruitment conditions' may encompass publicly made statements related to a specific hiring policy. It is not necessary that those statements come from the person responsible for the recruitment policy. Rather, it suffices that the actual employer fails to distance himself from those statements. It also is not required that at the time of the statements an actual recruitment procedure was taking place.[148]

However, the Court demands a sufficient link between the statements and the conditions for access to employment and to occupation with that employer. The existence of such a link is to be based on three relevant factors: (i) the status of the author of the statements in question – meaning that this person must have the ability to influence the hiring policy or at least be perceived as doing so; (ii) the type and content of the statements – meaning that they must reflect the intention to discriminate based on the criteria of Directive 2000/78; and (iii) the context of the statements – for example, whether they were made in a public or a private context or whether they were publicly broadcast.[149]

Finally, the Court clarifies that this interpretation of the directive does not conflict with the right to freedom of expression pursuant to Article 11 CFR, as it is not an absolute right and therefore may be restricted in accordance with Article 52 para. 1 CFR. As such, the restriction is provided for by law – the directive itself – and also respects the essence of the right to freedom of expression. In terms of proportionality, the Court stresses that the directive lays down the material and personal scope and the prohibited grounds of discrimination and that the limitation of the right to freedom of expression only concerns

146 Ibid., paras. 25–27.
147 Ibid., paras. 28–39.
148 Ibid., paras. 40–42.
149 Ibid., paras. 43–46.

statements that are discriminatory. The Court also stresses that the interference with the right to freedom of expression is necessary in order to secure the rights of persons belonging to one of the groups protected by Directive 2000/78. The Court emphasises that the essence of protection that is provided by the directive might become devoid of meaning if it were to exclude discriminatory opinions expressed by an employer or a person who is perceived to have influence on the recruitment policy, as these are likely to have a deterrent effect on potential applicants belonging to the discriminated group. Therefore, the Court concludes that statements falling within the scope of Directive 2000/78 cannot be excluded from that regime based on the fact that they were made in the context of an entertainment programme or reflect the personal opinion of its author.[150]

Concerning the first question, the Court states that the provisions of the directive are minimum requirements and therefore, that Member States are allowed to introduce higher standards. Consequently, even though Article 9 para. 2 of the directive refers to associations acting 'on behalf or in support of the complainant', Member States are not barred from allowing associations to take legal action where there is no identifiable victim of discrimination.[151]

7.4. COMMENT

The judgment, which is line with the opinion of the AG,[152] follows in the footsteps of two earlier cases: *Feryn* and *Asociaţia Accept*.[153] While the former case concerned statements made by a Belgian employer that he would not hire applicants of Moroccan origin, as this allegedly was not compatible with customers' wishes, the latter case dealt with statements made by the 'patron' of a Romanian football club who said in an interview that a contract with a specific player was not concluded due to the fact that this player was presented as homosexual. The existence of that case law has prompted some commentators to assert that the judgment in the present case does not offer much in the way of novelty.[154] However, this conclusion is to be contested, as in the present case there was neither a specific victim of discrimination (as was the case in *Asociaţia*

150 Ibid., paras. 47–58.

151 Ibid., paras. 59–65.

152 See CJEU (ECJ), *Associazione Avvocatura per i diritti LGBTI*, Case C-507/18, Opinion of AG Sharpston, 31.10.2019, ECLI:EU:C:2019:922.

153 CJEU (ECJ), *Feryn*, Case C-54/07, 10.07.2008, ECLI:EU:C:2008:397; CJEU (ECJ), *Asociaţia Accept*, Case C-81/12, 25.04.2013, ECLI:EU:C:2013:275.

154 See A. Tryfonidou, 'Case C-507/18 NH v Associazione Avvocatura per i diritti LGBTI–Rete Lenford: Homophobic speech and EU anti-discrimination law', (2020) 27(4), *Maastricht Journal of European and Comparative Law*, p. 518; U. Belavusau, 'The NH Case: On the "Wings of Words" in EU Anti-discrimination Law', (2020) 5(2), *European Papers*, pp. 1009–1011.

Accept) nor an ongoing recruitment procedure (as was the case in *Feryn*), but rather statements made by a senior lawyer without any link to a concrete recruitment process. As this means that the scope of application of Directive 2000/78 is remarkably wide, it is to be welcomed that the Court specified the criteria that have to be fulfilled in order to ensure that the nexus between the statements in question and the conditions for access to employment and to occupation is not merely hypothetical. While ensuring equality and combatting discrimination is undoubtedly a noble aim, there is no denying that there is an inherent tension with the right to freedom of expression[155] and, as one commentator put it, the danger of 'excessive censorship'.[156]

As is clear from the case law of the ECtHR, derogatory statements directed against sexual minorities are generally still covered by Article 10 para. 1 ECHR, but may be limited in accordance with Article 10 para. 2 ECHR.[157] Contrary to what has been asserted, however, it is not simply possible to afford '[...] more protection from homophobic speech [...]' by excluding that kind of speech from the scope of application of Article 9 CFR altogether,[158] as this would mean that the level of protection offered by Article 9 CFR would fall behind the level of protection offered by Article 10 ECHR, thus violating the convergence clause in Article 52 para. 3 CFR.[159]

8. CONCLUSION

The CJEU's jurisprudence in the field of EU fundamental and human rights law in 2020 partly shows a tendency towards emancipation from the jurisprudence of the ECtHR without, however, challenging or questioning the authority of the Strasbourg court as such. While the ECJ has established a traditionally high standard in the field of data protection, cases such as *FMS and Others* or *Commission v Hungary* show the Court's willingness to set a higher standard

155 See V. Passalacqua, 'Homophobic Statements and Hypothetical Discrimination: Expanding the Scope of Directive 2000/78/EC: ECJ 23 April 2020, Case C-507/18, Associazione Avvocatura per i diritti LGBTI', (2020) 16(3) *European Constitutional Law Review*, p. 523.

156 J. Miller, 'When Workplace Antidiscrimination Law Collides with Freedom of Expression: A Delicate Balancing Act', (2020) 6(3), *International Labor Rights Case Law*, p. 304.

157 See ECtHR, *Vejdeland and others v Sweden*, no 1813/07, 09.02.2012. See also ECtHR, *Liliendahl v Iceland*, no 29297/18, 12.05.2020, which was decided after the ECJ's judgment in *Associazione Avvocatura*. The only exception to this is when statements are so severe that pursuant to Article 17 ECHR, Article 10 of the Convention may not be invoked.

158 A. Tryfonidou (2020), 'Homophobic speech and EU anti-discrimination law', *supra* note 154, p. 520.

159 See S. Peers and S. Prechal, 'Article 52', in S. Peers, T. Hervey, J. Kenner et al. (eds.), *The EU Charter of Fundamental Rights. A commentary*, Hart Publishing, Oxford 2014, p. 1499, para. 52.133.

of protection also in other fields. In a similar manner, in *Centraal Israëlitisch Consistorie van België and Others*, the Court has demonstrated its readiness to pursue its own doctrinal path without crossing the boundaries of Article 52 para. 3 CFR. Generally, it can be positively stressed that the ECJ fairly extensively made reference to the case law of the ECtHR in the judgments discussed.

PART IV
HUMAN RIGHTS INSIGHTS

BUILDING BRIDGES BETWEEN LOCAL GOVERNMENTS AND THE SCIENTIFIC COMMUNITY TO PROMOTE HUMAN RIGHTS

Markus Möstl and Wanda Tiefenbacher

ABSTRACT

The Academy and Conference 'Human Rights Go Local – What Works: Field-proven Research Methods on Human Rights', held in February 2021, was the opening of an event series aiming to mobilise knowledge, moderate exchange and build bridges between all governance levels, disciplines and regions, with a focus on human rights at the local level. The event brought together human rights experts from local governments, international and regional organisations and the research community to discuss research methods that have proven successful to generate reliable human rights data for evidence-based policy-making at the local level. The practices, findings and proposals reported and discussed at the academy were synthesised into an Outcome Document, which was officially launched at the conference by high-level politicians, policy-makers and 200 human rights experts and international guests. This contribution presents the main challenges and solutions discussed by the participants of the academy and the Outcome Document's 14 'Encouragements' to local governments on how to reinforce their policies through evidence that is based on human rights research.

1. RESEARCH ON HUMAN RIGHTS AT THE LOCAL LEVEL: WHAT WORKS?

What research methods have proven successful to generate reliable human rights data for evidence-based policy-making at the local level? In February 2021, the Academy and Conference 'Human Rights Go Local – What Works: Field-proven Research Methods on Human Rights' brought together human rights experts from local governments, international and regional organisations and the research community to discuss exactly this question.[1] During five intensive academy days, over 40 experts from all over the globe met at eye level in ten interactive workshops and eight plenary sessions to exchange their expertise. As a kick-off event, a young researchers day gave next generation human rights experts the opportunity to present their research projects and receive feedback from participating experts and peers.

The online academy provided a unique platform for expert exchange and dissemination of proven methods to generate reliable human rights data for evidence-based urban policy making. The practices, findings and proposals reported and discussed at this event were synthesised into the 'Outcome Document and Explanatory Remarks on Building Bridges between Local Governments and the Scientific Community to Promote Human Rights'.[2] This tangible output of the event includes 14 'Encouragements' to local governments worldwide on how to reinforce their policies through evidence based on

1 The Academy and Conference was organised by the International Centre for the Promotion of Human Rights at the Local and Regional Levels under the auspices of the United Nations Educational, Scientific and Cultural Organization (UNESCO) and the UNESCO Chair in Human Rights and Human Security in cooperation with the UNESCO, the United Nations Office of the High Commissioner for Human Rights (OHCHR), UN-Habitat, the European Union Agency for Fundamental Rights (FRA), United Cities and Local Governments (UCLG), the Austrian Federal Ministry for European and International Affairs, the Provincial Government Styria, the City of Graz and the University of Graz. More information on this event is available at https://www.humanrightsgolocal.org/2021/02/17/building-bridges-between-local-governments-and-the-scientific-community-to-promote-human-rights/, last accessed 25.8.2021.

2 'Building Bridges between Local Governments and the Scientific Community to Promote Human Rights' Outcome Document and Explanatory Remarks 2021 of Human Rights Go Local: What Works – Academy and Conference on Human Rights at the Local and Regional Levels 2021 on Field-proven Research Methods on Human Rights, 1–9 February 2021, Graz, 9 February 2021.

human rights research. The addressees of these Encouragements are local level authorities, in particular mayors and the administrative staff of cities and smaller settlements around the globe.

The Outcome Document was launched on 9 February 2021 at the Conference on Human Rights at the Local and Regional Levels organised in the context of celebrating the 20th anniversary of Graz (Austria) as Europe's first Human Rights City, as well as officially opening the International Centre for the Promotion of Human Rights at the Local and Regional Levels under the auspices of the United Nations Educational, Scientific and Cultural Organization (UNESCO).[3] High-level politicians, policy-makers and human rights experts gathered online, together with 200 international guests, to lay the groundwork for the future of implementing human rights at the local level. Gabriela Ramos (Assistant Director-General for Social and Human Sciences of UNESCO), Nada Al-Nashif (United Nations Deputy High Commissioner for Human Rights) and Michael O'Flaherty (Director of the European Union Agency for Fundamental Rights) discussed the Outcome Document with Siegfried Nagl (Mayor of Graz) and Gerd Oberleitner (UNESCO Chair in Human Rights and Human Security at the University of Graz) under the moderation of Morten Kjærum (Director of the Raoul Wallenberg Institute of Human Rights and Humanitarian Law, Sweden).

In the following, the main challenges and solutions discussed by the participants of the academy and the related Encouragements to local level authorities adopted at the conference are presented. Due to the rich exchange during the event, this overview cannot mention all the results, nor does it aspire to fully substantiate all the statements made. Instead, the summary presents essential findings to be taken into consideration for research on human rights at the local level from a practical perspective.

2. CHALLENGES, SOLUTIONS AND ENCOURAGEMENTS

2.1. RESEARCH ON HUMAN RIGHTS AS A VALUABLE BASIS FOR EVIDENCE-BASED LOCAL POLICY-MAKING

Research on human rights at the local level can help mayors and city officials to better understand the situation of all city dwellers, and to plan, implement and evaluate human rights-based policies in almost every field of municipal activity

---

3 International Centre for the Promotion of Human Rights at the Local and Regional Levels under the auspices of UNESCO, https://www.humanrightsgolocal.org/, last accessed 25.08.2021.

accordingly. Beyond that human rights research is also a means to strengthen the accountability of local level governments.

A human rights-based approach to local governance is ideally always informed by the results of contextualised, high-quality research. Yet, in practice this is certainly not (yet) the case for many local governments. Local authorities sometimes perceive human rights as big ideas to live up to, which can be overstraining in everyday policy-making and service provision. While some local governments already do show a growing interest and commitment to human rights, *inter alia*, because of value based decisions or central state failures, other local governments still need to acknowledge that research on human rights is a useful foundation for evidence-based policy-making.

Specific local contexts call for other research questions and designs than human rights research covering the national level. There are established and field-proven research methods available that can be applied for research on human rights at the local level. Research based on these methods is necessarily highly context-specific in order to render meaningful results.

Participation is a key factor for the success of research on human rights. Such research should not be conducted *on* the local community but *with* the local community. The question 'what needs to be measured?' should serve as a starting point, while more traditional top-down approaches commencing with an analysis of international law and the localisation of international human rights instruments should only complement this approach. Explorative studies and the inclusion of researchers and mediators coming from the target group are suitable options to render research activities more participatory. Mediators can anticipate potential fears and the reluctance of the target group and react to them by providing reassurance to the individuals in order to ensure their participation.

Human rights research on the local level requires the engagement of the responsible politicians, representatives of the target group, non-governmental organisations (NGOs) and researchers. Understanding research as a joint effort among them can help the local administration, service providers, civil society, as well as the people concerned to find a common ground and a common language for local human rights concerns.

Local level governments worldwide are encouraged to:

(1) base the development of their key policies, programmes, and decision-making processes, as well as their monitoring and evaluation on research on human rights at the local level.

(2) resort to cooperate in, and promote research pursuing established and field-proven human rights research methods for the local level upholding highest quality standards and to refine them within their specific context, also by way of community-based needs assessment and participatory action research.

2.2. DEVELOPING HUMAN RIGHTS INDICATORS AT THE LOCAL LEVEL

Although human rights indicators giving account of the respect, the protection and the fulfilment of human rights, are a highly relevant instrument for research on human rights at the local level, practice shows that local policies are rarely informed by research that resorts to such indicators. In fact, there are no ready-made indicator schemes available for human rights research at the local level. Instead, existing indicator schemes usually apply to a particular region or city only and need to be contextualised for other settings.

Challenges for developing and applying human rights indicators that are relevant to the local level include: the methodological skills needed for human rights research are not always available to local governments; lack of political will; data accessibility and data quality; lack of financial resources; and the need to bring together different stakeholders, such as NGOs and local authorities.

Researchers and civil society do have the necessary methodological and technical knowledge to develop meaningful human rights indicators for the local level. However, indicators also need to be 'owned' by the local population. They have to be accessible and easy to use for people in the local administration as well as for members of the public. Therefore, human rights indicators should be developed on the basis of a participatory bottom-up approach, where local authorities and the relevant sectors of society are included in the development of indicators.

Pragmatic decisions might have to be taken when developing human rights indicators at the local level. The selection of the rights that are to be monitored, as well as the question which indicators should be used, is often a political decision made in view of other (national) commitments, such as national development plans or the Sustainable Development Goals (SDGs). Structural, process and outcome indicators are all important, but at the local level a focus should be put on process and outcome indicators.

Once indicators have been established, the human rights performance of cities can be measured by setting and reviewing benchmarks. Qualitative and quantitative methods need to be applied for assessing the performance of cities. Established methods include human rights reports, action research and monitoring. Performance assessments should be simple, practical and selective, as well as done frequently and in dialogue with the relevant stakeholders.

Local level governments worldwide are encouraged to:

(3) resort to or commission research building on human rights indicators giving account of the respect, the protection and the fulfilment of human rights, where methodologically adequate and feasible, as well as to commit to making local data on human rights publicly available.

2.3. LINKING LOCAL EFFORTS TO MEASURE HUMAN RIGHTS WITH THE SUSTAINABLE DEVELOPMENT GOALS

Human rights and the SDGs are closely interrelated, and practice shows that human rights policies can also be linked to the SDGs at the local level. As local authorities are often more aware of the global development goals than of human rights, the implementation of the SDGs is an operational opportunity for localising human rights. Human rights can be demystified in this context, for example, by pointing out that human rights are not only an abstract legal concept and making clear how municipalities already implement human rights in their daily work.

Not all SDG goals, targets and indicators are equally relevant, applicable and suitable to the local level. Some SDG indicators need to be prioritised, and new ones might need to be developed to be meaningful at the local level. The criteria for amendments should be based on local needs, local mandates and local capacities.

Despite the communalities between the SDGs and human rights, there are also conceptual and practical differences to be considered. In particular, the review process of the development agenda is clearly distinct from the traditional judicial and quasi-judicial review and monitoring mechanisms established for human rights treaties. In local practice, development policies might go into the same direction as human rights policies, but they do not necessarily seek to respect, protect and fulfil the human rights of all city dwellers. As a result, some residents could be left behind or the needs of specific groups could be neglected.

Local level governments worldwide are encouraged to:

(4) use the synergies between local efforts to measure the progress in the enjoyment of human rights by everyone and local efforts to measure the progress towards the achievement of the SDGs.

2.4. GENERATING HUMAN RIGHTS DATA RELEVANT TO THE LOCAL LEVEL

Human rights data is often scarcely available at the local level. Local statistical offices do not necessarily follow a human rights-based approach when collecting data on a regular basis, but they sometimes do produce data that is indeed relevant to human rights (policies). Public officials are to be made aware of how to access this existing data and statistics and how to use it as human rights information.

While large-scale surveys are helpful at the national level, they are not as useful at the local level, because more local particularities need to be considered.

Therefore, it is crucial to conduct smaller, more precise surveys at the local level (for example in each neighbourhood), in order to decide where to put consequent efforts and measures.

A combination of qualitative and quantitative data is necessary to complement existing data, particularly if sensitive issues are at stake. Even though policy-makers usually prefer data sets populated with quantitative data because of their supposed significance, they can be misleading in the case of marginalised groups. Qualitative data can reflect the situations of marginalised groups much better than mere quantitative data. Relying on only one research project or data source is not sufficient. Ideally, a mix of sources, studies and methods should be used to obtain a solid picture of the situation on the ground.

Data protection policies, as well as mistrust between public officials and civil society, often hinder the collection of meaningful data. Therefore, trust in valid data, trust in data protection and appropriate use of data and trust in the appropriate use of research outcomes for local policy-making needs to be built up. Obtaining data on sensitive issues is very difficult, takes time and requires trust building. As traditional data collection systems might be unable to fulfil these requirements, a human rights-based approach to data collection can help to overcome this problem, particularly as this approach calls for participation.

Local authorities are data providers and addressees of the research results that are based on this data. Not least due to this dual role, researchers need to closely collaborate with and involve local authorities also during data collection. The people who collect data and the people who develop policies based on the data might have very different interests. This gap has to be bridged, and strategic links need to be established between them. Formalised, collaborative platforms of the various stakeholders involved can help facilitate exchange of data needs, availability and accessibility. Standardised data collection mechanisms in different municipalities would allow for the sharing of data and mutual learning of local authorities.

Local level governments worldwide are encouraged to:

(5) review existing qualitative and quantitative data in light of the requirements for relevant human rights information and the call to leave no one behind.

(6) complement existing qualitative and quantitative data with information deemed necessary to fill data gaps, including data on groups left behind or at risk of being left behind.

(7) collect further relevant human rights data upholding the data protection provisions and respecting concerns of marginalised groups.

(8) strengthen collaborative platforms among the human rights communities, and statistics and data communities to implement and abide by the principles of a human rights-based approach to data, and to provide support for the consultation and participation of communities in data collection.

2.5. ESTABLISHING COOPERATION ON THE LOCAL, NATIONAL AND INTERNATIONAL LEVELS

Human rights research, education and communication should be regarded as an asset for cities and communities: human rights at the local level are not a set of restrictive norms, but can provide an area where the community comes together, discusses, becomes creative and induces human rights-based change and progress.

A broad collaboration with local, national and international research institutions and academia can help promote and strengthen human rights at the local level. National Human Rights Institutions often have access to the rights-holders and enjoy the trust of the population, which is why they are valuable partners to be considered.

The research community can act as a supporting structure to foster human rights at the local level. Higher education institutions have an important role in educating about human rights and training human rights trainers at the local level. Academia is active in preparing, creating, implementing and sustaining local authorities with scientific expertise. Since the results of a monitoring can also be (ab)used politically, the participation of local governments throughout the process is important.

Many institutions in the human rights landscape are engaged in research, advocacy and/or litigation. The engagement of such institutions as researchers, who are called on to implement participatory research methods, might attain a problematic role through this direct engagement with people concerned. This dual role could be problematic in the sense of taking sides with the target group. Yet, in practice, human rights researchers applying participatory approaches naturally have such a twofold role. The bias problem has to be overcome, since simply resorting to quantitative research without participation and direct engagement of the target group would not be satisfactory from a methodological point of view. Approaches to overcome the bias problem include transparency in respect to the methodology used for data collection; explanation of the limitations of data (data as such is not to be equated with knowledge); and taking responsibility for data by answering questions such as who produced this data? What was the purpose of its production? How can the data be used correctly without creating bias?

In all these efforts, scientific freedom is a prerequisite for the credibility and quality of research on human rights at the local level. Where human rights are not respected, there is also no respect for independent research.

Local level governments worldwide are encouraged to:

(9) acknowledge the benefits of a collaboration with local, national and international research institutions and academia to conduct research on human rights at the local level, including young researchers and innovative research methods.

(10) ensure transparency and availability of research data and respect and ensure the scientific freedom of researchers, as well as their freedoms of information, expression and association, which imply their rights to seek and receive information, to freely communicate research results to others and to publish and publicise them without censorship, as well as to collaborate with others both within and across the country's borders.
(11) strengthen the engagement with civil society, the local populations and all relevant stakeholders and create the space for them to participate in research on human rights at the local level.
(12) cooperate with national human rights institutions, as well as regional and international organisations to identify areas where existing research and results can benefit, promote and strengthen efforts at the local level.

2.6. EXCHANGING KNOWLEDGE AND INNOVATION WITH PEERS AND RESEARCHERS WORLDWIDE

Research on human rights at the local level needs to be multi-disciplinary and collaborative. In many cases, the expertise for conducting research on human rights is not available to local governments in-house. While some cities have thriving research communities with direct access to a university, a think tank or a national human rights institute, others do not. A broad exchange of knowledge and innovation is needed – particularly in order to support those local governments that do not have access to researchers working on human rights at the local level.

More cities are needed to ensure that the human rights city movement is moving forward and becomes an even bigger project. A more systematic exchange on positive examples of applications of human rights research is needed and can be achieved, *inter alia*, by joining or collaborating with dedicated city networks.

Local level governments worldwide are encouraged to:

(13) exchange knowledge and innovation with other local governments, including by joining and collaborating with city networks and human rights cities in order to promote human rights at the local level and globally.
(14) exchange knowledge and innovation with research institutions worldwide with the aim to build bridges between local governments and the scientific community in order to globally promote human rights at the local level.

3. COMING UP NEXT: THE ACADEMY AND CONFERENCE 2022

The Academy and Conference 2021 was the opening of an event series aiming to mobilise knowledge, moderate exchange and build bridges between all governance levels, disciplines and regions with a focus on human rights at the local level. The SDGs, the New Urban Agenda and the current volume of the 'Human Rights Go Local' publication series[4] regularly inform the selection of the event's annual thematic focus. The next 'Human Rights Go Local: What Works' Academy and Conference intends to take the aforementioned results further by focusing on successful strategies and initiatives for strengthening the commitments to human rights at the local level. Various approaches are currently developed and implemented around the globe with the intention to make human rights a more mandatory guideline for local policies. The Academy and Conference 2022 will provide a platform to collect and discuss regional and local approaches for strengthening the commitments to human rights at the local level and to disseminate practices that have been identified as successful by local governments.

Human rights experts from local governments, international and regional organisations and the research community as well as next-generation human rights experts are invited to this exchange of innovative approaches and proven practices for making cities and human settlements safe, resilient and sustainable, following a human rights-based approach.[5]

---

4 Two volumes of the 'Human Rights Go Local' publication have been published so far: K. Gomes and M. Möstl, 'Implementing Human Rights and the 2030 Agenda for Sustainable Development at the Local Level: Key Issues and Examples', in G. Oberleitner and K. Starl (eds.), *Human Rights Go Local Publications Series*, 1st edition, HRGL Publishing, Graz 2020. I. Meier, 'Research on Human Rights at the Local and Regional Levels: Methods, Practices, Approaches', in G. Oberleitner and K. Starl (eds.), *Human Rights Go Local Publication Series*, 2nd edition, HRGL Publishing, Graz 2021.

5 Visit the website of the 2022 Academy and Conference to register and get regular updates on the agenda: https://www.humanrightsgolocal.org/academy22/, last accessed 25.08.2021.

PART V
BOOK REVIEWS

Adina Gahr

Gwynne L. Skinner, Rachel Chambers and Sarah McGrath

Transnational Corporations and Human Rights

Cambridge, Cambridge University Press, 2020, 250 pages, €32.00

When committing human rights violations in developing countries, do transnational corporations stand above the law? During recent decades, there has been an exploding number of transnational corporations (TNCs). Due to this increase, TNCs have developed a complicated structure – and the legal system is not up-to-date. Laws no longer conform to the complex structures TNCs maintain, as there is not merely one main parent company, but a considerable number of subsidiaries behind it – sometimes owned by multiple corporations. In developing countries, TNCs benefit through their subsidiaries from low costs while posing a threat to the community on-site, especially people's health. The issue at hand is more pressing then ever: currently there are indicators that multiple giant TNCs (including Volkswagen (VW), Bayrische Motoren Werke AG (BMW), Hennes & Mauritz (H&M) and Adidas, to name only a few) are involved in the massive human rights violations against the Uighurs in China. This book examines the power imbalance between the profit TNCs make in developing countries and the very limited accountability parent companies have for human rights violations committed by their subsidiaries. Beyond this main objective, the book not only showcases our legal system's problems, but it also offers solutions.

The authors take a two-step approach to the issue of lack of accountability in TNCs. Part 1 of the book focuses on the barriers victims are facing when they seek compensation. First of all, seeking judicial remedies in the host country itself is typically almost impossible. As developing countries intend to attract TNCs, they accept insufficient regulations and oftentimes weak and corrupt judicial systems at the expense of their citizens. Additionally, local lawyers rarely take cases against corporations, either out of fear or a lack of resources. As a result, there seems to be a higher chance of being awarded compensation when bringing a claim before a court in another country, namely the home country of a TNC. However, even in these – often rich – home countries, plaintiffs are unable to achieve judicial remedy. This is where the authors' focus lies: the possibility of bringing human rights claims against TNCs in their home country. As these typically lie in either the United States (US), Europe or Canada, the book offers an insight into the issues that arise in these legal systems. The three main issues when examining these legal systems are the doctrine of limited liability of shareholders, subject matter jurisdiction and *in personam* jurisdiction. The aforementioned principles are the main barriers for claimants seeking judicial remedies in a TNC's home country. The authors not only re-examine these norms, but further stress that they are out-dated.

Therefore, in Part 2 of the book, the focus lies on possible theories to counter these obsolete principles. When evaluating each of the recent competing theories (namely enterprise liability, the due diligence approach, the parent corporation's duty of care and, lastly, the expanded tort law approach toward parental duty of care to foreseeable victims), the authors come to the conclusion that the best solution would be to ensure proper parent corporation liability through legislation. As a result, the authors propose specific legislative measures to first expand subject matter jurisdiction and, second also broaden personal jurisdiction regarding TNCs. In doing so, as continuously throughout the book, a special focus lies on the legal systems of the US, Canada and the European Union (EU, the Union). Lastly, Part 2 deals with other legal barriers victims face when seeking judicial remedies, including for example the 'choice of law' doctrine or the vast costs of litigation.

The book aptly lives up to the goal it seeks to reach: a display of the striking and unfair imbalance between a TNC's accountability for its actions and harm done to local communities. Skinner, Chambers and McGrath provide valuable insights into dealing with extraterritorial human rights violations – their book represents an essential read for legal scholars, theorists and especially for decision-makers.

The issue that the US, Canada and Europe must tackle is the impossibility for victims to seek judicial remedies in the TNC's country of origin. Clearly, TNCs profit immensely from cheap labour in poorer countries. Yet, when seeking judicial remedy for human rights violations, plaintiffs from developing countries often face obstacles, such as corruption and in general weak legal systems, subsequently rendering compensation in their home countries effectively impossible. Due to obsolete legal barriers, compensation cannot be reached in the TNC's country of origin, either. Thus, the authors call on states to take a stand against corporate immunity by imposing legislation – because an effective global enforcement of human rights requires judicial remedies for extraterritorial human rights violations, as well.

Stephanie GRASSER

Mario Viola de Azevedo Cunha, Norberto Nuno Gomes de Andrade, Lucas Lixinski and Lúcio Tomé Féteira (eds.)

New Technologies and Human Rights: Challenges to Regulation

London/New York, Routledge, 2020, 352 pages, £125.00 (Hardcover)

Human life is deeply affected and often reshaped by modern technology with 'enormous potential of providing better conditions of life' as well as 'damaging and disastrous effects'. Human integrity, autonomy, freedom and dignity are in danger. Therefore, long-established moral values need to be reassessed, and technological progress being subject to law to face the threats and dangers posed by new technologies. The most jeopardised under those are the most basic and primary rights – human rights (p. 1). Although significant progress has been made in terms of regulatory technological advancement, some aspects constitute a rather unexplored area of research, and a new legal framework needs to be discussed (p. 2).

The reviewed book is structured in 15 chapters and divided into seven parts: general legal and philosophical aspects of the interaction between human rights and new technologies; freedom of expression in the online environment; intellectual property, competition rules and new technologies; biobanks, bioethics and human rights; reproductive technologies and human dignity; balancing privacy and security; and emerging issues.

The first part, on general and philosophical aspects, consists of two contributions. The first discusses the value and risks of Information and Communication Technologies (ICTs) and concludes with considerations on constituting new human rights, such as the right to access the Internet as an 'explicitly recognised fundamental right' in international charters (pp. 11, 26). In the second contribution, the author eases the reader in the approach of 'new community-based ethics' as a consequence of nowadays crises. The participating citizen is the 'subject of rights' but even further the 'subject of duties', meaning to be not only a voting citizen but also a participating citizen (pp. 3, 27).

Part two, about freedom of expression, contains an article which tackles the issue of illegal or harmful content over the Internet. It is thus assessing the 'pan-European level of development and implementation of blocking policies' on the Internet (p. 47 et seqq.).

The first contribution of the third part, on intellectual property, competition rules and new technologies, discusses the context of intellectual property and human rights and how they are balanced, with regard to northern and southern perspectives. Connecting trade policy and intellectual property rights is the southern practice and can be seen as an advantage for a more balanced approach between these two rights (pp. 4, 79). The second text deals with the claim that 'development and access to technology should work in tandem, with the latter being considered a prerequisite'. The author is addressing the topic on the perspectives of the right to development, the international transfer of technology and competition law with the suggestion of 'the protection of competition as a global good' (pp. 4, 91).

Part four, on biobanks, bioethics and human rights, deals in its first text with 'possibilities and limits of a constitutional approach to the human bodiliness' with a focus on 'bioconstitution'. According to the author, many examples of the revolution of genetics, nanosciences and robotics (GNR) 'refuse the foundations' [...] 'of law as a whole' (pp. 4, 121 et seqq.). The following chapter focuses more on biobanks and the discussion about legal challenges of whom to protect and how to protect. A 'more careful distinction between personal and human, between our social-cultural and biological identities' is suggested. Our human samples are not equal with us as persons (pp. 143, 168).

Part five focuses on reproductive technologies and human dignity. The first author of this section discusses the philosophical concept of human dignity in a specific field of human embryo research (p. 169). The second author goes more into detail about the legal situation on embryonic stem cells, especially in Brazil. Fundamental and human rights are examined and brought into the context of 'the social and technical function of research'. Both conclude by 'defending a greater role of human dignity' (pp. 6, 185).

Privacy and security are the focus of the following two contributions in part six. The first deals with data protection and security and goes into detail about the 'risks posed to individual privacy' by electronic communications. Further tensions between information/network and community/identity are discussed and brought to a legal connection concerning human rights (pp. 6, 203 et seqq.). Based on the new technology for fighting crime, the next contribution is focusing on the conflict between privacy and security. A big challenge is the protection of the right to privacy when data is used for the purpose of public interest (fight against crime) (pp. 217, 230).

The final part deals with emerging issues concerning new technologies and consists of four contributions. It starts with a proposition of a right to personal identity. Doing so, the authors examine the changing of technological developments and their impact on identity. The discussion concludes with a human rights-based approach to the right to identity, its growing recognition and importance for implementation (pp. 231, 254). The second contribution takes a critical stance towards the privatisation of cyber warfare and its legal implications. The author claims a need for specific rules, as currently existing principles of international humanitarian law and human rights law 'fail to provide answers to all possible scenarios' (pp. 255, 272). The next contribution compares proposals for the restriction of freedom of expression in Argentina, Brazil, Chile, Colombia, Mexico and Venezuela. It focuses on content and removal cases in recent legislation (pp. 7, 273 et seqq.). The final contribution relates to the emerging potential and possible benefits of nanotechnology, especially to the Global South and the legal aspects of human rights. A special focus is then placed on nanotechnology and challenges brought up by this new technology concerning current patent rules. Nanotechnology, as a key developing field 'can bring hope to solve many of the major health problems that humanity is currently facing'. The challenges posed by the right to health need to be met by a 'more balanced approach to patent law' (pp. 8, 313).

Overall, the collected volume analyses and discusses emerging issues between new technologies and human rights, focusing on some relevant aspects in today's society. This book provides a good insight into the challenges posed by new technologies, not just raising legal questions, but also philosophical and social issues. Since this edition contains many different articles, it offers a good overview of the current debate, not only for those in the legal field but also for those in the political, social and philosophical fields, who are interested in human rights.

Helena Heck

Mariagiulia Giuffré

The Readmission of Asylum Seekers under International Law

Oxford, Hart Publishing, 2020, 408 pages, £72.00

When patriotic and populist politicians blame foreign nationals for the ill of their states and gain in popularity for it, states increasingly conclude bilateral or other agreements and arrangements for the readmission of people to their state of origin or habitual residence in order to simplify expulsion of irregular migrants. By design, such agreements can jeopardise the rights of a particularly vulnerable group of people – refugees. In particular, refugees' access to protection, meaning the protection from *refoulement*, the right to seek and enjoy asylum and the right to effective remedies before removal, might be endangered. Refugees often travel without identity and travel documents, as do mostly undocumented economic migrants. They therefore run risk of being assimilated with undocumented economic migrants (p. 1). Mariagiulia Giuffré's monograph illustrates the impact of such agreements on the rights of refugees by unpicking readmission agreements from a refugee and human rights perspective. The geographical focus of the work is on Europe, although its scope is not limited to it. The book is largely based on Giuffré's doctoral thesis and is divided into six chapters.

In the introductory chapter, the author clarifies that the research includes all kinds of cooperation agreements linked to the readmission of irregular migrants, such as development aid or visa facilitation agreements – all tools that make readmission more attractive for the requested states (p. 21). Moreover, Giuffré explains key concepts such as the right to seek asylum and the principle of *non-refoulement* and discusses the interrelation between international refugee and human rights law, as well as human rights protection in the context of the European Union (EU, the Union).

Chapter two focuses on the access to protection for refugees, especially in external migration control mechanisms. Giuffré examines several refugee and human rights instruments as well as EU law and concludes that the prohibition of direct and indirect *refoulement* applies to all EU Member States, including in the extraterritorial context and on the high seas. Regarding the right to asylum, the state of affairs is not abundantly clear in international law, but EU Member States are obliged to grant a right to asylum due to EU primary law (pp. 79, 125). Subsequently, the concept of a safe third country is critically analysed.

In the next three chapters, Giuffré analyses the main categories of agreements linked to readmission: bilateral standard readmission agreements, diplomatic assurances and agreements for technical and police cooperation. In chapter three, the author analyses the intersection between migration control through standard readmission agreements and core refugee rights and concludes that such agreements do not *per se* contradict fundamental rights of refugees (p. 131). However, there is a real risk that their rights are violated as a consequence of accelerated removal mechanisms that do not include separate provisions on refugees. Moreover, she criticises such agreements with states that cause refugee flows and the 'safe third country' rule (pp. 187, 188).

Chapter four challenges diplomatic assurances under Memoranda of Understanding, and the author claims that states should not rely on diplomatic assurances with states where torture and ill-treatment are still performed (p. 248). In the subsequent chapter, Giuffré discusses the impact of agreements aiming to perform readmission before the individuals enter EU territory and takes a closer look at such arrangements between Italy and Libya. Again, the author points out how these agreements can hamper the access to protection for refugees, especially since responsibility is shifted to third states, which often do not provide adequate access to protection (p. 309).

In the concluding chapter, the author summarises her findings. As readmission agreements are solely administrative tools, their texts are in theory compatible with refugee rights. In practice, however, refugees mostly travel alongside irregular migrants; therefore, refugees are at risk of being transferred to supposedly 'safe third countries' which can undermine refugees' access to protection. Giuffré once more stresses that European states must always guarantee the access to protection for refugees under their jurisdiction, be that within, at or outside their borders. To ensure the compliance of readmission agreements with refugees' rights, she firstly proposes that European states should never negotiate readmission agreements with states that do not properly protect the rights of refugees. Secondly, when European states negotiate extraterritorial migration control agreements, specific and effective clauses to protect the access to protection for refuges should be included in the agreement. Thirdly, all readmission agreements should keep in mind the risk that refugees may be treated as irregular migrants and should include non-affection clauses and procedural human rights clauses (pp. 314–315).

Giuffré deftly addresses the recent rise in bilateral readmission agreements, triggered by the political swing to the right in many European states. Governments tend to be silent about their refugee, human and European rights obligations toward refugees when they talk about irregular migration. In any case, this book is worth a read, not only for those interested and academics, but especially for policy-makers.

Anna Lena Hörzer

Jure Vidmar (ed.)

European Populism and Human Rights

Leiden/Boston, Brill Nijhoff, 351 pages, €127.00

'Populism [...] has come to dominate democratic politics' (p. 39). In recent years, rising populist movements, authoritarian regimes and shifts away from pluralism have undisputedly dominated the European political landscape. These trends pose imminent risks to democracy, its (liberal) values and institutions, the rule of law – and ultimately – human rights. *European Populism and Human Rights* is a comprehensive and valuable compendium that seeks to explore this political and legal tension between far-right populism, democracy and the existing human rights framework. The particular research interest hence lies in providing an understanding of the multifaceted phenomenon of populism, the ways it can potentially affect human rights in theory and practice and the extent to which instruments like the European Convention on Human Rights (ECHR) provide safeguards against such developments. While the analysis mainly focuses on legal aspects of this complex interrelation, the authors frequently also refer to interdisciplinary concepts and methodologies.

The collection, edited by Jure Vidmar, contains individual contributions from numerous renowned experts in the field of public international law and was published as a part of the *International Studies in Human Rights* series (Vol. 130). It is noteworthy that important impulses for the book stem from a congress held at the University of Maastricht in 2018, where some of the respective authors took part in panel discussions on 'Populism, Nationalism and Human Rights'.

In terms of structure, the book comprises 13 chapters and is subdivided into three parts, each addressing different levels of the analysis. Following an introductory contribution by the editor on 'Democracy and the European Public Order' (p. 1), the first part of the book is dedicated to the ambiguous notion of populism by framing it as a 'human rights problem' (p. 27) and considering its potential effects on democratic consolidation (chapters two to five). Part II theoretically addresses the effects, opportunities and existing political strategies of (transnational) populism in the context of human rights (chapters six to eight). Finally, Part III applies the theoretical basis in a practical context by focusing on concrete cases of freedom of expression and hate speech (chapter nine), genocide as an 'identity-based' (p. 319) hate crime (chapter 12) or case studies concerning backsliding into authoritarianism in Russia and challenges to judicial independence and the rule of law in Hungary and Poland (chapter 10).

Jure Vidmar's opening remarks serve as a crucial introduction which aims for a better understanding of the general role of democratic principles within the existing human rights framework. He highlights the essential difference between procedural and substantive definitions of democracy and examines whether certain democratic standards are guaranteed by human rights instruments such as the ECHR or the International Bill of Human Rights. In doing so, the author also focuses on the interpretations provided by various international courts, most notably in the *Handyside, Refah Partisi* and *Rekvenyi* cases of the European Court of Human Rights (ECtHR). Both in his opening and final contributions, Jure Vidmar concludes from the existing case law that 'democracy forms part of the European public order' (p. 25) and that 'a present-day European state needs to adhere to tenets of substantive democracy' (p. 25). It is this particular balance of human rights and democratic principles within the European public order that has increasingly been challenged by rising populism in recent years.

Based on these general considerations, the following chapters undertake the difficult attempt to define populism and to highlight its possible adverse effects on the democratic order guarantees found in human rights treaties. The wide variety of definitions introduced in the book is just symbolic of how contentious the concept is perceived among legal scholarship. Nevertheless, it appears that many authors have developed a common approach to populism as an 'anti-establishment' or 'anti-elitist' movement, claiming to represent 'the will of the people' (p. 257) and utilising an '"othering"-rhetoric' (p. 292) that often leads to marginalisation of minorities. This understanding is also reflected in recent prevalent definitions by Cas Mudde or Jan-Werner Müller.

In this light, it is, however, important to note that many of the authors suggest considering the utilisation of the term 'populism' with particular caution. For instance, Luigi Lonardo highlights potential counterproductive effects of such vague terms and pointedly stresses that 'The label of populism ought not to mark simply political opponents. "Populist" cannot be synonym of "person who disagrees with my views"' (p. 112). In a similar vein, Theo van Boven emphasises that it is important to distinguish between 'positive' and 'negative populism' (p. 36). Whilst the former manifests in global public campaigns in favour of human rights aims, the latter refers to policies that seek to undermine human rights causes. By the same token, Laura M. Henderson avers that transnational populist movements may have the potential to promote and expand human rights. Furthermore, Yota Negishi highlights the corrective power of populism fostering the re-emergence of '*fraternité*' (p. 141) values.

In general, *European Populism and Human Rights* is a well-structured, cohesive and highly topical compendium that presents a mandatory read not only for legal scholars, but also political theorists and decision-makers. It can furthermore be recommended to all individuals interested in one of the most serious political challenges of the upcoming years. What can be critically remarked is that the constraints mentioned in the concluding chapter have not always been adhered to very consistently throughout the contributions. The title of the book also suggests a broader approach to the topic, rather than the intended focus on far-right populism.

'Democracy […] can never be taken for granted' (p. 34), and it remains to be seen *whether* and *how* international organisations, regimes and citizens will manage to overcome the challenges far-right populism and democratic backsliding pose to human rights.

Marla MEILINGER

Bridget Lewis, Kelly Purser and Kirsty Mackie

The Human Rights of Older Persons: A Human Rights-Based Approach to Elder Law

Singapore, Springer, 2020, 338 pages, €96.00

In 2050, approximately two billion people worldwide will be at least 60 years old. It is predicted that the number of persons aged 60 and older will nearly double between 2015 and 2050, climbing from 12–22% of the global population. By then, there will be more elderly people than children and young adults aged 10 to 24. While the ageing population provides many benefits, such as pursuing higher education and spending more time with loved ones, it also comes with several hardships. As life expectancies rise and birth rates fall, the world is experiencing a demographic transition. Our societies face several challenges because of the associated economic and social developments, yet legislative responses so far have been insufficient or unsuitable, failing to adequately address systemic issues such as ageism and elder abuse. In many cases, legislation intended to help or protect older people inadvertently perpetuates human rights violations, either via poor design, lack of resources, limitation of access to justice or a combination of these elements. In *The Human Rights of Older Persons: A Human Rights-Based Approach to Elder Law*, authors Bridget Lewis, Kelly Purser and Kirsty Mackie argue that a human rights-based approach offers a stronger framework for the creation and implementation of all legislation that affects and interacts with the lives of the elderly. This approach promises to aid in changing community views about older people, moving away from conceptions focused on dependency and protection and toward a deeper appreciation of each individual's inherent dignity, autonomy and capability, regardless of age.

In light of the expanding population of senior citizens, this book could not be more timely or relevant. The authors start by explaining and defining basics like elder law and ageism, followed by an overview of the existing framework for protecting the human rights of older persons. Even though there is a framework that could protect the elderly, it often fails to do so. A human rights approach does offer a comprehensive and well developed set of standards to evaluate existing elder legislation, identify flaws and devise more acceptable solutions. This book calls for stronger domestic human rights protection so that older people in all jurisdictions have access to appropriate legal protections. As human rights are one of the most practical and positive ways to reframe elder law to better promote the autonomy, liberty and dignity of older persons, this book adopts and advocates a human rights-based approach.

In the subsequent chapters, the authors explain why the legal framework fails to protect the elderly. The book identifies threats to human rights, then outlines and applies a human rights framework to a series of legal areas and policy challenges. The authors begin by evaluating current human rights duties that relate to older people, before developing a unique, multidimensional human rights framework based on these laws, as well as numerous international instruments and multidisciplinary scholarship. They then apply this critical human rights perspective to several topics and areas in which senior citizens engage with the law and legal actors. Barriers to economic and social involvement, ageism and discrimination, legal capability, elder abuse, financial management, retirement and estate planning, housing, and health and elder care are just a few of them.

Individual autonomy in decision-making, as well as respect for dignity and liberty, are identified as essential elements of a human rights-based approach to elder law in this book. These principles should underpin all legislation affecting the elderly. Never has a book looked at these concerns through the prism of human rights and addressed them all before. This book advocates for a paradigm shift, suggesting that a human rights viewpoint may assist to overcome ageism and appreciate each individual's dignity and autonomy.

The book ends with proposals for strengthening elder law, both in specialised domains and more broadly, based on best practices from many jurisdictions and leading scholarship in the subject. The writers present a thorough human rights examination of significant areas of law that impact senior citizens and argue that a Convention on the Rights of Older Persons is an essential tool in achieving the paradigm shift. Because the challenges that arise in 'old age' are frequently the culmination of events that occur throughout one's life, a human rights-based approach to elder law must begin with a commitment to human rights for all ages.

This book is a unique contribution to the emerging body of elder law literature and can be recommended to everyone interested in elder law or human rights in general. Because we will all grow old(er), the book is relevant for everyone.

Katharina Michl

Michael Stohl and Alison Brysk (eds.)

A Research Agenda for Human Rights

Cheltenham, Edward Elgar Publishing, 2020, 208 pages, £85

Human rights are declared as one of the European Union's founding principles and are a collection of universal rights inherent to all human beings, without regard to race, ethnicity, nationality, gender, colour, religion, political opinion, birth or other status. Their purpose lies in preserving the equality, freedom, dignity and safety of all people. In 1948, the Universal Declaration of Human Rights was adopted by the United Nations (UN) General Assembly. This treaty was the first legal document that enshrined fundamental human rights to be universally protected. Since then, human rights scholarship has grown as an interdisciplinary field but currently stands at a crossroads – it is contracting in some directions while expanding in others.

A Research Agenda for Human Rights presents an accumulation of the historic path of scholarship in this field and the emergence of new practices, ideas and alternative methods and perspectives for future research. This 208-page publication is divided into an introduction, which provides an overview of the included topics and the applied methods, followed by 11 articles by acclaimed professionals in the field of human rights.

In the first article, 'The study of human rights history: A corpus-based linguistic approach to "human rights" in the nineteenth-century British press', Eetu Vento illustrates how the use of language plays a significant role in understanding the development of human rights ideas. He analyses the term 'human rights' using different methodologies and with that adds to the expanding literature dealing with the European provenance, meaning, dissemination and reception of principles regarding human rights. In 'Humanitarianism: Coping in the void', David Forsythe highlights human rights in connection with war crimes, the difficult dividing line between humanitarian values and politics and the resulting need for humanitarian help.

In the third article, Champa Patel outlines the need for more research in regard to internationally displaced persons (IDPs). She calls for more reliable and accurate data, a better understanding of the exact situations that cause the sizable amount of IDPs, a greater insight into multi-faceted and multi-staged displacement and the impact it has on host communities. 'International human rights law: Progress and prospects' highlights the development of international human rights law including treaties, parties and their obligations, and the challenges researchers will face in the future. In the fifth article, Iosif Kovras describes transitional justice and its expansion through grassroots initiatives led by civil society, non-governmental organisations (NGOs) and victim groups. This chapter is followed by 'Academic freedom as a human right', in which George Andreopoulos argues that academic freedom should be seen as its own human right instead of being subsumed under freedom of opinion and expression. He further explains the consequences the classification of academic freedom as a human right would have and calls for a more holistic approach to the topic.

The seventh article, by Inga T. Winkler, deals with socio-economic rights and their connection with the origins of human rights. She highlights the progress socio-economic rights have made in the last 25 years and drafts ideas for future research.

In the eighth contribution, Feryal Cherif shines a light on women's rights. In the past, gender discrimination was fought by small groups of activists, but over the years it has gained more and more attention from states, international law and human rights regimes. She outlines the evolution of women's rights and the increasing scholarship regarding the lives of women and the obstacles they have to face across the globe. In 'Inhumane environments: Global violence against environmental justice activists as a human rights violation', Feng, Mildenberger and Stokes summarise the violent acts directed against environmental and indigenous land rights activists. They argue that a tremendous amount of additional research needs to be conducted in order to understand the motives of such assassins and the effect these crimes have on society and the environment.

The penultimate article, by Janne Mende, deals with the role of businesses for human rights. She advocates for a threefold approach to the public, the private and the business-societal. This three-pole constellation implements a business responsibility for human rights as a new research agenda for human rights. This book closes with 'Understanding human rights at the local level'. In this article, Gerd Oberleitner and Klaus Starl outline the development of new practices and perceptions that aim to localise human rights at city and regional levels by applying different mechanisms such as multi-governance structures or multi-stakeholder processes.

In conclusion, it can be said that each contribution in this book is worth reading and well researched. It offers a wide-ranging overview into different areas of the human rights scholarship and an outlook of what can be expected from future research. However, this book would not be an easy read for those unfamiliar with the topics discussed. Nonetheless, *A Research Agenda for Human Rights* can be considered a valuable resource for practitioners and scholars of human rights law who intend to stay up-to-date with new methods, practices and ideas regarding the state of law and future developments within the field of human rights.

Julia PÖSCHL

Kyriaki Topidi (ed.)

Normative Pluralism and Human Rights: Social Normativities in Conflict

London, Routledge – Taylor & Francis, 2018, 306 pages, £120.00

In a globalised world, the contact between different cultural, religious and social communities has not only increased due to migration, but has to a certain extent always been part of the human experience in different parts of our world. Therefore, a mere one-sided contemplation of normative regimes is no longer appropriate. The complex legal situation that emerges from the coexistence of international and national law – as well as social, religious, cultural and societal norms in various forms depending on local circumstances – is often at the root of social conflicts and human rights violations.

In this four-part book, the authors analyse how normative conflicts influence the implementation and realisation of human rights in different socio-cultural settings and take up a stance on how the tension that typically arises from opposing social rules and legal norms could be eased or even resolved. The authors managed to examine this largely discussed topic from an entirely new point of view by taking an interdisciplinary and non-Eurocentric approach to normative pluralism, with the reoccurring theme of women's rights issues in different parts of the world. The authors also put a significant focus on normative pluralism as it is seen and practised in India, shifting the focus from Europe and at the same time recognising normative pluralism not as a 'problem' that is meant to be solved but as an integral part of society that needs to be acknowledged by the legal community.

Part I of the book commences with two chapters considering different methods of preventing conflict. Tommaso Amico Di Meane argues that 'conflict' can be studied through comparative law approaches and points out that a new, non-Eurocentric methodology focusing on non-Western legal traditions and diversity is required. In chapter three, Domenico Amirante confirms through a practical example how India manages its socio-cultural plurality, specifically by exploring the role of language in a multicultural society, which in respecting differences and by developing sensibility to pluralism the potential for conflict can be reduced significantly.

Part II contains four chapters on the articulation of conflict, focusing on Europe and Israel and talks about how conflicts, as seen by 'Western' decision-makers, are often based on religion and ethical values rather than social norms and culture. In this context, Kyriaki Pavlidou draws a comparison between the headscarf controversies in Turkey and Switzerland and the 'Crucifix' case in Italy, where the author calls out inconsistencies in the jurisdiction of the European Court of Human Rights (ECtHR) by describing the headscarf as a purely religious symbol and the crucifix as more of a 'socio-cultural' symbol, marking only one as 'problematic'. Author Melisa Vazquez addresses one specific law-related moral conflict, the refusal to perform an abortion, and how Sweden and Italy approach this subject. In chapter five, author Fabienne Bretscher discusses immigration and the development of 'new' minorities, as well as the special legal protection granted to such minorities and the conflicting approaches taken by international bodies (specifically the United Nations and the Council of Europe) in the debate on the inclusion of so-called new minorities. To illustrate the workings of legal pluralism in a multicultural system, author Kyriaki Topidi describes how religious diversity challenges public education, using Israel as an example.

In Part III, the authors illustrate how conflicts are handled at different levels and focus almost exclusively on India and Indian minority groups in Europe. Author Tanja Herklotz looks specifically at gender equality issues within the religion-based family and personal law system in India and elaborately compares two feminist approaches towards the reform of the Indian personal law system, and author Chiara Lapi sheds light on how Italy handles the gender equality issue regarding the inheritance law practices of Sikh Indian migrants living in Italy.

Lastly, Part IV discusses in four chapters how conflicts arising from legal pluralism may be resolved. To give the reader a vast understanding of the topic, the author (Pierluigi Consorti) first provides a comparison between the state-based multiculturalism approach to conflict management, which is ultimately a flawed construct according to the author, and the preferable and more flexible interculturalism approach, with its potential to provide cultural translation far beyond the regulations of formal law. Furthermore, author Peter Kirchschlaeger discusses in chapter 12 the justification of the universality of human rights and how this concept impacts different religious and worldview-based communities. With her illustration of Muslim divorce law and personal law in India, focusing on gender equality, author Gopika Solanki provides several practical examples and demonstrates how the relationship between religious law, customs and state law is constantly reformulated.

Overall, the book can be recommended to anyone interested in the relations among culture, religion and human rights as it offers a broad discussion of the topic not only in theory but also in practice. Especially by discussing normative pluralism in various contexts and under diverse circumstances and by shifting the focus from Europe, the authors manage to bring across numerous ideas on how to manage and best understand normative pluralism and its connection to human rights issues all over the world.

Isabella Noemi RAILE

Jonathan Herring

Domestic Abuse and Human Rights

Cambridge, Intersentia, 2020, 250 pages, €59.00

The COVID-19 pandemic served to pinpoint the existing problems within our society that had received only scant attention in previous years. Those who already found themselves in difficult circumstances prior to the outbreak of the virus often suffered even more from the consequences of this crisis than those who were in a financially and socially privileged situation. A serious problem that occurred during the numerous lockdowns all over the world was the increase of domestic abuse. This is one reason why Jonathan Herring's book *Domestic Abuse and Human Rights* is now perhaps even more topical than ever before.

Jonathan Herring systematically forges a link between domestic abuse and human rights, arguing that the state has an obligation to intervene and protect victims from abusive situations in their homes, as domestic abuse can no longer be seen as an exclusively private matter. According to the author, domestic abuse is characterised by three distinguishing features: coercive control; an intimate relationship between the perpetrator and the victim; and the dominating patriarchal structures in society. The last of these characterisations proclaims that Herring is in favour of a gendered approach to domestic abuse rather than a gender-neutral definition. This does not mean that the author turns a blind eye to abuse acted out by women or even children, as he dedicates one chapter to the abuse of parents by children. The reasons that Herring decides to follow a gendered approach are laid out in the second chapter, one of them being the differences between violence committed by men against women and violence committed by women against men. Not only do injuries caused by women tend to be less serious in the majority of cases, but also the origin of female violence is often found in self-defence. Apart from these rather detailed differences, it is genuinely eye-opening when Herring discusses the tremendous influence that patriarchal structures have on our private relationships and how in fact domestic abuse sustains the patriarchy, and vice versa. Domestic abuse and the patriarchy form an inseparable pair, reinforcing one another. As Herring states, for a man, becoming the victim of abuse is inconsistent with the image of masculinity anticipated by society. The role of being a victim will most likely not correlate with his self-perception. On the contrary, from a woman's perspective, the role of being the victim of abuse confirms the patriarchal messages sent by society, such as being inferior to men, or the belief that as a female she deserves domestic abuse. This tight connection among the external effects, the forces within the relationship and the influence of society on our private, intimate relationships should be a wake-up call fighting against patriarchal structures and paving the way for equality in all aspects of life.

Jonathan Herring focused on two human rights documents, namely, the European Convention on Human Rights (ECHR) and the Council of Europe Convention on preventing and combating violence against women and domestic violence, better known as the Istanbul Convention, in order to illustrate how human rights can be used as an instrument against domestic abuse. The main difference between these two treaties is that the ECHR is not designed to combat domestic abuse in particular, but is instead a general statement of human rights, whereas the purpose of the Istanbul Convention is to provide a document focusing explicitly on strengthening women's rights and combatting domestic abuse.

Nonetheless, the interpretation of the European Court of Human Rights, particularly Article 3, the prohibition of torture, and Article 8 ECHR, the right to respect for private and family life, can be used as sources of rights for victims of domestic abuse. Herring explicitly articulates his opinion that these two articles impose positive duties on the state, even when the victim does not want public authorities to intervene. This is the case because first, the public interest outweighs the interest of the victim, as domestic abuse should not be tolerated in any case. Second, an abuser can never rely on the right to private and family life in order to balance the wrong he does to the victim. Regarding the Istanbul Convention, Herring positively highlights that this human rights document recognises domestic abuse as a gendered phenomenon and stresses that non-legal interventions as well as societal changes in general must be considered in order to improve the situation of victims.

In conclusion, this book can be recommended to everyone who is interested in a structured approach to domestic abuse. Jonathan Herring succeeds in depicting the system behind this issue, regardless of whether the abuse constitutes violence against a partner, children, parents or the elderly. May it be read by many, so that the magnitude of domestic abuse will finally be understood and no longer seen as a problem occurring behind closed doors.

Agnes ROMANIN

Sara De Vido

Violence against Women's Health in International Law

Manchester, Manchester University Press, 2020, 272 pages, £80.00

In light of recent global developments – namely, the restriction of women's access to abortion – which call into question women's autonomy, as well as the high number of femicides (at least in Austria), violence against women's health is a present and highly relevant topic. *Violence against women's health in international law* deals with the issue of violence against women and the right to health, in particular reproductive health, and demonstrates the complex relationship between these two areas. Although there is already a rich body of literature of violence against women from different areas of research, the link between violence against women and the right to health introduces the new concept of violence against women's health from an international law perspective. The author, Sara De Vido, an Associate Professor of International Law at Ca' Foscari University of Venice, Italy, reconceptualises state responsibility to emphasise positive obligations of result, due diligence obligations and obligations to progressively take steps.

The book is structured according to the paradigm of medicine that has been circulating since Hippocrates, and the chapters are therefore divided into anamnesis, diagnosis, treatment and prognosis. Furthermore, every chapter analyses the connection between violence against women and the right to health on two different levels. On the one hand, the horizontal dimension of the problem is analysed, which covers interpersonal relations: 'violence between individuals, including "family and intimate partner violence and community violence" the former committed within the context of the family, "community" referring to "acquaintance and stranger violence," violence in workplaces and other institutions' (pp. 22, 23). On the other hand, the vertical dimension is examined, which includes state health policies and laws which might affect women's health and constitute a form of gender-based violence.

The book consists of four chapters. The first chapter (anamnesis) starts with a comprehensive overview of the jurisprudence of regional human rights courts, the activity of international human rights bodies and relevant national judgments and state practice regarding violence against women – in particular, violence against women's health and reproductive health. More than 70 decisions are analysed. A special focus is placed to the areas of 'domestic violence, rape committed in time of peace, including marital rape, and female genital mutilation/cutting' (p. 23). In chapter two (diagnosis) the author conceptualises the concept of violence against women's health and examines it from different perspectives.

Chapter three (treatment) analyses the structure of state obligations under international law and chooses the following appropriate scheme to conceptualise state obligations related to violence against women's health: 'positive obligations of result, positive obligations of due diligence and positive obligations to progressively take steps' (p. 195). The author conceptualises concrete state obligations while putting the vertical and horizontal dimensions of violence under the same umbrella, substantiating the statements with examples.

Chapter four (prognosis) summarises the main findings of the preceding analysis and assesses the higher significance of the issues discussed. The author concludes that violence against women causes a violation of the right to health and reproductive health and that state laws and policies in the area of health cause – or at least contribute to – violence against women. The author raises the critical question of whether international law itself is the cause of violence and mentions the weakness of monitoring mechanisms and the limited competences of United Nations treaty bodies and regional human rights courts. However, 'law as the cause and the cure' (p. 240) can be developed, improved and interpreted in the right way and can therefore help to change recent developments. The book hereby provides approaches to improvement, such as the need for positive obligations of result, due diligence obligations and obligations for the state to progressively take steps in the horizontal as well as on the vertical dimensions.

Moreover, *Violence against women's health in international law* is most certainly of fundamental value to academics and practitioners, as well as policy-making representatives alike. It offers a broad, yet in-depth insight into the resulting link between violence against women and the right to health, which enables a conceptualisation of the innovative idea of violence against women's health from an international law perspective. The concept enhances the definition of violence against women by revealing patterns of discrimination in state policies, considering women's specific needs and creating a human rights-based approach to women's autonomy.

INDEX